THE
WINES OF
BORDEAUX

THE
WINES OF
BORDEAUX

AND

VINTAGES AND TASTING NOTES 1952–2003

CLIVE COATES MW

WEIDENFELD & NICOLSON

DEDICATION

This book is dedicated to my son Ben, my daughter Emma, her husband Andy and my grandchildren Nicholas and Joshua.

First published in Great Britain in 2004
by Weidenfeld & Nicolson

Text copyright © Clive Coates, 2004
Design and maps © Weidenfeld & Nicolson, 2004
Original illustrations from Cocks & Féret
Photographed for this book by Martin Norris

A CIP catalogue record for this book is available from
the British Library.

ISBN 0 297 84317 6

Design director: David Rowley
Editorial director: Susan Haynes
Designed by Nigel Soper
Edited by Fiona Holman
Maps by Andrew Thompson
Indexed by Diana Lecore

Printed in Great Britain by Butler & Tanner Ltd,
Frome and London

Weidenfeld & Nicolson Ltd
The Orion Publishing Group
Orion House
5 Upper St Martin's Lane
London WC2 H 9EA

Title page illustration: Château Latour from Cocks et Féret

www.orionbooks.co.uk

CONTENTS

Maps

PREFACE

THIS IS THE THIRD BOOK I have written on Bordeaux, with the exception of a small, obscure part-work, a contribution to an edition (c. 1980) of *Mrs Beeton* and the chapter in my *Encyclopedia of the Wines and Domaines of France* (2000). What I wrote about Bordeaux in the *Encyclopedia* was of necessity truncated. My two previous books on Bordeaux (*Claret* and *Grands Vins, The Finest Chateaux of Bordeaux and their Wines*) were published in 1982 and 1993, respectively, and consisted of château profiles and vintage assessments.

This is a completely different book. While there is yet again a detailed section on recent vintages, complete with tasting notes, marks out of 20 and indications on when the wines should be drunk, the bulk of the book is concerned with the châteaux themselves, from the grandest estates in Pauillac to more modest properties in the Côtes de Bourg or Entre-Deux-Mers.

I have travelled even more extensively in Bordeaux in recent years than I normally do. I would like to thank all the various promotional organisations in the Gironde, from the CIVB downwards, for helping to set up tastings on the basis of which I made my selections of châteaux to then go and visit. My thanks also to Bill Blatch of Vintex, who organises an annual comprehensive tasting of the Médoc *crus bourgeois* and other wines. I must also note my appreciation to a group of professional friends in Britain who gather regularly to sample ranges of the top wines in bottle, and others based in Europe and the USA who are kind enough to invite me to join them.

Fiona Holman, my editor, has done her usual highly professional job in ironing out any discrepancies, and in ensuring that the detail is as precise and as up-to-date as possible: many, many thanks. Finally, I must acknowledge the immense help I have received from my personal assistant, Sonia Portalès. The bulk of this book was typed up, in her spare time, from my indifferent scrawl. Thank goodness she can read my writing. *Un grand merci.*

READERS' NOTES

My aim has been to cover every château of note. When it comes to the properties that have been classed in one of the many classifications I have not hesitated to be critical where I feel a lack of quality merits it. But at this level I have refrained from speaking about specific vintages at length. The notes in the Vintage Assessment pages, beginning on page 424, speak for themselves. In the châteaux profiles I have in general considered the performance of the wines produced since 1990 and have awarded the top châteaux star ratings: three stars for the absolute super-stars, then two stars for the very good and one star for good. No star but mentioned means the chateau is worthy of consideration. At the lower level, those of the *crus bourgeois* and *petits châteaux,* I have based my assessments on the vintages since 1995 and mention specific wines that have pleased me.

In the châteaux profiles that form the bulk of this book I have referred readers to *Grands Vins* and/or to articles in my monthly publication, *The Vine*, and elsewhere where they can find, if they wish, both a more detailed history of the château and an assessment of recent vintages.

I have used a marking system out of 20 all my working life – 20.0–19.0: Excellent, the best; 18.5–16.5: Very good to very fine indeed; 16.0–15.0: Good to very good; 14.5–13.5: Quite good; 13.0–12.0: Not bad, average; 11.5–10.0: Disappointing, if not poor; less than 10: Somewhat disagreeable, if not faulty. My value judgements expressed – fine, good, not bad, and so on – refer to the wine within the context of the vintage.

Optimum drinking: irrespective of when the tastings took place, the comments for when to drink the wines refer to their state of maturity in the autumn of 2003, as I was preparing this book.

The figures for maximum yield quoted for each appellation survey refer to what is called the *rendement de base*. This is a constant. On top of this the growers are permitted to add a percentage figure, normally 20 per cent. This is called the PLC (*plafond limite de classement*). Thus in Saint-Julien, for example, the figure given is 47 hl/ha. In most years the estates are permitted to make 56.4 hl/ha (47 plus 20 per cent).

BORDEAUX

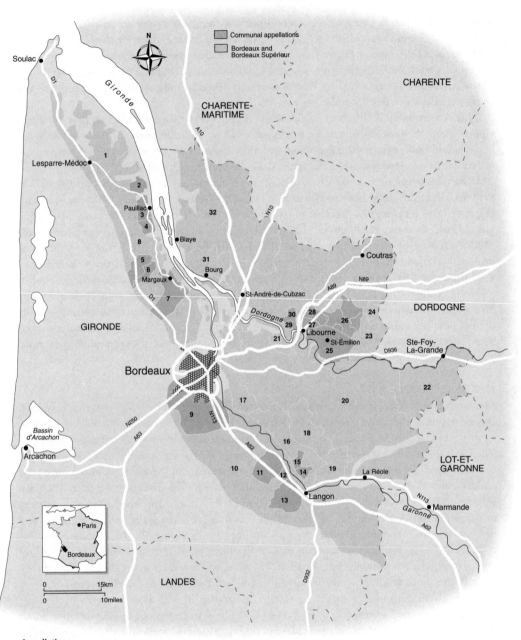

Communal appellations

Bordeaux and
Bordeaux Supérieur

CHARENTE

CHARENTE-MARITIME

Soulac

Gironde

Lesparre-Médoc

Pauillac

Blaye

Margaux

Bourg

St-André-de-Cubzac

Dordogne

Coutras

DORDOGNE

Libourne

St-Émilion

Ste-Foy-La-Grande

GIRONDE

Bordeaux

Bassin
d'Arcachon

Arcachon

La Réole

Langon

Marmande

Garonne

LOT-ET-GARONNE

Paris

Bordeaux

0   15km

0   10miles

LANDES

Appellations

1	Médoc	13	Sauternes	23	Côtes de Castillon
2	St-Estèphe	14	Ste-Croix-du-Mont	24	Bordeaux-Côtes de Francs
3	Pauillac	15	Loupiac	25	St-Émilion
4	St-Julien	16	Cadillac and Premières Côtes	26	St-Émilion satellites
5	Listrac-Médoc		de Bordeaux	27	Pomerol
6	Moulis-en-Médoc	17	Premières Côtes de Bordeaux	28	Lalande-de-Pomerol
7	Margaux	18	Bordeaux Haut-Benauge and	29	Canon-Fronsac
8	Haut-Médoc		Entre-Deux-Mers Haut-Benauge	30	Fronsac
9	Pessac-Léognan	19	Côtes de Bordeaux-St-Macaire	31	Côtes de Bourg
10	Graves	20	Entre-Deux-Mers	32	Côtes de Blaye and
11	Cérons	21	Graves-de-Vayres		Premières Côtes de Blaye
12	Barsac	22	Ste-Foy-Bordeaux		

INTRODUCTION

IN 2002 THE BORDEAUX WINE AREA – effectively the Gironde *département* minus the sandy, Atlantic coastal margins – measured 119,817 hectares and produced 5.61 million hectolitres of wine. This is the equivalent of 740 million bottles, 25 per cent of the *appellation contrôlée* harvest in France, 3 per cent of the total amount of wine produced in the world.

Bordeaux is by far the largest fine wine region in France. It produces four times as much as Beaujolais, Burgundy or Alsace, over twice as much as the Loire, just under twice as much as the Rhône.

Moreover Bordeaux produces – in both quantity and variety – all the three main types of wine: red, dry white and luscious sweet white. At the top levels these are the most aristocratic, the most profound, the most sumptuous and the most long-lasting of all table wines. Here the word breed, or *race* in French, used to describe wines of the greatest finesse and elegance, can be applied in the greatest number and with the most consistent regularity.

Whether Bordeaux is 'better' than, for instance, Burgundy, is a question of mood and personal taste. What is undeniable is that the world's fine wine market, measured by those wines which are sold *en primeur* for laying down, and subsequently traded through the auction and broking circuits, is dominated by Bordeaux.

It is the number and variety of its finest wines that, for me, makes Bordeaux the most impressive wine area of all. Burgundy has as many quality wine growers and top domaines, but production is on a very much smaller scale: a few casks rather than several dozen *tonneaux*. One single vineyard, itself much less extensive than a single Bordeaux estate, may in Burgundy be divided among a couple of dozen owners. In Bordeaux the vineyard will be in a single hand and the economies of scale make it much easier for the top growers to be as rigorous as possible in their selection of which *cuvées* will go into the *grand vin* and which will be rejected.

There are some 170 classed growths in Bordeaux; 60 Médocs, 28 Sauternes, 66 Saint-Émilions and 16 Graves. Add to this the top wines of Pomerol – which has never been classified – and the best of the *bourgeois* estates, many of whom produce wine of similar quality, and you have perhaps 220 single wine names producing at the highest level. Multiply that figure by the number of vintages drinkable or not yet mature that may be on the market, and you will have upwards of 5000 different wines. Each will be constantly changing as it gradually ages; and of all wines Bordeaux, whether red or sweet white – and indeed the top dry whites as well – has the greatest capacity to age, acquiring further profundity, complexity and uniqueness of character as it does so. Every year a new crop will unleash another substantial batch to be appreciated.

But this is only the tip of the iceberg. This cream will represent perhaps 5 per cent – but as much as 26 million bottles in total – of the annual harvest. Underneath that lies the unsung Bordeaux – good, if not fine, but still worthy of recognition. Not perhaps the sort of wines to which wine writers will devote pages of purple prose, nor drinkers any abject ceremony, but bottle after bottle of the most part solidly dependable wine at prices we can all afford to dispense regularly.

Bordeaux is both a city and the name of wine. The city, eighth largest in France, and until recently one of its major ports, lies on a bend of the river Garonne in south-west France. The Garonne flows north-westwards from the middle of the Pyrenees into the Atlantic Ocean. Some 10 kilometres north of Bordeaux it is joined by the last of its great tributaries, the river Dordogne. Together these form the estuary of the Gironde, from which comes the name of the *département* of which Bordeaux is the capital.

About 89 per cent of the AC Gironde harvest is red wine. This makes the Bordeaux area by far the largest quality red wine area of France. The Gironde's production of almost 6 million hectolitres of *appellation contrôlée* red wine dwarfs that of Burgundy's mere 660,000 hectolitres of Pinot Noir.

Unlike Burgundy – indeed, unlike much of the rest of France – Bordeaux is an area of largely proprietorial rather than peasant ownership and hence is one of relatively large estates, often long-established, self-sufficient in wine terms and which market their wines under their own 'Château' names. Cocks and Féret, the 'Bible of Bordeaux', lists some 4200 single vineyards and the proprietors thereof, and this itself is only the cream of around 11,500 growers who officially declare a crop each vintage.

HISTORY

IN OTHER BOOKS DEVOTED solely to the wines of Bordeaux, such as that of the late Edmund Penning-Rowsell (*The Wines of Bordeaux*), the history of the region and its wine has been covered with great depth and authority. I shall not attempt to emulate him. I refer readers to his lucid account and acknowledge my debt to him in preparing the *résumé* which follows.

It seems likely, says Penning-Rowsell, that Bordeaux was a wine-trading centre before it was a vine-growing region. The western side of the region is very flat, and in early Roman times it would have been marshy, covered in forest and infested with mosquitoes. The soil was poor and the climate less propitious for the cultivation of the vine than the higher ground, the *Haut Pays* further to the south and west. At the start Bordeaux was an *emporium*, important primarily as a port. It is therefore probable that it was not until the third century AD that the vine began to be widely planted in the locality. Ausonius, poet, consul and tutor to Roman emperors, owned vineyards in the area in the fourth century, though whether this was at Château Ausone is a matter for dispute. In one of his poems he refers not to the Dordogne but to the Garonne flowing gently at the bottom of his garden. Yet the most impressive Roman ruins outside Bordeaux are to be found in the grounds of Château La Gaffelière, at the foot of the Château Ausone escarpment.

Historical details during the next several hundred years, as elsewhere in the Europe of the Dark Ages, are sparse. There was an expansion of the vineyard in the eleventh century, but it was the arrival of the English after the marriage of the redoubtable Eleanor of Aquitaine to Henry Plantagenet, Henry II of England, in 1152 that had the profoundest effect. For three centuries the Bordeaux vineyards came under the jurisdiction of the English crown. England became the Gironde's most important export market, and each year, shortly after the harvest, before the winter had set in, a vast fleet would transport the cream of the crop, first chiefly to Bristol and Southampton, later to London. During the thirteenth, fourteenth and fifteenth centuries the vine gradually replaced all other forms of agriculture in the area, and though at first most of the wine shipped to England seems to have come from further north, from the Poitou and the Charente, Bordeaux soon became the major point of departure. For many hundreds of years, long after the departure of the English in 1453, wine was France's leading export, Britain its most important customer and Bordeaux the chief exporter.

Not all the wine exported was strictly 'Bordeaux', however; much was the produce of the *Haut Pays* – wine of the Dordogne, the Lot, the Tarn and the upper Garonne. These had to pay a tax, higher if from the French side of whatever was the border between the French and the English at the time, and faced other restrictions, such as being embargoed from shipment until after the Gironde harvest had left. Nevertheless, the whole of the South-West of France looked to England, and later to the Low Countries, Hamburg and the Baltic ports, for its market. Communications overland were cumbersome, hazardous and prolonged, and the French crown bought its wine from nearer at hand, from the upper Loire, Champagne and Burgundy.

Sensibly, even after the expulsion of the English after the battle of Castillon in 1453, the French kings took care not to disrupt the Bordeaux trade. The local inhabitants had never considered themselves anything other than Gascon, neither English nor French. The privileges the Bordeaux merchants had enjoyed under the English were confirmed, and after an initial bout of petty commercial warfare the French were forced to realise that they were now competing on their most important export market with wines from the Iberian peninsula and elsewhere.

The English remained customers for the finest Bordeaux wines even after the rise of the Dutch as an economic power in the seventeenth century and the various economic treaties discriminating against the French and in favour of Portugal which culminated in the Methuen Treaty in 1703. The Dutch became Bordeaux's major customer, but their requirements were for cheap wines, largely white, much of which was re-exported to Scandinavia and the Hanseatic ports.

The last quarter of the seventeenth and the first half of the eighteenth centuries was the period of the establishment of most of the great estates, what were to become the *crus classés* in 1855. Prior to this period the quality red wines had come from the upper Graves, surrounding the town of Bordeaux. Dutch engineers, with their experience in the Low Countries, drained the Médoc, formerly a land of marshes liable to widespread flooding at the time of neap tides, thus exposing the mounds of almost pure gravel, excellent for the vine, on which the great properties are centred to this day.

Château Haut-Brion in the Graves and then owned by the influential Pontac family, was the first of the Bordeaux estates to achieve renown and the first in English literature to be specifically named, Samuel Pepys enjoying the wine at the Royal Oak Tavern in 1663. Forty years later the London Gazette advertised the sale of Lafite, Margaux and Latour wines, as well as 'Pontac', looted from ships captured in the War of Spanish Succession. These estates were all owned by a new aristocracy, the *noblesse de la robe*. As the seventeenth century had progressed, a new breed of moneyed class had replaced the old *noblesse d'épée*. These families, of largely merchant origin, owed their power to their place in the Bordeaux *parlement*, their wealth to their land. Increasingly during the eighteenth century, suitable terrain in the Médoc was converted into monocultural vineyards, and after the French Revolution this expansion continued in Saint-Émilion, Pomerol and the Léognan part of the Graves.

The Revolution and the Napoleonic wars which followed, though serious for the wine trade, left the top growths relatively unscathed. A few proprietors – but there were not many – were guillotined, others emigrated and had their estates sequestered, as were those vineyards in ecclesiastical ownership. Though business suffered, there was little social upheaval. The great estates preserved their unity and remained the property of the moneyed classes. Bordeaux is a region of large domaines, vinously self-sufficient, *haute bourgeois* in ownership; Burgundy, originally owned by the church or the aristocracy until the Revolution, became a region of much fragmented vineyards in largely *petit bourgeois* or peasant possession. It is this which has caused the great difference between Bordeaux and Burgundy which continues to this day.

The nineteenth century saw three major scourges in the vineyard, the arrival of a new generation of proprietors, industrialists or those who had made their money out of the wine trade itself, and the beginning of the adoption of modern mechanical and scientific methods of tilling the land and making the wine.

The first of the great natural disasters was the arrival of oidium in the early 1850s. Oidium, or powdery mildew, is a cryptogamic disease which affects both leaves and grapes. The leaves shrivel and drop off; the fruit is split and dries up. Though the solution, the application of sulphur, was soon discovered, production was decimated and prices rose steeply, never to return to their previous levels.

Though phylloxera, a member of the aphid family, was first discovered in France in 1863, it did not make its appearance in the Gironde until 1869, and did not really begin to cause serious damage in the Médoc until a decade later. Phylloxera is the greatest pest of them all, for, unlike oidium and mildew, which, like a spring frost attack, bad weather during the flowering or hail in late summer, only affect a single year's harvest, the phylloxera kills the plant itself. Potentially its ravages are catastrophic. It is not for nothing that its cognomen is Vastastrix. Phylloxera arrived in Europe from America, and it was in America that the imagination of the Bordeaux viticulturalist Leo

Laliman found the solution to the problem, astonishingly as early as 1871. This was to graft the noble European varieties of the *vinifera* vine on to American non-*vinifera* rootstocks. Opposition to this radical proposal seemed solid until, despairing of finding an alternative solution, the growers had to face the inevitable. By 1882 97.5 per cent of the Gironde had been over-run by the louse, but it was only gradually, far more gradually in the top states than most people realise, that grafted vines began to be introduced. As late as the 1890s *vignes françaises* were still being planted. Château Latour did not begin to plant grafted vines seriously until 1901 and it took a couple of decades completely to replace the non-grafted old French vines.

Meanwhile Bordeaux had been hit by the third of its plagues. Downy mildew or peronospera arrived in the South of France in 1882, and seems to have spread rapidly west to the Gironde. Like oidium it is a cryptogamic disease, but affecting mainly the leaves. An antidote, copper sulphate solution, was soon discovered, and by 1888 the outbreak was under control.

As important as this succession of natural disasters were the economic consequences. Bordeaux, indeed the whole of France south of Paris, had many more hectares of land under vine in the 1850s than in 1900, even today. In hard-nosed financial terms the arrival of phylloxera could be termed salutary. Uneconomic vineyards were allowed to decay; their owners and their workers forced to seek alternative employment. The human corollary compounded by the Franco-Prussian War and by a recession in wine prices which remained until the mid-1950s, is incalculable. This cloud of misery that hung over the peasant *vigneron* for three successive generations still continues as a folk memory.

It was not just the smallholder who was affected by this lack of prosperity. Though Bordeaux was not in general as badly off as elsewhere in France, owing to the reputation of its wines and the fact that the majority of its reds could be held to mature in bottle, nevertheless it was more dependent than other areas on its export markets. Demand from Germany, a major customer for the cheaper wines, collapsed after the First World War, the British market was moribund before the war and declined afterwards, and sales to pre-Prohibition America were negligible. The world recession of the 1930s, followed by the Second World War, forced even well-known classed growths almost out of business. I have calculated that as much as one-quarter of the 1855 classed growths were virtually dormant in 1945.

All this seems hardly credible today. Rising standards of living, appreciation of wine as part of the art of good living, a widening of the consumer base and the emergence of the Far East as well as the United States as customers for the top growths have transformed the scene. At the bottom level of the pyramid a minor change in the ratio of the price of Bordeaux Rouge to Côtes du Rhône or Beaujolais, coupled with a plentiful harvest, can still cause problems. At the top end, a handful of proprietors seem to think they can get away with anything. Prices of First Growths and the best of the rest have been rising at an alarming rate alongside a succession of good but also highly plentiful vintages. It is now apparent that even the 'second best' Bordeaux are wines which most of us can only afford to drink rarely. And with prices of new wines almost as expensive as those now reaching maturity it hardly seems worthwhile to bother to buy them *en primeur*.

The price increases, however, have not been uniform across the board. Matched and even exceeded by subsequent performances on the auction/broking circuit, the gap between the properties at the top of the hierarchy and those at the bottom has widened and continued to widen further over the last 20 years. In 1981 Château Margaux opened at 125 Francs per bottle ex-cellars, the *bourgeois* growth Château Caronne Sainte-Gemme was offered at 14 Francs ; a ratio of one to nine. In 2000 Château Margaux cost the equivalent of 787.10 Francs while the price of Caronne Sainte-Gemme had risen to 40; a ratio of one to 20. Meanwhile brokers in London in the summer of 2001 were offering Château Margaux 1982 at £3650 a dozen. You could have obtained Caronne Saint-Gemme 1982 for less than £120; the ratio is now one to 30 (see Appendix Six).

These high prices, coupled with high death duties, have had their effect on the ownership of the top Bordeaux estates. Today only millionaires, insurance companies and multinationals can afford to buy classed growths. Fewer and fewer are owned and managed by individuals. Even fewer proprietors and their families live 'over the shop'. Most of the grander châteaux are used for ceremonial purposes only.

One benefit, though, has been that the whole of Bordeaux, from First Growths down to the regional co-operative, is making better wine. Scientific progress in vineyard and *chai*, the arrival of the trained *oenologue* (wine chemist), the financial means and the moral duty to make a rigorous selection of the *grand vin* have led to fewer poor vintages, more wine and a higher quality product. Some of those proprietors who produce the best wines may believe they can get away with murder. At least those who market them are fully aware of the competition from elsewhere.

THE WINES
RED WINES

There are two quite separate winemaking districts as far as the top red wines are concerned. West of the Garonne and Gironde, on a low-lying, gravel-covered peninsula, stretch the vineyards of the Graves and the Médoc, on either side of Bordeaux. The best Médoc wines come from six communes, each of which has its own particular character, described in detail in the following pages. The parishes of Margaux, Saint-Julien, Pauillac and Saint-Estèphe bordering the Gironde contain the majority of the most respected growths. In the Graves, the best wines are from Léognan, and closer to Bordeaux in Pessac and Talence in the conglomerate *appellation* of Pessac-Léognan.

Fifty kilometres away, north of the Dordogne river, lies a quite separate region covering the wines of Saint-Émilion and Pomerol which, in their own but different ways, are the equal of the Médoc and the Graves. Saint-Émilion itself is divided into an easterly section, known as the Côtes Saint-Émilion, on the slopes around the town of Saint-Émilion itself, and the Graves Saint-Émilion, four kilometres to the west on the border of Pomerol. Pomerol, north of the port of Libourne, only started to receive due recognition for the quality of its wines in the 1960s.

Médoc and Graves wines, based on Cabernet Sauvignon, are full, firm and tannic when young, even austere. Saint-Émilion wines may be equally abundant and rich, but lack the muscle and backbone of their westerly neighbours. Based on the Merlot, their wines are fruitcakey rather than blackcurranty in flavour, more aromatic in character. They mature faster and do not last as long. Pomerol wines, also Merlot based and from a clay rather than limestone soil, are fuller than those of Saint-Émilion. They can be rich and fat, heavier than Graves or Margaux (the two lightest regions of the Left Bank) and as long-lasting.

Adjacent to Saint-Émilion and Pomerol are the Libournais satellites. Lalande-de Pomerol, Fronsac and Canon-Fronsac produce lesser wines in the style of Pomerol. Surrounding Saint-Émilion are Montagne-Saint-Émilion, Saint-Georges-Saint-Émilion, Lussac-Saint-Émilion and Puisseguin-Saint-Émilion. Some of these wines are as good as ordinary Saint-Émilions themselves, but in the main those with a simple Saint-Émilion AC are more consistently reliable.

North-west of the Libournais, on the right bank of the Gironde estuary, lie the districts of Bourg and Blaye. Opposite the Graves, on the right bank of the river Garonne, is the Premières Côtes de Bordeaux. East of Saint-Émilion in the direction of Bergerac are the Côtes de Castillon and the Côtes de Francs. All these are now thriving areas, providing *petit château* wines of great interest at prices hardly far removed from that of Bordeaux Supérieur. These are wines that can be bought and drunk regularly, rather than being preserved for special occasions. Land in these areas is cheap compared with the astronomical prices now being paid for the Médoc classed growths. Able young winemakers, professionally trained, have moved in, or taken over from their less expert parents.

The remainder of the Gironde department, with the exception of the coastal area, is authorised for the production of Bordeaux and Bordeaux Supérieur. Entre-Deux-Mers is a white wine *appellation* only and any red wines produced there will be simply Bordeaux or Bordeaux Supérieur.

WHITE WINES

The Graves, stretching south from the suburbs of Bordeaux down the west side of the Garonne as far as Langon, produces the best dry white wines of Bordeaux as well as red wines; though to many people's surprise more red wine is made than white. Its northern half, from the city itself down to La Brède, is called Pessac-Léognan. For many years the dry white wines continued to be made by rustic, old-fashioned methods. Quite deservedly, they fell out of fashion. Recently there has been a dramatic improvement in the wine, and a revival of the region's fortunes.

Within the Graves, towards the southern end, is the enclave of Sauternes and Barsac, origin of the world's richest and most sumptuous sweet white wines. Lesser, medium-sweet white wines are made nearby at Cérons, and on the opposite bank of the Garonne at Sainte-Croix-du-Mont, Loupiac and Cadillac in the southern sector of the Premières Côtes de Bordeaux.

The peninsula between the Dordogne and Garonne rivers is known as the Entre Deux-Mers. This generic *appellation*, like that of Graves Supérieures, is used solely for white wines. Yet this is another source of good *petit château* red wine. Within the Entre-Deux-Mers are four more districts: Graves de Vayres, opposite Fronsac and the town of Libourne; Sainte-Foy-Bordeaux, at the extreme east below Montravel in the *département* of Dordogne; Côtes de Bordeaux Sainte-Macaire in the south, taking over where the Premières Côtes de Bordeaux ends; and Haut-Benauge, a sub-division of the Entre-Deux-Mers. In all, in 2002 there were 43 *appellations* within the Gironde.

PRODUCTION AND SURFACE AREA

The largest harvest of *appellation contrôlée* wine in the Bordeaux region took place in 1999. Of a total of 6.806 million hectolitres just over 87 per cent was red wine (including a little rosé). During the 1980s about 20 per cent of the crop was white, but as recently as the late 1960s more white wine than red wine was produced in the area. Most of the wine is sold as Bordeaux or Bordeaux Supérieur. The combined production of the 'quality' areas (the Médoc, Graves, Saint-Émilion, Pomerol, Sauternes and Barsac) was only some 1.8 million hectolitres, 26 per cent of the grand total – and it is arguable how much generic Graves, Saint-Émilion and Médoc is really 'quality' wine. Since the Second World War the total area under vine decreased from nearly 140,000 hectares – the peak was in 1950 – to under 100,000 in the late 1970s and early 1980s. It has since risen again to around 120,000 hectares. But the area producing AC wine has steadily climbed and now stands at 99 per cent of this total (see Appendix Three).

As well as increased surface area clonal selection and better vineyard husbandry have meant that the production of AC wine has more than tripled – the average yearly yield in the five years from 1945 to 1949 was just over 2 million hectolitres. In the five years between 1997 and 2001 it was almost 6.7 million. At the same time there has been a dramatic shift away from white to red wine – from one third of the harvest being Bordeaux rouge to about 87 per cent. In the five years from 1997 to 2001 more AC red wine was produced in the Bordeaux area than in the 20 vintages from 1945 to 1964.

It is the change from white to red, despite the increased fashion for white wine-drinking in the 1980s, which is the most curious and significant of these trends. Prior to the Second World War, oceans of generic Graves, Entre-Deux-Mers and Bordeaux Blanc, produced with various levels of sweetness from dry to almost luscious, provided France and its export markets with most of its staple white wine-drinking at a level of quality that was just above *ordinaire*. The fashion then changed to something a bit lighter and cleaner. The French lost their export market to Germany and Yugoslavia and the French domestic preference moved to Muscadet and Mâcon Blanc. White Bordeaux became almost un-saleable, fetching, at its cheapest level, no more than *vin ordinaire*. The growers began to switch to making red wines, and 1962 remains the only vintage when over 2 million hectolitres of white Bordeaux was harvested in the Gironde.

Production and Surface Area (2002 Harvest)

	SURFACE AREA (HA)		PRODUCTION (HL)	
REGIONAL WINES	**RED & ROSÉ**	**WHITE**	**RED & ROSÉ**	**WHITE**
BORDEAUX	41,775	6728	2,117,095	366,364
BORDEAUX SUPÉRIEUR	11,317	42	503,458	1379
BORDEAUX ROSÉ	2049	-	111,505	-
BORDEAUX CLAIRET	591	-	33,004	-
CRÉMANT DE BORDEAUX	17 (ROSÉ)	122	978 (ROSÉ)	7875
ENTRE-DEUX-MERS INCL HAUT-BENAUGE	-	1682	-	88,591
SAINTE-FOY-DE-BORDEAUX	344	47	14,417	1841
CÔTES				
BLAYE/CÔTES DE BLAYE				
PREMIÈRES CÔTES DE BLAYE	5773	348	267,923	16,937
CÔTES DE CASTILLON	3044	-	131,151	-
CÔTES DE FRANCS	506	9	21,674	246
BOURG	3951	22	181,680	960
GRAVES DE VAYRES	537	95	25,591	5224
PREMIÈRES CÔTES DE BORDEAUX	3496	310	150,188	10,553
MÉDOC/GRAVES				
GRAVES	2568	802	121,601	35,616
GRAVES SUPÉRIEURES	-	336	-	11,352
PESSAC-LÉOGNAN	1263	267	45,429	9721
MÉDOC	5358	-	278,474	-
HAUT-MÉDOC	4591	-	210,567	-
MARGAUX	1403	-	53,342	-
SAINT-JULIEN	909	-	35,978	-
PAUILLAC	1209	-	48,999	-
SAINT-ESTÈPHE	1254	-	52,872	-
LISTRAC	664	-	29,154	-
MOULIS	609	-	27,133	-
LIBOURNAIS				
CANON-FRONSAC	318	-	12,961	-
FRONSAC	843	-	32,571	-
POMEROL	764	-	27,300	-
LALANDE-DE-POMEROL	1131	-	47,251	-
SAINT-ÉMILION	1773	-	82,288	-
SAINT-ÉMILION GRAND CRU	3719	-	134,835	-
LUSSAC-SAINT-ÉMILION	1447	-	65,156	-
MONTAGNE-SAINT-ÉMILION	1594	-	70,270	-
PUISSEGUIN-SAINT-ÉMILION	745	-	33,783	-
SAINT-GEORGES-SAINT-ÉMILION	185	-	7812	-

REGIONAL WINES CONTINUED	SURFACE AREA (HA)		PRODUCTION (HL)	
	RED & ROSÉ	WHITE	RED & ROSÉ	WHITE
SWEET WHITE WINES				
SAUTERNES	-	1669	-	32,375
BARSAC	-	594	-	12,287
CÉRONS	-	63	-	1622
SAINTE-CROIX-DU-MONT	-	393	-	13,030
LOUPIAC	-	404	-	13,167
CADILLAC	-	215	-	5482
SAINT-MACAIRE	-	48	-	1427
TOTAL	105,737	14,080	4,976,441	636,051
	(88.2%)	(11.8%)	(88.7%)	(11.3%)
TOTAL RED AND WHITE WINES	119,817		5,612,492	

Source: CIVB.

THE STYLE OF THE WINE

THE NAME CLARET MEANS any red Bordeaux wine. The word is derived from the French *clairet*, indicating a lightish red wine as opposed to the fuller, more robust wines formerly produced in the hinterland beyond the Bordeaux area, but shipped through the same port.

Bordeaux, unlike many other top red French wines – Burgundy and Hermitage, for example – is made from a mixture of grapes. The red wines are produced from Cabernet Sauvignon, Cabernet Franc and Merlot, with Petit Verdot used in small proportions in many of the top Médoc estates, and Malbec found in some of the lesser properties of Saint-Émilion, Pomerol and the Libournais. Carmenère is also authorised in some *appellations*. Some years, such as 1998, favour the Merlot; others, such as 1996, the Cabernet. In general the wines of the Médoc are largely produced from Cabernet Sauvignon with some Cabernet Franc and Merlot. The Libournais wines are mainly made from the Merlot, with Cabernet Franc as the additional variety, but little Cabernet Sauvignon except in rare cases.

The quality of the final wine depends on the quality of these grapes at harvest time. The purpose of all viticultural procedures is to produce as much fruit as is consistent with quality – for, to a very large extent, quality is inversely proportional to quantity – in as perfect a condition as possible on the date that they are picked.

The character of a wine depends on a number of other things, most importantly the soil and, as vital in viticulture, the subsoil. Soils in the Bordeaux area combine, in one form and proportion or another, the following ingredients: gravel (of various types), sand, clay and limestone. The Médoc and the Graves are based on the first two, on a subsoil of gravel, *alios* (a hard, iron-rich sandstone), marl, clay or sand; Saint-Émilion and Pomerol soils contain more limestone, especially round the town of Saint-Émilion itself, and there is also more clay. Gravel and sand are present to a lesser extent. The subsoil consists of limestone, though in the Graves-Saint-Émilion and Pomerol there is gravel and clay.

Of equal importance to the chemical constituents of the soil is its aspect: the relation of the vineyard to the rays of the sun, and its protection from wind, hail and particularly frost; and the efficiency of its drainage. Unlike many other vineyards in France and Germany, most of the top Bordeaux vineyards lie on flat ground, not on a slope so much as a small mound, rarely more than a few metres above the surrounding countryside. Thus there is no natural protection from the prevailing weather, and severe frost can damage large tracts of vineyard, as it did spectacularly in Saint-Émilion and Pomerol in 1956 and throughout the region in 1977 and 1991. The Médoc is well drained and can withstand heavy rain better in wet years such as 1991, 1992 and 1993 than can the heavier clay or limestone soil of Pomerol and Saint-Émilion. On the contrary, these latter areas can cope with severe drought, as in 1989 and in 1985, better than the Médoc.

The climate in Bordeaux is conditioned by the nearby Atlantic Ocean, and is, in general, less extreme than in Burgundy, and better both in terms of a higher average temperature and less severe bouts of rainfall. Unlike in Burgundy, where the white wine harvest often runs concurrently with that of the red, and occasionally even afterwards, the harvest in Bordeaux always begins with the dry white wines. When the red wine vintage begins a week or so later, the Merlots are picked before the Cabernets, the Libournais area usually beginning a few days before the Médoc and the Graves. The sweet wine harvest commences last of all.

Compared with Burgundy, winemaking in Bordeaux is on a much larger scale: a domaine of 20 (or greatly more) hectares may make only two wines, the *grand vin* and a second wine; while in Burgundy an estate half the size or even smaller may have as many as 10 different wines to offer. In general in Bordeaux the vats are closed rather than open during fermentation, as is often the case in Burgundy, the fruit for red wines is almost invariably entirely destalked and vinification temperatures are high (30°C or so) for the top red wines. The malolactic fermentation seems to follow more easily, permitting an early *égalisage*, or blending of the vats of different grape varieties.

A relatively recent development in the leading estates has been the concept of a second wine. With increased prosperity and perfectionism only the very best vats are today assembled into the *grand vin*. The rejected wine, from younger vines or less successful parts of the vineyard, is bottled under another name. Today just about every top estate produces a second wine. These are mentioned in the château descriptions within each *appellation*.

WHEN TO DRINK THE WINES

Fine red Bordeaux is a much fuller, more tannic wine than red Burgundy. It has a deeper colour, the best wines remaining purple-hued for many years. It needs time to mature. Lesser red Bordeaux, the generic wines and the lightest *petits châteaux*, will be ready for drinking a couple of years or so after the harvest. The *bourgeois* wines will be mature at three to six years, the classed growths after five to ten years. The wines of lighter vintages, of course, will mature sooner than those of fuller years.

While there is a much smaller proportion of top dry whites than there is in Burgundy these too need time (a minimum of five years), though most of Bordeaux's dry white wine harvest is bottled early, having not been vinified or matured in oak, and is intended for early drinking. A good Sauternes has the capacity for long ageing. The best need to be kept for a minimum of a decade.

BORDEAUX VINTAGES

This is a brief summary of the most recent years. For further details see Part Two.

2003

A very hot, very dry year, indeed; and an unprecedently early harvest. Deeply coloured red wines with huge tannins, high alcohol levels and low acidity: uneven but some very fine results. The dry whites are heavy and lack zip. The Sauternes are very successful. It was a very small harvest.

2002

In contrast to the previous seven years, 2002 was a small crop, the result of a poor flowering. The summer continued largely inclement, and it was only the arrival of a splendid Indian summer from September onwards which rescued the vintage from disaster. Those who picked early – Saint-Émilion, Pomerol, the Graves, Margaux – made good wines; better, but not by much, than the 2001s. Those who picked last of all – Saint-Julien, Pauillac and Saint-Estèphe – made much better wines, close to the quality of 2000. These are full-bodied, firm, classic, nicely austere at present, promising wines of elegance which will last well. The Sauternes are very good, if not as outstanding as the 2001s. The dry whites are very good. Prices, in view of the general world economies, continued to fall, the First Growths coming out at half the levels of the 2000s.

2001

Once again a very large crop, though four per cent down on 2000 and 1999. The winter was wet, the spring was fine, July was dreary but August was warm, though not as hot as in 2000. The first three weeks of September were cool, but dry. There was then a thunderstorm, just before the red wine harvest commenced, after which it began to warm up. Crucially, despite the storm the rainfall in August and September and through until the end of the harvest was less than normal. Though by no means the quality of 2000, this is a good vintage for red wines, both consistent geographically across the Bordeaux area, and, as important, down the hierarchy from *cru classé* to *petit château*. They will mature in the medium term. The dry white wines are better balanced than in 2000. It was a great year for sweet wine. Red wine prices fell on the record 2000 levels, but not by much. And not enough.

2000

A very large crop. Overall almost exactly the same size as 1999. For once – the first since 1990 with the exception of 1997, which was flawed for other reasons – there was no excessive rain in September. Indeed, almost the reverse, for there was some hydric stress in the Libournais. This more than made up for a rainy, humid first half of the year. The result is a highly successful vintage, clearly the best since 1990, at its most successful in the Médoc. The wines have substance, tannin, concentration and richness. It is a Cabernet Sauvignon year. The warm, dry weather also ensured ripe, balanced wines all the way down the hierarchy. After 10 years of mediocre quality, a fine year for *petits châteaux*. The wines will need time, and keep well. Sadly, after the red grapes had been collected the weather broke. There is only a very small quantity of good sweet wine.

Prices were very high indeed, especially for the top, most fashionable wines.

1999

A huge crop, even larger than 1997, and currently the record, with over 6.8 million hectolitres produced. Overall it was wetter than normal, less sunny than normal, but strangely, significantly warmer than normal. This meant that when the rains arrived in September, which they did yet again, the fruit was ripe. The wines are only of medium weight but they are fresh, ripe and plump. They don't have much concentration, but they do have charm. They will evolve soon. Moreover, apart from vineyards round the town of Saint-Émilion which suffered hail damage just before the vintage was due to start, 1999 is geographically consistent. Very good Sauternes too.

1998

A very large crop, and an uneven one. After torrid weather in August the first two weeks of September were unsettled. There was then a 10-day period of fine weather during which most of the Libournais, as well as the dry white wines, enjoyed an easy harvest. Rain then set in again just as the Médoc-Graves harvest was getting into its stride. The result is the best Libournais vintage since 1990, very good dry white wines, very good Sauternes but only intermittently very good red wines in the Médoc and Graves. The wines were expensive.

1997

One of the largest crops in recent years, with nearly 6.7 million hectolitres produced, a record at the time. It was a very early harvest, but the most extended one in recent memory. After a very early bud-break the flowering commenced in mid-May, but the fruit-setting was prolonged by adverse weather, and this was reflected in the state of ripeness at vintage time. A variable result, therefore, for both red and dry whites, with the top properties proportionately more successful than the lesser estates. Some very good wines. They have less body but more charm than the 1994s. A very fine Sauternes vintage.

Continuing high prices made this a vintage of very questionable value.

1996

A large harvest: only just below the then record 1995. After fine weather during the flowering the summer was cool and wet, and the harvest was saved by a largely dry, sunny but cool September. Rain at the end of the month affected the Libournais. A fine October enabled the later-developing Cabernets in the Médoc to mature to an excellent ripe and healthy condition. The results therefore are variable: largely disappointing in Pomerol and Saint-Émilion, average in the Graves and southern Médoc, but very fine – up to 1990 levels – in Pauillac, Saint-Estèphe and Saint-Julien: where the wines will keep well. A fine vintage for Sauternes. An average vintage for dry wines. Prices were unprecedentedly high.

1995

For the first time the total crop exceeded 6.5 million hectolitres. The summer was largely dry, but, for the fifth year in succession, rain in September dashed hopes of a really spectacular quality harvest. Overall the results are more even than in 1996: good to very good in the Libournais, especially in Pomerol, good in the Graves for both red and dry white, good to very good in the Médoc, particularly in Saint-Julien, Pauillac and Saint-Estèphe. A quite good vintage in Sauternes. The red wines will evolve in the medium to long term, well in advance of the best 1996s. Prices were high.

1994

A splendid, hot, dry summer led everyone to hope for a high quality vintage. Sadly it was not to be. It began raining on 9th September and hardly ceased until the end of the month. Modern methods, however, can ensure at least acceptable wine, provided, as in 1994, there is no rot. The results are heterogeneous. Acidity levels are low; some of the tannins are not really properly ripe. But the wines, if lacking real character, are at least clean. They were largely ready by 2003. The dry whites

are adequate, the Sauternes disappointing. Overall, the yield was large.

1993

Another large vintage, and another where summer expectations were dashed by a rainy September. Indeed, there was even more rain than in 1994, though less than in 1992. At first the wines were lean and skinny. A year on they had taken up a bit more new oak from the cask than young Bordeaux usually does, and were pleasantly juicy if one-dimensional. By 2003, however, a lot of the fruit had dried out. An unexciting vintage, though with a little more substance than the 1992s. Again the dry whites were adequate. Again not a vintage for Sauternes. The wines are as good as ever they will be and should be drunk soon.

1992

This year saw the rainiest September of the 1990s: a record 279 mm. A large but poor vintage of hollow, watery wines which are now getting old. So are the dry wines, which were better. No Sauternes of note either.

1991

Following April frosts, a small vintage. The summer was fine, raising hopes of a small-but-beautiful vintage like 1961. But there was rain in the second half of September right through the harvest, which was late. Many Saint-Émilion and Pomerol estates did not produce a *grand vin*. The best wines – more interesting than those produced in 1992 and 1993 – come from those estates in the Médoc nearest to the Gironde and least affected by the frost. These are now fully ready, and worth investigating. The remainder are dull and now old. Some reasonable dry whites, but now past their best. No Sauternes of consequence.

1990

Very large, early and very fine quality harvest – for reds, dry whites and Sauternes. It was a hot summer, but the wines were not as stressed as in 1989, and the more mature tannins as a result are one of the reasons this vintage generally has the edge on 1989. The reds are big, rich and classy, and will be slow to mature, but will last well. Though not as expensive as the 1989s at the outset, prices are now the highest of recent years apart from the 1982s. Fine Sauternes.

1989

A very large, early vintage and a successful one, though a little uneven, and for the most part eclipsed by 1990. A hot dry summer produced fruit at the time of the vintage which was physiologically ripe (the sugar/acidity ratio) but was not completely phenolically ripe (i.e. the quality of the tannins). As a result, though the Saint-Émilions and Pomerols are fine, as are most Graves, some Médoc wines are a bit hard and astringent. Acidity levels are marginally lower than in the 1990 vintage too. A fine red wine vintage,nevertheless, which is only now fully ready. The dry whites, though rich, lacked a bit of zip and have aged fast. Very fine Sauternes. Prices at the outset were high.

1988

A medium-sized harvest. After a very rainy first half of the year the Cabernets struggled to achieve full maturity, and there was some rain at the end of September and in October. Medium to medium-full red wines that were rather austere at the outset. This higher than normal acidity has preserved the fruit and finesse, and at 15 years old the best wines are now mature and show a lot of interest, though the lesser wines are proportionately more boring. These best wines will keep well. Very good dry white wines. Fine Sauternes. Unjustly ignored at present, the best reds are now excellent value.

1987

A medium-sized vintage, spoiled by rain. In their prime the reds provided light, pleasant 'lunchtime' wines. Most are now far too old. Not of note in dry white or Sauternes either.

1986

A huge crop: in terms of yield per hectare the largest ever. There was a thunderstorm towards the end of September, just as the red wine harvest was due to start. This posed problems in the Graves and in the Libournais, where the rain was at its heaviest. Northern Médoc escaped unscathed. Concentrated, long-lasting wines in Saint-Julien and Pauillac, as good, if different, as 1982. This is where the 1986 harvest is at its best. These are à point. Good quality elsewhere in the Médoc, though there is inconsistency and now some age. In general the Graves and the Libournais wines are somewhat diluted and not as good as those of 1985. Fine elegant quality, too, in the dry white wines though these should now be drunk. Fine Sauternes.

1985

In general the wines evolved in the medium term and are now well into their prime. A very big crop, and an exceptionally dry end to the ripening season. In contrast to 1986, the Merlots were more successful than the Cabernets. Very good quality in Saint-Émilion and Pomerol. Also very good in the Graves and Margaux, though in Saint-Julien and Pauillac the 1996 vintage is very much better. This is not a heavyweight year but the wines have balance and elegance. Very good, dry white wines, fuller and richer than those of 1986 but now needing drinking up. Ripe Sauternes, though without nearly as much botrytis character as those of the 1986 vintage. Opening prices of this vintage were high.

Earlier Vintages

Red Wines

1983 is very good in the southern Médoc and the Graves, but disappointing elsewhere. 1982 is superb, but many of the Saint-Émilion and Pomerol wines lack grip. 1981 has held up surprisingly well. The best years prior to 1981 are: 1978, 1975, 1970, 1966, 1964 (Libournais only), 1961 and 1959.

Sauternes

After the magnificent trio of 1990, 1989, 1988, and then the 1986, the good years are 1983, 1976, 1975, 1971, 1967, 1962 and 1959.

Grape Varieties

THE GRAPE VARIETY – or mix of grape varieties – is the single most important contributor to both the flavour and the character of a wine. The soil is important, as is the expertise and techniques of vine-growing (*viticulture*) and winemaking (*vinification*). The weather is paramount in determining the quality of the vintage. But the grape variety contributes most to the style of the wine. These are the main quality varieties planted in Bordeaux.

Red Varieties

Cabernet Sauvignon

Though not the most widely planted grape in the Gironde, Cabernet Sauvignon is accepted as the classic claret grape. It is a vigorous but small producer, which develops late in the season – thus an advantage against spring frosts – and ripens late – a disadvantage if winter sets in too early. It flourishes on most types of soil, consistently showing its style and quality, as evidenced by the wide adoption of this grape outside the Bordeaux area, as a *cépage améliorateur* in the Midi, and in Australia and California. It is less susceptible to *coulure* (failure of the flower to set into fruit) or to *pourriture grise* (grey rot) than Merlot, but more so to powdery mildew. The grape cluster is cylindrical-conical, made up of small round berries, very black in colour. The variety is cane-pruned.

This is the grape that gives claret its particular blackcurrant taste. It provides the firmness, the tannin and the backbone. It gives the colour and the acidity, from whence comes the longevity, the depth, the finesse and the complexity of top Bordeaux wine.

Cabernet Franc

This vine is the 'poor country cousin' of Cabernet Sauvignon, and shares many of its characteristics, though the wine made from it is less positive and less distinctive. Though losing ground in the Médoc, it is widely preferred to Cabernet Sauvignon in Saint-Émilion and Pomerol (where it is called Bouchet), where it thrives better on the more limestone and clay-based soils and ripens earlier. Wine made from it is softer, more subtle, more aromatic than from Cabernet Sauvignon. It is for this reason, as well as its shorter growing cycle, that Cabernet Franc is the grape used further north for Chinon and Bourgueil in the Touraine. The bunch is looser, the grapes still small, but larger than Cabernet Sauvignon, and the resultant wine is more fragrant but less coloured, less full and less tannic. The variety is cane-pruned.

Merlot

The Merlot – or Merlot Noir to be pedantic – is the leading grape of the Dordogne side of the Bordeaux region and the most widely planted across the area as a whole. It is a vigorous, productive vine, which buds early – thus rendering it liable to spring frost damage – and ripens earlier than both the Cabernets. It is susceptible to *coulure*, downy mildew and botrytis (rot) which can cause considerable damage if there is rain at the time of harvest. It is less adaptable to different soils. The grape cluster is cylindrical, but looser than the Cabernets, and the berries are round, less thick-skinned, but larger and less intensely coloured. A Merlot wine is generally a degree or two higher in alcohol than the Cabernets, less acidic, less tannic and less muscular. It is softer, fatter and more aromatic in character, and it matures faster. The variety is cane-pruned.

Malbec

This is the principal grape of Cahors in South-West France, where it is called the Auxerrois, and is also grown in the Loire, where it is known as the Cot. In Bordeaux it is also authorized but it is little grown in the top properties, particularly in the Médoc, though it can be found in small proportions in the top estates of Saint-Émilion and Pomerol where it is known as the Pressac. The berries are large and the cluster loose. Malbec is prone to *coulure*, downy mildew and rot. The quantity of wine which results is large, compared to other Bordeaux varieties. Malbec is quite rich in tannin and colour, but with less intensity of aroma and with much less finesse. In Bordeaux the wine is only medium in body, though in Cahors the grape makes wine that is rather more beefy. The variety is cane-pruned.

PETIT VERDOT

This variety is of minor importance. Petit Verdot is a sort of super-concentrated Cabernet Sauvignon, which has all but disappeared except in some of the top Médoc estates (such as Château Pichon-Longueville-Lalande). It is difficult to grow, prone to disease and ripens last of all, often not completely successfully. Some growers swear by it, saying it brings finesse, acidity, alcoholic concentration and backbone. Others, like Monsieur Charmolüe at Château Montrose or Robert Dousson, late of Château de Pez, who carried out tests to discern the development of blends with or without wine from this grape, have decided it is not for them. As the late Peter Sichel of Château Palmer once ruefully pointed out, in the good vintages when everything ripens successfully, Petit Verdot is superfluous; in the poor years, when you need it, it does not ripen at all. Nevertheless, a mixture of grape varieties, each budding, flowering and ripening at a different time, acts as a kind of insurance against sudden attacks of frost, hail and other climatic hazards. It is rarely found outside the Médoc. The variety is cane-pruned.

CARMENÈRE

Carmenère is of even more minor importance than Petit Verdot. It was widely grown in the nineteenth century in the Médoc, before Merlot was in vogue here, but it was found to be susceptible to odium as well as to *coulure*. I know of only a handful of properties that still retain it today. The Carmenère gives a low yield of well-coloured, concentrated, rich, high-quality wine. It is rarely found outside the Médoc though it is a success in Chile. It is cane-pruned.

WHITE VARIETIES

SAUVIGNON BLANC

The Sauvignon Blanc, to differentiate it from other Sauvignons, is a vigorous variety which matures early, forming a compact, conical cluster of small round berries. According to leading ampelographers it is subject to *coulure*, but in my experience the size of the crop in Bordeaux does not seem to vary nearly as much as a result of poor flowering as does the Merlot, for example, and in the Loire crops suffer more as a result of frost, so no doubt more *coulure*-resistant strains have been developed. Oidium is more of a problem. It is also prone to botrytis, though not so much as Sémillon.

The Sauvignon grape produces a wine with a very individual flavour: steely, grassy, high in acidity, very flinty and aromatic. Words like gooseberry, blackcurrant leaf, even cat's pee are employed. As such the dry, stainless steel-aged, early-bottled Sauvignon is a wine now widely seen, though the Bordeaux version is somewhat fuller and less racy than that of the Touraine and Central Loire, and in Bordeaux many seemingly pure Sauvignons have a little Sémillon in the blend to round the wine off. Strange as it may seem for a white wine, this variety produces a wine with a certain amount of tannin, and as a result of this, fermentation and *élevage* (initial maturing) of pure Sauvignon in new oak is a procedure which needs to be handled with care. Combined with Sémillon in various proportions and aged in oak, Sauvignon produces the great white Graves. The Sauvignon is cane-pruned.

SÉMILLON

Sémillon is the most widely planted white grape variety in the Gironde and the base for all Bordeaux's great sweet wines, though its value for dry wine production is only just beginning to be appreciated once again. Sémillon is a vigorous, productive variety. It is spur-pruned; and pruned very hard in Sauternes to reduce the crop to a minimum. It produces a cylindrical bunch of round berries, noticeably larger than the Sauvignon Blanc. These tend to develop a pinkish shade at full maturity, turning to browny-purple with over-ripeness. It is a hardy variety but susceptible to rot, both *pourriture grise* and *pourriture noble*, as it has a thin skin.

Poorly vinified, dry Sémillon wines can lack freshness and bouquet, character, breed and acidity. The result is heavy, neutral and dull. Correctly vinified, as increasingly this variety is today by enterprising hands throughout the region, the results are totally different. The wines, though dry, are rich, fat and aromatic, with almost tropical, nutty fruit flavours and quite sufficient acidity. Good dry Sémillon is very classy, a far more interesting wine in my view than dry Sauvignon, and it has been under-rated in Bordeaux. It has taken the Australians, where for many years the variety has been grown in the Hunter Valley, to show the Bordeaux wine producers the potential for this grape.

MUSCADELLE

The Muscadelle has nothing in common, despite the similarity of spelling, with either the Muscadet of the Pays Nantais or the various varieties of Muscat. It is moderately vigorous but very productive, develops late, and produces a large, loose, conical cluster of sizeable round berries. It is susceptible to *coulure*, powdery mildew, *pourriture grise* and botrytis (*pourriture noble*) while being less prone to downy mildew. You will rarely come across the Muscadelle except in small proportions in the sweet white wine areas of Bordeaux. Even here it is frowned upon at the highest level, for it is considered to produce coarse wine, very perfumed, but lacking finesse. The variety is cane-pruned.

SAUVIGNON GRIS

For long considered a sub-variety of Sauvignon Blanc, it is now being realised that Sauvignon Gris is quite a distinct variety. The colour of the berry is much more apricot when mature and the flavour of the wine has a pronounced sweet-sour taste. A little goes a long way. But this little can add complexity to a blend.

The first three varieties above must make up 70 per cent of Bordeaux Blanc, 85 per cent of Bordeaux Blanc Supérieur and 100 per cent of all higher *appellations* such as Pessac-Léognan. For Bordeaux Blanc Ugni Blanc, Colombard and Merlot Blanc are also permitted, as are Ondenc and Mauzac. In practice these last two are no longer planted. For Bordeaux Blanc Supérieur the only accessory variety allowed is Merlot Blanc.

A YEAR IN THE VINEYARD

GOOD WINE IS PRODUCED from ripe, healthy, concentrated grapes. The object of viticulture is to produce fruit in as optimum a condition as possible at the time of the harvest, to produce as much as is compatible with the highest quality – but not too much, for quality is inversely proportional to quantity – and to mitigate the vagaries of the climate and the depredations of pests and diseases. Ninety per cent of a wine's eventual quality is produced in the vineyard.

SOIL AND ASPECT

The first element to consider is the soil. The vine will thrive on a wide range of geological structures and compositions, but some varieties do better on some soils than on others. Cabernet Sauvignon, for instance, while it has a tolerance for limestone and marl (limestone-clay mixtures), provided the soils are not too cool, performs to its most elegant capacity on well-drained gravel. Hence its preponderance in the Médoc and the Graves areas of Bordeaux. Here the soil is undulating but predominantly flat, the gravel mounds or *croupes*, rising gently above the interlying marshy land, drained by *jalles* or ditches. The subsoil of the Médoc and the Graves is an iron-rich sandstone rock, known as *alios*, and this itself lies over marl or limestone.

In the Libournais, the Saint-Émilion and Pomerol regions, the countryside is more hilly and the soil structure more varied. Round the town of Saint-Émilion itself the layer of surface soil is thin and marly, and lies on limestone rock; to the south the escarpment is steep, with more alluvial sandy soil on the valley floor. North and west of the town the limestone gives way to ancient weathered sand. Adjacent to the Pomerol border there are three ridges of gravel over sand and clay, the 'Graves Saint-Émilion'. This soil continues into Pomerol itself, where the soil is more clayey and is variously mixed with gravel and sand, on an iron-rich clay base known as *machefer*. Here the Merlot is the predominant grape, and the Cabernet Franc is preferred to the Cabernet Sauvignon.

The soil of Sauternes and Barsac is essentially limestone, mixed with gravels of various sizes, clay and siliceous elements. In Barsac the soil is richer in iron and deeper red in colour. It is lighter further away from the River Garonne in the communes of Fargues, Bommes and Sauternes itself. There is less clay and more sand than further north or across in the Libournais, and consequently white grape varieties perform better than red. Moreover the mesoclimate encourages the formation of noble rot.

In general the soil needs to be poor in nitrogenous matter. Above all it must be well-drained, particularly where the rainfall is higher.

Aspect is important, too, though the main quality wine areas of the Gironde are by no means hilly. Orientation of a vineyard towards the east or south-east is ideal. The first rays of the morning will warm up the ground, drive away the mist and ensure that maximum advantage is taken of the sun's heat.

MEASURES TO RESTORE THE LIFE OF THE SOIL

What is of equal importance is the life of the soil. Since the arrival of the tractor in the 1950s, together with the agro-chemical salesman willing to sell you anything from artificial fertilisers to insecticides and herbicides, the soil has been compacted between the rows, seriously so where there is a significant amount of clay in the composition, and the micro-flora and micro-fauna populations have been decimated. Analyses of viticultural soils have shown less life than in the Sahara desert. Herbicides have eliminated ploughing. Over-fertilisation has resulted in superficial root systems and an excess of potassium in the vineyard.

All this has reduced the vine's capacity to yield wine which unmistakably speaks of its origins. Wines have become neutral and standardised. Thankfully, the more enlightened growers have realised the danger. There has been a return to ploughing. Tractors with inflatable tyres, lightening the pressure on the soil, are being developed. Approaches to treatments have changed. Over-fertilisation has been stopped. We spray against mildew and oidium when an attack is due, not by rote. We counteract the pests by using predators, or interrupting their reproduction by means of little pheremone-containing containers (they are about the size of a small matchbox: the French call this sexual confusion). Everyone is becoming more ecological. Some estates are now run on bio-dynamic lines. This approach combines working according to the position of the moon and planets, with a quasi-homeopathic attitude to treatments.

WEATHER

In general the weather in Bordeaux is mild. Severe winter frosts are rare, as is severe summer heat, as the region's climatic extremes are cushioned by the effects of the Atlantic Ocean. It is both warmer in winter and more stable in summer than in Burgundy. Spring frost is less of a danger, as is hail. On the other hand, particularly in the Médoc and in the Graves where the drainage of the soil is super-efficient, drought can be a problem. In the driest years, the more water-retentive subsoils of the Libournais can keep the vine roots refreshed. But the reverse is also, of course, true.

Temperature, Precipitation and Sunshine

The average annual temperature in the Gironde is 12.5°C. It is rare, even in the deepest winter, for the thermometer to fall below minus 8°C. The last time temperatures fell low enough to kill the vines (−25°C) was in 1956, almost 50 years ago, though there was damage in 1985 in the Pomerol-Saint-Émilion border and isolated spots elsewhere. Equally summer temperatures rarely exceed 40°C. Years where there is a marked occurrence of leaves shrivelling and bunches being scorched are few and far between.

The average level of precipitation is around 955 mm a year, with 155 mm of this falling in the important months of August and September. In this respect the 1980s were drier than average, the 1990s wetter. The average amount of sun hours in the Gironde is 2060, with 1370 of this taking place between 1st April and 30th September. September is less sunny than May and only marginally more so than April. But it is usually drier in terms of the number of days of rain.

Rootstocks

Having chosen his site and prepared his land, if necessary by manuring and adjusting the chemical composition and certainly by ensuring that it is free of disease, the grower's next task is the choice of grape variety and clone or strain of that particular variety, and the selection of a rootstock to go with it. The former choice will, of course, be determined by the local *appellation contrôlée* laws. A permanent result of the phylloxera epidemic is that all vine varieties in France (except in one or two isolated pockets, particularly where the soil is predominantly sandy, for the aphid cannot thrive here) are today grafted on to American, phylloxera-resistant rootstocks.

A wide number of different rootstocks are on offer. The choice will be determined by, among other things, the resistance to chlorose (a disease where the leaves turn yellow and cease photo-synthesising). This in itself is dependent on the amount of active limestone and quality of extractable iron in the soil. The acidity of the soil, which will depend on its geological structure, the vigour of the vine, the adaptability between rootstock and *vinifera* variety, the drainage and the presence or deficiency of other minerals and trace elements, are also of importance. In general rootstock 3309 is popular, especially for Cabernet Sauvignon, 504 has declined from 50 per cent in its heyday in the 1970s to 20 per cent now (the vines are too vigorous and then race to maturity in September too fast); 101.14 is of interest as it makes Cabernet ripen a few days early; 420-A is the traditional Bordelais rootstock for Merlot, Cabernet Franc and Sémillon where the soils are less limestone-active; Fercal, which has replaced 41B, is for soils with more limestone; 161.49 is less resistant but of higher quality. The vine's vigour is reduced, but its maturity not retarded.

While it is fair to say that over the last 30 years developments in viniculture have outstripped those in viticulture, there has nevertheless been considerable research into the production of disease-resistant clones which can produce quantity without sacrificing quality, and the propagation of suitable rootstocks which are compatible, both with the clone and with the chemical and physical composition of the soil. Grafting normally takes place in the horticulturalist's greenhouse, not in the vineyard.

Vineyard Spacing

With considerations of mechanical tending of the vineyard, and, indeed, increasingly today, mechanical harvesting of the vintage, determining the space between the vines and the space between the rows, the vineyard is then planted. The amount of vines per given area varies greatly. Half as many vines can exploit the same amount of soil and produce as much wine as double the quantity. But in the better areas the density tends to be greater, such as in the Haut-Médoc. There the density is usually 10,000 vines per hectare, i.e. 1 metre x 1 metre. Elsewhere it can be as low as 3000 per hectare. The closer together, the more the vine is encouraged to develop a deeply penetrating root system. It will then extract the maximum complexity from soil and subsoil and be more resistant to temporary drought and floods.

PRUNING AND TRAINING

Over the next few years, as the vine slowly develops into a mature plant, it is carefully pruned and trained into a particular shape. There are, in essence, two basic pruning methods: long – or cane-pruning, and short – or spur-pruning; and two basic shapes. Cane-pruning lends itself to the ultimate formation of a hedge shape, the canes – one or two with about six buds on each – being tied to a series of horizontal wires stretched along the row of the vines. This is known as the Guyot system. Spur-pruning or the Gobelet method produces a free-standing bush shape. There are six or so short spurs, each with two or so buds. A compromise between the two, giving short spurs on horizontal branches which can be trained on wires, is the Cordon de Royat system. In the Bordeaux region the vine is almost invariably pruned to the Guyot system: in the Médoc a double Guyot is more common, in the Libournais, a single Guyot. Only in Sauternes, with Sémillon, is short-pruning adopted. Here the system is known as the Cot.

The vine flowers, and therefore will ultimately fruit, on the previous year's wood. The object of pruning is to select the best of this wood, to cut it back, eliminating all the rest, and to reduce the eventual crop to a potential of six to a dozen bunches of grapes per vine.

Viticulturalists have come to realise the significance of the leaf canopy as the 'engine' enabling the photosynthesis – the conversion of the carbon dioxide and water in the air into carbohydrates – to take place. Hence the leaf canopy has been raised and enlarged. The bigger the leaf system, the more efficient the photosynthesis. Moreover, the more one ploughs, eschewing herbicides, or indeed the more one plants the vineyard with special forms of grass, both of which force the root system deeper, the more one concentrates the must and promotes the conversion of character and individuality of the particular *terroir* into the eventual wine.

THE YEARLY CYCLE

The yearly cycle of the vine begins after the harvest. With the onset of the cold weather of winter the vine has become dormant, the sap has descended into the roots of the vine and the process of tidying up, cutting away the dead wood and preparing the vineyard for next year's harvest can begin. The roots will be earthed up to protect them against frost, manure and other fertilizers can be ploughed in, and stakes and wires can be renewed if necessary. This is the time to rip up old vines which are dead or beyond their useful life and to begin to prepare sections of the vineyard for replanting in the spring after a year or two's rest. Throughout the winter pruning takes place. It must be finished before the warmer weather returns again in the spring and the sap of the vine begins to rise anew.

SPRING

In March the vine begins to wake up from its winter dormancy. A further ploughing is undertaken, this time to weed and aerate the soil and to uncover the base of the vine. The buds begin to swell, and will eventually burst in late April to reveal a small cluster of tiny leaves. This is when the danger of frost in the vineyard is at its greatest. The vine itself can withstand winter temperatures as low as −20°C. The embryonic leaf-cluster is susceptible to just the slightest descent below zero.

COMBATTING PESTS AND DISEASES

There are three general ways in which the vine can be affected by outside influences – if we exclude the hand of man: by the weather, by insect depredation and by the outbreak of cryptogamic diseases such as oidium, mildew or botrytis (rot).

From the emergence of the leaves the vineyard is regularly sprayed: with sulphur against oidium, with copper sulphate (Bordeaux mixture) against mildew, and with other chemicals against red spider, moths and other insects. Later on the fruit may be sprayed to harden its skin and prevent the emergence of rot. Increasingly nowadays, Bordeaux's vineyards – and indeed the winemaking which follows – are run on organic and ecological principles.

'SEXUAL CONFUSION'

The most dangerous of the insects which can affect the fruit are the two moths Eudemis and Cochilis. In their caterpillar form (grape worm or *ver de la grappe*) a bad outbreak can cause havoc. During the 1990s more and more vineyards used the sexual confusion method to combat this danger. A small brown plastic container, roughly the size of a matchbox, is hung from every fifth vine and every fifth row. These exude pheromones which attract the male moth at the time when fecundation is due. The object is that the female moth is ignored and the next generation of Eudimis and Cochilis moths do not get born.

Other ways of combating insect depredation in as nature-friendly as possible involve the use of predators: the deliberate release of other insects or other predators which feed on those dangerous to the vine.

FLOWERING

In June the vine flowers, and this is one of the most critical times in the yearly cycle. Warm, dry weather is required to endure that the fruit setting, which follows the flowering, takes place swiftly and successfully. If the weather is cold and humid the flowers may not set into fruit (*coulure*) or the fruit may remain as small, green, bullet-hard berries and not develop (*millerandage*). Moreover, should the flowering be prolonged the result will be bunches of uneven ripeness at the time of the harvest.

Throughout the summer spraying continues, particularly if the weather is inclement; the vineyard is ploughed to aerate the soil and eliminate weeds; the shoots are trained on to the wires, so that they do not break off in the wind, and the vegetation is trimmed back so that the vine can concentrate its resources into producing fruit. This vegetation trimming is known in France as *rognage*. Some growers will tell you that it is wisest not to start this until the vine has finished flowering. In this way the production of second generation fruit, the *verjus*, which takes up vinous energy required elsewhere, will be discouraged.

STEPS TO CONSTRAIN THE HARVEST

With modern methods, disease-resistant clones, efficient spraying and so on almost every harvest risks being too prolific. A grower producing significantly less than the authorised limit in Bordeaux Supérieur (72hl/ha) will consider it, justly, as a financial disaster. But a top classed growth will not be living up to its duty to make the finest wine possible if it produces much above 50 hl/ha. In some vintages such as 1990 you can get away with it. Nature has decreed both quantity and quality. But in most, diminishing returns set in fast. Ten years ago, most top growers considered that jettisoning 50 per cent of the crop into the second wine was enough. They could still aim for 55-plus hl/ha in the vineyard. Today, led by the Libournais, interestingly – for in general the Merlot is more productive than the Cabernet Sauvignon – proprietors are reducing the crop to 45 hl/ha or even 35.

The earlier in the season you do this the better. Pruning is crucial. Thereafter *débourbage* (rubbing out the excess buds) before flowering, and eliminating double flowers from one bud just after flowering are equally important.

GREEN-HARVESTING

Much is made of green-harvesting – the *vendange verte*. Often today this is carried out twice: at the end of July before *véraison* and at the beginning of September. Many growers are sceptical. The crop is reduced but the wine is not more concentrated is the view of this lobby. The grapes just expand to fill the space available so you get *more* diluted wine, say some. The main utility of green harvesting, in my view, is to eliminate bunches which are less advanced, so ensuring an even ripening of the crop at harvest. In the view of Jean-Claude Berrouet, winemaker for the J-P Moueix wines (Châteaux Pétrus, Trotanoy and others) where they have been green-harvesting since 1973 one mustn't rely on the process. There are other procedures such as planting grass in the vineyard and changing from a double Guyot pruning system to a single Guyot as well as de-budding and, of course, pruning more severely in the first place, which should have priority.

YIELDS

It seems to have become a truism that 'Bordeaux over-crops'. Just as 'Burgundy over-chaptalises', or 'most wines are emasculated (or stripped) by over-fining and over-filtering,' these assertions have somehow been accepted as inescapable reality.

Does Bordeaux over-crop? At the lower level the answer is yes. But at the price supermarkets and others are prepared to pay it is not surprising. If the trade would persuade – or would be prepared to make the effort to convince the consumer to pay a little more for Bordeaux Rouge – we would soon see a difference in quality. There are said to be 300 branded Bordeaux wines. Few of these excite me. The consumer is better off sticking to very good vintages such as 2000 and buying up to a good Médoc *cru bourgeois*.

Does Bordeaux over-crop at the higher levels? A few years ago I would have said yes. In the mid-1990s even top growths like Château Latour were admitting to producing in excess of 55 hl/ha (and then assuring you that less than 50 per cent went into the *grand vin*). Things have changed. In 2002, admittedly a small vintage, Latour produced 32 hl/ha, Lafite 40 and Margaux 39.

It is a question of vintage and *encépagement*. It is clear that in some years like 2000 you can produce lots of wine and the wine can still be concentrated. Fifty hectolitres per hectare in 2000 will produce more substantial wine than 40 in 2002. Equally the Cabernet Sauvignon can be picked at a larger yield before dilution affects the crop than Merlot. For top Merlot 40 really is the limit – even in a vintage like 2000.

HIGH SUMMER

This colour change (*véraison*) takes place in August. Grapes as green as Granny Smith apples turn red and eventually black, or else soften into a greeny gold. From then it is seven weeks or so to the harvest (100 to 110 days after the flowering). Spraying must soon cease. The work in the vineyard is now over. All one can do is to pray for fine weather. Whatever might have happened earlier in the season the result will only have affected the quantity to be harvested. The weather from the *véraison* onwards is critical for the quality. What is required during these weeks is an abundance of sunshine, to ripen the fruit, an absence of excessive rain, which would only expand the grapes and dilute the wine, and an absence of humidity, which would encourage rot.

LEAF STRIPPING

Stripping off the leaves surrounding the fruit (*effeuillage*) is, though time-consuming, now widespread. The object is to allow freer air-circulation, thus eliminating the humidity which will cause the fruit to rot. Normally this is done in two stages, the side not exposed to the sun first, the other side later. This second *effeuillage*, though it risks the bunches being scorched by hot sun – which is why the procedure is undertaken early in September rather than in August – will help promote a deeper, more stable colour in the wine.

THE HARVEST

In about the third week of September the red wine harvest starts – picking of the white wine varieties might have started two weeks earlier or so. Preliminary tests (*prélèvements*) to establish the sugar and acidity content of the grapes will have taken place to endure that ripeness and concentration are at their optimum at the time of collection. The weather forecast is anxiously studied. A preliminary passage through the vineyard to eliminate the diseased or otherwise inadequate bunches or part of bunches, and therefore make the life of the picker easier, is often undertaken. And when the time is ripe the vintage begins. The result of a year's hard labour is soon evident.

MACHINE-HARVESTING

Today the majority of the Gironde vineyards, like the majority elsewhere, is harvested by machine. Only in the top estates of Bordeaux, or where the land is inappropriate – and of course in places which produce individual bunch-selected sweet wines such as Sauternes – does harvesting continue by hand. Fifteen years ago there were even mechanical harvesters in the vineyards of the classed growths of the Haut-Médoc. The proprietors then decided that there were two main disadvantages. The life of the vine was reduced and sorting out the best fruit from the bruised, rotten and unripe was much more difficult with machine-gathered grapes.

The advantage of mechanical harvesting is its convenience and its speed. One machine can do the work of 25 manual pickers and removes the stems from the bunches of grapes too. It can work 24 hours a day, if desired; and the new, second generation of machines, if correctly driven, does little harm to the vines. Mechanical harvesting can mean a later start to the harvest and a quicker conclusion, concentrating collection at the optimum state of the fruit's ripeness. This is the future at the level of everyday wine. Where perfectionism is the *sine qua non*, there is no substitute for hand-harvesting and the selection that goes with it.

BIODYNAMISM

As elsewhere, though not as yet in Bordeaux in any of the really top estates – the grandest is probably Château Pavie-Macquin in Saint-Émilion – vineyards are increasingly being run on biodynamic lines.

The principles behind biodynamism go even further than the bringing-life-back-to-the-soil ideas which drive ecological and biological systems, and were laid down by Rudolf Steiner. Steiner asserted that not merely the moon but the sun and the planets affect cycles on earth and their positions must be taken into consideration when activity in the vineyard is planned. There are auspicious days and inauspicious days. There are earth, air, fire and water days, which influence, respectively, the growth of roots, flowers, fruit and leaves. Treatments are natural and homeopathic, using very dilute and especially prepared distillations of, for instance, yarrow, camomile, nettle, oak, dandelion and valerian. Conventional agrochemicals and fertilisers, except sulphur and Bordeaux mixture (*bouillie bordelaise*), are absolutely forbidden as are weedkillers, pesticides and artificial yeasts, even clonal selection.

Does it work? The sceptical will say that biodynamists are usually very capable viticulturalists and winemakers in the first place, so would produce quality wine anyway. Others will merely be impressed with the number of top class domaines outside if not so far inside Bordeaux who now run their vineyards on this basis.

HOW WINE IS MADE

Wine is produced by fermenting the juice of freshly gathered grapes. It sounds simple. But in fact it is extremely complicated. Yeasts excrete enzymes which cause the sugar in the grape juice (or must) to turn into alcohol. The chemical process is very complicated. The reaction is exo-thermic, producing heat, so needs to be controlled. Carbon dioxide is also produced and there is an additional 3 per cent of other chemical by-products.

It is this 3 per cent of 'other' which is crucial. Alcohol has no flavour, nor does water – and the grape juice and therefore the wine is 85 per cent or so water. It is in the 3 per cent of other that you will find the colour and the flavour. The reason the fermentation process needs to be controlled is not only that at too high temperatures the process will 'stick' and the danger of acedifaction (the production of vinegar) will arise but that the flavour elements are very volatile. They need to be prevented from evaporating into the air. They must be preserved in the wine. Moreover the extraction and fixing of colour, tannins and flavour from the skins and pulp of the grape varies not only with the temperature, pressure and availability of oxygen and with the length of maceration of these skins with the fermenting must but with the increasing amount of alcohol as the must turns itself into wine.

There is a further problem. The effect of oxygen on wine will cause further chemical reactions to take place. Wine (alcohol) is only a halfway house between sugar and vinegar. While a little oxygenation is necessary for maturation, at all times in the vinification process, and during the time the wine is retained in bulk thereafter, evolving and undergoing the various treatments which take place before it is put in bottle, the winemaker must endure that the wine is uncontaminated by too much oxygen. He must not unduly expose the wine to air. Control, and the equipment with which to control, as well as a thorough knowledge of the process, is crucial.

What must not be forgotten, however, is that winemaking is not a creative process. The quality of the eventual wine, as I have said, is produced in the vineyard. The role of the winemaker is more one of preventive medicine: to allow the natural transformation of, we hope, fine quality fruit into wine, ensuring that nothing goes wrong on the way.

Making Red Wine

Picking at the Right Time

The choice of when to pick is perhaps the most crucial decision the winemaker has to make each year. In Bordeaux there are four parallel problems to be resolved. First the different grape varieties mature at different times. The Merlot is usually the first, followed in order by Cabernet Franc, Cabernet Sauvignon and, finally Petit Verdot, if planted. Normally, moreover, the Saint-Émilion and Pomerol areas are ripe before the Médoc and Graves. In the Médoc-Graves, in addition, the First Growths' vineyards are more forward than the *crus classés* which themselves are in advance of the lesser growths – one of the explanations of this hierarchy. Thus Latour will be four days or so in advance of Gruaud-Larose which itself will be four days ahead of Caronne Sainte-Gemme. One can see this very easily in April just by looking at the amount of vegetation in each vineyard. But it applies equally in September. To resolve the order in which he will pick his parcels the winemaker will constantly be analysing the ripeness of his fruit in the days before the harvest takes place.

Second, the bunches on a single vine, even the berries within a single bunch, may not be at an even stage of ripeness. Here crop-thinning (see above) and *triage* (see below) are essential. Third, less of a problem in Bordeaux than in hotter climates, but a problem in a dry, hot vintage such as 1989, the various elements which constitute 'ripeness' may not all evolve at the same pace, or arrive at optimum maturity at the same time. One measure of ripeness is the sugar-acidity ratio. As the sugar accumulates the acidity declines, turning from malic to tartaric. The rate this occurs is obviously very dependent on the climatic conditions. However the colour, aroma synthesis and tannin evolution, call it the phenolic maturity, progresses at a different rate, less dependent on whether it is hot or cold, wet or dry. Since 1991 Jean-Claude Berrouet, winemaker for J-P Moueix, has tested for phenolic maturity as well as the potential alcohol content. In vintages such as 1989, the sugar-acidity ratio suggested a harvest on a particular day, but the tannins were not sufficiently ripe.

Bordeaux's main problem is usually the reverse. In cooler vintages the advance to optimum maturity on all fronts is slow, and the longer one leaves the fruit to hung on the vine the more one risks the arrival of autumn rain, and hence dilution. What to do about this is discussed below.

There is, though, one major advantage in being at the cooler edge of winemaking. The long gestation, now regularly starting picking 110 days after flowering (it used to be 100) results, if weather conditions are benign, in more complex wines, all of whose components of maturity are ripe and in equilibrium. It is for this reason that Bordeaux, as far as the competition is concerned, is supreme. Much more rarely, elsewhere, do we find wines of such delicacy and complexity and finesse. Nor do the wines from elsewhere age as well, becoming mellow, dignified and even more subtle as they age.

It is for this reason that the internationalisation of Bordeaux wine is not just an error but a tragedy. There is a tendency in some quarters in Bordeaux to play up the market, to make wines which are to the palate of certain key critics such as the American, Robert Parker. These wines can be very well made. But if they stray too far in flavour from the character, personality and ageing ability of true Bordeaux, they will be betraying their origins. Bordeaux is a magic *terroir*. The wines must represent it.

I discuss various procedures which I consider deleterious to quality Bordeaux winemaking in the pages which follow. The first applies here, and that is a tendency to pick fruit, especially Merlot, at a state verging on over-ripeness (*sur-maturité*). As Jean-Claude Berrouet points out, Merlot is a septentrional variety. If it is too ripe it gets blowsy: it loses its class and freshness. As Allan Sichel says, waiting beyond the optimum maturity date often causes a loss of fruit and structure, as well as restricting ageing capacity. Why then do people do it? In order to get more alcohol and less acid. It would seem that their object is not the potential to age with dignity, for which a decent level of acidity is a prerequisite, but instant gratification: a fruit bomb with no hard edges.

TRIAGE

Triage is the sorting through of the fruit to eliminate all that is substandard. Inevitably it takes place in the vineyard if the grapes are hand-collected. Bad bunches will not be picked. In others rotten, unripe or bruised fruit will be cut out.

Most top proprietors now have a *tapis de triage* back in the winery. On arrival the plastic trays of fruit are poured onto a gently moving conveyor belt which leads to the destemmer/crusher. Each bunch is picked over a second time. Anything substandard, as well as leaves etc., is removed. A relatively new development is to *trier* a second time after the fruit has been de-stemmed. It is now in the form of individual grapes. One can be even more painstaking about only letting the perfect fruit progress through into the fermentation vat.

STEPS TO CONCENTRATE AND 'IMPROVE' THE MUST

If the weather turns nasty on you just as you are about to start picking you have little alternative, assuming that you cannot delay the harvest, than to curse and go out and collect the fruit in haste, before it turns soggy. You will then expect to get a must which is unbalanced: too much liquid in ratio to the solid matter, which will give you watery wine.

SAIGNER: One thing you can do is to *saigner* (bleed), i.e. to let 5, 10 or 15 per cent of the free-run juice, a pale pink, run off. The result will be a better ratio of liquid to solid. The downside will be that you will lose some of the aromatic matter. More than plain water will have been sidelined. You can only guess beforehand what is the optimum percentage of juice to *saigner*. A wine which has been over-concentrated in this way will be four-square, even austere and rustic.

CONCENTRATING MACHINES: A more recent approach is to concentrate by machine. These work on two principles: reverse osmosis or evaporation by vacuum distillation. The first method uses pressure to reverse the traditional tendency, where two liquids are separated by a semi-permeable membrane, for the more concentrated side to leak into the less concentrated side. By tangential, or cross-flow filtration, the excess water is squeezed out of the must. In the second method the concentrators heat the must under a vacuum to temperatures of between 25°C and 30°C. At this level the excess water is 'boiled' off. These machines are, however, more expensive than the reverse osmosis ones, though easier to maintain. A danger is that if the must is exposed to these temperatures for too long, the flavours and aromas will be affected. The wine will taste cooked.

Current EU regulations permit must concentration by one of these methods but limit the use to a 2 per cent increase in alcohol and/or a 20 per cent decrease in volume. If the concentratation method is used you cannot then chaptalise (see below).

How widespread is this practice in Bordeaux today? Many of the top estates now have one or other of these machines, some, such as Léoville-Las-Cases, have done for over a decade. Moreover, there are a number of contract companies who offer this service. It is a growing phenomenon. And as one of a battery of techniques, controls and procedures available to the winemaker I see nothing wrong with it, provided it is not abused. The proof, as always, is in the tasting of the finished wine. The danger, of course, is that a concentrating machine will concentrate the bad as well as the good. Must concentration is never going to make a silk purse out of a sow's ear.

CHAPTALISATION: Named after Napoleon's Minister of Interior, Jean-Antoine Chaptal, chaptalisation is the addition of cane or beet sugar to a must in order to raise the alcohol level of the resultant wine. EU regulations restrict the amount of chaptalisation allowable in Bordeaux to the equivalent of 2° of alcohol.

Is chaptalisation widespread? The answer, sadly, is yes. Almost all wines are chaptalised to a degree almost every year. Two per cent is excessive. The wine tastes artificial. But 1° or 1.5° which is more normal in the top estates is, say supporters, beneficial. The process 'knits the wine together'. Moreover, if the sugar is added towards the end of the fermentation process it will extend it, keeping high temperatures going on longer, which will aid the extraction of flavours from the pulp.

ACIDIFICATION: Acidification is rare in Bordeaux, but as it is more common elsewhere it must be mentioned. EU regulations do not permit the wine to be chaptalised and acidified at the same time.

VINIFICATION

On arrival at the *cuverie* or vinification centre, the grape bunches are dumped into a V-shaped trough and churned by means of a revolving vice through a *fouloir-égrappoir*. This pulls off the stalks and gently breaks the skin of the grape berry. The last property to vinify with the stems was probably Château Pétrus, and, unusually, some stems were added to the fermentation of the 1973 and 1974. Bordeaux grapes have enough tannin in the skins already.

The produce of different grapes, different sections of the vineyard, and, particularly, vines of different age, will be vinified separately. For red wines, there are two concurrent aspects to vinification: the fermentation itself – when the grape sugar is converted to alcohol – and maceration, the length of time the must is in contact with the skins, extracting tannin, colour and extract from the pulp. The temperature is important, for the reasons explained below.

FERMENTATION TECHNIQUES

COLD SOAKING: Cold soaking before fermentation is a technique Bordeaux has borrowed from Burgundy. In an aqueous solution colour and flavour are extracted more easily than tannin, so this is a procedure which is of great assistance to those seeking wines for early drinking. In most vintages, where one is not immediately heating up the fermenting must, this must will naturally 'cold soak' for three or four days while the temperature steadily mounts.

PIGEAGE: Treading down or *pigeage* is another Burgundian technique, the Bordelais having traditionally preferred pumping over (*remontage*). It results in fatter, heavier tannins and good colour, and these need to be stabilised. One way of doing this is to raise the post-fermentation temperature up to 38°C. All this results in a particular sort of wine: big and brawny. Not to everyone's taste.

Today the finer red wines are usually vinified at about 30°C, allowing the temperature to rise no higher than 33°C before cooling. Some estates, Léoville-Las-Cases for instance, prefer to ferment between 26°C and 28°C. The need for control of temperature, as well as the ability fully to clean and sterilize the fermenting receptacle, has led to a movement away from the more traditional oak to the use of stainless-steel fermentation vats, which are easily cooled by running cold water down the outside, by a heat exchanger inside or by means of an enveloping, thermostatically controlled 'cummerbund'.

It is important not to be too inflexible about fermentation and maceration temperatures. Anyone who pronounces that he always ferments at 31°C is a donkey, says the wine consultant Michel

Rolland. It shows he understand nothing about fermentation. As Jean-Bernard Delmas of Château Haut-Brion says: it is evident that the temperature we choose is a function of the vintage, the variety, the state of the berry, even the nature of the fermenting vat; whether the fruit is perfectly ripe or not, whether the skins are thick, whether the pips are large or small or more or less numerous. The length of the maceration also comes into it. High temperatures will in general raise the 'fat' of the wine to the detriment of the freshness of the aromas. And vice versa. The essence of Berrouet's approach, as he puts it, is not only to translate the character of the soil into the wine but also the personality of the vintage. In hot years like 1990, in order to protect the acidities you would ferment a little cooler, say at 28°C. Conversely in colder vintages such as 1994, to 'improve' the tannins, making them fatter and warmer, one would raise the temperature to 33°C, but not too long lest the tannins be too hard.

There are essentially two schools of thought about both temperatures and extraction times. The one, led by Michel Rolland, favours higher temperatures and longer extractions. Their results receive good press in America. The second school, what I term the classicist, is led by Jean-Claude Berrouet, winemaker of J-P Moueix and Jean-Bernard Delmas of Château Haut-Brion. They prefer lower temperatures and shorter fermentations and believe their results will produce better-balanced wines, more true to their origins and capable of longer ageing. However, as all will point out, the length of the maceration does not necessarily parallel the best extraction. High temperatures, says Michel Rolland, are not an obligation. It was a method which used to be employed at a period when the *matière première* was not at optimum and the desire was to extract as much as possible. It is still practicable but it is not essential.

ENZYMES: Enzymes are today widely used to help the extraction to take place. They are added to the fermenting must and are very efficient, especially when the must is the produce of young vines. But, says Jean-Claude Berrouet, I am not at all sure they are really necessary for great wines and old vines. Enzymes do, undeniably, help settle the lees. Clarification used to be much more difficult, says Michel Rolland. But he only uses enzymes to clarify the *vin de presse*.

BÂTONNAGE: *Bâtonnage*, or the stirring up of the fine lees, is a process that has been adapted from the production of white wines (see page 38). The principle is the same: that the wine can enrich itself by feeding off these lees, and periodically stirring them facilitates this effect. Today, with cleaner lees resulting from pneumatic presses, there is less danger that the lees will be tainted and impart unwholesome flavours.

ÉCOULAGE, VIN DE PRESSE: When fermentation is over, the juice is then run off into a clean, empty vat or barrel. This juice is the *vin de goutte*. The residue of skins is then pressed. The *vin de presse* that results is important. It will be firmer, more tannic and more acidic than the free-run juice, and a proportion will normally be blended back in varying quantities, or added periodically when the wine is later racked. No addition of *vin de presse* may result in a rather weak, ephemeral, wine, however enjoyable and supple it may be in its youth.

Usually the *vin de presse* is added when the blend is made (see below). Some châteaux – Léoville-Poyferré and Chasse-Spleen, for example – prefer to add it later, bit by bit, when topping up or when the wine is racked. This school of thought feels that a more exact assessment of how much *vin de presse* is required can be made after the wine has had a few months to develop. From the buyer's point of view it makes the precise judgement of the wine in cask in the April following the vintage, which is when it is put on the market, somewhat impossible.

ASSEMBLAGE, THE BLEND: The production of the blend, the creation of what in Bordeaux is called the *grand vin*, and the rejection of what is left to the second wine or a lesser *cuvée* is the winemaker's moment of truth. This is the point where the consultant oenologists earn their keep.

Most wines are blended surprisingly early. We outsiders may consider the job rather easier to do competently later, after the wine has been racked for the first time, after it has thrown off the harshness of its infancy, and there are some in Bordeaux who will agree. But most winemakers consider that the earlier it is done the better the constituent parts will meld with each other. Moreover it is believed that to do it before the wine goes into oak also facilitates the judgement.

I have been privileged to be a fly on the wall on a number of occasions. First, all the vats are assessed and marked as either A (certainly good enough to be in the *grand vin*, B (possible), or C (no). Financial considerations then come into play (in a poor vintage can one really afford to reject two-thirds of the crop?) Style comes into it (does the wine have the château signature? How do you compromise in a Cabernet-based vineyard in a year where the Merlots are all brilliant but the Cabernets weedy?) It may not at all be the case where all the As make an agreeable, balanced, finished wine. But it is on these decisions, taken perhaps in early December following the harvest, that the future reputation of the château will rest.

ÉLEVAGE

Once the fermentation process is complete the must is now wine and it must be looked after with meticulous care until it is ready for bottling, a process that must be done at the right time and with correct attention to detail. I am convinced that as much potentially good wine is ruined by incorrect or simply sloppy cellarwork or *élevage* as by poor vinification before or inferior storage afterwards.

Having made the blend (and we are assuming wine of some pretention here: lesser wines are stored in bulk), the wine is transferred to oak barrels – in which it may well have been lying before the *égalisage* – and allowed to mature and settle out its sediment, or lees. The barrels will need constant topping up, to make up for evaporation, particularly in the first few months, and for this reason they are first stored with the bung-hole upright, loosely covered by a glass stopper or rubber bung. Later, a wooden, more permanent bung will be driven into this hole, and the casks moved over so the bung is on the side.

MALOLACTIC FERMENTATION: After fermentation the first thing is to ensure that the wine is clean, in the sense of free of potential chemical or bacteriological contamination, and that it has completed its malolactic fermentation. This 'second' or malolactic fermentation, which also gives off carbon dioxide, often takes place immediately following the sugar-to-alcohol fermentation, and can be encouraged by warming the must or the surrounding area to between 18°C and 20°C, and the addition of an artificial malolactic bacterium to get the fermentation going. The result is to lower the apparent acidity by a degree or two; so rounding off the wine and softening it up.

MALOLACTIC FERMENTATION IN BARREL: This is now very fashionable in Bordeaux. Its adherents, while pointing out that all red Burgundy undergoes malo in barrel, will, like Michel Rolland, aver that you get more fat, more power, more roundness and a better integration of new wood. Those who are dubious will remind you that in Burgundy the malos take place in the spring, with the temperature of the wine at about 14°C. In Bordeaux the wine goes into the barrel warm. The result gives torrefaction (roasted) flavours. It makes the wines all taste similar, thus counteracting the subtlety of different *terroirs*. This would be what Jean-Claude Berrouet would say. I would personally add: who wants or needs, especially in a young wine 'more fat, more power, more roundness'? Let the wine proceed at its own pace. It has to be said, though, that these wines are well noted by certain American wine journalists.

OAK

One of the questions continually asked of a proprietor or his cellar manager is the proportion of new oak casks he uses each year. As a new one now costs upwards of 500 Euros, the provision of a large proportion of new oak is a major financial undertaking. Nevertheless, the extra muscle and tannin, coupled with the flavour the oak gives to a wine, is an essential ingredient in the taste of a fine red wine. A few of the very top estates invariably put their top wine entirely into new oak. For most producers, a proportion of between a quarter and a half, depending on the quality and style of the vintage, is normal. More would impart too much of a *boisé* (woody) flavour to the wine.

Nevertheless, there has been a trend toward the use of more new wood. On the other hand, together with more new wood has come a reduction in the time the wine spends there. Ageing used to be for a minimum of two years. Today it is frequently as much as six months less before bottling, and the wine may well have been run off into older casks or into vats after only a year to avoid taking up too much taste of the oak. The major French oak forests lie in the centre of the country. Limousin imparts a very marked oak flavour and is not used for fine wine. Tronçais, Nevers and Allier are widely found, the latter being the most delicate and favoured for white wines. The way in which the oak has been allowed to dry and its 'toast' will influence the flavours the wood imparts to the wine as much as its origin.

RACKING

During the first year of a wine's life, it will be racked to separate the wine from its lees, and also to transfer it from new to old oak and vice versa, so that all the wine spends an equal amount of time in wood of different ages. Big, full wines such as Bordeaux throw more sediment than lighter wines such as Burgundy. In Bordeaux the wine will be racked every three months in the first year, every four months thereafter. In principle the less you move or manipulate the wine the better. During the first winter of the second year, the wine is 'fined', traditionally with beaten white of egg for fine wines, to coagulate and deposit further unstable elements. Lesser wines are fined with isinglass, casein (milk powder), bentonite and other natural or proprietary substances.

MICRO-OXYGENATION

The dilemma is as follows: a little oxygenation, such as that which a wine receives while it is in cask, is very beneficial. But a lot is not. Every time you rack a wine, especially if you do it fast and in bulk, you are pumping it from here to there, and all such manipulations are deleterious. Moreover, with today's pneumatic presses giving much cleaner lees, is it really necessary to rack the wine six times between vinification and bottling?

The answer is micro-oxygenation, or *microbullage*. As the term suggests, the process entails a very gentle bubbling through of oxygen, as in a fish tank, over an extended period of time.

BOTTLING

The date of bottling is an important matter which has only received sufficient attention relatively recently. I still do not consider that it is flexible enough to allow for variations between one vintage and the next. A wine matures much quicker in cask than in bottle, and a variation of six or even three months in the date of bottling can hence have a decisive effect on the eventual date of maturity and on the balance of the wine.

A big, concentrated, tannic wine from a Bordeaux vintage such as 1990 or 2000 may need a full two years or even more in cask before it is ready for bottling, but equally a light vintage, particularly one that is feeble in acidity, such as 1997, needs early bottling. Currently, most top Bordeaux châteaux bottle during the spring and early summer of the second year, when the wine is between 18 and 20 months old. Wine which has been kept longer may dry out and become astringent, having lost some of its fruit before it is ready for drinking.

WHEN TO DRINK THE TOP WINES

Once a wine has been bottled, when will it be ready for drinking? And perhaps more important, how long will it be at peak after that? It has for long been the general rule held by the British that a wine such as a good Second or Third Growth Médoc from a fine vintage like 2000 requires ten years from the date of harvest to mature; a First Growth 15 or more; and lesser *cru bourgeois* Médocs, Saint-Émilions and Pomerols from five to ten years. *Petits châteaux* are at their best between three and six years after the harvest. These figures would be less in a softer, less tannic vintage such as 1999 or 1997, and proportionately more in a big, hard, tannic vintage. Thereafter, a well-made, well-stored wine will last for at least twice as long as it has taken to mature. The proportion between the time a wine will live once mature and the time it has taken to reach maturity increases with the quality of the wine and the vintage, so that a top wine from an excellent claret vintage, 1990, ready in 2000, instead of having thereafter a 20-year life at peak, may have as much as 40, or twice the length of time it took to mature, before beginning to go downhill.

Most white Bordeaux is at its peak within a year or so after bottling. Only the very best classed growth Pessac-Léognans are made for keeping more than five years. The best Sauternes, in the best vintages, though delicious at five years old, are even better after a decade's cellaring.

When you prefer to drink your wine is a matter of personal taste. While I personally incline more to the French taste – which to some in England and elsewhere seems a predilection for infanticide – I normally stick to the Bordeaux 10-year rule, and its equivalent elsewhere. Given the choice, however, I would prefer to drink a wine at the beginning of its 'at peak' plateau, rather than at the very end.

How to Make a Garage Wine

The last five years have seen an explosion in the amount of so-called 'garage wines' and special *cuvées*. These are usually produced in very small quantities, made from grapes verging on the over-ripe, strongly macerated and reared in wood. Most come from Saint-Émilion, Pomerol and their satellites. Many come from *terroirs* which would not normally be associated with classed growth wine. They are expensive and only a very few such wines are worth it. Readers searching for classical wines of elegance – as opposed to brute strength and lots of new oak – are advised to be wary.

Here is a list of the best-known. It is by no means exhaustive.

	APPELLATION	OWNER/WINEMAKER/GURU
D'AIGUILHE-QUERRE	CÔTES DE CASTILLON	EMMANUEL QUERRE/ JEAN-MARIE FERRANDEZ
L'ARCHANGE	SAINT-ÉMILION	PASCAL CHATONNET
BELLEVUE-MONDOTTE	SAINT-ÉMILION	GÉRARD PERSE
LA CLÉMENCE	POMEROL	CHISTIAN DAURIAC
LA CONFESSION	SAINT-ÉMILION	JEAN-PHILIPPE JANOUEIX
CLOS L'ÉGLISE	CÔTES DE CASTILLON	GÉRARD PERSE
EXCELLENCE DE BOIS PERTUIS	BORDEAUX	BERNARD MAGREZ
LA FLEUR DU BOUQUET	MOULIS	JEAN-LUC THUNEVIN
LA FLEUR MORANGE	SAINT-ÉMILION	VÉRONIQUE & FRANÇOIS JULIEN
LA FLEUR DE ROSE SAINTE-CROIX	LISTRAC	PHILIPPE PORCHERON/ JEAN-LUC THUNEVIN
GIROLATE	BORDEAUX	JEAN-LOUIS DESPAGNE
GRACIA	SAINT-ÉMILION	MICHEL GRACIA/ LUDOVIC POCHARD
LES GRAVIÈRES	SAINT-ÉMILION	DENIS BARRAUD
HOMMAGE DE MALESAY	CÔTES DE BLAYE	BERNARD MAGREZ
CLOS DU JAUGEYRON	MARGAUX	MICHEL THÉRON
CLOS DE LABRIE	SAINT-ÉMILION	MICHEL PUZIO
CLOS DES LUNELLES	CÔTES DE CASTILLON	GÉRARD PERSE
LUSSEAU	SAINT-ÉMILION	LAURENT LUSSEAU
LYNSOLENCE	SAINT-ÉMILION	DENIS BARRAUD
MAGREZ-FROMBRAUGE	SAINT-ÉMILION	BERNARD MAGREZ
MAROJALLIA	MARGAUX	JEAN-LUC THUNEVIN

PIERRE DE LUNE	SAINT-ÉMILION	TONY BALLU (MAÎTRE DE CHAI OF CHÂTEAU CLOS FOURTET)
LA SÉRÉNITÉ DE POUMEY	PESSAC-LÉOGNAN	BERNARD MAGREZ
SAINT-DOMINIQUE	SAINT-ÉMILION	CLÉMENT FAYAT
SANCTUS	SAINT-ÉMILION	STÉPHANE DERENONCOURT
DE VALANDRAUD	SAINT-ÉMILION	JEAN-LUC THUNEVIN

It all started with Château de Valandraud. In 1990 Jean-Luc Thunevin, a local merchant, found himself with 70 *ares* of old Cabernet Franc vines up on the plateau next to Château Pavie-Macquin. He noticed that the name of the wine appeared in old editions of Cocks et Féret. Having neither money nor premises, he sent his grapes to the co-operative.

The following year, encouraged by Alain Vauthier, co-owner of Château Ausone, and at a bit of a loose end at the time, he decided to make the wine himself. A friend lent him, yes, his garage. It was a cool autumn and having no heating equipment there was naturally a long period of cold soaking before the fermentation got under way. He had no money to buy a pumping-over machine so he had to tread down the cap to break it up.

The next summer, quite by chance, Thunevin met Michel Bettane, the highly respected French wine critic, in a local restaurant. Thunevin was with Vauthier, Bettane with Michel Rolland. Afterwards they went round the corner to taste the wine. Bettane wrote up the wine enthusiastically in the French *La Revue du Vin de France*. Stéphan von Neipperg of Château Canon-La-Gaffelière and Gérard Bécot of Château Beau-Séjour-Bécot also came to visit. Subsequently they developed their own non-*cru classé* super-star wines: La Mondotte and La Gomerie. Robert Parker was later introduced to the wines by Bordeaux merchant, Archie Johnston.

Most of the 'rules', as Jean-Luc Thunevin points out, are universal to the production of fine wine: old vines, a low yield, a long maceration, no fining, no filtering.

What is ironic, though, is that today most so-called garage wines are not made like Valandraud at all. Today we have long macerations but at high temperatures, lots of extraction, *bâtonnage*, micro-oxygenation, lots of new oak and malolactic fermentation in barrel. All this results in wines with a very deep colour, powerfully rich but roasted in flavour, impressively tannic but with these tannins very soft and fat, high in alcohol but with little acidity. It works best with the Merlot grape because this has less tannin and less acidity. Do they age well? No, not in my experience. Are they really Bordeaux in style? No, not at all. Bordeaux is a wine which has, above all, elegance. Elegance, or finesse, or breed – call it what you will – is the last thing you will find in most of these garage wines.

MAKING DRY WHITE WINE

VINIFICATION

The grapes for dry white wine normally reach maturity a few days before the red varieties, and the precise date for top quality is even more crucial in order that the exact balance between sugar and acidity can be obtained.

With the trend in the 1960s towards drier, crisper wines came an unfortunate move in Bordeaux and elsewhere towards picking a few days in advance of the optimum moment in order to make wines with a good refreshing acidity. This was sadly carried a bit too far and the results, too often, were wines with a rasping, malic acidity and a consequent lack of ripe fruit. The wines were too green. As the grape ripens the malic acidity changes into tartaric acidity. Now, with the help of mechanical harvesting, the grower can wait longer without the risk of prolonging the collection of the crop beyond the desired period. It is now appreciated that once the correct maturity in the grapes has been reached, provided the climatic conditions are favourable, the acidity, now essentially tartaric rather than malic, will not continue to diminish and may even concentrate further to give a wine with both ripeness and balance.

White wines are vinified without their skins, and the first procedure is to press them as soon as possible after arrival from the vineyard, normally in some form of horizontal, cylindrical apparatus. The juice is then run off and allowed to settle (a process called *débourbage*) for 24 hours so that the solid matter falls to the bottom before being vinified. Except in the top estates where fermentation takes place in oak barrels, vinification takes place in stainless steel vat or tank, often in anaerobic conditions and for white wines must proceed at a reduced temperature in order to prolong the process as long as possible, thus preventing loss of the volatile elements which impart flavour and aroma, and maximizing the intensity of the fruit. The common temperature for the controlled fermentation of most white wines is between 18°C and 20°C. For a long time it has been accepted that the lower the temperature of fermentation the more the volatile, flavour-enhancing chemicals in the fruit are preserved in the resulting wine. It is not the lower temperature *per se*, however, but the prolonging of the fermentation which is important. The longer the fermentation, the more complex the flavour. Today 'artificial' yeasts are widely employed, for they make the fermentation easier to control and produce wines of greater fruit definition and finesse.

Today in order to maintain a crisper acidity in the finished wine the second, malolactic fermentation is discouraged for most fine white wines in Bordeaux. Whether the wine is matured in cask or in tank, bottling takes place much earlier than for reds, often as early as the following spring. The object is to preserve the freshness and fruit and to minimize oxidation. Only the best, oak-vinified and oak-aged examples will develop in bottle.

Macération préfermentaire or skin contact before fermentation is a white-wine technique new to France. The principle which lies behind this idea of allowing white grape juice to remain in contact with the grape skins for a few hours before pressing is that it has been realized that most of the flavour-producing elements in the pulp of the grape lie near or within the skin. It is a process which needs to be handled with great care, for bruised or rotten berries will taint the whole wine. The results though are most rewarding: wines of greater complexity and depth of flavour, and it is a procedure which is spreading. Even more widespread is the idea of leaving the new white wine on its fine lees (*sur lie*) for as long as possible before the first racking. The wine feeds off this sediment, mainly dead yeast cells, and becomes richer and fuller in flavour. In some of the top estates in the Graves the wine might be kept on its lees until midsummer. An additional technique is to stir up these lees periodically, once a week or fortnight. This process is known as *bâtonnage*.

The bane of white wine has been the over-use of sulphur. Sulphur is a necessary ingredient in the preservation of wine. It protects it against oxidation and bacterial infection, but too heavy a hand with it will kill the wine. The sulphur will bind in with the wine, destroying the freshness, the nuances of the fruit and producing a sickly, heavy 'wet-wool' flavour. This used to be particularly prevalent in Bordeaux. Thankfully, after years of maltreating their white wines, the Bordeaux winemakers are beginning to realize – as their counterparts in the Loire and southern Burgundy did years ago – that, well-handled, dry and sweet white wine does not require as much sulphur to protect it as they thought. More careful winemaking, in anaerobic conditions and with a cleaner must, enables the winemaker to reduce his recourse to sulphur dioxide during the fermentation. The retention of the carbon dioxide produced by the fermentation also protects it. Healthy wine, correctly balanced, requires less sulphur thereafter. Modern equipment and sensitive *élevage* reduces its necessity even more. If the Loire and Burgundian winemakers can do it, why can't the Bordelais? The penny is beginning to drop. Fewer and fewer dry white Graves – though there are still far too many depressing examples – taste of nothing but sulphur dioxide.

ÉLEVAGE

The use of oak, new or newish, is another relatively recent development in white-wine production. Prior to the 1960s, wood – old barrels for the most part – was the most common receptacle for *élevage* and transport. The fashion then swung to the tank, enamelled or stainless steel, and the concrete vat. All the old, diseased, bug-infected barrels were burned, and probably a good thing too. Only the very top wine estates persisted with using oak for fermenting and aging their dry white wines.

But oak, new oak, adds weight, complexity of flavour, depth and class. Happily today, not only across the board of the nine white Pessac-Léognan classed growths but more widely elsewhere a proportion of new oak is *de rigueur*. And if you are using wood, the wine must be fermented in barrel. This is essential. The wood flavours derived thereby are more delicate and complex and exist in greater harmony with the rest of the flavour ingredients of the wine. Oak should be *de rigueur* for any white wine aspiring to quality status.

BOTTLING

White wines are generally bottled much earlier than reds: the vast majority, those not matured in oak, within six months of vinification. Most of the rest of the fine dry white wines are bottled the following autumn. Only the richest sweet wines such as those of Sauternes are given more than twelve months in cask.

WHEN TO DRINK THE WINE

When should you drink white wine? The lesser wines, like 'small' white wines all over the world, are essentially made one year for drinking the next. Within 12 months after bottling, i.e. 18 months after the harvest, they will begin to lose their youthful fruity freshness. This applies to most *petits* Graves and Entre-Deux-Mers.

Grander white wines – most of the *cru classé* Pessac-Léognans – those that have been fermented and matured in oak, can, and must, be kept. Often they enter a rather dumb phase after bottling, and for two or three years they will appear rather clumsy, particularly if they have been bottled with a little too much sulphur, as is still, sadly, often the case. Domaine de Chevalier is often a culprit. Lesser vintages will be at their best between three and eight years after the harvest. The best white wines, i.e. Châteaux Haut-Brion Blanc, La Mission-Haut-Brion, and Domaine de Chevalier, need longer before they are fully ready, and will keep for a further decade or more after that.

MAKING SWEET WHITE WINE

The world's greatest sweet wines are rare in number, highly prized, expensive to produce and infrequent in occurrence. That they appear at all is a tribute to the dedication and patience of the few wine growers who make a speciality of them, and is a consequence of a particular mesoclimate acting on a small number of specific grape varieties, the result of an Indian summer of misty mornings and warm balmy afternoons continuing long after the rest of the *vignerons* have cleared their vines and are busy in the cellars nurturing the birth of their new vintage.

The great sweet wines are not merely sweet. If this were all, the addition of sugar syrup to a finished dry wine would be all that was necessary. Indeed, this is how cheap sweet wines are made. But these the consumer will soon find bland and cloying.

NOBLE ROT

The finest dessert wines are the result of a particular phenomenon, the attack on the ripe, late-harvested fruit by a fungus known as *Botrytis cinerea*. It produces what is known in France as *pourriture noble* and in Germany and Austria as *Edelfaüle*, both of which can be translated as 'noble rot'. Leave any fruit on the tree after it has ripened and eventually it will rot. This rot (*pourriture grise*), however, will not be 'noble'; the fruit will be ruined and the taste disgusting. In certain parts of the vineyard areas of the world, though, in the right climatic conditions, the noble rot will occur. In Bordeaux the result is the great Sauternes and Barsacs, and occasionally similar wines in Cérons, Loupiac and Sainte-Croix-du-Mont.

What is required is a particular mesoclimate. The grapes are left on the vine after the normal harvesting time for the production of dry white wine. Noble rot needs a combination of warmth and humidity. It must continue fine and sunny long into the autumn but not be too dry. Most high-quality vineyard areas, however, are near the extremes of viable grape production; in poor years the fruit does not ripen sufficiently and the later the harvest the greater the risk that summer will have finished and autumn rains and chilly winter weather will have set in. This further complicates matters for the quality sweet wine producer. He needs not just a fine late summer but a prolonged and clement autumn. These ideal conditions occur rarely. Two years out of three, or even three out of four, are good years for red and dry white wines. For great sweet wines, the regularity is hardly one in three or even one in four. Sauternes has been exceptionally fortunate recently to have had three fine years – 1988, 1989 and 1990 – in a row. But since then nature has been less bountiful. More recently, only 1997 and 2001 come up to this level.

When noble rot attacks the ripe grapes, they will first darken in colour. From golden, they will turn a burnished, almost purple brown. Then the surface will appear to get cloudy, the skin will begin to wither and get mouldy as the spores of the fungus multiply, feeding on the sugar in the berry. Finally, the grape will become shrivelled like a raisin and completely decomposed. The noble rot does not have a very prepossessing appearance!

Unfortunately, it does not strike with equal regularity and precision over the whole vineyard or even over the whole of a single bunch of grapes. This necessitates picking over the vineyard a number of times in order to select each bunch, part bunch or even, at Château d'Yquem, each individual berry, separately. A prolonged harvest is therefore implicit in the production of noble rot wines. In some cases it will continue not just into November but even into December.

The effect of this noble rot attack is to alter the chemical and physical composition of the grape and therefore, obviously, the taste of the wine. First, the water content of the berries is considerably reduced. Second, the acidities are changed and, third, the quantity of higher sugars such as glycerine is increased. The net effect is to create a very small quantity of juice with a sugar content equivalent to a potential alcohol level which in a top Sauternes will be well above 20 degrees. This produces a wine with an actual alcohol level of 14 or 15 degrees or so and 4 or 5 degrees (higher in the most successful vintages) of unfermented sugar. This is the sweetness. The other effect of the noble rot is to combine this sweetness with a luscious, spicy, complex, individual flavour and a high, naturally ripe acidity level.

There is much talk in Sauternes today of a new technique called *cryo-extraction*. Briefly the principle is that juice heavy in sugars and glycerine freezes at a lower temperature than water. Thus, should you have a situation where it rains during the harvest, if you are able to freeze the grapes to a certain temperature and then press them carefully you should be able to capture the concentrated Sauternes-producing juice without it being diluted by the rain, for this rain will be frozen into ice-crystals and will not flow off during the pressing: a sort of artificial *Eiswein*, in fact.

Sauternes by its very nature is an aberration. Contrary to all normal agricultural principles and practices the grower deliberately allows his harvest to rot. He has to wait until he is at the mercy of the elements as autumn evolves into winter: 'We are playing poker with God', as one grower once told me. All too often a state of rot which was incipiently noble can be turned by bad weather into ignoble. This is where cryo-extraction comes in. It is not intended to replace normal harvesting and pressing in fine weather, but it will enable a grower to rescue his harvest if the climatic conditions turn against him. Of course, the majority of sweet and semi-sweet wines are made from grapes which, while ripe, are not affected by noble rot. They are merely dehydrated (*passerillé*). They are sweet because the fermentation process is arrested before all the sugar is converted into alcohol. This can be done by increasing the sulphur content and/or filtering out the active yeasts.

The fermentation of sweet white wine proceeds in general along the same lines as that for dry whites. Crushing has to be slow, repeated and gentle – often, paradoxically, the best juice does not come from the first pressing – and the wine is often chilled or centrifuged to eliminate the gross lees rather than being allowed to settle of its own accord. This is to prevent oxidation. The fermentation is slow, often difficult. It is important to preserve the correct balance between alcohol and sugar. A Cérons or Sainte-Croix-du-Mont wine in most vintages with, say 12.5 degrees of alcohol can support only a maximum 35 grams of sugar per litre. This wine would be called *moelleux* (medium-sweet) but not *doux* (very sweet). A *doux* Sainte-Croix, Cérons or Loupiac, such as were produced in 1989, with say 50 grams of sugar per litre, will need to be more alcoholic. A Sauternes with 14 to 15 degrees of alcohol needs to be really luscious or it will appear oily and heavy.

Once the sweet wine has been made it will take longer than a dry one to settle down and stabilize. Moreover the wine will be susceptible to further fermentation as, by its very nature, it will have a large amount of unfermented sugar in it. It needs therefore to be carefully nurtured, its sulphur level maintained at a relatively high level to preserve it. Exposure to the air must be avoided at all costs.

Nevertheless fermentation and maturation in (at least partially) new oak, and often for a year and a half or more, does wonders for the richest and most concentrated of these sweet wines. No classy Sauternes should be produced without oak. Sadly, most of the lesser sweet wines see no oak at all. They are vinified and aged in stainless steel.

Sweet white wines need aging. Though often delicious young they mature so well and can reach such levels of complexity that it is a tragedy to pull the cork too soon. A medium-sweet Cérons wine may be mature at five years. Ten is the minimum for a good Sauternes. And they will last. A 20-year-old Sauternes of a top vintage like 1997 will still be a virile teenager.

BORDEAUX CLASSIFICATIONS

BEFORE THE REVOLUTION

A group of Frenchmen will produce an argument; a group of Englishmen form a queue. So goes the old joke. If so, then a group of Bordeaux châteaux will form themselves into a classification, betraying both their French location and ancient English heritage. What could be a better amalgam of a queue and an argument?

There seems to be an instinctive desire – sometimes, these days, carried to excess – to collate, tabulate, classify and place into some sort of pecking order any miscellaneous collection of similar things. It is part of man's attempt to impose his meagre sense of order on a creation that is greatly more complicated than he is capable of comprehending. We classify the animal and vegetal worlds. The mineral is analysed down to its constituent parts. We even attempt to impose some sort of grid onto religion, philosophy and politics. Ever since the first Bordeaux châteaux emerged as individual wine-producing estates, they have been assessed and compared with one another and, largely by the price the wine has been capable of fetching on the open market, their quality has been assumed and its relative worth established. It is interesting, but no coincidence, that the first four properties to emerge as wines in their own right, the first estates to take up winemaking on a large scale, monocultural basis, the first individual château names to appear on the market, should be precisely those to be classified more than a hundred and fifty years later as *premiers crus*: Haut-Brion, Lafite, Margaux and Latour.

The wine of Château Haut-Brion, also known as Pontac, after the name of the owners in the seventeenth century, was the earliest to become established. The famous reference in Pepys' diary in 1663 to 'Ho Bryen' is probably the first to a wine of a specific estate. At the time, wines were matured for longer in cask, shipped when ready for drinking – and the wines were then vinified for consumption much sooner after the vintage – and drunk straight from the wood or bottled for immediate use in the locality of the wholesale purchaser. John Locke, who visited Haut-Brion in 1677, attests to the status and high prices of the wine and this is substantiated by the diarist John

Evelyn who met the proprietor in London in 1683. The latter was responsible for 'the choicest of our Bordeaux wines'.

Margaux, Lafite and Latour emerge towards the turn of the seventeenth century. During the War of Spanish Succession, a number of merchant ships conveying French wine to destinations in northern Europe were captured by the English and the contents put up for sale in London. These 'new French Clarets', when specifically named, were Haut-Brion or Pontac, Lafite, Margaux and Latour, the same wines as were imported by John Harvey, first Earl of Bristol, also in the first decade of the eighteenth century.

Perhaps the first classification of Bordeaux wines, as such, occurs in a letter written in 1723 from Bordeaux by J Bruneval to Henry Powell who was responsible for the cellar of the Prince of Wales. The same four wines are described as 'topping', i.e. the best. Bruneval also makes a favourable mention of Château d'Issan.

In his *Bottlescrew Days*, Andre Simon quotes from an anonymous French report dated 1730. 'The red wines (of the Graves and the Médoc) may be divided into three principal classes. The first comprises the growths of Pontac, Lafitte and Château de Margo (*sic*) which... sell for 1200 to 1500 *livres* per ton. It is the English who buy the greater part of this wine. The second class comprises a very large number of growths which... fetch from 300 to 500 *livres* per ton. They are shipped chiefly to England, Ireland, Scotland, Holland and Hamburg. The third class includes wines the usual price of which is only 100 to 200 *livres* per ton, the cheapest being shipped, as a rule, to Brittany, Normandy, Picardy and Dunkirk and the dearest to the north'.

It would be fascinating to have more specific information on the châteaux that were included in this second category. It would be instructive to see which, if any, of the other Graves estates were highly regarded at the time, for it seems unlikely that it was only Haut-Brion which made wines of renown; and it was the Graves area, in what are now the suburbs of the city, which was exploited for wine long before the marshy gravels of the Médoc were drained by the Dutch and became suitable for the vine. Moreover, it would give us concrete evidence of where in addition to the *premiers crus* there was large-scale wine production in the Médoc prior to the 1740s.

For it was not, in general, until the 1740s at the earliest that the vast majority of what are now the Médoc classed growths outside the *premiers crus* were intensively planted and started to take the form we know today. One or two had begun their existence earlier and the first records that we have, give us an indication of which they were.

For reasons which may have had as much to do with proximity to Bordeaux as anything else it seems to have been the communes of Margaux and Cantenac which came to the fore before those of Saint-Julien and Pauillac. With the exception of Château Calon-Ségur, Saint-Estèphe was long to remain a backwater.

An anonymous classification of 1745 shows that while Margaux, Latour, Lafite and Haut-Brion fetched 1500-1800 *livres tournois* the *tonneau*, the only others to top 1000, apart from La Mission Haut-Brion, were Rauzan, Dufort Vivens, Lascombes, d'Issan and Brane-Cantenac. Léoville and Calon-Ségur fell into the 800–1000 category. Pichon and Brane-Mouton (later Mouton-Rothschild) were less reputed at the time.

THE TASTET AND LAWTON ARCHIVES

Professor Pijassou, in his *Médoc*, delved further into the archives of the broking firm of Tastet and Lawton, founded in 1740, and has established a classification based on the average prices in *livres tournois* per *tonneau en primeur* from 1741 to 1774.

HAUT-BRION	1458
LAFITE	1278
CHÂTEAU MARGAUX	1275
LATOUR	1215
LÉOVILLE	810
BRANE-SAINT-JULIEN (LAGRANGE)	800
CALON-SÉGUR	775
LASCOMBES	768
MARQUIS-DE-TERME	766
GRUAUD (LAROSE)	734
BRANE-MOUTON (MOUTON-ROTHSCHILD)	716
GORSE (BRANE-CANTENAC)	686
MALESCOT	670
PETIT-CAZAUX, MARGAUX (LATER PART OF PALMER)	665
POUGET	654
PONTAC, MARGAUX (?)	605
RAUZAN	603
DESMIRAIL	540
ISSAN	537
PICHON-LONGUEVILLE	534
GISCOURS	506
DE GASQ (LATER PALMER)	494
LA CHESNAYE, CUSSAC (INCORPORATING LANESSAN)	492
LA COLONIE, MARGAUX (EVENTUALLY PART OF MALESCOT)	488
BERGERON (DUCRU-BEAUCAILLOU)	483
GOUDAL, CANTENAC (?)	459
BEYCHEVELLE	440
LA TOUR-DE-MONS	430
CITRAN	421
LYNCH-BAGES	400
DULUC (BRANAIRE)	394
PONTET-CANET	365
PAVEIL (DE LUZE)	361
PONTET-SAINT-JULIEN (LANGOA)	360
POMIES, LUDON	342
LAFON (ROCHET)	332
(FOURCAS) HOSTEN	310

Whether Tastet and Lawton dealt in the wines of the Graves other than Haut-Brion (and I don't see why not), I do not know, but the absence of any other Graves is significant. The explanation is perhaps that the next three top estates after Haut-Brion which remain today were at the time all in ecclesiastical hands: La Mission Haut-Brion, Pape-Clément and Carbonnieux. Today's main Léognan properties – de Chevalier, Haut-Bailly, Malartic-Lagravière and de Fieuzal – were not constituted until the nineteenth century. However, if La Mission and Pape-Clément were reserved for local use, the wine of the larger Benedictine Carbonnieux belonging to the Abbey of Bordeaux certainly was exported, for Simon has shown us evidence of a sale in 1762. This, however, could have been a white wine.

What is also interesting in the above list is the dominance of the wines of the commune of Margaux. No fewer than 19 of the 37 wines listed come from here or elsewhere in the southern Médoc. Cos d'Estournel and Montrose were formed later but significant by their absence are Batailley and the Grand-Puys, Talbot, then owned by the Marquis d'Aux, and Saint-Pierre.

Moreover, there are no wines from the Libournais. The wines of Saint-Émilion, Pomerol and Fronsac had more humble proprietors than the landed gentry and *parlementaires* of the Médoc, fetched greatly reduced prices and were traded directly out of Libourne. It was not until Napoleonic times that a bridge was built over the Garonne at Bordeaux and not until the 1830s that Libournais wines begin to appear in the Tastet and Lawton records.

THOMAS JEFFERSON

Thomas Jefferson, Minister in France for the new United States of America prior to the French Revolution, was a keen amateur of wine. He made an extensive tour of the French vineyards and visited Bordeaux in 1787. Here is his list of top wines:

FIRST GROWTHS

1500 LIVRES PER TONNEAU 'NEW'	CHÂTEAU MARGAUX
	LA TOUR
	HAUT-BRION
	LAFITTE (SIC)

SECOND GROWTHS

1000 LIVRES	RAUZAN
	LÉOVILLE
	GRUAUD-LAROSE
	KIRWAN (SPELT QUIROUEN)
	DURFORT

THIRD GROWTHS

800-900 LIVRES	CALON-SÉGUR
	MOUTON (ROTHSCHILD)
	GORSE (BRANE-CANTENAC)
	ARBOÈTE (LAGRANGE)
	PONTETTE (LANGOA-BARTON)
	DE TERME
	CANDALE (ISSAN)

Kirwan, curiously, does not appear in the Tastet and Lawton list. Otherwise, the list follows, very largely, that on page 43, only showing that the Second and Third Growth prices had begun to catch up those of the *premiers crus*.

ANDRÉ SIMON'S CLASSIFICATION OF 1800

Surprisingly, the French Revolution had little effect on the leading Bordeaux proprietors, their estates and the relative standing of their wines. Only a small number of château owners fell foul of the new authorities. Only one or two had to face the guillotine and it was only when a handful of others decided to emigrate that large domaines like that of Léoville were split up. The ecclesiastical properties were, of course, sequestered and there were a number of changes of ownership, but as winemaking concerns to top growths emerged largely unscathed.

In *Bottlescrew Days*, André Simon gives the following classification of the Médoc as it stood at the close of the eighteenth century:

FIRST GROWTHS	
(OPENING PRICE £24 PER HOGSHEAD)	MARGAUX
	LAFITTE (SIC)
	LATOUR

SECOND GROWTHS	
(£20 PER HOGSHEAD)	BRANE-MOUTON (ROTHSCHILD)
	RAUZAN
	LASCOMBES
	DURFORT (VIVENS)
	GORSE (BRANE-CANTENAC)
	LÉOVILLE
	GRUAUD-LAROSE

THIRD GROWTHS	
(£18 PER HOGSHEAD)	PICHON-LONGUEVILLE
	COS D'ESTOURNEL
	BERGERON (DUCRU-BEAUCAILLOU)
	BRANE-ARBOUET (LAGRANGE)
	PONTET-LANGLOIS (LANGOA)
	KIRWAN
	CHÂTEAU DE CANDALE (ISSAN)
	MALESCOT
	DE LOYAC – MARGAUX
	(EVENTUALLY PART OF MALESCOT)

FOURTH GROWTHS	
(£12 PER HOGSHEAD)	GISCOURS
	SAINT-PIERRE
	MANDAVIT (DUHART-MILON)
	PONTET-CANET
	DINAC (GRAND-PUY-LACOSTE)
	LA COLONIE, MARGAUX
	(EVENTUALLY PART OF MALESCOT)
	FERRIÈRE
	TRONQUOY-LALANDE
	(GRAND-PUY) DUCASSE
	POUGET
	DE TERME
	BOYD (CANTENAC)

There are several interesting omissions: Calon-Ségur, most importantly; de Gasq, later Château Palmer; the continuing absence of Talbot, Beychevelle and Branaire-Ducru; Lynch-Bages, despite the fact that the owner was a leading figure on the Bordeaux stage, also does not figure.

BORDEAUX AFTER THE RESTORATION

The 1820s saw the first comprehensive accounts of the wines of Bordeaux by Wilhelm Franck and the broker Paguierre and the first books on the wines of France and elsewhere, those of André Jullien, *Topographie de Tous les Vignobles Connus* and Alexander Henderson, *The History of Ancient and Modern Wines*. Jullien's first edition appeared in 1816 and his information on the hierarchy of the Bordeaux châteaux is reproduced in Henderson (1824). The first of many editions of Franck's *Traité sur les Vins du Médoc et les Autres Vins Rouges du Département de la Gironde* came out in the same year. Paguierre's *Classification et Description des Vins de Bordeaux* appeared in 1828.

At the same period Tastet and Lawton produced a detailed classification, publishing an extensive list down to Fourth Growths, from *Quatrièmes Purs* to *Quatrième et 7/8*. The late Ronald Barton once sent me a note of two classifications dated, so he said, 1824 and 1827, which I assumed might have hailed from the Barton and Guestier archives. The first is identical to the Simon classification and this may have been Simon's source. The second is the classification given in Wilhelm Franck's first edition, which is also reproduced by Paguierre.

LAWTON'S CLASSIFICATION OF 1815

Lawton was first in the field to produce his own classification. Involved in broking between the buyer and the seller, he was a man in the know. He produced a list of the Médoc containing 52 *crus*: three Firsts, six Seconds, twenty Thirds and twenty-three Fourths. Thirteen were in Saint-Julien, twelve in Cantenac, nine in Margaux, eight in Pauillac, five in Saint-Estèphe and one each in Ludon, Labarde, Arsac and Saint-Laurent.

LAWTON'S CLASSIFICATION OF 1815

FIRST GROWTHS	
	LAFITE
	LATOUR
	MARGAUX
SECOND GROWTHS	
	BRANE-MOUTON (ROTHSCHILD)
	RAUZAN (SÉGLA)
	LÉOVILLE-LAS-CASES
	LÉOVILLE-D'ABBADIE (LATER INCORPORATED INTO LAS-CASES)
	LÉOVILLE-BARTON
	LÉOVILLE-POYFERRÉ (AS IT WOULD BECOME)
	GRUAUD-LAROSE
	'CHEVALIER' (RAUZAN-GASSIES)
	MONTALAMBERT (DURFORT-VIVENS)
	LASCOMBES
	MONBRIZON (NOW ALSO DURFORT-VIVENS)
THIRD GROWTHS – 3 'PURS'	
	CALON-SÉGUR
	PICHON-LONGUEVILLE
	GORSE (BRANE-CANTENAC)
	KIRWAN
	BROWN
	CASTELNAU (ISSAN)
	CANDALE (ISSAN)
$3\frac{1}{8}$	LAGRANGE
	DUCRU-BEAUCAILLOU
$3\frac{3}{16}$	ROBOREL, MARGAUX
	LOYAC, MARGAUX
	LA COLONIE (ALL THREE LATER PART OF MALESCOT)
	MARQUIS D'ALESME
	FERRIÈRE
$3\frac{1}{2}$	LA TOUR-CARNET
	LANGOA, BEYCHEVELLE
	SAINT-PIERRE
	BRANAIRE, COS D'ESTOURNEL

	DAUX (TALBOT)
	GISCOURS
	POUGET
	DESMIRAIL
	PONTET-CANET
	MARQUIS-DE-TERME
	GRAND-PUY-LACOSTE
	GRAND-PUY-DUCASSE
	LYNCH-BAGES
4⅛	DUBOSC, SAINT-JULIEN
	DEYREM, SAINT-JULIEN
	POPP (CAMENSAC)
	COUTANCEAU (BELGRAVE)
	TRONQUOY, SAINT-ESTÈPHE
	MORIN, SAINT-ESTÈPHE
	DELEVEAU (LE BOSQ), SAINT-ESTÈPHE
4½	LA LAGUNE
	DU TERTRE
4¾	MASSAC, CANTENAC (NOW PART OF BOYD)
	LEROY, CANTENAC (?)
	MONBRUN, CANTENAC
	DURAND, (PRIEURÉ-LICHINE)
4⅞	LEGRAS (D'ANGLUDET)

Allowing for divisions and absorptions and the general ups and downs as a result of changes of ownership, this list is not that different from the 1855 Classification except in that some of the Thirds have moved up a place and the Fourth division was later sub-divided. One or two notable châteaux are missing: several Pauillacs and what was to become Château Palmer (then no doubt in a state of abeyance prior to the General's arrival as proprietor).

What is also noteworthy is that, even before the Rothschild arrival, Lawton unequivocally puts 'Brane-Mouton' at the head of his Second Growths.

ANDRÉ JULLIEN

Meanwhile, there was André Jullien, author of *Topographie de Tous Les Vins Connus*. The First Growths in his table below are the same consistent four wines which dominated Bordeaux from the start and would continue to remain unchallenged until the full emergence of Mouton soon after the arrival of the Rothschilds, and Cheval Blanc, Ausone and Pétrus a good while later. The Seconds consist of Rauzan, Durfort and Lascombes in Margaux, Gorse (Brane-Cantenac in Cantenac). Léoville and Gruaud-Larose in Saint-Julien, Brane-Mouton (Rothschild) in Pauillac and, interestingly, Pichon-Longueville. In the next category, more comprehensive than earlier tables, we find the following:

JULLIEN'S CLASSIFICATION OF 1816

CANTENAC	KIRWAN, ISSAN, POUGET, DESMIRAIL, DE TERME
MARGAUX	MALESCOT, D'ALESME-BECKER, DUBIGNON-TALBOT (A GROWTH CLASSIFIED IN 1855 WHICH WAS LATER TO DISAPPEAR), FERRIÈRE, AND LA COLONIE AND LOYAC, BOTH OF WHICH WERE TO BE ABSORBED INTO MALESCOT BEFORE OR SOON AFTER 1855

SAINT-JULIEN	DUCRU, LAGRANGE, SAINT-PIERRE, BRANAIRE, DAUCH (SIC) (TALBOT), BEYCHEVELLE
SAINT-LAURENT	(LA TOUR) CARNET, POPP (CAMENSAC), COUTANCEAU (BELGRAVE)
CUSSAC	LACHENAY, DELBOS, LEGALANT (LANESSAN AND ITS NEIGHBOURING DEPENDENT LACHESNAYE AND CARONNE-SAINTE-GEMME)
PAUILLAC	PONTET-CANET, GRAND-PUY-DUCASSE, GRAND-PUY- LACOSTE, LYNCH-BAGES, CROIZET-BAGES
SAINT-ESTÈPHE	CALON, COS D'ESTOURNEL, TRONQUOY, MERMAN (LE CROCK), MEYNEY, LAFON-ROCHET, COS-LABORY, 'MORIN', 'LEBOSC-DELAVEAU'
PESSAC	LA MISSION, PAPE-CLÉMENT, 'CANTELAUT', 'CHOLET'

Once again, there are some curious omissions: Giscours this time as well as de Gasq/Palmer, though the list is more comprehensive than most. What is interesting is the inclusion of four wines in Pessac for the first time and the large selection of Saint-Estèphes. Jullien's classification, it should be noted, was of all the red wines of Bordeaux. The Lawton list just covered the Médoc.

By the time we get to his third edition (1832) Jullien is even more ambitious. His red wine classification lists the names of 167 châteaux. La Mission-Haut-Brion and Pape-Clément are among 41 Seconds; Belair, Berliquet and Ausone together with various Fronsacs find their way into the Fourths, and there are several Bourgs and Blayes among the Fifths.

Interestingly, this third edition includes a white wine classification for the first time. Among the large number of Firsts we find most of the Sauternes and Barsacs we know today. The list is headed by Coutet and Climens (d'Yquem is eleventh). Curiously, among the Firsts are three dry white Graves châteaux, including Carbonnieux.

WILHELM FRANCK

We now come, said Wilhelm Franck in the preamble to his classification in the second (1845) edition of his book, '*to the most delicate part of our work*', and he goes on to make a point which has no less relevance today. A classification is an uncertain business; one broker's opinion will differ from another's; there is no unanimity. Moreover, wines vary from vintage to vintage. One year one château, however lowly, may produce wine better than its superior classed neighbour. The next year the reverse may be the case.

The hierarchy in Franck's first edition and the number of growths listed is much the same as that of André Simon quoted on pages 44–45. There are only the four consistent Seconds: Brane-Mouton, Rauzan, Léoville and Gruaud-Larose. Kirwan has been dropped to Fourth, Cos d'Estournel appears as a Third but Talbot and Beychevelle do not appear.

More interesting is a very much fuller classification in the 1845 second edition of Franck's *Traité*. This was the last important independent list before the 'official' assessment of 1855. Sixty-four wines are divided into five categories, with an honourable mention for a further eight *Bons Bourgeois*. Within each category, except for the First, the wines are in alphabetical order. (As I have given today's names this is not apparent below.) The prices of the First Growths fetched between 1800 and 3500 Francs and, allowing for a hypothetical 2400 Francs, the Seconds would obtain 2050-2100 Francs, the Thirds 1800 Francs, the Fourths 1200-1500 Francs and the Fifths 1000–1200 Francs. So a lowly *Cinquième* would earn 40 per cent of a Château Lafite. Today, the spread is greater. The First Growths open at 60–65 Euros (2002), and even a Fifth like Grand-Puy-Lacoste, which is patently above its 1855 station, fetches a mere 6–16 Euros or so, barely one-quarter of the price of the Firsts (See Appendix Six).

Here is the entire 1845 Franck classification, along with the production figures as well. Within each category, the wines were listed in alphabetical order. I use the château's current name where this has changed.

Wilhelm Franck's 1845 Classification

First Growths	Tonneaux
Château Margaux	100-120
Château Lafite	120-150
Latour	70-90
Haut-Brion	100-120

Second Growths	
Brane-Cantenac	50-60
Cos d'Estournel	70-80
Durfort-Vivens	30-35
Gruaud-Larose	100-150
Lascombes	15-20
Léoville-Las-Cases	80-100
Léoville-Poyferré	40-50
Léoville-Barton	50-70
Mouton (Rothschild)	120-140
Pichon-Longueville	100-120
Rauzan	50-70

Third Growths	
Desmirail	30-40
Dubignon-Talbot	15-20
Ducru-Beaucaillou	100-120
d'Issan	50-70
Brown (later Cantenac-Brown and Boyd-Cantenac)	60-70
Ganet, Cantenac (now part of Pouget)	20-25
Giscours	80-100
Kirwan	35-40
Lagrange	120-150
Langoa	100-120
Lanoire (now La Gurgue)	35-40
Montrose	100-120
Pouget	25-30
Malescot	60-70

Fourth Growths	
Talbot	70-80
Marquis d'Alesme	15-20
Beychevelle	100-120
Calon-Ségur	120-160
La Tour-Carnet	100-120
Duhart-Milon	40-50
Dubignon, Margaux (since disappeared)	12-15
Branaire	80-90
Ferrière	10-15
Lafon-Rochet	30-40
La Lagune	40-50
Clerc-Milon	25-30
Marquis-de-Terme	20-30

PRIEURÉ-LICHINE	25-30
PALMER	50-60
SAINT-PIERRE-BONTEMPS	25-35
SAINT-PIERRE-DUBARRY	25-35

FIFTH GROWTHS

BATAILLEY	60-80
BEDOUT-DUBOSQ, SAINT-JULIEN	
(SINCE DISAPPEARED: BEDOUT WAS A FORMER PROPRIETOR OF BATAILLEY)	50-55
DAUZAC	40-45
PONTET-CANET	100-120
CANTEMERLE	120-130
CHAILLET, PAUILLAC (NOW CORDEILLAN-BAGES)	15-18
CONSTANT, PAUILLAC (SINCE DISAPPEARED)	80-100
COS-LABORY	40-50
BELGRAVE	20-30
CROIZET-BAGES	50-60
GRAND-PUY-DUCASSE	80-90
GRAND-PUY-LACOSTE	50-60
LYNCH-BAGES	100-120
HAUT-BAGES-LIBÉRAL	20-25
LIVERSAN	40-50
LYNCH-MOUSSAS	30-40
LA MISSION HAUT-BRION	30-40
MOUTON-D'ARMAILHACQ	100-120
HAUT-BAGES-MONPÉLOU	25-30
CAMENSAC	30-40
SÉGUINEAU-DEYRIES, MARGAUX (MARSAC-SÉGUINEAU)	10-12

The *Bons Bourgeois* are: Marquis-d'Aligre-Bel-Air and Paveil in Soussans, Le Boscq, Morin, Le Crock and Tronquoy-Lalande in Saint-Estèphe, Lanessan in Cussac and Pedesclaux, later to become a Fifth Growth, in Pauillac.

How much does the 1855 Classification differ from that of Wilhem Franck? The 1855 Classification listed the wines in order of quality and not alphabetically within each section, so Mouton in 1855 is listed as top of the *deuxièmes*, Kirwan top of the *troisièmes*, Saint-Pierre top of the *quatrièmes* and Pontet-Canet top of the *cinquièmes*. Montrose and Ducru-Beaucaillou rise from Third to Second Growths. Châteaux Palmer, Ferrière, La Lagune, Marquis d'Alesme and Calon-Ségur are elevated to Third Growths. Pouget is relegated to a Fourth. Clerc-Milon is demoted to Fifth Growth. Out altogether goes La Mission, a surprising omission as Chiapella, the owner, was a notable *vigneron* and became *régisseur* of a number of important Médoc growths, Liversan and Haut-Bages-Montpélou, as well as a number of estates which have since disappeared. In come du Tertre and Pedesclaux.

BORDEAUX CLASSIFICATIONS: 1855 AND AFTER

'Too often' said Edmund Penning-Rowsell in his *Wines of Bordeaux* 'the 1855 Classification has, by inference, been presented either as the beginning of things – rather like the Creation – or, to use another Biblical simile, like the Tablets of the Law, handed down by the brokers of Bordeaux to Médocian proprietors....with Haut Brion's owner being smuggled in on the old boys network'.

What was so special about 1855 and why has no other 'official' classification of the top Médocs appeared since?

It is easier to answer the first part of this double-barrelled question than the second. The Victorian part of the nineteenth century was studded with grand, showy, universal exhibitions, the first of which was that held in Crystal Palace in London's Hyde Park in 1851. Not to be outdone, Napoleon III, the year after his proclamation as Emperor, set up a commission for an *Exposition Universelle de Paris* to take place in 1855. One of the attractions was to be a display of the best of Bordeaux wines and the commissioners invited the Bordeaux Chamber of Commerce to produce *une représentation complète et satisfaisante des vins du Département* – the Bordeaux region as a whole, it should be noted, not just the Médoc. The Chamber of Commerce decided that the wines of the Gironde should be represented by examples of communal wines except for those already referred to and accepted as *Crus Classés*. The drawing up of the list of *Crus Classés* they delegated to the *courtiers*, the brokers who acted as middle men between the proprietors and the *négoce*.

On 18th April 1855, the joint Committee of the Chamber of Commerce and the Syndicate of Brokers presented their classification of the red and white wines of Bordeaux. As Cyril Ray has put it in his *Lafite*, all the wines of the Gironde were called but, with the exception of Château Haut-Brion from Pessac in the Graves, none but the red wines of the Médoc and the white wines of the Sauternes were chosen. Therefore, not only were the rest of the red wines of the Graves as well as those of Saint-Émilion and Pomerol not considered up to *Cru Classé* standard but neither were any dry white wines. Moreover, the classifications, it is interesting to note, were based not only on the brokers' experience of the reputation and prices, past and present, of the wines in question, but on blind tastings of recent vintages submitted by the châteaux themselves. Further, the arrangement of the wines within the various levels of growth were in order of precedence, not alphabetical.

So the 1855 Classification was, first, the contemporary view of the best of all Bordeaux, not just the Médoc with Haut-Brion admitted as a sort of afterthought. Second, it was 'official' in that the joint considered view of the brokers had been authorised by the Bordeaux Chamber of Commerce. The hand-written list is stamped with their official seal. When the same bodies accepted the invitation to send a similar range of wines to yet another Universal Exhibition, this time in London in 1862, a duplicated list of wines was submitted with a statement that '*Les Vins désignés sous la dénomination de classes sont divisés en cinq catégories et leur rang est indiqué selon leur mérite*'. It is therefore misleading to reproduce the 1855 Classification in a different order. The late Alexis Lichine was guilty of this, promoting his beloved Prieuré to head of the Fourths. It is also an error to persist with the common misconception that it was a classification of the Médoc only and to repeat the myth that Ausone, for example, was only left out because its production was too small.

However, there was certainly no intention that the 1855 Classification should be permanent. I am sure it never occurred to anybody involved in its production that it would still be cited and discussed 150 years later. How did this happen? I would suggest that the original defect was the failure of those at the time to realise what a momentous object they had created. This lack of imagination only goes to prove the point I made in the previous paragraph. If they had had the foresight, the Joint Committee could have decreed that the classification should be reviewed every 25 years or so. They didn't; and since then nobody, official or otherwise, has had the legal or political authority nor the will to replace the 1855 Classification with anything else. The only change to the list has been the Presidential Decree of 1973 promoting Château Mouton-Rothschild to the ranks of the First Growths.

THE 1855 CLASSIFICATION
OF THE RED WINES OF BORDEAUX

This is the original list of 1855, with the incorporation of Château Mouton-Rothschild. It takes into account divisions and other changes since 1855. Surface areas and production figures are those quoted in the 16th (2001) edition of Cocks and Féret.

PREMIERS CRUS (FIRST GROWTHS)	COMMUNE	HECTARES	CASES
LAFITE	PAUILLAC	100	55,600
LATOUR	PAUILLAC	65	36,700
MOUTON-ROTHSCHILD (1973)	PAUILLAC	75	23,000
CHÂTEAU MARGAUX	MARGAUX	81	40,000
HAUT-BRION	PESSAC-GRAVES	43.2	16,000

DEUXIÈMES CRUS (SECOND GROWTHS)			
RAUZAN-SÉGLA	MARGAUX	51	23,300
RAUZAN-GASSIES	MARGAUX	28	13,300
LÉOVILLE-LAS-CASES	SAINT-JULIEN	97	47,200
LÉOVILLE-POYFERRÉ	SAINT-JULIEN	80	44,400
LEOVILLE-BARTON	SAINT-JULIEN	47	20,800
DURFORT-VIVENS	MARGAUX	30	6100
LASCOMBES	MARGAUX	50	24,400
GRUAUD-LAROSE	SAINT-JULIEN	82	51,000
BRANE-CANTENAC	CANTENAC-MARGAUX	90	12,500
PICHON-LONGUEVILLE-BARON	PAUILLAC	50	20,000
PICHON-LONGUEVILLE, COMTESSE DE LALANDE	PAUILLAC	85	50,000
DUCRU-BEAUCAILLOU	SAINT-JULIEN	50	19,000
COS D'ESTOURNEL	SAINT-ESTÈPHE	64	28,900
MONTROSE	SAINT-ESTÈPHE	68	37,100

TROISIÈMES CRUS (THIRD GROWTHS)			
KIRWAN	CANTENAC-MARGAUX	35	18,900
D'ISSAN	CANTENAC-MARGAUX	30	15,000
LAGRANGE	SAINT-JULIEN	109	66,700
LANGOA-BARTON	SAINT-JULIEN	17	7100
GISCOURS	LABARDE-MARGAUX	80	48,000
MALESCOT-SAINT-EXUPÉRY	MARGAUX	23.5	14,000
BOYD-CANTENAC	CANTENAC	18	8000
CANTENAC-BROWN	CANTENAC-MARGAUX	32	12,000
PALMER	CANTENAC-MARGAUX	50	20,000
LA LAGUNE	LUDON (HAUT-MÉDOC)	70	38,900
DESMIRAIL	MARGAUX	28	5000
CALON-SÉGUR	SAINT-ESTÈPHE	58	20,000
FERRIÈRE	MARGAUX	8	4000
MARQUIS D'ALESME-BECKER	MARGAUX	15.6	96,000

QUATRIÈMES CRUS (FOURTH GROWTHS)			
TALBOT	SAINT-JULIEN	102	54,200
SAINT-PIERRE-SEVAISTRE	SAINT-JULIEN	17	8000
BRANAIRE-DUCRU	SAINT-JULIEN	50	25,000

DUHART-MILON-ROTHSCHILD	PAUILLAC	67	37,200
POUGET	CANTENAC-MARGAUX	10	4400
LA TOUR-CARNET	SAINT-LAURENT (HAUT-MÉDOC)	45	20,000
LAFON-ROCHET	SAINT-ESTÈPHE	40	24,000
BEYCHEVELLE	SAINT-JULIEN	90	55,600
PRIEURÉ-LICHINE	CANTENAC-MARGAUX	69	38,300
MARQUIS-DE-TERME	MARGAUX	38	16,000

CINQUIÈMES CRUS (FIFTH GROWTHS)

PONTET-CANET	PAUILLAC	80	50,000
BATAILLEY	PAUILLAC	60	33,300
HAUT-BATAILLEY	PAUILLAC	22	10,000
GRAND-PUY-LACOSTE	PAUILLAC	50	16,700
GRAND-PUY-DUCASSE	PAUILLAC	40	11,000
LYNCH-BAGES	PAUILLAC	90	35,000
LYNCH-MOUSSAS	PAUILLAC	35	17,800
DAUZAC	LABARDE-MARGAUX	40	2000
D'ARMAILHAC	PAUILLAC	50	17,000
DU TERTRE	ARSAC-MARGAUX	50	25,500
HAUT-BAGES-LIBÉRAL	PAUILLAC	27	13,300
PÉDESCLAUX	PAUILLAC	12	5800
BELGRAVE	SAINT-LAURENT (HAUT-MÉDOC)	57	30,000
DE CAMENSAC	SAINT-LAURENT (HAUT-MÉDOC)	75	29,200
COS LABORY	SAINT-ESTÈPHE	18	10,000
CLERC-MILON	PAUILLAC	30	13,300
CROIZET-BAGES	PAUILLAC	28	15,600
CANTEMERLE	MACAU (HAUT-MÉDOC)	87	55,600

THE 1855 CLASSIFICATION OF THE SAUTERNES

This is the original list, but brought up to date to take account of divisions and other changes, together with current surface area and production figures.

PREMIER GRAND CRU (FIRST GREAT GROWTH)	COMMUNE	HECTARES	CASES
D'YQUEM	SAUTERNES	103	8300

PREMIERS CRUS (FIRST GROWTHS)

LA TOUR BLANCHE	BOMMES	35	4400
LAFAURIE-PEYRAGUEY	BOMMES	38.5	7900
CLOS HAUT-PEYRAGUEY	BOMMES	15	2000
DE RAYNE-VIGNEAU	BOMMES	78	7100
SUDUIRAUT	PREIGNAC	86	14,100
COUTET	BARSAC	38.5	5000
CLIMENS	BARSAC	29	2500
GUIRAUD	SAUTERNES	100	8500
RIEUSSEC	FARGUES	78	15,300
SIGALAS-RABAUD	BOMMES	14	2900
RABAUD-PROMIS	BOMMES	33	6700

MYRAT	BARSAC	22	3300
DOISY-VÉDRINES	BARSAC	27	3000
DOISY-DAËNE	BARSAC	15	6400
DOISY-DUBROCA	BARSAC	3.3	500
D'ARCHE	SAUTERNES	30	2200
FILHOT	SAUTERNES	60	10,000
BROUSTET	BARSAC	16	3800
NAIRAC	BARSAC	16	1300
CAILLOU	BARSAC	13	3600
CHÂTEAU SUAU	BARSAC	8	2200
DE MALLE	PREIGNAC	27	5000
ROMER-DU-HAYOT	FARGUES	10.9	3300
LAMOTHE-DESPUJOLS	SAUTERNES	7.5	1700
LAMOTHE-GUIGNARD	SAUTERNES	27	6000

CHANGES SINCE 1855

There have been, though, minor changes as a result of divisions and absorption of territory by one property of another. In 1855, Léoville, like Latour and Gruaud-Larose, is listed as one growth but with three owners. Rauzan, however, is shown as divided. Pichon, though, is still one single property.

Boyd, in Cantenac, is shown as being possessed by '*plusieurs propriétaires*'. Some 30 years later, after a legal wrangle, a new Third Growth, Cantenac-Brown, managed to demonstrate that it was entitled to be so classified as it origins lay in vineyards which had been Boyd in 1855. Batailley was split in the 1940s.

One château in the 1855 Classification no longer exists; another ceased to function but has since been resurrected; a Third almost disappeared. Dubignon, later Dubignon-Talbot, was always a tiny vineyard. It ceased production after the phylloxera epidemic but was later revived, the *courtiers* of Bordeaux admitting it to the ranks of the Bourgeois Supérieurs as '*ancien Troisième Cru*' in the 1949 edition of Cocks and Féret. In 1960, Cordier bought the brand name and the vineyard was divided between Ginestet of Château Margaux and Durfort-Vivens, and Zuger of Château Malescot-Saint-Exupéry.

Château Desmirail also disappeared from view, though more recently. In 1938, it was absorbed into Château Palmer, though earlier other sections had been sold off. In 1981, Palmer sold the brand name to Lucien Lurton of Château Brane-Cantenac and Lurton has since re-established the *cru*.

The vineyard of Château Ferrière was for a long time during the post-war period leased to Château Lascombes. The wine was supposed to have been produced separately. I tasted it a few times during this period and was unimpressed. In 1992 the Villars family acquired Château Ferrière. Instantly a very much better and quite different wine appeared under the Ferrière label.

Another wine which went through a curious period of half-existence was Pouget. For many years Châteaux Pouget and Boyd-Cantenac were made as one, the former being a selection of the vats of the latter. This too has been regularised.

OTHER CLASSIFICATIONS

With the arrival in the twentieth century of the laws of *appellation contrôlée* and a body, the INAO (*Institut National des Appellations d'Origine*) to administer and control them, the necessary authoritative machinery, in theory, for further classification was established. Sadly, the INAO has failed to tackle the roots of a plant which is now venerable, if not in parts diseased, and has merely been content with tinkering at the edges. The difficulty, I suggest, is the division of responsibility, if that is the correct word, between the INAO and bodies such as the CIVB in Bordeaux.

Meanwhile, there have been occasional rumours of a new classification of the Médoc. At one point in the 1950s, the classed growth owners conferred together, deciding by a majority that there should be a new classification, and in 1959 a committee was established to look into the matter. Their conclusions were sweeping. No fewer than 19 growths classified in 1855 were to be demoted, including all three in Saint-Laurent – La Tour Carnet, Belgrave and Camensac – as well as Lagrange, Dauzac and even Saint-Pierre, among others. A dozen *bourgeois* – Gloria, Lanessan, Siran, Labégorce and others – would be promoted according to the off-the-record reports. Not surprisingly, this radical re-adjustment caused such a furore that the proposals were dropped.

To counter these and later moves, several proprietors announced that they would boycott any attempts at a re-classification. Others, some *bourgeois* aspirants for elevation such as Gloria, for instance, boycotted the revision of the *bourgeois* list in 1978 and again in 2003 and so in theory are currently not classified at all. There were further proposals in the 1970s. In 1970, there was an official announcement that there would be a competition to establish a new hierarchy, this time embracing all the top wines of Bordeaux, those of the Libournais and Graves as well as the Médoc. In 1972, another decree was signed but this time the contest was just for Médoc proprietors alone.

Yet nothing has happened. A combination of inertia on behalf of those content with their 1855 position, antagonism from those threatened with de-classification, the lack of political will to establish an authority which could defend itself against the legal consequences of its actions and perhaps a feeling of doubt about how to establish an expert jury who would be seen to be 'expert' and independent enough, has all combined to preserve the old, creaky status quo.

THE 1959 CLASSIFICATION OF THE GRAVES

Château Haut-Brion did not wish to be included for its white wine as production was too tiny (currently 900 cases per annum).

	COMMUNE	HECTARES	CASES
CLASSIFIED RED WINES OF GRAVES		RED VINES ONLY	
BOUSCAUT	CADAUJAC	39	22,200
CARBONNIEUX	LÉOGNAN	50	27,800
DOMAINE DE CHEVALIER	LÉOGNAN	33	16,700
DE FIEUZAL	LÉOGNAN	38	13,300
HAUT-BAILLY	LÉOGNAN	28	14,000
HAUT-BRION	PESSAC	43.2	16,000
MALARTIC-LAGRAVIÈRE	LÉOGNAN	37	15,000
LA MISSION HAUT-BRION	PESSAC	20.9	7500
OLIVIER	LÉOGNAN	38	15,000
PAPE-CLÉMENT	PESSAC	30	12,800
SMITH-HAUT-LAFITTE	MARTILLAC	44	14,200
LA TOUR HAUT-BRION	TALENCE	4.9	8000
LATOUR-MARTILLAC	MARTILLAC	28	15,600
CLASSIFIED WHITE WINES OF GRAVES		WHITE VINES ONLY	CASES
BOUSCAUT	CADAUJAC	8	3300
CARBONNIEUX	LÉOGNAN	42	22,200
DOMAINE DE CHEVALIER	LÉOGNAN	5	2000
COUHINS	VILLENAVE-D'ORNON	4	2200
COUHINS-LURTON	VILLENAVE-D'ORNON	13	3000
LAVILLE HAUT-BRION	TALENCE	3.7	1100
MALARTIC-LAGRAVIÈRE	LÉOGNAN	7	3000
OLIVIER	LÉOGNAN	12	6000
LATOUR-MARTILLAC	MARTILLAC	10	5000

SAINT-ÉMILION

The wines of Saint-Émilion were first classified in 1959, and this classification was revised in 1967, in 1985 and again in 1996. The Premiers Grands *Crus classés* are divided into two sections, A and B.

PREMIERS GRANDS CRUS CLASSÉS

A	B
AUSONE	ANGÉLUS
CHEVAL BLANC	BEAU-SÉJOUR-BÉCOT
	BEAUSÉJOUR-DUFFAU-LAGARROSSE
	BELAIR
	CANON
	FIGEAC
	CLOS FOURTET
	LA GAFFELIÈRE
	MAGDELAINE
	PAVIE
	TROTTEVIEILLE

GRANDS CRUS CLASSÉS

L'ARROSÉE	FONROQUE	PETIT-FAURIE-DE-
BALESTARD-LA-TONNELLE	FRANC-MAYNE	SOUTARD
BELLEVUE	GRAND-MAYNE	LE PRIEURÉ
BERGAT	GRAND-PONTET	RIPEAU
BERLIQUET	LES GRANDES-MURAILLES	SAINT-GEORGES-CÔTE-
CADET-BON	GUADET-SAINT-JULIEN	PAVIE
CADET-PIOLA	HAUT-CORBIN	CLOS SAINT-MARTIN
CANON-LA-GAFFELIÈRE	HAUT-SARPE	LA SERRE
CAP-DE-MOURLIN	CLOS DES JACOBINS	SOUTARD
CHAUVIN	LANOITE (MOUEIX)	TERTRE-DAUGAY
LA CLOTTE	LARCIS-DUCASSE	LA TOUR-DU-PIN-FIGEAC
LA CLUSIÈRE	LARMANDE	(GIRAUD-BÉLIVIER)
CORBIN	LAROQUE	LA TOUR-DU-PIN-FIGEAC
CORBIN-MICHOTTE	LAROZE	(MOUEIX)
LA COUSPAUDE	LA MARZELLE	LA TOUR-FIGEAC
COUVENT DES JACOBINS	MATRAS	TROPLONG-MONDOT
DASSAULT	MOULIN-DU-CADET	VILLEMAURINE
LA DOMINIQUE	CLOS DE L'ORATOIRE	YON-FIGEAC
FAURIE-DE-SOUCHARD	PAVIE-DECESSE	
FONPLÉGADE	PAVIE-MACQUIN	

Classifications of the Crus Bourgeois of the Médoc and Haut-Médoc

In 1932 six properties in the Haut-Médoc were classified as *crus bourgeois exceptionnels*, and others in both the Haut-Médoc and the Bas-Médoc into *crus bourgeois* and *crus bourgeois supérieurs*. In the 1960s this list was expanded, and in 1978 was replaced by a division into the categories of *cru bourgeois, cru grand bourgeois* and *cru grand bourgeois exceptionnel*. Only properties in the Haut-Médoc could be considered for the latter category, and these wines had to be château-bottled. A number of the better growths (e.g. Château Gloria) declined to be considered for the 1978 classification, fearing that inclusion on this list would preclude consideration in a revision of the *crus classés*.

All this then changed in 1984. European law decreed that there should be one category only: that of *cru bourgeois*. Since then there has been an internal list of members of the Syndicat of Cru Bourgeois. In June 2003 the results of a new classification were announced (see Appendix Seven).

Clive Coates' Classification

The author's personal classification of Bordeaux's red wines can be found in Appendix Five.

PART

THE APPELLATIONS

ONE

AND THEIR CHÂTEAUX

MÉDOC

Surface Area (2002): 5358 ha.

Production (2002): 278,474 hl.

Colour: Red (the white wines are AC

Bordeaux or Bordeaux Supérieur).

Grape Varieties: Cabernet Sauvignon;

Cabernet Franc; Merlot; Petit Verdot;

Malbec; Carmenère.

Maximum Yield: 50 hl/ha.

Minimum Alcoholic Degree: 10%.

The *appellation* covers the following 16 communes (I list them roughly speaking from north to south): Vensac, Jau-Dignac-et-Loirac, Saint-Vivian-du-Médoc, Valeyrac, Queyrac, Bégadan, Saint-Christoly-Médoc, Conquèques, Civrac-en-Médoc, Prignac-en-Médoc, Gaillac-en-Médoc, Blaignan, Saint-Yzans-de-Médoc, Lesparre-Médoc, Ordonnac and Saint-Germain-d'Esteuil.

The Médoc (also called Médoc Maritime or Bas-Médoc to differentiate it from the Haut-Médoc) begins where the Haut-Médoc leaves off, north of Saint-Estèphe, and runs from Saint-Yzans and Saint-Germain d'Esteuil all the way up to Soulac at the tip of the peninsula. Viticulturally, as well as in terms of prestige, it is a minor area compared with its more famous neighbour to the south. There are 16 wine-producing communes, with a total area under vine of some 4800 hectares, producing some 300,000 hectolitres a year. The appellation covers red wines only. It is a part of the world which few outsiders tourists or foreign wine merchants ever visit. The countryside is low-lying, flat and open to the skies. Even more than the Haut-Médoc the atmosphere often resembles that of Holland. Fields of pasture cover the land more than vines, interspersed with copses, hamlets and the occasional wine-producing farmhouse surrounded by its dependent buildings. It is peaceful but bleak, rural and remote.

Nevertheless, the wines are well worth investigating, for they are inexpensive, and no serious list of Bordeaux *petits châteaux* will be without one or two of the better examples. As with the more famous estates to the south Cabernet Sauvignon and Cabernet Franc form the bulk of the plantings, together with Merlot and a little Malbec, and this mixture of varieties gives the wine body and backbone, albeit at a lower level of breed and concentration than in Pauillac or Margaux. The wines will have a similar blackcurranty taste, but without the oak element found in the better wines from further south.

An important thing to bear in mind in the Médoc is the date of the picking. The *crus bourgeois* of the Médoc and Haut-Médoc, and this

includes Moulis and Listrac as well as the Margaux wines of Arsac
and the inland vineyards of Cantenac, come in the main from colder,
less precocious soils than those on which the *crus classés* are sited:
vines at Château Caronne-Sainte-Gemme, for example, are four days
later in development than neighbouring Château Gruaud-Larose,
Gruaud-Larose is four days less advanced than Château Latour. Few
Médoc vintages offer fair weather right through September and
October, but it is obviously in these years that the *crus bourgeois* really
come into their own. Good *bourgeois* vintages include 1959, 1961,
1970, 1982, 1985 and 1986, though for the most part, the wines are
now tired; 1990 is a classic year and holding up well. Both 1995 and
1996 enjoyed an Indian summer in October, after rainy Septembers,
but 1998 did not. In 2000 the fine weather held for the first week of
October, but from then it was unsettled – yet this is a splendid vintage
for the *crus bourgeois*.

The *cru bourgeois* Médocs come from less fine soils, as well as their
mesoclimate being cooler. That is why they are *bourgeois* and not
classés. Almost inevitably, even if masked by new oak in the case of
some special *cuvées*, when young there will be an underlying element
of the rustic. In time this character will take over. My advice is not to
be too patient. Drink *cru bourgeois* Médocs soon after they have
softened up, i.e. five to eight years after the vintage. Only in
remarkable cases – 1970, 1982, 1990 and 2000 – will these *bourgeois*
ducklings turn out to be swans.

Châteaux ◆

Médoc AC
1. Noaillac
2. Laulan-Ducos
3. Lalande de Gravelongue
4. Lousteauneuf
5. Bellerive
6. Vieux Robin
7. La Clare
8. La Tour-de-By
9. Rollan de By
10. Greysac
11. Patache d'Aux
12. Laujac
13. d'Escurac
14. d'Escot
15. Inclassable
16. La Cardonne
17. Castéra
18. Fontis
19. Potensac
20. Tour-Haut-Caussan
21. Vieux-Chateau-Landon
22. Les Moines
23. Les Ormes-Sorbet
24. Tour St-Bonnet
25. Le Boscq
26. Les Grands Chênes
27. Tour-Blanche
28. Les Tuileries
29. Loudenne

Haut-Médoc AC
30. Coufran
31. Soudars
32. Verdignan
33. Bel Orme, Tronquoy de Lalande
34. Grandis, Pointoise-Cabarrus
35. Sociando-Mallet
36. Charmail
37. Lestage-Simon
38. d'Aurilhac
39. Cissac
40. Lamothe-Cissac
41. Hanteillan
42. Puy-Castéra
43. Ramage La Batisse
44. Peyrabon
45. Liversan
46. Bernadotte
47. Lieujean
48. Larose-Trintaudon
49. Belgrave
50. Camensac
51. La Tour Carnet

St-Estèphe AC
52. Le Boscq
53. Beau Site
54. Calon-Ségur, Faget
55. Valrose, Capbern-Gasqueton, Phélan-Ségur
56. Ségur de Cabanac
57. Domeyne, Haut-Beauséjour
58. Les Ormes de Pez
59. de Pez
60. Tronquoy-Lalande
61. Laffitte-Carcasset

MÉDOC & NORTHERN HAUT-MÉDOC

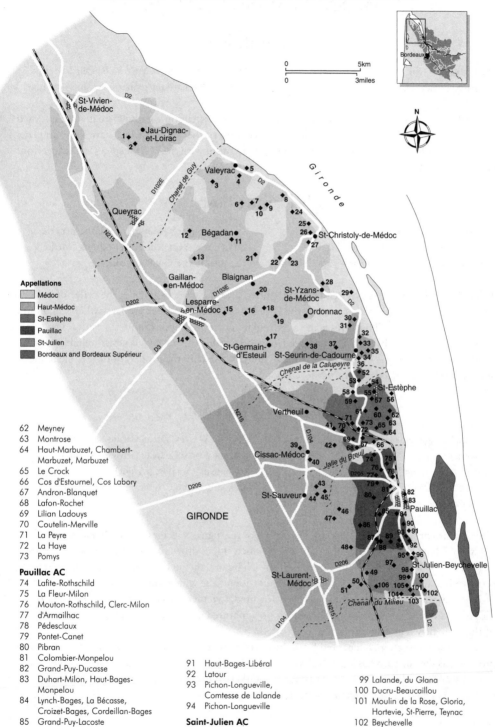

Appellations

- Médoc
- Haut-Médoc
- St-Estèphe
- Pauillac
- St-Julien
- Bordeaux and Bordeaux Supérieur

62 Meyney
63 Montrose
64 Haut-Marbuzet, Chambert-
   Marbuzet, Marbuzet
65 Le Crock
66 Cos d'Estournel, Cos Labory
67 Andron-Blanquet
68 Lafon-Rochet
69 Lilian Ladouys
70 Coutelin-Merville
71 La Peyre
72 La Haye
73 Pomys

Pauillac AC
74 Lafite-Rothschild
75 La Fleur-Milon
76 Mouton-Rothschild, Clerc-Milon
77 d'Armailhac
78 Pédesclaux
79 Pontet-Canet
80 Pibran
81 Colombier-Monpelou
82 Grand-Puy-Ducasse
83 Duhart-Milon, Haut-Bages-
   Monpelou
84 Lynch-Bages, La Bécasse,
   Croizet-Bages, Cordeillan-Bages
85 Grand-Puy-Lacoste
86 Lynch-Moussas
87 Batailley
88 Haut-Batailley
89 La Couronne
90 Bellegrave, Fonbadet

91 Haut-Bages-Libéral
92 Latour
93 Pichon-Longueville,
   Comtesse de Lalande
94 Pichon-Longueville

Saint-Julien AC
95 La Bridane
96 Léoville-Las-Cases,
   Léoville-Poyferré
97 Talbot
98 Langoa-Barton/Léoville-Barton

99 Lalande, du Glana
100 Ducru-Beaucaillou
101 Moulin de la Rose, Gloria,
    Hortevie, St-Pierre, Teynac
102 Beychevelle
103 Branaire
104 Gruaud-Larose
105 Terrey-Gros-Cailloux,
    Lalande-Borie
106 Lagrange

Médoc Leading Châteaux

Château Bellerive

OWNER: Guy Perrin.
COMMUNE: Valeyrac.

SURFACE AREA UNDER VINE: 13 ha – 60% Merlot;
30% Cabernet Sauvignon; 10% Cabernet Franc.

The is the most northerly of the top Médoc estates, and my attention was drawn to it when it scored rather well in a blind tasting of 1990s. I have enjoyed most of the vintages which have since come my way, particularly the 1996. The wine is encouragingly fresh, with the Merlot spices to the forefront and no lack of backbone.

Château Le Boscq

OWNER: Jean-Michel Lapalu.
COMMUNE: Saint-Christoly-de-Médoc.
SURFACE AREA UNDER VINE: 27 ha – 70% Cabernet

Sauvignon; 20% Merlot; 10% Cabernet Franc.
OTHER WINE: Château Patache d'Aux (Médoc).
CLASSIFICATION: Cru Bourgeois.

The imposing three-storey château is uninhabited and the wine is made in the cellar of nearby Château Patache d'Aux, also owned by the Lapalu family, and another property where cellar and château are separated. This gives a certain desolate air to matters in Saint-Christoly. The wine, from grapes harvested by machine, and aged in wood of which 20 per cent is new, is reliable, and the *vieilles vignes* bottling is even better. (N.B. Do not confuse with the property of the same name in Saint-Estèphe, or indeed with other Boscqs.)

Château La Cardonne

OWNERS: Les Domaines CGR; manager: Magali
  Guyon.
COMMUNE: Blaignan.
SURFACE AREA UNDER VINE: 87 ha – 50% Merlot;
  45% Cabernet Sauvignon; 5% Cabernet Franc.

SECOND WINE: Château Cardus.
OTHER WINES: Château Grivière (Médoc);
  Château Ramafort (Médoc).
CLASSIFICATION: Cru Bourgeois Supérieur.

The vineyard of Château La Cardonne lies on one of the highest *croupes* of the Médoc, south of the village of Blaignan, on a ridge of sandy gravel which slopes down towards the Gironde. Between 1973 and 1990 it belonged to the Rothschilds of Château Lafite, who increased the vineyard to its present size, and did much to establish the reputation of the wine today.

In the last decade a concentrator has been acquired, together with more sophisticated control of the temperature of fermentation. The wine is now matured in oak barrels for a year, and one-third of these are new. The fruit is machine-harvested.

The wine has certainly benefited from the decision to age it in wood; it has also become more profound as the vineyard has aged. Nevertheless the high percentage of Merlot shows. This is essentially a soft-centred wine with no hard edges. And there is nothing wrong with that. I have enjoyed the 1996, as I have of its associate Château Ramafort.

Château Castéra

OWNER: SNC Château Castéra; manager: Dieter Tondera.

COMMUNE: Saint-Germain-d'Esteuil.

SURFACE AREA UNDER VINE: 50 ha – 45% Cabernet Sauvignon; 45% Merlot; 7% Cabernet Franc; 3% Petit Verdot.

SECOND WINE: Château Bourbon La Chapelle.

OTHER WINE: Château Moulin de Buscateaux (Bordeaux Supérieur).

CLASSIFICATION: Cru Bourgeois Supérieur.

I first encountered this wine in the 1970s, when it belonged to Alexis Lichine et Cie. who sold it to the present owners in 1986. Though the property has a long history – there is a tower, still extant, which withheld a siege by the Black Prince in the thirteenth century – it was Lichine which put the property on the map. In the last decade the château and the winery have been entirely renewed. The fruit is collected both by hand and by machine, and it is now matured in cask, one-third of which is new. While not a wine with the greatest finesse – I find the tannins a little unsophisticated – Castéra can provide a good meaty bottle for the medium term.

Château La Clare

OWNER: Jean Guyon.

COMMUNE: Bégadan.

SURFACE AREA UNDER VINE: 15 ha – 45% Merlot; 35% Cabernet Sauvignon; 15% Cabernet Franc; 5% Petit Verdot.

SECOND WINES: Château Laveline; Château du Gentilhomme.

CLASSIFICATION: Cru Bourgeois.

The vineyard of La Clare lies on a ridge above the hamlet of Condissas and has belonged to the *pied-noir* Paul de Rozières since 1969. Today the older vines are picked by hand – and in better years these grapes are used for a Réserve du Château, matured entirely in new oak – and the rest are picked by machine. I find Château La Clare clear-cut, with a good Cabernet base to the flavour, with ripe tannins. It keeps well.

Chateau d'Escot

OWNER: M & Mme Hubert Rouy.

COMMUNE: Lesparre.

SURFACE AREA UNDER VINES: 18 ha – 75% Cabernet Sauvignon; 24% Merlot; 1% Petit Verdot.

SECOND WINE: Château Le Privera.

CLASSIFICATION: Cru Bourgeois.

The Rouy family bought Château d'Escot in 1991, since when quality has gone from strength to strength. The property lies somewhat off the beaten track, west of the main road to Bordeaux as you enter the town from the south, but the château itself, with its three slate turrets, is attractive, and the installations are up-to-date. Harvesting is both by machine and by hand. One-third of the barrels are renewed on an annual basis. The wine is marked by its Cabernet Sauvignon, and takes a little while to show its paces. But it is worth investigating. The 1996, in particular, shows promise.

Château d'Escurac

OWNER: Jean-Marc Landureau.
COMMUNE: Civrac-en-Médoc.
SURFACE AREA UNDER VINE: 20 ha – 50% Cabernet
  Sauvignon; 50% Merlot.

SECOND WINE: La Chapelle d'Escurac.
OTHER WINE: Château Haut-Myles (Haut-Médoc).
CLASSIFICATION: Cru Bourgeois Supérieur.

Until 1990 this wine was made by the local co-operative. Since Jean-Marc Landureau has taken over it is made on the spot, aged in 30 per cent new barrels and bottled unfiltered. The wine is stored in a renovated eleventh-century chapel. Good colour, ample fruit, balanced and stylish: a property to watch. The 2000 was particularly good, and so is the 2002.

Chateau Fontis

OWNER: Vincent Boivert.
COMMUNE: Ordonnac.
SURFACE AREA UNDER VINE: 10 ha – 50% Cabernet

Sauvignon; 50% Merlot.
CLASSIFICATION: Cru Bourgeois.

Situated in one block on the highest elevation in the Médoc, Château Fontis, called Château Hontemieux until 1995, was acquired by the 28-year-old Vincent Boivert in 1995. His parents, Jean and Hélène, are proprietors of Château Les Ormes-Sorbet in nearby Couquèques. Harvesting is by hand, with a *table de tri* in the winery and the wine is aged using one-third new wood. This has rapidly found a position as one of the Médoc's best *crus bourgeois*. The wine is of medium body, with juicy fruit, ripe tannins and plenty of flair.

Château Les Grands Chênes

OWNER: William Pitters International; director:
  Bernard Magrez.
COMMUNE: Saint-Christoly-de-Médoc.
SURFACE AREA UNDER VINE: 7 ha – 65% Cabernet
  Sauvignon; 30% Merlot; 5% Cabernet Franc.

SECOND WINE: Château Le Chêne Noir.
OTHER WINES: Château Pape-Clément (Pessac-
  Léognan); Château La Tour-Carnet (Saint-
  Laurent); Château Fombrauge (Saint-Émilion).
CLASSIFICATION: Cru Bourgeois Supérieur.

It was Madame Jacqueline Gauzy-Darricade, proprietor from 1981 to 1998, who put Les Grands Chênes, which lies in the middle of the village of Saint-Christoly-de-Médoc, on the map, but I have noticed no decline in quality since William Pitters International, owners of Château Pape-Clément and a number of other properties, took over in 1996. The vineyard is picked by machine, and one-third new oak is used for the main château wine. This is plump and medium-bodied with a good Cabernet flavour and stylish tannins. There is a 100 per cent new oak Cuvée Prestige. This can be too woody in lesser vintages. I prefer the 1989 to the 1990 for the moment, the latter still needs time, and the 1996 to the 1995. But this is a reliable estate, nevertheless.

Château Greysac

OWNER: Domaines Codem.

COMMUNE: Bégadan.

SURFACE AREA UNDER VINE: 60 ha – 45% Cabernet Sauvignon; 38% Merlot; 15% Cabernet Franc; 2% Petit Verdot.

SECOND WINE: Domaine de By.

OTHER WINES: Château des Bertins (Médoc); Château de Monthil (Médoc).

CLASSIFICATION: Cru Bourgeois Supérieur.

This is a *cru bourgeois* with a high profile. It is a member of the *Union des Grands Crus de Bordeaux* (otherwise almost entirely an association of classed growths) and it has been marketed for many years in the USA as an exclusivity of Seagram Château and Estate. Greysac lies in the hamlet of By, close to the estuary. The creeper-covered château is attractive; the *chais* are modern and neat and tidy. Harvesting is by machine and 20 per cent of the casks are new. I find the wine good, but rarely up with the best of the commune. I would like a bit more succulence. Admittedly there is plenty of competition in Bégadan.

Château Inclassable

OWNER: Rémy Fauchey.

COMMUNE: Prignac-en-Médoc.

SURFACE AREA UNDER VINE: 16 ha – 55% Cabernet Sauvignon; 30% Merlot; 5% Cabernet Franc;

10% Petit Verdot.

SECOND WINE: Château Fontaine de L'Aubier.

CLASSIFICATION: Cru Bourgeois.

Known as Château Lafon until it was renamed for the 2003 vintage, this property has a reputation that has steadily grown in the last few years. The 1995 is fine, and the subsequent vintages which have come my way have also impressed. One-third new oak is used in the cellar.

Château Lalande de Gravelongue

OWNER: SCEA Lalande de Gravelongue; managers: Christian & Nadine Nielsen.

COMMUNE: Valeyrac.

SURFACE AREA UNDER VINE: 15 ha – 50% Cabernet

Sauvignon; 38% Merlot; 10% Cabernet Franc; 2% Malbec & Petit Verdot.

SECOND WINE: Château Lalande Villeneuve.

In 2003 I was sent the 2000, 1999 and 1998 vintages of the *tête de cuvée* called La Croix. Harvesting is by hand, and this top wine is produced with a low *rendement* (25–30 hl/ha) from old vines and matured in new and one-year-old barrels. The 1998 was fruity but a little short. The 1999 was better, and the 2000 had good depth and grip although a slight absence of richness.

Château Laujac

OWNERS: Cruse family; manager: Alban Drion.

COMMUNE: Bégadan.

SURFACE AREA UNDER VINE: 50 ha – 60% Cabernet Sauvignon; 30% Merlot; 5% Cabernet Franc;

5% Petit Verdot.

SECOND WINE: Château La Tour Cordouan.

OTHER WINE: Château Laffitte Laujac (Médoc).

CLASSIFICATION: Cru Bourgeois.

Laujac is a real stately home of a château, and it sits in a large park of 350 hectares. The vineyard, rather like at Château Filhot, seems almost an afterthought, having dwindled from its pre-phylloxera proportions. The property has belonged to the Cruse family since 1852. Though the wine is rated highly by Cocks & Féret, I find it light: pleasant but somewhat one-dimensional.

Château Laulan-Ducos

OWNER: Ducos family.
COMMUNE: Jau-Dignac-Loirac.
SURFACE AREA UNDER VINE: 22 ha – 65% Cabernet

Sauvignon; 34% Merlot; 1% Cabernet Franc.
SECOND WINE: Insula Jovis.

Château Laulan-Ducos has changed hands only once, in 1911, since the fifteenth century. The property lies in the village of Sestignan, and since the death of her father François in 1997, has been run by Brigitte Ducos. The harvest is by machine and there are 20 per cent new barrels in the cellar. I have enjoyed both the 1990 and 1996 vintages in recent years.

Château Loudenne

OWNER: Jean-Paul & Marie-Claude Lafragette.
COMMUNE: Saint-Yzans-de-Médoc.
SURFACE AREA UNDER VINE: Red: 48 ha –
  50% Cabernet Sauvignon; 45% Merlot;
  5% Cabernet Franc; White: 14 ha –
  75% Sauvignon; 25% Sémillon.

SECOND WINE: Les Tours de Loudenne; Pavillon de
  Loudenne.
OTHER WINES: Château de l'Hôspital (Graves);
  Château de Rouillac (Pessac-Léognan).
CLASSIFICATION: Cru Bourgeois Supérieur.

The brothers Walter and Alfred Gilbey, London wine merchants, bought Château Loudenne in 1875. It was not just for the vineyard, but for the situation right alongside the estuary, perfect for shipping all their Bordeaux purchases from. Gilbey's became part of IDV (International Distillers and Vintners) in 1963, and Château Loudenne consequently became the centre for the group's purchases of Bordeaux and the maturation of its branded claret La Tour Pavillon. The charming pink château, beautifully restored in the 1960s, also serves as a School of Wine. In 2000 an era came to an end when Loudenne was sold by IDV to Jean-Paul Lafragette, producer of an alcohol-based drink, and owner of two properties in the Graves.

The wine itself can be termed a good honest *bourgeois*. The grapes are machine-harvested. The wine is medium-bodied, sometimes a little lean, but with decent balance and at least some finesse. What it lacks is richness and concentration. Most of the good vintages of the last 20 years, particularly as the vineyard, largely replanted in the early 1960s, has matured, are good at Loudenne. I note the 1996 particularly well. But the wine rarely excites me. The Loudenne *blanc* is a gently oaky but somewhat anonymous Bordeaux *blanc*.

See: *Victorian Vineyard*, Nicholas Faith.

Château Lousteauneuf

OWNER: Bruno Segond.

COMMUNE: Valeyrac.

SURFACE AREA UNDER VINE: 24 ha – 48% Cabernet Sauvignon; 36% Merlot; 10% Cabernet Franc;

6% Petit Verdot.

SECOND WINE: Le Petit Lousteau.

CLASSIFICATION: Cru Bourgeois.

The Segond family took over Château Lousteauneuf in 1962, and have gradually extended the vineyard. In 1993 they decided to château bottle. They now keep back the produce of the old vines, some picked by hand, mature it using 35 per cent new oak barrels, and label the wine *Cuvée Art et Tradition*. I find it rich, spicy and succulent.

Château Les Moines

OWNER: Claude Pourreau.

COMMUNE: Couquèques.

SURFACE AREA UNDER VINE: 30 ha – 75% Cabernet

Sauvignon; 25% Merlot.

SECOND WINE: Château Moulin de Brion.

CLASSIFICATION: Cru Bourgeois.

The soil here is marl, not gravel, and this, together with the high proportion of Cabernet Sauvignon, makes for a solid wine. Yet there is no lack of depth or richness here. M. Pourreau is a passionate winemaker. This is one of the better *cru bourgeois* in this part of the world, and it has the additional virtue of being consistent. There were very good wines in 1986, 1988, 1989 and 1990, and even better results in 1995 and 1996.

Château Noiallac

OWNER: Xavier & Marc Pagès.

COMMUNE: Jau-Dignac-et-Loirac.

SURFACE AREA UNDER VINE: 41 ha – 55% Cabernet Sauvignon; 40% Merlot; 5% Petit Verdot.

SECOND WINES: Château La Rose Noiallac; Château Les Palombes de Noiallac.

CLASSIFICATION: Cru Bourgeois.

Marc Pagès, owner of Château La Tour de By, and his son Xavier acquired Château Noiallac in 1983 from the Huillet family. Though in one of the more northern communes of the Médoc, the vineyard lies on a fine gravel mound and produces a neatly made wine I have often noted well, though it doesn't have quite enough personality to be included among the local super-stars. Château Noiallac supplies the French three star restaurant Taillevent in Paris with its house red Bordeaux. What is not disclosed is whether this is a special cuvée or whether it is the same wine sold under the château label.

Château Les Ormes-Sorbet

OWNER: Boivert family.

COMMUNE: Couquèques.

SURFACE AREA UNDER VINE: 22 ha – 60% Cabernet Sauvignon; 35% Merlot; 5% Cabernet Franc

& Petit Verdot.

SECOND WINE: Château de Conques.

CLASSIFICATION: Cru Bourgeois Supérieur.

Together with Châteaux Tour-Haut-Caussan and Potensac, Les Ormes-Sorbet is one of the bright stars in the Médoc firmament, and it has been for over 20 years. I remember buying the 1978. One of the reasons may be that Jean Boivert, who ran Les Ormes-Sorbet between 1969 and his death in 2004, was a trained *oenologue* (he also tasted for the *Répression des Fraudes*). Another is certainly the investment that has been continually ploughed back into vineyard and *chais*. But most important, I am convinced, is the hand harvesting, and the elimination of what is sub-standard that automatically goes with this. One-third new oak is used in the cellar. Of recent years the 1990 is fine; there was a remarkably pleasant 1991; the 1993 and 1994 were marked highly; and I have noted every vintage since 1996 as 'very good'. It keeps well too.

Château Patache d'Aux

OWNER: Jean-Michel Lapalu.
COMMUNE: Bégadan.
SURFACE AREA UNDER VINE: 43 ha – 60% Cabernet Sauvignon; 30% Merlot; 7% Cabernet Franc; 3% Petit Verdot.

SECOND WINE: Le Relais de Patache d'Aux.
OTHER WINES: Château Le Boscq (Médoc); Château Lacombe Noiallac (Médoc).
CLASSIFICATION: Cru Bourgeois Supérieur.

'Patache' was a local name for a stagecoach, and this is depicted on the label. The property was owned by the d'Aux family, descendants of the Comtes of Armagnac, before the French Revolution. The Lapalu family bought Patache d'Aux from the Delons of Château Léoville-Las-Cases in 1964. Today the château has been sold off and only the cellars remain, in which not only this wine but the Lapalus' Château Le Boscq is vinified and matured. Part of the harvest is still collected by hand. The wine, from 25 per cent new oak, can be a little sturdy in big hot years. But it just needs time. 1982, 1985, 1989 and 1990 were all very good for their *appellation*. The 1995 and 1996 are certainly quite good, but I found the 1998 a little short.

Château Potensac

OWNER: Jean-Hubert Delon & Geneviève d'Alton.
COMMUNE: Ordonnac.
SURFACE AREA UNDER VINE: 67 ha – 46% Cabernet Sauvignon; 25% Merlot; 16% Cabernet Franc;

2% Carmenère.
CLASSIFICATION: Cru Bourgeois Exceptionnel.

Château Potensac, jointly owned by a member of the Delon family who own Château Léoville-Las-Cases, is probably the best wine of the Médoc. It came into the hands of the Delon family through the female line. Georges Liquard was the late Michel Delon's maternal grandfather. According to Bernard Ginestet (*Médoc*, Jacques Legrand, 1989) the property has been in the same family since before the Revolution. Michel Delon told me that the Liquards arrived in France from Holland in the eighteenth century. Whether, and indeed when, they married with some local family in the Médoc is not clear. The first mention of the Liquards appears in Cocks et Féret in 1893.

What we do know is that Potensac was rather smaller in those days: it only produced 50 *tonneaux*. Expansion seems to have come in 1942. Michel Delon, who was born in November 1926, spent his youth at Potensac, a time he remembered vividly. Despite wartime privations, he looked back to this period with happiness. He explained how his grandfather Georges took up the opportunity to acquire three neighbouring vineyards, all virtually abandoned.

Michel took over from his father Paul in 1976. Much has been changed for the better since then. An entirely new *cuvier*, with stainless-steel vats for the fermentation of the wine, was constructed in the early 1980s. The local church, deconsecrated, is used as the barrel cellar, and once Léoville-Las-Cases has been cleared, the same team of pickers arrives to collect the harvest, normally a few days later, and therefore riper than most of the other local estates. Rarely for this part of Bordeaux the crop is not collected by machine.

Today the vines are more or less grouped together in one block and on the highest and most gravelly of the neighbouring soils. Most of the vineyard, rising to 33 m above sea level at its most elevated, lies north of the village, close to the boundary of Ordonnac with the commune of Blaignan.

The temperature of fermentation is relatively cool, at a maximum of 28°C, and there is 20 per cent new oak, supplemented with newish casks passed on from Léoville-Las-Cases.

This makes for a fullish, firm, well-coloured wine with the usual Cabernet Sauvignon tannins and austerity when the wine is young. It certainly needs keeping. Wines like the 1975 and 1970, let alone the 1982, are still fine and vigorous, though perhaps for not *that* much longer. What is apparent – for this, good as it is, is from the Médoc rather than Saint-Julien – is that a suggestion of the rustic can arrive as certain vintages age, plus an underlying astringency which will never soften to seductive mellowness. That is the *terroir* speaking. This is a very well-made *bourgeois*, not a classed growth. Nevertheless, Château Potensac was made an *Exceptionnel* – the only property in the Médoc to be given this accolade, in 2003.

Good recent vintages include a very good 2002, a splendidly concentrated, 2000, a 1999 which is rather better and more vigorous than most, a potentially lush, impressive 1998 and an ample and juicy 1995 (better than the 1996, as is the 1989 and even more so the 1988 to be preferred to the 1990 and the 1985 to the 1986).

See *The Vine* No 192, January 2001.

Château Rollan de By

OWNER: Jean Guyon.

COMMUNE: Bégadan.

SURFACE AREA UNDER VINE: 40 ha – 70% Merlot; 20% Cabernet Sauvignon & Cabernet Franc; 10% Petit Verdot.

SECOND WINE: Château La Clare.

OTHER WINES: Château Haut-Condissas (Médoc); Château Tour-Seran (Médoc).

CLASSIFICATION: Cru Bourgeois Supérieur.

The Burgundian Jean Guyon acquired Château Rollan de By, then with 2 hectares of vines, in 1989. He has since expanded the vineyard and established the wine as one of the area's best. He designed a cellar to his own specifications and installed 50 per cent new oak. The yield is limited to 45/50 hl/ha. Malolactic is partially undertaken in new oak barrels and the wine left to enrich itself on its lees for several months. For a decade now Rollan de By has consistently been one of the best wines of the Médoc.

Château Haut-Condissas is a special *cuvée* of Château Rollan de By. The yield is limited to 35 hl/ha and the wine vinified and matured in new oak. The first vintage was 1995. The wine soon came to prominence, beating most *crus classés* at blind tastings in France, the UK and elsewhere. The 1996 and subsequent vintages have also been well received, proving that this was no fluke. The 2002 is excellent.

Chateau Tour-Blanche

OWNER: Société des Vignobles d'Aquitaine; manager: Rémi Pradier.

COMMUNE: Saint-Christoly-Médoc.

SURFACE AREA UNDER VINE: 39 ha – 60% Merlot; 25% Cabernet Sauvignon; 10% Cabernet Franc;

5% Petit Verdot.

SECOND WINE: Château Guiraud-Peyrebrune.

OTHER WINE: Château Moulin-à-Vent (Moulis).

CLASSIFICATION: Cru Bourgeois.

I don't come across Tour-Blanche as often as I see Château Moulin-à-Vent, Dominique Hessel's other property. The vineyard is picked by machine. One-quarter of the barrels is new. The wine is nicely fresh, with a good backbone. This is not a real star of this part of the world, but a good honest bottle, nonetheless, after four or so years of ageing.

Château La Tour-de-By

OWNER: Marc Pagès and his children.
COMMUNE: Bégadan.
SURFACE AREA UNDER VINE: 74 ha – 65% Cabernet

Sauvignon; 30% Merlot; 5% Cabernet Franc.
SECOND WINE: Château La Roque de By.
CLASSIFICATION: Cru Bourgeois Supérieur.

This large and well-known property, a gravelly vineyard beautifully sited overlooking the Gironde estuary, was aquired by its triumvirate of *pied noir* owners in 1965. Marc Pagès, who runs it, lives in the substantial three-storey château. Nearby is the tower, once the lighthouse for the hamlet of By. The vineyard is picked by machine and there are 20-25 per cent new barrels in the air-conditioned *chai*. I have known, and regularly bought, this reliable wine for 35 years and can remember the vast majority of its vintages, especially those produced since the present-day stainless steel *cuvier* was added in 1973. Of recent years, the 1990 was fine for what it is, the 1996 is very good, still with a firm touch to it, the 1998 is rich, if a little short, and the 2000 impressive.

Château Tour-Haut-Caussan

OWNER: Philippe Courrian.
COMMUNE: Blaignan.
SURFACE AREA UNDER VINE: 17 ha – 50% Cabernet
  Sauvignon; 50% Merlot.

SECOND WINE: Château La Landotte.
OTHER WINE: Château Cascardais (Corbières).
CLASSIFICATION: Cru Bourgeois Supérieur.

The Courrian family can trace their history back to 1634, when they were already installed in Blaignan, but it was not until 1877 that they became associated with this property. It is named after the windmill depicted on the label which dominates the plateau on which lies one half of the vineyard (the remainder adjoins Château Potensac in Ordonnac). In 1981 Philippe Courrian was responsible for restoring the windmill, originally constructed in 1734, and he has refined and improved the quality of the wine, now with Château Potensac the best in the area. Unusually for the Médoc, the crop is harvested by hand. The Merlot is fermented at 33°C, the Cabernet at 28°, and one-third of the casks are new. This produces a lushness along with a concentration and vigour which is very impressive and allows the wine to mature satisfactorily.

Vintages are consistent here; even lesser ones such as 1997 and 1999 making pleasant bottles. The 2002 is one of the best Médocs. The 2000 is very impressive. I prefer the 1996 to the 1998. The 1995 is nicely succulent and fully mature. One of the super-stars of the *appellation*.

Château Tour Saint-Bonnet

OWNER: Pierre Lafon.
COMMUNE: Saint-Christoly-de-Médoc.
SURFACE AREA UNDER VINE: 40 ha – 45% Cabernet
  Sauvignon; 45% Merlot; 5% Malbec;

5% Petit Verdot.
SECOND WINE: Château La Fuie Saint-Bonnet.
CLASSIFICATION: Cru Bourgeois.

Tour Saint-Bonnet has been in the hands of the Lafon family since the turn of the nineteenth century, and can claim to be Saint-Christoly's senior estate. I have memories of the wine going back to the 1971 vintage. It is usually quite a compact wine, even a little hard at the outset, but it repays keeping. Most of the good vintages of the last decade or so can be recommended. The 1990 is very good. The 1995 is better balanced than the 1996 but both are good, as is the 1998, which was not a specially good year for *crus bourgeois*.

Château Les Tuileries

OWNER: Jean-Luc Dartiguenave.

COMMUNE: Saint-Yzans-de-Médoc.

SURFACE AREA UNDER VINE: 20 ha – 50% Merlot;
  50% Cabernet Sauvignon & Cabernet Franc.

SECOND WINE: Château Moulin-de-Bel-Air.

CLASSIFICATION: Cru Bourgeois.

M. Dartiguenave's ancestors were master-coopers, and they gradually built up their own domaine as life for the peripatetic artisan cooper became more difficult. No surprise, therefore, to find as much as one-third new oak in the cellar, even more for the Cuvée Prestige. I don't find this excessive though. Good vintages here include the 1990 and the 1996.

Vieux-Château-Landon

OWNER: Cyril Gillet.

COMMUNE: Bégadan.

SURFACE AREA UNDER VINE: 40 ha – 70% Cabernet
  Sauvignon; 25% Merlot; 5% Malbec.

SECOND WINES: Château Les Bernèdes; Château Le
  Bana.

OTHER WINE: Château Haut-Barrail (Médoc).

CLASSIFICATION: Cru Bourgeois.

This estate has been in the same family, though occasionally passing through the female line, for several centuries. As well as producing one of the commune's best wines, it is one of the show-pieces of Bégadan, the cellars being dotted with statuary and the place clean as a new pin. The crop is machine harvested, and there is 30 per cent new oak. I find the wine fullish, rich and reliable.

Château Vieux Robin

OWNER: Didier & Maryse Roba.

COMMUNE: Bégadan.

SURFACE AREA UNDER VINE: 19 ha – 60% Cabernet
  Sauvignon; 35% Merlot; 5% Cabernet Franc

& Petit Verdot.

SECOND WINE: Air de Vieux Robin.

CLASSIFICATION: Cru Bourgeois Supérieur.

Five generations of the same family have succeeded each other here, but the current generation has raised its reputation above that of the average. The mean age of the vines is now high, over 40 years old, and though the harvest is collected by machine there is a *triage* by hand before the fruit is moved up into the fermentation vats. The basic château wine is reared in 30 per cent new oak and is reliable. The Bois de Launier *cuvée*, named after a special parcel of vines in the vineyard, is both richer and quite a lot more oaky. This wine, as in most of the successful vintages of the last 15 years, can be very good.

Co-operatives

The co-operative movement is strong in the Médoc. There are establishments at Bégadan, Ordonnac, Prignac-en-Médoc, Queyrac, Saint-Yzans-de-Médoc (note the Grand-Saint-Brice bot-tling), Les Vieux Colombiers. Quality is reliable if rarely exciting.

HAUT-MÉDOC

SURFACE AREA (2002): 4591 ha.

PRODUCTION (2002): 210,567 hl.

COLOUR: Red (the white wines are AC

Bordeaux or Bordeaux Supérieur).

GRAPE VARIETIES: Cabernet Franc; Cabernet

Sauvignon; Merlot; Petit Verdot; Malbec;

Carmenère.

MAXIMUM YIELD: 48 hl/ha.

MINIMUM ALCOHOLIC DEGREE: 10%.

The *appellation* covers the following 19 communes (I list them roughly speaking from north to south): Saint-Seurin-de-Cadourne, Vertheuil, Cissac, Saint-Saveur, Saint-Laurent-de-Médoc, Cussac, Lamarque, Arcins, Castelnau, Avensan, Macau, Ludon-Médoc, Le Plan, Parempuyre, Saint-Médard-en-Jalles, Sainte-Hélène, Saint-Aubin, Le Taillan and Blanquefort. In addition parts of Soussans, Cantenac, Labarde and Arsac are AC Haut-Médoc rather than Margaux. Within the Haut-Médoc six communes have their own separate *appellation contrôlée*: Saint-Estèphe, Pauillac, Saint-Julien, Margaux (which includes the four communes listed above), Moulis and Listrac.

The Haut-Médoc begins at the Jalle de Blanquefort, north of Bordeaux, and continues to Saint-Seurin-de-Cadourne, a distance of some 50 kilometres as the crow flies. The vineyards stretch back from the Gironde estuary on a series of rippling mounds or *croupes* of gravel banks as far as the D1/N215, the main road from Bordeaux to Le Verdon and the ferry across the mouth of the estuary over into the Charente country.

This is the largest, greatest and most concentrated red wine area on earth. Once the traveller from Bordeaux reaches the first of the classed growths, Château La Lagune in the commune of Ludon some half an hour's drive away from the city centre, the vines and the great names continue almost uninterruptedly until you pass Château Coufran and Soudars in the hamlet of Cadourne and cross into the Bas-Médoc. To the right, particularly from Saint-Julien onwards, the great vineyards lie close to the water. The brown, sluggish, shallow estuary, within which lie long sandbanks or marshy islands, covered with tangled undergrowth, can clearly be seen. Behind, to the left, the vineyards continue until the gravel gives way to sand and pines. 'The best vines are those which can view the water' is a much repeated quotation and in general this is so. Those properties whose land lies on the first *croupe* facing the Gironde, produce the wines with the greatest complexity of character and depth of flavour. Those from the plateau behind often have more body, but less finesse. In principle those from the five communes which make up the Margaux *appellation* and those from Macau and Ludon in the south of the Haut-Médoc are more delicate than those further north.

This is a countryside dominated by fine wine. The estates are large, and can boast long histories. There are many fine parks and elegant buildings. It was in the Médoc that the *noblesse de la robe*, the wealthy Bordelais in the eighteenth century, established their country estates. During the nineteenth century a new breed of the moneyed classes, whose wealth was based in finance and industry or in wine, replaced those families which had died out or disappeared. These in their turn have been superseded by multinationals, insurance companies and other conglomerates in the post-Second World War era. The Haut-Médoc is not only more homogenous but more alive, more vigorous than the sleepy, more desolate countryside further north. The villages are larger and those who do not work in the *chais* and vineyards of the great estates commute to Bordeaux. There is an element of creeping suburbia, particularly close to the great city and the industrial developments that lie on its outskirts. The Haut-Médoc consists of 29 communes; some 10,100 hectares of vineyard produce a total of about 500,000 hectolitres of wine. Some 2800 hectares, one-third of the land under vine, is classed growth. The majority of these estates lie in Saint-Julien, Pauillac, Saint-Estèphe and the five communes which make up the Margaux *appellation*. Outside these, there are a further 19 communes whose *appellation* is simply Haut-Médoc. Most of these form a line behind the more famous parishes, lying on what one might term the third and fourth ridge of gravel mounds as they ripple away from the Gironde estuary. Two lie south of Margaux (Macau and Ludon); others (Cussac, Lamarque, Arcins) lie between Margaux and Saint-Julien. Saint-Seurin-La-Cadourne is north of Saint-Estèphe.

The Haut-Médoc is the Bordeaux heartland of the Cabemet Sauvignon grape. Together with the Cabemet Franc, balanced with a proportion of Merlot, and, in the best properties, combined with the flavour of new oak, this produces the blackcurrant-blackberry fruit, and the austere, firm, tannic, full-bodied character which is associated with the words 'claret' or 'Red Bordeaux' the world over.

What needs to be pointed out, however, is that Saint-Sauveur is not Pauillac nor is Saint-Laurent Saint-Julien or Avensan Margaux. The majority of the classed growths lie in the four great communes not just because the soil structure is better but because the mesoclimate is warmer. The vineyard in the Clos of Latour will mature four or five days in advance of that at Château Batailley three kilometres to the west. Batailley itself will be four or five days more in advance than Château Bernadotte, a further three kilometres to the west. The implications of this difference can be seen in the size of the harvest if the weather has changed during the flowering: in the relative quality of the wine if the summer ends too soon. These *bourgeois* growths need an even better September than the classed growths and a fine first half of October too. Not just because it will take longer to warm up their colder soils and properly ripen the fruit, but because at this level, for simple economic reasons, one needs to harvest to the limit and cannot afford to take the pains over *triage*, selection, new wood and the rest that the owners of the classed growths can.

This is why really good *bourgeois* and *petit château* wines occur only rarely, in a vintage such as 2000 (or, going back, 1990, 1985, 1982, 1970). In most of the vintages since 1990 over one and a half times the average amount of rain fell in September, and there was little improvement in October. The top classed growths in 1995, 1996, 1998, even 1997 and 1999, produced very good wine. In the lesser growths, sadly, the fruit was only just about ripe. Not surprisingly, the quality of the resulting wines was, proportionately, not nearly as good. Thankfully, there are always some honourable exceptions.

HAUT-MÉDOC LEADING CHÂTEAUX

Château d'Agassac

OWNER: Groupama Assurances.
COMMUNE: Ludon-Médoc.
SURFACE AREA UNDER VINE: 35 ha – 60% Cabernet
  Sauvignon; 40% Merlot.

SECOND WINES: Le Grand Verger d'Agassac;
  Pomiès d'Agassac.
CLASSIFICATION: Cru Bourgeois Supérieur.

Château d'Agassac is the second most important property in Ludon after Château La Lagune. It is a real castle, whose origins date back to the fourteenth century, replacing something even earlier. It was known in pre- and post-revolutionary days as Château Pomiès, after the owners from 1580 onwards, and appears as such in unofficial classifications of the time. Having reverted to the name Agassac and having passed through a number of hands since the outbreak of phylloxera the property was acquired by the Gasquetons of Château Calon-Ségur in 1960. The present proprietors took over in 1996, and have since invested much in the château and the *chais*. Like most wines from the southern part of the Haut-Médoc, Château d'Agassac is only a medium-bodied wine, and it has occasionally been a bit lean in the past. The 1996, though, had a pretty *petits fruits rouges* succulence and the vintages since 1998, especially the 2000, have both depth and class. This is now one of the top *crus bourgeois*.

Château d'Arche

OWNER: Ets. Mähler-Besse; manager: Franck
  Mähler-Besse.
COMMUNE: Ludon-Médoc.
SURFACE AREA UNDER VINE: 9 ha – 45% Cabernet
  Sauvignon; 40% Merlot; 5% Cabernet Franc;

  5% Petit Verdot; 5% Carmenère.
SECOND WINE: Château Egmont.
OTHER WINES: Château Palmer and others.
CLASSIFICATION: Cru Bourgeois Supérieur.

The Duchesne family, who bought Château d'Arche in 1890, sold it in the early 1990s to the Mähler-Besse family. The small vineyard lies between Château La Lagune and the village church. Before the takeover d'Arche was a reliable lesser *cru bourgeois*. There now seems to be a little more concentration (there is certainly a little more oak). To judge by the 1996 this may be a wine to watch. The vintages of the early 2000s continue this improvement.

Château Arnauld

OWNER: Theil and Roggy families; manager: François Theil.

COMMUNE: Arcins.

SURFACE AREA UNDER VINE: 38 ha – 50% Cabernet

Sauvignon; 45% Merlot; 5% Petit Verdot.

SECOND WINE: Comte d'Arnauld.

OTHER WINE: Château Poujeaux (Moulis).

CLASSIFICATION: Cru Bourgeois Supérieur.

The site was once the priory of Arcins, and the property is named after a long-standing family of Bordeaux *parlementaires*. It was acquired by M. & Mme Maurice Roggy in 1956, whose two daughters married the brothers François and Philippe Theil of Château Poujeaux. It is now François who manages the estate and since he took over in 1976 quality here has seen a distinct improvement. The grapes are gathered by hand and matured using 25 per cent new oak. Arnauld is quite a structured wine, but not without richness. It needs a good five years to come round. I have found it consistent, if not quite in the top flight.

Château d'Aurilhac

OWNER: SCEA Châteaux d'Aurilhac et La Fagotte; manager: Éric Nieuwaal-Grassin.

COMMUNE: Saint-Seurin-de-Cadourne.

SURFACE AREA UNDER VINE: 20 ha – 50% Cabernet

Sauvignon; 44% Merlot; 3% Cabernet Franc; 3% Petit Verdot.

SECOND WINE: Château La Fagotte.

CLASSIFICATION: Cru Bourgeois.

Aurilhac lies away from the river, about halfway between Châteaux Sociando-Mallet and Potensac, and was planted with vines as recently as the end of the 1980s. The cellars, though, are modern, the harvest is sorted through on a *table de tri*, the vinification is temperature-controlled and as much as half of the barrels are new. The result in the late 1990s – I have only known this wine since the 1996 vintage – are very promising. There is depth and style as well as concentration and richness. A future star, I'll bet.

Château Beaumont

OWNER: Grands Millésimes de France; director: Étienne Priou.

COMMUNE: Cussac-Fort-Médoc.

SURFACE AREA UNDER VINE: 113 ha – 53% Cabernet Sauvignon; 50% Merlot;

4% Cabernet Franc; 3% Petit Verdot.

SECOND WINE: Château d'Arvigny.

OTHER WINE: Château Beychevelle (Saint-Julien).

CLASSIFICATION: Cru Bourgeois Supérieur.

Château Beaumont takes its name from a former manager of Château Latour and was established in 1824; the château, vaguely Renaissance in style, was built in place of a former *manoir*, 30 years later. It passed through a number of hands before being acquired by Bernard Soulas in 1979. He drained the vineyard, renovated the *chais* and much extended the area under vine before selling out to GMF, a joint venture between the French insurance company Garantie Mutuelle des Fonctionnaires and the Japanese Suntory group.

Since the early 1980s this has been one of the leading Haut-Médoc *crus bourgeois* as it used to be in pre-phylloxera times. The fruit is machine harvested and 30 per cent new oak is used in the cellar. The wine is round, fruity and of medium weight, but can have good depth and elegance. Strangely, as the average age of the vines has matured in the 1990s, I have been less impressed with the wine. The 1986 and 1990 are better than anything since.

Château Belgrave

OWNER: Vignobles Dourthe; manager: Frédéric
    Bonnaffous.
COMMUNE: Saint-Laurent-Médoc.
SURFACE AREA UNDER VINE: 60 ha – 50% Cabernet
    Sauvignon; 40% Merlot; 7% Cabernet Franc;

3% Petit Verdot.
SECOND WINE: Diane de Belgrave.
OTHER WINE: Château La Garde (Pessac-
    Léognan).
CLASSIFICATION: Cinquième Cru (1855).

This is the first of three classed growth properties in Saint-Laurent which lie westwards of Château Lagrange on the western side of the Saint-Julien border. It was known as Coutenceau at the time of the 1855 Classification, when it was owned by M. Bruno-Devez who seems to have changed the name. The elegant if slightly sturdy château dates from the mid-eighteenth century.

Though Belgrave scraped in as a Fifth Growth in 1855 it never seems to have achieved the reputation of some of its peers. There have been a number of changes of ownership since the Bruno-Devez era, most accompanied by neglect of the vineyard. When the CVBG group took over in 1979 there were barely 20 hectares of productive vineyard, and 70 per cent of this was planted to Merlot. Both the château and *chais* were in serious need of restoration. A substantial investment was required.

This was put in hand, and, slowly but surely, an increase in quality back towards *cru classé* has been noticeable. If it has taken longer than expected it must be because the *terroir* is only just good enough. The ambition on the part of *oenologue*-winemaker Merete Larsen is clear, and Michel Rolland acts as a consultant. In 1998 the malolactic fermentation took place in barrel and the maceration was shortened to preserve the finesse. My initial reaction was 'bravo'. In fact, I have marked all the vintages since 1995 as 'good plus' or better. Château Belgrave is a medium-bodied wine with fresh acidity and a very Saint-Julien Cabernet-based character.

Sadly many of the trees in the drive and park surrounding the château were lost in the hurricane of Christmas 1999.

Chateau Bel Orme, Tronquoy de Lalande

OWNER: Jean-Michel Quié.
COMMUNE: Saint-Seurin-de-Cadourne.
SURFACE AREA UNDER VINE: 28 ha – 50% Merlot;
  40% Cabernet Sauvignon; 10% Cabernet Franc.

SECOND WINE: Château La Tour Carmail.
OTHER WINES: Château Croizet-Bages (Pauillac);
  Château Rauzan-Gassies (Margaux).
CLASSIFICATION: Cru Bourgeois.

Though the quality at the other Quié properties leaves much to be desired, since Jean-Louis Camp took over as *régisseur* in the mid-1990s Bel Orme has at least produced wine which can be considered 'quite good'. The early nineteenth-century château, both inside and out, continues however to be more impressive than the wine which is full, if not solid. The solution perhaps is to give up machine-harvesting, to age the wine using at least some new oak, and to make a more serious selection.

Chateau Belle-Vue

OWNER: Vincent Mulliez & Rémy Fouin; manager:
  Vincent Bache-Gabrielsen.
COMMUNE: Macau.
SURFACE AREA UNDER VINE: 9 ha – 42% Cabernet

Sauvignon; 38% Merlot; 20% Petit Verdot.
OTHER WINES: Chateau Bolaire (Bordeaux
  Supérieur); Château de Gironville (Haut-Médoc).

Since 1996 a separate wine has been produced from the best parcels of the Château de Gironville, which lies just south of Château Giscours on the border with the commune of Labarde, and this has rapidly achieved star status. The wine is medium-bodied, with a good base of depth, richness and oak. The 2000 was very good indeed.

Chateau Bernadotte

OWNER: May-Eliane de Lencquesaing; manager:
  Thomas Dô-Chi-Nam.
COMMUNE: Saint-Sauveur.
SURFACE AREA UNDER VINE: 35 ha – 50% Cabernet
  Sauvignon; 44% Merlot; 4% Cabernet Franc;

2% Petit Verdot.
SECOND WINE: Château Fournas-Bernadotte.
OTHER WINE: Château Pichon-Longueville,
  Comtesse de Lalande (Pauillac).

Curt Eklund, a Swiss, bought Château Fournas in Saint-Sauveur, plus 10 hectares of AC Pauillac, in 1973. In 1997 he sold both to May-Eliane de Lencquesaing. Mme de Lencquesaing has changed the name from Fournas to Bernadotte and transferred the 10 hectares of Pauillac vineyards to Chateau Pichon-Lalande, renovated both château and *chais* and spent her usual energies in improving and promoting the wine. I see no reason why this should not be the equivalent of what Château Lalande-Borie is to Ducru-Beaucaillou.

Château Cambon La Pelouse

OWNER: Jean-Pierre & Annick Marie; director: Olivier Pascaud.
COMMUNE: Macau.
SURFACE AREA UNDER VINE: 60 ha – 50% Merlot;

33% Cabernet Sauvignon; 15% Cabernet Franc; 2% Petit Verdot.
CLASSIFICATION: Cru Bourgeois Supérieur.

Château Cambon La Pelouse, which lies on one of the highest points of Macau between Giscours and Cantemerle, was well-known in the nineteenth century but was completely destroyed by frost in February 1956. The château then went out of business for a time before being acquired by the Carrère family in the late 1960s. They rented the estate out to David Faure in 1974 who continued the process of replanting. He sold out to Jean-Pierre Marie in 1996. Since then there has been rapid progress at this estate, culminating in a 2000 that was clearly of classed growth status: gently oaky, stylish and complex.

Château Camensac

OWNER: Forner family and Associates.
COMMUNE: Saint-Laurent-Médoc.
SURFACE AREA UNDER VINES: 65 ha – 60% Cabernet Sauvignon; 25% Merlot;

15% Cabernet Franc.
SECOND WINE: La Closerie de Camensac.
CLASSIFICATION: Cinquième Cru (1855).

Château Camensac was owned by, and the wine often named after, the Popp family in 1855. As with its *cru classé* Saint-Laurent neighbours, the twentieth century was not kind, and the estate was virtually derelict in 1964 when acquired by the present owners. The elegant *chartreuse*, eighteenth century in origin, standing amid umbrella pines, was restored; and the vineyard almost completely replanted.

In recent years I have made four major vertical tastings of Château Camensac, the first in 1987 when we sampled the vintages from 1983 back to 1970. Not surprisingly, the early vintages, even the 1982, were somewhat lacking in depth and character. In 1985 a corner was turned (80 per cent new wood) and this was confirmed in 1986 (100 per cent new wood). But that turned out to be a high tide. The 1988, 1989 and 1990 were barely 'quite good'. Better wines were made in 1995 and 1996, though, while prices remained dirt cheap for a classed growth. And the 1998 has continued this trend. The grapes are hand harvested, as one should expect, and between 35 and 80 per cent new oak, depending on the vintage, is employed. The wine is medium-bodied, round and with an agreeable earthy (in the best sense) spice.

See *Decanter*, March 1988, p.68.

Château Cantemerle

OWNER: SMABTP (Société Mutuelle d'Assurance du Bâtiment et des Travaux Publics); manager: Pascal Berteau.
COMMUNE: Macau.
SURFACE AREA UNDER VINE: 87 ha – 50% Cabernet Sauvignon; 40% Merlot; 5% Cabernet Franc; 5% Petit Verdot.
SECOND WINE: Les Allées de Cantemerle.
OTHER WINES: Château Haut-Corbin (Saint-Émilion); Château Le Jurat (Saint-Émilion).

Oh, dear. Poor old Cantemerle. In my formative years in the wine trade I sampled many a fine post-war bottle of Cantemerle: 1949, 1953, 1959, 1961.... The very essence of fragrance, elegance and delicacy. The wine then was made by Pierre Dubos and his son-in-law Henri Binaud and I was working for The Wine Society, which had a special relationship with Dubos, Binaud and their beloved Cantemerle. In the 1970s, sadly, Cantemerle ran into inheritance problems, and in 1980 it was sold. The firm of Cordier have an interest in the syndicate – the main shareholding belongs to the Société Mutuelle d'Assurance du Bâtiment et des Travaux Publics (SMABTP) – and it is they who are in charge of the wine. After a disappointing run from 1964 onwards I had high hopes when I saw the 1983. But since then nothing has excited me. Under the new regime, the vineyard, which had shrunk to about 20 hectares of old vines, has been considerably extended (20 hectares were additionally acquired from neighbouring Château de Malleret in 1999). But second wines are there to cope with the young vines. No, the heart seems to have gone out of Cantemerle, and that I find a tragedy.

P.S. I wrote the note above before sampling the 2002 in April 2003. This I marked 'very good plus'. It reminded me of the Cantemerles I was brought up on.

See *Grands Vins*, p.290.

Château Caronne-Sainte-Gemme

OWNER: Vignobles Nony-Borie; manager: François Nony.
COMMUNE: Saint-Laurent.
SURFACE AREA UNDER VINE: 45 ha – 60% Cabernet Sauvignon; 37% Merlot; 3% Petit Verdot.
SECOND WINE: Parc Rouge de Caronne.
OTHER WINE: Château Labat (Haut-Médoc).
CLASSIFICATION: Cru Bourgeois Supérieur.

Caronne-Sainte-Gemme lies south of Saint-Julien, across the Jalle du Nord and the Chenal du Milieu from Gruaud-Larose and Lagrange, and inland from Lanessan. The vineyard is in one piece, on a good gravel mound, but sadly it is a frost pocket. It is difficult to maintain old vines here. 'Caronne' comes from a Gallic word for a spring, while Sainte-Gemme derives, albeit in the feminine, from Saint James. We are *en route* to the shrine of Saint James at Compostella here. The

property was bought by Jean Nony's father in 1900 and is today run by him and his nephew François. Caronne-Sainte-Gemme is a wine I know well, and I have watched with interest the contest between Jean Nony, who held the purse strings, and who, as a wine merchant himself, saw no compelling reason to change things and François, who has seen the prices of Châteaux Sociando-Mallet and Haut-Marbuzet, and would like to invest in more new oak and a greater selection.

Meanwhile, despite the frost damage in 1956 and 1985, very good wines were made in 1961, 1962, 1966, 1970, 1982 and the trio of 1988, 1989 and 1990. More recently the 1995 and 1996 are 'quite good', the 1998 'good plus' but the 2000 and 2002 'very good'. In 2002 François Nony assumed full responsibility for Caronne-Sainte-Gemme. The wine is medium- to medium-full bodied, has good acidity and can have plenty of fruit and concentration. It has certainly shown that it can have class too: the will is now there to produce it.

See *The Vine* No 131, December 1995.

Château Charmail

OWNER: Olivier Sèze.
COMMUNE: Saint-Seurin-de-Cadourne.
SURFACE AREA UNDER VINE: 22 ha – 48% Merlot; 30% Cabernet Sauvignon; 20% Cabernet Franc.

SECOND WINE: Tours de Charmail.
OTHER WINE: Château Mayne-Vieil (Fronsac).
CLASSIFICATION: Cru Bourgeois Supérieur.

It is no coincidence that the Sèze family has a property in Fronsac. The histories of many of the top Saint-Émilion properties are littered with the names of this powerful and many-tentacled Libournais family. Roger Sèze bought Château Charmail in 1981, to add to his Fronsadais empire. I remember a sumptuous 1982, though Olivier Sèze, son of Roger, admitted that for the first decade the emphasis was on quantity rather than quality. More recently the 1996, 1997, 2000 and 2002 have been very successful. The vineyard is machine-harvested, the fruit is given 15 days of cold maceration before the fermentation starts and the wine matured using 25 per cent new oak. It is rich and plummy, showing the high amount of Merlot. This is one of the better *crus bourgeois* today.

Château Cissac

OWNER: Vialard family; director: Danielle Vialard.
COMMUNE: Cissac.
SURFACE AREA UNDER VINE: 50 ha – 75% Cabernet Sauvignon; 20% Merlot; 5% Petit Verdot.
SECOND WINE: Reflets du Château Cissac.

OTHER WINES: Château du Breuil (Haut-Médoc); Château Tour du Mirail (Haut-Médoc).
CLASSIFICATION: Cru Bourgeois Supérieur.

This is a very well-known and deservedly popular wine in Britain, Louis Vialard having lived what I might call a double life as head of a wine importing firm in London called French Wine Farmers. The property was created from a number of constituent parts by the Pauillac notary M. Mondon (he of Château Clerc-Milon-Mondon, as it once was) in 1885. The Vialards are descendants of M. Mondon.

The grapes are picked by hand, given a long vatting, and matured using 25 per cent new oak. Château Cissac is a medium-full, ample and juicy wine, though sometimes with a hard edge to it. Most of the vintages of the 1980s are at least 'good'. I prefer the 1988 and 1990 to the 1989. Since then I have similarly admired the 1995 and 1996, though the 1998 and 2002 not as much.

Louis Vialard once told me that he had to produce 55 hl/ha at Cissac to make ends meet. The 'official' statistics in Cocks & Féret show 267 *tonneaux* from the 50 hectares. That works out at just over 48 hl/ha!

See *The Vine* No 148, May 1997.

Château Citran

OWNER: Antoine Merlaut; director: Christian Schätzle.
COMMUNE: Avensan.
SURFACE AREA UNDER VINE: 90 ha – 58% Cabernet Sauvignon; 42% Merlot.
SECOND WINE: Moulins de Citran.

OTHER WINES: Château Chasse-Spleen (Moulis); Château Ferrière (Margaux); Château La Gurgue (Margaux); Château Haut-Bages-Libéral (Pauillac).
CLASSIFICATION: Cru Bourgeois Supérieur.

This is Avensan's most important estate, not that there is a lot of competition. It also has the potential to make wine of *cru classé* quality. It has always been a large property; indeed in the early 1900s it produced 800 *tonneaux*, which only Château Larose-Trintaudon can beat in today's rather more prolific days. It was acquired by the Miailhe brothers (of Château Pichon-Lalande etc.) in 1945, then passed to a brother-in-law, Jean Cesselin, in 1979. It then suffered a period of decline. The investment was not forthcoming. The vineyard evaporated. The fruit was machine-harvested. Then in 1987 the Japanese real estate company Touko-Haus took over. Their programme of investment was prodigious. The vineyard was drained. Neglected parts were replanted. A modern new vinification centre was constructed. It was all very exciting and very expensive. A new Citran with a newly designed label was launched. The 1990 was really fine for a *bourgeois*.

For some reason, which I imagine has a lot to do with accountants and the bottom line, Touko-Haus, after a decade's hard work, decided to pull out in 1997. The purchasers were the Taillan Group.

Claire Villars took over responsibility for the 1996 almost exactly a year after the wine was made. The joint effort resulted in a better wine than the predecessors had managed in 1995, though that was good too. Subsequently, in 2000, responsibility passed to another member of the Villars family, her uncle Antoine Merlaut.

Citran is a medium- to medium-full bodied wine, its flavours and elegance resembling those of Margaux more than Moulis (the vineyard lies halfway between these two villages). The best vintages have no lack of depth nor the ability to age.

Chateau Clément-Pichon

OWNER: Clément Fayat; manager: Patrick Daney.

COMMUNE: Parempuyre.

SURFACE AREA UNDER VINE: 20 ha – 50% Merlot; 40% Cabernet Sauvignon; 10% Cabernet Franc.

OTHER WINES: Château La Dominique (Saint-Émilion); Château Prieurs de la Commanderie (Pauillac).

CLASSIFICATION: Cru Bourgeois Supérieur.

The vast, richly Gothic extravaganza of a château was constructed in 1881 when it was known as the Château de Parempuyre. The name Clément-Pichon commemorates the present proprietor and the Pichon family (a branch of that in Pauillac) who were owners 150 years ago. My experience with today's wine dates only from Clément Fayat's acquisition in 1976, indeed with more recent vintages, as much of the vineyard had to be replanted, as well as the *chais* refurbished. Today the fruit is hand-harvested, subsequently picked over on a *table de tri* and aged in 25–40 per cent new barrels: a more than reliable, essentially soft-centred, fruity wine.

Château Coufran

OWNER: Miailhe family.

COMMUNE: Saint-Seurin-de-Cadourne.

SURFACE AREA UNDER VINE: 75 ha – 85% Merlot; 15% Cabernet Sauvignon.

SECOND WINE: Château La Rose Maréchale.

OTHER WINE: Château Verdignan (Haut-Médoc).

CLASSIFICATION: Cru Bourgeois Supérieur.

North of Saint-Seurin, this is the very last estate as one leaves the Haut-Médoc for the Médoc. Louis Miailhe bought it in 1924 and reconstituted the vineyard with this very high proportion of Merlot: 'the Pomerol of the Médoc' as the château puts it. The Merlot ripens early, is harvested by machine, and the wine matured using 25 per cent new wood. The result is a usually plump wine, of medium weight, and ready for drinking after three or four years. What it lacks, but that is the fault of the *encépagement* as well as the *terroir*, is class.

Château Dillon

OWNER: Ministry of Agriculture and Forestries.

COMMUNE: Blanquefort.

SURFACE AREA UNDER VINE: 35 ha – 48% Merlot; 44% Cabernet Sauvignon; 5% Cabernet Franc;

2% Petit Verdot; 1% Carmenère.

SECOND WINE: Château Breillan.

CLASSIFICATION: Cru Bourgeois.

Named after the Dillon family, owners before the French Revolution and originally of Irish extraction (no connection, please note, with today's Dillons at Château Haut-Brion), the estate was rented to the École Régionale d'Agriculture in 1923. This became the Lycée Viticole de Blanquefort in due course. When the original 30-year lease ran out the Ministry of Agriculture bought Château Dillon, which later absorbed neighbouring Château Breillan, now the name of the second wine.

The equipment is up to date. There is some hand-picking here, and there is one-third new wood. The wine, though competent and consistent – indeed proportionately better in the lesser vintages – rarely sings. It is soft, medium-bodied and matures reasonably quickly.

Château Grandis

OWNER: François-Joseph Vergez.
COMMUNE: Saint-Seurin-de-Cadourne.
SURFACE AREA UNDER VINE: 9.89 ha –
  50% Cabernet Sauvignon; 40% Merlot;

10% Cabernet Franc.
SECOND WINE: Château Maurac-Major.
CLASSIFICATION: Cru Bourgeois.

François-Joseph Vergez, who acquired Château Grandis in 1983, is the great, great-nephew of Eugène Vergez, responsible for most of the line drawings in Cocks and Féret, some of which are reproduced in this book. The Grandis family came over from Holland in the seventeenth century to help drain the Médoc, but lost their heads in the Revolution.

The wine is usually medium- to full-bodied, well coloured and quite tannic. But there can be good concentrated fruit underneath, as in the 1995. The 1996 is good too, as are vintages of the early 2000s but the wine needs five years to mature.

Château Hanteillan

OWNER: Catherine Blasco.
COMMUNE: Cissac-Médoc.
SURFACE AREA UNDER VINE: 82 ha – 52% Cabernet
  Sauvignon; 39% Merlot; 5% Cabernet Franc;

4% Petit Verdot.
SECOND WINES: Château Blagnac; Château
  Laborde.
CLASSIFICATION: Cru Bourgeois Supérieur.

Hanteillan is on the border of Saint-Estèphe, a few hundred metres along the Vertheuil road beyond Château Lilian Ladouys. It dates back to 1179, but as a result of phylloxera and the economic depression which followed, was virtually derelict when the current owners took over in 1972. Since then the château has been restored, the vineyard extended from 10 hectares and a new winery built. Harvesting is by machine. Thirty per cent new oak is used, with part of the wine stored in vat. The wine is medium-bodied, with fresh acidity, but could do with a bit more richness and depth.

Château La Lagune ★

OWNER: Ducellier family; manager: Patrick
  Moulin.
COMMUNE: Ludon-Médoc.
SURFACE AREA UNDER VINE: 80 ha – 55% Cabernet
  Sauvignon; 30% Merlot; 10% Petit Verdot;

5% Cabernet Franc.
SECOND WINE: Moulin de la Lagune.
OTHER WINE: Champagne Ayala.
CLASSIFICATION: Troisième Cru (1855).

The sprawl of the city of Bordeaux is such that it will take you a good half hour by car, going north into the Médoc, before you see any vines. The first major estate you reach is La Lagune in Ludon.

Known in pre-revolutionary times as Château Séguineau, after the family who owned it, La Lagune passed through a number of hands before being acquired by Jouffrey Piston, a wealthy Périgord landowner, in 1819. Piston seems to have put La Lagune on the map. The wine does not appear in classifications in the first quarter of the century, but was classed a *troisième cru* in 1855.

After the First World War the property fell on hard times and the vineyard declined. When it was acquired by Georges Brunet in 1954 it was practically derelict, and the château was a ruin. The American, Alexis Lichine had looked at it three years previously and declined the challenge. He bought the Prieuré, also dilapidated, instead.

Brunet replanted, only to have to sell up in 1962, the consequence of a messy divorce. He moved to Provence and created Château Vignelaure. La Lagune was bought by René Chayoux of Ayala Champagne, in whose hands it remains. Since 1964 the property has been run by ladies, Madame Boirie until 1986, followed by her daughter Caroline Desvergnes.

The wine can be a delight: soft, medium-bodied, fragrant and quite oaky, balanced and succulent. It has been remarkably consistent, as well as good value, from as early as the mid-1960s. More recently, as a result of replanting part of vines installed by Brunet, I have noticed a little weakness in the wine. All the vintages from 1995 to 2000 could have done with a bit more grip and punch. Château La Lagune will never be a blockbuster, but it needs to have length and depth of character. A new *cuvier* was constructed in 2003.

See *Grands Vins*, p. 286.

Chateau de Lamarque

OWNER: Gromand d'Evr family.
COMMUNE: Lamarque.
SURFACE AREA UNDER VINE: 35.5 ha –
    46% Cabernet Sauvignon; 25% Merlot;
    24% Cabernet Franc; 5% Petit Verdot.

SECOND WINES: D de Lamarque; Rose de Saignée
    Noblesse Oblige.
OTHER WINE: Château Cap de Haut (Haut-
    Medoc).
CLASSIFICATION: Cru Bourgeois Supérieur.

Château de Lamarque is one of the oldest buildings in the Médoc and is well worth a small detour. The oldest parts date from the eleventh century, and it has hardly been touched since the time of the Duc d'Épernon, proprietor in the seventeenth century. In 1841 the property passed to the Comte de Fumel, whose family had been owners of Château Margaux before the French Revolution. It remains in the same hands today.

Harvesting is by machine – the vineyard having been completely replanted in 1963 – and 30 per cent of the barrels are new. This is a dependable *cru bourgeois*: medium in weight, sometimes a little four-square but with decent fruit. It rarely excites me greatly but I liked the 1996.

Chateau Lamothe-Bergeron

OWNER: Cordier Mestrezat & Domaines.
COMMUNE: Cussac-Fort-Médoc.
SURFACE AREA UNDER VINE: 66 ha – 52% Cabernet
  Sauvignon; 34% Merlot; 14% Cabernet Franc.
SECOND WINE: Château Romefort.

OTHER WINES: Château Grand-Puy-Ducasse
  (Pauillac); Château Rayne-Vigneau (Sauternes)
  and others.
CLASSFICATION: Cru Bourgeois Supérieur.

The Bergeron family were owners here and at what subsequently became Château Ducru-Beau-caillou in Saint-Julien in the eighteenth century. 'Lamothe' means a *motte* or mound, on which, in 1868, the present château was constructed over a medieval ruin. The property passed into the Mestrezat empire in 1978.

Harvesting is partly by hand, partly by machine. There is 25 per cent new oak in the cellar. I find Lamothe-Bergeron a consistently attractive wine, regularly among the best in the commune – and there can be some stiff competition here. The wines have freshness and plenty of character, are of medium to medium-full weight, and can even be rich. The 2000, 1999, 1998, 1997 and 1996 were all 'good' or better, the 1995 a little less up to par, but the 1988, 1989 and 1990 trio again good or better.

Château Lamothe-Cissac

OWNER: Fabre family.
COMMUNE: Cissac-Médoc.
SURFACE AREA UNDER VINE: 33 ha – 76% Cabernet
  Sauvignon; 26% Merlot; 2% Petit Verdot;
  2% Cabernet Franc.

SECOND WINE: Château Fonsèche.
OTHER WINES: Château Landat (Haut-Médoc);
  Château La Tonnelle (Haut-Médoc).
CLASSIFICATION: Cru Bourgeois.

Built on Gallo-Roman ruins in 1912, Château Lamothe-Cissac and its vineyard was lost in a gambling debt in the casino at Biarritz, and was then abandoned until resurrected by the Fabre family in 1964. The first subsequent vintage was 1968. Progress since then has been considerable, and the wine is now second only to Château Cissac in the commune (coincidentally or not Éric Fabre is married to Hélène Vialard of Château Cissac). Harvesting is partly by hand, partly by machine; 20 per cent new wood is used and the wine given a long maceration. It is medium-full bodied and can be rich and satisfying. The 1995, 1996 and 2000 are above average.

Chateau Lanessan

OWNER: Bouteiller family.

COMMUNE: Cussac-Fort-Médoc.

SURFACE AREA UNDER VINE: 45 ha – 70% Cabernet
Sauvignon; 20% Merlot; 5% Cabernet Franc;
5% Petit Verdot.

SECOND WINE: Les Caliches de Lanessan.

OTHER WINES: Château Lachesnaye (Haut-
Médoc); Château Sainte-Gemme (Haut-Médoc).

CLASSIFICATION: Cru Bourgeois Supérieur.

In the early nineteenth century, Château Lanessan was sometimes listed under the name of Duboscq, after the owners prior to the French Revolution, who were themselves descendants of the Lanessan family. It often appeared in unofficial classifications of the time, albeit towards the end. It supposedly failed to make the 1855 Classification because the owner, Louis Delbos, could not be bothered to submit samples.

In 1907 a Delbos daughter married Étienne Bouteiller, the grandfather of Hubert and Bertrand Bouteiller who run Château Lanessan today. The Gothic-style château was constructed in 1878. There are extensive *chais*, part of which house a museum of carriages and related items.

I have had some very good Lanessans in the past. At a vertical tasting at the château in 1990 I noted the 1970, the 1979, the 1982 and the 1985 as being very good. Since then however I have been less impressed. The wine has lacked personality and richness.

See *Decanter*, December 1990, p.80.

Chateau Larose-Trintaudon

OWNER: AGF (Assurances Générales de France);
manager: Matthias von Campe.

COMMUNE: Saint-Laurent-Médoc.

SURFACE AREA UNDER VINE: 140 ha –
65% Cabernet Sauvignon; 35% Merlot.

SECOND WINES: Larose-Saint-Laurent; Les Hauts
de Trintaudon.

OTHER WINES: Château Larose-Perganson (Haut-
Médoc); Château La Tourette (Pauillac).

CLASSIFICATION: Cru Bourgeois Supérieur.

This is by quite some way the largest of the leading estates in Bordeaux, capable of producing 100,000 cases of wine a year. It has had an uneven history as well as a list of owners who read like the protagonists of some Ruritanian romance. It was derelict when replanted in 1965 by the Forner family, also of Château Camensac. In 1986 it was sold to AGF.

Inevitably, in view of its size, harvesting is largely by machine, but the winemaking equipment has continually been updated, and one-third of 2700 barrels are renewed each year. The wine is medium- to medium-full-bodied, fruity but occasionally, even with today's mature vines, a little lean. There is a lack of excitement here. Part of the vineyard extends into the commune of Pauillac. The wine from these parcels is bottled as Château La Tourette, which also lacks flair.

See *Decanter*, December 1998, p.62.

Château Lestage-Simon

OWNER: Union Française de Gestion; director: Merete Larson.
COMMUNE: Saint-Seurin-de-Cadourne.
SURFACE AREA UNDER VINE: 40 ha – 60% Merlot;

28% Cabernet Sauvignon; 11% Cabernet Franc.
SECOND WINE: Château Troupian.
CLASSIFICATION: Cru Bourgeois Supérieur.

Like its near neighbour, Château Coufran, Château Lestage-Simon is a Médoc-Merlot, and for the same reason: the soil is marl and not gravel. The wine is ripe and succulent and easy to drink. It is usually quite oaky, for one-third of the barrels are new each year. The wine is consistently of good quality, and in my view rather better than Château Coufran these days. In 1998 there was a major investment in the cellars. This is already noticeable in the quality of the wine.

Château Lieujean

OWNER: SC Garri du Gai; farmed by Domaines Lapalu; director: Patrice Ricard.
COMMUNE: Saint-Sauveur.
SURFACE AREA UNDER VINE: 38 ha – 69% Cabernet Sauvignon; 31% Merlot.

SECOND WINE: Château Lagrave.
OTHER WINES: Château Haut-Laborde (Haut-Médoc); Château La Tour de By (Médoc).
CLASSIFICATION: Cru Bourgeois.

This is yet another property which fell into hard times in the early twentieth century, and had to be replanted from scratch when the estate was bought in 1965 by André Baron. It has exchanged hands twice since then. Harvesting is both by hand and machine. Twenty to thirty per cent of the barrels are renewed annually. The wine is medium-bodied, plump, oaky and not without charm.

Château Liversan

OWNER: SC du Château Liversan; farmed by Domaines Lapalu; director: Patrice Ricard.
COMMUNE: Saint-Sauveur.
SURFACE AREA UNDER VINE: 39 ha – 49% Cabernet Sauvignon; 50% Merlot; 1% Cabernet Franc.

SECOND WINE: Les Charmes de Liversan.
OTHER WINES: Château Haut-Laborde (Haut-Médoc); Château La Tour de By (Médoc).
CLASSIFICATION: Cru Bourgeois Supérieur.

The somewhat dilapidated Château Liversan was taken over in 1984 by Prince Guy de Polignac. While the vineyard, thankfully, was of some age if not planted to the full, a considerable investment was made in the cellar. Good wines were produced in 1985, 1989 and 1990. In 1996 Liversan was sold to the Lapalu family of Château La Tour de By in the Médoc. More money has been invested. The 1998 and 1999 were certainly an improvement on the rather dull 1995 and 1996.

Château Malescasse

OWNER: Alcatel Alstom; managed by Groupe Taillan.
COMMUNE: Lamarque.
SURFACE AREA UNDER VINE: 37 ha – 46% Cabernet Sauvignon; 44% Merlot; 10% Cabernet Franc.
SECOND WINE: La Closerie de Malescasse.
CLASSIFICATION: Cru Bourgeois Supérieur.

Largely replanted in the early 1970s, having suffered from frequent changes of ownership, Malescasse was bought in 1979 by the Tesserons of Châteaux Pontet-Canet and Lafon-Rochet. They sold it in 1992 to Alcatel Alstom, owner until 2000 of Gruaud-Larose. It is still made by the same team. There is a new *cuvier*, an enlarged *chai* and one-quarter new oak. Picking is partly by hand. This has been one of the better, more consistent *bourgeois* Médocs for 20 years. It is usually medium-full, a little hard in its youth but acquires richness as it ages. The 1988, 1989 and 1990 were all very good. I am less impressed by the 1995, 1996 and 1998, but the 2000 and 2002 are good.

Château de Malleret

OWNER: du Vivier family.
COMMUNE: Le Pian-Médoc.
SURFACE AREA UNDER VINE: 31 ha – 60% Cabernet Sauvignon; 30% Merlot; 5% Cabernet Franc; 5% Petit Verdot.
SECOND WINE: Château Barthez.
CLASSIFICATION: Cru Bourgeois Supérieur.

Château de Malleret has belonged to the du Vivier family since 1827. It is an impressive estate of over 400 hectares, largely given over to racehorses. Between 1931, when, at the height of the slump, the vines were ripped up, and 1958, when Bertrand du Vivier took over, there were no vines. The fruit is partly hand-picked and there is 25 per cent new oak. The wines are medium-bodied, mature early, and can be elegant and fragrant. I have high marks for the 1990, 1995 and 1996.

Château Maucamps

OWNER: Tessandier family.
COMMUNE: Macau.
SURFACE AREA UNDER VINE: 18 ha – 55% Cabernet Sauvignon; 40% Merlot; 5% Petit Verdot.
SECOND WINE: Clos de May.
CLASSIFICATION: Cru Bourgeois Supérieur.

The Tessandier family bought Château Maucamps in 1954, since when they have sold the château itself, which is now a home for the elderly. The vintage is hand picked. Thirty per cent new oak is used for the maturation. After a succession of successes since the early 1980s– the 1986 and 1989 in particular – I regret I have been less enthused about the Maucamps in recent years.

Château Micalet

OWNER: Denis Fédieu.
COMMUNE: Cussac-Fort-Médoc.
SURFACE AREA UNDER VINES: 6 ha – 55% Merlot; 40% Cabernet Sauvignon; 7 Petit Verdot; 3% Cabernet Franc.
OTHER WINE: Château Moneins (Haut-Médoc).

From 1950 to 1970 the Micalet harvest was taken to the local co-operative. Today 'small is beautiful' is the call. The grapes are hand-picked and sorted. The percentage of new wood is gradually being increased – not so long ago there was none at all. And it is increasingly obvious that someone passionate is behind the winemaking. I am not the only person who was very impressed by the 1996: a lovely, fullish bodied, sensuous and flashy wine.

Château du Moulin Rouge

OWNER: Pelon & Ribiero families.
COMMUNE: Cussac-Fort-Médoc.
SURFACE AREA UNDER VINE: 15 ha – 50% Merlot;

40% Cabernet Sauvignon; 10% Cabernet Franc.
CLASSIFICATION: Cru Bourgeois.

Château du Moulin Rouge has long been one of the better *cru bourgeois*. The vineyard lies immediately south of the border with Saint-Julien and is hand-harvested. Ageing is partly in tank, partly in barrel of which 25 per cent is new. The wine is usually medium-full bodied, rich and ample, with a structure that needs five or six years to mellow – 1996 is the pick of the recent vintages. The 2002 is very good too.

Château Peyrabon

OWNER: Millesima; director: Xavier Michelet.
COMMUNE: Saint-Sauveur.
SURFACE AREA UNDER VINE: 56 ha – 62% Cabernet
  Sauvignon; 32% Merlot; 4% Cabernet Franc;
  2% Petit Verdot.

SECOND WINE: Château Pierbone.
OTHER WINE: Chateau La Fleur Peyrabon
  (Pauillac).
CLASSIFICATION: Cru Bourgeois.

Queen Victoria is said to have attended a concert in the ballroom of this handsome château, during the time when the estate belonged to the Marquis de Courcelles. The vineyard was smaller then, and until the late 1970s the wine was little seen, being sold privately.

He has enlarged the area under vines, at the expense of neighbouring Château Liversan, and established Peyrabon as one of the top wines of the commune. The domaine is harvested partly by hand. There is one-third new oak in the cellar. The wine is normally medium-full, quite sturdy and marked by the new oak in its youth. But it can mature satisfactorily.

Château Pontoise-Cabarrus

OWNER: Tereygéol family.
COMMUNE: Saint-Seurin-de-Cadourne.
SURFACE AREA UNDER VINE: 30 ha – 50% Cabernet
  Sauvignon; 45% Merlot; 3% Petit Verdot;

2% Cabernet Franc.
SECOND WINE: Les Hauts de Plaisance.
CLASSIFICATION: Cru Bourgeois.

The Cabarrus family, influential and wealthy both before the French Revolution, were owners here and at Château Lagrange. Thérèse de Cabarrus, mistress of Taillan,one of Napoleon's ministers, saved many from the fate of the guillotine. Subsequently they were both witnesses at the marriage of Napoleon to Joséphine.

When Émile Tereygéol bought Pontoise-Cabarrus in 1960, however, there were only 7 hectares under vine. Both château and *chai* were in dire need of renovation. The investment was made, and it was not long before the wine was acknowledged as one of the better examples of this commune. Harvesting is by machine. Maturation is partly in vat, partly in wood, with 20 per cent new barrels.

The wine is well-coloured, medium- to full-bodied, balanced and lush, needing five or six years to mature. I have liked nearly all the vintages that have come my way in recent years. Unlike many *crus bourgeois* the 1995, 1996 and 1998 seem as good as equivalent vintages of the 1980s.

Château Puy-Castéra

OWNER: Marès family; director: Alix Marès.
COMMUNE: Cissac-Médoc.
SURFACE AREA UNDER VINE: 28 ha – 57% Cabernet Sauvignon; 30% Merlot; 10% Cabernet Franc; 2% Malbec; 1% Petit Verdot.

SECOND WINE: Château Holden.
OTHER WINE: Mas de Bressandes (Costières de Nîmes).
CLASSIFICATION: Cru Bourgeois.

Puy-Castéra, meaning 'high camp', i.e. a Gallo-Roman military encampment – the ruins of which still remain – is another example of a wine estate which ceased to function in the 1930s as a result of the slump. Henri Marès, father of Roger, the head of the family today, arrived in 1973. By 1980 the entire 25 hectares had been planted and the wine had been decreed a *cru bourgeois*. As the vines age the wine is putting on weight and dimension. I liked the 1996.

In the Languedoc Roger's son Cyril makes one of the better Costières de Nîmes.

Château Ramage La Batisse

OWNER: MACIF.
COMMUNE: Saint-Sauveur.
SURFACE AREA UNDER VINE: 56 ha – 62% Cabernet Sauvignon; 33% Merlot; 3% Cabernet Franc; 2% Petit Verdot.

SECOND WINE: Château Touteran.
OTHER WINE: Château Belcier (Côtes de Castillon).
CLASSIFICATION: Cru Bourgeois Supérieur.

The small, elegant *chartreuse* of Ramage La Batisse is dominated by its *chai*, which is more like a bus garage than the traditional Médoc examples. Once again, here is a property created from nothing after decades of neglect – and as recently as 1961. François Monnoyier gradually enlarged the property, appointed a M. Picamoles to manage it – avoiding the Bordeaux *négoce*, Ramage La Batisse was sold direct – and soon established the wines as the leading example in the *commune*, before selling out to MACIF in 1986.

Harvesting is usually by machine – 1997 was an exception, owing to the fragility of the fruit. The malolactic fermentation now partly takes place in wood, of which there may be as much as 50 per cent new for the *grand vin*. The wine is usually medium-bodied, gently oaky, succulent and generous, and matures in the medium term. Of recent vintages I can recommend the 1996, 1997, 2000 and 2002. The 1990 was very good too, as, unexpectedly, was the 1991.

Château Sénéjac

OWNER: Thierry & Nancy Rustmann.
COMMUNE: Le Pian-Médoc.
SURFACE AREA UNDER VINE: 37 ha – 48% Cabernet Sauvignon; 37% Merlot; 11% Cabernet Franc; 4% Petit Verdot.

SECOND WINES: Artigues de Sénéjac; Comte de Sénéjac.
OTHER WINE: Karolus (Haut-Médoc).
CLASSIFICATION: Cru Bourgeois Supérieur.

The de Guigné family acquired this property as long ago as 1860 and sold it to the Rustmanns in 1999. Though well-known in pre-phylloxera years the château's reputation declined equally with a neglect of investment by subsequent generations, and it was not until the 1973 arrival of Charles de Guigné, who had been brought up in the USA, that fortunes were reversed. The wine's current renown is due to the New Zealand winemaker, Jenny Bailey-Dobson, who was in charge between 1983 and 1993. There is now an up-to-date winery to complement the elegant château. Harvesting is by hand, and 25 per cent new oak is employed. I fear Sénéjac does not quite have the flair today it expressed in the Dobson era, but it is still one of the better *bourgeois*: medium-bodied, balanced, fragrant and stylish. The 2002 is very good.

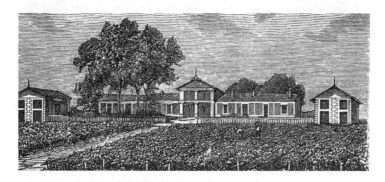

Château Sociando-Mallet ★

OWNER: Jean Gautreau.
COMMUNE: Saint-Seurin-de-Cadourne.
SURFACE AREA UNDER VINE: 72 ha – 55% Cabernet

Sauvignon; 40% Merlot; 5% Cabernet Franc.
SECOND WINE: La Demoiselle de Sociando-Mallet.

Château Sociando-Mallet is not just Saint-Seurin's leading growth but the main claimant of all the *bourgeois* wines to classed growth status. It sells for the same price as Third Growth Château La Lagune. The estate is the result of one man's obsession – now in his seventies, Jean Gautreau fell in love with the location, a splendid *croupe* of gravel commanding a gentle bend in the Gironde estuary, in the 1960s. He bought Sociando-Mallet, run down to 5 hectares of productive vines, in 1969. The *chais* were dilapidated, the modest château uninhabitable. Bit by bit the buildings were modernised and the vineyard enlarged, the last 8 hectares being planted in 1990. But the wine has been fine for many years.

Harvesting is by hand. Yields are low, and the wine can take the 80–100 per cent new oak in which it matures. A less concentrated product would be overwhelmed. This is a rich wine, full and Pauillac in character, with depth, finesse and staying power. I can think of few vintages no better than very good. The 1982, 1986 and 1990 are the best of that period. Since then the 1995, 1996 and 1998 have been noted very good indeed, or better, and the 2000 and 2002 are better still.

See *Grands Vins*, p. 305 & *The Vine* No 214, November 2002.

Château Soudars

OWNER: Éric Miailhe.

COMMUNE: Saint-Seurin-de-Cadourne.

SURFACE AREA UNDER VINE: 22 ha – 50% Merlot;

49% Cabernet Sauvignon; 1% Cabernet Franc.

CLASSIFICATION: Cru Bourgeois Supérieur.

Soudars is a recent creation. Éric Miailhe, son of Jean and grandson of Louis, responsible for Châteaux Coufran and Verdignan in the same commune, acquired 15 hectares of land *en friche* in 1973. The soil is largely a stony marl, rather than gravel, which explains the reason for a high percentage of Merlot in the vineyard as it suits this variety better.

Harvesting is by machine. There is one-third new wood in the cellar, sometimes of American origin which gives a rounder, more spicy flavour. The wine is plump but a little solid. The 1998 and 1996 are good, better than the 1995.

Château La Tour Carnet

OWNER: Bernard Magrez; director: Emmanuel Bonneau.

COMMUNE: Saint-Laurent-Médoc.

SURFACE AREA UNDER VINE: 48 ha – 53% Cabernet Sauvignon; 33% Merlot; 10% Cabernet Franc; 4% Petit Verdot.

SECOND WINE: Les Douves de Carnet.

OTHER WINES: Château Fombrauge (Saint-Émilion); Château Les Grands Chênes (Médoc); Château Pape-Clément (Pessac-Léognan).

CLASSIFICATION : Quatrième Cru Classé (1855).

La Tour Carnet is one of the oldest estates in the Médoc. Originally a proper castle, only the gatehouse, dating from the thirteenth century, still remains. The remainder of the château was constructed in the seventeenth and eighteenth centuries. The whole thing is surrounded by a moat. The owners in the nineteenth century were the de Leutkens family, wealthy Bordelais merchants.

As elsewhere fortunes dipped in the post-phylloxera period. The area under vine declined to 5 hectares, and the château was in ruins when it exchanged hands in 1962. The new owner was Louis Lipschitz, the manager of a local shipping line, and a gentleman of Polish origins.

From Lipschtz La Tour Carnet passed to Marie-Claire Pellegrin, his daughter (tragically her husband Guy-François was asphyxiated in a vat by carbon dioxide in 1988, having gone to the rescue of his cellar master). Mme Pellegrin sold out to Bernard Magrez of William Pitters International in 1999.

The soil at La Tour Carnet, which lies further west than Château Camensac and Château Belgrave, is cold. The vines largely face to the west and are more susceptible to frost than most *cru classé* vineyards. For this reason, perhaps, though there has been a considerable investment in the winemaking equipment in recent years, the wines still fail to reach *cru classé* standard. I made rather a dispiriting vertical tasting of the wines in 1991 and have called regularly since. Today the quality can be rated good. But that is not good enough, and with the Magrez penchant for lots of extraction and lots of new oak, quality seems to have swung from one side of the pendulum to the other: from the too lean to the too bulky.

Château Tour-du-Haut-Moulin

OWNER: Poitou family.
COMMUNE: Cussac-Fort-Médoc.
SURFACE AREA UNDER VINE: 31 ha – 50% Merlot;

45% Cabernet Sauvignon; 5% Petit Verdot.
CLASSIFICATION: Cru Bourgeois Supérieur.

Though the château itself is but a modest *maison bourgeoise*, Château Tour du Haut-Moulin is one of the best and most reliable of the *crus bourgeois*. The vineyard lies on a *croupe* of well-drained gravel close to the Gironde estuary and the Fort Médoc, a Vauban fortification down by the waterside. The château has been in the hands of the Poitou family for five generations. Picking is partly by hand, with 25 per cent new oak in the cellar. The wine is fuller than most, with ripe tannins, a lush texture and plenty of fruit. It lasts well. I have marked most of the vintages of the last 20 years either well or very well. The 2002 ('very good') continues this consistency.

Château Verdignan

OWNER: Miailhe family.
COMMUNE: Saint-Seurin-de-Cadourne.
SURFACE AREA UNDER VINE: 60 ha – 50% Cabernet Sauvignon; 45% Merlot; 5% Cabernet Franc.

SECOND WINE: Château Plantey de la Croix.
OTHER WINES: Château Coufran and Château Soudars (both Haut-Médoc).
CLASSIFICATION: Cru Bourgeois Supérieur.

Verdignan's vineyards lie east of the main vineyard road, opposite the Miailhe family's Châteaux Coufran and Soudars, and the soil is more gravelly here – hence a more classic *encépagement* and a sturdier, more masculine, more long-lasting wine. Verdignan has been owned by the Miailhes since 1972, originally with Jean Merlaut as co-stockholder, until he left to buy Château Chasse-Spleen in 1976. I find I usually prefer Château Verdignan to Coufran or Soudars, though I am rarely exceptionally enthused. The 1986 was better, as is the 1995 and 1998. The 2002 is very good.

Château Villegeorge

OWNER: Marie-Laure Lurton-Roux.
COMMUNE: Avensan.
SURFACE AREA UNDER VINE: 20 ha – 55% Cabernet Sauvignon; 44% Merlot.

SECOND WINE: Château du Peyremorin.
OTHER WINES: Château Duplessis (Moulis); Château Tour de Bessan (Margaux).
CLASSIFICATION: Cru Bourgeois Supérieur.

Apart from Citran, Villegeorge is the only notable *cru* in Avensan which is low-lying, filled with gravel pits and little ponds, and largely planted with pine trees. It had a good reputation in the latter part of the nineteenth century, when it belonged to the Clauzel family. In 1932 it was one of six estates classed as *cru bourgeois exceptionnel*. It was subsequently neglected, and when Lucien Lurton, of Château Brane-Cantenac, bought it in 1973, it was very run down. Lurton brought the vineyard back into shape, and renovated the *chais* before handing over to his daughter, a qualified oenologist. The vineyard is prone to frost, which explains the high proportion of Merlot, despite the gravel soil. Sadly I have to say that I have never found anything to substantiate its ranking in 1932. Things are improving, however, under the present regime.

SAINT-ESTÈPHE

SURFACE AREA (2002): 1254 ha.

PRODUCTION (2002): 52,872 hl.

COLOUR: Red (the white wines are *Appellation*

Contrôlée Bordeaux or Bordeaux

Supérieur).

GRAPE VARIETIES: Cabernet Franc; Cabernet

Sauvignon; Merlot; Petit Verdot; Malbec;

Carmenère.

MAXIMUM YIELD: 47 hl/ha.

MINIMUM ALCOHOLIC DEGREE: 10%.

S aint-Estèphe is the largest and most northerly of the four great Haut-Médoc wine communes. It has long suffered by comparison with the others. Writers extol the magnificence of Pauillac, the breed of Saint-Julien, the subtlety and fragrance of Margaux. Yet they do not warm to the wines of Saint-Estèphe. Saint-Estèphe can only boast five classed growths (two Seconds, a Third, a Fourth and a Fifth) and I do not consider would manage to scrape many more if there were to be a reclassification. The commune is dominated by a large cluster of good-but-never-great *bourgeois* growths, many extensive in size, with wines that are regularly exported and deservedly popular. But these are middle-class wines rather than aristocrats.

The soil in Saint-Estèphe is varied. In the south-east corner of the *appellation* it is heavy gravel on the hard sandstone base rich in iron known as *alios*, similar to that in Pauillac. Progressively west and north it contains more clay, less gravel, becomes heavier and more fertile. In parts there is limestone. Naturally the style of the wines varies too. Although in general there is more Merlot here than elsewhere in the Haut-Médoc, there are nevertheless many properties with 70 per cent or more Cabernet Sauvignon and Cabernet Franc.

Compared with Pauillacs the wines are in general tougher and denser, though not necessarily fuller. They are more aromatic and less elegant. They are solid rather than austere: firm, full and tannic but in a less distinguished way; less obviously richly blackcurrany in flavour, and more robust and spicy – even sweeter – in character. Some Saint-Estèphes do not age too gracefully. That said, the best wines – Cos d'Estournel clearly, and Montrose also – both from the south-eastern end of the parish, are as good, and can last as well, as the very greatest of their peers in Pauillac and Saint-Julien. Overall in the commune there has been an encouraging change for the better in recent years.

SAINT-ESTÈPHE LEADING CHÂTEAUX

Château Andron-Blanquet

OWNER: Audoy family.

SURFACE AREA UNDER VINE: 16 ha – 55% Cabernet Sauvignon; 30% Merlot; 15% Cabernet Franc.

SECOND WINE: Château Saint-Roch.

OTHER WINE: Château Cos Labory (Saint-Estèphe).

CLASSIFICATION: Cru Bourgeois.

Named after the village of Blanquet and M. Andron, proprietor in the nineteenth century, Château Andron-Blanquet has belonged since 1971 to the Audoy family of Château Cos Labory, and is vinified in the Cos *chais*. For much of this time Andron-Blanquet was effectively the second wine of Cos Labory. It was harvested partly by hand, stored in tank as well as barrel, and was a decent, quite sturdy example, if without much richness or finesse.

In 1994 Bernard Audoy decided to give it its own identity again. With a larger *chai* all the wine is now *barrique* aged (25 per cent is new each year) and it has become more sophisticated. As with many *bourgeois* Saint-Estèphes it can be brutal in its youth. I often find myself revising my opinion upwards when I see it for a second time alongside the new vintage, at 18 months of age.

Château Beau Site

OWNER: Héritiers Castéja.

SURFACE AREA UNDER VINE: 32 ha – 70% Cabernet Sauvignon; 30% Merlot.

SECOND WINE: Pavillon de Saint-Estèphe.

OTHER WINES: Château Batailley (Pauillac); Château Lynch-Moussas (Pauillac); Château Trottevieille (Saint-Émilion) and others.

CLASSIFICATION: Cru Bourgeois Supérieur.

There is a Beau Site (*tout court*) and a Beau-Site-Haut-Vignoble. This is the better property. Émile Castéja and his father-in-law Marcel Borie bought what had once been the major part of an estate called Morin in 1955. Following the terrible frosts of February 1956 they might have regretted their investment as much of the vineyard had to be replanted.

This is a fullish, dependable wine; a little harsh in its youth, but worth of patience. Cocks & Féret and other authorities claim it is reared in 50 per cent new wood. This is not obvious when you taste the wine. It is marketed exclusively by Borie-Manoux, the family firm of this branch of the Castéja family. The 2002 was good plus.

Château Le Boscq

OWNER: UFG; farmed by Dourthe-Kressmann.

SURFACE AREA UNDER VINE: 18 ha – 60% Merlot; 26% Cabernet Sauvignon; 10% Petit Verdot; 4% Cabernet Franc.

SECOND WINE: Heritage de Le Boscq.

CLASSIFICATION: Cru Bourgeois Supérieur.

This is one of the most northerly properties in Saint-Estèphe and lies on a *croupe* of gravel between châteaux Sociando-Mallet and Calon-Ségur. Though it once belonged to the Bartons of Château Langoa-Barton, it has only come to the fore in recent years, since being taken over by the UFG group in 1995. The wine is plump and without hard edges, with a pronounced hint of oak. A significant investment was made here between 1998 and 2002. From 1998 one can see this reflected in the wines which are very good, especially the 2000, 2001 and 2002.

Chateau Calon-Ségur ★

OWNER: Capbern-Gasqueton family.
SURFACE AREA UNDER VINE: 74 ha – 65% Cabernet
Sauvignon; 20% Merlot; 15% Cabernet Franc.
SECOND WINE: Marquis de Calon.

OTHER WINE: Château Capbern-Gasqueton
(Saint-Estèphe).
CLASSIFICATION: Troisième Cru (1855).

This is one of the oldest and most illustrious properties in the Médoc and since the beginning of monocultural winemaking the senior estate in the commune. Calon's history goes back to Gallo-Roman times: the name coming from the contemporary name for wood, *calon*, and the shallow boats used for fording the estuary, *calones*. In early medieval times it was the main fief of the Lords of Lesparre. Following the French conquest of the area after the Battle of Castillon in 1453, the estate passed through various hands, whose names would subsequently be recorded elsewhere in the vinous history of Bordeaux: Jean de Lur (later the Lur-Saluces of Château d'Yquem) and de Gasq (the predecessors of General Palmer at Château Palmer). Finally Nicolas-Alexandre de Ségur, president of the Bordeaux parliament and already owner of Château Lafite and Château Latour, received Château Calon through his marriage to Jeanne de Gasq in 1718. 'I make my wine at Lafite and Latour,' he is reported to have declared. 'But my heart is in Calon.' Hence the heart depicted on the label.

Following the break up of the Ségur empire – Nicolas-Alexandre was not well-served by his spendthrift successors – Calon-Ségur, as it was then known, passed to Étienne-Théodore Dumoulin, in 1778, and 36 years later to Firmin de Lestapis. Towards the end of the nineteenth century the Lestapis family experienced financial difficulties, and so sold Calon-Ségur to Georges Gasqueton and his uncle Charles Hanappier in 1894. It remains in the same family today. Philippe Capbern-Gasqueton took over in 1961 and at the same time the Gasquetons acquired the derelict Château du Tertre in Arsac. This was sold following Philippe's death in 1998.

The vineyard of Calon lies in one block north of the village of Saint-Estèphe. The château itself, set in a little garden, is an elegant, early eighteenth-century construction in creamy limestone with four curiously blunted mansard side towers. The light interior, housing the family's antique furniture and tapestries, is a delight.

Calon-Ségur made particularly good wines in the years between 1945 and 1961. Following the February 1956 frosts the proportion of Merlot in the vineyard was increased. This turned out to be a mistake, and so subsequently further replanting of Cabernet Sauvignon ensued. The *élevage* at this time, including a practice of leaving the wine a full two years before bottling, was not as it should have been. The quality of the wine declined; it often displayed rather rustic tannins. However, in the 1990s quality has improved. A new stainless *cuvier*, installed in 1999, improved things further, if the 2000, 2001 and 2002 are anything to judge by. Without being a Super-Second, Calon-Ségur certainly now merits its Third Growth classification.

See *Grands Vins*, p. 203.

Château Capbern-Gasqueton

OWNER: Capbern-Gasqueton family.

SURFACE AREA UNDER VINE: 35 ha – 65% Cabernet Sauvignon; 20% Merlot; 15% Cabernet Franc.

SECOND WINE: Château Grand Village Capbern.

OTHER WINE: Château Calon-Ségur (Saint-Estèphe).

CLASSIFICATION: Cru Bourgeois.

Château Capbern-Gasqueton has belonged to the same family for six generations. The handsome château lies in the middle of the village of Saint-Estèphe. The vineyard is split in two, one section adjoining Château Calon-Ségur, the remainder further south bordering Château Meyney.

    The wine, aged in barrels, of which one-quarter are new, is fullish, rich and earthy, with spicy tannins. It needs a good five years to soften in most vintages. It is made by the Calon-Ségur team, but must not be mistaken for Calon-Ségur's second wine.

Château Chambert-Marbuzet

OWNER: SF Dubosq & Fils; director: Henri Duboscq.

SURFACE AREA UNDER VINE: 7 ha – 70% Cabernet Sauvignon; 30% Merlot.

OTHER WINE: Château Haut-Marbuzet (Saint-Estèphe).

CLASSIFICATION: Cru Bourgeois Supérieur.

Chambert-Marbuzet is one of a number of small domaines associated with Henri Dubosq which are grouped round the hamlet of Marbuzet. Many of the names of these parcels are now used for second wines. However, Chambert-Marbuzet, acquired in 1962, is a wine in its own right. It is much more of a true Saint-Estèphe in character than Dubosq's celebrated Château Haut-Marbuzet. It is less new oaky, less lush. It is a bit hard in its youth, but usually worth keeping. The 1995, 1996, 1998 and 2002 are all very good.

Chateau Cos d'Estournel ★★

OWNER: Michel Reybier; director: Jean-Guillaume Prats.

SURFACE AREA UNDER VINE: 64 ha – 58% Cabernet Sauvignon; 40% Merlot; 1% Cabernet Franc;

1% Petit Verdot.

SECOND WINE: Les Pagodes de Cos.

OTHER WINE: Château Marbuzet (Saint-Estèphe).

CLASSIFICATION: Deuxième Cru (1855).

If Château Calon-Ségur is steeped in history, Cos d'Estournel, and even more so, Montrose, are upstarts. Vines do not seem to have been seriously planted here until Napoleonic times. Louis Gaspard d'Estournel had two original passions: horses and boats. He was a breeder and trainer of the former, and, helped by his shipping company a trader of horses and other goods in the Middle

East. Vines did not appear at Cos d'Estournel until 1810. The apochryphal story of how he shipped some of his wine to Arabia, hoping to exchange it for the local stallions, only to have to ship the wine home, for, being Muslim, the local sheiks failed to become customers – which longer journey convinced Estournel of the benefits of ageing his wine, appears in most books on Bordeaux. The story could be true. Quite a lot of wine 'returned from the Indies' was sold at this time.

The vineyard was much expanded in the 1820s, a period when Estournel acquired a number of adjoining properties. He lived at Pommiès, today's Château Pomys, which explains why there is no château at Cos. What there is instead is a vast *chai*, decorated with oriental arches and towers and surmounted by Chinese pagodas. The main door, exotically carved from African hardwood, was once the entrance to the harem of the Sultan of Zanzibar.

Towards the end of his life Louis Gaspard d'Estournel found himself in financial difficulties and was forced to sell up. The property changed hands a couple of times before being acquired by Fernand Ginestet in 1917. His daughter Arlette married into the Prats family, and one of Arlette's three sons, Bruno, took over in 1971 and established Château Cos d'Estournel as a Super-Second. The family sold Cos to the Taillan group in 1998 and they sold it on at the end of 2000 to Michel Reybier, a French businessman. Bruno's son Jean-Guillaume continues as managing director.

The wine is arguably the best wine of the commune, though not typically Saint-Estèphe in style. It is full but very lush and fruity, even exotic, but splendidly balanced. I have criticised some recent vintages for hardly tasting like Bordeaux at all, but I cannot deny its precision and intensity. Vintages, even in the minor years, have been remarkably consistent.

See *Grands Vins*, p. 188 & *The Vine* No 231, April 2004.

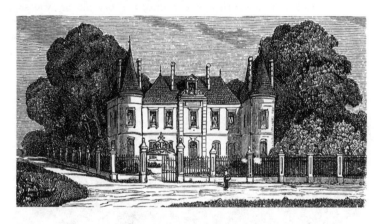

Château Cos Labory

OWNER: Audoy family.
SURFACE AREA UNDER VINE: 18 ha – 55% Cabernet Sauvignon; 35% Merlot; 10% Cabernet Franc.
SECOND WINE: Le Charme Labory.

OTHER WINE: Château Andron-Blanquet (Saint-Estèphe).
CLASSIFICATION: Cinquième Cru (1855).

Originally called Cos-Gaston, after both the hamlet of Cos and the proprietor prior to the French Revolution, this estate, whose château lies opposite the other Cos, and whose vineyards intermingle with it, passed through the female line to François-Armand Labory around the turn of the eighteenth and nineteenth centuries. Forty-five years later there was a family squabble over the succession, resolved only when Louis Gaspard d'Estournel (of the other Cos) stepped in and took charge. His successor, the Englishman Charles Cecil Martyns decided to dispose of a number of the estates his predecessor had acquired, in order to concentrate on his main domaine, and Cos Labory, somewhat smaller than it had originally been, was sold to Louis Peychaud in 1860. Subsequently there have been a number of changes of ownership. François Audoy married Cécile, *née* Loysel, shortly after the Second World War. Mme Audoy bought out her cousins, co-proprietors, in 1959. Cos Labory has been run by their eldest son, Bernard, since his father's death in 1984.

When the Audoys took over in 1959, there was much to do. The *chais* were cramped and dilapidated, the château needed renovation, and though the vines were old, there were gaps in the vineyard. Things have gradually been updated and enlarged, the last time being in 1999: *écoulage* is now by gravity direct from one stainless-steel vat into the one below. The wine has steadily improved too. It is a lighter wine than most Saint-Estèphes, merely Margaux-ish in size. But it has ripe tannins, succulent fruit and no lack of elegance.

Most of the recent vintages have been at least 'good plus'. The 1999, as at the more famous Cos d'Estournel, is a great success for the vintage. The 1998 is even better: subtle, harmonious and intense; and the 1995 and 1996 are very good, as are the trio of 2000, 2001 and 2002. All this deserves wider recognition. Meanwhile prices remain very reasonable.

See *The Vine,* No 71, December 1990.

Château Coutelin-Merville

OWNER: Bernard & François Estager.

SURFACE AREA UNDER VINE: 28 ha – 50% Merlot; 25% Cabernet Sauvignon; 23% Cabernet Franc;

2% Petit Verdot.

SECOND WINE: Château Merville.

CLASSIFICATION: Cru Bourgeois.

Château Coutelin-Merville, in the south-west corner of the *appellation*, was separated from Château Hanteillan, over the Haut-Médoc border in Cissac, in 1972. Both domaines had belonged to the Estager family since 1904. Guy Estager, then followed by his son François, have been in charge since the division and have made a stylish, generous wine, marked by the high percentage of Merlot. I have good marks on the 1995, even better on the 1996.

Château Le Crock

OWNER: Domaines Cuvelier; manager: Didier Cuvelier.

SURFACE AREA UNDER VINE: 32 ha – 60% Cabernet Sauvignon; 25% Merlot; 10% Cabernet Franc; 5% Petit Verdot.

SECOND WINE: La Croix-Saint-Estèphe.

OTHER WINE: Château Léoville-Poyferré (Saint-Julien).

CLASSIFICATION: Cru Bourgeois Supérieur.

The domaine of Le Crock is almost as famous for its fine and extensive château dating from around 1820, enclosed in a magnificent park, as for its wine. You can see both if you take the minor road between the two Cos properties up towards Château Montrose. Between 1788 and 1903, the estate belonged to the Merman family, from where they decamped to Château Marbuzet. It was then acquired by the Cuveliers. Since 1980, along with the revival of the fortunes of Léoville-Poyferré, the quality of Crock has similarly improved. Three vintages (1986, 1988 and 1989) have won the *Coupe des Crus Bourgeois*. The wine combines a certain Saint-Estèphe austerity with the more sophisticated fruit found further south in the Médoc and is balanced and reliable.

Château Domeyne

OWNER: Franchini family.
SURFACE AREA UNDER VINE: 7.2 ha – 60% Cabernet Sauvignon; 35% Merlot; 5% Cabernet Franc.

SECOND WINE: Château Haut-Vignoble-du-Parc (Haut-Médoc).
CLASSIFICATION: Cru Bourgeois.

A whole sheaf of medals, gold, silver and bronze, won at the *Concours Général* in Paris and elsewhere, dating back to 1979, attests to the consistency of quality here since the Franchini family took over in 1978. Harvesting is by hand and one quarter of the barrels are new. This is a good, solid wine. It repays keeping. The 1996 is the best of recent vintages.

Château Faget

OWNER: Lagarde family; managers: Marcel & Christian Quancard.

SURFACE AREA UNDER VINE: 4.5 ha – 60% Cabernet Sauvignon; 40% Merlot.

Formerly made by the local co-operative, the Marquis de Saint-Estèphe, the Quancard brothers took on a lease here in 1994, and the wine is now sold exclusively by the *négociants* Maison Cheval Quancard. This is a well-made, medium- to medium-full-bodied, fruity example, nicely underpinned by oak.

Château Haut-Beauséjour

OWNER: Champagne Roederer.
SURFACE AREA UNDER VINE: 18.7 ha – 52% Merlot; 40% Cabernet Sauvignon; 5% Petit Verdot;

3% Malbec.
OTHER WINE: Château de Pez (Saint-Estèphe).
CLASSIFICATION: Cru Bourgeois.

In 1992, three years before he acquired Château de Pez, Louis Rouzaud of Champagne Roederer came across this somewhat run-down estate belonging to the Brossard family. The wine was sold both as Beauséjour and also as Picard. Rouzaud bought the estate, renamed it as Haut-Beauséjour, and installed a programme of replanting and renovation of the vat house and cellars.

One-third of the barrels are new each year, and the vineyard is hand-harvested. I have been sampling this wine, at least initially, against de Pez, at the Château de Pez, for some years now. The vineyard lies east of Pez, near the village of Saint-Estèphe. The wine is a little less muscular but the fruit is more stylish. 'Good plus' would be my verdict for the time being. The 2002, though, I marked as 'very good'.

Château Haut-Marbuzet ★

OWNER: SF Dubosq & Fils; director: Henri Duboscq.
SURFACE AREA UNDER VINE: 58 ha – 50% Cabernet Sauvignon; 40% Merlot; 10% Cabernet Franc.

SECOND WINE: Château MacCarthy.
OTHER WINE: Château Chambert-Marbuzet (Saint-Estèphe).
CLASSIFICATION: Cru Bourgeois Exceptionnel.

Just as sometimes people really do resemble their pets, so do (rather more often) proprietors resemble their wines, and vice versa. This is more apparent in more hands-on wine regions such as

Burgundy. But it is certainly true here. Henri Dubosq is generous, warm-hearted, passionate and individual. So is the wine of Château Haut-Marbuzet. This, as he puts it, is a Dubosq wine which incidentally happens to be made in Saint-Estèphe. Château Chambert-Marbuzet, on the other hand, is a Saint-Estèphe made by Henri Dubosq.

The origins of the estate lie in the fragmentation and subsequent neglect of the vineyards on the Marbuzet plateau following the phylloxera epidemic. Hervé Dubosq, Henri's father, a smalltime *négociant*, acquired 7 hectares called Haut-Marbuzet in 1952. He managed to sell the entire 1953 crop to my predecessor at British Transport Hotels following a blind tasting of all the top Saint-Estèphes. Since then the domaine has expanded. The best is sold as Château Haut-Marbuzet, the rest under a number of names, those of other properties that have been absorbed in the interim. Henri joined his father in 1962, introduced 100 per cent new oak in 1970 and took over in 1973.

I have sampled all the main vintages since the famous 1953, many of them often, and have been a friend and admirer for years. This is by no means a classic wine: but it is delicious. And it lasts and lasts. Undoubtedly of *cru classé* status.

See *Grands Vins*, p. 209.

Château La Haye

OWNER: Georges Lecallier; manager: Alain Coculet.
SURFACE AREA UNDER VINE: 11 ha – 50% Cabernet Sauvignon; 42% Merlot; 3% Cabernet Franc; 5% Petit Verdot.
SECOND WINE: Fief de La Haye.
CLASSIFICATION: Cru Bourgeois Supérieur.

This is a wine of particular interest to the Dutch, for the name La Haye means Den Haag (The Hague); and it sells well in Holland. The property was a flourishing vineyard before the French Revolution. It was much larger then, belonged to the successful *négociants* Arbouet de Bernède, and was rated number two in Saint-Estèphe. The château itself is one of the few in the area which date from the seventeenth century or earlier. It was constructed, in fact, in 1557, and was said to have been a hunting lodge where Henri II paid court to his mistress, Diane de Poitiers. A monogram of their entwined initials adorns the label.

Today La Haye is managed by M. Coculet, *régisseur* of Château Phélan-Ségur. The vinification centre has been extended and modernised. The harvest is by hand and there is 30 per cent new wood. 'Quite good plus' is the verdict at present, but quality is improving.

Château Laffitte-Carcasset

OWNER: Philippe de Padirac.
SURFACE AREA UNDER VINE: 42 ha – 60% Cabernet Sauvignon; 40% Merlot.
SECOND WINE: Château La Vicomtesse.
OTHER WINE: Château Haut La Gravière (Haut-Médoc).
CLASSIFICATION: Cru Bourgeois.

Château Laffitte-Carcasset is a substantial eighteenth-century edifice lying between the co-operative and Château Tronquoy-Lalande. The property was bought by Vicomte Philippe de Padirac's father, Pierre, in 1956. After his death five years later the son acquired a neighbouring vineyard to increase his estate from 25 hectares to the present size, and installed an up-to-date winery, while his wife has occupied herself with restoring the château interior to its original elegance.

The selection is strict here, and one-third of the barrels is new. Quality of the wine is good, and dependable.

Château Lafon-Rochet

OWNER: Tesseron family; manager: Richard Bruno.

SURFACE AREA UNDER VINE: 40 ha – 55% Cabernet Sauvignon; 40% Merlot; 5% Cabernet Franc.

SECOND WINE: Les Pélerins de Lafon-Rochet.

OTHER WINE: Château Pontet-Canet (Pauillac).

CLASSIFICATION: Quatrième Cru (1855).

Château Lafon-Rochet's origins date back to 1658, when Pierre de Lafon, a councillor in the Bordeaux *parlement*, married an heiress called Antoinette de Guillemotte. She brought the land that was then called 'Rochette' with her as dowry. Lafon had the ground cleared and planted a vineyard. He is also said to have built an impressive château, but it must have been burnt down or been deliberately destroyed in later times, for the earliest illustrations that exist today show something very modest, almost like a bungalow.

The Lafon family, Lafon de Camarsac as they became (the estate passed to a collateral branch in 1820), remained owners until 1880. Subsequently there was a string of owners, most of whom neglected the property, until it was acquired by the late Guy Tesseron in 1959. There was much to be done. The vineyard had dwindled to 15 hectares, the *chais* and other outbuildings were badly in need of restoration and the '*château*', such as it was, was in such an appalling state it had to be raised to the ground. In its place a copy of an eighteenth-century *chartreuse* was constructed.

At first, Guy Tesseron made the mistake of planting too much Cabernet: 80 per cent. Eventually it was realised that this was an error, but not before 20 vintages of rather hard wines. Now there is 40 per cent Merlot, as at Cos d'Estournel, Lafon-Rochet's nearest neighbour, and the wine is both rounder and more sophisticated.

Quality in the 1990s has undergone a sea change: from dependable classed growth standard to something very much more exciting. The wine is full, warm-hearted and potentially rich and velvety. What is of interest is that today's *grand vin*, despite the *encépagement* in the vineyard, is made from 60 per cent or more Merlot, more often than not. There was a fine 1995, a very good 1996 , followed by even more progress in 2000 and 2002.

Château Lilian Ladouys

OWNER: SA du Château Lilian Ladouys; manager: Georges Pauli.

SURFACE AREA UNDER VINE: 42.7 ha – 58% Cabernet Sauvignon; 38% Merlot;

4% Cabernet Franc.

SECOND WINE: Le Devise de Lilian.

CLASSIFICATION: Cru Bourgeois Supérieur.

What was called plain Château Ladouys was a flourishing vineyard in the nineteenth century, sufficiently so for the proprietor, M. Barre, to commission an illustration in Cocks & Féret (see above). The estate then fell into bad times, lost part of its vineyard and the wine wound up being made by the co-operative. In 1989 it was acquired by Christian and Lilian Thiéblot – hence the change of name – who shortly afterwards managed to buy more vineyard land, planted with old vines.

Word soon got around that here was a new super-*bourgeois*, and despite a subsequent change of ownership (in 1996 it was acquired by a consortium of banks) and a change of winemaker – Georges Pauli of Château Gruaud-Larose and other Cordier estates in place of Jean-Jacques Godin, ex-Château Pichon-Lalande – progress has continued.

The *grand vin* is now often made with a majority of Merlot, despite the smaller percentage in the vineyard. There is cold maceration before fermentation and up to 60 per cent new wood. This is a rich, fullish bodied wine with none of the usual hard, even rustic elements of many *bourgeois* Saint-Estèphes. The 1995, 1996, 1998 and even the 1999 are all 'very good', if not better still, as is the 2002.

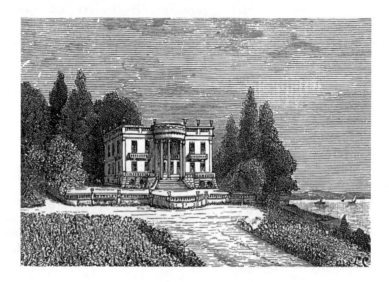

Château Marbuzet

OWNER: Michel Reybier; director: Jean-Guillaume Prats.

SURFACE AREA UNDER VINE: 7 ha – 46% Cabernet Sauvignon; 42% Merlot; 12% Petit Verdot.

OTHER WINE: Château Cos d'Estournel (Saint-Estèphe).

CLASSIFICATION: Cru Bourgeois.

Château Marbuzet – until recently called de Marbuzet – belonged in the latter half of the nineteenth century to the Merman family, owner of nearby Château Le Crock. Legend has it that the splendid château, Louis XVI in style, was built by Jules Merman for his mistress Régina Badet, a celebrated opera singer, and that the expense of the construction was so huge that it ruined him. Be that as it may, Fernand Ginestet bought the property at the same time as he bought Cos d'Estournel, in 1919.

With no château at Cos d'Estournel, Marbuzet has served as a location for entertaining ever since, and in recent years has been the name of Cos d'Estournel's second wine. This arrangement ceased in 1994 with the launch of Les Pagodes de Cos by Cos d'Estournel, and the wine can now be seen as a more than pleasant, medium-bodied example, with good fruit and no lack of elegance. It is quite a different wine to Cos d'Estournel. Both the 1995 and the 1996 are very good. The 2002 also shows promise.

Château Meyney

OWNER: Cordier Mestrezat & Domaines; director: Alain Duhau.

SURFACE AREA UNDER VINE: 51 ha – 70% Cabernet Sauvignon; 22% Merlot; 4% Cabernet Franc; 4% Petit Verdot.

SECOND WINE: Prieur de Meyney.

OTHER WINES: Château Grand-Puy-Ducasse (Pauillac); Château Lamothe-Bergeron (Haut-Médoc).

CLASSIFICATION: Cru Bourgeois Supérieur.

Château Meyney lies on its own gravel mound, facing the Gironde estuary, immediately to the north of Château Montrose. Once a monastery, it belonged in the early part of the nineteenth century to Jérôme Leutkens, proprietor of Château La Tour Carnet, and subsequently to the Sault and de Fumel families, when it was one of the largest growths in Saint-Estèphe.

In 1919, a year after acquiring Château Talbot in Saint-Julien, Meyney passed to Désiré Cordier. The château and the *chai*, covered in creeper, form a hollow square. One can easily picture the inside as a former cloister.

The wine is an archetypal Cordier wine: full, meaty, a little aggressively tannic in its youth, needing time to round off. I found it a bit lumpy in the 1970s and 1980s but in the last decade it has seemed to get richer and more sophisticated. Today it is not without merit. The 1994, 1995 and 1996 can all be recommended, as can the 2000 and 2002. The wine has been getting even more sophisticated in recent years.

Château Montrose ★

OWNER: Jean-Louis Charmolüe.

SURFACE AREA UNDER VINE: 68.5 ha – 65% Cabernet Sauvignon; 25% Merlot;

8% Cabernet Franc; 2% Petit Verdot.

SECOND WINE: La Dame de Montrose.

CLASSIFICATION: Deuxième Cru (1855).

Together with Château Cos d'Estournel, Montrose is the newest of Bordeaux's classed growths. The land was sold, along with the estate of Calon-Ségur, by the Ségur family, to Étienne Théodore Dumoulin in 1778. Calon-Ségur having been disposed of in the meanwhile, his son started planting a vineyard and constructing a château in 1815. Ten years later there were only 5 or 6 hectares of vines, but by 1832 there were 35, and by 1855, with 45 hectares of vines, it was a Second Growth, while Calon-Ségur was classed merely as *troisième*. Matthew Dolfus bought Montrose in 1866 and further enlarged the vineyard to its present size. After he died it was acquired by Jean Hostein who then passed it on to his son-in-law, Louis Charmolüe in 1896. The present owner, Jean-Louis Charmolüe, is Louis' grandson.

Though the Charmolües live mainly in Bordeaux – hardly any of the classed growth château owners live permanently in the Médoc – Château Montrose definitely has an inhabited air about it.

The château itself, overlooking the estuary, is a modest building, but houses a splendid collection of paintings. The family occupy it during the summer and at vintage time. A new stainless steel *cuverie* was constructed in 2000 to match the splendid first year cellar built a decade ago.

The wine is quite different either from Cos d'Estournel and from Calon-Ségur. What we have here is a clear-cut, almost Pauillac-y Cabernet based core to the wine, supported by quite a bit of tannin. Past vintages of Château Montrose: the 1961, the 1970, for instance, were too tannic for their own good. They never mellowed. They began to get it right in 1975 and 1978, but then erred on the too soft side in 1983 and 1985. Nineteen eighty-six was a great success, and an even better wine was produced in 1990. The vintages of the mid-1990s are merely good, but then in 1998 there came a change for the better. Both the 2001 and 2002 are clearly the best wines of the commune.

See *Grands Vins*, p. 195.

Château Les Ormes de Pez

OWNER: Cazes family; director: Stephen Carrier.
SURFACE AREA UNDER VINE: 33 ha – 60% Cabernet Sauvignon; 30% Merlot; 10% Cabernet Franc.

OTHER WINES: Château Cordeillan-Bages (Saint-Estèphe); Château Lynch-Bages (Pauillac).
CLASSIFICATION: Cru Bourgeois Exceptionnel.

More than 120 years ago, in the 1880s, during the time when Marcel Alibert was proprietor of Les Ormes de Pez, as he was briefly of Château Belgrave in Saint-Laurent, his *maître de chai* married Marie Cazes. He died soon after, and Marie became one of the first female managers of a Bordeaux estate. This began a family association with Château Les Ormes de Pez which resulted in Jean-Charles Cazes, her son, becoming proprietor in 1934, the same year as he took a lease on Lynch-Bages, which he was to acquire five years later.

The château is an elegant *maison bourgeoise*, set in a little park. The wine is made by the same team as at Lynch-Bages and is a dependable mediumweight wine, typical of the commune in that it can be pleasantly fruity if without any great elegance. I found the 2002 ('very good') rather better than usual.

Château La Peyre

OWNER: René Rabiller.
SURFACE AREA UNDER VINE: 7 ha – 50% Cabernet Sauvignon; 50% Merlot.

SECOND WINE: Le Mignot.
OTHER WINE: Chateau La Peyre (Haut-Médoc).

From 1989 to 1994 the Rabiller family produced an Haut-Médoc under the Peyre label. In this vintage they prized the Saint-Estèphe vineyard out of the clutches of the local co-operative. The full, oaky, succulent 1996 is a great success. There is more land still to develop which will bring the estate up to 12 hectares.

Chateau de Pez

OWNER: Champagne Roederer.
SURFACE AREA UNDER VINE: 24.1 ha – 45% Cabernet Sauvignon; 44% Merlot; 8% Cabernet Franc; 3% Petit Verdot.

SECOND WINE: Château La Salle de Pez.
OTHER WINE: Château Haut-Beauséjour (Saint-Estèphe).
CLASSIFICATION: Cru Bourgeois Exceptionnel.

Cocks & Féret and other authorities on Bordeaux cite Château de Pez as the best of the *bourgeois* Saint-Estèphes. While I admire what has been done here in the past, and what is being achieved today, I cannot agree. I would list Haut-Marbuzet, Phélan-Ségur, and if only potentially, Château

Meyney ahead of de Pez. That nevertheless still leaves this property firmly in the first division.

The property has a long history. It was part of the vast Pontac domaine in the seventeenth century, when the family owned Château Haut-Brion. It was already making a substantial amount of wine in the 1680s, making it one of the very first monocultural wine estates. At the time it must have been a great deal larger than today. It was sold off as a *bien national* during the French Revolution. In the nineteenth century it was known as La Salle de Pez and passed through a number of hands before being bought in 1920 by Jean Bernard. From 1955 to 1995 it belonged to Robert Dousson, Bernard's grandson, remaining one of the few sold exclusively by IDV after the crisis of 1973. It is now the property of Champagne Roederer.

The best way to describe Château de Pez, even now, when the edges have been refined a bit, is 'old fashioned' but in the best sense. There is certainly richness here. But the structure is tannic, and the fruit takes time to come through. Hence it was proportionately better in the biggest, most concentrated years. The new management has invested much, transforming the cellar. There has been a marked improvement since the 1996 vintage. The 2000 is especially good, as is the 2002.

See *The Vine*, No 105, October 1993.

Château Phélan-Ségur

OWNER: Xavier Gardinier & Fils.
SURFACE AREA UNDER VINE: 89 ha – 50% Cabernet
  Sauvignon; 47% Merlot; 3% Cabernet Franc.

SECOND WINE: Frank Phélan.
CLASSIFICATION: Cru Bourgeois Exceptionnel.

Bernard Phélan, of Irish extraction we are told, established himself in Saint-Estèphe right at the beginning of the nineteenth century. He was proprietor of an estate called Garamey. To this he added a much larger vineyard named Basterot in 1810, the lady proprietor (*née* Basterot) being the wife of one of the Ségurs. From this evolved Ségur-Garamey, as it was known in the first editions of Cocks & Féret. It was larger then than it is today, indeed the largest in the commune, producing 200 *tonneaux* in 1868.

Bernard Phélan was succeeded by his son Frank, and it was he who had the present, rather grand château constructed as well as building a very up-to-date winery. Frank had no heirs, after his death in 1883 his widow sold up. It subsequently passed into the hands of the Delon family, a branch of which today owns Château Léoville-Las-Cases. Following the Second World War, when the first generation of post-phylloxera vines were old, the quality of Phélan-Ségur was at *cru classé* level, but at the same time there was a lack of income and investment. After the death of Roger Delon in 1984, Château Phélan-Ségur, rather run down, was on the market.

It was acquired by the dynamic Xavier Gardinier, late of Champagne Lanson. But hardly had he taken over when customers started returning the 1983. The wine had a metallic taint. So would the 1984 and 1985, neither ever sold, until finely the cause was discovered: an insecticide spray had left a systematic residue in the fruit. Meanwhile a brand new vinification centre was built and the château, which lies in a large park between the village of Saint-Estèphe and the estuary, was cleaned and renovated.

Château Phélan-Ségur is today one of Saint-Estèphe's best *crus bourgeois*. The wine has typical Saint-Estèphe backbone but not the robustness. It is succulent and oaky (40 per cent new in the cellar) and has both depth and elegance. It was better in the 1990s than in the 1980s, when it was only quite good. The 1994, 1995 and 1996 are stylish but a little lightweight. The 1998 and 1999 are rather better, and this progress has been continued in 2000 and 2002.

See *The Vine*, No 113, June 1994.

Château Pomys

OWNER: François Arnaud.

SURFACE AREA UNDER VINE: 10 ha – 50% Cabernet Sauvignon; 30% Merlot; 20% Cabernet Franc.

SECOND WINE: Le Blason de Pomys.

OTHER WINE: Château Saint-Estèphe (Saint-Estèphe).

CLASSIFICATION: Cru Bourgeois.

A shadow of its former self, Pomys is not only a fraction of the size it was in the middle of the nineteenth century, but the domaine has lost its château. This is now a hotel.

Long associated with Château Cos d'Estournel, when its rather fine three-storey edifice served for Cos d'Estournel's lack of château, Pomys, or Pommies, as it was originally known, declined in size and reputation during the first half of the twentieth century. In 1951 the Arnaud family took over, and slowly but surely are reversing the process. They live nearby in Château Saint-Estèphe, which they acquired at about the same time. Pomys produces the better wine: medium-bodied, neat and fruity.

Château Ségur de Cabanac

OWNER: Guy Delon.

SURFACE AREA UNDER VINE: 6.3 ha – 60% Cabernet Sauvignon; 30% Merlot; 5% Cabernet Franc; 5% Petit Verdot.

OTHER WINE: Château Moulin de la Rose (Saint-Julien).

CLASSIFICATION: Cru Bourgeois.

Château Ségur de Cabanac is a splinter of Château Phélan-Ségur and was acquired by Guy Delon when he sold Phélan-Ségur after his father's death in 1984. This part of the vineyard has been called Ségur de Cabanac for 200 years. I find the wine plump and stylish and a good example of Saint-Estèphe. There is a decent structure without too much Saint-Estèphe muscle. The 2002 vintage is very good.

Château Tronquoy-Lalande

OWNER: Arlette Castéja Texier.

SURFACE AREA UNDER VINE: 17 ha – 48% Cabernet Sauvignon; 48% Merlot; 4% Petit Verdot.

SECOND WINE: Château Tronquoy de Sainte-Anne.

CLASSIFICATION: Cru Bourgeois Supérieur.

The impressive turreted nineteenth-century château and its small park lies in a sea of vines inland from Château Meyney and was a total ruin in 1969 when acquired by Mme Castéja and her husband Jean Texier, who died in 1973.

The property is named after the Tronquoy family who bought a vineyard called Lalande early in the nineteenth century. The wine is aged partly in barrel, partly in vat. It is ample and medium-bodied, with ripe tannins and attractive fruit. I enjoyed the 1996. It is an exclusivety of CVBG (Dourthe Kressmann).

Château Valrose

OWNER: Gerard Neraudau; director: Jean Trias.   25% Cabernet Sauvignon; 25% Cabernet Franc.
SURFACE AREA UNDER VINE: 5 ha – 50% Merlot;

Château Valrose has changed hands twice in recent years. Until 1998 it belonged to the Audoin family, owners of Château Houissant elsewhere in Saint-Estèphe. It was then bought by Jean-Michel Arcaute, owner of various properties in Pomerol and responsible for the current high reputation of Château Clinet. After his untimely death in a sailing accident in 2001, Valrose was sold to the present owners. I liked the 1996 under the old regime. Until recently I had only seen the 1999 vintage under the new regime. I was not particularly excited – but then it is not a particularly exciting vintage. But then in April 2003 I sampled the *tête de cuvée*, Cuvée Aliénor 2002, which I rather liked.

PAUILLAC

SURFACE AREA (2002): 1209 ha.

PRODUCTION (2002): 48,999 hl.

COLOUR: Red (the white wines are *Appellation*

Contrôlée Bordeaux or Bordeaux Supérieur).

GRAPE VARIETIES: Cabernet Sauvignon;

Cabernet Franc; Merlot; Petit Verdot;

Malbec; Carmenère.

MAXIMUM YIELD: 47 hl/ha.

MINIMUM ALCOHOLIC DEGREE: 10°.

THE COMMUNE OF PAUILLAC lies between Saint-Julien and Saint-Estèphe some 45 kilometres north of Bordeaux. The vineyards of the three communes are in fact contiguous, the vines of Léoville-Las-Cases in Saint-Julien marching with those of Latour in Pauillac, separated only by a narrow gully; those of Lafite in Pauillac facing those of Cos d'Estournel in Saint-Estèphe across a stream, the Jalle de Breuil. Pauillac is not the largest of the communal *appellations* – that honour falls to Margaux in size and to Saint-Estèphe in terms of volume of production; but it is the most important. Pauillac contains three of the four First Growths and no fewer than 15 other classified châteaux, almost a third of those in the 1855 Classification. It also boasts a number of good *bourgeois* properties.

The commune is split in two by a stream, the Chenal du Gaer, which flows diagonally across the parish in a north-easterly direction, debouching into the Gironde at the northern end of the town of Pauillac itself. North and west of this stream the land rises steeply (in Médocain terms) to some 27 metres above sea level, and includes the vineyards of both the Rothschilds and Pontet-Canet. South and east lie the Bages and Grand-Puy-Lacoste plateaux, the Batailleys, the Pichons and Château Latour. The Pauillac soil is heavy gravel, thicker to the north than to the south, based on a subsoil of larger stones, and iron-based sand. The wines of Pauillac are the archetype of Bordeaux and the taste of Cabernet Sauvignon, which in some cases – as at Château Mouton-Rothschild and Château Latour – forms the vast part of the *encépagement*. The wines are full-bodied, dense and tannic; austere when young, rich and distinguished when mature; and the longest-lived of all Bordeaux wines. At their best they are incomparable, the fullest, most concentrated and most profound of all red wines.

Pauillac Leading Châteaux

Château d'Armailhac

OWNER: Baronne Philippine de Rothschild.
SURFACE AREA UNDER VINE: 50 ha –
  50% Cabernet Sauvignon; 25% Merlot;
  23% Cabernet Franc; 2% Petit Verdot.

OTHER WINES: L'Aile d'Argent (Bordeaux
  Supérieur Blanc); Château Clerc-Milon
  (Pauillac); Château La Fleur-Milon (Pauillac);
  Château Mouton-Rothschild (Pauillac).
CLASSIFICATION: Cinquième Cru (1855).

The estate was owned by the eponymous Armand Armailhacq (with a 'q'), viticulturalist and chronicler of the local wines, at the time of the 1855 Classification. Having fallen on hard times it was sold to Baron Philippe de Rothschild, of neighbouring Mouton in 1933. He renamed the property Mouton Baron Philippe in 1956, and then changed this to Mouton Baronne Philippe, in honour of his second wife, in 1975. After his death, his daughter (by his first wife), Baronne Philippine, changed the name yet again.

    The vines lie between the châteaux of Mouton-Rothschild and Pontet-Canet, next to the curious Armailhac construction, which looks as if it has been chopped in half, vertically, and the south side discarded. The wine, made by the Mouton team, is more fragrant, and of a lighter texture than that of Château Clerc-Milon, its fellow Fifth Growth, and not as distinctive. It is nevertheless a good, attractive wine which fully merits its classification. Early in 2003 I preferred the 2000 to that of Clerc-Milon. The 1995, 1996, 1998 and 1999 are all good.

See *Grands Vins*, p. 111.

Château Batailley

OWNER: Castéja family.
SURFACE AREA UNDER VINE: 57 ha – 70% Cabernet
  Sauvignon; 25% Merlot; 3% Cabernet Franc;
  2% Petit Verdot.
SECOND WINE: Plaisance Saint-Lambert.
OTHER WINES: Château Beau-Site (Saint-Éstèphe);

Domaine de l'Église (Pomerol); Château Haut-
Bages-Monpelou (Pauillac); Château Lynch-
Moussas (Pauillac); Château Trottevieille (Saint-
Émilion).
CLASSIFICATION: Cinquième Cru (1855).

Batailley is said by some to commemorate a battle in the Middle Ages, by others to be named after a certain M. Batailley. Both are pure conjecture. Earliest records date from the French Revolution when it was owned by the Saint-Martin family. Over the next 70 years it passed through a number of hands, including that of the influential merchant Daniel Guestier, who did much to establish the reputation of the wine, as well as enlarging the vineyard. In 1866, after his death, the property passed to the banker Constant Halphen. His heirs sold Batailley in 1932 to the Borie brothers, who were already farming the vineyard. Ten years later the estate was split between them, giving rise

to the Haut-Batailley vineyard. Marcel Borie, the elder brother, retained Batailley itself, and his son-in-law, Émile Castéja, owns and lives in the château today.

The château, rebuilt early in the twentieth century, and set in a large park boasting a fine collection of mature trees, is one of the most attractive in the Médoc. It lies, surrounded by its vineyard in the south-west corner of the commune, on the road from Pauillac to Saint-Laurent-Médoc. The wine is a good, consistent, medium to medium-full bodied, fruity example which softens in the medium term. It lacks the distinction of a Super-Second. But – sold exclusively by the family firm of Borie-Manoux – it makes no attempt to sell for Super-Second prices. All vintages since 1990, especially the 1995 and 2000, are at least 'good plus'.

See *Grands Vins*, p. 92.

Château La Bécasse

OWNER: Roland Fonteneau.

SURFACE AREA UNDER VINE: 4 ha – 55% Cabernet Sauvignon; 36% Merlot; 9% Cabernet Franc.

The modest château lies in the hamlet of Bages, the vineyards being on the plateau to the east. This is a relatively new estate, being formed by an ex-*régisseur* of Château Ducru-Beaucaillou in 1966. The wine is full and sturdy, sometimes a bit solid, but with a good background of new oak. Some 30–40 per cent of the barrels are new.

Château Bellegrave

OWNER: Meffre family.

SURFACE AREA UNDER VINE: 3.3 ha – 80% Cabernet Sauvignon; 15% Merlot; 3% Malbec; 2% Petit Verdot.

OTHER WINES: Château du Glana (Saint-Julien); Château Lalande (Saint-Julien); Château Plantey (Pauillac).

The château is hidden in a park behind a large fence in the hamlet of Saint-Lambert, almost opposite Château Fonbadet, and for years has been one of the most obscure of the Pauillac *crus bourgeois*. The Meffre family took on a lease in 1977 and then bought Château Bellegrave from the Van der Voort family in 2000. Up to now the wine has been undistinguished, but the 2000 showed a distinct step in the right direction.

Château Clerc-Milon ★

OWNER: Baronne Philippine de Rothschild; director: Hervé Berland.

SURFACE AREA UNDER VINE: 30 ha –
46% Cabernet Sauvignon; 35% Merlot;
15% Cabernet Franc; 3% Petit Verdot;
1% Carmènere.

OTHER WINES: Château d'Armailhac (Pauillac); Château Mouton-Rothschild (Pauillac); L'Aile d'Argent (Bordeaux Supérieur Blanc); Château La Fleur-Milon (Pauillac).

CLASSIFICATION: Cinquième Cru (1855).

The origins of the name of this property lie with a M. Clerc, proprietor at the time of the 1855 Classification, and the *lieu-dit* Milon, a hamlet which lies inland from Château Lafite at the extreme north-west of the Pauillac commune. The history of the property is somewhat complex, and somewhat incompletely documented. It never seems to have been very large, nor very successful, and the 'château' is a simple *bourgeois* mansion in the village of Pouyalet. After some years of neglect earlier in the twentieth century, the property was acquired by Baron Philippe de Rothschild in 1970. The wine has improved considerably since then. It is now rich, full-bodied and concentrated, a more substantial example than its stablemate Château d'Armailhac, and frequently very good indeed. As prices are by no means (in Bordeaux terms) excessive, this is one of today's bargains. The 1990 is only the first of a succession of very good wines in the last decade and more.

See *Grands Vins*, p. 111.

Château Colombier-Monpelou

OWNER: Vignobles Jugla; manager: Bruno Marlet.

SURFACE AREA UNDER VINE: 24 ha – 60% Cabernet Sauvignon; 30% Merlot; 5% Cabernet Franc; 5% Petit Verdot.

OTHER WINES: Château Belle Rose (Pauillac); Château Grand-Duroc-Milon (Pauillac); Château Pedesclaux (Pauillac).

CLASSIFICATION: Cru Bourgeois Supérieur.

Château Colombier-Monpelou has been in the hands of the Jugla family, owners of the Pauillac Fifth Growth Château Pedesclaux, since 1970. The wine had a good reputation in the nineteenth century, when it was rated second after Château La Couronne among the non-classified estates. But it has slipped since. Harvesting is by machine. There is 40 per cent new oak. The wine is medium- to medium-full-bodied, with some fruit but rarely has finesse and excitement. The 1999 was better than usual though.

Château Cordeillan-Bages

OWNER: Cazes family; director: Stephen Carrier.

SURFACE AREA UNDER VINE: 2 ha – 80% Cabernet Sauvignon; 20% Merlot.

OTHER WINES: Château Lynch-Bages (Pauillac); Château Les Ormes de Pez (Saint-Estèphe).

The 2 hectares of Château Cordeillan-Bages come from the Lynch-Bages vineyard, the Cazes family having acquired both name and land some time ago. When the château was transformed into a Relais et Château hotel in the 1990s, the wine was resurrected and the vines vinified separately. It is a good, stylish Pauillac, rather better than what many suppose it to be, i.e. a separate labelling of Château Haut-Bages-Averous, Lynch-Bages' second wine. The 1998 and 2000 are particularly good examples.

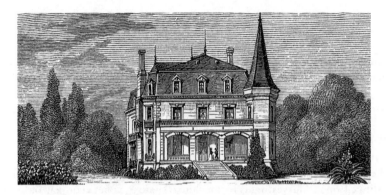

Château Croizet-Bages

OWNER: Jean-Michel Quié; manager: Lucien
Cintrat.

SURFACE AREA UNDER VINE: 30 ha – 54% Cabernet
Sauvignon; 38% Merlot; 8% Cabernet Franc.

SECOND WINE: La Tourelle de Croizet-Bages.

OTHER WINES: Château Bel Orme, Tronquoy de
Lalande (Haut-Médoc); Château Rauzan-Gassies
(Margaux).

CLASSIFICATION: Cinquième Cru (1855).

When Jean-Louis Camp, formerly of Château Loudenne, was appointed *régisseur* of the Quié properties in 1994 I hoped that at long last we would be able to cross the wines off our perennial list of under-achievers and begin to enjoy the wine. I am still waiting.

Its origins lie with the Croizet family who founded the estate in the mid-eighteenth century. By the time of the 1855 Classification it had passed to Julian Calvé in whose family hands it remained until acquired by Paul Quié, father of the present owner, in 1934. The château, now called La Tourelle, has become divorced from the property. The *chais* remain in the hamlet of Bages and have been recently modernised.

Château Duhart-Milon

OWNER: Domaines Barons de Rothschild;
manager: Charles Chevallier.

SURFACE AREA UNDER VINE: 71 ha – 69% Cabernet
Sauvignon; 28% Merlot; 3% Cabernet Franc.

SECOND WINE: Moulin de Duhart.

OTHER WINES: Château L'Évangile (Pomerol);
Château Lafite-Rothschild (Pauillac); Château
Rieussec (Sauternes).

CLASSIFICATION: Quatrième Cru (1855).

Until recently this was one of the more obscure Pauillac classed growths. The vineyards lie in the north-west corner of the commune, behind those of Château Lafite, in the hamlet of Milon. The proprietor in the 1830s was a M. Mandavi or Mandavit (there must have been a M. Duhart in pre-Revolutionary times, but records of him and his family have been lost). Thereafter the estate seems to have been divided, reunited by the Castéja family later in the century, but then allowed to run down until acquired by the Rothschilds of Lafite in 1962. Much of the vineyard had then to be replanted and it was not until 1982 (or, to those more charitable than I, 1978) that the wine came of age.

Today it is produced by the Lafite team in a separate cellar in the middle of the village of Pauillac – there is no 'château' as such – and is a full, occasionally four-square, but rich, masculine Pauillac: certainly classed growth quality, but not a Super-Second. The 1996, 1998 and 2000 are all very good.

See *Grands Vins,* p. 88.

Château La Fleur-Milon

OWNER: Baronne Philippine de Rothschild.
SURFACE AREA UNDER VINE: 12 ha – 70% Cabernet Sauvignon; 30% Merlot.
SECOND WINES: Château Buisson-Milon; Château Chanteclerc Milon.

OTHER WINES: L'Aile d'Argent (Bordeaux Supérieur Blanc); Château d'Armailhac (Pauillac); Château Clerc-Milon (Pauillac); Château Mouton-Rothschild (Pauillac).
CLASSIFICATION: Cru Bourgois.

The 'château', such as it is, and the rather larger, tidy *chai*, can be found in the village of Pouyalet. The vines lie on both sides of the main road between Pauillac and Saint-Estèphe. This is a good *bourgeois* example, having been built up to its present size by the late André Gimenez who bought 3 hectares in 1958. The wines are fermented in concrete vats and stored in wood, one-third of which are new. Since Yannick Gimenez, grandson of André, took over in 1996, standards have improved. The 1998 is very good. Early in 2003 La Fleur-Milon was bought by Baronne Philippine de Rothschild of Château Mouton-Rothschild.

Château Fonbadet

OWNER: Domaines Peyronie; director: Pascale Peyronie.
SURFACE AREA UNDER VINE: 20 ha – 60% Cabernet Sauvignon; 20% Merlot; 15% Cabernet Franc; 5% Petit Verdot.
SECOND WINE: L'Harmonie de Fonbadet.

OTHER WINES: Château Haut-Pauillac; Château Montgrand-Milon; Château Padarnac; Château Tour du Roc Milon (all Pauillac and all exclusive to various négociants).
CLASSIFICATION: Cru Bourgeois Supérieur.

The château of Fonbadet lies hidden in a little park between the hamlets of Saint-Lambert and Bages, with its scattered vines mainly on the plateau behind. The property was acquired by Pierre de Gères de Loupes in 1817, later disappeared entirely from the records, reappeared in the 1920s and was sold in the early 1960s to Pierre Peyronie.

The wine is aged partly in wood and partly in tanks. Since 1998, Pierre's daughter, Pascale, has been in charge, the percentage of new wood has been increased and a second wine introduced. Château Fonbadet has always been a full, rich, old-viney Pauillac. Often, however, it has been a bit too dense and solid for its own good. Things are rather better now. This is one of the best *bourgeois* growths of the area. The 2000 is undeniably firm but will soften.

Château Grand-Puy-Ducasse

OWNER: Cordier Mestrezat & Domaines; director: Alain Duhau.
SURFACE AREA UNDER VINE: 40 ha – 60% Cabernet Sauvignon; 40% Merlot.
SECOND WINE: Prélude à Grand-Puy-Ducasse.

OTHER WINES: Château Lamothe-Bergeron (Haut-Médoc); Château Marsac-Seguineau (Margaux); Château Meyney (Saint-Estephe); Château Rayne-Vigneau (Sauternes).
CLASSIFICATION: Cinquième Cru (1855).

The *chais* and handsomely restored château of Grand-Puy-Ducasse lie on the waterfront in the village of Pauillac. Its history is entwined with that of the other, more famous Grand-Puy (see below) and the Bordeaux parliamentarian, Pierre Ducasse, but though it featured in the 1855 Classification it was later to fall into bad times and lose most of such vineyards that lie on the Grand-Puy plateau. From 60 hectares in Napoleonic times the vineyard had declined to 10 hectares when the property was taken over in 1971. The *négociants* Mestrezat have administered it since 1982, since when the vineyard size has quadrupled.

The vineyard lies in three main parcels. One lies next to Grand-Puy-Lacoste, another near Château Pontet-Canet and a third adjoins Château Lynch-Moussas. During the 1980s the grapes were machine-harvested, and the wine was sub-standard. Today it is better: the grapes are hand-picked and the wine is of medium body and with reasonable style and depth. But, for a classed growth, it should be better still. Mestrezat have shown, in their other châteaux, that they do know how to make wine.

Château Grand-Puy-Lacoste ★★

OWNER: François-Xavier Borie.
SURFACE AREA UNDER VINE: 55 ha – 75% Cabernet
  Sauvignon; 20% Merlot; 5% Cabernet Franc.

SECOND WINE: Lacoste-Borie.
OTHER WINE: Château Haut-Batailley (Pauillac).
CLASSIFICATION: Cinquième Cru (1855).

Château Grand-Puy-Lacoste has a long history of consistently making excellent wine. Today it is justly regarded as a Super-Second. The name comes from François Lacoste, owner early in the nineteenth century, and Grand-Puy, being the plateau on which the vines are planted. *Puy*, like *tertre*, *fite* and *motte*, other names incorporated into Bordeaux domaine titles, is a word for mound or ridge. Raymond Dupin bought the estate in 1932 and sold it to the Borie family in 1978. Though somewhat smaller then, Dupin had jealously guarded his old vines. The vintages of the 1940s, 1950s and early 1960s are just as fine as they are today.

    The château is a substantial mid-nineteenth-century edifice, only partially restored. The Bories have renovated a section which was formerly an annexe, which is where François-Xavier Borie and his family live today when they are in the Médoc, but have concentrated on the *cuvier* and *chais*. The wine is full, firm, long-lasting, ripe and almost creamy-rich. It has a lot of breed. A classic Pauillac at a very high level of quality. A recent vertical in London marked all the major vintages back to 1982 as fine, if not better. The 1990 and 2000 particularly stood out.

See *Grands Vins*, p. 99.

Château Haut-Bages-Libéral

OWNER: Claire Villars Lurton.
SURFACE AREA UNDER VINE: 28 ha – 80% Cabernet
  Sauvignon; 20% Merlot.
SECOND WINES: La Chapelle de Bages; La Fleur de
  Haut-Bages-Libéral.

OTHER WINES: Château Chasse-Spleen (Moulis);
  Château Citran (Haut-Médoc); Château Ferrière
  (Margaux); Château La Gurgue (Margaux).
CLASSIFICATION: Cinquième Cru (1855).

The château and most of the vineyard of Haut-Bages-Libéral lie immediately to the north of Château Latour. Only a minor portion of the vines will be found on the Bages plateau to the east. M. Libéral, who gave his name to the title, was a broker and also owner of Château du Tertre in

Margaux. He was the proprietor here in Pauillac at the time of the 1855 Classification. From the 1870s onwards Haut-Bages-Libéral passed through a number of hands and its reputation evaporated. In 1960 it was sold to a consortium which included the Cruse family. They replanted the vineyard but incorporated part of it into Château Pontet-Canet. Not enough investment was made in the cellar, however, the wine being allowed to mature in vat, not cask, for instance. Quality remained humdrum until the Cruzes sold to the Merlaut family in 1983.

Bernadette Villars was entrusted with responsibility for the wine. She immediately embarked on an ambitious programme of renovation which included draining the vineyard for the first time, introducing a second wine, building a barrel cellar and insulating and temperature-controlling the entire *cuvier* and *chais*. Progress, especially in the 1990s, has been significant. Château Haut-Bages-Libéral is now a more than dependable classed growth. It is medium- to full-bodied, with good, rich Cabernet fruit and no lack of class. The 1990, 1995, 1996, 1998, 2000, 2001 and 2002 can all be recommended.

Château Haut-Bages-Monpelou

OWNER: Castéja family.
SURFACE AREA UNDER VINE: 15 ha – 70% Cabernet Sauvignon; 25% Merlot; 5% Cabernet Franc.
OTHER WINES: Château Batailley (Pauillac); Château Beau-Site (Saint-Estèphe); Domaine de L'Église (Pomerol); Château Lynch-Moussas (Pauillac); Château Trottevieille (Saint-Émilion).
CLASSIFICATION: Cru Bourgeois Supérieur.

This estate was once part of Château Duhart-Milon. The 15 hectares were split off from it in 1948 and sold to Marcel Borie, father-in-law of Émile Castéja, proprietor of Châteaux Batailley and Lynch-Moussas, both also in Pauillac. By coincidence, the property used to belong to ancestors of the Castéjas in the mid-nineteenth century, but was later dismembered.

This is a medium-bodied wine, soft and fruity, but without a great deal of distinction.

Château Haut-Batailley ★

OWNER: Françoise des Brest-Borie; director: François-Xavier Borie.
SURFACE AREA UNDER VINE: 22 ha – 65% Cabernet Sauvignon; 25% Merlot; 10% Cabernet Franc.
SECOND WINE: Château La Tour L'Aspic.
OTHER WINE: Château Grand-Puy-Lacoste (Pauillac).
CLASSIFICATION: Cinquième Cru (1855).

The Batailley estate was split in 1942, when the Borie brothers separated their assets. This is the southerly and smaller part of the vineyard. There is no château, as such, merely a Swiss chalet-like building which serves partly as the *chai* and also houses some of the vineyard workers.

The modest surroundings do not stop Haut-Batailley from producing a wine of a standard well above its Fifth Growth classification. The Borie family create something which is far different from their Castéja cousins alongside at Château Batailley. Château Haut-Batailley is fuller and firmer, a true Pauillac which takes time to mature. The flavour is rich and Cabernet Sauvignon-based. Occasionally it has almost been a little too austere. Today the tannins are rounder and the wine is very good indeed. Since 1990 the wines have climbed from 'good plus' to 'very good plus'. The 1998 and 2000 are delicious.

See *Grands Vins*, p. 96.

Château Lafite-Rothschild ★★★

OWNER: Domaines Barons de Rothschild; director: Charles Chevallier.

SURFACE AREA UNDER VINE: 103 ha – 71% Cabernet Sauvignon; 25% Merlot; 3% Cabernet Franc; 1% Petit Verdot.

SECOND WINE: Carruades de Lafite.

OTHER WINES: Château Duhart-Milon (Pauillac); Château L'Évangile (Pomerol); Château Rieussec (Sauternes).

CLASSIFICATION: Premier Cru (1855).

Château Lafite is the largest of the First Growths, and of late the most consistently fine of the three in Pauillac. The vineyard lies on both sides of the main road to Saint-Estèphe, and even includes a few hectares across the border in this commune.

Historical records date back to the early Middle Ages, but it was properly not until around 1670, the date the childless widow of Joseph Saubat de Pommiers, Jeanne de Gasq, took as her second husband Jacques de Ségur, that the property began to be transformed into a monocultural wine estate. Early in the next century the brand name Château Lafite was well established. It has rarely looked back. The Ségur dynasty lasted until 1784. After passing through various hands, Lafite, by this time first of the First Growths – the 1855 Classification is in order of preference – was sold to Baron James de Rothschild in 1868. The current member of the family who takes responsibility for Lafite is Éric, who took over from his uncle Elie in 1975.

It would be unsurprising if there had not been occasions when even a First Growth had to apologise for its poor quality, even one as potentially rich as Lafite. Here this period occurred in the late 1960s and early 1970s. After a run of magnificent vintages between 1945 and 1962, a rained-on 1964 was followed by a decade of under-achievement. In 1975 there was a double change: of *régisseur* as well as of Rothschild responsibility. Much was fine-tuned as a result. Subsequently the property gave up vinifying in large oak *foudres* and installed a new circular *cuverie* in 1989. This also serves as the second-year *chai*. The quality has been consistently top-class since 1978, though I confess I am no great fan of the 1994, made, as a result of the feebleness of the Merlot vats, almost entirely from Cabernet. On the other hand so was the magnificent 1961!

The château, which you can see through the fronds of weeping willows from the main road, as well as depicted on the label, is mid-sixteenth century in origin. Inside it retains the sombre, opulent, rather heavy Second Empire style of the time of the Rothschild purchase. It is surprisingly modest in scale.

The wine has been described as the epitome of elegance. The last 35 years have shown that, contrary to received opinion, which over-emphasised the grace and delicacy of the wine, Lafite is a classic Pauillac, as 'big' as Mouton-Rothschild or Latour. But underneath is finesse, plus the concentration, purity and definition of first class fruit. Lafite has been placed in the top three in every Bordeaux vintage I've surveyed since 1990. the 2000 is particularly fine: the wine of the vintage.

See *Grands Vins*, p. 42.

Château Latour ★★★

OWNER: François Pinault; director: Frédéric Engerer.

SURFACE AREA UNDER VINE: 67 ha – 76% Cabernet Sauvignon; 22% Merlot; 1% Cabernet Franc; 1% Petit Verdot.

SECOND WINE: Les Forts de Latour.

CLASSIFICATION: Premier Cru (1855).

Château Latour lies at the opposite end of the Pauillac commune from Château Lafite. Only a stream, converted into a drainage ditch, and the communal boundary, separates the Grand Clos de Latour from that of Château Léoville-Las-Cases in Saint-Julien.

Like Lafite, Latour has its origins in a medieval *seigneurie*. It was probably about the same time too, in the early 1670s, that vines were first planted on the land on a large scale. In 1670 it was purchased by a M. de Chavannes, a private secretary to Louis XIV, from whom it passed by marriage to a M. de Clauzel in 1678. Alexandre de Ségur, heir to Lafite, married Marie-Thérèse de Clauzel in 1695. Within a generation the Ségur family had acquired two of the greatest wine properties on earth!

For the next 82 years Lafite and Latour were run in tandem. But after the death of Nicolas-Alexandre de Ségur, son of the couple above, and not unsurprisingly known as the *Prince des Vignes*, the properties were split. Latour passed to the descendants of three of the Ségur daughters, and remained with their successors until 1962. The majority of the shares were then acquired by S Pearson and Sons Ltd., the family company of Lord Cowdray. Harvey's of Bristol took 25 per cent, leaving the rest in the hands of the Beaumont family, direct heirs of the Ségurs. In 1988 Allied Lyons, owners of Harvey's, took over the Pearson majority and much of the Beaumont equity. This was at the top of the market. They sold at a considerable loss to François Pinault in 1993.

The vineyard of Latour consists of the above-mentioned Grand Clos, between the estuary and the main road, and three smaller parcels inland. These had been fallow, and were only planted after the Pearson take-over. Naturally there had always been a selection, and therefore a second wine. In 1972 it was decided to launch Les Forts de Latour, the mainstay of which has its origin in these inland vines. Latour itself only comes from the Grand Clos.

The château of Latour is relatively recent, a Victorian edifice of no great distinction. Between this and the *chais*, recently extensively modernised, is the famous tower, built as a dovecote around 1625, and modernised since.

The wine has a reputation for being remarkably successful in lesser vintages, and consistent too. Some of the Latours in the 1980s were a little under par, but quality returned with a bang in 1990. At its best the wine is the most mineral, austere and dignified of all the First Growths; full, aristocratic, elegant, rich and complex. It is one of the longest lasting of all red wines, keeping in most vintages for 40 to 50 years, and for many it is the yardstick of fine claret.

See *Grands Vins*, p. 54.

Château Lynch-Bages ★

OWNER: Cazes family; director: Stephen Carrier.

SURFACE AREA UNDER VINE: 94.5 ha –
  73% Cabernet Sauvignon; 15% Merlot;
  10% Cabernet Franc; 2% Petit Verdot.

SECOND WINE: Château Haut-Bages Averous.

OTHER WINES: Le Blanc de Lynch-Bages (Bordeaux
  Supérieur); Château Cordeillan-Bages (Pauillac);
  Château Les Ormes de Pez (Saint-Estèphe).

CLASSIFICATION: Cinquième Cru (1855).

Château Lynch-Bages is the largest and most popular of the Fifth Growths. The attractive château, extensively restored in the 1980s, dates from the late 1820s, and dominates the plateau of Bages, just south of the village of Pauillac. The *chais* are extensive and it was from here that the affairs of AXA Millésimes were administered, as well as those of the Cazes domaines, until AXA relocated to Château Pichon-Longueville in 2000.

The Lynch family have their origins in Galway in Ireland. Following the Battle of the Boyne in 1690, John Lynch emigrated to Bordeaux. His descendants soon prospered, assimilated and, having turned from importing wool to exporting wine, acquired the Domaine de Bages in 1749. Michael Lynch was mayor of Pauillac during the French Revolution while his brother Count Jean-Baptiste was mayor of Bordeaux during the First Empire and Restoration. Lynch-Bages was sold in 1824, and the property then passed through a number of hands before the Cazes family, who had begun farming the run-down estate in 1934, acquired it in 1939. Jean-Charles Cazes, who died in 1972 at the age of 95, built up the vineyard and established the present reputation of the wine. Some excellent vintages were produced in the 18 years after the Second World War when many other châteaux were still in the doldrums. There have been many fine bottles since.

The wines of the 1990s, however, lack something. Lynch-Bages has always been a fullish, ample, slightly spicy wine, both rich and aromatic. The vintages are very competent, but fail in real excitement. As at Pichon-Longueville, which AXA Millésimes bought in 1986 and entrusted to Jean-Michel Cazes, the resources are there. But I feel the energy goes more into marketing than to the production of wines of the maximum breeding and flair. The 2000, 2001 and 2003 (especially) show an improvement.

See *Grands Vins*, p. 104.

Château Lynch-Moussas

OWNER: Castéja family.
SURFACE AREA UNDER VINE: 57 ha – 70% Cabernet Sauvignon; 30% Merlot.
SECOND WINE: Les Hauts de Lynch-Moussas.
OTHER WINES: Château Batailley (Pauillac); Château Beau-Site (Saint-Estèphe); Domaine de L'Église (Pomerol); Château Haut-Bages-Monpelou (Pauillac); Château Trottevieille (Saint-Émilion) and others.
CLASSIFICATION: Cinquième Cru (1855).

Not surprisingly, this property commemorates the same Lynch family as does the more famous Lynch-Bages. While Comte Jean-Baptiste Lynch owned the latter, Moussas was the estate of his younger brother Michael in Napoleonic times, at which time it was known as Château Peyronet. It was subsequently acquired by a Spanish merchant named Vasquez, owner at the time of the 1855 Classification, and remained in the hands of his successors until sold in 1919 to Jean Castéja. This generation of Castéjas neglected Lynch-Moussas, however, just as they did Duhart-Milon, and when Émile Castéja finally took over in 1969 the vineyard, *chais* and château were extremely run down, the former to such an extent that total replanting was necessary.

The main part of the vineyard lies west of Batailley, with the now restored eighteenth-century château over the border in the commune of Saint-Sauveur. The wine, for a long time rather lean and unappealing, is now finally showing signs of improvement. Castéja's son, Philippe, took over in 2001 and has transformed the vineyard. The 2002, finally, can be rated 'very good'.

Château Mouton-Rothschild ★★

OWNER: Baronne Philippine de Rothschild; director: Hervé Berland.
SURFACE AREA UNDER VINE: 82.5 ha –
77% Cabernet Sauvignon; 12% Merlot;
9% Cabernet Franc; 2% Petit Verdot.
SECOND WINE: Le Petit Mouton.
OTHER WINES: L'Aile d'Argent (Bordeaux Supérieur Blanc); Château d'Armailhac (Pauillac); Château Clerc-Milon (Pauillac), Château La Fleur-Milon (Pauillac).
CLASSIFICATION: Premier Cru (1973).

Mouton-Rothschild shares with the Barton châteaux in Saint-Julien the distinction of being the sole classed growths in the same family as in 1855. Though classed then at the top of the Second Growths, it was soon apparent that people would pay *premier cru* prices for Mouton. After half a century of lobbying the late Baron Philippe succeeded in persuading the French government to promote his beloved château to First Growth in 1973. The property was originally part of the Ségur estate, as was Lafite and Latour. Precisely when and how it was split off is not clear. It seems likely that this occurred about 1750, when it passed to Joseph de Brane, already the owner of vineyards in the hamlet of Pouyalet. By the 1770s Brane-Mouton, as it was then known, had firmly established itself as one of the leading Seconds if not quite up to the level of the *premiers crus*. In 1830 Hector de Brane, grandson of Joseph, sold Mouton to the banker Isaac Thuret. He in turn sold the property to Baron Nathaniel de Rothschild, of the English branch of the family, in 1853.

The modern history of Mouton begins with the arrival of Baron Philippe de Rothschild in October 1922, at the age of 20. As a teenager, he had been evacuated to the Médoc during the First World War, and had fallen in love with the place. While there was a modest château, constructed in the 1880s, the whole thing was somewhat dilapidated in appearance. The *chais* were just a collection of small farm outbuildings and there were neither water, electricity or proper roads. For the most part, the wines were matured and eventually bottled by the merchants in Bordeaux.

Baron Philippe de Rothschild was soon to change all that. From 1924 he insisted on château bottling the entire crop on the estate. This meant the construction of the magnificent first year *chai* which you pass through today, the first of many in the Médoc, but still the most impressive. Then there was the design of the Mouton-Rothschild label. That for the 1924 was so *avant-garde* it was deemed 'Bolshevist' by one wine writer. After 1945 he commissioned a new artist each year to design the top third of the label. After all the years when Mouton was run at arms length from Paris, as Lafite still is by one of the other branches of the Rothschild family, Baron Philippe was the man on the spot, and having bought out the other members of his family, he became the sole owner. Mouton was his passion. The wine, opulent, cedary, super-rich, and like its creator, somewhat larger than life, is unmistakable. The Baron died in 1988, and was succeeded by his only daughter, Baronne Philippine.

There is now a second wine: Le Petit Mouton; and a white wine, L'Aile d'Argent, a roughly 50:50 Sauvignon:Sémillon blend from a 4.5-hectare parcel of land lying west of the château.

Château Mouton-Rothschild today is the most irregular of the top wines of Bordeaux. It can be magnificent, as it was in 1949, 1961, 1982 and 1986, but often it is clearly the least exciting of the First Growths. At its best, however, it is full and concentrated, with a quite unmistakable opulence and a very seductive aromatic cedar-woody flavour which makes truly exhilarating drinking. Sadly it is now almost 18 years since we have seen a *grand vin* from Mouton, and it is for this reason that I award it two stars, not three.

Mention must also be made of the museum. This consists of an exquisite and eclectic collection of works of art, all with a vinous theme. In a part of the world where there is little else to see, though plenty to drink, a visit is a must.

See *Grands Vins*, p. 64.

Château Pédesclaux

OWNER: Jugla family.
SURFACE AREA UNDER VINE: 28 ha – 55% Cabernet Sauvignon; 40% Merlot; 5% Cabernet Franc.
SECOND WINE: Lucien de Pédesclaux.
OTHER WINES: Château Belle-Rose (Pauillac); Château Grand-Duroc-Milon (Pauillac); Château Haut-Padarnac (Pauillac); Château La Rose de Padarnac (Pauillac).
CLASSIFICATION: Cinquième Cru (1855).

This is one of the smallest and most obscure of the classed growths. It was founded around 1810 by E Pédesclaux, a wine broker, but does not appear in any of the unofficial classifications which preceed that of 1855. In 1930 Lucien Jugla took over the responsibility for running the estate, and his family bought Pédesclaux in 1950. The château, a modest *bourgeois* mansion depicted on the label, lies in Pouyalet; the vines occupy four parcels, two nearby and two north of Château Lynch-Bages. I have sampled Pédesclaux regularly *en primeur* in recent years, though less frequently in bottle afterwards. It is a round, medium-bodied wine, but of no more than *bourgeois* quality.

Château Pibran

OWNER: AXA Millésimes.

SURFACE AREA UNDER VINE: 9.5 ha – 60% Cabernet Sauvignon; 25% Merlot; 10% Cabernet Franc; 5% Petit Verdot.

OTHER WINES: Château Cantenac-Brown (Margaux); Château Petit-Village (Pomerol); Château Pichon-Longueville (Pauillac); Château Suduiraut (Sauternes).

CLASSIFICATION: Cru Bourgeois Supérieur.

Château Pibran lies just south of Château Pontet-Canet, where the gravel *croupe* descends gently southwards towards the railway and the little stream, the *chenal du Gaer*, which divides the commune of Pauillac in two. It was acquired by the insurance group AXA in 1987, from the Gauthier-Villa family, at the same time as Château Pichon-Longueville. The wine is plump, medium-bodied and gently oaky: pleasant but without compelling flair.

Château Pichon-Longueville ★

OWNER: AXA Millésimes.

SURFACE AREA UNDER VINE: 50 ha – 75% Cabernet Sauvignon; 25% Merlot.

SECOND WINE: Les Tourelles de Longueville.

OTHER WINES: Château Cantenac-Brown (Margaux); Château Petit-Village (Pomerol); Château Pibran (Pauillac); Château Suduiraut (Sauternes).

CLASSIFICATION: Deuxième Cru (1855).

Château Pichon-Longueville is the smaller but masculine section of the original Pichon estate. Since the AXA takeover in 1987 the Baron suffix has been repressed.

The Pichon domaine lies immediately inland from that of Latour at the southern end of the commune, in parts overlapping into Saint-Julien. It was founded by Pierre de Mazures de Rauzan in 1661. Twenty-three years later the estate passed as dowry when his daughter Thérèse married Jean-François de Pichon, Baron de Longueville. The Pichons, though ardent royalists, survived the Revolution, by which time there were two branches, one in Pauillac, the other in Parempuyre further south. Baron Raoul of Pauillac, who had no heirs, adopted his cousin, also Raoul, and the estate was then divided, two-fifths going to the two Raouls, three-fifths to the Baron's three sisters. This larger section became Pichon-Longueville, Comtesse de Lalande. The estate was officially divided in 1850 but the wines were not made separately until after the construction of the two châteaux in 1860. The heirs of the Barons remained at Pichon until 1933 when the property was sold to the Bouteiller family. Fifty-five years later the Bouteillers sold out to AXA, at a time when the reputation of Pichon-Baron had declined. The new regime built a new, attractive, largely underground *chai*, introduced a second wine, and with the 1990 vintage showed the Super-Second potential of the vineyard. This is a true Pauillac: full, rich, firm and masculine, with plenty of tannin but no lack of breed. Sadly, since then, as at Château Lynch-Bages, standards seemed to atrophy in the mid-1990s. The wine seemed to have lost its flair. The 2000, 2001 and 2003, however, show an improvement.

See *Grands Vins*, p. 82.

Chateau Pichon-Longueville, Comtesse de Lalande ★

OWNER: May-Eliane de Lencqesaing; manager: Thomas Dô-Chi-Nam.

SURFACE AREA UNDER VINE: 85 ha – 45% Cabernet Sauvignon; 35% Merlot; 12% Cabernet Franc;

8% Petit Verdot.

SECOND WINE: Réserve de la Comtesse.

OTHER WINE: Château Bernadotte (Haut-Médoc).

CLASSIFICATION: Deuxième Cru (1855).

None of the three daughters who inherited this part of Pichon in 1850 (see Pichon-Longueville above) had any children. Eventually the property passed to a niece, Elizabeth de Narbonne-Pelet, who like one of her aunts, Marie-Laure, was married to a Lalande. In 1925 Pichon-Lalande, as it is frequently contracted, passed to a consortium headed by Louis and Édouard Miailhe. May-Éliane de Lencquesaing, Édouard's daughter, took over in 1978.

It was the 1978 vintage which established Château Pichon-Lalande as a Super-Second. This was made by Jean-Jacques Godin, a protégé of Michel Delon of Château Léoville-Las-Cases, who had been briefly entrusted with management of Pichon in the mid-1970s. The advent of the unexhaustable promotional energy of Mme de Lencquesaing made sure that the world soon appreciated the revived quality of this Pichon. Subsequently there was a string of excellent wines, save only for the 1990, following which Jacques Godin departed. These showed the essence of Pichon-Lalande: a wine of intensity, splendid flair and elegance, richness and succulence; quite different from Château Pichon-Baron. The vintages of the late 1990s, however, including the 2000, are relatively unexciting. Château Pichon-Longueville, Comtesse de Lalande has lost its second star, for the time being.

See *Grands Vins*, p. 74.

Château Pontet-Canet ★

OWNER: Alfred & Gérard Tesseron.

SURFACE AREA UNDER VINE: 80 ha – 60% Cabernet
Sauvignon; 33% Merlot; 5% Cabernet Franc;
2% Petit Verdot.

SECOND WINE: Les Hauts de Pontet-Canet.

OTHER WINE: Château Lafon-Rochet (Saint-
Estèphe).

CLASSIFICATION: Cinquième Cru (1855).

Château Pontet-Canet can trace its history back to 1725 when the governor-general of the Médoc, Jean-François de Pontet, acquired an estate name 'Cannet', as it is spelled on a lintel in the cuverie. He was also proprietor of what is now Château Langoa-Barton. His successors sold Langoa to Hugh Barton in 1821, but held on to Pontet-Canet, this being acquired by the *négociant* Hermann Cruse in 1852, in, it would appear, rather a run-down condition. The Cruse family retained Pontet-Canet until 1975, when it passed to cousins, the Tesserons. Since then there has been a major and ongoing programme of investment in the *chai*, a reduction of the amount of Cabernet Sauvignon from 75 per cent to 63 per cent, the introduction of a second wine and a rise in the percentage of new oak. The result, noticeable from 1986 onwards and even more evident in the 1990s, has been a considerable increase in quality.

This is now one of the very best Pauillacs: full, rich, profound and stylish. The vineyard marches with that of Mouton-Rothschild and d'Armailhac on the southern side. The cellar is unusual in the Médoc in that not only is part of it underground but there is a lower second floor where the grapes, after passing through a *tapis de triage* (sorting table), can enter the vats from above, so avoiding unnecessary pumping. very good recent vintages include 1986, 1990, 1996, 1998 and 2000.

Co-operative La Rose Pauillac

60 members.

SURFACE AREA UNDER VINE: 60 hectares.

I have more notes on La Rose Pauillac, both *en primeur* and in bottle, than the other co-operatives in the Médoc. The wine is of medium body, fruity and if not very classy, at least pleasantly drinkable: a good wine of *bourgeois* standard for the medium term.

Saint-Julien

Surface Area (2002): 909 ha.

Production (2002): 35,978 hl.

Colour: Red (the white wines are *Appellation Contrôlée* Bordeaux or Bordeaux Supérieur).

Grape Varieties: Cabernet Franc; Cabernet Sauvignon; Merlot; Petit Verdot; Malbec; Carmenère.

Maximum Yield: 47 hl/ha.

Minimum Alcoholic Degree: 10°.

S aint-Julien lies immediately to the south of Pauillac and is the smallest of the four main Haut-Médoc communes in terms of its production. The commune is compact and dominated by its 11 classed growths, all of which produce excellent wine and many of which produce wine above their 1855 Classification level. There are five Second Growths, two Thirds and four Fourths.

At the northern end of the commune lie the three Léoville estates, at the southern end Beychevelle, Ducru-Beaucaillou and Gruaud-Larose. Langoa is in the middle, between the villages of Saint-Julien and Beychevelle; set back from the river are Châteaux Talbot and Lagrange. The Saint-Julien soil is predominantly gravel, particularly in those vineyards nearest to the Gironde, where it is based on a subsoil of the iron-based sandstone known as *alios* and clay. Further inland the soil has less gravel and more sand, and beneath this is a richer subsoil containing clay, *alios* and occasionally marl.

Saint-Julien wines are the closest to those of Pauillac in character, and like Pauillac they contain high proportions of Cabernet Sauvignon. Indeed, with the exception of such First Growths as Mouton-Rothschild, Latour and Lafite, there is not a great deal of difference in weight or style between the wines of the two communes. Properties such as Léoville-Las-Cases and Léoville-Barton can produce wine every bit as full-bodied and slow maturing as Lynch-Bages and Grand-Puy-Lacoste in Pauillac.

The quintessence of a wine from Saint-Julien is its balance and its finesse. The wines are well-coloured, have plenty of body, are full of fruit, rich and elegant. It is harmony rather than power which gives longevity; so Saint-Juliens, if without the firmness and reserve of a great Pauillac, nevertheless keep exceptionally well.

Château Beychevelle

OWNER: Grands Millésimes de France (GMF); manager: Philippe Blanc.

SURFACE AREA UNDER VINE: 74 ha – 62% Cabernet Sauvignon; 31% Merlot; 5% Cabernet Franc; 2% Petit Verdot.

SECOND WINE: Amiral de Beychevelle.

OTHER WINES: Château Beaumont (Haut-Médoc); Brulières de Beychevelle (Haut-Médoc).

CLASSIFICATION: Quatrième Cru (1855).

The splendid château of Beychevelle is one of the show-pieces of the Médoc, as befits its historical importance. It has its origins in a medieval *seigneurie,* a feudal castle owned by the Foix de Candale family. The estate passed to Jean-Louis de Nogaret de la Valette, soon to be first Duc d'Epernon, when he married Marguerite de Foix-Candale in 1587. Appointed Admiral of France, he ordered ships passing by on the Gironde estuary to lower their sails in salute. From *Baisse Voile* comes Beychevelle. Following the death without heirs of the second duke in 1661, the estate reverted to the crown, who sold it to pay off the Duke's debts. Part of the property was then split off, leading to the origins of what are now Branaire, Ducru-Beaucaillou and other well-known châteaux. It was probably under the ownership of the Marquis de Brassier (1740-1755) that Beychevelle became a commercial vineyard.

The property was sequestered during the French Revolution and then passed through a few hands before being acquired by Pierre-François Guestier in 1825, at the same time as his business partner Hugh Barton was acquiring Langoa and his part of Léoville. Following Guestier's death in 1874 Beychevelle was sold to the financier Armand Heine from which it passed to the Achille-Fould family, the first of which was Heine's son-in-law. The Achille-Foulds sold out in 1986.

The vineyards occupy much of the first gravel *croupe*, nearest to the river, at the southern end of the commune. The central part of the château dates from 1644, the wings from 1757, the date, it is said, of the planting of the venerable old cedar tree which dominates the front courtyard.

The authorities got it right when they classified Beychevelle as a Fourth Growth in 1855. The wine is good, even very good, but rarely fine. Why this should be, when Château Ducru-Beaucaillou, which occupies similar land, is so exceptional, remains a mystery. I can't help feeling Beychevelle could do so much better.

See *Grands Vins*, p. 179.

Château Branaire

OWNER: Patrick Maroteaux.

SURFACE AREA UNDER VINE: 52 ha – 70% Cabernet Sauvignon; 22% Merlot; 5% Cabernet Franc;

3% Petit Verdot.

SECOND WINE: Château Duluc.

CLASSIFICATION: Quatrième Cru (1855).

The origins of Château Branaire – formerly Branaire-Ducru – lie with the selling off of parcels of the Beychevelle estate in the 1660s (see left). In 1680 some of these were acquired by Jean-Baptiste Braneyre. One of his heirs, Jean du Luc, is credited with having established the reputation of the wine in the 1820s. It remained in the same family – Gustave Ducru, from whom the former suffix, was another relative – until the 1920s. After this fortunes declined, and both the buildings and the vineyard were in a ramshackle state when Jean Tapie bought the estate in 1952. The vineyard was gradually reconstituted, the cellars modernised and the elegant eighteenth century château and its exquisite *orangerie* restored. The Tapies, having done all the work, sold out in 1988.

The château faces Beychevelle at the southern end of the commune. Across a back road is a splendid modern winery, dating from 1991 and largely working by gravity. The vineyard lies in several sections behind the village of Beychevelle, between the plateaux of Châteaux Gruaud-Larose and Talbot. Because of this (do not forget the old adage about the best vines seeing the river.) Branaire lacks the distinction of Ducru-Beaucaillou or the Léovilles. But in most of the vintages since 1982 or so the wine has been full-bodied, rich and of reliably very good quality, if a little sturdy in its youth.

Château La Bridane

OWNER: Bruno Saintout.

SURFACE AREA UNDER VINE: 15 ha – 50% Cabernet Sauvignon; 36% Merlot; 10% Cabernet Franc; 4% Petit Verdot.

SECOND WINE: Château Moulin de la Bridane.

OTHER WINES: Domaine de Cartujac (Haut-Médoc); Château du Perier (Médoc).

CLASSIFICATION: Cru Bourgeois.

Most of the vines of this well-made *cru bourgeois* lie a kilometre or so inland from the château, itself in the village of Saint-Julien, behind Château Talbot. The proprietors themselves live in Saint-Laurent. Though the grapes are harvested by machine this is a neat little wine, matured using one-third new oak.

Château Ducru-Beaucaillou ★★

OWNER: Borie family; manager: Bruno-Eugène Borie.

SURFACE AREA UNDER VINE: 55 ha – 70% Cabernet Sauvignon; 30% Merlot.

SECOND WINE: La Croix de Beaucaillou.

OTHER WINES: Château La Couronne (Pauillac); Château Ducluzeau (Listrac); Château Grand-Puy-Lacoste (Pauillac); Château Haut-Batailley (Pauillac); Château Lalande-Borie (Saint-Julien).

CLASSIFICATION: Deuxième Cru (1855).

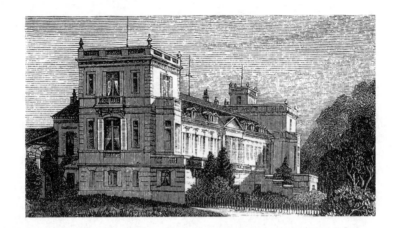

Like Branaire, the origins of Château Ducru-Beaucaillou lie with the dispersal of part of the Bey-chevelle *seigneurie* in the 1660s (see page 134). Nothing much is known about the wine or the estate during the following century, but at the time of the French Revolution it belonged to François de Bergeron, a councillor in the Bordeaux parliament. In 1795 the estate was acquired by Bertrand Ducru, under whose aegis the reputation of the wine slowly grew, as we can see from unofficial classifications at the time, from Fourth Growth to Second.

The Ducru family sold Beaucaillou to the Johnston family, famous Bordeaux merchants, in 1866, and it was then that the elegant Directoire-style *chartreuse* had two large Victorian double-storey wings added on either side – a desecration regretted by subsequent owners. The Johnstons remained at Château Ducru-Beaucaillou until 1928, when they sold the estate to M. Desbarats de Burke who sold it 13 years later to François Borie.

This is a property I have known, and a wine I have loved, since I first started drinking wine seriously. Much helped by the generosity of the late Jean-Eugène Borie, the first château profile I ever wrote was on Beaucaillou, back in the 1960s. Along with Château Palmer, Ducru-Beaucaillou was the first Super-Second: well-coloured, full-bodied, yet supple, elegantly fragrant, complex and classy. The quintessential claret. Apart from a problem with wood treatment taint which has troubled part of the 1988, 1989 and 1990 vintages Ducru-Beaucaillou has not put a foot wrong. The 1995 and 1996, let alone the 1998 and 2000, are every bit as lovely, in their own way, as are the 1953, 1959 and 1961.

See *Grands Vins*, p. 153.

Château du Glana

OWNER: Meffre family.
SURFACE AREA UNDER VINE: 42 ha – 65% Cabernet Sauvignon; 30% Merlot; 5% Cabernet Franc.
SECOND WINE: Château Sirène.

OTHER WINES: Château Bellegrave (Pauillac); Château Lalande (Saint-Julien); Château Plantey (Pauillac).
CLASSIFICATION: Cru Bourgeois Supérieur.

The late Gabriel Meffre and his brother Jean-Paul run Vignoble Meffre based in Gigondas; Gabriel's son Julien is based here in Bordeaux. This is one of the largest of Saint-Julien's non-classified growths, with vines which lie north of châteaux Gruaud-Larose and Lagrange and west of the village of Beychevelle, and a history which has its origins in the convoluted nineteenth-century goings on at Château Saint-Pierre. The Meffres bought it in 1961. The wine is good, if occasionally a rather sturdy, somewhat four-square example.

Up to 1999 the best *cuvées* were sold as Château du Glana, Vieilles Vignes, Du Glana *tout court* being a sort of second wine. This policy has now been changed.

Château Gloria

OWNER: Françoise Triaud; director: Jean-Louis Triaud.

SURFACE AREA UNDER VINE: 44 ha – 65% Cabernet Sauvignon; 25% Merlot; 5% Cabernet Franc; 5% Petit Verdot.

SECOND WINE: Château Peymartin.

OTHER WINES: Château Bel-Air (Haut-Médoc); Château Haut-Beychevelle-Gloria (Saint-Julien); Château Saint-Pierre (Saint-Julien).

Château Gloria is the creation of the late Henri Martin, father-in-law of Jean-Louis Triaud, who runs this and Château Saint-Pierre today. Martin's father was both a barrelmaker and a cellar-master at Saint-Pierre-Bontemps (the property was then divided). In 1923 he had a chance to acquire this half of Saint-Pierre but could not raise the money. Twenty years later Henri, then 40, began a series of land purchases which was to lead to Château Gloria: the vast majority of these were from Saint-Julien classed growths. From the late 1950s onwards it was clear that Château Gloria was a wine of classed growth quality. In 1983 he acquired Château Saint-Pierre-Sevaistre – by that time the Bontemps section had ceased to exist – and the properties have been run in tandem ever since. Tasted alongside each other it is clear that today, Château Saint-Pierre is superior. But Château Gloria is medium-bodied, balanced and stylish.

While not officially the second wine of Château Gloria, which is Château Peymartin, Haut-Beychevelle-Gloria is nevertheless a lesser wine from the Gloria stable. While the *grand vin* is given one-third new oak, this matures using one-fifth. It does not have the same distinction.

See *Grands Vins*, p. 167.

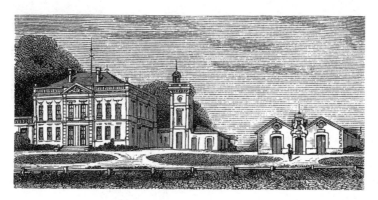

Château Gruaud-Larose ★

OWNER: Merlaut family; director: Georges Pauli.

SURFACE AREA UNDER VINE: 82 ha – 57% Cabernet Sauvignon; 31% Merlot; 7.5% Cabernet Franc; 3% Petit Verdot; 1.5% Malbec.

SECOND WINE: Sarget de Gruaud-Larose.

OTHER WINE: Château Malescasse (Haut-Médoc).

CLASSIFICATION: Deuxième Cru (1855).

Château Gruaud-Larose has for a long time been one of the most important classed growths in the commune of Saint-Julien. Historically it ranked second after the Léoville estate.

One part of the name comes from a local magistrate, M. Gruaud, who amalgamated three local properties in the 1750s. After his death the estate passed to his son-in-law, a local *parlementaire* called Joseph-Sébastien de la Rose. In 1812 the property was sold to a consortium, and this was to subsequently lead to a division of the estate between 1867 and 1935. Désiré Cordier, a local *négociant*, acquired one half in 1917, the remainder 18 years later. Since 1985 Gruaud-Larose has passed through the hands of a number of larger consortia, but until recently had continued to be made and marketed by the Cordier team. The vineyard lies in one piece at the southern end of the commune, directly inland from the village of Beychevelle.

The wine is fuller, more tannic, both richer and more muscular than a textbook Saint-Julien. At the outset it can not only be a bit burly but can exhibit rather green tannins. Underneath there is both depth and concentration, but it needs 10–12 years to soften up.

See *Grands Vins*, p. 146.

Château Hortevie

OWNER: Henri Pradère.
SURFACE AREA UNDER VINE: 3.5 ha – 70% Cabernet
  Sauvignon; 25% Merlot; 5% Petit Verdot.

OTHER WINE: Château Terrey-Gros-Cailloux
  (Saint-Julien).

A wine made in the cellars of Château Terrey-Gros-Cailloux, from a separate parcel of land containing slightly older vines. It has been an exclusivity of *négociants* Nathaniel Johnston & Cie. since 1955. This is an elegant, medium-bodied, very typical Saint-Julien matured in one-third new oak and is well worth seeking out.

Château Lagrange

OWNER: Suntory Group; director: Marcel Ducasse.
SURFACE AREA UNDER VINE: 113 ha –
  66% Cabernet Sauvignon; 27% Merlot;
  7% Petit Verdot.

SECOND WINE: Les Fiefs de Lagrange.
OTHER WINE: Les Arums de Lagrange (Bordeaux
  Blanc).
CLASSIFICATION: Troisième Cru (1855).

Château Lagrange is the largest of all the classed growths. It enjoyed a considerable reputation in the past, but was then allowed to decay for more than 100 years. In 1984 it was rescued by the Japanese Suntory Group, who after a considerable investment and sound direction on the spot, have succeeded in restoring Lagrange's reputation to its rightful place.

Lagrange first appears as an important vineyard in the 1740s under the name Brane-Saint-Julien, its owner being the same Joseph de Brane who owned Mouton (Rothschild). At the time, prior to the emergence of Gruaud-Larose, it was second only to the then undivided Léoville in the Saint-Julien hierarchy.

Lagrange then passed to M. Arbouet de la Bernède – appearing under the name Arbouet as a Third Growth in Thomas Jefferson's classification – before being sold to Jean-Valérie Cabarrus in 1796. Cabarrus was to become a count, and Napoleon's Finance Minister in Spain. He had constructed a large Italianate tower at one end of the classic eighteenth-century façade of the château, a piece of architectural desecration it is hard to forgive. The next major owner was the Comte

Duchâtel, Secretary for the Interior under Louis-Philippe, whose family were in charge from 1842 to 1875.

After this it was downhill all the way. There were a number of changes of ownership, but no one had the means to keep up the investment necessary to maintain the quality at Third Growth levels. Parts of the vineyard were sold off, what was left allowed to contract, and the quality declined. It needed someone with almost limitless resources to resurrect it. We can be grateful that Suntory – it took an amount of lobbying and soothing of ruffled feathers before the French government gave its approval – were eventually permitted to acquire the estate.

Château Lagrange lies immediately to the west of Château Gruaud-Larose at the southern end of Saint-Julien. The wine is a very good blend of classic Cabernet-blackcurrant, textbook Saint-Julien together with something a little bit solid and earthy which comes from the vineyard being on the second or third ridge of gravel away from the Gironde estuary. Quality is high these days and still improving and yet prices remain reasonable.

See *Grands Vins*, p. 161.

Château Lalande

OWNER: Meffre family.
SURFACE AREA UNDER VINE: 32 ha – 55% Cabernet Sauvignon; 40% Merlot; 5% Cabernet Franc.
SECOND WINE: Marquis de Lalande.

OTHER WINES: Château Bellegrave (Pauillac); Château Plantey (Pauillac); Château du Glana (Saint-Julien).
CLASSIFICATION: Cru Bourgeois.

This property was created in 1964 when Gabriel Meffre bought part of Château Lagrange (see above), and the vineyard lies between this château and that of Talbot. The wine is similar to that of its stablemate Château du Glana, whose cellars lie nearby in the hamlet of Beychevelle, being quite rich, but often a bit solid and earthy. It lacks the distinction of the best of Saint-Julien's *bourgeois* growths.

Château Lalande-Borie

OWNER: Borie family; manager: Bruno-Eugène Borie.
SURFACE AREA UNDER VINE: 18 ha – 65% Cabernet Sauvignon; 25% Merlot; 10% Cabernet Franc.
OTHER WINES: Château La Couronne (Pauillac); Château Ducluzeau (Listrac); Château Ducru-Beaucaillou (Saint-Julien); Château Grand-Puy-Lacoste (Pauillac); Château Haut-Batailley (Pauillac).

Château Lalande-Borie, like the estate above, has its origins in Château Lagrange, the late Jean-Eugène Borie having bought a parcel of fallow land in 1970, which he later replanted. The 1978 was the first vintage to be generally sold. Lalande-Borie has got better and better ever since, and it is now perhaps the best of all the Saint-Julien lesser wines: medium-bodied, fresh, succulent and well-balanced.

Château Langoa-Barton ★

OWNER: Barton family.
SURFACE AREA UNDER VINE: 17 ha – 74% Cabernet
  Sauvignon; 20% Merlot; 6% Cabernet Franc.
SECOND WINE: Lady Langoa.

OTHER WINE: Château Léoville-Barton (Saint-
  Julien).
CLASSIFICATION: Troisième Cru (1855).

Among the leading properties of Saint-Julien, Château Langoa-Barton has the distinction of being the longest in the same family's hands, having been bought by Hugh Barton in 1821. Barton acquired part of the Léoville estate four years later. The two vineyards have been run in tandem, from Langoa – there is no Château Léoville-Barton – ever since. The current proprietor, Anthony, took over from his uncle Roland in 1983.

The château, an elegant raised *chartreuse*, lies just south of the village of Saint-Julien, and was constructed in the late 1750s when the domaine belonged to Bernard de Pontet, whose family were later to concentrate on their property in Pauillac.

The two Barton châteaux exemplify the accuracy, where there has been no subsequent change, of the 1855 Classification. Langoa is never quite as concentrated or as distinctive as Léoville. It is nevertheless a lovely wine of medium-bodied, clean Cabernet fruit, balanced with its acidity and underpinned by new oak. As at Léoville there was a slight relaxation of standards at the end of Roland Barton's stewardship in the late 1970s and early 1980s. But since then, if anything, quality has been better than ever.

See *Grands Vins*, p. 136.

Château Léoville-Barton ★★

OWNER: Barton family.
SURFACE AREA UNDER VINE: 47 ha – 72% Cabernet
  Sauvignon; 20% Merlot; 8% Cabernet Franc.
SECOND WINE: La Réserve Léoville-Barton.

OTHER WINE: Château Langoa-Barton (Saint-
  Julien).
CLASSIFICATION: Deuxième Cru (1855).

Like the Lynchs of Château Lynch-Bages, the Bartons have their origins in Ireland. Unlike them, they are Protestant, and the family still has estates in Ireland to this day. Hugh Barton was the grandson of 'French Tom', who had arrived in Bordeaux in 1725 and rapidly became an important wine merchant (Barton & Guestier). Shortly after acquiring Langoa in 1821 (see above) he was able to make a down-payment on part of the Léoville estate. This had come onto the market in1794 as a result of one of the members of the Las-Cases family having emigrated. Five years later, in 1826, Hugh managed to acquire the remainder of this sequestered portion, some one-quarter of the original domaine, including some 35 hectares of vines. Both Langoa and Léoville have been made in the Langoa château ever since.

The Léoville-Barton vines lie in two main parcels, behind the château and a little to the north, behind the village, with the Langoa vines in a number of separate parcels both in front of the château and further inland towards Château Talbot. The *chais* have recently been considerably renovated.

Léoville-Barton is a full, Cabernet Sauvignon wine of considerable depth and distinction. It is not quite as austere as Château Léoville-Las-Cases, but more classic than Poyferré. While there was a brief eclipse at the end of the 1970s – Roland Barton, uncle of today's proprietor Anthony being old and disinclined to find the funds to keep the *chais* up to date – the results since have been very fine, equalling a splendid series of vintages both prior to and subsequent to the Second World War.

See *Grands Vins*, p. 136.

Château Léoville-Las-Cases ★★★

OWNER: Jean-Hubert Delon; director: Jacques Depoizier.

SURFACE AREA UNDER VINE: 97 ha – 70% Cabernet Sauvignon; 17% Merlot; 13% Cabernet Franc.

SECOND WINE: Clos du Marquis.

OTHER WINE: Château Potensac (Haut-Médoc).

CLASSIFICATION: Deuxième Cru (1855).

This is the nucleus of the original Léoville, now occupying about half of the original estate. Originally a dependency of the *seigneurie* of Lamarque, the territory gained its independence in 1707, being acquired by Jean de Moitié, president of the treasurers of France. His daughter married local parliamentarian Blaise Antoine Alexandre de Gasq de Léoville, also the founder of what is now Château Palmer. By the 1740s Château Léoville, as it was then known, was already one of the leading growths after the *premiers crus*. Blaise Alexandre had no children of his own, so in the 1770s Léoville passed to four of his nephews. It was one of these, fleeing the country at the time of the French Revolution – and therefore allowing his patrimony to be sequestered – which gave rise to the first dismemberment of Léoville and to Léoville-Barton. In 1840 there was a family feud between the then Marquis de Las Cases and his sister, the Baronne de Poyferré de Cerès, and a further portion was lost.

In 1900 Gabriel de Las Cases, the latest Marquis, was in financial difficulties. He sold some of the stock to various Bordeaux merchants as well as to Théophile Skavinski, manager of Léoville-Las-Cases as well as a number of other estates for absentee or disinterested landlords. Over the next 30 years Skavinski consolidated his position acquiring a majority share, a process continued by his successors, the Delon family.

The late Michel Delon took over from his father in 1975. By dint of a very severe selection (rarely does more than 40 per cent of the harvest go into the *grand vin*) and meticulous vinification he raised the quality from Super Second to First Growth level (and the prices too). The wine is almost

Pauillac-like (the origin of Léoville-Las-Cases' *grand vin*, its 53-hectare *Grand Clos*, lies immediately south of that of Château Latour), full-bodied, austere and tannic, needing time to mature but even in its youth showing aristocratic breeding. There are signs in the 2000 that Jean-Hubert, Michel Delon's son and successor, intends to reduce the austerity – without in any way loosening the concentration and depth. Château Léoville-Las-Cases has produced a glorious series of wines since 1975; those by Jean-Hubert since he took over in 2000 are every bit as good.

See *Grands Vins*, p. 122.

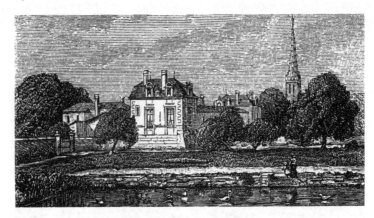

Château Léoville-Poyferré ★

OWNER: Domaines Cuvelier; manager: J-C Lepine.
SURFACE AREA UNDER VINE: 80 ha – 63% Cabernet Sauvignon; 27% Merlot; 8% Petit Verdot; 2% Cabernet Franc.

SECOND WINE: Château Moulin Riche.
OTHER WINE: Château Le Crock (Saint-Estèphe).
CLASSIFICATION: Deuxième Cru (1855).

Divided from Château Léoville-Las-Cases in 1840, Poyferré passed into the hands of the Baron d'Erlanger and Armand Lalande, the latter a respected Bordeaux *négociant*, in 1866. The Cuvelier family acquired it in 1920. At this time, and indeed subsequently, this was the Léoville with the highest reputation, vintages such as the 1874, the 1928 and the 1929, all of which I am happy to say have come my way, being legendary. There was a dip in standards in the 1960s and 1970s, at which time there was rather too much Merlot in the vineyard. But this was taken in hand by Didier Cuvelier after he assumed responsibility in 1979. Since then there has been major investment, including construction of an entirely new *cuverie* and first year barrel cellar. Experiments with a more 'modern' style of vinification were tried in the 1990s, but the 2000 saw a return to a more classic approach. Today Château Léoville-Poyferré is certainly rich and fine, but a lusher, more glossy wine than its Léoville neighbours.

See *Grands Vins*, p. 130.

Chateau Moulin de La Rose

OWNER: Domaines Guy Delon; manager: Hean-François Delon.
SURFACE AREA UNDER VINE: 4.8 ha – 60% Cabernet Sauvignon; 30% Merlot; 5% Petit Verdot;

5% Cabernet Franc.
OTHER WINE: Château Ségur de Cabanac (Saint-Estèphe).
CLASSIFICATION: Cru Bourgeois Supérieur.

Guy Delon has been the owner of the diminutive Moulin de La Rose since 1961, at which time he was co-owner of Château Phélan-Ségur in Saint-Estèphe. Though small, the domaine is scattered all over the *appellation*, and divided into no fewer than 25 different parcels. The cellar is in the hamlet of Beychevelle. This is one of the very best of all the *crus bourgeois*, a wine of medium weight but style and depth: well worth the effort of seeking out.

Château Saint-Pierre

OWNER: Domaines Martin; director: Jean-Louis Triaud.

SURFACE AREA UNDER VINE: 17 ha – 75% Cabernet Sauvignon; 15% Merlot; 10% Cabernet Franc.

OTHER WINES: Château Bel-Air (Haut-Médoc); Château Gloria (Saint-Julien); Château Haut Beychevelle-Gloria (Saint-Julien).

CLASSIFICATION: Quatrième Cru (1855).

Château Saint-Pierre's origins can be traced back to 1693. It was known then as Serançan and belonged to the Marquis de Chevevry. In 1769 the estate was acquired by the Baron de Saint-Pierre who, as was customary at the time, re-named the wine after himself. The property does not figure in pre-Revolutionary classifications, but by the time of the fall of Napoleon it was firmly established as a Third or Fourth Growth alongside Château Beychevelle and Château Langoa. Following the death of the Baron in 1796 the estate was divided between his two daughters, but the property was not physically split until 1832. Subsequently various sections were sold off but the bulk became two separate Saint-Pierre estates: that of Bontemps-Dubarry and Sevaistre.

In the early twentieth century a firm of Antwerp wine merchants called Van den Bussche arrived on the scene. They acquired the Sevaistre section and the majority of the Bontemps-Dubarry vineyard, though not the château itself, which had remained on this side. For a while a separate Bontemps-Dubarry wine continued to be produced, but eventually these vineyards were sold off. In 1981, Henri Martin, whose Château Gloria creation contained much land that had hitherto been Saint-Pierre, bought the château. Two years later he purchased Saint-Pierre-Sevaistre from the successor to the Van den Bussches, Paul Castelain. The wine is now simply Saint-Pierre.

When I first came across Château Saint-Pierre-Sevaistre, as it was then, in the 1970s, I found it a wine of substance and depth, with the sturdiness of those Saint-Juliens which come from vineyards away from the river Gironde tempered by the creaminess of old vines. It was good value and I was a regular customer. Martin's first vintage, the 1983, was promising. Since then, under the aegis of Jean-Louis Triaud, his son-in-law, quality has been a bit humdrum: the wine medium- to full-bodied, but lacking real richness and flair. It was not until the 1990 that I could once again get really enthused. The 1994 and 1995 were, in part, tainted as a result of wood treatment but the vintages since 1998, especially the 2000, have been very good indeed.

See *Grands Vins*, p. 167.

Château Talbot ★

OWNER: Lorraine Rustmann-Cordier & Nancy Bignon-Cordier; manager: Christian Hostein.

SURFACE AREA UNDER VINE: 102 ha – 66% Cabernet Sauvignon; 26% Merlot; 5% Petit Verdot; 3% Cabernet Franc.

SECOND WINE: Connétable de Talbot.

OTHER WINE: Caillou Blanc de Château Talbot (Bordeaux Blanc).

CLASSIFICATION: Quatrième Cru (1855).

Château Talbot is said to be named after John Talbot, Earl of Shrewsbury, commander of the English troops defeated at the Battle of Castillon in 1453, an event which marked the end of three centuries of English hegemony in Aquitaine and Gascony. There is, however, no documentary evidence to link Talbot with this piece of Saint-Julien land.

Known on old maps as Talabot ('talabot' is old Gascon for a sort of yoke with a suspended piece of wood which reaches down to the legs of the animal and prevents it from travelling too quickly) or Delage, after a former owner, modern history begins with the family of the Marquis d'Aux who possessed the domaine for nearly two centuries until 1899. After passing through the hands of a Monsieur A Claverie it was bought by Désiré Cordier in 1918. While the Cordiers have now sold their merchant business and their other properties such as Château Gruaud-Larose they have retained Château Talbot. It now belongs to the two daughters of Jean Cordier.

Talbot has always been a large domaine. The château and vineyards lie inland of the village of Saint-Julien. Since it has been 'independent' from the Cordier business quality has improved: from a dependable classed growth we now have a wine of considerable flair, and at prices which are not excessive. There is also a white wine, from 6 hectares of what used to be entirely Sauvignon but which is now 84 per cent Sémillon. This, too, is stylish.

See *Grands Vins* p. 175.

Château Terrey-Gros-Cailloux

OWNER: Annie Fort & Henri Pradère.

SURFACE AREA UNDER VINE: 15 ha – 70% Cabernet Sauvignon; 25% Merlot; 5% Petit Verdot.

SECOND WINE: Château Le Castagney.

OTHER WINE: Château Hortevie (Saint-Julien).

CLASSIFICATION: Cru Bourgeois Supérieur.

Unlike Margaux, practically all the land that is *appellation contrôlée* Saint-Julien is *cru classé*-worthy. As proof of this one only has to investigate the wines of Château Terrey-Gros-Cailloux (or Moulin de La Rose and others). Terrey-Gros-Cailloux has been enlarged since the 1950s by the Fort and Pradère families, and at the same time the wine has improved. There is good substance here, rich Cabernet fruit and a good base of oak: a lot of style for a reasonable price.

Château Hortevie is run from the same cellar in the middle of the hamlet of Beychevelle.

Château Teynac

OWNER: Philippe & Fabienne Pairault.
SURFACE AREA UNDER VINE: 12.5 ha –
  78% Cabernet Sauvignon; 20% Merlot;
  2% Petit Verdot.

SECOND WINE: Eléonore du Château Teynac.
OTHER WINES: Château Les Ormes; Château
  Corconnac; Château Caillou (all Saint-Julien).
CLASSIFICATION: Cru Bourgeois.

The origin of Château Teynac lies in Château Saint-Pierre. Indeed as 'Tenat' it appears in Wilhelm Franck's list of Third Growths in pre-Revolutionary times. In modern times it was re-established by Pierre Gauthier, formerly a buyer for the Bordeaux *négociant* Alexis Lichine, and for a long time was an exclusivity of the French mail-order business, the Savour Club. In the early 1990s it changed hands. The new proprietors have enlarged the vineyard and the wine is now available on the export market. It is a neatly made wine: medium-bodied, fruity, stylish and for relatively early drinking. The cellars are located in the back streets of the hamlet of Beychevelle.

MARGAUX

SURFACE AREA (2002): 1409 ha.

PRODUCTION (2002): 53,342 hl.

COLOUR: Red (the white wines are *Appellation*

Contrôlée Bordeaux or Bordeaux Supérieur).

GRAPE VARIETIES: Cabernet Franc; Cabernet

Sauvignon; Merlot; Petit Verdot; Malbec;

Carmenère.

MAXIMUM YIELD: 47 hl/ha.

MINIMUM ALCOHOLIC DEGREE: 10°.

While the other three great communes of the Haut-Médoc form a continuous chain of vineyard – from Beychevelle in Saint-Julien north to Calon-Ségur in Saint-Estèphe – Margaux lies separately to the south. In between, close to the estuary, much of the land is too marshy for vines, the gravel *croupes* are less well defined and no great properties are to be found. The *appellation* Margaux covers not one but five communes. As well as Margaux itself, Labarde, Arsac and Cantenac, the communes to the south, and Soussans, Margaux's neighbour to the north, all have the right, in whole or in part, to call their wines Margaux. This conglomeration of parishes boasts no fewer than 20 classed growths: one First (Château Margaux), five Seconds, no fewer than nine Thirds, three Fourths and two Fifths. Some of these, like some of Pauillac's Fifth Growths, are relatively obscure, small in production terms and little seen on the market or at auction. Others are very large, like Château Brane-Cantenac, or, like Château Palmer, deservedly extremely fashionable.

The soil varies within Margaux but is generally a sandy gravel, thinner than in Saint Julien and Pauillac and lighter in colour. This lies on a base which in Margaux itself is partly marl, partly clay. Elsewhere the subsoil is sometimes gravel, sometimes iron-rich sandstone *alios*, and in Labarde is sand and *graviers* (grit).

I find it difficult to generalise about the style of Margaux wines, for they vary greatly. While on the whole they are softer, have less backbone and develop sooner than Saint-Juliens, and also have less of the pronounced Cabernet Sauvignon-oak flavour (one is supposed to find a scent of violets in a Margaux), there are some Margaux wines – Lascombes for example – which are every bit as 'big' as wines from further north in the Haut-Médoc. The classic character of the commune, however, which many call feminine, can be found at Château Margaux and Palmer, and in wines like Ferrière. These have an inherent delicacy and elegance right from the start, which is not to say they do not have plenty of body and potential for ageing well.

On the whole the vineyards in the five Margaux communes are planted with more Merlot and less Cabernet than further north, and this gives a 'soft fruits' flavour, also found in wines of the Graves. In general, Margaux wines are less successful than those of Pauillac and Saint-Julien in lighter, poorer years.

Margaux is often a disappointing commune. There are more underachievers among the classed growths than in Pauillac, Saint-Julien and Saint-Estèphe combined. The consumer is usually better off directing their attention to the best of the *bourgeois* growths, such as Château Labégorce-Zédé and Château d'Angludet.

In part this is the result of a lack of cash, competence or the willingness to act, or a combination of all three. An additional explanation is that not all land which is *appellation contrôlée* Margaux is of classed growth quality. Much of it will never produce top class wine. The fact has been recognised by, *inter alia*, Châteaux Lascombes and Prieuré-Lichine. These are two estates which have been enlarged considerably since the 1950s. Detailed examination of the land, parcel by parcel, enabled René Vannetelle, *régisseur* at Château Lascombes in the early 1990s, to isolate 50 of the 100 hectares the château had under vine as capable of producing the *grand vin*. Only from this would the selection be made. That from the remainder would automatically go into the second wine. A similar procedure was carried out at Prieuré-Lichine when Stéphane Derenoncourt assumed responsibility for the wine in 1999.

Châteaux ◆

Listrac AC
1 Cap Léon Veyrin
2 La Lauzette
3 Fourcas-Loubaney
4 Fourcas-Dupré, Saransot-Dupré
5 Peyredon-Lagravette
6 Fourcas-Hosten
7 Clarke
8 Lestage
9 Fonréaud
10 Ducluzeau
11 Mayne-Lalande

Moulis AC
12 Moulin-à-Vent
13 Duplessis (-Hauchecorne)

14 Malmaison
15 Anthonic
16 Brillette
17 Dutruch Grand-Poujeaux, Chasse-Spleen, Branas-Grand-Poujeaux, Gressier-Grand-Poujeaux
18 Poujeaux, Bel Air Lagrave
19 Maucaillou

Margaux AC
20 Paveil-de-Luze
21 Tayac
22 Haut-Breton-Larigaudière
23 La Tour de Mons
24 Deyrem-Valentin, Marsac-Séguineau

25 Labégorce-Zédé
26 Labégorce
27 Bel Air Marquis d'Aligre
28 Lascombes
29 Ferrière, La Gurgue, Marquis d'Alesme-Becker, Malescot St-Exupéry
30 Margaux
31 Pontac Lynch
32 d'Issan
33 Durfort-Vivens, Marquis de Terme, Palmer, Rauzan-Gassies, Rauzan-Ségla
34 Cantenac-Brown
35 Martinens
36 Prieuré-Lichine

SOUTHERN HAUT-MÉDOC

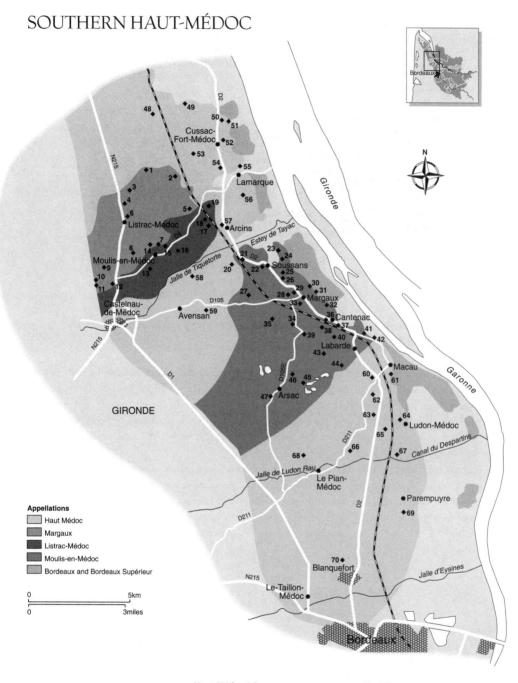

		Haut-Médoc AC			
37	Desmirail	48	Caronne-Ste-Gemme	59	Villegeorge
38	Kirwan	49	Lanessan	60	Cambon La Pelouse
39	Brane-Cantenac	50	du Moulin Rouge	61	Maucamps
40	Boyd-Cantenac, Pouget	51	Lamothe-Bergeron	63	Cantemerle
41	Siran	52	Micalet	63	Belle-Vue
42	Dauzac	53	Beaumont	64	d'Arche
43	d'Angludet	54	Tour-du-Haut-Moulin	65	La Lagune
44	Giscours	55	de Lamarque	66	de Malleret
45	Monbrison	56	Malescasse	67	d'Agassac
46	du Tertre	57	Arnauld	68	Sénéjac
47	d'Arsac	58	Citran	69	Clément-Pichon
				70	Dillon

Margaux Leading Châteaux

Château d'Angludet

OWNER: Sichel family; director: Benjamin Sichel.

COMMUNE: Cantenac.

SURFACE AREA UNDER VINE: 34 ha – 55% Cabernet Sauvignon; 35% Merlot; 10% Petit Verdot.

SECOND WINE: Ferme d'Angludet.

OTHER WINE: Château Palmer (Margaux).

CLASSIFICATION: Cru Bourgeois Supérieur.

The vineyard of Château d'Angludet lies in one block on an inland plateau where the commune of Cantenac marches with that of Arsac and Labarde. The property has a long history, dating back to the Middle Ages, long before it became a monocultural vineyard. In the eighteenth century it was regarded as a Fourth or Fifth Growth. But at the time of the 1855 Classification it was divided into four, its reputation had declined and it missed out. In 1932, however, it was deemed one of only six *crus bourgeois exceptionnels*.

Subsequently the vineyard and the château buildings fell into disuse. Angludet was derelict when Peter and Diana Sichel acquired it in 1961. Today the vineyard is mature and the *cuverie* has just been updated. Benjamin Sichel, the youngest of Peter and Diana's four boys, is in charge, and he produces wine which is certainly of classed growth quality. Angludet needs time as the tannins can be a bit hard and burly in the wine's youth. You need to wait 10 years. But patience is usually rewarded.

See *Grands Vins*, p. 271.

Château d'Arsac

OWNER: Philippe Raoux; director: Migeul Patxi.

COMMUNE: Arsac.

SURFACE AREA UNDER VINE: 112 ha – 60% Cabernet Sauvignon; 40% Merlot.

OTHER WINES: Château Le Montel d'Arsac (Haut-Médoc); Ruban Bleu d'Arsac (Haut-Médoc).

CLASSIFICATION: Cru Bourgeois Supérieur.

The history of Château d'Arsac vividly demonstrates the ups and downs in the fortunes of those who live and make wine in the Médoc. Records go back to the time of Eleanor of Aquitaine in the 12th century. In the sixteenth century the sisters Marguerite and Jacqueline d'Arsac were married to Étienne de la Boétie and Thomas de Montaigne respectively, best friend and brother to Michel, essayist and parliamentarian. A couple of centuries later the estate was part of the Ségur empire, and the proprietors of Château Lafite were also Barons d'Arsac. Then came the French Revolution. The château was destroyed. It was rebuilt in 1830 by the Rubichon family, as was the existing vat house. Under the aegis of the Hosteins the vineyard was enlarged to the extent that it became the largest in the Médoc,

Then, sadly, came phylloxera and the ensuing depression. When the *appellation* of Margaux was delimited in 1954 there was not a single vine at Château d'Arsac. The land was decreed *appellation contrôlée* Haut-Médoc.

The Raoux family took over in 1986, immediately made an application to have the vineyard re-classified as Margaux – this was granted in 1993 – and set about resurrecting the vineyard. There are now some 80 hectares in production, of which half is AC Margaux. Though the vines are relatively young the wine has a pleasant soft, oaky-fruity style and is worth investigating.

Chateau Bel Air Marquis d'Aligre

OWNER: Boyer family.
COMMUNE: Soussans.
SURFACE AREA UNDER VINE: 17 ha – 30% Cabernet Sauvignon; 30% Merlot; 20% Cabernet Franc;
10% Petit Verdot; 10% Malbec.
SECOND WINE: Château Bel Air Marquis de Pomereu.

There has always been something rather secretive about Bel Air. During the nineteenth century the Marquis d'Aligre and his successor the Marquis de Pomereu sold their wine directly to their friends or to Parisian restaurants, in a specially embossed bottle.

Today the wine sells on the Bordeaux market, yet is rarely seen, and Pierre Boyer is reluctant to receive visitors. The vineyard, which lies just north of Virefougasse, overlaps the Margaux-Soussans border. The vines are old – indeed, there are noticeable gaps in some of the parcels – and treated very organically. The wine is largely matured in tank and is bottled very late. It can have depth, but it can be a little dense. Old-fashioned would be an apt summary. Bel Air Marquis d'Aligre has hardly entered the twentieth century, let alone the twenty-first.

Château Boyd-Cantenac

OWNER: Guillemet family.
COMMUNE: Cantenac.
SURFACE AREA UNDER VINE: 17 ha – 68% Cabernet Sauvignon; 25% Merlot; 7% Cabernet Franc;
6% Petit Verdot.
SECOND WINE: Jacques Boyd.
OTHER WINE: Château Pouget (Margaux).
CLASSIFICATION: Troisième Cru (1855).

We have the precise date for the creation of Boyd-Cantenac. Jacques Boyd, a minor Bordelais aristocrat of British origin, bought the lands of Bernard Sainvincens in Cantenac on 11th August, 1754. Some 50 years later Jacques Boyd fell out with his son-in-law and presumptive heir, John Lewis Brown. Eventually the estate was divided, but this was not until after the 1855 Classification, and there was consequently a legal battle over who should be entitled to the Third Growth classification, Boyd-Cantenac or Cantenac-Brown (both, in the end).

In 1932, the Guillemet family, which already owned neighbouring Château Pouget, acquired Boyd. For many subsequent years the wines would be made jointly, Pouget being merely a selection of the lesser *cuvées* of Boyd. Since 1983 the two wines have been made independently and in 1993 a new separate *cuvier* was constructed. Boyd used to be partly picked by machine and was an old-fashioned, tannic, brutal wine. One felt that in most years it was both picked too early and then macerated for too long a time. There was subsequently a battle in the bottle between the tannins softening and the fruit holding up. Sadly the tannins usually won. Since 2000, after Lucien Guillemet took over, Boyd-Cantenac has shown a considerable improvement. The wine is richer and more supple without being weaker. The tannins are riper. The 2002 is a great success.

See *The Vine* No 128, September 1995.

Château Brane-Cantenac ★

OWNER: Henri Lurton.

COMMUNE: Cantenac.

SURFACE AREA UNDER VINE: 90 ha – 65% Cabernet
  Sauvignon; 30% Merlot; 5% Cabernet Franc.

SECOND WINE: Baron de Brane.

OTHER WINE: Château Notton (Margaux).

CLASSIFICATION: Deuxième Cru (1855).

This large and well-known Cantenac estate is named after its early nineteenth-century owner. In 1838 the Baron Hector de Brane, having earlier sold Mouton to concentrate his interests in the *appellation* of Margaux, announced in the local paper that henceforth the wine of his château Gorce-Gui would sail under the flag of Brane-Cantenac.

The Brane era ended in 1866, after which the estate passed through a number of hands before being acquired in 1926 by 'Père' Recapet, father-in-law of François Lurton, himself the grandfather of Henri. In the 1950s, Henri's father Lucien, having 10 children, set about enlarging his empire so that each one would have a château of his or her very own to look after when they grew up. Brane-Cantenac is the most prestigious, and this passed to his eldest son.

Despite the high Cabernet percentage, Château Brane-Cantenac is a typically fragrant Margaux, never a wine of great substance or tannic backbone. It would be an exaggeration to call it delicate though. The wine can have delicious intensity of fruit. Brane-Cantenac was fine in the heyday of Lucien Lurton up to 1966 – then standards fell. But now Henri Lurton is well-established, and following some major investment in the vineyard, the wine is back at Second Growth quality levels. Vintages of the late 1990s were very good. The 2000 is even better and the 2002 better still.

See *The Vine* No 126, July 1995.

Château Cantenac-Brown

OWNER: AXA Millésimes; director: Christian
  Seely.

COMMUNE: Cantenac.

SURFACE AREA UNDER VINE: 42 ha – 65% Cabernet
  Sauvignon; 30% Merlot; 5% Cabernet Franc.

SECOND WINE: Brio du Château Cantenac-Brown.

OTHER WINES: Château Petit-Village (Pomerol);
  Château Pichon-Longueville (Pauillac);
  Château Suduiraut (Sauternes) and others.

CLASSIFICATION: Troisième Cru (1855).

Brown was originally known simply as Château Cantenac and was part of the empire of Jacques Boyd (see above). It then passed to John Lewis Brown, his son-in-law, a painter whose family had been wine merchants. Brown was equally unsuccessful as a businessman as he was as a painter, and in 1843 the estate was sold, that which had been renamed Brown-Cantenac or Cantenac-Brown being acquired by the Lalande family. Armand Lalande had the present château (memorably described in *The Wines of Bordeaux* by Edmund Penning-Rowsell as resembling an English Home Counties' girls' boarding school) constructed in 1860.

Subsequently, via the Lawtons, successors to the Lalandes, Cantenac-Brown was sold to the du Vivier family. The du Viviers sold out the Compagnie du Midi in 1987, who installed a new winery and then sold on to AXA Millésimes in 1989.

I have to say that I have never found Cantenac-Brown an inspiring wine, and yet I must have had all the vintages of the last 40 years on several occasions. Neither the du Vivier nor the AXA style of winemaking has in my view succeeded in producing the wine of fragrance and finesse which the *terroir* suggests is possible (two-thirds of the vineyard lies on the very promising plateau between the château and the railway line). However, there is now a move at AXA to leave the individual properties more to get on with things themselves. I trust this will result in more interesting wines at Cantenac-Brown. The 2000 seemed to indicate a change for the better.

See *The Vine* No 128, September 1995.

Château Dauzac

OWNER: MAIF (Mutuelle d'Assurances des Instituteurs de France); manager: Philippe Roux.
COMMUNE: Labarde.
SURFACE AREA UNDER VINE: 45 ha – 58% Cabernet Sauvignon; 37% Merlot; 5% Cabernet Franc.

SECOND WINE: Château La Bastide Dauzac (Margaux).
OTHER WINE: Château Labarde (Haut-Médoc).
CLASSIFICATION: Cinquième Cru (1855).

Château Dauzac takes its name from Pétrus d'Auzac, who was granted the land in the twelfth century by Richard the Lionheart, King of England. Later it belonged to the Abbaye de Sainte-Croix in Bordeaux, owners also of Château Carbonnieux. Modern history begins in 1740 and the marriage of Elizabeth, daughter of Pierre Drouillard, to Comte Thomas Michel Lynch. Drouillard also owned an estate based at Bages, a hamlet just south of Pauillac. Both then became the property of the Lynch family.

The wine here, as opposed to that of their estate in Pauillac, had no great reputation, and is hardly mentioned at all in the classifications prior to that of 1855. The property was then owned by a M. Wiebrock and was alternatively known as Château Bellegarde, one of its best constituent parcels. In 1863 Nathaniel Johnston, a powerful wine merchant, and also owner of Château Ducru-Beaucaillou, arrived on the scene. Then followed the glory years for Dauzac. The wine soon achieved a high reputation, and following experiments in the Dauzac vineyard, 'Bordeaux mixture' (copper, sulphate and lime) was developed to counteract an outbreak of mildew in the 1880s.

The Johnstons sold up in the slump of the 1930s, as they were forced to at Château Ducru-Beaucaillou, and Dauzac passed to the Bernat family. Between 1954 and 1978 it belonged to the Miailhes, owners of nearby Château Siran and then, minus its Bellegrave vineyard, sold to the Chatelier family, proprietors of a Champagne house. They themselves sold out to MAIF in 1989.

In October 1992 MAIF made an imaginative choice when they invited André Lurton of Château La Louvière and much else besides to take an active role as wine consultant at Dauzac. The results have been decisive. Prior to 1990, it has to be said, Château Dauzac was one of Margaux's many underachievers. The new installations, which date from the Chatelier period, have been further modernised and the selection is more severe. The wine today is soft and fragrant and stylish and now fully merits its classification.

Château Desmirail

OWNER: Denis Lurton.
COMMUNE: Cantenac.
SURFACE AREA UNDER VINE: 30 ha – 60% Cabernet

Sauvignon; 39% Merlot; 1% Cabernet Franc.
SECOND WINE: Château Fontarney.
CLASSIFICATION: Troisième Cru (1855).

When a Mademoiselle Rauzan de Ribail married a Jean Desmirail, lawyer and parliamentary councillor in the 1720s, part of the Rauzan vineyard travelled with her as dowry and Château Desmirail was born. It remained in this family hands until about 1850, the wine having enjoyed a high reputation from the start of the records we have on such things, and which would be confirmed in 1855. By this time it had passed to a M. Sipière, *régisseur* of Château Margaux. He had the modest Desmirail château replaced by a more imposing pseudo-Louis XIII construction and seems to have enlarged the vineyard, though it subsequently shrunk back to 20 hectares or so.

After his death in the early 1870s, Robert Mendelssohn, a relative of the composer took over, but in the First World War saw his estate confiscated, as it was the property of an enemy alien. It was eventually sold at auction and acquired by a M. Michel. In 1938 Michel, in financial difficulties, wound up the estate. The château went to the Zugers, then managing Château Malescot-Saint-Exupéry and Marquis d'Alesme-Becker, and has since been used as the château of Marquis d'Alesme. The brand and the vines in Cantenac and Margaux were sold to Château Palmer (which in 1963 used the name Desmirail as a second wine having decided not to produce a *grand vin*). Part of the vineyard, 10 hectares in Arsac near Château Notton, was at first acquired by the Zugers but later sold to François Lurton of Brane-Cantenac.

In 1981, Lucien Lurton, son of François, bought the brand name of Desmirail from Château Palmer. He had already acquired cellar premises, though not a château, in the middle of the village of Cantenac, and onto the Arsac parcel, genuinely Desmirail, were grafted two other patches of vineyard. One lies between Châteaux Brane-Cantenac, Kirwan and the railway. The other is behind Brane-Cantenac's park. Château Desmirail was reborn.

The new Desmirail took its time to impress, being for much of the 1980s and early 1990s a little green and ungenerous, with neither fruit nor finesse. Since 1996 progress can be discerned. The 2000 is 'good plus'.

See *The Vine* No 128, September 1995.

Château Deyrem-Valentin

OWNER: Jean Sorge.
COMMUNE: Soussans.
SURFACE AREA UNDER VINE: 12 ha – 55% Cabernet
    Sauvignon; 45% Merlot.

SECOND WINES: Château Soussans; Château
    Valentin.
CLASSIFICATION: Cru Bourgeois.

Château Deyrem-Valentin is named after an owner who was a local councillor for Soussans during Napoleonic times. It was bought at auction by the grandfather of Jean Sorge, Maurice Blanc, in 1928. Sorge himself took over in 1972. The château and its dependent buildings, situated near the entrance to Château La Tour du Mons – though the vineyard is near Château Labégorce-Zédé to the south – are modest. But the wine is soft, balanced, full of fruit and with no lack of flair. It is one of a number of worthy *crus bourgeois* to be found at this end of the Margaux *appellation*.

Château Valentin is a 95 per cent Petit Verdot wine, the vineyard being Haut-Médoc, outside the Margaux *appellation* and is the only Bordeaux wine I know made almost entirely from this rare variety. The 2002 was very impressive.

Château Durfort-Vivens ★

OWNER: Gonzague Lurton.
COMMUNE: Margaux.
SURFACE AREA UNDER VINE: 30 ha – 70% Cabernet
Sauvignon; 15% Cabernet Franc; 15% Merlot.
SECOND WINE: Second de Durfort.
CLASSIFICATION: Deuxième Cru (1855).

Like many of the properties in the Médoc, Durfort's history is at times noble, at times murky. The name Durfort comes from a long-standing noble family in the Aquitaine area. As Durfort de Duras they had a base in the Lot-et-Garonne. But one Thomas de Durfort was the *seigneur* here at Château Margaux and the immediate locality in 1450.

The Durfort domaine, which included what is now Château Lascombes and other estates, passed into the hands of the Montalembert family in the seventeenth century. In 1768 the Marquise de Montalembert bequeathed her domaine to her two nephews and heirs, Monbrison and Vivens. The Viscomte de Vivens bought out his cousin and the wine has been called Durfort-Vivens ever since. It was one of a handful of growths specifically noted by Thomas Jefferson in 1787.

Durfort-Vivens changed hands several times in the nineteenth century until it was acquired by merchants Delor in 1895. Abel Delor sold it to Pierre Ginestet, proprietor of Château Margaux, in 1937, from which time it effectively became Margaux's second wine, a fact which only emerged later. In 1961 the Ginestets sold Durfort-Vivens, retaining the château, to Lucien Lurton. His son Gonzague has been in charge since 1992.

While the château (recently sold by Ginestet and then demolished to make way for more vines) and cellars face each other across a road at the southern end of Margaux, the wine really should be considered as a Cantenac, as the vineyards lie above and behind Château Brane-Cantenac. The wine is a sturdier form of Brane but one that for much of the last 40 years has been unexciting. Only since 1996 has it seriously merited its Second Growth position. The 2000, though, is very good – or even better.

See *The Vine* No 128, September 1995.

Château Ferrière ★

OWNERS: Claire Villars-Lurton.

COMMUNE: Margaux.

SURFACE AREA UNDER VINE: 8 ha – 80% Cabernet
Sauvignon; 15% Merlot; 5% Petit Verdot.

SECOND WINE: Les Remparts de Ferrière.

OTHER WINES: Château La Gurgue (Margaux);
Château Haut-Bages-Libéral (Pauillac).

CLASSIFICATION: Troisième Cru (1855).

History goes back to a Gabriel Ferrière, a royal broker in Bordeaux and the man in charge of Louis XV's hunting arrangements, who owned this estate and bequeathed it in 1777 to his first cousins, another Gabriel and a Jean Ferrière. Jean was imprisoned during the Terror but freed and elected Mayor of Bordeaux after the fall of Robespierre.

The property remained in Ferrière hands until 1914 when Henri Ferrière sold it to Armand Feuillerat, at the time the owner of Château Marquis de Terme. His daughter, Mme Armand Durand, leased the vineyard to Château Lascombes in 1954, after which the wine disappeared, emerging sporadically when someone required an exclusive label. In 1988 the Merlaut family bought the vineyard from the Durands and in 1991 negociated the end of the lease with Lascombes. The first vintage to emerge under the new regime was the 1992. The wine is made in the cellars of La Gurgue.

Very quickly, under the inspired direction of Claire Villars, Château Ferrière has been transformed into a sort of *petit* Palmer. It is not much above medium body, but is elegant, balanced and fragrant. And the price is still reasonable. A property to watch. The 2002 is quite delicious.

See *The Vine* No 174, July 1999.

Château Giscours

OWNER: Éric Albada Jelgersma; director:
Alexander van Beek.

COMMUNE: Labarde.

SURFACE AREA UNDER VINE: 80 ha – 55% Cabernet
Sauvignon; 40% Merlot; 5% Cabernet Franc &

Petit Verdot.

SECOND WINE: La Sirène de Giscours.

OTHER WINE: Château Duthil (Haut-Médoc).

CLASSIFICATION: Troisième Cru (1855).

Château Giscours, the leading estate in Labarde, is a substantial property with a long history. Records are said to go back to 1330, with details of vines grown on the land dating back to 1552. In November of this year it was sold by Gabriel Giraud, *seigneur* de la Bastide, to Pierre de L'Homme, a bourgeois Bordeaux merchant, for 1000 *livres*. A document specifically mentions land 'near the river' planted with vines. Around the turn of the eighteenth century the estate was acquired by a member of the Saint-Simon family. His successor, the Marquis Claude-Anne de Saint-Simon, fled to Spain during the Terror. Giscours was promptly confiscated and put up for sale as a *bien national* and was acquired by two Americans, John Gray Junior and Jonathan Davies, of Boston.

The American ownership proved to be brief. In 1825 Giscours sold to Marc Promis, a Bordeaux wine merchant. Promis pulled down the existing château and set about the construction of a new one. This was just about complete 22 years later when he decided to sell out to the Comte Jean-Pierre Pescatore, a Parisian banker. Pescatore soon had to re-build the château, for that built by Promis was largely destroyed by fire.

In 1875, to add to Château Pontet-Canet which they had acquired 10 years previously, the Cruse family, very successful Bordeaux wine merchants, became the proprietors. This they sold in 1913, after which the fortunes of Giscours went into decline. Such was the neglect that when Nicolas Tari, a grape-grower from Algeria, started buying into the estate in 1947 (a process he completed five years later) only 7 hectares of a possible 80 hectares were planted with vines.

Nicolas Tari, succeeded by his son Pierre in 1970, gradually replanted the vineyard and renovated the château. They even went as far as creating an artificial lake behind the woodland to the west of the estate. The motivation was to improve the drainage of the existing vineyard.

Though firmly in the list of the Third Growths in 1855, Château Giscours has rarely produced a wine to set the heart beating in the modern era, and towards the end of the Tari ownership (they sold out in 1995) standard dropped to the level of less than acceptable owing to a lack of both investment and selection. The new regime has introduced a second wine, embarked on a major renovation of the *chais* and improvements in the vineyard. I look forward to more exciting wines in the future.

See *Claret*, p. 211.

Château La Gurgue

OWNER: Claire Villars-Lurton.
COMMUNE: Margaux.
SURFACE AREA UNDER VINE: 10 ha – 70% Cabernet
  Sauvignon; 30% Merlot.

OTHER WINES: Château Ferrière (Margaux);
  Château Haut-Bages-Libéral (Pauillac).
CLASSIFICATION: Cru Bourgeois Supérieur.

Before the French Revolution, what is now La Gurgue was owned by a rich banker called Peixotto. It then passed in to the hands of Camille Lanoire (under which name it appears in a number of early classifications). His family remained at Lagurgue (one word – as it appears in Cocks & Féret) throughout the nineteenth century, after which it both changed ownership and was allowed to fall into neglect. When the Merlaut family took it on in 1978, the 1975 had been refused the *appellation* Margaux. Bernadette Villars, Claire's late mother, soon put the property back on the map. The vines are contiguous with those of Château Margaux. Today the wine echoes this proximity. It is one of the better *crus bourgeois* in the commune, with typically a bigger, more 'masculine' character, though less flair, than its stablemate Château Ferrière.

Château Haut-Breton-Larigaudière

OWNER: Jacques de Schepper.
COMMUNE: Soussans.
SURFACE AREA UNDER VINE: 14 ha – 65% Cabernet
  Sauvignon; 31% Merlot; 4% Petit Verdot.
SECOND WINE: Château du Courneau.

OTHER WINES: Château La Croizille (Saint-
  Émilion); Château Tayet (Bordeaux Supérieur);
  Château Tour Baladoz (Saint-Émilion).
CLASSIFICATION: Cru Bourgeois.

A hundred and twenty-five years ago the journalist and artist Bertall visited Château Haut-Breton-Larigaudière. He draws a vivid picture of the vintage at that time. The proprietor then was a M. Laudau and the property's reputation was high. In the 1930s and 1940s, as so often elsewhere, Haut-Breton-Larigaudière ceased to exist. In 1964 the merchant G. de Mour took it over and replanted the vineyard. This they passed on to the Belgian *négociant* Jacques de Schepper in 1992. Under this new management there has been much progress.

The *chais* and *cuvier* were renovated in 1993 and it was decided to introduce 80 per cent new oak, a high proportion for a *cru bourgeois*. The wine can sometimes not take this amount of oak abuse, but is usually very good. Like most Soussans-based wines (though some of the Haut-Breton-Larigaudière vines are actually in Arsac) the character is of medium body, fresh and succulent but with no hard edges.

Château d'Issan

OWNER: Cruse family; director: Emmanuel Cruse.
COMMUNE: Cantenac.
SURFACE AREA UNDER VINE: 30 ha – 70% Cabernet Sauvignon; 30% Merlot.

SECOND WINE: Blason d'Issan.
OTHER WINES: Château de Candale (Haut-Médoc); Moulin d'Issan (Bordeaux Supérieur).
CLASSIFICATION: Troisième Cru (1855).

Issan is one of the few real castles in the Médoc. It even possesses a moat. *Regum Mensis arisque deorum* (For the table of Kings and the altars of the Gods) is engraved on the lintel above the main entrance. Château d'Issan's history is long, complex and has attracted much that is apocryphal: that it was the wine served at the wedding breakfast of Henri II of England and Eléanor of Aquitaine; that it was the last stand of the English army defeated at the battle of Castillon in 1453 and that from the port nearby these soldiers fled, taking a large part of the 1453 crop with them.

Originally one of the two local *seigneuries* in the area (the other was what would become Château Margaux), the property was known as Théobon in the fifteenth century. In the seventeenth century it was acquired by a local parliamentarian called Thomas d'Essenhault, from which the name. It was Essenhault who constructed the present château. That the wine was already regarded highly in the eighteenth century is attested in a letter sent by a local merchant called Bruneval to Henry Powell, who looked after the cellar of the Prince of Wales, later George II. This refers to the Issan 1723. 'Never in my life have I tasted a Château d'Issan so good as this vintage'.

At the time of the French Revolution Issan belonged to the Castelnau and Foix de Candale families. The Candales then fled the country, leading to a division of the estate. But it was re-united in 1825 by Justin Duluc. It then passed through the hands of the Blanchy and Roy families before being allowed to decline in the 1930s. When Emmanuel Cruse took it over in 1945 it was virtually derelict. His son Lionel and grandson, also Emmanuel, are in charge today.

Sadly Château d'Issan, which produced some very good – if not exactly brilliant – wines in the 1980s, has failed to shine in the last decade, despite serious investment in the *cuvier* and *chais*. It seems to me to be too thin, too lean. I would like to see a fatter, richer, more succulent wine, plus, of course, the sort of depth and elegance one finds in nearby Château Palmer.

See *Grands Vins*, p. 239.

Château Kirwan

OWNER: Schÿler family; manager: Philippe Mottes.
COMMUNE: Cantenac.
SURFACE AREA UNDER VINE: 35 ha – 40% Cabernet Sauvignon; 30% Merlot; 20% Cabernet Franc; 10% Petit Verdot.

SECOND WINE: Les Charmes de Kirwan.
OTHER WINE: Château Fourcas-Hosten (Listrac).
CLASSIFICATION: Troisième Cru (1855).

The origins of Château Kirwan lie with a nobleman called Renard de Lassalle. At the beginning of the eighteenth century Lassalle sold his Cantenac vineyards to Sir John Collingwood, a British wine shipper. Collingwood augmented the estate with a further parcel called Ganet and the combined vineyard became his daughter's dowry when she married an Irishman from Galway, Mark Kirwan. Thomas Jefferson noted 'Quirouen' (sic) as a Third Growth in 1787.

The Kirwan family sold the estate to a M. Lanoix in 1828, and he passed it on to Camille Godard in 1856. Without heirs, Godard bequeathed the property to the city of Bordeaux in 1881. Schroder et Schÿler, Bordeaux merchants, took on a marketing role for Château Kirwan soon afterwards, and bought the estate in 1926.

Château Kirwan was decreed top of the Third Growths in 1855, and is one of the few in Margaux not to have changed its land since. There are two main parcels of vineyard; one behind the château as the land rolls away towards Brane-Cantenac; the other beyond Pouget towards Château d'Angludet.

The wine used to be somewhat rustic. Now that Jean-Henri Schÿler has retired from the *négociants* business to concentrate on Kirwan it is less burly and more civilised. It can be a bit 'hot' in its youth. I have found myself revising my notes upwards when I have encountered the vintages of the 1990s in bottle. The wines since 2000 have seen a distinct improvement.

See *The Vine* No 10, November 1985.

Château Labégorce

OWNER: Hubert Perrodo; director: Florent Granier.
COMMUNE: Margaux.
SURFACE AREA UNDER VINE: 36 ha – 48% Cabernet Sauvignon; 40% Merlot; 10% Cabernet Franc; 2% Petit Verdot.

SECOND WINE: Château Tour de Laroze.
OTHER WINE: Château La Mouline de Labégorce (Haut-Médoc).
CLASSIFICATION: Cru Bourgeois Supérieur.

The original history of both Labégorce and its neighbour Labégorce-Zédé (see page 160) is somewhat confused. On the one hand there is the Gorce family, owners in the early part of the eighteenth century of what has since become Brane-Cantenac. Then there is a *lieu-dit* overlapping the boundaries of the communes of Margaux and Soussans. Third there is the presence, or otherwise, of an Abbé. (There used to be a third property hereabouts – it doesn't exist any more, and the château burnt down in 1965 – called Château L'Abbé-Gorsse de Gorsse.) When Marie-Catherine de Mons married Jean-Baptiste de Secondat in 1740 her dowry made him *seigneur* of de Mons, Bessan, Marsac and Labégorce. Twenty years further on we have documentary evidence of the Gorsse (or Gorce) family's involvement with vines in Soussans. But not before. Is it just a coincidence that there were Gorces at Labégorce?

The split between the three estates, if they were ever one unit, seems to have been at the time of the Revolution. We know that Barthélémy Benoist acquired the 'Domaine de la Bégorce' in 1795. This became Labégorce-Zédé. Pierre Capelle owned a château called Marcadie in 1824 which also had its origins in the partly sequestered La Tour de Mons estate. This was enlarged by the acquisition of Gorsse land, changed its name, and passed into the hands of first M. Vastapani and then Fontuné Beaucourt in 1865. It was then that its present-day LouisXVI-style château was constructed. In 1918 the Rooryck family took over. Their heirs sold Labégorce to M. and Mme Robert Condom in 1965 and their son Jean-Robert was bought out by Hubert Perrodo in 1989.

Since then a major investment has taken place. The estate was a building site for six or seven years! The wine has improved and it is now one of the better Margaux *crus bourgeois*. But it does not have the aspiration to *cru classé* status of its neighbour Labégorce-Zédé.

Château Labégorce-Zédé

OWNER: Thienpont family; manager: Luc Thienpont.

COMMUNE: Soussans.

SURFACE AREA UNDER VINE: 27 ha – 50% Cabernet Sauvignon; 35% Merlot; 10% Cabernet Franc; 5% Petit Verdot.

SECOND WINE: Domaine Zédé.

OTHER WINES: Le Pin (Pomerol); Vieux Château Certan (Pomerol); Z de Zédé (Bordeaux Supérieur) and others.

CLASSIFICATION: Cru Bourgeois Exceptionnel.

Barthélémy Benoist (see above) had two daughters, the elder of whom married Jean-Émile Zédé, a merchant from Paris. In 1840, after a legal battle, their son Pierre Amadée took over. He and his wife Esther Henriette Chevassus had three children. They must have been a remarkable trio: the eldest Émile Hyppolyte became an admiral; Charles Jules went into the army and rose to be general; Gustave Alexandre became the inventor of the first propellor-driven submarine (he later blew himself up in a torpedo experiment that went tragically wrong).

The Zédés remained at their Labégorce until 1931. It subsequently changed hands five times in 30 years until acquired by Jean Battesti, an Algerian, in 1961. Battesti doubled the size of the vineyard, renovated the cellar, and as none of his children were interested in taking over, sold up to the Thienponts when he returned to Algeria in 1979.

With the arrival of Luc Thienpont, working on the good groundwork of Battesti, Labégorce-Zédé instantly began to make wine at least as good as the majority of Margaux *crus classes* if not better. The setting is modest, the château being a sort of Swiss chalet-style building stuck on to the side of the *chai* a couple of hundred yards along the road – which marks the Margaux-Soussans border – from the other Labégorce. But the wine, unforced, elegant, fragrant, harmonious, has real style and flair.

See *Grands Vins*, p. 276.

Château Lascombes

OWNER: Colony Capital; manager: Dominique Befve.

COMMUNE: Margaux.

SURFACE AREA UNDER VINE: 84 ha – 45% Cabernet

Sauvignon; 50% Merlot; 5% Petit Verdot.

SECOND WINE: Chevalier de Lascombes.

CLASSIFICATION: Deuxième Cru (1855).

Château Lascombes is probably the most blatant example of the wide disparity in location that can exist between the Classification of 1855 and the situation today. From its inception to 1952 Lascombes was never much larger than 15 hectares of vineyard. Now there are more than five times that amount.

Lascombes has its origins in the Durfort de Duras family. One can conjecture a piece of land passing by way of dowry. We hear of the name of Lascombes first in 1625, with the birth of the Chevalier Antoine de Lascombes. The wine is first mentioned in 1700. Two barrels a year, as feudal dues, were paid to Château Margaux, which used the wine for topping up purposes. The Lascombes era lasted until the French Revolution. The property then changed hands a few times before being sold to Gustave Chais-d'Est-Ange, secretary to the Gironde senate in 1867. It then covered 21 hectares. Chais-d'Est-Ange's son Jean-Jules Théophile was a famous lawyer in Paris. His interest in Lascombes fluctuated. Parts of the vineyard were sold off. Yet at the turn of the century he had the modest château pulled down and the rather ugly Gothic construction we see today built in its place. And he bought Marquis d'Alesme-Becker, intending to amalgamate the two. In 1923 he died, and subsequently a limited company was formed with the merchants Ginestet as major shareholders. By the late 1940s the Ginestets had sold their interest to concentrate on Château Margaux and Lascombes, somewhat run down, was up for sale. In 1952, having purchased the Prieuré on his own account the year before, Alexis Lichine organised a syndicate of Americans to buy the property.

Lichine modernised the château, built a swimming pool (which plays a second role as a reserve of water in case of fire), renovated the *chais* and considerably enlarged the vineyard. Bass, the British brewery group, having acquired Lichine's wine business in 1965, bought Lascombes in 1971. This later was sold to Colony Capital in 2001.

The big problem at Lascombes is that the 84 hectares covered by the vineyard today, while AC Margaux, are not necessarily capable of producing Second Growth wine. René Vannetelle, appointed manager in 1985, was quick to understand the problem. After an analysis of the soils, he decreed that only half would even be considered in the first place for the *grand vin*: even here there would be a selection. The following year an entirely new winery was installed. We held our breath. Sadly the spring to Super-Second quality was not immediately forthcoming. Bruno Lemoine, from Château Montrose, took over from Vannetelle when he retired in 1996, but resigned in disgust in 2001 when Alain Reynaud (of Château Quinault L'Enclos in Saint-Émilion) was brought in as consultant. Reynaud's first vintage (2001) was a disaster: over-extracted and clumsy. Since then he has changed his approach. The 2002 is much more civilised. Ironically, the 2000, made by Lemonine, was the best Lascombes for a generation.

See *Grands Vins*, p. 232.

Château Malescot Saint-Exupéry

OWNER: Roger Zuger and family; director: Jean-Luc Zuger.
COMMUNE: Margaux.
SURFACE AREA UNDER VINE: 23.5 ha –
50% Cabernet Sauvignon; 35% Merlot;
10% Cabernet Franc; 5% Petit Verdot.
SECOND WINES: La Dame de Malescot.
OTHER WINE: Domaine du Balardin (Bordeaux Supérieur).
CLASSIFICATION: Troisième Cru (1855).

According to tradition the Escousses family, notaries to Henri IV, founded what would become Malescot in 1610. On 1st August, 1697, the last of the line, Mlle Louise Escousses, sold the estate to Simon Malescot, Attorney General to Louis XIV and a member of the Bordeaux parliament. There were already vines on the property, in parcels which still exist today, and during the next 50 years Malescot became monocultural, and established itself as a Third Growth. The Malescots remained until the French Revolution, after which the domaine was split. In 1827 Comte Jean-Baptiste de Saint-Exupéry bought Malescot and re-united it. He added on a parcel called Loyac and amalgamated Malescot with an estate called La Colonie, which belonged to his wife's family, *négociants* in Bordeaux. (Antoine de Saint-Exupéry, the Second World War airman and author, was their grandson.)

After Jean-Baptiste's death in the 1840s his widow found herself in financial difficulties and was forced to sell out to a Bordeaux banker named Fourcaude. Fourcaude further enlarged Malescot, building it up to 100 hectares. Hardly had he completed this then he died, and once again the pendulum between success and failure began to swing the other way. Though his successors, a consortium of businessmen, continued the expansionist policies of Fourcaude they soon overreached themselves. Little by little the land was sold off. In 1900 Malescot Saint-Exupéry was sold to a Bremen businessman called Lerbs and would soon pass into the hands of the wine merchants Seignitz, also of Bremen.

As enemy property, Malescot Saint-Exupéry was confiscated during the First World War. It was acquired in a somewhat run down condition by an English firm who entrusted the local management to Edmund Ritz and his son-in-law Paul Zuger. Eventually they sold Malescot Saint-Exupéry (and Château Marquis d'Alesme-Becker, which they had also acquired) to the Zugers. Today the man in charge is Jean-Luc, Paul's grandson, who has been responsible for the wine since 1991.

Malescot Saint-Exupéry made some very fine bottles in the 25 or so years following 1945. Then, as elsewhere, something went missing. (It is no coincidence that in the late 1950s and early 1960s a major programme of replanting had taken place.) Since Jean-Luc's arrival there has been a major investment in the vineyard and in the cellars and things generally have been fine-tuned. The wine, fullish for a Margaux, rich and concentrated, built to last, is once more among the top half a dozen in the *appellation*.

See *Grands Vins*, p. 244.

Château Margaux ★★★

OWNER: Mentzelopoulos family; director: Paul Pontallier.

COMMUNE: Margaux.

SURFACE AREA UNDER VINE: 81 ha – 75% Cabernet Sauvignon; 20% Merlot; 3% Petit Verdot; 2% Cabernet Franc.

SECOND WINE: Pavillon Rouge du Château Margaux (Bordeaux).

OTHER WINE: Pavillon Blanc du Château Margaux (Bordeaux).

CLASSIFICATION: Premier Cru (1855).

The long and distinguished history of Château Margaux has its origins in a medieval *seigneurie* called La Motte (the mound) or Lamothe. In those days, before Dutch engineers drained the Médoc in the early seventeenth century, much of the land which was lower in elevation would spend parts of the year under water. Legend has it that there was a castle on this mound, and it was the home of Edward III, King of England, in the fourteenth century.

The manor and its domaine passed through a number of noble hands over the centuries. It was under those of the d'Aulèdes in the mid-seventeenth century that vines were first planted seriously on the estate. Records show that there were 70 hectares of vines in 1680. As soon as classifications began, early in the following century, Château Margaux was recognised as a First Growth.

Sequestered during the French Revolution, the estate was acquired in 1802 by the Marquis Douat de Colonilla who directed the demolition of the existing château and commissioned the one we know today. Then followed a succession of owners, all of them aristocrats, until the 1920s. Margaux was turned into a limited company with the Ginestets, merchants in Bordeaux, as significant stockholders. Over the years they bought the others out and by 1949 they were in charge. The Ginestets remained at Margaux until the scandal and slump of the early 1970s. In 1977 Château Margaux was sold to André Mentzelopoulos, a French supermarket group owner of Greek extraction. He died three years later, and subsequently his widow sold part of the equity to the Agnelli group. In 2003 Corinne Mentzelopoulos, his daughter, bought this shareholding back.

Some of the very loveliest bottles that have ever come my way have been produced by Château Margaux, but, as with other properties, and at the same time as Château Lafite, i.e. from 1964 to 1976, there was a period of under-achievement. Since the Mentzelopoulos family have been in charge, and under the inspired directorship of Paul Pontallier, who arrived in 1983, the property has not put a foot wrong. The wines, full but fragrant and subtle, rich and supremely elegant, are triumphantly First Growth, regularly indeed among the top three Bordeaux wines of the vintage.

See *Grands Vins,* p. 216 and *The Vine* No 215, December 2002.

Chateau Marquis d'Alesme-Becker

OWNER: Jean-Claude Zuger.
COMMUNE: Margaux.
SURFACE AREA UNDER VINE: 16 ha – 45% Merlot;
 30% Cabernet Sauvignon; 15% Cabernet Franc;

10% Petit Verdot.
SECOND WINE: Marquise d'Alesme.
CLASSIFICATION: Troisième Cru (1855).

Marquis d'Alesme-Becker has always been one of the smaller and most obscure of the Margaux classed growths. The Marquis in question flourished around the beginning of the seventeenth century. His descendents remained in charge until 1809, when they sold the estate to a Dutchman called Becker (or, sometimes, Bekker). At the time of the 1855 Classification it belonged to Mssrs Szjarderski and Rolland. There were then a mere 4 hectares. After Szjarderski's death Marquis d'Alesme-Becker was acquired by Arthur de Gassowski. He resold the estate to M. Chaix-d'Est-Ange of Château Lascombes who intended to join the two properties together. These plans came to nought with Chaix-d'Est-Ange's death just before the First World War, after which the British firm of W H Chaplin acquired it and run it jointly with their Château Malescot-Saint-Exupéry.

The Zuger family arrived as managers in the late 1930s, at which time they took over the château of Desmirail. This has since been the Marquis d'Alesme-Becker château. In 1955 they bought both Malescot-Saint-Exupéry and Marquis d'Alesme-Becker. In 1979 the two châteaux were split between the Zuger brothers and about 15 years later a transfer of some 10 hectares of land brought Marquis d'Alesme up to its present size. There has since been an enlargement and renovation of both *chai* and *cuvier*. Nevertheless the quality remains unexciting. The wine is rather light and thin. Not in my view up to *cru classé* level.

See *The Vine* No 124, May 1995.

Château Marquis de Terme

OWNER: Sénéclauze family; manager: Jean-Pierre
 Hugon.
COMMUNE: Margaux.
SURFACE AREA UNDER VINE: 38 ha – 55% Cabernet
 Sauvignon; 35% Merlot; 7% Petit Verdot;

3% Cabernet Franc.
SECOND WINE: Les Gondats de Marquis de Terme
 (Bordeaux Supérieur).
CLASSIFICATION: Quatrième Cru (1855).

The origin of this estate lies with that of Rauzan: François de Péliguilhan, Marquis de Terme, married Pierre de Rauzan's great-niece, a Mlle Ledoulx, in 1762. The Terme family remained until Napoleonic times. The property then changed hands a couple of times before being bought by Halvorous Sollberg, a Bordeaux *négociant* of Swedish origin, newly arrived in the Gironde, and newly married to a rich heiress from Calais. Subsequently he got himself into financial difficulties and disappeared, probably to Argentina, where he was presumed to have died. In 1834, having discharged some of Sollberg's debt, a M. Mac-Daniel acquired Marquis de Terme. He was the lover of the abandoned Mme Sollberg, and there is more than a suggestion that this was a sort of blind sale, keeping things warm, so to speak, while the widow's son Oscar worked to pay off the rest of his father's debts. This was achieved in 1845, at which time Oscar Sollberg took over at Marquis de Terme, now a domaine of some 45 hectares.

Sollberg – who was also to purchase Château Siran – had engaged Thomas Feuillerat as *régisseur* of his estate. Feuillerat had other interests locally, at Pontac-Lynch, and at a *cru* called Marian. His descendants took over at Marquis de Terme in 1898, and were to buy Château Ferrière in 1913. After the death of Armand Feuillerat in 1935 Marquis de Terme was sold to Pierre Sénéclauze, a wine merchant from Marseilles. An impressive new *chai* and *cuvier* were constructed in 1981.

Marquis de Terme is a wine more distinguished by its deep colour and rich, muscular structure than by its Margaux elegance. It has been refined since the new installations were built 20 years ago, and I usually mark it 'good', even 'good plus'. But it is still some way from being a wine of Château Rauzan-Ségla elegance, for example (the châteaux are close by). This is a puzzle, because the vineyards are well placed.

See *Grands Vins*, p. 266.

Château Marsac-Séguineau

OWNER: S C du Château Marsac-Séguineau; manager: Dominique Laux.
COMMUNE: Soussans.
SURFACE AREA UNDER VINE: 10 ha – 60% Merlot; 28% Cabernet Sauvignon; 12% Cabernet Franc.

SECOND WINE: Château Gravières de Marsac.
OTHER WINE: Château La Tour de Mons (Margaux).
CLASSIFICATION: Cru Bourgeois.

Located in the Marsac hamlet in Soussans, not far from Château La Tour de Mons, this is a well-made and individual wine, with a curious *encépagement* for a Margaux.

The seven-pointed crown on the label indicates a count, in this case Léon-Marie de Robien who in 1886 amalgamated the *bourgeois cru* Séguineau-Deyries with other parcels of land and renamed the estate. His successor Mme Vast further enlarged the property after she took over at the turn of the century. There followed a number of changes of ownership before the merchants Mestrezat assumed control in 1964. It has recently been sold again. Marsac-Séguineau is a wine of medium body, with plump attractive fruit, intended for the medium term. They made a particularly successful 1997 and the 1998, 1999 and 2000 were also very good.

Château Martinens

OWNER: Jean-Pierre Seynat-Dulos.

COMMUNE: Cantenac.

SURFACE AREA UNDER VINE: 30 ha – 54% Merlot; 31% Cabernet Sauvignon; 11% Petit Verdot; 4% Cabernet Franc.

SECOND WINE: Château Guyney.

OTHER WINES: Château Bois du Monteil; Château Corneillan (both Haut-Médoc).

CLASSIFICATION: Cru Bourgeois.

Martinens lies south-west of the village of Margaux, near Château Cantenac-Brown, with its vineyard in one piece – rare for the *appellation* – surrounding an attractive eighteenth-century château. It is said to have belonged to three unmarried English ladies called Anne, Jane and Mary White, who sold it to a local merchant, Pierre Changeur, in 1776. A century later, having passed through the hands of the Comte de Beauregard, it was acquired by Jules Jadouin, proprietor of Châteaux Vincent and Montbrun, spin-offs from the dismembered Château Palmer and Château d'Angludet. His son-in-law Jacques Lebègue was in charge until 1936. The Dulos-Seynat family took over the property in 1945.

I usually find the wine lacks sophistication. But the 2000 was very promising in cask.

Château Monbrison

OWNER: E M Davis & Fils; manager: Laurent Von der Heyden.

COMMUNE: Arsac.

SURFACE AREA UNDER VINE: 13 ha – 50% Cabernet Sauvignon; 30% Merlot; 15% Cabernet Franc;

5% Petit Verdot.

SECOND WINE: Bouquet de Monbrison.

OTHER WINE: Château Cordet (Médoc).

CLASSIFICATION: Cru Bourgeois Supérieur.

Over the last 20 years Monbrison has established itself as one of the very best of the non-classed growths of the entire Médoc, a tribute not so much to its position, which is in the backwoods of Arsac, as to the inspired winemaking, first by Elizabeth Davis' second son, Jean-Luc Vonderhoyden, and then after his death from leukaemia in 1992 by his brother Laurent.

The property was originally a subsidiary of the neighbouring Château d'Arsac. It belonged to the Copmartin family, Bordeaux councillors, from 1749 to 1818 when it was acquired by Paul Georges Conquère de Monbrison. At the time of the 1855 Classification Isidore Feuillebois, a local lawyer, was in charge. He sold Monbrison on to Gustave Chai-d'Est-Ange in 1866, the year before the latter was to acquire Château Lascombes. It subsequently passed into the hands of the Lavendier family, who also owned Château La Gurgue. Robert Meacham Davis, American protestant minister, poet, artist and journalist, who had fallen in love with Kathleen Johnston, of the well-known *négociant* family, bought Monbrison after the First World War. Elizabeth, their youngest daughter, took over, having to replant a derelict vineyard, after the Second World War. There was a period in the 1960s when the grapes were sold to Alexis Lichine's Château Prieuré-Lichine. This came to an end in 1976.

Firm, full, rich and increasingly sophisticated, Monbrison is clearly of *cru classé* quality.

See *Grands Vins*, p. 280.

Château Palmer ★★

OWNER: Mahler-Besse & Sichel families; manager: Bertrand Bouteiller.

COMMUNE: Cantenac.

SURFACE AREA UNDER VINE: 52 ha – 47% Cabernet

Sauvignon; 47% Merlot; 6% Petit Verdot.

SECOND WINE: La Réserve de la Général (to 1998); Alter Ego de Palmer.

CLASSIFICATION: Troisième Cru (1855).

Although the vineyard, under the name of Palmer, only dates from 1814 and the château from 1860, the origins of this celebrated property go back nearly a century earlier. They lie with the then substantial Issan estate, the senior *seigneurie* in Cantenac. In 1729 there was a division between the Foix-Candales and the Castelnau-Essenhault families. A further division between the Foix-Candales took place in 1748. This was the occasion, it seems, when a member of the many tentacled du Gascq family seized the occasion to buy some land and plant a vineyard. By the turn of the century there were 50 hectares under vine. The reputation of the wine, as yet, was not as high as some of the château's neighbours. That would be the creation of the next owner.

This was Major-General Charles Palmer. He bought the property from a recently widowed Madame de Gascq, changed its name, and over the next 15 years poured his fortune into the estate, trebling the size and establishing its name as a Third Growth. Eventually, sadly – he was no businessman and continually fleeced by his managers on the spot – he over-reached himself. The bank foreclosed in 1843. As quickly as it has been enlarged, Palmer was dismembered. When the Pereires, financiers of Portuguese-Jewish origin bought Palmer in 1853 there were only some 27 hectares of vines. In the Palmer heyday there had been 82. The Pereire era continued until 1938. Palmer was then sold to a consortium of four local names, two of which are left today.

Palmer has produced exquisite wines for decades, and has rarely put a foot wrong. It made particularly remarkable bottles in the 1960s, a period when neighbouring Château Margaux was under-achieving and before the emergence of other Super-Seconds such as Château Pichon-Longueville-Lalande. However, I find it not a wine which is very expressive in its youth. You have to wait. It is only when it begins to open out, generally after 10 years in the best vintages, that you can perceive the grace and finesse, delicacy and intensity which is Cantenac's contribution to the palette that is Margaux. Palmer is a very lovely wine. In recent years I have been particularly struck by 1983 (perhaps better than the 1982), 1985, 1986, 2000 and 2002.

See *Grands Vins*, p. 250 and *The Vine* No 208, May 2002.

Chateau Paveil-de-Luze

OWNER: Baron Geoffroy de Luze.
COMMUNE: Soussans.
SURFACE AREA UNDER VINE: 28 ha – 65% Cabernet
Sauvignon; 30% Merlot; 5% Cabernet Franc.
SECOND WINE: L'Enclos du Banneret.
CLASSIFICATION: Cru Bourgeois Supérieur.

Château Paveil de Luze lies on one site in the extreme north-west of the Margaux *appellation*, inland from the village of Tayat. The property dates back to the early eighteenth century when it passed as dowry from the Rauzan family to the Chevalier de Bretonneau. It was then that the attractive raised *chartreuse*-style château was constructed. Alfred de Luze acquired it in 1862. The wine is stored both in new wood and in vats and is relatively light and soft. It can be stylish and is meant for early drinking.

Château Pontac-Lynch

OWNER: Bondon family.

COMMUNE: Cantenac.

SURFACE AREA UNDER VINE: 10 ha – 60% Cabernet Sauvignon; 30% Merlot; 10% Petit Verdot.

SECOND WINE: Château Pontac-Faure.

OTHER WINE: Château Pontac Phénix (Haut-Médoc).

CLASSIFICATION: Cru Bourgeois.

Lying between Châteaux Margaux and Issan, behind Château Palmer, Pontac-Lynch was created by a member of the famous Pontac family in 1720. He subsequently sold out to Count Thomas Michel Lynch. At this time the wine was outselling most of what are today its more illustrious neighbours. It passed through a number of hands, including that of Alexandre Feuillerat (see Marquis de Terme) before being acquired and reconstituted by Jean-Pierre Bondon in 1952. His grand-daughter, Marie-Christine, has been in charge since 1987. Two versions of Pontac-Lynch are produced. The *grand vin* comes from 90 per cent Cabernet Sauvignon and 90 per cent new wood. The regular version more or less follows the *encépagement* in the vineyard and is given 40 per cent new oak. Recent vintages have been full, vigorous, rich and persistent. The cellar is rather untidy and seems disorganised but the wines are good.

Château Pouget

OWNER: Guillemet family.

COMMUNE: Cantenac.

SURFACE AREA UNDER VINE: 10 ha – 60% Cabernet Sauvignon; 30% Merlot; 10% Cabernet Franc.

SECOND WINE: Antoine Pouget.

OTHER WINE: Château Boyd-Cantenac (Margaux).

CLASSIFICATION: Quatrième Cru (1855).

Legend has it that the land that is now Pouget, like that of Château Prieuré-Lichine, once belonged to the Benedictine monks of Cantenac. Be that as it may, records show the owner in 1650 to be Étienne Monthil. His grand-daughter Thérèse, married to a M. Ducasse but childless, bequeathed the property to François-Antoine Pouget in 1748, about which time the château was constructed. Pouget's only child, Claire, married a well-to-do lawyer Pierre-François de Chavaille in 1771. It is under the name of either Pouget or Chavaille that the wine first appears in contemporary records.

One of the Chavaille children emigrated during the Terror. Part of the Pouget vineyard was sequestered and led an independent existence for some 70 years before being absorbed into Château Kirwan. Pouget remained in the Chavaille hands until 1906. It was then sold to Pierre Elie who was already owner of a vineyard called La Tour Massac. Elie's son-in-law was Louis Guillemet. Since he bought Château Boyd-Cantenac in 1932 the two (with La Tour Massac already absorbed into Pouget) have been run in tandem. Indeed, for many years until 1983 Pouget was but a selection of the Boyd vats.

Boyd-Cantenac and Pouget are still two very similar wines. Full in colour, hard, tannic and rather too tough for their own good. They rarely soften satisfactorily. Lucien Guillemet is now in charge and money has been spent on the cellar. Progress since 2000 has been considerable.

See *The Vine* No 128, September 1995.

Château Prieuré-Lichine

OWNER: Ballande Group.
COMMUNE: Cantenac.
SURFACE AREA UNDER VINE: 68 ha – 54% Cabernet Sauvignon; 40% Merlot; 5% Petit Verdot; 1% Cabernet Franc.

SECOND WINE: Le Cloître du Château de Prieuré-Lichine.
OTHER WINE: Château Brane Grand Poujeaux (Moulis).
CLASSIFICATION: Quatrième Cru (1855).

The estate we see today is the creation of the late Alexis Lichine. Prior to this it was small, and though a Fourth Growth in 1855, of no great consequence. Sequestered from its Benedictine owners during the French Revolution the property passed through a rapid succession of owners before Lichine bought it, in a very run down condition, in 1951.

Lichine increased Le Prieuré from 11 hectares to nearly 70, thereby creating a problem. *Appellation Contrôlée* Margaux is not necessarily *cru classé* land. The wine was competently made, but it rarely had the flair of the very best. It was 'good'. Was that really enough? Alexis Lichine died in 1989. Ten years later his son Sacha sould out to the present owners. The vineyard – it consists of up to 80 different parcels spread over the five villages entitled to the Margaux *appellation* – has been analysed. The *grand vin* will in future come only from the 40 hectares of 'best'. Stéphane Derenoncourt has also been asked to take charge of the winemaking. These are two very promising developments. I look forward to the wines of the new millennium, but so far have not been really impressed by the vintages of the 2000s.

See *Grands Vins*, p. 260.

Chateau Rauzan-Gassies

OWNER: Jean-Michel Quié; director: Jean-Louis Camp.
COMMUNE: Margaux.
SURFACE AREA UNDER VINE: 30 ha – 65% Cabernet Sauvignon; 25% Merlot; 8% Cabernet Franc; 2% Petit Verdot.

SECOND WINE: Chevalier de Rauzan-Gassies.
OTHER WINES: Château Bel Orme, Tronquoy de Lalande (Haut-Médoc); Château Croizet-Bages (Pauillac).
CLASSIFICATION: Deuxième Cru (1855).

This is the smaller of the two Rauzan properties, divided at the time of the French Revolution. During the nineteenth century it changed hands five times, and during the twentieth a few more before being acquired by the Quié family in 1943. Despite what has now been more than half a century of continuity, and moreover at a time when wine production has been profitable, Rauzan-Gassies has lagged behind. Occasionally, as with the 1996 and 2000, there was a hint of a change for the better when I first tasted the wine in cask. This usually turned out to be an illusion. There is no Second Growth quality here.

Château Rauzan-Ségla ★

OWNER: Chanel Inc./Wertheimer family; director: John Kolasa.
COMMUNE: Margaux.
SURFACE AREA UNDER VINE: 51 ha – 54% Cabernet Sauvignon; 41% Merlot; 4% Petit Verdot;
1% Cabernet Franc.
SECOND WINE: Ségla.
OTHER WINE: Château Canon (Saint-Émilion).
CLASSIFICATION: Deuxième Cru (1855).

Pierre de Mesures de Rauzan founded this estate in Margaux (which originally incorporated Châteaux Desmirail and Marquis de Terme, as well as both the Rauzans) in 1661. By the time of Thomas Jefferson's visit to Bordeaux in 1787 the wine had established itself at the top of the second growths. It was then owned by the formidable Madame de 'Rozan', who had two daughters. One married the Baron Pierre Louis de Ségla, the other a Seigneur de Gassies, and the domaine was split. The Ségla portion remained in this family hands until 1860, when it was sold to Eugène Durand-Dassier. From him, at the turn of the next century, it passed by marriage to the Cruse family. It was then that the château, a comfortable country house with interesting Dutch/Norman Shaw touches, was constructed.

The Cruse ownership lasted until 1956. M. Meslon held a brief tenure, during which he planted too much Merlot in a vineyard which was rather run down at the time. It then passed to John Holt and Sons of Liverpool, later part of the Lonrho group, who were also owners of the shippers Eschenhauer. There was a further interregnum at the end of the 1980s before Chanel, the luxury goods brand, bought the estate in 1994. The 1996, 2000 and 2002 can be particularly recommended.

The quality here has it seems always been better than at Rauzan-Gassies next door, but not in recent times of memorable quality until a new vinification centre and *chai* were built in time for the 1983 vintage. Today the wine is of Super-Second quality – not a blockbuster – more Palmer than Pauillac – but a wine of undoubted breed.

See *Grands Vins*, p. 226 & *The Vine* No 167, December 1997.

Château Siran

OWNER: William-Alain Miailhe de Burgh; director: Brigitte Miailhe.
COMMUNE: Labarde.
SURFACE AREA UNDER VINE: 24 ha – 43% Merlot; 38% Cabernet Sauvignon; 12% Petit Verdot;
7% Cabernet Franc.
SECOND WINE: S de Siran.
OTHER WINES: Bel Air de Siran (Haut-Médoc); Château Saint-Jacques (Bordeaux Supérieur).
CLASSIFICATION: Cru Bourgeois Exceptionnel.

The château of Siran lies next to that of Dauzac, along the road between Labarde and Macau, and shares with it and Château Giscours much of the fine plateau that lies in front of them. It has been in the same family's hands since 1848, when Léo Barbier, an ancestor of the Miailhes, acquired it from Count J B Lynch, who also owned Château Dauzac at the time. Coincidentally, come a century later, the two properties would again, if briefly, be under the same ownership.

Château Siran produced some very good wines in the 1960s, when it was a contender for *cru classé* status. Sadly, things have gone off the boil since then. It was awarded Exceptionnel status in 2003 but does not merit it in my view.

See *The Vine* No 128, September 1995.

Château Tayac

OWNER: Favin family; manager: Nadine Portet.
COMMUNE: Soussans.
SURFACE AREA UNDER VINE: 37 ha – 65% Cabernet
Sauvignon; 33% Merlot; 2% Petit Verdot.
SECOND WINE: Château du Grand Soussans.
CLASSIFICATION: Cru Bourgeois.

In 1847 the vineyard, at the extreme north-west of the Margaux *appellation*, was part of Château Desmirail. Between 1875 and 1891 'Haut-Tayac et Siamois *réuni*' was owned by a A H Holagray but the vinification of the wine undertaken in Margaux by M. Mellet, proprietor of the defunct Dubignon-Talbot, once a Third Growth. It was then divided. André Favin arrived in 1960, reunited some of the best bits, acquired others such as Château Grand Soussans, and did much to establish the present reputation of the wine.

It is a fairly sturdy wine, the fruit being picked both by machine and by hand. In recent years the new wood has been increased to one-third and the wine has become more sophisticated.

Chateau du Tertre

OWNER: Éric Albada Jelgersma; director:
  Alexander van Beek.
COMMUNE: Arsac.
SURFACE AREA UNDER VINE: 50 ha – 40% Cabernet
  Sauvignon; 35% Merlot; 25% Cabernet Franc &
Petit Verdot.
SECOND WINE: Les Hauts du Tertre.
OTHER WINES: Château Duthil (Haut-Médoc);
  Château Giscours (Margaux).
CLASSIFICATION: Cinquième Cru (1855).

'Tertre' – like 'fite' and 'mothe' – is another local word for mound, or hill. This is exactly how you could describe the vineyard of Château du Tertre, which lies inland and borders that of Angludet and Giscours at its highest point.

The land belonged to the *seigneurs* of the Château d'Arsac – one of whom was Michel de Montaigne's brother Thomas, and another the Ségur family of Château Lafite – until just before the French Revolution. There were a number of different owners in the nineteenth century. It was then left to decay in the first half of the twentieth, and was derelict when taken in hand by the Gasqueton family of Château Calon-Ségur and their Belgian partners in 1961. Philippe Gasqueton and his son-in-law Alain de Baritault did a very good job. The 1978 vintage Château du Tertre was certainly of *cru classé* level and it continued to improve thereafter. It is a full, backward, tannic wine, which needs time. Austere when young, the best vintages show no lack of richness underneath. After the death of Philippe Gasqueton in 1996 du Tertre was sold to the proprietor of Château Giscours. Quality, sadly, has since declined.

See *The Vine* No 70, November 1990.

Chateau La Tour de Mons

OWNER: SAS Château La Tour de Mons; manager: Dominique Laux.

COMMUNE: Soussans.

SURFACE AREA UNDER VINE: 43 ha – 58% Merlot; 36% Cabernet Sauvignon; 6% Petit Verdot.

SECOND WINE: Château Marquis de Mons.

OTHER WINE: Château Marsac-Séguineau (Margaux).

CLASSIFICATION: Cru Bourgeois Supérieur.

What was originally Château La Tour Marsac was once the largest *seigneurie* in the Soussans area, and a proper fortress. Though still there on the label, this château was destroyed by fire in 1895.

The de Mons family arrived from Belgium early in the seventeenth century and probably gained control of the estate by marriage. Their successors continued at La Tour de Mons, as it had become, until very recently, the property passing by marriage again into the hands of M. de Gastebois in the nineteenth century and the Dubos and Claudel families since the 1920s, at which time it was run jointly with Château Cantemerle. The present proprietors took over in May 1997.

Since then the cellars have been renovated and a major programme of installing a drainage system in the vineyard has been carried out. The wine was *cru classé*-worthy in the 1950s and 1960s, but then lost its flair. The vintages since 1998 have shown an improvement, but so far only to 'quite good' levels. However, the average age of the vines is currently still quite young.

See *The Vine* No 128, September 1995.

MOULIS & LISTRAC

SURFACE AREA (2002): MOULIS 607 ha;

 LISTRAC 664 ha.

PRODUCTION (2002): MOULIS 27,113 hl;

 LISTRAC 29,154 hl.

COLOUR: Red (the white wines are *Appellation*

 Contrôlée Bordeaux or Bordeaux Supérieur).

GRAPE VARIETIES: Cabernet Franc; Cabernet

 Sauvignon; Merlot; Petit Verdot; Malbec;

 Carmenère.

MAXIMUM YIELD: 47 hl/ha.

MINIMUM ALCOHOLIC DEGREE: 10°.

Moulis and Listrac lie inland, adjacent to one another in the Haut-Médoc between Margaux and Saint-Julien. Both produce fairly full-bodied wines, often with a somewhat hard, 'chewy', tannic structure. Sometimes these tannins can be a bit green. Often the wines are a bit too tough for their own good. The soil is varied: a clayey-siliceous mixture on a gravel base in the northern part of Listrac, clay-limestone with gravel on a base of ironstone or Saint-Estèphe limestone south of the village and in the western part of Moulis. Round the hamlet of Grand Poujeaux on the eastern side of Moulis the geology is more classic, as at Saint-Julien, with more gravel, on a sandstone-clay base. It is here that the best wines are to be found. Those properties to the west and those in Listrac tend to benefit proportionately more from a warm, dry September. Their terroirs are colder.

With Châteaux Chasse-Spleen and Poujeaux, Moulis contains two growths of *cru classé* quality, but mostly these two *appellations*, produce, at best, wines of substance rather than great finesse.

A recent development in Listrac has been the production, in small quantities, of stylish white wine. Though merely Bordeaux Blanc, they can be clean, fruity, gently oaky and not a bit without interest. Two of the best are Saransot-Dupré and Fonréaud's Le Cygne.

Moulis Leading Châteaux

Château Anthonic

OWNER: GFR Château Anthonic; director: Jean-Baptiste Cordonnier.

SURFACE AREA UNDER VINE: 28 ha – 58% Merlot; 40% Cabernet Sauvignon; 2% Petit Verdot.

SECOND WINE: Les Aigles d'Anthonic.

OTHER WINES: Château Le Malinay (Moulis); Château La Grave de Guitignon (Moulis).

CLASSIFICATION: Cru Bourgeois Supérieur.

This property went through three changes of name in 75 years, only finally emerging as Anthonic in 1922. It has been in the hands of Pierre Cordonnier since 1997 and he has done much to establish this property as one of the best of those Moulis estates whose vineyards do not lie on the Grand Poujeaux plateau. His brother, François, owns Château Dutruch Grand-Poujeaux and they share the same vineyard manager. Good sturdy wines here.

Château Bel Air Lagrave

OWNER: Jean-Paul Bacquey.

SURFACE AREA UNDER VINE: 9 ha – 60% Cabernet Sauvignon; 35% Merlot; 5% Petit Verdot.

SECOND WINE: Château Peyvigneau.

OTHER WINES: Château Haut-Franquet (Moulis); Château La Closerie du Grand-Poujeaux (Moulis).

CLASSIFICATION: Cru Bourgeois.

The vineyard, in the process of being enlarged, lies on the Grand Poujeaux plateau. The estate, which has belonged to the same family for 150 years, is run on biological lines, the wine being matured in one-third new oak. There is more character and less of a four-square tendency here than is found at many of its neighbours. A wine to watch.

Château Branas-Grand-Poujeaux

OWNER: Justin Onclin/Ballande Group.

SURFACE AREA UNDER VINE: 6 ha – 50% Cabernet Sauvignon; 45% Merlot Noir; 5% Petit Verdot.

OTHER WINES: Clos des Demoiselles (Listrac); Château Prieuré-Lichine (Margaux).

Jacques de Pourquery, who sold out to the owners of Prieuré-Lichine in 2002, bought Château Branas-Grand-Poujeaux in 1963. The fruit here is picked by hand and the wine vinified in one-third new barrels. My experience of Branas-Grand-Poujeaux is not extensive, but what I have seen I have admired: a Moulis with more flair and succulence than most.

Château Brillette

OWNER: Erwan Flageul; manager: Anne-Laurence Chauvel.

SURFACE AREA UNDER VINE: 40 ha – 48% Merlot; 40% Cabernet Sauvignon; 9% Cabernet Franc;

3% Petit Verdot.

SECOND WINE: Château Berthault-Brillette.

CLASSIFICATION: Cru Bourgeois Supérieur.

Brillette was a thriving estate in the nineteenth century but then was neglected, the area under vine declining to a mere 3 hectares in 1960. It was acquired in 1976 by supermarket millionaire Raymond Berthault. He died in 1981 following which his widow Monique took over until 1994. Château Brillette is now run by Jean-Louis Flageul, her son.

Brillette is distinct from other Moulis wines in being lighter and more supple than most: it is oaky and stylish in the best years such as 2000, but somewhat lean in the years when the sun does not shine sufficiently.

Château Chasse-Spleen ★

OWNER: SA Chateau Chasse-Spleen; director: Dominique Lafuge.

SURFACE AREA UNDER VINE: 107 ha – 65% Cabernet Sauvignon; 30% Merlot; 5% Petit Verdot.

SECOND WINE: L'Oratoire de Chasse-Spleen.

OTHER WINE: Château Gressier-Grand-Poujeaux (Moulis).

CLASSIFICATION: Cru Bourgeois Exceptionnel.

This is the super-star of the *appellation*, and has been for quite some time – long before the arrival of the Merlaut family and then later Bernadette Villars in 1976. Chasse-Spleen was one of six properties decreed a *Cru Bourgeois Supérieur Exceptionnel* in 1932.

The estate was formerly known as Château Grand-Poujeaux but divided into Château Gressier-Grand-Poujeaux and Château Chasse-Spleen in the 1860s, one Gressier daughter having married Jean-Jacques Castaing. The château, garden and outbuildings were also divided in two. Chasse-Spleen passed to the Lahary family after the First World War. Chasse-Spleen was gradually but decisively refined and improved under Bernadette Villars' inspired direction. The cellars were renovated, the vineyard drained and the selection made more severe. This was carried on after her death in November 1992 by her eldest daughter Claire. Since 1999, leaving Claire with three other properties to look after, responsibility has passed to the second daughter, Céline.

The wine today is full-bodied, firm and long-lasting, but with a richness and quality of tannins rare in a Moulis wine. There have been few, if any, disappointments in the last 25 years.

See *Grands Vins*, p. 295.

Château Duplessis (-Hauchecorne)

OWNER: Marie-Laure Lurton-Roux.

SURFACE AREA UNDER VINE: 18.5 ha – 62% Merlot; 24% Cabernet Sauvignon; 12% Cabernet Franc; 2% Petit Verdot.

SECOND WINE: Château La Licorne de Duplessis.

OTHER WINES: Château Villegeorge (Haut-Médoc); Château La Tour de Bessan (Margaux).

CLASSIFICATION: Cru Bourgeois.

Château Duplessis is named after the family of Armand du Plessis, better known as Cardinal Richelieu. In the middle of the nineteenth century it was divided between the two Fabre brothers. That which became Duplessis-Fabre is now owned by Philippe Dourthe of Château Maucaillou. This one here takes its suffix from a later owner in the nineteenth century. It was acquired by Lucien Lurton jointly with Mestrezat in 1971, Lurton taking over total control in 1983. The wine has body and is quite firm, but I find it lacks flair.

Château Dutruch Grand-Poujeaux

OWNER: François Cordonnier.

SURFACE AREA UNDER VINE: 25 ha – 50% Merlot; 45% Cabernet Sauvignon; 5% Petit Verdot.

SECOND WINE: Château La Gravière Grand Poujeaux.

CLASSIFICATION: Cru Bourgeois Supérieur.

As the name suggests, this is one of the many estates which have their base on the much divided Grand Poujeaux *croupe*. It has had but three owners in recent times: the eponymous M. Dutruch, then M. Lambert, and, since 1967, François Cordonnier, who was for some time in charge of the vineyard at the Château de Chenonceau in the Loire. The château dates from 1863 and the *chai* from 1869. There is an attractive stone vinous *bas relief* with this date on the door of the cellar. The wine is fullish-bodied, firm, ripe and spicy: a more than satisfactory bottle in the good vintages, such as 1990, 1996, 2000 and 2002.

Château Gressier-Grand-Poujeaux

OWNER: Bertrand de Marcellus.
SURFACE AREA UNDER VINE: 22 ha – 60% Cabernet

Sauvignon; 30% Merlot; 10% Cabernet Franc.
CLASSIFICATION: Cru Bourgeois Supérieur.

This is, to my knowledge, the only leading estate in Bordeaux which has remained in the same family hands since its inception. It is, though, only half the size it once was.

It is named after a M. Gressier who created the domaine in 1760. In the 1820s – though the estate was not formally split until 1860 – the property was divided between two Gressier daughters, and one half became what is now Château Chasse-Spleen. Zamé Zaire Gressier, who retained the Gressier portion, had married Alphonse de Saint-Affrique in 1850. Their descendant, Philippe de Saint-Affrique, who also owned Château Fourcas-Hosten in Listrac until 1971, was succeeded by his grandson, Bertrand de Marcellus in 1989.

Gressier has a long history of making one of the better wines of the area, with the typical Moulis power tempered by the richness and elegance coming from its location on the Grand Poujeaux plateau. It is a wine built to last.

Château Malmaison

OWNER: Baronne Nadine de Rothschild; director:
Otto Bertrand.
SURFACE AREA UNDER VINE: 24 ha – 80% Merlot;
20% Cabernet Sauvignon.

SECOND WINE: Les Granges des Domaines Edmond
de Rothschild.
OTHER WINES: Château Clarke (Listrac); Château
Peyre-Lebade (Listrac).

Edmond de Rothschild bought the almost derelict Château Malmaison when he acquired neighbouring Château Clarke in Listrac in 1973. At the time there was one productive hectare of vines. The vineyard was replanted between 1974 and 1978, and, now that the vines are reasonably mature – the first vintage was 1978 – one can perceive a round, quite civilised and gently oaky example. It comes forward in the medium term.

Château Maucaillou

OWNER: Philippe Dourthe.
SURFACE AREA UNDER VINE: 68 ha – 55% Cabernet
Sauvignon; 36% Merlot; 7% Petit Verdot;
2% Cabernet Franc.
SECOND WINE: Château Cap de Haut-Maucaillou.

OTHER WINES: Château Duplessis-Fabre (Moulis);
Château Maucaillou-Felletin (Haut-Médoc);
Domaine de Maucaillou (Listrac).
CLASSIFICATION: Cru Bourgeois Supérieur.

This is the third best wine of Moulis after Châteaux Chasse-Spleen and Poujeaux, as well as the largest estate. The huge *chais* were constructed in 1871 by M. Petit-Laroche, who was also a wine merchant. The château, a glorious hodge-podge of different styles, followed in 1875, a birthday present, it is said, for the wife of M. Petit-Laroche.

Roger and André Dourthe bought the property, which was rather run down at the time, in 1929. Philippe Dourthe, the current proprietor, and erstwhile director of *négociants* CVGB, took over after his uncle Roger's death in 1984. A number of local proprietors use Château Maucaillou's bottling facilities. Vinified at low temperatures: 22°C to start with rising to 29°C at the end, Maucaillou is a soft, oaky wine which develops earlier than most in the area, after four to five years.

Château Moulin-a-Vent

OWNER: Dominique & Marie-Hélène Hessel.

SURFACE AREA UNDER VINE: 25 ha – 60% Cabernet Sauvignon; 38% Merlot; 2% Cabernet Sauvignon.

SECOND WINE: Château Moulin de Saint-Vincent.

OTHER WINE: Château Tour Blanche (Médoc).

CLASSIFICATION: Cru Bourgeois Supérieur.

The vineyards of Moulin-à-Vent straddle the inland D1 road, the main thoroughfare between Bordeaux and Lesparre to the north. The château is by the crossroads at Bouqueyran. The Hessels took over in 1977 and have gradually restored the château, renovated the vat house and the cellars and improved the winemaking. Moulin-à-Vent is clearly the best of the inland Moulis estates, but it is overshadowed by many of those whose fruit comes from the Grand Poujeaux plateau.

Château Poujeaux ★

OWNER: Theil family.

SURFACE AREA UNDER VINE: 55 ha – 50% Cabernet Sauvignon; 40% Merlot; 5% Cabernet Franc; 5% Petit Verdot.

SECOND WINE: La Salle de Poujeaux.

OTHER WINE: Château Arnauld (Haut-Médoc).

CLASSIFICATION: Cru Bourgeois Exceptionnel.

While sixteenth-century records show Château Poujeaux as belonging to Gaston de L'Isle, proprietor also of Château Latour, documentation of winemaking on the estate dates from the mid-eighteenth century, when it formed part of the landholdings of the Marquis de Brassier, owner of Château Beychevelle. It was acquired by André Castaing on 18th July 1806. The Castaings rechristened the wine as Poujeaux and it remained in their hands until 1920, by which time the estate had been split into three. (Meanwhile a younger son, Jean-Jacques had married into what was to become Château Chasse-Spleen.) François Theil bought one-third of Château Poujeaux in 1920. His son Jean later acquired another segment, but it was not until 1957 that the last part was purchased and the domaine reunited into its pre-1880 proportions.

Poujeaux is a wine of deep colour and determined structure, fuller, more opulent than Chasse-Spleen: perhaps less classically elegant. Similarly, it has been splendidly consistent in recent years. It is always one of the best two in the *appellation*. Which you prefer depends as much as anything else on personal taste.

See *Grands Vins*, p.301.

LISTRAC LEADING CHÂTEAUX

Château Cap Léon Veyrin

OWNER: Alain Meyre.

SURFACE AREA UNDER VINE: 15 ha – 55% Merlot; 40% Cabernet Sauvignon; 5% Petit Verdot.

SECOND WINE: Château Les Hauts de Veyrin (Haut-Médoc).

CLASSIFICATION: Cru Bourgeois Supérieur.

Cap Léon Veyrin – the curious name refers to two parcels of Listrac land on which the vineyard is based – is situated in the extreme north of the commune, the château being in the hamlet of Donissan. It has been in the same family since 1810, two brothers, Antoine and Jean Meyre, having married two sisters, Zélia and Elina Curat, towards the end of the nineteenth century.

The wine is rich, meaty and robust, proportionately better, like so many *crus bourgeois*, in the warmer vintages.

Chateau Clarke

OWNER: Baron Benjamin de Rothschild; manager: Otto Bertrand.

SURFACE AREA UNDER VINE: 54 ha – 70% Merlot; 30% Cabernet Sauvignon.

SECOND WINE: Les Granges des Domaines de

Edmond de Rothschild.

OTHER WINES: Château Peyre-Lebade (Listrac); Château Malmaison (Moulis).

CLASSIFICATION: Cru Bourgeois Supérieur.

The name of this estate comes from a Toby Clarke, a ship owner, based in Nantes, but one imagines, of British origin, who acquired the property, then 230 hectares in size, in 1771. In 1820, the Saint-Guirons family of Château Grand-Puy-Lacoste became proprietors, and their successors remained here until 1955. It was then sold, but abandoned until 1973 when Edmond de Rothschild arrived on the scene.

As with the neighbouring *cru*, Malmaison, the vines are still quite young, but with up-to-date vinification methods and plenty of new oak a medium-bodied wine with no lack of refinement is produced. It matures in the medium term, after four to five years. The adjoining Rothschild estate, Château Peyre-Lebade, produces a similar wine.

Château Ducluzeau

OWNER: Mme Jean-Eugène Borie; director: Bruno-Eugène Borie.

SURFACE AREA UNDER VINE: 5 ha – 90% Merlot; 10% Cabernet Sauvignon.

OTHER WINES: Château Ducru-Beaucaillou (Saint-

Julien); Château Grand-Puy-Lacoste (Pauillac); Château Haut-Batailley (Pauillac); Château Lalande-Borie (Saint-Julien).

CLASSIFICATION: Cru Bourgeois.

Following its founding by M. Ducluzeau early in the nineteenth century this small estate has been passed on down through the female side. Mlle Hugon, daughter of the owner in 1870, married a M. Astein. They had a daughter who became the wife of André Rochette. Monique, daughter of André, married Jean-Eugène Borie of Château Ducru-Beaucaillou. The grapes were sold to the Listrac co-operative for 40 years until 1976, since when the wine has been made independently.

As you can imagine, today made by François-Xavier Borie, a man of intelligence and perfectionism, the wine is very stylish. Being 90 per cent Merlot, the fruit is to the fore; yet it keeps well. The somewhat divided vineyard lies to the south of the *appellation* near Château Fonréaud.

Château Fonréaud

OWNER: Chanfreau family; director: Jean Chanfreau.

SURFACE AREA UNDER VINE: 34 ha – 58% Cabernet Sauvignon; 38% Merlot; 4% Petit Verdot.

SECOND WINES: La Tourelle de Château Fonréaud.

OTHER WINES: Château Lestage (Listrac); Château Caroline (Moulis); Château Chemin Royal (Moulis); Le Cygne (Bordeaux Blanc).

CLASSIFICATION: Cru Bourgeois Supérieur.

Fonréaud comes from 'Font Réaux', meaning Royal Fountain. In the eleventh century a king of England is said to have stayed here and discovered a spring nearby. Be that as it may, the vineyard occupies the highest slope in the Médoc at 43 metres above sea level, surmounted by the handsome château, constructed in 1859. The property was owned by the Durantou family before the French Revolution and by *négociants* of Danish origin after it. It passed through many owners before emerging in the hands of Léo and Marcel Chanfreau, lately returned from Algeria, in 1962.

The wine is a classic, sturdy Listrac; a bit tough in its youth; a bit stringy in lesser vintages. There is also a small amount of white wine, Le Cygne, mainly from Sauvignon Blanc which has become interesting in recent years.

Château Fourcas-Dupré

OWNER: GFA du Château Fourcas-Dupré; manager: Patrice Pagès.

SURFACE AREA UNDER VINE: 46 ha – 54% Cabernet Sauvignon; 44% Merlot; 10% Cabernet Franc;

2% Petit Verdot.

SECOND WINE: Château Bellevue Laffont.

CLASSIFICATION: Cru Bourgeois Supérieur.

The word Fourcas not only comes from this *lieu-dit* north of the village of Listrac, where this and other Fourcas properties are to be found, but, it is suggested, from a hand-held plough called a *fourcat*. The property owes its suffix to Adolphe Dupré, who bought it in 1843. After passing through a number of owners and being allowed to run down it was taken in hand by Paul and Michel Delon, owners of Château Léoville-Las-Cases, in 1967. The Delons replanted the vineyard, restored the buildings – vinifying the wine in Saint-Julien – but then sold out to Guy Pagès, father of Patrice, in 1970. Pagès also has an interest in nearby Château Fourcas-Hosten.

Despite the similarities in *encépagement* I find the Merlot shows more here at Fourcas-Dupré. There is an attractive smoky, cedary, aromatic character once the tannins have rounded off.

Château Fourcas-Hosten

OWNER: SC du Château Fourcas Hosten; managers: Peter M F Sichel & Patrice Pagès.

SURFACE AREA UNDER VINE: 47 ha – 45% Cabernet Sauvignon; 45% Merlot; 10% Cabernet Franc.

SECOND WINE: Les Cèdres de Hosten.

CLASSIFICATION: Cru Bourgeois Supérieur.

The château of this Fourcas, an attractive, early nineteenth-century *chartreuse*, lies to the south of Fourcas-Dupré, in the middle of the village of Listrac. The vineyard, however, is divided. Half lies opposite that of Fourcas-Dupré, the rest west of the château. M. Hosten was the owner in the eighteenth century. The property then passed into the hands of the Saint-Affrique family, who owned it from 1810 to 1971 when it was acquired by Bernard de Rivoyre, a Bordeaux *négociant*.

Fourcas-Hosten is a firmer, more austere wine than Fourcas-Dupré. It takes longer to soften up in the best vintages (around eight years). In good years there is no lack of depth and elegance to be appreciated once this happens, placing the property among the top handful in the *appellation*.

Château Fourcas-Loubaney

OWNER: Altus Finances.

SURFACE AREA UNDER VINE: 50 ha – 60% Cabernet Sauvignon; 30% Merlot; 10% Petit Verdot.

SECOND WINES: Château La Bécade; Château Moulin de Laborde; Château La Fleur-Bécade; La Closerie de Fourcas-Loubaney.

CLASSIFICATION: Cru Bourgeois Supérieur.

Fifteen years ago Fourcas-Loubaney was a mere 4-hectare vineyard. Today there are 50 hectares. Since the arrival of first the Novalliance group in 1989, and subsequently Altus Finances, which belongs to the Crédit Lyonnais bank, a number of neighbouring Listrac estates have been absorbed, giving rise, among other things, to two grades of second wine: La Bécade and Moulin de Laborde being superior to the remaining pair. Only some 20 per cent of the production is sold as Fourcas-Loubaney.

It is a rich, concentrated wine, matured using 50 per cent new wood. It is today probably Listrac's best wine.

Château La Lauzette

OWNER: Jean-Louis Declercq.

SURFACE AREA UNDER VINE: 15 ha – 45% Cabernet Sauvignon; 45% Merlot; 8% Petit Verdot; 2% Cabernet Franc.

SECOND WINE: Les Galets de La Lauzette.

CLASSIFICATION: Cru Bourgeois.

Formerly known as Château Bellegrave, until a law suit instigated by a rival château forced a change of name from the 1993 vintage, Château La Lauzette has belonged to Jean-Louis Declercq since 1980. This change seems to have given it a new lease of life. The wine is full-bodied, but lush and oaky (40 per cent new wood each year) with good succulent fruit.

Château Lestage

OWNER: Chanfreau family.

SURFACE AREA UNDER VINE: 44 ha – 52% Merlot; 46% Cabernet Sauvignon; 2% Petit Verdot.

SECOND WINE: La Dame de Coeur du Château Lestage.

OTHER WINES: Château Fonréaud (Listrac); Château Caroline (Moulis); Château Chemin Royal (Moulis).

CLASSIFICATION: Cru Bourgeois Supérieur.

Lestage is an impressive mid-nineteenth-century pile, about a kilometre north-west of the Chanfreaus' other château, Fonréaud, and the two have been run in tandem ever since their purchase in 1962. Lestage is a fullish-bodied, robust wine. It can be pleasantly fruity but lacks real refinement.

Château Mayne-Lalande

OWNER: Bernard Lartigue.

SURFACE AREA UNDER VINE: 20 ha – 45% Cabernet Sauvignon; 45% Merlot; 5% Cabernet Franc; 5% Petit Verdot.

SECOND WINE: Château Malbec Lartigue.

OTHER WINE: Château de Mayne de L'Énclos (Moulis).

CLASSIFICATION: Cru Bourgeois Supérieur.

Bernard Lartigue managed to extract his family estate from the claws of the local co-operative. This was in the 1982 vintage, and the wine met with great acclaim. He hasn't looked back. Today there are two versions of Mayne-Lalande, as well as the second wine. The regular is matured using 30 per cent new oak. The Grande Réserve uses more new wood and is bottled later.

Château Peyredon-Lagravette

OWNER: Paul Hostein.

SURFACE AREA UNDER VINE: 7 ha – 65% Cabernet Sauvignon; 35% Merlot.

SECOND WINE: Château Cazeau-Vieil.

CLASSIFICATION: Cru Bourgeois.

This is one of the best domaines in the *appellation* and the wine has more personality than most Listracs. Paul Hostein recently celebrated his 50th vintage, having taken over at the age of 19 after his father's sudden death in 1950. The tannins are ripe and the fruit concentrated.

Château Saransot-Dupré

OWNER: Yves Raymond.

SURFACE AREA UNDER VINE: 12 ha – 62% Merlot; 28% Cabernet Sauvignon; 8% Cabernet Franc; 2% Carmenère.

SECOND WINE: Château Pérac.

OTHER WINE: Château Saransot-Dupré Blanc (Bordeaux Supérieur).

CLASSIFICATION: Cru Bourgeois Supérieur.

This is the same Adolphe Dupré who gave his name to the neighbouring Fourcas estate. The Raymond family acquired the property in 1875. A high proportion of Merlot is used because the land is clayey-limestone rather than gravel. This gives an ample wine which is less hard and austere than the majority of Listracs. The white wine, too, has become increasingly stylish in the last few years.

GRAVES & PESSAC-LÉOGNAN

The Graves region commences a few kilometres north of Bordeaux – though nowadays few vineyards here have survived the increasing sprawl of suburbs, industrial estates and shopping precincts – and continues south, round the back of the sweet wine areas of Cérons, Barsac and Sauternes, as far as the town of Langon. This is a much more interesting landscape than the Médoc, and far richer in history. There is more for the tourist to see – the ancient fortress at Roquetaillade, castles at Villandraut and Budos, the cathedral at Bazas and the early Gothic church at Uzeste, where Clément V, the Gascon Pope, lies buried. And, of course, there is the lovely moated Château de La Brède, home of the seventeenth-century French statesman and philosopher, Montesquieu, and perhaps the greatest tourist attraction in the entire Gironde.

The Graves is both hillier and more wooded than the Médoc. The countryside becomes gradually more undulating as you travel south, oak and silver birch progressively giving way to pine as you approach the forests of the Landes, whose sandy soils form a natural limit to the vineyard area. The soil within the Graves is similar to that of the Médoc. As might be expected from its name, the area is composed of ridges of gravel rippling away from the river Garonne. This is for the most part combined with and based on sand or sandstone although there is also clay. The soil to the south nearer Langon contains more limestone and is perhaps more suitable for white wines than red, though both are made in the area.

The vine shares the cleared landscape with pasture and arable land. There are fields of maize and market gardens. In the northern part of the Graves, immediately outside the motorway which encircles Bordeaux and extending down to Léognan and Cadaujac, the region is heavily populated. In the south further away from Bordeaux the atmosphere is more pastoral. This is a larger area than the Haut-Médoc – 55 kilometres from north to south and 20 kilometres at its widest east to west point. But there are fewer vines. Much of the best vineyard area close to Bordeaux has disappeared in the expansion of the city and the creation of the airport at Mérignac. At the turn of the nineteenth century there were 168 properties or individual growers recorded in the Mérignac-Pessac-Talence-Gradignan sector in what are now the suburbs of the city. Today there are only nine. Production in the Graves is less than half that of the Haut-Médoc.

The Graves is commonly thought to be a white wine region even though more red wine is actually produced. Certainly the generic wine, hugely popular a generation or two ago before the rise of Liebfraumilch and the vogue for Muscadet and Mâcon, was, and still is, a white wine – though there is nothing to stop red wines being labelled simply as Graves. Today if a white wine is labelled 'Graves', the wine will be dry, and probably in a dark green glass bottle. If labelled 'Graves Supérieures' it can only be a medium, almost medium-sweet wine and will be in a clear bottle.

Château Haut-Brion was included in the Bordeaux red wine Classification of 1855, at a time when the rest of what are now the leading estates further south, with the exception of Château Carbonnieux, had only recently been formed. After the Second World War, like those of Saint-Émilion, the Graves proprietors lobbied for a separate classification, and this was granted in 1953 and revised in 1959, adding a white wine section. There is one category only, that of *cru classé*. Sadly, unlike the classification of Saint-Émilion, no clause was included ensuring a periodic revision. This is now long overdue. There are not only one or two red wine *bourgeois* Graves estates such as Château La Louvière which deserve promotion to *cru classé* status, but, more importantly, many white wines which deserve recognition.

In 2003 the Syndicat Viticole des Graves announced plans to introduce a three tier classification, like that in Saint-Émilion: *grand cru*, *grand cru classé* and *premier grand cru classé* which would be renewable every 10 years. At the time of writing this is just a proposal. It has not yet been sanctioned by the INAO.

While a re-classification might generally be welcomed by outsiders and might focus attention onto a currently neglected part of Bordeaux, it will be bound to be viewed with suspicion by the existing Graves *crus classés*. One can argue that growths such as La Louvière, Larrivet-Haut-Brion and Les Carmes-Haut-Brion deserve promotion. But this would only serve to underline more heavily the difference between the top wines – Haut-Brion, La Mission Haut-Brion, Domaine de Chevalier – and the rest. I doubt that these rest would accept a classification into two Graves, A and B, as in Saint-Émilion, which would be a logical solution to the problem. Equally I do not see any justification in promoting the remainder of the Pessac-Léognan estates together with the top wines of the Graves du Sud into a *grand cru classé* band. Their wines are merely of *cru bourgeois* quality.

PESSAC-LÉOGNAN

RED

SURFACE AREA (2002): 1263 ha.

PRODUCTION (2002): 45,429 hl.

COLOUR: Red.

GRAPE VARIETIES: Cabernet
   Sauvignon; Cabernet-Franc; Merlot;
   Malbec; Petit Verdot.

MAXIMUM YIELD: 45 hl/ha.

MINIMUM ALCOHOLIC DEGREE: 10°

WHITE

SURFACE AREA (2002): 267 ha.

PRODUCTION (2002): 9721 hl.

COLOUR (DRY): White.

GRAPE VARIETIES: Sauvignon Blanc;
   Sauvignon Gris; Sémillon;
   Muscadelle.

MAXIMUM YIELD: 48 hl/ha.

MINIMUM ALCOHOLIC DEGREE: 10°

In 1984 the INAO issued a decree permitting the classed growths in the communes of Pessac and Léognan to add the name of their commune to that of Graves on the labels of their wines. (For some time there had been an insistence by the growers in the 'Graves du Nord' that their wine was superior to that of their neighbours to the south, and they lobbied for an official distinction between the two parts of the region similar to that between the Haut and Bas-Médoc.) Three years later this was changed again. Instead of two separate sub-*appellation*s only relative to the communes in question, there is now a single denomination, that of Pessac-Léognan. The *appellation* covers 10 communes – Pessac and Léognan, plus Talence, Gradignan, Villenave d'Ornon, Cadaujac, Martillac, Mérignac, Canéjan and Saint-Médard d'Eyrans. The Graves has been cut in two, and all the classed growths of the Graves are found in Pessac-Léognan.

While historically the northern Graves can claim to be the cradle of the Bordeaux vineyard area, apart from Château Haut-Brion and three or four estates in ecclesiastical hands prior to the French Revolution, such as La Mission Haut-Brion and Carbonnieux, the area was much later to become monocultural. For some reason the entrepreneurs looked north rather than south during the first half of the eighteenth century. This may simply have been because there was less forest to clear. The development of the Pessac-Léognan area as a vineyard not only does not appear to have started until well into the nineteenth century, but seems to have been more of a *petit bourgeois* movement. We have a few grandiose, confident châteaux, but the size of the estates are for the most part much smaller than in the Médoc.

How do the wines differ from those of the Médoc? Just as violets is the word everyone applies to the wines of Margaux, the simile for Graves is warm brick. By this I assume one means a certain earthiness, a dryness which is not astringent. Most Graves *rouges*, moreover, are only medium rather than substantial in structure. In body, therefore, a red Graves is similar to a Margaux. It should be full of fruit rather than diffuse and loose-knit, and it should have an underlying richness. Sadly in many cases red Graves fail to excite because they lack this richness as well as succulence and personality. A glance at a sample of *en primeur* lists will show that the buyers have gone to the Médoc for their *petits châteaux* and *bourgeois* Cabernet-based wines, but rarely to the Graves. At the lower price levels it seems the Graves is not providing what people want.

The white wines, similarly, paint a disappointing picture. There are even fewer really top-class white Graves than there are red. Only three, to be precise, Laville Haut-Brion, Haut-Brion and Domaine de Chevalier. These are high quality wines, built to last: the Bordelais equivalent of *grand cru* Burgundy.

In the southern Graves and across the Garonne river in the Premières Côtes and beyond into the Entre-Deux-Mers, you will find an increasing number of enterprising properties producing cask vinified, easy-to-drink dry white wines: the equivalent of Mâcon Blanc-Villages at Mâcon prices. It is therefore logical to look to the Pessac-Léognan for the equivalent of village Puligny and Meursault and to the *crus classés* for something at *premier cru* level: a wine with the depth and concentration to require three or four years' bottle age to mellow into complexity; one which could be kept a decade.

Sadly, this would be a futile search. Most Pessac-Léogan white, including most the *crus classés*, are almost as ephemeral as the better wines of the Entre-Deux-Mers. And the Entre-Deux-Mers are less expensive.

It was only 15 years ago, following, and reluctantly, one felt, what had been going on elsewhere – in Australia, in Burgundy, by flying winemakers, by foreigners on the spot – that the Pessac-Léognan châteaux began to vinify their white wines correctly. Now the techniques are there, they must begin to make more serious wine.

GRAVES & PESSAC-LÉOGNAN

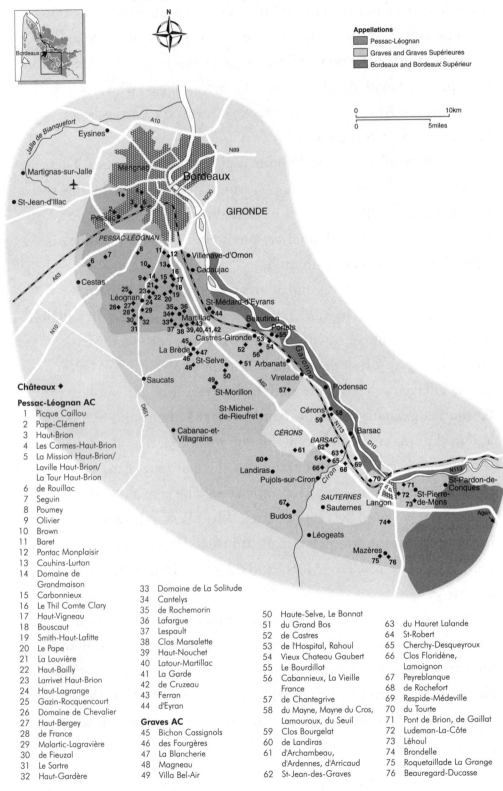

Appellations

- Pessac-Léognan
- Graves and Graves Supérieures
- Bordeaux and Bordeaux Supérieur

Châteaux ◆

Pessac-Léognan AC

1 Picque Caillou
2 Pape-Clément
3 Haut-Brion
4 Les Carmes-Haut-Brion
5 La Mission Haut-Brion/
Laville Haut-Brion/
La Tour Haut-Brion
6 de Rouillac
7 Seguin
8 Poumey
9 Olivier
10 Brown
11 Baret
12 Pontac Monplaisir
13 Couhins-Lurton
14 Domaine de
Grandmaison
15 Carbonnieux
16 Le Thil Comte Clary
17 Haut-Vigneau
18 Bouscaut
19 Smith-Haut-Lafitte
20 Le Pape
21 La Louvière
22 Haut-Bailly
23 Larrivet Haut-Brion
24 Haut-Lagrange
25 Gazin-Rocquencourt
26 Domaine de Chevalier
27 Haut-Bergey
28 de France
29 Malartic-Lagravière
30 de Fieuzal
31 Le Sartre
32 Haut-Gardère

33 Domaine de La Solitude
34 Cantelys
35 de Rochemorin
36 Lafargue
37 Lespault
38 Clos Marsalette
39 Haut-Nouchet
40 Latour-Martillac
41 La Garde
42 de Cruzeau
43 Ferran
44 d'Eyran

Graves AC
45 Bichon Cassignols
46 des Fourgères
47 La Blancherie
48 Magneau
49 Villa Bel-Air

50 Haute-Selve, Le Bonnat
51 du Grand Bos
52 de Castres
53 de l'Hospital, Rahoul
54 Vieux Chateau Gaubert
55 Le Bourdillot
56 Cabannieux, La Vieille
France
57 de Chantegrive
58 du Mayne, Mayne du Cros,
Lamouroux, du Seuil
59 Clos Bourgelat
60 de Landiras
61 d'Archambeau,
d'Ardennes, d'Arricaud
62 St-Jean-des-Graves

63 du Hauret Lalande
64 St-Robert
65 Cherchy-Desqueyroux
66 Clos Floridène,
Lamoignon
67 Peyreblanque
68 de Rochefort
69 Respide-Médeville
70 du Tourte
71 Pont de Brion, de Gaillat
72 Ludeman-La-Côte
73 Léhoul
74 Brondelle
75 Roquetaillade La Grange
76 Beauregard-Ducasse

Château Baret

OWNER: Héritiers Ballande.

COMMUNE: Villenave d'Ornon.

SURFACE AREA UNDER VINE: Red: 13 ha – 60% Cabernet Sauvignon; 35% Merlot; 5% Cabernet Franc. White: 5 ha – 60% Sauvignon; 35% Sémillon; 5% Muscadelle.

SECOND WINE: Château de Campiran.

Château Baret was the property of the Baret family for nearly two centuries before passing to a son-in-law, André Ballande. After his death in 1981 Philippe Castéja took over the management, and sales since then have been exclusive to Castéja's firm, Borie-Manoux. I find the red wine light and decent if without much personality. The white is correctly oaky and a pretty wine, but also a little slight. The attractive, eighteenth-century *chartreuse*, illustrated above, was gutted by fire in the 1930s. The central portion, reconstructed after the fire, is two storey, with a slate mansard roof: a bit of a desecration, really.

Château Bouscaut

OWNER: Louis Cogombles & Sophie Lurton-Cogombles.

COMMUNE: Cadaujac.

SURFACE AREA UNDER VINE: Red: 39 ha – 55% Merlot; 40% Cabernet Sauvignon; 5% Malbec. White: 7 ha – 50% Sémillon; 50% Sauvignon.

SECOND WINE: La Flamme de Bouscaut.

OTHER WINES: Château Lamothe-Bouscaut; Château Valoux (both Pessac-Léognan).

CLASSIFICATION: Cru Classé for both red and white (1959).

Château Bouscaut is Cadaujac's sole growth of importance and takes up most of the land under vine. It is not an isolated vineyard though. Château Carbonnieux lies nearby in one direction and Château Couhins in another. It seems to have been a M. Courtade de Moussaron who built up the estate in the early nineteenth century. From him it passed to the Chabanneau family, who enlarged it further and who sold on to Victor Place, a Belgian, and the Comte de Rivaud. Place bought out his partner soon afterwards. After a serious fire gutted the château in the early 1960s Place's son, Robert, starved of the means necessary to repair and maintain Bouscaut, put it on the market. It was sold to an American syndicate who invested heavily but failed to find the return they were looking for. In 1975 it passed to Lucien Lurton and it is now run by daughter-in-law, Sophie.

Château Bouscaut was for a long time one of the dullest of the *crus classés*: the red diffuse and lacking quality fruit, and the white dull if not coarse. A corner for the former was turned in 2000: at least quite good. The 2002 was even better: 'very good'. The white has been at least of reasonable quality since they started vinifying it in wood at the beginning of the 1990s. The 1999 and 2000 are attractive, crisp and flowery. The 2001 and 2002 are even more interesting.

See *The Vine*, No 72, January 1991.

Château Brown

OWNER: Bernard Barthe.
COMMUNE: Léognan.
SURFACE AREA UNDER VINE: Red: 23.5 ha –
49% Merlot; 48% Cabernet Sauvignon; 3% Petit

Verdot. White: 4.5 ha – 67% Sauvignon;
33% Sémillon.
SECOND WINE: Le Colombier de Château Brown.

The Brown is the same British wine-shipper John Lewis Brown who gave his name to Château Cantenac-Brown in the 1840s. The estate was enlarged in the next generation by a M. Blanc and then passed to a M. Sesboué at the turn of the century. Like many proprietors Brown's fortunes then went into decline. It was not until 1974 that it was taken in hand by Jean-Claude Bonnel. He replanted 15 hectares, built an entirely new winery and began a one-third per year rotation of new wood. The Barthe family arrived from deeper in the South-West of France in 1994 and have continued the good work.

The vineyard of Château Brown extends north and west of that of Château Olivier, a *terroir* of great potential. The red is quite oaky, with a good succulent fruity spiciness. The white is fat and exotic and also marked by new wood. The owners haven't quite realised the full possibilities of the site. But when they do Château Brown will a candidate for classed growth status.

Château Cantelys

OWNER: GTA Malice/Daniel Cathiard.
COMMUNE: Martillac.
SURFACE AREA UNDER VINE: Red: 10 ha –

50% Cabernet Sauvignon; 50% Merlot.
White: 5 ha – 50% Sauvignon; 50% Sémillon.

Daniel Cathiard of nearby Château Smith-Haut-Lafitte has leased Cantelys since 1994, and his team make the wine. The red is light and fruity but a little dull. The white has more interest, but it evolves soon. The 1998 was already showing some age in April 2000.

Château Carbonnieux

OWNER: Perrin family.
COMMUNE: Léognan.
SURFACE AREA UNDER VINE: Red: 47 ha –
60% Cabernet Sauvignon; 30% Merlot;
7% Cabernet Franc; 2% Malbec; 1% Petit
Verdot. White: 37 ha – 65% Sauvignon;

34% Sémillon; 1% Muscadelle.
SECOND WINE: Château La Tour Léognan.
OTHER WINES: Château Haut-Vigneau (Pessac-Léognan); Château Le Sartre (Pessac-Léognan).
CLASSIFICATION: Cru Classé for both red and white (1959).

Carbonnieux is the largest property in the Pessac-Léognan *appellation* and the only one making a serious amount of white wine. The vineyard straddles the boundaries between Léognan and Villenave d'Ornon, and marches with that of the commune of Cadaujac.

The property is named after a Ramon Carbonnieux, *seigneur* in 1234. It belonged to the Ferron family, local parliamentarians, between 1519 and 1740, when it was sold to the local Abbaye of Sainte-Croix. The monks were already making commercial amounts of wine at Sainte-Croix. Once they had replanted and extended the vineyard at Carbonnieux they began to do so here as well. What these two religious establishments specialised in, indeed pioneered, was high-quality dry white wine.

Carbonnieux was sequestered during the French Revolution. It was already a large estate, and was to expand further. It passed through a number of hands before being allowed to decline after the Second World War. The Perrins arrived during the terrible February 1956 frost to find a château that had not been inhabited for 50 years and a vineyard which required almost total replanting.

Vintages such as 1964 and 1970 demonstrate that Carbonnieux *rouge* can be a wine of fragrance and elegance, though rarely above medium weight. Too often in recent years, though, there has not been enough depth and concentration. The white is one of the fuller Graves, and since 1988, correctly vinified, one of the better of the *crus classés*. It can be kept for 10 years or more in the best vintages.

See *The Vine* No 72, January 1991.

Château Les Carmes-Haut-Brion

OWNER: Chantecaille/Furt families; director: Didier Furt.

COMMUNE: Pessac.

SURFACE AREA UNDER VINE: Red: 4.5 ha –

55% Merlot; 30% Cabernet Franc; 15% Cabernet Sauvignon.

SECOND WINE: Le Clos des Carmes.

Les Carmes lies immediately to the north of Château Haut-Brion itself, its vineyard hardly much larger than the park which surrounds the château. It was once part of the Haut-Brion estate, but the land was donated by one of the members of the Pontac family, lords of Haut-Brion, to the local order of the Carmelites in 1584.

It continued in Carmelite hands until 1791 when the land was confiscated and put up for sale. It then seems to have passed rapidly through a number of owners before the estate was acquired by Léon Colin in 1850. Having passed down through the female line it remains in the same family hands today.

Much has changed for the better since 1984 when Didier Furt took charge. The wine used to be somewhat rustic. There was no selection, no new oak and bottling was carried out in the merchant cellars of the Chantecailles elsewhere in Bordeaux. Furt has changed all that, modernised the *cuverie*, installed a new barrel cellar, brought in a second wine and even managed to enlarge the vineyard slightly.

We have now a wine of depth, richness and balance; one which is a little firm at the outset; but a definite contender for *cru classé* status.

See *The Vine* No 128, September 1995.

Domaine de Chevalier ★★

OWNER: Bernard family; manager: Olivier Bernard.

COMMUNE: Léognan.

SURFACE AREA UNDER VINE: Red: 33 ha – 65% Cabernet Sauvignon; 30% Merlot;

2.5% Cabernet Franc; 2.5 Petit Verdot.

White: 5 ha – 70% Sauvignon; 30% Sémillon.

SECOND WINE: L'Esprit de Chevalier.

CLASSIFICATION: Cru Classé for both red and white (1959).

Of all the top Pessac-Léognan properties Domaine de Chevalier is the most hidden away, at the western extremity where the Graves gives way to the pine forest of the coastal area. It is, however, very good '*graves*' and the wine that is made here is very fine indeed.

On the map drawn up by the geographical engineer, Pierre de Belleyme in the 1770s the area is called 'Cibaley'. But if there was a family called Cibaley their records have been lost. The map indicates that there were vines on the estate. But legend has it that they were pulled up in favour of pine trees at the beginning of the nineteenth century. It was not until 1852, after Jean Ricard had acquired what was now called Domaine de Chevalier, that a vineyard was planted anew. Ricard was also proprietor of Châteaux Haut-Bailly and Malartic-Lagravière.

While these were subsequently sold, the family continued at Chevalier, Ricard being succeeded by a son-in-law, Gabriel Beaumartin, and then by his grandson, also Jean Ricard. The reputation of the estate had now been established, only to be further enhanced by Claude, son of the second Jean, who took over in 1945. Claude was super-perfectionist, following his pickers round the vineyard, which was only a third of its present size at the time, like a bloodhound, ensuring that only the finest fruit found its way into the baskets and therefore eventually into the fermentation vat. Claude Ricard also instigated the process of picking the white grapes by *passages*, as in Sauternes, visiting each row several times to pick each bunch at its optimum.

In 1983, wary of future inheritance problems, the property, jointly owned by Claude, his three brothers and two sisters, was sold to the Bernard family. Olivier Bernard arrived to understudy Claude until he retired five years later and continuity was ensured. A brand new winery was constructed, the red wine vineyard tripled in size – it was felt that one could not enlarge the white wine production without sacrificing the perfectionistic Ricard-inspired way of running it – and more efficient frost protectors were installed. Hitherto, in a small vineyard entirely surrounded by pine trees, spring frost had been a major problem.

Today the red Chevalier (if not the white, though that is cheap by comparison with *grand cru* Burgundy) is one of Bordeaux's major bargains. Though only of medium to medium-full weight, it is a wine of finely balanced fruit, excellent grip, elegance and intensity. It can be a little tight, even austere in its youth, even a shade herbaceous in a leaner vintage. But it has indisputable class, and it lasts well, up to 20 years in the best vintages. Recent successful vintages include the 1983 (the 1982 is uneven), 1985, 1986, 1989, 1990, 1995, 1998, 1999, 2000 and 2002. The white wine, like the other two great Bordeaux whites, Laville Haut-Brion and Haut-Brion, while delicious out of cask, can go into an adolescent phase after bottling. Do not write it off if this happens. Leave it for a few years and go back to it. It won't collapse on you in a hurry.

See *Grands Vins*, p. 335 and *The Vine* No 198, July 2001.

Château Couhins-Lurton ★

OWNER: André Lurton.
COMMUNE: Villenave d'Ornon.
SURFACE AREA UNDER VINE: Red: 18 ha –
  50% Cabernet Sauvignon; 40% Merlot;
  10% Cabernet Franc; White: 5.5 ha –
  100% Sauvignon.
SECOND WINE: Château Cantebau.

OTHER WINES: Château Bonnet (Entre-Deux-
  Mers); Château de Cruzeau (Pessac-Léognan –
  see below); Château La Louvière (Pessac-
  Léognan); Château de Rochemorin (Pessac-
  Leognan).
CLASSIFICATION: Cru Classé for white (1959).

The divided Château Couhins is the only Graves property classed solely for white wine. Its early origins are obscure but by 1874 it was owned by J B Sérès and produced 25 *tonneaux* of wine. The wine was, however, red. The daughter of M. Sérès married the *négociants* Victor Hanappier and the property, enlarged in 1945, remained in the Hanappier, later Hanappier-Gasqueton, family until 1970. By this time it was a Graves *cru classé en blanc*. It is not clear when white grapes were first planted. In 1949 there were 20 hectares under vine producing 15 *tonneaux* of red wine and 40 of white, plus another 15 *tonneaux* of white, under the Cantebau label. But 30 years on all this had been reduced to a mere 5 hectares, which Mme Gasqueton was proposing to rip up.

In 1967 André Lurton had only recently bought the derelict La Louvière, and was in a poor position to make a further serious investment, but he was anxious not to let a classed growth disappear. He managed to persuade Mme Gasqueton to lease him the vineyard. Three years later, however, Mme Gasqueton sold up. The estate was acquired by the French organisation SAFER, who split up the vineyard, and sold the château off separately. Eventually the majority passed to the agricultural research establishment INRA. The wine they produce is of little consequence and not commercially available. André Lurton managed to hold on and eventually purchase his bit, and in 1992 purchased the original château. Most of the vineyard dates from 1983–1985, which was when the wine began to be vinified in wood and aged with less recourse to sulphur. The white is classy: fullish-bodied, often quite marked by the oak when young and it keeps well. At present it is clearly on a higher level than all the *crus classés* except the top three: Domaine de Chevalier, Laville Haut-Brion and Haut-Brion. The red wine is not *cru classé* and the vines are young. I have never tasted it.

See *The Vine* No 90, July 1992.

Château de Cruzeau

OWNER: André Lurton.
COMMUNE: Saint-Médard-d'Eyrans.
SURFACE AREA UNDER VINE: Red: 42 ha –
  55% Cabernet Sauvignon; 43% Merlot;
  2% Cabernet Franc. White: 18 ha –

  85% Sauvignon; 15% Sémillon.
SECOND WINE: Château de Quantin.
OTHER WINES: Château Bonnet (Entre-Deux-Mers);
  Château Couhins-Lurton (Pessac-Léognan);
  Château La Louvière (Pessac-Léognan);

Château de Cruzeau lies directly south of Château Latour-Martillac. It was already a thriving wine estate before the French Revolution. In 1873 it possessed 30 hectares of vines. Like many properties it was allowed to run down until being wholly restored after André Lurton bought it in 1973.

The vines are now of a respectable age. Though the red is of only lesser *bourgeois* interest the white – clean, crisp and gently oaky – is a very good example of second tier Graves. It is today just as good as most of the *crus classés*.

Château d'Eyran

OWNER: de Sèze family; manager: Patrick Valette.
COMMUNE: Saint-Médard-d'Eyrans.
SURFACE AREA UNDER VINE: Red: 10 ha –
50% Cabernet Sauvignon; 50% Merlot.
SECOND WINE: Château Haut L'Artigue.

The Sèze family have been here since 1796. After the phylloxera epidemic the vines were uprooted, however, and no wine was produced here until the 1950s. In 2000 the Sèze family entrusted the estate to Patrick Valette. His arrival has led to a transformation in quality. What was a rather lean, stringy wine is now balanced and stylish and not without depth. Worth watching.

Château Ferran

OWNER: Hervé Beraud-Sudreau.
COMMUNE: Martillac.
SURFACE AREA UNDER VINE: Red: 19 ha –
60% Merlot; 40% Cabernet Sauvignon.
White: 4 ha – 55% Sémillon; 45% Sauvignon.
SECOND WINE: Château de Belloc.

The property takes its name from Robert de Ferran, a seventeenth-century Bordeaux parliamentary lawyer. Together with other surrounding land such as that of Château Rochemorin it was part of the dowry which Jeanne de Lartigue brought with her when she married the philosopher Montesquieu, lord of neighbouring Château La Brède, in 1715. Subsequently, while the Montesquieus continued at Rochemorin, Lartigue and Ferran were sold off. But it was already an important vineyard at the time of the French Revolution. The current proprietor's family has been here since 1883.

The red is of medium weight, clean but without much personality. The white, too, is clean and gently oaky, but it lacks depth. Perhaps the most interesting about a visit here is an attractive pigeon tower, constructed in 1749. The château itself, a solid, five-light construction with a mansard roof, looks as if it was built a century later.

Château de Fieuzal

OWNER: SC Château de Fieuzal; directors:
  Lochlann Quinn & Jean-Luc Marchive.
COMMUNE: Léognan.
SURFACE AREA UNDER VINE: Red: 35 ha –
  63% Cabernet Sauvignon; 31% Merlot;
  5% Cabernet Franc; 1% Petit Verdot. White: 9 ha
– 50% Sauvignon; 50% Sémillon.
SECOND WINE: L'Abeille de Fieuzal.
OTHER WINES: Château Haut-Gardère
  (Pessac-Léognan); Chateau d'Hourcat (Graves).
CLASSIFICATION: Cru Classé in red (1959).

Before the French Revolution Château de Fieuzal belonged to the Rochefoucaulds. There were almost certainly some vines around, but it was by no means a serious wine estate. It emerged as a vineyard at the end of the First Empire. One can hazard that there was a M. de Fieuzal, though there are no records of him, save the sign of the bee, Napoleon's own emblem, which is still shown on the bottle capsules. Subsequently the estate passed to Albert de Griffon, who also owned Château Malartic-Lagravière, and then to Abel Ricard in 1893.

After this it was somewhat neglected. It was left to Ricard's son-in-law, the Swede Éric Bocké, to resurrect de Fieuzal after the First World War. After his wife's death in 1973 Bocké sold the estate to Georges Négrevergne who appointed his son-in-law, Gérard Gribelin to run it. The vineyard was enlarged, the *chais* entirely rebuilt and the wine improved, for the first time being sold on the open market. De Fieuzal was subsequently acquired by Fructivie, a subsidiary of the Banque Populaire in 1994. But Gribelin remained as managing director. In the spring of 2001 Château de Fieuzal changed hands again. The new owner is Lochlann Quinn, an Irish industrialist.

The Fieuzal *rouge* is a bigger, sturdier wine than most Graves. It can be a bit hard in its youth. It needs time to round off. There is usually no lack of richness. What can be missing, if you attack it early, is finesse. The non-classed white wine – they didn't make it commercially in the 1950s – is fuller and richer and oakier than most. It can be very good. And it keeps well.

See *Grands Vins*, p. 343.

Château de France

OWNER: SAS Thomassin; director: Bernard
Thomassin.
COMMUNE: Léognan.
SURFACE AREA UNDER VINE: Red: 36 ha –

60% Cabernet Sauvignon; 40% Merlot. White:
2.5 ha – 70% Sauvignon; 30% Sémillon.
SECOND WINE: Château Coquillas.

Château de France lies immediately north of Château de Fieuzal. A century ago it belonged to the Lacoste family. Henri Lacoste is the first recorded proprietor, in 1874. The wine seems to have enjoyed a high reputation. From the beginning of the twentieth century onwards the estate passed through a number of hands, the last time when it was acquired by the present proprietor in 1971.

At the time the vines were very young. Now that they have grown up a bit we can rate the red wine as usually one of the best of the non-*crus classés* (though perhaps not the 2000, which didn't sing on the only occasion, out of cask, that I have sampled it). The white wine is clean and fruity, but forward.

Château La Garde

OWNER: Vins et Vignobles Dourthe; manager:
Caroline Debelmas.
COMMUNE: Martillac.
SURFACE AREA UNDER VINE: Red: 56 ha –

60% Cabernet Sauvignon; 40% Merlot. White:
1.8 ha – 100% Sauvignon.
SECOND WINE: La Terrasse de La Garde.

Château La Garde was created as a wine estate in the middle of the nineteenth century by a family named Lacoste, who constructed what was at the time a very up-to-date winery. They sold out to the merchants Eschenauer in 1926. Since Dourthe Frères took over La Garde from Maison Eschenhauer in 1990, major investments have been made, and this is now the leading non-classified growth in this commune.

There is a red *tête de cuvée*, Réserve du Château. All the white wine, a very stylish example, is bottled as Réserve du Château. Well worth seeking out. As to the red wine, I loved the 2000 when I first saw it in cask, and was most impressed by the 1999 and 1998. I prefer the 1999 to the 1996.

Chateau Gazin-Rocquencourt

OWNER: Jean-Marie Michotte & Françoise Baillot-Michotte; manager: Jean-Michel Fernandes.
COMMUNE: Léognan.
SURFACE AREA UNDER VINE: 14 ha – 65% Cabernet Sauvignon; 35% Merlot.
SECOND WINE: Château Gazin-Michotte.
OTHER WINE: Les Granges de Gazin (Pessac-Léognan).

The Michotte-Fourès team rescued the derelict Château Gazin-Rocquencourt in the early 1970s and replanted the vineyard, which lies in one block on the eastern side of the commune, in 1973. The wine was a bit thin and ungenerous a decade ago but recent vintages have shown an improvement. Gazin-Rocquencourt can be an attractive bottle for the medium term. I liked the 1995. The 2000 is also promising.

Domaine de Grandmaison

OWNER: Jean Bouquier.
COMMUNE: Léognan.
SURFACE AREA UNDER VINE: Red: 16 ha – 50% Cabernet Sauvignon; 50% Merlot.
White: 3 ha – 80% Sauvignon; 20% Sémillon.

Grandmaison was a well established growth in the nineteenth century, when it was owned by the Moreau-Berton and then the Danguilhem families. The Bouquiers became the owners in 1939. The vineyard is on the left bank of the Eau Blanche river opposite those of Châteaux La Louvière and Carbonnieux. The red is of medium weight, but without much in the way of style or personality. The white is pretty but ephemeral.

Château Haut-Bailly ★

OWNER: Robert G Wilmers; director: Véronique Sanders.
COMMUNE: Léognan.
SURFACE AREA UNDER VINE: 32 ha – 65% Cabernet Sauvignon; 25% Merlot; 10% Cabernet Franc.
SECOND WINE: La Parde de Haut-Bailly.
CLASSIFICATION: Cru Classé in red (1959).

Château Haut-Bailly is the Graves' sole *cru classé* for red wines only, and the quality of these reds has been consistently of a very high standard for many years. The vineyard lies in one block on either side of the road immediately south of Château La Louvière, and contains some 15 per cent of 100-year-old mixed vines whose exact variety is uncertain.

The estate seems to have been founded in the 1830s by a M. Ricard, but not the same Ricard who was the owner of Domaine de Chevalier. In 1872 these Ricards sold out to Alcide Henri Bellot de Minières, a man of flamboyant energy with a scientific training. It was Bellot de Minières who put Haut-Bailly on the map, gaining Second Growth prices for the wine. One of his secrets was to disinfect the vats with several litres each of Grande Fine Champagne Cognac, which was then left there, and not drained away. He termed the wine *Premier Grand Cru Exceptionnel*.

The 1930s, followed by the Second World War, were an unhappy time for Haut-Bailly, as elsewhere, but in 1955 the estate was bought by a Belgian wine merchant called Daniel Sanders. Sanders carefully replanted those sections of the vineyard which had been abandoned, and his son Jean continued the good work after Daniel retired. In 1998 the Sanders family sold out to the American Robert J Wilmers.

Haut-Bailly is a full-bodied, rich but supple wine. Though obviously showing a tannic structure when young, it is never hard. Moreover, it has considerable depth and finesse. I regularly note it as 'fine'.

See *Grands Vins*, p. 349.

Château Haut-Bergey

OWNER: Sylviane Garcin-Cathiard.
COMMUNE: Léognan.
SURFACE AREA UNDER VINE: Red: 15.5 ha – 70%
Cabernet Sauvignon; 30% Merlot. White: 2.5 ha

– 70% Sauvignon; 30% Sémillon.
SECOND WINE: Château Ponteilh-Monplaisir.
OTHER WINES: Château Barda-Haut (Saint-
Émilion); Clos L'Église (Pomerol).

Haut-Bergey lies south-west of the village of Léognan, on the way towards Domaine de Chevalier. It belonged in the eighteenth century to Jean-François Cresse, member of the local parliament and treasurer to the Guyenne, and in the nineteenth century to the Ferrié d'Estang family. Sylviane Garcin, sister of Daniel Cathiard of Château Smith-Haut-Lafitte, acquired it from Jacques Deschamps in 1991. The wine in Deschamps' day had a good reputation. Mme Garcin has modernised the *chai* and château – a solid, late nineteenth-century pile – and planted some white grape varieties. Today the red wine is rich and oaky, one of the better of the non-classed Léognan growths. The white wine vineyard is still young but the wines are promising.

Chateau Haut-Brion ★★★

OWNER: Domaines Clarence Dillon; manager:
Jean-Philippe Delmas.
COMMUNE: Pessac.
SURFACE AREA UNDER VINE: Red: 43.2 ha –
45% Cabernet Sauvignon; 37% Merlot;
18% Cabernet Franc. White: 2.7 ha –
63% Sémillon; 37% Sauvignon.
SECOND WINE: (red) Bahans de Haut-Brion;

(white) Les Plantiers du Haut-Brion.
OTHER WINES: Château Laville Haut-Brion
(Pessac-Léognan); Château La Mission Haut-
Brion (Pessac-Léognan); Château La Tour Haut-
Brion (Pessac-Léognan).
CLASSIFICATION: Premier Cru (1855); Cru Classé
for red (1959).

The vineyard of Château Haut-Brion, which is now found in the middle of the western suburbs of Bordeaux, was the first in the whole of Bordeaux to be established as a monocultural, high quality wine enterprise, in the mid-seventeenth century. The wine is mentioned in Samuel Pepys' diary, the first such reference to a single-estate Bordeaux, in 1663. It also appears in an inventory of King Charles II's cellar in 1663.

At the time the domaine belonged to the wealthy Pontac family. Where they led, others were soon to follow, at Lafite, Latour and Margaux, later in the century, and by a host of what would later become classed growths in the first half of the eighteenth.

Château Haut-Brion passed through the female line: firstly to Thérèse, wife of the owner of Château Margaux, Jean-Denis d'Aulède; then to their daughter Catherine, who married Comte Louis de Fumel. For a time the vineyard was divided. Joseph de Fumel, son of Louis, received Thomas Jefferson on 25th May 1787.

This Fumel was guillotined in July 1794. After briefly passing through the hands of Talleyrand, Foreign Minister of France, the property was bought by a Parisian banker, Joseph-Eugène Larrieu, who subsequently succeeded in reuniting the vineyard. Haut-Brion remained in the Larrieu family until 1924. Clarence Dillon, an American financier, bought Haut-Brion in 1935. Today his granddaughter, Jean, Duchesse de Mouchy and her son Robert, Prince de Luxembourg, represent the Dillon family. The estate is run by the much respected Jean-Bernard Delmas and his son Jean-Philippe. In 1983, the Dillons acquired neighbouring Château La Mission Haut-Brion.

Haut-Brion was the first leading wine of Bordeaux, even before Château Latour, to be fermented in stainless steel, in 1961. Here the vats are quite squat, maximising the juice to *marc* ratio. This was followed by a new *cuverie* 30 years later. As Delmas had pioneered at La Mission four years earlier the fermentation vats sit on top of one another, facilitating *écoulage* when the juice is run off the *marc* after maceration.

The red wine is fullish – not as big as some of the Pauillac *premiers crus* – ripe, concentrated, balanced, elegant and intense. Quality is very high, and the wine has been remarkably consistent. I cannot recall a single disappointment. The 1989 is the wine of the vintage.

There is also a small quantity of an exquisite white wine. This proves that at best, a Sémillon-Sauvignon blend can rival what can be produced at the very top level, in Burgundy. Sadly there is little of it.

See *Grands Vins*, p. 310 and *Decanter*, April 2002.

Chateau Haut-Gardère

OWNER: SC Château de Fieuzal; directors: Lochlann Quinn & Jean-Luc Marchive.
COMMUNE: Léognan.
SURFACE AREA UNDER VINE: Red: 18.5 ha – 60% Cabernet Sauvignon; 35% Merlot; 5% Cabernet Franc. White: 5.3 ha –
50% Sauvignon; 49% Sémillon; 1% Muscadelle.
SECOND WINE: Le Reflet de Haut-Gardère.
OTHER WINES: Château Le Bonnet (Pessac-Léognan); Château de Fieuzal (Pessac-Léognan); Château d'Hourcat (Graves).

The vineyard of Haut-Gardère lies opposite that of Château de Fieuzal at the southern end of the commune of Léognan. The estate was founded by a M. Guiserix in the middle of the nineteenth century and then expanded by Comte Alfred de Griffon, the Pope's consul in Bordeaux. Griffon was also proprietor of Château de Fieuzal. In 1894, like de Fieuzal, Château Haut-Gardère passed into the hands of the Ricard family, owners also of Domaine de Chevalier and neighbouring Château Malartic-Lagravière. Marcel Ricard developed an experimental vineyard here in order to study the performance of the Bordeaux grape varieties on phylloxera-resistant rootstock. Up to 1935 the wine sold for the same price as the other Ricard châteaux. Haut-Gardère was subsequently neglected, and the vineyard replaced by conifers.

In 1979 it was resurrected by Bernadette and Jacques Lesineau. The Lesineaus sold out to Château de Fieuzal in 1995. Since then we have been able to see that Haut-Gardère's erstwhile reputation was well deserved. This is a fullish, rich, quite oaky, meaty wine, similar to Château de Fieuzal. It keeps well. The vintages since 1996 have been very good. The white wine is equally satisfactory. A contender for *cru classé* status.

Château Haut-Lagrange

OWNER: Francis Boutemy.
COMMUNE: Léognan.
SURFACE AREA UNDER VINE: Red: 18 ha –

55% Cabernet Sauvignon; 45% Merlot.
White: 3.3 ha – 50% Sauvignon; 50% Sémillon.
OTHER WINE: Clos Marsalette (Pessac-Léognan).

Though Château Haut-Lagrange appears on the famous Cassini map of 1764, there is no trace of the name in any of the wine books of the nineteenth and twentieth centuries until very recently. Francis Boutemy, who had hitherto been responsible at Château Larrivet Haut-Brion, planted the vineyard in 1989. The vineyard is well sited and Boutemy is an able winemaker. The wines already have finesse. The 2000 vintage showed richness as well. I am sure that in a decade or so, when the vines approach maturity, we will have a wine of *cru classé* quality.

Château Haut-Nouchet

OWNER: Louis Lurton.
COMMUNE: Martillac.
SURFACE AREA UNDER VINE: Red: 28 ha – 72%
  Cabernet Sauvignon; 28% Merlot. White: 8 ha –

78% Sauvignon; 22% Sémillon.
SECOND WINE: Orangerie de Haut-Nouchet.
OTHER WINE: Château Doisy-Dubroca
  (Sauternes).

The Haut-Nouchet estate spreads between that of Latour-Martillac and Château de Cruzeau at the southern end of the Pessac-Léognan *appellation*. It was created in the 1830s, owned in the 1860s by the Tandonnet family and then bought by Marcel Vayssière, Senator for the Gironde. Subsequently the vineyard was neglected, the estate was sold to a speculative builder and only a last minute reprieve prevented it being turned into a housing estate. Lucien Lurton acquired the land in 1973, replanted the vineyard and built a new *chai* and *cuverie*. His son Louis is now in charge.

The white wine is very good, and, unlike elsewhere in Pessac-Léognan, there is a reasonable amount of it; certainly it is a contender for classed growth status. The red is ample and generous, certainly well-made; but it lacks a little depth.

Château Haut-Vigneau

OWNER: Perrin family.
COMMUNE: Martillac.
SURFACE AREA UNDER VINE: Red: 12 ha –

70% Cabernet Sauvignon; 30% Merlot.
OTHER WINES: Château Carbonnieux (Pessac-
  Léognan); Château Le Sartre (Pessac-Léognan).

There was a small vineyard here in the 1860s, owned by the Bornel family, but it seems to have not survived the phylloxera epidemic. In the 1980s the land was acquired and replanted by the Perrin family of Château Carbonnieux.

Éric Perrin is in charge today. It is of course early days. But I have found nothing yet to get excited about, even in potential. The vines are still young.

Château Lafargue

OWNER: Jean-Pierre Leymarie.
COMMUNE: Martillac.
SURFACE AREA UNDER VINE: Red: 16 ha –
40% Cabernet Sauvignon; 40% Merlot;
16% Cabernet Franc; 2% Malbec; 2% Petit
Verdot. White: 4.2 ha – 70% Sauvignon;
30% Sémillon.
SECOND WINE: Château Haut-de-Domy.
OTHER WINE: Domaine de Blayés (Pessac-
Léognan).

The vineyard of Château Lafargue lies partly in Martillac, on clayey-limestone, and partly in the neighbouring commune of Saint-Médard-d'Eyrans, on deep gravel. It has been in the hands of the Leymarie family since 1927. Jean-Pierre Leymarie also produces lilies of the valley. The red wine is full bodied and oaky, quite extracted, sometimes with rather unsophisticated tannins. The white comes in a *tête de cuvée* form under the label of Cuvée Alexandre. My sole experience of this so far was the 2000. I was unimpressed.

Château Larrivet Haut-Brion

OWNER: Philippe Gervoson.
COMMUNE: Léognan.
SURFACE AREA UNDER VINE: Red: 45 ha –
50% Cabernet Sauvignon; 50% Merlot.
White: 8.5 ha – 50% Sauvignon; 48% Sémillon;
2% Muscadelle.
SECOND WINE: Domaine de Larrivet.

Château Larrivet Haut-Brion is one of Léognan's oldest and most distinguished estates, and a prime contender for *cru classé* status. Prior to the French Révolution it was known as the Château de Canolle. The Canolles, also connected with Château Belair in Saint-Émilion, were the descendants of an English family called Knollys who had remained in France after the Hundred Years War. They survived the Revolution, but then ran out of male heirs in the middle of the nineteenth century. What was in 1824 a large estate – it produced 75–100 *tonneaux* and occupied 125 hectares – was gradually dismembered. It changed its name to Haut-Brion-Larrivet, the stream La Rivette running across the vineyard and serving to drain the land, and then, following a court case in 1929 with Château Haut-Brion, to Larrivet Haut-Brion. The vineyard had dwindled to a 3-hectare rump by 1940, the date it was sold to Jacques Guillemaud. After the Second World War Guillemaud, succeeded by his grandson, Francis Boutemy, expanded the vineyard to 16 hectares. In 1987 Jacques Guillemaud's widow sold out to the firm of Andros, important jam manufacturers.

Francis Boutemy supervised the purchase and replantation of a further 26 hectares, part of which had been Larrivet's originally and part to the south-east, near Château Smith-Haut-Lafitte. He then departed to concentrate on his newly acquired Château Haut-Lagrange.

The new team, under the direction of Philippe Gervoson, son of the owner of Andros, have enlarged the *chais* to accommodate the increased production, and introduced a second wine. At first quality seemed to slip from what it had been under Boutemy in the 1980s. But the 1996 and 2000 red wines, if not the 1998, are very good. White wines need a more delicate touch, however. I don't think the new team have got this right yet.

See *Grands Vins*, p. 370.

Château Latour-Martillac

OWNER: Kressmann family.

COMMUNE: Martillac.

SURFACE AREA UNDER VINE: Red: 30 ha –
60% Cabernet Sauvignon; 35% Merlot; 5% Petit
Verdot. White: 10 ha – 55% Sémillon;
40% Sauvignon; 5% Muscadelle.

SECOND WINE: Château La Grave-Martillac.

OTHER WINES: Château Langlet (Graves); Château
Lespault (Pessac-Léognan).

CLASSIFICATION: Cru Classé in both red and white
(1959).

La Tour Martillac or Latour-Martillac – spellings vary: it is the former in the Graves classification, the latter in the latest Cocks & Féret – is the senior estate in the commune. The tower, now isolated, was originally a staircase of a small twelfth-century fort. The rest of the fort, or the remains thereof, was used to construct the present château at the end of the eighteenth century.

The domaine, like much of the surrounding area, was once part of the vast estates of the Château La Brède, which lies some four kilometres to the south. The first mention of any wine dates from the mid-nineteenth century when it was owned by a leading Bordelais jurist, a M. Charropin. The Kressmanns arrived on the scene in 1871, soon after Edouard Kressmann, of German extraction, had founded his firm in Bordeaux. At first they distributed the wine. Subsequently they farmed the estate. In 1929 they bought it. Much of their energies here for the next 40 years was in the production of their branded wine: Graves Monopole Dry.

It was not until the late 1980s, and the arrival of the brothers, Tristan and Loïc Kressmann, who appointed Denis Dubourdieu (for the white wine) and Michel Rolland (for the red) as consultant oenologists, that quality here was anything more than merely humdrum. The 1990s have seen a renaissance. In both colours Latour-Martillac is now one of the best of the *crus classés*. The white has more depth and staying power than most. The red is fullish-bodied, plump and succulent.

See *Grands Vins*, p. 365.

Château Laville Haut-Brion See Château La Mission Haut-Brion.

This is the white wine of Château La Mission Haut-Brion.

Château Lespault

OWNER: SC Bolleau-Lespault; manager:
Kressmann family.

COMMUNE: Martillac.

SURFACE AREA UNDER VINE: Red: 5 ha –
70% Merlot; 25% Cabernet Sauvignon;
5% Malbec. White: 1 ha – 100% Sauvignon.

The tiny Lespault estate, leased to the Kressmann family of Château Latour-Martillac, lies on the other side of the village of Martillac on rather higher ground. In the nineteenth century, owned by the Bentéjac family, though never very large, the vineyard enjoyed a high reputation. For a time in the 1980s, the name was used for the second wine of Latour-Martillac.

Today, independent again, the red is pleasant but light. The white is rather more interesting.

Château La Louvière

OWNER: André Lurton.

COMMUNE: Léognan.

SURFACE AREA UNDER VINE: Red: 35 ha – 64% Cabernet Sauvignon; 30% Merlot; 3% Cabernet Franc; 3% Petit Verdot. White: 13.5 ha – 85% Sauvignon; 15% Sémillon.

SECOND WINE: L de La Louvière.

OTHER WINES: Château Bonnet (Entre-Deux-Mers); Château Couhins-Lurton (Pessac-Léognan); Château de Cruzeau (Pessac-Léognan); Château de Rochemorin (Pessac-Léognan).

La Louvière occupies the land between Haut-Bailly and Carbonnieux on the same ridge of gravel. The sole reason why it is not a classed growth is that in the 1950s it was derelict, having fallen into the same hard times as so much of the Bordeaux *vignoble* in the first half of the twentieth century.

Château La Louvière has a long and well documented history, taking its name from a Guilhem de la Louvière, abbot of Sainte-Croix, owner of a white wine vineyard whose reputation was very high in pre-revolutionary times. This ecclesiastic lived around the year 1200.

After belonging to a number of members of the local gentry, La Louvière was bequeathed to the Carthusian monastery in Bordeaux in 1620. Sequestered by the state in 1791 it was auctioned off to Jean-Bernard Mareilhac, at the time mayor of Bordeaux. The elegant château, designed by François Lhote, was constructed soon afterwards. During the next century La Louvière enjoyed a good reputation, but then in the twentieth it was neglected. André Lurton bought a derelict vineyard and a shell of a château in 1965.

La Louvière is the best of the non-classed Graves in both colours, and the most consistent. Indeed, I would rate it higher in both colours than quite a few of the classed growths. It is very sad that the authorities in the 1950s were so short-sighted that they failed to put in a regular revision clause to the Graves classification. André Lurton has more cause to be aggrieved at this omission than most.

See *The Vine*, No 72, January 1991.

Château Malartic-Lagravière

OWNER: Alfred-Alexandre Bonnie.

COMMUNE: Léognan.

SURFACE AREA UNDER VINE: Red: 41 ha – 50% Merlot; 40% Cabernet Sauvignon; 10% Cabernet Franc. White: 6 ha –

80% Sauvignon; 20% Sémillon.

SECOND WINE: Le Sillage de Malartic.

CLASSIFICATION: Cru Classé in both red and white (1959).

The vineyard of Malartic-Lagravière is in one block south of the village of Léognan, with the château and the *chai* lying below the vineyard, which is on a distinct ridge. The first Malartic was Pierre, who was sold a property known as La Gravière in 1803. Some 45 years later the domaine changed hands twice, the second occupant being Mme Arnaud Ricard. The Ricards had been bar-relmakers in the area for several generations, and various members of the family crop up in the history of a number of estates, chiefly Domaine de Chevalier.

Château Malartic-Lagravière remained with the Ricards until 1908, when it passed to Lucien Ridoret, who had married Angèle Ricard in 1876. The Ridorets were master mariners, and left their wives to supervise the vineyards. Jacques Marly married André Ridoret's only daughter Simone and took over in 1947. In contrast, this marriage produced 10 children. In 1997 Malartic-Lagravière was sold to Alfred-Alexandre Bonnie, having belonged to Champagne Laurent Perrier since 1990.

It is clear that Malartic-Lagravière had suffered from a lack of investment for much of the twentieth century. The red wine was rather dense and inky, and the white, at the time make only from Sauvignon, hard and sulphury. In the 1990s a major scheme of renovation took place, including the installation of an up-to-date winery, then the introduction of a second wine and a progressive switch towards more Sémillon in the white wine plots. Under the management of Bruno Marly, youngest son of Jacques, the property is now producing wines worthy of their *cru classé* status. The 2002 was a major step forward.

See *The Vine*, No 44, September 1988.

Clos Marsalette

OWNER: Francis Boutemy, Stephan von Neipperg & J P Sarpoulet.
COMMUNE: Martillac.
SURFACE AREA UNDER VINE: Red: 6 ha – 55% Cabernet Sauvignon; 45% Merlot.

White: 0.6 ha – 50% Sauvignon; 50% Sémillon.
OTHER WINES: Château Canon-La-Gaffelière (Saint-Émilion); Château Haut-Lagrange (Pessac-Léognan); Clos de L'Oratoire (Saint-Émilion) and others.

This is a recent joint venture – it dates from 1993 – between two of Bordeaux's younger leading lights. The wines are made at François Boutemy's Château Haut-Lagrange. Like this property, the vines are still young. But the results are promising.

Château La Mission Haut-Brion ★★

Château Laville Haut-Brion ★★

Château La Tour Haut-Brion ★

OWNER: Domaines Clarence Dillon; manager: Jean-Philippe Delmas.

COMMUNE: Talence.

SURFACE AREA UNDER VINE: Red: (La Mission Haut-Brion): 21 ha – 48% Cabernet Sauvignon; 45% Merlot; 7% Cabernet Franc. White: (Laville Haut-Brion): 3.7 ha – 70% Sémillon; 27% Sauvignon; 3% Muscadelle. Red: (La Tour Haut-Brion): 4.9 ha – 42% Cabernet Sauvignon; 35% Cabernet Franc; 23% Merlot.

SECOND WINE: La Chapelle de la Mission Haut-Brion.

OTHER WINE: Château Haut-Brion (Pessac-Léognan).

CLASSIFICATION: Cru Classé in red (1959): Châteaux La Mission Haut-Brion and La Tour Haut-Brion. Cru Classé in white (1959): Château Laville Haut-Brion.

It would seem logical to assume that these three properties, contiguous with that of Haut-Brion itself – the Talence-Pessac communal boundary passes between them – were once part of Haut-Brion. There is, however, no record of any separation. What is now the combined vineyard of La Mission and Laville belonged to Dame Olive de Lestonnac, widow of Antoine de Gourges, a leading parliamentarian, in 1650. She bequeathed the land to the local church who in their turn handed it to a missionary order, the Lazarite *Précheurs de la Mission*. As at this time the Pontac family owners of Château Haut-Brion, were busy expanding their domaine, as they had been doing for a century or more, it seems unlikely that La Mission should ever have been in their hands.

The Lazarite ownership lasted until the French Revolution, when the estate was confiscated and sold as a *bien national*. There were some 15 hectares under vines, producing around 25 *tonneaux*, and the price the land fetched attests to the reputation of the wine. The new owner was Martial Victor Vallant.

After two further changes of ownership La Mission passed into the hands of the Chiapella family, progressive winemakers and managers of other grand estates which had absentee landlords. Though listed in various unofficial classifications, La Mission did not make it into the hierarchy of 1855.

Following the Chiapellas the estate again had a series of different owners until acquired by wine-merchant Henri Woltner in 1919. It was he who saw to the planting of white grape varieties in part of the vineyard. His wife inherited the adjacent, tiny La Tour Haut-Brion, and this name was used for the second wine of the combined estate for the following 60 years or more.

On the death of Henri Woltner in 1974, management passed to a son-in-law, the Belgian Francis Dewavrin. Despite stunning wines in both colours in 1975, it was a period of no investment and a decline in standards. Laville, particularly, is over-sulphured and of poor quality in the 1976–1982 period. Following family disputes among the Woltner successors the three properties were sold to the Dillons of Château Haut-Brion in the autumn of 1983.

Under the able direction of Jean-Bernard Delmas, and now his son, Jean-Philippe, the three estates are now producing excellent wine once again. La Tour Haut-Brion is now a wine in its own right (the second wine of La Mission being named La Chapelle de la Mission Haut-Brion) and a brand new winery was constructed in 1987. What is fascinating is that despite the proximity – often the vineyards dove-tail with one another – let alone the same management team, La Mission and Haut-Brion itself remain two entirely distinctive wines.

La Mission, despite its much higher proportion of Merlot, is always the more minerally, the more austere, the more apparently tannic, the more Médocian. Haut-Brion, by contrast, exhibits from the start what one might call the true Graves character: warm brick, aromatic flavours, roundness and spice. Both are very fine. Perhaps Haut-Brion is the more complex, the more profound, the more elegant. Terroir will out!

See *Grands Vins*, p. 323 & *The Vine* No 227, December 2003.

Château Olivier

OWNER: Jean-Jacques de Bethmann.

COMMUNE: Léognan.

SURFACE AREA UNDER VINE: Red: 30 ha –
50% Cabernet Sauvignon; 45% Merlot;
5% Cabernet Franc. White: 14 ha –

50% Sémillon; 50% Sauvignon.

SECOND WINE: Seigneurerie d'Olivier.

CLASSIFICATION: Cru Classé in both red and white
(1959).

Château Olivier is a proper castle. Partly a feudal bastion, partly Renaissance, encircled by a moat, it dates back to early medieval times. In the late fourteenth century the owner was a local noble named Rostang d'Olivey (sic). He played host to the Black Prince, who resided in Bordeaux between 1362 and 1375. Duguesclin was another guest, in 1374.

The Olivier estate is large, over 200 hectares, and it still derives most of its income from forestry, cereals and the rearing of cattle. At the time of the start of the Etchegoyen family ownership in 1846 the vineyard was modest. The Etchegoyens enlarged the surface area under vines, doubling the production in a couple of decades. Their successors, the Wachters, from whom the present proprietor is descended, continued the expansion.

For much of the twentieth century the vineyard of Château Olivier was leased out to the *négociants* Eschenhauer, who were chiefly concerned with producing a branded white wine from it. In 1987, Jean-Jacques de Bethmann who had bought out his siblings, was finally able to end this arrangement. The lease had ended in 1981, but Eschenhauer continued to retain the exclusivity for the wine. It is only from this date that Château Olivier has been a wine worthy of note.

Château Olivier has a very special terroir. This has now been analysed to reveal the potentiality of a major parcel at present covered in pine trees. This will be replaced with vines over the next few years. When these are mature Olivier will be able to rival any wine in the commune.

See *Grands Vins*, p. 355.

Château Le Pape

OWNER: Monjanel family.

COMMUNE: Léognan.

SURFACE AREA UNDER VINE: Red: 5 ha –

75% Merlot; 25% Cabernet Sauvignon.

SECOND WINE: L'Émule du Pape.

The vines of Château Le Pape were planted in the early 1970s, and lie on fairly high ground for the Graves just to the south of Château Carbonnieux. Anthony Perrin, owner of the latter property, was farmer here between 1983 and 1997. The château is a small, elegant, First Empire *chartreuse*. The vines are now mature and the wine today is round, soft and well-balanced. The 2000 is a most attractive example.

Château Pape-Clément ★

OWNER: Bernard Magrez; director: Éric Larramona.

COMMUNE: Pessac.

SURFACE AREA UNDER VINE: Red: 30 ha – 60% Cabernet Sauvignon; 40% Merlot. White: 2 ha – 45% Sauvignon; 45% Sémillon; 10% Muscadelle.

SECOND WINE: Le Clémentin du Château Pape-Clément.

OTHER WINES: Château Fombrauge (Saint-Émilion); Château Les Grands Chênes (Médoc); Château Poumey (Pessac-Léognan); Château La Tour Carnet (Haut-Médoc) and others.

CLASSIFICATION: Cru Classé in red (1959).

The *pape* or Pope in question is Clément V, elevated to the Papacy in 1306: fearful of the strained relations between the Vatican and the King of France, he decided to relocate from Rome to Avignon. He was born Bertrand de Goth at Villandraut, a castle south of Sauternes. When he was appointed in 1299 to the Archbishopric of Bordeaux his elder brother Béraud made over a property which was to become Château Pape-Clément. On Bertrand's elevation to the papacy seven years later he bequeathed the land back to his successors as Archbishop of the city.

The first reference to the wine, and its quality, dates from 1619, though it never seems to have been commercially traded until it passed into lay hands following the French Revolution. During the next 150 years ownership changed and fortunes rose and fell a number of times: high under Monsieur J B Clerc in the 1860s and his successor J Clinto, a stockbroker, who had the present, rather ugly château constructed; low in the slump of the 1920s and 1930s. On the verge of being wound up, and the land sold for development, Pape-Clément found a champion in Léo Montagne, who bought it in 1939. His successors progressively sold out to Bernard Magrez in the 1990s.

The red wine – the white wine production is tiny, and a relatively new introduction – was fine in the 1950s and 1960s, and then went into decline until 1984, when a new *régisseur*, Bernard Pujols, was appointed. Since then until 2000 it was consistently one of the very best in the *appellation*. The wine is firm, rich and long-lasting. If Château Haut-Bailly and Domaine de Chevalier, in their different ways, have characters which approach that of Haut-Brion, Pape-Clément is like La Mission Haut-Brion.

In 2000 Bernard Magrez took over completely. M. Magrez likes modern wines. The wines since, in my view, are over-extracted and they do not speak of their terroir. They are full-bodied and rich and very oaky. Do they taste like Graves? Will they age with dignity? They are not to my style and I fear that age will only transform them into lumpy grape-juice.

Château Picque Caillou

OWNER: Paulin & Isabelle Calvet.
COMMUNE: Mérignac.
SURFACE AREA UNDER VINE: Red: 19 ha –
  50% Merlot; 40% Cabernet Sauvignon;
  10% Cabernet Franc. White: 1 ha –

50% Sauvignon; 50% Sémillon.
SECOND WINE: La Réserve de Picque Caillou.
OTHER WINE: Château Chênevert (Pessac-
  Léognan).

Picque Caillou is the last surviving wine-producing estate in the commune of Mérignac, better known as the site of Bordeaux's airport. For three generations it belonged to the Denis family before Paulin Calvet and his wife took over in 1997. The white wine vines are still very young, being planted in 1993. Since 1997 the quality has improved. The 2000 red is most attractive, as are both the 2001 and 2002.

Château Pontac Monplaisir

OWNER: Jean & Alain Maufras.
COMMUNE: Villenave-d'Ornon.
SURFACE AREA UNDER VINE: Red: 7 ha –
  50% Cabernet Sauvignon; 50% Merlot.

White: 8 ha – 60% Sauvignon; 40% Sémillon.
SECOND WINE: Duc de la Grace d'Ornon.
OTHER WINE: Château Limbourg (Pessac-
  Léognan).

The origins of this property lie in a hunting lodge owned by Jacques de Pontac, of the family which owned Château Haut-Brion. It belonged to the Lalanne family in the nineteenth century, when part of the vineyard was planted with Pinot Noir, and another plot with Riesling.

The estate was acquired by August Maufras in 1920, allowed to run down somewhat, but then resurrected by his son Jean who took over in 1955. The château is an elegant *chartreuse*, forming, with the *chais*, three sides of a hollow square. It lies behind some rather impressive wroughtiron gates in an attractive park on the R113, the main *route nationale* going south from Bordeaux to Langon. Sadly the wines do not live up to their stylish origins. The red wine lacks flair and the white character.

Château Poumey

OWNER: Bernard Magrez; director: Éric
  Larramona.
COMMUNE: Gradignan.
SURFACE AREA UNDER VINE: 8 ha – 60% Cabernet
  Sauvignon; 40% Merlot.

OTHER WINES: Château Fombrauge (Saint-
  Émilion); Château Les Grands Chênes (Médoc);
  Château Pape-Clément (Pessac-Léognan);
  Château La Tour Carnet (Haut-Médoc) and
  others.

Twenty years ago this property, the sole surviving wine estate in Gradignan, measured 2 hectares of vineyard and belonged to the Trouvé family. In 1995 the Pape-Clément team took over. The wine is now made and reared in their cellars. I have not seen the white, but up to the 2000 vintage the red was balanced and attractive with a gentle oaky background: well worth investigating. Since then, like Pape-Clément, I find it is over-extracted.

Château de Rochemorin

OWNER: André Lurton.

COMMUNE: Martillac.

SURFACE AREA UNDER VINE: Red: 47 ha –
60% Cabernet Sauvignon; 40% Merlot.
White: 17 ha – 90% Sauvignon; 10% Sémillon.

SECOND WINE: Château Coucheroy.

OTHER WINES: Château Bonnet (Entre-Deux-
Mers); Château Couhins-Lurton (Pessac-
Léognan); Château de Cruzeau (Pessac-Léognan);
Château La Louvière (Pessac-Léognan).

Like Château de Cruzeau to the south-west on the other side of the village of Martillac, Rochemorin has a considerable history but was derelict as a vineyard when André Lurton bought it in 1973. Rochemorin was a dependency of Château La Brède. Tradition has it that the famous Montesquieu was born here, on 10th January 1716, and not at La Brède. The family owned it until 1919, when it was sold to foresters.

The red wine is now one of the most dependable of the non-classified growths, though not up to the standard of its stablemate Château La Louvière. I particularly liked the 2000. The white wine, gently oaky, clean and stylish, is even better.

Chateau de Rouillac

OWNERS: Jean-Paul & Marie-Claire Lafragette.

COMMUNE: Canéjan.

SURFACE AREA UNDER VINE: Red: 10 ha –
60% Cabernet Sauvignon; 40% Merlot.

White: 2 ha – 63% Sauvignon; 33% Sémillon.

SECOND WINE: Moulin de Rouillac.

OTHER WINE: Château de Cassiot (Pessac-
Léognan).

Château de Rouillac is one of only two properties left in Canéjan, south-west of Bordeaux beyond Gradignan. There were 20 in 1893. The great town planner Baron Georges Haussmann was given Château de Rouillac by Napoleon III in 1869. In the 1930s the vineyard was ploughed up but it was replanted in 1970 by the present owners. The château is large and impressive, the installations modern, but the wine, sadly, is not very inspiring.

Château Le Sartre

OWNER: Perrin family.

COMMUNE: Léognan.

SURFACE AREA UNDER VINE: Red: 18 ha –
65% Cabernet Sauvignon; 35% Merlot.
White: 7 ha – 65% Sauvignon; 35% Sémillon.

OTHER WINES: Château Carbonnieux (Pessac-
Léognan); Château Haut-Vigneau (Pessac-
Léognan).

Château Le Sartre lies south of Château de Fieuzal and is the last important vineyard in Léognan before vines give way to forest. It was established in the mid-nineteenth century by a M. Rouannet. Subsequently abandoned, the land – there is an attractive creeper-covered, modest château joined by outbuildings on either side – was purchased and replanted by Anthony Perrin in 1981. The first vintage was 1984. The red is pleasant but a little slight. The white is now a very stylish example of early-drinking, modern Graves.

Château Seguin

OWNER: Darriet family.

COMMUNE: Canéjan.

SURFACE AREA UNDER VINE: Red: 30 ha –

50% Cabernet Sauvignon; 50% Merlot.

SECOND WINE: L'Angelot de Seguin.

A century ago this was a thriving property. It stretched over 61 hectares at the highest point of the commune of Canéjan of which 16 were vineyard. Thirty years later production had evaporated to next to nothing. The vines were finally pulled up in 1944. In 1987 the land was taken over by the present owners and the vineyard replanted. The vines are still young, therefore, and so far I have not found anything to get excited about. The 1997 red was better than most non-classed growths though, and the 2000 is not bad. There used to be a white wine, but production has ceased.

Chateau Smith-Haut-Lafitte

OWNER: Daniel & Florence Cathiard.

COMMUNE: Martillac.

SURFACE AREA UNDER VINE: Red: 45 ha –
55% Cabernet Sauvignon; 30% Merlot;
13% Cabernet Franc; 2% Petit Verdot.

White: 11 ha – 95% Sauvignon; 5% Sémillon.

SECOND WINE: Les Hauts de Smith.

OTHER WINE: Château Cantelys (Pessac-Léognan).

CLASSIFICATION: Cru Classé in red (1959).

The vineyard of Smith-Haut-Lafitte lies at the northern end of the commune of Martillac, not far from Châteaux Carbonnieux and Bouscaut. In the Middle Ages there was a manor house on the site owned by a family called du Bosq. This lay on a gravel mound for which the local name was *la fitte*. When a Scotsman, Georges Smith bought the estate in 1720 there was already an established vineyard here.

The next important proprietor was Sadi Duffour-Dubergier in the 1850s. Duffour-Dubergier was mayor of Bordeaux and president of its chamber of commerce. He and his successors expanded the vineyard, updated the cellar and improved the reputation of the wine. Up until then, wines from Martillac were considered second-division Graves. In the latter third of the nineteenth century Smith Haut Lafitte sold for the price of a Médoc Fourth Growth.

The Duffour-Dubergier era came to an end in 1902, and the firm of Eschenhauer stepped in: firstly as distributors, from 1914 as farmers, and finally from 1958 as owners. In 1991 they sold Smith-Haut-Lafitte to Daniel and Florence Cathiard.

The Cathiards have done much to improve the quality of the wine, and they are certainly very energetic, if not relentless, in promoting it. In 1999 a new hotel-de-luxe-cum-spa, Les Sources de Caudalie, was constructed at the southern end of the vineyard.

The white Smith-Haut-Lafitte suffers, in my view, from being principally Sauvignon in origin. It is stylish and fruity, but it lacks depth and staying power. The red, too, is no more than medium-bodied. The fruit is good and the oak well integrated but it lacks a little richness, breeding and originality.

See *The Vine* No 72, January 1991.

Domaine de La Solitude

OWNERS: Communauté Religieuse de La Sainte Famille; farmed by Domaine de Chevalier.
COMMUNE: Martillac.
SURFACE AREA UNDER VINE: Red: 24 ha – 35% Merlot; 10% Cabernet Franc; 35% Cabernet Sauvignon. White: 7 ha – 60% Sauvignon; 40% Sémillon.
SECOND WINE: Prieuré La Solitude.

Tucked away in the western extremes of the commune of Martillac is a convent which seems to have escaped the Revolutionary Terror of the late eighteenth century. In the middle of the nineteenth century the religious order was named the Dames de Lorette. Since 1920 the estate has belonged to another, La Sainte Famille.

In 1993 the Soeurs asked Olivier Bernard of Domaine de Chevalier to take over responsibility for the vineyard. The cellar installations have been modernised and the wine put on the map. My experience of the wine is confined to the post-1993 era. The white has lots of depth and personality. It is more of a keeper than most Graves. The red is medium-bodied with plenty of grip, style and vigour, without being a blockbuster. Both are well worth searching for.

Château Le Thil Comte Clary

OWNERS: de Laitre family.
COMMUNE: Léognan.
SURFACE AREA UNDER VINE: Red: 14 ha – 70% Merlot; 30% Cabernet Sauvignon.
White: 3.1 ha – 50% Sauvignon; 50% Sémillon.
SECOND WINE: Reflets du Château Le Thil Comte Clary.

Château Le Thil is located in the woods between Châteaux Carbonnieux and Smith-Haut-Lafitte. It was founded by Jeanne Clary about a century ago whose ancestors had been closely associated with the first Napoleon, one of them marrying Bernadotte, one of Napoleon's marshals and created king of Sweden. The property today continues to belong to a branch of the Clary family.

I have not tasted on the spot here, merely at gatherings of the non-*cru classé* Pessac-Léognans I ask to have set up for me every April. Nor do I have much experience of the wines in bottle. What I have seen has not encouraged me to beat a path to the door.

GRAVES DU SUD

RED

SURFACE AREA (2002): 2568 ha.

PRODUCTION (2002): 12,1601 hl.

COLOUR: Red.

GRAPE VARIETIES: Cabernet
Sauvignon; Cabernet Franc;
Merlot; Malbec; Petit Verdot.

MAXIMUM YIELD: 50 hl/ha.

MINIMUM ALCOHOLIC DEGREE: 10°.

WHITE

SURFACE AREA (2002): 802 ha.

PRODUCTION (2002): 35,616 hl.

COLOUR: White, dry.

GRAPE VARIETIES: Sauvignon;
Sémillon; Muscadelle.

MAXIMUM YIELD: 50 hl/ha.

MINIMUM ALCOHOLIC DEGREE: 9.5°.

WHITE GRAVES SUPÉRIEURES

SURFACE AREA (2002): 336 ha.

PRODUCTION (2002): 11,353 hl.

COLOUR: White, semi-sweet.

GRAPE VARIETIES: Sauvignon;
Sémillon; Muscadelle.

MAXIMUM YIELD: 50 hl/ha.

MINIMUM ALCOHOLIC DEGREE: 9.5°.

Officially, the wines of Pessac-Léognan are Graves, and many of them call themselves *Grand Vin du Graves* on their labels as well as *appellation* Pessac-Léognan. Those which are merely Graves come from the southern part of the region. To avoid confusion I call them the *Graves du Sud*.

This forested area with few vines commences at the southern end of Léognan and Martillac and continues south to encircle – on all but the river Garonne side – the sweet wine districts of Cérons, Barsac and Sauternes, until it reaches Saint-Pardon de Conques beyond Langon. The area occupies approximately three times the surface of the Pessac-Léognan *appellation contrôlée*.

Most of the vineyards lie fairly close to the river, but isolated ones can be found as far inland as Cabanac, Landiras, Budos and Mazères. *Appellation* Graves can be produced in the commune of Cérons – indeed this is a very good source for dry white wine – but not in Barsac or Sauternes. Three wines are produced in the Graves du Sud: simple Graves, red or (dry) white, and the richer Graves Supérieures, which is semi-sweet.

As well as the 10 Pessac-Léognan communes, Graves and Graves Supérieures can come from the following 33 communes (roughly from north to south): Bégles, Cestas, Saint-Jean-d'Illac, Martignac, Labrède, Ayguemortes-les-Graves, Beautiran, Cabanac-et-Villagrains, Castres, Isle Saint-Georges, Saint-Morillon, Saint-Selve, Saucats, Podensac, Arbanats, Budos, Cérons, Guillos, Illats, Landiras, Portets, Pujols-sur-Ciron, Saint-Michel de Rieufret, Virelade, Eysines, Toulenne, Langon, Saint-Pierre de Mons, Roaillan, Mazères, Léogats, Saint-Pardon and Le Haillan. Cocks & Féret list no growths in Bégles, Cestas, Saint-Jean-d'Illac or Martignac, all in the suburbs of Bordeaux, while Isle Saint-Georges, which is mainly alluvial land close to the river, produces only Bordeaux and Bordeaux Supérieur.

Sadly, the Graves du Sud area tends to be prone to frost. Any vineyard inland in the middle of the pine forests, such as Château de

Landiras, needs to take steps to combat it. Absurdly the use of smoke pots has now been banned. They are said to pollute the air. In addition, all the way along the N113, the Bordeaux-Langon highway, down to and including Barsac and Preignac in Sauternes, there are vineyards regularly affected by frost.

The soil is much more varied here than in the Médoc or Pessac-Léognan. Yes, there is gravel, of course. But here it is more likely to be mixed with sand, limestone and clay. And instead of the iron-rich sandstone sub-soils of further north, subsoils range from pure sand, iron-pan (a sand aggregate), tuff and other calcareous soils to rock.

The wines vary likewise. The reds are rarely more than medium-bodied, usually for early drinking, and seldom more than decent *petits châteaux*. They are priced accordingly. Some of the more successful are the 100 per cent Merlot *primeur* examples such as are found in Langon and beyond.

The whites are not only more interesting but possess much the greater potential. There are a number of different styles. Happily it is now rare to come across the rather sulphury brews of yesteryear. In the last 15 years the growers have cleaned up their individual acts. At the base level we have *primeur* wines, gently oaky, not far different from those found in the Premières Côtes de Bordeaux across the Garonne and beyond in the Entre-Deux-Mers. Increasingly now we have more concentrated, more serious examples. These can just as easily be based on Sémillon, now more widely recognised for its possibilities as a dry white wine variety, as Sauvignon. Many are just as good as the more loose-knit, forward Pessac-Léognans, even the lesser *crus classés*. Production of white wine is declining in the Graves and there has been a tendency in the last 50 years or so to replant the best bits of what had been a white vineyard with red vines.

None of the properties in the Graves du Sud were included in the 1959 classification of the Graves.

THE GRAVES DU SUD LEADING CHÂTEAUX

Château Archambeau

OWNER: Jean-Philippe Dubourdieu.
COMMUNE: Illats.
SURFACE AREA UNDER VINE: Red: 19 ha –
  50% Merlot; 40% Cabernet Sauvignon;

10% Cabernet Franc. White: 9 ha –
50% Sauvignon; 50% Sémillon.
SECOND WINE: Château Mourlet.

These Dubourdieus are cousins of those at Château Doisy-Daëne and Clos Floridène. I find the white more interesting than the red here. It is exemplary: only lightly oaked, flowery, crisp, balanced and stylish. It is for early drinking. The 1999 was deliciously *à point* early in 2002.

Château d'Ardennes

OWNER: François Dubrey.
COMMUNE: Illats.
SURFACE AREA UNDER VINE: Red: 43.6 ha –
  $5% Merlot; 40% Cabernet Sauvignon;

10% Cabernet Franc; 5% Petit Verdot.
White: 17.8 ha – 65% Sémillon; 30% Sauvignon;
5% Muscadelle.
SECOND WINE: Château La Tuilerie.

Both colours of wine are successful here. The red wine is matured using between a quarter and a third new wood, and quite soon becomes soft and cedary. The white is quite *primeur*, with an interesting touch of the tropical as a result of the goodly proportion of Sémillon. Here the new oak is less in evidence.

Château d'Arricaud

OWNER: Bouyx family; manager: Isabelle
  Laharthe.
COMMUNE: Landiras.
SURFACE AREA UNDER VINE: Red: 14 ha –

57% Merlot; 40% Cabernet Sauvignon; 3% Petit
Verdot. White: 11 ha – 70% Sémillon;
20% Sauvignon; 10% Muscadelle.
SECOND WINE: Château du Portail.

This is a fine property, with a château dating from pre-revolutionary times, enlarged in 1825. It belonged then to the Royalist Comte Joachim de Chalup, who, though interned during the Terror, managed to escape the guillotine. Though in Landiras, d'Arricaud is a near neighbour of Châteaux Archambeau and d'Ardennes. Three wines are produced: red, dry white Graves and Graves Supérieures. The last, now increasingly rare elsewhere, is more than noteworthy. The red, the Merlot to the fore, is juicy and succulent and the dry Graves is good too.

Château Beauregard-Ducasse

OWNER: GPA de Gaillote; farmed by Jacques
  Perromat.
COMMUNE: Mazères.
SURFACE AREA UNDER VINE: Red: 30 ha –

50% Merlot; 40% Cabernet Sauvignon;
8% Cabernet Franc; 2% Petit Verdot.
White: 12 ha – 60% Sémillon; 40% Sauvignon.
SECOND WINE: Château Ducasse.

This estate is set well back from the river Garonne on the highest point of the Graves (a veritably mountainous 112 metres above sea level). Having belonged to the Jeanduduran family for several generations, it came into the hands of Jacques Perromat, the son-in-law, in 1981.

Château Beauregard-Ducasse's red wine is sub-titled Albert Duran and the white Albertine Peyri. The lesser *cuvées* are sold off under the second wine label. The top wines, neatly oaky, are balanced and stylish.

Château Bichon Cassignols

OWNER: Jean-François Lespinasse.
COMMUNE: La Brède.
SURFACE AREA UNDER VINE: Red: 7.5 ha –

58% Merlot; 42% Cabernet Sauvignon.
White: 5 ha – 74% Sémillon; 26% Sauvignon.
SECOND WINE: Le Petit Bichon.

We are almost in Pessac-Léognan here. The château lies on the northern edge of La Brède, with the vineyards stretching up towards the Martillac boundary. The vineyard was established in 1981 and it is only in recent years that it has achieved any reputation. The Lespinasses, Jean-François and Marie, are very ecologically conscious, and today make neat wines in both colours. The superior 'Grande Réserve' is normally worth the extra. I particularly liked the red 1998. The white 1999, oaky and quite exotic, was good too.

Château La Blancherie

OWNER: SCEA La Blancherie.
COMMUNE: La Brède.
SURFACE AREA UNDER VINE: Red: 11 ha –
   55% Merlot; 40% Cabernet Sauvignon;

5% Cabernet Franc. White: 10 ha –
   50% Sauvignon; 50% Sémillon.
SECOND WINE: Château La Pageante.
OTHER WINES: Chateau Lestinette (Graves).

The château is said to be haunted, the ghosts being the unquiet remains of the Labadie brothers, guillotined in 1794. The property came into the hands of the Coussié family in 1934. The white, crisp, clean, appealing and juicy, with not a vestige of oak and best drunk young, is the wine I know the best here. It is aged in stainless-steel tanks, on its lees, and is supervised by the well known *oenologue* Professor Denis Dubourdieu. The red is sold as La Blancherie-Peyret.

Château Le Bonnat

OWNER: Jean-Jacques Lesgourgues.
COMMUNE: Saint-Selve.
SURFACE AREA UNDER VINE: Red: 20 ha –
   50% Cabernet Sauvignon; 50% Merlot.

White: 6 ha – 50% Sauvignon; 50% Sémillon.
OTHER WINES: Château Cadillac (Cadillac &
   Premières Côtes de Bordeaux); Château Haute-
   Selve (Graves).

Between 1987 and 1997 Le Bonnat was farmed by the team of Château de Fieuzal in Léognan, and it was there that I first encountered it. It now belongs to Vignobles Jean-Jacques Lesgourgues, owner, *inter alia*, of the modern Château Haute-Selve, a kilometre to the north. My experience of Bonnat since this changeover is not extensive. Under the previous regime the red was full and succulent and the white juicy and aromatic, with a good base of oak.

Château Le Bourdillot

OWNER: Patrice Haverlan.
COMMUNE: Virelade.
SURFACE AREA UNDER VINE: Red: 17 ha –
   65% Cabernet Sauvignon; 35% Merlot.
   White: 5 ha – 70% Sémillon; 30% Sauvignon.

SECOND WINE: Tentation du Château Le
   Bourdillot.
OTHER WINES: Château La Gravette des Luques
   (Graves); Domaine des Luques (Graves); Château
   Monet (Sauternes).

The property was founded in 1818, the date the small but elegant *chartreuse* was constructed. It has belonged to four successive generations of Haverlans since 1906. This is an exemplary set up: up-to-date, tidy and efficient. There is 50 per cent new wood for the red wine, 30 per cent for the white. The best white is called Tentation, and is delicious. It has grip and depth. The 2000 is one of the few examples of this vintage in the Graves *appellation* which showed the potential to age in February 2002. The 1998 red 'Prestige' was also fine. I was less enamoured of the somewhat charmless 1999.

Clos Bourgelat

OWNER: Dominique Lafosse.
COMMUNE: Cérons.
SURFACE AREA UNDER VINE: Red: 6.7 ha –
  51% Merlot; 46% Cabernet Sauvignon;

3% Cabernet Franc. White: 7.6 ha –
  83% Sémillon; 15% Sauvignon; 2% Muscadelle.
SECOND WINE: Château Barthé.

Red wine is a relatively new addition to the range at this long-established property, said to be a hunting lodge of the Duc d'Épernon. The non-oaky, dry Graves is clean, fruity, light and early maturing. The Cérons can be very good.

Château Brondelle

OWNER: Jean-Noël Belloc & Philippe Rochet.
COMMUNE: Langon.
SURFACE AREA UNDER VINE: Red: 25 ha –

60% Cabernet Sauvignon; 40% Merlot.
White: 15 ha – 60% Sémillon; 35% Sauvignon;
  5% Muscadelle.

Great improvements have been evident here since the brothers-in-law, Jean-Noël Belloc and Philippe Rochet, took over in 1985, built a brand new *chai* and changed their cellarmaster in 1998. *Cuvées* Damien (red) and Arneis (white), named after Philippe Rochet's children, are special bottlings. These *cuvées* age well in bottle. One of the best addresses in the commune.

Château Cabannieux

OWNER: Régine Dudignac-Barrière.
COMMUNE: Portets.
SURFACE AREA UNDER VINE: Red: 14 ha –
  50% Merlot; 45% Cabernet Sauvignon;

5% Cabernet Franc. White: 6 ha – 80% Sémillon;
  20% Sauvignon.
SECOND WINES: Château Haut Migot; Château de
  Curcier.

Cabannieux, not to be confused, of course, with Château Carbonnieux, lies away from the main Bordeaux to Langon road on the highest ground in the commune of Portets. It appears in Cocks & Féret in 1874 and still belongs to the same family. Perhaps as a result, progress has been slower to evolve here than at other estates. The red wine is given 20 per cent new oak and is medium-bodied and fruity, but not special. Though the white wine is now matured in new oak, the sulphur levels are still somewhat excessive. The best *cuvées* are labelled 'Réserve du Château'.

Château de Castres

OWNER: José & Brigitte Rodrigues-Lalande.
COMMUNE: Castres.
SURFACE AREA UNDER VINE: Red: 16 ha –
  50% Merlot; 45% Cabernet Sauvignon;
  5% Cabernet Franc. White: 4 ha – 55% Sémillon;

40% Sauvignon; 5% Muscadelle.
SECOND WINE: Château Tour de Castres.
OTHER WINE: Château Lalande-Poitevin
  (Bordeaux Supérieur).

The Château de Castres, a well-established but somewhat neglected vineyard, set back in forest near Saint-Selve, was bought by the Rodrigues-Lalande family in 1996. José Rodrigues' father has a vineyard in Portugal. His wife's family are viticulturalists in nearby Portets.

The vineyard, which will be shortly extended to 32 hectares, has grown from 7.5 hectares, so much of it is still young. But it is treated biodynamically, the cellar is up-to-date and Rodrigues himself is clearly both able and ambitious. The 2001s confirm rising progress. Malolactic fermentation for the red wines now takes place partly in barrel and there is also now *bâtonnage*. For the time being these are wines for consumption in the medium term. Watch this space, though. I have a feeling this is going to be a yardstick address.

Château de Chantegrive

OWNERS: Henri & Françoise Lévêque.
COMMUNE: Podensac.
SURFACE AREA UNDER VINE: Red: 60 ha –
  50% Cabernet Sauvignon; 50% Merlot;
  10% Cabernet Franc. White: 40 ha –

50% Sémillon; 50% Sauvignon.
SECOND WINES: Benjamin de Chantegrive; Château
  La Rose Nouet.
OTHER WINES: Château d'Anice (Graves); Château
  Bon Dieu des Vignes (Graves).

This large and well-known property extends over the communes of Cérons, Podensac, Illats and Virelade and is the senior estate in the area. The large *chai* can hold 800 barrels at ground level and a further 240 (for the superior Cuvée Caroline Blanc), underground. I find the wines well made, but even the Cuvée Caroline is not up with the very best in this part of Bordeaux. In appropriate vintages, some Cérons is made.

Château Cherchy-Desqueyroux

OWNER: Francis Desqueyroux.
COMMUNE: Budos.

SURFACE AREA UNDER VINE: White: 5.5 ha –
  80% Sémillon; 20% Sauvignon.

This is one of the very best examples of that semi-sweet wine, Graves Supérieures. Indeed, in the best years here the sweetness can rival a lesser Sauternes; there can even be some *pourriture noble*. It is priced accordingly.

Clos Floridène

OWNER: Denis & Florence Dubourdieu.
COMMUNE: Pujols-sur-Ciron.
SURFACE AREA UNDER VINE: Red: 17 ha –
  70% Cabernet Sauvignon; 30% Merlot.

White: 13 ha – 50% Sémillon; 45% Sauvignon;
  5% Muscadelle.
SECOND WINE: Château Montalivet.

Professor Denis Dubourdieu, Bordeaux's paramount white wine guru, acquired Clos Floridène in 1982. It comprises one piece enclosed by a wall, on soil which is very similar to that in nearby Barsac. The red is good, but it is the white wine which excites me here: rich, but dry, capable of taking bottle age, and with a depth and class which prove that the Graves du Sud can produce a quality which is every bit as high as all but the very best of Pessac-Léognan.

Château des Fourgères

OWNER: Henri de Secondat, Baron de
Montesquieu; manager: Benoît Labuzan.
COMMUNE: La Brède.
SURFACE AREA UNDER VINE: Red: 4.5 ha :

80% Merlot; 20% Cabernet Sauvignon. White: 4
ha –
70% Sauvignon; 30% Sémillon.
SECOND WINE: Les Personnes de Montesquieu.

The vineyard here was replanted in the late 1980s, the first vintage being 1991. The white wine is sold under the Clos Montesquieu label. It can develop in bottle. The château itself is located near that of Château La Brède, residence of the current Baron's famous ancestors. It dates, in part, from the sixteenth century.

Château de Gaillat

OWNER: Coste family.
COMMUNE: Langon.
SURFACE AREA UNDER VINE: Red: 12.5 ha –

65% Cabernet Sauvignon; 30% Merlot;
5% Malbec.
SECOND WINE: Château de Carrelesse.

This property, once a white wine estate, was replanted with black grapes between 1968 and 1972 by the erstwhile merchant Pierre Coste, father of the current manager, his daughter Hélène. Gaillat has been in the hands of the Coste family since the 1890s. Château Gaillat is deliberately produced to be soft and juicy and agreeable when young.

Since 1996 an additional 3-hectare parcel in the neighbouring communes of Saint-Pierre du Mons and Saint-Pardon has been used. This produces, from 45-year-old vines, the rather superior Cuvée Courreges-Seguès.

Château du Grand Bos

OWNER: André Vincent.
COMMUNE: Castres.
SURFACE AREA UNDER VINE: Red: 12 ha –
47% Cabernet Sauvignon; 44% Merlot; 7% Petit
Verdot; 2% Cabernet Franc. White: 0.75 ha –

60% Sémillon; 30% Sauvignon;
10% Muscadelle.
SECOND WINE: Cadet du Grand Bos.
OTHER WINE: Château Plégat-La-Gravière
(Graves).

Deep into the woods, beyond Château de Castres, is Château du Grand Bos; as the name indicates it is entirely surrounded by trees. Having sold Saint-Estèphe's Château La Haye, André Vincent arrived here in 1989, when almost all the vineyard (but not the white wine section) was replanted. It had been allowed to go to waste following the phylloxera epidemic.

The château is modest, dating from 1771. There is a small, neat, two-storey barrel cellar on one side, the modern stainless-steel *cuvier* on the other; the whole thing making three sides of a hollow square. Red wine is the chief concern here and this is one of the best examples in the Graves du Sud. Despite the relatively young age of the vineyard, the wine has real flair.

Domaine du Hauret Lalande

OWNER: Jean-Frédéric Lalande.
COMMUNE: Barsac.
SURFACE AREA UNDER VINE: Red: 5 ha –
70% Cabernet Sauvignon; 30% Merlot.

White: 18 ha – 65% Sémillon; 30% Sauvignon;
5% Muscadelle.
OTHER WINES: Domaine du Hauret-Lalande
(Cérons); Château Piada (Sauternes – Barsac).

This is a relatively recent creation. Jean-Frédéric Lalande bought various plots in Illats in 1988, part of which he then replanted with black vines. The red wine has not come my way, but the white Graves, aged partly in tank and partly in barrel, is fullish, stylish, ample and juicy: for early drinking. The Barsac is also excellent.

Château Haute-Selve

OWNER: Jean-Jacques Lesgourgues.
COMMUNE: Saint-Selve.
SURFACE AREA UNDER VINE: Red: 35 ha –
  50% Merlot; 50% Cabernet Sauvignon.

White: 8 ha – 50% Sauvignon; 50% Sémillon.
OTHER WINES: Château Cadillac (Cadillac &
  Premières Côtes de Bordeaux); Château Le
  Bonnat (Graves).

Château Haute-Selve comes as a bit of a shock. Here in the centre of the artisanal, small family estate countryside of the Graves du Sud you suddenly come across a vast vineyard, all in one block, in the middle of which is a very large modern *chai*. This is guarded by two giant statues, Castor and Pollux. There is no château as such. The vineyard was planted in 1992. It is pre-pruned by machine. The first vintage was 1996.

The approach is undeniably commercial – the aim being to bring out the fruit rather than making very weighty wines. But the quality is good and the wines continue to improve.

Château de L'Hospital

OWNER: Lafragette family.
COMMUNE: Portets.
SURFACE AREA UNDER VINE: Red: 11 ha –
  78% Merlot; 12% Cabernet Sauvignon and
  10% Cabernet Franc. White: 4 ha –

65% Sémillon; 30% Sauvignon; 5% Muscadelle.
SECOND WINE: Château Thibault-Ducasse.
OTHER WINE: Château de Rouillac (Pessac-
  Léognan).

This property takes its name from Jacques de L'Hospital, one of Louis XIV's councillors, though the château dates from 1787, the last days of the Ancien Régime. In 1989 it was acquired by the Swiss Marcel Disch, who sold to the Lafragette family in 1998.

The reds and whites of this and the following year are good, if for early drinking. I have not tasted any subsequent vintages.

Château Lamoignon

OWNER: Michel Pascaud.
COMMUNE: Pujols-sur-Ciron.
SURFACE AREA UNDER VINE: Red: 12 ha –
  60% Merlot; 30% Cabernet Sauvignon;

10% Cabernet Franc. White: 5 ha –
70% Sémillon; 30% Sauvignon.
OTHER WINES: Château de Carles (Sauternes –
  Barsac); Château Hounade (Graves).

The original Lamoignon was a companion of musketeer d'Artagnan. This vineyard, owned for 250 years by the Guiasse family, has been a subsidiary of the Château de Carles since the end of the nineteenth century. It makes a delicious modern-style, gently oaky white wine, best drunk quite soon after bottling. The red wine, sold as Château Hounade, has not come my way.

Château Lamouroux

OWNER: Olivier Lataste.

COMMUNE: Cérons.

SURFACE AREA UNDER VINE: Red: 4.5 ha –
70% Cabernet Sauvignon; 30% Merlot.

White: 5.5 ha – 70% Sémillon; 20% Sauvignon;
10% Muscadelle.

OTHER WINE: Grand Enclos du Château de Cérons
(Cérons).

Château Lamouroux is the name for the red and dry white Graves produced in this Cérons estate. The best of these is the superior *cuvées* of the white wine, sold as Cuvée de L'Enclos. This is well worth looking out for. It improves in bottle.

Château de Landiras

OWNER: SCA Domaines La Grave; manager:
Marie-Hélène Levêque.

COMMUNE: Landiras.

SURFACE AREA UNDER VINE: Red: 15.5 ha –

75% Merlot; 25% Cabernet Sauvignon.

White: 4 ha – 50% Sémillon; 50% Sauvignon.

SECOND WINES: Domaine La Grave; Notre Dame
de Landiras.

Isolated in the forest, hard by the ruins of an early fourteenth-century fortress, once the home of Jeanne de Lestonnac, founder of the order of Notre Dame, and later of the Montferrand family, lies the château de Landiras. Partly destroyed by the frosts of 1956, the vineyard was carefully reconstituted in the late 1980s and early 1990s by Peter Vinding-Diers. Peter made wonderful wines, but the vineyard was hail-prone, and it proved impossible to make the efforts financially viable. The red is decent. It was the white wine, made with Vinding-Diers' own selected yeast R2, which put Landiras on the map. It has since changed ownership twice.

Château Léhoul

OWNER: Serge Fonta.

COMMUNE: Langon.

SURFACE AREA UNDER VINE: Red: 7 ha –

50% Cabernet Sauvignon; 45% Merlot;
5% Cabernet Franc. White: 2.5 ha –
50% Sauvignon; 50% Sémillon.

The best white wine here comes under the label 'Plénitude' and is medium to medium–full-bodied, rich and concentrated, with an individual spiciness. A good Graves Supérieures is also produced. I have little experience of the red wine.

Château Ludeman-La-Côte

OWNER: SCEA Chaloupin-Lambrot; manager:
Murielle Belloc-Lambrot.

COMMUNE: Langon.

SURFACE AREA UNDER VINE: Red: 9 ha –

60% Cabernet Sauvignon; 35% Merlot;
5% Malbec. White: 6 ha – 80% Sémillon;
20% Sauvignon.

SECOND WINE: Clos Les Majureaux.

Since the arrival of Murielle Belloc-Lambrot, the third lady in succession to be responsible here, in 1990, the area under vine has been doubled, new oak has been used in the maturation and quality has improved. I have not had much experience of the white wine, which is fresh and fruity, reared in tank, but the red, if a little over-oaky sometimes, has depth and personality. Both the 1998 and 1999 can be recommended.

Château Magneau

OWNER: Henri Ardurats & Fils.
COMMUNE: La Brède.
SURFACE AREA UNDER VINE: Red: 14 ha –
  50% Merlot; 45% Cabernet Sauvignon;
  5% Cabernet Franc. White: 26 ha –
50% Sauvignon; 40% Sémillon;
20% Muscadelle.
OTHER WINES: Château Coustaut (Graves);
  Château Guirauton (Graves).

This is the senior estate in the commune, as well as the largest. Its vineyard overlaps into Saint-Morillon to the south-west. It has been in the hand of the Ardurats family and their ancestors since the time of Henri IV, at the beginning of the seventeenth century. Today it is run by the brothers Bruno and Jean-Louis.

The red wine is balanced and stylish, medium-bodied and early maturing. The basic white is good. The Cuvée Julien, introduced in 1985, is made from 60 per cent Sémillon and 40 per cent Sauvignon and vinified and matured in barrel, one-third of which is new. This is one of the best examples in the region.

Château du Mayne

OWNER: Jean Perromat.
COMMUNE: Cérons.
SURFACE AREA UNDER VINE: Red: 9 ha –
  70% Cabernet Sauvignon; 25% Merlot;
  5% Cabernet Franc. White: 4 ha –
  60% Sémillon; 30% Sauvignon;
10% Muscadelle.
SECOND WINE: Château de Bessanes.
OTHER WINES: Château de Cérons (Cérons);
  Château Prost (Sauternes); Domaine de Terrefort
  (Bordeaux Supérieur); Château du Vieux Moulin
  (Loupiac).

Progress is being made here, as more and more of the wine is oak aged. The red, strongly Cabernet, is matured for three years before bottling; the white for 24 months in a mixture of barrel and *cuve*. This may sound a bit bizarre today – most white Graves are bottled after six to nine months, and the reds after 12–18 months – but the results are very satisfying. The 1998 white, with little if any evidence of new oak, was splendidly profound, concentrated and vigorous when I tasted it in February 2002.

Château Mayne du Cros

OWNER: Michel Boyer.
COMMUNE: Cérons.
SURFACE AREA UNDER VINE: Red: 5 ha –
50% Cabernet Franc; 40% Cabernet Sauvignon;
10% Merlot. White: 4 ha – 50% Sémillon;
40% Sauvignon; 10% Muscadelle.

Very good wines, both red and white, are made here and they are matured using new oak. They are rich, ripe, intense and succulent. The lesser wines are sold as Château Haut-Mayne, which is rather confusing, as there is another Château Haut-Mayne close by.

Château Peyreblanque

OWNER: Médeville family.
COMMUNE: Budos.
SURFACE AREA UNDER VINE: Red: 7 ha –
90% Cabernet Sauvignon; 10% Merlot.
White: 1 ha – 80% Sémillon; 20% Sauvignon.
OTHER WINE: Château Fayau (Cadillac).

The Médeville family, merchants as well as vineyard proprietors, acquired Château Peyreblanque in 1900. The wine is made and matured at Château Fayau in Cadillac. The white wine here (I have not come across the red) is vinified and matured in wood, of which one-third is new. It is rich and fat and has good grip and energy: individual and exotic; very good.

Château Pont de Brion

OWNER: Molinari & Fils.
COMMUNE: Langon.
SURFACE AREA UNDER VINE: Red: 14 ha –
  60% Cabernet Sauvignon; 35% Merlot; 5% Petit

Verdot. White: 6 ha – 66% Sémillon; 34%
Sauvignon.
SECOND WINE: Château Ludeman Les Cèdres.

The concept of first and second wine is taken seriously here: fully 50 per cent of the production is sold as Château Ludeman Les Cèdres. One-third new oak is used for the Pont de Brion *rouge* which is a decidedly stylish, medium- to full-bodied example. I have less experience of the white wine.

Château Rahoul

OWNER: Alain Thiénot.
COMMUNE: Portets.
SURFACE AREA UNDER VINE: Red: 22 ha –

70% Cabernet Sauvignon; 30% Merlot.
White: 5 ha – 80% Sémillon; 20% Sauvignon.

The property is named after Guillaume de Rahoul, under whose ownership the château, an elegant *chartreuse*, was constructed in 1646. The white wine was put on the map by Peter Vinding-Diers who managed the estate on behalf of absentee landlords in the 1980s. This is one of the best examples in the region. More recently, the red has become more serious. I liked the 2000.

Château Respide-Médeville

OWNER: Christian & Andrée Médeville.
COMMUNE: Toulenne.
SURFACE AREA UNDER VINE: Red: 7.7 ha –
  60% Cabernet Sauvignon; 40% Merlot.
  White: 5.4 ha – 50% Sauvignon; 38% Sémillon;

12% Muscadelle.
SECOND WINE: Dame de Respide.
OTHER WINES: Château Gilette (Sauternes);
  Château Les Justices (Sauternes).

There are good red and white wines here. The white is gently oaky, and is ready quite early. The red is medium-bodied, fresh and succulent: again for the medium term.

Château de Rochefort

OWNER: Jean-Christophe Barbe.
COMMUNE: Preignac.
SURFACE AREA UNDER VINE: White: 2 ha –

80% Sémillon; 15% Sauvignon; 5% Muscadelle.
OTHER WINE: Château Laville (Sauternes).

From a small vineyard lying outside the Sauternes boundaries, the Barbe family produce a stylish, clean and juicy Graves Supérieures: one of the very best examples of the *appellation*.

Château Roquetaillade La Grange

OWNER: Bruno, Dominique & Pascal Guignard.

COMMUNE: Mazères.

SURFACE AREA UNDER VINE: Red: 30 ha –
60% Cabernet Sauvignon; 30% Merlot;
8% Cabernet Franc; 2% Malbec. White: 15 ha –

50% Sémillon; 25% Sauvignon; 25% Muscadelle.

SECOND WINE: Château de Carolle.

OTHER WINES: Château Rolland (Sauternes –
Barsac); Château Lamothe-Guignard
(Sauternes).

The land here was once part of the Roquetaillade estate, being separated from it in 1962. The impressive *donjon*, dating from 1306 and built by Gaillard de la Motte, is close by. I have admired the white wine in the past. It was never very serious, but it was an agreeably clean, fresh, gently oaky example at a time when most of its peers were more rustic. Sadly it is still no better than that. It has not moved with the times. The red, too, is decent at best.

Château Saint-Jean-des-Graves

OWNER: Jean-Gérard David.

COMMUNE: Pujols-sur-Ciron.

SURFACE AREA UNDER VINE: Red: 11 ha –

70% Merlot; 30% Cabernet Franc. White: 9 ha –
50% Sémillon; 50% Sauvignon.

OTHER WINE: Château Liot (Sauternes).

While the red is juicy, pleasant and for early drinking, it is the white wine which is the star here. This is quite delicious, with an harmony and a depth of interest which is rare in the region. It is one of the few which can age gracefully.

Château Saint-Robert

OWNER: Foncier Vignobles; director: Michel
Garat.

COMMUNE: Pujols-sur-Ciron.

SURFACE AREA UNDER VINE: Red: 29 ha –
55% Merlot; 25% Cabernet Sauvignon;
20% Cabernet Franc. White: 5 ha –

80% Sauvignon; 20% Sémillon.

SECOND WINE: Les Baillots de Saint-Robert.

OTHER WINES: Château Bastor-Lamontagne
(Sauternes); Château Beauregard (Pomerol);
Château du Haut-Pick (Sauternes).

Records here date back to 1686 and the Duroy family, parliamentarians in Bordeaux. Following the Revolution it was acquired by M. Poncet-Deville who did much to establish the reputation of the wines. It has belonged to the Crédit Foncier de France bank since 1879. The basic wines, both red and white, are good here, but what is especially of note is the Cuvée Poncet-Deville. Here old vines and new oak come into play. The wines are ripe, balanced, profound and stylish.

Château du Seuil

OWNER: Robert Watts.

COMMUNE: Cérons.

SURFACE AREA UNDER VINE: Red: 8 ha –
50% Cabernet Sauvignon; 40% Merlot;

5% Cabernet Franc; 5% Malbec. White: 4.6 ha –
80% Sémillon; 20% Sauvignon.

SECOND WINE: Domaine du Seuil.

This elegant eighteenth-century château, acquired by the Welshman Robert Watts in 1988, lies between the main road and the river Garonne, set in a little park. The vines are to the north. Both colours are of note, but it is the white, matured in new oak and bottled after six months, which I think they get absolutely right. It is intense and fruity and is ready for drinking quite early.

Château du Tourte

OWNER: Hubert Arnaud.
COMMUNE: Toulenne.
SURFACE AREA UNDER VINE: Red: 6 ha –

65% Merlot; 35% Cabernet Sauvignon.
White: 4 ha – 85% Sémillon; 15% Sauvignon.
OTHER WINE: Tourte des Graves.

Hubert Arnaud has been in charge here since 1994, since when, supervised by Professor Denis Dubourdieu and his team, the white wine has been fermented and aged on its lees in wood, a goodly proportion of which is new, with regular *bâtonnage*. This is good. The red is less exciting.

Château La Vieille France

OWNER: Michel Dugoua & Fils.
COMMUNE: Portets.
SURFACE AREA UNDER VINE: Red: 19.1 ha –
  75% Merlot; 20% Cabernet Sauvignon;

5% Petit Verdot. White: 4.4 ha – 70% Sémillon;
25% Sauvignon; 5% Muscadelle.
SECOND WINE: Château Cadet de la Vieille France.

Château La Vieille France has belonged to the Dugoua family since 1610. It is run today by the brothers Bertrand and François, sons of Michel, the eleventh generation to be in charge. The reds are good, marked with the Merlot. The white (called Cuvée Marie – there is no basic *cuvée*) is gently oaky, ripe and stylish.

Vieux Château Gaubert

OWNER: Dominique Haverlan.
COMMUNE: Portets.
SURFACE AREA UNDER VINE: Red: 20 ha –
  50% Cabernet Sauvignon; 45% Merlot;
  5% Cabernet Franc. White: 4 ha – 50% Sémillon;

45% Sauvignon; 5% Muscadelle.
SECOND WINE: Benjamin de Vieux Château
  Gaubert.
OTHER WINE: Château Grand Bourdieu (Graves).

There were vines here before the French Revolution but it was the Gaubert family, who had made their fortune in the weapons industry, who enlarged the vineyard and had the château constructed from 1796 onwards. Dominique Haverlan acquired the estate, then somewhat run down, in 1988. It is now one of the major properties in the area. The white wine is clean and for early drinking; the red a little more serious.

Villa Bel-Air

OWNER: Jean-Michel Cazes.
COMMUNE: Saint-Morillon.
SURFACE AREA UNDER VINE: Red: 24 ha –
  50% Cabernet Sauvignon; 40% Merlot;
  10% Cabernet Franc. White: 22 ha –

45% Sémillon; 40% Sauvignon;
15% Muscadelle.
OTHER WINES: Château Lynch-Bages (Pauillac);
  Château Les Ormes de Pez (Saint-Estèphe).

This is the main estate in Saint-Morillon, though of recent origin, having been pieced together by Jean-Michel Cazes in the 1980s. The red wine has good depth, and is rich in the more successful vintages. The white wine, vinified and aged using a high proportion of new wood, can be too oaky for my taste, but there is good ripe fruit underneath.

SAUTERNES

SURFACE AREA (2002): 1669 ha (SAUTERNES) plus

594 ha (BARSAC): 2263 ha in total.

PRODUCTION (2002): 37,375 hl.

COLOUR & STYLE: Sweet white.

GRAPE VARIETIES: Sémillon; Sauvignon;

Muscadelle.

MAXIMUM YIELD: 25 HL/HA.

MINIMUM ALCOHOLIC DEGREE: 12.5°.

In the south of the Graves, on the left bank of the river Garonne just above the town of Langon, lies the Sauternes district, home of the greatest, richest and most luscious sweet wines of the world. Surrounding Sauternes on either side of the river are the other, lesser sweet wine areas of Bordeaux: Cérons, Loupiac and Sainte-Croix-du-Mont. Here the wines are less intensely sweet, less concentrated, less honeyed, but they can nevertheless be fine wines in their own right.

Sauternes and the region's other sweet wines are the result of botrytis-affected grapes. The harvest is deliberately put off until late in the season, allowing the grapes to become affected by noble rot (*pourriture noble* in French). What produces the mesoclimate necessary for its production is a little river, hardly more than a stream, called the Ciron. This arises out of a spring deep in the Landes and flows into the Garonne between Barsac and Preignac. The waters are cold; when they meet the warmer Garonne the atmosphere becomes suffused in mist, particularly in the early autumnal mornings. This creates the humidity necessary for the *Botrytis cinerea* fungus.

There are three grape varieties used for Sauternes: Semillon, Sauvignon Blanc and Muscadelle, but it is Semillon which is the basis of the wine, for it is this grape which is the most susceptible to rot. It is very rigorously pruned to reduce the yield, more so than the Sauvignon (Muscadelle is present to only a very small extent, and disapproved of by the leading châteaux), and so while the average *encépagement* in the vineyard might be 85 per cent Semillon to 15 per cent Sauvignon the blend in the wine might be 75 to 25 per cent.

Sauternes consists of five communes. Of these the largest, and an *appellation* in its own right, is Barsac. Barsac lies to the north, on the bank of the Garonne, its vineyards stretching back to the autoroute. To the south is Preignac, also on the river bank, but with its best vineyards inland from the *autoroute* where it marches with the commune of Sauternes. On the other sides of Sauternes are the communes of Fargues and Bommes.

The Sauternes is a laid-back region, seemingly one of the backwaters of Bordeaux, despite the worldwide fame of its wines. The region is attractive, undulating and well-wooded. Each of the important classed growths occupies its own little hillock, the less well-exposed valleys being left to pasture or planted with maize and wheat rather than with vines. The roads in between the fields and vineyards are narrow and winding and it is easy to lose one's way.

Authorities are divided on if not how and why, exactly when Sauternes began to be the luscious, properly botrytised wine we know today. In the old days, *vignerons* were not allowed to start their harvest until the *Ban des Vendanges* had been announced. Authority to pronounce the date was usually vested in some local lord, ecclesiastical or lay. It has been suggested that on occasion the noble in question was delayed at court or on other official duties, and as a result the *Ban* was not declared until noble rot had set in. Instead of the crop being ruined, as feared, the resultant wine was found to be delicious, so slowly but surely the date of the harvest was delayed while growers and proprietors waited for the fungus to arrive.

My suggestion is that *all* white wines, and I have sampled nineteenth-century Montrachets which were definitely botrytis-affected, were harvested in ancient times in the same way as Vouvray is today. A little dry wine was made from early gathered grapes as an insurance policy. The remaining fruit was left to ripen further. In those days wines with a higher alcoholic degree and the resultant residual sugar were always more highly prized than dry wines. Before the days of importing sugar practically the only ingredient to hand to sweeten food or drink was honey. Inevitably, white winemakers would find themselves with rotten grapes, noble or ignoble, at the end of the season, and would discover the delight of botrytised wine.

It used to be said that the man responsible for introducing noble rot to the Sauternes district was a M. Focke who had arrived from the Rhineland to take over at Château La Tour Blanche in the 1830s. The

Germans were already making botrytised wines. Focke merely brought the idea with him and introduced it to an area already making semi-sweet, late-harvest white wines. To support this thesis one can site André Jullien who in the first edition of his *Topographie de Tous Les Vignobles Connus*, 1816, refers merely to *très moelleux* or *semi-liquoreux* wines when he discusses Sauternes: not properly *liquoreux* or *doux*, please note. His description of the harvest refers to several passages over as much as two months, to rot and to the colour of the grapes being brown, but not to fungal growth. Elsewhere, while there is little if any equivalent reporting of the sweet wines of Germany, he does refer to Tokaji as being *doux*, known as *rayon de miel* (ribbon of honey), and the wine being a *vin de liqueur*. It would seem that he considered that there was a difference in intensity.

The crucial difference, however, is not so much between degrees of sweetness – wines have been made out of dried grapes (*vin de paille* and so on) since biblical times – but with wines made from grapes infested with noble rot or not. Richard Olney (*Yquem*) provides ample evidence at this property of picking by *tri* and not usually starting the harvest until mid-October, from as far back as 1666, from which he deduces that the fruit must have been rot-infested. He argues plausibly. But we nevertheless do not have definite proof.

The heyday of the fashion for Sauternes can be said to begin with 1847. The Grand Duke Constantine, brother to the Tsar of Russia, paid 20,000 Francs for a 900-litre tun of the Yquem of this vintage. In the 1920s a minor Barsac such as Château Broustet would sell for as much as a First Growth Médoc (8000 Francs). A wine like Climens would be 50 per cent more (12,000 Francs), with Yquem fetching twice as much again (24,000 Francs). Even as late as the 1940s Rieussec would sell for the same price as Château Margaux. Then a slump set in. Sweet wines went out of fashion. The result was a vicious spiral of low prices, lack of profit, underinvestment and a temptation to cut corners.

After a fine run of vintages between the end of the Second World War and the early 1960s, successful years became sparse. The market for sweet wines evaporated. Life became increasingly uneconomic. One Second Growth, Château de Myrat, grubbed up its vines and gave up entirely (though it has been recently resurrected). Others gave up even the pretence of producing serious wine. Many changed hands – four classed growths in 1971 alone. Not only was production unprofitable, but the owners seemed to have lost faith in their product. There was no combined marketing effort, indeed little communication between one owner and another. I remember as late as 1982 introducing one château proprietor to his neighbour. In the 10 years one had lived in the region (he was one of the 1971 arrivals, the other had been resident far longer) they had never actually met!

Today the position is different. There is a new mood of buoyancy, profitability and confidence in the air. In part this is a question of new blood and new brooms, the arrival of a new generation and outsiders such as the Rothschilds at Rieussec and AXA Millésimes at Suduiraut. They were helped by one good (1985) and five excellent (1983, 1986, 1988, 1989, 1990) vintages in eight years for which they asked and readily obtained economically realistic prices (sadly, there have only been three excellent vintages – 1997, 2001 and 2002 – since). These prices enabled investment in new oak and refrigerated stabilisation equipment, made it a commercial possibility to wait for the arrival of an abundance of *pourriture noble* and to pick over each row of vines a number of times, and allowed for a severe selection of only the best *cuvées* for the *grand vin*. While not all the top properties were in a financial position to profit fully from the quality of the 1983 vintage, there has been a revolution in Sauternes since the mid-1980s, equivalent to that which has taken place in the Graves with the dry white wines. For the first time for a generation most of the classed growths – indeed nearly every single one of them – are making fine wine. The future looks exciting.

Sauternes will always be expensive. If in the Médoc and the Graves a yield of one bottle of wine per vine is the norm in the top properties, in the Sauternes the yield will be only one-third or less. One glass of wine per vine, they will tell you at Château d'Yquem. In the Sauternes collection costs are higher and successful vintages rarer. For these reasons we must be prepared to pay high prices for good Sauternes or the wine will cease to exist.

There are significant differences between the style of wines produced in the five Sauternes communes. Sauternes itself is the fullest, the richest, the most concentrated, especially at Château d'Yquem, but potentially, at least, also in the other top estates. Fargues, nearby, as characterised by Château Rieussec, Yquem's immediate neighbour, produces wines the closest in character. Those of Bommes (Lafaurie-Peyraguey, Rayne-Vigneau, Sigalas-Rabaud and Rabaud-Promis) and Preignac (Suduiraut) are ample and plump, marginally less honeyed, a little more flowery. Barsac is an *appellation* in its own right and the estates have a choice whether to label their wines Sauternes or Barsac: Climens, Coutet, Doisy-Daëne and Nairac) are the most racy of them all, the least luscious. But it is in fact difficult, as well as dangerous, to generalise. Because of the drawn-out harvest, where one grower may wait and have his patience rewarded, or his neighbour pick early and avoid the terrible consequences of a change in climate, Sauternes is not only much less consistent from vintage to vintage but also between one château and its neighbour.

WHEN TO DRINK THE WINES

When should you drink your fine Sauternes? The wines are full-bodied, alcoholic, high in sugar and high in balancing acidity. They are big wines, in short. It is infanticide to drink the richest, best-balanced vintages too early; before 10 years old in fact. Château d'Yquem, however, is an exception. The wines are twice as concentrated as the rest of Sauternes and so the timescale needs to be doubled. On the other hand, I consider lesser vintages are at their best young. The wines may be sweet but they will not be as honeyed and luscious, the harmony may not be what it should be. As a result, wines from these years may get coarse as they age. Drink them young, at the age of five years or so, and you will enjoy their youthful freshness and fragrance.

SAUTERNES VINTAGES

2002: A small vintage as a result of poor flowering but a successful one. The wines are medium-full bodied, pure, racy and flowery with plenty of botrytis. Not as powerfully concentrated as the 2001s, though. Drink from 2010.

2001: Excellent weather conditions have produced a potentially great vintage. The wines are full-bodied, rich, very concentrated and very powerful, but have fine balancing acidity. The best will need 15 years to reach their peak.

2000: Climatic conditions were favourable in September, and the grapes collected in the first couple of *tris* were of high quality. After 11th October the weather deteriorated, the *pourriture* rapidly becoming *grise*. Most of what came in after this has been declassified.

1999: The last week of September was extremely wet, and the weather did not really improve until 5th October. It was then fine. The vintage is a success. Better than 1998 but not as good as 1997.

1998: Certainly potentially a very good vintage. The wines showed well in April 1999, with no lack of either noble rot nor balancing acidity. A year later I found the majority of the wines ample and generous if without the grip and intensity of a really fine vintage.

1997: The first really fine vintage since 1990. At its very best inland in the communes of Sauternes, Fargues and Bommes than nearer the river Garonne in Barsac. Needs a decade to mature.

1996: The wines showed well in April 1997, indicating a lighter vintage but one with style and at least some botrytis. A year on many seemed a bit coarse and clumsy. Now mature. Some good wines, but overall inconsistent.

1995: A vintage of medium-sweet wines with only a little botrytis. Some interesting wines at the best levels but not really a serious sweet wine year. For drinking soon.

1994 to 1991: Rainy weather at vintage time induced the wrong sort of rot. One or two properties such as Climens produced the odd pleasant sweetish wines. But none with any real Sauternes character.

1990: The last and perhaps greatest of a magnificent trio: 1988, 1989 and 1990. Never before have we had three top Sauternes vintages in a row. Full, rich, very concentrated wines with excellent supporting acidity and real finesse. The complete Sauternes vintage. Will last 50 years or more. The best wines are only just ready.

1989: Splendidly ripe, rich wines, luscious and honeyed. Perhaps the 1990s have a little more elegance, but it is a close run thing. The wines are similar in size and should be consumed over the same timescale.

1988: A slightly lighter vintage with very good noble rot and an excellent supporting acidity. The wines have a delightful flowery fragrance and real breed and length All but the very biggest wines are now just beginning to mature. Drink over the next 30 to 40 years.

1987: Not a Sauternes vintage.

1986: A vintage much in the mould of 1988 but not quite as fine. There are nevertheless some very lovely wines which are now just about ready. Drink over the next 20 years.

1985: A vintage of full, sweet wines but without much noble rot flavour. Now ready. Drink until 2010.

1984: Not a Sauternes vintage.

1983: A potentially great vintage, but not all the top properties were performing as well as they do today, so the results are spotty. The best are rich and full with plenty of botrytis. They are ready now and will last another 20 years.

Good earlier vintages: 1976, 1975, 1971, 1967, 1962 and 1959.

What is important to bear in mind is that the expression 'off-vintage Sauternes' is a bit of an oxymoron. The concept of a second wine or a *bourgeois* example is also suspect. A Sauternes, by its very nature, must be a wine with recognizable botrytis, vinified in newish oak: something rich and intense and concentrated. This you won't find in a lesser vintage, or in wine declassed from the *grand vin*. Nor, for reasons of economics, are you likely to come across this sort of quality in a *bourgeois* growth.

The top Sauternes growths – with the exception of those in Barsac – occupy or share their own little hill. Lower down the slope are the vineyards of the normally smaller, lesser properties. Often these latter estates promote their wines by pointing out that their vines touch those of Yquem or one of the other *crus classés*. There is no harm in doing this but the consumer should be aware that the terroirs are not exactly as promising.

SAUTERNES & OTHER SWEET
WHITE WINE AREAS

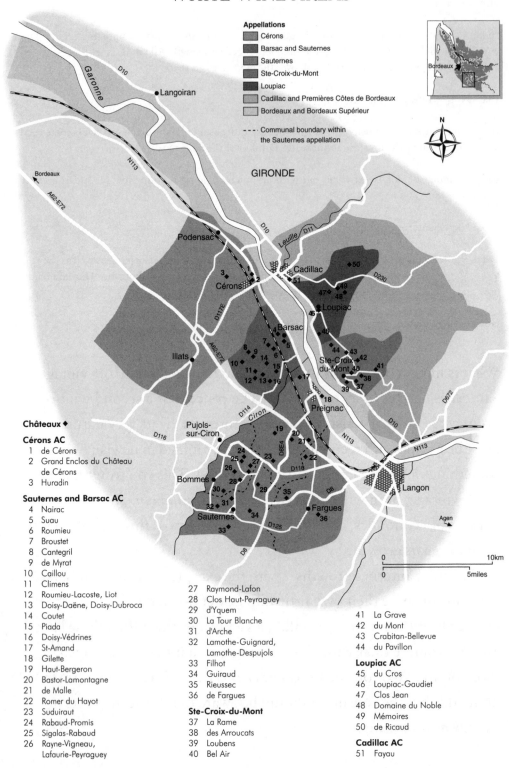

Appellations

- Cérons
- Barsac and Sauternes
- Sauternes
- Ste-Croix-du-Mont
- Loupiac
- Cadillac and Premières Côtes de Bordeaux
- Bordeaux and Bordeaux Supérieur

- - - - Communal boundary within
the Sauternes appellation

Garonne

D10

Langoiran

Bordeaux

N113

A62-E72

GIRONDE

Podensac

Leuille D11

D10

Cadillac

50

Cérons
3   2
Cérons

47 49
48

Loupiac

46

Illats

Barsac
7   6
8   9
10   14 5
11   15
12   13 16
17

46

44 43
42
Ste-Croix-
du-Mont 40
39 37
38
41

D230

D117E

A62-E72

D114

Ciron

Preignac
18

Pujols-
sur-Ciron

D116

D8E4

19
20
21   22
23
24
25   27
26   28   29
30
32   31
33   34
Sauternes
35
29

Bommes

D118

Fargues
36

D8

Langon

N113

N113

D10

D672

Agen

D125

D8

0   10km
0   5miles

N

Châteaux ◆

Cérons AC
1 de Cérons
2 Grand Enclos du Château
   de Cérons
3 Huradin

Sauternes and Barsac AC
4 Nairac
5 Suau
6 Roumieu
7 Broustet
8 Cantegril
9 de Myrat
10 Caillou
11 Climens
12 Roumieu-Lacoste, Liot
13 Doisy-Daëne, Doisy-Dubroca
14 Coutet
15 Piada
16 Doisy-Védrines
17 St-Amand
18 Gilette
19 Haut-Bergeron
20 Bastor-Lamontagne
21 de Malle
22 Romer du Hayot
23 Suduiraut
24 Rabaud-Promis
25 Sigalas-Rabaud
26 Rayne-Vigneau,
    Lafaurie-Peyraguey

27 Raymond-Lafon
28 Clos Haut-Peyraguey
29 d'Yquem
30 La Tour Blanche
31 d'Arche
32 Lamothe-Guignard,
    Lamothe-Despujols
33 Filhot
34 Guiraud
35 Rieussec
36 de Fargues

Ste-Croix-du-Mont
37 La Rame
38 des Arroucats
39 Loubens
40 Bel Air

41 La Grave
42 du Mont
43 Crabitan-Bellevue
44 du Pavillon

Loupiac AC
45 du Cros
46 Loupiac-Gaudiet
47 Clos Jean
48 Domaine du Noble
49 Mémoires
50 de Ricaud

Cadillac AC
51 Fayau

Sauternes Leading Châteaux

Château d'Arche

OWNER: Héritiers Bastit Saint-Martin; manager:
Pierre Perromat.
COMMUNE: Sauternes.
SURFACE AREA UNDER VINE: 30 ha – 90% Sémillon;

10% Sauvignon;.
SECOND WINE: Cru de Braneyre.
CLASSIFICATION: Deuxième Cru (1855).

Formerly known as Braneyre, which name is now reserved for the second wine, this estate was acquired by the Comte d'Arche, a Bordeaux parliamentarian, in 1727. Following the French Revolution, the domaine was sequestered, sold to a M. Dublanc, but subsequently divided into three sections. One of these, d'Arche-Vimeney, was eventually sold to the Cordiers of Château Lafaurie-Peyraguey in 1980. the other two were not reunited until 1960. This was at the time of Armand Bastit Saint-Martin, who had succeeded his father-in-law in 1925. Pierre Perromat, a former director of the INAO, has managed d'Arche since 1981. The château, a much restored, raised eighteenth-century *chartreuse*, is largely covered in creeper, and seems unoccupied.

As with many properties in the area, the wine has shown a renaissance since 1983. One-third new wood is used. The vineyard lies between Châteaux Guiraud and La Tour Blanche. Stylistically too, the wine is a halfway house, both honeyed and *liquoreux* and peachy: certainly one of the better *deuxièmes crus*.

See *The Vine*, No 93, October 1992.

Château Bastor-Lamontagne

OWNER: Foncier Vignobles; manager: Michel
Garat.
COMMUNE: Preignac.
SURFACE AREA UNDER VINE: 56 ha – 80% Sémillon;
17% Sauvignon; 3% Muscadelle.

SECOND WINE: Les Remparts de Bastor.
OTHER WINES: Château Beauregard (Pomerol);
Château du Haut-Pick (Sauternes); Château
Saint-Robert (Graves).

Bastor-Lamontagne lies on the western side of Preignac, across the autoroute, heading up towards Château Suduiraut. A large estate, it has enjoyed few changes of ownership in its long history, has been very consistent over the last 40 years and is one of the leading contenders for promotion to the ranks of the classed growths.

In the eighteenth century it belonged to a councillor in the Bordeaux parliament, François de Lamontagne. A predecessor, one assumes, must have been a M. Bastor. By the 1830s the proprietor had changed to Joseph-Eugène Larrieu, a Parisian banker who a decade later was to acquire Château Haut-Brion. Joseph-Eugène's grandson, Eugène, died just before the turn of the century, by which time the reputation of the estate was well-established. Even in 1874, after the 1855 Classification, Cocks & Féret persist in listing it under the heading '*autres deuxièmes crus*'.

This last Larrieu had no direct heirs. Before too long the estates were sold off, and in 1936 Bastor-Lamontagne passed to a bank, the Crédit Foncier de France who own Château Beauregard in Pomerol and one or two other estates. The Crédit Foncier have remained the owners ever since.

The wine is fermented in stainless steel and matured using 25 per cent new oak. I sampled as far back as 1971 in October 1990, and have tasted subsequently on a regular basis: there are very few failures, if any.

See *The Vine* No 76, May 1991.

Château Broustet

OWNER: Didier Laulan.

COMMUNE: Barsac.

SURFACE AREA UNDER VINE: 16 ha – 70% Sémillon; 20% Sauvignon; 10% Muscadelle.

SECOND WINE: Les Charmes du Château Broustet.

OTHER WINE: Château Saint-Marc (Sauternes).

CLASSIFICATION: Deuxième Cru (1855).

Where the name Broustet comes from we do not know. In the early nineteenth century the estate belonged to Bernard Capdeville, as did Château Nairac, and in the 1855 Classification the two are regarded as a single entity. After Capdeville's death in 1861 the properties were divided. Mademoiselle Capdeville had married Henri Moller, owner of Château Myrat, senior of the Second Growths. She took charge of Broustet which was then run in tandem with Château Myrat.

Following the phylloxera epidemic, Mme Moller, now widowed, sold both estates: Château Broustet to Gabriel Supeau. He was more interested in the convenience of the proximity of the *chais* to the Barsac railway station – his main business being that of barrelmaker – and he did not get round to replanting the vineyard until 1900.

Through Gabriel Supeau's daughter, Château Broustet passed into the hands of the Fournier family. They were also owners of Château Canon in Saint-Émilion. When Éric Fournier took over in 1972 there was much to do at Canon, and this received priority in terms of funds and attention. Several of the lesser vintages of the 1970s and 1980s were not declared, the quality of production being a bit hit and miss. Not until 1984 was the cellar modernised, cold stabilisation installed and the percentage of new wood what it should be. Sadly internal family disagreements and inheritance taxes forced the Fournier family to sell Château Broustet in 1992.

The quality of Broustet, both before and after the Fournier sale, has been uneven: the 1970 is good, as is the 1975, but the 1971 is better still. Thereafter the results are unexciting until you get to 1985. But the 1988–1990 trio are even better. The 1990s was not a great decade for Sauternes, but even the 1997, the only fine vintage between 1990 and 2001, is a bit common. At its best Château Broustet can be rich and honeyed for a Barsac. What it tends to lack is Barsac's typical raciness.

Château Caillou

OWNER: Michel & Marie-Josée Pierre.

COMMUNE: Barsac.

SURFACE AREA UNDER VINE: 13 ha – 90% Sémillon; 10% Sauvignon.

SECOND WINE: Les Erables de Caillou.

OTHER WINES: Graves Rouge du Château Caillou (Graves); Château Petit Mayne (Sauternes).

CLASSIFICATION: Deuxième Cru (1855).

The Caillou vineyard lies close to those of Châteaux Myrat and Climens on the western side of Barsac. The turreted château, imposing from the front, but absurdly shallow when seen from the side, is fronted by what looks to be a cannon: it is in fact a large concrete bottle.

The name comes, it is logical to think, from the pebbles (*cailloux*) in the soil. The first recorded owners, proprietors from the late eighteenth century until 1909, were the Sarraute family. After the arrival of phylloxera their fortunes declined, as did the size of the vineyard. When it was sold to Jean Ballan early in the twentieth century, only 3 hectares were in production. Joseph Bravo married Ballan's daughter Reine, and the property is today run by his son Jean-Bernard, founder of the Sauternes Jazz Quartet, and daughter Marie-José Pierre.

The wine, vinified in tank and aged using 20 per cent new wood – Jean-Bernard Bravo is not in favour of very oaky wines – is full and rich: Climens-like. Quality is very good. Where I take exception is Caillou's policy of declaring a small amount of the best of the crop as *Private Cuvée*. Eliminating the cream surely diminishes the remainder of the *grand vin*. These *Private Cuvée* bottles are fine. But the standard bottlings in vintages such as 1990, 1989 and 1988, all splendid years in Sauternes, I find only average.

Château Cantegril

OWNER: Pierre & Denis Dubourdieu.
COMMUNE: Barsac.
SURFACE AREA UNDER VINE: 29 ha –
  80% Sémillon; 20% Sauvignon.

OTHER WINES: Château Cantegril (Graves);
  Château Doisy-Daëne (Sauternes – Barsac &
  Bordeaux Blanc); Clos Floridène (Graves);
  Château Reynon (Bordeaux Supérieur).

There are remains of a medieval fortified castle, occupied later by the Duc d'Épernon and the Lords of Cantegril, on the site here. One of the latter married Mlle Myrat. In 1854 Château Cantegril and what was to take on an independent existence as Château Myrat were separated. Cantegril was acquired by M. Ségur Montagne. Subsequently the estate changed hands several times before being acquired by M. Mansencal, Mme Pierre Dubourdieu's father.

The Dubourdieus will tell you that it should have been Château Cantegril which was classed top of the Second Growths in 1855, not Château Myrat. They look after this wine with the same care as they do at Doisy-Daëne, vinifying using one-third new oak. The wine is plump, clean, flowery and succulent. The 1997 and 2001 are very good indeed.

Château Climens ★★

OWNER: Bérénice Lurton.
COMMUNE: Barsac.
SURFACE AREA UNDER VINE: 31 ha –

100% Sémillon.
SECOND WINE: Cyprès de Climens.
CLASSIFICATION: Premier Cru (1855).

Climens is one of the great Sauternes estates: for many the very best, save for Yquem. In some vintages it is even better.

Its history goes back as far as the sixteenth century, when a deed of sale in favour of Guirault Roborel, King's Prosecutor at Barsac refers to the estate as Climens. In fact, the name of a Jean

Climens crops up in a document from 1462. But no direct connection between this individual and Barsac has yet been established. The Roborel family continued at Climens until 1800, when the estate was sold to Jean Bineaud. The deed of sale mentions three parcels of vines, totalling 27 hectares. At the time of the 1855 Classification Climens was owned by Eloi Lacoste. He passed it on in 1871 to Alfred Ribet, who sold out in his turn in 1885, at the height of the phylloxera epidemic, to Henri Gounouillhou, a publisher, who had recently married Mlle Dubroca, heiress to Doisy-Dubroca, a small Second Growth.

Climens' reputation had already been established before the French Revolution. Under the Gounouillhou regime it was to rise even further, becoming the only real rival to Château d'Yquem. This has not changed since its acquisition in 1971 by Lucien Lurton of Château Brane-Cantenac and other Médoc estates. It is now owned by one of Lurton's 10 children.

The château is a modest single-storey *chartreuse*, unoccupied for most of the year. Next door, in the *chai*, the wine is vinified and matured in oak, 35 per cent of which is new. The wine is full, rich, needing time to mature, and long-lasting. It is invariably one of the top three in the whole of Sauternes, vintage after vintage.

See *Grands Vins*, p. 555.

Château Coutet ★

OWNER: Baly family.

COMMUNE: Barsac.

SURFACE AREA UNDER VINE: 38.5 ha – 75% Sémillon; 23% Sauvignon; 2% Muscadelle.

SECOND WINE: La Chartreuse de Coutet.

OTHER WINE: Vin Sec de Château Coutet (Graves).

CLASSIFICATION: Premier Cru (1855).

Château Coutet, with its square crenellated tower, fourteenth-century chapel and other vestiges of early medieval architecture which date back even earlier, provides ample evidence that the area was a thriving region well before anyone thought of developing the land in the Médoc. In the eighteenth century it belonged to President Pichard, one of the senior figures in the Bordeaux parliament. In 1786 Pichard was able to step in when cousins of his, the Ségurs, were forced to sell Lafite. Shortly afterwards he decided to sell Château Coutet, which then passed to Gabriel Barthélémy Romain de Filhot, a neighbour in Sauternes. Filhot (Pichard suffered the same fate) was one of only a few Bordeaux nobles who fell foul of the French Revolution, being guillotined in 1793. One would have assumed his properties would be sold off as *biens nationaux*. However, some 14 years later his orphaned daughter Marie-Geneviève married Antoine-Marie de Lur-Saluces of Château d'Yquem. He was well in with the new regime, being Napoleon's chamberlain. By 1810 Marie-Geneviève was able to re-acquire her patrimony.

The Lur-Saluces family retained Château Coutet until 1922. Three years later it changed hands once again, being bought by a Lyonnais industrialist, Henri-Louis Guy. Guy's daughter married, for the second time, Edmond Rolland, once tutor to her children, and an *abbé* (he obviously had to renounce his priesthood). They remained at Coutet until the death of Mme Rolland in 1977, when the property was sold to Marcel Baly.

It was during the Rolland-Guy era, beginning in 1943, that a special bottling, the Cuvée Madame, was produced from a particularly good vat in the best vintages. All the wine is vinified and matured in wood, one-third of which is new.

The Cuvée Madame, which represents perhaps 5 per cent of the harvest, in the vintages when it is produced, is a wine of immense concentration, intensity and class. The *grand vin* is not quite as full-bodied or as dense (in the best sense of the word) as Climens. It is both more floral and more peachy. I do not find it as consistent as Climens. But it certainly merits its classification. The 1989 is the star of the more recent vintages.

See *Grands Vins*, p.550.

Château Doisy-Daëne ★

OWNER: Pierre & Denis Dubourdieu.
COMMUNE: Barsac.
SURFACE AREA UNDER VINE: 15 ha –
80% Sémillon; 20 Sauvignon.

OTHER WINES: Château Cantegril (Sauternes &
Graves); Clos Floridène (Graves); Château
Reynon (Bordeaux Supérieur).
CLASSIFICATION: Deuxième Cru (1855).

The origin of the three Doisy estates belongs with the Védrines family (see below). Some time in the 1830s or 1840s the property was split, and one part – the parts were by no means equal – passed into the hands of a M. Daëne. He remained the proprietor until the 1870s. A decade later the estate changed hands again. It was acquired by a M. Dejean of the *négociants* Cazelet & Fils. The Dejeans held it until 1924 when Georges Dubourdieu, grand and great-grandfather of Pierre and Denis, took over.

The Dubourdieus are widespread in the area. A cousin owns Château Roumieu-Lacoste, another Château Archambeau in Illats, and that is not all. This branch of the Dubourdieus also owns Château Cantegril, detached from Château Myrat in 1856. Denis Dubourdieu and his wife Florence own Château Reynon in the Premières Côtes, while his main occupation is that of a very influential professor of oenology at Bordeaux University.

The Sauternes is vinified in stainless steel, cold treated and then matured in oak, one-third of which is new. The wine is less luscious than Doisy-Védrines, but very pure and refined in a flowery-peachy sort of way. It has great elegance and is usually the best of the Second Growths. A dry wine, one of the best in the area, is made from roughly half Sémillon and half Sauvignon, by selective picking, from overripe grapes not affected by noble rot. This is both original and delicious. In 1990, a super-*cuvée* of the sweet wine was launched to be made only in the best years: L'Extravagance, 100 cases of it.

See *Grands Vins*, p. 581.

Château Doisy-Dubroca ★

OWNER: Louis Lurton.
COMMUNE: Barsac.
SURFACE AREA UNDER VINE: 3.3 ha –

100% Sémillon.
SECOND WINE: La Demoiselle de Doisy.
CLASSIFICATION: Deuxième Cru (1855).

When the Doisy domaine was split the smallest part passed to Mlle Faux, owner at the time of the 1855 Classification. It was then sold to Mlle Dubroca. In 1880 this lady married Henri Gounouillhou of neighbouring Château Climens. The two estates have been allied ever since, though in the 1920s, after the death of Gounouillhou, the proprietor here is listed as a Marcel Dubroca.

Now that Lucien Lurton has divided up his empire among his many children, Climens and Doisy-Dubroca are separately owned again. Here the *chai* and *cuvier* have recently been renovated.

Up to a decade ago, the wine was made at Château Climens. Doisy-Dubroca is vinified and matured in cask, one-third of which is new. The wine is clean, concentrated and intense: very like Climens, if not quite so full-bodied.

Château Doisy-Védrines ★

OWNER: Castéja family; manager: Olivier Castéja.
COMMUNE: Barsac.
SURFACE AREA UNDER VINE: 28 ha – 80% Sémillon;

15% Sauvignon; 5% Muscadlle.
SECOND WINE: Château Petit Védrines.
CLASSIFICATION: Deuxième Cru (1855).

This is the original element of the Doisy domaine, and is named after Jean Védrines who arrived in the area from Agen in 1704, marrying into the Raymond family, Bordeaux lawyers. The estate was from the start one of the most important in Barsac. The wine is listed in the earliest classifications immediately after Châteaux Coutet and Climens, its nearest neighbours. In 1828 the Dubos or Dubosq family seem to be co-owners of Doisy alongside the Védrines. Sometime after this it was split, the Védrines-Dubosq retaining the largest portion. This they sold to a local family called Boireau in 1851. Through the female line it subsequently passed to the Castéjas.

Vinification starts in stainless steel and finishes in barrel, half of which is new. There are up-to-date *passage à froid* installations as well as cryo-extraction facilities. The wines are rich and honeyed and rather fuller than the peaches and cream character of Doisy-Daëne: equally lovely, equally consistent.

See *Grands Vins*, p. 577.

Château de Fargues ★

OWNER: Lur-Saluces family; manager: François
  Amirault.
COMMUNE: Fargues.
SURFACE AREA UNDER VINE: 14.5 ha –

80% Sémillon; 20% Sauvignon.
SECOND WINE: Guilhem de Fargues (Bordeaux
  Blanc).

The southern part of the Bordeaux region is rich in medieval fortifications. Some have ecclesiastical connections, as at Château Villandraut. Others are proper castles, what the French term *donjons*. Most – at Budos, Castets, La Brède, Landrias and Roquetaillade – date from immediately after the elevation of Bertrand de Goth to the Papacy, as Clément V, in 1306, as he flexed the muscles of his patronage by liberally bestowing the red hat of cardinalship among his friends and relations. One such was Raymond Guilhem, a nephew. This is the origin of the fortress of Château de Fargues. As a wine estate, though, it only dates from 1942. Prior to this the land was not vineyard but pasture and pine trees.

In 1472 Isabelle de Monferrand, heiress to Fargues, married Pierre de Lur. Some 114 years later their descendant Jean married Catherine Charlotte, only child of the Marquis de Saluces. Jean inherited the marquisate and changed his name to Lur-Saluces. It has been in the hands of the same family ever since and remains theirs even though Château d'Yquem has been sold to LVMH. The château, though, is now but a shell. Ghostly, it looms over the neighbouring village. Unconcerned, the locals play soccer on the nearby football pitch.

While some red wine was produced in the late nineteenth century, it was not until 1935 that it was decided to produce Sauternes at Fargues, and Sémillon and Sauvignon were planted. The wine continues to be made by the Yquem team, with the same attention to detail, and 100 per cent new oak. Taste it by itself and you might well think it as Yquem. Taste the two side by side, and the extra class and sheer magic of the latter is clearly apparent.

See *Grands Vins*, p. 589.

Château Filhot

OWNER: Comte Henri de Vaucelles.

COMMUNE: Sauternes.

SURFACE AREA UNDER VINE: 60 ha – 50% Sémillon; 45% Sauvignon; 5% Muscadelle.

SECOND WINE: Château Pineau du Rey (Bordeaux Blanc).

CLASSIFICATION: Deuxième Cru (1855).

Filhot is in many ways the odd man out among the top Sauternes châteaux. While all the others have used the prosperity of the post-1983 period to go back to new or newish oak for the maturation, if not for the vinification as well, Filhot, which abandoned oak barrels for fibre-glass tanks in the 1960s, has refused to budge. More important, for a wine which comes from the commune as well as the *appellation* of Sauternes, it is merely light and gently sweet, rather than rich and luscious; it is not a wine with an intense noble rot character. It could be a Cérons, or a Sainte-Croix-du-Mont.

The Filhot family, parliamentary councillors, arrived in Sauternes in 1709, developed an important *vignoble* and from 1735 onwards had constructed a very grand château – a proper stately home in a large English-style park. By the 1780s the wine was fetching as much as Yquem.

Though Gabriel-Barthélémy-Romain de Filhot, born in 1750, was guillotined in the French Revolution, as was his wife, and his properties confiscated (he also owned Château Coutet), his daughter Marie-Geneviève, having married into the Lur-Saluces family, was eventually able to reclaim her inheritance. As I have pointed out (see Château Coutet) the Lur-Saluces were well connected with the Napoleonic elite.

Château Filhot remained in Lur-Saluces hands, until, somewhat neglected, it was acquired by a son-in-law, de Lacarelle, in 1935. His daughter married into the Vaucelles family. A son of hers, Henri, has been in charge since 1974.

Today, Filhot is one of the dullest of the Sauternes classed growths. Something needs to be done here.

See *The Vine* No 113, June 1994.

Château Gilette

OWNER: Médeville family.

COMMUNE: Preignac.

SURFACE AREA UNDER VINE: 4.5 ha – 90% Sémillon; 8% Sauvignon; 2% Muscadelle.

OTHER WINES: Château Les Justices (Sauternes); Château Respide-Médeville (Graves).

The Médeville family, who have been in Preignac since 1710, produce a very curious wine at Château Gilette. Instead of being matured in cask for a year or two, it is kept in epoxy resin-lined concrete vats for 15 or more years before being bottled. Only the best years are declared. This has been the Médeville way of producing Sauternes since the 1930s, when it was an economy measure, barrels being prohibitively expensive.

The results are very odd: quite alcoholic and often more sweet than obviously botrytised, but with this high sugar level subdued by the long ageing process. Sometimes they lack zip and complexity. Moreover, there are often two *cuvées* of the same vintage, the better labelled *crème de tête*. I find Château Gilette a bit hit and miss, but some of the older wines, such as the 1949 and 1950, are certainly fine for a non-classed growth.

A more traditional Sauternes is made at the 14-hectare Château Les Justices.

Château Guiraud

OWNER: Narby family.

COMMUNE: Sauternes.

SURFACE AREA UNDER VINE: 100 ha –
  65% Sémillon; 35% Sauvignon.

SECOND WINE: Le Dauphin du Château Guiraud.

OTHER WINE: G du Château Guiraud.

CLASSIFICATION: Premier Cru (1855).

Formerly known as Château Bayle, and associated in pre-revolutionary times with the Essenhault family, owners of Château d'Issan, and later with the Mons of La Tour du Mons, this estate was acquired by Pierre Guiraut, as it was spelled at the time, son of a Bordeaux *négociant*, in 1766. The Guiraud family, as they later became, retained the property until 1846. In 1862 it passed to the wealthy Bernards, who enlarged the vineyard, modernised the *chais* and constructed the present elegant two-storey château. Having passed by marriage into the hands of James Maxwell, of Irish origin, the domaine was sold to Paul Rival in 1932. Though at first he did not neglect it, as he grew older Rival became a recluse, and both vineyard and château became more and more dilapidated. The quality of the wine suffered accordingly. Moreover, a large part of the estate was replanted with the more productive Sauvignon. For many years, from the 1960s onwards, Château Guiraud was said to be for sale. Eventually it passed to the Narby family in 1981. A major investment had to be made. Happily the 1980s saw a string of very good Sauternes vintages.

Guiraud is the sole *premier cru* in the commune of Sauternes with the exception of Château d'Yquem and its vineyards lie immediately to the south. Like Château Rieussec the wine is usually one of the deepest in colour of the classed growths. Guiraud is full-bodied and rich, usually with good botrytis, but often a little heavy: very good rather than fine. The best of the recent vintages, 1997 and 2001, show an improvement on 1988, 1989 and 2000 though.

See *Grands Vins*, p. 560.

Château Haut-Bergeron

OWNER: Lamothe family.

COMMUNE: Preignac.

SURFACE AREA UNDER VINE: 25 ha – 90% Sémillon;
  5% Sauvignon; 5% Muscadelle.

SECOND WINE: Château Fontebride.

OTHER WINE: Château Farluret (Sauternes –
  Barsac).

The hospitable Lamothes, Hervé and Patrick and their father Robert, look after one of Preignac's best non-classed growths which their family have owned since the seventeenth century. The estate is scattered, with parcels in Sauternes and Bommes as well as Preignac. Older bottles used to announce '*contigu d'Yquem*'. The château lies beyond the *autoroute*, coincidentally in a hamlet called Lamothe.

Plenty of new wood is employed here, the selection is severe and the vines are old. There are cryo-extraction facilities. This is a very good domaine, though not seen as much on the export market as it might be, large volumes being sold to domestic private clients. The 1988 is delicious. The 1990 came top of a blind tasting of *crus bourgeois* organised for me in April 1999. Fine wines were made in 1997 and 2001.

Clos Haut-Peyraguey

OWNER: Pauly family; manager Martine Langlais-Pauly.
COMMUNE: Bommes.
SURFACE AREA UNDER VINE: 15 ha – 90% Sémillon;

10% Sauvignon.
OTHER WINE: Château Haut-Bommes.
CLASSIFICATION: Premier Cru (1855).

Clos Haut-Peyraguey came into existence in 1879 when Château Lafaurie-Peyraguey was split up. This section, smaller than that which continues as Château Lafaurie, is on higher land, but was without château or *chai*. It was acquired by a M. Grillon, a Parisian pharmacist, and already owner of Château de Veyres in Preignac. Grillon had the present *chai* constructed – there is no château, as such – and did much to establish his new brand. In the 1893 Cocks & Féret it is classed second only to Rayne-Vigneau in the commune of Bommes, above Lafaurie. In 1914 Clos Haut-Peyraguey passed to Eugène Garbay and the merchant Fernand Ginestet. The Ginestet interest lasted until 1937. The Paulys, who live in the château of Haut-Bommes, are successors of the Garbays.

Until 1985 the wine was decent without being very exciting, occasionally a little sulphury. In this vintage Jacques Pauly decided to vinify at least part of the crop in wood. Since then the wine has improved. It is now usually of medium weight, both elegant and luscious, as Bommes wines should be, with plenty of complexity in the expression of the fruit. The 1988 and 1997 are fine.

Château Lafaurie-Peyraguey ★★

OWNER: Groupe Suez; manager: Yannick Laporte.
COMMUNE: Bommes.
SURFACE AREA UNDER VINE: 41 ha –

90% Sémillon; 8% Sauvignon; 2% Muscadelle.
SECOND WINE: La Chapelle de Lafaurie.
CLASSIFICATION: Premier Cru (1855).

The crenellated walls and corner towers of Château Lafaurie-Peyraguey make it look like a medieval fort. In fact, though there is a thirteenth-century porch, most of the buildings were constructed in the seventeenth century. A hundred years later the proprietor was Nicolas-Pierre de Pichard, owner of Château Coutet, and for a short while, Château Lafite. He was guillotined in

1793, and Château Pichard, as it was then called, was put up for auction by the state. The purchasers were two gentlemen, M. Lafaurie and M. Mauros. The latter does not seem to have been involved for long, but M. Lafaurie remained until just after the Classification of 1855, when the estate was rated third in the entire Sauternes area.

In 1865 Lafaurie-Peyraguey passed into the hands of Comte Duchatel, a former Minister of the Interior under Louis-Philippe, and owner of Château Lagrange in Saint-Julien. He died shortly afterwards, and when his widow passed away a decade later, their heirs failed to agree on the succession. For some reason the estate was divided as well as put up for sale. In 1879 the large part, including the château, that which would continue as Lafaurie-Peyraguey, was acquired by another pair of gentlemen, MM. Farinel and Grédy. In 1917 it passed to Désiré Cordier.

Following a period when the wine was largely matured in glass-lined tanks (1967–1975), and was sweet rather than luscious, the decision was taken to ferment it, as well as age it, in wood. Forty per cent of this is new. Following the installation of cold-treatment tanks in the early 1980s, there is less recourse to sulphur, and the wine is more sophisticated. It is now one of the very best Sauternes, full-bodied, rich and concentrated, with very good balancing acidity and plenty of class.

See *Grands Vins*, p. 536.

Château Lamothe-Despujols

OWNER: Guy Despujols.
COMMUNE: Sauternes.
SURFACE AREA UNDER VINE: 7.5 ha – 85% Sémillon;
10% Sauvignon; 5% Muscadelle.
SECOND WINE: Les Tourelles de Lamothe.
CLASSIFICATION: Deuxième Cru (1855).

The hill of Lamothe (the mound) occupies the south-west corner of the Sauternes *appellation*. Once upon a time it was fortified in order to protect the local inhabitants from brigand incursion from the forests of the Landes beyond.

Modern history of the estate begins with Jean-François de Borie who sold a property then called Lamothe-d'Assault to an English merchant named Dowling in 1814. In 1820 Dowling sold it to the brothers Baptiste, and it was in the hands of a Veuve Baptiste at the time of the 1855 Classification. Shortly afterwards the property was split. The larger portion went to a son-in-law, M. Massieux, and would eventually become Lamothe-Guignard. The rump passed to a M. Dietz, then to a local family called Espagnet and eventually to M. Bastit Saint-Martin. This important gentleman, president of the Crédit Agricole and member of the French senate, had inherited neighbouring Château d'Arche, then also divided. He was, moreover, the proprietor of the other part of Lamothe, but for some reason failed to unite them. In 1961 he sold this Lamothe to the Despujols, parents of Guy, who has been responsible since 1989.

For most of the time I have known Château Lamothe-Despujols I have been unimpressed. The wine has had little flair and has been decidedly over-shadowed by its neighbour. Even the 1988, 1989, 1990 trio were poor. Since Guy Despujols' arrival things have improved though. M. Despujols did not send his wine for a blind tasting I made of the 1997s in bottle in April 2000, but I had marked it 'very good plus' in cask two years previously, and also complimented the 1996.

See *The Vine* No 92, September 1992.

Château Lamothe-Guignard

OWNER: Philippe & Jacques Guignard.
COMMUNE: Sauternes.
SURFACE AREA UNDER VINE: 17 ha – 90% Sémillon; 5% Sauvignon; 5% Muscadelle.

OTHER WINES: Clos du Hez (Graves); Château de Rolland (Sauternes – Barsac); Château Roquetaillade La Grange (Graves).
CLASSIFICATION: Deuxième Cru (1855).

Following the split (see Lamothe-Despujols above), this Lamothe passed into the hands first of M. Massieux, then to Charles Joseph Bergey at the turn of the nineteenth century, and finally to Bergey's daughter, Marie-Angèle Tissot. In the 1950s, with the estate somewhat run down, M. Bastit Saint-Martin, by this time owner of the other part of Lamothe, was approached by Mme Tissot's heirs who wanted to dispose of their domaine. He took it on, only to lease it to M. Duscombes. In April 1981 he sold this Lamothe to the Guignard brothers.

The Guignards arrived at an opportune moment. Sauternes was on the brink of a revival and there were to be plenty of good vintages in the following few years. They were young and enthusiastic. They had learned their *métier* at the family property in Barsac. Very soon they had put Lamothe-Guignard back on the map.

The buildings and cellars adjoin that of Despujols – though you approach by a separate road – but are merely functional. The wine though, more Bommes or Preignac than Sauternes in style, is normally medium- to full-bodied, ripe, succulent and flowery rather than very luscious. It is clean and has good botrytis. One of the better, yet more modestly priced of the Second Growths.

See *The Vine* No 92, September 1992.

Château Liot

OWNER: Jean-Gérard David.
COMMUNE: Barsac.
SURFACE AREA UNDER VINE: 20 ha – 85% Sémillon; 10% Sauvignon; 5% Muscadelle.

SECOND WINES: Les Graves de Liot; Château du Levant.
OTHER WINE: Château Saint-Jean-des-Graves (Graves).

This is one of the more reliable of Sauternes' non-classed properties. It has belonged to the David family for five generations. The vineyards adjoin those of Château Climens in Haut-Barsac, up near the *autoroute*, and the rather *petit* château, with outbuildings running on either side of it, lies opposite. As with many properties in the neighbourhood, the wines have been cleaned up in the last 15 years or so: less sulphury, more elegant. The 1990 is especially good.

Château de Malle ★

OWNER: Comtesse Nancy de Bournazel.
COMMUNE: Preignac.
SURFACE AREA UNDER VINE: 27 ha – 75% Sémillon; 23% Sauvignon; 2% Muscadelle.
SECOND WINE: Château de Sainte-Hélène.

OTHER WINES: Château Cardeillan (Graves); Chevalier de Malle (Bordeaux Blanc); M. de Malle (Graves blanc, matured in barrel on its lees); Château Tour de Malle (Graves).
CLASSIFICATION: Deuxième Cru (1855).

Château de Malle is one of the loveliest buildings in the Bordeaux region. Dating from the beginning of the seventeenth century it is a stunning mixture of Renaissance and classical styles, standing in an Italianite park populated by numerous pedestalled sculptures.

There were Malles at Preignac as early as the fourteenth century. It was Jacques de Malle, a president in the Bordeaux parliament, who commissioned the present day château. Three generations later, a successor, Pierre, was counsellor to Louis XIV and Keeper of the Seals for the Guyenne region. He had one child, a daughter, Jeanne. When she married Alexandre-Eutrope de Lur-Saluces in 1702, the Malle dynasty came to an end.

Following the union between Louis-Amédée de Lur-Saluces and Jeanne de Sauvage, which brought Yquem into the family, it was usually younger branches which resided at Malle. The last of one of these was the childless Pierre de Lur-Saluces. He bequeathed de Malle to his nephew and godson, Pierre de Bournazel. Not only were things somewhat run down, but hardly had Bournazel arrived when the vineyard was almost completely destroyed by the notorious February 1956 frost. Bournazel had to start from scratch.

Pierre, an electrical engineer by profession, recently married and with a young family, remained in Paris at first while the vineyard, *chais* and château were reconstructed and renovated. The Bournazels finally moved in in 1981. Sadly Pierre passed away in 1985, but his wife Nancy has proved a dynamic and highly talented successor.

The quality of de Malle up to the mid-1980s was uninspiring at best, merely sweet, often sulphury. Since then there has been a remarkable improvement. You could date it from 1986, the first year the wine was vinified in wood (50 per cent new) or from the arrival of the capable Alain Pivonet as *maître de chai* in 1983. Château de Malle is now clean, flowery, racy and with no lack of botrytis. It is more Barsac than Sauternes. Above all it is elegant. Today it is one of the best of the Second Growths. The 1988 and 1989 are very good indeed. The 1990 is a little heavy. The 1997 is fine and the 2002 is delicious. The other wines produced here can also be firmly recommended.

See *The Vine* No 81, October 1991.

Château de Myrat

OWNER: de Pontac family.
COMMUNE: Barsac.
SURFACE AREA UNDER VINE: 22 ha – 88% Sémillon;
  8% Sauvignon; 4% Muscadelle.

OTHER WINE: Château Peychaud (Bordeaux
  Supérieur).
CLASSIFICATION: Deuxième Cru (1855).

The elegant château dates from the 1720s and is situated in a park with the vineyard in one piece surrounding it. Once larger than it is today, for it incorporated what is now Château Cantegril, it was classed top of the Second Growths in 1855. It was owned then by M. Perrot. Subsequently it passed to Henri Moller, who acquired Château Broustet by marriage. In 1853 it was sold to the Martineau family. They then sold to the Pontacs who once owned Château Haut-Brion and other estates. The proprietor, Comte Maximilien de Pontac, restored the estate and replanted much of the vineyard, which the Martineaus had neglected.

Sauternes became more and more unprofitable in the 1960s and 1970s. In 1971 four classed growths changed hands. In 1976 the Comte decided that enough was enough. He ploughed up the Myrat vines.

Maximilien died in April 1988. His heirs Jacques and Xavier had been urging him to replant. They did not have much time before they would lose their rights to resurrect the vineyard. Sadly for the new generation, the new vineyard would not enjoy the best of the weather. There was a severe frost in April 1994, and no really successful vintages before 1997. Even this, at Myrat, is no more than quite good. The vintages since have seen no improvement. Château de Myrat is today an underachiever, one of the least impressive of the Second Growths.

Château Nairac ★

OWNER: Nicole Tari-Heeter; director: Nicolas Heeter.

COMMUNE: Barsac.

SURFACE AREA UNDER VINE: 15 ha – 90% Sémillon; 6% Sauvignon; 4% Muscadelle.

CLASSIFICATION: Deuxième Cru (1855).

The Nairac château, restrained, elegant, Victor-Louis inspired, dating from 1777, lies in a little park on the N113 Bordeaux to Langon road. The bulk of the vineyard lies directly behind, just north of the village of Barsac.

The property has its origins in André Duranceau in the mid-seventeenth century. After several changes of ownership the estate passed in 1777 to Élysée Nairac, from a family of shipowners and politicians, who immediately set about constructing today's château. Élysée died young, but his two daughters, neither of whom were to marry, remained at Nairac until the 1840s. The domaine was then sold to Bernard Capdeville, owner of Château Brousset and farmer elsewhere, probably at Château Nairac as well. On Capdeville's death in 1861 his estate was divided and Nairac and Brousset separated. There were to be a number of changes of ownership here over the following century, and fortunes rose and fell. The château was neglected but at least the vineyard was replanted after the frosts of February 1956.

In August 1971, Nairac was up for sale. The purchasers were a young couple: Tom Heeter, from Dayton in Ohio, and his wife Nicole, née Tari, whose family owned Château Giscours in Margaux. With an almost maniacal energy, attention to detail and perfectionism Heeter set about restoring the vineyard, modernising the *chai* and improving the wine. Every single *passage* became a different wine, each element was treated differently, lodged in different new oak barrels as Heeter strove for perfection. The eventual creation of the *grand vin* involved a rigorously painstaking selection. The results, almost from the word go, were remarkable.

Sadly the marriage came to an end. In 1986 the Heeters divorced, Tom ceding his interest in Nairac to Nicole and the children. Son Nicolas is now in charge. He is continuing the good work.

Nairac lies on the lower ground of Barsac, risking floods if the river Garonne bursts its banks. This happened in 1981. From its location you would expect a light, supple wine. Not so. Nairac is not only very woody, sometimes to excess, but powerful, full-bodied and concentrated, ageing slowly, keeping well. It is bottled later than most. What is missing is a little delicacy. The wine is so in-your-face that it lacks elegance. Very good indeed, then, at best. But not fine.

See *Grands Vins*, p. 584.

Château Piada

OWNER: Jean-Fréderic Lalande.

COMMUNE: Barsac.

SURFACE AREA UNDER VINE: 9.5 ha – 98% Sémillon; 2% Sauvignon.

SECOND WINE: Clos du Roy.

OTHER WINES: Château Piada-Lalande (Bordeaux); Domaine du Hauret-Lalande (Graves & Cérons).

There is a record of the Piada domaine in an archive dating from 1274. Subsequently it became part of the Coutet estate, which it adjoins, regaining independence when the Lur-Saluces sold it in 1809 to the Pisan-Lataste family. They retained Piada for much of the century before it passed by marriage to E Brunet. Jean Lalande bought it in 1940 and his heirs own the estate today.

Château Piada is one of the better and more consistent of the non-classed growths. The wine is barrel-fermented, the selection is rigorous, and the wine is ripe, succulent and flowery with good balancing acidity. The 1997 can be recommended.

Château Rabaud-Promis ★

OWNER: Déjean family; manager: Philippe Déjean.
COMMUNE: Bommes.
SURFACE AREA UNDER VINE: 33 ha – 80% Sémillon; 18% Sauvignon; 2% Muscadelle.

SECOND WINES: Sauternes par Rabaud-Promis.
OTHER WINE: Allegría (Bordeaux Blanc).
CLASSIFICATION: Premier Cru (1855).

Château Rabaud, as it was originally called, is named after an ancient noble family. In 1660 Marie Peyronne de Rabaud married Arnaud de Cazeau. The estate remained in the hands of the Cazeaus until 1819 when Pierre-Hubert de Cazeau sold it to Gabriel Deyme. It is under the name of either Deyme or Cazeau that the wine first appears in the records of contemporary writers. In 1864 the property was sold to Henri Drouillet de Sigalas. Sixteen years later it absorbed the 10 hectares of neighbouring Château Pexiotto, a Second Growth which had belonged to the owners of Climens.

In 1903 the property was divided. Part of the estate passed to Adrien Promis. In 1930 it was united again, a company having been formed by the shareholders of both parts plus the firm of Ginestet who were to market the wine. This arrangement lasted until 1950 when the Promis shares were acquired by Raymond-Louis Lanneluc. Philippe Dejean, who married Lanneluc's grand-daughter, arrived in 1972 and has since bought out the other members of his wife's family.

Château Rabaud-Promis was an underachiever for years, the wine not seeing a stick of oak, being merely sweet and sulphury and inelegant to boot. As with many neighbouring châteaux there has been a major renaissance since the mid-1980s. The wine is now made as it should be and is now a genuine *premier cru*. Château Sigalas-Promis remains more concentrated, and usually finer. The Rabaud-Promis is rich and ample, however. The 1988, 1989, 1990 trio are all fine, though I found the 1997 when I tasted it in bottle in April 2000 less exciting than the other Bommes First Growths.

See *Grands Vins*, p. 572.

Château Raymond-Lafon

OWNER: Meslier family; manager: Charles-Henri Meslier.
COMMUNE: Sauternes.
SURFACE AREA UNDER VINE: 16 ha – 80% Sémillon;

20% Sauvignon.
SECOND WINES: Château Lafon-Laroze; Le Cadet de Raymond-Lafon.

At the foot of the Yquem hill, between the Yquem vineyards and those of the two Peyragueys, lies the château and domaine of Raymond Lafon. A century and a half ago the immediate area was rich in Lafons, who seem to have farmed their land jointly. Cocks & Féret in 1850 refers to Lafon cousins, while there were two others Lafons based in Preignac. One of the Lafons was Raymond, who was mayor of Sauternes. By 1868 he had his own vineyard, while Désir Lafon, no doubt a brother or cousin, was listed at Château Lafon (*tout court*).

Following several changes of ownership Château Raymond-Lafon, in a rather dilapidated state, was acquired by Pierre Meslier, at the time *régisseur* at Yquem, in 1972. Meslier expanded the vineyard, and decided to make the wine in the same way and with the same attention to detail as Yquem.

It was not long before his efforts were recognised, and demand for the wine exceeded supply, even at what were very high prices for a non-classed growth, in the 1980s higher even than Climens and Rieussec. This is certainly a very good wine, though more Bommes or Preignac than Sauternes in style. It lacks the lusciousness. It is only when you put it up against one of the top *premiers crus* that you see that, like Château Fargues, in the final analysis it lacks a little breed.

The 1985, 1989 and 1990 are all good as are the 2001 and 2002. Some of the 1983, which was otherwise a great success, suffered secondary fermentation in bottle, a rare problem.

See *The Vine*, No 19, August 1986.

Château Rayne-Vigneau ★

OWNERS: Cordier Mestrezat & Domaines;
  manager: Patrick Eymery.
COMMUNE: Bommes.
SURFACE AREA UNDER VINE: 80 ha – 74% Sémillon;
  24% Sauvignon; 2% Muscadelle.
SECOND WINE: Madame de Rayne.

OTHER WINES: Gemme de Rayne-Vigneau
  (Bordeaux Blanc); Château Grand-Puy-Ducasse
  (Pauillac); Château Lamothe-Bergeron (Haut-
  Médoc); Le Sec de Rayne-Vigneau (Bordeaux
  Blanc).
CLASSIFICATION: Premier Cru (1855).

This estate commemorates the names of two of its early proprietors: Gabriel de Vigneau in the late seventeenth century and Catherine Marie de Rayne who acquired the domaine in 1834. In between it belonged to the Duffour family, Bordeaux wine merchants. Catherine de Rayne was childless, and on her death 'Vigneau' passed to her brother, Vicomte Gabriel de Pontac. It was then named Vigneau-Pontac. It was re-christened Rayne-Vigneau in 1892 by Albert, son of Gabriel, in honour of his aunt. The next change of ownership was in the 1920s, when after Albert's death the estate was administered by a son-in-law, the Vicomte de Roton. This gentleman's son, François still owns the château. It has been divorced from the vineyard. Roton was mayor of Bommes, vice-president of the local growers' syndicate and a geologist. He found the soils of the steeply rising hill of Château Rayne-Vigneau a veritable mine of precious and semi-precious soils: agate, onyx, sapphire, cornalian, amethyst, jasper, opal....

In 1961 the vineyard was bought by Georges Raoux. It was a sad time for the Sauternes area. Ten years later it was acquired by the *négociants* Mestrezat. This was the lowest ebb for Château Rayne-Vigneau. Most of the vineyard needed replanting. The cellars needed renovation. Everything was in a sorry state. It was not really until 1982, when Patrick Eymery arrived as *régisseur*, that money and energy was spent at Rayne-Vigneau, cryo-extraction and cold treatment facilities installed and the wine once again fermented in barrel. Now there is a second wine and 50 per cent of the casks are renewed annually.

As with so many Sauternes estates one can date the rebirth of quality wine, not from 1983, that potentially excellent vintage, but 1986. The 1988, 1989 and 2000 trio are equally fine, if not better. The 1997 is currently very closed-in, almost monolithic.

Today it comes as no surprise to see that back in 1855 Château Rayne-Vigneau was rated in third position among the First Growths. The wine is a typical high-class Bommes, combining the richness of Sauternes with the racy peachiness of Barsac, yet with an intensity, and in this case a finesse all of its own.

See *Grands Vins*, p. 541.

Château Rieussec ★★

OWNER: Domaines Barons de Rothschild (Lafite).
COMMUNE: Fargues.
SURFACE AREA UNDER VINE: 75 ha – 90% Sémillon; 7% Sauvignon; 3% Muscadelle.
SECOND WINES: Clos Labère.

OTHER WINES: Château Duhart-Milon (Pauillac); Château L'Évangile (Pomerol); Château Lafite-Rothschild (Pauillac); R de Rieussec (Bordeaux Blanc).
CLASSIFICATION: Premier Cru (1855).

Rieussec lies immediately to the south of Yquem, on its own little hill, the third highest (after Yquem and Rayne-Vigneau) in the area, and the wine is perhaps the closest to it in character. It belonged to the Carmelites before the French revolution (they also owned Château Les Carmes Haut-Brion in Pessac) and, after sequestration, was bought as a *bien national* by Jean-Bernard Mareilhac, also proprietor of Château La Louvière in the Graves. From 1846 to 1971 Rieussec had no fewer than nine different owners. Despite periodical under-investment the reputation for the wines seems to have remained high. Older vintages that have come my way, such as the 1928, 1929, 1937, 1949 and 1959, are all fine: rich and sweet, if quite heavy and alcoholic.

In 1971 Albert Vuillier, once shareholder in Champagne Lanson, arrived on the scene. Much needed to be done. Vuillier was *sympa*, intelligent and perfectionistic, but his means had their limits. Moreover, there was extensive hail damage in 1973, 1974 and again in 1977. In 1984 he sold out to the Rothschilds of Château Lafite.

At long last the finances were in place. Pneumatic presses were installed, as were cold treatment facilities, the cellars were enlarged, modified and air-conditioned; more new oak was employed, and harvesting procedures and the eventual selection tightened up. Vuillier remained as a consultant for a few years, retiring in 1986.

In the past Château Rieussec had a tendency to be a bit four-square. It was intense and concentrated but it could have been better balanced. Moreover, the colour darkened fast. Today it is cleaner and fresher, without having abandoned its essential size and power. Vintages since 1983 (where I was present at the initial tastings for the *assemblage*) have been consistently of very high quality. Yet they only started fermenting in barrel in 1996. A new vinification cellar was constructed in 2000. It is a Sauternes which needs patience.

See *Grands Vins*, p. 567.

Château Romer du Hayot

OWNER: André du Hayot.
COMMUNE: Fargues.
SURFACE AREA UNDER VINE: 16 ha plus 5 en fermage – 70% Sémillon; 25% Sauvignon;

5% Muscadelle.
SECOND WINE: Château Andoyse du Hayot.
OTHER WINE: Château Guiteronde.
CLASSIFICATION: Deuxième Cru (1855).

One of the more obscure of the Sauternes classed growths, Romer du Hayot is two estates, yet made as one wine. The château was demolished when the *autoroute* was built. The vines lie across this *autoroute* from Château de Malle, about as far away from Rieussec and Château de Fargues as you can get and still remain within the commune. The wines are made at Château Guiteronde, near Caillou in Barsac.

Romer first appears as Château Montalier in the accounts of Wilhelm Franck and Cocks & Féret prior to 1855. It was owned by Comte de la Myre-Mory. By 1855 itself the name Romer has arrived. Montalier we know now was a one-time proprietor. Romer we assume was a predecessor. The property was split between the Comtesse's heirs in 1881. In 1937 the larger sector was acquired by the mother of André du Hayot. Meanwhile in 1911 the Farges family had bought a 5-hectare rump owned by other heirs of the Myre-Morys. Since 1976, following the death of Roger Farges, André du Hayot has farmed this parcel. He now treats Romer as one single estate.

When I first came across the wine it was not the product of a rigorous botrytis-seeking selection, and it was both vinified and matured in vat. It was bottled early. It was usually clean, but it was merely a sweet wine. M. Hayot would rarely send a sample along to my annual blind vintage tastings on the spot in April.

Today the wines are aged in cask, though still fermented in stainless steel. The cellars are clean and air-conditioned. But there was still no noble rot discernable in the 1997 where there should have been.

Château Roumieu

OWNER: Catherine Craveia-Goyaud.
COMMUNE: Barsac.

SURFACE AREA UNDER VINE: 16.3 ha – 89%
Sémillon; 10% Sauvignon; 1% Muscadelle.

The place-name Roumieu means a stopping-off point on the pilgrim's way to the shrine of Saint James of Compostella. Consequently there is a scallop shell (the emblem of Saint James) depicted on the label. The property belonged to the Dubourg and Mercier families in 1868, and passed to the Dubourgs a dozen years later, but seems to have been divided in the 1890s. The largest element passed to the Goyauds. Mme Craveia succeeded her father Pierre in 1983.

Château Roumieu has a high reputation. Both Bernard Ginestet and Cocks & Féret class it as the best of Barsac's non-classed growths. Potentially, at least, this is fully justified. The wine is both fermented and aged in wood and the vines are well placed, adjoining those of Château Doisy-Védrines in Haut-Barsac. What I have seen of post-1986 vintages I have liked. But I have not seen mature Roumieus very often.

Château Roumieu-Lacoste

OWNER: Hervé Dubourdieu.
COMMUNE: Barsac.
SURFACE AREA UNDER VINE: 11 ha –

100% Sémillon.
SECOND WINE: Château Ducasse.
OTHER WINE: Château Graville-Lacoste (Graves).

As mentioned above, the Roumieu estate was divided in the 1890s, when a section passed to Léon Lacoste, Hervé Dubourdieu's great-grandfather. Hervé's uncle is Pierre Dubourdieu of nearby Château Doisy-Daëne. The château lies opposite to Château Climens with the vines surrounding it, a substantial element of which are quite old.

Roumieu-Lacoste is produced in an up-to-date winery complete with a pneumatic press and temperature-controlled, stainless steel tanks. The wine is aged in a mixture of vat and newish barrels, and is clean, plump and of good style. Dubourdieu also produces a commendable cask-fermented white Graves from vines at Pujols-sur-Ciron.

Château Saint-Amand

OWNER: Anne-Mary Facchetti-Ricard.

COMMUNE: Preignac.

SURFACE AREA UNDER VINE: 20 ha – 85% Sémillon; 14% Sauvignon; 1% Muscadelle.

SECOND WINE: Château Solon.

OTHER WINE: Château de La Chartreuse (Sauternes).

Saint Amand was Bishop of Bordeaux in 404 AD. He is the patron saint of brewers. On this estate, which lies close to both the river Ciron and the river Garonne, there are the remains of a ninth-century chapel dedicated to him. The Ricards have been owners here for more than 300 years.

I have known this wine longer than most. For many years it was shipped and bottled in England by Sichel, who sold it as Château La Chartreuse. Today, as then, it is fermented in tank, given a short time in wood and bottled early. It is an agreeable wine, plump and fruity. I have also found it consistent.

Château Sigalas-Rabaud ★

OWNER: Lambert des Granges family; managed by Cordier Mestrezat & Domaines.

COMMUNE: Bommes.

SURFACE AREA UNDER VINE: 13 ha – 85% Sémillon;

15% Sauvignon.

CLASSIFICATION: Premier Cru (1855).

Following the final split between this estate and its neighbour Château Rabaud-Promis, Sigalas-Rabaud passed to the Marquis René Lambert des Granges, who had married one of Gaston Drouillet de Sigalas' daughters. He has been succeeded by his son, Comte Emmanuel. At the end of 1994 Cordier, owners of neighbouring Château Lafaurie-Peyraguey, took a minority interest. They now manage the estate.

In contrast to its neighbour Rabaud-Promis, Sigalas-Rabaud produced better wine than most during Sauternes' doldrums of the 1960s and 1970s. The 1962, 1967 and 1971 are among the successes of the vintage, as is the 1975 (the 1976 aged fast, lacking grip). Though at the time the wine was both fermented and partially aged in tank, yields were small and the fruit properly botrytised. Today, both vinification and maturing is in oak, 60 per cent of which is new, and the wine is even better. This is the most powerful of the Bommes wines, often 14.5° or more. The 1997 is very fine, so is the 2002.

See *Grands Vins*, p. 572.

Château Suau

OWNER: Roger Biarnes.

COMMUNE: Barsac.

SURFACE AREA UNDER VINE: 8.1 ha – 80% Sémillon;
10% Sauvignon; 10% Muscadelle.

OTHER WINES: Château du Coy (Sauternes);
Château de Navarro (Graves).

CLASSIFICATION: Deuxième Cru (1855).

This is an obscure classed growth, and, it has to be said, justifiably so. It takes its name from Élie de Suau, a court official to Louis XIV. The property passed by marriage to the Lur-Saluces family, who sold it in 1793. In the early nineteenth century it belonged to the Pédesclaux family, Bordeaux brokers who gave their name to a Fifth Growth in Pauillac. Later it was sold to Émile Garros, estate manager at Yquem, whose successors passed it on to Daniel Biarnes in 1960, but retained the château. It is now run by Daniel's son, Roger. The wine is made at Château de Navarro in Illats, the vines lying alongside the *route nationale* at the southern end of Barsac, and is vinified in tank. It is no more than medium-sweet, without much botrytis, and often a bit sulphury, though reasonably clean underneath. Even in the great Sauternes vintages (1988, 1989, 1990, 1997) it never scores better than 'quite good'.

Château Suduiraut ★★

OWNERS: AXA Millésimes; director: Christian
Seely.

COMMUNE: Preignac.

SURFACE AREA UNDER VINE: 90 ha – 90% Sémillon;
10% Sauvignon.

SECOND WINE: Castelnau de Suduiraut.

OTHER WINES: Château Cantenac-Brown
(Margaux); Château Petit-Village (Pomerol);
Château Pichon-Longueville (Pauillac) and
others.

CLASSIFICATION: Premier Cru (1855).

Suduiraut lies north of Yquem on the highest slopes of Preignac. It is an impressive château, dating from the time of the Suduirauts in the seventeenth and eighteenth centuries. The extensive park is said to have been laid out by Le Nôtre, the renowned French architect and garden designer. At the beginning of the nineteenth century it passed to the du Roy family who enlarged it. At the time of the 1855 Classification it belonged to the Guillot brothers. There was then a series of owners, during which time things were allowed to decline, before Léopold Fonquernie, a rich industrialist from the north of France, took over in 1940. AXA Millésimes bought Suduiraut from Fonquernie's daughters in 1992.

I have had some magnificent older bottles, notably the 1899 and 1949, but for much of the latter half of the twentieth century I felt Suduiraut was over-cropped, picked too early and lacked real *premier cru* concentration. It was flowery and elegant but had no real depth or botrytis intensity. Moreover the *crème de la crème* was siphoned off to a Cuvée Madame in suitable vintages from 1982 onwards. There has been a distinct improvement since AXA Millésimes arrived in 1992. The 1997, 2001 and 2002 are excellent while the 1988–1990 trio are no better than 'good'.

See *Grands Vins*, p. 546.

Château La Tour Blanche ★

OWNER: Ministry of Agriculture; director: Corinne Reulet.

COMMUNE: Bommes.

SURFACE AREA UNDER VINE: 40 ha – 80% Sauvignon; 15% Sémillon; 5% Muscadelle.

SECOND WINE: Les Charmilles de Tour Blanche.

OTHER WINES: Isis (Bordeaux Blanc); Osiris (Bordeaux Blanc).

CLASSIFICATION: Premier Cru (1855).

Though there is an isolated tower on the estate, it is not the one depicted on the label. In fact the property is named after Jean Saint-Marc de Latourblanche, treasurer general at the time of Louis XIV. There is then a historical hiatus until the arrival of M. Focke from the Rhineland in the 1830s. Focke is said in all the older books to have introduced the idea of botrytised wines to the Sauternes area. It has now been established that, at least at Yquem, nobly-rotten wines were being produced as early as the 1750s. But no doubt M. Focke played his part. We can see that elsewhere in the region yields fell in the second quarter of the nineteenth century, which would indicate a general move to the luscious wines we expect today.

Following Focke's death his widow sold La Tour Blanche in 1860. It then passed to Daniel Osiris, financier, umbrella-maker and amateur oenologist. Focke bequeathed his property to the state on condition that it should be used as an agricultural school. At first the French government were more interested in the school than the wine, and from 1924 to 1955 the vines were leased out on a share-cropping basis to the Cordiers of Château Lafaurie-Peyraguey. It was not until the arrival of a new director, Jean-Paul Jausserand, in 1983, however, that the wine began to justify its position as top of the First Growths (Yquem is a *Premier Grand Cru*, in a category of its own). Since then progress has been significant. The 1990 can be particularly recommended.

See *Grands Vins*, p. 532.

Château d'Yquem ★★★

OWNER: LVMH (Louis Vuitton-Moët-Hennessy).

COMMUNE: Sauternes.

SURFACE AREA UNDER VINE: 108 ha –

80% Sémillon; 20% Sauvignon.

OTHER WINE: Ygrec (Bordeaux Blanc).

CLASSIFICATION: Premier Grand Cru (1855).

Château d'Yquem is the apex qualitatively and the centre geographically of the Sauternes area. Each major property occupies its own little hill. Yquem's is the highest. It is also the largest estate, the most perfectionistic, the most consistent. Unlike the rest of the region there was no cutting of corners, no lack of investment, no dip in quality in the sad days of the 1960s and 1970s.

Until the recent acquisition by LVMH, Yquem could boast that it was the sole leading property in Bordeaux which had belonged to the same family, the Lur-Saluces, since before the French Revolution. Indeed there has only been a single change of ownership, and that through marriage, since 1593, when Jacques de Sauvage, local treasurer to the king, an ancestor of whom was mayor of Bordeaux in the fourteenth century, took over as tenant of what was then the royal property of

Yquem. The château, conceived as a medieval fortified *manoir*, has its origins before this time, though largely rebuilt in the Renaissance style somewhat later.

On 6th June 1785 a magnificent wedding, uniting two of the leading families in the area, took place. Joséphine de Sauvage d'Yquem married Louis-Amédée de Lur-Saluces of Château de Fargues. Their descendants married into and became involved in a number of local Sauternes estates: Filhot, Coutet, de Malle and others over the next couple of centuries. In 1999, rather against the will of Comte Alexandre de Lur-Saluces, who lives at Yquem and ran the estate on behalf of his extended family, Yquem was sold to LVMH. Nothing, however, seems to have changed as far as the production of the wine is concerned.

At Yquem we have Sauternes winemaking at its most perfectionistic. The vines are pruned to yield 9 hl/ha – one glass of wine per vine (as opposed to a full bottle in a classed growth red wine château). Collection of the grapes is berry by botrytised berry, rather than by bunch or half-bunch elsewhere. The grapes are crushed in a small horizontal hydraulic press in three stages. Unlike in Champagne, for example, the first pressing does not necessarily give the best wine. There is no *débourbage* before the wine is put into cask. Fermentation and ageing is in new oak, of course, the latter taking place in a splendid underground cellar, constructed in 1987. The *assemblage* is late and the wine is not bottled for three years or more. Only then is it put on the market.

Yquem has been criticised occasionally for offering off-vintages, such as 1963 or 1968, which should have been beneath its dignity to sell. If non-botrytised Sauternes is an oxymoron it is even more so at Yquem prices, which are three times that of its nearest competitor. A glance at the château's statistics over the last generation shows, however, the rigour that is applied. In 1973 and 1978, perfectly ripe years, 85 per cent was rejected in the make-up of the *grand vin*; in 1979 60 per cent. Often there is no *grand vin*. Nor is there a second wine. What is not required is sold off anonymously in bulk.

There is something very special, and indeed very consistent, about Yquem. The wine is more oaky than most in its youth. It is by quite some way the richest, most concentrated, most intense wine of its kind. In great years – I have a marginal preference for 1989 over 1990 and 1988 – it is nectar: the liquid quintessence of concentrated sunbeams, to quote Thomas Love Peacock. In vintages which lack botrytis it is one of the few sweet wines of interest: though I would not personally fork out the cost of a bottle.

There is also a dry wine, called Ygrec. This used to be dry, hard and rather charmless. In 2000 the the vinification was changed to produce a *demi-sec* wine. It was still a bit rigid, but in 2002 it was vinified entirely in old wood. This version is a great success.

See *Grands Vins*, p. 524.

THE LESSER
SWEET WHITE
WINE AREAS

Medium-sweet white wines – less luscious, less botrytis-affected, less concentrated and earlier maturing than those of Sauternes and Barsac – are found on the left bank of the river Garonne, immediately north of Barsac in the commune of Cérons, and on the opposite side of the river in Sainte-Croix-du-Mont and Loupiac. These are all *appellations* which date from the early days of proper laws on wine place names in the mid-1930s. In addition, more recently, a new *appellation*, Cadillac, was created in 1973 to cover the similarly sweet wines of the southern end of the Premières Côtes de Bordeaux.

It is important to note, when reviewing the economics and fortunes of these *appellations*, that growers in Cérons are equally entitled to produce Graves, red, white and Supérieures, from their vineyards, and those in Cadillac can also make Premières Côtes de Bordeaux. The only alternative for Sainte-Croix-du-Mont and Loupiac growers is Bordeaux Supérieur or Bordeaux.

Looking at the figures one can see that Cérons is a declining *appellation*. In the early 1970s production averaged 15,000 hectolitres a year. By the later 1980s this had fallen to 2650 hl per annum, one-sixth of what it had been. Cadillac, meanwhile, has never really caught on. The quality of Loupiac and Sainte-Croix-du-Mont, however, remains what it was 20 years ago. But one wonders what the figures would be if a fancier alternative was on offer.

For sadly, despite three great vintages – 1988, 1989 and 1990 – at the end of the 1980s, and successful vintages such as 1997 and 2001 more recently, there is little interest in these wines. This lack of fashion leads to a vicious declining spiral. No interest is followed by prices too low to make sufficient profit to be invested in things like new oak, fine-tuned selection and numerous *passages* though the vineyard. This leads to inferior quality in all but the most altruistic estates, which in turn leads to a reduction in quality, even less interest and even lower prices. Given in addition the failure of the climate to produce years conducive to the preparation of sweet wine more regularly than one year in three, on average, it is a surprise to find anyone bothering at all. And a relief to find that there are, in fact, a good dozen or so estates where you *can* find good wines in good vintages.

There is not a lot of difference between Loupiac and Sainte-Croix-du-Mont, adjacent *appellations* up on the plateau on top of a steep hill above the Garonne on its right bank. The soil here is essentially clay-limestone, a relatively cool environment for the vine. The fruit concentrates as much by dehydration as by noble rot. As a result the wines have a tendency to be a little four-square. This applies equally to the little amount of Cadillac produced a little further north.

On the opposite side of the river, in Cérons, not only is the soil different, being a sandy gravel on a limestone base, but the vineyards can benefit, as do those in the nearby Sauternes region, from the morning-mist and afternoon-sun mesoclimate engendered by the nearby river Ciron. Noble rot or *pourriture noble* is more common.

The wines are not dissimilar to lesser Sauternes and Barsacs. Moreover, with the advantage of the Graves *appellations* to fall back on in less good years, growers can confine their sweet wine production to just the old vines in the best sites. As a result, perhaps, Cérons is the most interesting of these lesser sweet wines.

In general, however, I find the wines fall between two stools. They are not intense and rich enough to make dessert wines. But they are too sweet to accompany food. Perhaps their best role is as aperitif wines. My palate usually prefers something drier, sadly. They are best drunk young, between the ages of three and eight years. Few properties and few vintages produce anything capable of ageing well for any longer.

CÉRONS

SURFACE AREA (2002): 63 ha.

PRODUCTION (2002): 1622 hl.

COLOUR & STYLE: Sweet white.

GRAPE VARIETIES: Sémillon; Sauvignon; Muscadelle.

MAXIMUM YIELD: 40 hl/ha.

MINIMUM ALCOHOLIC DEGREE: 12.5°.

The name Cérons derives from the Gallo-Roman 'Sirione' (as may well also the name Ciron, the famous morning mist-producing tributary of the Garonne, which enters the main river some 5 kilometres to the south). This denotes a place where the Garonne could be forded at low tide.

The *appellation* covers the inland parish of Illats as well as the commune of Podensac to the north. All this covers some 1000 hectares, but the locals have the option of producing Graves *rouge*, *blanc sec* and the medium-sweet Graves Supérieures as well as the sweet Cérons. Some 80 per cent of the local production is, in fact,

Graves. Only some 80 hectares of vines produce the average of around 2500 hectolitres of Cérons.

The soil, a sandy gravel on a limestone base, is very similar to the other adjoining communes, whether Graves or Sauternes. The underlying rock is particularly hard at Cérons, and the remains of local quarries can be seen. This soil, plus the local mesoclimate, produce wines which if a little less *liquoreux*, can have the elegance of a Sauternes. The top wines are not unlike, and can rival, the lesser wines of Barsac and Preignac. It should be noted that, at 40 hl/ha, plus the possibility of PLC, that the official *rendement* is ridiculously high for the production of quality sweet wines.

CÉRONS LEADING ESTATES

Château de Cérons

OWNER: Jean Perromat.
COMMUNE: Cérons.
SURFACE AREA UNDER VINE: 12 ha – 85% Sémillon;
15% Sauvignon.
OTHER WINE: Château du Calvimont (Graves).

This is the senior estate in the *appellation*, though it is not the size it used to be, having been cut in two when the main Bordeaux to Langon highway was constructed in the late 1840s, after which the divided parts were sold off separately. The elegant château was built at the end of the seventeenth century, and faces Cérons' twelfth-century church in the middle of the village. It has been in Jean Perromat's hands since 1958. Perromat picks by *tris*, up to a dozen *passages* through the vineyards between late September and late November, vinified in wood (50 per cent new), and bottles late, more than three years after the vintage. The wines are rich, concentrated, profound and elegant, at least the equal of a Sauternes Second Growth. They also age well. The 1983 was still young in February 2002.

See *The Vine*, No 211, August 2002.

Grand Enclos du Château de Cérons

OWNER: Olivier Lataste.
COMMUNE: Cérons.
SURFACE AREA UNDER VINE: 6 ha – 70% Sémillon;
20% Sauvignon; 10% Muscadelle.
OTHER WINE: Château Lamouroux (Graves).

This is the 'other half' of the Château de Cérons, separately sold off in 1855. For much of the following century it was considered the better estate. This may not be currently true but the wine can nevertheless be a great success. The vines are old. The 1990 is delicious.

Château Huradin

OWNER: Daniel & Catherine Lafosse.
COMMUNE: Cérons.

SURFACE AREA UNDER VINE: 2.3 ha –
100% Sémillon.

This estate has come down to Daniel Lafosse through his wife's family. Older vintages, of which there are still some for sale, are labelled Yves Ricaud, the previous proprietor. No oak is used here at all, but despite this the wines are good; and in the case of the 1997 and 1985, very good.

The following estates also produce good Cérons on a regular basis, even if in limited quantities, (see the Graves chapter for further details): in Cérons: Château du Seuil; in Illats: Château Archambaud; Château Arnicaud; Domaine du Hauret-Lalande.

SAINTE-CROIX-DU-MONT & LOUPIAC

The regulations for Sainte-Croix-du-Mont and Loupiac are identical. Note that the maximum yield is 40 hl/ha. In fact, as the figures will show, as at Cérons, the actual yield is below 30 hl/ha.

SURFACE AREA: (2002): Sainte-Croix du Mont: 393 ha; Loupiac: 404 ha.

PRODUCTION: (2002): Sainte-Croix du Mont: 13,030 hl; Loupiac: 13,167 hl.

COLOUR & STYLE: Sweet white.

GRAPE VARIETIES: Sémillon; Sauvignon; Muscadelle.

MAXIMUM YIELD: 40 hl/ha.

MINIMUM ALCOHOLIC DEGREE: 13°.

These two *appellations* lie side by side – Sainte-Croix du Mont to the south – opposite Barsac and Preignac. The land rises steeply away from the river. The vines are effectively on the clay-limestone soil of the plateau above. From the summit you get a splendid view west over the Sauternes region (Château d'Yquem is unmistakable) and into the forests of the Landes beyond. Like the Premières Côtes de Bordeaux, of which these vineyards are effectively an extension, and the Entre-Deux-Mers further inland, this is undulating countryside, the vines being reserved for the more favourable sites. With all the clay in the soil, this is a cool place to plant a vineyard. As a result, the wines concentrate as much by dehydration as by being affected by noble rot and they can be a bit pedestrian, lacking the raciness of a true Barsac while never reaching the luscious richness of a true Sauternes. There is little difference between the wines of the two communes.

Sainte-Croix-du-Mont Leading Châteaux

Château des Arroucats

OWNER: Annie Lapouge.
SURFACE AREA UNDER VINE: 30 ha – 80% Sémillon;
15% Sauvignon; 5% Muscadelle.
SECOND WINE: Château Dorléoc.

Mme Lapouge inherited Arroucats from her father Christian Labat who created the estate. No wood is used in the *élevage* but the grapes are harvested by *tris successifs* and the wine is clean, sweet and succulent. Prices are reasonable.

Château Bel Air

OWNER: Michel & Jean-Guy Méric.
SURFACE AREA UNDER VINE: 12 ha – 90% Sémillon; 10% Sauvignon.
OTHER WINES: Château Croix de Bern (Premières Côtes de Bordeaux); Château Haut-Valentin (Cadillac).

Jean-Guy Méric has now taken over from his father, and, in contrast to hitherto, part of the crop is fermented and aged in wood, of which one-third is new. This *cuvée* is called Prestige. This replaces Crème de Tête, a description no longer permitted. The 1997 is very good.

Château Crabitan-Bellevue

OWNER: Bernard & Nicolas Solane.
SURFACE AREA UNDER VINE: 22 ha – 91% Sémillon;
8% Sauvignon; 1% Muscadelle.
SECOND WINE: Clos de Crabitan.

Bernard Solane's ancestors were coopers. They took over half the old Crabitan estate in 1970 and have since enlarged it. A further 22 or so hectares nearby produce Premières Côtes de Bordeaux. The best Sainte-Croix-du-Mont, only produced in the good vintages, is the *Cuvée Spéciale*. It is vinified and aged entirely in wood, one-third of which is new. The oak flavour is very obvious in the wine when it is young. But it can handle it. It ages well.

Château La Grave

OWNER: Jean-Marie Tinon.
SURFACE AREA UNDER VINE: 11 ha – 90% Sémillon; 10% Sauvignon.
OTHER WINE: Château Grand-Peyrot (Sainte-Croix-du-Mont).

Look out here for the special *cuvée* called Sentiers d'Automne. This is vinified and aged in wood, part of which is new, while the basic *cuvée* is not. M. Tinon also produces good sweet wine at the 5-hectare Château Grand-Peyrot.

Château Loubens

OWNER: Arnaud de Sèze.
SURFACE AREA UNDER VINE: 15 ha – 95% Sémillon;
5% Sauvignon.
SECOND WINE: Château de Tours.

Château Loubens can boast a history which dates back to the sixteenth century, when it belonged to a Bordeaux parliamentarian called Pierre de Spens de Lancre. In 1620 Louis XIII, hunting in the area, spent the night here. In the nineteenth century it came into the hands of the Sèze family, who rebuilt the château, and established the wine's reputation as the leading *cru* in the *appellation*, a position it still holds today, shared with Château La Rame. The vast cellars, hewed out of the rock, which is formed here out of a bank of fossilised oysters, descend to a depth of 70 metres. The wine does not see any wood, being matured in tank for three years before bottling. Yet it is rich, profound, classy and with no lack, usually, of noble rot. It will keep well.

Château du Mont

OWNER: Paul & Hervé Chouvac.
SURFACE AREA UNDER VINE: 15 ha – 70% Sémillon;
20% Sauvignon; 10% Muscadelle.

This estate has been producing very good sweet wine, vinified and aged in wood, one-third of which is new, for some years. In 1999 they introduced a *tête de cuvée*: Cuvée Pierre. This is really most impressive: both splendidly concentrated and splendidly elegant.

Château du Pavillon

OWNER: Alain & Viviane Fertal.
SURFACE AREA UNDER VINE: 4.5 ha – 85% Sémillon;
15% Sauvignon.
OTHER WINE: Château Les Roques (Loupiac).

Alain and Viviane Fertal arrived at Pavillon in 1994, having purchased this and the neighbouring Château Les Roques from the d'Arfeuille family. The Sainte-Croix-du-Mont is vinified in tank. Only 10 per cent is aged in wood. The wine has reasonable class and dimension. The château itself is most attractive, and the view across the Garonne excellent.

Château La Rame

OWNER: Yves Armand.
SURFACE AREA UNDER VINE: 20 ha – 80% Sémillon;
20% Sauvignon.

One of the largest and one of the best estates in the *appellation*, La Rame lies at the southern end of the commune and has been in the hands of the Armand family since 1956. Great progress has been made here since 1986, when Yves Armand took over. Since then the property has been enlarged, three different *cuvées* produced and cryo-extraction facilities acquired.

The best wine is the Réserve du Château, vinified and aged in wood of which one-third is new. This wine has no lack of botrytis and it ages well. M. Armand also produces a good Blanc Sec, La Caussade and he used to produce a Premières Côtes de Bordeaux *rouge*, Domaine de la Barrail Charmille. These are also good. From the 2002 vintage the Domaine de Barrail wine has been bottled as Château La Rame.

LOUPIAC LEADING CHÂTEAUX

Château du Cros

OWNER: Michel Boyer.

SURFACE AREA UNDER VINE: 38.5 ha –
70% Sémillon; 20% Sauvignon;
10% Muscadelle.

SECOND WINE: Fleur de Cros.

OTHER WINES: Château Lépine (Sainte-Croix-du-Mont); Château des Lucques (Barsac); Château Mayne du Cros (Cérons); Clos L'Olivier (Loupiac); Château des Roches (Loupiac).

South of the village, on top of the escarpment above the Garonne, where the cliff is almost vertical, is the Château du Cros, a stronghold constructed in the thirteenth and fourteenth centuries. In 1921, François Thevenot, grandfather of Michel Boyer, bought the estate from the Comte de la Chassaigne, a descendant of the philospher, Michel de Montaigne.

The wine is vinified and matured in wood, the proportion of new oak varying with the quality of the vintage. It is fresh and elegant rather than intensely sweet and luscious, but is still one of the best examples of the *appellation*. There is a very good, dry white, Le Cros Bois et Tradition.

Clos Jean

OWNER: Lionel Bord.

SURFACE AREA UNDER VINE: 13 ha – 80% Sémillon;
15% Sauvignon; 5% Muscadelle.

SECOND WINE: Château Loustalot.

OTHER WINE: Château Rondillon (Loupiac).

Clos Jean has belonged to the Bord family since 1813. The château is a pretty *maison girondine* and it lies on a little hill above its vines. Nearby, a brand new *chai* and vinification centre have been constructed. The wines from the 9-hectare Château Rondillon in Loupiac are made here as well. Fermentation of both wines is in tank, and 50 per cent of the wine is matured in oak. The wines are clean and floral, Clos Jean having a bit more richness and depth. There is a good dry white, Clos Jean, Bordeaux Blanc.

Château Loupiac-Gaudiet

OWNER: Marc Ducau; manager: Daniel
Sanfourche.

SURFACE AREA UNDER VINE: 25 ha – 80% Sémillon;
20% Sauvignon.

The elegant château, a *chartreuse* flanked by two *pavillons*, approached through an avenue of plane trees, lies near Loupiac's fine twelfth-century Romanesque church. It has belonged to the Ducau family for four generations. The basic wine is not wood-aged, and is clean and fresh. The *tête de cuvée*, Château de Loupiac, is a more serious, oaky example which needs five years to mature.

Château Mémoires

OWNER: Jean-François Menard.

SURFACE AREA UNDER VINE: 55 ha (6 ha of Loupiac

– 80% Sémillon; 15% Muscadelle;
8% Sauvignon).

Château Mémoires is located in the commune of Saint-Maixant, south of Sainte-Croix-du-Mont. As well as Loupiac, Cadillac and Premières Côtes de Bordeaux *rouge* are produced, as is a dry white wine, Fleur d'Opile. Today there are two levels of the two sweet wines on offer, the lesser examples of which are only aged, not vinified, in wood. The top *cuvée*, Grains d'Or, can have as much as 80 per cent new wood. No Grains d'Or Loupiac was produced between 1996 and 2001, which seems a bit odd as certainly, on the face of it, 1997 and 2001 were most successful. Quality is, therefore, variable.

Domaine du Noble

OWNER: Patrick Dejean.
SURFACE AREA UNDER VINE: 13 ha – 85% Sémillon; 15% Sauvignon.
SECOND WINE: Château du Gascon.

This is an unpretentious set-up, but still produces some very good wines. Vinification and *élevage* are in wood, one-quarter of which is new. The wine is clean, rich, elegant and harmonious. It will keep well.

Château de Ricaud

OWNER: Alain Thienot; manager: James François.
SURFACE AREA UNDER VINE: 20 ha – 80% Sémillon; 15% Sauvignon; 5% Muscadelle.

Records here date back to 1451 when the estate belonged to Bernard de Lamensans, a colleague of Gaston Le Foix. Today's château, surrounded by a little park set back from the village of Loupiac, dates from the mid-nineteenth century. It is a splendidly absurd Gothic folly. Since 1980 the property has belonged to the Champenois Alain Thiénot. Fermentation is in tank, maturation in oak. There has been much progress here in the last 20 years and today the wines are very good. The Premières Côtes de Bordeaux is also good – here the estate has 55 hectares under vines.

Château Les Roques

OWNER: Alain Fertal.
SURFACE AREA UNDER VINE: 4 ha – 85% Sémillon; 15% Sauvignon.
OTHER WINE: Château du Pavillon (Sainte-Croix-du-Mont).

There is no château, as such, this name referring to the vines of Alain Fertal which lie over the border in Loupiac. The two wines are made at Château du Pavillon. The Cuvée Frantz, first made in 1999, is the superior one. Rich, honeyed and classy, it is very good indeed. Drink it after five years.

CADILLAC

SURFACE AREA (2002): 215 ha.

PRODUCTION (2002): 5482 hl.

COLOUR & STYLE: Sweet white.

GRAPE VARIETIES: Sémillon; Sauvignon; Muscadelle.

MAXIMUM YIELD: 40 hl/ha.

MINIMUM ALCOHOLIC DEGREE: 12°.

The *appellation* Cadillac was created in 1973 and revised significantly in 1980 to embrace the sweet wines of the southern half of the Premières Côtes de Bordeaux. This *appellation* covers the following 22 communes: Baurech, Béguey, Cadillac, Capian, Cardan, Donzac, Gabarnac, Haux, Langoiran, Laroque, Lestiac, Le Tourne, Monprimblanc, Omet, Paillet, Rions, Saint-Germain-de-Grave, Saint-Maixant, Semens, Tabanac, Verdelais and Villenave-de-Rions.

The most northerly is Baurech, which lies opposite Portets; the most southerly Saint-Maixant, opposite Langon. Throughout, growers have the option between making Cadillac, sweet wine, Premières Côtes de Bordeaux, red, or, if they wish to produce dry white wine, Bordeaux or Bordeaux Supérieur. In practice some 240 hectares are given over to the sweet wine, about 2000 hectares to red wine, and 1000 to dry white.

Very few estates make more than a token quantity of Cadillac and then only in the best vintages. Many of the growers in Loupiac and Sainte-Croix-du-Mont also have land in the Cadillac *appellation*.

CADILLAC LEADING CHÂTEAU

Château Fayau

OWNER: Jean Médeville & Fils.
SURFACE AREA UNDER VINE: 10 ha – 90% Sémillon;
   10% Sauvignon.
SECOND WINE: Réserve Jean Médeville.

OTHER WINES: Château Barbier (Sauternes);
   Château Boyrein (Graves); Château Gréteau-Médeville (Bordeaux Supérieur); Château du Juge (Bordeaux Blanc); Château Pessan (Graves).

This is the leading Cadillac estate, and the centre of the Médeville family's 180-ha wine empire. Fayau in fact is 36 hectares, but only some 6–10 hectares are devoted to sweet wines. One of these is vinified and stored in tank, bottled at three years old. A superior *cuvée* is fermented and reared in wood. It is concentrated more by *passerillage* (evaporation) than botrytis but is rich and ripe, if rather oaky in its youth. Even the basic wine, in good years such as 1997, is wholly admirable.

Other Cadillacs of note include the following: Château Carsin (Juha Berglund, Rions); Château de Cèdres (Vignobles Larroque, Paillet); Château du Juge (Pierre Dupleich, Cadillac); Château Reynon (Denis & Florence Dubourdieu, Béguey); Château Peybrun (Catherine de Loze, Cadillac); Clos Sainte-Anne (Francis Courselle, Capian).

PREMIÈRES CÔTES DE BORDEAUX

SURFACE AREA (2002): Red: 3496 ha. White: 310 ha.

PRODUCTION (2002): Red: 150,188 hl. White: 10,553 hl.

COLOUR & STYLE: Red & medium-sweet white.

GRAPE VARIETIES: Red: Cabernet Sauvignon; Cabernet
Franc; Carmenère; Merlot; Malbec; Petit Verdot.

White: Sémillon; Sauvignon; Muscadelle.

MAXIMUM YIELD: Red & White: 50 hl/ha.

MINIMUM ALCOHOLIC DEGREE: Red: 10.5°; White: 11.5°.

The Premières Côtes de Bordeaux *appellation* run northwards on the right bank of the river Garonne between Saint-Maixant, south of Loupiac, to Bouliac, opposite Bordeaux, plus an isolated sector outside the Bordeaux suburbs of Lormont, between the A10 *autoroute* and the N89 Bordeaux-Libourne highway. This consists of 37 communes (in alphabetical order) – Bassens, Baurech, Béguey, Bouliac, Cadillac, Cambes, Camblanes, Capian, Carbon-Blanc, Cardan, Carignan, Cénas, Cenon, Donzac, Floriac, Garbanac, Haux, Langoiran, Laroque, Latresne, Lestiac-sur-Garonne, Lormont, Monprimblanc, Omet, Paillet, Quinsac, Rions, Saint-Caprais-de-Bordeaux, Sainte-Eulalie, Saint-Germain-de-Grave, Saint-Maixant, Semens, Tabanac, Le Tourne, Verdelais, Villenave de Rions, Yvrac. The name of the commune can be added to that of the *appellation* for reds with a natural alcohol level of 11.5° or higher. I have yet to see an example.

The southern half of the Premières Côtes, from Baurech southwards, is equally entitled to the *appellation* Cadillac: a semi-sweet white wine. Not all the growers declare under the Premières Côtes label. Many find the wine easier to sell as plain Bordeaux, which is the designation they have to use for their dry white wine. It is estimated that, in addition to what is declared as Premières Côtes, a further 2740 hectares of red and 1500 hectares of white produce Bordeaux or Bordeaux Supérieur.

The soil structure is variable. To the north there is gravel and sand mixed with clay; to the south more marly soil, all on a limestone base. The plateau at the top of the slope plus the slopes themselves are the best locations for vines. Most of the more alluvial soil, down-slope from the D10 road which runs along close by the river Garonne, is excluded from the *appellation*. The further one journeys inland, the more clay there is in the soil, and the less distinguished the wine. Hence the border, some 5 kilometres inland, between Premières Côtes and Entre-Deux-Mers.

This is a region which has seen a welcome renaissance in the last decade. There has been the arrival of enterprising outsiders such as Juha Berglund at Château Carsin, with his Australian winemaker, Mandy Jones. Others, such as the d'Halluins at Clos Bourbon, have arrived from elsewhere in France. Most producers now offer a *cuvée prestige*, aged with a proportion of new oak. Frequently we now find Libournais *oenologues* such as Louis Mitjaville (at Château Carignan) involved in the production of the red wines. Professor Denis Dubourdieu, who has his own estate in Béguey, Château Reyon, is another major influence.

The white wine under the Premières Côtes de Bordeaux label, being medium sweet, is in my view a neither-one-or-the-other sort of wine, and of minor interest. Prior to 1973, before the imposition of appellation laws in the UK and before the invention of Cadillac, much Premières Côtes left France to re-emerge in Britain as generic Sauternes. Happily those days are long behind us. But only a few estates make a noteworthy example of this wine. For most if they make a sweet wine it is Cadillac or nothing.

Good addresses include: Clos du Moine (Jean-Michel Barbet at Sainte-Croix-du-Mont); Château Crabitan-Bellevue (Bernard Solane & Fils at Sainte-Croix-du-Mont); Château Haut-Moulin (Vignobles Sanfourche at Donzac); Château Margoton (Francis Courrèges at Saint-Caprais-de-Bordeaux); and Château de Teste (Laurent Réglat at Monprimblanc).

Premières Côtes de Bordeaux Leading Châteaux

Château La Bertrande

OWNERS: Anne-Marie Gillet.
COMMUNE: Omet.
SURFACE AREA UNDER VINE: Red: 9.5 ha –

40% Merlot; 30% Cabernet Sauvignon;
20% Cabernet Franc; 10% Petit Verdot. White:
2 ha – 70% Sémillon; 30% Sauvignon.

The commune of Omet is set away from the river, above Cadillac. Mme Gillet produces a rich, ripe, medium to medium- to full-bodied red wine with plenty of personality. The 1998 is particularly good. Cadillac is also produced when the vintage permits. But sadly it has not come my way.

Château de Birot

OWNER: Éric & Hélène Fournier-Castéja.
COMMUNE: Béguey.
SURFACE AREA UNDER VINE: Red: 17 ha –
64% Merlot; 20% Cabernet Sauvignon;

11% Cabernet Franc; 5% Malbec. White: 4 ha –
66% Sémillon; 30% Sauvignon; 4% Muscadelle.
SECOND WINE: Enclos de Birot.

In 1989 the charming Éric Fournier, the man behind Château Canon in its pre-Chanel days, bought Château de Birot, one of the most elegant buildings in the Bordeaux region, dating from the second half of the eighteenth century. The red wine is firmer than most, with plenty of fruit and depth. There is also a neat fresh white Bordeaux, briefly aged in barrels, and Cadillac, in suitable years.

Clos Bourbon

OWNER: SCEA Clos Bourbon; director: Catherine
d'Halluin.
COMMUNE: Paillet.
SURFACE AREA UNDER VINE: Red: 4 ha –

70% Merlot; 15% Cabernet Sauvignon;
15% Cabernet Franc. White: 1 ha –
80% Sémillon; 15% Sauvignon; 5% Muscadelle.
SECOND WINE: Château La Rose Bourbon.

Clos Bourbon, which lies halfway up the hill above Paillet, was bought in 1994 by Michel Boyer of Château du Cros in Loupiac for his daughter and her husband. The château, which dates from the seventeenth century, has been restored, at least in part, but with the d'Halluins' increasing family, is definitely a home rather than a museum piece. I like the wines. The Cuvée Vieillie en Fût de Chêne 2000 is soft, juicy, balanced and gently oaky. The 1998, slightly more austere, is very good too.

Château Brethous

OWNER: François & Denise Verdier.
COMMUNE: Camblanes-et-Meynac.
SURFACE AREA UNDER VINE: 13.7 ha – 67% Merlot;

23% Cabernet Franc; 5% Cabernet Sauvignon;
5% Malbec.

The Verdiers arrived at this charming, eighteenth-century chartreuse in 1964, totally replanted the vineyard and constructed an attractive, vaulted *chai*. The harvest is gathered by machine and largely vinified in tank. The Cuvée Prestige is partly aged in new oak (about one-third) and is a rich, fullish wine which ages well. The 1998 is an excellent example.

Château Carignan

OWNER: Philippe Pieraerts.
COMMUNE: Carignan.
SURFACE AREA UNDER VINE: 65 ha – 70% Merlot;
20% Cabernet Sauvignon; 10% Cabernet Franc.
SECOND WINE: L'Orangerie de Carignan.

The château dates from 1452. Philippe Pieraerts, who is now assisted by consulting *oenologue* Louis Mitjaville, acquired the property in 1981. There is a Cuvée Prima, from the young vines and for early drinking. The Château Carignan itself has long been one of the Premières Côtes' very best reds. It is lush and fat, even chocolatey in its youth. There is one-third new wood here. The 1998 came out top at a tasting of the vintage in February 2002.

Château Carsin

OWNER: Juha Berglund.
COMMUNE: Rions.
SURFACE AREA UNDER VINE: Red: 9.7 ha –
37% Cabernet Sauvignon; 36% Cabernet Franc;
27% Merlot. White: 17.7 ha – 56% Sémillon;
44% Sauvignon.
SECOND WINE: Domaine de L'Esclade.

The Finn Juha Berglund acquired Château Carsin in 1990 and has since enlarged it significantly. The wines are well made, consistent and sell for competitive prices. The Cuvée Noire, alternatively labelled as Cuvée Prestige *rouge*, is aged partially in new wood and needs three years' ageing. The five different white *cuvées*, all sold as Bordeaux Blanc, are also very good. There is a less oaky basic *cuvée*, a more oaky Cuvée Prestige, occasionally a 100 per cent Sauvignon Gris and a Cadillac.

Château de Chelivette

OWNER: Jean-Louis Boulière.
COMMUNE: Sainte-Eulalie.
SURFACE AREA UNDER VINE: 2.1 ha – 65% Merlot;
25% Cabernet Sauvignon; 10% Cabernet Franc.

A small vineyard, but an ancient domaine, with buildings dating from the sixteenth century, a chapel and a dovecote as well as a château. This is a round, gently oaky, essentially soft-centred wine, but it has no lack of finesse.

Château La Chèze

OWNER: Jean-François Rontein & Vincent Priou.
COMMUNE: Capian.
SURFACE AREA UNDER VINE: Red: 9.5 ha –
50% Merlot; 30% Cabernet Sauvignon;
20% Cabernet Franc. White: 1 ha –
100% Sauvignon.

This sixteenth-century *maison noble* was acquired in 1986 by Jean-Pierre and Claire Sancier who replanted the vineyard and sold on to the current owners, both qualified *oenologues*, in 1997. They make a stylish, succulent wine, gently oaky red in the *Élevé en fûts de chêne* version. The 1999 is good. The 2000 even better.

Château du Grand Plantier

OWNER: Albucher family.
COMMUNE: Monprimblanc.
SURFACE AREA UNDER VINE: Red: 11 ha –
70% Merlot; 25% Cabernet Sauvignon;
5% Cabernet Franc. White: 12 ha – 80%
Sémillon; 10% Sauvignon, 10% Muscadelle.

I have not had much experience of the red wines here, but I do know the white, and it is often delicious. Even in 2000, a vintage where a lot of whites lacked a certain sparkle, this was ripe and flowery, crisp and racy; for drinking quite soon.

Château du Juge

OWNER: Chantal David Dupleich.
COMMUNE: Cadillac.
SURFACE AREA UNDER VINE: Red: 14 ha –

70% Merlot; 30% Cabernet Sauvignon.
White: 10.4 ha – 70% Sémillon; 30% Sauvignon.
SECOND WINE: Cru Quinette.

It is the white wine which interests me most here. This is ripe and forward, with interesting quasi-tropical flavours which come from the high percentage of Sémillon: it is individual and well-balanced.

Château Langoiran

OWNER: SC Château Langoiran; manager: Nicolas
   Filou.
COMMUNE: Langoiran.
SURFACE AREA UNDER VINE: Red: 20 ha –

66% Merlot; 27% Cabernet Franc; 7% Cabernet
Sauvignon. White: 0.5 ha – 40% Sémillon;
30% Sauvignon; 30% Muscadelle.

Just south of the village of Langoiran lie the ruins of the twelfth-century château, a national monument. Hard by, an elegant, eighteenth-century *chartreuse* is the present Château Langoiran. The *chais,* carved into the hillside, are approached through the remains of the old chapel. The Cuvée Prestige here is rich and oaky, with no lack of weight. It has been improving in recent years. I prefer the 1999 to the 1998.

Château Laroche

OWNER: Julien & Martine Palau.
COMMUNE: Baurech.
SURFACE AREA UNDER VINE: Red: 21.7 ha –

60% Merlot; 20% Cabernet Sauvignon;
20% Cabernet Franc. White: 2.2 ha –
60% Sémillon; 40% Sauvignon Blanc.

Martine Palau is the driving force here. She and her husband bought Laroche in 1976 and have since enlarged the vineyard. The eighteenth-century château, with its sixteenth-century tower, is fine. The red grapes are picked mechanically and the wine, aged partly in wood, is very well made. Even the basic wine is very good. The more oaky Château Laroche Bel Air is complex and delicious. I have little experience of the white wine.

Château Lezongars

OWNER: Priac Holdings SA; manager: Philip Iles.
COMMUNE: Villenave-de-Rions.
SURFACE AREA UNDER VINE: Red: 39.2 ha –
   76% Merlot; 17% Cabernet Sauvignon;

7% Cabernet Franc. White: 6.1 ha –
90% Sauvignon; 10% Sémillon.
SECOND WINE: Château de Roques.

Next to a jumble of buildings which form the *cuvier* and *chais* here stands a most delightful, square Palladian villa designed by the architect Dutheil, a former owner, in the nineteenth century. The estate has tripled in size since 1955. As elsewhere in the region, the harvest is both by machine and by hand, maturation both in tank and vat.

The wine is of good standard if without being one of the top examples of the *appellation*. The special *cuvée*, L'Enclos de Lezongars, offers more interest and depth. I have enjoyed both the 2000 and 2001.

Château de Malherbes

OWNER: Jean-Pierre & Claire Sancier.
COMMUNE: Latresne.
SURFACE AREA UNDER VINE: Red: 11.5 ha –
  58% Merlot; 15% Cabernet Franc;

26% Cabernet Sauvignon; 1% Malbec.
White: 1 ha – 55% Sémillon; 45% Sauvignon.
SECOND WINE: Château de Rambal.

When Jacques Fritz was sole owner here the wine was made by the Quinsac co-operative, of which he was chairman, and then aged here at the Château de Malherbes. When the Sanciers left Château Le Chèze to join him in 1997 a new *cuvier* was built and the *chais* modernised, since when the wine has been worth noting. As well as the basic wine, there is a Cuvée Élevé en Fûts de Chêne. Both are good. The 2000s are better than the 1999s, which themselves are superior to the 1998.

Château Mont-Perat

OWNER: Thibault Despagne.
COMMUNE: Capian.
SURFACE AREA UNDER VINE: Red: 70 ha –
  45% Cabernet Sauvignon; 41% Merlot;
  14% Cabernet Franc. White: 28 ha –

63% Sémillon; 21% Sauvignon;
16% Muscadelle.
OTHER WINES: Château Franc-Perot; Château Le
  Lucat; Château Rauzan Despagne (Bordeaux &
  Entre-Deux-Mers).

Château Mont-Perat is the Premières Côtes end of the Despagne family's commanding empire. The wines here are made with the same passion and attention to detail as in the Entre-Deux-Mers at Château Rauzan Despagne in Naujan-et-Postiac. The best *cuvées* here are labelled as Mont-Perat, but even the other label, Franc-Perot, is better than most. The white wines are excellent, too.

Château Plaisance

OWNER: Patrick & Sabine Bayle.
COMMUNE: Capian.
SURFACE AREA UNDER VINE: 1.2 ha – 65% Merlot;
  45% Cabernet Sauvignon; 5% Cabernet

Franc. White: 4 ha – 80% Sémillon;
20% Sauvignon.
SECOND WINE: Château Florestan.

The château is a raised *chartreuse* dating from the eighteenth century surrounded by its vineyards, all in one block. It has belonged to Patrick and Sabine Bayle since 1985. The wine is matured in cask in a splendid underground cellar and comes in four versions: a light, Merlot-based wine labelled Château Florestan, a Cuvée Tradition, a Cuvée Spéciale, and from the oldest vines, Cuvée Alix. All are of interest: the two top wines are very good indeed. A small amount of 35-year-old Sémillon makes good dry white wines, both Tradition and Cuvée Alix, and even a little Cadillac when weather conditions permit.

Château Puy Bardens

OWNER: Yves Lamiable.
COMMUNE: Cambes.
SURFACE AREA UNDER VINE: 20 ha – 60% Merlot;

30% Cabernet Sauvignon; 10% Cabernet Franc.
SECOND WINE: Le Clos de La Chapelle.

Commanding a splendid view over the Garonne, Château Puy Bardens is an architectural hodge-podge, having been ruined in the 1860s by a Dr Barincou, who owned it at the time. The basic wine is stored half in cask, of which one-third are new, half in tank. The Cuvée Prestige sees more wood and is a rich wine with plenty of depth. I much enjoyed the 1999.

Château La Rame

OWNERS: Yves Armand.
COMMUNE: Monprimblanc.
SURFACE AREA UNDER VINE: 15 ha – 65% Cabernet

Sauvignon; 35% Merlot.
OTHER WINES: Château La Rame (Sainte-Croix-du-Mont); Château La Rame (Bordeaux Rouge).

As you might expect from the proprietor of one of the best wines in Sainte-Croix-du-Mont – Château La Rame – this is a very good example of the local red wine. I have only seen the *tête de cuvée*, which used to be called Domaine du Barrail La Charmille until it was renamed as Château La Rame from the 2002 vintage. The 1999 was a plump, gently oaky, forward wine with no hard edges. The 2000 was rather more serious, demanding five years in bottle. There is no lack of balance and elegance here.

Château Reynon

OWNER: Denis & Florence Dubourdieu.
COMMUNE: Béguey.
SURFACE AREA UNDER VINE: Red: 18 ha –
75% Merlot; 20% Cabernet Sauvignon;

5% Cabernet Franc. White: 19 ha –
70% Sauvignon; 30% Sémillon.
SECOND WINE: Clos de Reynon.

Today's Château Reynon was built in 1848, but in the classical style, on the site of the old Château de Béguey. Jacques David, father of Florence Dubourdieu, bought it in 1958. Denis Dubourdieu, the distinguished Professor of oenology at Bordeaux University, took over when he married Florence in 1976. The red wine is rich and succulent, but what is of more interest to me is the Bordeaux Blanc Sec, Vieilles Vignes. Rare in the region for being Sauvignon- rather than Sémillon-based, it was one of the first white Bordeauxs to be made by modern methods – skin contact, *élevage sur lie*, *bâtonnage* and so on, and with recourse to a minimum of sulphur. For this, if for nothing else, Denis Dubourdieu deserves a medal, or even a statue. Cadillac is produced in appropriate vintages.

Château Suau

OWNER: Monique Bonnet.
COMMUNE: Capian.
SURFACE AREA UNDER VINE: Red: 52 ha –
50% Merlot; 30% Cabernet Sauvignon;

20% Cabernet Franc. White: 7 ha –
40% Sémillon; 40% Sauvignon;
20% Muscadelle.
SECOND WINE: Château Maubert.

Once a hunting lodge for the Duc d'Épernon, governor of Bordeaux in the seventeenth century, and having belonged to the Guenant family ever since, Château Suau, not to be confused with its Barsac eponym, was acquired in 1986 by Claude Bonnet, father of the present proprietor. Since then it has been completely renovated, both in the vineyard and in the *chai*. The results speak for themselves: a rich, gently oaky, really quite profound red, *élevé en fûts de chêne*, and a delicious white wine, vinified in cask which is one of the best in the region.

BETWEEN THE RIVERS

etween the rivers Garonne and Dordogne is some of the
loveliest countryside in the whole of the Gironde *département*.
It is an undulating landscape, full of attractive country houses
of just the right size and proportions to tempt one to go and live there.
These lie in little parks, abutting onto vineyards and pastureland
interspersed with woods, rushing streams and country paths. Most of
the larger villages can boast a Romanesque church and a medieval
market square. There is even the odd real castle, what the French call a
donjon, though not as many as you will find in the southern Graves.

Most of the wine is red and merely Bordeaux *Appellation
Contrôlée*, the vinous breadbasket of the Bordeaux area. This will be
destined for little more than someone's brand name house Bordeaux,
and can often be really rather ordinary. In some parts, especially in the
Premières Côtes de Bordeaux, overlooking the Garonne and running
from Bordeaux to Langon, better red wines can be found. Both within
and without the Premières Côtes area there are enterprising growers
who have led the way – well ahead of their counterparts in the Graves
– in the production of clean dry white. These are of equal interest.

Most of what is not Premières Côtes in this region is in the Entre-
Deux-Mers, an *appellation* for white wines only. The red wine from
here, of which there is more than white, is Bordeaux or Bordeaux
Supérieur. Many of the locals prefer to label their white wine also as
simple Bordeaux, as they find the wine easier to sell under this
appellation.

The Entre-Deux-Mers has a subsidiary, the Haut-Benauge. This
occupies the land roughly between the towns of Targon and Gornac.
Peripheral to the Entre-Deux-Mers are three further *appellations*: the
Graves de Vayres, both red and white, which faces Fronsac on the other
side of the river Dordogne; Sainte-Foy-Bordeaux, red and white, which
is situated adjacent to the Dordogne *département* to the east; and
Côtes de Bordeaux Saint-Macaire, white only, which lies to the south,
just above Langon. Sadly, it is hard to find anything to get excited

about in these last three areas. Nor do I quite see the logic of Haut-Benauge. There are some good addresses in Targon, but the focal point of new-wave white Bordeaux stretches further north, to cover the communes of La Sauve and Créon as well.

Entre-Deux-Mers

Surface Area (2002): 1571 ha of which 111 ha is Entre-Deux-Mers, Haut-Benauge.

Production (2002): 88,591 hl of which 6250 hl is Entre-Deux-Mers, Haut-Benauge.

Colour & Style: Dry white wine for early drinking.

Grape Varieties: Sémillon; Sauvignon; Muscadelle; plus Merlot Blanc (30% maximum); Colombard; Mauzac; Ugni Blanc (10% maximum).

Maximum Yield: 60 hl/ha.

Minimum Alcoholic Degree: 10°.

Take away the Premières Côtes de Bordeaux, including Cadillac, Sainte-Croix-du-Mont, Loupiac and the three minor *appellations* of Sainte-Foy, Graves de Vayres and Saint-Macaire, and what you have left between the rivers Garonne and Dordogne is Entre-Deux-Mers. This is exclusively a white wine *appellation*. With white wine in decline throughout the Bordeaux region, this part of the world, in fact, produces far more red wine than white: 78 per cent of what is planted here is black grapes making generic Bordeaux Rouge. Much of the rest is declared as Bordeaux Blanc rather than Entre-Deux-Mers, the growers finding it easier to sell the wines as plain Bordeaux. The total area under vine in this part of the Gironde is around 32,500 hectares.

Nevertheless it is the white wine which is the more interesting. The geology varies, but is essentially clay mixed in with limestone, with pockets of sand elsewhere. In the northern part of the region there are gravel parcels; in the south loam. This yields red wines which are decent at best. Where the region has scored in the last 15 years is through an ever-expanding number of enterprising producers who make what I call new-wave white Bordeaux. Francis Courselle at Château Thieuley in La Sauve was one of the pioneers, André Lurton at Château Bonnet in Grazillac another, Jean-Louis Despagne with various estates in Naujan-et-Postiac a third. These producers showed what could be done by modern methods and to an affordable price-point. Hitherto, white Bordeaux had usually been something off-dry and far too sulphury. One reaction to this led to rather green, hard, dry-as-a-bone Sauvignon wines. Then, from the early 1980s a few producers began to get it right. Vinification at low temperatures, yes, but not that low that nothing was extracted but thin, green fruit; *maceration préfermentaire* (skin contact) to obtain more flavours; the use of selected yeasts; maturation on the fine lees; stirring them up occasionally (*bâtonnage*); the use of the carbon dioxide produced by the fermentation, and/or inert gas to protect the wine without having to use too much sulphur, and various other techniques: all this plus the new pneumatic presses and temperature control resulted in wines which were not only clean but full of interest – a Bordelais equivalent to Mâcon Blanc-Villages. It was a long time coming, but it was worth the wait.

The Entre-Deux-Mers, including Haut-Benauge, covers the following *cantons* in whole or in part: Carbon-Blanc, Lormont, Cenon, Floriac, Créon, Targon, Libourne (left bank of the Dordogne only), Branne, Pujols, Pellegrue, Sauveterre, Monségur and La Réole.

The following châteaux produce new-wave white Bordeaux, either under the Entre-Deux-Mers or Bordeaux Blanc labels. Most of these properties produce red wine, too – simple Bordeaux Rouge, largely from Merlot, and sometimes in large quantities. These wines are only of marginal interest. I have always used what time I had in the region to concentrate on the white wines which are of much greater interest. I have, therefore, only given the planting figures for the white grape varieties.

PREMIÈRES CÔTES DE BORDEAUX & ENTRE-DEUX-MERS

Appellations

- Entre-Deux-Mers
- Premières Côtes de Bordeaux
- Bordeaux Haut-Benauge and Entre-Deux-Mers Haut-Benauge

0   15km

0   10miles

Châteaux ◆

Premières Côtes de Bordeaux AC
1 de Chelivette
2 Carignan
3 de Malherbes
4 Brethous
5 Puy Bardens
6 Laroche
7 Langoiran
8 Plaisance, La Chèze
9 Mont-Perat
10 Suau
11 Lezongars

12 Clos Bourbon
13 Carsin
14 Reynon, de Birot
15 du Juge
16 La Bertrande
17 du Grand Plantier
18 La Rame

Entre-Deux-Mers AC
19 Nardique la Gravière
20 Bauduc
21 de Fontenille
22 Thieuley
23 Turcaud

24 Toutigeac
25 Sainte-Marie
26 Mylord
27 Reynier
28 Ninon
29 Bonnet
30 Fondarzac
31 Tour de Mirambeau
32 Mayne-Cabanot
33 Roquefort
34 Moulin de Launay
35 Bellevue
36 Gayon

Château Bauduc

OWNER: Gavin Quinney.
COMMUNE: Créon.

SURFACE AREA UNDER VINE: White: 7 ha –
50% Sémillon; 50% Sauvignon.

The wine of this estate was put on the map by the Welshman David Thomas who took over in 1981. Thomas retired in 1999 and sold up to the Englishman Gavin Quinney. The pearl here is the *cuvée* Trois Hectares, vinified in cask and made from 100 per cent Sémillon. This is consistently delicious and remains so despite the change of ownership. The 2002 is delicious.

Château Bellevue

OWNER: d'Amécourt family; director: Yves
d'Amécourt.
COMMUNE: Sauveterre.

SURFACE AREA UNDER VINE: White: 7.4 ha –
54% Sémillon; 46% Sauvignon.

Château Bellevue was constructed in the seventeenth century by the Lestelle family. Bruno and Marguerite de Ponton d'Amécourt acquired the estate in 1973, and doubled the size of it by buying the neighbouring Château Saint-Germain in 1986. Most of the production here (62 hectares) is red wine. There are two *cuvées* of white, however, the Cuvée Classique and the Cuvée Aquarelle, the second of which is the oaky version. Both were very good in 2001.

Château Bonnet

OWNER: André Lurton.
COMMUNE: Grézillac.
SURFACE AREA UNDER VINE: White: 105 ha –
45% Sémillon; 45% Sauvignon;
10% Muscadelle.

OTHER WINES: Château Couhins-Lurton
(Pessac-Léognan); Château de Cruzeau
(Pessac-Léognan); Château La Louvière
(Pessac-Léognan); Château de Rochemorin
(Pessac-Léognan).

This is an imposing château – it dates from 1778 – a vast estate – there are another 100 hectares of black vines – and an impressive set-up. From here the wines of the Lurton empire are despatched. The property was acquired by Lurton's grandfather in 1897. When André Lurton took over in 1956 there were a mere 30 hectares of vineyard. The white wine comes in two versions, as it does in most places: a basic and a more oaky Réserve. In 2000 it was decided to suspend the Réserve as it was interfering with sales of Rochemorin and the like. I hope they change their minds. It is a very good example, perhaps the best in the entire Entre-Deux-Mers.

Château Fondarzac

OWNER: Claude Barthe.
COMMUNE: Naujan-et-Postiac.

SURFACE AREA UNDER VINE: White: 50 ha –
40% Sémillon; 40% Sauvignon;
20% Muscadelle.

This well-established estate has been producing good white wine for some time. *Macération pelliculaire* (cold soaking) and temperature-controlled fermentation have been in place for 15 years or more, though it was only in 1999 that a bladder press was acquired, and only in this vintage that a Cuvée Claude Barthe, vinified in oak, was introduced. Some of the white wine is sold as Château Darzac. Both the 2000 and the 2001 under this label are good.

Château de Fontenille

OWNER: Stéphane Defraine.
COMMUNE: La Sauve.
SURFACE AREA UNDER VINE: White: 5 ha –

40% Sauvignon; 30% Sémillon;
30% Muscadelle.

The Belgian Stéphane Defraine arrived in Bordeaux in 1997, worked for David Thomas at Château Bauduc for a while and set up here in 1999. He has 30 hectares of black vines as well. There is just one version of each colour. The 2001 and 2002 white were delicious; the 2000 a little more four-square.

Château Gayon

OWNER: Jean Crampes.
COMMUNE: Caudrot.

SURFACE AREA UNDER VINE: White: 1.7 ha –
90% Sauvignon; 10% Sémillon.

This property lies within the Saint-Macaire *appellation*, but sells its wine as Bordeaux. Most of it is red, of which there is a surface area of 27 hectares. But a little white wine is made, half vinified in barrel, half in vat. It is elegant, racy and forward. The château, which dates from the seventeenth century, is worth a visit too. There are some interesting frescoes.

Château Mayne-Cabanot

OWNER: GFA Corbières.
COMMUNE: Rauzan.

SURFACE AREA UNDER VINE: White: 5.6 ha –
76% Sauvignon; 24% Sémillon.

The wine is produced by the Cave Coopérative de Rauzan, one of the largest in the Bordeaux area. No wood. But crisp, definitive and stylish. Drink it young.

Château Moulin de Launay

OWNER: Claude Greffier.
COMMUNE: Soussac.

SURFACE AREA UNDER VINE: White: 75 ha –
45% Sémillon; 35% Sauvignon;
20% Muscadelle.

This is a thoroughly modern set up producing almost entirely white wine (there is one hectare of black grapes) by up to date methods. There is no oak, the wine is forward, but it is inexpensive.

Château Mylord

OWNER: Michel Alain Large.
COMMUNE: Grézillac.

SURFACE AREA UNDER VINE: White: 25 ha –
34% Sémillon; 33% Sauvignon;
33% Muscadelle.

The Large brothers produce a good, reliable non-oaky white wine. Starting with the 2000 vintage, they also ferment 10 barrels' worth of the same must in wood. This wine was certainly good, though it could have had, like so many 2000s, a little more zip. I look forward to further progress at Château Mylord.

Château Nardique La Gravière

OWNER: Christian & Philippe Thérèse.
COMMUNE: Saint-Genès-de-Lombaud.

SURFACE AREA UNDER VINE: White: 16 ha –
50% Sémillon; 40% Sauvignon;
10% Muscadelle.

About half of this 30-hectare domaine is given over to white grapes. This is another early-maturing example. But there is good fruit and plenty of depth and length. I enjoyed the 2001. The 2002 is good, too.

Château Ninon

OWNER: Pierre Roubineau.
COMMUNE: Grézillac.

SURFACE AREA UNDER VINE: White: 3 ha –
40% Sémillon; 40% Sauvignon;
20% Muscadelle.

Most of the production here is of red wine, but I have had delicious examples of a soft, stylish, even complex white. The 2000 is particularly good.

Château Rauzan Despagne

Château Tour de Mirambeau

Château Bel Air Perponcher

OWNER: Jean-Louis Despagne.
COMMUNE: Naujan-et-Postiac.
SURFACE AREA UNDER VINE: White: Tour de
Mirambeau: 59 ha; Rauzan d'Espagne:51 ha;

Bel Air Perponcher: 35 ha.
ENCÉPAGEMENT: 40% Sémillon; 40% Sauvignon;
20% Muscadelle.

Jean-Louis Despagne has been a pioneer of good, inexpensive, clean white Bordeaux, and that is exactly what the basic *cuvées* of these three properties are. But note that there are several *cuvées*: a pure Sauvignon, an Entre-Deux-Mers and a Bordeaux Blanc. It is all a bit confusing. Quite separate is something quite different: the Cuvée Passion. This is from old vines, 70 per cent Sauvignon and 30 per cent Sémillon, and is vinified in wood. I love it. Jean-Louis Despagne's reds, supervised by Michel Rolland, are good too.

Château Reynier

OWNER: Marc Lurton.
COMMUNE: Grézillac.
SURFACE AREA UNDER VINE: White: 7 ha –

50% Sauvignon; 45% Sémillon; 5% Muscadelle.
OTHER WINE: Château de Bouchet La Rentière
(Bordeaux & Entre-Deux-Mers).

Hard by Château Bonnet, and purchased at the same time 110 years ago, is another Lurton estate, inherited from his father Dominique by Marc Lurton, brother of Pierre who is responsible at Château Cheval Blanc. The building dates from the fifteenth century, the vineyard from the late 1950s, having been entirely destroyed by the 1956 frosts. Most of the 28-hectare estate produces red wine which is good and succulent. The white wine in the main is not oak-matured but is balanced, ripe and stylish. Following a very good 2000, the 2001 can be singled out. There is a small *cuvée* of gently oaky white produced for a client in Belgium.

Château Roquefort

OWNER: Frédéric Bellanger.
COMMUNE: Lugasson.

SURFACE AREA UNDER VINE: White: 32 ha –
65% Sauvignon; 30% Sémillon; 5% Muscadelle.

This is a large estate – there are an additional 56 hectares for red wine – with a long history. A castle was built here in 1291, a *manoir* in the fifteenth century and today's château in the eighteenth century. Modern wine began with a new cellar in 1987 which was further modernised in 1994. The basic white Cuvée Tradition is clean, crisp and flowery and there is a more oaky Cuvée Spéciale.

Château Sainte-Marie

OWNER: Gilles & Stéphane Dupuch.
COMMUNE: Targon.
SURFACE AREA UNDER VINE: White: 13.8 ha –

60% Sauvignon; 30% Sémillon;
10% Muscadelle.
SECOND WINE: Château La Gravelle.

About 40 per cent of the production is white wine. There are three *cuvées*: the basic, the Vieilles Vignes, crisp, Sauvignonny and not oaky, and the richer, more exotic Cuvée Madlys which shows signs of oak ageing. The red is good, too.

Château Thieuley

OWNER: Francis Courselle.
COMMUNE: La Sauve.

SURFACE AREA UNDER VINE: White: 30 ha –
60% Sauvignon; 40% Sémillon.

Château Thieuley is a benchmark for all modern white Bordeaux. Francis Courselle's parents bought the estate in 1950. Francis, a trained oenologist, has been in charge since the early 1970s, and in 1986 he first began to ferment part of the white wine crop in new oak: this is the Cuvée Francis Courselle, a lovely wine. The basic white is very good too – just gently oaky – and the red (from 40 hectares of vines) is rich, complex and succulent.

Château Toutigeac

OWNER: Philippe Mazeau.
COMMUNE: Targon.

SURFACE AREA UNDER VINE: White: 6.8 ha –
60% Sauvignon; 30% Sémillon;
10% Muscadelle.

Toutigeac was acquired by the Mazeau family in 1928. It has been run by Philippe Mazeau, one of the pioneers of modern white Bordeaux, since 1985. There is no oak, and the wine is destined for early drinking, but it is fresh, clean and fruity. Production here is mainly of red wine, for which there are 44 hectares of vines. It is supple, forward and full of fruit.

Château Turcaud

OWNER: Maurice & Simone Robert.
COMMUNE: La Sauve-Majeure.

SURFACE AREA UNDER VINE: White: 45 ha –
50% Sauvignon; 45% Sémillon; 5% Muscadelle.

One-third of the yield here is white wine, of which there are two *cuvées*. The Entre-Deux-Mers is light, fruity and forward, with no oak. The Bordeaux Blanc, Cuvée Vinifiée et Élevée en Fûts de Chêne is rather more complex, concentrated and interesting, but also for fairly early drinking.

CÔTES DE BORDEAUX–SAINT-MACAIRE

SURFACE AREA (2002): 48 ha.

PRODUCTION (2002): 1427 hl.

COLOUR & STYLE: Medium-sweet white wine.

GRAPE VARIETIES: Sémillon; Sauvignon; Muscadelle.

MAXIMUM YIELD: 50 hl/ha.

MINIMUM ALCOHOLIC DEGREE: 11.5°.

The rare *appellation* of Côtes de Bordeaux–Saint-Macaire continues on from where the Premières Côtes leaves off on the righthand side of the river Garonne opposite Langon. The undulating countryside is typical of that of the Entre-Deux-Mers and the soils are similar, too: essentially clay, mixed with limestone and sand. The vine shares the terrain with maize, pasture and fruit trees.

The *appellation*, for a gentle, sweet wine in the style of Graves Supérieures, is confined to the following 10 communes: Saint-Macaire, Saint-Pierre-d'Aurillac, Saint-Martin-de-Sescas, Caudrot, Le Pian-sur-Garonne, Saint-André-du-Bois, Sainte-Foy-La-Longue, Saint-Laurent-du-Plan, Saint-Laurent-du-Bois and Saint-Martial. Fifty-one hectares, out of a total of some 2800 hectares under vine, are declared as Saint-Macaire, most locals preferring to produce generic Bordeaux, red and dry white. I have rarely come across the wine.

Graves de Vayres

Surface Area (2002): Red: 537 ha; white: 95 ha.

Production (2002): Red: 25,591 hl; white: 5224 hl.

Colour & Style: Merlot-based, medium-weight reds; dry whites.

Grape Varieties:Red: Cabernet Sauvignon; Cabernet Franc; Merlot; Malbec; Petit Verdot; Carmenère. White: Sémillon, Sauvignon, Muscadelle, Merlot Blanc.

Maximum Yield: Red: 50 hl/ha; White: 60 hl/ha.

Minimum Alcoholic Degree: Red: 10°; White 10.5°.

Graves de Vayres is rather obscure. The *appellation* lies on both sides of the Bordeaux-Libourne highway, the N89, opposite Fronsac on relatively flat land whose soils are largely sandy, mixed with gravel and clay on a gravel subsoil, and extends over two communes, Vayres and Arveyres. Not all growers take advantage of the *appellation*, however. In total the area under vine is 935 ha of red varieties and 165 ha white.

Graves de Vayres is not a wine I have encountered often. In my experience the reds are a little thin and the whites somewhat neutral. Château Lesparre (Michel Gonnet) at Beychat-et-Caillou and Château La Chapelle Bellevue (Lisette Labeille) at Vayres are two of the best.

Sainte-Foy-Bordeaux

Surface Area (2002): Red: 199 ha; white: 49 ha.

Production (2002): Red: 9941 hl; white: 1905 hl.

Colour & Style: Light, Merlot-based reds; dry and medium-sweet *moelleux* whites.

Grape Varieties: Red: Cabernet Sauvignon; Cabernet Franc; Merlot; Petit Verdot; Malbec. White: Sémillon; Sauvignon; Muscadelle; plus Merlot Blanc; Colombard; Mauzac; Ugni Blanc (10% maximum).

Maximum Yield: Red: 50 hl/ha; white 55 hl/ha.

Minimum Alcoholic Degree: Red: 10°; dry white: 10.5°; Moelleux: 11°.

East of Castillon the vines on the north bank of the river Dordogne find themselves in the *département* of that name and produce Bergerac and Montravel, rather than Bordeaux. On the opposite bank the departmental boundary and the town of Sainte-Foy, across which is the Dordogne *appellation* of Saussignac, are not reached for a further 20 kilometres. Here, at the extreme eastern end of the Gironde is another little known *appellation*: Sainte-Foy-Bordeaux.

Sainte-Foy-Bordeaux comprises the following 19 communes: Sainte-Foy, Saint-Avit-Saint-Nazaire, Saint-Philippe-de-Seignal, Eynesse, Pineuilh, Pessac-sur-Gironde, Saint-André-et-Appelles, Saint-Avit-de-Soulège, Gensac, Les Lèves-et-Thoumeyragues, La Roquille, Ligueux, Saint-Quentin-de-Caplong, Caplong, Massaugas, Riocaud, Margueron, Landerrouat and Pellegrue.

The area is pretty, if somewhat of a backwater. As in the Entre-Deux-Mers the countryside is undulating and not monocultural, which makes it more varied. The soils are a mixture of limestone and clay plateau interspersed with gravel, more or less sandy depending on location. In total there are some 6500 hectares under vine, of which 1100 are planted with white vines. Despite having their own *appellation*, most growers prefer to make generic Bordeaux.

Once again this is an *appellation* which rarely comes my way, and when it does fails to persuade me to investigate further. One property I can recommend is Patrick de Coninck's Château Martet in Eynesse. His Réserve de Famille is worth searching for. A second is Château des Thibeaud at Caplong. At Château Pierrail in Margueron the Demonchaux family make a delicious, gently oaky white wine.

SAINT-
ÉMILION

SAINT-ÉMILION

SURFACE AREA (2002): 1773 ha.

PRODUCTION (2002): 88,288 hl.

COLOUR: Red.

GRAPE VARIETIES: Merlot; Cabernet Franc
(Bouchet); Cabernet Sauvignon;
Malbec (Pressac).

MAXIMUM YIELD: 45 hl/ha.

MINIMUM ALCOHOLIC DEGREE: 10.5°.

SAINT-ÉMILION GRAND CRU

SURFACE AREA (2002): 3719 ha.

PRODUCTION (2002): 134,835 hl.

COLOUR: Red.

GRAPE VARIETIES: Merlot; Cabernet Franc
(Bouchet); Cabernet Sauvignon; Malbec
(Pressac).

MAXIMUM YIELD: 40 hl/ha.

MINIMUM ALCOHOLIC DEGREE: 11°.

Some 40 kilometres east of Bordeaux, across the peninsula of the Entre-Deux-Mers, is the sizeable, bustling town of Libourne, centre both geographically and commercially of the Right Bank. The portmanteau phrase Dordogne or Libournais wines means those of Saint-Émilion, Pomerol, Fronsac and their satellites. For centuries this region was, literally, a backwater. The wines were the poor country cousins of those of the Graves and the Médoc. Holdings were small and ownership in the hands of the peasants or local *petite bourgeoisie*. Communications with Bordeaux were tedious – there was neither a bridge across the Dordogne at Libourne nor one across the Garonne at Bordeaux until 1820 or so. And the wines had little impact on the Bordeaux marketplace as a result. While the aristocrat-owned *châteaux* of the Médoc, monocultural estates from the 1740s, found equally well to-do customers in Britain and Ireland, the artisanal produce of the Libournais was shipped as generic wine to the burghers of Holland, Bremen and the Hanseatic ports. The area remained one of mixed farming until much later than the Médoc and the Graves, few domaines having any individual reputation until the 1830s or 1840s.

Not surprisingly, when the Bordeaux brokers drew up the 1855 Classification, the wines of the Libournais were ignored. It was not until post-phylloxera times, towards the end of the nineteenth century, that prices began to match those of even the lesser Médoc classed growths, and only since the Second World War that there has been parity. The Libournais remains a wine region of small estates, of charming but largely architecturally undistinguished dwellings, but often with surprisingly lengthy family histories of ownership.

Some six kilometres north-east of Libourne lies the ancient walled town of Saint-Émilion. In contrast with Libourne Saint-Émilion is almost too self-consciously picturesque. Wine has been made here since Gallo-Roman times. Whether the Roman poet and statesman, Ausonius, after whom one of the area's most prestigious estates is named, ever had a vineyard in Saint-Émilion is a matter for dispute, but there is plenty of archaeological evidence to support a history of almost two millennia of continuous vine cultivation. Above Château Ausone on the plateau you can see ancient trenches excavated out of the limestone bedrock. These were filled with earth and planted with fruit trees such as apples, pears, cherries and peaches. Vines were then trained up the trees and onto overhanging trellises in a sort of pergola system. Not long ago, not at Ausone but in the vineyard of Château La Gaffelière, another Saint-Émilion First Growth, an impressive Gallo-Roman mosaic showing a vineyard scene was partially uncovered. This is no longer on view to the tourist, sadly, having been earthed up to await a more comprehensive dig in 25 years' time or so when techniques are yet more advanced.

The town is named after the hermit, Aemilianus, who lived in the eighth century. Deciding to retire from life completely he sought a quiet spot where he could calmly meditate on the cares of the world. He found his site, a grotto in a limestone bluff above the valley of the Dordogne. Today this is Saint-Émilion. Above the hermit's cell, excavated deep into the rock, is a vast, underground monolithic church, the largest in Europe. Surrounding this the steep, cobbled streets and houses cling to the sides of a defile in the slope. The narrow alleys are filled with shops selling the celebrated local macaroons as well as wine and cans of *confit d'oie*, *cèpes* and *pâté de foie gras*.

From the Église Collégiale and Place Pioceau at the top of the town the view south is spectacular: the celebrated classed growths on the plateau and the slopes, lesser vineyards on the valley floor and finally the Dordogne, glinting away in the distance. You can also look directly down to the Place du Marché. Here, outside the Église Monolithique, the Jurade of Saint-Émilion congregate four times a year in their red ceremonial robes to proclaim the start of the harvest in September and command the ritual burning of an old wooden barrel, commemorating the old days when the Jurade (and not some bureaucrat in Paris or Brussels) held power over the legislation of the local wines.

Saint-Émilion, though by no means the largest in overall surface area, is the most compact and the most intensely cultivated *appellation* in Bordeaux. There is hardly a spare field which is not covered in neat rows of vines. The area forms a rough rectangle only ten kilometres by five, yet there are more than 5400 hectares of vines. By comparison, the entire Haut-Médoc (measuring 50 kilometres from Blanquefort north to Saint-Estèphe) has not even double the amount under cultivation, about 10,200 hectares of vines.

In contrast to the rolling gravel plateaux of the Médoc, where the châteaux holdings are large and the atmosphere is aristocratic, Saint-Émilion is a region of the small peasant proprietor. The 5400 hectares are divided among a thousand or more different owners, some 25 per cent of whom are members of the thriving local co-operative.

Geographically and also in the style of its wines, Saint-Émilion can be divided into three main areas. South of the town itself, the land falls away abruptly towards the river Dordogne. The best vineyards lie either on these slopes or occupy the plateau on the other three sides of the town. This is the area known as the Côtes-Saint-Émilion. Here the soil consists of a thin layer of limestone debris on a solid limestone rock base, into which many a quarry has been hewn and is now used for cellaring the wine. Mixed with the limestone is a certain amount of clay. There is more sand as you descend down the slope into the valley. All but two of Saint-Émilion's First Growths lie in the Côtes.

To the west of the Côtes, adjacent to Pomerol, is the smaller area of Graves-Saint-Émilion. As the name suggests, there is gravel in the soil. There is less limestone and clay than in the best sites of the Côtes but more sand. The subsoil is of the same composition. This area is almost entirely occupied by two First Growths, Châteaux Cheval Blanc and Figeac.

Between these two areas, but largely north and west of the town itself, lies an area of old weathered sand known as the *sables anciens*, similar to that found in the Graves-Saint-Émilion, but without the gravel and on a base of limestone. The sand here is distinct from the more alluvial soil to the south of Saint-Émilion. Wines from here are good, if not of the very highest quality. There are no First Growths.

The wines of Saint-Émilion – and indeed the whole of the Libournais – are made from the three great red varieties of the Bordeaux area, but in a different proportion to that used in the Médoc. In the Médoc the Cabernet Sauvignon is king, occupying between 60 and 80 per cent of the vineyards; Merlot is an important subsidiary; Cabernet Franc is out of favour. In Saint-Émilion the Merlot, known locally as the Bouchet, is the most widely planted variety, with Cabernet Franc the main additional grape, while Cabernet Sauvignon is hardly used at all. The reason for the choice of this Cabernet is the difference in soil structure. Cabernet Sauvignon thrives in the gravelly soils of the Médoc but Cabernet Franc performs far better in the predominantly limestone but colder soils of the Saint-Émilion area, where it is known locally as the Bouchet. It also matures sooner than the Cabernet Sauvignon.

The two main areas of Saint-Émilion, the Côtes and the Graves, produce quite different wines; though with the exception of Château Cheval Blanc and Château Figeac the top growths have similar *encépagements*, roughly 50 to 80 per cent Merlot and 20 to 50 per cent Cabernet Franc or Bouchet.

The Côtes wines can vary depending whether the vineyard is largely or indeed entirely on the plateau or mostly on the slope. Some of the plateau wines can be very full and sturdy like Château Canon and Clos Fourtet. Mostly, though, all these Côtes wines start off well-coloured, quite full, without being particularly densely structured, and develop quickly, being ready for drinking a few years earlier than a Médoc or Graves of similar standing. In character they are loose-knit, somewhat warmer and sweeter than in the Médoc, with a spicy, fruit-cakey flavour which derives from the predominant Merlot grape. A good First Growth from a successful vintage needs to be kept eight years or so before it is ready for drinking. It will keep well for at least a decade after that if properly stored. The wines of the *sables anciens* are similar but both less intense and less stylish.

The Graves-Saint-Émilion really needs to be considered as a quite separate area. The wines have more power and are fuller and more concentrated, richer and firmer than those of the Côtes. These Saint-Émilions are more similar to Pomerols, their nearest neighbours. They tend to require a couple of years longer to mature and last better.

The lesser wines of the Saint-Émilion area, and this applies to the satellites as well as to Saint-Émilion itself, are predominantly Merlot-based, loose-knit, gentle wines without a great deal of grip. In weaker years they can rapidly become attenuated – but, at least, unlike a lesser Médoc in a poor year, they do not have unpleasant unripe tannins. Personally I find Fronsacs and lesser Pomerols have more interest.

It is commonly but erroneously believed that the famous 1855 Classification of Bordeaux was of the Médoc only, with Château Haut-Brion being smuggled in on the old-boy network because it was too important to be left out. In fact, the Classification was of all the red wines of Bordeaux. It was simply that the Libournais wines were not then considered fashionable and fetched low prices at that time. Indeed, at the time it was the wines of Fronsac which fared better.

Anxious not to be left out for ever, the local growers lobbied for their own separate classification in the 1950s. This is under the ultimate control of the INAO and is supposed to be revised every 10 years. In fact the original classification of 1954 was revised in 1969, 1985 and in 1996. The wines and growths are divided into four categories: *premiers grands crus classés* (itself subdivided into A and B), *grands crus classés*, *grands crus* and plain or generic Saint-Émilion.

The two Category 'A' First Growths are Château Ausone in the Côtes and Château Cheval Blanc in the Graves-Saint-Émilion. These sell for almost double the price of the others. Prices are equivalent to those of Château Haut-Brion and the First Growths in the Médoc.

Of the *premiers grands crus classés* (B) I would class Canon, Figeac and Magdelaine in a class above the rest and equivalent to the Super-Seconds of the Médoc, wines such as Châteaux Ducru-Beaucaillou, Léoville-Las-Cases, Palmer and Pichon-Longueville, Comtesse de Lalande. Châteaux Angélus, Beauséjour-Duffau-Lagarrosse and Pavie (until it changed hands in 1998) are very good, Belair is elegant if somewhat unconcentrated and Clos Fourtet is fuller and improving. In my view the remaining properties should be demoted into a lower division with the best châteaux from the next category.

This list of *grands crus classés* is far too cumbersome, not least because many of the properties are very small and their wines rarely encountered. The highfliers ought to be separated out into a superior classification (and into which Châteaux Trottevieille and others should be demoted from *premiers grands crus classés*). These high-fliers are, in alphabetical order: L'Arrosée, Bellevue, Berliquet, Cadet-Piola, Canon-La-Gaffelière, La Couspaude, Dassault, La Dominique, Fonplégade, Fonroque, Larcis-Ducasse, Larmande, Laroze, Clos de L'Oratoire, Pavie-Macquin, Rol Valentin, La Serre, Soutard, Tertre-Daugay, Tertre-Roteboeuf and Troplong-Mondot. Three of these, La Mondotte, Rol Valentin and Tertre-Roteboeuf, are

Châteaux ♦

Lussac-St-Émilion AC
1 Bel-Air
2 Croix de Rambeau
3 de Bordes
4 de Barbe Blanche
5 Lucas
6 Lyonnat
7 Haut-Piquat

Montagne-St-Émilion AC
8 Faizeau
9 Calon
10 Béchereau
11 Maison-Blanche
12 Vieux Chateau Saint-André
13 Montaiguillon
14 La Couronne
15 Roudier
16 L'Envie
17 de Musset
18 Le Clos Daviaud

Saint-Georges-St-Émilion AC
19 Saint-André-Corbin
20 Troquart

21 Saint-Georges
22 Tour du Pas Saint-Georges

Puisseguin-St-Émilion AC
23 Chêne-Vieux
24 Fayan
25 Lafaurie
26 Guibeau-la-Fourvieille
27 Branda

St-Émilion AC
28 Rolland-Maillet
29 Grand-Corbin-Despagne
30 Corbin-Michotte
31 Corbin
32 Chauvin, Haut-Corbin
33 Ripeau
34 La Dominique
35 Cheval Blanc
36 La Tour du Pin Figeac (Giraud-Bélivier), La Tour du Pin Figeac (Moueix)
37 La Tour Figeac
38 Figeac
39 Quinault l'Enclos
40 Trianon
41 Yon-Figeac

42 Laroze
43 Franc-Mayne, Grand-Mayne, Clos des Jacobins
44 La Gomerie
45 Rol-Valentin
46 Fonroque, Laniote, Cap de Mourlin
47 Moulin du Cadet
48 Cadet-Bon, Cadet-Piola
49 Larmande
50 Soutard
51 Dassault
52 Laplagnotte-Bellevue
53 Faurie-de-Souchard
54 Clos de l'Oratoire, Petit-Faurie-de-Soutard
55 Haut-Sarpe
56 Balestard-La-Tonnelle
57 La Couspaude
58 Sansonnet
59 Trottevieille
60 Le Prieuré
61 Pavie-Macquin
62 Bergat
63 La Clotte, La Serre, de Valandraud, Villemaurine

SAINT–EMILION & SATELLITE AREAS

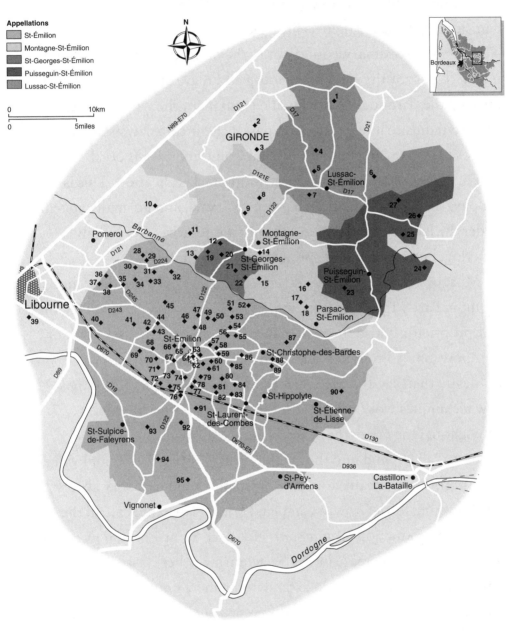

Appellations

- St-Émilion
- Montagne-St-Émilion
- St-Georges-St-Émilion
- Puisseguin-St-Émilion
- Lussac-St-Émilion

0 10km
0 5miles

N

GIRONDE

Lussac-St-Émilion

Pomerol

Barbanne

Montagne-St-Émilion

St-Georges-St-Emilion

Puisseguin-St-Émilion

Parsac-St-Émilion

Libourne

St-Emilion

St-Christophe-des-Bardes

St-Hippolyte

St-Étienne-de-Lisse

St-Laurent-des-Combes

St-Sulpice-de-Faleyrens

St-Pey-d'Armens

Castillon-La-Bataille

Vignonet

Dordogne

Bordeaux

64	Couvent des Jacobins, Guadet Saint-Julien	
65	Clos Fourtet, Les Grandes Murailles	
66	Beau-Séjour-Bécot, Grand-Pontet	
67	Beauséjour (Duffau-Lagarrosse), Canon, Clos Saint-Martin	
68	Bellevue	
69	Le Dôme	
70	Angélus	
71	Matras	
72	Tertre-Daugay	
73	Berliquet	
74	Ausone, Belair, Magdelaine	
75	L'Arrosée, Fonplégade	
76	Canon-La-Gaffelière	
77	La Gaffelière	
78	Saint-Georges-Côte-Pavie	
79	Moulin Saint-Georges	
80	La Mondotte	
81	Pavie, Pavie-Decesse	
82	Larcis-Ducasse	
83	Bellefont-Belcier	
84	Le Tertre-Roteboeuf	
85	Troplong-Mondot	
86	Barde-Haut	
87	Fombrauge	
88	Clos Dubreuil	
89	Laroque	
90	Faugères	
91	Clos Badon	
92	Ferrand Lartigue	
93	Monbousquet	
94	Plaisance	
95	Teyssier	

in fact not even *grands crus classés* but merely *grands crus*.

The next category below *grands crus classés* is *grands crus*. This is a misleading title, for there is little *grand* about most of these wines. The wines are ordinary, equivalent to the *petits châteaux* found in the northern part of the Médoc, in Bourg and Blaye and the other lesser areas of the Gironde. To be classified *grand cru* the wines have to attain a requisite level of alcohol, pass a chemical analysis and be approved by a tasting panel. There are some 200 *grands crus*.

Finally there is the simple Saint-Émilion classification. This is simple generic wine, without a property name, and normally appears under the label of a local merchant or co-operative. Good daily drinking, but nothing more pretentious than that.

Most of Bordeaux's new-wave garage wines originated in Saint-Émilion. Partly this is because it is a more hands-on, personal region. The proprietor is also the winemaker. To some extent, as a result of the above, Saint-Émilion is a less stuffy, less traditional part of Bordeaux than say, the Médoc. It is also because a number of these new techniques work better with Merlot than with Cabernet Sauvignon. One factor, however, is the INAO laws. In Pauillac a property can expand into the neighbouring vineyard without losing its classification. Château Mouton-Rothschild could in theory absorb the neighbouring Fifth Growth Château Pontet-Canet and call all the combined production *premier cru*. Not so in Saint-Émilion. A classed growth can only increase in size by acquiring other classed growth land. A *premier* cannot even extend into a mere *grand cru classé*. The reason is that the terroirs are of different *appellations*. Once fixed, they remain until the next re-classification. This hasn't stopped the acquisitions of course. But has led to an increasing number of new, separate, non-*cru classé* wines which are sold at the same price or indeed higher than their *cru classé* stablemates. Examples include La Mondotte, La Gomerie and Le Dôme. These have no official status. They are the super-*grands crus* of Saint-Émilion.

Saint-Émilion Leading Châteaux

Château Angélus ★

OWNER: de Boüard de Laforest family.
COMMUNE: Saint-Émilion.
SURFACE AREA UNDER VINE: 23.4 ha – 50% Merlot; 47% Cabernet Franc; 3% Cabernet Sauvignon.
SECOND WINE: Le Carillon de L'Angélus.

OTHER WINES: Château La Fleur de Boüard (Lalande-de-Pomerol); Château de Francs (Côtes de Francs).
CLASSIFICATION: Premier Grand Cru Classé B.

Château Angélus is a Saint-Émilion success story. In 1996 it became only the second property in Bordeaux (Mouton-Rothschild is the other) to be promoted into the ranks of the First Growths. As recently as 1980 the wine was rustic, matured entirely in concrete vats and hardly worthy of being even *grand cru classé*. This was the year Hubert de Boüard de Laforest, later joined by his elder cousin Jean-Bernard Grenié, began to take over. The excellence of Angélus today is their creation.

The nucleus of Angélus is 13 hectares of vineyard, known then as the Domaine de Mazerat, which were inherited by Hubert's great-grandfather Comte Maurice de Boüard de Laforest from his aunt, the widow of the Chevalier Charles Souffrain de Lavergne. This was in 1909. In 1924 3 adjoining hectares entitled Clos de l'Angélus were purchased from the Gurchy family. After the Second World War the family decided to rename the wine Château L'Angélus (the definitive article has since been dropped). The neighbourhood is said to be the only place in the area where one could hear the angelus, rung at dawn, midday and sunset, from all three of Saint-Émilion's churches. Further acquisitions followed, and the vineyard now measures nearly 24 hectares, all in one piece, at the foot of the slope below Château Beauséjour-Duffau-Lagarrosse.

For almost 10 years, from 1982 onwards, Angelus was a bit of a building site, as investment was gradually poured into the property: stainless steel vats, a temperature-controlled barrel cellar, *tapis de triage*, new wood, new reception area and so on. The wine, of course, steadily improved. The price was raised as a consequence – 1985, better than the 1982, was the first really serious Angélus. From 1989 and 1990 onwards Angélus was clearly of First Growth quality: fine in a rich, well extracted, new wood, glossy sort of way; big, generous and concentrated. Today it is regularly one of the top three of the *premiers grands crus classés B*.

See *Grands Vins*, p. 423.

Château L'Arrosée ★

OWNER: Caille family; director: Jean-Philippe Caille.
COMMUNE: Saint-Émilion.

SURFACE AREA UNDER VINE: 9.4 ha – 60% Merlot; 20% Cabernet Sauvignon; 20% Cabernet Franc.
CLASSIFICATION: Grand Cru Classé.

The L'Arrosée vineyard – there is no château as such, merely the *chai* with a vineyard worker's cottage attached at the side – lies on a sheltered, south-facing slope next to Château Fonplégarde and below Château Berliquet. Like the latter, the wine used to be made by the local co-operative. While it enjoyed a high reputation a century ago, it is only since 1956, when the present proprietor, the charming 70-year-old François Rodhain managed to terminate the contract, that L'Arrosée has once again been independent, and the quality of the wine has assumed its rightful place.

A hundred and fifty years ago L'Arrosée was one of a number of properties owned by Pierre Magne, Napoleon III's finance minister. At the time, and subsequently, the land was tended by the Dupuch family, owners of adjoining vineyards and elsewhere. They were able to acquire L'Arrosée from successors of Pierre Magne in 1911. François Rodhain is a direct descendant.

Rodhain divided his vineyard into three: from the top of the slope comes wine of power, from the middle richness, from the lower parts finesse. He is a believer in very low yields, late harvesting, essential given the high proportion of Cabernet Sauvignon, in plenty of new oak, and, if appropriate, late bottling, normally 18–24 months after the harvest. I find the wine full-bodied, rich, masculine and long-lasting for a Saint-Émilion, concentrated and splendidly classy. A major pretender to First Growth status.

François Rodhain sold L'Arrosée to the Caille family of Lyon in July 2002.

See *Grands Vins*, p. 427.

Château Ausone ★★

OWNER: Vauthier family.
COMMUNE: Saint-Émilion.
SURFACE AREA UNDER VINE: 7 ha – 55% Cabernet
   Franc; 45% Merlot.
SECOND WINE: Chapelle d'Ausone.

OTHER WINES: Château Moulin Saint-Georges
   (Saint-Émilion); Château de Fonbel (Saint-
   Émilion).
CLASSIFICATION: Premier Grand Cru Classé A.

Ausonius, the fourth-century Roman academic, poet, consul and tutor to future emperors, is commemorated in the name of this famous property, though it is doubtful if he ever lived on this site. The villa that he inherited from his father, in which he lived after his retirement, which he describes in his poems, was on the banks of the Garonne. Nevertheless there is ample evidence of Gallo-Roman activity in the Saint-Émilion area, not least at the foot of the vineyard below Ausone where a substantial mosaic has been discovered.

Ausone is the smallest of the Bordeaux First Growths and the only one whose vineyard lies on a slope. Modern history begins with the Cantenat family, owners from 1718 until the latter third of the nineteenth century. In the 1868 Cocks & Féret, Ausone is rated fourth in the area. The property then passed to a nephew, M. Lafargue, already managing Château Belair on the part of absentee landlords, and subsequently to a niece of his, Mlle Challon who had married Édouard Dubois in 1891. By 1878 Ausone is top of the Saint-Émilions. It is to Édouard Dubois-Challon – who bought neighbouring Belair in 1916 – that we must accord the credit for the reputation of the wine in the twentieth century.

The quality of Ausone diminished after the Second World War, the wine remaining elegant, but rather light. But after the death of Jean Dubois-Challon, son of Édouard, in 1974, his widow took things in hand. She made the bold choice of appointing the richly bearded, 19-year-old Pascal Delbeck as *régisseur*. Things began to improve. Yet all too frequently the wine in bottle did not live up to its apparent potential when judged in cask at the age of six months.

By this time Ausone was *en indivision*, its shares divided between Mme Dubois-Challon and her cousins, the Vauthier family. Eventually in 1995, Mme Dubois-Challon relinquished control, and Alain Vauthier took over. She died in 2003. He is now the owner, with his sister, of Ausone. Pascal Delbeck remains at Château Belair, which was wholly owned by Mme Dubois-Challon, but is no longer responsible for Ausone, where Michel Rolland is now employed as consultant. The wine is now made in a new *cuvier*, constructed in 2002, but retaining the oak vats and stainless-steel tanks of the previous cellar, and matured in an extensive – but no longer as damp as it once was – cavern, hewn out of the rock beneath the ruins of the old Chapelle Madelaine. Judging by the wines since 1997, the quality of Ausone in bottle now merits its place as one of Saint-Émilion's two *Premiers Grands Crus Classés A*.

See *Grands Vins*, p. 376.

Clos Badon

OWNER: Jean-Luc Thunevin.
COMMUNE: Saint-Sulpice-de-Faleyrens.
SURFACE AREA UNDER VINE: 6.5 ha – 70% Merlot;
   30% Cabernet Franc.

OTHER WINE: Château de Valandraud (Saint-Émilion).
CLASSIFICATION: Grand Cru.

The vines lie between those of Château Pavie and Château Larcis-Ducasse and the D670, the Libourne-Bergerac road, the first vintage being 1998. It is made with the same *garagiste* attention to details plus 100 per cent new oak as at Château de Valandraud, but it is rather less expensive. It is not quite as concentrated though.

Château Balestard-La-Tonnelle

OWNER: Capdemourlin family.
COMMUNE: Saint-Émilion.
SURFACE AREA UNDER VINE: 10.6 ha – 70% Merlot;
   25% Cabernet Franc; 5% Cabernet Sauvignon.
SECOND WINE: Chanoine de Balestard.

OTHER WINES: Château Cap de Mourlin (Saint-Émilion); Château Petit Faurie de Soutard (Saint-Émilion); Château Roudier (Montagne Saint-Émilion).
CLASSIFICATION: Grand Cru Classé.

The history of Balestard-La-Tonnelle, whose vineyards lie between those of Châteaux Soutard and Trottevieille, goes back a long way. The wine is named after a local ecclesiastic, and extolled by the poet François Villon in the fifteenth century. Villon's poem is depicted on the label: the wine is described as a 'divine nectar'. The other part of the name refers to a tower somewhat similar to that Château Latour, an ancient mill, which stands in the grounds. In 1868 the property belonged to the Courrech family. It then passed to M. Bertauts-Coulure, who sold it to M. Berthon in 1923. Roger Capdemourlin, already the owner of the château that bears this name, married M. Berthon's daughter, and ran both for 30 years before retiring in favour of his son Jacques.

    Balestard-La-Tonnelle is a reliable, second division Saint-Émilion: full-bodied, often quite sturdy, rich and spicy. I score it moderately well, both from cask in the spring after the vintage, and later when I see it in bottle. But it has never suggested itself as a contender for promotion. The 2000 was better than usual, though.

Château Barde-Haut

OWNER: Sylviane Garcin-Cathiard.
COMMUNE: Saint-Émilion.
SURFACE AREA UNDER VINE: 17 ha – 80% Merlot;
   20% Cabernet Franc.

SECOND WINE: Le Vallon du Château Barde-Haut.
OTHER WINES: Clos L'Église (Pomerol); Château Haut-Bergey (Pessac-Léognan).
CLASSIFICATION: Grand Cru.

Château Barde-Haut's vineyard overlooks the neighbouring commune of Saint-Laurent-des-Combes. It was acquired by Mme Garcin in 2000. Since then there has been a lot of investment in the cellar, not least a change to 100 per cent new oak. It is already clear that this is a rising star.

Château Beauséjour (Duffau-Lagarrosse) ★

OWNER: Duffau-Lagarrosse family; manager: Jean-Michel Dubos.
COMMUNE: Saint-Émilion.
SURFACE AREA UNDER VINE: 7 ha – 70% Merlot;

20% Cabernet Franc; 10% Cabernet Sauvignon.
SECOND WINE: La Croix de Mazerat.
CLASSIFICATION: Premier Grand Cru Classé B.

This is the smaller part of the Beauséjour vineyard, divided in 1869, the date this section was acquired by the Duffau-Lagarrosse family, who still own it today. Prior to this the site had belonged to the Gerès and Carle de Figeac families before coming into the hands of a lawyer Pierre-Paulin Ducarpe. Ducarpe had a son, Léopold, and a daughter who became Mme Duffau-Lagarrosse.

For many years, despite being rated fifth in the commune in 1868, this Beauséjour was an under-achiever. The vineyard is found next to that of Château Canon, west of the town itself, above that of Château Angélus. But the wine was rather too solid, even dense, for its own good – there was rather more Cabernet Sauvignon then. Jean-Michel Dubos arrived to manage the estate in 1983, and since then things have improved considerably. The wine still has volume, but there is now rather more richness, concentration and class. It keeps well.

See *Grands Vins*, p. 388.

Château Beau-Séjour-Bécot ★

OWNER: Gérard & Dominique Bécot.
COMMUNE: Saint-Émilion.
SURFACE AREA UNDER VINE: 16.5 ha – 70% Merlot; 24% Cabernet Franc; 6% Cabernet Sauvignon.

SECOND WINE: La Tournelle de Beau-Séjour-Bécot.
OTHER WINES: La Gomerie (Saint-Émilion); Château Grand-Pontet (Saint-Émilion).
CLASSIFICATION: Premier Grand Cru Classé B.

North of Château Beauséjour-Duffau-Lagarrosse, on its own little promontory overlooking the lesser vineyards below, is Beau-Séjour-Bécot. After Beauséjour was divided in 1869 Léopold Ducarpe constructed an elegant mansion in a little park, with a separate *chai* nearby. In 1924 his heirs sold out to Dr Jean Fagouet. In their turn Fagouet's heirs sold this Beauséjour to Michel Bécot, father of the present owners, in 1969. A major investment then followed, the old *chais* being replaced by a state-of-the-art *cuvier* underneath which is a substantial barrel cellar. New oak was intro-duced, and the vineyard drained. Subsequently the Bécots acquired the neighbouring Château Grand-Pontet from Barton and Guestier, which they retained as a separate wine, and the 4.5-hectare Château Les Trois Moulins whose vineyard they added to Beau-Séjour-Bécot, as it had now become, as they did the land of Château La Carte which they already owned.

It was this latter act which got them into difficulties with the authorities. Argue, quite justifi-ably, as they did, that the terroirs were very similar, the fact remained that the original section was *appellation contrôlée Premier Grand Cru Classé*, while Trois-Moulins and La Carte were simply *appellation contrôlée Grand Cru Classé*. It was illegal to combine the three and call the result a First Growth. Beau-Séjour-Bécot was demoted. Ironically it was only from this time – 1982 – that the wine, unexciting in the Fagouet era, could be considered of First Growth quality.

Years of legal appeals followed, to no avail. In 1989, Michel Bécot, no doubt somewhat embit-tered, decided to retire. His sons took over. They subsequently acquired a piece of land called La Gomerie, from which they produce an excellent, non-classed wine. And in 1996 Beau-Séjour-Bécot was re-admitted to the top rank of Saint-Émilions.

The wine, however, is quite unlike the other Beauséjour, or indeed neighbouring Canon. It is rich and oaky, ripe and succulent and with an agreeable spicy, toffee-mocha flavour, but it is essen-tially soft-centred. And it has continued to improve.

See *The Vine* No 82, November 1991.

Château Belair ★

OWNER: The heirs of the late Mme Helyett
  Dubois-Challon; manager: Pascal Delbeck.
COMMUNE: Saint-Émilion.
SURFACE AREA UNDER VINE: 12.6 ha – 70% Merlot;
30% Cabernet Franc.
OTHER WINE: Château Tour du Pas Saint-Georges
  (Saint-Georges Saint-Émilion).
CLASSIFICATION: Premier Grand Cru Classé B.

Belair, which lies next to Château Ausone, but which has as much of its vineyard on the plateau above as on the slopes below, can claim to be the oldest Libournais wine estate of all. For most of the nineteenth century it was regarded as making the best wine.

We have to go back to the Middle Ages and the Hundred Years War between the French and the English, and a family called Knollys. Robert de Knollys was governor of the Guyenne, captain of the local English army, and owner of considerable land holdings in the area. Following the Battle of Castillon in 1453, and the departure of the English, the Knollys, like many who had been established in the area for generations, decided to remain. Their name gradually transformed into Canolle, they became French, a successor was raised to the marquisate by the youthful Louis XIV as a result of successful exploits during the Fronde, and their descendants were one of the first to establish a monocultural vineyard at Belair. It was already an old vineyard, measuring 11 hectares in 1752. The Canolles remained at Belair until 1916.

This was the year Château Belair was acquired by Édouard Dubois-Challon, already the proprietor of Château Ausone next door. Ausone has passed to one branch of his successors. His daughter-in-law, Mme Helyett Dubois-Challon, remained at Belair until her death early in 2003.

Belair has never been the sort of muscular wine one finds at Château Canon, despite sharing much of the plateau above the château with this growth. Elegance, fragrance and delicacy are the keynotes. Nevertheless there are times when I have Belair a little slight. It could do with a bit more power and concentration, and I am sure it could retain its breed and quality of fruit even if it were a little more substantial.

See *Grands Vins*, p. 392.

Château Bellefont-Belcier

OWNER: SA B J L & Partners; manager:
  Dominique Hébard.
COMMUNE: Saint-Laurent-des-Combes.
SURFACE AREA UNDER VINE: 12.4 ha – 83% Merlot;
10% Cabernet Franc; 7% Cabernet Sauvignon.
SECOND WINE: Marquis de Bellefont.
CLASSIFICATION: Grand Cru.

Château Bellefont-Belcier is situated just across the border with Saint-Émilion in the commune of Saint-Laurent-des-Combes. The vineyard lies on a continuation of the Pavie slope. For many years this property belonged to the Faure family, successive generations being christened Pierre, before being sold to the present owners in 1994. They appointed Louis Mitjaville, son of François of nearby Château Tertre-Roteboeuf as *régisseur*, and he did much to put Bellefont-Belcier on the map. Château Bellefont-Belcier is now a medium-bodied, fresh, juicy, oaky Saint-Émilion, worthy of *grand cru* status.

Château Bellevue ★

OWNER: de Coninck & Horeau families.
COMMUNE: Saint-Émilion.
SURFACE AREA UNDER VINE: 6.2 ha – 67% Merlot; 16.5% Cabernet Franc; 16.5% Cabernet Sauvignon.

SECOND WINE: Château Ramonet.
OTHER WINES: Château Canon (Canon-Fronsac); Château Junayme (Canon-Fronsac); Château Vrai-Canon-Boyer (Canon-Fronsac).
CLASSIFICATION: Grand Cru Classé.

This is a long-established and well-sited property. It belonged to the Lacaze family from 1642 until sold by Gaston Lacaze to his cousin Louis Horeau, in 1938. It lies below the Beauséjours, next to Château Angélus. Until recently it was one of the more obscure of the classed growths, in danger, perhaps, of being demoted. But in 2000 the owners invited Nicolas Thienpont and Stéphane Derenoncourt, who had worked wonders at Château Pavie-Macquin, to take charge. The result? A transformation of quality. The vineyard is now run according to biodynamic principles, as at Pavie-Macquin but rare in the Bordeaux region.

Château Bergat

OWNER: Castéja family; director: Philippe Castéja.
COMMUNE: Saint-Émilion.
SURFACE AREA UNDER VINE: 4.5 ha – 50% Merlot; 40% Cabernet Franc; 10% Cabernet Sauvignon.

OTHER WINES: Château Batailley (Pauillac); Château Trottevieille (Saint-Émilion); Domaine de L'Église (Pomerol).
CLASSIFICATION: Grand Cru Classé.

The vineyard of Bergat lies between Château Trottevieille and the town of Saint-Émilion, and is run by the same team. Having been farmers of the estate for many years the Castéjas bought the property in 1990 from the Clausse-Bertin family, who had owned it for more than a century. The wine is soft and fruity, but lacks real depth and concentration.

Château Berliquet ★

OWNER: Vicomte Patrick de Lesquen; manager: Patrick Valette.
COMMUNE: Saint-Émilion.
SURFACE AREA UNDER VINE: 10 ha – 70% Merlot;

25% Cabernet Franc; 5% Cabernet Sauvignon.
SECOND WINE: Les Ailes de Berliquet.
CLASSIFICATION: Grand Cru Classé.

The vineyard of Berliquet is particularly well-situated, lying half on the plateau, half on the slope between Châteaux Magdelaine and Canon. One hundred and fifty years ago it was one of the top wines in the area. In the eighteenth century it belonged to the influential de Sèze family. It then passed to the Perez family for more than a century before being sold in 1918 to the last descendant of another of Saint-Émilion's most influential dynasties, Comte Louis de Carles. Patrick de Lesquen's mother, Giselle, was Comte Louis' daughter. An aviator, then a banker, de Lesquen entrusted the management of Berliquet to the local co-operative in 1950.

Approaching retirement, de Lesquen began to take a more personal interest in Berliquet. In 1978 he entered into a new contract with the co-operative. They would continue to produce the wine, but it would be vinified separately in a new winery at the property. In 1996, when the lease finally ran out, he took charge himself, appointing Patrick Valette, son of the former owner of Château Pavie, as manager. Since then the improvement in quality has been startling. The wine is full and rich, cool and elegant: a definite contender for First Growth status.

See *The Vine* No 190, November 2000.

Château Cadet-Bon

OWNER: Guy Richard.
COMMUNE: Saint-Émilion.
SURFACE AREA UNDER VINE: 4.65 ha – 70% Merlot;
  30% Cabernet Franc.

SECOND WINE: Château Vieux Moulin du Cadet.
CLASSIFICATION: Grand Cru Classé.

Legend has it that this estate is named after a younger son (*cadet*) of one Jacques Bon, mayor of Saint-Émilion in the fourteenth century. As there are other estates with a Cadet prefix or suffix in the immediate area one wonders whether Cadet is in fact not a *lieu-dit* (place name). This vineyard belonged to Justin Bon in 1868, to the Pineau family at the end of the nineteenth century and then to François Gratadour. It was bought by the present owners, Bernard and Marcelline Gans in 1986, who have since succeeded in getting the property promoted to *Grand Cru Classé* in 1996, a position it lost at the previous classification. The vineyard lies between Châteaux Soutard and Cadet-Piola north of the town of Saint-Émilion. Since its reclassification the wine has improved, losing a certain rustic touch it possessed previously. It is now a good wine, worthy of its status.

The same owners also owned Château Curé-Bon from 1992 to 2000. This has now been incorporated into Château Canon.

Château Cadet-Piola

OWNER: Jabiol family.
COMMUNE: Saint-Émilion.
SURFACE AREA UNDER VINE: 7.1 ha – 51% Merlot;
  28% Cabernet Franc; 18% Cabernet Sauvignon;
  3% Malbec.

SECOND WINE: Chevaliers de Malte.
OTHER WINE: Château de Pasquette (Saint-Émilion).
CLASSIFICATION: Grand Cru Classé.

This property is named after a nineteenth-century mayor of Saint-Émilion, Albert Piola, a pioneering viticulturalist responsible for introducing the Guyot method of pruning as well as the Cabernet Sauvignon grape into the Libournais. From him the estate passed to Robert Villepigue, proprietor of Château Figeac. The Jabiols arrived as farmers in 1952 and bought Cadet-Piola from M. Villepigue's successors 10 years later. There is no château here, as such; merely the winery above some extensive underground vaulted cellars, hewn out of the rock. In the vineyard one can still see traces of the trenches cut out of underlying limestone which was the Gallo-Roman method of planting vines, a tradition which persisted late until the Middle Ages.

Cadet-Piola is usually quite a full-bodied wine, sometimes at the expense of being a little solid. But it is well worthy of its ranking.

Château Canon ★★

OWNER: Chanel Inc./Wertheimer family; director:
  John Kolasa.
COMMUNE: Saint-Émilion.
SURFACE AREA UNDER VINE: 22 ha – 75% Merlot;

  25% Cabernet Franc.
SECOND WINE: Clos Canon.
OTHER WINE: Château Rauzan-Ségla (Margaux).
CLASSIFICATION: Premier Grand Cru Classé B.

Château Canon produces one of the very best wines of the Libournais region. The vineyard occupies most of the plateau west of the town, enclosed by a wall, and unchanged since the estate was founded in the eighteenth century. It is well possible that this is the oldest monocultural property in the area.

The owner then was Jean Biès. In 1760 he sold what was then called the Domaine de Saint-Martin, after the name of the local church, to Jacques Kanon, a retired naval captain. The Kanon era lasted a mere 10 years, yet he had the château constructed, invested substantially in the vineyard and *chais*, and established the wine as one of the leading labels in the area. His successor was Raymond Fontémoing, an important local merchant. Canon remained in the hands of his successors until 1857 – when it took up its present title – subsequently passed through a number of hands before being acquired by Gabriel Supeau for his daughter Henriette and her husband André Fournier, in 1919.

It was the Fournier family, André, his son Pierre and one of the latter's children, Éric, who ensured the reputation of Château Canon in modern times: full-bodied, rich, concentrated, classy and long-lasting. Eventually, sadly, and to Éric's deep regret, the family decided to sell up, and Château Canon was bought by the American end of Chanel, who had already acquired Château Rauzan-Ségla, in 1996.

Much needed to be done. There had been a lack of investment in the vineyard, parts of which required wholesale replanting. Moreover the woodwork in the *chais* had been infected by a treatment, and this had to be replaced. This was soon put to rights. After a brief blip in the mid-1990s the quality of Canon is back where it should be.

In 2000 Canon acquired the 4 hectares of the adjoining *grand cru classé* Château Curé-Bon. Following discussion with the authorities, these vines have been incorporated into the *premier grand cru classé*. An equivalent 4 hectares of less well-regarded vineyard has been downgraded and sold off.

See *Grands Vins* p. 397 and *The Vine* No 200, September 2001.

Château Canon-La-Gaffelière

OWNER: Comtes von Neipperg.
COMMUNE: Saint-Émilion.
SURFACE AREA UNDER VINE: 19.5 ha – 55% Merlot;
40% Cabernet Franc; 5% Cabernet Sauvignon.
SECOND WINE: Neipperg Sélection.

OTHER WINES: Château d'Aiguilhe (Côtes de
Castillon); Clos Marsalette (Pessac-Léognan);
La Mondotte (Saint-Émilion); Clos de L'Oratoire
(Saint-Émilion).
CLASSIFICATION: Grand Cru Classé.

The bulk of the Canon-La-Gaffelière vineyard lies below that of Château La Gaffelière itself (the word Gaffelière indicating that this was once the site of a leprosarium) above the railway, with the château and *chais* on the other side. For a century or so, following the French Revolution, the owners were the Boitard de La Poterie family, who were also proprietors of Château Grand-Barrail--Lamarzelle-Figeac. In 1890 it passed to the Peyraud family, whose successors were to sell it on to

Pierre Meyrat, mayor of Saint-Émilion in 1953. In 1971 the estate was sold to Joseph-Hubert Von Neipperg, a Count of the Holy Roman Empire from the Neckar valley in Württemberg.

It is really since 1983, when Stephan von Neipperg took over, that Château Canon-La-Gaffe-lière has risen to its present position, a contender for First Growth status. Stephan had the vineyard drained, started pruning more drastically, as well as green harvesting, had a sophisticated pumping-over machine installed, and increased the percentage of new oak. Moreover, he engaged the services of Stéphane Derenoncourt as consultant oenologist. More recently he has expanded his empire.

Canon-La-Gaffelière is, above all, a wine of elegance and personality. Today it is one of the best of the *grands crus classés*.

See *The Vine* No 82, November 1991.

Château Cap de Mourlin

OWNER: Capdemourlin family; director: Jacques Capdemourlin.
COMMUNE: Saint-Émilion.
SURFACE AREA UNDER VINE: 14 ha – 65% Merlot; 25% Cabernet Franc; 10% Cabernet Sauvignon.
SECOND WINE: Capitan de Mourlin.

OTHER WINES: Château Balestard-La-Tonnelle (Saint-Émilion); Château Petit Faurie de Soutard (Saint-Émilion); Château Roudier (Montagne Saint-Émilion).
CLASSIFICATION: Grand Cru Classé.

Though the Capdemourlin family are said to have been vineyard workers in the neighbourhood for nearly 500 years, their name does not crop up in Cocks & Féret until 1899. This is alongside their eponymous château, declared to have a previous existence under the name of Artuzan or Artugon (if so there is a considerable lack of the name in earlier editions of Cocks & Féret).

Cap de Mourlin, divided between rival members of the family from 1936 to 1982, was reunited in 1983. The wine is generally less well-regarded than Château Balestard-La-Tonnelle. I find it no less good. I enjoyed the 2000 in the spring of 2001. The vineyard lies opposite that of Château Larmande, north of the town of Saint-Émilion.

Château Chauvin

OWNER: Marie-France Février & Béatrice Ondet.
COMMUNE: Saint-Émilion.
SURFACE AREA UNDER VINE: 15 ha – 75% Merlot;

20% Cabernet Franc; 5% Cabernet Sauvignon.
SECOND WINE: La Borderie de Chauvin.
CLASSIFICATION: Grand Cru Classé.

The origins of Château Chauvin lie with the Fourcaud-Laussac family of Château Cheval-Blanc, who also possessed a property about a kilometre to the east at the time of the Second Empire. In 1891 part was acquired by Victor Ondet. Fifteen years later Ondet increased his holding by another 7 hectares. Today it is the fourth subsequent generation, two sisters, who run this admirable estate. The wine is fullish-bodied, ample and quite oaky. It fully merits its classification.

Château Cheval Blanc ★★★

OWNER: Bernard Arnault & Albert Frère; manager: Pierre Lurton.
COMMUNE: Saint-Émilion.
SURFACE AREA UNDER VINE: 35.5 ha –

60% Cabernet Franc; 39% Merlot; 1% Cabernet Sauvignon.
SECOND WINE: Le Petit Cheval.
CLASSIFICATION: Premier Grand Cru Classé A.

Château Cheval Blanc is Saint-Émilion's greatest wine. It is also the only great wine in the world made principally from Cabernet Franc. The property lies in superficially gravelly soil on the Pomerol border, marching with Château La Conseillante and Château L'Évangile. Indeed Château Pétrus is hardly a kilometre away as the crow flies.

Once part of the great Figeac estate, what became Cheval Blanc was detached in two stages between 1832 and 1838 and acquired by a family called Ducasse. In 1852 Jean Laussac Fourcaud married Henriette Ducasse. There were then 31.5 hectares under vine. At first these Graves-Saint-Émilions, as they are known, were considered less classy than those wines made around the town itself, though Château Cheval Blanc was always first in the list. Gradually, during the rest of the nineteenth century they became more and more fashionable. By the beginning of the next the price of Cheval Blanc was on a par with those of Châteaux Ausone and Belair, considered the best of the 'Côtes' wines. By the 1960s Cheval Blanc was selling for the price of the Médoc First Growths. Today it is often even more expensive. The property remained in the hands of the Fourcaud-Laussac family until 1988 when it was sold to the present owners. Pierre Lurton, the current manager, was appointed in 1991.

The wine is splendidly concentrated, without the least suspicion of over-extraction, rich, full bodied, oaky and profound. It has also been remarkably consistent. While not, on past form, being able to register the 75-, even 100-year life of Latour or some of the other Médocs, it will keep for at least 50 years, which I suggest is enough for most of us.

See *Grands Vins*, p. 382, and *The Vine* No 204, January 2002.

Château La Clotte

OWNER: Chailleau family; manager: Nelly Moulierac.
COMMUNE: Saint-Émilion.
SURFACE AREA UNDER VINE: 4 ha – 80% Merlot;

15% Cabernet Franc; 5% Cabernet Sauvignon.
SECOND WINE: Les Combes de Laclotte.
CLASSIFICATION: Grand Cru Classé.

This tiny *cru* lies next to Château Pavie-Macquin below the eastern walls of the town of Saint-Émilion. From 1747 to 1913 it belonged to the Grailly family from whom it was acquired by Sylvain Chailleau. I used to see this wine regularly – at least *en primeur* – for between 1969 and 1989 the land was farmed by Ets. J-P Moueix. It was then taken back in hand by a new generation of the

Chailleau family. This change of direction has not caused the wine to suffer though. If anything, since 1997, it has improved. I now find it rich, ample, succulent and positive. One of the better *grands crus classés*.

Château Corbin

OWNER: Bardinet family; manager: Anabelle Bardinet.
COMMUNE: Saint-Émilion.

SURFACE AREA UNDER VINE: 12.7 ha – 80% Merlot; 17% Cabernet Franc; 3% Cabernet Sauvignon.
SECOND WINE: Château Corbin Vieille Tour.
CLASSIFICATION: Grand Cru Classé.

Corbin, north of Château Figeac, was with it one of the two *maisons nobles* in the area in the Middle Ages. This is the extreme north-west of the Saint-Émilion commune, near the border with Montagne Saint-Émilion and Lalande-de-Pomerol as well as Pomerol itself. In the nineteenth century much of the land here belonged to the influential Chaperon family, including neighbouring Château Jean Faure. In the 1920s Corbin was acquired by the Giraud family, who also owned Château Certan-Giraud in Pomerol. When the latter was sold to Ets J-P Moueix in 1999 it enabled Mme Blanchard and her granddaughter to buy out the other members of the family and make much-needed investment in the vineyard and in the *chai*. Until then Corbin had not been much to shout about. Now things are changing.

Château Corbin-Michotte

OWNER: Jean-Noël Boidron.
COMMUNE: Saint-Émilion.
SURFACE AREA UNDER VINE: 6.7 ha – 65% Merlot; 30% Cabernet Franc; 5% Cabernet Sauvignon.

SECOND WINE: Château Les Abeilles.
OTHER WINES: Château Calon (Montagne Saint-Émilion); Château Cantelauze (Pomerol).
CLASSIFICATION: Grand Cru Classé.

Corbin-Michotte lies next door to Château Corbin. The vineyard is farmed without fertilisers, insecticides and herbicides, and leaf removal is carried out in the run-up to the vintage. My experience of Corbin-Michotte is not extensive. Sadly I was not impressed by his 2000, nor by the 2002.

Château La Couspaude

OWNER: Aubert family.
COMMUNE: Saint-Émilion.
SURFACE AREA UNDER VINE: 7 ha – 70% Merlot;

20% Cabernet Franc; 10% Cabernet Sauvignon.
SECOND WINE: Junior de la Couspaude.
CLASSIFICATION: Grand Cru Classé.

Designated La Gouspaude in the 1868 Cocks & Féret, when it belonged to the Commandant Lolliot, Couspaude lies next to Château Trottevieille on the plateau north-east of the town of

Saint-Émilion. The Aubert family has owned it since 1908. Château La Couspaude was demoted from *grand cru classé* to *grand cru* in 1985, apparently because the wine was not *mise au château* (the Auberts have several other minor estates).

This led, as it has done elsewhere, to a change of direction and a positive improvement in quality, with, *inter alia*, the introduction of a second wine in 1994 and a move to 100 per cent new oak. Promoted once more in 1996, Château Couspaude is now one of the best of the *grands crus classés*: full-bodied, rich, oaky and concentrated.

Château Couvent des Jacobins

OWNER: Joinaud-Borde; managers: Denis
Pomarède & Denis Borde.
COMMUNE: Saint-Émilion.

SURFACE AREA UNDER VINE: 10.5 ha – 70% Merlot;
30% Cabernet Franc.
SECOND WINE: Le Menut des Jacobins.
CLASSIFICATION: Grand Cru Classé.

The Jacobins were a monastic order of Dominicans, so named because one of their original hospices was in the Rue Saint-Jacques in Paris. They should not be confused with the political Jacobins at the time of the French Revolution! The convent is situated in the middle of the town; the vineyard, in three pieces, on the south-eastern side. It was sequestered in 1793 and came into the hands of the Joinaud-Borde family in 1902. I find the wine variable: soft, generous and oaky at best, as in 1995 and 2000, but a little weak in other years such as 1998 when they should have done better.

Château Curé-Bon (La Madelaine)

In the middle of the nineteenth century the local priest or *curé*, named Bon, planted 4 hectares of vine on the plateau above Châteaux Ausone and Belair. After his death in 1874 the domaine passed to his nephew Camille Lapelletrie. Maurice Landé, proprietor in the 1970s and 1980s (I remember a delicious 1978), sold out to Bernard and Marceline Gans, co-incidentally proprietors of Château Cadet-Bon, in 1992. In 2000 the 4 hectares of Curé-Bon were sold to Château Canon, into which it has been absorbed.

Château Dassault

OWNER: Dassault family; Manager: Laurence
Brun-Vegriette.
COMMUNE: Saint-Émilion.
SURFACE AREA UNDER VINE: 24 ha – 65% Merlot;

30% Cabernet Franc; 5% Cabernet Sauvignon.
SECOND WINE: D de Dassault.
CLASSIFICATION: Grand Cru Classé.

Victor Fourcaud Beylot, wine merchant and elder brother of Jean Fourcaud Laussac of Château Cheval Blanc united three small properties under the name Château Couperie in 1862. The wine was an immediate success, but under later owners, particularly a Jewish family called Reynard, who were forced to seek refuge in Switzerland during the Second World War, fortunes declined. When Marcel Dassault, founder of the aircraft manufacturers who produce the Mirage jet, acquired it in 1953 it was a total ruin.

Though he visited rarely, he put forward all the investment that was necessary to recreate things from scratch, and the wine was promoted to *grand cru classé* in 1969. The estate is situated beyond that of Château Soutard in the north-east sector of the *appellation* and makes a reliable, fullish, oaky wine which is one of the best and most consistent of the classed growths.

See *The Vine* No 22, September 1986.

Le Dôme ★

OWNERS: Jonathan & Lyn Malthus.
COMMUNE: Vignonet.
SURFACE AREA UNDER VINE: 2.85 ha –
75% Cabernet Franc; 25% Merlot.

OTHER WINES: Clos Nardian (Bordeaux Blanc);
Château Laforge (Saint-Émilion Grand Cru);
Château Teyssier (Saint-Émilion Grand Cru).
CLASSIFICATION: Grand Cru.

Le Dôme comes from two parcels of old vines bought by Jonathan Malthus in 1998 and 2001 which lie near Château Angélus. This is a more classically made wine than Château Laforge, Malthus' other *tête de cuvée*. It has heaps of fruit and lots of dimension and class. A splendid recruit to the ranks of the super-stars. The first vintage was 1998.

Château La Dominique

OWNER: Clément Fayat; directors: Emmanuel
Villega & Étienne Priou.
COMMUNE: Saint-Émilion.
SURFACE AREA UNDER VINE: 22.5 ha – 80% Merlot;
15% Cabernet Franc; 5% Cabernet Sauvignon.
SECOND WINE: Saint-Paul de Dominique.

OTHER WINES: Château Clément-Pichon (Haut-
Médoc); Château Prieur de la Commanderie
(Pomerol).
CLASSIFICATION: Grand Cru Classé.

The vineyard of Château La Dominique marches with that of Château Cheval Blanc in the Graves-Saint-Émilion and is said to have been given its name as a souvenir of a former proprietor's sojourn in the West Indies. This charming story may well be true. On the other hand, as the area lies on the pilgrim route to Santiago de Compostella, the name may have religious connotations.

The first known owners were the Chaperon family in the 1840s, merchants who were important proprietors all over the Libournais. Henri Greloud, a relation by marriage, took over some 10 years later. His successors sold La Dominique to Louis Soualle, who was also buying Château Gazin at the same time, in 1918. From M. Soualle succession passed to the Baillencourt family in 1933. Following problems with death duties, at the same time as the Baillencourt successors sold 5 hectares of Gazin to Pétrus in 1969, they also decided to sell La Dominique. It was acquired by the civil engineer and businessman Clément Fayat, the first of his ventures in the Bordeaux area. Much-needed investment was then put in – the vineyard was drained, a new winery installed and a *chai à barriques* constructed. It was decided to use 50 per cent new wood. Soon La Dominique began to be talked about. From the early 1980s La Dominique has been one of the better *grands crus classés*. The wine is plump and oaky, with smooth ripe tannins; an easy-to-drink wine. Sometimes I wish, though, it had a bit more bite.

See *The Vine* No 82, November 1991.

Clos Dubreuil

OWNER: Benoît Trocard.

COMMUNE: Saint-Christophe-des-Bardes.

SURFACE AREA UNDER VINE: 1.4 ha – 90% Merlot;
10% Cabernet Franc.

SECOND WINE: Anna.

OTHER WINE: Chateau La Croix-Bellevue
(Lalande-de-Pomerol).

CLASSIFICATION: Grand Cru.

This microscopic property dates from 1996. The wine, from old vines, is made by Louis Mitjaville, and is full-bodied, intense, concentrated and very classy. It is also rather expensive.

Château Faugères

OWNER: Corinne Guisez.

COMMUNE: Saint-Étienne-de-Lisse.

SURFACE AREA UNDER VINE: 28 ha – 70% Merlot;
25% Cabernet Franc; 5% Cabernet Sauvignon.

SECOND WINE: Les Roses du Château Faugères.

OTHER WINE: Château Cap de Faugères (Côtes de
Castillon).

CLASSIFICATION: Grand Cru.

Faugères lies at the eastern end of the Saint-Émilion *appellation* (the family's Castillon estate is
next door) and has belonged to the Guisezes since 1823. Since the latest generation took over in
1987 major investment has been made: the vineyard has been drained, a new *cuvier* built, new oak
introduced and the yield reduced. The wine is plump and succulent and not over-oaked: a very
good example. Péby-Faugères is a 100 per cent Merlot, 100 per cent new oak super-*cuvée*.

Château Faurie-de-Souchard

OWNER: Jabiol Sciard family; manager: Françoise
Sciard.

COMMUNE: Saint-Émilion.

SURFACE AREA UNDER VINE: 11.5 ha – 65% Merlot;
26% Cabernet Franc; 9% Cabernet Sauvignon.

SECOND WINE: Château Souchard.

OTHER WINE: Château Cadet-Peychez (Saint-
Émilion).

CLASSIFICATION: Grand Cru Classé.

Faurie evokes a local battle during the Hundred Years War and Souchard the name of a wealthy
family of landowners and parliamentarians in the eighteenth century. The property belonged to
the Lavaud family in 1868. Later on, owners included a M. Raby and a Charles Jean, who also was
proprietor of neighbouring Château Trottevieille, and, from 1933, the Jabiol family. Mme Françoise
Sciard, *née* Jabiol, took over in 1983. The wine is pleasant, but on the soft side. It lacks depth, concentration and class.

Château Ferrand Lartigue

OWNER: Pierre & Michèle Ferrand.

COMMUNE: Saint-Sulpice-de-Faleyrens.

SURFACE AREA UNDER VINE: 6 ha – 90% Merlot;

8% Cabernet Sauvignon; 2% Cabernet Franc.

CLASSIFICATION: Grand Cru.

The property lies on the Dordogne side of the main Libourne–Bergerac road in the commune of
Saint-Sulpice-de-Faleyrens. The consultant oenologist is Louis Mitjaville, son of François of
Château Tertre-Roteboeuf. Like all his wines the fruit is to the fore and there is plenty of depth
and balance, without exaggeration. Ferrand Lartigue has justly become one of the best of the new-
wave *grands crus*.

Château Figeac ★★

OWNER: Manoncourt family; manager: Éric d'Aramon.
COMMUNE: Saint-Émilion.
SURFACE AREA UNDER VINE: 40 ha – 35% Cabernet Franc; 35% Cabernet Sauvignon; 30% Merlot.

SECOND WINE: La Grange Neuve de Figeac.
OTHER WINES: Château de Millery; Château Petit Figeac; Château Fleur-Pourret (all Saint-Émilion).
CLASSIFICATION: Premier Grand Cru Classé B.

Figeac and its great rival, neighbouring Château Cheval Blanc, occupy much of the famous gravel mounds which have given their name to the Graves-Saint-Émilion sector on the Pomerol border of the commune.

A medieval manor occupied the site until it was razed to the ground in 1590. This was replaced by an elegant Renaissance mansion by the Cazes family who controlled an estate of some 400 hectares. In 1694 Marie de Caze married François de Carles. Figeac was to remain in the hands of their successors until 1838, by which time much of the outlying land, including what is now Cheval Blanc, had been sold off. During the next half-century there were further changes of ownership, and the estate was further dismembered, reducing the vineyard to more or less its present size, and giving rise to a number of neighbouring domaines which incorporated the name Figeac into their title. In 1892 the property was acquired by Henri de Chevremont and for a time was managed by the celebrated viticulturalist Alfred Macquin, who hoped to acquire it. From de Chevremont Figeac has passed through the female line to the Manoncourts, today's owners.

Figeac is noteworthy for being planted with a large proportion of Cabernet Sauvignon, a policy inaugurated by Thierry Manoncourt in the 1950s and unusual in Saint-Émilion. This creates a wine which is somewhat austere in its youth, but gives it a welcome acidity in hot vintages such as 1982 and 1989, and the staying power to last. There are years such as 1964 when Figeac is every bit as good as Cheval Blanc. If normally Cheval Blanc is clearly superior, Figeac is nevertheless one of the better First Growths.

See *Grands Vins*, p. 403 and *The Vine* No 219, April 2003.

Château Fombrauge

OWNER: Bernard Magrez.
COMMUNE: Saint-Christophe-des-Bardes.
SURFACE AREA UNDER VINE: 56 ha – 71% Merlot;
  18% Cabernet Franc; 11% Cabernet Sauvignon.
SECOND WINE: Le Cadran de Fombrauge.

OTHER WINES: Château Pape-Clément (Pessac-
  Léognan); Château La Tour Carnet (Haut-
  Médoc) and others.
CLASSIFICATION: Grand Cru.

Château Fombrauge is the largest important estate in the Libournais, one of only a handful of Médoc proportions. The vineyards overlap into the neighbouring communes of Saint-Étienne-de-Lisse and Saint-Hippolyte. The château itself has its origins in a Carthusian monastery.

During my time as a wine merchant Fombrauge was owned by the Bygodt family. In 1985 it passed to a consortium based on the firm of Hans Just of Copenhagen. In 1999 it was acquired by the present owners. Fombrauge has always been a very good example of a minor Saint-Émilion, soft, full of fruit and gently oaky. The new owners have more ambitious intentions which I will watch with interest. Château Magrez-Fombrauge is a very oaky super-*cuvée*.

Château Fonplégade

OWNER: Marie-José Moueix & Nathalie Moueix-
  Guillot.
COMMUNE: Saint-Émilion.
SURFACE AREA UNDER VINE: 18 ha – 60% Merlot;
  35 Cabernet Franc; 5% Cabernet Sauvignon.

SECOND WINE: Château Côtes Trois Moulins.
OTHER WINES: Château La Croix Bellevue
  (Lalande-de-Pomerol); Château Moulinet
  (Pomerol).
CLASSIFICATION: Grand Cru Classé.

Château Fonplégade lies next to Château L'Arrosée on the southern flank of the Saint-Émilion *côte* below the vineyard of Château Magdelaine. It has a long history as one of the top estates of Saint-Émilion. In 1868 it was rated sixth in the area, and belonged to the Comtesse de Gallard, sister of the Baron de Marignan, proprietor of Château Belair. She had acquired the property in 1863. Following her death Fonplégade passed to Paul Boisard. Boisard had no children but appointed a Mlle Roquefort as his successor. During her tenure, however, a time of world wars and economic depression, the estate was neglected, and much needed to be done when Armand Moueix took over in 1953.

Fonplégade is quite a good wine, fairly elegant, soft and fruity. But until the last couple of vintages it lacked depth and vigour and real class. Given its excellent location and past reputation, I used to say it could do better. However, a new generation took over in 2002 and things are now beginning to improve.

Château Fonroque

OWNER: Alain Moueix.

COMMUNE: Saint-Émilion.

SURFACE AREA UNDER VINE: 17.6 ha – 87% Merlot;
13% Cabernet Franc.

SECOND WINE: Château Cartier.

OTHER WINES: Château Magdelaine (Saint-Émilion); Château Trotanoy (Pomerol).

CLASSIFICATION: Grand Cru Classé.

A date, 1756, on a lintel at the entrance to the cellar indicates that wine has been made here, just north of the town of Saint-Émilion itself, for two and a half centuries. In the mid-1800s the property belonged to the Malet de Roquefort family, owners then and now of Château La Gaffelière. Subsequently it was taken over by Hubert Chatonnet and then, in 1925, by Elie Laporte, a wine merchant. In 1931 Fonroque was acquired by Jean Moueix, founder of Ets J-P Moueix. This was his first venture into château ownership. It has now passed down to Alain Moueix.

Château Fonroque is a thoroughly reliable Saint-Émilion, favouring the Merlot grape as is the practice *chez* Moueix. The wine is medium- to full-bodied, balanced, plump and fruity. It is even better since a second wine was introduced in 2000.

See *The Vine* No 82, November 1991.

Clos Fourtet

OWNER: Philippe Cuvelier; manager: Tony Ballu.

COMMUNE: Saint-Émilion.

SURFACE AREA UNDER VINE: 20 ha – 80% Merlot;

15% Cabernet Sauvignon; 5% Cabernet Franc.

SECOND WINE: Closerie de Fourtet.

CLASSIFICATION: Premier Grand Cru Classé B.

Clos Fourtet occupies much of the plateau adjoining Château Canon immediately outside the town of Saint-Émilion. The word means a small fort, the land being a garrison for troops of soldiers billeted in the area in the eighteenth century. The château and *chais* date from 1790. Logic would indicate that this is the time that the area was first seriously planted with vines. The extensive cellars, hewn out of the rock, date from earlier. The first owner in the records was a M. Leperche, in the middle of the nineteenth century. It remained in the hands of his successors until 1919, when it was acquired by the merchant Fernand Ginestet. In 1947, in order to complete the purchase of Château Margaux, the Ginestets sold Clos Fourtet to the Lurton family, André (of Château Couhins and others), Lucien (of Château Brane-Cantenac and others), Dominique and their sister Simone Noël. It was Dominique, the youngest, who managed it at first, later succeeded by his son Pierre, who is now at Château Cheval Blanc. In 2001 the Lurtons sold Clos Fourtet to Philippe Cuvelier, a French businessman.

Clos Fourtet has never, in my experience, been one of the high fliers among the First Growths, and I have often suggested it to be no better than many *grands crus classés* which should be considered for promotion. Things began to improve in the late 1980s, in the time of Pierre Lurton. He left in 1991 and this progress was not sustained. The wine is ripe, but lacks dimension and class. It is not really worthy of its classification. Let us hope the new ownership soon puts this to rights. The 2002, tasted out of cask in April 2003, showed an improvement.

See *The Vine* No 60, January 1990.

Château Franc-Mayne

OWNER: Georgy Fourcroy and Associates.
COMMUNE: Saint-Émilion.
SURFACE AREA UNDER VINE: 7.02 ha – 90% Merlot;

10% Cabernet Franc.
SECOND WINE: Les Cèdres de Franc-Mayne.
CLASSIFICATION: Grand Cru Classé.

Château Franc-Mayne is well situated below Beau-Séjour-Bécot and was once part of a larger estate that included the neighbouring Château La Gomerie. In the nineteenth century it belonged to Edmond Fourcaud and the Baron des Cordes, before being sold to the Libournais merchant Jean Theillassoubre. It was acquired by the insurance group AXA from M. Theillassoubre's successor Mme Butard in 1984, but she continued to run it. In 1996 AXA Millésimes sold Franc-Mayne to Georgy Foucroy and his associates. The wine was decent but a little dull in the AXA era. It has improved since and the 2000 was fat, rich, concentrated and oaky.

Château La Gaffelière

OWNER: Comte Léo de Malet-Roquefort.
COMMUNE: Saint-Émilion.
SURFACE AREA UNDER VINE: 22 ha – 80% Merlot;
  10% Cabernet Franc; 10% Cabernet Sauvignon.

SECOND WINE: Clos La Gaffelière.
OTHER WINE: Château Tertre-Daugay (Saint-Émilion).
CLASSIFICATION: Premier Grand Cru Classé B.

Château La Gaffelière lies at the foot of the slope below the Châteaux of Belair and Ausone. In 1969 an important Gallo-Roman mosaic depicting a vine covered in fruit was uncovered in part of the estate, leading to renewed speculation about Ausonius (310–395 AD) and his connection with the area. The de Malet-Roquefort family have owned the property, on the site of a former leprosarium, since the sixteenth century.

I have had some magnificent Gaffelières of the 1945–1961 era. More recently the wine has not really been one of the stars among the First Growths. It is certainly good: medium- to full-bodied, fruity and positive. Sometimes it is very good but it is rarely fine. Is it just that its situation, the bulk of the vineyard being behind the château, below that of Pavie, is not as fine as the First Growths properly on the slope? Or could a greater attention to detail do the trick?

See *Grands Vins*, p. 409.

Château La Gomerie ★

OWNER: Gérard & Dominique Bécot.
COMMUNE: Saint-Émilion.
SURFACE AREA UNDER VINE: 2.5 ha – 100% Merlot.
SECOND WINE: Mademoiselle de La Gomerie.

OTHER WINES: Château Beau-Séjour-Bécot (Saint-Émilion); Château Grand-Pontet (Saint-Émilion).
CLASSIFICATION: Premier Grand Cru.

The land that is now La Gomerie was formerly part of the holdings of the Abbaye de Fayze. This was sold off at the time of the French Revolution. Even though it was divided in mid-century – part being absorbed into neighbouring Château Franc-Mayne for a time – it was nevertheless quite a large estate, registering 45 *tonneaux* in 1909, when it belonged to Maurice Despujol and Raymond Paillet. Forty years later, by this time in the hands of the Lescure family, production was down to 10 *tonneaux* (1000 cases). The Bécot brothers, who bought the estate from Marcel Lescure in 1995, make 750 cases of *grand vin*.

La Gomerie, like other wines including the *vins garagistes*, is what one could term a super-*grand cru*: non-classified, made with obstinate and often misguided perfectionism in tiny quantities with lots of new wood and all sorts of new techniques in order to garner maximum points in magazines six months after the vintage. Many of these new-wave wines are not, in fact, very good, just superficially attractive. La Gomerie is not one of these. It is, in fact, very fine, with intensity, concentration and a lot of depth and class. Dare I suggest it is a better wine than the Bécots' *premier grand cru*? It certainly trades for more money.

Château Grand Corbin-Despagne

OWNER: Despagne family; manager: François Despagne.

COMMUNE: Saint-Émilion.

SURFACE AREA UNDER VINE: 26.5 ha – 75% Merlot;

20% Cabernet Franc; 4% Cabernet Sauvignon; 1% Malbec.

SECOND WINE: Petit-Corbin-Despagne.

CLASSIFICATION: Grand Cru.

There have been Despagnes in the Saint-Émilion area for 500 years, says the château brochure, viticulture beginning here in the Corbin *lieu-dit* in the north-west of the *appellation* with one Louis Despagne in 1812. It still belongs to the same family. Grand-Corbin-Despagne was appointed *grand cru classé* in 1954 but was subsequently demoted. Since 1996 a new generation has breathed life into the property, and things have improved. The wine is lush and oaky. It now deserves to be upgraded.

Château Grand-Mayne

OWNER: Jean-Pierre Nony.

COMMUNE: Saint-Émilion.

SURFACE AREA UNDER VINE: 19.1 ha – 76% Merlot;

13% Cabernet Franc; 11% Cabernet Sauvignon.

SECOND WINE: Les Plantes du Mayne.

CLASSIFICATION: Grand Cru Classé.

Well placed on the gentle inclines below the Beauséjours, this estate produces one of the very best of the classed growths. It can trace its history back to the Laveau family, who bought it in 1685. The Laveaus were a powerful family who owed their fortune to trade with the West Indies. Between 1811 and his death in 1836 Grand-Mayne, rather bigger then than now, belonged to Jean Laveau, who with Soutard and other châteaux under his belt was one of the leading landowners in the area. Having no direct heirs, his empire was then divided. In 1868 the property was owned by the Puchaud family. Adrien Puchaud was succeeded by L Massip and then by the Termes-Dubrocas, owners in 1909. It was acquired by Jean Nony, father of the present proprietor, in 1934.

I find the wine consistent and wholly admirable: rich and full-bodied without being over-extracted, balanced and oaky. It keeps well.

Château Grand-Pontet

OWNER: Pourquet-Bécot families.

COMMUNE: Saint-Émilion.

SURFACE AREA UNDER VINE: 14 ha – 75% Merlot; 25% Cabernet Franc.

SECOND WINE: Dauphin de Grand-Pontet.

OTHER WINES: Château Beau-Séjour-Bécot (Saint-Émilion); Château La Gomerie (Saint-Émilion).

CLASSIFICATION: Grand Cru Classé.

The domaine is said to have been founded by an army officer named d'Estien in 1415, and to have remained in the hands of his descendants for 550 years. The present estate was formed by Gabriel Combruze, mayor of Saint-Émilion and *député* for the Gironde, who united two properties, La Carte and Petit Bois at the beginning of the twentieth century. Grand-Pontet was owned by the merchants Barton & Guestier between 1965 and 1980, when it was acquired by the present owners.

The vines lie downslope from Château Beau-Séjour-Bécot, and, though now made independently by the Bécot sisters, the wines have much in common: rich, round and oaky, with no hard edges. This is usually one of the better *grands crus classés*.

Château Les Grandes Murailles

OWNER: Reiffers family; manager: Sophie
  Fourcade.
COMMUNE: Saint-Émilion.
SURFACE AREA UNDER VINE: 2 ha – 95% Merlot;

5% Cabernet Franc.
OTHER WINES: Château Côte de Baleau (Saint-
  Émilion); Clos Saint-Martin (Saint-Émilion).
CLASSIFICATION: Grand Cru Classé.

Just outside Saint-Émilion is a large wall, the last remains of a twelfth-century Benedictine convent. This lies in the vineyard of the diminutive Grandes Murailles and is depicted on their label. There is no château, the wine being made at Château Côte de Baleau.

Les Grandes Murailles has been the property of the same family since 1643, the Reiffers succeeding the Malens in the 1950s. In 1985, two of their three properties, Les Grandes Murailles and Côte de Baleau, were demoted to simple *grand cru*. Les Grandes Murailles has since been promoted. It is not one of the highfliers, however. I find it lacks depth and finesse.

Château Guadet Saint-Julien

OWNER: Lignac family.
COMMUNE: Saint-Émilion.
SURFACE AREA UNDER VINE: 5.5 ha – 75% Merlot;

25% Cabernet Franc.
SECOND WINE: Le Jardin.
CLASSIFICATION: Grand Cru Classé.

The château and *chais* of Guadet-Saint-Julien are at the top end of the town of Saint-Émilion, with the vines along the road to Montagne-Saint-Émilion to the north. The Guadets were a noble Libournais family, one of whom was guillotined in 1794. Their successors, the Lacombes, sold the estate to the Gantey family in 1874. The Lignacs are their direct descendants.

Guadet-Saint-Julien is a wine I see regularly on my April visits to Bordeaux. It has never inspired me. I find it rather weak for a *grand cru classé*. The 1998 is no more than an agreeable fruity wine. The 2000 is thin. The 2002 lacks charm.

Château Haut-Corbin

OWNER: SMABTP (Société Mutuelle d'Assurance
  du Bâtiment et des Travaux Publics); director:
  Philippe Dambrine.
COMMUNE: Saint-Émilion.
SURFACE AREA UNDER VINE: 6 ha – 65% Merlot;

25% Cabernet Franc; 10% Cabernet Sauvignon.
OTHER WINES: Château Cantemerle (Haut-
  Médoc); Château Le Jurat (Saint-Émilion).
CLASSIFICATION: Grand Cru Classé.

Château Haut-Corbin lies north of Château Chauvin, within a few hundred metres of the Montagne-Saint-Émilion border. It was upgraded to classed growth in 1969 and sold by its proprietor Édouard Guinaudie to the present owners in 1985. I find the wine fully worthy of its place among the *grands crus classés*. It is a wine of good colour, juicy fruit, depth and grip, showing the vineyard's proximity to Pomerol.

Château Haut-Sarpe

OWNERS: Jean-François & Marie-Antoinette
  Janoueix.
COMMUNE: Saint-Christophe-des-Bardes.
SURFACE AREA UNDER VINE: 21 ha – 70% Merlot;
  30% Cabernet Franc.

SECOND WINE: Château Vieux Sarpe.
OTHER WINES: Château La Croix (Pomerol);
  Château La Croix-Saint-Georges (Pomerol) and
  others.
CLASSIFICATION: Grand Cru Classé.

Despite being no more than 500 metres from the town walls, the vineyard of Château Haut-Sarpe is not in Saint-Émilion but in the neighbouring commune of Saint-Christophe-des-Bardes. The wine was already well-known in 1750 when the property belonged to Jacques-Amedée de Carles, lieutenant general to the king. In fact the 'cru de Sarpe' is the first specific Saint-Émilion wine to be mentioned in the records. In the nineteenth century the estate belonged to the Comte d'Allard and then to successive Barons du Foussat de Bogeron, the last of whom sold Haut-Sarpe to Joseph Janoueix in 1930.

The château and its surroundings are splendid. Sadly, I find the wine lacks structure and distinction.

Clos des Jacobins

OWNER: Gérard Frydman; manager: Hubert de Boüard de Laforest.
COMMUNE: Saint-Émilion.
SURFACE AREA UNDER VINE: 8.4 ha – 70% Merlot; 30% Cabernet Franc.
SECOND WINE: Prieuré des Jacobins.
CLASSIFICATION: Grand Cru Classé.

Ecclesiastical land sequestered at the time of the French Revolution, Clos des Jacobins was owned by the Cordes and then the Vauthier families before being acquired by Domaines Cordier in 1964. They sold it to Gérard Frydman in 2001. Frydman has engaged Hubert de Boüard de Laforest of Château Angelus as overall manager. Since then the vineyard has been drained, the winemaking equipment has become more sophisticate, a more exacting selection is taking place and the proportion of new oak increased. The new team did not make the 2000, which did not impress me (I had never been particularly struck by Clos des Jacobins, however). But I wait developments with interest. The vineyard, between Châteaux Franc-Mayne, Grand-Mayne and Laroze, is well sited. I marked the 2002, out of cask in April 2003, as 'good plus'.

Château Laforge

OWNER: Jonathan & Lyn Malthus.
COMMUNE: Saint-Émilion.
SURFACE AREA UNDER VINE: 5.7 ha – 92% Merlot; 8% Cabernet Franc.
OTHER WINES: Le Dôme (Saint-Émilion); Château Teyssier (Saint-Émilion).
CLASSIFICATION: Grand Cru.

Château Laforge is a recent creation. It comes from five different parcels illustrating the three main soil types of the Saint-Émilion commune, all neighbours to *grands crus classés* vineyards. The wine is made by modern methods at Château Teyssier, including *microbullage* and *bâtonnage* of the lees, and is splendidly rich and concentrated, yet complex and classy. Top classed growth quality here. The first vintage was 1998.

Château Laniote

OWNER: Arnaud & Florence de la Filolie.
COMMUNE: Saint-Émilion.
SURFACE AREA UNDER VINE: 5 ha – 70% Merlot; 20% Cabernet Franc; 10% Cabernet Sauvignon.
SECOND WINE: Chapelle de Laniote.
CLASSIFICATION: Grand Cru Classé.

The château of Laniote lies just north of Fonroque and has belonged to the Freymond-Rouja family, of which the Filolies are direct descendants, for seven generations. This is a satisfactory, middle-of-the-road Saint-Émilion *grand cru classé*, quite weighty, usually with well-balanced fruit, occasionally a little bulky. The label depicts, not the modest château but the Chapelle de la Trinité which is built above Saint-Émilion's grotto. This is owned by the same family.

Château Laplagnotte-Bellevue

OWNER: Henri & Claude de Labarre.

COMMUNE: Saint-Christophe-des-Bardes.

SURFACE AREA UNDER VINE: 6 ha – 70% Merlot:
20% Cabernet Franc; 10% Cabernet Sauvignon.

SECOND WINE: Archange de Laplagnotte.

OTHER WINE: Château La Croix-Lartigue (Côtes de Castillon).

CLASSIFICATION: Grand Cru.

Château Laplagnotte-Bellevue is in the northern part of the commune of Saint-Christophe-des-Bardes, only a few metres from the Montagne-Saint-Émilion border. It was bought by the Labarres in 1989 from the Biais family and is now run by their son Arnaud. On his arrival in 1998 the *chais* and vat-house were extensively modernised, and it is from this period that the property has been one to watch. The wine is clean, balanced, juicy and succulent, with a good base of oak.

Château Larcis-Ducasse

OWNER: Hélène Gratiot Alphandey & Jacques-Olivier Gratiot.

COMMUNE: Saint-Laurent-des-Combes.

SURFACE AREA UNDER VINE: 10.9 ha – 65% Merlot;
25% Cabernet Franc; 10% Cabernet Sauvignon.

CLASSIFICATION: Grand Cru Classé.

The property adjoins Château Pavie but is situated across the border in the commune of Saint-Laurent-des-Combes. It was the only property outside Saint-Émilion to have been classified right from the beginning. There is a long history here. The wine was already well regarded before the French Revolution. In the early part of the nineteenth century the property belonged to Adolphe Pigasse, who owned neighbouring Château Pavie. He subsequently disposed of it, and it was then divided between a M. Ducasse and a M. Bergey. In 1893 both halves were acquired by Henri Raba. Henri was succeeded by his son André. The current proprietors are the children of his niece. Nicolas Thienpont, who runs Château Pavie-Macquin, Bellevue and other estates, has been in charge here since 2002.

Larcis-Ducasse has been a good, full-bodied, generous, accessible wine, gently oaky on the finish: among the best of the *grands crus classés*. It has now improved even further.

Château Larmande

OWNER: Groupe d'Assurances La Mondiale; manager: Pascal Maniez.

COMMUNE: Saint-Émilion.

SURFACE AREA UNDER VINE: 25 ha – 65% Merlot;

30% Cabernet Franc; 5% Cabernet Sauvignon.

SECOND WINE: Le Cadet de Larmande.

CLASSIFICATION: Grand Cru Classé.

Château Larmande lies on the plateau north of the town of Saint-Émilion. In the nineteenth century it belonged first to the Pion de Case family and then to a M. Saint-Genis. Towards the end of the century the *régisseur* was Gaston Meneret. Together with his friend Amedée Capdemourlin he acquired Château Larmande around the time of the First World War. Gaston's son, Germain, married Alice de Capdemourlin, and Larmande became theirs in 1935. Their son Jean-Fernand, known simply as Jean, ran Larmande until it was sold to the present proprietors in 1990.

I have long considered Château Larmande one of the very best of the *grands crus classé*. Yields are low, the average age of the vines is high and the cellar equipment is up to date. Quality has not declined under the new regime. We have a splendidly rich, profound, long-lasting wine here. It is consistent too.

See *Grands Vins*, p. 430.

Château Laroque

OWNER: Beaumartin family.
COMMUNE: Saint-Christophe-des-Bardes.
SURFACE AREA UNDER VINE: 58 ha – 88% Merlot;
10% Cabernet Franc; 2% Cabernet Sauvignon.
SECOND WINES: Les Tours de Laroque; Château Peymouton.

Like Château Haut-Sarpe, this classed growth is situated in Saint-Christophe-des-Bardes, not in Saint-Émilion itself. Like another neighbour, Château Fombrauge, this is a very large domaine by Libournais standards. The château befits the size of the estate. There is an eleventh-century *donjon* next to the château, which has a splendid Louis XIV façade. In 1868 it belonged to the Marquis de Rochefort-Lavie and was managed by Paul Boisard, later owner of Château Fonplégade. The *cuvier* measured 28 metres by 16 and there were three barrel cellars capable of holding a total of 6000 barrels. As they made only some 1200 casks-worth of wine each year this indicates a later bottling than today. But Laroque was not all the Rochefort-Lavies owned.

The property was acquired by the Beaumartin family during the 1930s. By this time it had fallen into neglect. Some 40 hectares needed to be replanted and a major investment was required in the *chais*. It was not until the 1960s that quality was again what it had been 100 years before. Since then there has been further progress, and in 1996 Laroque was promoted to *grand cru classé*. This applies only to a specific 27 hectares out of the 58 under vine. The wine from the remaining vineyards is sold under the name of Château Peymouton. Château Laroque is of medium weight and usually well-made. What it seems to lack, however, is a bit of personality.

Château Laroze

OWNER: Meslin family.
COMMUNE: Saint-Émilion.
SURFACE AREA UNDER VINE: 27 ha – 59% Merlot:
35% Cabernet Franc; 6% Cabernet Sauvignon.
SECOND WINES: Clos Yon Figeac; Lafleur Laroze.
CLASSIFICATION: Grand Cru Classé.

Following the assembly of various parcels in the Mazerat area into what became the Clos L' Angélus in the early 1880s, the Gurchy family combined two properties lower down the slope: Camus La Gommerie and Lafontaine, into a domaine which they called Laroze. The château was constructed soon after. Dr Meslin acquired it in the 1920s. Today's owner is his grandson Guy. Since 1993 Guy Meslin has made a serious investment, draining the vineyard, entirely renovating the *cuverie*, lowering the yield and so on. His intention is to increase the Merlot percentage in the vineyard to 70 per cent, which is what is usually in the *grand vin* blend. This is now one of the very best of the *grands crus classés*. A full-bodied, rich wine with real depth, grip and style.

Château Magdelaine ★★

OWNER: Ets J-P Moueix.

COMMUNE: Saint-Émilion.

SURFACE AREA UNDER VINE: 11 ha – 90% Merlot; 10% Cabernet Franc.

SECOND WINE: Château Saint-Brice.

OTHER WINES: Château Fonroque (Saint-Émilion); Château Trotanoy (Pomerol) and others.

CLASSIFICATION: Premier Grand Cru Classé B.

In the sure hands of the J-P Moueix family and their very able winemaker, Jean-Claude Berrouet, Château Magdelaine is frequently these days the third best Saint-Émilion wine after Cheval Blanc and Ausone. For two centuries it belonged to the Chatonnet family, one of whom, in the 1860s, made the smart move of acquiring 5 hectares at the top of the slope from neighbouring Château Fonplégade, at the time when the original domaine was being split up as a result of the rules of succession to give rise to what became Curé Bon de la Madelaine (without the 'g') and other properties no longer extant. After the First World War, the estate passed to a son-in-law, Georges Jullien. In 1952, his son Jean, a professor of law, sold Château Magdelaine to Jean-Pierre Moueix.

The vineyard lies more or less 50:50 on the plateau next to Châteaux Belair and Ausone and on the slope above Fonplégade and L'Arrosée. It is planted with the highest proportion of Merlot among the First Growths. The wine has marvellous fruit, depth, balance and class. I can only simply say: Bravo.

See *Grands Vins*, p. 414 & *The Vine* No 233, July 2004.

Château Matras

OWNER: Véronique Gaboriaud-Bernard.

COMMUNE: Saint-Émilion.

SURFACE AREA UNDER VINE: 8 ha – 34% Merlot; 33% Cabernet Franc; 33% Cabernet Sauvignon.

SECOND WINE: L'Hermitage de Matras.

OTHER WINES: Château Bourseau (Lalande-de-Pomerol); Château L'Hermitage de Mazerat (Saint-Émilion).

CLASSIFICATION: Grand Cru Classé.

Château Matras is located below Beauséjour-Duffau-Lagarrosse next to Château Angélus in a sheltered amphitheatre ideally situated facing to the south and west. A 'matras' was a crossbowman, and the name is said to derive from some soldier who retired here after fighting in the Hundred Years War. In 1868 the property belonged to a M. Bourricaud. It then passed to Romain Chaperon and by the turn of the century to Chaperon's son Albert. Some time after the First World War it was sold to the Comte Louis de Carles, who was also proprietor of nearby Château Berliquet. It subsequently passed to his daughter Mme de Frémond, at which time it was farmed by a M. Vauthier, who, we are told, forgot to apply for the original classification of the 1950s. (Matras was finally admitted in 1969.) Mme de Frémond sold the estate to Jean Bernard-Lefebvre in 1962 and the property is now run by his daughter.

This is not a wine which has come my way very often in bottle. In recent years I have only tasted the 2000. I found it a bit hard. The 2002, from cask, was plump, fruity and oaky: quite good. Château L'Hermitage is an old wine, 100 per cent new oak, super-*cuvée*, first produced in 1997.

Château Monbousquet

OWNER: Gérard & Chantal Perse.
COMMUNE: Saint-Sulpice-de-Faleyrens.
SURFACE AREA UNDER VINE: 32 ha – 60% Merlot; 30% Cabernet Franc; 10% Cabernet Sauvignon.
SECOND WINE: Château Angelique de

Monbousquet.
OTHER WINES: Château Pavie (Saint-Émilion); Château Pavie-Decesse (Saint-Émilion).
CLASSIFICATION: Grand Cru.

Château Monbousquet is the principal growth in Saint-Sulpice-de-Faleyrens, the commune on the Dordogne side of the Libourne-Bergerac road. For many years it belonged to the ebullient Querre family predominant in the local Jurade. The château itself is an elegant construction resting in a quiet *parc anglais*. In 1993 this château became the first of Gérard Perse's forays into the Libournais. The wine which was well-made, soft and gently oaky, if without great depth or character, is now very extracted: not my cup of tea at all.

La Mondotte ★

OWNER: Comtes von Neipperg.
COMMUNE: Saint-Laurent-des-Combes.
SURFACE AREA UNDER VINE: 4.5 ha – 80% Merlot; 20% Cabernet Franc.

OTHER WINES: Château d'Aiguilhe (Côtes de Castillon); Château Canon-La-Gaffelière (Saint-Émilion); Clos de L'Oratoire (Saint-Émilion).
CLASSIFICATION: Grand Cru.

The vineyard which produces La Mondotte lies up on the plateau east of the town of Saint-Émilion near Château Troplong-Mondot and the Pavies Decesse and Macquin. It was acquired by the Neipperg family when they bought Château Canon-La-Gaffelière in 1971.

The wine was first made separately in 1996 and met with instant critical approval. It now sells for prices higher than most of the First Growths. The vines are old and yields are kept to below 30 hl/ha. Extraction is by means of *pigeage* (treading down); malolactic fermentation takes place in barrels and 100 per cent new oak is employed. This is perhaps the best of all the new-wave Saint-Émilions. There is a depth and complexity which only a fine terroir can give.

Château Moulin du Cadet

OWNER: SAS Blois Moueix; manager: Pierre & Isabelle Moueix.
COMMUNE: Saint-Émilion.
SURFACE AREA UNDER VINE: 4.3 ha – 90% Merlot; 10% Cabernet Franc.

OTHER WINES: Château Fonroque (Saint-Émilion); Château Magdelaine (Saint-Émilion); Château Trotanoy (Pomerol).
CLASSIFICATION: Grand Cru Classé.

Château Moulin du Cadet lies among the other Cadet estates, north of the town, conveniently next door to Château Fonroque. The *moulin* or 'mill' in the title reminds us of the days when Saint-Émilion was not as vinously monocultural as it is today.

This Cadet is likely to have been a spin off one of the others as a result of inheritance divisions. The first proprietor I can find is a Lucien Brissaud in 1909. It eventually passed to the Mouliérac family, owners of Château La Clotte. They entered into a farming arrangement, as they did with La Clotte, with Ets J-P Moueix. In 1989 they sold the estate to the Moueix family.

It is interesting to compare Moulin du Cadet with Fonroque today. The properties are adjacent, the *encépagement* is identical, the winemaking must be pretty similar. Yet the wines are quite different. I find Château Fonroque has more structure, but Moulin du Cadet has more flair.

Château Moulin Saint-Georges

OWNER: Alain Vauthier.

COMMUNE: Saint-Émilion.

SURFACE AREA UNDER VINE: 7 ha – 80% Merlot;
20% Cabernet Franc.

OTHER WINE: Château Ausone (Saint-Émilion).

CLASSIFICATION: Grand Cru.

The vineyard lies on the slope opposite Ausone and marches with Saint-Georges-Côte-Pavie, La Gaffelière and Pavie-Macquin. The wine is certainly good enough to be upgraded to *grand cru classé*. It is soft and oaky with rather more grip and depth than most minor Saint-Émilions.

Clos de L'Oratoire ★

OWNERS: Comtes von Neipperg.

COMMUNE: Saint-Émilion.

SURFACE AREA UNDER VINE: 10.2 ha – 85% Merlot;
15% Cabernet Franc.

OTHER WINES: Château d'Aiguilhe (Côtes de
Castillon); Château Canon-La-Gaffelière (Saint-Émilion); Château Peyreau (Saint-Émilion).

CLASSIFICATION: Grand Cru Classé.

Clos de L'Oratoire lies next to Château Soutard on the plateau north-east of the town of Saint-Émilion. It was originally part of Château Peyreau, an estate founded by the *négociant* Charles Beylot in the middle of the nineteenth century and successfully enlarged so that by 1909 there were 52 hectares under vine producing 100 *tonneaux*. Much reduced it passed to Michel Boutet in the 1960s, who decided to divide the estate in two. He called the better section Clos de L'Oratoire and was successful in getting this elevated to classed growth status in 1969. Both halves were bought by Stephan von Neipperg in 1991.

In Neipperg's capable hands Clos de L'Oratoire has gone from strength to strength. This is a full-bodied, rich, concentrated wine with even more depth and quality than Château Canon-La - Gaffelière. A sure contender for First Growth status.

Château Pavie

OWNER: Gérard & Chantal Perse.

COMMUNE: Saint-Émilion.

SURFACE AREA UNDER VINE: 37 ha – 70% Merlot:
20% Cabernet Franc; 10% Cabernet Sauvignon.

OTHER WINES: Château Pavie-Decesse (Saint-Émilion); Château Monbousquet (Saint-Émilion).

CLASSIFICATION: Premier Grand Cru Classé B.

Pavie is the largest of the *Côtes* Saint-Émilion *premiers crus*. It occupies most of the south-facing slope east of the town, with its sister Château Pavie-Decesse up above on the plateau.

In the early nineteenth century this area was divided between a number of different owners, the largest holdings belonging to Adolphe Pigasse, who also owned what is now Château Larcis-Ducasse, and the Talleman family. In 1855 a Bordeaux merchant, Ferdinand Bouffard, arrived on the scene. During the following few years he succeeded in uniting most of the land. For some reason, though it belonged to him, he retained the Pigasse section as a separate vineyard: this became Pavie-Decesse. The only plot he did not acquire was what is now Pavie-Macquin, also up on the plateau. Bouffard did much to raise the reputation, and hence the price, of Pavie. Shortly after the First World War ownership passed to Albert Porte. In 1943 it was bought by Alexandre Valette, who also acquired Château Troplong-Mondot. The Valettes, particularly Jean-Paul, Alexandre's grandson, who managed the property from 1967 onwards, continued Ferdinand Bouffard's good work. They sold out to Gérard Perse in 1998.

Since his arrival Gérard Perse has made a considerable investment in Pavie. Certain parcels of vines have been replanted. The concrete fermentation vats have been replaced by stainless steel, a new barrel cellar has been constructed and the yield has been cut to 25 hl/ha. Sadly the winemaking methods have also been changed. Pavie is now a rather over-extracted wine. It has lost its elegance.

See *Grands Vins*, p. 418.

Château Pavie-Decesse

OWNER: Gérard & Chantal Perse.
COMMUNE: Saint-Émilion.
SURFACE AREA UNDER VINE: 3.65 ha – 90% Merlot: 10% Cabernet Franc.

OTHER WINES: Château Monbousquet (Saint-Émilion); Château Pavie (Saint-Émilion).
CLASSIFICATION: Grand Cru Classé.

Château Pavie-Decesse lies on the plateau above the slope of Château Pavie. From the new *salle de réception* there is a splendid view south over the valley of the Dordogne. When Pavie was sold following Ferdinand Bouffard's death after the First World War, Pavie-Decesse was acquired by Marcel Larget, from whom it passed to R Marzelle. The Valettes bought it in 1970, and sold it to the Perses in 1997, the year before they sold Château Pavie.

During the Valette era Pavie-Decesse was a good succulent wine, sometimes a little robust, but meriting its classification. Today, like Pavie itself, I find it rather overdone.

Château Pavie-Macquin ★

OWNER: Corre-Macquin family; director: Nicolas Thienpont.
COMMUNE: Saint-Émilion.
SURFACE AREA UNDER VINE: 15 ha – 70% Merlot;

25% Cabernet Franc; 5% Cabernet Sauvignon.
SECOND WINE: Les Chênes de Macquin.
CLASSIFICATION: Grand Cru Classé.

This part of Pavie has, it would seem, always been independent. It was owned in the first part of the nineteenth century by a M. Chapuis. Albert Macquin, expert viticulturalist and propagator of vines – who introduced the Bordelais to grafting onto American rootstocks as the solution to phylloxera – bought the estate in 1887. Macquin was succeeded by his son-in-law, Antoine Corre. The property has been run since 1990 according to biodynamic principles by Nicolas Thienpont. The wine is now made by Thienpont and oenologist Stéphane Derenoncourt.

Pavie-Macquin is fullish, rich, profound and classy: one of the very best of the *grands crus classés*.

Château Petit-Faurie-de-Soutard

OWNER: Françoise Capdemourlin & Vignobles Aberlen.

COMMUNE: Saint-Émilion.

SURFACE AREA UNDER VINE: 8 ha – 65% Merlot; 30% Cabernet Franc; 5% Cabernet Sauvignon.

SECOND WINE: Petit Faurie de Soutard Deuxième.

OTHER WINES: Château Balestard-La-Tonnelle (Saint-Émilion); Château Capdemourlin (Saint-Émilion).

CLASSIFICATION: Grand Cru Classé.

Immediate neighbour to its stablemate Château Balestard-La-Tonnelle, this estate was split off from the larger Château Soutard in 1851 owing to inheritance problems. Following several changes of owner, the Aberlen family bought it in 1936. In 1977 Jacques Capdemourlin took charge, the property having been inherited by his wife. The wine is reasonably stylish. But it lacks depth.

Château Plaisance

OWNER: Xavier Mareschal; manager: Patrick Valette.

COMMUNE: Saint-Sulpice-de-Faleyrens.

SURFACE AREA UNDER VINE: 17 ha – 85% Merlot;

15% Cabernet Sauvignon.

SECOND WINE: Château La Fleur Plaisance.

CLASSIFICATION: Grand Cru.

In the capable hands of Patrick Valette, this is one of the best wines of this rather sandy part of Saint-Émilion. Recent vintages have been generous, gently oaky, rich and stylish.

Château Le Prieuré

OWNER: Olivier Guichard.

COMMUNE: Saint-Émilion.

SURFACE AREA UNDER VINE: 6.3 ha – 60% Merlot; 30% Cabernet Sauvignon; 10% Cabernet Franc.

SECOND WINE: Château L'Olivier.

OTHER WINES: Château Siaurac (Lalande-de-Pomerol); Château Vray-Croix-de-Gay (Pomerol).

CLASSIFICATION: Grand Cru Classé.

Formed by the dismemberment of the vineyards belonging to the Cordeliers, a Franciscan order, during the French Revolution, Le Prieuré was acquired in 1899 by a M. Brisson, a retired *député* for the region. He was already owner of Château Siaurac in Lalande-de-Pomerol. Brisson's daughter became the Baronne Guichard. The property remains in the hands of her descendants.

The vineyard is well placed between Châteaux Trottevieille and Troplong-Mondot, east of the town. The wine, which is marketed like the other Guichard properties, by Ets J-P Moueix, is positive, structured and clean. It could do with a bit more personality.

Château Quinault L'Enclos

OWNER: Alain & Françoise Raynaud.

COMMUNE: Libourne.

SURFACE AREA UNDER VINE: 18 ha – 70% Merlot; 15% Cabernet Franc; 10% Cabernet Sauvignon; 5% Malbec.

SECOND WINE: La Fleur de Quinault.

OTHER WINES: Château La Croix de Gay (Pomerol); Château La Fleur de Gay (Pomerol).

CLASSIFICATION: Grand Cru.

Château Quinault L'Enclos lies in the eastern suburbs of Libourne. The vineyard was under threat from developers when rescued by the Raynauds in 1997. The soil is a sandy gravel here. The vines are old, averaging 45 years. Until the 2002 vintage Quinault L'Enclos was produced by modern 'garage' methods, including too long a period of extraction for my taste, but in this vintage Reynaud relaxed the style considerably. It now tastes like real wine. I shall watch how this wine ages with interest.

Château Ripeau

OWNER: Françoise de Wilde.
COMMUNE: Saint-Émilion.
SURFACE AREA UNDER VINE: 15.5 ha – 65% Merlot;

30% Cabernet Franc; 5% Cabernet Sauvignon.
SECOND WINE: La Garenne de Ripeau.
CLASSIFICATION: Grand Cru Classé.

Château Ripeau owes its origins to the *maison noble* at Corbin, in the north-east corner of the *appellation*. There were vines here before the French Revolution, according to contemporary maps. It was owned by a M. Pailhas in 1868. It then passed to the Buller family, and, after the First World War, to Marcel Loubat, who for a time also owned neighbouring Château Jean Faure, and from him it passed to Michel Janoueix de Wilde. Françoise de Wilde has been in charge since 1976. There was a dip in quality here in the early 1990s, following a family tragedy, but since 1997 we have seen a change of direction for the better. Improvements in the cellar have been made and the yield in the vineyard reduced. The wine is full-bodied and rich, with, appropriately, a Pomerol touch.

Château Rolland-Maillet

OWNER: Michel & Dany Rolland.
COMMUNE: Saint-Émilion.
SURFACE AREA UNDER VINE: 3.6 ha – 75% Merlot;
25% Cabernet Franc.

OTHER WINES: Château Bertineau Saint-Vincent
(Lalande-de-Pomerol): Château Le Bon Pasteur
(Pomerol); Château Fontenil (Fronsac).
CLASSIFICATION: Grand Cru.

Rolland-Maillet is the Saint-Émilion element in Michel and Dany Rolland's collection of four estates, and comes from land just across the Pomerol border from Château Le Bon Pasteur itself. As you would expect, knowing the winemaking skill of Michel Rolland, this is an excellent example for a minor *appellation* with good fresh fruit, ripe tannins and no lack of complexity.

Château Rol-Valentin

OWNER: Éric & Virginie Prissette.
COMMUNE: Saint-Émilion.
SURFACE AREA UNDER VINE: 4 ha – 85% Merlot;

15% Cabernet Franc.
SECOND WINE: Les Valentines.
CLASSIFICATION: Grand Cru.

While an estate called Côtes de Rol Valentin used to exist, this is effectively a new creation, dating from the arrival of the Prissettes in 1994. The nucleus of the vineyard is 1.8 hectares of vines on the *sables anciens* between La Gomerie and Château Chauvin. Until 1998 this was blended with the wine from 2 hectares on gravelly soil in Saint-Sulpice-de-Faleyrens. From 1999 this land has been replaced by 2.5 hectares in the commune of Saint-Étienne-de-Lisse. The wine is supervised by Stéphane Derenoncourt, responsible for such wines of flair as La Mondotte and Pavie-Macquin. Rol-Valentin is medium- to full-bodied, succulent, rich and oaky. One of the new super-*grands crus*.

Château Saint-Georges-Côte-Pavie

OWNER: Masson family.
COMMUNE: Saint-Émilion.
SURFACE AREA UNDER VINE: 5.5 ha – 80% Merlot;

20% Cabernet Franc.
SECOND WINE: Côte Madeleine.
CLASSIFICATION: Grand Cru Classé.

The vineyard lies between La Gaffelière and Pavie, opposite Château Ausone: a promising position. It has belonged to the Masson family for over a century. The wine has a good reputation, being soft, fresh, fruity and developing in the medium term. As the owners are not members of any of the various promotional groups in the area this is a wine I have not met as often as most.

Clos Saint-Martin

OWNER: GFA Les Grandes Murailles; manager: Sophie Fourcade.
COMMUNE: Saint-Émilion.
SURFACE AREA UNDER VINE: 1.3 ha – 70% Merlot; 20% Cabernet Franc; 10% Cabernet Sauvignon.

OTHER WINES: Château Côte de Baleau (Saint-Émilion); Château Les Grandes Murailles (Saint-Émilion).
CLASSIFICATION: Grand Cru Classé.

The tiny Clos Saint-Martin is found by the church of that name, surrounded by Château Canon and the two Beauséjours. It is the only one of the three Reiffer estates that has not suffered the ignominy of being declassified. (The other two were downgraded, one understands, because all three were made at Côte de Baleau. Since then Les Grands Murailles has been reinstated.) As at Les Grandes Murailles, the Reiffers succeeded the Malen family here in the 1950s. When I first started tasting the wine regularly in the 1980s vinification was supervised by François Boutemy, at the time also responsible for Château Larrivet Haut-Brion in Léognan. He produced a good, quite firm, oaky wine which is still the style today.

Château Sansonnet

OWNER: Patrick d'Aulan.
COMMUNE: Saint-Émilion.
SURFACE AREA UNDER VINE: 6.3 ha – 70% Merlot;

25% Cabernet Franc; 5% Cabernet Sauvignon.
SECOND WINE: Château Lasalle.
CLASSIFICATION: Grand Cru.

Having been owned by the Robin family for more than a century, Château Sansonnet was bought by the d'Aulans, formerly of Champagne Piper-Heidsieck, in 1999. I found the 2000 rather forced and oaky, lacking grace. But the new owners are only at the start of a learning curve. Until 1996 Sansonnet was a *grand cru classé*. Its vineyard is adjacent to Trottevieille so there is potential.

Château La Serre

OWNER: Luc d'Arfeuille.
COMMUNE: Saint-Émilion.
SURFACE AREA UNDER VINE: 7 ha – 80% Merlot; 20% Cabernet Franc.

SECOND WINE: Les Menuts de La Serre.
OTHER WINES: Château La Pointe (Pomerol); Château Toumalin (Fronsac).
CLASSIFICATION: Grand Cru Classé.

La Serre lies between Châteaux Villemaurine and Trottevieille on the north-eastern outskirts of the town of Saint-Émilion. The château dates from the end of the seventeenth century when the property was owned by Romain de Labeyme, descendant of a long line of Bordeaux parliamentarians. In 1868 La Serre belonged to the Marcon family. It then come into the hands of the celebrated Albert Macquin, owner of Château Pavie-Macquin and manager of Château Figeac. In 1949 a M. de Coulon, a Swiss businessman, sold La Serre, and also the Pomerol château of La Pointe to the *négociant* Paul Delahoutre. These passed to his son-in-law, Bernard d'Arfeuille in 1956. Château La Serre has consistently been one of the top *grands crus classés*. I have notes going back to the 1959. It is concentrated, harmonious and classy. It lasts well.

See *The Vine* No 96, January 1993.

Château Soutard

OWNER: de Ligneris family.
COMMUNE: Saint-Émilion.
SURFACE AREA UNDER VINE: 22 ha – 70% Merlot;

30% Cabernet Franc.
SECOND WINE: Clos de La Tonnelle.
CLASSIFICATION: Grand Cru Classé.

Château Soutard is one of the most individual wines as well as one of the most ecologically run properties in the Bordeaux area. The wine is made for the long term. For some reason the malos do not take place here until the late spring or early summer following the vintage – elsewhere in Bordeaux this fermentation usually follows the sugar-alcohol fermentation back in the late autumn. This makes Soutard difficult to judge in April when the campaign for the new vintage opens. Normally François de Ligneris, who makes the wine, withholds Soutard for tasting. He does not sell it through the usual Bordeaux channels anyway.

The vineyard was created by Jean Combret de Faurie in about 1762, at the same time as the elegant château was built. His heir, a nephew, sold the estate to Jean Laveau, possessor of several other estates in the area in 1811. When Laveau died without direct male heirs in 1836 the estate was divided, giving rise to Château Faurie de Souchard and Petit Faurie de Soutard. The nucleus passed to a granddaughter, and then to her son Adolphe d'Allard, mayor of Saint-Émilion in the time of Napoleon III. From him, Soutard came into the hands of the Ligneris family.

The wine is full-bodied, somewhat austere, even hard in its youth. It seems to lack generosity. This arrives later, when the richness and concentration are also more apparent. It needs time, but it is usually worth waiting for.

See *Grands Vins*, p. 433.

Château Tertre-Daugay

OWNERS: de Malet-Roquefort family.
COMMUNE: Saint-Émilion.
SURFACE AREA UNDER VINE: 16 ha – 60% Merlot;
40% Cabernet Franc.

SECOND WINE: Château de Roquefort.
OTHER WINE: Château La Gaffelière (Saint-Émilion).
CLASSIFICATION: Grand Cru Classé.

Tertre means hill, in this case a splendid promontory south-west of the town, giving a spectacular view of the Dordogne valley from Libourne almost to Castillon. In 1868 there were three proprietors in the area: Henri Greloud, Philippe Azélias and a M. Bourricaud, the latter working with his son-in-law, R. Chaperon. These are names which crop up frequently in the histories of the Saint-Émilion estates. The senior part, dignified as Château Daugay in 1909, came into the possession of L Alix. In 1949 the proprietor was Léon Galhaud. Subsequently Tertre-Daugay was neglected. In 1978, it was pretty well derelict when bought at auction by Léo de Malet-Roquefort . The old vines have been conserved, however, and in a new *chai* and with 50 per cent of the casks renewed annually, we have quite a substantial wine with plenty of class and depth. The wine is made by the same team as at La Gaffelière.

Château Tertre-Roteboeuf ★

OWNER: François & Émilie Mitjaville.
COMMUNE: Saint-Laurent-des-Combes.
SURFACE AREA UNDER VINE: 6 ha – 85% Merlot;
   15% Cabernet Franc.

OTHER WINE: Château Roc de Cambes (Côtes de
   Bourg).
CLASSIFICATION: Grand Cru.

South-east of Saint-Émilion, above Château Bellefont-Belcier, where what one might call the Pavie slope finally comes to its end, lies the vineyard of Tertre-Roteboeuf. This is the origin of one of the Saint-Émilion's most brilliant and original wines: one that would be a *grand cru classé* if not a *premier grand cru classé* if only François Mitjaville had been bothered to apply for promotion.

The vineyard comes from Miloute Mitjaville's side of the family. The couple were working in Paris, but decided to take over their inheritance in the 1970s. After a two-year *stage* at Château Figeac François Mitjaville installed himself in 1977. It was a struggle at first. Money was tight. But after the 1982 had come top in a blind tasting the orders began to flow. From 1989 everything was in place and the wine began to show class as well as depth and concentration. Today Tertre-Roteboeuf is as good as all but one or two of the *premiers* and sells for even higher prices. It needs a decade to mature. The 'Le' was dropped at the beginning of the name a few years ago.

See *Grands Vins*, p. 438.

Château Teyssier

OWNER: Jonathan & Lyn Malthus.
COMMUNE: Vignonet.
SURFACE AREA UNDER VINE: 21 ha – 70% Merlot;
   30% Cabernet Franc.

SECOND WINE: L'Esprit de Teyssier.
OTHER WINES: Le Dôme (Saint-Émilion); Château
   Lafarge (Saint-Émilion).
CLASSIFICATION: Grand Cru.

Although the château is situated in Vignonet, south of Saint-Émilion, two-thirds of the vineyards which produce Teyssier now lie in the better adjoining commune of Saint-Sulpice-de-Faleyrens. Jonathan Malthus bought the estate, much smaller then than it is today, in 1991, and he has gradually built it up since. In 2001 he acquired the neighbouring property, Château Destieux Berger, and has merged this with Château Teyssier. This is intelligent, up-to-date winemaking, and the result is a wine with plenty of fruit and no lack of depth and substance: a very good example of a *grand cru*. His other wines, from better land surrounded by classed growths, are even better.

Chateau La Tour du Pin Figeac (Giraud-Bélivier)

OWNER: Giraud-Bélivier family.
COMMUNE: Saint-Émilion.
SURFACE AREA UNDER VINE: 11 ha – 75% Merlot;
   25% Cabernet Franc.

SECOND WINE: Château La Tournelle du Pin Figeac.
OTHER WINES: Château Le Caillou (Pomerol);
   Domaine du Vieux Manoir (Lalande-de-Pomerol).
CLASSIFICATION: Grand Cru Classé.

The origins of this property and the two below are the same. Until 1879 they were part of Château Figeac. Then in 1882 the broken-off section was divided into three parts. Part of the name comes from a tower which was located in this part of the Figeac vineyard before the French Revolution. The property was acquired by Gérard Bélivier in 1923 and transferred to Lucien Giraud, a son-in-law, in 1972. It is now run by André Giraud. Divided into three sections this La Tour du Pin Figeac lies close to the D244 road from Libourne to Montagne-Saint-Émilion, with one of these sections directly opposite La Conseillante. The wine is matured partly in cask and partly in cement vats. It is improving, but it is not yet in the top league of the *grands crus classés*.

Château La Tour du Pin Figeac (Moueix)

OWNER: Vins Jean-Michel Moueix.

COMMUNE: Saint-Émilion.

SURFACE AREA UNDER VINE: 9 ha – 80% Merlot;
  20% Cabernet Franc.

SECOND WINE: Clos La Fleur Figeac.

OTHER WINES: Château Taillefer (Pomerol) and
  others.

CLASSIFICATION: Grand Cru Classé.

Jean-Marie Moueix, son of Armand Moueix and father of Jean-Michel, bought this estate in 1947. Like the above, the vines lie between Châteaux Cheval Blanc and Figeac. As with Château Fonplégade, which this branch of the Moueix family also own, I find the wine quite good but it should be a good deal better. There seems to be more substance here than in the wine above.

Château La Tour Figeac

OWNER: Rettenmaier family.

COMMUNE: Saint-Émilion.

SURFACE AREA UNDER VINE: 14.6 ha – 60% Merlot;

40% Cabernet Franc.

SECOND WINE: L'Esquisse de la Tour Figeac.

CLASSIFICATION: Grand Cru Classé.

After the split (see La Tour du Pin Figeac left), this estate was first owned by a M. Corbière. It then passed to his son-in-law, Émmanuel Boiteau, who sold it to Mme La Veuve Lassèverie in 1918. For 20 years after 1973 it was managed by Michel Boutet, who had been running Château Canon-La-Gaffelière and Clos de L'Oratoire until Stephan von Neipperg took over on behalf of a consortium of German and French shareholders. Otto Rettenmaier bought the property in 1994. Since 1997 La Tour Figeac has been transformed. The vineyard is now run biodynamically. Stéphane Derenoncourt is the consultant oenologist. There is *pigeage*, *microbullage*, malolactic fermentation in barrel and the wine is worked on its lees. The wine is full-bodied, oaky, intense and delicious. La Tour Figeac is now a major contender for elevation to First Growth status. A nice touch: the vats are named after famous composers and musicians.

Château Trianon

OWNER: Dominique Hébrard.

COMMUNE: Saint-Émilion.

SURFACE AREA UNDER VINE: 10 ha – 80% Merlot;
  10% Cabernet Franc; 5% Cabernet Sauvignon;

%5 Carmenère.

OTHER WINE: Château de Francs (Côtes de Francs).

CLASSIFICATION: Grand Cru.

Château Trianon lies on the western side of the *appellation* near the outskirts of Libourne. Hubert Lecointre sold it to Dominique Hébrard in 2001. Hébrard has drained the vineyard, reduced the yield and built a new vat room and barrel cellar. The first releases under the new regime are promising.

Château Troplong-Mondot ★

OWNER: Christine Valette.

COMMUNE: Saint-Émilion.

SURFACE AREA UNDER VINE: 30 ha – 90% Merlot;

5% Cabernet Franc; 5% Cabernet Sauvignon.

SECOND WINE: Mondot.

CLASSIFICATION: Grand Cru Classé.

Due east of Saint-Émilion, on the highest point in the area, is an ugly water-tower. This stands on the edge of a park which surrounds Château Troplong-Mondot. The property's vineyard occupies the best part of this hill, and from the time records begin the wine was acknowledged as being one of the leading examples in the area. The owners in the eighteenth century were the influential and many-tentacled de Sèze family. In the 1830s the Troplong family arrived, Gérus, his son Raymond, followed by Raymond's nephew Édouard. They were to remain proprietors until 1918. In the Cocks & Féret of 1869, Troplong-Mondot is rated second in the area after Château Belair.

The estate was acquired in 1921 by Georges Thienpont, a wine merchant from Etikhove in Belgium who was to buy Vieux Château Certan three years later. In the middle of the depression, in 1936, Thienpont was forced to sell one of his estates. Troplong was the larger, and then more prestigious. It had to go. The buyer was Alexandre Valette.

Christine Valette, granddaughter of Alexandre, took over in the early 1980s, abandoned the harvesting machine and engaged Michel Rolland as advisor. Since then standards have risen impressively. The wine is full-bodied, concentrated, complex and elegant. One of my favourite contenders for *premier grand cru classé* status.

See *Grands Vins*, p. 442.

Château Trottevieille

OWNER: Castéja family; manager: Philippe Castéja.
COMMUNE: Saint-Émilion.
SURFACE AREA UNDER VINE: 10 ha – 50% Merlot; 45% Cabernet Franc; 5% Cabernet Sauvignon.

OTHER WINES: Château Batailley (Pauillac); Domaine de L'Église (Pomerol); Château Lynch-Moussas (Pauillac) and others.
CLASSIFICATION: Premier Grand Cru Classé B.

While the other *Côtes* Saint-Émilion First Growths form a south-east to south-west-facing band south of the town itself, Trottevieille is isolated among a sea of plain *grands crus classés* on the plateau to the north-east. You could well ask: what has Trottevieille got that Châteaux Troplong-Mondot, La Serre, and Soutard, all high-flying neighbours, have not got.

The owners before the French Revolution were the Laveau family, merchants who would be involved with Château Soutard a generation or two later. By the 1840s, though, the proprietor at Trottevieille was a M. Isambert, owner of Château L'Évangile. There were then several changes of ownership, and at one time the domaine was split but by 1893 it had been reunited and belonged to Édouard Jean. It remained in the hands of the Jeans and their successors, the Gibauds, until acquired by Marcel Borie in 1949. The heirs of Borie are the Castéjas.

Trottevieille is today an elegant wine, but never one with a great deal of depth or concentration. Whether it deserves to be a First Growth when the above three proprieties and a good half-dozen more are not is a moot point.

See *The Vine* No 22, November 1986.

Château de Valandraud ★

OWNER: Jean-Luc Thunevin & Murielle Andraud.
COMMUNE: Saint-Émilion.
SURFACE AREA UNDER VINE: 12 ha – 70% Merlot; 25% Cabernet Franc; 2.5% Malbec;

2.5% Cabernet Sauvignon.
SECOND WINE: Virginie de Valandraud.
OTHER WINES: Clos Badon (Saint-Émilion).
CLASSIFICATION: Grand Cru.

Valandraud was the original garage wine, or *vins garagistes* as they were dismissively referred to in the French press. Jean-Luc Thunevin and his sister Murielle Andraud, having created a successful *négociant* business, began building a wine estate in 1990. The first vintage was the 1991, when the surface area was so small it could literally be made in a friend's garage. Helped by Alain Vauthier and Michel Rolland this quickly became a great success. Bit by bit, especially with the addition of 5.5 hectares in Saint-Étienne-de-Lisse in 1999, the original surface area, one 70-*ares* piece of old Cabernet Franc which lies near Château Troplong-Mondot, has been enlarged.

The wine has developed over the last decade. At first Thunevin trod down the cap (*pigeage*), not having the equipment to pipe over (*remontage*). 100 per cent new oak is used, with the malolactic fermentation taking place in barrel. This followed a period of pre-fermentation cold maceration, and the wine was not racked, reduction being avoided by using *microbullage* and stirring up the lees (*bâtonnage*).

The wine is certainly impressive. Whether it is good, and whether it will mature with dignity is another matter. Three years after the vintage, when I make an annual comprehensive bottle tasting I find my notes say 'very good' at best. The prices, however, suggest it should be brilliant. The 1998, though, I *do* think is a fine wine.

Château Villemaurine

OWNER: Vignobles des Robert Giraud; manager: Jean-Luc Duwa.
SURFACE AREA UNDER VINE: 7 ha – 79% Merlot; 11% Cabernet Franc; 10% Cabernet Sauvignon.

OTHER WINES: Château du Castillon (Haut-Médoc); Clos Larcis (Saint-Émilion); Château Timberlay (Bordeaux Supérieur) and others.
CLASSIFICATION: Grand Cru Classé.

The huge underground cellar of Villemaurine is situated on the north-east edge of the town of Saint-Émilion, with the vineyard stretching towards Château Trottevieille beyond. The name has Moorish connections. Jean Combret de Faurie of Château Soutard farmed the estate before the French Revolution and Jean Laveau, his successor there, owned Château Villemaurine in the 1830s. By 1868 the estate had been divided. Half belonged to Pierre Jean, whose widow Mathilde managed to reunite the property only to sell it to Raoul Passemard in 1893. In 1949 it belonged to Mme Raoul Passemard and Dr Jacques Vauthier. The merchant Robert Giraud bought it in 1970.

The vineyard is distinctive for being planted with Cabernet Sauvignon rather than Cabernet Franc as the accessory variety to the Merlot. The wine is decent, with plump fruit and plenty of oak but it could have more personality.

Château Yon-Figeac

OWNER: Bernard Germain; manager: Nicolas Dabudyk.
SURFACE AREA UNDER VINE: 25 ha – 80% Merlot;

20% Cabernet Franc.
SECOND WINE: Château Yon Saint-Martin.
CLASSIFICATION: Grand Cru Classé.

Château Yon-Figeac lies between Château Laroze and Château Lamarzelle on the weathered sand between the Côtes and Graves parts of the Saint-Émilion commune. The suffix denotes its proximity to Château Figeac, not that it was ever part of the domaine. In the last third of the nineteenth century Yon-Figeac belonged to the Gurchy family, active elsewhere in the immediate vicinity. It then passed through a couple of hands before being acquired by the Collets and their successors the Lussiez. In 1985 they sold to the merchants Germain. A new *cuvier* was installed in 1987, followed by temperature- and humidity-control in a renovated barrel cellar in 1999. Hitherto Château Yon-Figeac had been a decent medium-weight, fruity wine, but never in the top rank. The 2000 saw a change to something rather over-extracted which I did not like.

SAINT-ÉMILION SATELLITES

T he river Barbanne, a tributary of the Isle, runs in an east-
westerly direction and separates Saint-Émilion from its
satellites to the north. There are four of these: Saint-Georges-
Saint-Émilion, Montagne-Saint-Émilion, Lussac-Saint-Émilion and
Puisseguin-Saint-Émilion. At their best the wines from these areas are
every bit as good as a Saint-Émilion *grand cru*. At their worst they are
attenuated and rustic. But, as elsewhere, the last few years have seen an
encouraging increase in quality. Attitudes have changed. Investments
have been made. The locals have come to realise that in an increasingly
competitive world the mediocre is just simply not good enough.

This is a large area: collectively, at approaching 4000 hectares under
vine, about three-quarters as large as Saint-Émilion itself; much larger
than Pomerol (800 hectares) or its satellite, Lalande-de-Pomerol
(1000 hectares). The countryside is more undulating than on the Saint-
Émilion plateau, and less extensively planted, the vines being
interspersed with woodland, even the odd field of pasture. There are
some important estates, grand buildings surrounded by parks, but at

the same time many of the properties are very small, tended at the weekends by part-time *vignerons* who are members of the local co-operatives.

When the *appellation contrôlée* regulations were drawn up in 1936, there was a fifth satellite: Parsac-Saint-Émilion. In 1973 this was absorbed into Montagne. In the same year the growers in Saint-Georges-Saint-Émilion were offered the choice of remaining as Saint-Georges or of using the better-known Montagne *appellation*. This right to use either name still exists.

In such a large area, it would be surprising if the soil structure was not varied. Nearest to Saint-Émilion, in Montagne and Saint-Georges, the geology is a similar clay-limestone on a limestone base (*calcaire à astéries*). Even here, however, there are parts which are siliceous clay or even loam, and now on a more iron-rich base. Further north in Lussac you will find a gravel plateau mixed with sand on the western side, cold heavy clay to the east. While in Puisseguin, where the altitude rises to 89 metres above sea-level, the clay-limestone on the surface rests on a stony, well-drained subsoil.

All this, of course, affects the style of the wines. The vineyards resting on the clay-limestone are the more classic, potentially the most elegant. On very sandy soils the wines will have a tendency to be a bit slight, on very clayey compositions a bit dense. As important will be the attitude of the winemakers. While the *encépagement* does not greatly vary – a 70:20:10 ration between Merlot, Cabernet Franc and Cabernet Sauvignon being the norm – different viticultural and vinicultural methods can have a crucial effect on style as well as quality. Most vineyards are picked by machine. Much wine is made entirely in tank. As elsewhere there are basic and *têtes de cuvée*. At a handful of properties the wines are made with the same dedication as at a top Saint-Émilion *cru classé*. These are the wines worth seeking out. Drink the lesser examples at between three and six years old, the better wines from five to ten.

Saint-Georges-Saint-Émilion

Surface Area (2002): 185 ha.

Production (2002): 7812 hl.

Colour: Red (the white wines are *Appellation Contrôlée* Bordeaux or Bordeaux Supérieur).

Grape Varieties: Merlot; Cabernet Sauvignon; Cabernet Franc; Malbec.

Maximum Yield: 45 hl/ha.

Minimum Alcoholic Degree: 10°.

Saint-Georges is the smallest of the Saint-Émilion satellites (the growers have the option of labelling their wine as Montagne-Saint-Émilion) and lies nearest to the town of Saint-Émilion. The village of Saint-Georges has a fine early Romanesque church on a little hill, above the splendidly extravagant Louis XVI-château Saint-Georges.

With one or two honourable exceptions I find Saint-Georges the least exciting of the satellites. At a tasting of a dozen examples of both the 1998 and 2000 vintages in February 2002 I found it hard to be enthusiastic about the wines of more than a couple of estates. Most of the wines were weak and rustic.

Château Saint-André Corbin

Owner: Robert Carré; farmed by Alain Moueix.
Surface Area Under Vine: 19 ha – 77% Merlot;
  23% Cabernet Sauvignon.

Other Wine: Château Fonroque (Saint-Émilion).

The more than reliable firm of Ets. Jean-Pierre Moueix is behind this wine, so not surprisingly it is one of the stars of the *appellation*. Moreover, archeological excavations here suggest this might have been the site of Ausonius' villa Luccanius. A double reason for pursuing this medium-bodied, fruity, stylish example.

Château Saint-Georges

Owner: Desbois family.
Surface Area Under Vine: 50 ha – 60% Merlot;

20% Cabernet Sauvignon; 20% Cabernet Franc.
Second Wine: Château Puy-Saint-Georges.

The setting here is aristocratic. The magnificent château, designed by Victor Louis and constructed in 1770, is fronted by a large formal garden. This garden would not be out of place in the Loire Valley. It is somewhat incongruous to find it here in one of the lesser outlying areas of Bordeaux.

The vineyard, enclosed within a brick wall, is by far the largest in the *appellation*. Though harvesting is by machine, 50 per cent new oak is used for the aging. This is a rich, succulent wine which lasts well.

Château Tour du Pas Saint-Georges

OWNER: The heirs of the late Mme Jean Dubois-Challon; manager: Pascal Delbeck.
SURFACE AREA UNDER VINE: 15 ha – 50% Merlot;
35% Cabernet Franc; 15% Cabernet Sauvignon.
SECOND WINE: La Cuvée du Pas.
OTHER WINES: Château Belair (Saint-Émilion).

Château Tour du Pas Saint-Georges has been in the hands of the Dubois-Challon family since 1885 and managed by Pascal Delbeck since 1976. Delbeck's style is for light, elegant wines. Sometimes this example is too ethereal, verging on the weedy, which is curious given the large amount of Cabernet in the *encépagement*. Drink early.

Château Troquart

OWNER: Grégoire family.
SURFACE AREA UNDER VINE: 5.5 ha – 70% Merlot;
20% Cabernet Franc & Cabernet Sauvignon;
10% Malbec.

Château Troquart lies in the hamlet of Troquard (*sic*) across a little valley from the village of Saint-Georges. The Grégoire family produce quite a sturdy wine, matured using 15 per cent new oak, but one of richness and depth if you are prepared to wait a year or two longer than most. One of the stars of the *appellation*.

MONTAGNE-SAINT-ÉMILION

SURFACE AREA (2002): 1594 ha.

PRODUCTION (2002): 70,270 hl.

COLOUR: Red (the white wines are *Appellation Contrôlée* Bordeaux or Bordeaux Supérieur).

GRAPE VARIETIES: Merlot; Cabernet Sauvignon; Cabernet Franc; Malbec.

MAXIMUM YIELD: 45 hl/ha.

MINIMUM ALCOHOLIC DEGREE: 10°.

Montagne is the largest of the Saint-Émilion satellites. It stretches under Lussac and Puisseguin all the way from Lalande-de-Pomerol to the Côtes de Castillon and arguably contains the best properties in this whole satellite area. The village of Montagne lies in the middle, hardly a kilometre from that of Saint-Georges. Here the Saint-Émilion satellites have their headquarters, next to the carefully restored twelfth-century church of Saint-Martin, and a restaurant which the syndicate sponsors which (unless it has changed hands by the time you read this) I can thoroughly recommend.

Château Béchereau

OWNER: Bertrand-Dupas families; director: Joël Dupas.
SURFACE AREA UNDER VINE: 11 ha – 80% Merlot; 10% Cabernet Franc; 10% Cabernet Sauvignon.

SECOND WINE: Château Vieux Potana.
OTHER WINE: Château Becherau (Lalande-de-Pomerol & Bordeaux Supérieur).

Harvesting is by machine here, but there is a double *table de tri*, and about one-sixth of the harvest is declared as a Cuvée Spéciale. Made in wood, of which 30 per cent is new, and bottled without prior filtration, this is a wine of medium weight with good fruit and dimension.

Château Calon

OWNER: Jean-Noël Boidron.
SURFACE AREA UNDER VINE: 36 ha – 70% Merlot; 15% Cabernet Franc; 12% Cabernet Sauvignon; 3% Malbec.

SECOND WINE: Château Fonguillon.
OTHER WINES: Château Calon (Saint-Georges-Saint-Émilion); Château Cantelauze (Pomerol); Château Corbin-Michotte (Saint-Émilion).

This is a large property just outside Montagne in the cellar of which M. Boidron's other Château Calon (5.5 hectares) is also made. Harvesting, unusually, is by hand, and the wine is held partly in new barrels, partly in tank. These wines have a good reputation, and old vintages are widely available, as M. Boidron's policy is only to sell a part of his production *en primeur*. Despite good notes from others I find both these Calons rather weak and rustic.

Château Le Clos Daviaud

OWNER: SCEA Mirambeau; managers: Bernard Banton and Philippe Lauret.

SURFACE AREA UNDER VINE: 5 ha – 60% Merlot; 20% Cabernet Franc; 20% Cabernet Sauvignon.

The estate lies in the village of Parsac, on the Castillon boundary of the Montagne *appellation*. The label shows Parsac's eleventh-century church. Since 1994 a Cuvée de la Trilogie has been produced, aged in oak, one-third of which is renewed each year. Harvesting is by hand. This is a plump, positive, stylish example.

Château La Couronne

OWNER: Thomas Thiou.
SURFACE AREA UNDER VINE: 11.5 ha – 95% Merlot;

4% Cabernet Franc; 1% Cabernet Sauvignon.
SECOND WINE: Château La Rousselerie.

Thomas Thiou bought this estate from Edgard Ginestet in 1994 and in 1998 created a super-*cuvée* called Reclos. This is 100 per cent Merlot and matured in 100 per cent new wood. M. Thiou harvests by hand and uses micro-oxygenation techniques during the fermentation. The wine is stored in a mixture of barrel and wood *foudres*. I find both the Reclos and the basic wine are very well-made examples of what they set out to be: rich, fat, ample, fruity and long on the palate.

Château L'Envie

OWNER: Vignobles Despagne & Fils.
SURFACE AREA UNDER VINE: 2 ha – 90% Merlot;
10% Cabernet Sauvignon.

These Despagnes are cousins of those at Château Maison-Blanche (see below) and Château Corbin (Despagne). Château L'Envie is an old-vine *cuvée* of Château Vieux Bonneau. The first vintage was in 1998. The grapes are mechanically harvested and the wine reared entirely in new wood. The oak is not obtrusive though. I find the wine rich and concentrated with plenty of depth: a very good example of the *appellation*.

Château Faizeau

OWNER: Chantal Lebreton.
SURFACE AREA UNDER VINE: 12 ha – 100% Merlot.
SECOND WINE: Chants de Faizeau.

OTHER WINES: Château La Croix de Gay (Pomerol); Château La Fleur de Gay (Pomerol).

Chantal Lebreton is the daughter of the Raynauds of Châteaux La Croix de Gay and La Fleur de Gay in Pomerol. She has been making the wine here at Faizeau since 1983, and in 1999 became the sole proprietor following a division of the family property. Since 1989 a 100 per cent Merlot wine, from 50-year-old or more vines and aged in 50 per cent new oak, has been bottled as Château Faizeau Vieilles Vignes; the remainder becoming Château Chants de Faizeau. This is the best of all the satellite Saint-Émilion wines, regularly the richest, the most concentrated and the most elegant of all of them: delicious stuff.

Château Maison-Blanche

OWNER: GFA Despagne-Rapin; director: Nicolas Despagne.
SURFACE AREA UNDER VINE: 32 ha – 50% Merlot; 50% Cabernet Franc.
SECOND WINE: Les Piliers de Maison Blanche.

OTHER WINES: Château Hautes Graves Beaulieu (Pomerol); Château Lamarsalle (Montagne-Saint-Émilion); Château La Rose Figeac (Pomerol); Château Tour de Corbin Despagne (Saint-Émilion).

Maison-Blanche is an attractive château, the main floor of which is raised up over the cellar, and reached by a double balcony. It lies close to the Lalande-de-Pomerol border on the western side of the *appellation*. The main interest here is the Cuvée Louis Rapin, first launched in 1985. The grapes for this are hand-harvested and aged in 50 per cent new wood. This is a rich, quite sturdy wine with no lack of depth. It keeps well.

Château Montaiguillon

OWNER: Amart family; manager: Chantal Amart.
SURFACE AREA UNDER VINE: 28 ha – 60% Merlot;
20% Cabernet Franc; 20% Cabernet Sauvignon.
SECOND WINE: Chateau du Haut-Mont.

Château Montaiguillon is located close to the river Barbanne in the south-west corner of the *appellation* and has been in the Amart family's hands since 1949. The *encépagement* includes 60 per cent Cabernet (both Sauvignon and Franc) which is unusually high for these parts, but the wine is sound, with positive fruit and plenty of depth. There is more to this than in most of the neighbouring wines. It keeps well. The grapes are picked by both hand and machine, and storage is in wood, of which one-third is new.

Château de Musset

OWNER: Gadenne family; director: Patrick Valette.
SURFACE AREA UNDER VINE: 7.5 ha – 70% Merlot;
20% Cabernet Franc; 10% Cabernet
Sauvignon.
SECOND WINE: Domaine de Petit Musset.

Technically, Patrick Valette, who is winemaker at Saint-Émilion's Château Berliquet and elsewhere, is the leaseholder here. He took over in 1991. The property is in the south-east corner of Montagne-Saint-Émilion, in a little hamlet of the same name, and the château, which Valette has nothing to do with, is impressive. A large vaulted cellar lies underneath. This is one of Montagne's best wines: pure, elegant and succulent.

Château Roudier

OWNER: Capdemourlin family.
SURFACE AREA UNDER VINE: 30 ha – 65% Merlot;
25% Cabernet Franc; 10% Cabernet Sauvignon.
SECOND WINE: As de Roudier.
OTHER WINES: Château Balestard-La-Tonnelle (Saint-Émilion); Château Capdemourlin (Saint-Émilon); Château Petit-Faurie de Soutard (Saint-Émilion).

Château Roudier is close to the river Barbanne and the Saint-Émilion *appellation,* a few kilometres to the north of the Capdemourlins' other properties. Harvesting is by hand, and, as at their other estates, quality has perked up here in the last few years.

The basic Château Roudier is tank-aged. It is round and ripe, with no hard edges, and early maturing. A super-*cuvée*, L'As de Roudier, was first made in the mid-1990s. Sixty per cent of this is aged in one- or two-year-old barrels. This is an impressive wine: rich and fat with plenty of depth.

Vieux Château Saint-André

OWNER: Jean-Claude Berrouet.
SURFACE AREA UNDER VINE: 6 ha – 80% Merlot;
15% Cabernet Franc; 5% Cabernet Sauvignon.
OTHER WINE: Château Samion (Lalande-de-Pomerol).

As you would expect from the winemaker of Ets J P Moueix this is an impeccable example: pure, cool and unforced, with delicious fruit. I have never tasted Jean-Claude Berrouet's other wine, but then again Château Samion's surface area in Lalande is only 30 *ares*, enough to make a mere six barrels of wine!

LUSSAC-SAINT-ÉMILION

SURFACE AREA (2002): 1447 ha.

PRODUCTION (2002): 65,156 hl.

COLOUR: Red (the white wines are *Appellation Contrôlée* Bordeaux or Bordeaux Supérieur).

GRAPE VARIETIES: Merlot; Cabernet Sauvignon; Cabernet Franc; Malbec.

MAXIMUM YIELD: 45 hl/ha.

MINIMUM ALCOHOLIC DEGREE: 10°.

Lussac is the second largest and most northerly of the Saint-Émilion satellites, and sprawls above Montagne-Saint-Émilion. The area is in the shape of a lozenge, with a north-south ridge running through the middle. As with the other satellite areas, there is only a handful of really good estates; rather more, sadly, whose wines remain rustic.

Château de Barbe Blanche

OWNER: André Lurton & André Magnon.
SURFACE AREA UNDER VINE: 28 ha – 65% Merlot; 25% Cabernet Franc; 10% Cabernet Sauvignon.

OTHER WINES: Château Bonnet (Entre-Deux-Mers); Château La Louvière (Pessac-Léognan) and others.

Château de Barbe Blanche was acquired by the Crédit Foncier bank, owner *inter alia* of Château Bastor-Lamontagne in Sauternes and Château Beauregard in Pomerol, in 1985. Fifteen years later they sold it to André Lurton and André Magnon. Quality was decent prior to 2000, and has improved significantly since. The superior bottling, Cuvée Henri IV, is one of Lussac's best wines.

Château Bel-Air

OWNER: Jean-Noël Roi.
SURFACE AREA UNDER VINE: 21 ha – 70% Merlot;

15% Cabernet Franc; 15% Cabernet Sauvignon.

Château Bel-Air is a handsome, eighteenth-century building with a winery attached. It has belonged to the Roi family for more than a century. The soil here is clay with iron-pan underneath, 'as at Pomerol' you are told, and the wine is rich, succulent and very good. From 1998 there has been a superior Cuvée Jean-Gabriel, commemorating two Roi ancestors. This is even better.

Château de Bordes

OWNER: Paul Bordes.
SURFACE AREA UNDER VINE: 0.3 ha – 100% Merlot.
OTHER WINES: Chateau des Huguets (Bordeaux

Superieur); Château Lafaurie (Puisseguin-Saint-Émilion).

One could almost consider this a *tête de cuvée* of M. Bordes' 5-hectare Bordeaux Supérieur Château des Huguets, which it adjoins just over the border in the commune of Les Artigues-de-Lussac on the western side of the *appellation*. The wine is full, fleshy, oaky and very good indeed. I have especially admired the 1998 and the 2000.

Château Croix de Rambeau

OWNER: Jean-Louis Trocard.
SURFACE AREA UNDER VINE: 6.3 ha – 80% Merlot; 15% Cabernet Franc; 5% Malbec.

OTHER WINES: Château La Croix des Moines (Lalande-de-Pomerol); Château Trocard (Bordeaux Supérieur).

The château of Croix de Rambeau is situated north of Château Bordes, outside the *appellation* but the vines are in Lussac. The wine from those vines outside the appellation are used for the

Château Trocard label. The wine here is quite firm and needs more aging time than most. There is depth and good acidity, but it can be a little four-square.

Château Haut-Piquat

OWNER: Jean-Pierre Rivière.
SURFACE AREA UNDER VINE: 30 ha – 75% Merlot;
15% Cabernet Sauvignon; 10% Cabernet Franc.

Lying on one site just outside the village of Lussac, the handsome château and its vineyard were acquired by M. Rivière in 1971. Unlike many of his neighbours, M. Rivière picks his grapes by hand. The wines here have both depth and fruit.

Château Lucas

OWNER: Marcel and Frédéric Vauthier.
SURFACE AREA UNDER VINE: 22 ha – 60% Cabernet
Franc; 40% Merlot.

There are three vrey good wines here: Lucas is matured 90 per cent in vat, Grand Lucas has 50 per cent barrel-aging and L'Esprit de Lucas comes from 100 per cent new wood. Harvesting is by hand. Frédéric Vauthier is the brother of Alain of Château Ausone.

Château Lyonnat

OWNER: Jean Milhade.
SURFACE AREA UNDER VINE: 48 ha – 70% Merlot;
15% Cabernet Franc; 15% Cabernet Sauvignon.
SECOND WINE: Château La Rose Perruchon.

The Lyonnat estate is in the south-east corner of the *appellation* just outside the village of Lussac. It has been one of the most reliable satellite Saint-Émilions for some years. The wine is rich and ripe and ages well. Both the 1998 and the 2000 are very good.

PUISSEGUIN-SAINT-ÉMILION

SURFACE AREA (2002): 745 ha.

PRODUCTION (2002): 33,783 hl.

COLOUR: Red (the white wines are *Appellation Contrôlée* Bordeaux or Bordeaux Supérieur).

GRAPE VARIETIES: Merlot; Cabernet Sauvignon; Cabernet Franc; Malbec.

MAXIMUM YIELD: 45 hl/ha.

MINIMUM ALCOHOLIC DEGREE: 10°.

Puisseguin borders the Côtes de Castillon and is roughly half the size of Montagne and Lussac. The nucleus of the area, above the village of Puisseguin, is fairly hilly. Though smaller and less well-known there are as many good properties here as in Lussac-Saint-Émilion.

Château Branda

OWNER: Arnaud Delaire, Yves Blanc, Guy Benjamin.
SURFACE AREA UNDER VINE: 8.5 ha – 70% Merlot;
15% Cabernet Franc; 15% Cabernet Sauvignon.
OTHER WINE: Vieux Château Chambeau (Lussac-Saint-Émilion).

Messrs Delaire (who is responsible for the winemaking), Blanc and Benjamin bought Château Branda and Vieux Château Chambeau from Jean-Michel Biehier in July 1998. The new team first got it right with the 2000 vintage. Harvesting is by hand, the wine is aged entirely in new wood and it is profound, rich, seductive and classy.

Château Chêne-Vieux

OWNER: Yvonne Foucard.
SURFACE AREA UNDER VINE: 11.5 ha – 70% Merlot; 20% Cabernet Sauvignon; 5% Cabernet Franc;
5% Malbec.
OTHER WINE: Château du Musset (Lalande-de-Pomerol).

Château Chêne-Vieux has been in the hands of the Foucard family since 1937. Harvesting is largely by machine, and the wine is only partly reared in wood. But it is usually soft and agreeable. The 2000 marked a distinct improvement on previous years, having real depth.

Château Fayan

OWNER: Philippe Mountet.
SURFACE AREA UNDER VINE: 10.7 ha – 80% Merlot;
10% Cabernet Franc; 10% Cabernet Sauvignon.

There are two *cuvées* here. Naturally the best is that Élevé en Fût de Chêne. This has good weight, depth, grip and succulence. Both the 1998 and the 2000 can be recommended.

Chateau Guibeau-La Fourvieille

OWNER: Henri Bourlon.
SURFACE AREA UNDER VINE: 34 ha – 70% Merlot;
15% Cabernet Franc; 15% Cabernet Sauvignon.

Château Guibeau-La Fourvieille, the amalgamation of two estates, lies on the extreme eastern end of the *appellation*. It has been passed down from father to son since as far back as 1709, which must be a record for the Bordeaux area. The wines are of medium weight with good rich fruit and an attractive base of oak.

Château Lafaurie

OWNER: Paul Bordes.
SURFACE AREA UNDER VINE: 5 ha – 80% Merlot; 10% Cabernet Franc; 10% Cabernet Sauvignon.
SECOND WINE: Enclos des Prieurs de Lafaurie.
OTHER WINE: Château de Bordes (Lussac-Saint-Émilion).

Paul Bordes produces one of the best wines of the *appellation*: rich and fresh with a good oaky base and plenty of personality. It was the best of a range of 2000s I tasted in February 2002. The 1998 was very good too.

POMEROL

SURFACE AREA (2002): 764 ha.

PRODUCTION (2002): 27,300 hl.

COLOUR: Red.

GRAPE VARIETIES: Merlot; Cabernet Franc

    (Bouchet); Cabernet Sauvignon; Malbec

    (Cot or Pressac).

MAXIMUM YIELD: 42 hl/ha.

MINIMUM ALCOHOLIC DEGREE: 10.5°.

P omerol is a strange area. If one excludes the vineyard of its greatest domaine, Château Pétrus, it has no focus. Travelling north out of Libourne along the road which leads to Montagne-Saint-Émilion you pass a few vineyards and then come to the village of Catusseau. At this point the road forks. Between these two roads, about half a kilometre away on the highest ground of the area, lies Château Pétrus surrounded by most of the rest of the top Pomerol domaines. This is the nucleus of the area. A little further on, to the left, there is a church and a few houses. This is all there is of Pomerol as a village.

The Pomerol *vignoble* is by far the smallest of the top-quality wine regions of Bordeaux. It is a compact commune of relatively small estates, many of which are now owned, managed or marketed by the excellent firm of Jean-Pierre Moueix in Libourne. The heart of the area is a gravel and clay plateau which lies on a hard, iron-rich base known as *crasse de fer* or *machefer* and which slopes down to the more alluvial sandy soils of the Dordogne, Isle and Barbanne rivers on three sides, and adjoins the Graves-Saint-Émilion vineyards on the east. The area measures barely three kilometres by four and consists of some 800 hectares of vines. This is hardly one-seventh of the whole of Saint-Émilion, and roughly comparable with the smallest of the great Médoc communes, Saint-Julien.

Pomerol's fame is recent. While a number of Pomerol's leading growths can trace their history back to before the French Revolution, the vineyards were neglected until very recently indeed. Pomerol was only recognised as an area in its own right in 1923 and as late as 1943 when a list of comparative prices was produced for the Vichy Government, Pétrus could only command the price of a Second Growth Médoc and the next category of top Pomerols below Pétrus, Vieux Château Certan and La Conseillante, for example, were rated the equivalent of Giscours and La Lagune. It took two people – Mme Loubat, owner of Château Pétrus, and her ally Jean-Pierre Moueix –

plus two enthusiastic English disciples, Ronald Avery and Harry Waugh, to transform the situation. Yet Pomerol still remains a small, sleepy, bourgeois backwater, with few imposing estates.

Despite its size, Pomerol is today renowned the world over. If 40 years ago the wines were barely recognised as being part of the Bordeaux pantheon, today they are much in demand. The name of Pétrus, its prodigious auction prices, and the quality of the other top wines hardly need pointing out any longer. On the other hand, as the vast majority of the individual properties are so tiny, barely a dozen hectares in surface at their largest, some wines are rarely encountered and difficult to acquire. Look at any list of old wines: plenty of Médocs, few Pomerols. The main grape is Merlot, the principal subsidiary variety Cabernet Franc (here, as in Saint-Émilion, called the Bouchet). You may also find a few rows of Malbec (here known as the Pressac). One or two properties such as Vieux Château Certan even have Cabernet Sauvignon, but in general this variety does not do as well on this side of the Gironde as Cabernet Franc.

Pomerol wines are subtly different from those across the border in Saint-Émilion, particularly those from the limestone rock and *sables anciens* (weathered sandstone) around the town of Saint-Émilion

Châteaux ◆

Lalande-de-Pomerol AC
1 Laborde
2 des Annereaux
3 Sergant
4 La Borderie-Mondésir
5 Jean de Gué
6 La Croix des Moines
7 L'Ancien
8 Haut-Goujon
9 Perron
10 Pont de Guestres
11 Moulin de Sales
12 de Viaud
13 de Bel-Air
14 Les Cruzelles
15 La Fleur du Boüard
16 Siaurac
17 Haut-Surget
18 Belles-Graves
19 Tournefeuille

20 La Croix Saint-André
21 Haut-Chaigneau
22 Moncets
23 Bertineau Saint-Vincent
24 Les Hauts-Conseillants

Pomerol AC
25 Beauchêne
26 Mazeyres
27 Bellegrave
28 Prieurs de la Commanderie
29 de Sales
30 Moulinet
31 L'Enclos
32 Clos René
33 Montviel
34 Rêve d'Or
35 Haut-Cloquet
36 Bel Air
37 Feytit-Clinet
38 Latour-à-Pomerol

39 La Grave à Pomerol
40 Rouget
41 Clos L'Église
42 Clinet
43 L'Église-Clinet
44 du Domaine de l'Église
45 La Croix-de-Gay
46 Le Gay
47 Vray Croix de Gay
48 Lafleur
49 La Fleur-Pétrus
50 Lafleur-Gazin
51 Gazin
52 La Bon Pasteur
53 Haut-Maillet
54 Pétrus
55 Hosanna
56 Lagrange
57 Gombaude-Guillot
58 La Cabanne
59 Bourgneuf-Vayron

60 Trotanoy
61 Haut-Tropchaud
62 Vieux Château Certan
63 L'Évangile
64 La Conseillante
65 Le Pin
66 Guillot
67 Guillot-Clauzel
68 La Violette
69 La Pointe
70 Marzy
71 Bonalgue
72 Plince
73 Nénin
74 La Croix
75 Petit-Village
76 Beauregard
77 Clos du Clocher
78 Clos Beauregard
79 Beau Soleil
80 La Croix du Casse

POMEROL & LALANDE-DE-POMEROL

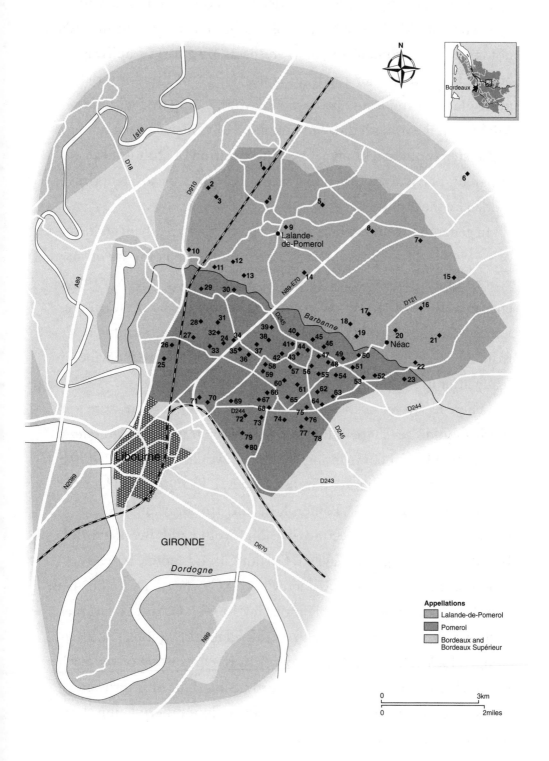

N

Bordeaux

Isle

D18

D910

1

2

3

4

5

6

9

Lalande-
de-Pomerol

8

7

A89

10

11

12

13

14

N89-E70

15

D121

16

29

30

17

Barbanne

18

19

20

Néac

21

28

31

D245

39

40

45

46

22

23

27

32

24

34

38

41

44

47

49

50

51

52

26

33

35

37

42

43

48

54

53

25

36

58

57

56

55

60

59

66

61

62

63

71

70

69

67

65

64

D244

68

75

D244

72

73

74

76

D245

79

77

78

D243

80

Libourne

N2089

GIRONDE

D670

Dordogne

N89

Appellations

Lalande-de-Pomerol

Pomerol

Bordeaux and
Bordeaux Supérieur

0   3km

0   2miles

itself. Saint-Émilions are in general soft, aromatic, plump, fleshy and slightly spicy. Compared with the deeper-coloured, intense, firm, blackcurranty Médocs they are looser-knit, quicker to mature and do not last as long. Pomerols in many respects are a sort of halfway house. They are fresher and more solid than Saint-Émilions, richer, more plummy and less fruitcakey in flavour. Compared with the Médocs on the other hand, they are more obviously velvety but have less austerity and backbone. The concentration of fruit is more apparent, particularly when the wines are young, because it is less hidden by the tannin.

In general, I would expect a top Pomerol to be ready in eight years or so, while all but the greatest Saint-Émilions need only six or seven years. Equally they will keep longer. However, there is a large difference in both backbone and the potential for longevity between the wines from the central Pomerol plateau and the looser-knit wines from the more sandy outskirts of the appellation. Here the wines are ready after five years or so.

There has never been a Pomerol classification. If there were to be one it should site Château Pétrus first and separately, as a *premier grand cru*, like Yquem. Among the Firsts I would include, in alphabetical order: La Conseillante, L'Église-Clinet, L'Évangile, La Fleur-Pétrus, Lafleur, Latour-à-Pomerol, Le Pin, Trotanoy and Vieux Château Certan. In the second division I would add: Beauregard, Le Bon Pasteur, Bourgneuf-Vayron, Certan-Giraud (now Château Hosanna), Certan de May, Clinet, Clos du Clocher, La Croix de Gay, Clos L'Église, L'Enclos, La Fleur de Gay, Le Gay, Gazin, La Grave, Lafleur-Gazin, Lagrange, Nenin, Petit-Village, La Pointe, Clos René, Rouget, La Violette and Vray Croix de Gay. One or two of these where recent changes of ownership show promising signs of improvement (Clos L'Église, Hosanna, Nenin) would no doubt merit being classed in the premier league before too long.

Pomerol Leading Châteaux

Château Beauchêne

OWNER: MM. Leymarie & Fils.
SURFACE AREA UNDER VINE: 9.7 ha – 60% Merlot; 40% Cabernet Sauvignon.

OTHER WINES: Château Bodet (Canon-Fronsac); Château Panet (Canon-Fronsac); Clos de Vougeot (Burgundy).

The vineyard lies near Château Mazeyres in the extreme south-west of the *appellation* and owes its origins to the division of this estate at the end of the nineteenth century. It has belonged to the Leymarie family since the 1940s. Part of the crop is sold as Clos Mazeyres. The wine is quite extracted and new oaky, but there is no lack of fruit and attraction. For reasonably early drinking.

Château Beauregard

OWNER: Foncier Vignobles; manager: Michel Garat.
SURFACE AREA UNDER VINE: 16 ha – 70% Merlot; 30% Cabernet Franc.

SECOND WINE: Le Benjamin de Beauregard.
OTHER WINES: Château Bastor-Lamontagne (Sauternes); Château du Haut-Pick (Sauternes); Château Saint-Robert (Graves).

In the twelfth century the Knights Hospitaliers of Saint John of Jerusalem possessed a *manoir* here. This was replaced by a grander edifice built by the Beauregard family in the seventeenth century. The estate was sold to a local merchant with the name of Bonaventure Berthomieux (for all that, a member of a well-established Saint-Émilion family) in 1793, following which today's rather elegant *chartreuse* was constructed. It was around this time that the vineyard was established.

Following neglect by Berthomieux's son, Château Beauregard was acquired by M. Durand-Desgranges, a local broker, in 1854. By 1863, this gentleman had raised the reputation of his wine, according to Cocks & Féret, to thirteenth position in the commune, a position it has occupied, by and large, ever since. In 1922 the estate was bought by a local lawyer, M. Brulé, on behalf of his god-daughter, Henriette Giraud. She married Raymond Clauzel. Their successors sold Beauregard to the Crédit Foncier de France in 1991, but remain in the château for the time being.

The vineyard is well sited on the eastern edge of Pomerol's central plateau, between Château Petit-Village and the commune boundary with Saint-Émilion, across which are the two Tour du Pin Figéacs. There are three terraces, the one closest to the château being the best. The wine used to have a tendency to sturdiness, but since the appointment of Michel Rolland as consultant in 1987 there is now a second wine, the Cabernets are picked riper and there is more new oak. Beauregard has improved and is now a good second-division Pomerol.

See *Grands Vins*, p. 456.

Clos Beauregard

OWNER: Jean-Michel Moueix.
SURFACE AREA UNDER VINE: 3.6 ha – 60% Merlot; 30% Cabernet Franc; 10% Cabernet Sauvignon.

The vineyard lies on the third terrace below Château Beauregard and was split off from it in 1935, when it was acquired by Antoine Moueix, grandfather of the present owner. This is a light wine for early drinking.

Château Beau Soleil

OWNER: Mme Arcaute.
SURFACE AREA UNDER VINE: 3.8 ha – 70% Merlot; 30% Cabernet Franc.
OTHER WINE: Château La Croix du Casse (Pomerol).

This small estate consists of several parcels in the vicinity of Château La Croix du Casse, and was acquired by the late Jean-Michel Arcaute, who already owned that property, in 1996 from the Rambaud-Béguin family. I don't know the wines of the old regime, but today we have an agreeably plump and fruity wine with no lack of style for drinking in the medium term.

Château Bel Air

OWNER: Sudrat family.
SURFACE AREA UNDER VINE: 13 ha – 95% Merlot; 5% Cabernet Franc.
OTHER WINE: Château Beauséjour (Fronsac).

The château and its surrounding vineyard, which have been in the hands of the Sudrat family since 1914, are situated close to the N89 road from Libourne to Périgueux. I do not have a lot of experience of the wine but what I have seen was a pleasant, round, fruity wine which evolves in the medium term.

Château Bellegrave

OWNER: Jean-Marie Bouldy.
SURFACE AREA UNDER VINE: 7.8 ha – 70% Merlot; 25% Cabernet Franc; 5% Cabernet Sauvignon.
SECOND WINE: Château des Jacobins.

Bellegrave lies on the western edge of the *appellation*, just south of Château de Sales. It has belonged to the Bouldy family for several generations. The wine is a typical Pomerol of this part of the *appellation* with its silico-gravel soils: medium weight, no great backbone but with agreeable fruit. Here 50 per cent of the casks are renewed annually and this gives the wine more dimension than some of its neighbours.

Château Bonalgue

OWNER: Pierre Bourotte SA.
SURFACE AREA UNDER VINE: 6.5 ha – 80% Merlot; 20% Cabernet Franc.
SECOND WINE: Château Burgrave.
OTHER WINES: Château du Courlat (Lussac-Saint-Émilion); Château Les Hauts Conseillants (Lalande-de-Pomerol).

Bonalgue is both a château and a small hamlet. It lies just outside Libourne, where the bypass meets the N89 road to Périgueux. It belonged to the Rabion family through both Revolutionary and

Napoleonic times, the château being constructed in 1815 by Antoine Rabion, a retired soldier. It was acquired by the Bourotte family in 1926. Today it belongs to Pierre Bourotte, *Président Directeur Général* of merchants J B Audy in Libourne.

The wine, despite its good colour, is of medium body only, and often a bit too diffuse. I liked the 1999, though.

Château Le Bon Pasteur

OWNER: Michel Rolland.
SURFACE AREA UNDER VINE: 6.7 ha – 75% Merlot; 25% Cabernet Franc.
OTHER WINES: Château Bertineau Saint-Vincent (Lalande-de-Pomerol); Château Fontenil (Fronsac); Château Rolland-Maillet (Saint-Émilion).

Le Bon Pasteur lies on the Pomerol–Saint-Émilion–Lalande de Pomerol border above Château Gazin. Michel Rolland's maternal grandfather, Joseph Dupuy, built up Le Bon Pasteur in the 1920s. After the untimely death of his father, Serge, Michel took over in 1978. One of the first to be temperature-controlled in Pomerol, the winery serves as the vinification centre for two of the other Rolland properties, the vineyards of Rolland-Maillet and Bertineau Saint-Vincent being close by.

This is the best of Rolland's own wines – he is consultant to a multitude of others, in Bordeaux and elsewhere. It is full-bodied, rich and generous, gently oaky and keeps well. This is definitely a contender for *cru classé* status, should one ever be proposed.

See *The Vine* No 128, September 1995.

Château Bourgneuf-Vayron

OWNER: Xavier Vayron.
SURFACE AREA UNDER VINE: 9 ha – 90% Merlot; 10% Cabernet Franc.

This property was originally called just plain Château Bourgneuf, and has been in the hands of the Vayron family for six generations. It was considerably enlarged in 1931 by the purchase of a parcel of vines from the Gombault family. During the 1980s the Vayron suffix was incorporated to differentiate it from Château Bourgueneuf (*sic*), a neighbour. The vines are sited in one block between those of Château Trotanoy and the main (N89) road. Bourgneuf-Vayron is normally a plump, sturdy wine, with no lack of richness and substance. It can occasionally be a bit too solid.

Château La Cabanne

OWNER: Jean-Pierre Estager.
SURFACE AREA UNDER VINE: 10 ha – 92% Merlot; 8% Cabernet Franc.
SECOND WINE: Domaine de Compostelle.
OTHER WINES: Château Haut-Maillet (Pomerol); Domaine de Gachet (Lalande-de-Pomerol); Domaine des Gourdins (Saint-Émilion); Château La Papeterie (Montagne-Saint-Émilion); Château Plincette (Pomerol).

Château La Cabanne is the star in the extensive portfolio of the diminutive Jean-Pierre Estager. Its history can be traced back to the fifteenth century, when it was part of a larger domaine which included the land which is now châteaux Bourgneuf-Vayron, Clinet and Trotanoy. La Cabanne's somewhat scattered vineyard today occupies land around the elegant, intelligently restored *chartreuse*, which dates from the beginning of the nineteenth century.

At the time it belonged to the Berthomieu family, associated also with Château Beauregard. By the 1860s it had passed to the Destrilles, who sold on to the Laveau brothers in the early 1890s.

François Estager, originally from the Corrèze department, acquired it from the successors of Dr François Audy in 1951. His son Jean-Pierre took over in 1966.

La Cabanne is a good second-division Pomerol which has been steadily improving over the years: medium to medium- to full-bodied, ripe and succulent with no hard edges, and today ripe, balanced, intense and positive. The 1998, 1999, 2000 trio can be warmly recommended.

Château Certan de May de Certan ★

Owner: Odette Barreau-Badar; manager: Jean-Luc Badar

Surface Area Under Vine: 5 ha – 70% Merlot; 25% Cabernet Franc; 5% Cabernet Sauvignon.

Château Certan de May, as it is often referred to, lies directly opposite Vieux Château Certan, from which it was detached in 1858. At first known as Petit Certan, it remained in the hands of the Demay (*sic*) family, originally of Scottish origin, but established in Pomerol since the end of the sixteenth century, until they finally ran out of heirs in 1925. It was then bought by Mme Barreau's father, André Badar.

Older vintages here, such as the 1947, have been superb. But in the late 1960s and early 1970s there was a falling off. André Badar was in bad health and Certan de May was farmed by Ginestet, at the time owners of neighbouring Château Petit-Village. Jean-Luc Badar took over in 1975, following which the cellars were renovated, the percentage of new wood increased and the quality restored. Despite one or two disappointing results recently (neither the 1998 nor the 1999 are really up to the usual standard, and the 2000, 2001 and 2002 could have been yet better) Certan de May since 1978 has established itself firmly among the top wines of the commune.

See *Grands Vins*, p. 467.

Château Clinet ★

Owner: Jean-Louis Laborde.
Surface Area Under Vine: 9 ha – 75% Merlot; 15% Cabernet Sauvignon; 10% Cabernet Franc.

Second Wine: Fleur de Clinet.
Other Wines: Château La Croix du Casse (Pomerol).

Clinet, L'Église-Clinet and Clos L'Église are all situated adjacent to each other overlooked by Pomerol's church. Clinet's vineyards are behind the *chais* and run down towards those of Château La Grave. Back in the 1830s the property was owned by the Arnauds of Château Pétrus. In the 1860s it passed to the Constant family, who were also involved with Lafleur-Pétrus. At the beginning of the twentieth century, after two more changes of ownership, the estate was bought by J P Lugnot. Lugnot's daughter married into the Ets. GAM Audy family, merchants in Libourne, and Clinet was to remain in their hands until the bulk of the equity was transferred to the GAN assurance group in 1991. Jean-Louis Laborde bought it in 1998.

The people responsible for today's high reputation of Château Clinet are the late Jean-Michel Arcaute, Georges Audy's son-in-law, and consultant Michel Rolland. The vineyard was almost entirely destroyed by the terrible 1956 frost. Though replanted, it was then neglected. It was only when the Arcaute/Rolland duo arrived in 1985 that the winemaking was taken in hand. Machine-harvesting was abandoned, picking was delayed until as late as possible, the grapes were sorted and the vatting period was extended. Moreover the amount of new wood was increased and a second wine introduced. While the 1982 is negligible, the 1989 and 1990 are fine. Today's Château Clinet is a big wine. It can be a bit too 'international' in style and lack refinement. But it is usually, if not fine, very good indeed.

See *Grands Vins*, p. 470.

Clos du Clocher

OWNER: Ets. J B Audy.
SURFACE AREA UNDER VINE: 5.7 ha – 80% Merlot;
  20% Cabernet Sauvignon.

SECOND WINES: Esprit du Clocher; Château
  Monregard La Croix.

Clos du Clocher is located behind Château Beauregard and the village of Catusseau on the edge of the main Pomerol plateau and belongs to the 'other' Audy merchant family (see Château Clinet). The vineyard, though, is better sited, being a number of parcels nearer Pomerol's village church, in the best part of the commune. It was assembled and created in 1931 by the ancestors of the present owners.

Michel Rolland consults, 50 per cent new wood is used, and the label is both distinctive and attractive. This is one of the best of the lesser Pomerols, and it is consistent too.

Château La Conseillante ★

OWNER: Nicolas family; manager: Arnaud de
  Lamy.

SURFACE AREA UNDER VINE: 12 ha – 65% Merlot;
  30% Cabernet Franc; 5% Malbec.

La Conseillante, château, separate *chai* in the middle of the vineyard, and the vines themselves, march with Château Pétrus on the south-eastern side. Across the road is the vineyard of Château Cheval Blanc. It could hardly be better placed.

The estate is named after Catherine Conseillan (*sic*) who inherited a domaine of mixed farming in 1735. She was one of the pioneers of the development towards monocultural vineyards which began in the late 1750s alongside her neighbours at Vieux Château Certan and L'Évangile. La Conseillante, the *dame de fer* (iron lady) as she was known, appears not to have had any children. The estate passed to a favourite niece, Marie Despujol, married to Jean Fourcaud, a merchant (whose family were later to marry in to Cheval Blanc) and their son Pierre took over in the 1820s. The next records relate to the Leperche-Princeteau family in the 1840s. In 1871 they sold La Conseillante to

Louis-Nicolas. His successors, the brothers Bernard, a retired insurance agent, formerly mayor of Libourne and François, a retired doctor, run La Conseillante today.

The wine here should, as it is very often, be superb. The vintages of the post-war period were fine, right up to 1978. Since then, as other Pomerols have joined the ranks of the super-stars, La Conseillante has sometimes been off the boil: the wine has elegance and fruit, but there can be an absence of concentration and depth. This was particularly evident in the mid-1990s. Happily I can report that the 1999 and 2000 are delicious and this improvement has continued with the 2001 and 2002 vintages.

See *Grands Vins*, p. 474.

Château La Croix

OWNER: Jean Janoueix family.
SURFACE AREA UNDER VINE: 10 ha – 60% Merlot; 20% Cabernet Franc; 20% Cabernet Sauvignon.
SECOND WINE: Château Le Cabachot.

OTHER WINES: Château La Croix Saint-Georges (Pomerol); Château Haut-Sarpe (Saint-Émilion); and others.

La Croix lies at the eastern end of the village of Catusseau, the vines adjoining those of Château Beauregard and those of the other neighbouring château belonging to this branch of the merchant Janoueix, Château La Croix Saint-Georges. Another branch, that of Jean-François Janoueix, owns Château La Croix-Toulifaut.

All these crosses (*croix*), and there is a stone one in the vineyard, allude to the Knights Hospitaliers of Saint John of Jerusalem who were prominent in the area in the Middle Ages, when Pomerol lay on the important pilgrim route to Santiago de Compostella, the shrine of Saint James, in northern Spain. More recently, before the Revolution, La Croix belonged to the Sèze family who also owned Château Berliquet, and were active as merchants, lawyers and ecclesiastics. The Janoueix family bought Château La Croix in 1960 from Ulysse Nadeau.

The château is an elegant, two-storey mansion in the Directoire style. Sadly I have never been particularly struck by the wine. It lacks both dimension and refinement.

Château La Croix-de-Gay

OWNER: Raynaud family.
SURFACE AREA UNDER VINE: 12 ha – 80% Merlot; 10% Cabernet Franc; 10% Cabernet Sauvignon.

OTHER WINES: Château Faizeau (Montagne-Saint-Émilion); Château La Fleur de Gay (Pomerol).

The château of La Croix-de-Gay is in the hamlet of Pignon, opposite Domaine de L'Église. The vineyard, however, is in eight parcels, both nearby and on the central plateau. It was enlarged in the 1970s when Noël Raynaud, father of the generation in charge today, acquired a 1.5-hectare parcel of land near Château Trotanoy.

The Raynauds are direct descendants of the Barraud family, mentioned as owners of a *métairie* in documents dating from 1477. In the middle of the nineteenth century the proprietor of La Croix-de-Gay was B Larroucaud, from whom it passed to J H Angle. J M Barraud was his son-in-law and owner in 1901; a M Ardurat married Barraud's daughter, and incorporated a neighbouring vineyard known as Vieux Château Groupey into the estate. From Ardurat La Croix-de-Gay passed to the present proprietors.

Much has been achieved here since the early 1980s. In 1985 the *cuverie* was renovated. Three years earlier, with the 1982 vintage, it was decided to isolate the grapes of a 1.75-hectare parcel lying close to Château Lafleur, and planted to 100 per cent Merlot. This was matured in 100 per cent new oak and given the name La Fleur de Gay. It proved an instant success. Progress has continued. If La Fleur de Gay (800–1000 cases per year) has been a bit too oaky for my taste in the past, it is less so now. La Croix-de-Gay has become more and more sophisticated too. The wine should not be confused with its near neighbour, Château Vray Croix de Gay.

Château La Croix du Casse

OWNER: GAN.
SURFACE AREA UNDER VINE: 9 ha – 70% Merlot; 30% Cabernet Sauvignon.

SECOND WINE: Domaine de Casse.
OTHER WINE: Château Clinet (Pomerol).

La Croix du Casse occupies land south of Château Nénin on the sandy-gravelly lower terrace. It was acquired by Georges Audy when the previous owners decided to sell up after the 1956 frosts. The vineyard had to be almost entirely replanted. Subsequent responsibility passed to Audy's son-in-law, the late Jean-Michel Arcaute. He and his friend Michel Rolland did much to raise the standard of quality here.

Château La Croix du Casse is a wine of no more than medium body, for enjoying in the medium term. It is full of fruit, however, and not without elegance. The château is now for sale.

Clos L'Église ★

OWNER: Sylviane Garcin-Cathiard.
SURFACE AREA UNDER VINE: 5.9 ha – 57% Merlot; 36% Cabernet Franc; 7% Cabernet Sauvignon.

OTHER WINE: Château Haut-Bergey (Pessac-Léognan).

Clos L'Église was owned in the 1860s, when serious records of the individual châteaux in Pomerol began to be kept, by the Rochut family, who were influential in the area, and were also owners of what is now Château Plince. A brief liaison with the Constant family of neighbouring Château Clinet spawned Château L'Église-Clinet in 1882, which reduced the size of both the older châteaux. In the 1920s it passed by marriage to the Moreau family who sold it in 1997 to Sylviane Garcin-Cathiard.

Two-thirds of the vines surround the château (which is effectively the *chai*) with the rest in two parcels which lie elsewhere. This makes a big, rich wine. Prior to Mme Garcin's arrival it had a tendency to be a bit four-square. Now the winemaking has been refined, and it is one of the best examples in the commune.

See *The Vine*, No 81, October 1991.

Château du Domaine de L'Église

OWNER: Castéja family.
SURFACE AREA UNDER VINE: 7 ha – 90% Merlot;
10% Cabernet Franc.

OTHER WINES: Château Batailley (Pauillac);
Château Trottevieille (Saint-Émilion) and others.

The name and the Maltese cross on the handsome label indicate that this property once belonged to the Knights Hospitaliers of Saint John of Jerusalem. It was sequestered by the state in 1793 and eventually came into the hands of the Bertin family, owners by the 1870s. Émile Castéja, proprietor of the Bordeaux merchants Borie-Manoux, bought it from Simon Landard, nephew of a Mme Bertin, in 1973. It now belongs to his son, Philippe and daughter Mme Prébend-Hason.

The château adjoins various other properties which incorporate L'Église into their title, and its vineyard, in three parts, lies nearby. The vineyard, largely destroyed in the 1956 frost, is now once again mature. Sadly the wine, though it has improved in the 1980s, is eclipsed by the best of its neighbours such as those above and below. It needs more depth and concentration.

Château L'Église-Clinet ★★

OWNER: Denis Durantou.
SURFACE AREA UNDER VINE: 5.5 ha – 80% Merlot;
20% Cabernet Franc.
OTHER WINES: La Chenade (Lalande-de-Pomerol –

a merchant's blend); La Petite Église (Pomerol –
partly second wine, partly bought in); Saintayme
(a branded Saint-Émilion).

L'Église-Clinet was formed by the separation of parts of Clos L'Église and Château Clinet in 1882. A Mauléon Rochut of the former had married Mlle Constant of the latter, and it was time to divide their combined inheritance among their children. Denis Durantou's grandmother was *née* Rabier. Her father Paul, had married the daughter of Mauléon Rochut.

For 40 vintages, up to and including 1982, L'Église-Clinet was farmed by Pierre Lasserre of Clos René, Mme Rabier having been widowed during the Second World War, and her son-in-law, Jacques Durantou, Denis' father and the local *préfet,* not wishing to take an active role. The wine at this stage was old-fashioned, solid and tannic, a bit like Château Lafleur. It was often fine. But it did not realise the full potential of the vineyard. Since 1985, and particularly since 1990, Denis Durantou has established L'Église-Clinet as one of the very best wines in the commune. The 1998 is particularly fine. Despite being expensive it is much sought-after. Denis Durantou also has a flourishing merchant business based next door to the château.

See *Grands Vins*, p. 479.

Château L'Enclos

OWNER: Marc-Weydert family; manager: Hugues Weydert.

SURFACE AREA UNDER VINE: 9.5 ha – 82% Merlot; 17% Cabernet Franc; 1% Malbec.

OTHER WINE: Domaine du Chapelain (Lalande-de-Pomerol).

The origins of this estate lie with the Larroucaud family towards the end of the nineteenth century. Pierre Larroucaud grouped a number of parcels of vines together, built himself a new château, rather like a Swiss chalet in appearance, in the hamlet of Grand Moulinet, on the west side of the Libourne-Périgueux road, and christened it L'Enclos after the name of the land on the local register. Through the female line it passed first to a J F Carteau, then to his daughter Mme Xavier Marc and hence to her daughter, Catherine and husband Hugues Weydert who has been responsible for the wine since 1989.

The vines are in several parcels. While the château and much of the land is on the 'wrong' side of the main road, on sandy-gravelly soils which run down to Château de Sales, one significant section lies near Château Pétrus. I have much enjoyed older vintages of L'Enclos, including the 1959, 1948 and 1929, and the 1982 is lovely. Since Hugues Weydert took over standards have improved even more. This is one of the best of the second tier Pomerols.

See *Grands Vins*, p. 483.

Château L'Évangile ★★

OWNER: Domaines Barons de Rothschild (Lafite).

SURFACE AREA UNDER VINE: 14.8 ha – 65% Merlot; 35% Cabernet Sauvignon.

SECOND WINE: Blason de L'Évangile.

OTHER WINES: Château Duhart-Milon (Pauillac); Château Lafite-Rothschild (Pauillac); Château Rieussec (Sauternes).

Château L'Évangile and its vineyard, all on one site, lie between Château Pétrus and Cheval Blanc on Pomerol's high plateau. It is one of the oldest in the area, emerging as a monocultural wine estate as early as the mid-eighteenth century, alongside its neighbours.

It was then called Fazilleau and belonged to the Libournais family called L'Église. Subsequently it passed to a lawyer named Isambert who changed the name to L'Évangile (the Gospel), and in 1862 it was acquired by Paul Chaperon. Chaperon also owned Châteaux Grand Corbin and Tertre Daugay in Saint-Émilion. He had the present Second Empire château constructed and soon raised the reputation of the wine to the high standard it enjoys today. Chaperon died in the 1870s, to be succeeded eventually by his daughter Mme Paul Ducasse. The Domaines Barons de Rothschild of Lafite bought 70 per cent of the equity from the widow of Mme Paul Ducasse's son, Louise, in 1990.

Up to the Rothschilds' arrival L'Évangile had a tendency, while undoubtedly full-bodied and rich, to be a bit solid. I normally found it less exciting than Vieux Château Certan, La Conseillante and Trotanoy, to cite only three of its main rivals. The 1985 was fine though, as was the 1990 and this progress has continued. Since then both the quality and the consistency have risen considerably. Now it definitely is one of the very best Libournais super-stars. The 1998 is outstanding, and this has been followed by fine wines in 2000, 2001 and 2002.

See *Grands Vins*, p. 487.

Château Feytit-Clinet

OWNER: Michel Chasseuil (until the 2000 vintage the estate was managed by Ets J-P Moueix).

SURFACE AREA UNDER VINE: 6.3 ha – 85% Merlot; 15% Cabernet Franc.

The château and *chais* of Feytit-Clinet are opposite Latour-à-Pomerol downslope from Pomerol's church near the N89 road. However, while Latour's vineyard includes a large section on the plateau immediately south of the church, Feytit-Clinet lies towards the bottom of the slope near the N89.

In the middle of the nineteenth century the estate belonged to the Cajus family. Mme Henry Tane was the owner in 1929. Her successors, the Tane-Domergue family, asked Ets J-P Moueix to take over in 1967. In 2000 Michel Chasseuil, himself a descendant of the Domergues, rescinded this arrangement. It is obviously a bit too early to tell what effect this change will have on the wine. In the capable hands of Ets J-P Moueix Feytit-Clinet was of medium weight, yet with plenty of character and balance: one of the best of the second-division Pomerols.

Château La Fleur-Pétrus ★★

OWNER: Jean-Pierre Moueix.

SURFACE AREA UNDER VINE: 13 ha – 90% Merlot; 10% Cabernet Franc.

OTHER WINES: Château La Grave à Pomerol (Pomerol); Château Magdelaine (Saint-Émilion); Château Pétrus (Pomerol); Château Trotanoy (Pomerol) and others.

The château of La Fleur-Pétrus is sited, appropriately, between that of Lafleur and Pétrus itself, with its vineyard to the north, stretching away to the woods on the commune boundary. In 1996 the vineyard was enlarged, and its average age extended, by the addition of 4 hectares of old vines bought from Mlle Robin of neighbouring Château Le Gay.

Mention of La Fleur-Pétrus first appears in the 1874 edition of Cocks & Féret. It belonged to A Constant, one of at least three members of his family active in the area at the time, one of whom was proprietor of Château Clinet. This Constant had a son called Ernest, and, one assumes, a son-in-law called O Pineau. It was through the latter that the succession passed. The last of the Pineaus, Fabien sold up in the 1930s. After briefly being in the hands of an old French family called Mountouroy it was acquired by a M. Garet. He sold the estate to Jean-Pierre Moueix in 1952.

La Fleur-Pétrus is one of the very best Pomerols, third in the Moueix stable after Trotanoy and Pétrus, and only surpassed by four or so other properties (Vieux Château Certan, Lafleur, L'Évangile and L'Église-Clinet). Without the power of Pétrus itself it is nevertheless fullish bodied, and it is certainly rich, intense and balanced. Above all it is elegant. With the exception of a period in the mid-1980s when the average age of the vineyard dipped somewhat – a repercussion of the 1956 frosts – La Fleur-Pétrus has also been very consistent.

See *Grands Vins*, p. 491.

Château Le Gay

OWNER: Yves & Catherine Péré-Vergé.

SURFACE AREA UNDER VINE: 6 ha – 60% Merlot; 40% Cabernet Sauvignon.

OTHER WINES: Château La Croix des Templiers (Pomerol); Chateau La Gravière (Lalande-de-Pomerol); Domaine de Montvent (Lalande-de-Pomerol); Château Montviel (Pomerol).

Château Le Gay lies just outside the hamlet of Pignon, with its vineyard to the north of it on the central plateau of Pomerol, a soil of clayey-gravel. Until recently the property had been in the same family since the 1840s, first the Grelouds, and since the 1920s, their descendants, the Robins. After

Marie-Geneviève Robin's death in 2002 it was sold to the present owner. Unlike at Château Lafleur, where the late Mlle Robin's cousins, Sylvie and Jacques Guinaudeau, are responsible, the vineyard and wine of Le Gay had been entrusted from 1982 to Ets Jean-Pierre Moueix.

Le Gay has always been a full-bodied, sturdy wine, needing time to come round. In recent years, though still built for the long term, it has become more refined, less solid, allowing the inherent richness to come out. This is a very good Pomerol.

The *chais* were demolished and rebuilt in 2003.

See *The Vine* No 113, June 1994.

Château Gazin ★

OWNER: de Bailliencourt family.
SURFACE AREA UNDER VINE: 24 ha – 85% Merlot;

10% Cabernet Franc; 5% Cabernet Sauvignon.
SECOND WINE: L'Hospitalet de Gazin.

Château Gazin is one of the larger properties in the area, and occupies the land immediately to the north of Château Pétrus, on a single site. Its history begins with Antoine Feuilhade (1699–1776), lawyer, local politician and wealthy landowner. He owned a number of properties in the area and was one of the area's pioneers in the transfer from mixed farming to serious viticulture. In 1772, towards the end of his life, he bought Gazin.

Following his death Gazin was acquired by M. Capitain-Bayonne. This individual constructed the nucleus of the present château and subsequently took on another reasonably-sized Pomerol estate, Château Rouget. Rouget and Gazin were run in tandem for more than a hundred years. In 1885 the combined estate was divided, the Gazin section passing to the merchant Louis Quenedey. It was to remain with Quenedey until 1917 when it was sold to another wine merchant, Louis Soualle. Through Soualle's daughter Château Gazin came into the hands of the Bailliencourts. The following 60 years were an unhappy and unprofitable time to be in the wine business, either as merchant, or as proprietor. The Bailliencourts' other property, Château La Dominique, across the border in Saint-Émilion, was abandoned, and sold, almost derelict, in 1969. Ten years later, in order to pay death duties, the family was forced to sell 5 hectares of Gazin to Château Pétrus. For a time, at this period, the Gazin vineyard was picked by machine.

Despite these problems, I have good notes on many of the Gazin vintages of the 1960s and 1970s. But it is really since the arrival of Nicolas de Bailliencourt in 1987 that things have been transformed. He abandoned the harvesting machine, entered into a marketing arrangement with Ets. J-P Moueix, who additionally provide consultancy advice, and decided to introduce a second wine. Since then Gazin has been able to hold its head up among the first division in Pomerol. The wine has a good colour, is full of succulent fruit and is elegant and harmonious. The 1998 is the best of recent vintages.

See *Grands Vins*, p. 495.

Château Gombaude-Guillot

OWNER: Laval family.

SURFACE AREA UNDER VINE: 6.9 ha – 67% Merlot;

30% Cabernet Franc; 3% Malbec.

SECOND WINE: Cadet de Gombaude.

This is a château whose location I know well, for I often pass it near the church in the centre of the *appellation* after I have visited sundry Clinets and L'Églises. I am not, however, very familiar with the wine. The vineyard is in three parcels. Two of these are on the high plateau near the château and other Guillot properties, the other is on sandier land in a *lieu-dit* called Plantey. Château Gombaude-Guillot has belonged to the same family, the Darbeau Lavals, for at least four generations. The wine is full-bodied and rich but lacks a little refinement.

Château La Grave (à Pomerol) ★

OWNER: Christian Moueix.

SURFACE AREA UNDER VINE: 8.3 ha – 85% Merlot;
  15% Cabernet Franc.

SECOND WINE: Domaine Trigant de Boisset.

OTHER WINES: Château Pétrus (Pomerol); Château Trotanoy (Pomerol); Château La Fleur-Pétrus (Pomerol); Château Magdelaine (Saint-Émilion) and others.

Château La Grave à Pomerol sits within a little park, surrounded by its vineyard which is all in one piece, at the bottom of the main Pomerol plateau as the land declines gently towards the N89 Libourne-Périgueux road. It used to be known, somewhat cumbersomely, as La Grave-Trigant-de-Boisset, after its owners in the mid-nineteenth century. Mlle Trigant married a lawyer called Dubourg, and from the Dubourgs it passed, again through the female line, to Mme Edgard Bouché. It was from her that Christian Moueix bought La Grave in 1971. He simplified the name in 1986.

The wine is plump and fleshy, of medium body: elegance rather than power being the keynote. It has for long been one of the best of the second tier Pomerols. The introduction of a second wine in 2000 has produced a greater degree of intensity and refinement in the *grand vin*. I noted this as 'very good indeed'.

See *The Vine* No 81, October 1991.

Château Guillot

OWNER: Luquot family.

SURFACE AREA UNDER VINE: 4.7 ha – 70% Merlot;
  30% Cabernet Franc.

OTHER WINE: Château Gruzeau (Saint-Émilion).

The vineyard is well sited, on the western end of the plateau near Château Trotanoy, on clay-gravel soil. The Luquots, also *négociants*, have owned the estate since 1937. I do not have a great deal of experience of this wine but what I have seen suggests that its character is forward and fruity, but without enormous finesse.

Château Guillot-Clauzel

OWNER: Clauzel family; manager: Stéphane Asséo.　　40% Cabernet Franc.
SURFACE AREA UNDER VINE: 1.7 ha – 60% Merlot;

Formerly called Château Graves-Guillot, and situated next to Château Trotanoy, this used to be owned by the Savinien Giraud family, owners of this latter property. One assumes this small section was once part of this famous estate. The Clauzels are direct descendants of the Savinien-Girauds. Most of the wine is sold to private clients. What I have seen I have rated 'average to good'. My friend, the author Hubrecht Duijker is more complimentary.

Château Haut-Cloquet

OWNER: François de Lavaux.
SURFACE AREA UNDER VINE: 3 ha – 50% Merlot;
　30% Cabernet Sauvignon; 20% Cabernet Franc.
OTHER WINES: Château des Bordes (Pomerol);
Clos des Galevesses (Lalande-de-Pomerol);
Château Martinet (Saint-Émilion); Château de Renaissance (Pomerol).

François de Lavaux runs the merchant Horeau-Beylot in Libourne. He took over here in 1971. This is the best of his own Pomerols (he also markets Clos du Vieux Plateau Certan). The vineyard is well sited with a gravel, iron-pan base. The wine has good substance and fruit, but could do with more refinement.

Château Haut-Maillet

OWNER: Jean-Pierre Estager.
SURFACE AREA UNDER VINE: 5 ha – 70% Merlot;
　30% Cabernet Franc.
OTHER WINES: Château La Cabanne (Pomerol);
　Domaine du Gachet (Lalande-de-Pomerol);
　Château Plincette (Pomerol) and others.

This is another element in Jean-Pierre Estager's empire, and is located beyond Château Le Bon Pasteur in the extreme north-west of the *appellation*. Like many of Estager's wines I have noticed a distinct improvement in the latter part of the 1990s: this is now a good, plump, medium-bodied wine for the medium term.

Château Haut-Tropchaud

OWNER: Michel Coudroy.
SURFACE AREA UNDER VINE: 2.1 ha – 90% Merlot;
　10% Cabernet Franc.
OTHER WINES: Château de Maison Neuve (Montagne-Saint-Émilion); Château La Faurie Maison Neuve (Lalande-de-Pomerol).

This is yet another of the fairly obscure and tiny domaines on the Pomerol plateau. Its vines adjoin those of Vieux Châteaux Certan. Again I cannot boast that I am very familiar with this property or its wines, but what I have seen I have liked very much: the wine is rich, fullish-bodied and with plenty of depth and character.

Château Hosanna ★

OWNER: Ets Jean-Pierre Moueix.
SURFACE AREA UNDER VINE: 4 ha – 80% Merlot;
20% Cabernet Franc.
OTHER WINES: Château La Fleur-Pétrus (Pomerol);
Château Lagrange (Pomerol); Château La Grave
à Pomerol (Pomerol); Château Magdelaine
(Saint-Émilion); Château Pétrus (Pomerol);
Château Trotanoy (Pomerol) and others.

Following the first split up of Vieux Château Certan in 1858, which led to the emergence of Certan de May, there was a further division in the early 1890s. The first mention of what was to become Château Certan-Giraud appears in the Cocks & Féret of 1893. Here we have 'Certan' owned by one Talazac Junior. Why this further piece should have been cut off the land of the senior château we do not know. To distinguish it from its neighbours a later proprietor, M. Marzelle, added his name to the title. In 1949 it belonged to M Ecognère, who passed it on to the Giraud family in 1956. They changed the name again but continued to market part of the crop as Certan-Marzelle.

In 1998 the Girauds sold the estate to Ets J-P Moueix. Christian Moueix disposed of certain lower-lying parcels around Bourgneuf to Château Nénin, thus reducing the size of the vineyard from 7.5 hectares to 4, and changed the château name to Hosanna.

The vineyard marches with that of Vieux Château Certan on its western side and is very well placed on the plateau. The wine should be fine. Under the previous ownership Certan-Giraud was never very inspiring. Under the Moueix regime early signs show that we have another Pomerol superstar: combining substance, richness and flair. The 2000, 2001 and 2002 are all very good.

Château Lafleur ★★

OWNER: Jacques & Sylvie Guinaudeau.
SURFACE AREA UNDER VINE: 4.6 ha – 50% Merlot;
50% Cabernet Franc.
SECOND WINE: Pensées de Lafleur.
OTHER WINE: Château Le Gay (Pomerol).

Sometime in the early 1870s, the Gay vineyard was split between the two sons of the Veuve Greloud. Henri took what was at first termed the Domaine Lafleur; his brother Émile received the truncated Le Gay. André Robin, a son-in-law, was the sole survivor of this generation, and took over both estates in the early 1920s. The late Marie-Geneviève Robin (her sister Thérèse died in 1984) was the last of the line, neither of these sisters ever having married. Today Mlle Robin's cousins, Jacques Guinaudeau and his wife Sylvie, have managed to acquire total control of Lafleur.

Château Lafleur lies in one piece immediately north-east of Pétrus, marching with châteaux Hosanna and La Fleur-Pétrus on other sides. In general the soil is very gravelly, but Jacques Guinaudeau has analysed five distinct types within his minuscule vineyard. This suits his five vats, two of concrete and three of stainless steel.

Up to Jacques Guinaudeau's arrival in 1985 Lafleur was a very powerful wine: sometimes too much so for its own good. Underneath the size there was plenty of richness and intensity. When it was good it was magnificent, the nearest thing to Pétrus. But at times it was a bit too solid: fine but not great. Guinaudeau dispensed with the stems, introduced a second wine and since 1995 has been deliberately trying to produce a lighter, more elegant and intense wine, to bring the fruit to the forefront, as he puts it. I have found this change noticeable in the wine from the 1997 vintage onwards. Today's Lafleur is a remarkably lovely wine.

See *Grands Vins*, p. 499.

Château Lafleur-Gazin

OWNER: Delfour family; manager: Ets J-P Moueix.
SURFACE AREA UNDER VINE: 7.8 ha – 80% Merlot; 20% Cabernet Franc.

As you might expect from its name, this property lies between châteaux Lafleur and Gazin. The soil is partly the clayey-gravel of the high plateau but partly quite sandy as the land descends towards the river Barbanne. As a result of this I have always felt that the introduction of a second wine here, and a really serious selection of the vats preceeding this, would do wonders for the quality and reputation of the *grand vin*. As it is, we have a medium-bodied, supple, succulent wine which is a good second-division Pomerol and which matures in the medium term.

For three generations Lafleur-Gazin was the property of the Borderie family. Mme Delfour is Maurice Borderie's daughter. Ets Jean-Pierre Moueix took over management of the estate in 1976.

Château Lagrange

OWNER: Ets Jean-Pierre Moueix.
SURFACE AREA UNDER VINE: 8.2 ha – 95% Merlot; 5% Cabernet Franc.
OTHER WINES: Château La Fleur-Pétrus (Pomerol); Château Magdelaine (Saint-Émilion); Château Pétrus (Pomerol); Château Trotanoy (Pomerol); and others.

In the nineteenth century this estate was known as Lagrange-Tropchaud and it belonged to the Jaurias family, proprietors also at the time of vineyards in the sandy soils of what are now the suburbs of Libourne. In the twentieth century ownership passed to a company called Vignobles Grand-Corbin. Ets J-P Moueix acquired it in 1959. In 1999 part of the vineyard was transferred to Château Hosanna.

The vineyard is well sited on the plateau. The wine tends to be quite full-bodied and sturdy, a characteristic repeated elsewhere in the immediate locality, but there is plenty of richness and depth underneath. It needs time, but lasts well. This is one of the best of the second tier Pomerols.

Château Latour (à-Pomerol) ★★

OWNER: Lily Lacoste; manager: Ets J-P Moueix.
SURFACE AREA UNDER VINE: 7.9 ha – 90% Merlot; 10% Cabernet Franc.

Château Latour is indisputably one of Pomerol's first division estates, and has been so long before the estimable firm of Ets J-P Moueix were asked to take over as managers in 1962. In the middle of the nineteenth century the proprietors of what was then a much smaller vineyard were a family name Chambaud. In 1875 their only daughter married Louis Garitey. Garitey died in 1914 and his estate was divided up between his three daughters, Latour going to Mme Édouard Loubat, who was later, progressively, to acquire Château Pétrus. During the 1920s Mme Loubat considerably enlarged the estate, improving it by adding two parcels on the high plateau, including the Clos des Grandes Vignes next to the church. The château, together with its pointed little tower from which the estate gets its name, and part of the vineyard, are further downslope opposite that of Feytit-Clinet. After Mme Loubat's death in 1961 her daughter entrusted the management to J-P Moueix.

Latour is a bigger wine than La Fleur-Pétrus (its stablemate, and usually sold at the same price) but not as refined. The wines of the 1970s were real blockbusters. It has been consistent, not having to sustain the replanting necessary at La Fleur-Pétrus, and today is rich and creamy, even opulent: a very satisfying wine.

See *Grands Vins*, p. 505.

Château Marzy

OWNER: Romain-Maison family.
SURFACE AREA UNDER VINE: 7 ha – 80% Merlot;
20% Cabernet Franc.

I don't know a great deal about this property or its wine, having first come across it when I sampled the 1999 in the tasting room of Michel Rolland's laboratory in Catusseau. I liked this very much . It was smooth and seductive, balanced and persistent and stood out among a rather depressing collection of dreary third-division Pomerols. The vineyard lies in the Libourne suburbs near the local racecourse.

Château Mazeyres

OWNER: Caisse de Retraite de la Société Générale; manager: Alain Moueix.
SURFACE AREA UNDER VINE: 19.49 ha –
80% Merlot; 20% Cabernet Franc.
SECOND WINE: Château L'Hermitage-Mazeyres.

Mazeyres and its vineyard lie on the other side of the railway line in the sandy soils of the extreme south-west of the Pomerol *appellation*. The fine Directoire château, recently renovated, stands on the site of a Gallo-Roman villa, and some interesting pottery of the period has been unearthed. The estate was bought by the Querre family around the turn of the nineteenth and twentieth centuries and acquired from them by the Pension Fund of the Société Générale bank in 1988. Since then the vineyard has been much extended and a new *cuverie* constructed. Regrettably the wine remains commonplace.

Château Montviel

OWNER: Yves & Catherine Péré-Vergé.
SURFACE AREA UNDER VINE: 5 ha – 70% Merlot; 25% Cabernet Franc; 5% Cabernet Sauvignon.
SECOND WINE: Château Bellevue.
OTHER WINES: Château La Croix des Templiers (Pomerol); Château Le Gay (Pomerol); Château La Gravière (Lalande-de-Pomerol); Domaine de Montvent (Lalande-de-Pomerol).

The château of Montviel is in the hamlet of Grand Moulinet, opposite that of Clos René. It has belonged to the Péré-Vergés since 1985. The sandy-gravelly soil yields a lightish wine which can be pretty but which rarely has much dimension, or, indeed, real class. The 2001, I was happy to note, showed a distinct improvement though. In late 2002, the Péré-Vergés bought Château Le Gay.

Château Moulinet

OWNER: Domaines V Armand Moueix.
SURFACE AREA UNDER VINE: 18 ha – 60% Merlot; 30% Cabernet Sauvignon; 10% Cabernet Franc.
SECOND WINE: La Grange Chatelière.
OTHER WINES: Château La Croix-Bellevue (Lalande-de-Pomerol); Château Fonplégade (Saint-Émilion); Château Taillefer (Pomerol).

Château Moulinet lies on sandy-clayey soil in the north-western sector of the *appellation*, between the Libourne–Périgueux road and Château de Sales. A stone engraved with a Maltese cross shows the presence of the knights of Saint John of Jerusalem in the Middle Ages. The wine is light but fruity but not among the first division of Pomerols. Armand Moueix bought the property in 1971.

Château Nénin ★

OWNER: Delon family.

SURFACE AREA UNDER VINE: 28 ha – 70% Merlot; 20% Cabernet Franc; 10% Cabernet Sauvignon.

SECOND WINE: Les Fugues de Nénin.

OTHER WINES: Château Léoville-Las-Cases (Saint-Julien); Château Potensac (Médoc).

Château Nénin is one of the larger and grander estates in Pomerol, the elegant, two-storey château standing in a large park south of the village of Catusseau, opposite Château La Pointe. Nineteenth-century owners included M. Viard-Delzé and several generations of Paillets. The Despujol family sold it, somewhat run down, to Michel Delon of Château Léoville-Las-Cases in 1997. Since 1998 the *cuvier* has been reconstructed, the *chais* modernised and the vineyard enlarged by 3 hectares of vines lying near Château Bourgneuf acquired from Château Certan-Giraud after the latter's sale to Ets J-P Moueix.

I have had plenty of fine old Nénins: full-bodied, rich and succulent. The new regime has swiftly put the wine back into the first division of Pomerol châteaux.

Château Petit-Village

OWNER: AXA Millésimes.

SURFACE AREA UNDER VINE: 11 ha – 80% Merlot; 10% Cabernet Franc; 10% Cabernet Sauvignon.

OTHER WINES: Château Cantenac-Brown (Margaux); Château Pichon-Longueville (Pauillac); Château Suduiraut (Sauternes).

Lying between Vieux Château Certan and Château Beauregard, on the gravelly soil of the central plateau, the triangular vineyard of Petit-Village is very well placed. Its long history dates back to the Dufresne family, merchants before the French Revolution. In the middle of the nineteenth century, owned by the Séguins, it was rated fifth in the commune. Subsequent owners include the Buidin-Buffins and Jean-Paul Héron.

In 1919, amid some consternation, for a Bordeaux-based merchant had never before bought into Saint-Émilion or Pomerol, Petit-Village was bought by Fernand Ginestet. From the Ginestets, the vineyard having been completely destroyed by the 1956 frost, Petit-Village passed through the female line to Bruno Prats, who sold it to AXA Millésimes in 1989.

I have had good pre-1956 frost Petit-Villages, invariably bottled or shipped by Ginestet (there was little if any château-bottling at the time) and I have had good wines since. Since the AXA takeover, however, the wine has lacked personality. Now that the vineyard is fully mature again it should be producing better than this. The 2000, however, shows merit.

See *Grands Vins*, p. 509.

Château Pétrus ★★★

OWNER: Ets J-P Moueix.
SURFACE AREA UNDER VINE: 11.4 ha – 95% Merlot;
  5% Cabernet Franc.
OTHER WINES: Château La Fleur-Pétrus (Pomerol);
Château Magdelaine (Saint-Émilion); Château
Lagrange (Pomerol); Château Trotanoy
(Pomerol) and others.

Pétrus is the most sought after and most expensive of all the top Bordeaux châteaux, its price at auction or on the broking circuit easily outstripping the rest of the First Growths. It is, in a sense, a unique wine. It lies in the centre of the Pomerol plateau where the soil is almost pure clay, on an iron-rich base, while in the vineyards which surround it there is much more gravel, mixed with an increasing percentage of sand the more the land slopes downwards. The wine is made with an almost obsessive dedication to quality.

The vineyard was the creation of the Arnaud family towards the end of the eighteenth century. It remained in their hands until after the First World War, being gradually acquired from 1925 onwards by Mme Edmond Loubat and one of her nieces, her successor. In 1969, Pétrus was enlarged by the acquisition of 5 hectares from neighbouring Château Gazin.

The wine is effectively 100 per cent Merlot, gathered in two consecutive afternoons by the Moueix team at the optimum point of ripeness. It is vinified in concrete vats, until the early 1980s with a percentage of the stems, macerated for 18 to 25 days, and bottled after one and a half to two years. At the outset the wine is full-bodied, powerful, very concentrated, tannic, rich and sturdy, not immediately suggesting Merlot. It often needs 15 or more years to mature. When it is mature it can be truly great: certainly the best Merlot-based wine in the world, and that by a long way. Yet its origins are modest. Just a small, light blue-painted, empty farmhouse. No statues, no flags, no immodesty.

See *Grands Vins*, p. 446 & *The Vine* No 233, July 2004.

Le Pin ★★

OWNER: Thienpont family.
SURFACE AREA UNDER VINE: 2 ha – 92% Merlot;
  8% Cabernet Franc.
OTHER WINES: Château Labégorce-Zédé
  (Margaux); Vieux Château Certan (Pomerol) and
  others.

Sometimes today Le Pin sells for even more than Pétrus. Yet it is a recent phenomenon. Though there was a little wine in 1979 and 1980, the first commercial vintage was 1981.

Mme Loubie acquired the small vineyard that is now the nucleus of Le Pin in 1924. She sold its produce in bulk as generic Pomerol. After her death in 1979, the property was sold to the Thienpont family, owners *inter alia* of neighbouring Vieux Château Certan. There was one hectare of vines. In 1985 another hectare was bought from the local blacksmith. The vines lie below those of Vieux Château Certan and Petit-Village, surrounding a plain modern house, the cellar of which is the *cuvier* and *chai* of Le Pin.

Like Pétrus, but there the resemblance ends, the wine is 100 per cent Merlot. It is vinified in stainless steel, but undergoes malolactic fermentation and ages in 100 per cent new wood. The wine is very Merlot, medium-bodied, lush and oaky, voluptuously appealing in an upfront sort of way. I love it: but given the choice I would rather cellar Vieux Château Certan, a third of the price at the outset and even less 10 years on.

See *Grands Vins*, p. 524.

Château Plince

OWNER: Moreau family.
SURFACE AREA UNDER VINE: 8.3 ha – 68% Merlot;
24% Cabernet Franc; 8% Cabernet Sauvignon.

Plince faces Château La Pointe on the road between Libourne and Catusseau, the rather top-heavy château in a small park. Like its former stable companion, Clos L'Église (now sold), its origins lies with the Rochut family in the nineteenth century, ancestors of the Moreaus.

Plince is not in the top tier of Pomerols, but, like its neighbour, Château La Pointe, is carefully made and consistent. A plump, medium- to full-bodied example which is one of the best of Pomerol's second division.

Château La Pointe

OWNER: d'Arfeuille family.
SURFACE AREA UNDER VINE: 23 ha – 75% Merlot;
  25% Cabernet Franc.
SECOND WINE: La Pointe Riffat.
OTHER WINES: Château La Serre (Saint-Émilion);
  Château Toumalin (Canon-Fronsac).

Château La Pointe is a large property by Pomerol standards, and the Directoire-style mansion is one of its better buildings, isolated behind its vines in a little park off the Libourne-Catusseau road, just before you reach Château Nénin.

It was already well established in 1868, when it belonged to a M. Grandet. It was sold in the 1930s to a M. Ducolon, already the proprietor of Château La Serre in Saint-Émilion. The properties have been twinned ever since. In 1949 Ducolon sold both estates to Paul Delahoutre and they passed to his son-in-law, Bernard d'Arfeuille in 1956.

Medium-bodied, balanced, pure and succulent, with a gentle oaky base, La Pointe is consistently one of the best of the second-tier Pomerols.

Château Prieurs de La Commanderie

OWNER: Clément Fayat.
SURFACE AREA UNDER VINE: 4 ha – 80% Merlot;
  20% Cabernet Franc.
SECOND WINE: Château Saint-André.
OTHER WINES: Château Clément-Pichon (Haut-
  Médoc); Château La Dominique (Saint-Émilion).

Prieurs de la Commanderie – the name commemorating the Knights of Saint John of Jerusalem – is on the sandy soils on the western side of the *appellation*, near Château de Sales. It has belonged to Clément Fayat since 1984. The wine is soft and fruity, occasionally dominated by new wood, of which the property employs 50 per cent each vintage. I often find it rather weak. M. Fayat makes better wine at Château La Dominique.

Clos René

OWNER: Pierre Lasserre; manager: Jean-Marie Garde.

SURFACE AREA UNDER VINE: 12 ha – 70% Merlot; 20% Cabernet Franc; 10% Malbec.

The château is situated in the hamlet of Grand Moulinet, a couple of hundred metres from that of L'Enclos, and makes one of the better wines in this western sector of the *appellation*, below the main Libourne-Périgueux road.

The property has belonged to the Lasserre family for six generations and is now managed by Jean-Marie Garde, Pierre Lasserre's grandson. The wine is quite full, with good acidity for a Pomerol, occasionally a little robust: but it keeps well. Part of the crop is sold as Château Moulinet-Lasserre.

Château Rêve d'Or

OWNER: Vigier family.
SURFACE AREA UNDER VINE: 7 ha – 67% Merlot; 33% Cabernet Sauvignon.

SECOND WINE: Château du Mayne.
OTHER WINE: Château La Croix-Blanche (Lalande-de-Pomerol).

The château of Rêve d'Or lies on the main Libourne-Périgueux highway below that of Château Bourgneuf. The vines are sited either side of this road and higher up on the main plateau. The property was created by a Vigier ancestor, Pierre, in 1886. The wine is plump and of good substance, if not always of the greatest elegance, but not too hard, despite the high proportion of Cabernet Sauvignon in the blend.

Château Rouget

OWNER: Société des Grands Vins de Pomerol; manager: Labruyère family.
SURFACE AREA UNDER VINE: 16 ha – 85% Merlot;

15% Cabernet Franc.
SECOND WINE: Vieux Château des Templiers.

This is one of the oldest properties in the region, belonging to Pierre Bayonne, mayor of Pomerol, at the beginning of the nineteenth century. Later, it was run in tandem with Château Gazin and was owned by David Fabre. By the end of the century it has regained its independence and was in the hands of M. Dupuy de la Grand' Rive. It then passed to Marcel Bertrand in 1925 and to Bertrand's nephew, Jean Brochet, in 1974. The Labruyères, from the Mâconnais, purchased Rouget in 1992.

There always seemed to be plenty of old Rougets available on the Bordeaux market when I was a merchant, and I have sampled my fair share. Some were good but the overall impression they gave me was of inconsistency. Things have improved since the new owners took over. Today the wine is full-bodied, ripe, elegant, rich and complex: at the top of the second tier or even in the first division, depending on where you draw the line. The 2000, 2001 and 2002 show even further progress.

Château de Sales

OWNER: Bruno de Lambert.
SURFACE AREA UNDER VINE: 47.5 ha – 70% Merlot;
15% Cabernet Franc; 15% Cabernet Sauvignon.
SECOND WINE: Château Chantalouette.

This is by far the largest estate in Pomerol, with rows of vines in some cases 850 metres long. It lies on sandy soils in the north-west corner of the *appellation*, the quietly beautiful château, dating from the sixteenth century, in an extensive park which descends to the river Barbanne. De Sales has been in the hands of the same family since 1550, though the names have changed when it passed through the female line. Alexandre de Laage was the proprietor in the middle of the nineteenth century. Bruno de Lambert, a great, great-grandson, took over in 1982.

Partly harvested by machine, matured without using new oak, de Sales is only of medium body, deliberately intended for relatively early drinking: supple and fruity at best, a bit feeble in lesser vintages but decent enough in years such as 1998 and 2000.

Château Trotanoy ★★

OWNER: Ets J-P Moueix.
SURFACE AREA UNDER VINE: 7.2 ha – 90% Merlot;
10% Cabernet Franc.
OTHER WINES: Château La Fleur-Pétrus (Pomerol);
Château Lagrange (Pomerol); Château La Grave (Pomerol); Château Magdelaine (Saint-Émilion); Château Pétrus (Pomerol) and others.

The vineyards of the other contenders for the title 'number two in Pomerol' after Château Pétrus – L'Évangile, Lafleur, Vieux Château Certan – adjoin those of Château Pétrus. Trotanoy lies a kilometre away to the south-west on a deep, gravelly-clay soil underneath which is limestone. It has been one of the top estates in the area from the very beginning of the move to monocultural wine production in the last third of the eighteenth century when it belonged to the Giraud family. It remained in their hands until the 1940s. It was then bought by a M. Pecresse, who sold it on to Jean-Pierre Moueix in 1953.

The château is an elegant construction, if with no particular architectural distinction, dating from 1890 and approached through an avenue of cypress trees.

The wine is excellent: profound, classy, creamy and richly concentrated, fullish-bodied but not massive, unlike Pétrus. Sometimes, as in 1975 and 1982, it is ready earlier than some of its peers, but it nevertheless keeps very well. Recent outstanding vintages include 1989, 1990, 1995, 1996, 1998, 2000 and 2002.

See *Grands Vins*, p. 517 and *The Vine* No 210, July 2002.

Vieux Château Certan ★★

OWNER: Thienpont family.
SURFACE AREA UNDER VINE: 13.5 ha – 60% Merlot;
   30% Cabernet Franc; 10% Cabernet Sauvignon.

OTHER WINES: Château Labégorce-Zédé
   (Margaux); Le Pin (Pomerol).

Vieux Château Certan lies immediately to the south of Château Pétrus and for a long time, for much of the nineteenth century, was the leading estate in the area. It was not quite the first to be planted entirely with vines, but quickly followed the Girauds at Château Trotanoy and Catherine Conseillan at neighbouring Château La Conseillante, probably in the 1780s. The owners then were the Demay family. In 1858, holding on to what is now Château Certan de May, the family sold the bulk of the estate to Charles de Bousquet, a Parisian. He enlarged and reconstructed one end of the château, but failed to complete the other end, giving it the curious lopsided look which exists today. The successor to Charles de Bousquet remained at Vieux Château Certan until 1924 when it was sold to Georges Thienpont, a Belgian wine merchant. His grandson, the fervently perfection-istic Alexandre, lives on the spot and makes the wine today.

I have had, I am happy to say, more than my fair share of all the great Vieux Château Certan vintages of the Thienpont era, and almost without exception they have been mightily impressive. If anything, they are even better today than they were 20 or 40 years ago. The wine is full-bodied and firm, with an almost Saint-Julien-like austerity in its youth. It is quite the opposite of its lush, flamboyant stable companion Le Pin, for which Alexandre Thienpont is at least 50 per cent respon-sible. Vieux Château Certan has class, complexity, depth and distinction and it is one of my favourite Bordeaux wines. Since the fine 1982, Vieux Certan has produced lovely wines in 1985, 1989, 1990, 1995, 1996 and every vintage between 1998 and 2002.

See *Grands Vins*, p. 460.

Clos du Vieux Plateau Certan

OWNER: de Lavaux family.
SURFACE AREA UNDER VINE: 50 ares –
100% Merlot.
OTHER WINES: Château Haut-Cloquet (Pomerol);
Château Martinet (Saint-Émilion); Château La
Renaissance (Pomerol); Château Saint-Pierre
(Pomerol).

A dozen or so years ago, a couple of wine merchants appeared in London, installed themselves in
a hotel, and invited various members of the trade and sundry journalists to come and sample 'a
new Pomerol sensation'. It turned out to be the 1989 and 1990 vintages of this microscopic vineyard,
suitably lying between Vieux Château Certan and Le Pin and, like the latter, hitherto sold in bulk.
The site might have had potential, but the wines were somewhat artisanal, as are the rest of the
wines in the Lavaux portfolio. The 1998 and 1999 were rather better, sampled out of cask in the
cellars of Château Martinet in the suburbs of Libourne. But I have not seen them in bottle.

Château La Violette

OWNER: Servant-Dumas family.
SURFACE AREA UNDER VINE: 4.5 ha – 80% Merlot;
15% Cabernet Franc; 5% Cabernet Sauvignon.
SECOND WINE: Le Pavillon de Violette.
OTHER WINES: Château L'Église (Montagne-Saint-
Émilion); Château Les Templiers (Lalande-de-
Pomerol); Château Teysson (Lalande-de-
Pomerol).

While the château lies in the village of Pomerol, the vines are well-placed on the gravel of the central plateau near those of Trotanoy and Le Pin. It belonged to Ulysse Bélivier a century ago and is
today run by his successors, who are merchants based in Arveyres on the other side of the Dordogne. This is a good meaty wine with plenty of fruit and depth: definitely worth of inclusion
among the second tier of Pomerols.

Château Vray Croix de Gay

OWNER: Baronne Guichard family.
SURFACE AREA UNDER VINE: 3.7 ha – 80% Merlot;
15% Cabernet Franc; 5% Cabernet Sauvignon.
OTHER WINES: Château Le Prieuré (Saint-Émilion);
Château Siaurac (Lalande-de-Pomerol).

This small estate is well placed, up on the central plateau between the vineyard of Château Lafleur
and the Pomerol church. It seems to have been independent from the other Gay properties for well
over a century. The wine has good substance and ample fruit if without having the greatest distinction. But it merits being included among the second tier of Pomerols.

LALANDE-DE-POMEROL

SURFACE AREA (2002): 1131 ha.

PRODUCTION (2002): 47,251 hl.

COLOUR: Red.

GRAPE VARIETIES: Merlot; Cabernet Sauvignon;

Cabernet Franc; Malbec.

MAXIMUM YIELD: 42 hl/ha.

MINIMUM ALCOHOLIC DEGREE: 10.5°.

North of Pomerol, across a little stream called the Barbanne, lies the up-and-coming area of Lalande-de-Pomerol, based on two communes, Lalande and Néac. In the same way as Montagne, Lussac and Puisseguin are satellites of Saint-Émilion, Lalande is an echo of Pomerol: lesser wines, earlier-maturing, and not so expensive. Yet this expanding area is certainly worth investigation. The wines are increasingly respectable and Lalande now has its own promotional *confrèrie*, *Les Baillis de Lalande de Pomerol*.

Until 1954 this was not one *appellation* but two, split by the Libourne-Périgueux road into Lalande to the west and Néac to the east. The land of Néac is on a higher plateau. The gravel soils are older and deeper, and mixed with clay on a limestone, iron-rich base, similar to that in the heart of Pomerol itself. The gravels in the original Lalande are thinner and mixed with sand. Generally speaking – but it all depends on the winemaker – the best properties are in Néac. In all there are some 1100 hectares under vine, producing about 56,000 hectolitres of wine a year. Twenty years ago 800 hectares produced some 40,000 hectolitres of wine annually.

This is an agreeable part of Bordeaux, not as high nor with as spacious a view as at Fronsac, nor as attractively undulating or woody as at Bourg and Blaye, but nevertheless there are a number of elegant mansions and carefully tended parks and gardens. There is more of an atmosphere of life at a slow pace than in the determinedly monocultural, not-a-square-metre-left-unplanted compactness that you find in Saint-Émilion. In the village of Lalande itself there is a fine thirteenth-century church which once belonged to the Knights of Saint John of Jerusalem. Néac, too, has a church which is worth a visit. You can see its spire from the vineyard of Château Pétrus.

Lalande-de-Pomerol wines are positioned at the same price level as those of Fronsac. Fronsac has established a reputation for itself in recent years, and Lalande seems set to follow suit. The wines are brisker and plumper than those of the Saint-Émilion satellites and I find them more interesting, but then I find lesser Pomerols have more to offer, in general, than lesser Saint-Émilions. It all boils down to a question of taste.

In recent years the *appellation* has attracted a number of the region's high fliers. Hubert de Boüard of Saint-Émilion's Château Angélus is now installed at La Fleur de Boüard. Denis Durantou of Château L'Église-Clinet in Pomerol offers Les Cruzelles as well as a surprisingly good merchant generic Lalande-de-Pomerol called La Chenade. The brightest of the new generation on the spot, Pascal Chatonnet, shows with his Château La Sergue what his neighbours could do on their estates. Progress is being made. Sadly, elsewhere, there are still too many who produce up to the legal limit, harvest by machine, make no meaningful *grand vin* selection and store their wine entirely in tank. But this is true for almost all the *appellations* in Bordeaux.

Lalande-de-Pomerol produced very good wines in both 1998 and 2000, and good wines in 2001 and 2002. These in general are better than the 1999s and 1997s, which are somewhat dilute. In general, Lalande-de-Pomerols are ready for drinking reasonably early, say within three or four years after the vintage, and they are at their best for a similar spell after that. Only the very best wines, and in the very best vintages, have much to offer after a decade's cellaring.

LALANDE-DE-POMEROL LEADING CHÂTEAUX

Château L'Ancien

OWNER: Vignobles Léon Nony; director: Simone
Nony.
COMMUNE: Néac.
SURFACE AREA UNDER VINE: 4 ha – 100% Merlot.

OTHER WINES: Château Garraud (Lalande-de-
Pomerol); Château Treytins (Lalande-de-
Pomerol).

L'Ancien is both the smallest and the most recently acquired of the Nonys' three Lalande-de-
Pomerol estates, but it is clearly the best. Established at Château Garraud since the 1930s, the
Nonys bought L'Ancien in 1997. The vineyard contains nothing but very old Merlot. The wine is
concentrated, intense, rich and oaky.

Château des Annereaux

OWNER: Milhade family.
COMMUNE: Lalande-de-Pomerol.
SURFACE AREA UNDER VINE: 22 ha – 70% Merlot;
30% Cabernet Franc.

SECOND WINE: Château des Biscarrats.
OTHER WINE: Château Sergant (Lalande-de-
Pomerol).

The Milhades are direct descendants of the Annereaux family, who date back to the fifteenth century. Harvested both by hand and by machine, but matured in 50 per cent new oak, this is a good
middle-of-the-road Lalande, made for drinking in the medium term. Another branch of the family owns Château Sergant.

Château de Bel-Air

OWNER: Jean-Pierre Musset.
COMMUNE: Lalande-de-Pomerol.
SURFACE AREA UNDER VINE: 16 ha – 75% Merlot;

15% Cabernet Franc; 5% Cabernet Sauvignon;
5% Malbec.

Château de Bel-Air adjoins Château de Viaud in the south-west of the *appellation*, just above the
Barbanne river. The vineyard lies in one block around the pleasant, square, two-storey château.
The estate has been in the hands of the Musset family since 1961, and is now run by Dominique
Musset, son of Jean-Pierre. This is a good, soft, dependable, oaky wine which is ready for drinking
early.

A couple of kilometres to the north of Bel-Air is both the hamlet and a château called Musset,
owned by the Foucard family.

Château Belles-Graves

OWNER: Theallet-Piton family; manager: Xavier
Piton.
COMMUNE: Néac.

SURFACE AREA UNDER VINE: 16 ha – 80% Merlot;
20% Cabernet Franc.
SECOND WINE: Chevalier de Caselys.

Château Belles-Graves, an attractive, eighteenth-century *chartreuse* surrounded by its vineyard on
a south-facing slope, was bought by Jean Theallet, grandfather of Xavier Piton, in 1938. The wine
is fullish-bodied, if not quite sturdy, with plenty of fruit. A little more new oak would give it a bit
more flair.

Château Bertineau Saint-Vincent

OWNER: Michel & Dany Rolland.

COMMUNE: Néac.

SURFACE AREA UNDER VINE: 4.2 ha – 75% Merlot; 25% Cabernet Franc.

OTHER WINES: Château Le Bon Pasteur (Pomerol); Château Fontenil (Fronsac); Château Rolland-Maillet (Saint-Émilion).

The village of Bertineau lies in the north-east corner of the *appellation*. But the wine itself is made at Château Le Bon Pasteur in Pomerol. As you might expect, the winemaker guru Michel Rolland produces an exemplary wine here: rich, succulent, ripely fruity and gently oaky. It lasts well.

Château La Borderie-Mondésir

OWNER: Jean-Marie Rousseau.

COMMUNE: Lalande-de-Pomerol.

SURFACE AREA UNDER VINE: 2.1 ha – 50% Merlot; 50% Cabernet Sauvignon.

Situated just outside the village of Lalande-de-Pomerol, the Rousseau family's tiny estate produces a delicious wine: with style, ripe tannins, plump fruit and fresh harmonising acidity. A Cuvée Excellence was produced in 2001.

Château La Croix des Moines

OWNER: Jean-Louis Trocard.

COMMUNE: Lalande-de-Pomerol.

SURFACE AREA UNDER VINE: 8 ha – 80% Merlot;

10% Cabernet Franc; 10% Cabernet Sauvignon.

OTHER WINE: Château La Croix de Rambeau (Lussac-Saint-Émilion).

Harvesting is both manual and mechanical here, but the wine is stored in oak, of which 35 per cent is new. In 2002, a *tête de cuvée* called L'Ambroisie (ambrosia) was made. This was very good indeed, but the basic wine I still noted as 'good plus'. The property has been in the hands of the Trocard family for several generations.

Château La Croix Saint-André

OWNER: Carayon & Vecchierini families; manager: Francis Carayon.

COMMUNE: Néac.

SURFACE AREA UNDER VINE: 16.5 ha – 80% Merlot;

10% Cabernet Franc; 10% Cabernet Sauvignon.

SECOND WINE: Château La Croix Saint-Louis.

OTHER WINE: Château Chabiran (Bordeaux Supérieur).

The vines of Château La Croix Saint-André are old, and very well placed on a plateau above the village of Néac. Following a careful analysis of each of the 33 parcels of individual vineyard belonging to the estate, each plot is treated separately. *Cuvaisons* are long, and the wine is full-bodied and rich and repays keeping. The pianist Arthur Rubenstein used to be a customer. Following his death the 1982 vintage was dedicated to his memory.

Château Les Cruzelles

OWNER: Christian Pichon; rented by Denis Durantou.

COMMUNE: Lalande-de-Pomerol.

SURFACE AREA UNDER VINE: 8.8 ha – 60% Merlot; 40% Cabernet Franc.

OTHER WINE: Château L'Église-Clinet (Pomerol).

The vines lie in roughly one square block, bordering the N89, the main road from Libourne to Périgueux. Denis Durantou, of Pomerol's Château L'Église-Clinet, has taken on a lease here – his first vintage was 2000. This wine is a splendid success: rich, full-bodied, fresh, concentrated and classy; a wine for keeping. The 2001 and 2002 are also fine examples. Durantou also produces the Lalande-de-Pomerol brand called La Chenade from wine he buys in bulk.

Château La Fleur de Boüard

OWNER: Hubert de Boüard.

COMMUNE: Néac.

SURFACE AREA UNDER VINE: 17 ha – 75% Merlot;
  25% Cabernet Franc.

SECOND WINE: Château La Fleur Saint-Georges.

OTHER WINE: Château Angélus (Saint-Émilion).

The nucleus of this new estate (Hubert de Boüard's first vintage was 1998 – the year he acquired what had been Château La Fleur Saint-Georges from the insurance group AGF) is a 7.5-hectare plateau of almost pure, dense gravel. The basic wine is stylish, profound and complex. In 2000 4000 bottles of a *tête de cuvée*, called La Fleur de Boüard Plus, were made from old vines planted on this gravel. This is truly excellent.

Château Gachet

OWNER: Pierre Brisson.

COMMUNE: Néac.

SURFACE AREA UNDER VINE: 8.3 ha – 60% Merlot;
  30% Cabernet Sauvignon; 10% Cabernet Franc.

Pierre Brisson produces a good, meaty, old-vine Lalande-de-Pomerol which is exclusively sold by Maison Sichel in Bordeaux rather than being château-bottled. The vineyard is well-sited on the south-west-facing slopes of the main plateau of Néac.

Château La Gravière

OWNER: Yves & Catherine Péré-Vergé.

COMMUNE: Lalande-de-Pomerol.

SURFACE AREA UNDER VINE: 6.5 ha – 70% Merlot;
  30% Cabernet Franc.

OTHER WINES: Château La Croix des Templiers
  (Pomerol); Château Le Gay (Pomerol); Domaine
  de Montvent (Lalande-de-Pomerol); Château
  Montviel (Pomerol).

Château Montviel is a small but improving château in Pomerol down by the N89, the main road from Libourne to Périgueux. A kilometre or two to the north the Péré-Vergés have this domaine. I have only seen the 2001 and 2002 La Gravière. I found both the wines rich and surprisingly sophisticated.

Château Haut-Chaigneau

OWNER: André & Jeanine Chatonnet.

COMMUNE: Néac.

SURFACE AREA UNDER VINE: 21 ha – 70% Merlot;
  15% Cabernet Franc; 15% Cabernet Sauvignon.

SECOND WINES: Château Tour Saint-André;

Château La Croix Chaigneau.

OTHER WINES: Château La Pignière de La Sergue
  (Lalande-de-Pomerol); Château La Sergue
  (Lalande-de-Pomerol).

Château Haut-Chaigneau is no more than a grand, high-ceilinged, curved reception room which connects with an equally impressive underground barrel cellar. I have often done tastings of the *appellation*'s wines here. The curve of the walls conducts sound, like the circular whispering gallery at the top of Saint-Paul's cathedral in London. All were constructed in 1991.

The wine itself is rich and sturdy and generally one of Lalande-de-Pomerol's best. It normally has sufficient weight and richness but it can sometimes also be a bit rustic. I prefer the 1998 (and at this early stage the 2001) to the 1999 and 2000.

Chateau La Sergue is a *tête de cuvée* of Château Haut-Chaigneau produced by Pascal, son of André Chatonnet. Since it first appeared in 1996 it has consistently been one of the *appellation*'s best wines: full-bodied, rich and oaky, it is a wine of real flair and harmony. It comes from a particular 5-hectare plot on the Haut-Chaigneau estate and is made from 90 per cent Merlot and 10 per cent Cabernet Sauvignon. The *rendement* is 30 hl/ha and the wine is matured entirely in new oak. There is now a further wine called Château La Pignière de La Sergue from an adjoining vineyard which is equally as good.

Château Les Hauts-Conseillants

OWNER: Pierre & Monique Bourotte.
COMMUNE: Néac.
SURFACE AREA UNDER VINE: 10 ha – 80% Merlot;
   12% Cabernet Franc; 8% Cabernet Sauvignon.

SECOND WINE: Château Les Hautes Tuileries.
OTHER WINES: Château Bonalgue (Pomerol); Clos du Clocher (Pomerol); Château du Courlat (Lussac-Saint-Émilion).

This is the family property of Pierre Bourotte, *Président Directeur Général* of *négociants* Jean-Baptiste Audy in Libourne. The vineyard is mainly in Néac, near the hamlet of Chevrol, but partly also across the main road in Lalande-de-Pomerol. The wine is of medium body, supple, fruity and consistent and is a good example of the *appellation*.

Château Haut-Goujon

OWNER: Henri Garde.
COMMUNE: Lalande-de-Pomerol.
SURFACE AREA UNDER VINE: 8.5 ha – 70% Merlot;

25% Cabernet Sauvignon; 5% Cabernet Franc.
OTHER WINE: Château Haut-Goujon (Montagne-Saint-Émilion).

The hamlet of Goujon straddles the N89, the main Libourne-Périgueux road. The wine is soft and medium-bodied, but fresh, stylish and early maturing. One-third of the casks are new.

Château Haut-Surget

OWNER: Patrick Fourreau.
COMMUNE: Néac.
SURFACE AREA UNDER VINE: 40 ha – 70% Merlot;

15% Cabernet Franc; 15% Cabernet Sauvignon.
SECOND WINE: Château Lafleur Vauzelle.
OTHER WINE: Château Grand Moulinet (Pomerol).

Château Haut-Surget, one of the larger properties in the region, is in the village of Chevrol. The château itself is merely the façade for the *chai* and reception room. The estate has been in the hands of the Fourreau family for five generations, Patrick having built up the area of vines cultivated from 8 hectares in 1969. He claims to be the first in the area to have installed a *table de tri*. The fruit is picked by hand, and matured using one-third new barrels. This is a wine of flair and balance, regularly one of Lalande's best. The 2000 is lovely.

Château Jean de Gué

OWNER: Jean-Claude Aubert.

COMMUNE: Lalande-de-Pomerol.

SURFACE AREA UNDER VINE: 10 ha – 65% Merlot; 25% Malbec; 10% Cabernet Franc.

SECOND WINE: Domaine de Musset.

OTHER WINE: Château La Couspaude (Saint-Émilion).

Château La Couspaude is one of the best of the Saint-Émilion *grands crus classés*, so it is not surprising that Jean-Claude Aubert's other estate, Château Jean de Gué, is among the top properties in the Lalande-de-Pomerol *appellation*. Harvesting is by hand, there is a *table de tri*, *cuvaisons* are long, and maturation takes place using 50 per cent new oak. This is a full-bodied, rich wine that benefits from some ageing. I was particularly impressed by the 2000.

Château Laborde

OWNER: Jean Trocard.

COMMUNE: Lalande-de-Pomerol.

SURFACE AREA UNDER VINE: 21 ha – 90% Merlot;

10% Cabernet Franc.

SECOND WINE: Château Le Bousset.

This reasonably large property has been in the hands of the Trocard family since the time of the French Revolution. The wine is medium-bodied, ample and fruity. One-quarter of the barrels are new each year.

Château Moncets

OWNER: Jerphanion family.

COMMUNE: Néac.

SURFACE AREA UNDER VINE: 18.6 ha – 60% Merlot; 30% Cabernet Sauvignon; 10% Cabernet Franc.

SECOND WINE: Château Gardour.

OTHER WINE: Château La Bastidette (Montagne-Saint-Emilion).

The château of Moncets is a fine, nineteenth-century construction which serves as a winery for both the estates above, the vineyards being adjacent just above the river Barbanne on the Néac-Montagne border. The wine, from hand-picked fruit and matured using 20 per cent new wood, is rich and stylish. I particularly liked the 2002.

Château Moulin de Sales

OWNER: Alain Chaumet.

COMMUNE: Lalande-de-Pomerol.

SURFACE AREA UNDER VINE: 10 ha – 70% Merlot; 20% Cabernet Sauvignon; 10% Cabernet Franc.

SECOND WINE: Château L'Ancestrale.

OTHER WINE: Château L'Évêché (Lalande-de-Pomerol).

Both Alain Chaumet's properties make reliable, second-division Lalande-de-Pomerols. Harvesting is both by hand and machine, maturation partly in tank, partly in cask. These are lightish wines which mature early.

Château Perron

OWNER: Bernard Massonie.
COMMUNE: Lalande-de-Pomerol.
SURFACE AREA UNDER VINE: 15 ha – 80% Merlot; 10% Cabernet Sauvignon; 10% Cabernet Franc.

SECOND WINES: Château Pierrefitte; Clos de Malte.
OTHER WINES: Château Perron La Fleur (Lalande-de-Pomerol); Château La Valette (Lalande-de-Pomerol).

Perron is a handsome château, dating from 1645 and situated in the middle of the village of Lalande-de-Pomerol. The vineyards are harvested by hand. For the Château Perron wine, one-third of the barrels are new. There is also special *cuvée*, Perron La Fleur, for which 80 per cent of the wood is new. Both wines have plenty of fruit and backbone, and age well. Bernard Massonie took over from his father in 1998.

Château Pont de Guestres

OWNER: Rémy Rousselot.
COMMUNE: Lalande-de-Pomerol.
SURFACE AREA UNDER VINE: 3.5 ha – 100% Merlot.

SECOND WINE: Château Au Pont de Guitres.
OTHER WINE: Château Les Roches de Ferrand (Fronsac).

My experience of this estate is limited to the 2000. This is a wine with good weight, richness and ripe tannins, which is long on the palate. One-third of the barrels are renewed annually.

Château Sergant

OWNER: Jean Milhade.
COMMUNE: Lalande-de-Pomerol.

SURFACE AREA UNDER VINE: 18 ha – 80% Merlot; 10% Cabernet Sauvignon; 10% Cabernet Franc.

This is a good, middle-of-the-road Lalande-de-Pomerol from a property largely built up by M. Milhade over the last 20 years. The vines lie on Lalande's central gravelly plateau. The harvest is partly mechanised and part of the wine is matured in tank. The result is something which may lack a little finesse, but is still balanced and reliable, for early drinking. The 1997 was a lot better than most Lalandes and I much liked the 2002. Cousins run the nearby Château des Annereaux.

Château Siaurac

OWNER: Olivier Guichard.
COMMUNE: Néac.
SURFACE AREA UNDER VINE: 33 ha – 60% Merlot;
35% Cabernet Franc; 5% Cabernet Sauvignon.
OTHER WINES: Château Le Prieuré (Saint-Émilion);
Château Vray Croix de Gay (Pomerol).

Château Siaurac, with its extensive park, is the nearest Lalande-de-Pomerol can offer to a stately home. The château is grand and imposing, and dates from the Directoire period. The wine is supervised and marketed by Ets. Jean-Pierre Moueix, alongside the Guichard family's other estates. Siaurac is full-bodied and rich and an excellent example of the *appellation*.

Château Tournefeuille

OWNER: Petit & Cambier families.
COMMUNE: Néac.
SURFACE AREA UNDER VINE: 15.5 ha – 70% Merlot;
30% Cabernet Franc.

The Petit and Cambier families took over here in 1998 and have improved the quality at this south-facing domaine overlooking the river Barbanne. The 2000 was rich, concentrated and backward. One-third of the barrels are renewed annually.

Château de Viaud

OWNER: SAS du Château de Viaud; director:
Philippe Raoux.
COMMUNE: Lalande-de-Pomerol.
SURFACE AREA UNDER VINE: 19 ha – 80% Merlot;
14% Cabernet Franc; 6% Cabernet Sauvignon.
SECOND WINE: Les Dames de Viaud.
OTHER WINE: Château d'Arsac (Margaux).

Not to be confused with the adjacent Domaine de Viaud, property of the Bielle family, this Château de Viaud is in the south-west corner of the *appellation*. There were vines here well over two centuries ago, as is shown by the Belleyme map. A group of wine-lovers bought the estate in 1986, completely renovated the cellars and then sold out to the present owners in 2002. The wine is full-bodied, rich and oaky (using 50 per cent new wood). It lasts well.

FRONSAC & CANON-FRONSAC

SURFACE AREA (2002): Fronsac: 843 ha;

CANON-Fronsac: 318 ha.

PRODUCTION (2002): Fronsac: 32,571 hl;

Canon-Fronsac: 12,961 hl.

COLOUR: Red.

GRAPE VARIETIES: Merlot; Cabernet Franc

(Bouchet); Cabernet Sauvignon; Malbec

(Pressac).

MAXIMUM YIELD: 47 hl/ha.

MINIMUM ALCOHOLIC DEGREE: 10.5°.

Fronsac lies west of Pomerol, across the river Isle, a tributary of the Dordogne which it joins at Libourne. Viewed from the river or from the opposite bank in the Entre-Deux-Mers, you can see the land rising sharply. The Fronsac vineyards are on this limestone bluff, the Tertre de Fronsac, and on the land behind it descending gradually towards the village of Galgon. The Fronsac plateau dominates a bend in the Dordogne and the surrounding countryside. Over twelve centuries ago, Emperor Charlemagne commanded a fortress to be built to control the area and to defend the Libournais against marauding pirates. The site was known as Fransiacus.

In 1623 the fortified castle which had evolved from Charlemagne's stockade was razed to the ground. Ten years later the great Cardinal de Richelieu bought the land – and the title of Duke of Fronsac – for the children of his younger sister. The area has many elegant eighteenth- and early nineteenth-century buildings. The countryside is also attractive, with neat vineyards interspersed with woodland and small, formal parks surrounding the larger mansions. The views from the higher ground across to the Entre-Deux-Mers and along the Dordogne in both directions are well worth a detour.

Two and a half centuries ago Fronsac's leading wines were the stars of the Libournais. References to Canon meant Fronsac's most famous wine owned by the Fontemoing family and not the Saint-Émilion *premier cru*. Indeed, the very first Bordeaux wine to appear in a Christie's catalogue refers to 'a hogshead of Canon Claret'. This can only be the Fronsac wine, for what is now the Canon estate in Saint-Émilion was known as the Domaine de Saint-Martin until 1857.

The rise in fame of Saint-Émilion wines in the mid-nineteenth century and those of Pomerol somewhat later was paralleled by a decline in the prestige of Fronsac. By the end of the century, a good Fronsac wine could fetch between 500 and 1000 Francs a *tonneau*, roughly equivalent to a Pomerol satellite or Saint-Émilion *grand cru*, but by the 1950s the price was little more than that of Bordeaux

Supérieur. Most wines were sold in bulk, standards were poor and the wine rustic. After the frost disaster of 1956 when Fronsac, because of its higher elevation, was affected the least of all the Libournais wine areas – but still severely enough – an organised effort was made to improve standards and promote the wines.

The real progress has begun more recently and is still accelerating. More and more estates now vinify under controlled conditions, invest in new oak casks and produce wine to be reckoned with. Fronsac has also begun to attract the real estate investor. The excellent Libourne company of Jean-Pierre Moueix was for a long time a source of good Fronsac wines. Sadly they have recently sold their Fronsac estates. Others important in the area include the d'Arfeuilles, erstwhile *négociants* and owners of Château La Pointe in Pomerol. Other Libournais merchants such as Horeau-Beylot, Janoueix, Armand Moueix and René Germain are also owners or farmers of wine estates in the Fronsac area.

Fronsac consists of two *appellation*s spread over six communes. The better of the two, in theory if not necessarily in practice, is Canon-Fronsac, which covers the communes of Saint-Michel-de-Fronsac and Fronsac. Surrounding Canon-Fronsac and producing about two-and-a-half times as much wine is the plain Fronsac *appellation* which covers part of the commune of Fronsac plus La Rivière, Saint-Germain-La-Rivière, Saint-Aignan, Saillans and part of Galgon. The soil is clayey-limestone, with some sand on the lower-lying land nearest to the Dordogne, on a limestone base, the Molasses de Frondasais. Like Saint-Émilion, the area is honeycombed with quarries and man-made caves, many of which are now used for the cultivation of mushrooms as well as for the storage of wine.

The wines have fruit character and charm and are increasingly well made. The area has value for money on its side, too, as the wines usually cost less than a Médoc *cru bourgeois* or Saint-Émilion *grand cru classé*.

FRONSAC & CANON–FRONSAC

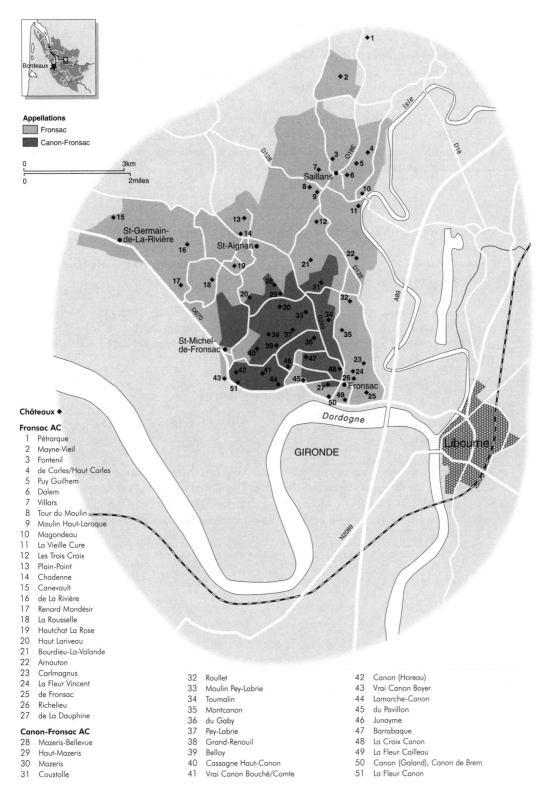

Appellations
- Fronsac
- Canon-Fronsac

Châteaux ◆

Fronsac AC
1 Pétrarque
2 Mayne-Vieil
3 Fontenil
4 de Carles/Haut Carles
5 Puy Guilhem
6 Dalem
7 Villars
8 Tour du Moulin
9 Moulin Haut-Laroque
10 Magondeau
11 La Vieille Cure
12 Les Trois Croix
13 Plain-Point
14 Chadenne
15 Canevault
16 de La Rivière
17 Renard Mondésir
18 La Rousselle
19 Hautchat La Rose
20 Haut Lariveau
21 Bourdieu-La-Valande
22 Arnauton
23 Carlmagnus
24 La Fleur Vincent
25 de Fronsac
26 Richelieu
27 de La Dauphine

Canon-Fronsac AC
28 Mazeris-Bellevue
29 Haut-Mazeris
30 Mazeris
31 Coustolle

32 Roullet
33 Moulin Pey-Labrie
34 Toumalin
35 Montcanon
36 du Gaby
37 Pey-Labrie
38 Grand-Renouil
39 Belloy
40 Cassagne Haut-Canon
41 Vrai Canon Bouché/Comte

42 Canon (Horeau)
43 Vrai Canon Boyer
44 Lamarche-Canon
45 du Pavillon
46 Junayme
47 Barrabaque
48 La Croix Canon
49 La Fleur Cailleau
50 Canon (Galand), Canon de Brem
51 La Fleur Canon

Canon-Fronsac Leading Châteaux

Château Barrabaque

OWNER: Bernard Noël; manager: Nicole Noël.
COMMUNE: Fronsac.
SURFACE AREA UNDER VINE: 7.5 ha – 70% Merlot;

20% Cabernet Franc; 10% Cabernet Sauvignon.
SECOND WINE: B de Barrabaque.

Barrabaque is a substantial château up on the hill above Fronsac overlooking the river Dordogne. Achille Noël acquired it from the Craby family in 1936. Mme Nicole Noël and her team produce a nicely fullish, sometimes rather four-square wine under the basic Barrabaque label. Rather better is the more new oaky Cuvée Prestige.

Château Belloy

OWNER: Travers family; manager: Hélène Texier-
  Travers.
COMMUNE: Fronsac.
SURFACE AREA UNDER VINE: 6.85 ha – 60% Merlot;

40% Cabernet Franc.
SECOND WINE: Pavillon de Belloy.
OTHER WINE: Château Queyrau Le Haut (Canon-
  Fronsac).

The vines are well sited, and the château is an elegant, early nineteenth-century construction, with a rather less stylish Second Empire wing to the side. The wine has until recently been undistinguished. Since Mme Texier has been in charge, however, there has been a change for the better. The 2000 was promising.

Château Canon

OWNER: Jean Galand.
COMMUNE: Fronsac.

SURFACE AREA UNDER VINE: 1.4 ha – 100% Merlot.

This is one of two châteaux Canons in Fronsac. Note that there are additionally a dozen or so which incorporate the name Canon into their title. This Canon used to belong to a M. Marc before being bought by Ets Jean-Pierre Moueix in 1971. Under their ownership it became the leading Fronsac estate. In 2000 they sold it on to a local *pharmacien*, Jean Galand. Recent vintages indicate no fall in standards.

Château Canon

OWNER: Henriette Horeau & de Coninck family.
COMMUNE: Saint-Michel de Fronsac.
SURFACE AREA UNDER VINE: 10 ha – 90% Merlot;
  5% Cabernet Franc; 5% Cabernet Sauvignon.

SECOND WINE: Château Canon Lange.
OTHER WINES: Château Bellevue (Saint-Émilion);
  Château Junayme (Canon-Fronsac); Château
  Vray Canon Boyer (Canon-Fronsac).

For many years this larger Château Canon estate belonged to the de Laage family. It was bought by Louis Horeau, father of Henriette, who combined two properties he had acquired separately, in the 1930s. The vineyard lies in two sections on either side of Château Vray Canon Boyer, one facing south, the other west, and contains some venerable old vines. The wine can be fruity, but lacks distinction. It is not aged in cask. Canon is exclusively marketed by the Conincks' *négociant* firm, Horeau Beylot.

Château Canon de Brem

OWNER: Jean Halley.
COMMUNE: Fronsac.
SURFACE AREA UNDER VINE: 8.7 ha – 85% Merlot;

15% Cabernet Franc.
OTHER WINES: Château La Croix Canon (Canon-
  Fronsac); Château La Dauphine (Fronsac).

Château Canon de Brem lies on the main road between Fronsac and Saint-Michel with its vineyard in front of it on the hill. On the flatter land behind the château is the vineyard of Château La Dauphine, part of the same property, but in the *appellation* of Fronsac. The estate was bought by Ets Jean-Pierre Moueix in 1984 and sold by them to Jean Halley, a shareholder in the supermarket group Carrefour in 2000; but Moueix continue to market the wine. In old editions of Cocks & Féret, the front of the house illustrated Canon de Brem while the garden side was used for La Dauphine. Prior to the Moueix takeover, part of Canon de Brem was sold to private clients as Château Pichelèbre. Subsequently Christian Moueix isolated a separate parcel and called it, confusingly, Canon-Moueix. Following the recent sale this name no longer exists (the last vintage was the 2000) and the vines have been incorporated back into Canon de Brem.

Canon de Brem is rich and generous, consistently one of the very best wines of the *appellation*. Let us hope this continues despite Moueix no longer being responsible for the wine. A huge new winery was built for M. Halley's new estates in 2002.

Château Cassagne Haut-Canon

OWNER: Jean-Jacques Dubois.
COMMUNE: Saint-Michel-de-Fronsac.

SURFACE AREA UNDER VINE: 15 ha – 70% Merlot;
25% Cabernet Franc; 5% Cabernet Sauvignon.

Cassagne means 'oak' in old Gallic. The property is above Saint-Martin, on top of the hill. From the terrace of the late nineteenth-century château, the view over the Dordogne valley is remarkable. The estate was formed towards the end of the nineteenth century by General Thorel. The simple château wine can be a bit solid. The special *cuvée*, La Truffière, contains a higher proportion of Cabernet Sauvignon, sees more new oak and is worth the extra cost.

Château Comte

OWNER: Mme Desobeau; manager: Françoise
  Roux.
COMMUNE: Fronsac.

SURFACE AREA UNDER VINE: 4 ha – 80% Merlot;
20% Cabernet Franc.

The elegant château was built between the sixteenth and eighteenth centuries. It stands in a splendid park high up on the plateau behind the village. Originally belonging to Dr Goizet, who was also the owner of Château Canon, it is now farmed by Mme Roux and sold through the Palais du Fronsadais organisation of Arnaud Roux-Oulié. The first successful vintage of the new regime was the 2000: an oaky, substantial, backward wine.

Château Coustolle

OWNER: Alain Roux.
COMMUNE: Fronsac.
SURFACE AREA UNDER VINE: 20 ha – 60% Merlot;
  35% Cabernet Franc; 5% Malbec.

OTHER WINES: Château Bourdieu La Valade
  (Fronsac); Château Capet Bégaud (Canon-
  Fronsac).

This is a large property by Fronsac standards, lying in the north-east corner of the *appellation*, adjacent to and above M. Roux's other estates giving him 40 hectares in total. The vines are partly picked by machine and the wine is matured also partly in tank. There is certainly potential here. Until recently, in bottle, the wines had a tendency to be somewhat rustic. I noted a distinct improvement with the 1998 and 2000 vintages, both of which I marked 'very good', as I did the 2002.

Château La Croix Canon

OWNER: Jean Halley.
COMMUNE: Fronsac.
SURFACE AREA UNDER VINE: 12.4 ha – 80% Merlot;
  20% Cabernet Franc.

OTHER WINES: Château La Dauphine (Fronsac);
  Château Canon de Brem (Canon-Fronsac).

Formerly called Château Bodet, this estate was acquired by Ets Jean-Pierre Moueix in 1995. They changed the name first to Château Charlemagne and then to La Croix Canon, and sold it along with their other Fronsac domaines to M. Halley in 2000, though they continue to market the wine. Potentially it could be the best of the three, the vineyard being in a south-east-facing amphitheatre above the river Dordogne and most of the vines are of a considerable age. In the late 1990s this was a rich, generous, fruity and very classy wine. Vintages since the changeover have maintained the Moueix standards.

Château La Fleur Cailleau

OWNER: Paul Barre.

COMMUNE: Fronsac.

SURFACE AREA UNDER VINE: 4.4 ha – 88% Merlot;
10% Cabernet Franc; 2% Malbec.

SECOND WINE: Château Vigne.

OTHER WINE: Château La Grave (Fronsac).

La Fleur Cailleau lies close to Château La Croix Canon above the village of Fronsac and was once part of a larger estate, becoming independent when it was sold to Paul Barre in 1982. Right from the start the wine was a success: oaky, creamy-rich and succulent. The viticulture is conducted on organic lines.

Château La Fleur Canon

OWNER: Alain de Coninck.

COMMUNE: Saint-Michel-de-Fronsac.

SURFACE AREA UNDER VINE: 7 ha – 70% Merlot;
30% Cabernet Sauvignon.

OTHER WINES: Château Canon (Canon-Fronsac); Château Junayme (Canon-Fronsac); Château Vrai Canon Boyer (Canon-Fronsac).

This is one of several Fronsac properties associated with the Horeau/de Coninck family. The wines are ripe and medium-bodied, but they lack a little succulence of fruit and real definition. Maturation here is in tank.

Château du Gaby

OWNER: Khayat family.

COMMUNE: Fronsac.

SURFACE AREA UNDER VINE: 7.5 ha – 85% Merlot;
10% Cabernet Sauvignon; 5% Cabernet Franc.

SECOND WINE: Château La Roche Gaby.

Antoine Khayat bought the somewhat run-down La Roche Gaby, as it was then known, in 1999 from Mme Marie-Madelaine Frouin. The vineyard is well sited on the top of the plateau. The *chais* date from 1661. The first vintages under the new ownership show a lot of promise. The 2000 is a wine of real character and flair, and the 2002 is very good indeed.

Château Grand-Renouil

OWNER: Michel Ponty.

COMMUNE: Saint-Michel-de-Fronsac.

SURFACE AREA UNDER VINE: 6 ha – 85% Merlot;
15% Cabernet Franc.

SECOND WINE: Château Petit Renouil.

OTHER WINES: Château Canon Feydieu (Canon-Fronsac); Château du Pavillon (Canon-Fronsac).

The château of Grand-Renouil is up a west-facing valley below Château Cassagne Haut-Canon, with its vineyards behind. Michel Ponty inherited it from his father in the 1980s. This is a richer, more profound wine than M. Ponty's du Pavillon, with a little more new oak. I find this a reliable château, but marked it as 'good plus' as in 1998 and 1990, rather than 'very good'.

Château Haut-Mazeris

OWNER: M Bleynie & Mme Ubald-Bocquet.
COMMUNE: Saint-Michel-de-Fronsac.
SURFACE AREA UNDER VINE: 6 ha –
   60% Merlot; 20% Cabernet Franc;

20% Cabernet Sauvignon. (There are a further
4.9 ha across the border in the Fronsac commune
of Saint-Aignan.)

This estate, on perhaps the highest point of the *appellation*, is surrounded by the other estates with Mazeris as part of their name. *Élevage* is shared between tank and new oak. The introduction recently of a *tête de cuvée*, Cuvée Capucine, has effectively reduced the basic Haut-Mazeris to the status of a second wine. But the Capucine, if the 2002 is anything to go by, is very good.

Château Junayme

OWNER: de Coninck-Horeau family.
COMMUNE: Fronsac.
SURFACE AREA UNDER VINE: 16 ha – 80% Merlot;
   15% Cabernet Franc; 5% Cabernet Sauvignon.

SECOND WINE: Château La Tour Canon.
OTHER WINES: Château Canon (Canon-Fronsac);
   Château La Fleur Canon (Canon-Fronsac);
   Château Vrai Canon Boyer (Canon-Fronsac).

The vineyard of Château Junayme stretches half a kilometre on either side of the Coninck-Horeau's other Canon-Fronsac châteaux on slopes which face south-east overlooking Le Port de Fronsac. The wine is matured partly in *cuve*, partly in barrel. The wine is of medium body, but like the rest of the family's wines, uninspiring. Neutral when young, it attenuates rapidly.

Château Lamarche-Canon

OWNER: Éric Julien & Vignobles Germain.
COMMUNE: Fronsac.

SURFACE AREA UNDER VINE: 5 ha – 90% Merlot;
   10% Cabernet Sauvignon.

The château of Lamarche-Canon lies on the main road at the small junction which runs up to the château of Junayme. Since 1992 a special cuvée called Candelaire has been produced from the older vines and given longer in oak. This has effectively relegated what is bottled as Lamarche-Canon to a second wine. I used to find Candelaire a bit oaky, Lamarche-Canon a bit slight. But recent vintages have shown a distinct improvement. The Cuvée Candelaire 2002 was 'very good plus'.

Château Mazeris

OWNER: de Cournuaud family.
COMMUNE: Saint-Michel-de-Fronsac.
SURFACE AREA UNDER VINE: 24 ha – 85% Merlot;

15% Cabernet Franc.
SECOND WINE: Château Lafund.

The property has been in the same family since 1800. The vines adjoin Mazeris and Mazeris-Belle-vue on the plateau near the *appellation* boundary. Mazeris is one of the better Fronsacs, a wine I see regularly on the tasting table of Ets J-P Moueix. It is firmer than, say, Canon de Brem, and takes longer to open out but is rich and succulent. Since 1994, Patrick de Cournuaud has produced an old vine super-*cuvée* called La Part des Anges: this is quite oaky, but very good indeed.

Château Mazeris-Bellevue

OWNER: Jacques & Monique Bussier.
COMMUNE: Saint-Michel-de-Fronsac.
SURFACE AREA UNDER VINE: 9.3 ha – 45% Merlot;
35% Cabernet Franc; 15% Cabernet Sauvignon;
5% Malbec.

This Mazeris estate has been owned by the same family since 1848. As a result of the high Cabernet content the wine is full-bodied and backward, sometimes a bit hard, needing time to show itself. I always feel a little more new oak, or, today, micro-oxygenation, would help. But there is good depth underneath. It is worth waiting for.

Château Montcanon

OWNER: Marcel Durant.
COMMUNE: Fronsac.
SURFACE AREA UNDER VINE: 1.5 ha – 95% Merlot;
5% Cabernet Franc.
OTHER WINE: Château Toumalin-Joncquet
(Canon-Fronsac).

This is, in effect, a super-*cuvée* of M. Durant's Château Toumalin-Joncquet. Durant, in his early sixties, looks after the vineyard while his son-in-law, Arnaud Roux-Oulié, makes the wine. The first vintage was 2000. Old vines, 100 per cent new oak: all rather good! The 2002 also showed promise.

Château Moulin Pey-Labrie

OWNER: Hubau family.
COMMUNE: Fronsac.
SURFACE AREA UNDER VINE: 6.7 ha – 70% Merlot;
20% Cabernet Sauvignon; 10% Cabernet Franc.
SECOND WINE: Château Le Moulin.
OTHER WINES: Château des Combes Canon
(Fronsac); Château Haut-Lariveau (Fronsac).

This reliable property (not to be confused with its neighbour, Château Pey-Labrie) is situated on the top of the plateau behind Château Gaby. One-third new wood is used each year, and the wine is medium- to full-bodied, ripe, opulent and balanced. The 2002 was very good indeed.

Château du Pavillon

OWNER: Michel Ponty.
COMMUNE: Fronsac.
SURFACE AREA UNDER VINE: 4 ha – 100% Merlot.
OTHER WINE: Château Grand-Renouil (Canon-Fronsac).

This is M. Ponty's lesser (and certainly cheaper) Fronsac. The wine has decent substance and fruit but not much dimension or staying power. When I first encountered it, alongside Château Grand-Renouil, I assumed it was the second wine. I was quickly corrected. The Pavillon vineyard is quite separate, and is located further down the slope from Château Junayme.

Château Pey-Labrie

OWNER: Éric Vareille.
COMMUNE: Fronsac.
SURFACE AREA UNDER VINE: 9.2 ha – 75% Merlot;
15% Cabernet Franc; 10% Cabernet Sauvignon.
SECOND WINE: Château Haut Pey-Labrie.
OTHER WINE: Château Caillou (Canon-Fronsac).

This well-sited vineyard has been in the hands of the Vareille family since 1961, and can date its history back to the early 1800s. The fruit is hand-picked and the wine matured partly in tank, partly in barrel, of which 10 per cent is new. Since 1995 there has been a special *cuvée* called Coeur Canon, which is entirely reared in wood. The wines here are nicely substantial, firm and fresh. The basic Pey-Labrie can be a bit solid at first but the Coeur Canon has plenty of interest. It was good in both 2000 and 1998.

Château Roullet

OWNER: Michel Dorneau.
COMMUNE: Fronsac.
SURFACE AREA UNDER VINE: 26 ha – 65% Merlot; 25% Cabernet Franc; 10% Cabernet Sauvignon.

OTHER WINES: Château La Croix (Fronsac); Château Haut Gros Bonnet (Canon-Fronsac); Château Pontus (Fronsac).

The vineyards are situated above those of M. Dorneau's other properties on the eastern side of the *appellation*, and the wine is made at the combined premises of Châteaux Pontus and La Croix. The wine of Roullet is gently oaky (some one-third of the barrels are new), ripe, succulent, medium-bodied and stylish. I liked both the 2000 and the 1998.

Château Toumalin

OWNER: d'Arfeuille family.
COMMUNE: Fronsac.
SURFACE AREA UNDER VINE: 8 ha – 75% Merlot; 25% Cabernet Franc.

OTHER WINES: Château La Pointe (Pomerol); Château La Serre (Saint-Émilion).

The d'Arfeuille family inherited Château Toumalin, as they did their other interests, from the father-in-law of Bernard d'Arfeuille, Paul Delahoutre, who, incidentally, was also the owner of Château Pey-Labrie, Toumalin's neighbour, in the 1940s. This is a good, reliable, gently oaky (25 per cent new each year), medium-bodied Fronsac with plenty of personality. It keeps well.

Château Vrai Canon Bouché

OWNER: Françoise Roux.
COMMUNE: Fronsac.
SURFACE AREA UNDER VINE: 15 ha – 90% Merlot; 10% Cabernet Franc.

SECOND WINE: Château Les Terraces de Vrai Canon Bouché.
OTHER WINE: Château Vincent (Fronsac).

The vines of Château Vrai Canon Bouché are on the celebrated Canon plateau above extensive *caves* hacked out to provide stone for local houses, which now provide an admirable environment to store the wine. The property takes part of its name from a former owner, Edgard Bouché. It was acquired by Ernest Roux in 1953. This is a fullish-bodied, rich, oaky wine, that needs a year or two more than other Fronsacs to mature. I liked the 1998, but wonder whether the 2000 (50 per cent new oak) was a little over-oaked. The 2002 is not excessively woody though. The wine is distributed by Arnaud Roux-Oulié's Palais du Fronsadais.

Château Vrai Canon Boyer

OWNER: de Coninck family.
COMMUNE: Saint-Michel-de-Fronsac.
SURFACE AREA UNDER VINE: 8.5 ha – 90% Merlot;
   5% Cabernet Franc; 5% Cabernet Franc.

OTHER WINES: Château Bellevue (Saint-Émilion);
   Château Canon (Canon-Fronsac); Château
   Junayme (Canon-Fronsac).

The château is a large, clumsy, late nineteenth-century example. It lies in a park with the *chai* at the bottom of the garden on the Canon plateau. Sadly, as at the other Coninck estates, the problems of *indivision* and lack of investment are all too apparent in both the cellar and the wine. The former lacks a single oak barrel. The latter could, indeed should, be very good. But it lacks class.

FRONSAC LEADING CHÂTEAUX

Château Arnauton

OWNER: Xavier & Jean-Pierre Hérail.
COMMUNE: Fronsac.
SURFACE AREA UNDER VINE: 24 ha – 85% Merlot;

10% Cabernet Sauvignon; 5% Cabernet Franc.
SECOND WINE: Château de Montahut.

The vineyards of Arnauton are situated to the east of the road from Fronsac to Saillans, with a good view back to the Gironde. The wine is good and sturdy. It is worth trading up to the superior *cuvée*, Grand Sol. This is full-bodied, rich and nicely oaky (25 per cent new wood). I marked the 2000 as 'very good'. But the basic wine in both 2000 and 1998 were no better than 'quite good'.

Château Bourdieu-La-Valade

OWNER: Alain Roux.
COMMUNE: Fronsac.
SURFACE AREA UNDER VINE: 13 ha – 80% Merlot;
   20% Cabernet Franc.

SECOND WINE: Château La Cournelle.
OTHER WINES: Château Capet Bégaud (Canon-
   Fronsac); Château Coustolle (Canon-Fronsac .

This is a good middle-of-the-road Fronsac: medium- to medium-full-bodied, with decent fruit and personality. As at Château Coustolle, Alain Roux's Canon-Fronsac flagship, there has been an improvement here in recent years.

Château Canevault

OWNER: Jean-Pierre & Sylvie Chaudet.
COMMUNE: Fronsac.

SURFACE AREA UNDER VINE: 1.9 ha – 70% Merlot;
   20% Cabernet Franc; 10% Cabernet Sauvignon.

The Chaudets have 6 hectares of Bordeaux Supérieur vines at Lugon, 8 kilometres away to the north-east, also called Château Canevault. And this is where this Fronsac is made. The 2000 had good weight, fruit and balance.

Château Carlmagnus

OWNER: Arnaud Roux-Oulié.
COMMUNE: Fronsac.
SURFACE AREA UNDER VINE: 2.26 ha –

100% Merlot.
OTHER WINE: Chateau Carlmagnus (Fronsac).

Arnaud Roux-Oulié bought this property, then called Château Carolus, in 1998 and has since established it as one of the very best of the *appellation*. Modern methods are used: the vineyard is partly planted with grass to reduce the vigour of the vines and partly ploughed. The vines are routinely debudded, green harvested and the leaves stripped to expose the fruit to the sun. The wine is fermented and macerated at 28°C with the malos taking place in barrel (100 per cent new wood). This results in a lush, oaky wine, but one with good acidity and class. The 2000 was one of the Fronsacs of the vintage. In 2002, there being another Château Carolus in the Médoc, Arnaud Roux decided to change the name to Carlmagnus. I marked this vintage very good plus.

Château de Carles

OWNER: Antoine Chastenet de Castaing &
  Stéphane Droulers.
COMMUNE: Saillans.

SURFACE AREA UNDER VINE: 20 ha – 80% Merlot;
  15% Cabernet Franc; 5% Malbec.
SECOND WINE: Château Couperat.

The Château de Carles, a fine building with a fifteenth-century façade, stands outside Saillans overlooking the valley of the river Isle. It has belonged to the Chastenet de Castaing family since the early 1900s. The vineyard is hand-picked and the wine aged in a mixture of wood (two-thirds new) and tank. The basic wine, sold by Ets J-P Moueix, is round, ripe and medium-bodied. The *tête de cuvée*, Haut-Carles, is fat, rich and oaky. The last decade has seen both consistency and good quality here, the 2000 being particularly successful.

Château Chadenne

OWNER: Philippe & Véronique Jean.
COMMUNE: Saint-Aignan.
SURFACE AREA UNDER VINE: 4 ha – 75% Merlot,

25% Cabernet Franc.
OTHER WINE: Chateau Haut-Picat (Bordeaux).

Philippe and Véronique Jean, Corrèzien in origin, acquired Château Chadenne from the Crabit family towards the end of 1999. The 2000 vintage was their first effort. The grapes are hand-picked, but presently the maturation takes place in tank as well as in wood. The Jeans also own the adjacent 5-hectare Château Haut-Picat (AC Bordeaux).

Hitherto Chadenne has not been one of Fronsac's high fliers. I have now seen the first three vintages under the new ownership and things are looking up.

Château Dalem

OWNER: Michel Rullier.
COMMUNE: Saillans.
SURFACE AREA UNDER VINE: 14.7 ha – 65% Merlot;

25% Cabernet Sauvignon; 10% Cabernet Franc.
SECOND WINE: Château La Longua.
OTHER WINE: Château de La Huste (Fronsac).

Michel Rullier's Château Dalem has been one of the top Fronsacs for at least the last couple of decades. The elegant, eighteenth-century château lies in the middle of the village of Saillans. Winemaking is up-to-date, with around one-third new wood being used for the maturation. Dalem is fullish-bodied, firm, ripe and very well balanced. The 2000 is a fine example of a Fronsac and the 2002 was my favourite Fronsac in April 2003. Sadly I am rather less impressed with the stable-companion, Château de La Huste.

Château de La Dauphine

OWNER: Jean Halley.
COMMUNE: Fronsac.
SURFACE AREA UNDER VINE: 8.9 ha – 85% Merlot;
15% Cabernet Franc.

OTHER WINES: Château Canon de Brem (Canon-
Fronsac); Château La Croix Canon (Canon-
Fronsac).

This is effectively the same property as Canon de Brem, the vines behind the château on the flatter more sandy soil being Dauphine, Fronsac, those across the road on the slope being Canon de Brem, Canon-Fronsac. The château dates from 1750. Along with Canon de Brem, La Dauphine was sold by Ets J-P Moueix to Jean Halley in 2000. The wine is less structured than Canon de Brem, but round, balanced and succulent. Under the Moueix regime it was regularly one of Fronsac's best wines. The 2002, under the new regime, was most attractive.

Château La Fleur Vincent

OWNER: M. & Mme Stéphane Oulié.
COMMUNE: Saint-Aignan.

SURFACE AREA UNDER VINE: 0.93 ha –
100% Merlot.

This small property was acquired in 1999 by Stéphane Oulié, and is marketed by his brother Arnaud Roux-Oulié's Palais du Fronsadais. The 2000 was a good, gently oaky example.

Château Fontenil

OWNER: Michel & Dany Rolland.
COMMUNE: Saillans.
SURFACE AREA UNDER VINE: 9 ha – 85% Merlot;
15% Cabernet Franc.
SECOND WINE: Tilet Rouge.

OTHER WINES: Château Bertineau Saint-Vincent
(Lalande-de-Pomerol); Château Le Bon Pasteur
(Pomerol); Château Rolland-Maillet (Saint-
Émilion).

Michel Rolland, consultant winemaker to many estates worldwide, bought Fontenil together with his wife Dany, also a qualified oenologist, in 1986, since when they have enlarged Fontenil by about a half. This is also where they live. As you might expect, the wine is a real star: rich, succulent and gently oaky. The 2000 is quite delicious; and the 2002 one of my Fronsacs of the vintage.

Château de Fronsac

OWNER: M. & Mme Paul Seurin; rented to Arnaud
Roux-Oulié.
COMMUNE: Fronsac.

SURFACE AREA UNDER VINE: 8 ha – 80% Merlot;
20% Cabernet Franc.
OTHER WINE: Château Carlmagnus (Fronsac).

There was a Roman villa here, followed by a fortified camp built by Emperor Charlemagne. The Duc de Richelieu, governor of Guyenne in the eighteenth century, had a pleasant château built on the site, but this burned down in 1993. The château today is a reconstruction. Arnaud Roux-Oulié added the property to his expanding portfolio of wine estates in 2000 and suffixed the title with 'Panorama du Tertre'. The wine is quite oaky, but good. The vines are 40 years old.

Château Hautchat La Rose

OWNER: Jean-Bernard Saby.
COMMUNE: Saint-Aignan.
SURFACE AREA UNDER VINE: 6.5 ha – 80% Merlot;

15% Cabernet Franc; 5% Cabernet Sauvignon.
OTHER WINE: Château Rozier (Saint-Émilion).

A major improvement in quality has taken place here since M. Saby's two sons, both *oenologues*, have made their presence felt. Both viticultural and vinicultural procedures have been tightened up and new oak introduced. The 2002 was impressively good.

Château Haut Lariveau

OWNER: Grégoire & Bénédicte Hubau.
COMMUNE: Saint-Michel-de-Fronsac.
SURFACE AREA UNDER VINE: 4.4 ha – 100% Merlot.

OTHER WINES: Château des Combes (Canon-Fronsac); Château Moulin Pey-Labrie (Canon-Fronsac).

The château occupies the site of a twelfth-century hospital, part of the Order of Saint John of Jerusalem. Grégoire and Bénédicte Hubau, originally from the Nord *département*, make as reliable a wine here as they do at Moulin Pey-Labrie.

Château Magondeau

OWNER: Goujon family.
COMMUNE: Saillans.

SURFACE AREA UNDER VINE: 18 ha – 80% Merlot;
10% Cabernet Franc; 10% Cabernet Sauvignon.

Château Magondeau has been in the hands of the friendly Goujon family since 1882. Harvesting is partly by machine and the wines reared in both tank and barrel. The basic Magondeau is clean and fruity, the *tête de cuvée* Château Magondeau Beau-Site is a gently oaky, quite meaty wine with good depth. I liked both the 2002s.

Château Mayne-Vieil

OWNER: Sèze family; managers: Marie-Christine Boyé & Bertrand Sèze.
COMMUNE: Saillons.

SURFACE AREA UNDER VINE: 32 ha – 90% Merlot;
10% Cabernet Franc.

This substantial property lies at the northern edges of the Fronsac *appellation*. In addition to the Fronsac there are 13 hectares of Bordeaux *rouge* over the border. The estate belonged to the de Paty family for 300 years before being acquired by Jean-Raymond Fontemoing, of the major Libournais *négociant* dynasty, in 1809. Fontemoing's successors constructed the present château, an elegant *chartreuse*, in 1860. Bertrand Sèze's grandfather bought Mayne-Vieil in 1918. This is a reliable wine, machine-harvested and matured partly in wood. The Cuvée Aliénor is excellent, regularly one of the best Fronsacs of the vintage.

Château Moulin Haut-Laroque

OWNER: Jean-Noël Hervé.
COMMUNE: Saillans.
SURFACE AREA UNDER VINE: 15 ha – 65% Merlot;
20% Cabernet Franc; 10% Cabernet Sauvignon;
5% Malbec.
OTHER WINE: Château Cardeneau (Fronsac).

Moulin Haut-Laroque is one of a number of reputed Saillans properties whose wines are marketed by L'Expression de Fronsac group (others include Dalem, Fontenil, Villars and La Vieille Cure). It has been in the hands of Jean-Noël Hervé's family since before the phylloxera outbreak. The fruit is collected by hand, sorted through both before and after de-stemming, and the wine aged in one-third new oak casks. The wine is ripe, gently oaky, medium- to full-bodied and succulent. It is regularly one of the best wines of the *appellation*. The 2002 was very good indeed.

Château Pétrarque

OWNER: Francis Carayon.
COMMUNE: Saillans.
SURFACE AREA UNDER VINE: 2.5 ha – 80% Merlot;
10% Cabernet Franc; 10% Cabernet Sauvignon.

This small estate, up on the Saillans plateau, is owned by Francis Carayon, who manages Château La Croix Saint-André in Lalande-de-Pomerol for the Chabiran family. I have only met this wine recently, but I have liked what I have seen: it has stylish fruit and good freshness.

Château Plain-Point

OWNER: Michel Aroldi.
COMMUNE: Saint-Aignan.
SURFACE AREA UNDER VINE: 17 ha – 75% Merlot;
15% Cabernet Sauvignon; 10% Cabernet Franc.
SECOND WINE: Château La Métairie.

North of the hamlet of Saint-Aignan, the vineyard of Château Plain-Point surrounds the ivy-covered château in one single block. It is the senior property in the commune in both age and quality. The harvest takes place by hand, and there is 50 per cent new oak. This is a medium- to full-bodied wine, ripe, succulent, elegant and well-made. It keeps well.

Château Puy Guilhem

OWNER: Jean-François & Annie Enixon.
COMMUNE: Saillans.
SURFACE AREA UNDER VINE: 11 ha – 90% Merlot;
10% Cabernet Franc.
SECOND WINE: Château Puy Saint-Vincent.

Jean-François and Annie Enixon bought Château Puy Guilhem in 1995, since when we have seen a renaissance. The estate lies on south-east-facing slopes overlooking the valley of the river Isle and today produces a good, fullish-bodied, gently oaky wine, with good grip and no lack of ripe fruit.

Château Renard Mondésir

OWNER: Xavier Chassagnoux.
COMMUNE: La Rivière.
SURFACE AREA UNDER VINE: 7 ha – 85% Merlot;
15% Cabernet Franc.
SECOND WINE: Château Renard.

The vineyard of Château Renard Mondésir occupies a south-west-facing slope above the rather elegant Directoire-style château. It was acquired by Amédée Chassagnoux, grandfather of Xavier, in 1978. Since about 1990 this property has been one to note. The wine is fullish-bodied, succulent and gently oaky; one of the best in the commune.

Château Richelieu

OWNER: Jean-Bernard Fraikin.
COMMUNE: Fronsac.

SURFACE AREA UNDER VINE: 12.5 ha – 75% Merlot;
25% Cabernet Franc.

There is a direct line here to the famous Richelieu family, the seventeenth-century Cardinal who built the elegant château, and his grand-nephew, the soldier and diplomat. Jean-Bernard Fraikin bought the estate in 1996. The vineyard is well sited on the slopes in the south-east corner of the *appellation*, and the wine is an attractive, plummy example, partly reared in new oak, partly in tank. The 2002 is very good.

Château de La Rivière

OWNER: Jean Leprince; managers: Xavier & Valérie Pénaud.
COMMUNE: La Rivière.
SURFACE AREA UNDER VINE: 59 ha – 75% Merlot;

12% Cabernet Sauvignon; 8% Cabernet Franc;
2% Malbec.
SECOND WINE: Prince de la Rivière.
OTHER WINE: Aria de la Rivière (Fronsac).

La Rivière is the largest estate in the commune, and its oldest wine estate. The splendid château dates in part from the fourteenth century and is built on the ruins of an even earlier *donjon*. The present reputation of the wine is largely due to the previous owner, the irrepressible Jacques Boirie (he once organised a blind tasting of his wines against various Bordeaux First Growths, and did not come out the second). Boirie sold out to the current proprietor in the early 1990s. Hand harvesting; one-third new wood; and now a *tête de cuvée*, Aria de la Rivière. I enjoyed the 2002.

Château La Rousselle

OWNER: Viviane & Jacques Davau.
COMMUNE: La Rivière.
SURFACE AREA UNDER VINE: 4.6 ha – 60% Merlot;

20% Cabernet Franc; 20% Cabernet Sauvignon.

Purely by chance, the three top growths in the commune of La Rivière follow each other in this list. This estate has come from nowhere in just the space of 15 years. The vineyard was completely replanted in 1971 when the Davaus took over. Since then there has been a succession of good wines: nicely oaky (50 per cent of the barrels are renewed each year), plump and attractive. Stéphane Derenoncourt is now consulting. The 2001 was a splendid success.

Château Tour du Moulin

OWNER: Vincent & Josette Dupuch.
COMMUNE: Saillans.
SURFACE AREA UNDER VINE: 7 ha – 81% Merlot;
12.5% Cabernet Franc; 6.5% Cabernet Sauvignon.

This estate has undergone a renaissance since being taken over by new owners in 1987. Major replanting has taken place, and although the vines are still young, the 2000 and 2001 show promise. Debudding and leaf-stripping are routine, the harvest is by hand and 25 per cent of the barrels are new. For the time being stick to the superior Cuvée Particulière. The 2002 was very good.

Château Les Trois Croix

OWNER: Patrice Léon & family; managers: Stéphane & Bertrand Léon.
COMMUNE: Fronsac.
SURFACE AREA UNDER VINE: 14 ha – 90% Merlot; 10% Cabernet Franc.
SECOND WINE: Château Lanolière.

Château Les Troix Croix lies at the junction of the communes of Fronsac, Saillans and Saint-Aignan, from where no doubt three church towers are visible. At 80 metres above sea level this is one of the highest spots on the Fronsac plateau. The Léon family took over in 1995, and have since introduced a barrel cellar (50 per cent new oak each year). Prior to that the wine was aged in tank. Though the average age of the vines is 40 years, I am so far more impressed by other Fronsacs in the area (such as La Vieille Cure). However, the 2000 and 2001 showed a bit more backbone and concentration.

Château La Vieille Cure

OWNER: Colin Ferenbach & Partners.
COMMUNE: Saillans.
SURFACE AREA UNDER VINE: 19 ha – 80% Merlot;
15% Cabernet Franc; 5% Cabernet Sauvignon.
SECOND WINE: Le Calice de la Vieille Cure.

There was already an established vineyard here in 1780. The vines are situated in one site on a south-east-facing slope above the river Isle. The estate has belonged to Colin Ferenbach and his American associates since 1986 and the wine is generous, fruity and usually good value for money.

Château Villars

OWNER: Jean-Claude & Brigitte Gaudrie.
COMMUNE: Saillans.
SURFACE AREA UNDER VINE: 29 ha – 73% Merlot;
18% Cabernet Franc; 9% Cabernet Sauvignon.
SECOND WINE: Château Moulin Haut-Villars.

Jean-Claude represents the seventh generation of Gaudries at Château Villars, the estate having come into the family at the beginning of the nineteenth century. The grapes are hand-picked and then vinified in cement vats. The wine is aged in barrel, one-third new. For a long time this was one of the very best and most reliable of Fronsacs: rich, fat, concentrated and gently oaky. But, sadly, more recent vintages (2001 and 2002) suggest something has gone off the boil here.

CÔTES DE CASTILLON & CÔTES DE FRANCS

CÔTES DE CASTILLON

SURFACE AREA (2002): 3044 ha.

PRODUCTION (2002): 13,151 hl.

COLOUR : Red only.

GRAPE VARIETIES: Merlot; Cabernet
Sauvignon; Cabernet Franc; Malbec.

MAXIMUM YIELD: 50 hl/ha.

MINIMUM ALCOHOLIC DEGREE: 10.5°.

CÔTES DE FRANCS

SURFACE AREA (2002): Red: 506 ha;
white: 9 ha.

PRODUCTION (2002): Red: 21,674 hl;
white: 246 hl.

COLOUR: Red & White.

GRAPE VARIETIES: Red: Merlot; Cabernet
Sauvignon; Cabernet Franc; Malbec.
White: Sémillon; Sauvignon; Muscadelle.

MAXIMUM YIELD: 50 hl/ha (red and dry
hl/ha (*blanc liquoreux*).

MINIMUM ALCOHOLIC DEGREE: 10° (red and
dry white); 12.5° (*blanc liquoreux*).

East of Saint-Émilion and its satellites, above the town of Castillon near the border between the Gironde *département* and that of the Dordogne, lie the Côtes de Castillon and the Côtes de Francs. Both these regions were formerly Bordeaux Supérieur. In 1989 – having been plain Bordeaux Supérieur until 1955 – what was then Bordeaux Supérieur, Côtes de Castillon, was upgraded to Côtes de Castillon Contrôlée. This consists of the following nine communes: Castillon-La-Bataille, Saint-Magne-de-Castillon, Belvès-de-Castillon, Sainte-Colombe, Monbadon, Gardegan et Tourtirac, Les Salles de Castillon, Saint-Genès de Castillon and Saint-Philippe-d'Aiguilhe.

To the north, three further communes – Francs, Saint-Cibard and Tayac, were given their own special Appellation Contrôlée Bordeaux, Côtes de Francs in 1967. Here, white wine as well as red is permitted. Côtes de Castillon is an appellation for red wines only. In both areas the dominant grape variety is the Merlot.

This is an attractive part of Bordeaux. The landscape can be sleeply undulating, rising to 100 metres above sea level, dividing the countryside into woodland, pasture and vineyards. The latter are usually sheltered sites facing southwards over the Dordogne valley, protected from the north. Few of the estates can boast large vineyards, though areas under vine are normally larger than across the border in Saint-Émilion. An all important co-operative at Gardegan accounts for the wine of some 150 of the smaller estates and is responsible for one-fifth of the total production. There is a second, smaller co-operative in the Côtes de Francs.

The soil structure is similar to that further west. Down by the river there is rich alluvial matter. In the valleys clay mixes with sand. Better soils contain gravel as well, while on the top of the slopes you will find clay-limestone soils and marl.

Both areas have expanded in recent years. Castillon has risen from around 2450 hectares to 3000 since 1982. At the same time the Francs has grown from 300 hectares to 500 today. In the meanwhile both the communes of Monbadon and Les Salles de Castillon have mysteriously been promoted from Francs to Castillon.

At the same time there has been an injection not just of the equipment and controls necessary to produce better wine, but the willingness to improve standards. As elsewhere this has come about by means of changes of generations of existing families and the arrival of outside investors. One of the first were the Thienpont family, owners of Vieux Château Certan in Pomerol. Georges Thienpont, one of the sons of the original Georges, who bought Certan in 1924, settled in the Côtes de Francs as a cattle farmer. He and his son Nicolas began planting vines at Château Puygueraud in 1979, expanding later into other estates. Château Puygueraud remains one of the top wines of the *appellation*. Elsewhere in the Côtes de Francs Patrick Valette, son of Jean-Paul, late of Saint-Émilion's Château Pavie, bought Château La Prade, Hubert de Boüard (Angélus) and Dominique Hébrard (Cheval Blanc) renovated Château de Francs and Jean-Marie Chardonnier, a Bordeaux *négociant*, purchased Château Marsau.

More recently, in the Côtes de Castillon, Stephan von Neipperg has acquired Château d'Aiguilhe, his *oenologue* consultant Stéphane Derenoncourt has founded Domaine de L'A, while British wine merchant Tony Laithwaite makes wine at Château La Clairière.

Both the Francs and the Castillon are happy hunting grounds for those looking for well-made minor Bordeaux. There are lots of good wines in both 1998 and 2000 and some more than satisfactory examples from 1999. They are ready after some four to seven years, depending on the vintage. Many châteaux produce a basic, non-oak-aged *cuvée*, and then one or two superior, increasingly oaky versions. These, if not too excessively priced, are usually well worth the extra premium.

CÔTES DE CASTILLON & CÔTES DE FRANCS

DORDOGNE

Tayac
◆ 2
1 ◆

Francs
◆ 3
4 ◆

Monbadon ●
◆ 5
7 ◆ 8 ◆
6 ◆
9 ◆
10 ◆

Puisseguin ●
◆ 13

St-Philippe-
d'Aiguille ◆ 12

le Salles
◆ 11

◆ 14

Theolat

◆ 15

St-Genès-
de-Castillon

GIRONDE

◆ 16

◆ 24
22 ◆
17 ◆
18 ◆ Ste-Colombe ● 23 ◆ Belvès-de-
Castillon
19 ◆ 21 ◆
20 ◆ 25 ◆
30 ◆ 29 ◆ ◆ 26
◆ 27
28 ◆
Castillon-la-
Bataille
31 ◆

D936

Dordogne

Appellations

Bordeaux-Côtes de Francs
Côtes de Castillon

0   3km
0   2miles

Châteaux ◆

Côtes de Francs AC

1   Marsau
2   de Francs
3   Laclaverie
4   Les Charmes-Godard
5   La Prade
6   Puygueraud

Côtes de Castillon AC

7   Cantegrive
8   Terrasson
9   Grand Tuillac
10   Les Hauts de Granges
11   de Belcier
12   Grimon
13   Joanin-Bécot

14   d'Aiguilhe
15   de Pitray
16   Domaine de l'A
17   Arthus
18   Cap de Faugères
19   Haute Terrasse
20   Lapeyronie
21   Poupille

22   Clos Puy Arnaud
23   Côte Montpezat
24   Les Rochers
25   La Croix Lartigue
26   Robin
27   de Chainchon
28   Clos L'Église
29   Fontbaude
30   Roque Le Mayne/La Bourrée
31   Grand Peyrou

Côtes de Castillon Leading Châteaux

Domaine de L'A

OWNER: Stéphane & Christine Derenoncourt.
COMMUNE: Sainte-Colombe.

SURFACE AREA UNDER VINE: 4.2 ha – 60% Merlot;
25% Cabernet Franc; 15% Cabernet Sauvignon.

The well-known and highly regarded *oenologue* Stéphane Derenoncourt founded this small estate in 1999. It is now run on biodynamic lines. The first three vintages are delicious: lush, balanced and stylish. Stéphane Derenoncourt also makes Clos Puy Arnaud (see page 405) and is consultant to Stephan von Neipperg at Château d'Aiguilhe and elsewhere.

Château d'Aiguilhe

OWNER: Comtes von Neipperg.
COMMUNE: Saint Philippe d'Aiguilhe.
SURFACE AREA UNDER VINE: 40 ha – 90% Merlot;
10% Cabernet Franc.

SECOND WINE: Château Fourtanet.
OTHER WINES: Château Canon-La-Gaffelière (Saint-Émilion); Château Clos de L'Oratoire (Saint-Émilion); Château La Mondotte (Saint-

The château is a picturesque ruin, but the cellars are modern and the site is magnificent: a large vineyard in an even larger park. Stephan von Neipperg of Saint-Émilion's Château Canon-La-Gaffelière and Clos de L'Oratoire bought the estate from a Catalan family in 1999. Yields are low, the winemaking is supervised by Stéphane Derenoncourt (see above) and the wines matured using 80 per cent new wood. The wine is fullish-bodied, plump, rich and classy: one of the stars of the *appellation*.

Arthus

OWNER: Richard & Danielle Dubois.
COMMUNE: Sainte-Colombe.
SURFACE AREA UNDER VINE: 11.5 ha – 70% Merlot;

30% Cabernet Franc.
OTHER WINES: Clos de la Vieille Église; Vieux Grean (both Côtes de Castillon).

Richard and Danielle Dubois are both oenologists. Arthus, a special selection from old vines and matured entirely in new oak, is one of three Côtes de Castillon wines they produce. Despite this the wine is not over-oaked. Indeed it is pleasantly rich, balanced and positive.

Château de Belcier

OWNER: MACIF; manager: Gilbert Dubois.
COMMUNE: Les Salles de Castillon.
SURFACE AREA UNDER VINE: 52 ha – 57% Merlot;
28% Cabernet Franc; 9% Cabernet Sauvignon;

6% Malbec.
SECOND WINE: Château de Monrecueil.
OTHER WINE: Château Ramage La Batisse (Haut-Médoc).

Having acquired Ramage La Batisse in 1986, the insurance company MACIF took over at Château Belcier, Les Salles de Castillon's senior estate, which was rather run down at the time. A large scale renovation then took place, not only in the *chai*, but in the château and its park, without, thankfully, having to lose a magnificent pine tree, said to be over a hundred years old, which stands in the central courtyard. The wine is of medium weight, fruity and stylish. There is a *tête de cuvée*, Le Pin de Belcier, which is rich and oaky.

Château La Bourrée

OWNER: Meynard family.
COMMUNE: Sainte-Magne-de-Castillon.
SURFACE AREA UNDER VINE: 20 ha –
  60% Merlot; 30% Cabernet Franc;

10% Cabernet Sauvignon.
SECOND WINE: Château du Vieux Montpezat.
OTHER WINE: Château Roque Le Mayne (Côtes de
  Castillon).

Jean-François Meynard, a youthful ex-champion rower, runs an efficient family set-up from this château down on the plain. Château La Bourrée, a good, basic wine, is machine-harvested and aged in one-third new wood. Of more interest is the Roque Le Mayne which comes from a 10-hectare vineyard he acquired in 1996 on the Montpezat *côte*. This is made using such techniques as *bâtonnage*, malo in barrel and upwards of 50 per cent new oak. The first harvest was 1998. Jean-François made a better wine in 1999 and an even better one in 2000.

Château Cantegrive

OWNER: Doyard brothers.
COMMUNE: Monbadon.
SURFACE AREA UNDER VINE: 17 ha – 65% Merlot;

20% Cabernet Sauvignon; 15% Cabernet Franc
OTHER WINE: Château Gasquerie (Côtes de Francs).

The Doyard brothers, Pascal and Yannick, who are also vineyard owners in Vertus, in Champagne's Côte de Blancs, produce a decent wine under the Cantegrive label, and a *tête de cuvée* called De l'An 1453. Matured entirely in new wood, this is rich, succulent and, not surprisingly quite oaky. This is perhaps the best address in the commune.

Château Cap de Faugères

OWNER: Corinne Guisez and family.
COMMUNE: Sainte-Colombe.
SURFACE AREA UNDER VINE: 30 ha – 70% Merlot;

30% Cabernet Franc.
SECOND WINE: Château Palenquey.
OTHER WINE: Château Faugères (Saint-Émilion).

Cap de Faugères rests on a plateau which overlaps from Castillon's Sainte-Colombe into the Saint-Émilion *commune* of Saint-Étienne-de-Lisse. The Guisez family have roughly half of their estate in each *appellation*. When Corinne and her late husband Péby, a film producer, acquired Cap de Faugères from cousins in 1987, there were only some 28 hectares under vine. Now there is a combined total of 60. The Castillon is hand-harvested, and stored partly in barrel, partly in tank, to preserve its freshness. The secret, though, is that the harvest is restricted to 36–40 hl/ha. This is an admirable modern set up. The wines are ripe, meaty, quite substantial and gently oaky: highly commendable.

Château de Chainchon

OWNER: André & Patrick Erésué.
COMMUNE: Castillon-La-Bataille.
SURFACE AREA UNDER VINE: 20 ha – 70% Merlot;

20% Cabernet Franc; 10% Cabernet Sauvignon.
OTHER WINE: Vlamy Dubourdieu Lange (Côtes de
  Castillon).

Château de Chainchon has been in the hands of the Erésué family since 1846. In modern times the Erésués were members of the local co-operative but André Erésué managed to extricate himself in 1980. He ran the estate until he retired in 1996, when his son Patrick, who had been *régisseur* at Château Canon-La-Gaffelière in Saint-Émilion, took over. This was the first year the property made its *tête de cuvée*, Valmy Dubourdieu Lange, named after a grandfather. This is made using such modern techniques as *microbullage*, *bâtonnage* and malo in barrel, with 50 per cent new wood, as well as being from old vines in the best parts of the estate. It is a full-bodied, quite firm, rich, 100 per cent Merlot wine with no lack of flair. There are two other *cuvées*, the non-oak-aged basic and a Cuvée Prestige. The Prestige *cuvée* is quite good; but it lacks a bit of generosity.

Château Clos L'Église

OWNER: Gérard Perse & Dr Alain Raynaud.
COMMUNE: Sainte Magne-de-Castillon.
SURFACE AREA UNDER VINE: 52 ha – 60% Merlot;
20% Cabernet Franc; 20% Cabernet Sauvignon.
OTHER WINES: Château Pavie (Saint-Émilion);
Château Quinault L'Enclos (Saint-Émilion).

Gérard Perse and Alain Raynaud bought Clos L'Église in 1999, and have since enlarged the surface area under vine. Production is low, in the order of 38 hl/ha, there is a sorting table, the wine is macerated for as much as six weeks, and matured using 100 per cent new oak. This is modern winemaking at an intervention level I find excessive. The resulting wines are rich but dense. They take ages to mature, by which time the fruit has largely disappeared.

Château Côte Montpezat

OWNER: Dominique Bessineau.
COMMUNE: Belvès de Castillon.
SURFACE AREA UNDER VINE: 30 ha – 70% Merlot;
15% Cabernet Franc; 15% Cabernet Sauvignon.
SECOND WINE: Château de Brousse.
OTHER WINE: Château Haut-Bernat (Puisseguin-Saint-Émilion).

This is one of the best and most highly regarded estates in the area. There is a medieval well and the château dates from the early seventeenth century. Dominique Bessineau acquired the property in 1989, since when it has been thoroughly modernised. Harvesting is by hand, and the wine is matured roughly one-third in new barrels, one-third in one-year-old barrels and one-third in tank. I was not too excited by the 2000 on the only occasion I have seen it. But the track record of Château Côte Montpezat during the 1990s has been admirable, as well as consistent.

Château La Croix Lartigue

OWNER: Claude de Labarre; manager: Arnaud de Labarre.
COMMUNE: Belvès de Castillon.
SURFACE AREA UNDER VINE: 8.2 ha – 70% Merlot;
30% Cabernet Franc.
OTHER WINE: Château Laplagnotte-Bellevue (Saint-Émilion).

The Labarre family acquired this estate in 1999, and immediately set about constructing a brand new winery. Harvesting is by hand and maturation is partly in barrel, partly in tank. The basic wine is good: clean, fruity and quite stylish. A lot more personality and oak will be found in the *tête de cuvée*: Les Cîmes de Lartigue.

Château Fontbaude

OWNER: Sabaté Zavan family.
COMMUNE: Sainte-Magne-de-Castillon.
SURFACE AREA UNDER VINE: 20 ha – 60% Merlot;
30% Cabernet Franc; 10% Cabernet Sauvignon.

Château Fontbaude, then only 4 hectares, was bought by the present owners' parents in 1967. It is now run by the brothers, Christian and Yannick Sabaté, together with their brother-in-law Patrick Zavan. The château is merely a modern farmhouse at the foot of the vineyard, with a new, small *chai à barrique* adjoining the winery. Harvesting is mechanical. There are three *cuvées*: the Tradition, non-oak-aged; the Vieilles Vignes, with one-third new wood, and, first produced in 1999, L'Ame de Fontbaude. This latter is full-bodied and rich, quite oaky, but concentrated and stylish.

Château Grand Peyrou

OWNER: Christian Laguillon.
COMMUNE: Sainte-Magne-de-Castillon.

SURFACE AREA UNDER VINE: 7 ha – 70% Merlot; 25% Cabernet Franc; 5% Cabernet Sauvignon.

I cannot speak with much experience of this wine, but both the 1999 and the 2000 were ripe, positive and succulent: very good quality.

Château Grand Tuillac

OWNER: Philippe Lavigne; managers: Laurent & Sylvie Poitevin.
COMMUNE: Saint-Philippe d'Aiguilhe.

SURFACE AREA UNDER VINE: 24 ha – 75% Merlot; 20% Cabernet Franc; 5% Cabernet Sauvignon.
OTHER WINE: Château Grand Bert (Saint-Émilion).

Château Grand Tuillac stands on one of the highest points of the *appellation*. Harvesting is by machine, and the wine is aged partly in wood, partly in tank. The standard *cuvée* is unexciting but the Cuvée Élégance is fullish, new woody, generous and supple. The Lavignes have been here for six generations.

Château Grimon

OWNER: Gilbert Dubois.
COMMUNE: Saint Philippe-d'Aiguilhe.
SURFACE AREA UNDER VINE: 5.4 ha – 60% Merlot;

40% Cabernet Franc.
SECOND WINE: Château Dubois-Grimon.

This is a relatively new estate, having been built up during the first half of the 1980s. Ten per cent of the casks are new, and the wine is quite substantial, with good tannins and plenty of fruit.

Château Les Hauts de Granges

OWNER: Luc Vincent.
COMMUNE: Les Salles de Castillon.
SURFACE AREA UNDER VINE: 16.5 ha – 64% Merlot; 26% Cabernet Sauvignon; 10% Cabernet Franc.

SECOND WINE: Château La Blaude.
OTHER WINE: Château du Vieux Chêne (Côtes de Francs).

On the plateau on the border between Castillon and the Côtes de Francs lies a scruffy farmhouse set up next to an elegant *maison girondine*. The estate has belonged to Luc Vincent, otherwise a farmer near Lille, since 1989. He is somewhat of an absentee landlord, visiting one week per month. Most of the wine is sold off in bulk, or aged in tank prior to estate bottling. The traditional *cuvée* lacks sophistication. Better is the Cuvée Réserve, aged in barrel of which one-third is new. I have marked this well. The 2001 was supervised by a newly-appointed *oenologue* and I believe this is the start of a major improvement here.

Château Haute Terrasse

OWNER: Pascal Bourrigaud.
COMMUNE: Sainte-Magne-de-Castillon.
SURFACE AREA UNDER VINE: 2.5 ha – 50% Merlot;
25% Cabernet Franc; 25% Cabernet Sauvignon.
OTHER WINE: Château Champion (Saint-Émilion).

The splendid south-facing slope of Haute Terrasse is a recent acquisition by the Bourrigaud family, long established in Saint-Émilion. I have only sampled the 2000. If this is anything to go by we have a new super-star. The wine is full-bodied, rich, concentrated and stylish.

Château Joanin-Bécot

OWNER: Juliette, Gérard & Dominique Bécot.
COMMUNE: Saint-Philippe-d'Aiguilhe.
SURFACE AREA UNDER VINE: 9.9 ha – 75% Merlot;
25% Cabernet Franc.
SECOND WINE: Le Secret de Joanin.

Joanin is a hamlet in Saint-Philippe-d'Aiguilhe and it was here that the Bécots of Château Beauséjour-Bécot in Saint-Émilion bought 5.4 hectares in 2000, and another 4.5 the following year. The vines are of a respectable age, the yield is restricted to 42 hl/ha, and 60 per cent of the barrels are new. The first results are promising.

Château Lapeyronie

OWNER: Jean-Frédéric & Hélène Lapeyronie.
COMMUNE: Sainte-Colombe.
SURFACE AREA UNDER VINE: 8.5 ha –
70% Merlot; 15% Cabernet Franc;
15% Cabernet Sauvignon.
SECOND WINE: Château Le Font du Jeu (Côtes de Castillon).
OTHER WINE: Château Vignoble d'Alfred (Côtes de Francs).

The estate is admirably situated on a south-west-facing slope, not far from the Saint-Emilion border. The Lapeyronies believe in low yields, plenty of new oak and malolactic fermentation in barrel. The result is a rich and succulent wine which ages well in barrel. Château Le Font du Jeu comes from a separate part of the estate and is equally attractive.

Château de Pitray

OWNER: Mme de Boigne; manager: Pierre Chiberry.
COMMUNE: Gardegan-et-Tourtirac.
SURFACE AREA UNDER VINE: 30 ha – 68% Merlot;
32% Cabernet Franc.
SECOND WINE: Château de Parsac.

In the middle of a 100-hectare domaine, most of which is a park with some splendid venerable trees – 100-year-old oaks and cedars – lies an absurdly magnificent mock Gothic-Renaissance pile, built in 1868. The same family, descendants both of the Ségurs, once owners of Château Lafite, and the original Seigneurs of Pitray, have owned this estate since the seventeenth century. The vineyard lies in one piece, on slopes which face south, and is harvested mechanically. There are two *cuvées*. The basic one is aged in tank; the Première in wood, of which one-third is new. This latter wine, if not the greatest Castillon, is certainly worthy of note.

Château Poupille

OWNER: Carrille family; manager: Philippe Carrille.
COMMUNE: Sainte-Colombe.
SURFACE AREA UNDER VINE: 16 ha – 97% Merlot;
3% Cabernet Franc.
OTHER WINES: Château Haut Cardinal (Saint-Émilion); Château Robin des Moines (Saint-Émilion).

At the eastern side of the commune of Sainte-Colombe, just off the road that runs north from Castillon-La-Bataille up to the Côtes de Francs, you will find Castillon's best estate. Jean-Marie Carrille bought it in 1967 and his son Philippe took over in 1993. There were 10 hectares originally, but the vineyard has been extended since. The vines are closer together than is normal in these parts, hand-harvested and the wine aged in wood, using one-third new. Philippe Carrille has tried *microbullage*, malo in barrel and *bâtonnage*, but has reverted to more traditional methods, considering that the results are more elegant. The best wine is called simply Poupille. It is a wine of real flair, quality and finesse: rich and succulent, intense and harmonious. It is not sold *en primeur*.

Clos Puy Arnaud

OWNER: Thierry Valette.
COMMUNE: Belvès-de-Castillon.
SURFACE AREA UNDER VINE: 7.5 ha – 70% Merlot; 20% Cabernet Franc; 10% Cabernet Sauvignon.

The first vintage of this wine, supervised by *oenologue* Stéphane Derenoncourt (whose Domaine de L'A is close by), was the 2000: an instant success; concentrated, new oaky, remarkably stylish and even quite powerful. Before the 2000 vintage the château produced a wine called Château Pervenches Puy Arnaud. The vineyard itself, up at an altitude of 75–100 metres above Belvès, on the way to Tourtirac, is admirably situated and cultivated biodynamically.

Château Robin

OWNER: Stéphane Asséo & family; manager: Jean-Michel Ferrandez.
COMMUNE: Belvès-de-Castillon.
SURFACE AREA UNDER VINE: 12.6 ha – 80% Merlot; 15% Cabernet Franc; 5% Cabernet Sauvignon.
SECOND WINE: Château Fleur de Robin.

This is a highly regarded property, but one whose set up is artisanal in the extreme. M. Asséo, the proprietor, lives in California, where he has a vineyard. There is certainly nowhere for him to stay on the spot. The fruit is collected by hand, vinified in concrete vats and undergoes malolactic fermentation and further ageing in barrel, one-third of which is new wood. The wines are rich, meaty, profound and vigorous, with plenty of succulent fruit. Recommended.

Château Les Rochers

OWNER: Jacques & Patricia Aroldi.
COMMUNE: Belvès-de-Castillon.
SURFACE AREA UNDER VINE: 14.5 ha – 70% Merlot;
15% Cabernet Franc; 15% Cabernet Sauvignon.
SECOND WINE: Château Font-Bonne.

Jacques Aroldi produces an ample, rich, gently oaky (one-third new barrels) wine with plenty of generosity. The 2000, the only vintage I have seen, is very good.

Château Terrasson

OWNER: Mialon family; farmed by Christophe Lavau.

COMMUNE: Monbadon.

SURFACE AREA UNDER VINE: 14 ha – 75% Merlot;

15% Cabernet Franc; 10% Cabernet Sauvignon.

OTHER WINE: Château Terrasson (Côtes de Francs).

The vineyard here overlaps from Castillon into the Côtes de Francs. This is a neat set-up, manual harvesting being followed by oak-ageing, one-third in new barrels. The *tête de cuvée* is named Cuvée Pervenche.

CÔTES DE FRANCS LEADING CHÂTEAUX

Château Les Charmes-Godard

OWNER: Thienpont family; manager: Nicolas Thienpont.

COMMUNE: Francs.

SURFACE AREA UNDER VINE: Red: 3.5 ha – 70% Merlot; 20% Cabernet Franc; 10% Cabernet Sauvignon. White: 1.6 ha –

65% Sémillon; 20% Sauvignon Gris; 15% Muscadelle.

OTHER WINES: Château Laclaverie (Côtes de Francs); Le Pin (Pomerol); Château La Prade (Côtes de Francs); Château Puygueraud (Côtes de Francs); Vieux Château Certan (Pomerol).

Les Charmes-Godard was the third and last of the Thienpont family's Côtes de Francs purchases, in 1988. The red is a neatly-made, medium-bodied, fruity example, but not, however, as interesting as the Puygueraud (see below). But here is the Francs' best white wine. It is vinified in barrel, most of which is new or newish oak, with subsequent *bâtonnage* over a period of eight months. Drink it reasonably young.

Château de Francs

OWNER: Hubert de Boüard & Dominique Hébrard.

COMMUNE: Francs.

SURFACE AREA UNDER VINE: Red: 28 ha – 60% Merlot; 40% Cabernet Franc. White: 2.9 ha –

50% Sémillon; 50% Sauvignon.

SECOND WINE: Château Les Doures de Francs.

OTHER WINES: Château Angélus (Saint-Émilion); Château La Fleur de Boüard (Lalande-de-Pomerol).

Hubert de Boüard of Château Angélus, and Dominique Hébrard, whose family used to be owners of Château Cheval Blanc, friends since their schooldays, acquired Château de Francs in 1985. They have since established it as the leading property in the *appellation*. The red wine is full-bodied, rich and generous. Substantial parts of the original medieval château, plus later Renaissance additions, still remain.

Château Laclaverie

OWNER: Nicolas Thienpont.

COMMUNE: Saint-Cibard.

SURFACE AREA UNDER VINE: 9 ha – 50% Merlot; 25% Cabernet Franc; 25% Cabernet Sauvignon.

OTHER WINES: Château Les Charmes-Godard

(Côtes de Francs); Le Pin (Pomerol); Château La Prade (Côtes de Francs); Château Puygueraud (Côtes de Francs); Vieux Château Certan (Pomerol).

Georges Thienpont, father of Nicolas, created and began to modernise this estate in the 1970s, the process being continued by his son after he retired. The first vintage was the 1985. As with Les Charmes-Godard the wine is plump, fruity and medium-bodied: a balanced wine for reasonably early drinking.

Château Marsau

OWNER: Jean-Marie & Sylvie Chadronnier.
COMMUNE: Francs.

SURFACE AREA UNDER VINE: 10 ha – 100% Merlot.

The Chadronniers (Jean-Marie is a Bordeaux *négociant*) took over here in 1994, since when there has been a positive renaissance. The wine is matured using 50 per cent new oak, and is medium-bodied, round and supple.

Château La Prade

OWNER: Nicolas Thienpont.
COMMUNE: Saint-Cibard.
SURFACE AREA UNDER VINE: 4.5 ha – 80% Merlot; 20% Cabernet Franc.
OTHER WINES: Château Les Charmes-Godard (Côtes de Francs); Château Laclaverie (Côtes de Francs); Le Pin (Pomerol); Château Puygueraud (Côtes de Francs); Vieux Château Certan (Pomerol).

Château La Prade used to belong to Patrick Valette, son of the late Jean-Paul of Saint-Émilion's Château Pavie. He made one of the best Côtes de Francs wines during the 1980s, but then sold out to Nicolas Thienpont in 2000. Under the latter's able management high quality continues. There is both more substance and more depth than in the majority of the neighbouring wines.

Château Puygueraud

OWNER: Thienpont family; manager: Nicolas Thienpont.
COMMUNE: Saint-Cibard.
SURFACE AREA UNDER VINE: 32 ha – 55% Merlot; 25% Cabernet Franc; 15% Cabernet Sauvignon; 5% Malbec.
OTHER WINES: Château Les Charmes-Godard (Côtes de Francs); Château Laclaverie (Côtes de Francs); Le Pin (Pomerol); Château La Prade (Côtes de Francs); Vieux Château Certan (Pomerol).

Château Puygueraud was the late Georges Thienpont's original Côtes de Francs base. He arrived here in 1946. For 30 years he reared cattle and occupied himself with other farming activities on the site. It was not until the late 1970s that he started planting vines. His first, vintage, the 1983, the year his son Nicolas joined him, was an instant success, which almost single-handedly put the *appellation* on the map, encouraging others to invest in the locality. Château Puygueraud remains the Côtes de Francs' best red wine: full, rich, classy and succulent.

Georges Thienpont died in 1997. In his memory, a super-*cuvée* labelled 'Georges' was launched in 2000. It contains more Cabernet than the basic château wine, and plenty of Malbec, an *assemblage* of which Georges Thienpont would have approved. I find this delicious too.

BOURG & BLAYE

I gnored by the media – for few, myself usually included, bother to set foot into the area when we descend to survey the new vintage *en primeur* – neglected by the trade, whether external or Bordeaux merchant, the regions of Bourg and Blaye have been calmly been getting on with things, improving the product and fine-tuning the value for money of their wines over the last decade.

This quiet revolution is exemplified by a new quality *appellation* in the Blaye, which was supposed to take place from the 2000 vintage, but so far nothing has happened. Bourg is likely to adopt a similarly enhanced code of winemaking practice in the near future. In the meanwhile prices have remained stable, indeed in real terms are hardly higher than they were a decade ago, while levels in more fancy *appellations* have risen considerably. With the excellent 2000 vintage now approaching maturity, readers should remind themselves to take a look at what is on offer from Bourg and Blaye today. They will not be disappointed.

The port of Bourg lies on a steep slope at the point where the Garonne and Dordogne rivers combine to form the estuary of the Gironde. Hardly more than a large village, it is an attractive location, with many fine buildings and narrow stairways descending to river level. It is crowned by the Château de la Citadelle, originally a fortification constructed by the English in 1153 and later the summer palace of the Archbishops of Bordeaux.

The compact vineyard of the *appellation* Côtes de Bourg stretches out behind it over 15 communes in a single canton occupying some 3850 hectares (up from around 3300 in 1991). It is spread across three crests of hillsides, one behind the other, parallel to the estuary. This is a more severely accentuated countryside than the more gently undulating Blaye, but more intensely planted with vines. The soils are largely clay-limestone, mixed with gravel over harder limestone rock. Below ground there are many quarries, used as cellars or for growing mushrooms. The essential variety is the Merlot (55 per cent) but blended more with Cabernet Sauvignon (35 per cent) than Cabernet Franc or Malbec (10 per cent) as might be thought more appropriate for these cool soils. Some 50 hectares produce a Sauvignon-based white wine, which usually leaves something to be desired.

North and east will be found the vineyards of Blaye. Blaye, like Bourg, a port, is dominated by an important Vauban-inspired defensive fortification constructed in 1685–1689. The vineyards of the local *appellations* cover the districts around the town on clay and limestone soil, to the north in the canton of Saint-Ciers-sur-Gironde, where there is more gravel and less clay, and further south and east, on the opposite side of the *autoroute* at Saint-Savin where the clay-limestone and clay-gravel hillsides alternate with plateaux of clay and flint. The subsoil consists of iron hardpan.

This is a gentler, more rolling, pastoral landscape, less intensely monocultural, though the vineyard plantation has grown from 3480 hectares in 1991 to 5800 hectares in 2001. Historically, too, this was a white wine area. Though more important than Bourg, a meagre 200 hectares of Sauvignon-based white wine vineyard exist today. The principal *appellation* for both reds and whites is Premières Côtes de Blaye, and the red vine *encépagement* is similar to that of the Bourg.

Until the last decade or so, both Bourg and Blaye were major contributors to *négociants'* branded Bordeaux Rouges. Most of the production never saw any casks and was sold off in bulk. Even what remained separate under a château name was bottled in Bordeaux rather than at the estate. As the better domaines have moved to château-bottling they have found less of a market on the usual Bordeaux circuit. Many now sell direct and I get the feeling many more are open to direct negociations.

Traditionally, most of the vineyards in both wine regions have been machine-harvested; most of the wine reared in tank. Increasingly today a number of *cuvées* are produced – the traditional basic one, a gently woody example, and a *tête de cuvée*, from a reduced crop, the fruit collected by hand from selected old vine parcels, and matured using new oak. Many of these are highly commendable, and remain good value, though priced perhaps a quarter as much on the shelves.

With this comes a new, higher quality red wine *appellation* for the Côtes de Blaye. To be labelled Blaye *tout court* the grapes will in future be riper (11° rather 10.5°), must come from a reduced harvest (a base of 51 hl/ha in 2000 rather than 61 hl/ha) and in new plantations from a more concentrated number of vines per hectare (6000 rather 4500). A similar move is under discussion for white Blaye. Bourg is expected to follow.

While the wines of Bourg and Blaye are largely similar, there is nevertheless a difference, though this is more marked when comparing basic blends than special *cuvées*. The Blayes are less tannic, and mature sooner. Today the 2000s are drinkable. Bourgs are sturdier, more what the French call *sauvage*. But they have more definition and more interest. The properties are also larger, the châteaux more imposing. One can see that this was a prosperous area in pre-phylloxera times.

Generalisations such as these, however, can be quickly exploded by the reality of samples. In both areas there has been an influx of new owners from the outside and changes of generation within existing wine families. Yields have been cut, vineyards are regularly now green-harvested, leaves are stripped to allow the fruit to ripen more efficiently, the date of the harvest has been postponed, the fruit is sorted in order to reject the substandard, new equipment and temperature control have been installed, and new oak introduced. Standards have improved. Much of this is very recent. A comparison of the 1998 vintage with the 2000 is telling.

Historically the difficulty the consumer has had with Bourgs and Blayes is the unripeness of their tannins in all but rare vintages such as 2000. Why the growers chose the more tannic Cabernet Sauvignon rather than the softer (and earlier maturing) Cabernet Franc as chief accessory to the Merlot, as in Fronsac and Saint-Émilion, I cannot imagine.

When François Mitjaville, of Saint-Emilion's high-flying Tertre-Roteboeuf, bought Château Roc de Cambes in 1988, he commanded his man on the spot, an Arab with the impossible name of Tayat Abderrahmane, not to pick until the grapes were what Mitjaville considered fully ripe. His poor employee found himself the object of derision in the local *cafés*. Everyone else had long finished their harvest before Roc de Cambes had even begun. But when they tasted the wine…

CÔTES DE BOURG

SURFACE AREA (2002): Red: 3951 ha; white: 22 ha.

PRODUCTION (2002): Red: 181,680 hl; white: 960 hl.

COLOUR: Red & white.

GRAPE VARIETIES:Red: Cabernet Sauvignon; Cabernet Franc; Merlot; Malbec.

   White: Sémillon; Sauvignon; Muscadelle; Merlot Blanc; Colombard.

MAXIMUM YIELD: Red: 50 hl/ha. White: 60 hl/ha.

MINIMUM ALCOHOLIC DEGREE: Red: 10°; white: 9.5°.

The vineyards of the Côtes de Bourg are spread over the following 15 communes within the *canton* of Bourg: Bayon-sur-Gironde, Bourg, Comps, Gauriac, Lansac, Mombrier, Prignac-et-Marcamps, Pugnac, Saint-Ciers-de-Canesse, Saint-Seurin-de-Bourg, Saint-Trojan, Samonac, Tauriac, Teuillac and Villeneuve. It is the only Bordeaux *appellation* to be located within a single canton.

BOURG & BLAYE

CHARENTE-MARITIME

GIRONDE

N

Bordeaux

Gironde

St-Ciers-sur-Gironde

Reignac

D253

A10

N137

D225

D18

D23

1

2 ● St-Paul

D22 6

St-Girons-d'Aiguevives

St-Savin

4 ● Cars

St-Christoly-de-Blaye

7

St-Mariens

Blaye

3 5

Berson

N137

9

Cezac

● Plassac

D250

8

10

11

12 13

St-Trojan

Pugnac

Villeneuve 14

A10

N10

Bayon-sur-Gironde 15

19

21

23

22

Lansac

D23

16 18

20

17 Bourg

D669

D251

St-André-de-Cubzac

Garonne

Dordogne

D937

D669

Appellations

Côtes de Blaye and Premières Côtes de Blaye

Côtes de Bourg

0   10km

0   5miles

Châteaux ◆

Côtes de Blaye AC
1 Segonzac
2 Les Jonqueyres
3 Graulet
4 du Grand Barrail
5 Bel-Air La Royère
6 Les Grands Maréchaux
7 Les Graves

8 Garreau
9 Tayat
10 Bertinerie, Haut-Bertinerie

Côtes de Bourg AC
11 Haut-Guiraud
12 Mercier
13 L'Hospital
14 Repimplet
15 Falfas

16 Le Clos du Notaire
17 Roc de Cambes
18 de La Grave
19 Martinat
20 Guionne
21 Lamothe
22 Fougas
23 Nodoz

Côtes de Bourg Leading Châteaux

Château Le Clos du Notaire

OWNER: Roland & Marie-Sylvette Charbonnier.
COMMUNE: Bourg-sur-Gironde.

SURFACE AREA UNDER VINE: 20 ha – 65% Merlot;
30% Cabernet (both); 5% Malbec.

This estate, situated on limestone rock almost over-hanging the estuary of the Gironde has been making increasingly good wine in recent years, culminating in a splendid 2000. The vineyard is partly machine-harvested, the wine being matured partly in tank, partly in wood.

Château Falfas

OWNER: John & Véronique Cochran.
COMMUNE: Bayon-sur-Gironde.
SURFACE AREA UNDER VINE: 22 ha – 55% Merlot;

30% Cabernet Sauvignon; 10% Malbec;
5% Cabernet Franc.
SECOND WINE: Les Demoiselles de Falfas.

The château is really fine: a superbly elegant construction dating from the fourteenth and fifteenth centuries, the home of the Saigneurs de Lansac. It has been owned since 1988 by an American lawyer, John Cochran and his wife Véronique. The vineyards are cultivated biodynamically and hand-harvested, producing a splendidly rich, opulent *cuvée* called Le Chevalier. Made from 70-year-old vines, the wine is 65 per cent Cabernet Sauvignon and aged in 100 per cent new oak. There is also a basic *cuvée*. The Cochrans are also ardent music lovers and host chamber concerts in their lovely château.

Château Fougas

OWNER: Jean-Yves Béchet.
C OMMUNE: Lansac.

SURFACE AREA UNDER VINE: 11 ha – 50% Merlot;
25% Cabernet Sauvignon; 25% Cabernet Franc.

Located on the road between Bourg and Pugnac, and on the site of an ancient monastery, razed to the ground during the French Revolution, Fougas is an elegant, First Empire-style *chartreuse* on either side of which are the winery buildings. It reminds me a little of Château Camensac in the Médoc. Back in 1983 Jean-Yves Béchet had the sensible idea of inviting clients to become bond-holders, payment being in wine. There is quite a lot of new oak here, especially in the Cuvée Maldoror, but the wine is rich and concentrated enough to take it.

Château de La Grave

OWNER: Philippe & Valérie Bassereau.
COMMUNE: Bourg-sur-Gironde.
SURFACE AREA UNDER VINE: Red: 43 ha –

80% Merlot; 20% Cabernet Sauvignon. White:
1.7 ha – 70% Sémillon; 30% Colombard.
SECOND WINE: Château Maine d'Armour.

The château is a nineteenth-century, mock-Louis XIII hotch-potch. It has been in the hands of the same family since 1889. The Bassereaus offer bed-and-breakfast, so you can stay here if you wish. Unusually, the vines are entirely hand-harvested. The basic *cuvée*, called Caractère, is admirable. Cuvée Nectar, first produced in 1995, is nicely substantial, gently oaky, rich, balanced and positive.

Château Guionne

OWNER: Alain & Isabelle Fabre.
COMMUNE: Lansac.

SURFACE AREA UNDER VINE: 20 ha – 55% Merlot;
25% Cabernet Sauvignon; 20% Malbec.

The year 2000 saw two changes of ownership at Château Guionne, culminating with the Fabres who arrived from the Corbières in the summer. One of the first things they did was to engage Libournais-based guru Michel Rolland as consultant. He told them to acquire a sorting table, a pneumatic press and a new destemmer-crusher. Until 1998 no wood was to be seen at Guionne. The Fabres have introduced new oak. Top quality really starts with the 2001 here. There are two *cuvées*, a non-woody basic (not unsophisticated) and the *cuvée élevée en fûts de chêne*, which is obviously better still. The vineyard is hand-picked.

Château Haut-Guiraud

OWNER: Jean Bonnet-Grimard; manager:
  Christophe Bonnet.
COMMUNE: Saint-Ciers-de-Canesse.
SURFACE AREA UNDER VINE: 28 ha – 70% Merlot;

30% Cabernet Sauvignon.
OTHER WINES: Château Castaing (Côtes de
  Bourg); Château Haute-Tuilerie (Côtes de Blaye).

The property has been in the hands of the Bonnet family for some time, and it has been producing consistently good quality since I first came across it in the mid-1980s. Picking is by machine but there is a sorting table. Maturation is 15 per cent in barrel, mostly new and 85 per cent in tank. The Merlot-based wine is opulent and generous, particularly in a vintage such as 2000.

Château L'Hospital

OWNER: Bruno & Christine Duhamel.
COMMUNE: Saint-Trojan.
SURFACE AREA UNDER VINE: 6 ha – 80% Merlot;

10% Cabernet Sauvignon & Cabernet Franc;
10% Malbec.
SECOND WINE: Château de Laplace.

Bruno and Christine Duhamel have only been at Château L'Hospital since 1997, but have already managed to place their wine in a number of three star restaurants. Both 'château', a simple farmhouse, and *chais* remain to be completely renovated. There is a basic *cuvée* and a selection *élevé en fûts de chêne*, as well as the charmingly juicy, forward second wine. I feel the 2000 vintage represented the coming of age here. In this vintage the wines have proportionately more depth and interest. Some of the grapes are picked by hand.

Château Lamothe

OWNER: Pessonnier & Pousse families; manager:
  Anne Pousse.
COMMUNE: Lansac.

SURFACE AREA UNDER VINE: 23 ha – 60% Merlot;
25% Cabernet Sauvignon; 10% Malbec;
5% Cabernet Franc.

Lamothe is a small but gracefully imposing château dating from the middle of the eighteenth century. The estate was acquired by the Pessonnier family in 1990. Paul Pessonnier has now retired, and his daughter, Anne Pousse, is in charge today. While picking is by machine, all the wine is reared in wood, there being a Cuvée Classique and a Grande Réserve, the latter using new wood in part. These are elegant wines, not a bit tiring to drink, individual and well balanced. Recent vintages have been very good and the 1999 was a conspicuous success for the year.

Château Martinat

OWNER: Stéphane & Lucie Donze.
COMMUNE: Lansac.
SURFACE AREA UNDER VINE: 10 ha – 60% Merlot;
  30% Cabernet Sauvignon; 10% Malbec.

OTHER WINES: Château Les Donats (Côtes de
  Blaye); Château Grand Chemin (Côtes de Bourg);
  Château Les Lys (Bordeaux Blanc).

Stéphane and Lucie Donze arrived at Château Martinat in 1994. It is only since 1998 that they feel they have really begun to get things right. Working with *oenologue* Christophe Veyrey, a 'graduate' of Michel Rolland's laboratory, they introduced a super-*cuvée* called Epicuria to much acclaim in 1999: a parcel selection, 100 per cent new wood, malolactic fermentation in barrel, stirring up the lees – all the usual. Happily the wine is not over-extracted. In fact, it is rich, smoky-oaky, voluptuous and very good indeed; unlike many of these new-wave wines which you feel are produced more to get good marks after six months rather than marry well with food after 5 or 10 years, Epicuria does have good acidity. It will age with dignity.

Château Mercier

OWNER: Chéty family.
COMMUNE: Saint-Trojan.
SURFACE AREA UNDER VINE: Red: 21.5 ha –
  45% Merlot; 25% Cabernet Sauvignon;
  25% Cabernet Franc; 5% Malbec. White: 1.5 ha –

60% Sauvignon; 20% Sémillon;
  20% Muscadelle.
SECOND WINE: Philippe de Navarre.
OTHER WINE: Clos du Piat (Côtes de Bourg).

The tall, bearded Philippe Chéty and his equally tall and bearded son Christophe represent the twelfth and thirteenth generations of the same family at Château Mercier, an ownership which dates back to the eighteenth century. They have been practising *lutte raisonnée*, the environmentally friendly attitude to viticulture since 1984. The fruit is harvested by machine, after a cleaning-up passage through the vines, and as elsewhere there are two *cuvées*: a non-oaked version for early drinking and an oaky (25–33 per cent new wood) Cuvée Prestige. This latter wine was particularly good in 1999 and 2000. Christophe Chéty also personally owns the 4-hectare Clos du Piat, also in Côtes de Bourg, which I can also recommend.

Château Nodoz

OWNER: Jean-Louis Magdeleine.
COMMUNE: Tauriac.
SURFACE AREA UNDER VINE: 45 ha – 60% Merlot;

35% Cabernet Sauvignon; 5% Cabernet Franc.
SECOND WINE: Château Galau.

The estate takes its name from the Comte de Nodoz, owner in pre-revolutionary times. The Magdeleine family have been owners since 1930. What used to be the top floor of the *cuverie* is now a splendidly vaulted tasting room. A modern vat house lies next door. There are three *cuvées* here. The 'Spéciale' matures entirely in new wood. In 2001 malos took place in barrel and the wine was worked on its lees. Second is the yellow label 'Cuvée en barriques de chêne' (50 per cent new oak), and then there is the non-woody basic wine. Magdeleine and his *oenologue*, the celebrated Michel Guiraud, have succeeded in retaining the best of traditional methods while utilising all the benefits of modern ones.

Château Repimplet

OWNER: Michèle & Patrick Touret.
COMMUNE: Saint-Ciers-de-Canesse.
SURFACE AREA UNDER VINE: 14.5 ha – 60% Merlot;

40% Cabernet Sauvignon & Cabernet Franc.
SECOND WINE: Château des Trois Moulins.

Patrick Touret used to be a petrol engineer until he bought this derelict estate in 1982. 'Repimplet', in old Gascon, means a good place to rest. Certainly there is an impressive view from here. We are at one of the highest points of the *appellation*. As Patrick Touret points out, 'All the top Bourg estates can see the estuary'. The basic wine shows no lack of personality. The Cuvée Amélia Julien is splendidly rich and was very good indeed in both 1999 and 2000.

Château Roc de Cambes

OWNER: François Mitjaville.
COMMUNE: Bourg.
SURFACE AREA UNDER VINE: 14 ha – 60% Merlot;
    25% Cabernet Sauvignon; 10% Cabernet Franc;

5% Malbec.
OTHER WINE: Château Tertre-Roteboeuf (Saint-
Émilion).

François Mitjaville bought Roc de Cambes, whose vineyards lie in two natural amphitheatres close to the water just north of Bourg, in 1988. The wine is made in cement *cuves* and matured in 50 per cent new wood in a troglodyte cellar. François was quick to realise the importance of patience. 'One of the reason why Roc de Cambes is better than its peers is that the rest are simply picked too early', he says. On might also point out the lower yields here. Roc de Cambes is expensive for a Bourg. But it is worth it: full-bodied, robust, tannic, rich and long-lasting.

Other good Bourg estates: Clos Alphonse Dubreuil (see Château Jonqueyres in Blaye), Châteaux Bégot, Garreau, Haut-Macô, Haut-Mondésir, Montaigut, Puy d'Amour and de Rousselet.

CÔTES DE BLAYE

SURFACE AREA (2002): Red: 5773 ha; white: 345 ha.

PRODUCTION (2002): Red: 267,923 hl; white: 16,939 hl.

COLOUR : Red & white.

GRAPE VARIETIES: Red: For Premières Côtes de Blaye and Blaye: Cabernet Sauvignon; Cabernet Franc; Merlot; Malbec. White: For Blaye: Ugni Blanc (90%). For Côtes de Blaye: Colombard (60–90%). For Premières Côtes de Blaye: Sémillon; Sauvignon; Muscadelle plus (max 30% in total) Merlot Blanc; Colombard; Ugni Blanc.

MAXIMUM YIELD: Red: Premières Côtes de Blaye: 61 hl/ha. Blaye: 51 hl/ha. White: Premières Côtes de Blaye: 61 hl/ha. Blaye: 61 hl/ha.

MINIMUM ALCOHOLIC DEGREE: Red: 10.5°. White: Blaye & Côtes de Blaye: 9.5°; Premières Côtes de Blaye: 10°.

The Blaye *appellations* cover some 40 communes in the cantons of Blaye, Saint-Savin and Saint-Ciers-sur-Gironde.

CÔTES DE BLAYE LEADING CHÂTEAUX

Château Bel-Air La Royère

OWNER: Xavier & Corinne Loriaud.

COMMUNE: Cars.

SURFACE AREA UNDER VINE: 13.5 – 80% Merlot;

20% Malbec.

OTHER WINE: Château Les Ricards (Premières Côtes de Blayes).

Bel-Air La Royère and its sister Château Les Ricards were taken over by the Loriauds in 1995. With the help of consultant *oenologue* Christian Veyry they have quickly put the two properties on the map. The 1998, 1999 and 2000 vintages are all very good. Bel-Air La Royère is vinified in concrete vats, and undergoes malolactic fermentation in barrel of which 90 per cent is new. Les Ricards is produced using a little Cabernet Sauvignon. Here the new wood element is only 20 per cent. There is a difference in the yield too: 30 hl/ha for Bel-Air as opposed to 42. Château Les Ricards is a good everyday Bordeaux: clean, plump and unpretentious. Bel-Air La Royère is quite different. It is modern: oaky and glossy. But not too much so. I think it will keep well.

Château Bertinerie & Château Haut-Bertinerie

OWNER: Daniel Bantegnies.

COMMUNE: Cubnezais.

SURFACE AREA UNDER VINE: Red: 42 ha – 65% Merlot; 35% Cabernet Sauvignon for

Château Haut-Bertinerie. White: 18 ha – 100% Sauvignon for Château Haut-Bertinerie.

SECOND WINE: Château Manon La Lagune (Premières Côtes de Blaye).

Bertinerie is the leading Côtes de Blaye estate in the canton of Saint-Savin, east of the Bordeaux-Tours motorway. It is a substantial estate, having been built up during the last 40 years from 17 hectares to its present size. From 1987 onwards the vineyard has been converted to the Lyre (double curtain) form of training, this gaining a week of maturity over traditionally trained vineyards. The *tête de cuvées* are bottled as Haut-Bertinerie; the white fermented in 100 per cent new wood, the red matured 80 per cent in new wood, 20 per cent in tank, to preserve freshness. The lower tiers are labelled Bertinerie. This is neat, perfectionistic winemaking, producing elegantly balanced wines for the medium term. The white is one of the few successes of the *appellation*.

Château Garreau

OWNER: Jean-Patrick Massé.

COMMUNE: Pugnac.

SURFACE AREA UNDER VINE: 2.7 ha – 75% Merlot; 15% Cabernet Sauvignon; 10% Cabernet Franc.

This is a small estate on the Bourg/Blaye border which produces a very well-made, juicy, gently oaky wine with a good colour and plenty of potential to age in bottle. The 2000 was particularly good.

Château du Grand-Barrail

OWNER: Denis Lafon.

COMMUNE: Cars.

SURFACE AREA UNDER VINE: Red: 35 ha – 65% Merlot; 25% Cabernet Sauvignon; 10% Malbec.

White: 2 ha – 50% Sauvignon; 50% Sémillon.

OTHER WINES: Château Graulet; Château Gardut Haut-Cluzeau; Château du Chevalier (all Premières Côtes de Blaye).

Denis Lafon bought this property in 1967. The vines, in fact, are in the commune of Plassac, but the office is in Cars. As with many other properties here there are three *cuvées*: the non-oaky basic, the gently oaky Prestige and Révélation, the new oaky *cuvée* first made in 1998 from hand-picked selected parcels of old vines. Across the range these are well-made, clean wines. The Révélation (of which there is also a good white version) is rich and intense, and not over-oaked.

Château Les Grands Maréchaux

OWNER: Étienne Barre & Christophe Reboul-Salze.

COMMUNE: Saint-Girons-d'Aiguevives.

SURFACE AREA UNDER VINE: 20.5 ha – 70% Merlot; 15% Cabernet Franc; 15% Cabernet Sauvignon.

SECOND WINE: Château Les Maréchaux.

Barre and Reboul-Salze, both wine professionals in Bordeaux, bought Château Les Grands Maréchaux in 1997 and have since put this property on the map. Harvesting is by hand, and the wine is matured approximately one-third in new wood, one-third in older barrels and one-third in tank. The best *cuvées* are sold as Château Les Grands Maréchaux. This is stylish, plump wine with no lack of interest, evolving in the medium term.

Château Graulet

OWNER: Riesterer family; farmed by Denis Lafon.

COMMUNE: Cars.

SURFACE AREA UNDER VINE: Red: 28 ha – 55% Merlot; 30% Cabernet Sauvignon; 15% Malbec.

White: 2 ha – 34% Sauvignon; 33% Sémillon; 33% Muscadelle.

SECOND WINE: Château La Croix de Graulet.

As with Château du Grand-Barrail above, the vineyard is, in fact, in Plassac, but Denis Lafon, who rents this vineyard from a Swedish industrialist, has his headquarters inland in the commune of Cars. There are two *cuvées* of red wine, a basic and a Prestige, aged in oak, where the Merlot content is 70 to 80 per cent. I like the 1998 but was less enthused by the 1999 on a recent visit. The 2000 was not offered.

Château Les Graves

OWNER: Jean-Pierre Pauvif.

COMMUNE: Saint-Vivien-de-Blaye.

SURFACE AREA UNDER VINE: Red: 13 ha – 80% Merlot; 15% Cabernet Sauvignon;

5% Cabernet Franc. White: 3 ha – 80% Sémillon; 15% Muscadelle; 5% Sauvignon.

SECOND WINE: Château La Grave Julien.

There are three red wines here, for as well as the second wine there is a superior Cuvée Elevée en Fûts de Chêne. This is produced from 5 hectares of the oldest vines, so is available in reasonable quantity, and is one of the best in the region. The fruit is to the fore, the wine is really quite concentrated, especially in a vintage such as 2000, and the wood does not dominate.

Château Les Jonqueyres

OWNER: Pascal & Isabelle Montaut.

COMMUNE: Saint-Paul-de-Blaye.

SURFACE AREA UNDER VINE: 15 ha – 90% Merlot; 5% Cabernet Franc; 5% Malbec.

SECOND WINE: Domaine de Courgeau.

OTHER WINE: Clos Alphonse Dubreuil (Côtes de Bourg).

This is the home of one of the region's superstars. Pascal Montaut inherited (and had to replant) 5 hectares from his maternal grandfather in 1977, took over his father's vines in 1982, and has since further built up his domaine. From the start he has restrained the production and sorted through the fruit – the vineyards have always been hand-harvested – twice, at the vine and in the winery. The *chais* are disarmingly ramshackle; the wine, though, has splendid subtlety and originality.

A recent addition to the portfolio is a microscopic (50 *ares*) vineyard in the Côtes de Bourg called Clos Alphonse Dubreuil. Old vines and 100 per cent new oak produce one of the best wines of the *appellation*.

Château Segonzac

OWNER: Thomas & Charlotte Herter-Marmet.

COMMUNE: Saint-Gènes-de-Blaye.

SURFACE AREA UNDER VINE: 30 ha – 60% Merlot;

20% Cabernet Sauvignon; 15% Malbec; 10% Cabernet Franc; 5% Petit Verdot.

Just north of Blaye, atop a hill commanding a fine view over the Gironde estuary, is a rather solid square château with a mansard roof, constructed towards the end of the nineteenth century by the estate's founder, French Minister for Agriculture Jean Dupuy. This is Segonzac, the property of the Marmet family, managed since 2000 by the son-in-law, Thomas Herter. The wine is produced in a large winery nearby, the basic one aged in tank, the Vieilles Vignes in older oak and the Cuvée Prestige, a new addition to the range, in 100 per cent new wood. This has been a good source for some time. Recent vintages show even further improvement.

Château Tayat

OWNER: Guy Favereaud.

COMMUNE: Cézac.

SURFACE AREA UNDER VINE: Red: 24 ha –

70% Merlot. White: 6.8 ha – 80% Sémillon; 20 % Sauvignon.

The Favereaud family arrived at this rather impressive, early nineteenth-century château in 1972. From 2 hectares of old vines Guy Favereaud produces a Cuvée Tradition Élevée en Fûts de Chêne. This is a firmer wine than those of his neighbours, but worth waiting for. I find it proportionately better in the really warm vintages like 2000.

Other good Blaye estates include: Châteaux Canteloup, Destourtes, Ferthis, Haut-Vigneau, Maison Neuve, Mayne-Guyon, Mondésir-Gazin, Sociondo, Roland-La-Garde and Terre-Blanque.

Apart from Châteaux du Grand-Barrail and Haut-Bertinerie (see above), good white wines include Château Charron, Cuvée Acacias.

THE REST OF BORDEAUX

Finally do not forget that east of Bourg and Blaye, north of Saint-Émilion and its satellites, lies an expanse of the Gironde department almost as large in area as the Entre-Deux-Mers. Not all of it is planted with vines, but Guîtres and Coutras are important centres with some 1640 hectares between them. Around Saint-André-de-Cubzac there are a further 1700 hectares while in the eight communes around Libourne which do not enjoy a more famous *appellation* there is another thousand. All this produces some 250,000 hectolitres of wine a year, almost all of it lightish, Merlot-based red. One of the few châteaux here to have made a reputation on the international scene is Château Méaume which belongs to the Englishman, Alan Johnson-Hill. This lies in the commune of Maransin, west of Guîtres. Two others in Saint-André-de-Cubzac are the Quancard family's Château de Terrefort-Quancard and Robert Giraud's Château Timberlay.

PART

TWO

VINTAGE ASSESSMENTS

VINTAGE ASSESSMENTS

Vintage assessments have been provided in the following pages for every year between 2003 and 1985. Prior to 1985 I have only selected good vintages.

The notes on the following pages are based on comprehensive group tastings, not on one-offs. It is only in these situations, I believe, that you can accurately mark wine as exactly as within half points out of 20 (or out of a hundred) one within another. I have noted where certain bottles do not meet up to the consensus of the rest of the occasions when I have sampled the bottles recently – or where, in the case of older wines, I feel that they were better a few or more years ago. A group of us in England congregate in January every year at The Crown Inn in Southwold, Suffolk, an agreable small hotel/high class pub, with all the benefit of Adnams' admirable wine list, to make a three-day, three-year-on survey of the latest Bordeaux vintage. This opportunity is substantiated by a similar range of wines of the same vintage offered by the Institute of Masters of Wine, sponsored by the Union des Grands Crus, the following November. The same group meets regularly to taste the vintage 10 years on. Other opportunities, as readers will see, have been kindly provided to me by groups of collectors and wine lovers in Austria, France, Germany and the USA.

Wines are marked out of 20, and are *within the context of the vintage*. This may seem complicated, but how else do you adequately rate a very good example of a poor year? Optimum Drinking assessments have been updated to reflect the wines' standing in 2004, the date of publication of this book, i.e. Drink Now means drink from 2004 to about 2007. The rest of the tasting note, however, has not been updated and is just as I wrote it at the time of the tasting.

Prices, both opening and current, are largely based on the list and archives of Farr Vintners. Rather than compare, for instance, the ex-château price in French Francs or, now, Euros, or an average of the different *tranches*, with Pound Sterling prices in London, I have, as much as possible, tried to compare like with like: the going rate then, per case in bond, with the similar going rate as this book went to press in late autumn 2003. All dollar figures for current prices are based on the conversion rate of £1 sterling = $1.80 (2004).

2003 VINTAGE

SIZE OF THE CROP:	6,511,094 HECTOLITRES.
VINTAGE RATING:	14.0/18.5 (RED WINES).
	12.0 (DRY WHITE WINES)
	17.5 (SWEET WINES).

602,701 hl (8 per cent) of the harvest was white wine. As a result of the poor flowering and the great heat and intermittent drought, this was the smallest harvest for many years, though only 2 per cent less than 2002. It is also the most variable red wine crop, quality ranging from the merely average to very fine, with little consistency even within the various communes. A vintage to choose with care.

For the winemakers of most of western Europe, 2003 – and Bordeaux was no exception – was a quite extraordinary year. It was extremely hot; it was extremely dry; and the harvest began in the middle of August, a full month earlier than the average.

After a cold start to the year the weather soon warmed up. Right from the beginning it was both sunnier and drier than the norm. Overall the spring was 4°C warmer. There were 62 hours more sunshine and the rainfall deficit was 47 mm. Budbreak occurred in the last 10 days of March. April and May continued dry, warm and sunny, and the first flowers were observed on 21st May around 15 days earlier than usual, indicating a harvest which would begin around 5th September.

From the flowering onwards it began to get really hot. The average June to August temperature was a full 6°C above normal. It continued very dry apart for a hailstorm on 24th June which affected some 6000 hectares in a swathe which ran from the Graves, across Entre-Deux-Mers into Saint-Émilion. Earlier, on 28th April vineyards in the Libournais had also suffered from hail. And on 15th July a further 3000 hectares in the Médoc and the Blaye would be affected.

The *véraison* took place in July. By now the fruit was three weeks in advance. From now on the temperatures averaged 32°C and, until the harvest began – 13th August for the white grapes and 19th August for the red varieties – it was completely dry.

After 19th August, though still warmer and drier than average, the heatwave began to relax its grip. The temperature in September was only 1.4°C above the average and there was even a little rain – 32 mm of it, 24 mm during the first two days. This was to have a very important effect.

Overall 2003 is the driest year in Bordeaux since 1961. It was the sunniest ever, and there were no fewer than 53 days where average temperatures exceeded 30°C. It was over 40°C in the shade on the 5th and 13th August at Haut-Brion.

While many in the Libournais were picking by the 20th August, and had finished by the end of the month, vineyards in the Médoc/Graves did not commence until much later, and even some in the Libournais were prepared to wait. The Moueix domaines (Châteaux Magdelaine, Trotanoy, Pétrus etc.) were cleared between 1st and 19th September. Cos d'Estournel picked between 12th and 25th September, Léoville-Las-Cases over the same span: so here the harvest was not too precocious at all and the state of the fruit has benefited from the odd showers and cooler weather which had taken place since the beginning of the month.

Yields are low: half the normal crop *chez* Moueix, 35 per cent less at Haut-Brion, 27 hl/ha at Léoville-Las-Cases, but hopes for the red wines are high. Despite the hydric stress the tannins are ripe and the acidities not as low as feared. The colours are enormous, and the amount of tannin huge. Alcohol levels are also high. Overall quality varies with the soil structures and the age of the vines. Selection will play a vital part. One or two of the more excitable producers are already talking about a great vintage.

The dry white wines are rich, tropical and exotic. Many will have had their acidities adjusted. This is not something the Bordelais are used to doing. How well will they have succeeded we shall see.

In the Sauternes the little rain which had fallen between 1st and 10th September had launched an attack of botrytis, on fruit already magnificently ripe and even slightly *passerillé* (dried out). The harvest began on 16th September and ran through until the second week of October. Expectations are high.

This book went to press before the wines were available for tasting. For my report of the wines in barrel in April 2004 see *The Vine*, No 232, May 2004.

2002 VINTAGE

SIZE OF THE CROP:	5,612,492 HECTOLITRES.
VINTAGE RATING:	15.5/20 (RED WINES OF THE LIBOURNAIS, GRAVES, MARGAUX AND SOUTHERN MÉDOC).
	17.5 (RED WINES OF SAINT-JULIEN, PAUILLAC AND SAINT-ESTÈPHE).
	16.0 (DRY WHITE WINES).
	17.0 (SWEET WINES).

After seven record-breaking harvests the 2002 yield is well down. It is the smallest crop since the frost-affected 1991 and 22 per cent less than the 1997–2001 five-year average (6,686,600 hectolitres). 11.3 per cent (63,651 hl) of the 2002 harvest was white wine. With 119,817 hectares under production the overall yield was 46.8 hl/ha.

These figures hide the reality as far as the top wines are concerned. Many of the better growths, those who green-harvested and later sorted the fruit at the entry to the winery, produced half a normal crop, less than half a bottle of wine per vine. The last time, apart from the frost-reduced 1991 vintage, that the overall yield was below 50 hl/ha, was 1988.

Two thousand and two was doubly blighted. The world's economies had ground to a halt. Neo-conservative American reaction to Jacques Chirac's refusal to join the 'crusade' against Saddam gave rise to an encouragement of a US boycott of things French. Robert Parker (for personal reasons, I gather, not political ones) did not make his usual March/April visit to judge the *primeurs*. Without this most Americans were lost, unable to make a decision about the vintage. But meanwhile they had the much hyped 2000 vintage, now in the shops, to occupy their energies. Moreover initial reports before the Bordeaux doors opened at the end of March seemed unconvinced about the 2002 quality. Despite price reductions there seemed to be little initial demand for the wines, apart from the First Growths and one or two Super-Seconds.

This lack of interest, however, did the quality of the best 2002s an injustice. While the red wines of Saint-Émilion and Pomerol and their satellites, the Graves, and Margaux and the southern Médoc are largely very competent, they were not *that* much better than the 2001s (which incidentally had had a good winter and were showing well). But from Saint-Julien northwards we have a very much better vintage. One that can be judged 'fine'.

Assisting these wines' charms were their prices. First Growths fell from €120 ($145) for the 2000s, via €85 ($100) in 2001 to €65 ($80) (Latour) and €60 ($70) for other châteaux. This means British wine merchants were able to offer them at £680 ($1220) plus. This was cheaper than the current prices of all other current vintages, even 1992 and 1997. This position applied to many other 'names'. Château Léoville-Barton (a splendid wine this year) was £215 ($380). Gruaud-Larose was as low as £140 ($250). Growers and proprietors, whom I have often hitherto accused of living in cloud cuckoo-land, were realistic. Long may it continue. Fine Bordeaux, eventually, will be drunk. Let's hope not by label hunters, speculators and cork dorks but by those who can appreciate them. They can afford the 2002s.

THE WEATHER

To summarise: 2002 was very nearly a complete disaster, but it was rescued at the last minute, as was 1978, by an almost perfect September and first half of October. In this fine Indian summer, while the Merlots benefited, it was the Cabernets, particularly the Cabernet Sauvignons, which really ripened and concentrated, and those who picked the latest who could really profit. This is the essential reason for the proportional excellence of Saint-Julien, Pauillac and Saint-Estèphe.

It was a dry winter, and a cold one, especially over Christmas (unusually, it was a white Christmas in Bordeaux), apart from a spell between 21st January and 13th February. March continued very dry. It was cold at first, but then things warmed up, leading to bud-break at more or less the normal time. April was largely cool, continuing dry for the most part, but not offering much threat of frost. By this time it was already obvious that the *sortie* of embryonic bunches was naturally low. In 2001 and 2000 the *sortie* had been normal. In 1999 it had been prolific. Moreover very few counter-buds evolved in 2002.

The 2002 flowering was catastrophic. The first two weeks of May were cold and miserable. Then there was a heatwave, the temperature reaching 31°C on one occasion. Subsequently, with the flowers just beginning to appear it suddenly went cold and wet, remaining so for a full week. A little rain during flowering is not too bad, provided it is warm. A couple of cool days is also not a problem, if it stays dry. But both! Almost no flowers of this period germinated. What was lost was most of the Saint-Émilion and Pomerol Merlots.

The calamity continued. The weather began to alternate between periods of high heat and storms and cold. Erratic conditions continued right through the rest of the flowering and beyond. There was more *coulure*, throughout the region, followed by widespread *millérandage*. All the Merlots were affected to some extent by the former; most of the Cabernets, both Franc and Sauvignon, by the latter. One point to make, however, and this is the first deviance with on the face of it similar conditions in 1978 and 1984, is that, while the flowering was long and drawn out, this irregularity was between bunches and not within the bunch. This was to prove a decisive advantage.

From 20th or so of June right through to 1st September the weather settled down. It was largely cool – only twice did temperatures rise above 30°C, and largely dry, apart from a down-pour on 19th August followed by showery days to the end of the month. Despite the loss to the potential crop most of the top domaines crop-thinned, if only to eliminate the very backward bunches and those so close together that rot might develop. They leaf stripped too, aiding aera-tion and the bunches' direct exposure to the sun. Others, however, performed neither of these expensive tasks. Why crop-thin one's Cabernets when most of the Merlot had been lost? And if one did not crop-thin one didn't de-leaf either. This meant that these growers found themselves exposed to rot after the storms of 19th August. Luckily for them the rest of the summer was dry!

The end of season miracle began on 10th September. With the major exception of Friday 20th, when as well as a thunderstorm there were isolated outbreaks of hail in the Gironde, plus a much more severe attack in the vineyards of the adjoining Lot-et-Garonne *département*, the weather continued fine, sunny and warm, though cool at night, until Wednesday 9th October. This put an end to the rot (those bunches badly affected could easily be eliminated). It brought a marvellous finishing touch to the fruit which, nature being what it is, had quietly if slowly been progressing throughout the summer, abysmal though conditions might have seemed on the surface. Despite the weather the red wine grapes on 23rd September, the date the Merlot harvest began to get seriously under way, showed no lack of ripeness: the Merlots were at 12–12.5°, the

Cabernets, which would begin to be picked a week later, were 10.5–11°. Moreover the tannins were high, but also ripe.

This was an important week. The Merlots were ready. They were good but not exciting. It was warm, but cold at night, preserving the acidity and ensuring that there was no need to hurry to harvest the Cabernets. September had seen, apart from what fell on 20th, a mere 32 mm of rain. As October approached the Cabernets, both Franc and Sauvignon, arrived at fruition, as did, unusually, the small amount of Petit Verdot still to be found in the Médoc. Those vineyards which had been looked after properly, especially those properly de-leafed, found that their fruit began to dry up and concentrate as the final push to maturity arrived. Those with the best drained soils and those with vines the latest to mature, so that they could enjoy all the fine weather offered in the first eight days of October, found themselves with a trio of excesses: high alcohol, high but very ripe tannins and high acidities. It is from these excesses that great wines can be made. By the time the weather changed for the worse the harvest was all but over. Nature had timed the fine weather practically to the second!

THE WHITE WINES

Meanwhile, down in the Graves and the Entre-Deux-Mers the combination of sunny days and cool nights resulted in some very good dry whites, largely picked between 9th and 18th September. They are full-flavoured, with proper ripeness and very good acidities. They should keep well. The size of the white wine harvest is not as low as that of the red wines.

In the Sauternes a cleaning up *tri* in mid-September was followed by a *premier tri* of botrytised grapes, mainly Sauvignon. There was then a wait, as it was too dry for noble rot to develop until the beginning of October, followed by third and fourth *passages* until the end of the month. By and large these pickings consisted of fruit which had already reached physiological ripeness before being attacked by rot. This is always a good thing. The 2002 Sauternes do not have the power and intensity of the 2001s, but are nevertheless fullish-bodied, pure, racy and flowery. I am reminded of the 1986s.

THE RED WINES

There is, as I have said, a very large difference in quality between the wines of Saint-Julien, Pauillac and Saint-Estèphe (and one or two estates further north) and the rest of the region. It is a Cabernet Sauvignon vintage. Everywhere, blends have more Cabernet and less Merlot than is planted in the vineyard. Even where there were no lack of Merlot vats, some were rejected in the composition of the *grand vin*. They were simply not good enough.

There are various reasons for the superiority of the northern Haut-Médoc.

• The Merlots, and particularly those earlier to ripen, suffered more from the storm of 20th September.
• Northern Haut-Médoc soils, particularly those in Saint-Julien, Pauillac and the close-to-the-estuary vineyards of Saint-Estèphe (the best in this commune) drain the most efficiently.
• There was less rain here on 20th September than elsewhere.
• Bordeaux's highest proportions of Cabernet Sauvignon, and Petit Verdot, are here.

The wines of Saint-Émilion, Pomerol and their satellites have a good colour, medium to medium-full weight and are fresh, ripe and succulent, without suggesting any serious concentration or grip. With the exception of the arch-over-extractor Gérard Perse (of Château Pavie and others) 2002, as everyone stressed right from the outset, is emphatically *not* a year for over-extraction; the Merlots just couldn't take it – the vintage is a success. But only up to 'good plus' or 'very good' levels. It is better than 2001 and 1999, a great deal better than 1997, but a long way from 2000 and 1998.

The red wines of the Graves are, by and large, a little more interesting. Graves are unfashionable, sadly. But for those seeking refinement there are some very good wines. Avoid, however, the too-extracted wines of M. Magrez (Pape-Clément etc.).

In Margaux and the southern Médoc we have the most irregular results from the 2002 vintage. This is not only because of the habitual under-achievement of many of the classed growths (some of which, hitherto disgraceful, have now pulled their socks up) but because, I feel, wary of the effect of over-extraction, some winemakers have erred by not prolonging the maceration enough. Many are pleasant but a little weak, even some of the great names. Some 'very good' wines but overall 'good plus': much closer to 2001 than 2000.

From Beychevelle and its neighbours in Saint-Julien north to Sociando-Mallet in Saint-Seurin we have 2002 at its sometimes very exciting best. Here we have properly concentrated, vigorous wines, with structures approaching those of 2000, and in many cases levels of tannin, alcohol and acidity, especially the latter, in excess of this great vintage. There are certainly some wines which, in their own way, are as good. They are also substantially cheaper. This is where you should concentrate your purchases.

2002 – Opening Prices

Having been reduced from those of 2000 in 2001, prices fell further in 2002, the First Growths offering their wine at €60–65 (2001 €85, 2000 €120). A year later, in May 2004, these price levels still largely remain on the Bordeaux marketplace.

The Stars of the Vintage

As Tasted in April 2003

	MÉDOC/GRAVES	SAINT-ÉMILION/POMEROL
WINES OF THE VINTAGE	LAFITE, LATOUR	AUSONE
VERY FINE AND MORE	DUCRU-BEAUCAILLOU; HAUT-BRION; LÉOVILLE-BARTON; LÉOVILLE-LAS-CASES; MARGAUX; MONTROSE	
FINE AND MORE	DOMAINE DE CHEVALIER; COS D'ESTOURNEL; FERRIÈRE; GRAND-PUY-LACOSTE; GRUAUD-LAROSE; LANGOA-BARTON; LÉOVILLE-POYFERRÉ; MALESCOT-SAINT-EXUPÉRY; LA MISSION HAUT-BRION; PALMER; PICHON-LONGUEVILLE-LALANDE; SOCIANDO-MALLET; TALBOT	CHEVAL BLANC; L'ÉGLISE-CLINET; L'ÉVANGILE; LE PIN; VIEUX CHÂTEAU CERTAN
VERY GOOD AND MORE (AND well priced)	BOUSCAUT; BOYD CANTENAC; D'ESCURAC; HAUT-BAGES-LIBÉRAL; HAUT-BAILLY; HAUT-BATAILLEY; HAUT-CONDISSAS; MALARTIC-LAGRAVIÈRE; MOULIN DE LA ROSE; DE PEZ; ROLLAN DE BY; TERREY-GROS-CAILLOUX/HORTEVIE; TOUR HAUT-CAUSSAN	
THE BEST SAUTERNES	PREMIERS CRUS CLIMENS; RIEUSSEC; SUDUIRAUT AND PERHAPS, BEST OF ALL, SIGALAS-RABAUD	DEUXIÈMES CRUS DE MALLE; DOISY-DAËNE; DOISY-VÉDRINES

2001 VINTAGE

SIZE OF THE CROP:	6,560,628 HECTOLITRES.
VINTAGE RATING:	15.0/20 (RED WINES).
	16.0/20 (DRY WHITE WINES).
	18.5/20 (SWEET WINES).

This is 4 per cent less than the record-breaking harvests of 1999 and 2000. It represents a yield of 55.4 hl/ha. The white wine harvest was 701,496 hectolitres (10.7 per cent of the total), the lowest ever. Forty years ago it was half.

To generalise, with the exception of 2000, 2001 is the best red wine vintage since 1990. This is not to deny that there were some very fine wines in Saint-Émilion and Pomerol in 1998, and in Saint-Julien and Pauillac in 1996. But the progress in winemaking since then is very evident. All the way down the hierarchy from First Growth to *petit château* wine is being made with more flair and competence than hitherto. Vineyard management – de-budding, green harvesting, leaf trimming – has never been more widespread. Vinification practices have also improved. With a few unfortunate exceptions there are less over-macerated, *siliconé* wines than in past vintages. The overall quality has never been higher. And the vintage is consistent from Pomerol to Pauillac, Saint-Émilion to Saint-Estèphe.

So, the reds are good. Of less importance commercially (sadly), 2001 is a brilliant Sauternes vintage, and the dry white wines are crisper and better balanced than 2000.

A REDUCTION IN RENDEMENT AT THE TOP LEVELS

On the face of it, 2001 would seem to be another large crop. It was not so long ago that three million hectolitres of red wine was considered abundant. But these statistics are misleading. Five or six years ago the yield even among the First Growths in the Médoc was 55 hl/ha or more. Led by the example of the Libournais, who have been actively reducing their crop for a decade, the classed châteaux on the Left Bank have followed suit. A relatively humble property in Pomerol such as Château L'Enclos has aimed for 45 hl/ha for some years (in fact Hugues Weydaet produced 39 hl/ha in 2001, owing to *millerandage*); L'Évangile produced 40 hl/ha, the same as in 2000. So did Vieux Château Certan. Ausone, however, produced 30 per cent less than in 2000.

These sort of yields are rare in the Médoc/Graves. Yet both Lafite and Latour made 47 hl/ha in 2001, a lot less than in 1995 and 1996. Elsewhere the 2001 crop was even lower: 42 hl/ha at Mouton-Rothschild and Château Margaux; as low as 37 hl/ha at Pontet-Canet, 36 hl/ha at Brane-Cantenac, 35 hl/ha at Malescot-Saint-Exupéry, 32 hl/ha at Montrose and 31.62 hl/ha (what precision!) at Léoville-Las-Cases. That it was as high as 54 hl/ha at Beychevelle helps to explain why this château, which could be fine, is merely, boringly 'good'.

THE WEATHER

Alain Vauthier of Château Ausone summed it up: three negative factors – a wet winter, a wet July and a storm on 22nd September – and three positive aspects – a fine spring, a fine flowering and a good August. Crucially, despite this September storm, the August-September precipitation was rather less than average. Though not as dry, overall, as 2000, the rainfall in the three weeks before the harvest started was a mere 12 mm and in the important three weeks while picking took place was 109 mm, as against 107 in 2000, most of this falling on the fabled 22nd September, a few days before the collection started in Saint-Émilion and Pomerol and a full week before even the Merlots were harvested in the Médoc and the Graves.

The year began with the washout of the latter half of the 2000 Sauternes harvest. It went on raining almost non-stop until the end of January, producing twice the usual precipitation for these months. And, while it was wet, it was also warm.

Following a cold end of February, but with, thankfully, no serious frost, March was warm, and bud-burst occurred ahead of schedule, only for further development to be held back by a cool April. There was a little frost damage, mainly on the night of the 20th. The beginning of May continued grey and miserable. It was not until the 9th that weather conditions improved. Until the first week of July it remained dry and warm, with one or two exceptions. During this fine weather the vines caught up, flowered successfully and promised well.

Most of July was seriously cold and wet, the middle 10 days being 5°C cooler and twice as rainy as normal. But as August approached the heat returned. It was hotter at the beginning than at the end of the month, however, and this is where the 2001 weather pattern, having up to now uncannily echoed that of 2000, began to diverge. 2000 had been made by a really hot August. In 2001 it was more warm than hot, and while the first three weeks of September were dry, and indeed sunnier than 2000, temperatures were a full 2°C cooler. There were only three days, between 1st and 21st September, when the thermometer hit 25°C, as against 11 in 2000.

The dry white wine harvest commenced on 10th September and took place without interruption, finishing by the weekend of the 22nd. The Merlot harvest on the Right Bank had been due to start on Monday the 24th. Following a storm, which unleashed 41 mm of rain in Pomerol – though less in the Médoc – growers delayed. Most waited three or four days and were then able to pick their entire crop in good conditions. While there were isolated showers the only serious rainfall until the red wine harvest had long been completed was on 2nd October. Moreover, in contrast to 2000, admittedly an earlier harvest, it began to get warmer. The Médoc, which generally started to pick its Merlots on 1st October and its Cabernets between the 4th and the 14th, seems to have had the best of it though at the end the fruit began to deteriorate, which has effected the *bourgeois* growths of the northern Haut Médoc and Médoc. The fine weather continued, and some Sauternes of real power and concentration, the noble rot arriving after the fruit was fully physiologically ripe, were made.

THE WINES

While there was not the August-September warmth of 2000, which would produce the rich, abundantly ripe and fruity wines of this vintage, and their tannic structure too, 2001 has a lot of other good things going for it.

First, it was a late harvest. 'It's rare these days', said Frédéric Ardouin, technical director at Château Latour, 'for us not to start until 1st October.' In fact it was the first time for 15 years. So the 'hang' was prolonged. This long gestation, other things being equal, brings added complexity.

Second, in the absence of great heat and drought, the leaf canopy remained green. Photosynthesis was taking place right up to the last minute. Moreover, if August had been wetter than in 2000 (though a lot drier than average), September was very dry, only 36 mm being recorded in Bordeaux, though more in Pomerol. There was therefore no risk of dilution.

The year 2001, like 2000, was not one which required concentrating, chaptalisation or much in the way of *saignée*. Vinifications were slow, intentionally, growers realising immediately that 2001 should be a year favouring the fruit rather than the structure, and prolonging the cold soaking process and reducing the fermentation temperatures accordingly.

Some growers were confident in their 2001s from the start and able to draw out macerations after fermentation so that the resultant wines have concentration and intensity as well as fruit.

Elsewhere I feel some could have decided to go for more vigour. Their wines are elegant but lack a bit of real thrust at the end. Examples of the latter include Palmer, Pichon-Lalande, Rauzan-Ségla and Cheval Blanc, among what are usually high fliers. Examples of the former include Ausone, Lafite, Malescot-Saint-Exupéry, Calon-Ségur, Montrose and Saint-Pierre.

Others were less excited at the outset. Indeed the majority of the producers only began to come round to a higher view of the vintage in the late spring of 2002. Some are still dubious. One reason was the level of acidity. As it turned out the acidities are ripe and very good, not a bit too malic, nor too green. But such is the panic in many Bordeaux circles for making a wine which is too austere at the time the gates open for tasting at the end of March – because certain influential critics don't like acidity – that too many growths err in the opposite direction, producing wines which are rich, soft and bland: nice at six months, for some, but useless for keeping.

The Style of the 2001s

The best – and there is a lot of best – of the 2001 reds have a medium-full structure, plenty of ripe (sometimes almost jammy), but not over-ripe fruit, good balancing acidities, ripe tannins, and a frank, pure, classic temperament. They will come forward in the medium to long term: *bourgeois* growths from 2006–2007, most classed growths when they are eight or nine years old, only a few of the most concentrated not before 2012.

Where are the Best Wines?

As in 2000, it would not appear that one side of Bordeaux, or indeed one commune, has the edge over the rest. There are very good wines throughout Bordeaux. What is particularly noteworthy is the progress that has been made throughout the region since even as recently as 1998. It is pleasing to be able to report that out of the 48 *grands crus classés* Saint-Émilions I sampled (there are 53 in total) only seven were less than quite good. Only a decade ago it would have been 27. This improvement is echoed everywhere in Bordeaux, from the Blaye to the Graves, from Fronsac to Saint-Estèphe.

Prices

Prices fell. It could be argued that they should have fallen further, but the net effect in the summer of 2002 was that First Growths, at below £1000 ($1800) a dozen, were less, not only than the 1999s, but then the going rate for 1998, 1996 and 1995. Some properties did not reduce their prices, others such as Lascombes, even increased them (a pity, as the 2000 was splendid, the 2001 merely, though competently, 'international'). If you compare something like Château Cantemerle, it came out at £115 ($200) as opposed to £150 ($270) for the 2000. Château Potensac was £89 ($160) rather than £115 ($200). Not unreasonable.

Given the collapse of share prices, uncertainty in general in not only the economic but the political field, plus the fact that after 2000, 2001 was almost destined to be ignored, it was difficult to foresee an investment opportunity for the 2001s. The quality of subsequent vintages, and the future of the world's financial markets will show if I am right.

There is no investment value in Sauternes. Prices for the top 2001s in the summer of 2002 varied from £145 ($260) per dozen for d'Arche to £300 ($540) for Rieussec. Château d'Yquem is not on the market yet.

THE STARS OF THE VINTAGE

	MÉDOC/GRAVES	SAINT-ÉMILION/POMEROL
THE WINE OF THE VINTAGE	LAFITE	
NEARLY AS GOOD	HAUT-BRION; MARGAUX	PÉTRUS; TROTANOY
VERY FINE	DOMAINE DE CHEVALIER; DUCRU-BEAUCAILLOU; LATOUR; LÉOVILLE-BARTON; LÉOVILLE-LAS-CASES; LA MISSION HAUT-BRION; MONTROSE; MOUTON-ROTHSCHILD	AUSONE; L'ÉGLISE-CLINET; L'ÉVANGILE; LA FLEUR-PÉTRUS
FINE	CALON SÉGUR; COS D'ESTOURNEL; DUHART-MILON; GRAND-PUY-LACOSTE; HAUT-BAILLY; LÉOVILLE-POYFERRRE; MALESCOT SAINT-EXUPÉRY; SAINT-PIERRE; TALBOT	ANGÉLUS; L'ARROSÉE; BELLEVUE; BERLIQUET; CANON; CERTAN DE MAY; CHEVAL BLANC; LA CONSEILLANTE; FIGEAC; LA FLEUR DE BOÜARD LE PLUS; HOSANNA; LAFLEUR; MAGDELAINE; LA MONDOTTE; CLOS DE L'ORATOIRE; PAVIE-MACQUIN; LE PIN; TERTRE-ROTEBOEUF; TROPLONG-MONDOT; VIEUX CHÂTEAU CERTAN

UNEXPECTED NEWCOMERS PLUS VALUE FOR MONEY

THE BEST RED WINES	
POMEROL	BON PASTEUR; L'ENCLOS; LA GRAVE; VRAI CROIX DE GAY
SAINT-ÉMILION	LA FLEUR CARDINALE; PLAISANCE; SAINTAYME; CLOS VILLEMAURINE
SAINT-ÉMILION GRANDS CRUS CLASSÉS	LA COUSPAUDE; FRANC MAYNE; GRAND MAYNE; LARMANDE; LAROQUE; TERTRE DAUGAY; LE PRIEURÉ; VILLEMAURINE
LALANDE-DE-POMEROL	LA CHÉNADE; LES CRUZELLES; LA SÈGUE
MONTAGNE-SAINT-ÉMILION	FAIZEAU
CÔTES DE CASTILLON	D'AIGUILHE; CAP DE FAUGÈRES; POUPILLE
CÔTES DE FRANCS	LA PRADE
FRONSAC	CANON DE BREM; DALEM; FONTENIL; GABY; MAYNE VIEIL, CUVÉE ALIÉNOR; MOULIN HAUT-LAROQUE; VILLARS
MÉDOC	MAURAC; PONTENSAC; ROLLAN DE BY; VIEUX CHÂTEAU LANDON; LES VIGNES DE CABELEYRON
HAUT-MÉDOC	CANTEMERLE; CHASSE-SPLEEN; LAMOTHE-BERGERON; POUJEAUX
MARGAUX	DAUZAC; DEYREM VALENTIN; L'ENCLOS GALLIAN; FERRIÈRE
SAINT-JULIEN	GLORIA
PAUILLAC	FONBADET; HAUT-BAGES-LIBÉRAL
SAINT-ESTÈPHE	COS LABORY; SÉGUR DE CABANAC; HAUT-MARBUZET

THE BEST DRY WHITE WINES

VERY FINE	HAUT-BRION
FINE PLUS	DOMAINE DE CHEVALIER
FINE	LAVILLE HAUT-BRION; COUHINS
VERY GOOD INDEED	LATOUR-MARTILLAC; PAPE-CLÉMENT

THE BEST SAUTERNES

VERY FINE	CLIMENS; LAFAURIE-PEYRAGUEY; RAYNE-VIGNEAU; RIEUSSEC; SIGALAS-RABAUD; SUDUIRAUD
FINE	COUTET; DOISY-VÉDRINES; CLOS HAUT-PEYRAGUEY; LA TOUR-BLANCHE
VERY GOOD INDEED	BASTOR-LAMONTAGNE; CRU BORDENAIRE; DOISY-DAËNE; DE MALLE; NAIRAC

2000 VINTAGE

SIZE OF THE CROP:	6,804,476 HECTOLITRES.
VINTAGE RATING:	18.5/20 (RED WINES).
	15.0/20 (DRY WHITE WINES).
	13.0 (SWEET WINES).

This is, marginally after 1999, the largest harvest ever, an average yield of 57.6 hl/ha. The white wine harvest was 815,868 hectolitres (12 per cent of the total).

What is the definition of a great vintage? I would postulate that at least one of the ingredients is that it should be consistent hierarchically; that the lesser wines should be ripe, rich, balanced and full of fruit; that one should be able to pick with confidence among the ranks of the *bourgeois*, the *petits châteaux*, and in the satellite *appellations*.

Bordeaux has had four such great years in the last 30: 1970, 1982, 1990 and, now 2000. In these vintages not only are there great wines at the top of the hierarchy, not only is the vintage a success across the whole region, from Saint-Émilion and Pomerol to Pauillac and Saint-Julien, but there are delicious examples to be found in the lesser areas such as Côtes de Bourg, Lalande-de-Pomerol, Fronsac, Montagne-Saint-Émilion and Côtes de Castillon, as well as in the Médoc north of Saint-Estèphe.

Moreover, 2000 has two extra advantages. First, the wine is made better today than it has ever been. Today everyone is properly equipped, most are conscientious, even lesser properties crop-thin, and make a selection, isolating a *grand vin* from the rest. But even at the top of the tree, at First Growth and Super-Second level, standards have improved. Even at Lafite and Pétrus they produce better wine than they did in 1990, as in 1990 the wines were better than they were in 1982.

Second, despite exaggerated price increases among the fashionable wines – the First Growths 500–600 per cent higher than in 1990; Super-Seconds such as Pichon-Lalande and Ducru-Beaucaillou 450 per cent up – the prices of the lesser wines remain reasonable. A good *bourgeois* such as Château Caronne-Sainte-Gemme sold ex-château for 30 Francs in 1990, for 40 Francs for its 2000, an increase of a mere 33 per cent. Here is Bordeaux value.

There is, of course, another way of looking at the proposition. Are the top 2000s going to be as good as the top 1990s, 1982s or 1961s? Here the question is moot, the response almost impossible. We won't really be able to answer until the 2000s are themselves mature. And we still need to wait for the 1990s to reach their peak. My gut feeling is that nothing will surpass the finest 1961s. They seem to be unique. But I am perfectly happy to agree that 2000, at its best, is as good as 1982 and 1990. The trouble is that the top wines are horrendously expensive.

Yet, despite that, the interest in the vintage was huge. Never has a vintage sold out so fast. This enthusiasm extended all the way down to the consumer, despite a falling stock market, despite the horrors of 11th September.

THE WEATHER

A year of excesses and opposites, was how one grower put it to me. The first half of the year was distinctly unpromising. The second half was, if not totally perfect, at least more than enough to compensate. Thankfully, for unsettled conditions early in the season often leave their mark to be felt later on, this was not the case in 2000.

The story of 2000 has to begin with the hurricane which arrived on 27th December 1999. It was not so much that it had an effect on the 2000 crop, which it didn't, but that it set the scene for what would be a very difficult and depressing first half of the year. The result of winds which were measured at 144 km/hour in Bordeaux and 198 km/hour on the coast (hurricane force starts at 117 km/hour) was a major destruction of the local pine forest, serious losses in châteaux parks and a millennium celebration in the cold and by candle.

The winter, however, was overall a great deal warmer than usual, with only one really cold spell, from 11th to 28th January. The first 10 days of January, and the whole of February and March were all warmer than the average, and though January and March were dry, February was 63 per cent wetter than usual.

April was cold and wet, but not cold enough to cause any frost damage. The threat was mildew, and with the vineyards too humid to allow the tractors to pass through treatments got delayed and the disease rapidly spread throughout the region.

May was mixed. Hot at first, then cool, then warm again with even more but intermittent rain. Altogether April and May precipitated 200 mm. There was more to come in the beginning of June, by which time the vines had begun to flower, a few days ahead of the average, but a week later than 1999.

Despite seesaw climatic conditions in June: cool one minute, very hot the next, and 65 mm of rain during the flowering, most of it on 3rd and 4th June, the fruit-set, surprisingly, was over very quickly, and without much *coulure* damage. This was followed by two weeks of fine dry weather. For the first time the *vignerons* allowed themselves to smile. The mildew had dried up, and it looked as if the majority of the fruit would arrive at maturity at the same time. Recalcitrant bunches anyway are now the first to be eliminated during the green-harvesting.

Following the 3rd/4th June thunderstorm it then remained largely dry for the rest of the summer. July was averagely warm, with a little rain at the beginning of the month. But August was hot, with 11 days over 30°C, and this fine weather continued into September. The fruit, which had seemed rather water-engorged in July, now concentrated, developing thick skins and accumulating sugar. In some cases the net result, despite the precipitations earlier in the year, was a threat of the phenolic development becoming blocked. This was especially felt in Pomerol and the Graves-Saint-Émilion, particularly as this side of the Gironde missed a much-needed storm on the night of 25th August, which eased the problem in the Médoc and the Graves.

For the first time since 1990 it didn't rain – or almost didn't – during the harvest. September saw 43 mm of rainfall, most of it during the night of the 19th, as against an average of 75 mm. Some growers had already begun to crop their Merlots, the harvest commencing on the Right Bank on 14th September. Others, in the Médoc, just delayed picking until the effect of this storm had evaporated. Many Merlots came in at 14°. Even more noteworthy, for the first time ever in some cases, Cabernets Sauvignons were harvested at 13°. The weather was unsettled during the weekend of 30th September – 1st October, but otherwise the rain held off until 11th October. By this time the red wine harvest was very largely complete. Sadly for the Sauternais, the rain continued. There are wines resulting from one or two *passages* made prior to 11th October in the Sauternais cellars, and these are good. Those made from later-picked grapes have in most cases been declassified.

THE WINES

The fruit was healthy. It was concentrated. Alcohol levels, and perhaps surprisingly, acidity levels as well, were high. The skins were thick. The potential tannins very high. All the elements were in place for a great red wine vintage. What was vitally important was not to overdo the winemaking process. Only a light hand on the tiller, control over temperatures (30°C maximum), a reduction in pumping over and a shortening of the macerating process would result in wines of elegance and *terroir* definition. 'In 2000 the key was infusion rather than maceration', said Christian Moueix. Sadly, in some parts of Bordeaux, especially in the Saint-Émilion/Pomerol area, winemaking fashions dictate otherwise. There were in fact rather fewer over-cooked wines than I feared. But there are some. This is not a vintage for *vins garagistes*.

Elsewhere, right across Bordeaux both geographically and hierarchically, we have wines of very good colour, considerable but at present largely hidden ripe tannins, deliciously concentrated, very pure, intense fruit and very good acidity. The wines have volume, dimension, class and complexity. There are many châteaux which make wine considerably better than they had done a decade earlier. Overall the selections have been severe. A much smaller proportion of the total has been declared as *grand vin* than in similar years a decade or more ago. So in many cases we have a better result than has ever been achieved before. Others have made the best wine since 1990. Overall it is a splendid vintage.

Where are the Best Wines?

This is indisputably a Cabernet Sauvignon vintage. So as you would expect the best wines are to be found in the Médoc and the Graves. All the way from Haut-Bailly and Domaine de Chevalier in Pessac-Léognan to Sociando-Mallet in the north of the Haut-Médoc the vintage is consistently good. There are only three major disappointments (see below). A number of erstwhile underachievers in Margaux are now members of the starry firmament. Even Rauzan-Gassies is good! Even Château Bouscaut, a Graves *cru classé* notorious for having been given 69 or something out of 100 in an American journal (equivalent to undrinkable) in 1999 (I did not like it either), and on which it based its advertising campaign, is also 'good'.

Strangely the Cabernet Franc on the Médoc-Graves side did not turn out as well. Most properties only used a small proportion, or rejected it entirely, as happened also with the late-picked Petit Verdot, collected after the weather broke on 11th October.

On the other side of the Gironde the picture is mixed. First in Pomerol and the Graves area of Saint-Émilion the 1998 vintage was very successful. Whether the 2000 or the 1998 is better at, say, Cheval-Blanc, Trotanoy, L'Église-Clinet and Vieux Château Certan is a question of taste and opinion. Here, say some but not all, the Cabernet Franc, in contrast to the Médoc, was very successful. Second, we need to bear in mind the greater amount of hydric stress felt here as a result of the lack of rain at the end of August. What this meant was that the fruit ripened as much by dehydration as maturation. Third, there is the effect of over-extraction, either un-witting, or deliberate, in the belief that it will attract higher points in American journals. Despite this there are many delicious Libournais wines. But 2000 remains a Médoc vintage.

Prices – Then and Now

The earlier the wine came out on the market, and the more modest its place in the hierarchy, the cheaper it was. At the top levels many wines were 50 – even 100 – per cent up on those of 1999. At the bottom the increases were in the order of 5 or 10 per cent. On the one hand, then, as I have said, the 2000s were alarmingly expensive. But at the less fashionable end, given the quality of the *bourgeois* wines, the 2000s were excellent value. Château Caronne-Sainte-Gemme was offered by Farr Vintners in July 2001 at £70 ($120) a dozen in bond.

Despite the high opening prices, the top 2000s showed a healthy growth in the years which followed, the only Bordeaux vintage to increase in value during this period. Lafite and Latour, which had opened at £1880 ($3380), sold for £2850 ($5130) in July 2003. Pichon-Longueville, Comtesse de Lalande and other Super-Seconds rose by 50 per cent or more. 2000, like 1982, seems destined to be recession-proof.

Conclusion

Three years on, the wines safely in bottle, it is time to put aside the millenium hype, forget the fearfully high prices, and ask ourselves the question: how good are the 2000 reds? Is it, as some have claimed, the best ever – because there is a larger quantity of good wines than ever before?

My feeling, having tasted the wines noted on the following pages over three days in January 2004, was more one of frustration than satisfaction: exasperation, that, as usual, the majority of the wines were no more than 'good', rather than joy at the fact that the usual suspects – all the First Growths except Mouton-Rothschild, all the Super-Seconds save Pichon-Longueville, Comtesse de Lalande – have produced lovely wines.

There are some splendid 2000s. What is sad is that there are so few, though in general the wines at bourgeois and petit château level are more than satisfactory. Where the vintage disappoints is in the middle, properties with classed growth terroir who fail, year in, year out, even given the weather advantages of 2000, to produce classed growth wine.

The Stars of the Vintage

	MÉDOC/GRAVES	SAINT-ÉMILION/POMEROL
THE WINES OF THE VINTAGE	LAFITE; MARGAUX	
VERY FINE INDEED	DUCRU-BEAUCAILLOU; HAUT-BRION; LATOUR; LÉOVILLE-BARTON; LÉOVILLE-LAS-CASES	CHEVAL BLANC; PÉTRUS
VERY FINE	GRAND-PUY-LACOSTE; LA MISSION HAUT-BRION; PALMER	ANGELUS; AUSONE; LA CONSEILLANTE; L'EGLISE-CLINET; L'ÉVANGILE; FIGEAC; LA FLEUR-PÉTRUS; LAFLEUR; LE PIN; TROTANOY; VIEUX CHÂTEAU CERTAN
GOOD VALUE	D'AURILHAC; CARONNE SAINTE-GEMME; COUFRAN; CHASSE-SPLEEN; DOMAINE DE CHEVALIER; D'ESCURAC; FERRIÈRE; LABÉGORCE-ZÉDÉ; LARRIVET HAUT-BRION; LA LOUVIÈRE; DE PEZ; ROLLAN DE BY	BERLIQUET; BERTINEAUT SAINT-VINCENT; CANON DE BREM; LA CROIX CANON; LES CRUZELLES; DALEM; LA FLEUR DE BOUARD; LA GRAVE-À-POMEROL; FONTENIL; LA SERGUE; LA SERRE
DISAPPOINTMENTS	COS D'ESTOURNEL; MOUTON-ROTHSCHILD; PICHON-LALANDE	PAVIE

THE TASTING

The following range of red wines were sampled over three days by the usual team of British wine trade professionals at The Crown Inn, Southwold in January 2004.

SAINT-EMILION

CHÂTEAU ANGÉLUS

2012-2030	18.0

Full colour. Rich, full, concentrated, high quality nose. Backward. Full-bodied, concentrated and tannic on the palate. But not over-extracted. Very fine grip. Lots of depth and class. Impressive quality. Lovely long finish. Fine plus.

CHÂTEAU L'ARROSÉE

2012-2024	15.5

Fullish colour. Slightly lumpy on the nose. But decent weight and grip underneath. Medium-full body. A little tannin. Rather ungainly. Yet good acidity and nice ripe fruit. It lacks a bit of flair. Good plus.

CHÂTEAU AUSONE

2011-2030	19.0

Full colour. Rich, very classy, understated nose. Lovely fruit. Great harmony. Fullish body. Backward. Subtle, concentrated and really multi-dimensional and elegant. A very lovely example.

CHÂTEAU BARDE-HAUT

2009-2019	14.0

Full colour. Dense, quite prominently oaky nose. Slightly dry. Not a lot of weight underneath. Medium-full body. Not much depth, nor much sophistication. A little over-extracted. Not very long.

CHÂTEAU BEAU-SÉJOUR-BÉCOT

2008-2015	14.0

Full colour. Soft, ripe, fruity nose. Gently oaky underneath. Medium weight. Not a lot of grip. Quite oaky. The follow-through is better than the attack though. The finish is more positive. Quite good.

CHÂTEAU BEAUSÉJOUR-DUFFAU-LAGARROSSE

2012-2030	17.0

Full colour. Attractive nose. Classy, balanced fruit here. Fullish body. Some tannin. Backward. But very good depth and class. Not hot at the end. Long, complex and promising.

CHÂTEAU BELAIR

2008-2018	14.5

Fullish colour. Elegant, balanced nose. But not a lot of weight. Nor on the palate a lot of personality. Medium-full body. Decent acidity. A lack of richness and dimension. But balanced and long. Quite good plus.

CHÂTEAU BELLEVUE

2008-2024	17.0

Fullish colour. Ripe, rich, succulent nose. Medium-full body. Round, ripe, soft, balanced and well made. Lovely fruit. Plenty of personality. Long. Quite forward but very good indeed.

CHÂTEAU BERLIQUET

2009-2022	15.0

Fullish colour. Ripe, generous nose. Not a lot of weight, but balanced and gentle. On the palate this shows medium body and good fruit. Not short but it lacks a little zip and interest and dimension. Good.

CHÂTEAU CANON

2010-2024	16.5

Full colour. Ripe, fresh, balanced nose. Not a blockbuster but cool and classy. Medium-full body. Good fruit. Good balance. Longer and more interesting than it seems at first. Very good plus.

Château Canon-La-Gaffelière

2009-2018	15.5

Full colour. Just a little forced on the nose. But balanced and more relaxed on the palate. Medium-full body. Good fruit if not that sophisticated. It lacks a little personality. But positive finish. Good plus.

Château Cheval Blanc

2012-2035	19.0

Full colour. Full nose. Tannic and backward. But very, very concentrated. Full body. Ample. Very, very rich and very, very concentrated. This is as good as Ausone (which I didn't think at first). Lots and lots of depth. Very finely balanced and very classy.

Le Dôme

2012-2025	16.0

Full colour. Rich, fullish, ample nose. Decent acidity and concentration. Nicely fresh. Not over-extracted. Well-made. Full-bodied on the palate. Rich and ripe. Balanced and well-made, following through nicely. It just lacks a little personality and class. Very good.

Château La Dominique

2009-2020	15.0

Fullish colour. Soft, oaky nose. Slightly bland. Medium to medium-full weight. Decent acidity. Quite nice, ripe, plump fruit. Good.

Château Figeac

2010-2025	16.5

Full colour. As often in its youth slightly green on the nose. But good depth underneath. Medium-full body. Good grip. Individual. You can taste the Cabernet Sauvignon. Backward. Long. Very good plus.

Clos Fourtet

2009-2020	15.0

Full colour. Ripe and rich but a bit lumpy on the nose. Medium-full body. Slightly bland. Fruity and quite rich but it lacks a bit of class and freshness. Good at best.

Château Grand-Mayne

2010-2020+	16.5

Full colour. Fresh, ripe nose. Good fruit here. Medium-full weight. Balanced. Medium to medium-full body. Very good fruit. Long and positive and fresh and stylish on the follow-through. This is very good plus.

Château Larcis-Ducasse

2007-2012	13.0

Medium to medium-full colour. Robust on the nose. Quite ripe but no great class. Medium body. Rather short. Not much style. A bit fruitless. Unexciting.

Château Magdelaine

2010-2025	17.0

Fullish colour. Lovely rich, fresh nose. Very good fruit. Not a blockbuster. Medium-full body. Rich and plump. Fresh and balanced. Plenty of depth, personality and class. Lovely finish. Very good indeed.

Château Monbousquet

2007-2014	13.5

Full colour. Ripe, round nose. A bit bland but not too forced. Quite oaky on the palate. Not much acidity. Nor much depth or concentration. Forward. Dull. It lacks zip.

La Mondotte

2010-2025	17.5

Full colour. Splendid rich fruit on the nose. Plus some oak. Fullish body. Rich. Some tannin. Quite tannic. This has a lot more personality than Clos de L'Oratoire. Harmonious. Profound. Fine.

Château Moulin St-Georges

2007-2016	15.5

Full colour. Attractive, plump, plummy, balanced nose. Not a blockbuster but fresh and classy. Decent attack. Only medium bodied and indeed quite forward. But juicy and fresh. Good plus.

Clos de l'Oratoire

2011-2028   16.5

Full colour. Rich, generous, succulent, ripe nose. Youthful. Fullish body. Just a little forced. Some tannin. Good fruit. Good grip. Good concentration. Slightly dense at present. Very good plus. It needs time.

Château Pavie

2012-2025   15.0

Very full colour. Full, extracted, oaky nose. Fullish body. Some tannin. Quite a lot of oak. Lumpy. Yet good grip if a bit hot. I find it unstylish.

Château Pavie-Decesse

2010-2020   14.0

Full colour. Rich, very oaky nose. Rather dense and over-extracted on the palate. High in alcohol too. Full-bodied but clumsy. The finish is hot and ungainly and rather short.

Château Pavie-Macquin

2010-2030   17.5

Full colour. Balanced, rich, succulent nose. Fullish body. A little tannin. This is profound and classy. Lovely fruit. Very good grip. Lot of depth. Lovely finish. A fine example.

Château Quinault L'Enclos

2008-2020   15.5

Full colour. Ripe, quite fresh but slightly bland nose. Medium body. A balanced, stylish second division Saint-Émilion. Good long finish. Good plus.

Château Rol-Valentin

2011-2025   16.0

Full colour. Quite a full sturdy nose. But good fruit and grip. Fullish body. Ripe. Some tannin. Good grip. Not a great deal of class but balanced, long and well-made. Very good.

Château Soutard

2011-2025   16.0

Medium-full colour. Decent fruit but a lack of concentration and richness and oak. Good acidity but a little one-dimensional. Medium weight. More oak on the palate. Balanced but no real depth. A bit dull.

Château Tertre-Roteboeuf

2010-2022   16.0

Full colour. Ripe, individual, slightly austere nose. Fullish body. Some oak. Good grip. Nicely cool. Balanced. Long. It lacks a little class but very good.

Château Troplong-Mondot

2012-2032   17.5

Full colour. Splendid rich nose. Gently oaky. Opulent. Succulent. Full-bodied. Concentrated. Impressive on the palate. Lovely multi-dimensional fruit. Very good acidity. Lots of dimension and class. Very long. Fine.

Château Trottevieille

2009-2020   15.0

Medium-full colour. Soft, plump nose. Fresh but not a great deal of depth. Medium-full body. It lacks a little richness. Good acidity though. Positive at the end. Good.

Château de Valandraud

2008-2016   15.0

Full colour. (Slightly corked.) Not too much of a blockbuster. Ripe and balanced on the nose. Not an over-extracted garage wine any more. Good acidity. It lacks a little concentration and depth. Good at best.

Pomerol

Château Beauregard

2010-2020   16.0

Full colour. A little over-extracted on the nose. Better on the palate. Fullish body. Good grip. Attractive fruit without being too dense or hot. Indeed very positive, even elegant at the end.

Château Bon Pasteur

2010-2024   17.0

Full colour. Attractive, ripe, oaky, fruity nose. This is most appealing. Medium-full body. Fresh and balanced. Lovely fruit. Very harmonious and plenty of class. Very good indeed.

Château Bourgneuf

2009-2017   14.0

Medium-full colour. Slightly lumpy on the nose at first. It improved in the glass. Medium-full body. Fruity. Reasonably balanced. But no great style or personality. Quite good.

Château Certan de May

2007-2014   14.0

Full colour. Ripe and stylish, but by no means a blockbuster on the nose. Ripe but no great concentration or volume. It lacks a dimension and a drive and class. As so often these days a disappointment.

Château Clinet

2012-2025   17.0

Medium-full colour. Rich, fat, oaky nose. Quite full but not too over-extracted. Fullish body. Good richness. Good grip. Not the greatest elegance. But very good indeed. It finishes long.

Château La Conseillante

2010-2025   15.0

Full colour. Elegant nose. Balanced. Not a blockbuster. Medium-full body. Very good grip. Lovely fruit. Rich, ample and elegant. An improvement on recent vintages. But still not up to snuff.

Château La Croix du Casse

2007-2014   14.0

Medium-full colour. Fresh nose. Quite stylish, but not much depth or concentration. Medium body. A decent second division brew. Balanced. Fresh. Good for what it is. Forward.

Château La Croix de Gay

2008-2018   14.0

Medium-full colour. Quite oaky and a little over extracted on the nose. Medium to medium-full body. Slightly astringent. Not much class or depth yet decent grip and so a positive finish. Quite good.

Clos L'Église

2010-2020   15.0

Full colour. Rich, fat, oaky nose. Slightly over-extracted. Fullish body. Oaky. It lacks a little grip. A little lumpy. Good at best.

Château L'Église-Clinet

2012-2030   18.0

Full colour. Classy nose. Cool, balanced and fullish. An ample, quite full-bodied wine on the palate. Very good grip. Lots of concentration and style. Lovely fruit. Lovely finish. This is fine if not very fine.

Château L'Évangile

2012-2035   19.0

Full colour. Brilliant nose. Excellent fruit, depth, class and harmony. Lots and lots of dimension. Balanced, cool, rich and very concentrated. Splendidly classy and very, very long and lovely. Excellent.

Château La Fleur de Gay

2008-2016   16.5

Full colour. Rich, fat, oaky, positive nose. Good depth here. Medium-full body. Ripe and balanced. Stylish. Lovely fruit. Very long. This is very good plus.

Château La Fleur-Pétrus

2009-2018   15.5

Full colour. (Slightly corky.) Medium-full weight. Ripe, stylish, balanced and cool. Medium-full body. It lacks a little richness and personality. The bottle was slightly corked but I still don't find it as good as it should be.

Fugue de Nénin

2007-2015   14.0

Medium-full colour. Lightish, fruity, gently oaky nose. This is better within its context than the *grand vin*. Ripe. Medium to medium-full body. Good balance. Good for what it is.

Château Gazin

2008-2016   15.0

Full colour. Cool nose. Not a great deal of depth. But balanced and quite elegant. On the palate it lacks a little fat and richness at first. Balanced. It finishes better than it starts. Good but not great.

Château La Grave à Pomerol

2008-2016   16.5

Full colour. Ample, ripe, fresh and balanced. Medium to medium-full body. Succulent. Nicely rich. Harmonious. Very good plus.

Château Hosanna

2010-2025   17.5

Full colour. Ripe, ample, generous nose. Fullish-bodied and succulent. Some tannin. This is rich and seductive. Very well balanced. Better than La Fleur-Pétrus and Latour-à-Pomerol today.

Château Lafleur

2012-2030   17.5

Full colour. Fullish, concentrated, slightly earthy and tannic nose. A backward wine. Fullish body. Ripe. Some tannin. A little ungainly. Yet balanced and concentrated. This will get better and better. Fine but not great.

Château Lagrange

2010-2020   15.5

Full colour. Rich, meaty nose. Good grip though. Medium-full body. Ripe. Quite sturdy. But fresh and balanced. Positive finish. Good plus.

Château Latour à Pomerol

2010-2025   17.0

Full colour. Succulent, cool, classy fruit on the nose. Fullish body. Rich, balanced and very good indeed on the palate. Slightly raw at present.

Château Nénin

2008-2014   14.0

Full colour. Ripe and balanced but without a lot of depth, richness or interest. Medium body. Not a great deal of grip or dimension. Very dull. But reasonably balanced. Bigger but no better than its second wine, the Fugue.

Château Petit-Village

2008-2014   13.5

Full colour. Not a great deal of interest here on the nose. It seems a bit green and lean. Medium body. It lacks concentration and personality. It lacks richness and depth too. Decent grip at least.

Le Pin

2009-2024   17.0

Very full colour. Very Merlot, very succulent nose. Medium-full body. Ripe and quite sweet. Not a great amount of acidity or dimension but stylish, fresh and with very good length. Very good indeed but not great.

Château Rouget

2008-2018   14.5

Full colour. Ripe fruit, quite sweet on the nose. Good freshness though. Medium-full body. Decently succulent but slightly dull on the palate. Balanced nevertheless. Quite good plus.

CHÂTEAU TROTANOY

2012-2030	18.5

Full colour. Very lovely ample, rich, concentrated, classy nose. This is very delicious. Fullish body. Very lovely, plump, ripe fruit. Rich and concentrated. Excellent grip. Very cool. Excellent. Very, very long and lovely at the end.

VIEUX CHÂTEAU CERTAN

2012-2030	18.0

Full colour. Rich, concentrated, backward nose. Similar on the palate. Fullish body. Some tannin. Very good acidity. Still a little dumb. The finish is most impressive though. Very, very long. This is needs time. Fine plus.

PESSAC-LEOGNAN

CHÂTEAU BAHANS HAUT-BRION

2007-2019	15.5

Medium-full colour. Soft, elegant, ripe nose. Medium weight. Stylish fruit. Balanced. Quite forward but very attractive. Good plus.

CHÂTEAU BOUSCAUT

2007-2017	15.0

Medium-full colour. Soft nose. Cool. Good fruit. Medium weight. Medium body on the palate. Ripe and balanced. Positive follow-through. Attractive.It finishes well. Good. Quite forward.

CHÂTEAU CARBONNIEUX

2009-2019	15.0

Full colour. Soft nose. A little oak. Plump fruit. Not a lot of style. Medium-full body. Decent fruit and rather more finesse and interest than on the nose at first. Good.

CHÂTEAU LES CARMES HAUT-BRION

2009-2019	15.0

Full colour. Quite rich and succulent on the nose. Some oak. Attractive. Medium-full body. A little tannin. Slightly ungainly but this will go. Good fruit and depth. Good grip. Positive finish. Good.

DOMAINE DE CHEVALIER

2010-2030	18.0

Full colour. Very refined, gently oaky, complex nose. Very lovely. Fullish body. Very harmonious. Very lovely fruit. Long and persistent and very, very elegant. Fine plus.

CHÂTEAU DE FIEUZAL

2008-2014	13.5

Medium-full colour. Quite firm, succulent, slightly robust nose. Medium-full body. Slightly lacking class and richness. It lacks charm too. Rather lumpy.

CHÂTEAU HAUT-BAILLY

2010-2028	17.0

Full colour. Rich, balanced, silky, stylish nose. Lots of depth here. Medium-full body. Harmonious. Ripe and gently oaky. Very elegant. Long. Very good indeed.

CHÂTEAU HAUT-BERGEY

2008-2014	13.0

Fullish colour. Slightly robust on the nose. A little over-extracted. Lumpy and rustic on the palate. Some tannin. A bit astringent. Unbalanced.

CHÂTEAU HAUT-BRION

2010-2030	19.0

Full colour. Marvellous expression of very classy fruit on the nose. Fullish body. Ample. Complex. Excellent harmony. This is rich, discreet, profound and complex. Very lovely indeed.

CHÂTEAU LARRIVET HAUT-BRION

2007-2015	14.0

Full colour. Just a little green on the nose. Medium body. Quite well balanced but not much depth. Slightly astringent at the end. Only quite good.

CHÂTEAU LATOUR-MARTILLAC

2008-2016	15.0

Fullish colour. Decent nose. Cool. But it lacks a little richness. Better on the palate. Medium to medium-full body. Quite ripe. Harmonious. No lack of interest. Good.

CHÂTEAU LA LOUVIÈRE

2008-2016   14.5

Fullish colour. Quite rich but at the same time a little austere on the nose. Medium to medium-full body. As with so many of these lesser Graves there is reasonable balance but a lack of character. Quite good plus.

CHÂTEAU MALARTIC-LAGRAVIÈRE

SEE NOTE

Full colour. Badly corked. Impossible to taste.

CHÂTEAU LA MISSION HAUT-BRION

2010-2030   18.0

Full colour. Lovely nose. Backward. But rich and profound. Fullish body. Not too austere. Very good tannins. Lovely fruit. Long and persistent and very classy. Fine plus.

CHÂTEAU PAPE-CLÉMENT

2012-2025   15.5

Full colour. Fullish nose. Backward. Quite firm. Full body. Some tannins. It needs time. Not too over-extracted. But quite a meaty example. Rich. It lacks a little finesse but good plus.

CHÂTEAU SMITH-HAUT-LAFITTE

2008-2017   15.5

Full colour. Soft, ripe, gently oaky nose. Quite attractive. Medium to medium-full body. More interesting fruit than most of the lesser Graves flight. Balanced. Quite stylish.

CHÂTEAU LA TOUR HAUT-BRION

2008-2016   15.5

Fullish colour. Ripe, fullish, elegant nose. Medium-full body. It starts well but then it tails off a bit. Good fruit. Not short. Certainly elegant. But it lacks a little grip and backbone. Merely good plus.

MÉDOC AND OTHER WINES

CHÂTEAU BIBIAN

2008-2014   13.0

Full colour. A bit tense and forced on the nose. Medium-full body. Not a lot of grip. Slightly over-macerated. Ungainly.

CHÂTEAU CAMENSAC

2008-2014   13.5

Fullish colour. Soft, oaky, pleasant but a lack of depth and class. Medium body. A bit dull, but quite fresh. Slightly bitter at the end.

CHÂTEAU CANTEMERLE

2007-2012   13.0

Fullish colour. Light, slightly green nose. It lacks succulence. Medium body. Rather thin, vegetal and one-dimensional. Decent acidity but no depth and no charm.

CHÂTEAU CHASSE-SPLEEN

2010-2025   16.5

Full colour. Rich, ripe, concentrated and oaky on the nose. This has class and depth. Fullish body. Very good tannins. Lovely rich, ripe, expansive fruit. Very good grip. This is very lovely. An excellent result.

ESSENCE DE DOURTHE

2008-2014   13.0

Very full colour. It smells Californian. Alcoholic. Oaky. Quite macerated. Ungainly. Medium-full body. Some tannin. Very modern. Unstylish.

CHÂTEAU HAUT-CONDISSAS

2009-2020+   16.0

Full colour. Fullish nose. Rich, ample, oaky and quite profound. Fullish body. Good grip and depth. Rich and oaky. Old viney aspects. Long, positive and stylish. This is very good.

CHÂTEAU LA LAGUNE

2008-2016	15.0

Fullish colour. Soft, gently oaky nose. No great grip or concentration but quite classy. Medium body. Balanced, fruity and attractive on the palate. But only one and a half dimensions. Good but no better.

CHÂTEAU LANESSAN

2008-2014	13.0

Full colour. Nice ripe Cabernet nose. A little oaky. But no real depth or class. Medium to medium-full body. Good acidity. It lacks a bit of richness and style. It lacks charm too. The tannins could have been riper.

CHÂTEAU LATOUR-HAUT-CAUSSAN

2009-2016	14.0

Medium-full colour. Rather forced on the nose. Slightly green and harsh. Better on the palate. Medium to medium-full body. Good grip. Quite sophisticated fruit and a positive finish. Quite good.

CHÂTEAU POTENSAC

2008-2014	13.5

Full colour. It smells a bit of old tea. Some size but not much fruit or charm. Medium body. Some unripe tannins. It lacks generosity. Only fair. Good grip though.

CHÂTEAU POUJEAUX

2009-2018	14.5

Full colour. Slightly harsher than Chasse Spleen on the nose. But good depth underneath. Not as good though. Less body. Less ripe tannins. Less dimension and richness. Only quite good plus.

CHÂTEAU ROC DE CAMBES

2009-2012	13.0

Fullish colour. Quite sturdy nose. Ripe and with some tannin. It lacks a bit of sophistication. Medium to medium-full body. A bit of unripe tannin. Good acidity but a lack of grace and charm.

CHÂTEAU SOCIANDO-MALLET

2008-2016	14.0

Full colour. Ripe, rich, oaky but rather austere on the nose. Medium-full body. Decent tannins. But it doesn't really sing today. Decent fruit and balance. But no better than quite good. I have better bottles than this.

CHÂTEAU LA TOUR-CARNET

2007-2011	12.5

Full colour. Some volume on the nose but not much character or style. Medium body. A little short. It lacks fruit. Very dull.

MARGAUX

CHÂTEAU D'ANGLUDET

2011-2022	14.0

Medium-full colour. Quite firm on the nose. A little sturdy and four-square. Medium-full body. It lacks a little richness and complexity. And sex appeal.

CHÂTEAU BEL AIR MARQUIS D'ALIGRE

2006-2010	13.5

Medium colour. Soft and rustic on the nose. Medium body. No tannin. Fruity but rather hollow and unsophisticated. Original. But not special. Not bad plus.

CHÂTEAU BOYD-CANTENAC

2010-2025	15.0

Medium-full colour. A little sturdy but good fruit on the nose. Medium-full body. Good grip and good ripe fruit. It lacks a little nuance but good. The Pouget is fresher and more interesting.

CHÂTEAU BRANE-CANTENAC

2008-2020	16.0

Fullish colour. Good class and nice ample fruit on the nose. Medium to medium-full body. Good tannins. By no means a blockbuster but fresh, harmonious, complex and sophisticated. Positive finish.

Château Cantenac-Brown

2008-2018   13.5

Medium to medium-full colour. Soft and
rather boiled sweet fruity on the nose.
Medium body. Rather simple. No depth.

Château Dauzac

2007-2012   13.0

Full colour. Slightly austere on the nose.
There is a touch of chlorine – as in a
swimming pool – here. Medium to medium-
full body. It lacks a little richness and
sophistication. Not bad.

Château Deyrem-Valentin

2008-2015   14.5

Medium-full colour. Nicely soft and ripe on
the nose if without any great sophistication.
Medium to medium-full body. Quite good
fruit and balanced but not a lot of depth.

Château Durfort-Vivens

See Note

Medium-full colour. The nose has a slight
taint to it. Medium body. It doesn't seem to
be very concentrated. To be re-tasted.

Château Ferrière

2010-2028   17.0

Fullish colour. Complex, complete and classy
on the nose. Lovely fruit. Very silky.
Medium-full body. Balanced, concentrated,
fresh and very elegant. Lovely long finish.
Very good indeed.

Château Giscours

2007-2014   14.5

Full colour. Pretty nose. Fruity but not very
concentrated or profound. Forward as well
as a bit superficial. Pleasant ripe attack. But
not much to show after. Yet it is fresh. Quite
good plus.

Château La Gurgue

2010-2026   15.5

Medium-full colour. Slightly robust on the
nose. Ripe but a little unsophisticated. Better
as it evolved. Medium-full body. Good fruit
and grip. Good depth. Good plus.

Château Haut-Breton-Larigaudière

2009-2017   14.0

Medium-full colour. Ripe but quite oaky
nose. Medium-full body. A little tense. But
balanced and fruity. Quite good.

Château d'Issan

2007-2015   14.5

Full colour. A little lightweight but
reasonably fruity on the nose. Not as weedy
as usual. Pleasant. Even elegant. But short
attack. Only medium body. It lacks a bit of
concentration. Only quite good plus.

Château Kirwan

2010-2025   15.5

Full colour. Decent ripe fruit with a touch of
oak on the nose. Medium-full body. Rich. A
little unrelaxed but some very good fruit
underneath. Balanced too. Good plus.

Château Labégorce-Zédé

2009-2024   16.0

Fullish colour. Attractive, plump fruit on the
nose. Medium to medium-full body.
Balanced. Smooth. Nicely fresh. This has a
good long finish. Very good.

Château Lascombes

2012-2030   17.0

Medium-full colour. Fullish, rich, quite
sturdy nose. Yet good smooth style on
aeration. Fullish body. Very well balanced.
Rich, concentrated and sophisticated. Lots of
depth. Very good indeed.

Château Malescot-St-Exupéry

2010-2025   16.5

Medium-full colour. Quite a full, firm, rich
nose. Still a bit hidden. Fullish body. Rich.
Good tannins. Harmonious. Lots of depth.
This is very good plus. Lovely finish but not
enough for for fine.

Château Margaux

2012–2040	19.0

Full colour. Quite closed but immensely impressive on the nose. Very lovely fruit. Real depth of character here. Full body. Excellent balance. Great purity and splendid multi-dimensional flavours. Very, very long. Very fine plus.

Château Marquis de Terme

2008–2018	15.0

Full colour. Slightly earthy but plummy, gently oaky and even old viney on the nose. Underneath only medium body and not a lot of grip. Good but it lacks a bit of nuance at the end.

Château Monbrison

2009–2020	15.5

Fullish colour. Only medium weight, but ripe and stylish on the nose. Medium body. Good tannins. Ample, fruity attack. Attractive if no real complexity. But nice and fresh. Good plus.

Château Palmer

2010–2030	18.5

Full colour. This is very lovely. Ripe and rich, velvety and harmonious, complex and profound on the nose. Fullish body. Very good grip. Very good tannins. Backward. Very, very elegant, complex flavours. Very complex and harmonious. Lovely long finish.

Pavillon Rouge du Château Margaux

2010–2020	16.0

Medium-full colour. Quite classy. Good oak. Balanced nose. Very good indeed for a second wine. The class of its origin shines through. Medium-full body. Very good grip. Lovely fruit. Will keep well. Very good.

Château Pouget

2010–2028	15.5

Fullish colour. Good depth and fruit on the nose. Not too dense nose as it was in the past. Medium-full body. Rich and plump. Good tannins. Harmonious. Even some depth. Good plus.

Château Prieuré-Lichine

2008–2015	14.0

Fullish colour. Plump and fruity but not very classy on the nose. Medium to medium-full body. The ample fruit of the vintage but a lack of elegance. Reasonable balance. Quite good at best.

Château Rauzan-Gassies

2006–2010	12.5

Medium-full colour. Soft fruity nose. Not much depth or class. Medium body. Nothing much on the palate and not very sophisticated either. Forward.

Château Rauzan-Ségla

2010–2028	17.5

Fullish colour. Classy nose. Rich and concentrated. Fullish but with true Margaux velvet. Medium-full body. Ripe, balanced and stylish. Long. This has real depth. Fine.

Château Ségla

2005–2010	14.0

Medium-full colour. Soft but classy on the nose. Forward. Round. Medium body. Good fruit if no real depth. Very good for a second wine.

Château du Tertre

2008–2015	15.0

Fullish colour. Good fruit here but slightly forced on the nose. Medium body. Ripe but ungainly. Sweet but bitter as well. It lacks class. Not a great deal of acidity either. As it got more relaxed it showed rather better.

Château La Tour du Mons

2007–2013	13.5

Medium-full colour. Fruity nose but not a lot of depth and sophistication. Medium body. Pleasant but rather dull. One-dimensional. Forward.

SAINT-JULIEN

Château Beychevelle

2010–2024	15.5

Fullish colour. Ripe nose. Quite plump. Some style. But no great magic on the nose. Medium-full body. Ripe and balanced. But only one and half dimensions and amount of finesse. Good plus.

Château Branaire-Ducru

2010–2023	15.0

Fullish colour. Ripe but not very concentrated and powerful on the nose. Stylish though. Medium-full body. Ripe Cabernet fruit. Not a lot of grip. Nor depth. Correct but a bit dull.

Clos du Marquis

2010–2023	15.0

Fullish colour. A slight touch of mint on the nose. Good fruit. Fullish body. Balanced. It lacks a little character and complexity but balanced and well made. Good.

Château Ducru-Beaucaillou

2012–2030	19.0

Full colour. Very lovely nose. Very pure and classy. Still very youthful. Excellent fruit. Full body. Complete and very elegant. Multi-dimensional. Really very, very lovely. Very, very complex.

Château Gloria

2009–2018	14.5

Full colour. Ample and ripe on the nose if no great depth or class. Strangely this is more relaxed than the Saint-Pierre. Pleasant fruit if a little short. Quite good plus.

Château Gruaud Larose

2015–2035	18.0

Full colour. A big wine on the nose. Slightly clumsy. The tannins are a little green and vegetal. But there is richness underneath. Full body. Tannic. Very good grip. Very concentrated. Lots of substance here. Very long. Powerful. Fine plus.

Château Lagrange

2010–2023	15.5

Full colour. Ripe Cabernet nose. Good style here. Fullish body. Good grip. Not the greatest complexity or finesse. But good plus. A little forced at the end.

Château Langoa-Barton

2010–2030	16.5

Full colour. Seductive, ripe, feminine but concentrated and harmonious on the nose. Medium to medium-full body. Very aromatic. Balanced and stylish. But by no means a blockbuster. Lovely finish. Very good plus.

Château Léoville-Barton

2012–2030	18.5

Full colour. Splendid fruit on the nose. Rich, backward and profound. A very lovely fragrant, full bodied Cabernet wine. Much less austere than Léoville-Las-Cases. Very splendid, very ripe, concentrated fruit. Very fine.

Château Léoville-Las-Cases

2015–2035	19.0

Full colour. Rather austere but most impressive. Very lovely Cabernet fruit on the nose. Full body. Backward. Tannic. Most impressive fruit. Very good grip. This is not singing but it is potentially lovely.

Château Léoville-Poyferré

2010–2028	16.5

Full colour. Ample, ripe and oaky. More 'modern' in style than Léoville-Las-Cases (Michel Rolland rather than Jean-Claude Berrouet in a Saint-Julien context). Slightly more extracted. Good fruit but less class and less relaxed. Very good plus.

Château Saint-Pierre

2009–2016	13.5

Full colour. Slightly driven on the nose. Medium to medium-full body. Not a lot of grip. The fruit is a little bitter. Only a little tannin. This is disappointing. Raw at the end.

Château Talbot

2012-2028	16.5

Full colour. Lots of depth and style here. Lovely Cabernet fruit. Fullish bodied, tannic, ripe and concentrated. Lots of flavour at the end. Ample. Very satisfactory. This is very good plus.

PAUILLAC

Château d'Armailhac

2010-2025	16.0

Full colour. Ripe nose but surprisingly soft. It seems to lack grip. On the palate medium- to full-bodied, ripe, balanced and rather more exciting. Stylish too. Slightly bitter at the end but this will go. Very good.

Carruades de Lafite

2009-2018	14.5

Fullish colour. Fullish, meaty, rich nose. Medium weight. Some fruit. Some grip. But rather anonymous. There is class here though.

Château Clerc-Milon

2010-2025	15.5

Full colour. Like the d'Armailhac not very forceful on the nose. It lacks richness too, it seems. On the palate a little raw. But reasonably balanced and stylish. I prefer the d'Armailhac today.

Château Croizet-Bages

2008-2014	13.5

Full colour. Slightly bland on the nose. But reasonably pleasant style. Medium body. Not much tannin. Decent fruit but it lacks distinction. But at least not rustic.

Château Fonbadet

2010-2015	12.5

Full colour. Slightly lumpy and four-square on the nose. A bit over-macerated. Tough. Too much unripe tannin here. Not enough fruit. Ungenerous. Will it ever round off?

Les Forts de Latour

2009-2025	16.5

Full colour. Quite firm and Cabernet/Pauillac-y on the nose. Cool but not too austere. Fullish body. Ripe and classy. Much better than the Carruades. Well mannered. Full of interest. Very good plus.

Château Grand-Puy-Lacoste

2010-2030	18.0

Fullish colour. Relaxed, harmonious, ripe and generous on the nose. Very stylish. Medium-full body. Balanced, intense, nice and classy. Long and lovely. Not a blockbuster but fine plus.

Château Haut-Bages-Libéral

2010-2025	15.5

Full colour. Slightly raw but ripe nose. Good depth underneath. Medium-full body. A little tannin. Very good ripe fruit. This has good grip and plenty of style. Good plus.

Château Lynch-Bages

2011-2030	17.5

Full colour. A bit closed-in on the nose but plump and ripe and full. Full body on the palate. Some tannin. Vigorous. Rich and well balanced. Plenty of depth. Fine.

Château Pichon-Longueville

2012-2030	17.5

Full colour. Rich and meaty on the nose. Full body. Some tannin. Quite a big wine. A proper Pauillac. Good depth. Backward. Closed-in. Good grip. Long and positive. Fine.

Château Pichon-Longueville, Comtesse de Lalande

2008-2018	15.5

Full colour. Decent fruit on the nose. But a lack of the usual intensity and silkiness. Medium-full body. A slight touch of astringency. No middle palate here. It lacks concentration. Disappointing. No better than good plus.

Château Pontet-Canet

2011-2030   16.5

Full colour. Fullish, meaty, rich nose. Plenty
of substance and plenty of style here. Fullish
body. Good grip. Plenty of depth. Indeed
concentrated. Very good fruit. Long. Very
good plus.

SAINT-ESTÈPHE

Château Calon-Ségur

2009-2016   14.5

Medium-full colour. Ripe, caramelly and
chocolaty on the nose. Medium-full body.
The attack lacks a bit of class and
concentration. And the finish is a little
empty. Unsophisticated.

Château Cos d'Estournel

2010-2028   17.5

Full colour. Lots of concentration on the
nose. Lots of depth too. Fullish body. Rich.
Very ripe, almost exotic. Yet good grip.
Montrose is much more classic. This is much
more seductive. Fine.

Château Cos Labory

2008-2016   14.0

Fullish colour. Ripe and balanced if not very
sophisticated on the nose. Medium to
medium-full body. Slightly sturdy. Decent
fruit. It lacks elegance. Quite good at best.

Château Haut-Marbuzet

2009-2022   16.0

Medium-full colour. Rich, ripe and sexy on
the nose. Medium to medium-full body.
Oaky, ripe and succulent. Well balanced
fruit. An attractive example.

Château Lafon-Rochet

2012-2022   14.0

Full colour. Quite firm on the nose. But not
hard. Just a little austere. Medium-full body.
Some tannin. It lacks a bit of charm. It seems
a little green. Will this disappear as it rounds
off?

Château Lilian Ladouys

2008-2018   15.0

Fullish colour. Succulent nose. Reasonably
stylish. Nice and ripe. Slightly astringent on
the palate. Medium to medium-full body.
Good fruit. Easy to enjoy. It finishes well.
Good.

Château Montrose

2011-2030   17.5

Full colour. Classy Cabernet nose. Not a
blockbuster. But balanced and very ripe.
Fullish body. Very well balanced. Very lovely
cool Cabernet. Harmonious and long. Very
complete.

Château Les Ormes de pez

2010-2025   16.0

Full colour. Good richness on the nose. Some
style too. Medium-full body. Rich, ripe and
balanced. Rather more sophisticated than
usual. Lovely finish. Very good.

Château Phélan-Ségur

2008-2018   15.5

Fullish colour. Classy nose. Good fruit.
Only medium weight though. Medium-full
body. It could have done with a little more
richness on the attack but it finishes long and
positively. It has class too. Good plus.

FIRST GROWTHS AND SIMILAR

TASTED SEPARATELY (AND SOMETIMES FOR THE SECOND TIME)

CHÂTEAU AUSONE

2012-2040   19.0

Full colour. Very fine fruit on the nose. Ripe, rich, abundant and profoundly classy. Full-bodied. Some tannin. Very good grip. This is a big, concentrated example with a lot of quality and dimension. Very fine plus.

CHÂTEAU CHEVAL BLANC

2012-2040   19.0

Full colour. Rich and ample but on this occasion, at first, not as exciting as the Ausone. Fullish body. Some tannins. Plump and rich. Very good grip. Excellent follow-through. Very long. Very fine plus.

CHÂTEAU HAUT-BRION

2012-2040   19.0

Full colour. Very, very elegant, fragrant nose. Very lovely style and harmony. Fullish body. Very intense. Multi-dimensional. Not a blockbuster but very, very lovely fruit. Very long.

CHÂTEAU LAFITE

2012-2040   19.5

Very full colour. Very, very rich and still quite closed-in on the nose. Full body. Very, very rich. Marvellous fragrance and poise. Excellent harmony. Very, very long and lovely. Splendid finish. Very fine indeed.

CHÂTEAU LATOUR

2012-2040   20.0

Full colour. Exciting, concentrated, vigorous, fresh fine fruit on the nose. Full and firm. Full body. Very, very lovely pure Cabernet fruit. Great vigour and energy here. This is the wine of the vintage. Splendid depth and class. Marvellous finish.

CHÂTEAU MARGAUX

2012-2040   19.0

Full colour. Plump, ripe, rich and fragrant on the nose. Gently oaky. Really quite oaky on the palate. Fullish body. Very good fruit. Lots of dimension but not quite the grip and personality of the very best Pauillacs.

CHÂTEAU MOUTON-ROTHSCHILD

2012-2040   17.5

Full colour. Ample and ripe. Quite rich on the nose. Not as vigorous as the wines above though. Nor as concentrated. Fullish body. Some tannin. Fine but it lacks that extra excitement and completeness the other First Growths possess. Disappointing, as so often these days.

CHÂTEAU PÉTRUS

2014-2040   18.5

Full colour. Very concentrated. Very Merlot. Full and backward on the nose. Rich and full-bodied but not too dense or tannic on the palate. Very, very ripe. Almost sweet. Lush and seductive. Very fine.

1999

SIZE OF THE CROP:	6,806,674 HECTOLITRES.
VINTAGE RATING:	14.0 (RED WINES).
	16.0 (DRY WHITE WINES).
	15.0 (SWEET WINES).

Absolutely the largest harvest ever, though 2000 would come within a cellar-ull of it. The yield for the red wines was at 59.1 hl/ha, less than 1997. The white wine harvest was 879,133 hl (12.9 per cent of the total).

In the months after the harvest reports first began to circulate about the amount of rain in the 1999 vintage. Some two and a half times the norm (185 mm) had fallen in September, most of it right in the middle of the vintage. We were not led to expect very much. Growers' confidence in their wines, as they racked them off their pips and skins, was at a low ebb. Once again a rainy September had ruined the chances of a fine vintage. With the exception of 1997, blighted for other reasons, every vintage since 1990 had been at least to some extent washed out by a rainy September. Not since 1990 had the weather played fair, giving the growers a chance to make a great wine.

But as the wines settled down, and the blends were made, separating the *grand vin* from the rest, it began to be apparent that 1999 was by no means a disaster. By no means great, and certainly of no compelling justification whatsoever for buying *en primeur*, but not as poor as 1997. In the Médoc/Graves the 1999 vintage is not that far short of 1998 (1998 is a fine vintage in Saint-Émilion and Pomerol but only 'good' in the Médoc/Graves). On the Libournais side, especially in Pomerol, it is perhaps in general better than in 1996. The wines have no great structure, nor depth, concentration and grip. But they *do* have fruit, and this fruit, in the best examples, is balanced and attractive.

Unlike many vintages, the wines were easy to appreciate in cask. One could see where they were going: pleasant bottles, useful for restaurant lists, which would evolve in the medium term. Prices though, remained high. Unless you insisted on buying every vintage, or had to have every super-Pomerol in short supply in your cellar, there was no reason to buy 1999s *en primeur*.

THE WEATHER

It was a curious year. Usually when it is warm, it is dry and sunny; when it is wet it is often cold and windy. In 1999 it was wetter than normal, less sunny than normal, but it was still a full 2 °C warmer than normal. Thus, when the rains arrived in September, the fruit was ripe or almost ripe from the sugar/acid point of view, depending on location, and the phenols were nearly there as well.

After a rainy end to the 1998 growing season the winter was dry and reasonably cool. March was warm and largely dry; April wet, very warm at first, cool in the middle of the month and hotter later. This humid, almost tropical weather continued into May, necessitating serious spraying to prevent mildew – a continual fight against diseases, mainly cryptogamic, would be a pattern throughout the summer – and growth galloped ahead. The vine was ready to flower when the weather cleared up to give a week of hot, dry days between 23rd May and 1st June, the same as 1998 and 10 days ahead of the average.

The Merlot flowering was rapid and efficient, that of the Cabernets, which followed a week later in colder weather, a little more drawn out.

The *sortie*, however, had been prolific. The vine's nature is to produce fruit, and, left to itself, it would in 1999 have made 120 hl/ha without raising a sweat. Most serious growers pruned to six to eight buds, rubbed off the double buds on the reverse side of the cane, crop-thinned after the flowering and green-harvested twice, first when they de-leafed on one side, second, when they de-leafed on the other. Yet overall Bordeaux still produced over 59 hl/ha, excluding what Allan Sichel estimates as some 600,000 hl surplus to the legal limits, which would have been sold off for distilling. Yields among the classed growths and their equivalents range from 42 hl/ha in some of the most perfectionistic Libournais properties, to 58 hl/ha in the Médoc – before selection.

The remainder of June and most of July were dry and warm: isolated showers, but no real 30°C heat. With August and the *véraison* however, the humid conditions, plus the threat of mildew, returned again. Then, and this was the saving of the 1999s, warm dry weather set in again, and for almost a month, from shortly after Europe's eclipse of the sun on 11th August to early September, the conditions were perfect, temperatures up in the high 20s to low 30s every day. If only it had continued...

After the anticipation, the reckoning. The most brutal was in Saint-Émilion, on the west side of the plateau adjacent to the town (Clos Fourtet, Canon) and the vineyards below and to the north (the Beauséjours, Angélus, Fonroque etc.). Here a severe hailstorm on 5th September literally shredded the vineyards. Some 550 hectares were affected: 60 châteaux had, it seemed, lost most if not all of their crop.

Everyone rallied round, the remaining properties donated workers and harvesting machines. The solutions on offer were either to pick the lot, before the grapes went volatile, or pick the ripest and worst affected and spray the rest against rot (which would mean waiting a further fortnight before one was legally allowed to collect the remainder). Ets J-P Moueix took the noble decision to declassify their Château Fonroque and adjacent estates. In retrospect, other properties should have followed suit.

Meanwhile, the white wine harvest had already commenced: at the end of August at Haut-Brion, on the 3rd or 4th September in the rest of Pessac-Léognan, during a warm and sunny week which started on 6th September elsewhere. These dry white wines are very fine.

There was rain on Monday 14th, but after that a few days of sun. The red wine harvest got into full swing in Saint-Émilion and Pomerol, and some Merlots were collected in the Médoc, especially in Margaux, and in the Graves. Thanks to the fine end of August weather, and despite subsequent showers, sugars were high and the fruit was healthy. Many had Merlots vats of 14° alcohol and above. The concentrating machines were redundant.

Most growers on the Left Bank, however, had pencilled in Monday 20th September as their date to start the harvest. On this day as much as 100 mm of rain was recorded at the central weather forecasting and monitoring station at Bordeaux University. There was more rain on the Tuesday and Wednesday, and the weather continued unsettled for the remainder of the month. Not until Tuesday 5th October did it turn fine and sunny again. After the dry Graves, it was the Sauternes proprietors who would enjoy the best of the weather.

THE WINES

On the face of it, then, 1999 sounds like a bit of a washout as far as the red wines are concerned: more 1992 or 1993 than 1995, 1996 and 1998. In many ways this is perfectly correct. The wines do not have the structure of the finest of the Libournais of the previous year nor the best of the Médoc/Graves of the mid-1990s.

On the other hand, if one eliminates the 100 mm of rain which fell on 20th September, and puts the effect of the Saint-Émilion hailstorm aside, the September rainfall was not more than the 75 mm average. Add to that the very fine weather from mid-August to the beginning of

September (*août fait le moût*: August makes the must, as the locals say), and the fact that the gravelly soil of the Médoc and the Graves drains very efficiently, one can begin to get a different picture, one that is reflected in the character of the wines: no great depth, concentration, grip or structure, but in many cases very pleasant, even attractive fresh, ripe, plump fruit, at least a decent acidity, and, rather than a 'hole in the middle', the signature of most weaker vintages, a core of succulence, even of fat. Given the choice between a vintage with a lot of fruit and only medium weight (the 1999s) or the reverse, I know which I would choose.

REGIONAL VARIATIONS

A surprising feature of the 1999 red wine vintage is its consistency, and this coherence applies both geographically and hierarchically. There are no great wines, indeed few very fine wines, but encouragingly few very poor examples. Equally – the devastated sector of Saint-Émilion aside – and even here there are some worthy results – it is hard to single out a commune much better or seriously worse than the overall pattern. In April 2000 I sampled some very good *petits châteaux* at the laboratory of Michel Rolland in Catusseau and at the offices of Bill Blatch of Vintex, and at the table of other gurus such as Stéphane Derenoncourt and Louis Mitjaville in Saint-Émilion. There are some welcome if belated improvements noticeable among the lesser growths in Pomerol, if not in Saint-Émilion. If L'Arrosée, Clos Fourtet and Patrick Valette at the newly resurrected Château Berliquet can make very good wines in 1999, why are Fonplégarde, La Gaffelière and Trottevieille, all of which escaped the hail, so uninspiring? If Tertre-Roteboeuf, Troplong-Mondot and Pavie-Macquin are wines you would consistently earmark to purchase, why are so many of the rest of their peers not just dull, but rustic? There are some very good wines at the top levels in Pomerol, except that in 1999 they did not justify their high prices, good-value-for-money in Fronsac, on the other hand, and, by and large, good results in the Graves, with Château Haut-Brion simply stunning.

Which brings us to the Médoc. For very many years, if not for ever, the flights of Margaux and the southern Médoc, i.e. everything from Château Chasse-Spleen to Château La Lagune, have been the most heterogeneous of every single major Bordeaux vintage appreciation I have attempted. In the last few years this has begun to change. Perennial under-achievers have pulled their socks up: Brane-Cantenac, Durfort-Vivens, Boyd-Cantenac, Kirwan, and especially Ferrière. Given that Margaux, Palmer, Rauzan-Ségla and Malescot are always consistent, and the clutch of super-*bourgeois* (Chasse-Spleen, Poujeaux, Labégorce-Zédé, Angludet etc.) are usually noteworthy, the result is that 1999 in this part of the world (even at La Lagune and Cantemerle) is a welcome success. There are some enjoyable wines here for the medium term. Ferrière, Deyrem-Valentin and Labégorce-Zédé are my stars at sensible prices. The standout is Château Palmer, which I rate higher than Château Margaux in 1999.

Saint-Julien (and I include the classed growths in Saint-Laurent), as always, is consistent, and here are two of my three wines of the vintage, Léoville-Las-Cases and Léoville-Barton. Most of the rest are good too. Château Saint-Pierre, a bit of an under-performer recently, Langoa-Barton and Talbot all scored well. Ducru-Beaucaillou is elegant but a little light.

Pauillac, home to three of the *premiers crus*, is inconsistent. I love the class of Lafite, my fourth wine of the vintage with Châteaux Haut-Brion, Palmer and Léoville-Las-Cases. Latour is fine and was the group's first choice. Pichon-Lalande is disappointing for the second year in a row, so surprisingly is Grand-Puy-Lacoste. But Pontet-Canet is surprisingly good.

Saint-Estèphe offers no disappointments, but, as elsewhere with 1999, there were no stand-outs either. Cos-Labory is delicious and underrated. Phélan-Ségur is the pick of the *bourgeois*, with more personality than most, and Sociando-Mallet and Haut-Condissas showed well.

It is among the dry and sweet whites that 1999 finally reaches a level beyond the acceptable. The dry whites were gathered before the rain came in to dilute the effects of the fine weather in the four weeks after 15th August.

There are some great wines at the very top levels; wines which combine power, alcohol, richness and acidity. There are some very good wines all the way down the scale to the new-wave wines of the Premières Côtes and Entre-Deux-Mers.

The Sauternes are also very good. Not as splendid as the 1997s but better than 1998. The best of all? Climens, Rieussec, Sigalas-Rabaud and de Malle.

Prices

What worries me are the high prices now being asked for the top Bordeaux wines. Having been relatively stable during the 1991–1994 period, levels soared in 1995, again in 1996 and ridiculously so for the 1997s (Bordeaux goes mad, I commented at the time). They fell in 1999, but not by much, only to soar ahead in 2000.

Logic – but logic, as followers of the Bordeaux market will know, is not a concept which enters easily into the Bordelais' mentality – would suggest that for a decent but not special vintage such as 1999, and while there were still stocks of 1998 available (and even more of the less sought after 1997s) prices should fall. Buyers need an inducement to buy. Sellers outside Bordeaux need something to help encourage a market. What was required in 1999, might have been, in the case of the more fashionable wines, only a gesture, 15 per cent or so, which together with a 7.0 Dollar/Franc ratio and a 10.8 Pound/Franc ratio would have added up to a 25 per cent decrease on opening prices for the 1998s.

The difficulty is that, naturally, it is the high fliers, the First Growths, Super-Seconds and super-Libournais which tend to decide the market. These are precisely the properties which can sell all they produce, in all but the most disastrous vintages, at almost any price level they care to command. You could even have made a profit, albeit small, buying First Growth 1997s *en primeur*. What is forgotten, by those whose vineyards are outside this privileged sector, is that they live in quite a different world.

A gesture *was* made, by Jean Merlaut of Château Gruaud-Larose. Early in April this property came out at 136 Francs, a drop of 15 per cent on 1998s' 160FF. Lafon-Rochet followed, down from 85FF to 77FF. Until the Easter weekend (April 2000) that was about it, apart from the fact that, ominously, both Sociando-Mallet and Haut-Marbuzet, both super-*bourgeois*, came out at 100 Francs: the previous year's price. Meanwhile Ets. J-P Moueix, one of the few proprietors who remain logical and sensible, had, as well as deciding to declassify Fonroque and others, also made a gesture in the right direction.

As the days moved on, a pattern began to emerge. The less fashionable made a token gesture; those with bigger heads, delusions of glory or greater ability to blackmail the Bordelais merchants did not. Nor did many good-value-for-money minor châteaux, whose prices had remained more stable over recent years.

The net result – which would be even more exaggerated in 2000 – was a further widening of the price gap between the 30 or 40 fashionable wines and the rest.

Today in the autumn of 2003, prices remain what they were in June 2000. There is little interest in the vintage.

The Tasting

The following range of red wines were sampled at The Crown Inn, Southwold in January 2003.

Saint-Émilion

Château L'Arrosée

2006–2014   16.0

Fullish colour. Good restrained style here on the nose. Fullish body. Good ripe tannins. Meaty and ripe on the palate. Good substance. Very good.

Château Ausone

2010–2025   18.5

Full colour. Full, rich and concentrated on the nose. Just a bit solid. Splendid on the palate. Medium-full body. Rich and intense. Very good fruit. Slightly oaky. Very good grip. This has vigour, depth and class. Very fine.

Château Barde-Haut

NOW–2011   15.0

Fullish colour. Ripe, mellow, quite oaky nose. Good acidity and class. On the palate it lacks a bit of grip. Medium-full body. Slightly flat at the start. Better on the finish. Good.

Château Beau-Séjour-Bécot

NOW–2010   14.0

Full colour. Slightly corked on the nose. Rich and fullish bodied nevertheless. Underneath decent fruit and grip. Slightly one-dimensional but quite good.

Château Belair

DRINK SOON   11.0

Medium-full colour. Quite elegant but light and slightly lean, if fragrant on the nose. Weak on the palate. Forward. Feeble.

Château Berliquet

NOW–2011   15.0

Medium-full colour. Good rich nose. Good grip too. Stylish and well-made. A slight bitterness on the attack. But medium-full body and with good tannins. At least some acidity. Good.

Château Canon

DRINK UP   11.0

Full colour. Slightly thin and lean on the nose. Unexciting. Light and astringent on the palate. It should have been declassified.

Château Canon-La-Gaffelière

NOW–2012   16.0

Fullish colour. Round, ripe, attractive nose. Medium-full body. It lacks a bit of zip and personality. But good fruit. It finishes better than it starts. Very good.

Château Cheval Blanc

2008–2018   17.5

Fullish colour. Rich, full, mocha-flavoured on the nose. Quite light on the palate after the Ausone. Good classy, balanced fruit but an absence of real concentration, grip and vigour. Fine at best.

Le Dôme

2006–2017   16.0

Full colour. Rich but solid, tannic nose. Good depth underneath. Fullish body. Quite tannic. But good concentrated fruit. Very good grip. Long finish. This is very good.

Château La Dominique

NOW–2009   13.5

Fullish colour. Slightly flat on the nose. It lacks zip and real richness. Boring. Medium to medium-full body. Slightly lacking acidity too. Quite ripe and fruity but it lacks zip and personality. Fair.

Château Figeac

NOW–2013   16.0

Fullish colour. Good clean, pure nose. Not a great deal of weight but classy. Medium to medium-full body. Ripe and quite fat. Not a lot of vigour but balanced, classy and long. Very good.

Château Fombrauge

NOW–2009	13.5

Medium to medium-full colour. Ripe but slightly anonymous nose. Some substance but not much depth. Medium weight. Not much tannin, nor grip. Quite pleasant but boring. No character. Not bad plus.

La Forge

2006–2016	15.0

Full colour. A rich but quite solid nose. Oaky. Fullish body. Meaty. This is slightly forced but it is good. Ripe and positive at the end.

Clos Fourtet

NOW–2012	15.0

Full colour. Decently fresh and stylish and substantial. A good effort for a vineyard that got the brunt of the hail. Medium-full body. Good tannins. Decent fruit. Good positive finish.

Château Grand-Mayne

NOW–2011	14.0

Full colour. Some substance here but a bit anonymous on the nose. Medium body. A little bitter. A little astringent. But decent fruit and grip. Quite good.

Château Magdelaine

DRINK SOON	12.0

Medium to medium-full colour. Light, fruity nose. No great weight or depth here. Rather light and wimpy. It will get astringent. It should have been declassified. Short and non-descript.

Château Monbousquet

NOW–2010	14.0

Full colour. Aromatic nose. A touch of nutmeg and orange peel. Medium body. Very perfumed. Quite oaky. But all make-up and nothing underneath. Pleasant though. Not too extracted. Quite good.

La Mondotte

2006–2016	16.5

Full colour. Good depth and richness here on the nose. Fullish body. Ripe. Good tannins. Decent grip. Very ample, concentrated fruit. This is very good plus.

Château Pavie

2006–2014	14.0

Fullish colour. Solid and lumpy on the nose. Fullish body. Good tannins. A lot of oak. At the limit of over-extraction. Hot at the end. Ungainly. Quite good at best.

Château Pavie-Decesse

NOW–2009	11.0

Fullish colour. Ripe nose but rather perfumed and superficial. Very tannic on the palate. Rather stewed. Ungainly and unbalanced. It will get astringent.

Château Pavie-Macquin

2006–2015	17.0

Full colour. Fullish, quite profound nose. Very good style. Fullish body. Concentrated. Good tannin. Very good grip. Lots of depth here. Rich, complex and long. Very good indeed.

Château Quinault L'Enclos

NOW–2009	13.5

Fine colour. Plump, oaky nose. Medium body. Rather one-dimensional on the palate. A little flat at the end. It lacks depth. Not bad plus.

Château Rol Saint-Valentin

NOW–2011	15.0

Full colour. Rich and oaky but not a lot of depth and class on the nose. Fullish body. Getting soft. Ripe and with plenty of charm on the palate. A well-made wine from a so-so terroir. Good.

Château Soutard

NOW–2008	13.0

Medium-full colour. Good nose. Nicely austere. But rather dilute and astringent on the palate. This is only medium-bodied. It lacks grip and definition. Not special.

CHÂTEAU TERTRE-ROTEBOEUF

NOW–2017	17.0

Medium-full colour. Ripe, rich and with very good depth on the nose. Fullish-bodied without being dense. Very good grip. Lovely fruit. Individual and long. Very good indeed.

CHÂTEAU TROPLONG-MONDOT

2006–2015	15.5

Fullish colour. A slightly reduced/sweaty nose. A bit dense and tannic, if not stewed on the palate. This hides the fruit. The finish is positive though. Indeed ripe and vigorous. Good plus. It needs time.

CHÂTEAU TROTTEVIEILLE

DRINK SOON	12.5

Full colour. Slightly thin and sweaty on the nose. Rather light and fruitless on the palate. No class. No concentration. Nothing here. Poor.

CHÂTEAU DE VALANDRAUD

NOW–2012	15.0

Full colour. Fresh on the nose. Good rich fruit. Attractive. It even has depth. Brettanomyces flavours though. It is ample and fruity on the attack but then it tails off a bit. There could have been more grip. Good at best.

POMEROL

CHÂTEAU BEAUREGARD

2007–2015	14.0

Fullish colour. Slightly ungenerous but balanced and fruity on the nose. It lacks just a bit of richness. Fullish body. Some tannin. A bit sturdy. No depth and not enough grip. Nor richness. Four-square. Quite good at best.

CHÂTEAU LE BON PASTEUR

2006–2016	17.0

Very full colour. Cool and very ripe indeed. Lovely grip. This is very well made. The nose is most impressive. Medium-full body. Very good tannins. Very good grip. Fresh and alive. Lovely. Hats off for what it is!

CHÂTEAU BOURGNEUF

2007–2016	15.0

Medium-full colour. Slightly dense on the nose but plenty of fruit. Slightly tough and tannic on the palate. As much astringency. Yet good grip. Not dense. Good fruit too. It needs time. Good.

CHÂTEAU CLINET

2007–2014	14.0

Full colour. Slightly solid. Slightly four-square nose. Quite substantial. Rather dense. Medium-full body. Rather astringent on the follow-through. Plenty of fruit but rather unbalanced. Quite good.

CHÂTEAU LA CONSEILLANTE

NOW–2010	15.0

Fullish colour. Round, ripe, stylish and ample on the nose, but not as big as most in this flight. Medium to medium-full body. Not much tannin. Good fruit but it tails off and it lacks depth and personality on the follow-through. Merely good.

CHÂTEAU LA CROIX DE GAY

NOW–2010	13.5

Full colour. Frank, fruity nose. Medium body. A bit simple. Fruity and pleasant. But no real depth. Forward too. Not bad plus.

CHÂTEAU LA CROIX DU CASSE

NOW–2008	13.0

Medium-full colour. Light and slightly weedy on the nose. Light and slightly astringent on the palate. Slightly fruity but not that much. Forward. Fair at best.

CLOS L'ÉGLISE

2007–2016	16.0

Full colour. Full and oaky on the nose. Slightly solid. Slightly dense. Slightly four-square. Medium to medium-full body but rather tannic on the attack. Better on the finish where there is some very good ripe fruit. Slightly unbalanced but very good.

Château L'Église-Clinet

2009–2025　　　　　　　　　　18.5

Full colour. Fine nose. Lots of concentration. Splendid depth. This has lovely fruit and is really very impressive. Full-bodied and backward. Fat and impressive. A lot of substance here. Yet not a bit over-concentrated or over-macerated. Very fine.

Château L'Évangile

2008–2025　　　　　　　　　　19.0

Full colour. Very lovely, rich, concentrated, balanced, classy nose. This is really excellent. This is delicious. Full body. Very poised. Rich, concentrated, classy and very long and complex. Very fine plus.

Château La Fleur de Gay

2006–2016　　　　　　　　　　17.5

Full colour. Ripe, oaky, generous and surprisingly stylish and balanced on the nose. Medium-full body. Very Merlot. Very ripe and rich. Good follow-through. Long. Fine.

Château La Fleur-Pétrus

2008–2020　　　　　　　　　　17.5

Fullish colour. Good style and good concentration. Very lovely fruit on the nose. Fullish body. Very good tannins. This is balanced and classy. Quite firm still. Good grip. Fine.

Château Gazin

NOW-2013　　　　　　　　　　16.0

Full colour. Fresh, plump, stylish nose. Medium-full body. Not the greatest of depth and concentration but ripe, long, harmonious and classy. Very good.

Château La Grave

2006–2018　　　　　　　　　　15.5

Medium-full colour. Plump, balanced and attractive on the nose. Medium-full body. Ripe and ample. Very good grip. Good tannins. Positive. Quite concentrated. No lack of class. Quite good plus.

Château Lafleur

2007–2020　　　　　　　　　　18.0

Medium-full colour. Very lovely fruit on the nose. Rich, profound and very classy. Medium-full body. Not as big as it has been. Ripe and rich, balanced and intense. Very long. Fine plus.

Château Latour-à-Pomerol

2006–2016　　　　　　　　　　16.0

Fullish colour. Rich, fat, classy and quite concentrated on the nose. Not as much zip or as much fruit as La Fleur-Pétrus. But medium- to full-bodied and ample. Not much better than the Château La Grave today on the palate. Yet the finish is good.

Château Petit-Village

2007–2014　　　　　　　　　　15.5

Very full colour. Quite extracted but not very ample. Four-square. Fullish weight. Some tannin. Ripe but slightly anonymous. Better than it has been though. Rich, in fact, at the end. Good plus.

Le Pin

2006–2015　　　　　　　　　　16.0

Full colour. Very Merlot on the nose. Rich and almost sweet. Only medium body. Ripe. Violet and raspberry flavours. Not a lot of tannin. Not enough depth though. Very good but not special.

Château Rouget

2007–2015　　　　　　　　　　14.0

Full colour. Rich but quite substantial, even solid on the nose. Rich and fullish-bodied and tannic on the palate. Slightly tough. A bit ungainly. Decent fruit underneath though. Quite good.

Château Trotanoy

2007–2020　　　　　　　　　　18.5

Fullish colour. Lovely fruit on the nose. Really classy and really concentrated. Fullish weight. Very, very ripe. Splendid fruit. Very good acidity too. This is rich and complete, long and very stylish. Very fine.

VIEUX CHÂTEAU CERTAN

2009–2025	19.0

Full colour. Impressive nose. Very, very lovely concentrated fruit. Very good tannins. Ripe, rich and concentrated. Fullish body. Very good tannins. Very lovely profound fruit. Splendid depth. Multi-dimensional. Very fine.

GRAVES

BAHANS HAUT-BRION

2006–2016	16.0

Fullish colour. Gently fruity, classy nose. Complex. Medium weight. Ripe and quite flowery. Good grip. Long and stylish. Very good.

CHÂTEAU BOUSCAUT

NOW-2010	13.5

Medium-full colour. Decent fruit on the nose, and a little oak. Medium body. A little astringent, but fruity and quite forward. Better on the finish than on the attack. Not bad plus.

CHÂTEAU CARBONNIEUX

NOW-2009	13.5

Medium-full colour. Soft, round, quite evolved nose. Medium body. A little neutral. Some fruit but rather one-dimensional. It lacks grip. Forward. Not bad plus.

DOMAINE DE CHEVALIER

2008–2020	18.0

Full colour. Subtle, cedary-rich nose. Lovely balance. Medium-full body. Lovely, complex, unaggressive but persistent flavours. Very good fruit. Long and sophisticated. Fine plus.

CHÂTEAU DE FIEUZAL

2007–2016	15.0

Full colour. Rich, ample, succulent nose. Fullish body. Good oakiness. Rich but a little raw on the palate. Good grip. It lacks a little class but good.

CHÂTEAU HAUT-BAILLY

2008–2018	16.5

Full colour. Lots of depth here. Rich. Very good acidity. Medium-full body. Ripe tannins. Very good grip. Lovely concentrated fruit. Rich, long and classy. Very good plus.

CHÂTEAU HAUT-BERGEY

2006–2012	14.0

Medium-full colour. Some oak on the nose. Some substance but it lacks a little richness. A bit four-square. Medium body. Decent ripe fruit on the palate. Quite sweet, in fact. Balanced. It lacks a bit of real finesse but quite good.

CHÂTEAU HAUT-BRION

2009–2030	19.5

Fullish colour. A nose of great distinction. Not a blockbuster but rich, concentrated, classy and very, very lovely fruit. This is substantiated on the palate. Fullish body. Very intense. Very poised, very long and of very high class.

CHÂTEAU LA LOUVIÈRE

2006–2013	15.0

Medium-full colour. Plump, attractive, accessible fruit on the nose. Medium to medium-full body. Good style. A little oak. Quite rich. Good grip and depth. Good.

CHÂTEAU MALARTIC-LAGRAVIÈRE

2007–2014	15.5

Fullish colour. Good depth here on the nose. Nice touch of oak as well. Medium-full body. Rich. Good depth. Even some concentration. Good grip too. This has style. Good plus.

CHÂTEAU LA MISSION HAUT-BRION

2010–2025	18.5

Very full colour. Very lovely, classy, concentrated fruit on the nose. Lots of depth. Full body. Very good tannins. Excellent grip. Very elegant, concentrated fruit. Splendid harmony. This has real depth. Very long and complex. Very lovely. Very fine.

Château Pape-Clément

2008–2018	16.0

Full colour. Full, oaky, quite macerated nose. Not too overstated. Fullish body. Rich. A little four-square. Good depth and grip though. It finishes well. Very good.

Château Smith Haut-Lafitte

NOW-2010	13.5

Medium-full colour. Quite oaky on the nose. Not a great deal of concentration though, or weight. Medium body. Not much depth or succulence. Decently balanced but essentially boring. Quite forward. Not bad plus.

Château La Tour Haut-Brion

2008–2020	17.5

Good full colour. Full, rich, classy, gently oaky nose. Medium-full body. Good tannins. Lovely fruit. Distinctly elegant. Very long and harmonious. Delicious. Fine quality.

Haut-Médoc & Moulis

Château Camensac

2006–2012	13.5

Fullish colour. Ripe and oaky but not much finesse on the nose. Medium-full body. The tannins are a little astringent and the wine lacks grip. Some fruit but a bit short and dry. Unexciting.

Château Cantemerle

2006–2013	14.0

Medium-full colour. Quite substantial but not a lot of distinction on the nose. On the palate medium body, a little tannin but not a lot of grip. Pretty fruit but it lacks a little distinction. Quite good at best.

Château Chasse-Spleen

2007–2014	15.0

Fullish colour. Full, rich, aromatic and gently oaky on the nose. Good depth here. Medium-full body. Quite ripe, but not as promising on the palate. Good grip. It just lacks a bit of freshness. Good though.

Château La Lagune

2006–2016	15.5

Medium-full colour. Soft, quite developed nose. Quite oaky but not much concentration. Medium body. Easy to drink. Nicely fruity and harmonious. Good length and style. But not as much depth as usual. Good plus.

Château Lanessan

2006–2012	13.5

Medium-full colour. Some fruit and some substance on the nose. But not much depth or class. Medium body. Rather unsophisticated and with slightly unripe tannins. Decent acidity. But no distinction. Not bad plus.

Château Sociando-Mallet

2009–2021	16.0

Fullish colour. Rich, Cabernet-flavoured, ripe, slightly oaky nose. Good grip. Most impressive. Medium-full body. Nice and rich and balanced on the palate. Ripe tannins. Good energy. Very good.

Château La Tour Carnet

2006–2012	13.5

Full colour. Rich and full on the nose. Good backbone. On the palate this is a little dense and tannic. Medium to medium-full body. Slightly dry and it lacks charm.

Margaux

Château d'Angludet

2008–2017	14.5

Medium-full colour. Good rich nose but slightly sturdy. Fullish body. Well-made. Just a little tough still. The tannins could have been a little riper. But good grip and good fruit. Quite good plus.

Château Boyd-Cantenac

2009–2019	16.0

Fullish colour. Nice rich nose. Not too stewed for once. Better than it has been for years. Fullish body. Good grip. Plump, fruity and long. Plenty of depth. Very good.

CHÂTEAU BRANE-CANTENAC

2008–2015	16.5

Full colour. Good succulent, classy fruit on the nose. Fullish body. Good oak. Rich and succulent. Good freshness. It doesn't have the class of the very best but good length and complexity. Very good plus.

CHÂTEAU CANTENAC-BROWN

2007–2012	13.5

Medium-full colour. Slightly solid, slightly ungainly on the nose but some fruit. Medium-full body. It lacks grace and personality. It also lacks a bit of grip. Boring.

CHÂTEAU DAUZAC

NOW-2009	12.0

Medium-full colour. Slightly lean on the nose. Medium body. Rather astringent. This has dried out. Not special.

CHÂTEAU DEYREM-VALENTIN

2007–2015	15.0

Fullish colour. Good plump nose. No great weight but attractive fruit. Medium to medium-full body. Ripe. Good fruit. Decent balance. Lots of charm. It finishes long. This is good.

CHÂTEAU DURFORT-VIVENS

2007–2017	15.5

Full colour. High-toned nose. Good fruit. Good style. Medium-full body. Ripe and plump. It lacks a little nuance but clean, fresh and positive at the end. Good plus.

CHÂTEAU FERRIÈRE

2008–2020	17.0

Full colour. Good oaky, subtle fruit on the nose. Medium-full body. Ripe tannins. Very good acidity. Fresh and with good richness and complexity on the palate. Long. Very good indeed.

CHÂTEAU GISCOURS

NOW-2009	13.0

Medium-full colour. Thin on the nose. Neither depth nor class. Light on the palate. Some fruit but no backbone. Not much distinction either. Forward. A disappointment.

CHÂTEAU LA GURGUE

2008–2018	15.0

Medium-full colour. Quite rich. Just a little solid on the nose. Medium-full colour. Not too solid on the palate. Good fruit. Not as subtle as Château Ferrière but long and satisfying. Balanced and with good depth. Good.

CHÂTEAU D'ISSAN

DRINK SOON IF AT ALL	11.0

Full colour. Light, slightly anonymous nose. Some volatile acidity. Thin. Astringent. Horrid.

CHÂTEAU KIRWAN

2008–2017	15.5

Full colour. Plump nose with a touch of new oak if not much class. Medium to medium-full weight, fresh, balanced and gently oaky. Stylish and charming. Good positive finish. Good plus.

CHÂTEAU LABÉGORCE-ZÉDÉ

2007–2016	14.5

Full colour. Plump, ripe and quite full on the nose. Medium to medium-full body. Ripe and round. A little tannin. It lacks a little grip. But the fruit is good and the wine is not short. Quite good plus.

CHÂTEAU LASCOMBES

2006–2010	12.5

Medium to medium-full colour. Slightly farmyardy on the nose. Medium-full weight. Unclean. A little astringent. It tails off on the palate. Even if this is not a true bottle I don't think this will ever excite.

CHÂTEAU MALESCOT SAINT-EXUPÉRY

2009–2021	16.0

Full colour. Sturdy nose. Good richness. Fullish on the palate. Rich. Plenty of grip and depth. Not that classy though, but the finish is long and generous. Very good.

CHÂTEAU MARGAUX

2008–2018	17.0

Full colour. A bit edgy on the nose. Rather pinched at present. This is fullish-bodied, but it lacks a bit of energy and concentration. There is plenty of fruit. Yet it is all a bit flat and even, by First Growth standards, dilute and short. Merely very good indeed.

CHÂTEAU MONBRISON

2007–2017	16.0

Medium to medium-full colour. Ripe, stylish and fruity on the nose, though no great weight. Medium-full body. Round, ripe, balanced and stylish. Very well-made. Long and complex. Lovely fruit. Very good.

CHÂTEAU PALMER

2009–2025+	19.0

Full colour. Very lovely nose. Gently oaky. Rich and complex, profound and elegant. This is super. Medium-full body. Quietly complex and composed. Really splendid ripe, rich, concentrated, multi-dimensional fruit. Very harmonious. Very long. Very fine plus.

CHÂTEAU POUGET

2008–2016	14.0

Full colour. Fullish nose. Not as oaky or as attractive as Boyd-Cantenac though. This sample is a bit corked. Some fruit and quality. Good balance. Quite good at best perhaps.

CHÂTEAU PRIEURÉ-LICHINE

2006–2011	13.0

Medium-full colour. Slightly anonymous on the nose. Some fruit. Some substance. Medium body. It lacks grace. A little astringent. Dull and a little short. Disappointing.

CHÂTEAU RAUZAN-SÉGLA

2008–2021	17.5

Medium-full colour. Refined, cool, complex, balanced nose with a touch of oak. Very well balanced. Medium-full body. Very classy. Very harmonious. This is long and complex. Lovely finish. Fine quality.

CHÂTEAU DU TERTRE

NOW–2010	13.0

Full colour. Some fruit on the nose. Not much character, class or depth though. Light-medium body. Not much grip or character on the palate. Boring. Rather short.

CHÂTEAU LA TOUR DE MONS

2006–2011	13.5

Fullish colour. Soft nose. Ripe. But not much grip. Medium body. A little unsophisticated. Reasonable length on the palate. But it lacks definition and class.

CHÂTEAU VINCENT

2007–2012	13.0

Fullish colour. Fullish nose. A little pinched but some fruit here. Medium-full body. Slightly astringent. A little stewed. It lacks charm and balance. Some fruit though. Not bad.

SAINT-JULIEN
CHÂTEAU BEYCHEVELLE

2007–2016	14.0

Full colour. Pleasant, ripe, medium-full nose. It lacks a little distinction. Medium body. Some tannin. Not much depth or concentration. Nor zip. Fruity but boring. Quite good at best.

CHÂTEAU BRANAIRE

2009–2020	16.0

Full colour. Good fullish, rich Cabernet Sauvignon nose. Fullish body on the palate. Good tannins. Good grip. Not quite the individuality and personality of the top Saint-Juliens but fresh, balanced and very good.

Château Ducru-Beaucaillou

2009–2025   17.5

Full colour. Rich, complete, very elegant nose. Not a blockbuster by any means, it seems. This is very discreet at first. But underneath it is very intense, very harmonious and very classy. Medium-full body. Very long, lingering finish. But not enough punch for better than fine.

Château Gloria

2008–2014   13.0

Full colour. Good stylish, medium-full, fruity nose. This has a slight chemical taint the Saint-Pierre does not have. Medium-full body. Slightly astringent. Decent fruit and grip underneath. Not bad.

Château Gruaud-Larose

2012–2030   17.5

Full colour. Tight and tannic on the nose. Very backward. Big, full bodied, sturdy and tannic on the palate. Plenty of rich fruit. Good grip. It needs time, as always. And slightly solid at present, as always. But the tannins are not too austere. Fine.

Château Lagrange

2009–2022   16.5

Medium-full colour. Not a blockbuster but good, ripe Cabernet Sauvignon nose. Fullish body. Very good grip. Very good fruit and very good tannins. This is pure and clean and very impressive. Very good plus.

Château Langoa-Barton

2009–2022   17.5

Fullish colour. Lovely perfumed nose. Very Cabernet Sauvignon. Very ripe. Surprising intensity. Medium-full weight. Splendidly balanced. This is a very lovely, harmonious, classy example. Very long. Fine.

Château Léoville-Barton

2011–2028   18.5

Full colour. Less backward than Léoville-Las-Cases. Very lovely, concentrated Cabernet fruit. Very classy. Fullish body. Very harmonious. Excellent tannins. Very concentrated, very classy finish. Very fine.

Château Léoville-Las-Cases

2012–2030   19.0

Full colour. Very profound, very Cabernet Sauvignon nose. Very Latour-ish. Splendid class. Lovely balance. Really very impressive. Full-bodied, tannic, rich and profound. This is backward but splendid. Very, very long and lovely. Very fine plus.

Château Léoville-Poyferré

2008–2020   17.0

Medium-full colour. Good fruit but a slight touch of over-solid tannins on the nose – too much *vin de presse*? Better on the palate. Fullish body. Some tannin. Good grip. Not the concentration of Léoville-Las-Cases or Léoville-Barton but balanced and very attractive. It just lacks a little zip. Very good indeed.

Château Saint-Pierre

2009–2025   17.0

Fullish colour. Rich, fullish, oaky nose. Medium-full body. Round, ripe, very elegant, harmonious fruit. Not too big. Quite accessible. Creamy rich at the end. Very good indeed.

Château Talbot

2009–2022   16.5

Full colour. Rich, ample, fullish nose. Fullish body. Good oak. Lovely concentrated, classy fruit. Very good attack. The finish is rich and long. Very good plus.

Pauillac
Château d'Armailhac

2007–2014   15.0

Fullish colour. Ample nose. A touch dry. But good substance. Medium-full body on the palate. Pleasantly fruity. But no great grip or depth. Slightly dry at the end. Yet not short. Merely good.

Carruades de Lafite

2008–2019   16.0

Fullish colour. Quite substantial, but good ripe fruit on the nose. Medium-full colour. Good tannins. This is ripe, generous and has good acidity. Long finish. Very good.

CHÂTEAU CLERC-MILON

2007–2014	15.0

Medium-full colour. Good ripe succulent fruit on the nose if without much depth. Medium to medium-full body. Accessible, pretty fruit but one dimensional, even slightly short. Good at best.

CHÂTEAU CROIZET-BAGES

2006–2010	13.0

Medium-full colour. Some development. Rather artisanal on the nose. Some fruit on the palate. Medium body. A little astringent and not very classy. But not bad.

CHÂTEAU DUHART-MILON

2009–2021	16.0

Medium-full colour. Rich, chunky, quite oaky nose. Fullish body on the palate. Good tannins. Fresh and if quite sturdy, certainly of very good quality. Good length. Nicely rich and ample. Just needs time.

CHÂTEAU FONBADET

2006–2010	12.5

Medium-full colour. Some development. Rather artisanal on the nose. A bit lumpy and tannic. Coarse and angular. Clumsy, dry and pretty poor on the palate.

LES FORTS DE LATOUR

2009–2021	16.0

Fullish colour. Classy nose. Firm and backward. Not a bit green though. Good Cabernet Sauvignon flavours. Medium-full body. Good tannins. Nicely ripe and with good acidity. Slightly four-square at the end. Very good.

CHÂTEAU GRAND-PUY-LACOSTE

2008–2018	16.0

Fullish colour. Not as impressive on the nose as it should be. It seems a bit weak. Yet ripe and full of fruit. Medium-full body. This has very good fruit but it lacks a bit of grip and backbone. Yet long and classy at the end. But too slight. Very good at best.

CHÂTEAU HAUT-BAGES-LIBÉRAL

2009–2018	15.5

Full colour. Slightly chunky and tannic on the nose. But good fruit underneath. Slightly tough on the palate. Medium to medium-full body. Some tannin. Good grip. It lacks a little distinction. But good plus.

CHÂTEAU HAUT-BATAILLEY

2007–2015	15.0

Medium-full colour. A bit lightweight on the nose but fresh and balanced. Like the Grand-Puy-Lacoste this is classy but rather wimpy. The finish is long and ripe and even rich. But there is not enough structure and grip. Good at best.

CHÂTEAU LATOUR

2009–2025	19.0

Full colour. The nose is unexpectedly clumsy. Curiously curate's egg. On the palate the attack doesn't disclose much quality but the follow-through is delicious. Is this just a phase? Splendidly classy fruit and very long at the end.

CHÂTEAU LYNCH-BAGES

2008–2018	15.5

Full colour. Chunky nose. But not a lot of distinction. Medium-full body. Quite fat, spicy-mocha flavours. It lacks a bit of zip. Some astringency. It lacks flair too. Ample and sexy though. So good plus.

CHÂTEAU MOUTON-ROTHSCHILD

2009–2020	17.5

Full colour. Rich and concentrated if not that distinctive on the nose. Medium-full body. Good tannins. Quite alive and vigorous. Good fruit if not that concentrated. Yet long and complex. Fine.

CHÂTEAU PICHON-LONGUEVILLE

2009–2020	17.0

Full colour. Rich and full and with some tannin, but rather more class on the nose than Lynch-Bages. Fullish body. Nicely fresh. This has good Cabernet fruit and a lot more class and distinction than Lynch-Bages. Long. Very good indeed.

CHÂTEAU PICHON-LALANDE

2008–2016   16.0

Medium-full colour. Fragrant on the nose. Very good fruit but not much depth or intensity. Medium weight. Ripe tannins. But curiously one dimensional for Pichon-Lalande. Forward. Classy but a little weak. Very good at best.

CHÂTEAU PONTET-CANET

2010–2022   16.0

Very full colour. Ripe, rich, stylish nose. Not a blockbuster but very good poised fruit. Quite full-bodied. Good tannins. Very good acidity. Fresh, ripe, long and vigorous. Very good.

SAINT-ESTÈPHE

CHÂTEAU CALON-SÉGUR

2007–2018   15.0

Medium-full colour. Good fresh, balanced, classy nose. But not a great deal of depth or complexity. Medium-full body. Good tannins. Decent fruit. But it lacks zip. Rather dul. Good balanced though and a positive finish. Good.

CHÂTEAU COS D'ESTOURNEL

2009–2025   18.0

Full colour. Ripe, complex, classy nose. Lots of lush, succulent fruit. Fullish, complex, rich and voluptuous. Good tannins. Long and complex. Excellent balance. Very fine finish. Fine plus.

CHÂTEAU COS LABORY

2007–2017   14.5

Fullish colour. Ripe, plump, quite stylish nose. Medium to medium-full weight. Soft, fruity and gentle. It could have had a bit more zip though. Quite good plus.

CHÂTEAU HAUT-MARBUZET

2007–2017   15.5

Full colour. Rich, lush, oaky nose. Similar on the palate. Medium-full body. Ripe tannins. Sweetish. Exotic. Long. Balanced. Individual. Good plus.

CHÂTEAU LAFON-ROCHET

2009–2019   15.0

Fullish colour. Full, Cabernet nose. Good depth and class. Fullish body. Good tannins. Quite concentrated. But just a little one-dimensional. A little stewed perhaps too. Yet the finish is positive. Good.

CHÂTEAU MONTROSE

2009–2022   17.0

Fullish colour. Fresh, quite Cabernet nose. Good depth and class. Full body. Good tannins. Ripe and rich. This is elegant and has very good grip. Sophisticated. Long. Very good indeed.

CHÂTEAU LES ORMES DE PEZ

2007–2015   14.0

Medium to medium-full colour. Aromatic. Slightly loose-knit. Slightly spicy nose. Medium-full body. Slightly astringent. Not a lot of class. But decent balance. A little mean at the end. It lacks charm. Quite good.

CHÂTEAU PHÉLAN-SÉGUR

2007–2019   15.5

Full colour. Soft, ripe, oaky nose. Good class and plenty of charm. Medium-full body. Ripe fruit. Good style. Essentially gently but balanced and stylish. Good plus.

1998 VINTAGE

SIZE OF THE CROP:	6,583,034 HECTOLITRES.
VINTAGE RATING:	15.0 – 18.5 (RED WINES – SEE BELOW).
	16.0 (DRY WHITE WINES).
	15.0 (SWEET WINES).

This was the fourth vintage in a row to register above 6 million hectolitres, an average yield of 58.1 hl/ha. White wines represented 884,386 hl (13.4 per cent of the total).

Nineteen ninety-eight is a vintage which, like many in the last decade, began well and promised much. That it did not in the end turn out to be the 'great one' we had all been waiting for since 1990 can be blamed variously on an August which was too hot and too dry, to rain which fell on and off from the beginning of September onwards, and increasingly so after the 26th, to a continuing but misguided trust that green-harvesting and the increasingly available concentrating machines will do what a rather more draconian pruning and de-budding earlier in the season should have done, and to what is patently a lack of will in the vast majority of châteaux below the top 30 or so (though there are of course some honourable exceptions) to make wine of a quality which justifies their existence in one of the many classifications.

There are, however, some great wines in Saint-Émilion and Pomerol, but alongside these few there are many which are less than competent. There are some nearly great wines in the Médoc and the Graves, but rather more disappointments. It was, in general, a very good year for both dry white wines and for Sauternes. But 1998 is a variable vintage. Years such as 1970, 1982 ,1990 and 2000 (even 2001, but at a lesser level) provided good wines across the board geographically and hierarchically. Nineteen ninety-eight does not.

Moreover, despite, at least in the Médoc-Graves, decreases in prices over 1997 – and a return at least in the direction of sanity should be gratefully acknowledged – the 1998s were still expensive. Many Saint-Émilions and Pomerols came out at levels *higher* than 1997. This could have been justified if the 1997s had been correctly priced. But the 1997s were double what they should have been.

THE WEATHER

After a dry, sunny and indeed quite warm start to the year, bud-break was early, as it had been in 1997. Growth was brought to a stop during a cold, very wet April, but thankfully Bordeaux was spared the frosts which struck eastern France from Burgundy right down to the Corbières on the night of 13/14th. Fine weather from 7th May onwards enabled the vines to catch up their progress, and the flowering around the end of the month was swift, even and successful – and one week earlier than the norm.

A meteorologically normal June led into a July and August which were both very dry and sunny and very hot. There were 515 hours of sunshine against a 1995-to-1997 average of 414, 58 mm of rain against 143, 27 hot days (25–30°C) and 19 very hot days (plus 30°C). While the *véraison* passed off speedily and satisfactorily around 1st August, the vines soon began to suffer thereafter.

This was the first element in the 1998 vintage's undoing, and it shows, as Allan Sichel points out in his Vintage Report 'what a fine balance is required for the vine to produce the magical nectar we strive for each year'. '*Août fait le moût*', August makes the must, is a well-known Bordeaux saying. Great vintages are made by fine Augusts as well as dry picking times. We need hot weather in August to produce the concentration, the high and ripe levels of tannins and anthocyans. But if, as happened, it was *too* hot, causing leaves to shrivel and drop off, exposing fruit to be grilled by the sun, shutting off sap within the plant and therefore arresting the photosynthetic process of creating sugar, then August was undermining the potential quality. This stress, naturally, was felt more in the stony, well-drained Graves-Médoc, than in the cooler, more water-retentive, clay-limestone soils of Pomerol-Saint-Émilion. In the Médoc many resulting blends would wind up without any Cabernet Franc in the *grand vin*, this being the variety which had carried the brunt of the stress.

As August melted into September the weather cooled and it began to rain. For the first week the weather was mainly sunny. There were then three days of storms followed by another week of very good weather, and it was largely at this time that the dry white wine varieties were collected. Château Haut-Brion, always the first to pick, because of its very beneficial mesoclimate, picked its white wine fruit from the 7th to the 9th. It even made a start on its Merlots on the 15th, while most of the rest, even in Saint-Émilion and Pomerol, had to wait until the 21st or later.

The weather continued fine until the weekend of 26th September. The following Monday to Wednesday saw intermittent showers, but cold drying winds to sop up some of the moisture. But then on 1st October, the funeral of Jean-Eugène Borie of Château Ducru-Beaucaillou, 60 mm fell in one day. It continued to rain, on and off, for the next fortnight.

In all, at least 300 mm of rain fell in the Bordeaux region between 1st September and the end of the picking. There was, however, less rain in September in Pomerol (101 mm) than at Bordeaux's Mérignac Airport in the centre of the Left Bank (183 mm). As the growers in Pomerol also had the advantage of more Merlot and an earlier date of starting the harvest one can understand why people are calling 1998 a Libournais or Right Bank vintage.

THE SIZE OF THE CROP

Individual yields vary from château to château. Surprisingly, given that Merlot is more prolific than either of the Cabernets and that in the gravelly soils of the Médoc and Graves many bunches shrivelled up and dropped off in the heat of August, figures are much higher on the Left Bank than on the Right.

Here are some examples: La Mondotte 22 hl/ha; de Valandraud 30; Beauséjour-Bécot 32; Canon-la-Gaffelière 32; Vieux Château Certan 34; Ausone 35; Tertre-Roteboeuf 35; L'Église-Clinet 35; L'Évangile 37; La Conseillante 44; Léoville-Las-Cases 39; Lafite 48; Montrose 48; Pichon-Lalande 50; Léoville-Barton 50; Haut-Brion 51; Latour 54; Cos d'Estournel 58.

THE WINES

Nineteen ninety-eight, then, is a vintage which favoured those able to pick early. That a number of Saint-Émilion and Pomerols do not shine in 1998 must be put down to the current fad for sur-maturity. There is a tendency – and it goes with a desire for super-extraction – to delay the harvest. Merlot, however, is a fragile grape, compared with Cabernet. Its skin is thinner, its acidity lower. I quote Allan Sichel again. 'Merlot must not be allowed to over-ripen. Waiting beyond the optimum maturity date often causes loss of fruit and structure, as well as restricting ageing capacity.' In 1998, this policy proved a disaster, and it was particularly sad to taste some of the top Pomerols and Saint-Émilions and then to discover that they were not joined by hosts of others. The top wines, however, are delicious. They rival, and in many cases surpass, what was to come in 2000.

On the other hand, when you look at the rainfall figures as they affected the Cabernets (one and half times the average, the same as in 1994, in the Médoc-Graves in September; three and a half times the average in the first days of October) it is remarkable that these wines were not affected more. The Cabernet Sauvignons on the Left Bank have preserved much of their dignity. Tannin levels are high, colours are good, acidities are not too bad, and the resultant wines – or at least the top ones – have good fruit. The grapes may have been collected in moist conditions, but thankfully this variety rarely reaches over-maturity, and in 1998 it was only at the very end that rot became a serious problem. Moreover, though I do not have figures directly related to Saint-Julien and Pauillac, where you will find the best Médocs, it would seem that rainfall figures, overall, were less here than that quoted from the Mérignac airport.

One of the potential dangers with the 1998 vintage was that of over-extraction and prolonged maceration. Had the wines been made to rote, many more would have had the aggressive tannins of the 1975 vintage. That so few do in fact possess this trait is a tribute to modern winemaking. We do indeed make better wines today.

Some, however, have erred on the other side, and the wines are light and pretty, but a bit hollow. Château Pichon-Lalande is an example here, having made the same mistake it did in 1990. There are one or two others, like Certan de May and La Conseillante, where you wish the wine had had a bit more power and backbone. But there are many more on the Right Bank whose fault is simply a lack of clean rich fruit: they are as much rustic as unconcentrated.

To summarise, then, we have wines on the right bank, the Saint-Émilion and Pomerol area, which range from quite clearly the best since 1989 and 1990 (and some are better still) to boring wines no better than the average of 1994, 1995, 1996 and 1997. The Graves range from high quality at Château Haut-Brion (the same statistical figures as 1989 and 1990, but fresher on the palate, less sur-maturity, less cooked fruit flavours), via better than the last four years average in the rest of the classed growths, to mundane elsewhere.

There are good wines, disappointing wines and disasters throughout the Médoc. In general they are better than 1994, but not as good as 1996, where the 1996s were really special. Indeed in character they are much like a cross between the two. There are many with an appealing fruit, which gives them more definition than 1994, but few with the real concentration, richness and high-toned personality of a really individual wine. The vintage lacked that final week of splendid weather that would have given the last push towards greatness.

As in 1997 this is neither a year for second wines – the vast majority are very wishy-washy, making one relieved that there is today such a rigorous selection between the *grand vin* and the rest – nor a vintage where the *vin de presse* has been of much use. In general, 1998 is proportionately better the higher up the hierarchy you go. The lower down the scale the more the vintage resembles 1994 rather than anything more encouraging.

Sauternes, for the third year in succession, produced a successful vintage. There was a first *tri* collected between 16th and 26th September of very good ripe botrytised fruit, a second, probably later rejected, around the end of the month, and a third, also questionable, picked early in October. Those who held on were able to produce much improved lots from fourth and even fifth visits to the vineyard after the weather had improved from 10th October onwards. The wines have balance and fruit, and are on the fresh rather than the luscious side: not as fine as 1997, nor as concentrated as the 2001s, but a good vintage nonetheless.

PRICES THEN AND NOW

Very stupidly, Bordeaux proprietors had raised prices the previous year. In the spring of 1999 they realised they had made a mistake. Most prices came down, some by as much as 30 per cent. This made the best wines, especially the riches which would be found in Saint-Émilion and Pomerol, very good value. At a Super-Second level, wines such as Vieux Château Certan were on offer for £550 ($990) a dozen. Château Cheval Blanc, my wine of the vintage, was £1250 ($2250). Prices of these sort of wines have risen significantly since. Cheval Blanc is £2000 ($3100). Vieux Château Certan is now £750 ($1350) and is now £950 ($1710). Prices for the more modest wines of the Libournais and the Médoc-Graves at even up to Super-Second levels have hardly moved at all since the summer of 1999, though Médoc-Graves First Growths have risen (Château Margaux from £750/$1350 to £900/$1620 a case for instance).

THE TASTING

The following wines were tasted in Southwold in January 2002. I have had added a few notes on 1998s which I tasted the following month while in Bordeaux.

SAINT-ÉMILION

CHÂTEAU ANGÉLUS

2007–2020   17.5

Full colour. Ample and very rich. Succulent and yet balanced and stylish on the nose. Full body. Very good tannins. Very Merlot fruit. Not too oaky. Very good grip. This has concentration and definition. Long. Fine.

CHÂTEAU L'ARROSÉE

2008–2020   16.5

Fullish colour. Full, backward nose but with good ripe tannins underneath. Fullish body. Quite structured. Good grip. Plenty of fruit. Very good length and style. It just needs time. Very good plus.

CHÂTEAU AUSONE

2008–2028   18.5

Fullish colour. Full and concentrated. Quite rich blackberry fruit. Some oak. Is it a bit over-done? Fine on the palate. Full-bodied but not over-extracted. Good grip. Concentrated and tannic. Good Libournais class. Eclipsed by Cheval-Blanc but very fine.

CHÂTEAU BALESTARD-LA-TONNELLE

NOW–2018   16.0

Fullish colour. Good concentration. Good grip. Sophisticated tannins. This has depth. Better than its stablemate Cap de Mourlin. Very good.

CHÂTEAU BARDE-HAUT

NOW–2015   14.5

Good colour. Plump, fruity nose. Not much depth underneath but ripe and stylish. Medium weight. Ample. A little tannin. Decent grip. Well-made. Not that long on the finish though. Quite good plus.

CHÂTEAU BEAU-SÉJOUR-BÉCOT

NOW–2014   15.0

Medium-full colour. Plump, oaky, ripe, medium-full nose. Medium weight. Ripe tannins. Decent fruit. Not a lot of personality. A slight lack of real depth. Good merely.

CHÂTEAU BEAUSÉJOUR-DUFFAU-LAGARROSSE

2008–2028   17.5

Very good colour. Full and firm on the nose. Very good fruit. Quite backward but not a bit too dense and solid. On the palate fullish, rich, ample and gently oaky. Good tannins. Very good grip. Not a bit four-square. It needs time but fine quality. Lovely finish.

CHÂTEAU BELAIR

NOW–2013   15.5

Medium colour. Soft nose. Elegant, but a bit light. Medium body. Not a great deal of tannin, nor of vigour. This is forward. Plump and succulent and quite stylish nevertheless. But not very serious given the terroir. Good plus.

CHÂTEAU BERLIQUET

NOW–2018   17.0

Good colour. Lovely fruit on the nose. Ripe and stylish. Intense and classy. But not a blockbuster. Excellent balance. Medium weight. Some oak. Very ripe tannins. Excellent fruit and balance. Lots of style. Quite accessible. Lovely finish. Very good indeed.

Château Cadet Piola

NOW–2018   17.0

Very good colour. This is delicious. Full but no hard edges. Good grip. Lovely profound, fresh fruit. Very good balance. Lots of depth. Very good indeed.

Château Canon

NOW–2020   16.5

Good colour. A little four-square on the nose. Good tannin but not enough richness to the fruit. Ripe on the palate though. Full body. Some tannin. Good acidity. Just a touch rigid at present but it has good length and depth. A wine for food. Very good plus.

Château Cap de Mourlin

NOW–2012   15.5

Medium-full colour. Rich and ripe. Good grip. Stylish plummy fruit. Again an enormous improvement on previous vintages. It needs two to three years to round off. Good plus.

Château Cheval Blanc

2008–2028   20.0

Full colour. Splendidly concentrated fruit on the nose. Marvellously rich, ripe and opulent. A brilliant result. Full body. Hugely concentrated. Yet cool and composed. Very good grip. Excellent fruit. Real depth. Magnificent!

Château Corbin

NOW–2010   15.0

Medium to medium-full colour. Good succulent example. Not quite as sophisticated as Château Corbin is today but balanced, fresh and beginning to round off.

Château Corbin Michotte

NOW–2010   14.0

Made by Jean-Noël Boidron. Good colour. Brettonamyces on the nose. Not much new oak, if any. Medium body. This I find disappointing. It is medium-bodied, fresh, drinkable and fruity. But neither stylish, nor profound, nor rich. Quite good at best.

Le Dôme

2007–2020   17.0

Fullish colour. Impressive nose. Rich and concentrated. Lots of depth. Not too much oak. This is really rather fine. Fullish body. Very good, ripe tannins. Good depth of fruit. This is well-made. Some oak. The finish is lush and long. Very good indeed.

Château Figeac

NOW–2012   14.0

Fullish colour. Perfumed nose. A bit tarty. Medium body. Plump. Some oak. Ripe. Not enough grip. A bit simple but stylish nevertheless. No depth here. Quite good at best.

Clos Fourtet

NOW–2018   17.5

Very good colour. Subtle nose. Gently succulent. Quite classy. Just a hint of wood. This is really rather sophisticated. On the palate the wine is medium- to full-bodied, balanced and very fresh. Cool, long, complex and elegant. Not a blockbuster. But very lovely long finish. Fine.

Château Franc-Mayne

2006–2018   17.0

Good colour. Rich, fullish nose. Very good oak. This is meaty, succulent and very stylish. Full body. Quite a lot of tannin but these tannins are very ripe. Excellent classy fruit. Really profound. This is a splendid example. As good as the 2000.

Château La Gaffelière

NOW–2015   15.0

Fullish colour. Balanced, stylish nose. Good ample fruit without being a very big wine. Medium weight. Ripe tannins. Good succulence and balance. But no better than good. It lacks a little personality. Good length though.

LA GOMERIE

NOW–2018   16.0

Fullish colour. Plump, ripe but really quite oaky on the nose. Medium-full body. Not a lot of backbone. But good grip. Lush and quite exotic. Not that long but very good.

CHÂTEAU GRAND CORBIN-DESPAGNE

NOW–2010   13.0

Good full colour. Medium weight on the nose. Ample fruit but not a lot of grip. Medium body. Quite forward. A pretty wine but a bit short. Will get astringent. Not bad at best.

CHÂTEAU GRAND-MAYNE

2007–2020   16.0

Good colour. Quite firm on the nose. Good structure. Backward. Some tannin. Good grip. A touch astringent at present but I think this will go. Good fruit. It finishes positively. Very good.

CHÂTEAU LES GRANDES MURAILLES

NOW–2011   13.0

Good colour. Ripe, positive, balanced and attractive, if without First Growth depth. On the palate this is a bit one-dimensional and a little short. Boring. Medium body. It got greener and greener as it developed. Not bad.

CHÂTEAU LAFORGE

2006–2018   15.5

Fullish colour. Good fresh nose. Some oak. No outstanding depth but balanced and harmonious. Well made. Quite oaky on the palate. But ripe and stylish and cold and really quite long. Very good.

CHÂTEAU LARCIS-DUCASSE

NOW–2012   15.5

Cooler than the 2000 which I tasted alongside. Good ample wine nevertheless if not quite so sophisticated. Ripe and balanced. It lacks a bit of concentration. But decent length. Good plus.

CHÂTEAU MAGDELAINE

2006–2026   18.0

Medium-full colour. Classy. A lot of concentration and depth. Nothing exaggerated here. Lovely ripe, complex Merlot fruit. A touch of oak. Very good grip and concentration. Elegant. Cool and composed. Long. Fine.

CHÂTEAU MONBOUSQUET

NOW–2010   12.5

Good colour. Very ripe fruit. Very cassis/blackberry. Lush and succulent. Quite oaky. Yet a bit of a confection. On the palate a bit over-extracted. Perfumed. Slightly astringent at the end. This will not age gracefully. Poor.

LA MONDOTTE

2007–2020   17.0

Very full colour. Very rich, almost perfumed. Quite oaky too on the nose. Fullish body. Some tannin. Almost over-ripe. Very lush and succulent. Good grip. Ample and potentially very seductive and silky. Not the grip of Angélus or sheer class of Magdelaine. But very good indeed.

CHÂTEAU MOULIN SAINT-GEORGES

2006–2016   13.0

Good vigorous colour. Firm, backward, tannic nose. A little hard. Slightly corked but at the same time rather forced and dry at the end. A bit top heavy.

CHÂTEAU DE CLOS L'ORATOIRE

2007–2020   17.0

Good colour. Lots of lovely, lush fruit here on the nose. Concentrated and balanced. Fullish body. Good tannins. Ripe. Very good grip. A lot of depth. Classy fruit too. Long. Very good indeed.

Château Pavie

2007–2012	15.0

Full colour. Quite high volatile acidity. Good oak. Lots of ripe fruit. All giving it a slightly sweet sour aspect on the nose. Medium-full body. Quite oaky on the palate. Good grip. But it lacks a bit of real concentration for fine. Long though. And some class. But curious. A little concocted. Good.

Château Pavie-Macquin

2008–2025	17.0

Good colour. Rich, concentrated nose. Some oak but not excesively so. Lots of depth. Full, fat, rich and concentrated. Very good grip. This is very impressive. Quite structured. Good tannins. Long. It needs time. Very good indeed.

Château Petit Faurie de Soutard

NOW–2012	15.0

A medium-bodied, fresh, plump, stylish wine. A lot better than it has been in the past. Good fruit. This is really the first year that the wine has not been lean and rustic. One-third new oak. It needs two to three years. Good.

Château Quinault L'Enclos

NOW–2015	14.5

Medium-full colour. Soft, lush, modern nose. Good Merlot fruit. Not a lot of depth underneath. Medium weight. Mellow and succulent. Very ripe and lush. Not a lot of grip. Well-made. Pleasant second devision Saint-Émilion. Quite good plus.

Château Ripeau

NOW–2010	14.0

No more concentration than the 1999 (which was ripe, quite rich and had good fruit and good substance). But a little more rustic. This was the last vintage of the 'old regime'. Quite good only. Alain Reynaud helps here, *à titre d'amitié*.

Clos Saint-Martin

NOW–2012	13.5

Good colour. Rather lean and herbaceous on the nose. Medium to medium-full body. Fresh but slight ungenerous. Better on the follow-through. Not bad plus.

Château Sanctus

NOW–2009	13.5

A super-cuvée of Château de Bienplaisance. Medium-full colour. Plump and fruity but a bit shallow on the nose. Light. Unexciting. Not much backbone. Boring.

Château Soutard

NOW–2012	13.5

Medium colour. Slightly lean on the nose. Good acidity. Medium weight. It lacks a bit of flesh and generosity. Decent length. But unexciting. Not bad plus.

Château Le Tertre-Roteboeuf

2008–2020	15.0

Full colour. Firm nose. Quite a bit drier than the usual modern style of Saint-Émilion. Some tannin. But good depth. Some Brett. A Châteauneuf-du-Pape made out of Merlot. If it wasn't for the Brett this would be fine because it is full and concentrated and the acidity is excellent. Backward. Long. Quite alcoholic. Good.

Château La Tour Figeac

2006–2018	15.5

Good colour. Oaky, plump, ripe and with attractive personality on the nose. Fullish body. Some tannin. Good grip. This has plenty of character. Very good length. Ripe and quite concentrated. Good plus.

Château Troplong-Mondot

2008–2020	17.0

Good colour. Quite a full, tannic, sturdy wine on the nose. Full body. Some tannin. This is quite a solid example at present. But there is no lack of richness, grip or depth. Just needs time. Very good indeed.

Château Trottevieille

NOW–2009   14.5

Medium to medium-full colour. Fresh, stylish and fruity on the nose. Ample and attractive if without great weight. Medium body. Not much tannins. Nor much grip. But fruity and pleasant and quite good plus.

Château de Valandraud

2007–2017   16.0

Full colour. Very perfumed and concentrated on the nose. Very rich on the palate. Quite full. Some tannin. Plenty of substance here. But it doesn't add up to a great deal, curiously. There is no great deal of grip. Merely very good.

Pomerol

Château Beauregard

2007–2019   16.0

Good colour. Quite firm on the nose. A little austere perhaps. Fullish body. Some tannins. Best at the end. Good ripe fruit. Good grip. This will last well. The finish is even quite classy. Long. Very good.

Château Le Bon Pasteur

2006–2018   16.0

Fullish colour. Lush nose. Ripe, balanced, clean as a whistle. Good soft tannins. Very well made. Fullish body. Ample. Good tannins. Warm, rich and generous. Not great but very good.

Château Cantelauze

NOW–2010   14.5

Made by Jean-Noël Boidron. Good colour. Plump, plummy, rich and without brettanomyces (see Château Corbin Michotte). No great class underneath and there are rustic hints. But quite good plus.

Château Certan de May

NOW–2009   13.5

Medium to medium-full colour. Pleasantly fruity but somewhat lacking grip and depth on the nose. Quite elegant but forward. Only medium body. A bit weak. It lacks concentration and structure. Forward. Only average.

Château Certan-Marzelle

NOW–2009   12.0

Medium-full colour. Rustic nose. Medium body. The tannins are not very ripe. The wine is edgy. Some fruit – you could hardly avoid it in 1998 – but no class. Thank God this property is now in better hands! It now belongs to Ets J-P Moueix.

Château Clinet

2008–2020   16.5

Medium-full colour. Rich, smooth and oaky on the nose. Very creamy. But it lacks a little grip and individuality. Medium-full body. Certainly very ripe. Some tannin. A little solid and inflexible. Slightly over-extracted and over-oaked. Decent finish. But no nuance. Merely very good plus.

Château La Conseillante

NOW–2010   12.5

Fullish colour. Slightly weak and vegetal on the nose. It lacks richness. Weak and already astringent. Medium body. A feeble wine. No future.

Clos L'Église

2006–2018   16.0

Fullish colour. Plump and rich and quite oaky on the nose. A little obvious perhaps. Medium-full body. The oak dominates a bit. Decent length. Good fruit. But a bit tiring to drink. Very good at best.

Château L'Église-Clinet

2007–2025   18.5

Very good colour. Splendid rich nose. Good structure and very good acidity. But above all very luscious fruit. Full body. Very rich and really quite oaky on the palate. Yet the length and grip are there. The tannins are ripe and will integrate properly leaving an intensely flavoured wine of succulence and complexity and good class. Very fine.

Château L'Enclos

NOW–2010   14.0

Good colour. Ripe but just a little dry and diffuse on the nose. Medium to medium-full body. Slightly astringent on the palate too. There is a little attenuation lurking here. Decently fruity but it lacks a little freshness. Merely quite good.

Château L'Évangile

2008–2030   19.0

Full colour. Splendid nose. Concentrated and very classy. Splendid expression of mature fruit. Excellent harmony. Very elegant. This is seriously good wine. Very harmonious. Really intense at the end. Very fine plus.

Château La Fleur de Gay

NOW–2015   15.0

There was little wine as a result of hail damage. But there is no hail taste (this can leave a metallic taint in the wine). Medium-full colour. Plump, ripe, oaky nose. Very attractive. Lots of immediate appeal. Medium weight. The tannins are ripe and the wine isn't too oaky. What it lacks is a little depth and a little real classy. Good at best.

Château La Fleur-Pétrus

2006–2024   18.0

Good colour. Ample nose. Plumper than Latour-à-Pomerol. Rich and quite fat. Good class. Fullish body. Very Merlot. Very fresh. This gives the finish an intensity and a length not present in the bigger, oakier, more 'modern style' wines. Long and complex and classy. Fine plus.

Château Guillot

NOW–2011   14.0

Fullish colour. Plump, perfumed, oaky nose. Medium body. Fruity and balanced but a little one-dimensional. It lacks concentration and only has a fair amount of style. Good length though. Quite good.

Château Lafleur

2009–2025   17.0

Medium-full colour. Quite solid on the nose. Tannic and dense. Inflexible. A full, even tough example. There is some fine concentrated fruit here and very good grip. But is it a little top heavy? It doesn't sing. Very good indeed at best.

Château Latour-à-Pomerol

2006–2020   17.5

Medium-full colour. Ripe, cool, composed and elegant on the nose. Lovely fruit and very well balanced. Medium-full body. Lovely fruit. Ripe but very well balanced. Very long. Very harmonious. Really intense at the end. Fine.

Château Nénin

2006–2011   13.5

Medium-full colour. A little austere. Good grip. Some fruit. Not quite enough richness and depth. Medium body. Rather too neutral. Some tannin. Decent balance. It lacks dimension and charm. Not bad plus.

Château Pétrus

2010–2030   19.5

Fullish colour. Big, full, sweet nose. Quite a monster underneath. Lots of tannin. Quite bulky. On the palate this is excellently concentrated. Heaps and heaps of concentrated fruit. Not quite as brilliant as Cheval Blanc but very impressive. Very fine indeed.

Le Pin

NOW–2010   17.0

Fullish colour. Lush. Very Merlot. Not up to Vieux Château Certan on the nose. It seems a little overblown. Medium-full body. Very ripe and lush. Nicely fresh. Very plump and very rich. But it doesn't have the backbone and depth of a great wine. Very good indeed at best.

CHÂTEAU LA POINTE

NOW–2011   14.5

Medium-full colour. Soft, stylish, well-made lesser Pomerol nose. Forward. Fruity. Easy to enjoy. Medium body. Forward. A little oaky but not much tannin. Four-square. Good fruit and balance though. Attractive. Quite good plus.

CLOS RENÉ

2006–2011   14.0

Medium-full colour. Quite firm and chunky on the nose. Medium-full body. Some tannin. A little too much. Not over-extracted in the modern sense though. Some fruit. Good grip. Best with food. It may mellow satisfactorily. Quite good.

CHÂTEAU ROUGET

2006–2018   16.0

Full colour. Quite full. Good firm nose. Good depth here. A little oak. Fullish body. Ripe, balanced and succulent. Quite acceptible. Long and attractive. Very positive finish. Very good.

CHÂTEAU TROTANOY

2007–2025   18.5

Full colour. Lots of depth here on the nose. Excellent fruit. Rather more volume and grip than Château Magdelaine. Fullish body. Rich, concentrated and profound. Very lovely fruit. Long and intense and classy. A delicious example. Very fine.

VIEUX CHÂTEAU CERTAN

2008–2030   19.5

Fullish colour. Lovely nose. Excellent acidity. Very super-concentrated fruit. Very classy. Real depth here. Full body. Fresh. Marvellously concentrated. Excellent balance. This is a real beauty. I can't fault this. Total harmony and great majesty. Very fine indeed.

GRAVES

DOMAINE DE CHEVALIER

2007–2025   17.5

Medium to medium-full colour. Harmonious, elegant, poised nose. Lovely fruit. Medium-full body. Very good ripe tannins. Lovely concentrated fruit. By no means a blockbuster but very, very long and very, very complex at the end. Real elegance here. Fine.

CHÂTEAU DE FIEUZAL

NOW–2020   15.5

Medium-full colour. Good fresh nose. Some substance but not too burly. Medium-full body. Good cool, quite fruity attack. Good tannins. This has style and balance and the follow-through is clean and positive. Good plus. From 2005.

CHÂTEAU LA GARDE

2006–2012   14.5

Good colour. Good nose. Ripe and positive. Medium body. Only a little tannin. Not as classy as the 2000. But a decently made, balanced example. Quite good plus.

CHÂTEAU HAUT-BAILLY

2006–2020   18.0

Good colour. Soft, round, plump and rich on both nose and palate. Not quite the structure of the 2000 but the same very lovely, supple, concentrated fruit. Very good grip. Very elegant. Very long. Fine plus for 1998.

CHÂTEAU HAUT-BERGEY

2007–2020   16.0

Medium-full colour. Some maceration, some oak and some fruit on the nose. A ripe wine. Good depth and good grip. Fullish body. Meat, positive and stylish. It finishes well. Very good.

CHÂTEAU HAUT-BRION

2008–2028	19.0

Full colour. Fragrant, classy nose. Not a blockbuster but very lovely fruit. Composed. Pure and intense. On the palate this is rich and fruity. Rather more generous, opulent and concentrated than La Mission Haut-Brion. Very classy. Long. Very fine plus.

CHÂTEAU LATOUR-MARTILLAC

2006–2015	15.5

Medium-full colour. Slightly green but good depth and personality here. More generous on the palate. Good fruit. Medium-full body. Some tannin. It lacks a bit of real flair. Good plus.

CHÂTEAU MALARTIC-LAGRAVIÈRE

2008–2020	16.5

Very good colour. Nicely elegant on the nose. Not a bit too tough or solid. Fullish body. Good tannins. Quite structured but fresh, balanced, vigorous and full of fruit. Intense even. Lovely long finish. This is very good plus.

CHÂTEAU LA MISSION HAUT-BRION

2008–2028	18.0

Medium to medium-full colour. Good acidity. Lots of fruit and lots of depth. Very classy. Very well balanced, complex fruit. Full but not too extracted. Very long. Lovely finish. This has a lot distinction. Very fine.

CHÂTEAU PAPE-CLÉMENT

2007–2028	16.5

Medium to medium-full colour. Rich, full, meaty nose. Fullish body. Some tannin. Plenty of substance here but not enough grip and dimension. Not as long or as stylish as Domaine de Chevalier by some way. Very good plus at best.

CHÂTEAU PICQUE CAILLOU

2007–2020	17.0

Good colour. Plenty of depth and class here. Medium to medium-full body. Very good tannins. Excellent acidity. Fresh. Nicely ripe and generous. Classy and long. Very complex. Very good indeed.

CHÂTEAU SMITH-HAUT-LAFITTE

NOW–2015	15.5

Good colour. Mellow on the nose. Attractive. Medium to medium-full body. Very lovely fruit. Medium body. Ripe and juicy. Gently oaky. This is very seductive. It is only medium- to medium-full-bodied though. Promising as it is on the attack it tails off slightly and as a result it finishes a bit shallow. It lacks just a bit of grip. Good plus though.

MÉDOC/HAUT-MÉDOC

CHÂTEAU D'AGASSAC

NOW–2012	15.0

Good colour. Cool nose. Medium structure. A little ungenerous. Medium to medium-full body. A little tannin. Not a great deal of concentration. Nor the style of the 2000 which I tasted alongside it. But decent fruit and balance. More attractive on the palate than the nose would suggest. Good.

CHÂTEAU ARNAULD

NOW–2015	15.5

Good colour. The tannins are a little hard here, but there is also good ripe fruit. Medium to medium-full body. A touch of astringency to the tannins. But enough grip and succulence to balance them: more than enough. This is ripe, long and positive. Lovely finish. Much more civilised than heretofore. Good plus.

CHÂTEAU D'AURILHAC

NOW–2015	15.0

Good colour. Slightly dry, austere nose but good fruit underneath. Decent fruit on the palate but a little astringency. On the one hand fresh, especially on the finish. But a bit hard on the attack. This is the right way round, so good.

CHÂTEAU BEAUMONT

NOW–2008	14.0

Good colour. Medium weight. Pretty fruit. Decently balanced. Quite forward. This is a good honest bottle but what it lacks is a bit of concentration and a bit of flair. No hard edges. And clean and decent. Quite good.

CHÂTEAU BELGRAVE

2006–2018   15.5

Good colour. Slightly hard on the nose. This is bigger and firmer than the 2000 but less classy. Nevertheless there is good fruit here and good grip and depth of character. The tannins are ripe enough. Good plus.

CHÂTEAU BELLE-VUE

NOW–2012   15.0

Very good colour. Rich, full and meaty on the nose. A little oak. Creamy. This has good depth on the attack. Just a little tannin. Medium-full body. Oaky. Decent grip. But it tails off a little. Good.

CHÂTEAU CAMENSAC

2007–2017   15.0

Fullish colour. Ample, plump, soft, gently oaky nose. Medium-full weight. A little raw. Decent balance. Quite stylish. Slightly astringent at the end. Good though.

CHÂTEAU CANTEMERLE

2006–2018   15.0

Medium-full colour. A little development. Slightly dry on the nose. A little spicy too. No great weight or concentration behind it. Medium to medium-full body. Decent fruit and some charm. The finish is ripe and succulent. In the middle there is a lack of charm, but the follow-through is better. Balanced and quite stylish. Decent length. This is better without doubt than the 2000. Good.

CHÂTEAU LA CARDONNE

NOW–2010   14.5

Medium to medium-full colour. Medium weight. Quite fresh. But a little hard on the nose. Medium body. Round, plump and fruity on the attack. Decent follow-through. No real depth or personality but well made. Quite good plus.

CHÂTEAU CHARMAIL

NOW–2012   16.0

Medium-full colour. Rich, plump, Christmas-cakey nose. Medium to medium-full body. Some tannin to round off. Good

grip. Accessible and open on the palate. Plump and generous. Good long positive finish. This is very good.

CHÂTEAU CITRAN

NOW–2012   14.0

Good colour. Smoky-burnt nose. This character rather gets in the way on the palate. Medium body. Only a little tannin. Some fruit but also a little astringent. Quite good at best.

CHÂTEAU CLÉMENT-PICHON

NOW–2011   14.0

Good colour. Good nose. Rich and less Merloty than the 1999, which I also tasted on the same day. On the palate medium-full body, some tannin and good grip. Again not the greatest of style though. But ripe and balanced. Quite good.

CHÂTEAU COUFRAN

NOW–2008   15.0

Good colour. Ripe and fresh and quite concentrated and classy on the nose. The attack is ample, fresh and fruity. Medium body. There is a little astringency at the end. A little one-dimensional but very pleasant. Good. Drink quite soon.

CHÂTEAU D'ESCURAC

NOW–2013   16.5

Good colour. Rich and oaky on the nose. Nicely austere but not a bit hard. Ample and generous, yet with very good grip. Still a bit of tannin to mellow. Profound and classy. Very good plus.

CHÂTEAU GREYSAC

NOW–2009   14.5

Good colour. Slightly hard on the nose. A lack of charm here. Medium to medium-full body. Some tannin. A little astringent. Decent fruit and balance underneath. Not short. Quite good plus.

CHÂTEAU HAUT CONDISSAS

NOW–2012	17.5

Very good colour. Lovely elegant nose.
Opulent, oaky, rich and plump. Long. Fullish
body. Quite meaty. But very good depth.
Good weight. This is impressive. No
weakness. Although slightly astringent at the
end. A fine example.

CHÂTEAU LA LAGUNE

2006–2015	14.0

Medium-full colour. Accessible, plump, oaky
nose. Pleasant but rather anonymous.
Medium body. Decent fruit and balance and
some oak. Quite clean. But it lacks real depth
and character. Quite good at best.

CHÂTEAU LAMOTHE-BERGERON

NOW–2010	14.5

Very good colour. Good rich, vigorous nose.
Slight touches of stems. Medium to medium-
full body. Good, if not up to 2000 and 2001
standards. Ample, fresh, ripe fruit. Good
energy underneath. Quite rich. Quite
harmonious. It lacks just a little zip. Quite
good plus.

CHÂTEAU LANESSAN

NOW–2010	13.0

Medium-full colour. Some fruit on the nose.
But some astringency too. Dull. On the
palate a little fruit but no real depth or
concentration. It finishes flat. It will get
attenuated. Not bad.

CHÂTEAU MALESCASSE

2008–2018	16.0

Medium-full colour. Quite plump and fruity.
Good grip. Fresh. Medium-full body. Some
tannin. Not too hard. At present neither the
concentration of the 2000 or the charm of the
1999 which I tasted alongside. But good
depth and good freshness. Quite elegant.
Very good.

CHÂTEAU MAUCAMPS

DRINK SOON	13.0

Medium to medium-full colour. Fruity nose
but not a lot of concentration or depth. This
is really a bit thin. Already rather astringent.
One-dimensional. Not good enough. Ready.

CHÂTEAU DU MOULIN ROUGE

NOW–2012	14.5

Slightly hard tannins here. This is taking its
time. Slightly astringent. Not quite enough
grip or richness to balance it. Medium to
medium-full body. Quite good plus.

CHÂTEAU ROLLAN DE BY

2006–2016	16.0

Full colour. Quite soft, flexible nose and
without being a bit weak. Indeed medium-
full-bodied, ripe and well put together.
Classy for a *bourgeois*. Good fruit. More
advanced than the rest of the mainly Saint-
Estèphe flight. Very good.

CHÂTEAU SAINT-PAUL

NOW–2009	13.5

Good colour. The tannins are a little dry on
the nose. Here the wine is a little empty.
There is not enough grip or concentration of
fruit on the palate. The 1999 which I tasted
alongside is proportionately much better
(15.0). This is only fair.

CHÂTEAU SOCIANDO-MALLET

2008–2025	17.0

Fullish colour. Lovely fruit on the nose. A
hint of mint, a little oak. Fullish body. Quite
firm. Some tannin. This needs time. Fine on
the follow-through. Very good indeed.

CHÂTEAU SOUDARS

NOW–2012	16.0

Good colour. Medium weight. Balanced and
stylish. Good depth. Good ripe tannins and
very good acidity. Good grip and freshness.
Ripe and ample. Still needs time but no lack
of depth. Not up to the 2000 in its definition
and class this is nevertheless very good.

CHÂTEAU LA TOUR-DU-HAUT-MOULIN

NOW–2012   16.0

Good colour. Quite a firm, backward nose. Not too structured nor that concentrated on the nose. A touch of astringency here as well as tannin. Good fruit underneath but a certain lack of charm and excitement. Merely good. Yet no lack of elegance and length at the end. It improved in the glass. Very good.

CHÂTEAU VERDIGNAN

NOW–2011   15.5

Good colour. I get a certain hard edge to the tannins here. This is more old-fashioned than the three more recent vintages. But it is still good. Even if there is a suspicion of astringency on the attack. Underneath ripe, fresh, succulent fruit. Better on the palate than on the nose. Good plus.

LISTRAC-MÉDOC
CHÂTEAU CLARKE

NOW–2015   16.0

Good colour. Slightly hard on the nose like a lot of *crus bourgeois* 1998s. But this has good depth and balance, grip and fruit. Better acidity than most. So it will age well. Stylish. Very good.

CHÂTEAU FONRÉAUD

NOW–2009   13.5

Good colour. Nothing much on the nose. Slightly hard tannins. Decent fruit but no succulence. Not enough acidity to prevent it getting astringent in due course. Not bad plus.

CHÂTEAU FOURCAS-DUPRÉ

NOW–2015   15.0

Good colour. Good depth and richness on the nose without being too hard. Medium-full body. Not hard on the palate, but a slightly masculine structure. Decent acidity. Long and stylish but with a hint of astringency on the follow-through. A good 1998.

CHÂTEAU FOURCAS-HOSTEN

NOW–2009   13.5

Good colour. Quite evolved but not in a very satisfactory way. Rather astringent. Slightly hard. A lack of both fruit and grip. Only fair.

CHÂTEAU LESTAGE

NOW–2009   14.0

Good colour. Slightly softer and more evolved than Château Fonréaud, the Chanfreau's family other property. Quite good fruit and acidity. For once this is more satisfactory. More positive at the end. Quite good.

MOULIS
CHÂTEAU CHASSE-SPLEEN

NOW–2020   16.0

Good colour. Still quite youthful on the nose. Decent fruit but it lacks a little concentration. Quite persistent though. Medium to medium-full body. Just a little tannin. A small wine after the 2000 and 2001 but very good quality. There is elegance and balance here.

CHÂTEAU POUJEAUX

2007–2017   14.5

Fullish colour. Quite sturdy on the nose. A lack of real succulence. Better on the palate. A little tough but good fruit and good grip. Fullish body. Decent length. It lacks a bit of class though. Quite good plus.

Margaux

Château d'Angludet

NOW–2018   15.0

Medium-full colour. Slightly pinched, dry and stemmy on the nose. A certain lack of charm. Better on the palate. Medium to medium-full body. Now accessible. Decent, plump fruit. Good acidity. It lacks a bit of concentration. But positive at the end. Good.

Château Brane-Cantenac

2006–2020   16.5

Fullish colour. Classy nose. Clean, pure and balanced. Not a blockbuster. Medium-full body. Ripe, balanced and stylish. Quite elegant. Good fresh finish. Long on the palate. Very good plus.

Château Dauzac

2007–2018   17.5

Good colour. Good youthful nose. Slightly spicy but also cedary. Fresh. Palmer-ish. Very elegant. Very complex. Medium-full body. Lovely harmony. Great style. Very good depth. Not a blockbuster but long and full of finesse. Very well balanced. Very vigorous. Fine.

Château Deyrem Valentin

NOW–2016   15.5

Good colour. High-toned nose. Just a touch lactic. Medium body. A fragrant wine with no lack of depth, class and balance. But a bit more loose-knit than the 2001. Ripe and quite intense. Good definition. Positive at the end. Good plus.

Château Durfort-Vivens

2006–2014   15.0

Medium-full colour. Firmer and chunkier than Brane-Cantenac. Slightly harder too. Less sex appeal. On the palate it lacks a bit of grip. Medium-full body. Some fruit. But a little astringent. It doesn't sing. A little flat at the end. Merely good.

Château Ferrière

2007–2020   17.5

Good colour. Very sophisticated ripe fruit on the nose. Gently oaky. Real breed and very Margaux in style. Disarmingly lovely fruit on the palate. Balanced, fragrant, intense and very, very lovely. Medium-full body. Very harmonious. Very good tannins. This is really fine.

Château Giscours

NOW–2009   14.0

Medium colour. Lightish nose with a suggestion of mocha. Light to medium body. Decent, quite sweet, ripe fruit. Slightly cedary on the follow-through. A little feeble but quite charming. It has some finesse and character. Not short. Quite good.

Château La Gurgue

NOW–2015   15.0

Medium-full colour. Lovely ripe fruit on the nose. No hard edges. Medium body. Not a lot of tannin. Ripe and plump. Fresh, balanced and quite classy. The finish is long, fresh and complex. This is good.

Château d'Issan

NOW–2012   14.0

68 per cent Cabernet Sauvignon, 32 per cent Merlot. 47 per cent new wood. Good colour. Light on the nose but clean, pure and elegant if no real depth or structure. Just a little thin and green. Light to medium body. There isn't much tannin. Decent grip. Ripe fruit yet at the same time a little weedy. Forward. Quite good at best.

Château Kirwan

2006–2018   16.5

Good colour. A little subdued on the nose. Slightly dry. Not a lot of personality. Better on the palate. Medium body. Good fruit. Quite oaky. Reasonable grip and depth. Positive finish. This is very good plus.

Château Labégorce-Zédé

2007–2020   15.5

Full colour. Very good fruit on the nose. Plump and gently oaky. Medium-full body. Good grip and tannins. Nice fruit. A good wine but not quite enough concentration and personality and above all real Margaux class. Good plus.

Château Lascombes

2007–2014   13.5

Medium-full colour. Fullish but slightly herbaceous on the nose. A bit burly on the palate. Medium-full body. Some tannin. A bit astringent too. There is fruit here but no grace. Essentially lumpy. Not bad plus.

Château Malescot Saint-Exupéry

2008–2024   17.0

Fullish colour. Good rich, full, concentrated nose. This has class and depth. Fullish body. A big wine for Margaux. Concentrated and very well balanced too. Very good fruit. Some oak. Lots of depth. Very good indeed.

Château Margaux

2010–2030   19.0

Full colour. Closed-in, oaky nose. High quality. Lots of lovely plump fruit. Fullish body. Quite some tannin. Some from the oak. This is more backward than Latour. Underneath ripe, rich and classy. Very good grip. Long and vigorous. Very fine indeed.

Château Marquis de Terme

2007–2019   16.0

Fullish colour. Plump nose. Ripe and succulent. No great elegance but not a bit too tough. Unexpectedly attractive on the palate. Fullish body. Ripe and ample. Good tannins. This is long and even quite classy. Very good.

Château Monbrison

2007–2020   16.0

Fullish colour. Soft, ripe, succulent, oaky nose. Good class. Medium-full body. Good balance. Attractive fruit. Ripe tannins and good grip. This is well-made. Not too hard or 'Arrières Côtes'. It finishes well. Very good.

Château Palmer

2008–2025   18.0

Fullish colour. Quietly successful. Very intense and classy fruit on the nose. Lovely balance. Very composed. A really lovely wine, head and shoulders above its peers. Very pure. Velvety fruit. Very intense. Long, complex and with real distinction. Fine plus.

Pavillon Rouge du Château Margaux

2007–2017   16.0

Medium to medium-full colour. Classy nose. Good oak. Good depth. Lots of dimension. This shows very well. A little austere on the palate. But nevertheless there is plenty of fruit, grip and class. The finish is very good.

Château Prieuré-Lichine

2006–2012   13.0

Fullish colour. Some fruit on the nose but a little pinched and coarse. A bit astringent on the palate. Not the class for a classed growth. Medium body. Coarse and lumpy. Not bad.

Château Rauzan-Ségla

2006–2020   17.0

Full colour. Lovely nose. Real breed. Persistent and gently oaky. Very good fruit. Medium-full body. Ripe tannins. This is a classy wine. Long, fresh, pure and very harmonious. Real Margaux class. Very good indeed.

Château Tayac

2006–2016   14.0

Good colour. Soft nose. Good crisp, ripe fruit. An elegant wine. Very Margaux in style. Good attack. Just a little weak on the follow-through. Still fresh. The tannins are well *fondus*. Quite good.

CHÂTEAU DU TERTRE

NOW–2012   14.5

Medium colour. Light nose. A little raw. Not much depth or strength here. Light to medium body. Just a little tannin but evolving fast. Decent ripe fruit, like the Giscours, but not much depth. Again charming but not really serious, nor very elegant. Not bad plus. Ready quite soon.

CHÂTEAU LA TOUR DE MONS

NOW–2010   14.0

Good colour. Slightly weedy on the nose. It lacks concentration and zip. Better on the palate. Light to medium body. Fresh. Quite plump fruit. No great structure. But slight and positive. Quite good.

SAINT-JULIEN

CHÂTEAU BEYCHEVELLE

2008–2020   16.0

Fullish colour. Fullish, oaky, just a touch reduced. This blew off after a minute. Fullish body. Good grip. Not a great deal of dimension but good Cabernet fruit and some depth. It finishes well. Very good.

CHÂTEAU BRANAIRE-DUCRU

2009–2020   15.5

Medium-full colour. Ripe, soft but quite extracted on the nose. Fullish body. Slightly dry and earthy *arrières côtes* aspects. Good rich fruit. Positive finish. Good plus.

CHÂTEAU LA BRIDANE

NOW–2010   13.0

Less colour and leaner on the nose than the two previous vintages. This one is a bit thin and it suggests astringency. Forward. Not bad at best.

CHÂTEAU DUCRU-BEAUCAILLOU

2009–2025   17.5

Medium-full colour. Very elegant on the nose. Ripe. Not a blockbuster. But good depth. Excellent expression of fruit. Fullish body. Classy and balanced. Still young. Very good length. This is complex and quite concentrated. It needs time. Fine.

CHÂTEAU GLORIA

NOW–2010   15.0

Medium-full colour. Quite full but it lacks a little zip and personality. Quite an evolved, medium-bodied wine. Reasonably fresh, fruity and stylish. But slightly anonymous and not enough grip. Good but a bit dull.

CHÂTEAU GRUAUD-LAROSE

2009–2024   16.5

Full colour. Rich and full and sturdy on the nose. But good class here. Full and tannic but lots of ripe fruit. It needs time. But there is quality here. Good depth. Good grip. Positive and impressive at the end. Very good plus.

CHÂTEAU LAGRANGE

2006–2011   15.0

Good colour. Not a great deal of finesse on the nose. Slightly sweaty. Medium to medium-full body. Ripe and fruity. A little astringency from the tannins and from the oak because it lacks a bit of acidity. Lagrange tends to be a little too over-ripe these days and hence lacks zip and flair. A meaty wine. Good but not great.

CHÂTEAU LANGOA-BARTON

2008–2020   17.0

Full colour. Lovely quite oaky nose. Very good class here. Fullish body. A little more austere than Talbot. Slightly dry at first. But lovely balanced, elegant fruit on the after taste. Very long. Very positive. Very good indeed.

CHÂTEAU LÉOVILLE-BARTON

2010–2030   18.0

Full colour. Richer and fuller than the Langoa Barton. The oak is not so evident on the nose. Lots of class. Very good concentration. High quality. Full body. Very profound. Lovely fruit. Excellent grip. This is long and very classy. Fine plus.

CHÂTEAU LÉOVILLE-LAS-CASES

2010–2030	19.0

Very full colour. This shows real First
Growth class and depth. Good as the
Léoville-Barton is this is more profound. Full
body. Splendid extraction of very aristocratic
fruit here. Ripe tannins. Marvellous grip.
Very, very long. Complex and aristocratic.
Very fine plus.

CHÂTEAU LÉOVILLE-POYFERRÉ

2008–2024	17.5

Fullish colour. Lush and oaky and very ripe
on the nose. Less austere than Léoville
Barton or Léoville-Las-Cases. Fullish body.
Very exotic, almost sweet fruit. Yet no lack
of class. Quite oaky on the palate but not
excessively so. Long and complex. Fine.

CHÂTEAU SAINT-PIERRE

2006–2020	16.0

Good colour. Nice and plump on the nose if
without a great deal of depth and
personality. Accessible. Medium to medium-
full body. Plump and ripe. Good style if
without the greatest grip and depth. Yet the
finish is positive. Very good.

CHÂTEAU TALBOT

2008–2020	16.5

Full colour. Good Cabernet fruit on the nose.
Balanced and well put together. Not too
sturdy. Fullish body. Lovely civilised, ripe
fruit. Good balance and depth. Good grip.
Ample and long. Most attractive. It sings
more than most Saint-Juliens today. Very
good plus.

PAUILLAC

CHÂTEAU D'ARMAILHAC

NOW–2010	13.5

Good colour. Just a little dry and even dilute
on the nose. Medium body. Rather diffuse
on the palate. Quite fruity. But an absence of
grip and depth. Slightly astringent. Will it get
attenuated? Slightly dry and short on the
finish. It doesn't convince me. Not bad plus.

CHÂTEAU BATAILLEY

2006–2018	15.5

Fullish colour. Soft, ripe, accessible and
seductive on the nose. An attractive,
mediumweight example. Good fruit. Fresh
and balanced. Good elegance if no great
intensity and dimension at the end. Good
plus.

CARRUADES DE LAFITE

2006–2018	16.5

Medium-full colour. Cool and pure on the
nose. Restrained but classy. Medium body. A
little tannin. It doesn't quite have the fat and
concentration, but it shows a lot of quality
fruit. Well balanced too. The tannins are ripe
and the acidity is very good. Very good plus.

CHÂTEAU CLERC-MILON

2007–2012	15.0

Very good colour. A bit more to it than
d'Armailhac, but the tannins are a bit
attenuated. Medium body. Some richness.
Some grip. Decent finish. This is good but
the fruit, though ripe, is not very
concentrated.

CHÂTEAU DUHART-MILON

2006–2011	14.5

Good colour. Quite earthy on the nose in a
dead leaves sort of way. This detracts from the
finesse on the palate. Medium to medium-full
body. Some tannin. Decent fruit underneath,
but this twiggy flavour is present all the way
through. Slightly astringent. Slightly spicy.
Will it throw this off? Only quite good plus.

CHÂTEAU FONBADET

NOW–2011	13.5

Good colour. The wines have become more
sophisticated since Pascale Peyronie took
charge in 1998. This has a good positive nose
and no lack of fruit. Medium to medium-full
body. A little rustic at the end but not bad
plus. From 2005.

CHÂTEAU GRAND-PUY-DUCASSE

2006–2012   14.5

Very good colour. Soft, plump nose. Decent
attack but as so often with this vintage in the
Médoc, a lack of zip. So it finishes flat.
Decent fruit and decent oak nevertheless. It
finishes reasonably. Quite good plus.

CHÂTEAU GRAND-PUY-LACOSTE

2008–2028   17.5

Fullish colour. Very lovely fruit on the nose.
Very ripe and concentrated. Fullish body.
Classy. Gently oaky. Very impressive. Fullish
body. Excellent fruit. Very ripe and rich. Not
too rigid. Very, very long. Intense and classy.
Very lovely. As good as Ducru-Beaucaillou,
also owned by the Bories. Fine.

CHÂTEAU HAUT-BAGES LIBÉRAL

2007–2025   16.5

Good colour. Very good Cabernet fruit on
the nose. Lots of depth. Classy and
concentrated. Medium to medium-full body.
Good tannins. Good fruit. Ample, ripe and
quite profound. Harmonious. It finishes well.
Very good plus.

CHÂTEAU HAUT-BATAILLEY

2008–2020   16.0

Medium-full colour. More austere than the
Grand-Puy-Lacoste but lovely fruit
underneath. Just a touch of oak. Very good
quality here. Decent weight and very good
fruit. Some personality and plenty of length.
Good tannins. Very good.

CHÂTEAU LAFITE

2010–2030   19.5

Fullish colour. Very classy nose. Gently
oaky, profound, rich fruit. Almost old viney
in its creamy richness. Full body. Great
distinction. Excellent grip. Splendid balance.
This is very, very lovely. I prefer it to
Margaux and Latour. It has real definition.
Very, very long. Very fine indeed.

CHÂTEAU LATOUR

2008–2028   19.0

Fullish colour. Pure, ripe, Cabernet fruit.
Firm and austere on the nose. High quality
here. Fullish body. Some tannin. Very lovely
balanced fruit. The finish is long, ripe and
very classy. An impressive wine if not the
usual austere blockbuster. Very fine plus.

CHÂTEAU LYNCH-BAGES

2008–2018   16.0

Full colour. Ripe on the nose but a bit lumpy
and inflexible. Fullish body. Slightly rigid.
Good grip and good fruit. But it does add up
to something very sophisticated. Nowhere
near Grand-Puy-Lacoste in quality. Merely
very good.

CHÂTEAU MOUTON-ROTHSCHILD

2008–2028   16.5

Full colour. Rather reduced on the nose.
Even when this disappeared the wine was
unremarkable by First Growth standards.
Fullish body. Good tannins. Oaky. Good
grip. But a lack of richness, concentration
and flair. Merely very good plus.

CHÂTEAU PICHON-LONGUEVILLE

2008–2024   16.5

Medium-full colour. Good Cabernet depth
on the nose. Proper Pauillac size. Backward.
Better class and depth than Lynch-Bages.
Fullish body. Ripe. Quite classy. Positive
finish. Not brilliant but very good plus.

CHÂTEAU PICHON-LONGUEVILLE-LALANDE

NOW–2015   16.0

Medium to medium-full colour. Soft, ripe
and stylish on the nose. But it seems to lack
strength, grip and depth. Forward. Pretty.
Somewhat hollow in the middle. It lacks real
structure and it doesn't have the intensity it
normally has. A disappointment. Essentially
a little weedy, but the fruit is attractive. Very
good.

CHÂTEAU PONTET-CANET

2008–2020   16.0

Fullish colour. Quite soft, but plump and
nicely intensely fruity on the nose. Fullish on
the palate. Good tannins. Good ripe fruit. It
lacks a little personality and class compared
with Grand-Puy-Lacoste but there is plenty
of length. Very good.

Saint-Estèphe

Château Calon-Ségur
2008–2025	17.5

Fullish colour. Rich and ample on the nose. Fullish body. Good tannins. Ample, rich and balanced. Long. This has class and personality and very good fruit. The best Calon-Ségur since 1959. Fine.

Château Cos d'Estournel
2008–2024	17.0

Fullish colour. Good nose. Ripe and fresh. Medium-full weight. Reasonable richness and concentration. Good grip. This is classy, but it doesn't quite have the depth and concentration for 'fine'.

Château Cos Labory
2008–2018	16.0

Very good colour. Good nose. Clean pure fruit. Not a blockbuster but ripe, elegant and individual. Medium body only. Ripe tannins though and good acidity. Attractive, ripe raspberry fruit. Long and stylish. Very good.

Château Haut-Marbuzet
2007–2020	16.0

Medium-full colour. Lush and oaky and seductive on the nose. Medium-full body. Some tannin. Ripe fruit. No great depth or class but long and attractive. Great charm. Very good.

Château Lafon-Rochet
2007–2016	15.5

Good colour. Quite austere on the nose. Medium-full body. Some tannin. The tannins are quite well covered. Good, slightly hard, plummy fruit. Balanced. Quite juicy on the follow-through. This will round off and get more generous. The finish is positive. Good plus.

Château Lilian Ladouys
2006–2015	16.0

Good colour. Elegant, balanced and fresh on the nose. This is ripe and attractive. Medium-full body. Plump. Very good acidity. Plenty of energy. Good ripe, balanced fruit. No hard tannins. Long, seductive and succulent. Very good. Rather better than the 2000 and 2001.

Château Meyney
2007–2016	14.0

Very good colour. Good richness and no weakness on the nose. Decent plump, quite meaty fruit on the attack, then a little hollow. Then the wine comes back. Slightly astringent but otherwise no worse for wear. Quite good.

Château Montrose
2008–2024	17.0

Full colour. Firm, rich, classy nose. Plenty of depth. Fullish body. Some tannin. Very good concentrated, ripe, stylish fruit. Long. Very good character. Not too hard for once. Very good indeed.

Château Les Ormes de Pez
NOW–2015	15.0

Good colour. Ripe nose. Just a little artisanal. Medium-full body. Good grip. Good balance. The tannins are ripe and round and the wine has plenty of fruit. But at the end there is something a little rustic. But good.

Château Phélan-Ségur
2007–2017	15.5

Good colour. A little dry and pinched on the nose. Better on the palate. Yet there is a hard edge here. Medium body. Good grip and nice plump fruit. It finishes well so I think this hardness will become more generous as it evolves. Good plus.

Château Tronquoy-Lalande
NOW–2009	13.0

Medium-full colour. Fresh nose. Decent fruit. A bit *sauvage* and rather astringent on the palate. Decent grip but rather unbalanced. Not bad.

1997 Vintage

Size of the Crop :	6,682,605 hectolitres.
Vintage Rating :	13.5 (red wines).
	12.5 (dry white wines).
	18.0 (sweet white wines).

Another very large harvest, indeed one of the highest ever in terms of yield per surface area at 59.2 hl/ha. The white wine crop was 933,917 hl (14 per cent).

When the 1997 Bordeaux vintage came on the scene it was savagely attacked. The proprietors were castigated for charging excessive prices: increases on 1996 (themselves a lot higher than 1995) for a vintage which wasn't nearly as good. The wines were criticised for – well, not being very good. With the usual either pure white or darkest black tendencies of most media generalisations this was quickly glossed from not very good to very disappointing. My three-year-on tasting, however, showed that there is much to commend, much to enjoy, plenty which is more than respectable. It is a tribute to today's conscientious winemaking that at the top level some very pleasant 1997s should have come out of what were really not very auspicious climatic conditions.

The Weather

It was a very extraordinary year. The result was that the poor old vines, buffeted this way and that by changeable conditions, as well as overloaded with fruit, lost their flexibility to adapt, almost as if their basic natural urge to produce ripe fruit come what may had been undermined.

After a very brief winter – it was only really cold from Christmas to mid-January – the weather was very mild. November 1996 had been wet, and an average rainfall in February, plus temperatures over 3°C warmer than usual both in this month and the next, led to a bud-break which took place a full two weeks earlier than 1996, itself a precocious vintage. On the one hand this promised an early harvest. On the other it meant that almost inevitably there would be a risk of frost.

Thankfully it continued mild, and as March moved into April, it was indeed hot, temperatures reaching 25°C on 11th April. Development of the vine raced ahead at first, but was then retarded by drought, no rain falling in April until the 25th. Frost by then had ceased to be a problem (temperatures rose to 29°C on 2nd May). The vine was ready to flower.

Some six weeks earlier than usual, the first flowers began to appear over the weekend of 3rd/4th May. Sadly the weather then changed for the worse, a series of cold squally spells spun out the fecundation process, especially in the Merlots, the first red grape variety to develop. The result was that not only on the same vine, but even within the same bunch, you had berries which were several weeks apart in their cycle. This problem would persist right up until the harvest.

Towards the end of May the weather improved, allowing the later developing varieties such as Cabernet Sauvignon to flower better. But nevertheless the flowering had extended over a month (1996: 12 days). This is an irregularity unprecedented in Bordeaux. There have always been patches of vineyard with cooler microclimates where the vines were later to develop. Merlots ripen before Cabernet Francs which ripen before Cabernet Sauvignons. But to have individual grapes within the same bunch flowering and ripening at different times, several weeks apart, was clearly going to present a major problem to those in charge of picking the fruit in September.

The weather continued to be uneven. Fine at the beginning of June, chilly and showery for the rest of the month. Cool and humid for most of July. Very hot indeed for almost the whole month of August: but still humid. Normally, after the *véraison*, the wine forgets about its leaf growth, and sets about to bring the fruit to fruition. In these tropical conditions, this change of events never took place. Despite measures to thin out the leaves to expose the fruit to the sun (helping to increase the colour as well as mature the grapes) which took place amidst unprecedented crop-thinning – one of the few ways to regularise the uneven state of maturity – all this heat did not result in a concentration of the emerging fruit. The sugar-acid ripening process proceeded, if sluggishly, but the phenolic ripening process shut down almost altogether.

The Harvest

With a great fanfare, the top Graves properties started picking their white grapes on 18th August. Legendary and exceptional, said the press release, pointing out that this was perhaps the earliest harvest ever, or if not the earliest since 1893. Even Jean-Bernard Delmas of Château Haut-Brion, normally a man of sanguine restraint, got really quite excited. And the Haut-Brion Blanc *is* exceptional, with both a high natural alcohol level of 13°, and acidities to match. But here they can, and did, afford to pick through their small amount of vineyard three, four, even five times to select the best at their optimum point. Elsewhere, sadly, the ripest grapes, both red and white, had been attacked by vinegar flies, and the danger of *pourriture aigre* meant that these, in theory the prime fruit, had to be jettisoned.

Worse was to come. The humid August weather finally erupted. In the last week there were several violent thunderstorms, unleashing a total of as much as 80 mm of rain between 25th August and 1st September.

As far as the white wines were concerned this caused much of the fruit to begin to rot before it was fully ripe. A lot depended on how the vines had been looked after in July and August, but it resulted in whites which, for the most part, were somewhat anonymous: correct at best, and for early drinking.

As to the reds, such improvement that had occurred prior to the storms was quickly seen to be fool's gold. The early Merlots, though with decent potential alcoholic degrees, began to collapse, and had to be collected prematurely. Acidities were low and the wines were light in colour. Some châteaux kept the must cool for fermentation eventually with fruit with tougher (and more highly coloured) skins.

Thankfully this was to be the last of the rain. What looked like a total disaster was rescued by a September which would be almost rainless (a shower or two on the 12th and 13th), with more or less uninterrupted sun right through until 5th October.

'Rescued', note. Not really 'improved'. Despite this fine weather, the fruit did not respond as it should have done, as indeed it had done the previous year. The later-ripening Merlots were, of course, better than those from the earlier-ripening vineyard plots. But a policy of waiting further still resulted only in a lack of freshness, not an increase in concentration.

The Cabernets gained by being late to develop and not having suffered so much from the end-of-August storms. Yet the same thing happened here as with the Merlots: the fruit concentrated, but the development of the anthocyanins remained blocked. Only at the very end of the vintage, and this meant those châteaux whose fruit was able to continue on the vine until October (125 days and more after the flowering; normally a grape is ripe after 100 days) did we get an element of real concentration. Only a few Saint-Julien and Pauillac estates were able to benefit fully.

In all it was the longest, most drawn-out, most never-racking vintage in history. Some white grapes were picked on 18th August, most Merlots from 8th to 22nd September, most Cabernets from 16th September to 4th October, but some as late as 16th October, almost two months after the first Sauvignon grapes were picked at Château Haut-Brion!

Meanwhile, however, things were looking up in the Sauternes. The first *tris*, early in September, were unpromising. I firmly hope that none of these grapes found their way into the *grand vin*. Subsequent fruit was decidedly promising. The harvest continued into November, producing wines which had a richness and a power not seen since 1990. Here at least we have a success.

RED WINEMAKING AND ÉLEVAGE

Fermentations extended the problems the Bordelais had suffered throughout the growing season. Firstly there was the need for a severe *triage*, to sort through and eliminate the unripe fruit. Despite what had often been two successive green-harvests in the field – or to be precise a green harvest before *véraison* and a *rosé* harvest thereafter – there was still much that was green and unripe in the fruit. There were other complications. There was a lot of it. The grapes were large, with a high liquid to solid ratio. Acidities and tannins were low. And very often the fruit was coming in at 30°C, the ambient temperature in the vineyard. On the one hand it was necessary to *saigner*, or to use one of the new concentrating machines. Then there was the question of whether to macerate short and risk a lack of colour and depth, or to macerate long and risk a greenness from the unripe fruit getting into the wine. The *vin de presse* wasn't going to be a help this year. It was as exhausted as the winemakers. In general most producers opted for a shorter maceration process, or had the problem taken out of their hands by the speed at which the fermentation took place. There are a few over-macerated wines on the Right Bank (Saint-Émilion and Pomerol), hardly any in the Graves and Médoc.

THE WINES

Faces were long in November, when the new wine was racked off its lees. Opinions had improved slightly by April, when the doors were opened for the world to come and taste. Twelve months on, when the 1998s were first offered, it was apparent that the 1997s had benefited from a year in cask (as I had predicted when I first reported on them). Now, safely in bottle, it is clear there is much to enjoy, particularly in the Médoc and Graves. And don't forget the Sauternes.

PRICES THEN AND NOW

As I have said, prices were irrationally excessive at the beginning. If they have moved since, it is in a downwards direction, apart from one or two garage wines from Saint-Émilion and Pomerol. Today the First Growths will cost you £700–£750 ($1260–$1350) a dozen, the Super-Seconds anything from as low as £185 ($330) for Léoville-Poyferré to £350 ($630) for La Mission Haut-Brion. Much of the wine has been sold at a loss. One Bordeaux merchant complained to me that in order to shift his Léoville-Las-Cases he was forced to sell it for 100 Francs less than he had originally paid for it. Many of the wines were sold in 2003 at prices as much as 50 per cent less than their opening prices in 1998.

Sauternes are rarely wines which give a profit to those buying early. Prices of the 1997s have hardly moved from the outset. Currently they range from £150 ($270) for Château Filhot to £300 ($540) for Rieussec, much the same as currently asked for the 2001s. Château d'Yquem is £1750 ($3150). Prices of the 1989 and 1990 vintages are only a little higher.

THE TASTING

The following wines were tasted in Southwold in May 2001. My thanks to Alastair Marshall, Rob Chase and the rest of the Adnams team for all their work and background organisation.

SAINT-ÉMILION

CHÂTEAU ANGÉLUS

NOW–2013   17.5

Very good colour. Full, rich, ample, concentrated nose. Fullish body. Lots of depth and grip. Unexpectedly ripe, even rich. Good grip, vigour and intensity. Classy and very promising.

CHÂTEAU L'ARROSÉE

NOW–2008   15.5

Medium colour. A little lean on the nose. But decent, clean fruit and acidity. Medium-full body. Good tannins. It lacks a little depth but good weight and style. Very good.

CHÂTEAU AUSONE

2006–2020   18.5

Fine colour. Opulent nose. Luscious and succulent and very ripe. Full bodied and oaky. Quite some tannin but the tannins are ripe. The wine is quite substantial yet without hard edges. Very good grip. Plenty on the follow-through. Very lovely fruit. Very fine.

CHÂTEAU BEAUSÉJOUR-DUFFAU-LAGARROSSE

NOW–2008   14.0

Good colour. Just a little hot and over-macerated on the nose. Medium-full body. Some tannin. Decent fruit and grip at first but rather too astringent later. Yet there is some style here. Fresh finish. Quite good.

CHÂTEAU BEAU-SÉJOUR-BÉCOT

NOW–2006   13.5

Good colour. Sweet, spicy and oaky on the nose. Really quite succulent without being too forced. Medium body. A little tannin. A little over-macerated. The wine is a little short. But decent fruit and style. Not bad plus.

CHÂTEAU BELAIR

NOW–2006   15.5

Medium to medium-full colour. Clean, pure, ripe and elegant. Lovely fruit. By no means a blockbuster. But all the better for it. Medium body. A little slight but a lot of finesse.

CHÂTEAU BERLIQUET

NOW–2006   15.0

Good colour. Lovely gentle, fruity-oaky nose. Soft. No hard edges. Very stylish. Medium weight. Stylish. Ripe. Harmonious. Quite oaky. But very good in this context. Ready now.

CHÂTEAU CHEVAL BLANC

2007–2020   18.5

Medium-full colour. Not a lot on the nose. Still a little tight and a bit austere. More generous on the palate. Medium-full body. A touch of astringency. This is rich and very fine but rather closed at present. Very good grip though. I think it will improve as it ages.

LE DÔME

NOW–2006   13.5

Medium colour. Quite weighty on the nose. A little over-done. But ripe it has to be said. Medium-full body. Some oak. Not much dimension here. Decent but a bit superficial at the end. Not bad plus.

CHÂTEAU MAGDELAINE

NOW–2006   14.0

Medium to medium-full colour. Clean and pure on the nose if a little lean. Elegant though. Medium weight. No great depth. No tannin. But fruity and stylish and positive at the end. Quite good.

CLOS DE L'ORATOIRE

DRINK SOON   13.0

Good colour. Ripe and sweet on the nose. Not exactly elegant. But a good effort for the vintage. Thinner and more undergrowthy on the palate. Medium body. A little tannin. Unexciting.

CHÂTEAU PAVIE

NOW–2006   12.0

Medium to medium-full colour. Rather stewed and artificial on the nose. Lumpy and astringent and coarse on the palate. Some weight. But far too extracted and the fruit is unripe.

Château Pavie-Decesse

NOW–2006   12.5

Very good colour. An odd bit of volatile acidity on the nose. Ripe though, in a slightly artificial sweet/sour way. Some tannin. Medium-full. Lumpy and coarse and a bit stewed. Already astringent. Seriously unbalanced. No.

Château Quinault L'Enclos

NOW–2006   13.0

Good colour. Succulent fresh nose. Up-front fruit. Nothing much underneath. Decent start. Then it tails off. Medium body. A little tannin. Rather one-dimensional. Fair.

Château Le Tertre-Roteboeuf

NOW–2008   16.0

Good colour. Fullish, rich and generous on the nose. There is depth and character here. Medium-full body. Oaky, generous and ripe. Not over-extracted. Positive and long. Very good. Nearly there.

Château Troplong-Mondot

NOW–2007   13.5

Good colour. Rather stewed on the nose. Lumpy. A little too much maceration here for the vintage. L'Arrosée got it about right. Some depth. But the structure dominates here. Quite good at best.

Château de Valandraud

NOW–2006   15.5

Medium-full colour. Really quite stylish on the nose. Good Cabernet Franc. Not forced. Medium to medium-full body. Quite ripe. Attractively balanced. Good length. Good class. Unexpectedly good. Positive finish. If slightly hot at the end.

Pomerol

Château Beau Soleil

DRINK SOON   12.5

Medium colour. Soft, pretty but somewhat one-dimensional nose. Light and pretty but now a bit astringent at the end. A point. Nothing special. Drink soon.

Château Certan de May

NOW–2006   14.5

Medium colour. Plump, attractive nose. No great depth but good stuff. Medium-full body. No tannin. A little simple. But fresh and charming. Quite good plus.

Château La Conseillante

DRINK SOON   14.0

Medium-full colour. Ripe and pretty on the nose, though not a lot of depth. Light to medium body. Some oak. Pretty but weak. Stylish but a little short. Quite good.

Clos L'Église

NOW–2010   16.5

Medium-full colour. Ripe, slightly spicy, gently oaky nose. Medium-full body. Good acidity. This is an attractive example with just a little tannin to resolve and no lack of character. Positive finish. Very good plus.

Château L'Évangile

NOW–2015   18.0

Fine colour. Rich nose. Lots of depth. This is fine and concentrated. Good backbone. Nice ripe tannins. Fullish body. Some acidity. Clean and pure and intense if a little austere at present. Good weight. Fine plus.

Château La Fleur de Gay

NOW–2008   16.0

Medium-full colour. Rich Merlot, oaky nose. Good class and depth. Medium-full body. Decent grip. Ample and fruity if without any great character or definition. Very good.

Château Gazin

NOW–2007   15.0

Fullish colour. Succulent and ripe on the nose. An attractive wine. Not over-done. A little more to it than Certan de May. Fresh. Just about ready. Balanced, stylish and positive. Good.

CHÂTEAU LATOUR-À-POMEROL

NOW–2010   17.0

Medium-full colour. Rich, succulent nose.
Very clean and pure. Very good depth for the
vintage. Medium to medium-full body. Rich
and impressive. Lovely fruit. The tannins are
just about absorbed. Long and profound at
the end. This is very good indeed if not fine.

CHÂTEAU PETIT-VILLAGE

NOW–2006   13.0

Very good colour. Earthy nose. A bit over-
extracted. Medium to medium-full colour. It
lacks grip. Superficial. The tannins are still
astringent. Unexciting.

CHÂTEAU PÉTRUS

NOW–2020   18.5

Fine colour. Soft, ripe and flowery. But not
the depth of some, nor the weight, on the
nose. Just a touch dry as it developed. Very
ripe and fresh on the palate. Good grip.
Quite oaky. Quite intense. Lots of
concentration at the end. Very fine.

LE PIN

NOW–2007   16.0

Fullish colour. Ripe, succulent Merlot nose.
Not the dimension or depth of Vieux
Château Certan though. On the palate a little
slight. Not quite enough concentration and
grip. Very attractive though. The finish is
positive. Very good.

CHÂTEAU TROTANOY

NOW–2010+   18.0

Medium-full colour. Rich, concentrated for a
1997, very impressive nose. Lots of substance
here. But very clean and pure. Not a bit over-
macerated. Fullish body. Very harmonious.
Very classy. Very good tannins. A super
example. Splendid concentrated fruit. Very
long. Very fine.

VIEUX CHÂTEAU CERTAN

NOW–2010+   17.5

Medium-full colour. Splendidly rich,
concentrated nose. Lovely fruit. Real – and
unexpected for a 1997 – depth. Fullish body.
Very concentrated. Splendid tannin. Not as
fine a fruit as the Trotanoy but a fine wine
nevertheless. Very good grip. Still needs time.

GRAVES

DOMAINE DE CHEVALIER

NOW–2013+   17.5

Good colour. Classically elegant nose. Lots
of depth. Finely balanced. Medium-full
body. Some tannin. Lovely cool, balanced
fruit. Ripe and balanced and complex. Very
stylish. Lovely long finish. Fine quality.

CHÂTEAU HAUT-BAILLY

NOW–2011   16.5

Very good colour. Lovely succulent, fullish
nose. Ripe and gently oaky. Not a bit tough
but plenty of substance and depth. Medium-
full body. Round and fat. Still a little tannin.
Not the grip of Domaine de Chevalier or La
Mission Haut-Brion, or the quality of the
tannins in these wines, but very good plus.
Long and succulent.

CHÂTEAU HAUT-BRION

2007–2020   16.5

Fine colour. Some substance on the nose. But
a little herbaceous. It lacks flair. Better on the
palate but a little overdone. The follow-
through is astringent and the fruit lacks fat.
The effect is slightly lumpy. The tannins
aren't ripe enough.

CHÂTEAU LA MISSION HAUT-BRION

NOW–2015+   18.5

Very good colour. Fullish nose. Lots of wine
here. Concentrated and classy. Backward but
the tannins are certainly ripe enough. Fullish
body. Very lovely, elegant, finely balanced
fruit. This has real breed. Very good grip.
Excellent for a 1997.

Margaux and Southern Médoc

Château Brane-Cantenac

NOW–2012	16.5

Medium-full colour. Rich and classy on the nose. This is very stylish on the palate. Medium body. Very good acidity. Positive and very well balanced. Even better than the Durfort-Vivens.

Château Chasse-Spleen

NOW–2012	16.0

Medium-full colour. Elegant nose. Very good, classy, ripe fruit. Medium to medium-full body. Good oak. Laid-back and harmonious. Long and positive. Lovely finish. This is very good.

Château Durfort-Vivens

NOW–2011	16.0

Medium-full colour. Nice, rich and fat on the nose. Good oak. Medium-full body. Ripe. Plenty of depth. Elegant and well balanced. Very good.

Château Giscours

NOW–2008	13.5

Medium colour. Lighter on the nose than du Tertre. But similarly a lack of style. Medium to medium-full body. But a little raw. Not bad plus.

Château Kirwan

NOW–2011	14.0

Good colour. Ripe nose. A little oak. Just a little overdone. Medium-full body. A little astringent. Good fruit and grip though. So the finish is positive. Quite good.

Château Labégorce-Zédé

NOW–2011	16.0

Medium-full colour. Classy nose with a touch of wood. Clean, pure and harmonious. Quite soft on the palate. Medium body. But good grip. This has length, complexity and elegance. Very good.

Château La Lagune

NOW–2009	14.5

Medium-full colour. Pleasant nose. Soft and fruity if not very intense or very profound. Medium to medium-full body. Well made. But a little dull. Forward. Good at best.

Château Margaux

NOW–2015	17.5

Medium-full colour. Fresh. Medium to medium-full weight. Not the greatest depth or concentration but balanced, ripe and stylish. Medium-full body. Good tannins. Ripe and stylish and harmonious. Good positive finish. Not the weight of Lafite. A classy wine though. Fine.

Château Marquis de Terme

NOW–2008	14.0

Medium-full colour. Good fruit here on the nose. Ripe but a little bland. Pleasantly balanced. Medium to medium-full body. But it lacks a bit of zip and flair. Quite forward. Quite good.

Château Palmer

NOW–2012	17.5

Medium to medium-full colour. Lovely nose. The wine is quite forward but the fruit is ripe. Cedary background. Soft. Promising. Very stylish. Very lovely fruit. Medium-full body. Rich and intense on the palate. Lots of dimension and finesse. Fine.

Château Poujeaux

NOW–2010	15.0

Good colour. Ripe, generous, fleshy nose. Not as classy as Chasse-Spleen, also from Moulis. Medium-full body. Good substance. Spicy. Balanced. It lacks a little finesse but good.

Château Rauzan-Ségla

NOW–2012+	17.0

Good colour. Classy, laid-back nose. Lovely fruit. Medium to medium-full body. Very lovely, soft cedary fruit. Finely balanced. Very Margaux in character. Not a bit forced. Very good indeed.

Château Sociando-Mallet

NOW–2012   16.0

Medium-full colour. Succulent, quite firm nose. Good Cabernet. Good tannins. Medium-full body. Ripe and stylish. Good depth and very good grip. Very good.

Château du Tertre

NOW–2008   13.0

Medium-full colour. A bit lumpy and rather reduced on the nose. Rather forced. A hard wine on the palate. Ripe but also a bit astringent. Ungainly. Fair.

Saint-Julien

Château Branaire-Ducru

NOW–2015   17.0

Medium-full colour. Very lovely nose. There is a lot of ripeness and flair here. Medium-full body. Not a bit aggressive. This is unexpectedly stylish. Long and complex and very lovely.

Château Ducru-Beaucaillou

NOW–2018+   18.5

Medium-full colour. Marvellous nose. Very lovely ripe, silky Cabernet fruit. Great class. Succulent and oaky. Lots of flair. Fullish body. Splendid tannins. Really very lovely. Lots of fruit. Excellent balance. Very intense. Splendid.

Château Gruaud-Larose

NOW–2012   14.5

Medium-full colour. Slightly muscular on the nose. A bit lumpy. Slightly herbaceous tannins. Fullish body. Tannic. Ripe but a little unsophisticated. The tannins are a bit clumsy. Merely good. Needs time.

Château Lagrange

NOW–2013   16.0

Good colour. Full, firm, very Cabernet nose. Almost Pauillac-y. Medium-full body. Ripe. Good tannins. The attack is positive. The wine is well made. Not the greatest of dimension but very good.

Château Langoa-Barton

NOW–2013   16.0

Good colour. Ripe, graceful, soft and elegant on the nose. Youthful. Medium-full body. A little raw on the palate. But good Cabernet underneath. Balanced and classy.

Château Léoville-Barton

NOW–2018   18.0

Good colour. Splendid nose. Ripe. Not as backward as Las-Cases. Fullish body. Very good tannins. Concentrated and ripe. Lovely Cabernet fruit. Very good grip. Lots of character. Lots of finesse. Fine plus.

Château Léoville-Las-Cases

NOW–2020+   18.5

Good colour. Full, firm, Cabernet-Pauillac nose. Lots of depth. Really quite backward still. Marvellous fruit on the palate. Not as silky as Ducru-Beaucaillou but as profound. Very long. Very classy.

Château Saint-Pierre

NOW–2012   15.0

Medium-full colour. Just a little green on the nose. There is certainly class here. Very good old viney Cabernet. Good grip. Quite oaky. But it is also just a touch austere. It finishes well though. I'll give it the benefit of the doubt.

Pauillac

Château d'Armailhac

NOW–2008   15.0

Medium-full colour. Light, fruity and pretty on the nose. Pleasant fruit plus some oak. It lacks a bit of depth and concentration. But it has plenty of charm. Forward. Some elegance. Good.

Château Duhart-Milon

NOW–2008   13.5

Good colour. Full, raw, slightly reduced nose. A bit lumpy on the palate. Just a little too tannic. Raw rather than rich. And the reduction is still here. Fair only.

Château Grand-Puy-Lacoste

NOW–2011   16.0

Medium-full colour. Ripe, rich, Cabernet-ish and succulent on the nose. Good class but not a patch on Ducru-Beaucaillou. Medium to medium-full body. Good sophisticated and harmonious fruit. Not much underneath but long and positive. Very good.

Château Haut-Batailley

NOW–2012   15.5

Good colour. It seems more substantial than Grand-Puy-Lacoste on the nose if a little raw and less ripe. Medium to medium-full body. Less evolved but a good positive follow-through. Good plus.

Château Lafite

2008–2023   19.0

Fine colour. Very lovely concentrated fruit. Very good oak as well. Rich and classy and finely balanced. Fullish body. Fragrant. Rich and very finely balanced. Very lovely classy fruit. Very complex and classy. Not quite as concentrated as Latour at the end. Very fine plus.

Château Latour

2008–2023   19.5

Fullish colour. Full, rich and ripe on the nose. More so than Mouton-Rothschild. This is a more succulent wine. Full, rich, fat and aristocratic. This is very lovely. Splendidly balanced, intense and elegant. Marvellous finish. Very lovely.

Château Lynch-Bages

NOW–2009   15.0

Good colour. Some fruit but not a lot of weight and succulence on the nose. Only medium weight. Not a lot of tannin and grip. Pleasant but it lacks a bit of interest and refinement. Good only.

Château Mouton-Rothschild

2008–2023   19.0

Fine colour. Slightly austere Cabernet on the nose. Lots of class on the palate. Very fine fruit. Very pure. Very intense. Full body. Fine grip and very good tannins. Long and impressive. Excellent intensity at the end. Very classy.

Château Pichon-Longueville

NOW–2010   15.5

Medium-full colour. Some tannin. More depth and richness than Lynch-Bages on the nose. Slightly suave. Medium-full body. Some tannin. Not quite enough grip but good plus.

Château Pichon-Longueville, Comtesse de Lalande

NOW–2009   16.0

Medium-full colour. Light, ripe and charming on the nose. There is class here if not much weight. Medium body. A little tannin. Slightly better grip than Pichon-Longueville. But not up to Lalande's top flight reputation. Very good at best.

Château Pontet-Canet

NOW–2014   16.0

Very good colour. Classy nose. Good concentrated fruit. Some oak. Medium-full body. Good tannins. Lots of finesse. This has grip, depth and balance. Plenty of personality. Very good.

Saint-Estèphe

Château Calon-Ségur

NOW–2010   15.0

Medium colour. Just a little lumpy and unripe on the nose but basically good substance. A little rustic on the palate. But quite ripe and well balanced. Fullish body. Typical chewy Saint-Estèphe. Good but not great.

CHÂTEAU COS D'ESTOURNEL

NOW–2010	13.5

Very good colour. Strangely four-square on the nose. Full but lumpy. Some tannin. But these tannins are not very ripe. Fullish body. Quite meaty. Not a bit slight. But rather too lumpy. Not hot. But a little unstylish. It needs time. This is a bit of a disaster.

CHÂTEAU HAUT-MARBUZET

NOW–2010	16.0

Good colour. Rich, oaky, opulent and spicy on the nose. No lack of substance but it misses a bit of elegance. Fullish body. Round and quite concentrated. Good tannin. Good grip. Highly satisfactory.

CHÂTEAU MONTROSE

NOW–2007	16.0

Medium to medium-full colour. Not a great deal on the nose here. Good Cabernet fruit. Good balanced. Ripe and stylish. Not short but a little lightweight. Yet positive and long. Lovely finish. Good plus. Just about ready.

CHÂTEAU PHÉLAN-SÉGUR

NOW–2008	14.5

Medium-full colour. Classy and balanced on the nose if a slight lack of weight. Slightly astringent on the palate. But the wine is elegant. Medium to medium-full body. Good positive finish.

SAUTERNES

CHÂTEAU D'ARCHE

NOW–2015	16.0

Cool nose. Flowery and slightly herbal. Not much botrytis evident. Medium weight. An attractive, sweet wine with intensity and balance. Clean, dry and fresh. This is still youthful. Some botrytis. Long finish. Very good.

CHÂTEAU BROUSTET

NOW–2009	15.0

Soft, sweet, mellow nose. Attractive fruit. Some botrytis if not the greatest intensity. Stylish though. As it evolved a quite minty-herbal flavour became apparent. Medium-full body. Complex. Quite sweet. Good racy acidity. This is an individual wine. I would not rate it as a yardstick Sauternes but I find it rather attractive.

CHÂTEAU CAILLOU

NOW–2020	17.0

Lovely nose. Intense and racy. Lemon sherbet flavours. Fullish, ample and concentrated on the palate, with very good balancing Barsac acidity and a mineral finish. This is very good indeed. Still young.

CHÂTEAU CLIMENS

NOW–2030	17.0

Good rich nose. Fat, sweet and ripe on the nose. Very honeyed. Some evolution. Very good botrytis. Not as powerful or as much grip as the 1999. Full, rich and slightly four-square at present. Rather adolescent. Good botrytis. Needs time. Very good indeed at least.

CHÂTEAU COUTET

NOW–2008	15.0

Lacks a little zip but quite good botrytis here on the nose. A little sulphur too. Medium weight. Plump and forward. No great depth but a pleasant wine which will be ready soon.

CHÂTEAU DOISY-DAËNE

NOW–2012	14.0

Round and ripe and sweet on the nose. No enormous concentration of botrytis. Indeed it is slightly heavy. Lacks raciness. Fullish and sweet. Some noble rot. Quite good but slightly four-square. Still young though. This might yet improve with age.

Château Doisy-Védrines

(SEE NOTE)

High-toned nose. Curious, almost maderised touch. Even higher volatile acidity than usual. As it evolved the maderised element disappeared, to be replaced by a chemical smell. Good sweetness on the palate. Medium body and some botrytis and grip. But this now has almost a chemical flavour. It makes it barely drinkable. Judgement deferred.

I asked the château to send me another bottle, which they duly did: This is quite different. Concentrated, youthful, closed nose. Fresh. Good botrytis. Full and racy as all good Barsacs should be. Rich, balanced, complex and honeyed on the palate. Long. Very good indeed. 17/20. Now-2025.

Château Filhot

DRINK SOON   13.0

Light colour. Not very sweet on the nose. Not much noble rot either. More like a Cérons than a Sauternes. Reasonably clean though. Medium weight. Clean and fresh. But a lack of concentration. Appley-peachy fruit makes this an agreeable drink. But it is not a true Sauternes. Forward. Ready.

Château Guiraud

(SEE NOTE)

Quite a golden colour. This has gone off. Definitely maderised. Medium weight. No intensity. Not much fatness or botrytis either. I can't mark this.

Clos Haut-Peyraguey

NOW–2020   17.5

Rich, full and honeyed on the nose. Still quite backward. Good noble rot. Full, fat, youthful and concentrated on the palate. Lots of botrytis. This has a fine potential. Plenty of wine. Plenty of vigour. Fine.

Château Lafaurie-Peyraguey

NOW–2025   18.5

High-toned, flowery nose. Some botrytis at least. Slightly hidden. A lot of attraction here. Very good grip. Full, youthful and gently oaky. Very rich and concentrated. Vanilla pods. Really intense noble rot on the palate. This is most impressive and very classy. Marvellous finish.

Château Lamothe-Guignard

NOW–2007   12.0

Slightly heavier colour than some in this first flight. Heavy on the nose too. Not much botrytis. Rather coarse and sulphury. Sweet and fullish on the palate. A little short. There is a little noble rot here but the wine is a disappointment.

Château de Malle

NOW–2020   17.5

Subtle nose. Reserved and backward. Medium to medium-full weight. Lots of botrytis here. This is impressive. Fullish body. Very intense. Very concentrated. This is flowery and finely balanced. Youthful. Long. Lovely.

Château de Myrat

NOW–2008   14.0

Some botrytis on the nose. Some substance. A little heavy and a touch sulphury. There are some burnt flavours here. Quite full. Honey and toffee. Good acidity. Reasonable depth. Not exactly the greatest or flair but quite good.

Château Rabaud-Promis

NOW–2012   15.0

Clean and fullish. Some botrytis, but not a lot. Just a little sulphur at the end. Better on the palate. Flowery and plump. Medium intensity. Good fresh fruit. Still needs time. Good but not great.

CHÂTEAU RAYNE-VIGNEAU

NOW–2015   16.5

Quite a high-toned nose. But not exactly very concentrated or very intense: curious. On the palate this has reasonable weight, and it is nicely fresh. It is quite sweet and honeyed too. Yet strangely monolithic. Needs time. Certainly very good plus.

CHÂTEAU ROMER DU HAYOT

NOW–2007   12.0

Medium-sweet but little botrytis on the nose. Medium structure, a little four-square. A lack of real flair. Medium-sweet, medium-bodied and rather one-dimensional on the palate. No noble rot. Quite a clean dry finish. But rather disappointing in the context of the 1997 vintage.

CHÂTEAU RIEUSSEC

2007–2030   19.0

Full, backward, rich and fat on the nose. Still very much an infant. Lots of wine here, but it is not singing today. Plenty of botrytis, but all closed-in. A very full, powerful, backward and intense wine. It is all here. But it is an infant. Splendid potential. This is very fine.

CHÂTEAU SIGALAS-RABAUD

NOW–2020   18.0

A very lovely nose. Very elegant and very concentrated. High botrytis levels and very excellent acidity. Absolutely yardstick. Medium weight. Honeyed. Rich and sweet and smooth and harmonious. Good intensity. Lots of class. Fine plus.

CHÂTEAU SUAU

NOW–2007   13.0

A bit sulphury on the nose. I don't think there is much botrytis here. The sulphur blew off after a while leaving a medium-bodied, medium-sweet wine. A little neutral. On the palate there is some botrytis. Decent grip and the wine is clean. There is an absence of real flair but the wine is not bad. A bit heavy on the finish.

CHÂTEAU SUDUIRAUT

NOW–2025   18.5

A very fine nose here. Excellent grip. Flowery and fruity and very intense. Lots of botrytis. Very youthful still. Very harmonious. Full, ample, multi-dimensional, yet cool and racy at the end. I find this immensely seductive. Long. Very fine.

CHÂTEAU LA TOUR-BLANCHE

NOW–2025   18.0

Slightly deeper colour than some. A more broad-backed, evolved nose than some. Was it bottled later? Full, abundant, vanilla and toffee flavours. Very full on the palate. Rather more backward than it appears on the nose. A vigorous, concentrated wine with very good acidity. This will last very well. Rich and quite powerful. Fine plus.

The d'Yquem and de Fargues 1997 were released on the market in the summer of 2002. I tasted them for the second time in April 2003.

CHÂTEAU DE FARGUES

2006–2028   16.5

Quite closed on the nose. A broad flavour which is fat and full-bodied, ripe and rich, but which lacks a little grip and nuance.

CHÂTEAU D'YQUEM

2015–2050   20.0

Still very youthful on the nose, but very concentrated and impressive. Full-bodied and rich, fat and complex: indeed quite powerful. Splendid vigour and grip. Marvellous classy fruit. Profound and excellent.

1996 VINTAGE

SIZE OF THE CROP:	6,413,570 HECTOLITRES.
VINTAGE RATING:	14.0 – 18.5 (RED WINES – SEE BELOW).
	16.0 (DRY WHITE WINES).
	14.0 (SWEET WINES).

Another very large crop, the yield per hectare being 57.2 hectolitres. The white wine harvest measured 979,816 hl (15.3 per cent).

After the successes of the 1980s, culminating in the very fine 1990 vintage, we had to wait a long time for a vintage of comparable quality. Nineteen ninety one was short, and a wash-out. The next two years were large but rained on. In 1994 it rained a little less and the wines are acceptable. The following year it rained less still, and there are some very good wines. Which brings us to 1996. Here we have some fine wines in absolute terms, though only in Saint-Julien and Pauillac, plus a much larger number of very good wines throughout the Médoc and the Graves, though to a lesser extent in Saint-Émilion and Pomerol. Even in Margaux, hitherto, outside the top three or four, a boring series of wines, we can rate most of the usual suspects as good. The big disappointment is largely in the portfolio of Ets Jean-Pierre Moueix, but they were brave enough to admit at the outset that they had underachieved, and reduced prices, while others were increasing them. Nineteen ninety-six was not a cheap vintage to buy *en primeur*.

THE WEATHER

The winter was mild but wet, and this encouraged an early budding towards the end of March. After a cold snap at the beginning of April the weather warmed up again, but most of May was cool and miserable, and the vines began to lose their original precocity. Then, just as they were due to flower, winter changed to summer overnight. The first three weeks of June were splendidly hot and sunny. All the three main black grape varieties were able to flower within a very short period – a mere twelve days rather than a more usual 24 between the first Merlots and the last Cabernets. This suggested not only an early harvest, but, more importantly, one of uniform ripeness. However, despite *millerandage* in the Merlots, it was apparent that it was going to be another very large vintage.

Thereafter, the summer was one of contrasts. July started cool and wet. The last three weeks and the first 10 days of August were unsettled. The amount of rain which fell during this period – for it varied between Bégadan in the Médoc (21 mm) and Pauillac (36 mm) down to Margaux (54 mm), and 120 mm in Mérignac, near to the top Graves vineyards; while 103 mm fell in Sauternes and 87 mm in Saint-Émilion – was to have a telling effect on the quality of the vintage. By this time the *véraison* had occurred, and it was spun out. Ripeness was no longer homogenous. Neither was the harvest going to be *that* early. What the rapid *floraison* had promised the summer weather had frittered away.

In fact, faces were long at the beginning of September. There was a serious risk that the rain-inflated fruit would begin to rot before it was fully ripe.

Thankfully the first 17 days of September were very sunny and dry, though cool at nights. The water in the grapes evaporated. Sugar contents rose dramatically, though the acidity levels, mainly malic, remained high for the time being. (This was to change later.) The *Ban des Vendanges* was announced on 12th September, and the Sauvignon grapes were gathered in ideal conditions, giving a very good base to the white wines. Top Graves properties also gathered their Semillons during this fine spell.

The red wine harvest was due to commence on 23rd September. On the 17th, with just under a week to go, the weather changed. The next week was inclement, intermittent showers or periods of more prolonged rain fell throughout the region. Once again, however, the brunt fell in the Entre-Deux-Mers and the Right Bank. Once again the northern Médoc had the best of the weather.

The Merlot harvest began on Monday 23rd September. It was overcast but dry. Growers rushed to collect as much as possible before a forecasted thunderstorm on the Wednesday. Again the Médoc was spared the worst of this. The rain fell mainly in the Graves, slightly less in Saint-Émilion and Pomerol.

Following this rainy Wednesday the weather remained unsettled: fine over the weekend, rain on the 27th and again between the 30th and 2nd and on the 4th October, this time uniformly across the region. But after that the skies cleared, the barometer rose, and a splendid Indian summer set in which was to last throughout the rest of the month. Inevitably those with more Cabernet, which ripens later, had more interesting vats to play with than those with more Merlot. Those who were able to pick latest of all picked the healthiest, most concentrated grapes. All this, together with the rain pattern earlier (65 mm for September in Pauillac, 117 mm in Mérignac in the Bordeaux suburbs, a similar figure in Saint-Émilion) points inexorably to the three great communes of the northern Haut-Médoc: Saint-Julien, Pauillac and Saint-Estèphe. Here there are some excellent wines. Elsewhere the 1996 harvest is no better than average.

THE WINES

I wrote the following in June 1997: Two periods saved 1996 from ignominy: the weather between 1st and 17th September, and the weather after 4th October. Despite the unsettled period in between sugar readings were very high – it was not a year where excessive chaptalisation was called for – the fruit was generally very healthy, and the colour of the resulting wine is very impressive.

Acidities, however, are low. But then they were low in 1982, so this of itself is no bad thing. But in 1996 this does lead, in the case of many of the Merlot-based wines of Pomerol and Saint-Émilion (the Fronsacs are, in fact, proportionately rather good this year), to a lack of definition.

Moreover the quality of the tannins in the early-picked Merlots is somewhat less desirable. While the sunny first two and a half weeks of September did wonders for the photosynthesis, it requires heat to round off and sophisticate the phenolic elements in the grape. And this period, though sunny, was really rather cool. On only one day did temperatures rise beyond 26° C. There is therefore a certain rusticity in the character of many of the wines of the Right Bank which together with a certain fluidity and the lack of real definition makes for few really exciting wines. The 1995s are to be preferred. The 1996s aren't bad. But they are boring.

With a few honourable exceptions one can say the same for the red Graves, both *crus classés* and *bourgeois*. Here the 1995s are less exciting. So it is a moot point which is the better vintage.

The 1996 vintage comes to life in the Médoc, and gets better and better as one travels north. Margaux, as always, is heterogeneous, but even at its best not as exciting as Saint-Julien, Pauillac and Saint-Estèphe. Yet both the Merlots as well as the Cabernets (mainly of course Cabernet Sauvignon) provided superior vats to across the river, and the benefit of both less rain and the better-drained gravel soils is manifest. There are some very good wines.

Across the board in the Médoc the final blends show a higher proportion of Cabernet than in the bare vineyard statistics, or in the 1995 wine: 65 per cent (as against 50) at La Lagune; only

10 per cent Merlot (18–20 usually) in Château Margaux; 75 per cent Cabernet Sauvignon (45 in 1995) in Pichon-Lalande. Almost invariably all the Petit Verdot was blended into the *grand vin*. In 1995 most was rejected.

I also compared the 'soft, charming and oaky 1995s' with 'austere yet rich in puppy-fat 1996s'. The former showed well. Would the latter in a year's time?

Re-tasting the 1996s in cask in the spring of 1998 was a revelation. During the twelve months they had undergone a sea-change. It was a reminder that a number, being late-assembled, being more Cabernet than usual, were slow to show their true character, and were rather closed-in in April of 1997. Twelve months on and they were transformed. I not only upgraded my assessment of the vintage as a whole, but decided that some of the top wines, such as Léoville-Las-Cases, were as good, possibly even better, than they had been in 1990. This judgement has been substantiated in further tastings of the wines in bottle.

Here are my favourites:

SAINT-ÉMILION	L'ARROSÉE; CANON-LA-GAFFELIÈRE; PAVIE-MACQUIN; TROPLONG-MONDOT
POMEROL	L'ÉGLISE-CLINET; VIEUX CHÂTEAU CERTAN
GRAVES	DOMAINE DE CHEVALIER; HAUT-BAILLY; PAPE-CLÉMENT
MÉDOC	SOCIANDO-MALLET
MARGAUX	MALESCOT-SAINT-EXUPÉRY; PALMER; RAUZAN-SÉGLA
SAINT-JULIEN	DUCRU-BEAUCAILLOU; LÉOVILLE-BARTON; LÉOVILLE-LAS-CASES (THE WINE OF THE VINTAGE); LÉOVILLE-POYFERRÉ
PAUILLAC	GRAND-PUY-LACOSTE; PICHON-LONGUEVILLE; PICHON-LONGUEVILLE, COMTESSE DE LALANDE; PONTET-CANET.

And the First Growths? Strangely, while Ausone, Cheval-Blanc and Haut-Brion are all very fine, as is Margaux, none of the three Pauillacs is quite as impressive as I might have expected after sampling the rest of the Pauillacs and Saint-Juliens. This is yet another of those vintages where you are much better off buying widely at Super-Second level, than less profusely and more expensively among the *premiers crus*.

PRICES THEN AND NOW

Prices opened at high levels: well above 1995, themselves well above those of 1994. Back in June 1997 the First Growths opened at £700–£800 ($1260–$1440) while Super-Seconds such as Pichon-Longueville, Comtesse de Lalande and Ducru-Beaucaillou were £300 ($540) or so. Today the market seems to have decided that Haut-Brion (£1100/$1980), Mouton-Rothschild (£1200/$2160) per dozen dpd, and Cheval Blanc (£1200/$2160) are the under-achievers; Lafite (£2000/$3600), Margaux (£2000/$3600) and Latour (£1750/$3150) the super-stars. Léoville-Las-Cases is £1150 ($2070), Pichon-Longueville, Comtesse de Lalande (£600/$1080)and Ducru-Beaucaillou (£600/$1080). Bargains, relatively speaking, include Grand-Puy-Lacoste (£360/$640), Langoa-Barton (£215/$380), Léoville-Barton (£360/$640), Léoville-Poyferré (£300/$540), Pichon-Longueville (£300/$540), Pontet-Canet (£240/$430), Rauzan-Ségla (£285/$510), Sociando-Mallet (£250/$450) and Talbot (£240/$430). Here, and even more so among the more minor wines, prices are hardly any more in July 2002 than they were five years earlier in June 1997, when the market for the 1996s opened.

THE TASTING

This report is based on two comprehensive tastings. The first took place over several days in January 2000. The second was the Institute of Masters of Wine 1996 tasting in November 2000.

Saint-Émilion

Château Angélus

NOW–2013   17.0

Fine colour. Lush nose, without much in the way of zip. Generously ripe, aromatic and oaky on the palate. Medium-full body. Good ripe integrated tannins. An ample, almost voluptuous example, with a lot more to it, and in a much more attractive way, than most Saint-Émilions. Good acidity if not the greatest length. But a long, satisfactory finish. Very good indeed.

Château L'Arrosée

NOW–2015   16.5

Medium-full colour. Some development. Plenty of depth on the nose. Rich, concentrated and balanced. Rather more to it than most Saint-Émilions. Fullish body. Good tannins. Good grip. More dimension than most. Ripe, long and opulent at the end. Very good plus.

Château Ausone

NOW–2025   18.5

Very full colour. Rich, lush, oaky nose. Just a bit bland perhaps? Fat and very succulent. Full and oaky on the palate. Very ripe. Good grip. Not bland on the palate after all. Plenty of drive and intensity. Very long. Very fine.

Château Beau-Séjour-Bécot

NOW–2011   15.0

Fine colour. Rich, meaty, quite extracted nose. Plenty of new oak here. Ripe and attactive but a little obvious. It lacks real flair. Fullish though. Succulent and balanced. Very good.

Château Beauséjour-Duffau-Lagarrosse

NOW–2010   14.5

Medium-full colour. Firm, cool nose. Good tannins and quite a lot of them. Strange aromas as it developed but these disappeared on aeration. Slightly vegetal. High volatile acidity. Medium-full body. A bit austere on the palate. Good grip but a little solid. May soften well.

Château Canon

SEE NOTE   10.0

Medium-full colour. Some development. Soft nose with a slightly metallic taint. Thin on the palate. Weedy and tainted.

Château La Gaffelière

NOW–2013   16.0

Good firm, full colour. Good rich nose. Good concentration. Some oak. An attractive, succulent example. Fullish, quite extracted but not overly so. Fat and opulent. Quite oaky. Good depth and balance. Very good.

Château Cheval Blanc

2005–2020   18.5

Full colour. Good fresh nose. Plenty of depth and class if not the greatest concentration and depth. Medium-full body. Quite oaky. This is quite forward. Good acidity. Fresh and classy. Unexpectedly long. Very fine indeed.

Château La Couspaude

NOW–2007   14.5

Fullish colour. Quite extracted, opulent and succulent on the nose. Medium-full body. It lacks a bit of grip on the palate. It lacks a bit of class too. Slightly lumpy. Quite good plus at best.

Le Dôme

NOW–2012   15.0

Fullish colour. Fresh, plump and fruity on the nose. An ample, Merlot-based wine on the palate. Not dilute. Indeed, well put together. Rather anonymous though for all the fruit. Good though. It may pick up more personality as it evolves.

Château La Dominique

NOW–2010   15.5

Fullish colour. No development. Ripe nose. Good depth. A little oak and a little tannin. Just a bit hard at present. Medium body. Quite oaky on the palate. Good fruit and balance. Reasonable concentration but it lacks First Growth flair. Good plus.

Château Figeac

DRINK UP   12.0

Medium-full colour. Some development. Rather sweet and concocted on the nose. On the palate this is dilute. Lacks grip and backbone. Really a bit of a disgrace for Figeac. Short and watery.

Château Fonroque

DRINK SOON   12.5

Medium colour. Some development. Predominantly Merlot. Ripe, slightly loose-knit nose. Medium body only. No tannin. Soft but a little watery. Unexciting. Lacks freshness.

Clos Fourtet

NOW–2009   14.0

Full colour. Plump nose. Slightly four-square on the palate but decent grip. The oak dominates a bit. Slightly astringent. Medium body. A little tannin. But slightly lumpy. Some fruit. Decent follow-through. Quite good.

Château Larmande

NOW–2010   (15.0)

Fullish colour. Still youthful. Slightly sweety on the nose. Not entirely clean. Indeed, as it developed, clearly corky. Seems fullish, with good depth and fruit but perhaps not quite enough grip. Good (?).

Château Magdelaine

DRINK SOON   13.0

Medium to medium-full colour. Soft nose. Ripe Merlot base. Lacks depth and grip on the palate. Disappointing for what it is. Short and weedy. Not much better than Château Fonroque.

La Mondotte, 1996

NOW–2015   17.0

This was the first vintage. A separate plot of vines cultivated by Stephan von Neipperg of Canon-La-Gaffelière. Very full colour. Full, firm, rich and concentrated on the nose. There is plenty of quality wine here. Full, oaky and abundant on the palate. Still some tannin. This is remarkably good for a first effort. Firm, long and backward. Really quite extracted but a very good example.

Château Pavie

NOW–2013   16.0

Very good colour. Rich and plump and full of ripe fruit on the nose. Not the greatest flair but plenty of wine here. Fullish body. Some tannin. The tannins are not *that* well covered but there is good acidity and the wine is fat. Finishes well. Very good.

Château Pavie-Macquin

NOW–2016   17.0

Medium-full colour. Closed-in. Concentrated, rich, backward nose. Fullish. Good ripe tannins. Nice, cool and oaky. This is classy as well as profound and balanced. Unexpectedly good. Very good grip. Laid-back and subtle. This has real length, which is rare in Saint-Émilion in this vintage. Will keep well. This is very good indeed.

Château Pavie-Decesse

NOW–2010   14.5

Fullish colour. Ripe, slightly uncomplicated nose. But clean and plenty of fruit. Medium to medium-full body. Fresh and fruity. Nicely balanced if no real depth or concentration. Stylish though. Positive finish. Quite good plus.

Château Le Tertre-Roteboeuf

NOW–2011   15.5

Medium-full colour. Some development. The nose is a little closed but promising. Medium-full body. Plump and fruity. Attractive and ripe without having the greatest body and depth. Fresh and positive at the end though. Good plus.

CHÂTEAU TROPLONG-MONDOT

NOW–2015	17.0

Good full, youthful colour. Classy nose. Very fine fruit here. Fullish body. Cool character. Good tannins. Good grip. This is harmonious and elegant. Plenty of depth. One of the best Saint-Émilons of the vintage. Very good indeed.

VIRGINIE DE VALANDRAUD

NOW–2007	13.5

Medium-full colour. Plump nose. Not a lot of depth. But there is attractive fruit here. Plump and oaky on the attack. Medium to medium-full body. A bit short on the finish. One-dimensional. Fresh and enjoyable though. Not bad plus.

POMEROL

CHÂTEAU BEAUREGARD

NOW–2010	15.0

Fullish colour. Some tannin. Some concentration. A little lumpy though. The nose lacks grace. Fullish body. Some tannin. Decent grip. A competent wine with a positive follow-through. Quite oaky. But it lacks a bit of personality and flair. Good though.

CHÂTEAU BEAU SOLEIL

NOW–2006	13.0

Fullish colour. Fresh nose. Pleasant if no real depth. Medium body. No tannin. Short and one-dimensional on the palate. Reasonable balance though. Forward. Pleasant. Not bad.

CHÂTEAU CERTAN DE MAY

NOW–2006	13.5

Medium colour. Some development. Rather reduced on the nose. Got more agreeable as it developed. Plump and ripe on the palate but not very big or profound. Slightly simple. Not very stylish. Medium body. Unbalanced. A little stewed. Not bad plus.

CHÂTEAU CLINET

NOW–2010	13.5

Medium-full colour. Some development. Ripe, fullish, oaky, stylish nose. Quite extracted but not too much so. On the palate it lacks charm though. Fullish body. A little lumpy and astringent. Good acidity. But it lacks class. Not bad plus.

CHÂTEAU LA CONSEILLANTE

NOW–2008	14.0

Medium-full colour. Soft, ripe, pleasant, gently oaky nose. Not a blockbuster. Has charm but no depth. Medium body. Just a little tannin. Fresh, slightly jammy fruit. Quite attractive if not serious. Quite good.

CHÂTEAU LA CROIX DU CASSE

NOW–2006	13.0

Medium-full colour. Not a lot of depth on the nose. Fruity but a little simple. Medium body. No tannin. Rather weak on the follow-through. Forward. Unexciting. Fresher than Château Fonroque. Not bad.

CHÂTEAU L'ÉGLISE-CLINET

NOW–2012	16.5

Fullish colour. Light, fresh, fruity nose. No great depth though. On the palate fullish, oaky, stylish and complex. This has very good fruit and more to it than at first appears. Balanced and elegant. Finishes well. Very good plus.

CHÂTEAU L'EVANGILE

NOW–2007	14.0

Medium-full colour. Some development. Slightly over-macerated on the nose. But reasonable grip and fruit. What it lacks is a bit of fat. Slightly four-square. A little tannin. Medium body. Decent follow-through. Quite positive but lacks charm. Quite good.

CHÂTEAU LA FLEUR DE GAY

NOW–2006	12.5

Medium-full colour. Pleasant but a little weak and nondescript on the nose. Not the usual dominance of oak. Lacks grip and thrust on the palate. Medium body. Slightly astringent. Some new oak. Not special. Essentially unbalanced.

CHÂTEAU LA FLEUR-PÉTRUS

NOW–2005	13.0

Medium-full colour. Some development. Some fruit but not much depth and grip on the nose. Rather short and weedy on the palate. Some fruit. Getting attenuated fast. Not bad at best.

CHÂTEAU GAZIN

NOW–2007	15.5

Medium-full colour. Ripe, positive, stylish nose. Medium to medium-full body. Attractive fruit. Gently oaky. Quite positive. A little superficial but well-made. Plenty of charm. Good plus.

CHÂTEAU LA GRAVE (À-POMEROL)

NOW–2007	13.5

Medium to medium-full colour. Non-descript nose. No real depth, grip or flair. Fresher than some of the other Moueix wines but rather short and one-dimensional nevertheless. Will not age well. Slight unripe touches underneath. Not bad plus.

CHÂTEAU LAFLEUR

NOW–2015	17.0

Medium-full colour. Rich, backward, concentrated, slightly dense and solid nose. Good depth here. This is one of the better Pomerols. Fullish body. Good concentration. Good grip. A little oak. Quite vigorous. This will keep and improve. Very good indeed.

CHÂTEAU LATOUR-À-POMEROL

DRINK SOON	12.0

Medium-full colour. Some development. Rather weedy and sweet on the nose. Less good than the La Fleur-Pétrus. Lighter and even worse on the palate. Disappointing.

CHÂTEAU NÉNIN

NOW–2006	13.0

Medium-full colour. Rather four-square, dense and solid on the nose. Similar on the palate. Lacks grip. Not much charm here. Short. Will get astringent.

CHÂTEAU PÉTRUS

2005–2015	17.5

Fullish colour. Lovely, poised, succulent fruit here. Not a blockbuster. Complex, classy and fragrant. Medium-full body. Some oak. A gentle wine without the real strength of a First Growth. But long and classy. Fine.

CHÂTEAU LE PIN

NOW–2012	17.0

Very fine, full colour. Soft, plump and ripe on the nose. No weakness. A lot of attraction. Medium body. Abundant and ripe and reasonably balanced if without real structure and grip. Attractive, long, stylish at the end. Very good indeed.

CHÂTEAU DE SALES

NOW–2007	13.0

Medium-full colour. Better than the Croix du Casse on the nose. Plump and fruity. Good charming personality. Medium body. Still a little raw. Not much tannin. Some fruit on the palate. Lacks a bit of class though. Not bad.

CHÂTEAU TROTANOY

NOW–2007	13.5

Medium-full colour. Soft, sweet and mawkish on the nose. Hot and cloying. Medium body. Weedy again but better than La Fleur-Pétrus. At least something at the end. Forward. Not bad plus.

VIEUX CHÂTEAU CERTAN

NOW–2015+	18.0

Good full colour. A nose of real quality here. Full, concentrated and rich. Very fine vigour and grip. And nicely cool. Not a bit over-extracted. One of the very few really serious 1996 Libournais wines. Fullish body. Ripe tannins. Excellent intensity and harmony. Cool and classy. Fine plus.

GRAVES

CHÂTEAU BOUSCAUT

NOW–2008   13.5

Medium to medium-full colour. Reasonably ripe and stylish on the nose. A bit anonymous and a bit short on the palate. Medium body only. Quite pretty fruit. Reasonably positive at the end. Not bad plus.

CHÂTEAU CARBONNIEUX

DRINK SOON   12.0

Medium colour. A little thin and lightweight on the nose. Very thin and forward on the palate. No backbone. A bit of a disgrace.

DOMAINE DE CHEVALIER

NOW–2018   17.5

Fullish colour. Cool and restrained and classy on the nose. Medium-full body. Very lovely ripe, concentrated fruit. Long and harmonious too. This is classy. Very long. Very lovely. Fine.

CHÂTEAU DU CRUZEAU

NOW–2010   14.0

Medium-full colour. Fresh, plump nose. No great distinction but a well-made, fruity, balanced wine. Quite good.

CHÂTEAU DE FIEUZAL

NOW–2010   14.5

Fullish colour. Quite a fat, sweet, almost tawny nose. Quite extracted. Fullish body. Slightly raw. Plenty of wine here. Some tannin. But the tannins are not as sophisticated as some. Just a little clumsy. Needs time. May improve if it softens. Seems to lack fruit. Only quite good plus today.

CHÂTEAU HAUT-BAILLY

NOW–2018   17.0

Fullish colour. Gently oaky. Ripe, plummy, quite concentrated nose. Plenty of depth and style. Fullish body. Old viney. Some tannin. Lots of wine here. More backward than most at present. Very long and succulent. Very good plus.

CHÂTEAU HAUT-BRION

2006–2018   18.5

Full colour. Attractive if not massive. Ripe fresh fruit on the nose. Medium-full body. Very good tannins. An intensely-flavoured, rich, complex wine. Lovely fruit. Persistent. Cedary at the end. Very fine.

CHÂTEAU LA LOUVIÈRE

NOW–2010   15.0

Fullish colour. Plump and fruity on the nose if without any great depth or flair. Just a little oak. On the palate ripe and plummy. Medium-full body. Good tannins. Good grip. Good but needs a little excitement.

CHÂTEAU MALARTIC-LAGRAVIÈRE

2005–2015   16.0

Fullish colour. Plump, fullish, quite oaky nose. This is a surprise. Medium-full body. Fresh, positive, ample fruit. Good grip. Balanced and really quite intense. Very good.

CHÂTEAU LA MISSION HAUT-BRION

2004–2018   17.5

Medium-full colour. Soft, elegant, gently oaky nose. This is more evolved than I would have expected at this stage. Softer too. Very classy though. Medium-full body. Some tannin. Really lovely intense fruit. Very long. Fine.

CHÂTEAU OLIVIER

NOW–2015   16.5

Good full colour. Stylish nose. No great substance but the fruit is ripe and intense and the wine gently oaky and composed. Medium to medium-full weight. Just a little tannin. Elegant complex fruit. Long and positive. This is very good plus.

CHÂTEAU PAPE-CLÉMENT

2005–2018   17.0

Fullish colour. Fullish, rich, oaky, quite concentrated nose. More backward than some. A meaty example. Classy and complex. Full body. Some tannin. Lovely fruit and lots of depth. Needs time. Intense and satisfying. Very good indeed.

Château de Rochemorin

NOW–2008   13.5

Medium to medium-full colour. Soft nose. Some fruit. Light and softer and with less grip than the du Cruzeau. But reasonably positive at the end. Quite stylish.

Château Smith-Haut-Lafitte

NOW–2010   15.0

Fullish colour. A little green on the nose. Lacks succulence. Soft and oaky underneath. Medium to medium-full body. Quite ripe and stylish. Decently balanced too. But not enough character for more than 'good'. Quite oaky on the palate and the finish.

Château La Tour Haut-Brion

NOW–2012   16.0

Medium-full colour. Good rich nose. Oaky. Distinctive. Plenty of depth. Medium-full body. Ripe and stylish. Not a blockbuster but elegant and balanced. Very good.

Moulis

Château Chasse-Spleen

NOW–2015   16.0

Medium-full colour. Good nose. There is depth and style here and just about the right aspect of new oak. Medium-full body. Balanced and elegant. Very good fruit. A classy, harmonious example. Long and complex. Finishes very well. Very good.

Château Poujeaux

2005–2018   16.0

Fullish colour. Rich, meaty, robust nose. Quite sizeable. Quite refined on the palate. Good fruit. Fullish body. Tannic. Good grip. This has plenty of depth. Long and satisfying in a spicy, meaty sort of way. Very good.

Haut-Médoc

Château Belgrave

NOW–2009   13.0

Medium-full colour. A little thin on the nose. Not much distinction here. Medium to medium-full body. Slightly herbaceous/farmyardy. A bit astringent at the back too. Uninspiring.

Château de Camensac

NOW–2010   13.5

Medium-full colour. Slightly sweaty on the nose. Some sweetness, some oak on the palate but rather short. Medium body. It lacks distinction. Better than Belgrave though. More positive at the end.

Château Cantemerle

NOW–2009   13.0

Full colour. Ripe nose if with no great depth. Medium body. A little tannin. Pleasantly fruity but rather commonplace attack. The finish lacks richness and concentration as well as real class. Cantermerle should do better than this. Only fair.

Château La Lagune

NOW–2012   15.0

Full colour. Soft, ripe, mellow, oaky nose. Medium body. A gentle wine. Well-made. Oaky and fruity and balanced. But a lack of real depth. Just a little one-dimensional. Quite forward. Good.

Château Sociando-Mallet

2006–2020   18.0

Very full colour. Splendidly full but lush, ripe nose. Oaky too. Fullish and complex. Very good grip. Ripe tannins. This has class and length. Very lovely. Plenty of wine here. Really fine finish. This is fine.

Château La Tour-Carnet

NOW–2011   14.0

Medium-full colour. Just a bit hard on the nose. Not much class evident underneath. Medium to medium-full body. Decent fruit and decent acidity. Not much dimension but quite good.

Margaux

Château d'Angludet

2005–2011   14.0

Full colour. Firm, sturdy nose. Just a little dense. Fullish body. Some tannin. Typical solid Angludet. Lacks a bit of grip. Yet a positive finish. Good fruit. Only average though.

CHÂTEAU BOYD-CANTENAC

NOW–2012   14.0

Medium-full colour. Rather hard and vegetal on the nose. Riper on the palate. Medium-full body. A little one-dimensional but good grip and a positive finish. Quite good.

CHÂTEAU BRANE-CANTENAC

NOW–2012   15.0

Fullish colour. Plump, ripe, attractive nose. A little less substantial than Durfort-Vivens, another Lurton property in Margaux. Good fruit. Nicely balanced and attractive fruit but it could have done with a bit more depth and grip. Good though.

CHÂTEAU CANTENAC-BROWN

NOW–2010   13.5

Medium to medium-full colour. Soft nose. Nothing much here. Quite pretty fruit but medium body. Some oak. It has charm but not much depth. Forward. Not bad plus.

CHÂTEAU DAUZAC

NOW–2012   14.0

Good colour. Ripe and positive on the nose. Medium to medium-full body. Gently oaky. Fresh. Not the greatest depth but stylish. Quite forward. Quite good.

CHÂTEAU DESMIRAIL

NOW–2007   13.0

Medium to medium-full colour. A small wine. Not a great deal of depth and richness on the nose. Medium body on the palate. Not much grip. It tails off. Boring. Forward.

CHÂTEAU DURFORT-VIVENS

NOW–2015   15.5

Full colour. Good ripe, quite Cabernet nose. There is style and depth here. Oaky too. Medium-full body. Just a little tannin. This is elegant and quite intense. Not a blockbuster but good grip and long positive finish. Good plus.

CHÂTEAU FERRIÈRE

2005–2018   16.0

Good colour. Full, rich and concentrated on the nose. Gently oaky. Medium-full body. Quite structured. It needs time. Rich. Plenty of depth. Lots of dimension at the end. Very good.

CHÂTEAU GISCOURS

DRINK SOON   12.0

Medium colour. Thin on the nose. Aspects of tobacco. Medium body. Thin and weedy. It lacks grip. Already a bit astringent. Short. A bit of a disgrace.

CHÂTEAU D'ISSAN

NOW–2008   13.0

Medium to medium-full colour; some development. Soft nose. Quite pleasant fruit, gently cedary, but a bit on the light side. As it evolved it lost its puppy fat and became more and more lean. A lightish wine. Not much backbone or tannic structure. Reasonable fruit. But no depth. Unexciting.

CHÂTEAU KIRWAN

2005–2015   15.5

Very full colour. Good oaky nose. Fullish body. Ripe and concentrated, if not a little over-extracted. Good tannins. Quite rich. Very good grip at the end. Needs time. Good plus.

CHÂTEAU LABÉGORCE-ZÉDÉ

NOW–2009   13.5

Full colour. Lightish, not very pronounced nose. Good fruit but rather closed. Not much sign of oak. It lacks a bit of class. Not really very long either. Medium-full body. A little clumsy. Lacks flair. Not bad plus.

CHÂTEAU LASCOMBES

2005–2011   13.5

Fullish colour. Full and sturdy on the nose. A little four-square. Fullish on the palate. Some tannin. Fruity and reasonably balanced but there is neither personality nor flair here. Commonplace.

Château Malescot-Saint-Exupéry

NOW—2018   16.0

Fullish colour. Attractive, accessible nose.
Very good balanced, stylish fruit. Not the
greatest of strength though. A touch of oak.
More to it on the palate. Medium-full body.
Good grip. Ripe, indeed almost a touch of
sweetness. Stylish and long on the follow-
through. Very good.

Château Margaux

2006—2026+   18.5

Full colour. Fine nose. Very classy fruit.
Quite firm and closed but not a blockbuster.
Very lovely fruit. Concentrated. Fullish
body. Very good ripe tannins. This is long
and complex and lovely. Very classy.

Château Marquis de Terme

NOW—2012   15.0

Medium-full colour. Ample, fat, but quite
sturdy nose. Fullish body. Good tannins.
Rich and ripe. A little raw still. But good
acidity. It is a little burly, as Marquis de
Terme often is, but it is a good wine with a
positive conclusion.

Château Palmer

2005—2020   17.0

Full colour. Lovely classy fruit on the nose.
Really fine. Fullish, the tannins very
integrated. A concentrated, intense wine.
Cool and nicely aloof. Very long on the
palate. This is discreetly fine.

Château Pouget

NOW—2009   13.0

Medium-full colour. Fresh on the nose.
Quite sturdy but not inky. Slightly vegetal on
the attack. It lacks class, dimension and
richness. Not bad.

Château Prieuré-Lichine

NOW—2011   14.0

Very full colour. Ripe but slightly non-
descript on the nose. Lacks a bit of elegance.
Medium-full body. Good tannins. The attack
is promising but then it tails off a bit. Plump
but just a little short. Quite good.

Château Rauzan-Gassies

DRINK SOON   12.0

Good colour. Burly nose. Not much
distinction here. Medium body. Short and
already astringent. No breed. A disgrace.

Château Rauzan-Ségla

NOW—2015   16.5

Fullish colour. Quite firm. Fullish, oaky
nose. Plenty of depth here. Fullish on the
palate. Some tannin. Good grip. Quite oaky.
The attack is good, the follow-through even
better. Long. This will keep well. Not
brillant but very good plus.

Saint-Julien
Château Beychevelle

2005—2015   15.5

Fullish colour. Good ripe Cabernet nose.
Attractive wine if with no great
concentration or depth. It lacks a bit of
succulence. Good acidity but not enough
flair, concentration or class or complexity.
Medium-full body. Good plus.

Château Branaire

NOW—2010   14.5

Medium-full colour. Ample, fullish, slightly
earthy nose. Plenty of wine here, but it lacks
high tones. Fullish body. Some tannins.
There is richness but at the same time a
certain solidity, with the tannins not very
ripe, and somewhat astringent. Reasonable
acidity. Somewhat ungainly. But good plus.

Château Ducru-Beaucaillou

2006—2020   18.5

Fullish colour. Very classy nose indeed.
Splendid depth of fruit. Lovely harmony and
real intensity. Gently oaky. Very refined.
Fullish body. Very fine grip. The tannins are
very ripe and integrated. Splendid follow-
through. Excellent, multi-dimensional finish.
Very fine plus.

CHÂTEAU GRUAUD-LAROSE

2006–2020	17.0

Medium-full colour. Some development. Plump nose. Not the usual blockbuster. Ample and fruity but some evolution. A somewhat unsophisticated element to the tannins though there are plenty of them. Fullish body. Good oak. Riper and more classy on the palate than on the nose. Plenty of wine here. Finishes well. Very good indeed.

CHÂTEAU LAGRANGE

NOW–2015	16.0

Fullish colour. Very cassis on the nose. Good oak. A well-made example. Medium-full and classy on the palate but it lacks a little grip and concentration. Quite oaky at the end. Decent acidity. Plenty of style and harmony. Very good.

CHÂTEAU LANGOA-BARTON

2005–2025	17.0

Fullish colour. Slightly softer nose than some but revealing very lovely fruit. Quite oaky. A very lovely wine. Excellent fruit. More open and more accessible than Léoville-Barton, offering more enjoyment today. Ripe and generous. Delicious.

CHÂTEAU LÉOVILLE-BARTON

2006–2025	18.0

Medium-full colour. Some development. Rich, backward, profound nose. Lots of depth. Lots of class. Very finely balanced. Fullish colour. Very concentrated. Excellent grip. Lovely fruit here. Very long. Really classy and complex at the end. Very fine.

CHÂTEAU LÉOVILLE-LAS-CASES

2006–2026	19.0

Full colour. Very profound and very aristocratic on the nose. Backward but immaculate. A much bigger, more tannic wine than Ducru-Beaucaillou. Much less developed. This is truly excellent. Very fine ripe, rich fruit. Very fine grip. Lots of lovely fruit. This is still a bit awkward. It is the Ducru-Beaucaillou which sings today. But this will be the greater wine eventually.

CHÂTEAU LÉOVILLE-POYFERRÉ

2005–2025	18.0

Fullish colour. Rich, fat, almost opulent nose. Medium-full body. Very fine tannins. This has grip and depth and a very seductive character. Long and satisfying at the end. Very fine.

CHÂTEAU SAINT-PIERRE

NOW–2010	14.5

Fullish colour. Good nose. There is depth here, and at least some style, and a satisfactory underpinning of oak. Medium to medium-full body. A little tannin. Decent ripe fruit if without any real quality and depth and concentration. Quite good plus.

CHÂTEAU TALBOT

2006–2026	17.0

Full colour. Full ample nose. Slightly robust. Elements of eucalyptus. Fullish body but quite tannic. The wine has good grip and there is plenty of depth. Very good indeed. But not great.

PAUILLAC

CHÂTEAU D'ARMAILHAC

2005–2017	16.0

Fullish colour. Ample nose. Just a little stewed and lacking zip. Good substance on the palate. No lack of grip. Ample fruit. Ripe tannins. Positive at the end. This is very good.

CARRUADES DE LAFITE

NOW–2012	13.5

Medium-full colour. Soft, round, rich, oaky nose. Medium to medium-full body. Quite elegant, but a slightly green metallic touch. Not tainted, but it lacks a bit of generosity and fat. Good at best. But it seemed to collapse in the glass. On aeration it was less marked.

CHÂTEAU CLERC-MILON

2005–2017	(16.5)

Fullish colour. Firm but juicy on the nose. Very Cabernet. Nicely ripe. As it developed it became more and more corky. Underneath more class and personality than the d'Armailhac. Very good plus if in good condition.

CHÂTEAU CROIZET-BAGES

DRINK SOON	13.5

Medium colour. Soft nose. Not much distinction. On the palate medium body. Not enough grip. Not much class. Better than Rauzan-Gassies but not by much.

CHÂTEAU DUHART-MILON

2006–2018	15.5

Full colour. Rich but slightly dense, slightly solid on the nose. Full and rich on the palate. Quite a lot of tannin. The solidity of the usual Duhart-Milon is still there. Big but inflexible. Yet good length. Good plus.

LES FORTS DE LATOUR

2005–2015	15.5

Very full colour. Rich and ripe and ample on the nose. Accessible, classy bramble berry fruit. Medium-full weight. Not a lot of tannin. Just a little short at the end. Very attractive though. Good plus.

CHÂTEAU GRAND-PUY-DUCASSE

NOW–2008	14.0

Medium-full colour. A little rigid on the nose. On the palate medium to medium-full body. A little astringent. Quite pretty fruit, but not enough grip. Quite good at best.

CHÂTEAU GRAND-PUY-LACOSTE

2006–2026	18.0

Full colour. Very fine fruit on the nose. Full and concentrated. Very Cabernet. Full but not solid. Ripe integrated tannins. Very fine grip. Above all lovely rich, ripe fruit. Long and elegant. Harmonious. Classic. This is fine.

CHÂTEAU HAUT-BAGES-LIBÉRAL

2005–2015	15.0

Very good colour. Less substance, less concentration, less class on the nose than the Grand-Puy-Lacoste, for instance. But good plummy fruit. Medium-full body. Good oak. Nice fruit. Not the greatest concentration and style but ripe and enjoyable. Good.

CHÂTEAU HAUT-BATAILLEY

2005–2015	16.0

Full colour. Not *that* big a wine. But full of Cabernet fruit and quite oaky. Less austere than usual. A medium-weight, elegant wine. Rather less concentrated than Grand-Puy-Lacoste or Ducru-Beaucaillou but attractive, balanced and accessible. Long on the finish. Very good.

CHÂTEAU LAFITE

2005–2012	17.5

Very full colour. Full and rich, concentrated and backward on the nose. Rather an adolescent, tannic, monolithic wine and a little lumpy at that. As much astringent as tannic in fact. This is not that brilliant. Sweet. Merely fine.

CHÂTEAU LATOUR

2006–2015	18.0

Very full colour. Quite oaky and quite high-toned on the nose. This is slightly looser-knit than you might expect. But there is lovely intense fruit here and very good balance. Fullish body. Fine plus.

CHÂTEAU LYNCH-BAGES

2005–2015	15.5

Fullish colour. Ample, ripe nose. But lacks both a little personality and a bit of zip. Quite full and quite sweet on the palate. Some tannin. But a little jammy. It lacks real grip. Superficially attractive. Essentially lacks class as well. Good plus only.

Château Mouton-Rothschild

2008–2025   18.0

Full colour. Slightly monolithic. At first you think this has great structure and depth. It is certainly big and tannic but it is a little solid. Classy but adolescent. Backward. Fullish on the palate. Rich and concentrated. Not totally convincing but fine plus.

Petit-Mouton

NOW–2011   14.5

Very full colour. Ample nose. Fat, but strangely one-dimensional. This is really a bit dull. Medium body. A little astringent. Lacks flair. Some fruit. Decent acidity. But only quite good plus.

Château Pichon-Longueville

2006–2018   17.0

Full colour. Nice cool fruit on the nose. Good style and good acidity. Quite different from Lynch-Bages. Fullish body. Balanced. Good tannins. Nice and complex. Then on the follow-through not *that* long nor that much class. This is fine all the way through except at the very end.

Château Pichon-Longueville, Comtesse de Lalande

2005–2020   18.0

Very full colour. Very lovely complex nose. Chocolate and coffee and all sorts of fruit. This is very lovely. Fullish body. Very concentrated. Almost sweet. Very long. Very fine lovely fruit. Very classy. Fine plus.

Château Pontet-Canet

2005–2018   17.0

Full colour. A ripe wine. Stylish too. But quite a lot of oak. The wine itself is not that big or concentrated. Medium-full body. Ripe, rich and classy. Good length and depth. Not a blockbuster but lovely and very long. Very good indeed.

Saint-Estèphe

Château Calon-Ségur

NOW–2010   13.5

Full colour. Slight vegetal elements on the nose. Rather raw. Not that much grip. Medium-full body. Rather loose and short. Fruity but it lacks style. Not bad plus.

Château Cos d'Estournel

2008–2020   17.0

Full colour. Quite extracted nose. Spicy and very concentrated though. Full body. Very concentrated. Some tannin but the tannins are very well covered. This is intense and though 'modern' not short of interest and class. But very good indeed rather than fine.

Château Haut-Marbuzet

NOW–2015   15.5

Fullish colour. Very oaky. Very succulent ripe fruit on the nose. A fullish, rich, very oaky wine. Spicy and opulent. Seductive. But the oak is a bit too much. Good plus.

Château Lafon-Rochet

2005–2015   15.5

Fullish colour. Fullish, slightly austere, very Cabernet nose. But flexible enough. Medium-full body. Some tannin. A little one dimensional but good grip here. Positive at the end. Good plus.

Château Montrose

NOW–2012   15.0

Full colour. Slight touch of reduction over a quite austere Cabernet nose. Just a little sweaty. Medium-full body. Slightly astringent as well as tannic. Some acidity but not really enough. Ripe but not very long and stylish. Good merely. Tails off a bit at the end.

Château de Pez

NOW–2012   14.0

Fullish colour. Quite austere on the nose. Good concentration. Full body. Quite tannic. This is a typically brutal Saint-Estèphe. Lacks suppleness. Good fruit and girp if a bit sturdy. Better with food. Quite good.

1995 VINTAGE

SIZE OF THE CROP:	6.538 HECTOLITRES.
VINTAGE RATING:	15.5 (RED WINES).
	15.0 (DRY WHITE WINES).
	14.0 (SWEET WINES).

A record crop at the time, the total crashing through the 6 million hectolitres barrier. The yield also was high, though not the record at 57.7 hl/ha. The white wine harvest produced 1,044,454 hl (16 per cent of the total).

I was not convinced by the 1995s at the outset. The quality of the vintage did not strike me as very special, merely very good, and the prices were high. Inflation had set in at the auction houses. Collectors seemed to be prepared to pay increasingly crazy money for anything proven as fine in the vintages of the 1982 to 1990 period. This was reflected in the opening prices offers of the 1995s, the first commendable vintage since 1990, but across the board, not just in the wines which would subsequently be judged as fine.

This hike in price levels required a hype on the part of the properties, the Bordeaux *négoce* and the rest of the wine trade if they were to be successful in selling the vintage right down to the consumer. This I considered inappropriate.

THE WEATHER

Meanwhile, however, back to 1995. The first half of the year was superb. A mild winter and an early spring without serious frost damage produced a flowering which was 10 days in advance of the norm (*demi-floraison* 4th June, the same date as in 1994) and this flowering took place in perfect conditions, ensuring little *coulure*, a large harvest and probability of an early one.

After an almost totally dry June there was a wet start to July, but this was the last extensive amount of rain many of the vineyards would see until vintage time. It was also very warm indeed. As a result the progress towards maturation was delayed: many vines became *bloquées* by the drought. The *demi-véraison* took place four days later than in 1994 (10th August) but was nevertheless eight days ahead of the average. Further progress depended on where you were, and the type of soils your vines were planted in. The August precipitation varied from 8 mm to 108 mm. While it rained in Saint-Laurent (60 mm on 23rd August) it did not rain in nearby Saint-Julien or the easterly vineyards of Pauillac. Saint-Émilion and Pomerol, as well as Barsac and Sauternes received 70 mm or more earlier in the month, but in Bordeaux itself, at the weather station in Mérignac, the month's precipitation was a mere 22 mm, and in Saint-Julien, only 25 mm was measured from 1st June to 1st September.

As you might expect, the young vines, planted in the very well-drained, gravelly soils of the Médoc and the Graves, suffered more than older vines, and vines planted in the clay-limestone soils of the Libournais.

Yet again, for the fifth year in succession, it rained in September just as the red wine harvest was about to get under way. But, in relation to 1991, 1992, 1993, and 1994 the amount of rain was less, and, crucially, after the equinox the weather dried up. The total September rainfall at Mérignac was 145 mm (1994: 175 mm; 1993: 275 mm) and most of this fell between the 9th and the 19th. However, it was only on three or four of these days that the rain was really hard; the rest were showers, easy enough to avoid. And temperatures had fallen, so there was little danger of rot.

And once again this rainfall was uneven. If the measurement was 145 mm in Mérignac it was 100 mm or less throughout most of the Médoc, and similarly in Saint-Émilion and Pomerol. The largest amounts of rain fell in the Graves and in Sauternes but even here 145 mm represents an upper, not a lower limit.

THE HARVEST

The vintage began as early as 28th August for the Sauvignons on the most precocious sites in the Graves. The weather had retreated from the summer heat. It was cool but stable. The lesser whites hit the worst of the vintage conditions, starting on 7th September, just as the weather was beginning to break up and continuing through to the 20th, just as it was becoming dry again.

By the time the dry white wine harvest was drawing to its end, that for the red was beginning: the Merlots on both sides of the Bordeaux wine area from 16th September onwards, the Cabernet Francs from the 19th in the Libournais, the Cabernet Sauvignons on the left bank a week later in the best of the weather.

TAKING STEPS TO REDUCE THE CROP

For many years châteaux proprietors have taken great pains to assure you of the sacrifices they have made in the name of quality at the time the *grand vin* blend was being created. And they continue to do so today. In 1995 at Latour only 59 per cent of the production was bottled as Château Latour; at Labégorce-Zédé, Phélan-Ségur and Pontet-Canet, 50 per cent; at Rauzan-Ségla 45 per cent; at Lagrange and Léoville-Las-Cases 35 per cent. When you idly asked, in a polite sort of way, what they had produced overall, you were looked at as if you had asked something rude. When you suggested that maybe if they had made 45 hl/ha overall instead of 60 that perhaps more of the wine would be suitable for the *grand vin*, you were regarded as being seriously impertinent.

In 1995, for the first time, total yields, and a reduction to sensible ones, were taken seriously. At Château Mouton-Rothschild they pruned to one bud per cane less, and made 25 per cent less volume than in 1994, 35 hl/ha, while at Château Latour it was 50.6 hl/ha. At Léoville-Poyferré the yield was 49 hl/ha, at L'Évangile 34 hl/ha, at Belair 37 hl/ha.

Green harvesting had suddenly become very fashionable, and as a result, in the top châteaux at least, yields were much lower than in 1994, though only Saint-Julien and Pauillac, overall, produced a smaller crop in 1995.

THE WINES THEN

This was what I wrote in June 1996:

Overall, then, it was a crop of very good Cabernet (mainly Franc) in Saint-Émilion, plus good Merlot, and very good Cabernet (mainly Sauvignon) in the Médoc and Graves, plus again good Merlot. In many cases in the Médoc, however, a larger proportion of Merlot than usual has found its way into the *grand vin*. The explanations are various: that the younger vines were so stressed that the phenolic elements were not totally ripe in all the Cabernets, despite the fine end to the growing season; that the Cabernet berries, in general, were unusually small, resulting in overly tannic wines, which needed more Merlot than usual in the blend to soften them up; and, in some cases, by the fact that late-harvested Merlot *cuvées* were in fact just as good as the Cabernets.

The result is red wine which has something of 1985 about it, though in the case of many examples – particularly those from up-and-coming estates where yields were as much as 25 per cent less than a decade ago – of greater intensity. The wines have rather more tannin though, an aspect largely hidden at present, and in the best cases they have better acidity too: so the spectrum is from a 1985 look-alike to a cross between 1985 and 1986, or 1985 and 1990.

So there is a large number of very good wines indeed. But, *au fond*, as in 1985, there is an absence of anything which really stands up in the glass and says '*grand vin*'. Consequently, good as the vintage is, it is merely very good to very good indeed. Not fine. Not classic. Not as good as 1982, 1986 and 1990 – or indeed, in Saint-Émilion and Pomerol, as 1989 either. The best required a decade, but no longer, to mature.

THE WINES NOW

Nineteen ninety-five was succeeded by 1996. In 1996 we have a few – merely the top dozen – very fine wines in the Northern Médoc, as good as anything we can select from the 1982–1990 period. The Saint-Émilions and Pomerols were not as good, indeed less good than the 1995s. In consequence, 1995 has been generalised as a Merlot or Right Bank vintage and 1996 as the opposite.

The first thing to consider is whether this description is apt. The answer is apart from the top few, no. After Château Cheval Blanc and Château Ausone, the standard of the Libournais rapidly descends, with a few honourable exceptions such as L'Angélus, L'Arrosée and Figeac, in Saint-Émilion, and Vieux Château Certan, Trotanoy, Le Pin and Clinet in Pomerol, into the banal. Moreover there are some conspicuous failures among generally well-touted estates: Châteaux Canon and Pavie are definitely under par, the nearly fabulous Valandraud is so over-oaked it is already astringent. L'Évangile is short, Lafleur burly and graceless; Certan de May vegetal if not tainted, and neither La Fleur-Pétrus nor Latour-à-Pomerol, thoroughbreds of the Moueix stable, are as good as they should be. Many wines, indeed, have not lived up to the promise they showed in cask.

No, this is not a Saint-Émilion or Pomerol vintage. There are some lovely wines in the Graves: La Mission Haut-Brion and Haut-Brion are really fine. Châteaux Pape-Clément and Haut-Bailly are both sumptuous. The commune of Margaux is as irregular as usual (avoid Giscours, Issan and, from further south, Cantemerle), and the Saint-Estèphes are dull and short. Where the vintage is at its best, as so nearly always, is in Saint-Julien and Pauillac. Ducru-Beaucaillou and Léoville-Las-Cases are of top First Growth quality, Léoville-Barton and Léoville-Poyferré are fine. Only Château Saint-Pierre, tainted, is to be avoided in the top Saint-Juliens. In Pauillac, Duhart-Milon and Lynch-Moussas are not as good as they should be and Carruades de Lafite is a disaster. Neither Lynch-Bages nor Pichon-Longueville are very interesting. Pichon-Longueville, Comtesse de Lalande and Mouton-Rothschild do not sing. But Grand-Puy-Lacoste is splendid, Pontet-Canet, d'Armailhac and Clerc-Milon lush, rich and promising, while Lafite is very fine and Latour the wine of the vintage.

I threw a ringer into one of the Pauillac flights. This is a new wine called Château Haut-Condissas. The property lies in the Bas-Médoc and the wine is made by Claire Pecqueux of Château Rollan de By. It has aspirations to be a new Sociando-Mallet. Château Haut-Condissas is just a little over-extracted, but I marked it well nevertheless, giving it the same mark as Sociando-Mallet (16.5/20).

To sum up, there are some very good wines in the 1995 vintage, and it is still widely available. But though the vintage is better than 1991, 1992, 1993, 1994, 1996 (in Saint-Émilion and Pomerol) and 1997 that doesn't make it a great year. For 10–15 per cent more you can still acquire the gems of the 1990 and 1986 vintages, which, from the investment point of view will almost certainly show greater growth (better wines, shorter supply, more ready for drinking from now onwards). The price of wine does occasionally move in mysterious ways. But overall there is a certain logic behind it.

PRICES THEN AND NOW

I advised my readers not to invest in the 1995s at the outset. Like many years – all the years of the 1980s with the exception of 1982, indeed – I felt the vintage would be available at the same prices or less in real terms a few years on. Buy only the *recherché* Pomerols and Saint-Émilions, if you must. But nothing else.

Was I right? Well, I have to admit, not entirely. The Médoc-Graves First Growths opened at £600 ($1080) a case in Britain, Super-Seconds such as Châteaux Pichon-Longueville, Comtesse de Lalande and Ducru-Beaucaillou at £280 ($500), Palmer, Lynch-Bages and Cos d'Estournel at a little less, Léoville-Las-Cases at a little more. Two and a half years later the First Growths were being offered at £1000–£1200 ($1800–$2160): £1400 ($2520) for Château Latour; Ducru-Beaucaillou, Pichon-Longueville, Comtesse de Lalande and Léoville-Las-Cases were available at £700 ($1260), Cos d'Estournel at £530 ($950), but Lynch-Bages at a mere £280 ($500). So some wines had more than doubled in two and half years; others, and there were rather more of them as you go down the hierarchy, had barely moved.

Obviously I underestimated the continuing demand for the First Growths and top Super-Seconds. You can see this sort of rise on the prices of Châteaux L'Église-Clinet, Clinet, L'Angelus and Le Tertre-Roteboeuf too, and especially in that of Lafleur. But, while not denying that many of these are excellent wines, there are others, equally good, whose prices, as I maintained they would be, were no more in real terms then than they were at the outset. Moreover, the general market in stocks and shares, let alone specialised PEPs and other investment schemes, increased handsomely in this same period. Fine wine was not unique.

The climb in prices since the beginning of 1999 has been much less marked. The spread for the First Growths is £1000 ($1800) for Haut-Brion to £2000 ($3600) for Margaux. The Super-Seconds have not moved and with one or two exceptions the market for the lesser wines has remained static.

The Tasting

Once again these notes are based on two comprehensive tastings: the first in January 1999, the second the Institute of Masters of Wine tasting the following November.

Saint-Émilion

Château L'Angélus

2005–2018	16.5

Very full colour. Rich and voluptuous on the nose. A little over-extracted perhaps. Yet the fruit is very concentrated. Rich and full but definitely new wave. Good grip. This is certainly a great success. There is no lack of depth. Very good plus. Needs time.

Château L'Arrosée

NOW–2015	17.0

Fullish colour. Interesting spice here. Quite Cabernet. A bit of liquorice and bitter chocolate. Good individuality. Fullish. Good structure. I like the slight austere touch. Rich. Good grip. This has class. Long. Very good indeed.

Château Ausone

NOW–2020	18.5

Full colour. Very lovely, lush, refined fruit on the nose. Sweet, rich and ripe. Not a blockbuster. Seductive and complex. Good touch of spice. Very lovely fruit. Discreetly complete. Lovely finish. Very long. Very fine.

Château Beauséjour-Bécot

NOW–2015	16.0

Fullish colour. Stylish, oaky nose. Lovely fruit here. But not a blockbuster. Great charm. Fullish. Good ripe tannins. Good acidity. Delicious fruit. Most seductive. Good length. Very good.

Château Beauséjour-Duffau-Lagarrosse

DRINK SOON   14.0

Medium to medium-full colour. Plump and fresh on the nose. But on the light and forward side. Medium body. Forward, pleasant and quite ample and ripe. Reasonable length. Very pleasant but not serious. Quite good.

Château Belair

NOW–2012   16.0

Medium to medium-full colour. Fresh and fruity. Interesting damson fruit. Not that sweet. Medium-full. Quite rich, but it lacks a little acidity so though it is very good the follow-through doesn't add much.

Château Belfont-Belcier

NOW–2015   16.5

Medium-full colour. Stylish, quite plump, ample and fruity nose with good depth and a touch of oak. Fullish. Good ripe tannins. Good grip too. This is cool and quite concentrated. Finishes well. Very good plus.

Château Berliquet

NOW–2008   15.0

Medium colour. Some evolution. Soft and fruity. But no real backbone on the nose. Medium body, ripe and fruity. A touch of oak. A wine of charm if no real depth. Forward. Good.

Château Cadet-Piola

NOW–2015   16.0

Good full colour. Ripe, fresh Merlot nose. Good acidity. Good depth on the nose. Fullish, rich and opulent on the palate. Good grip. A nice but not exaggerated touch of oak. Long. Very good.

Château Canon

DRINK SOON   13.0

Medium colour. Thin. Fruity but a bit light and weedy. Light on the palate. Will get astringent. Pleasant, indeed some style but nothing underneath to support it. Should have been better than this. But no taint.

Château Canon-La-Gaffelière

DRINK SOON   13.5

Fullish colour. Quite oaky on the nose. New wave and succulent. On the palate rather masked by the oak. Even a bit astringent. It seems to lack fat. And the oak is too dominant. Not bad plus at best.

Château Cheval Blanc

NOW–2015   17.5

Fullish colour. Very ripe and lush and Libournais on the nose. Aromatic and spicy. Lush and voluptuous, but it doesn't have the grip of Ausone or Pétrus. Fine but marginally disappointing for Cheval Blanc.

Château Curé-Bon (La Madelaine)

DRINK SOON   13.5

Medium-full colour. Soft Merlot nose. Lacks a bit of zip and concentration. Medium to medium-full body. Rather one-dimensional as a result of the lack of acidity. Pleasant at best. Not bad plus.

Château Dassault

NOW–2012   16.0

Medium-full colour. Good ripe nose and better acidity than some in this flight. Decent substance here. Medium-full. Good grip. This has good depth and indeed balance and class. Finishes well. Very good.

Château La Dominique

DRINK SOON   12.0

Fullish colour. Sweet but a little shallow on the nose. Jammy but superficial. Nothing here on the palate. Short and inconsequential. Poor for what it is.

Château Ferrand Lartigue

NOW–2012   15.5

Medium-full colour. Slightly raw on the nose still. It lacks a bit of fat and generosity. Medium-full. Some tannin. A bit more succulence on the palate but good grip. The tannins show. But this has a good finish. Good plus.

CHÂTEAU FIGEAC

NOW–2018   17.5

Medium-full colour. Fresh but slightly lean
on the nose. Good class. This is fullish and
has a lot of depth. Nicely cool. Good grip.
Long and complex. Really stylish. Really
long on the palate. This is fine.

CHÂTEAU FONROQUE

NOW–2008   13.0

Medium-full colour. Chemical nose. Metallic.
This blew off after a bit. But underneath,
though there is some grip, the wine is still a
little hard. Lacks succulence. No charm.
Unclean, really – but is this a bad bottle?

CHÂTEAU LARMANDE

NOW–2008   14.5

Medium-full colour. Ripe, new wave, sweet
and oaky. Very seductive but no real depth.
Did not hold up in the glass. Medium to
medium-full. A little tannin. Slightly over-
extracted. Quite good plus at best.

CHÂTEAU MAGDELAINE

NOW–2008   15.5

Medium to medium-full colour. Fresh nose
but it lacks a bit of ripeness and charm. Very
Merlot. Plump but it lacks a bit of zip. Quite
concentrated. Not really for the long term.
Good plus.

CHÂTEAU MONBOUSQUET

NOW–2008   14.0

Very full colour. Rich and fat on the nose.
This has good depth. On the palate a
medium-full, spicy, toasty wine. It lacks a
little grip and elegance. But it is quite good.
Slightly one-dimensional.

CHÂTEAU PAVIE

DRINK SOON   12.5

Medium-full colour. Somewhat metallic, thin
and attenuated on the nose. A great
disappointment. Short. Already empty and
astringent. Château Pavie-Decesse is much
better for once.

CHÂTEAU PAVIE-DECESSE

NOW–2011   15.0

Fullish colour. Ripe nose. Good definition.
Not an enormous amount of weight though.
Yet on the palate good substance. Ripe.
Good grip. Decent fruit. Good but lacks a
little definition. Reasonable finish.

CHÂTEAU PAVIE-MACQUIN

DRINK SOON   14.0

Medium colour. Smells of paper and rustic
and a little farmyardy at that. Too dry. A bit
one-dimensional but has a little freshness at
the end and reasonably ripe fruit. Medium
body. Quite good.

CHÂTEAU LE TERTRE-ROTEBOEUF

NOW–2010   15.5

Medium-full colour. Some oak. But a lack of
grip on the nose. Medium body. New wave.
Very oaky wine. Nice ripe fruit but only
medium weight and grip so the finish seems a
little astringent. And a touch short. Good
plus.

CHÂTEAU TROPLONG-MONDOT

NOW–2015   16.0

Full colour. Rich, fat, spicy, oaky nose. Good
depth. On the palate fullish. Some tannin.
Quite solid. This has weight and class, and is
very good. But it is a little adolescent.

CHÂTEAU VALANDRAUD

DRINK SOON   12.0

Very full colour. Hugely new oaky. Ripe. But
what is underneath? Full and fat but no
dimension or class. And the oak dominates
to the extent that it is astringent. Not for me.

POMEROL
CHÂTEAU BON PASTEUR

NOW–2009   14.0

Medium colour. Some development. Soft,
ripe and oaky but no real depth. A little
lacking in grip. On the palate a lot of oak.
Quite classy fruit. Quite good.

Château Bourgneuf

DRINK SOON   12.0

Full youthful colour. Ample nose. Juicy fruit. But is there a slight taint? On the palate this is a little awkward with a metallic end to it. Unexciting.

Château Certan de May

DRINK SOON   13.0

Medium-full colour. Reasonable depth and grip. But rather too vegetal. Only medium body and not much dimension at that. Somewhat artificial. Dull. This is disappointing.

Château Clinet

NOW–2015   16.5

Fullish colour. Good freshness and substance. Still youthful. Rich, full, ample and balanced. Good fruit and plenty of depth. Just lacks a little real sparkle for fine. But very well made. This is very good plus.

Clos L'Église

NOW–2010   15.5

Medium body. Some development. Slightly artificially fruity. Good substance. Nice fresh fruit. Decent grip. Not the greatest of distinction but good plus.

Château L'Église-Clinet

NOW–2011   16.0

Full colour. Rich, concentrated and solid. Still young. Fullish. Quite some tannin. Rich and fruity. Quite oaky. Lacks a little zip. A modern wine. Very good but not great.

Château L'Évangile

DRINK SOON   14.0

Medium-full colour. Somewhat solid and stewed on the nose. Even a bit of H2S. On the palate medium body. Rather sweet. Rather short. This doesn't sing. Quite good at best.

Château Feytit-Clinet

DRINK SOON   12.5

Medium to medium-full colour. Light and fruity. Neutral otherwise on the nose. A bit green and empty. Light, short and forward. Not bad at best.

Château La Fleur-Pétrus

DRINK SOON   12.5

Medium-full colour. Weedy, rather attenuated nose. Nothing here. Lacks grip on the palate. Sweet but inconsequential, and will get attenuated. No. Disappointing.

Château Gazin

NOW–2008   15.0

Medium to medium-full colour. Nice ripe nose. Good oak and substance. Good depth. Medium body. Nicely fruity, but not enough grip or depth for better than 'good'.

Château La Grave (-à-Pomerol)

DRINK SOON   12.0

Medium to medium-full colour. Not entirely clean on the nose. Muddy and indeterminate. A bit forced on the palate. Medium body. Indifferent. Ugly finish.

Château Lafleur

NOW–2013   16.0

Medium-full colour. A little stewed on the nose. Rather four-square on the palate. Reasonable fruit. Some tannin. But a lack of grace and real grip. A bit solid. But then it always is. Very good but not great.

Château Lagrange

NOW–2010   15.0

Medium-full colour. A little closed on the nose. Some substance but perhaps a little over-extracted. Fullish and ripe. Decent acidity. A good middle of the road Pomerol. Lacks a little grace. But long enough. Good.

Château Latour-à-Pomerol

DRINK SOON   14.0

Fullish colour. A bit stewed and rustic on the nose. Thin too. Medium body. Rather classless. Some grip. Some fruit. Quite good at best.

CHÂTEAU MAZEYRES

DRINK SOON   12.5

Medium to medium-full colour. Rather hard and driven on the nose. Lacks charm and doesn't seem to have that much depth. Slightly sour on the palate. Medium body. Unexciting. Lacks class and charm.

CHÂTEAU PÉTRUS

NOW–2025   18.5

Fullish colour. Very concentrated Merlot fruit on the nose. Lots of depth here and the grip missing in most Libournais wines too. Quite a big wine, thought not *that* huge. Very, very concentrated and very, very fine grip at the end. Lovely fruit. Very fine.

CHÂTEAU LE PIN

NOW–2012   16.5

Fullish colour. Fullish and quite oaky on the nose. Very good fruit on the palate. Good, fresh acidity. Real charm. But not enough real concentration for fine. Very good plus.

CHÂTEAU TROTANOY

NOW–2011   17.0

Fullish colour. Full and rich and classy on the nose. Ample. Medium-full. Good ripe tannins. Lovely fruit here. Not the greatest depth but very good indeed. Quite classy. Positive finish.

VIEUX CHÂTEAU CERTAN

NOW–2018   17.5

Medium-full colour. Ample, fat and plump nose. Good depth. Fullish. Concentrated. Very good grip. Still some tannin. This has real depth and class. A fine example.

GRAVES

DOMAINE DE CHEVALIER

NOW–2011   15.0

Medium colour. Some development. A little austere and stalky on the nose. Lacks charm. A strange mixture of rather sophisticated and concentrated, oaky *petits fruits rouges* and a certain thin stalkiness. Better on the palate than on the nose. But only good.

CHÂTEAU HAUT-BAILLY

NOW–2015   17.0

Medium colour. Fat, rich, 'old viney' nose. Quite full. Certainly concentrated. Good oaky base. This is plump and has a very good follow-through. Very good indeed.

CHÂTEAU HAUT-BRION

2005–2020   19.0

Medium-full colour. Marvellously complex, elegant, intense nose. Splendid fruit. Real class. Real depth. Fullish. Splendidly subtle and harmonious. Plus really excellent fruit. Very fine plus.

CHÂTEAU LA MISSION HAUT-BRION

NOW–2020   18.5

Medium-full colour. Depth and class here. Quite Médoc-y. Still youthful. Fullish. Quite tannic but very good tannins. Backward but splendidly promising. Ripe and concentrated and profound. Very fine.

CHÂTEAU PAPE-CLÉMENT

NOW–2018   17.0

Medium-full colour. Very Graves in style. Nice plump fruit. Good substance. Fullish, rich and earthy in a good sense. Good grip and very good tannins. Plenty of wine here. Very good indeed.

MARGAUX & SOUTHERN MÉDOC

CHÂTEAU D'ANGLUDET

NOW–2015   16.0

Medium-full colour. Good structure and depth here, and nice plump fruit. Quite a solid, meaty wine. But the tannins are ripe and the fruit concentrated. This is very good.

CHÂTEAU BRANE-CANTENAC

NOW–2010   15.0

Fullish colour. Ripe, rich and quite fat on the nose. Medium-full. Some tannin. A little raw at present. But there is reasonable class and depth. Good.

Château Cantemerle

DRINK SOON   12.5

Medium colour. Light and rather thin and undistinguished on the nose. And similar on the palate. Rather short. Poor.

Château Dauzac

DRINK SOON   12.5

Fullish colour. Slightly raw nose. A bit anonymous. Rather thin and astringent on the palate. This is a bit of a disappointment for Dauzac has been making progress recently.

Château Desmirail

NOW–2009   14.0

Fullish colour. Slightly raw on the nose. Lacks a little class and generosity. Medium body. Some tannin. Reasonable grip. Somewhat anonymous but the balance is OK. Quite good.

Château Durfort-Vivens

DRINK SOON   14.0

Medium colour. Light nose. Indeed a little thin perhaps. Lacks weight. Quite fruity. Medium to medium-full body. A little neutral though. Nothing really to fault it, but nothing to commend it either.

Château Giscours

DRINK SOON   10.0

Fullish colour. Slight volatile acidity on the nose. Seems a little dead underneath. Sweet. Oxidised. Astringent. No. A bad bottle?

Château Ferrière

NOW–2010   15.5

Full colour. Soft, charming, oaky nose. Medium-full body. Good ripe tannins. Good grip, even quite concentrated. This has attractive fruit. Not a blockbuster but a true Margaux in character. Good plus.

Château Haut-Breton-Larigaudière

DRINK SOON   14.0

Medium-full colour. Fruity nose but a little bland. Medium body. Quite juicy. Some oak. This has charm if not *that* much depth. Reasonable balance. Quite good.

Château d'Issan

DRINK SOON   13.0

Medium-full colour. A little raw on the nose. Lacks definition. Vegetal. A little coarse on the palate. The fruit lacks class and the wine, only medium bodied, is a little short. Dull.

Château Kirwan

DRINK SOON   14.0

Medium colour. Some oak on the nose. Quite attractive fruit, but forward and without great strength. On the palate medium body. Not a great deal of grip. Quite attractive but certainly oaky. This tends to dominate. Astringent finish.

Château Labégorce-Zédé

DRINK SOON   13.0

Medium-full colour. Lightish, somewhat raw nose. Not much class. Medium body. A little coarse and raw on the palate. The fruit lacks charm. Undistinguished. This is a disappointment for this usually reliable property.

Château La Lagune

DRINK SOON   14.5

Medium colour. Pleasantly oaky but no great depth on the nose. A small wine, but respectable fruit, balance and length. Good oak support. Lacks real depth and concentration. Quite good plus.

Château Lascombes

NOW–2009   14.5

Medium-full colour. Slightly corky but oaky and plump on the nose. Is there enough grip underneath? Medium to medium-full body. Attractive fruit. Quite dominated by the oak because there isn't really enough grip and concentration. Lots of charm though. Quite good plus.

Château Malescasse

DRINK SOON   12.5

Medium to medium-full colour. Light nose. Lacks fat and concentration. Strangely sweet and confected on the palate. Not much grip or tannin. Medium body. Coarse.

CHÂTEAU MALESCOT-SAINT-EXUPÉRY

NOW–2008	15.0

Full colour. Plump and fruity on the nose but not much grip or strength. Medium to medium-full body. Good fruit and good balance. More to it than seems on the nose. This has good weight. A little adolescent at present. Finishes positively. Good.

CHÂTEAU MARGAUX

2005–2025	19.0

Full colour. Big, backward, quite pro-nounced oak. Fine fruit underneath. Fullish and tannic and oaky. Quite powerful. This has real class and real intensity. Splendid finish. Very fine plus.

CHÂTEAU MARQUIS DE TERME

NOW–2009	14.0

Fullish colour. Big, raw and solid on the nose. Tannic but with really quite good fruit underneath. Yet a bit stewed I think. We shall see. The finish is positive rather than negative. Quite good.

CHÂTEAU MONBRISON

NOW–2008	15.0

Medium-full colour. Soft, pleasant, oaky nose. Medium weight. Nice rich fruit. Good tannins. This is long and positive without being *that* concentrated. Good.

CHÂTEAU PALMER

NOW–2020	18.0

Fullish colour. Classy nose. Complex, concentrated and quite backward compared with most. Fullish body. Impressive fruit here. Lovely balance. This has real class and depth. Very, very long. Undoubtedly fine.

PAVILLON ROUGE DU CHÂTEAU MARGAUX

NOW–2015	17.0

Medium-full colour. Fragrant nose. Classy. Some oak. Not a blockbuster but smooth and well-made. Most attractive fruit. Medium-full. Very good grip. This is succulent and delicious. Very good indeed.

CHÂTEAU PRIEURÉ-LICHINE

NOW–2010	14.5

Medium-full colour. Supple and fruity on the nose. No great distinction or depth. Medium weight. Good tannins. Attractive and well-made if with no real class. Quite good plus.

CHÂTEAU RAUZAN-SÉGLA

SEE NOTE

Noted very good indeed (17.0) and (Now-2018) at a vertical tasting I presided over at the Boston Vinexpo in February 1998.

SAINT-JULIEN
CHÂTEAU BEYCHEVELLE

2005–2018	16.5

Very good colour. Firm, full Cabernet nose. A little solid and ungainly at present but there is depth here, I think. Round and ripe. Full and tannic. But a little lacking grip. Yet a better effort than they have made for years. This really does have concentration for once. Long. Very good plus.

CHÂTEAU BRANAIRE-DUCRU

NOW–2012	16.0

Very good colour. High toned. Very rich, spicy, voluptuous nose. But it seems to lack a little zip and grip. Better on the palate. Fullish body. Very good round tannins. Ripe and with good if not great acidity. Fat and seductive. Very good.

CHÂTEAU DUCRU-BEAUCAILLOU

NOW–2020	19.0

Fullish colour. Very lovely intense, refined fruit here. Essence of really high quality Saint-Julien without being a blockbuster. This has real class. Fullish. Gently oaky. Exquisite fruit. Real poise. Real breed. Very, very long on the palate. This is very fine.

CHÂTEAU GRUAUD-LAROSE

2005–2020	17.0

Medium-full colour. Fullish, quite rich and tannic but slightly ungainly nose. A little less lumpy as it evolved. Full, rich and Cabernet-y. Good grip. Quite a sizeable wine. This is backward but very good indeed. It will last well: it has got the acidity.

Château Lagrange

NOW–2015 16.5

Full colour. Classy Saint-Julien nose if not with the intensity of Ducru-Beaucaillou. Balanced. Medium-full weight. Lovely ripe fruit. Other wines are bigger, but this is balanced and has great attraction. In the final analysis only very good plus because it is only medium-bodied. But a very well-made example.

Château Langoa-Barton

NOW–2015 16.5

Fullish colour. Soft, aromatic, but essentially very classy Cabernet on the nose. Fullish. Lovely fruit. Very good Cabernet-oak-Saint-Julien flavour. Ripe. Very good grip. Not a blockbuster but a classy example. Finishes well. Very good oaky underpinning.

Château Léoville-Barton

2005–2020 18.0

Full colour. Very fine, rich, concentrated nose here. Open and ripe. Lots of class and depth. Chocolate and *crème patissière*. Fullish. Excellent fruit. A lot of grip as well. This is profound and lovely. Long, subtle and harmonious at the end. Fine plus.

Château Léoville-Las-Cases

2006–2025 19.0

Very good colour. Still quite closed. But enormous depth here. Fabulous fruit. Real intensity. A full backward, complete wine. Very lovely and very classy. Still underdeveloped but potentially a wine of very fine quality. Full. Very good tannins. Really fine Cabernet fruit. Very long. Very fine indeed.

Château Léoville-Poyferré

2005–2020 17.5

Very good colour. Lovely aromatic but essentially Cabernet fruit here. This has real concentration and very high quality. Fullish, balanced and fine. Not quite the class, the concentration or the originality of Léoville-Las-Cases or Léoville-Barton but a fine wine.

Château Saint-Pierre

NOW–2006 10.0

Very good colour. There is a taint here, I think. The nose has a metallic hint, and is rather astringent. No better on the palate. Medium body. Spicy, stalky and dry. Undistinguished. Don't touch it.

Château Talbot

NOW–2018 16.0

Fullish colour. Nice, ripe, quite high-toned (even a suggestion of H2S at first) nose. Medium full body. Ripe. Nicely classy Saint-Julien. Good depth. Not quite the concentration, intensity and class of some but very good.

Moulis
Château Chasse-Spleen

NOW–2012 15.0

Medium-full colour. Ample, plump, ripe and attractive on the nose. Medium- to full-bodied and attractive. A slight lack of grip. But ample and ripe and of good style. Good.

Château Poujeaux

NOW–2015 16.0

Fullish colour. Ample, ripe and jammy on the nose. Fullish. Very good tannins. Lovely fruit. Better acidity than Chasse-Spleen. Long. Very good.

Pauillac
Château d'Armailhac

NOW–2018 16.5

Good colour. Nicely plummy, even violety nose. Nice fruit. Not a blockbuster. Medium-full. Good grip and intensity. Stylish and harmonious. Long. Very good plus.

Château Batailley

NOW–2014 15.5

Fullish colour. Ripe but lacks a little zip and depth. Good commercial stuff here. Fullish body. Nicely rich. Better acidity than appeared at the start. Finishes well. Very good.

CARRUADES DE LAFITE

DRINK SOON   11.0

Fullish colour. This is a little tough and
rustic on the nose. Forced and vegetal. Also
rather sulphury. Something went wrong here!

CHÂTEAU CLERC-MILON

NOW–2018   16.5

Good colour. Fat, rich, opulent and plummy
on the nose. Lots of depth. Most attractive.
Rather more backward than d'Armailhac.
Fullish. Some tannin. Good depth. Perhaps
just a little more grip.

CHÂTEAU DUHART-MILON

NOW–2008   13.0

Medium-full colour. Quite closed on the
nose. A little dense, as so often. A chunky
wine. Some fruit. But no grace. I am not
excited. But it is not bad, I suppose.

LES FORTS DE LATOUR

NOW–2010   15.0

Full colour. Nicely perfumed on the nose. Not
a blockbuster. Balanced and stylish. Slightly
corky as it developed. But, disregarding this,
fruity and easy to drink. Good.

CHÂTEAU GRAND-PUY-LACOSTE

2005–2020   18.0

Full colour. Quite backward but quite lovely.
Super concentrated fruit. Well put together.
Very harmonious. Very elegant. This is full
and rich, subtle and very well balanced. Very
classy. Very long. Not a blockbuster but with
a quite splendid finish.

CHÂTEAU HAUT-BAGES-LIBÉRAL

NOW–2009   15.0

Fullish colour. Oaky and cedary on the nose.
Good stylish blackberry fruit. Quite
accessible. Only medium to medium-full
body. Good fruit. Possibly slightly lacking in
grip. Pleasant but slightly one-dimensional.
Good.

CHÂTEAU HAUT-BATAILLEY

NOW–2018   16.0

Full colour. Rich, full and concentrated.
Very good class. Medium-full. Quite tannic.

Quite extracted. Warm and rich. This is not
brilliant but it is unexpectedly good. Not as
hard as it often is. Good plus.

CHÂTEAU LAFITE

2005–2020   18.5

Fullish colour. Backward, austere, indeed
even a little vegetal at the beginning. Fullish,
tannic and closed at first. The follow-
through however is most impressive. Rich,
really classy and really long. Very fine.

CHÂTEAU LATOUR

2005–2025   19.5

Fullish colour. Very good fruit. Quite oaky.
Excellent grip. Not too austere. Fullish and
backward. Very lovely fruit. Very complete.
This is really excellent. Marvellous breed.
Splendid intensity. Very fine indeed.

CHÂTEAU LYNCH-BAGES

NOW–2013   15.0

Fullish colour. Soft and fruity. Quite attractive but not much depth. Medium body. No
selection here. It is pleasant, indeed ripe,
fruity and not short. But it is a little bland.
Good though.

CHÂTEAU LYNCH-MOUSSAS

DRINK SOON   13.0

Full colour. Plump, attractive fruit on the
nose. But without much weight underneath.
Yet weedy on the palate. This tails off. The
fruit was there but with nothing to support
it. Not bad.

CHÂTEAU MOUTON-ROTHSCHILD

NOW–2013   16.0

Fullish colour. Ample fruit. Cedary oak, but
slightly bland. A certain lack of
concentration. In a First Growth context this
is a bit of a disappointment. Pretty, elegant
and balanced. But where is the size and
concentration, the grip and staying power?
Very good only.

CHÂTEAU PICHON-LONGUEVILLE

NOW–2012   14.0

Full colour. Full nose. But a little over-
extracted. Some oak. But little depth or

excitement. Just rather dull. Medium-full. Reasonable grip. Neutral.

Château Pichon-Longueville, Comtesse de Lalande

NOW–2015	15.0

Medium-full colour. Quite closed. But a lot of concentration here. Good weight. Still backward. Yet on the palate it doesn't quite sing. Quite full. Quite intense but rather disjointed. Not special this year.

Château Pontet-Canet

NOW–2015	16.0

Full colour. Very lovely ripe fruit on the nose. Rich and opulent. Classy and balanced. But quite open and accessible. Fullish. This is getting to be a true Pauillac. Rich, harmonious and very good.

Saint-Estèphe

Château Calon-Ségur

NOW–2008	14.0

Fullish colour. Full on the nose. Slightly rustic. But some new oak. Plenty of substance. A fullish wine, but bland. The acidities are low. Will it get astringent? Slightly short. And not very classy either. Quite good.

Château Cos d'Estournel

NOW–2015	16.5

Fullish colour. Aromatic, concentrated, intense nose. This is an impressive example. Fullish, rich and intense. Very good tannins. Very fine grip. Lots of oak. This is complex and very well-made. And yet it lacks a little real Médoc definition. Very complex. Very good plus.

Château Haut-Marbuzet

NOW–2007	15.0

Fullish colour. Lush, expansive nose. Good oak. But a hint of oxidation. Almost sweet on the palate. Medium-full. Very oaky. Not quite the grip. Or the class for fine. But good.

Château Lafon-Rochet

DRINK SOON	14.0

Fullish colour. No great weight on the nose.

Nor class, but fresh and pretty. Similar on the palate. A little short at the end. A decent wine for early drinking. The fruit is quite stylish. Quite good.

Château Meyney

DRINK SOON	13.0

Fullish colour. Lacks a little ripeness and charm on the nose. Medium body. Neutral, vegetal and short. Fair at best.

Château Montrose

NOW–2009	15.5

Fullish colour. Chocolaty flavours plus some new oak on the nose. Good depth. Fullish. Good fruit. Not quite the grip for better than good plus though. I think this will get astringent.

Château de Pez

NOW–2012	15.0

Medium-full colour. Vanilla fruit and oak on the nose. Medium-full. Good ripe fruit here. Not a bit burly. Round and rich in fact. Finishes well. Good.

Château Phélan-Ségur

DRINK SOON	14.0

Fullish colour. On the lighter side but the nose shows elegant fruit. Well-made but only medium body. Acidity is on the low side. A pleasant wine for drinking soon. Attractively ripe. Quite good.

Médoc & Haut-Médoc

Château Haut-Condissas

2005–2020	16.5

Fullish colour. Full, rich, sizeable and very concentrated. This is impressive on the nose. Quite oaky. Is it a bit over-extracted? Fullish. On the palate lacks a little zip and grip so slightly four-square. Very good plus though.

Château Sociando-Mallet

NOW–2018	16.5

Medium-full colour. Good Cabernet fruit. Straight. Balanced. Oaky. Fullish, ample, rich and highly satisfying. Nicely fresh at the end. This is a classy example. Very well put together. Very good plus.

1994 VINTAGE

SIZE OF THE CROP:	5,676,859 HECTOLITRES.
VINTAGE RATING:	14.0 (RED WINES).
	14.0 (DRY WHITE WINES).
	13.0 (SWEET WINES).

This was to be the last time the Bordeaux harvest produced less than 6 million hectolitres until 2002. The yield was 50.2 hl/ha. 846,787 hectolitres of white wine was produced (14 per cent of the total).

The 1994 vintage followed the disappointing, indeed frustrating pattern of the early 1980s. After a nice, hot August everything looked very promising, but everyone's hopes were swept aside by a rainy September.

Yet, it was not quite so wet as in 1993 and 1992. The effect of the dilution was less. The resultant crop was at least OK, and with nothing else since the 1990 vintage to get excited about, an effort was made to sell 1994s as futures. The campaign was only moderately successful, and with both 1995 and 1996 proving to be better vintages, interest in the 1994s sank into oblivion and has never re-emerged.

By current standards the wines are good value. They have a decent colour, not a lot of tannin – and what there is is ripe and supple rather than hard and green – at least adequate balance and in many cases no shortage of charm. There are no great wines; indeed few fine ones; but a lot which will give pleasure. Use them to lead into something older and more interesting. The majority are now ready. Indeed some of the *bourgeois* wines are now losing their fruit.

THE WEATHER

It was a mild but rainy winter. Indeed hardly a winter at all, with December, January and February all two to three degrees above normal. In March it was warmer still. But the end of the month the shoots were well advanced, inducing on the one hand a fear of a repeat of the 1991 frost, and on the other the probability of an early, and therefore possibly exceptional harvest. Already it could be seen that the *sortie* was not huge. It would not, other things being equal, be an enormous crop.

There *was* frost. April was cool and unsettled, and in the middle of the month the temperature descended. Nearly everybody was affected to some extent, but the only serious damage occurred in the middle and southern Médoc – Caronne-Sainte-Gemme in Saint-Laurent down through Moulis and Avensan to Arsac and Le Pian – and in the southern Graves and Barsac. Here some growers found themselves, eventually, as much as a third short of a normal harvest, as at Caronne, or even more, as at Montalivet in Pujols in the Graves.

The first of May brought back the sun and the warmth, and the bedraggled shoots began to revive. Despite some hailstorms, which seem to have caused little damage, the vines flowered early and speedily. The local Wine Institute dated the *mi-fleur* at 4th June, 10 days ahead of the average and the sixth equal earliest since 1952. (The order goes 1952 and 1990, 1989, 1960 and 1961, 1976 and 1994, then 1982, 1993 and 1959.) The weather during the flowering was unsettled, but despite this there was very little *coulure* and almost no *millerandage*, and once the flowering had completed Bordeaux relaxed into a splendid, and sometimes very hot, June, July and August. July produced an average temperature of 22.8°C, only just less than the record

1989. August offered 22.6°, a full 2° above average. And there was sufficient rain to prevent any blockage in the development of the grapes. The *mi-véraison* was set at 6th August: very early, indicating a harvest which would start on 14th September or thereabouts, or on the 19th for those who like to begin on a Monday.

In 1993 the rain began on the 9th September; in 1994 it began on the 7th. In both cases the precipitation was sometimes relentless, sometimes intermittent, but nevertheless more or less continual, in 1994 not finally giving up until the end of the month.

The question was, what to do? The Merlots were certainly ripe by the 7th September, at 11.5°, and in most cases up to 12° a week later. Was there any point in waiting? With the weather forecasts pessimistic most producers decided to pick. Those who did so during the weekend before Monday 19th, when there was a brief respite from the rain, and during the three days which followed, got the best of it. In retrospect those who followed immediately into the Cabernets did well too. Unfortunately the weather forecasters got it wrong. The week of 26th September, when a return to fine weather had been promised, in fact produced yet more rain, and lots of it, and those who were caught in these downpours produced inferior vats.

It was, in fact, a vintage where those who were prepared to grab what they had did better than those who sat it out waiting for better times to turn up. It was equally a vintage where those who were favoured with a precocious site were able to reap the benefit. And it was a year where those with lots of early-harvesting Merlot, and, in some cases Cabernet Franc (though this is a moot point) benefited over those with a majority of late-maturing Cabernet Sauvignon and Petit Verdot.

THE SIZE OF THE CROP

Until the rains arrived 1994 promised to be a smaller crop than it eventually turned out to be. Despite the statistics above many châteaux were at pains to assure me that this year, at the very least, their yields were down to 40 hl/ha overall, much less than in 1993. Sometimes you have to take these protestations with a pinch of salt, as in the past – and I have checked – they do not correspond with the figures available at the *Marie* for all to see, if they wish. Some proprietors have a tendency, when asked for their yield, to divide what they have produced as *grand vin* by their area under production, conveniently forgetting second wines and the rest, and turning a deaf ear to the word 'overall'. Château Latour, at least, comes clean: 58 hl/ha, with 52 per cent of the production going in to the *grand vin*. At Haut-Brion they produced 160 *tonneaux* of *grand vin* and 70 of Bahans, which I calculate overall as 49.3 hl/ha. But at the end of July they had green harvested on the basis of 40 hl/ha. You can see the effect of the rain.

THE WINES

Given the appalling September, the inevitable dilution that the rain produced in the resulting wine, the quality of the 1994s is a tribute to modern vinification methods and château perfectionism. Growers resisted the temptation to prolong the maceration to add a bit of extra weight. They compensated for the not-too-special Cabernet by adding a bit of extra Merlot to the blends, and they did not hesitate to bottle a little earlier than usual to preserve what freshness the wines possessed. In all this they were helped by the fact that September was cool, so the incidence of rot was not much of a threat, and by the fact that the fine July and August had at least given a base of quality which could not be entirely washed out by the downpours that were to come. We could, after all, have had a second 1975.

Acidities, however, are on the low side. This is fine in that the wines are soft, the tannins are low. It allows the fruit to sing out. But it means that the 1994s are medium-term wines which, while pleasant, are essentially simple. Rarely do you find a 1994 with real length, dimension and complexity. As I said in the summer of 1995: they are good, but they are by no means great.

PRICES THEN AND NOW

As futures in June 1995, the First Growths were offered at £375–£400 ($670–$720) per case in bond, while the Super-Seconds were £165–£200 ($290–$360). Seven years on prices had more or less doubled. The First Growths can be had for £750–£800 ($1350–$1440). Cos d'Estournel is £335 ($600), Pichon-Longueville, Comtesse de Lalande is £395 ($700), and Léoville-Las-Cases is £400 ($720). A perfectly decent, if not desperately exciting *cru bourgeois*, such as Château Potensac, is £100 ($180).

THE STARS OF THE VINTAGE

	MÉDOC/GRAVES	SAINT-ÉMILION/POMEROL
VERY FINE	HAUT-BRION; LATOUR; MARGAUX	PÉTRUS
FINE	DUCRU-BEAUCAILLOU; LAFITE; LÉOVILLE-LAS-CASES; MOUTON-ROTHSCHILD; PICHON-LONGUEVILLE, COMTESSE DE LALANDE	L'ANGÉLUS; CHEVAL BLANC; FIGEAC; LE PIN; LATOUR-À-POMEROL; VIEUX CHÂTEAU CERTAN
VERY GOOD INDEED	RAUZAN-SÉGLA; CLERC-MILON; LE PETIT MOUTON	LA FLEUR DE GAY

THE TASTING

The majority of the following wines were sampled in Southwold in January 1998. Sadly, a number of bottles were either corked or bore traces of contamination by oxytetracloranizole, a problem which was evident at Ducru-Beaucaillou in the 1988, 1989 and 1990 vintages and which was noticeable here in Saint-Pierre and Gloria, and in Les Forts de Latour and one or two other wines. This is a curious taint, not, if the wine is substantial, very noticeable at first. But like corkiness, it gets worse with oxidation. The Canon 1994 is perhaps the worst example, which is why we did not bother with it.

SAINT-ÉMILION

CHÂTEAU L'ANGÉLUS

NOW–2012	17.5

Full colour. Rich, backward, good depth on the nose. This is a big full wine. Rich, concentrated and tannic. A lot of depth. Needs time. Fine long finish. This is very classy. The second time in two months I have noted this well: much better than in cask.

CHÂTEAU L'ARROSÉE

NOW–2010	16.5

Fullish colour. Firm, oaky and concentrated on the nose. Backward. Fullish, ripe, even rich. This has plenty of depth and class. Properly long and stylish at the end. Very good plus.

CHÂTEAU AUSONE

NOW–2008	14.0

Medium-full colour. Ripe but a little dry and astringent on the nose. Like many Ausones of this period it has not lived up to the promise it showed in cask. Medium to medium-full body. Decent acidity. But a lack of succulence. Quite good at best.

CHÂTEAU BEAUSÉJOUR-BÉCOT

NOW–2007	14.5

Full colour. Plenty of ripe fruit. Really quite rich on the nose. An opulent wine on the attack. Medium-full. It lacks a little grip, which is a pity. Quite good plus though but the finish is less good than the nose, which is a bad sign.

Château Beauséjour-Duffau-Lagarrosse

DRINK SOON   13.0

Medium-full colour. Quite high acidity. Not really enough ripeness. Medium body. Not much tannin. A little short and rather one-dimensional. Boring.

Château Bellefont-Belcier

DRINK SOON   14.0

Fullish colour. Quite ripe, soft, a little dry on the nose. A little neutral. Medium to medium-full, ripe and plummy. Quite backward. Good grip. This is quite good: a bit burly now, but will develop. Quite good.

Château Canon-La-Gaffelière

DRINK SOON   13.0

Full colour. Some oak here. Quite spicy. More supple than some on the nose. On the palate only medium body. And not enough grip. Finishes a little astringent. Not much joy here. Rather empty and one-dimensional at the end.

Château Cheval Blanc

NOW–2010   17.5

Medium to medium-full colour. A little stewed on the nose. Not much oak either. Improved on aeration. Medium-full, ripe and plump. Good balance. Positive finish. There is good grip here. And the finish is very good indeed. Long. Fine but not great.

Château La Couspaude

DRINK SOON   15.0

Medium-full colour. Soft nose. Quite oaky making it rounder and riper than some. Medium body. Well-made but forward. Good fruit here. Balanced and elegant. Good length. Good.

Château La Dominique

DRINK SOON   14.0

Fullish colour. Good depth here on the nose. Class too. Gamey on the palate. Some tannin. Medium full. A little bitter. Doesn't live up to its early promise. Yet positive at the end. Quite good.

Château Ferrand-Lartigue

DRINK SOON   13.5

Medium-full colour. Ripe, open, plummy and raspberry nose. Not a lot of tannin. Good acidity. There is some tannin but more astringency here. A lot of Merlot. A lack of acidity. And a lack of consistency.

Château Figeac

NOW–2012   17.5

Fullish colour. Good oak. Firm, classy nose. Plenty of depth here. Medium-full. Very good stylish fruit. Balanced, complex. Nicely spicy. Lovely finish. This is fine.

Clos Fourtet

DRINK SOON   14.5

Full colour. Reasonable fruit and substance. Medium-full, a touch of oak. Quite elegant. Balanced and agreeable. Quite stylish and long on the finish. Quite good plus.

Château Grand-Mayne

DRINK SOON   12.5

Medium to medium-full colour. Attractively balanced but not *that* substantial on the nose. Unripe fruit and rather too astringent on the palate. Lacks charm. Medium body. Unexciting.

Château Grand-Pontet

DRINK SOON   13.0

Medium colour. A little development. A little light and nondescript on the nose. But what there is is reasonably attractive. Forward. On the palate there isn't enough fruit. But there is at least some style. Finishes positively. Not bad.

Château Larcis-Ducasse

DRINK SOON   12.0

Medium colour. A little development. Rather dank on the nose. A little stewed. Thin and forward. This is little better than a generic. One-dimensional. Very dull.

Château Larmande

NOW–2009   16.0

Full colour. Ripe, mulberry and spice on the nose. Not a blockbuster but nicely balanced. Medium-full. Good balance. Fruity. This has length and depth. Stylish. Long. Very good.

Château Magdelaine

DRINK SOON   12.0

Medium-full colour. Fullish, a bit dense on the nose. On the palate a little sweet and a little ungainly. The tannins are not very ripe. A curious, rather artificial wine.

Château Monbousquet

NOW–2009   15.0

Fullish colour. Just a little dark and stewed on the nose. Got better as it evolved. Quite full. Good grip. Nice rich fruit. The finish is long and lush. But essentially the wine lacks class and definition. Good.

Clos de L'Oratoire

DRINK SOON   13.0

Fullish colour. A little raw on the nose. Possibly a bit stewed. Medium-full. Somewhat coarse. Good acidity but the fruit is more burly than ripe. Slightly vegetal and bitter on the finish but reasonably long. Not bad at best.

Château Pavie

DRINK SOON   15.5

Medium-full colour. Medium weight on the nose. No real depth or class but attractive fruit and balance. A small wine. Neat but forward. Not a lot of concentration. But balanced and attractive fruit here. Good length. Good plus.

Château Pavie-Decesse

DRINK SOON   14.0

Fullish colour. Nice ripe blackberry fruit on the nose. A little astringent on the palate. Medium-full. Somewhat dense and neutral. Quite good though.

Château Pavie-Macquin

NOW–2008   16.0

Fullish colour. Good ripe plummy fruit on the nose. Round, plump, ripe and fruity. This is stylish. Finishes well. Very good.

Château Soutard

DRINK SOON   12.0

Medium colour. A little development. Somewhat foursquare and sweaty on the nose. Lumpy. Medium body. Classless. Slightly unripe at the end. Poor.

Château Le Tertre-Roteboeuf

DRINK SOON   15.0

Medium-full colour. Gently, new oaky, ripe nose. A small, but stylish, forward wine. On the palate very pleasant, nicely balanced. But good as it is somewhat neutral. Almost ready.

Château Troplong-Mondot

NOW–2015   16.0

Good colour. Quite burly at first on the nose, but plenty of richness underneath. Fullish bodied, meaty, succulent and with very good grip on the palate. Really quite structured. It needs food.

Château de Valandraud

DRINK SOON   15.0

Fullish colour. A little dense and stewed on the nose. Better on the palate but a bit bitter and earthy nonetheless. Fullish. Quite tannic. Slightly hard. The finish is quite long and ripe. So good. But will it ever have much charm?

Château Vieux-Fortin

DRINK SOON   13.0

Medium to medium-full colour. Quite pleasant plummy fruit on the nose. Not enough ripeness or depth on the palate. Reasonable balance but dull. Medium body. Forward.

POMEROL

CHÂTEAU LE BON PASTEUR

NOW–2009   16.0

Fullish colour. Nice meaty fruity nose. Balanced and with good depth. Nice ripe tannins here. Medium-full, quite tannic. Good fruit on the palate. Just a touch dense. But needs time. Very good.

CHÂTEAU CERTAN DE MAY

NOW–2010   16.5

Fullish colour. Plump, fat, ripe nose. Attractive juicy fruit here. Quite full. Good accessible wine here. Fresh and balanced. Positive, stylish and long. Not great but very good plus.

CHÂTEAU CLINET

NOW–2010   14.0

Fullish colour. A little vegetal on the nose. On the palate it is fullish and ripe but rather tough and astringent. And it lacks fat. A bit ungainly. Good fruit though. Quite good.

CHÂTEAU LA CONSEILLANTE

NOW–2012   16.0

Fullish colour. A little stewed on the nose. On the palate this has size and grip. This is a little inflexible but it is better than Clinet and I think it will resolve itself. Good fruit. Very good.

CHÂTEAU LA FLEUR-PÉTRUS

DRINK SOON   13.0

Full colour. The tannins are a bit hard and dense here. A bit dense and stewed on the palate. Hard at the end. This is tough going. Will it ever soften up? I doubt it.

CHÂTEAU LA CROIX-DE-GAY

DRINK SOON   14.0

Fullish colour. Slightly stewed. A bit oxidised, a bit hard on the nose. On the palate medium body but rather astringent tannins. And not the class of Gazin. This doesn't excite me though it is reasonably balanced. Quite good.

CHÂTEAU LA CROIX DU CASSE

DRINK SOON   14.0

Fullish colour. Ripe on the nose. But it lacks a little zip. Medium body. Not a lot of depth. Reasonable balance. Pleasant, forward. A little one-dimensional. Clean though. But a bit simple. Quite good.

CHÂTEAU L'ÉGLISE-CLINET

NOW–2010   16.5

Full colour. Classy, balanced nose. Very good depth. Medium-full. Quite firm. Still some unresolved tannin. Underneath a stylish wine, not a blockbuster with lots of charm. Very good plus.

CHÂTEAU L'ÉVANGILE

NOW–2012   18.5

Full colour. Full, rich, concentrated, chocolaty nose. Fine quality. Lots of depth. Fullish. Very lovely fruit here. Ripe and succulent. Long. This is generous and luscious and juicy. Lovely finish. Very fine.

CHÂTEAU LA FLEUR DE GAY

DRINK SOON   17.0

Full colour. Gentle. Quite oaky. Plump. Only medium-body. Markedly oaky on the palate. Fresh Merlot fruit. Not as complex as some but very seductive. Surprising length. Very good indeed.

CHÂTEAU LE GAY

DRINK SOON   15.0

Medium-full colour. Soft, fruity, quite forward on the nose. Not serious, but attractive. Chocolatey, black cherry flavours. Not that much grip. But a good, medium- to full-bodied wine. Reasonable finish.

CHÂTEAU GAZIN

NOW–2009   15.0

Full colour. A little dense and stewed on the nose. Inflexible. Medium-full. Good fruit. But something a little green about the tannins. Yet there is class here. Highish acidity. Needs time. Good.

Château Lafleur

DRINK SOON   14.0

Fullish colour. Very aromatic, almost perfumed ripeness on the nose. A very up front wine. Behind the lushness there seems to be a slight lack of grip. Curious. Will it get a bit astringent?

Château Petit-Village

DRINK SOON   16.0

Fullish colour. Quite backward on the nose but good depth and grip. This is clean, quite classy, reasonably balanced. Medium-full. Lacks a bit of real personality. Very good if not great.

Château Pétrus

NOW–2015   18.5

Full colour. Backward nose. Balanced, rich and concentrated. Lovely fruit here and very good acidity. Fullish, splendidly ripe tannins. Very lovely concentrated fruit. This is a splendidly balanced, concentrated, classy wine. Really fine. Lovely finish.

Le Pin

NOW–2015   17.5

Full colour. Firm, full, backward, oaky nose. This is an unexpectedly big wine. Full, rich and concentrated. Needs time. Still quite a lot of unresolved tannin. Very lush fruit underneath. Very long. Fine.

Château La Pointe

NOW–2012   14.0

Fullish colour. Lovely lush fruit here. Ripe and balanced but dried out quickly. A fullish, opulent wine. Smooth. Ripe tannins but a little four-square. Died in the glass. Quite good.

Château Latour-à-Pomerol

NOW–2015   17.5

Fullish colour. Plenty of depth and rich ripe fruit on the nose. Good backbone too. Full, concentrated, very ripe. Very lovely old viney, creamy-rich fruit. Long, complex, classy finish. Impressive. This is very fine.

Château Trotanoy

NOW–2012   17.5

Good colour. Fullish, oaky and quite tannic on the nose. Good weight, and above all good acidity on the palate. At present a little adolescent. But there is good richness underneath. Fine.

Vieux Château Certan

NOW–2011   17.5

Fullish colour. Plump nose. High acidity. Quite backward. Medium-full. This has good plump fruit and is nice and fresh on the attack. Then the finish is long and subtle and classy. Essentially gentle. Fine.

Graves

Château Carbonnieux

DRINK SOON   16.0

Medium-full colour. Soft nose. Quite oaky. Medium-full. The tannins are quite absorbed and there is good acidity. Plump, elegant, long. Just about ready. Very good.

Domaine de Chevalier

DRINK SOON   14.5

Medium colour. Fresh nose but a little pinched. Medium body. Lacks a little grip and depth but pleasant and quite succulent. Forward. Quite good plus.

Château de Fieuzal

DRINK SOON   13.5

Medium to medium-full colour. Ripe, spicy nose. Lightish. Lacks a bit of real richness. A little astringent. Unexciting. Forward.

Château La Garde

DRINK SOON   16.0

Medium-full colour. Quite rich and cedary on the nose. Good weight. Fullish, quite concentrated. Good grip. This has richness and style. Again by no means a blockbuster. And quite forward. Very good.

Château Haut-Bailly

DRINK SOON   12.5

Medium-full colour. Fruity nose but not a lot of depth or strength. Light. No fat. A bit thin. Not weedy. Just a bit dull. Astringency lurks. Unexciting.

Château Haut-Brion

NOW–2018   18.5

Full colour. Quite oaky, quite open on the nose. Very lovely concentrated fruit here. Splendid grip. This is lush, ripe and very seductive. Fullish. Very intense. Very fine.

Château Larrivet Haut-Brion

DRINK SOON   (13.5)

Medium-full colour. Quite evolved on the nose. But not a lot of grip. Corked. Medium-bodied. Reasonably fruit but no real concentration. Average. Forward. The wine was corked.

Château Latour-Martillac

DRINK SOON   13.0

Medium-full colour. Neutral nose, but without much power on the nose. Nondescript palate. Lacks fruit. A bit astringent. No personality. Boring.

Château La Louvière

DRINK SOON   14.5

Medium-full colour. Ripe, succulent nose. Reasonably clean. Some substance. Neat fruit. This has good depth and length. Quite good plus. But lacks real drive and personality.

Château La Mission Haut-Brion

NOW–2011   16.5

Full colour for the vintage. Fresh nose, with a touch of mint. But slightly four-square. Medium-full body. Reasonable balance and class but no better than very good plus. It lacks excitement.

Château Pape-Clément

DRINK SOON   13.0

Medium colour. Soft nose. A little pinched. Light on the palate, a bit astringent. Lacks depth. Dull.

Château Smith Haut-Lafitte

DRINK SOON   16.5

Medium-full colour. Oaky nose. This has weight and depth. And above all personality. Medium-full, elegant and balanced. Long and complex. Very good plus.

Haut-Médoc

Château Belgrave

DRINK SOON   14.0

Medium to medium-full colour. Some development. A bit evolved and weedy on the nose. Medium body. Little tannin. Quite good fruit and balance but rather one-dimensional though the finish is reasonably positive. Quite good only.

Château Cantemerle

DRINK UP   12.5

Medium to medium-full colour. Some development. A bit pinched on the nose. Light weight. Little tannin. Rather short. Too weedy and no class either.

Château La Lagune

DRINK SOON   15.0

Medium to medium-full colour. Medium weight and quite oaky on the nose. A gentle wine. Good fruit. Good oak support. Reasonable balance. But a little lightweight. Good finish though.

Château Sociando-Mallet

NOW–2009   16.0

Medium-full colour. Quite sturdy on the nose. Rich and nicely oaky on the palate. There is depth here. Very good fruit and good grip. Long. Will keep well. Very good.

Château La Tour-Carnet

DRINK SOON   13.5

Medium to medium-full colour. Slightly sweety on the nose. Lacks real succulence. On the palate though it is curiously sweet. Medium to medium-full. A little tannin. Good grip. But strangely artificial.

Moulis

Château Chasse-Spleen

DRINK SOON   12.5

Medium-full colour. A bit pinched on the nose. A thin green line of vegetal tannin. Rather weedy and very astringent on the palate. Poor.

Château Poujeaux

NOW–2008   15.0

Fullish colour. Quite substantial on the nose. Fullish, ripe and balanced on the palate. There is depth and substance here. But what it lacks is real class. This is good.

Margaux

Château Brane-Cantenac

DRINK SOON   13.0

Medium to medium-full colour. A little burly on the nose. Rather suave on the palate. Medium weight. No class. Has neither fruit, balance nor interest. Boring.

Château Cantenac-Brown

DRINK SOON   12.0

Medium to medium-full colour. Malic on the nose. Astringent on the palate. Unbalanced. Medium-full weight. Raw. Not for me.

Château Desmirail

DRINK SOON   11.5

Medium colour. A bit thin on the nose. Soft, quite fruity, but loose-knit and one-dimensional on the palate. Insipid finish. Forward. Very poor.

Château Giscours

DRINK SOON   14.0

Medium-full colour. Some substance on the nose and palate if not a lot of class or personality. This has reasonable weight and balance, even length. But not enough interest for better than quite good.

Château La Gurgue

NOW–2012   16.5

Fullish colour. Quite substantial but no hard edges in the mouth. Plump and succulent. Good oak. Medium-full. Sophisticated. Balanced. Long. This is very good plus.

Château d'Issan

DRINK SOON   13.5

Fullish colour. Rather hard on the nose. A bit over-extracted. Better on the palate. Good substance. Quite rich if not very stylish. Yet rather astringent at the end. I can't get excited.

Château Lascombes

DRINK SOON   11.5

Medium colour. Rather thin and vegetal on the nose. Medium body. Soupy. Sweet. Coarse. Short. Poor.

Château Margaux

NOW–2020   18.5

Fullish colour. Full, rich, concentrated oaky nose. This is a profound wine. Backward. Substantial. Fullish, real depth here. This has real intensity even power. Fine ripe tannins. Long, backward but lush. Very fine.

Château Palmer

DRINK SOON   15.0

Medium-full colour. Soft cedary nose. Very oaky on the palate. And not enough grip. Medium to medium-full. Stylish. Gentle – a little too gentle really. It lacks vigour. Forward.

Château Prieuré-Lichine

DRINK SOON   12.5

Medium-full colour. Rather rough-and-ready on the nose. A bit astringent. On the palate it is beginning to lose its fruit, and it never had much finesse in the first place. Unexciting.

Château Rauzan-Gassies

DRINK SOON   12.0

Medium-full colour. Gentle oaky nose. But the fruit behind it is not very ripe. Nor has the wine much substance. On the palate a little astringent. Rather insipid at the end and a bit artificially sweet in the middle. Fell apart in the glass. Poor.

Château Rauzan-Ségla

NOW–2012   17.0

Fullish colour. Full, rich, quite opulent, classy nose. Oak and very good fruit. This is fullish, very Margaux, with lovely fruit.

Delicately balanced. Rich, complex, classy, long. Very good indeed.

Château du Tertre
DRINK SOON   13.0

Medium colour. A little attenuated on the nose. Medium body. Sweet but unstylish. Not bad at best.

Saint-Julien
Château Beychevelle
NOW–2008   13.5

Fullish colour. Something a bit unripe and attenuated on the nose here. On the palate as much astringent as tannic. A little lean. Quite substantial but a lack of richness and real elegance. A bit dry on the palate.

Château Branaire-Ducru
NOW–2018   16.0

Medium-full colour. Fine stylish, composed nose. On the palate this is quite austere. There is size and fruit, but not quite the grip perhaps? Quite classy and certainly long enough. Very good.

Château Ducru-Beaucaillou
NOW–2015   18.0

Fullish colour. Closed nose. Classy but backward Cabernet. Fullish, quite tannic. The fruit is ripe and concentrated. Most satisfactory. Long. Just needs time. Fine plus.

Château Gloria
NOW–2006   13.0

Medium-full colour. Slightly pinched on the nose. Rather coarse and astringent on the palate. Better at the end. Medium-full body. Good grip. But unattractive. Only fair. And a slight taint. This is also noticeable in the Saint-Pierre, Gloria's stablemate.

Château Gruaud-Larose
NOW–2008   15.0

Medium-full colour. Earth and spice on the nose. Some tannin. On the palate quite full and oaky. Fruity but a bit rustic. Reasonable grip. Lacks succulence as well as elegance. But good.

Château Lagrange
NOW–2018   16.0

Full colour. Backward nose. Full and firm. Rich, tannic, concentrated. There is good depth and quality here. Proper Cabernet fruit. Very good grip. And a proper *vin de garde*. Very good.

Château Langoa-Barton
NOW–2008   15.0

Medium-full colour. Nicely fresh on the nose. Medium body. Good fruit and balance. It has charm if not much depth. Good.

Château Léoville-Barton
NOW–2009   16.0

Fullish colour. Quite oaky on the nose. Not a very full-bodied wine underneath. Rather more forward than most of these Saint-Juliens. Medium-full. Round, balanced but a slight lack of concentration. Pretty though. Very good.

Château Léoville-Las-Cases
NOW–2015   18.5

Fullish colour. Quite a solid wine on the nose. Backward. Full, rich and tannic. This is quite a big wine, certainly quite a macerated wine. Fat and spicy. Very closed at first. Yet it improved considerably in the glass. There is real depth here – and class. A sleeper. Very fine.

Château Léoville-Poyferré
NOW–2010   16.5

Fullish colour. Elegant Cabernet nose without being a blockbuster. Medium-full. Good tannins. Nice ripe fruit. This is a stylish, balanced example with a neat, elegant finish. Very good plus.

Château Saint-Pierre
NOW–2018   (16.0)

Full colour. Lots of oak on the nose. Like the Gloria a slight taint. Classy concentrated fruit too. Is it a little too oaky? Otherwise fullish, very ripe and concentrated. Lovely balance. Very long. Very good apart from the taint.

Château Talbot

NOW–2015   16.0

Fullish colour. Stylish nose but not a blockbuster. Good fruit and a nice touch of oak. Medium-full body. A little tannin. Very good, ripe, elegant fruit. Long, balanced. Very good.

Pauillac

Château d'Armailhac

NOW–2012   15.0

Fullish colour. Round and plump on the nose. Not a blockbuster. Some oak. Medium full. A little forced. A slight bit over-macerated. Good grip. Lacks a little elegance. Good though.

Carruades de Lafite

DRINK SOON   15.0

Fullish colour. Rather reduced on the nose. And sulphur here as well as H2S. A lighter wine than some underneath. Medium-full. Not a lot of tannin. Good balanced fruit. Pretty.

Château Clerc-Milon

NOW–2018   17.5

Full colour. Rich, ample, backward nose. This is full. A true Pauillac. Classy Cabernet fruit. Very good grip. Rich, succulent and long. Real elegance. Fine. Needs time.

Château Duhart-Milon

NOW–2008   14.5

Medium-full colour. A little tough on the nose. Medium-full. A bit vegetal. There is not enough ripeness and succulence here. Good grip. The finish is better than the start. So quite good plus.

Les Forts de Latour

NOW–2018   (17.5)

Fullish colour. Soft, elegant, seductive nose. Fullish, oaky, very well balanced, very succulent. Not a blockbuster but a wine of real intensity and depth. Very lovely. Very classy. As it developed a slight taint as in the Ducru-Beaucaillous of 1988 to 1990. Fine otherwise.

Château Grand-Puy-Ducasse

NOW–2007   13.5

Full colour. Quite a big wine, but rather forced and solid on the nose. Full, tannic and stewed and astringent. Raw. Rustic.

Château Grand-Puy-Lacoste

NOW–2012   16.5

Full colour. Quite a masculine nose after Petit-Mouton and Haut-Batailley. Not as much depth or concentration as some or as much class. Medium full. Good tannins. Good balance. Good ripe fruit. But if less dimension, at least very good plus.

Château Haut-Bages-Libéral

NOW–2015   16.5

Fullish colour. Classy but quite firm Cabernet nose here. Fullish on the palate. Very good tannins. Good grip. This is clean, classy, not quite a blockbuster but a most attractive and splendidly balanced example. Very good plus.

Château Haut-Batailley

NOW–2015   16.5

Medium full colour. Caramel and sweet oaky nose. Vanilla as well. Medium-full. Ripe, stylish and balanced. An elegant wine. Quietly successful. Not the biggest, but very well poised. Long. Very good plus.

Château Lafite

NOW–2018   17.5

Full colour. Fragrant, classy nose. No undue oak. Quite gentle. But certainly intense. Medium-full. The tannins are ripe – or certainly by 1994 standards. Good grip. Classy fruit. Lovely intensity. Fine but not great. Lacks the complexity a bit of Merlot would have given it (all the Merlot was declassified into the Carruades).

Château Latour

NOW–2018   17.5

Fullish colour. Somewhat astringent and ungenerous on the nose but riper and more concentrated on the palate. No great grip but plenty of the Latour class. Fine.

Château Lynch-Bages

DRINK SOON   13.5

Fullish colour. A bit lean and unripe on the nose. A green touch. Medium-full, quite ripe and indeed even a little sweet. But as much astringent as tannic. A bit ungainly. Coarse.

Château Mouton-Rothschild

NOW–2020   18.0

Full colour. Rich, fat, ripe, opulent nose. Oaky. Quite full. Fullish. Does it lack just a little grip for a First Growth? Ripe fruit. Good freshness. But lacking a little intensity compared with Château Margaux. Fine plus.

Petit-Mouton

NOW–2015   17.5

Full colour. Succulent, vanilla oak here. Lots of ripe fruit on the nose. On the palate medium-full. Elegant, balanced. Good intensity. Generous and attractive. Very stylish finish. A fine example.

Château Pichon-Longueville

DRINK SOON   13.5

Fullish colour. Slightly ungainly tannins on the nose. On the palate medium-full, as much astringent as tannic. Slightly raw and disjointed. Only fair.

Château Pichon-Longueville, Comtesse de Lalande

NOW–2018   18.0

Full colour. Toasted oak here on the nose. Full, rich, but quite tannic, quite backward. At first a little brutal. But proper Pauillac size and depth here. Long finish. Needs time. This is fine plus.

Château Pontet-Canet

NOW–2012   16.0

Full colour. Opulent and oaky on the nose. Very seductive. Fullish, very rich fruit. This is most attractive. It is balanced too. Long, charming. Very good indeed.

Saint-Estèphe

Château Calon-Ségur

NOW–2008   14.0

Medium colour. A little more backward on the nose than most. Rather raw. Not too spicy. Good grip. Slightly edgy. But there is promise here. Quite good.

Château Cos d'Estournel

DRINK SOON   16.0

Fullish colour. Clumsy nose. Fullish, spicy, sweet. Quite oaky. A very good wine, because it is succulent and ripe and balanced. But not a great wine. It seems to lack the style and the concentration of the best Pauillacs and Saint-Juliens. I must see this again. I have fond memories of it in cask.

Château Haut-Marbuzet

DRINK SOON   13.5

Medium colour. A bit diffuse and rustic on the nose. Some oak. Medium body. Not much tannin. This is fruity and pleasant but it lacks depth. And there is a lack of style. Not bad plus.

Château Lafon-Rochet

DRINK SOON   13.5

Medium to medium-full colour. Sweaty ungainly nose. Not much weight or depth. Forward. Not bad plus.

Château Montrose

NOW–2012   16.0

Full colour. Fat, intense, very ripe – almost luscious – oaky nose. A fullish, ample wine that is almost too seductive. Almost overblown. But I like it.

Château Les Ormes de Pez

NOW–2008   15.5

Medium colour. Ripe, oaky nose. Not too brutal. Medium-full, ripe and sweet. Not the greatest of class but succulent and balanced. Good plus.

Château Phélan-Ségur

NOW–2009   15.5

Fullish colour. Quite tannic on the nose. But the tannins are ripe. Fullish, quite substantial. This has depth and weight. Good fruit and grip. Better than it seemed in cask.

1993 VINTAGE

SIZE OF THE CROP:	5,779,088 HECTOLITRES.
VINTAGE RATING:	12.0 (RED WINES).
	12.0 (DRY WHITE WINES).
	12.0 (SWEET WINES).

A smaller crop than 1992 but still a large one, the yield being 51.1 hl/ha. The white wine harvest was 938,804 hl (16.2 per cent of the total).

For the second vintage in a row rain undermined what promised to be an exciting one at the beginning of September. And, how it did rain! There are limits even to what magicians can do. So from the start 1993 was destined to be no better than a stop-gap vintage. There are a few honourable wines such as Latour and Léoville-Las-Cases, and Pauillac and Saint-Julien are the best appellations. Otherwise the wines were rather charmless at the outset, and have never satisfactorily softened up. Most were sold through the French supermarket system, their customers being less picky about their vintages than the average reader of this book.

THE WEATHER

Up to the second week of September 1993 promised much. Though overall it was a cool summer – but so was 1985 – and one deficient in sunshine, the flowering progressed early and swiftly, and the *véraison* was also smooth and successful. The bunches were small, though numerous, but well spaced out, this latter factor helped by judicious crop-thinning. It could have been an exciting vintage.

But then came the rains. Only in 1992 did it rain more. At Bordeaux's main weather station in Mérignac 248 mm of rain fell in September. In the best vintages the total for August and September is normally less than 100 mm. While the Mérignac figure exaggerates the problem (for example, only 152 mm fell in Pauillac) it was certainly wet. Thankfully it was cool, and rot was slow to develop.

The red wine harvest began around 14th September, with the Merlots in the Libournais. It was raining, and it would continue to rain, on and off, throughout the month and well into October. By the 21st the Médoc had commenced picking: there was no point in delaying. And by the first week of October it was all over, most Sauternes producers, even with cryo-extraction facilities, not being able to create anything noble. Only from the dry white wine vineyards, where at least some of the fruit was collected before the rains began to have a serious effect, was anything better than average produced.

THE WINES

Superficially the weather pattern suggests 1974, a justly forgotten vintage, as a parallel. The 1974s, though were hard and fruitless at the beginning, and hard and fruitless at the end. More sophisticated winemaking has made 1993 pleasant and drinkable, if nevertheless short and boring, and attenuating quickly in the glass. But there are some nice wines. And the colours, at least, are surprisingly good. What is disappointing overall is that the Merlot-based wines of Saint-Émilion and Pomerol should be so dull. In principle these should have done better out of the weather pattern than the later-ripening, and therefore in principle, more bedraggled Cabernets. Most 1993s are already showing age. Drink the rest soon.

Prices Then and Now

There was no *en primeur* market for the 1993s. Prices were announced (£290/$520 per case in bond for the First Growths, £125–£145 ($220–$260) for the Super-Seconds) but there were few takers. Ten years on the *premiers crus* range from £750 ($1350) for Latour to £1000 ($1800) (Château Margaux). Gruaud-Larose is £265 ($470), Cos d'Estournel £285 ($510) and Léoville-Las-Cases £360 ($640). These levels are ridiculous, and only show what ignorant people are prepared to pay for a fashionable labels.

The Stars of the Vintage

The best	Latour; Léoville-Las-Cases
Also Recommended	
Saint-Estèphe	Cos d'Estournel; Calon-Ségur; Cos Labory; Haut-Marbuzet
Pauillac	Clerc-Milon; Lafite; Pichon-Longueville, Comtesse de Lalande
Saint-Julien	Lagrange; Langoa-Barton; Léoville-Barton; Léoville-Poyferré
Margaux	Malescot-Saint-Exupéry; Margaux; Palmer
Other Médocs	None
Graves/Pessac-Léognan	Haut-Bailly; Haut-Brion; Pape-Clément
Pomerol	Trotanoy; Vieux Château Certan
Saint-Émilion	L'Angélus; Canon-La-Gaffelière; Pavie; Pavie-Decesse

1992 Vintage

SIZE OF THE CROP:	6,272,449 HECTOLITRES.
VINTAGE RATING:	11.0 (RED WINES).
	12.0 (DRY WHITE WINES).
	11.0 (SWEET WINES).

This was by some way – 250,000 hectolitres – the largest crop of Bordeaux Appellation Contrôlée since modern records began. The yield was a whopping 55 hl/ha. 1,234,138 hectolitres were declared as white wine (19.7 per cent of the total crop).

Inevitably it is the sad role of one vintage to be labelled as the 'worst of...' or 'worst since...'. Someone has to be last. Of recent Bordeaux vintages the wooden spoon falls to the 1992s. It was, after all, the wettest summer for over 50 years, and the sun didn't shine much either. The vintage also followed the commercial disaster of the 1991 harvest, short as a result of spring frost, and in most cases not very exciting either. After the abundance of the 1980s decade, fortune was not smiling on the Gironde in the early 1990s.

Even so, 1992 was by no means a disaster on a par with 1963, 1965, 1968 and 1969. The wines were for the most part short and dilute, but they are not rotten. They lacked definition, but they were healthy and fruity. Provided they were cheap – and that was an important proviso – they had a role as lunch wines, and as an opportunity for the general public to acquire big names they would not normally be able to afford.

The reason all this is in the past tense is that, 12 years on, the vintage is now old. Only the First Growths – and these, strangely, are uniformly disappointing in quality – plus a few others such as Léoville-Las-Cases, Ducru-Beaucaillou, Pape-Clément and Domaine de Chevalier are still alive. Even these should be drunk soon.

Prices Then and Now

There was no futures campaign for the 1992s. Most, like the 1993 would be, were eventually disposed of through the French *grandes surfaces*. Prices in the autumn of 2003 range from Chasse-Spleen and de Fieuzal at £135 ($240) per dozen to Lafite at a ridiculously inflated £750 ($1350). £750 ($1350) will buy you 18 bottles of Grand-Puy-Lacoste 1986. I know which I'd rather drink!

1991 VINTAGE

SIZE OF THE CROP:	2,588,094 HECTOLITRES.
VINTAGE RATING:	10.0–12.0 (RED WINES – SEE BELOW).
	12.0 (DRY WHITE WINES).
	11.0 (SWEET WINES).

1991 was the smallest crop since 1984, the yield being a mere 24.3 hl/ha. The white wine harvest was 429,181 hectolitres (16.6 per cent).

After the years of plenty, the years of famine. After the riches of the 1980s decade the first few vintages of the 1990s would prove to be disappointing in Bordeaux. And the 1991s, blighted by frost, seemed at the time to have the least reputation of all.

In fact, as tastings showed, 1991 was by no means the least good of the 1991–1993 trio. It *was* very short. Many properties in Saint-Émilion and Pomerol declassified their entire crop, and there are quite a few other wines which are so poor that they should have been declassified too. But, increasingly as I journeyed north in tastings through the Médoc and also and in other spots as well, I found no lack of wines of interest. The best of these were clearly more interesting than those of 1992 and in their own way could equal the best of the 1993s. But even these, nearly 15 years on, are now tired.

THE WEATHER

After a crisp winter, a mild March and a mini-heatwave at the beginning of April encouraged an early development of the vines. By 20th March the Merlot shoots were well advanced. One could even begin to count the embryonic flower clusters. The Cabernets were just ready to burst into life. But that night it froze.

I remember waking up in the morning of the 21st in Saint-Émilion, scraping the ice off the windscreen of my car without much of a thought and setting off back to London at the end of my trip to sample the 1990s. The sky was blue, the vineyards were white with frost. It was only a few days later, back in London, that I began to realise the extent of the devastation. The Merlot crop had been more or less wiped out. Only a few vineyards close to the Gironde, in Bourg and in the Médoc from Saint-Julien to Saint-Estèphe had escaped relatively unscathed. The only hope for at least an adequate crop would be the possibility of a second generation of buds ripening to fruition.

The weather in May and June did not provide much encouragement. It was damp and cold, and the flowering was late and drawn out. July, however, was warmer, and August hotter still, with an average temperature a whole degree above that of 1990, which itself had been a record. Hopes rose of a small but beautiful vintage, another 1961.

It continued warm into September, but there were also a number of heavy local thunderstorms especially towards the end of the month. This increased the problems. Not only were the growers waiting for the second generation of fruit to ripen fully. There was also now a fear that the first generation would begin to rot. As it turned out the weather improved in the first two weeks of October. It wasn't particularly warm, but there was little further rain. Those who wished to do so could wait, at least until more heavy rain on 14th and 15th October effectively marked the end of the harvest. What was not in by then was no longer worth collecting.

THE WINES

There were three ingredients to the 1991 red wine recipe: first generation fruit which was ripe and in good condition thanks to the August heat; second generation fruit which was less ripe, but difficult to distinguish from the first; and fruit affected by rot. Success depended on the ability to separate the three. Fortune favoured the Médoc, where there was less frost damage and so a smaller second generation of fruit. Indeed, some parcels at Château Latour had been totally spared from frost and even had to be crop-thinned in order not to over-produce. Moreover, because of the efficiently-draining gravel soils, rot was less of a problem on the Left Bank. This is where the wines were at their best.

At worst, the 1991s were thin, washed out and herbaceous. They attenuated quickly. Some were already astringent after a year in bottle. This applied even in the minor classed growths in the Graves and in Margaux. These properties should have done better here, particularly as there was no shortage of worthy examples such as Pavie and Le Tertre-Roteboeuf in the Libournais.

There were, though, some good, even very good wines further up the Graves hierarchy. I have no doubt that the warmer air of the city of Bordeaux helped protect the vineyards of Haut-Brion, La Mission and Pape-Clément from frost damage. Domaine de Chevalier, despite being in a frost pocket, was very good too. In Margaux only Angludet, d'Issan, Lascombes, Malescot, Palmer and Château Margaux itself were worthy of consideration, but once north of here the position is rosier. There were plenty of interesting wines in Saint-Julien, Pauillac and Saint-Estèphe. These included Ducru-Beaucaillou, Lagrange, Langoa and Léoville-Barton, Saint-Pierre, Cos d'Estournel, Montrose, Batailley, Clerc-Milon, Duhart-Milon, Lafite, Latour, Mouton-Rothschild, Pichon-Longueville, Comtesse de Lalande, Pichon-Longueville and Pontet-Canet. The wine of the vintage was Léoville-Las-Cases.

These wines had good structure and balance, no lack of fruit and class, and even a dimension and character. There was an interesting aspect of spice. Here the 1991s were clearly more interesting than 1987 or 1984, for instance. They were at their best at the end of a decade. Few believed a wine with such an agreeable personality could have come from such a denigrated vintage.

PRICES THEN AND NOW

There was no *en primeur* campaign for the 1991 vintage. When they were put on the market, after bottling, the First Growths were sold on at around £250 ($450) or so, the Super-Seconds at half that. Today prices are similar to the 1992s: up to £900 ($1620) for Latour for the First Growths, £225 ($400) for Gruaud-Larose. As with the 1992s, this is far too high.

1990 VINTAGE

SIZE OF THE CROP:	6,007,966 HECTOLITRES.
VINTAGE RATING:	18.5 (RED WINES).
	18.5 (DRY WHITE WINES).
	18.5 (SWEET WINES).

Nineteen ninety was a record harvest at the time, though soon to be superceded (by 1992). The overall yield was 59.5 hl/ha, again huge, but for once the vintage showed that you could produce both quality and quantity at the same time. It is curious that for the three undisputedly fine vintages in recent times – 1982 and 2000 are the others – this should be the case. Bordeaux's white wine harvest was 1,102,305 hectolitres, representing 18.3 per cent of the total.

Nineteen ninety ended a most remarkable Bordeaux decade. Never before had there been such a regular succession of fine vintages – only two out of ten less than very good; never before had the quantities of these fine vintages been so plentiful. In 1970 Bordeaux produced over 2 million hectolitres of *appellation contrôlée rouge* for the first time. It was considered rather excessive. In only one year in the decade of the 1980s were 2 million hectolitres of red Bordeaux *not* produced; and this failure, in 1984, was only by a whisker. In eight years out of ten the figure was over 3.5 million hectolitres: in three of the vintages over 4.5 million. Quantity, it seemed, was no longer inversely proportional to quality.

Following the hype which had surrounded the 1989s it came as something of a surprise when comparing the 1990s alongside the 1989s in cask to find that the later vintage was better. This was confirmed three and a half years later, when I first made a comprehensive in-bottle tasting of the 1990s. And is even more true today, 14 years on. The vintages are superficially similar, in that they were both early, plentiful and the products of hot and dry summers. But the 1990s are both better across the board – with certain exceptions – and more consistent at the lower levels. The tannins are riper, acidities are higher, and harmony, fruit and elegance all superior. And the vintage was cheaper. It was the cheapest in real terms since 1982, and a vintage to purchase *en primeur*.

THE WEATHER

Climatically 1990 proved to be quite as extraordinary as 1989. It was a very mild winter, with only three light frosts between 1st November and 28th February. A heatwave in February, the thermometer on one afternoon reaching 26°C, produced a very early start to the vegetative cycle, the first shoots being visible by 12th March, and a prolific *sortie* of embryonic bunches of grapes. If it continues like this, growers were heard to say, we'll be starting the harvest on 20th August, 10 days earlier even than 1989, which itself was the earliest since 1893.

The temperatures then cooled, and over the next 10 days there was a little frost damage – but light, isolated and in no way of the scale which was to follow a year later. The rest of April was mild and wet, and with the benefit of all this rain the vegetation galloped ahead during a mini heatwave in the first fortnight of May, starting to flower by the week of 14th May, a full 10 days ahead of 1989, and still on schedule for a 20th August harvest.

Then, right in the middle of the flowering, the weather changed. Unsettled conditions prolonged the fruit-setting. The weather was not bad enough to cause *coulure*, but sufficient to create, especially in the Cabernet grapes, an enormous variation from château to château, parcel to parcel, vine to vine, and even grape to grape. These irregular Cabernet bunches were to prove a worry right to the very end of the harvest.

The weather continued to alternate between warm and cool and wet and dry until 10th July, by which time it was clear that the harvest was going to be abundant. But if the humid weather were to continue there would be a major danger of rot. At the same time the authorities announced that the maximum harvest level for 1990, including the PLC, would be 60 hectolitres per hectare, reduced by 5 hl/ha from the 1989 figure. All this encouraged many growers to perform a crop-thinning or *éclaircissage*. Almost every property of note seems to have made a *vendange verte* in 1990. Yet even with severe crop-thinning, a conscientious cutting out of poorer-quality fruit at the time of the harvest, and, in some cases, a *saignée* or bleeding of the vats before the fermentation commenced, yields were nudging the 60 hl/ha maximum. And I am talking about at perfectionist properties like Pichon-Longueville, Comtesse de Lalande and Malescot. It seems crazy that in a temperate part of the world like Bordeaux, it should be necessary to worry (and indeed have to absorb the expense of) restraining Nature's bounty rather than eking out her frugality, as the late Peter Sichel put it in his annual Vintage Report, in March 1991.

From 11th July onwards the weather was exceptionally hot and dry. The two months of July and August were the driest since 1961. July was the sunniest ever, and August, with an average temperature of 23.1°C, the hottest in Peter Sichel's records which went back to 1928. Even though September was cool and June had been unremarkable, the summer of 1990 was overall slightly hotter, slightly sunnier and slightly drier than 1989, and that vintage had been the warmest since 1949.

The extreme heat, however, occurred towards the latter half of July, reaching 40°C on the weekend of 21st/22nd. The effect was to block the vegetative cycle – without water the vine simply turns itself off – delaying the onset of the *véraison*. Exposed leaves got scorched; exposed berries, where the vegetation had been thinned out to assist air circulation as a preventive anti-rot measure earlier in the month, were also scorched. If you vinify scorched berries you impart a metallic flavour to the wine, so it would become absolutely necessary to cut these out at the time of the harvest.

While there were the usual odd thunderstorms in August, rainfall was barely a third of the norm and the vines continued to suffer. The more uniform Merlot grapes were looking good, especially where the soils were more water-retentive, but the Cabernets were still looking patchy.

Then, thankfully, there was rain. To quote from the detailed vintage report of Bill Blatch of Vintex, to whom this account is much indebted: 'On the night of 29th/30th August, it rained hard: 10 mm in most places, up to 20 in the Graves, and 35 in the Entre-Deux-Mers. The whole Bordeaux vineyard, red as well as white, suddenly woke up from its lethargy and a proper ripening cycle started again.'

The white wine harvest commenced just after this rainstorm, and was completed during the week of 9th September, Haut-Brion collecting its Sauvignons and Sémillons on 3rd September, and towards the end of this week one or two Libournais growers began to fill up a few vats of Merlot. By the following week the red wine harvest was fully under way, most Merlots being collected before a weekend of rain on 22nd/23rd September, and most of the more competent growers then waiting until the Cabernets were fully ripe a week or so later. The harvest was prolonged, it being necessary to move the picking teams around from parcel to parcel, even to working over the same rows of vines more than once, in order to ensure that each plot was collected at an optimum state of ripeness.

Happily, not only were the grapes high in sugar, but the fruit was also physiologically ripe. This had been a problem in 1989. Moreover, apart from the September 22nd/23rd intermission there was little interruption as a result of rain. The growers could take their time. It was not until 20th October that the weather broke. By then, even the most recalcitrant Cabernets had fully ripened and the must was happily fermenting away in the proprietors' cellars.

THE WINES

While it was clear from the outset that the 1990 vintage was better than that of 1989 in the Médoc and the Graves, with the exception of Château Haut-Brion and one or two other properties, the earlier vintage was generally preferred in Saint-Émilion and Pomerol. Today this is a closer call. It boils down to a question of acidity levels. The Merlot grape, on which most Libournais wines are based, has a lower level of acidity than the Cabernet. Given a vintage such as 1989 (and indeed 1982), where the acidities are on the low side in the first place, you would expect some wines to lack grip, and not to have aged as impressively as originally hoped. The 1989s are full and fleshy but only a handful have this defining grip.

The 1990s *do* have this grip, and so have preserved their elegance. Indeed, often when sampling 1990, 1989 and 1988 of the same château side by side I find myself preferring not only the 1990 but the 1988 to the 1989. So if, as I suggest in the next chapter, 1989 is better than 1982, not least because the wines are better made, then 1990 is better still. In the words of one of the participants at our annual 10-year-on tasting: 'This is the best vintage since 1961.' Most wines are barely ready, and will keep a further 10 years, if not 20.

PRICES THEN AND NOW

Opening prices in France fell by around 10 per cent on 1989 levels. In Britain, helped by an improved rate of exchange, they were cheaper still. This meant that the First Growths were on offer at £350 ($630) per case in the late spring of 1991. The Super-Seconds were £160–£180 ($280–$320). La Lagune and Sociando-Mallet were £80 ($140).

The 1990s have always been desirable, or certainly were following a subsequent report by Robert Parker when he upgraded his original impressions and scores. In retrospect the vintage was excellent value at the outset. Today the *premiers crus* fetch up to £3800 ($6840) for Château Margaux, Cheval Blanc and Latour though Haut-Brion is half that. Léoville-Las-Cases is £1025 ($1840), Lynch-Bages is £920 ($1650), Léoville-Barton is £700 ($1260) and La Lagune and Domaine de Chevalier are £450 ($810). Even Cissac sells for £200 ($360). This is, though there are exceptions, some 20–25 per cent more than the prices for the equivalent 1989s.

THE STARS OF THE VINTAGE

	MÉDOC/GRAVES	SAINT-ÉMILION/POMEROL
EXCELLENT	LAFITE; LATOUR	
VERY FINE	HAUT-BRION; LÉOVILLE-BARTON; LÉOVILLE-LAS-CASES; MARGAUX	CHEVAL BLANC; PÉTRUS; LE PIN; VIEUX CHÂTEAU CERTAN; TROTANOY
FINE	COS D'ESTOURNEL; DUCRU-BEAUCAILLOU (IF NOT TAINTED); GRAND-PUY-LACOSTE; LANGOA-BARTON; LÉOVILLE-POYFERRÉ; MONTROSE; MOUTON-ROTHSCHILD; PICHON-LONGUEVILLE	CANON; L'ÉVANGILE; LA FLEUR-PÉTRUS; LAFLEUR; PAVIE

VERY GOOD AND BETTER	CARRUADES DE LAFITE; CHASSE-SPLEEN; DOMAINE DE CHEVALIER; CLERC-MILON; LES FORTS DE LATOUR; HAUT-BAGES-LIBÉRAL; HAUT-BAILLY; LABÉGORCE-ZÉDÉ; LAGRANGE; LYNCH-BAGES; MALESCOT-SAINT-EXUPÉRY; LA MISSION HAUT-BRION; PALMER; PAPE-CLÉMENT; PAVILLON ROUGE DU CHÂTEAU MARGAUX; PICHON-LONGUEVILLE, COMTESSE DE LALANDE; POUJEAUX; RAUZAN-SÉGLA; SAINT-PIERRE; SOCIANDO-MALLET	ANGÉLUS; BEAUSÉJOUR-DUFFAU-LAGARROSSE; BON PASTEUR; CALON-SÉGUR; CANON-LA-GAFFELIÈRE; CERTAN DE MAY; CLINET; L'ÉGLISE-CLINET; FIGEAC; LA FLEUR DE GAY; GAZIN; HAUT-MARBUZET; LATOUR-À-POMEROL; MAGDELAINE; PAVIE-DECESSE; LE TERTRE-ROTEBOEUF; TROPLONG-MONDOT

DISAPPOINTMENTS

There are few disappointments. The notable châteaux that should have done better include Mouton-Rothschild and Ausone (not up to First Growth standard), Pichon-Longueville, Comtesse de Lalande (a disappointment given the rest of its excellent vintages in the 1980s), d'Issan, Giscours, du Tertre, Beychevelle, Le Gay and La Dominique.

THE TASTING

The following wines were sampled in London in September 2000.

SAINT-ÉMILION GRANDS CRUS CLASSÉS & LESSER LIBOURNAIS

CHÂTEAU L'ANGÉLUS

NOW–2015   17.0

Very full colour. Still young. Quite closed on the nose. Full, tannic, sweet, rich and extracted. Is it going to soften? Certainly impressive. The finish is very intense. Very good indeed.

CHÂTEAU L'ARROSÉE

NOW–2008   15.0

Medium-full colour. Still youthful. Quite firm on the nose. Good depth but a little austere. On the palate I feel they picked a little too early. Slight green aspect throughout. High acidity. Merely good. Drink with food.

CHÂTEAU BEAUSÉJOUR-BÉCOT

NOW–2008   15.5

Medium colour. Some maturity. Ample nose. Soft and seductive. Still nice and fresh. Medium to medium-full body. Good fruit and balance. Open and accessible. Stylish. Good plus.

CHÂTEAU CANON-LA-GAFFELIÈRE

NOW–2012+   17.0

Fullish, immature colour. Good rich concentrated, youthful nose. Fullish body. Still some tannin. Very good grip. Ripe and balanced. Plenty of depth. Still young. Very good indeed.

CHÂTEAU LA DOMINIQUE

DRINK SOON   13.5

Fullish colour. Some maturity. Quite evolved. Merlot-oak nose. No great depth. Not enough grip. Fruity and not astringent. But superficial and losing its freshness and interest.

Château Larmande

<u>NOW–2007</u>   14.0

Medium colour. Still young. A little rustic on the nose. But decent fruit and balance underneath. On the palate very similar. Good grip. Even rich. But it lacks elegance. Quite good at best.

Clos de l'Oratoire

<u>DRINK SOON</u>   13.0

Full colour. A little development. A little oxidised on the nose. Dirty but chocolatey-spicy and rather astringent on the palate. This is unexciting.

Château Pavie-Decesse

<u>NOW–2010+</u>   16.0

Fullish colour. Still youthful. Ripe and intense fruit. Unexpectedly classy. On the palate quite full, and it will still improve. Good grip and concentration. Quite stylish. Plenty of substance here. Very good.

Clos Saint-Martin

<u>DRINK SOON</u>   15.5

Full colour. Still youthful. Quite oaky on the nose. Fresh and ripe and attractive, if small scale. Medium body. *À point*. Fresh. More-ish. Good plus.

Château Le Tertre-Roteboeuf

<u>NOW–2015</u>   16.0

Fullish, youthful colour. Very good nose. Lovely concentrated fruit. Very good grip too. This is impressive. Full, concentrated and individual on the palate. Rich but still solid. Very good grip. Plenty of depth. Very good.

Château Troplong-Mondot

<u>NOW–2013</u>   16.0

Fullish colour. A little development. Rich and succulent. Good weight and depth. Fullish body. Slightly over-ripe (cooked fruit, mocha etc.). It lacks a little size but there is lots of substance here. Very good.

Saint-Émilion Premiers Grands Crus Classés

Château Ausone

<u>DRINK SOON</u>   13.0

Fullish colour. Some development. Pretty on the nose but no great excitement. Dull, flat, weedy palate. No zip. Quite clean but a bit astringent. Unexciting.

Château Beauséjour-Duffau-Lagarrosse

<u>NOW–2013</u>   16.0

Fullish, youthful colour. Rather tough and tannic on the nose, if not a bit hard. Rich underneath. But a certain lack of flexibility. Solid, full and astringent. This is too big for its boots. Yet very rich, if not very classy underneath. Very good.

Château Canon

<u>NOW–2015+</u>   17.5

Medium-full, mature colour. Full, rich and concentrated. Slightly solid, slightly tannic nose. Plenty of depth here. Medium-full body on the palate. The tannins are now almost absorbed. Very good grip. Lovely fragrant fruit. Very long. Very subtle. Fine.

Château Cheval Blanc

<u>NOW–2015+</u>   17.5

Medium colour. A little development. This is less impressive on the nose as I would have expected. It is quite forward, and it lacks grip and concentration. Ripe though. Better on the palate. Very rich and succulent. Full bodied, ample and concentrated. Fine but not the intensity and class for better.

Château Figeac

<u>NOW–2013</u>   16.0

Fullish colour. Some development. An attractive and indeed stylish nose if no great concentration or depth. The tannins are a little chunky. Quite a high extraction. Good grip. Needs time. Slightly solid at present. Certainly very good.

Château Magdelaine

NOW–2009   16.0

Fullish colour. Some development. Very Merlot on the nose. Ripe and opulent. The attack shows a touch of rubber but the follow-through is rich, fat and shows very good grip. Long at the end. Very good but not fine.

Château Pavie

NOW–2012+   17.5

Fullish colour. Some development. Ripe, balanced, stylish and attractive. Plenty of depth. Plenty of class. 'Old viney'. Medium-full body. Good concentration and depth. Just about ready. Lots of interest here. Classy too. Fine.

Pomerol

Château Le Bon-Pasteur

NOW–2007   16.0

Full colour. Still youthful. Modern style. Rich, spicy and opulent on the nose. Common origins but well made. This is a little astringent on the follow-through but the wine is rich and opulent. Very good.

Château Certan de May

NOW–2007   16.0

Medium colour. Not a lot of development. Good plump, fresh nose. This has good balance. Good plump Pomerol. Not the greatest length or depth. But stylish fruit. Very good.

Château Clinet

NOW–2012+   17.0

Full but mature colour. Full, rich and opulent. For once with Clinet not over the top. Simply very concentrated. Good fresh acidity stopping it from being too hot. On the palate a little astringent. Ripe and plump but just not quite enough grip for better than very good indeed.

Château La Conseillante

DRINK SOON   15.0

Fullish, mature colour. Plump, fruity nose. Pretty but no great depth. Medium-full body. Ready now. It lacks a bit of concentration and grip. Indeed intensity too, but it is plump and enjoyable. Good.

Château L'Église-Clinet

DRINK SOON   16.0

Very full mature colour. A touch solid and even inky on the nose. Rich and ripe but a little clumsy. Fullish body. A little astringent. Not enough grip. This has very good, opulent fruit but not the acidity to balance it. Very good though.

Château L'Enclos

DRINK SOON   14.5

Full colour. Still youthful. Slight earthy aspect to the tannins. But ripe and rich if a bit hidden. Still needs time. On the palate a little dull. But fresh enough. Quite good plus. Ready.

Château L'Évangile

NOW–2015   17.5

Full, mature colour. Rich, fat, concentrated and surprisingly opulent on the nose. High quality here. Medium-full body. Ripe and balanced and stylish. Not quite the concentration and intensity of Vieux Château Certan but certainly fine. Lovely classy finish.

Château La Fleur de Gay

NOW–2010+   16.0

Full colour. A little maturity. Lots of new wood over a sturdy wine. Very pleasant. But what it lacks is depth and balance. Medium-full body. Fruity and ripe. Very good. Ready.

Château La Fleur-Pétrus

NOW–2015+   17.5

Very full colour. A little mature. Ripe and plump and succulent on the nose. Medium-full body. No hard edges. Ample and rich and mellow and easy to drink. Very good grip underneath. Moueix's Pomerols are rather better than his Magdelaine today. Fine plus. Now ready.

Château Le Gay

DRINK SOON   13.5

Fullish colour. Not a lot of development. Just a little solid on the nose. Ripe but four-square on the palate. Slightly astringent. Average quality only.

Château Gazin

NOW–2007   16.0

Full colour. Still youthful. Medium to medium-full weight on the nose. Stylish, fresh and balanced. Medium body. Good fruit. Quite complex. Good style. Very good.

Château Lafleur

NOW–2015   16.0

Full colour. This is a sturdy, muscular, somewhat over-extracted brute of a wine. Lots of tannin. Full-bodied, rich and concentrated but a little stewed and astringent. At best with food. It lacks grace.

Château Latour-à-Pomerol

NOW–2012+   17.0

Very full colour. A little maturity. As often slightly fresher than La Fleur-Pétrus if not so fat and concentrated. I like this a lot. But the La Fleur-Petrus has better class and balance. Very good indeed.

Pensées de Lafleur

DRINK SOON   13.0

Medium colour. Some development. Light but pleasant nose. Not much grip or length. Pretty. But needs drinking soon.

Château Pétrus

2006–2030   19.0

Very full colour. Little sign of maturity yet. Very fine nose. Concentrated and backward without being too dense. On the palate very full. Still some unresolved tannin. Fat, rich and opulent. Very good grip. Above all excellent concentration. Very long. Still adolescent. Very fine indeed. Could be even better than I judge it today.

Château Le Pin

NOW–2015+   18.5

Full colour. Still youthful. Marvellously perfumed nose. Very concentrated and very delicious. Medium-full body. Very fine fresh fruit. Not as Merlot-y as usual. Excellent.

Château Trotanoy

NOW–2015+   18.5

Very full colour. A little mature. Good depth here. Very concentrated and still not yet ready. Particularly lovely fruit. Rather more concentrated, substantial and tannic than La Fleur-Pétrus or Latour-à-Pomerol. Very intense at the end. Very lovely.

Vieux Château Certan

NOW–2018+   18.5

Fullish, mature colour. Full, rich and concentrated on the nose. Lots of depth here. Still quite youthful. High quality here. Full body. Very fine fruit. Very complex and intense. Splendid grip. Excellent fruit. This is still young. Potentially very fine.

Graves
Château Bouscaut

DRINK SOON   13.0

Fullish colour. Some brown. Slightly lumpy, earthy nose. Medium to medium-full body. Reasonably juicy but it lacks real class and finishes astringent. Not bad at best.

Domaine de Chevalier

NOW–2012+   17.0

Medium-full colour. Some maturity. Mellow, classy nose. Understated. Harmonious. It seems ready. Medium to medium-full body. This is undeniably classy. It lacks the personality for fine. But it is very good indeed .

Château de Fieuzal

NOW–2008   14.0

Fullish colour. Just a little maturity. Rather hard on the nose. A little over-extracted. Medium-full body. Rich but burly. Still some tannin to resolve. Good fruit and finish but a little over-weight. Lacks real class. Quite good merely.

Château Haut-Bailly

NOW–2012+   16.0

Medium-full colour. A little mature. Soft, seductive nose. Good base of ripe fruit here. Medium-full body. Ample and balanced. Very good grip. Old viney. Fine positive finish. Just needs time. Very good.

Château Haut-Brion

NOW–2023   19.0

Full colour. Still young. Sweet on the nose and more mulberry in flavour than the Médocs. Equally refined. Like Lafite this is now opening out. Fullish body. Rich. Very good tannins. Lovely balance. This is very complex and very lovely.

Château La Mission Haut-Brion

NOW–2015+   17.0

Medium-full colour. Some maturity. Rich, ripe, quite firm, very classy nose. Still immature. Very La Mission in style. Fullish body. Still some tannin. Complex, ripe and nicely spicy. Not great but very good indeed.

Château Pape-Clément

NOW–2012+   16.5

Medium-full colour. A little mature. Quite a burly sort of nose. But rich enough. Fullish body. Quite sweet. Some tannin. Rich and exotic. But very good acidity. Long and positive. Very good plus.

Haut-Médoc

Château Cantemerle

NOW–2010   14.0

Medium colour. Not much brown. Soft, quite stylish nose. This is now ready. Mellow. Medium-bodied. Balanced and quite elegant. Decent finish if no great complexity. Quite good.

Château Caronne-Sainte-Gemme

NOW–2008   13.0

Good fullish colour. Glowing. Some maturity. Slightly solid, rustic nose. But some weight and some fruit. Medium-full body. A good *bourgeois* example. But it lacks a little class. Will still improve though. Not bad.

Château La Lagune

NOW–2010   15.5

Fullish colour. Still immature. More austere than Poujeaux or Chasse-Spleen. But good depth and very good grip. Some tannin to resolve on the palate. Medium-full body. Slight lack of dimension but good plus.

Château Sociando-Mallet

NOW–2015+   17.0

Full colour. Very youthful. Splendidly rich nose. High quality Cabernet Sauvignon here. Medium-full body. Still some tannin. A little oak. Very finely balanced fruit. This is high class. Still needs time. Very Pauillac-y. Very good indeed.

Moulis

Château Chasse-Spleen

NOW–2012+   16.0

Fullish colour. Still immature. Rich nose. Still a little solid though. Some tannin to resolve. Medium-full weight. Some oak. Balanced and attractive. Good grip. More classic than Poujeaux. This still needs a little while but it is very good.

CHÂTEAU POUJEAUX

NOW–2012+   16.5

Fullish colour. Still immature. Rich, fat, roast-chestnutty nose. Plenty of depth and quality here. Medium-full body. Quite new oaky. A seductive, ripe, harmonious wine. Finishes long. Very good plus. Just about ready.

MARGAUX

CHÂTEAU BRANE-CANTENAC

NOW–2010   13.5

Medium to medium-full colour. A little maturity. Ripe nose. Just a little clumsy. Some substance but not enough class. Better on the palate. Medium-full body. A little tannin. Good balance and good fruit. Just needs the finesse. Not bad plus.

CHÂTEAU GISCOURS

DRINK SOON   11.0

Medium-full colour. Some maturity. Rather thin. Something chlorine about the nose. Weedy and attenuated on the palate. Very one-dimensional. No backbone. Poor.

CHÂTEAU D'ISSAN

DRINK SOON   11.0

Medium colour. Still youthful. A little thin on the nose. Lacks succulence. Corked. But nevertheless weedy and rather poor for what it is.

CHÂTEAU LABÉGORCE-ZÉDÉ

NOW–2012+   16.0

Fullish colour. Some maturity. Some tannins to resolve on the nose but ripe underneath. Fullish, rich, fat and quite concentrated on the palate. Good grip and style too. Long. Finishes well. Very good.

CHÂTEAU LASCOMBES

NOW–2008   14.0

Fullish colour. Some maturity. Rich, full and fat. But not much class on the nose. Medium body only. Fruity but a bit one-dimensional. Just about ready.

CHÂTEAU MALESCOT-SAINT-EXUPÉRY

NOW–2010+   16.0

Full colour. A little matured. Slightly rigid and tannic on the nose. But good fruit underneath. Still needs time. There is depth here. A little solid but very good.

CHÂTEAU MARGAUX

NOW–2025   18.5

Full colour. Still young. Very classy, refined nose. Splendid balance. Not too oaky. On the palate a little solid. The tannins not quite integrated. Time will tell. The fruit and intensity are impressive. Very fine.

CHÂTEAU MONBRISON

NOW–2010   15.0

Fullish colour. Some maturity. A little tough on the nose still but good fruit and depth if a little hard essentially. Medium-full body. The tannins are now resolved. Attractive, balanced fruit if without any real distinction. Good.

CHÂTEAU PALMER

NOW–2020   18.0

Fullish colour. A little maturity. Class at last, was what I said when I came to this within the Margaux flight. Balance and elegance on the nose. Medium-full body. Very lovely fruit here. Splendid harmony and complexity. Long and intense. Lovely.

PAVILLON ROUGE DU CHÂTEAU MARGAUX

NOW–2012+   16.5

Fullish colour. Little maturity. Still just a little tannin to resolve but the nose shows classy fruit and some oak underneath. Medium-full body. Balanced and attractive. The *terroir* shows though. Long. Very well made. Very good plus.

CHÂTEAU PRIEURÉ-LICHINE

NOW–2010   14.5

Fullish colour. Little maturity. Ripe, slightly one-dimensional, a little common on the nose. Decently balanced though. Quite attractive. Medium to medium-full body. The tannins are good. Quite good plus.

CHÂTEAU RAUZAN-SÉGLA

NOW–2015	16.0

Fullish colour. A little maturity. Quite mellow on the nose. Plenty of depth and finesse here. A little more tannins to resolve compared with Château Palmer. Slightly more substance. Are the tannins really ripe? Good grip. Plenty of quality. Very good.

CHÂTEAU DU TERTRE

NOW–2007	13.0

Fullish colour. Some maturity. Plenty of structure, plenty of ripe fruit. Good balance if no real Margaux distinction on the nose. On the palate a bit attenuated. This will not age well. A pity.

SAINT-JULIEN

CHÂTEAU BEYCHEVELLE

NOW–2008	14.0

Good colour. Decent nose but an absence of real style and balance. Medium to medium-full body. Some fruit, but only quite good. Fully ready.

CHÂTEAU BRANAIRE-DUCRU

NOW–2012	14.5

Fullish colour. Still youthful. Ample and rich and fullish but not very classy on the nose. A little attenuated on the palate. Medium-full bodied and plump. Ripe but it lacks distinction. Quite good plus.

CHÂTEAU DUCRU-BEAUCAILLOU

NOW–2020	17.5

Full colour. A little mature. This is a little tight but doesn't seem tainted on the nose. Classic Saint-Julien with just a touch of oak. Still young. Fullish body. Lovely balance. Subtle and intense. Splendid finish. Fine.

CHÂTEAU GRUAUD-LAROSE

NOW–2020	16.5

Very full colour. Still youthful. Big nose. The tannins are a little green and hard. But the wine is still very young. Typical Gruaud-Larose. Tough and earthy and tannic. Yet full and rich. Enough substance here for very good plus, if not the class for fine.

CHÂTEAU LAGRANGE

NOW–2015	16.0

Full colour. Still youthful. Fullish, a little austere, a touch green on the nose. Still very young though. Medium-full body. Quite some tannin. It needs to round off. The follow-through is promising. Very good.

CHÂTEAU LANGOA-BARTON

NOW–2020	17.0

Full colour. Still youthful. Very lovely fruit without being a blockbuster on the nose. Understated. Medium body. Balanced and classic. Just a little tannin. Excellent fruit. Very composed. Very good indeed.

CHÂTEAU LÉOVILLE-BARTON

NOW–2025	18.5

Full colour. Still youthful. Classy, concentrated, complete nose. Excellent grip and harmony. A splendid example. Full, rich, concentrated, intense and very harmonious. Splendid ripe tannins. Very integrated. Really long and classy. Very fine.

CHÂTEAU LÉOVILLE-LAS-CASES

2005–2025	18.5

Very full colour. Still youthful. Backward. Very classic. Excellent structure. Very classy fruit on the nose. Still very youthful. Still very closed-in on the palate, even compared with Léoville-Barton. Very concentrated. Very lovely. Still quite a lot of tannin. Needs time. Very fine.

CHÂTEAU LÉOVILLE-POYFERRÉ

NOW–2020	17.5

Full colour. Still youthful. Ripe, succulent, oaky nose. A plump, rich, exotic wine. Fullish body. The tannins are just about resolved. Fat and opulent. Very full of fruit. Long. Fine.

CLOS DU MARQUIS

NOW–2015	15.0

Full colour. A little maturity. Soft but classy Cabernet nose. A touch green on the palate. Medium-full body. Good balance. A touch neutral. Good though. And it will get more generous.

Château Saint-Pierre

NOW–2012   16.5

Fullish colour. Still youthful. Rich, sweet but not very weighty nose. Does it have enough grip? Medium body. The tannins are just about resolved. Ripe and balanced if without enough weight and class for fine. But very good plus. Still needs two years.

Château Talbot

NOW–2015   15.5

Full colour. A little mature. The tannins are a little hard and stalky on the nose. Talbot is classier and cleaner than this today. Plenty of ripe balanced fruit though but the palate is a little astringent and a little tough. Enough substance and richness here to come through. Good plus.

Pauillac

Château d'Armailhac

NOW–2010+   15.5

Fullish colour. Some development. Ripe, mellow and gently oaky. Quite stylish. Attractive nose. Medium body. Just about ready. Ripe, juicy and balanced. Finishes well. Good plus.

Carruades de Lafite

NOW–2010+   17.0

Full colour. Still immature. Fragrant, classy, intense nose. Medium body. Lots of elegance. Very well balanced. But the wine lacks a little substance. Full marks for the harmony and the breed.

Château Clerc-Milon

NOW–2012   17.0

Fullish colour. Some development. Richer and fuller than d'Armailhac on the nose. More intense fruit. Fullish body. Very good tannins. Lots of lovely ripe fruit here. Old viney. Very well balanced. This is very lovely, really seductive. And ready now.

Les Forts de Latour

NOW–2012+   17.0

Full colour. Very youthful. Very ripe, oaky, immediately attractive on the nose. On the palate very good fruit. Medium to medium-full body. Slightly raw. But the tannins are now resolved. This is very good indeed. Ready soon.

Château Grand-Puy-Lacoste

NOW–2020   17.5

Full colour. Still very youthful. Rich, very concentrated and very classy on the nose. This has old-vine intensity. On the palate it was still austere. The tannins still need resolving. But there is promise here. Intense at the end.

Château Haut-Bages-Libéral

NOW–2015+   16.5

Fullish colour. Still immature. Slightly solid on the nose. But ripe Cabernet. A true Pauillac. Medium-full body. Good tannins on the palate. Good fruit and grip too. This is unexpectedly good. Fine positive finish. Approaching maturity.

Château Haut-Batailley

NOW–2010   14.0

Medium-full colour. Still youthful. Some development on the nose. Ripe and balanced but gentle. Is there enough acidity? Slightly attenuated. And a lack of real personality. Medium-full body. Slightly raw rather than tannic. Long enough but it lacks a bit of sex appeal.

Château Lafite

NOW–2025   19.5

Full colour. Still young. Very lovely fruit on the nose. A little more open and a little riper and more accessible than Latour and Margaux. Higher toned than the latter. This is most impressive. Real intensity and depth. Splendid harmony. Fullish. Excellent. Very fine indeed.

CHÂTEAU LATOUR

2005–2030   20.0

Full colour. Still young. The nose is still closed, even more so than the Margaux. Marvellous poise and essence of fruit. Still an infant but not aggressive. Full body. Excellent tannins. Marvellously concentrated. Real breed. This has everything. A great wine.

CHÂTEAU LYNCH-BAGES

NOW–2015   17.0

Full colour. Still youthful. Mellow, slightly spicy nose. Full, ample and attractive. Medium-full body. Slightly raw. Not quite the grip it could have had. Yet ripe and enjoyable. Very good indeed. Nearly ready.

CHÂTEAU MOUTON-ROTHSCHILD

NOW–2018   17.5

Full colour. Still young. Rich, opulent nose. But neither the intensity or the class of the other first growths. On the palate this is confirmed. The wine has generous fruit and good acidity but the tannins are not as sophisticated nor is there the dimension for better than fine.

CHÂTEAU PICHON-LONGUEVILLE

NOW–2020   18.0

Full colour. Some development. Quite a big tannic nose. Still rather adolescent. Rather better on the palate. This is full with very good tannins and a very good grip. Rich and fat. Not the greatest breed but fine plus.

CHÂTEAU PICHON-LONGUEVILLE, COMTESSE DE LALANDE

NOW–2010   16.5

Full colour. Some development. A gentle nose. Slightly unripe tannins. Not quite enough depth. Medium body. Ripe, pleasant, round and stylish. Good long finish. But not really as serious as it should be. Very good plus.

SAINT-ESTÈPHE

CHÂTEAU CALON-SÉGUR

NOW–2015   16.0

Full colour. Some development. Fullish nose. Good grip. Not rustic but slightly four-square. On the palate this is medium-full, balanced and quite classy. Classic compared to Cos d'Estournel. Good length. Very good.

CHÂTEAU COS D'ESTOURNEL

NOW–2018   17.5

Full colour. Little sign of maturity. Opulent, oaky, ripe and exotic. Full body. Rich and chocolatey. Still some tannin to resolve. But open, balanced and with plenty of personality and good grip. Fine.

CHÂTEAU HAUT-MARBUZET

NOW–2015   16.5

Fullish colour. Some development. Very sexy nose. Rich, opulent and oaky. Medium full body. Still a little tannin. Ripe. Very good grip. This is very seductive. Long and most attractive. Very good plus.

CHÂTEAU MEYNEY

NOW–2010   14.5

Good colour. Ripe, plummy, meaty nose. Fullish body. Very ripe, almost over-ripe palate. Decent acidity. It lacks a little style. Quite good plus.

CHÂTEAU MONTROSE

NOW–2020   17.5

Very full colour. A little development. Rich, full, firm and concentrated on the nose. Still backward. Fullish body. Tannic and backward. Very good fruit. Undeniably impressive. Much more classic than the Cos d'Estournel. The tannin just a little too much. Needs time.

CHÂTEAU LES ORMES DE PEZ

NOW–2007   12.5

Fullish colour. Still youthful. A little tough and rustic on the nose. Slightly spicy, slightly sweet behind. Yet good grip. Rather too tough and astringent and rustic on the palate. Not much enjoyment here.

1990, 1989 AND 1988 SAUTERNES

To have had two fine vintages (1989 and 1988) in a row was almost unprecedented. For this to be followed by a third is unique. I have records going back to the eighteenth century. Never before has a hat-trick been achieved.

1990

The climatic conditions were quite different from the rest of the region, in the main that there was a thunderstorm on 13th August, which released 50mm of rain to keep the maturation cycle ticking over, followed by a further 23 mm on the 22nd and 23rd of the month, ideal to kick-start the incidence of botrytisation. The result was that the grapes were already physiologically ripe before the noble rot set in, and when it did it did so with a rapidity and uniformity that meant a swift collection without the necessity to pick over the same row of vines more than a couple of times. Incredibly the harvest began ? on 11th September? even before some of the red wine châteaux had started their collection. From 8th September a very hot southerly wind intensified the concentration of the fruit, and potential alcohol levels in excess of 25o in some pressings were announced by some astonished growers. The harvest was finished by 16th October, well before the weather broke. At Guiraud it was over by 29th September.

Nineteen ninety is the richest, in terms of its sugar and alcohol levels, of all these three recent vintages. It is also a plentiful crop. As to which of the three is the best, it is difficult to generalise. Compared with the 1989s the wines are more backward than one year's difference would suggest. They are fuller too. Some are richer and better. In other cases the alcohol shows and I prefer the greater finesse of the 1989s. In general the lighter wines – the lesser Barsacs for instance – are better in 1989. In the rest of the appellation the position may be the reverse.

1989

As in 1990, the 1989 Sauternes vintage was an early one, but unlike it the noble rot was slow to establish itself. The August and early September heat produced very ripe fruit but the season was dry and the botrytis spread only gradually and spasmodically. Luckily the weather remained fine and the proprietors could take their time to instruct their pickers to make a number of *passages* through the vines.

The vintage began around 18th September, and lasted until the final days of October. The grapes were exceptionally rich, a full degree of potential sugar above that of 1988. This has produced very powerful, concentrated, *liquoreux* wines which are more burnt in taste ? toffees rather than fruit salad ? than those of the previous year, and which will take rather longer than the 1988s to mature. Perhaps some grapes were harvested a little early, and these wines lack real botrytis character. These and others will not have the elegance or the balance of those of the previous vintage. The best though, and this must at this stage remain a tentative judgement, look to combine the finesse of the 1988s with the structure and richness of the 1990s. Perhaps at the topmost levels, therefore, this is the best vintage of the three.

Despite some hail damage it was once again a plentiful crop.

1988

The rain which hit Bordeaux on 12th October provided the spur to that recalcitrant fungus, the *Botrytis cinerea*, and this ensured a splendid 1988 Sauternes harvest. The spread of the fungus was faster than in 1989, though not as swift as it had been in 1986. Once again the weather remained fine throughout the harvest, and as in the other recent successful vintages, nearly everyone made good wine. In style the wines are richer and more luscious than the 1986s, but not as honeyed, as alcoholic or as powerful as the 1989s. They have a splendid, complex, elegant flavour of peaches and apricots: indeed fruit salad in general. Acidities are very good. The wines will evolve sooner than the 1989s, but after the 1986s. This is a delicious vintage, full of breed. The wines will keep well. Marvellously balanced. Again the harvest was plentiful. God was certainly smiling on the Sauternais in the late 1980s.

THE STARS OF THE VINTAGE

In general the best of the three vintages is 1989, as it is at Château d'Yquem. But there are plenty of exceptions. The best of the three vintages at Château de Fargues is the 1990. The best Climens is also the 1990. Likewise at Coutet, Doisy-Védrines, Guiraud, Sigalas-Rabaud and La Tour-Blanche. At Clos Haut-Peyraguey and Rayne-Vigneau it is the 1988 which is the best of the three.

1990

EXCELLENT	CLIMENS; D'YQUEM
VERY FINE	COUTET; LAFAURIE-PEYRAGUEY; SIGALAS-RABAUD; LA TOUR-BLANCHE
FINE	DOISY-VÉDRINES; DE FARGUES; RAYNE-VIGNEAU; RIEUSSEC
VERY GOOD INDEED	DOISY-DUBROCA; GUIRAUD

1989

EXCELLENT	COUTET (CUVÉE MADAME); D'YQUEM
VERY FINE	CLIMENS; COUTET; DOISY-VÉDRINES; DE FARGUES; LAFAURIE-PEYRAGUEY
FINE	RIEUSSEC; SUDUIRAUT (CRÈME DE TÊTE); LA TOUR-BLANCHE
VERY GOOD INDEED	DOISY-DAËNE; DOISY-DUBROCA; LAMOTHE-GUIGNARD; RABAUD-PROMIS; RAYNE-VIGNEAU

1988

EXCELLENT	D'YQUEM
VERY FINE	LAFAURIE-PEYRAGUEY; RAYNE-VIGNEAU
FINE	CLIMENS; DE FARGUES; CLOS HAUT-PEYRAGUEY; DE MALLE
VERY GOOD INDEED	DOISY-DUBROCA; SIGALAS-RABAUD

PRICES

Prices of the three vintages are very similar. Yquem currently sells for £1780 to £2100 ($3200-3780) per dozen, Rieussec and Climens just under £400 ($720); middle-ranking classed growths such as La Tour-Blanche and Guiraud are £240 ($430), Filhot is £195 ($350).

If you compare these prices with 1997 and 2001, the only subsequent vintages which are comparable, you will find that they are no more than 20 per cent higher. Not much of a premium, I would suggest, for proven wines of full maturity.

1989 VINTAGE

SIZE OF THE CROP:	5,904,558 HECTOLITRES.
VINTAGE RATING:	18.0 (RED WINES).
	15.0 (DRY WHITE WINES).
	19.0 (SWEET WINES).

As the 1990 would be, 1989 was a record crop at the time, the only other 5 million-plus harvest being 1986. The yield, at 60.1 hl/ha, was the second highest in modern times, after 1986, and has not been surpassed since. The white wine vintage produced 1,034,673 hectolitres which was 17.5 per cent of the total.

The 1989 harvest was plentiful and it was early, some Merlots being gathered as early as 31st August. It followed one of the best summers – both hot and dry – that Bordeaux had enjoyed since the 1940s. The wines showed a fine colour, natural degrees of alcohol and concentration that were very promising and plenty of rich fruit. Not surprisingly it was hailed as a great vintage. It sold well, despite high prices, and has been much in demand since. Today the wines are 15 years old and fully ready. Time for a sober reassessment. Is it a great vintage? Is it consistent? Which are the best wines?

THE WEATHER

Climatically, it was certainly an extraordinary year. For a start, it was not just an early but an unprecedentedly early harvest. Not since 1893 has the collection of the red wine grapes commenced in August.

A mild, indeed warm, and largely dry winter, followed by torrential rain at the end of February, and only partly influenced by a cooler March, produced a bud-break before the end of this month. This is three weeks earlier than the average. April was miserable: very wet indeed and decidedly chilly, though thankfully not so inclement as to produce frost damage. It can be said that this was exactly what was needed, that the vine's development was retarded, except that there is always the danger that this sort of climatic see-sawing renders the poor old vine susceptible to *coulure*. This did not happen in 1989, largely because May, in total contrast to April, was gloriously sunny and warm. No less than 316 hours of sunshine were recorded – an average of 10 hours a day – fully 50 per cent above normal. It was also, naturally, more than 4° warmer than the average. This produced an early flowering. It began before the end of the month – and despite a cold snap between 30th May and 4th June (which caused much crossings of fingers and biting of finger nails, especially over the Cabernets), this flowering was over by 12th June, the date it usually begins. All the red varieties flowered successfully; the whites less so. The weather continued excessively warm – indeed it was decidedly uncomfortable in the non-air-conditioned tents of the Vinexpo held in Bordeaux every second year – and the stage was set for a large harvest, and an early one.

It was to end up as the second hottest summer since the Second World War. The average temperature from June to September was 20.9°C, the same as 1947, and only surpassed by 1949 (21.3°C). It was also very dry. The yearly rainfall was again the lowest since 1949. The May to September rainfall measured 195 mm against an average of 332 mm but the crucial month of August – and it was August which was the prologue to the harvest rather than September – was by no means a record-breaking drought. The rain fell mainly in short, sharp, violent storms, on 7th August, 16th, and particularly on the 19th and 20th. Moreover, there had been a savage hailstorm on 7th July which ran from the north of the village of Sauternes across the vineyards of Bommes before petering-out by the autoroute, so avoiding damaging the vineyards of Barsac, but severely reducing the crop at Rayne-Vigneau, Clos Haut-Peyraguey and neighbouring estates.

As August entered its final week, the grapes were approaching ripeness. Or were they? How do you measure ripeness? The normal, time-honoured procedure is to determine the sugar (and therefore the potential alcohol) content of the fruit, and to measure the acidity. At some moment, at about 12–13° of potential alcohol, depending on the variety, the balance between the sugar and acidity will be correct. For a period, indeed, just after this stage of maturity, the grape will concentrate both in sugar *and* alcohol if the weather is fine. This is the period to pick.

But this is only the opportune time if the grape is additionally phenolically ripe; if the tannins are mature. What happened in 1989 was that the grapes were analytically ripe, indeed even threatening to produce acidities which were too low for comfort, but that the tannins were unripe. This is a problem unprecedented in Bordeaux, but more common in the more torrid climates of the New World. It was illustrated by a charming anecdote related by Peter Sichel in his annual Vintage Report. Sichel writes of a grower who complained that he usually knew when to start picking his grapes. He would kick the vines. It the grapes fell off, it was time to start. 'This year I don't understand. The sugar is high, the acidity is low, but my toes are black and blue from kicking the vines and nothing happens!' This factor left the grower with a perplexing problem, and gave rise to an argument about picking dates which continued well into the New Year. The problem was further exacerbated by the sheer size of the crop; some 20 per cent up in red wine on the previous record, that of 1986.

With the white grapes, the problem was one of speed rather than of the ripeness of the tannins. Most white wine producers, fearing a repetition of 1982 – high alcohol, low acidity and hence rather heavy, inelegant wines – started on Monday 29th August and had finished by the following weekend. Some lingered into the first full week of September, and were helped by temperatures which were in the upper 20s by day but were cool at night.

Some red wine growers, and not just in the Libournais, normally the first to crop, also started picking before the end of the month. Alexandre Thienpont at Vieux Château Certan began collecting his Merlot on 31st August, so did Jean Delmas at Haut-Brion. Latour also started on this date. Elsewhere, in the Médoc as well as in Saint-Émilion and Pomerol, the harvest commenced on 4th September – at Palmer and Rauzan-Ségla – on the 5th at Las-Cases and Calon-Ségur, on the 6th at Cheval Blanc, or on the 7th at Cos d'Estournel. Pétrus was collected on the 6th and 7th. Some started later, and will confess they should have begun sooner. Others claim they hit it just right. Some were forced to wait because their last vineyard treatments had been too recent in mid-August, and to pick any earlier would leave a taint in the wine. Many will accuse their neighbours of leaving the Merlots too late with the result that the acidity was too low. Others, who picked later, will maintain their tannins were ripe and those of the early pickers were not.

With the Merlots, the main problems were the size of the crop, the over-sufficiency of alcohol (nearly everybody had a *cuve* of over 14°), and the low level of acidity. A tendency to big, hot, flabby wines with a 'hole in the middle', in short. Levels of tannin were also higher, much higher, than in most vintages. But if you have merely tannin and alcohol, and no acidity and concentration, you will hardly have wines of character, let alone elegance.

Picking then turned to the Cabernets. And what followed was one of the longest drawn-out harvest of recent times. With the difficulties over the ripeness of the tannins, all vineyards *should* have waited perhaps as much as a week between picking the last of the Merlots and the first of the Cabernets. Not all the châteaux could afford to leave their pickers lying around idle.

Some, indeed, collected some of their youngest Cabernets and vinified them together with the last (potentially 15°, but with consequent low acidity) of their Merlots. At Lascombes, one of these properties, I was told that this mixture produced the best *cuvée*.

The harvest was only occasionally interrupted by rain. There was quite a bit in the southern Médoc, the Graves, the Entre-Deux-Mers and the Libournais on Sunday 10th September. It was then virtually dry until Friday 22nd when there were storms. But fine weather returned after the 25th. Most had completed their harvest by then. Others lingered on. At Haut-Bailly the last grapes were not cleared until 6th October.

THE WINES

Fifteen years on, there is much that is highly commendable about the 1989s. The colours are impressive; the wines are full, rich and fleshy; in most cases, contrary to what was feared at the time, the tannins are ripe enough and not too obtrusive. But it is elegance which is the *sine qua non* of a great wine, and elegance is dependent not only on concentrated fruit but its balancing acidity. There are only a handful of 1989s, good as the vintage is, which have this defining grip. These can be safely relied on to keep for another decade. The remainder should be consumed by 2010 or so.

That said, the vintage is better, overall, than 1982. Not perhaps because it was inherently superior, but because the wines were better made. There are more wines which show the vigour that will take them comfortably into their third decade. Compared with the 1982 vintage at this stage the general picture is of more freshness, more style and more consistency. And of course it is a great Sauternes vintage. However, based on a wide range of vertical tastings, with one or two exceptions, (Haut-Brion, some top Saint-Émilions and Pomerols), 1990 is the better vintage. Acidity levels are higher in 1990 and the wines have greater length.

PRICES THEN AND NOW

The first growths, having kept prices stable at 170–180 Francs ex-château since 1983, bounced them up to 225–250 Francs. This translated to £430 ($770) upwards on the British market. The Super-Seconds were more restrained and could be had for around £210–£230 ($370–$410). La Lagune and Sociando-Mallet were £95–£100 ($170–$180). I must point out that the rate of exchange had fallen from the British point of view by 15 per cent on the figures applicable for the 1988s. The ratio would have improved when it came to calculating the prices for the 1990s.

Today the First Growths sell for between £1050 ($1890) for Ausone and £3100 ($5580) for Haut-Brion. Super-Seconds are £600–£1000/$1080–$1800 (Palmer and Lynch-Bages); Gruaud-Larose is £450 ($810), La Lagune £420 ($750), Sociando-Mallet is £360 ($640), Angludet is £265 ($470) and Cissac is £220 ($390).

THE STARS OF THE VINTAGE

	MÉDOC/GRAVES	SAINT-ÉMILION/POMEROL
GREAT	HAUT-BRION	
VERY FINE	MARGAUX; LA MISSION-HAUT-BRION; PALMER	CHEVAL BLANC; LAFLEUR
FINE	DOMAINE DE CHEVALIER; COS D'ESTOURNEL; GRAND-PUY-LACOSTE; LAFITE; LATOUR; LÉOVILLE-BARTON; LÉOVILLE-LAS-CASES; MOUTON-ROTHSCHILD; PICHON-LONGUEVILLE; PICHON-LALANDE	ANGÉLUS; CERTAN DE MAY; CLINET; L'ÉGLISE-CLINET; PÉTRUS; LE PIN; TROTANOY; VIEUX CHÂTEAU CERTAN

VERY GOOD	CLERC-MILON; DUCRU-BEAUCAILLOU (IF A GOOD BOTTLE); LES FORTS DE LATOUR; GRUAUD-LAROSE; HAUT-BAILLY; LAGRANGE (SAINT-JULIEN); LANGOA-BARTON; LÉOVILLE-POYFERRÉ; LYNCH-BAGES; PAPE-CLÉMENT	FIGEAC; LA FLEUR DE GAY; GAZIN; LAGRANGE (POMEROL); LATOUR-À-POMEROL; MAGDELAINE; LE TERTRE-ROTEBOEUF;

DISAPPOINTMENTS

Margaux and the southern Médoc in general; Saint-Estèphe in general. d'Armailhac, Ausone, Batailley, La Conseillante, La Dominique, L'Évangile, La Gaffelière, Gloria and Saint-Pierre. As so disappointingly often, the second and third rank wines in Saint-Émilion and Pomerol provide little enjoyment.

THE TASTING

The following wines were sampled in London in September 1999.

SAINT-ÉMILION

CHÂTEAU ANGÉLUS

NOW–2009	17.5

Full, immature colour. Oaky and eucalyptus on the nose. Very impressive attack. Rich and full and opulent and very ripe. Good grip too. Lovely warm, ripe finish. This is fine.

CHÂTEAU L'ARROSÉE

DRINK SOON	14.5

Medium to medium-full, mature colour. Attractive, ripe nose. Good fruit and balance. Medium body. Pleasant but no great depth. Good grip. Quite good plus.

CHÂTEAU AUSONE

DRINK SOON	14.0

Medium-full, mature colour. A bit thin and over-developed on the nose. Lacks grip. Medium body. A little dry and astringent. A little attenuated. No depth or class. Poor for what it is.

CHÂTEAU CANON

DRINK SOON	18.0

Medium-full colour. Ripe, spicy, succulent nose. Rich, fat, generous and with plenty of depth. Splendid Merlot fruit. Very good grip. This is a lovely example. Fine plus.

CHÂTEAU CHEVAL BLANC

NOW–2020	18.5

Full, rich, immature colour. Splendid nose. Rich, concentrated, opulent and still youthful. Full. Some tannin. Lovely rich fruit. Very good acidity. I don't think this has the complexity or the elegance of Haut-Brion but it is very impressive. Needs time.

CHÂTEAU LA DOMINIQUE

DRINK SOON	13.0

Full colour, just about mature. Strange aspect of garden mint on the nose. Rather astringent on the palate. Medium body. The fruit is a bit one-dimensional and the finish a bit attenuated. Not bad at best.

CHÂTEAU FIGEAC

NOW–2007	17.0

Fullish colour. Mature. Quite spicy nose. Good freshness. Quite substantial. Fresh. Still quite youthful. Medium-full. The tannins are now soft. Subtle. Long. Not a blockbuster but classy. Very good indeed.

CHÂTEAU LA GAFFELIÈRE

DRINK UP	11.0

Medium-full colour. Fully mature. Slightly four-square on the nose. Ripe enough. A bit stewed and astringent. Lacks class. Short. Unpleasant.

Château Magdelaine

NOW–2008   16.5

Fullish colour. Just about mature. Ripe, opulent nose. Holding up well. Very Merlot. Medium to medium-full body. Round, ripe and plump. Decent grip. Good follow-through. Ample. Very good plus.

Château Pavie

DRINK SOON   15.0

Medium-full colour, now mature. Ripe but a little dense on the nose. Lacks grace. Medium-full body. This still has a little tannin. Slightly 'hot' but decent fruit and grip. Lacks a bit of class. Decent grip. Good follow-through. Ample. Very good plus.

Château Le Tertre-Roteboeuf

NOW–2010   17.0

Full, immature colour. Austere, backward nose. Good depth. Smells of smoky bacon. Fullish and quite tannic on the palate. A little too much, perhaps. Yet the follow-through is ripe and long. Good grip. Very good indeed.

Château Troplong-Mondot

NOW–2007   15.5

Fullish colour. Still youthful. Classic nose. Ripe, backward and concentrated. Medium-full body. Ripe and ample. Succulent. Very good but lacks a little grip. Just a little lacking personality. Good plus.

Pomerol

Château Le Bon Pasteur

DRINK SOON   15.0

Full colour. Still immature-looking. Ripe, ample and attractive. On the palate this is juicy and well made if without much class. But good.

Château Certan de May

NOW–2008   17.5

Medium-full, well-matured colour. Fine nose. Lots of class. Very good acidity, concentration and depth here. Fullish. Good tannins. Good fresh fruit. Long and harmonious on the follow-through. Classy. Fine.

Château Clinet

NOW–2015   17.5

Full colour. Still youthful. Full and abundant, but not the balance and class of say Vieux Château Certan. Full on the palate. Rich and fat. More depth and grip on the palate than I thought on the nose. Still some tannin. Good positive finish. Fine. Will still improve.

Clos du Clocher

DRINK SOON   14.0

Fullish colour. Just about mature. Very Merlot. Ample but not much class. Medium weight. Quite round and juicy. Pleasant and reasonably fresh. Quite good.

Château La Conseillante

DRINK SOON   13.0

Full colour. Just about mature. High-toned nose. Ripe and abundant. Quite Merlot. Lacks just a little concentration and grip. A bit attenuated as it developed. Unexciting. Poor. Astringent at the end.

Château La Croix-de-Gay

DRINK SOON   13.0

Medium-full colour. No undue age. Ripe but slightly lumpy on the nose. Fullish, astringent palate. Lacks grip as well as flair. Hot finish.

Château L'Église-Clinet

NOW–2009   17.5

Medium-full, fully mature colour. Ripe and abundant and easy to enjoy on the nose. Plump and succulent. Medium to medium-full body. Very abundant. Almost over-ripe. Quite spicy. Good grip though. Impressive but not quite the finesse for better than fine.

Château L'Enclos

DRINK SOON   14.5

Fullish, mature colour. Ripe, balanced, attractive nose. A small wine. Very Merlot, but a wine with charm and fruit and a positive finish. Quite good plus.

Château L'Évangile

DRINK SOON   13.0

Fullish, mature colour. Rather more slightly unripe Cabernet than most on the nose. Slightly rigid. Similar on the palate. Slightly astringent. This is not impressive. Quite full. But too dense and solid.

Château La Fleur de Gay

NOW–2010   17.0

Full colour. Still youthful. Full, rich, concentrated, oaky nose. Slightly solid on the palate. Good clean, ripe fruit though. Balanced. Good grip. Fullish. Very good indeed.

Château La Fleur-Pétrus

DRINK SOON   14.0

Medium-full, mature colour. Some Merlot on the nose. Not as fat or as much grip as Latour-à-Pomerol. Medium body. A touch attenuated on the palate. A little one-dimensional. Not too short but only quite good.

Château Le Gay

DRINK SOON   14.0

Fullish colour. Still youthful. Full, dense, slightly solid nose. Good fruit underneath. Medium-full. Some fruit. But a bit astringent. Quite good.

Château Gazin

NOW–2007   16.0

Full colour, still immature. Stylish, balanced, medium-weight nose. Good fruit here. Medium to medium-full body. Attractive and positive. Very good.

Château Lafleur

NOW–2015   19.0

Full colour. Still youthful. Splendidly full, rich and concentrated on the nose. Still backward. On the palate this is most impressive. Full. Excellent grip. Lush, abundant, concentrated, rich fruit. Lots of depth and dimension. Very fine indeed.

Château Lagrange

NOW–2008   16.0

Full colour. Barely mature. Good rich nose. Plenty of substance if no great class here. Quite full. Balanced, quite rich and satisfying. Shows well. Finishes positively.

Château Latour-à-Pomerol

NOW–2012   17.0

Medium colour, mature. Rich, ripe, concentrated nose. Plenty of depth. Similar palate. Fullish. Will still improve. Very good indeed.

Château Petit-Village

DRINK SOON   14.0

Full colour. Still immature-looking. Dense nose. Some substance but no flair. Fullish. A bit stewed. Lacks grip. Decent, even concentrated, ripe fruit but no balance. Only quite good.

Château Pétrus

NOW–2020   19.0

Full colour. A little maturity. Very rich and concentrated. No undue tannin but still youthful and slightly closed. Impressive. Rather better than a 1990 sampled three days previously. Fullish, very rich and slightly tannic. Slightly adolescent. Very fine but not really great. It lacks real complexity and class.

Château Le Pin

NOW–2009   18.0

Fullish colour. A little mature. Lush, ripe, oaky and abundant on the nose. Very generous fruit. A fullish, seductive wine. Rich and abundant. No hard edges. Good acidity. Not too Merlot. Fine plus.

Château La Pointe

DRINK SOON   14.0

Medium colour. Well matured. Soft, ripe, almost sweet cedary fruit on the nose. Medium body. No great class or grip. But a pleasant wine.

CLOS RENÉ

DRINK SOON   13.5

Fullish, mature colour. Quite substantial, but good richness. A little four-square. Solid, stewed palate. This is over-macerated. Decent grip underneath.

CHÂTEAU DE SALES

DRINK SOON   13.0

Medium to medium-full colour. Still quite youthful. A little non-descript on the nose. But some substance. A bit stewed on the palate. Slightly cooked fruit. Now a bit astringent. Lacks grace.

CHÂTEAU TROTANOY

NOW–2012   18.0

Fullish colour. Just about mature. Splendidly concentrated nose. This is very classy and very ripe and rich. Fullish. Very lovely, concentrated 'old viney' fruit. Good grip. Will still improve but just about ready. Very long, complex and classy.

VIEUX CHATEAU CERTAN

NOW–2012   18.0

Medium-full, fully mature colour. Fine nose. Cool and classy and concentrated. Lovely fruit. Still young. Fullish. Very good grip. This is potentially very, very classy. Very, very complex. Very lovely, long finish and excellent fruit. Fine plus.

GRAVES

BAHANS-HAUT-BRION

DRINK SOON   14.5

Medium-full colour. Mature. Plump nose. Well mannered. Good fruit. Slightly astringent on the palate. But good ripeness and reasonable acidity. Some class. Good length. Lacks a bit of personality.

DOMAINE DE CHEVALIER

NOW–2010   17.5

Medium-full colour. Mellow, cedary, classy and discreet on the nose. Lovely. Medium-full, ripe, balanced and complex. Very good class. Very good length. Fine. *À point* now.

CHÂTEAU HAUT-BAILLY

NOW–2008   16.0

Medium-full colour. Just about mature. Plump, ripe, mature mellow nose. Lots of attraction. Medium-full to fullish body. A little astringent. Not quite the grip and flair of Domaine de Chevalier. Very good.

CHÂTEAU HAUT-BRION

NOW–2015+   19.5

Fullish colour. Some maturity. Opulent and cedary on the nose. Very ripe and seductive. Living up to its reputation. Full, complex, very classy, very long and multi-dimensional. Not quite magnificent but very impressive.

CHÂTEAU LA MISSION HAUT-BRION

NOW–2018   18.5

Medium-full, mature colour. Quite unlike Haut-Brion but very lovely, composed, cool, classy nose. Real balance and complexity. Backward, full, rich and very lovely. Still needs time. Splendidly classy finish.

CHÂTEAU PAPE-CLÉMENT

NOW–2010   16.5

Medium, mature colour. Quite full and firm compared with Haut-Bailly and Domaine de Chevalier on the nose. Ripe and concentrated. Fullish body. Lacks a little grip and personality but sufficiently fresh and complex to be very good plus. Positive finish.

MARGAUX

CHÂTEAU BRANE-CANTENAC

DRINK SOON   13.5

Medium-full colour. Now ready. Reasonable depth on the nose. A little pinched though. Some fruit but more astringent on the palate. The Merlot shows. Medium body. Some depth but a dry finish.

CHÂTEAU CANTENAC-BROWN

DRINK SOON   13.5

Medium-full colour. Still quite youthful. Quite fresh on the nose. But light and fruity. No real concentration. Medium body. A little dry. Some fruit and interest but no real class. Quite positive at the end. Not bad plus.

Château Giscours

DRINK SOON   12.0

Medium-full colour. Now ready. Reasonable substance on the nose but some attenuation. On the palate a bit thin. More attenuated. No astringency but a cheap effort.

Château Labégorze-Zédé

NOW–2008   15.5

Fullish, immature colour. Slightly dry on the nose but acceptable fruit. Fullish. Good concentrated blackberry fruit and reasonable grip. A little astringent overall but certainly good plus. Better with food.

Château Margaux

NOW–2015   18.5

Very full backward colour. Fullish, backward nose. Good Cabernet fruit. Not the greatest of depth and complexity though. Fullish. Some tannin. Very good fruit. A little rigid. But this will improve.

Château Palmer

DRINK SOON   15.0

Medium to medium-full colour. Now ready. Soft, mellow, quite sweet nose. One of the few wines in this flight which is not astringent. Medium-full body. Ripe. Good grip. Good but not great. Lacks real class.

Pavillon Rouge du Château Margaux (Bordeaux)

DRINK SOON   13.5

Medium to medium-full colour. Just about ready. Some fruit in a slightly pinched sort of way on the nose. Medium body. Reasonable palate if not very long. Some fruit. But a lack of definition and class.

Château Prieuré-Lichine

DRINK SOON   14.0

Full, immature colour. Good rich fruit on the nose. Still youthful. Fullish. Still a bit of unresolved tannin which I think will always be there. Some acidity. Quite rich. But overlaid by astringency. Better with food. 1975 in style. Quite good.

Château Rauzan-Ségla

DRINK SOON   13.0

Medium to medium-full colour. Just about ready. Quite fat and mellow on the nose. Some substance. Not much class. Medium body. Some fruit but a little dry on the palate, and a bit short. Not bad.

Haut-Médoc & Moulis
Château Cantemerle

DRINK UP   12.0

Fullish colour. Still youthful. Rather dried out nose. Poor quality. Medium to medium-full body. Lacks grip. Attenuated fruit and now astringent as well. Poor.

Château Caronne-Sainte-Gemme

DRINK SOON   13.0

Light to medium colour. Fully mature. Rather dry on the nose. Not a lot of succulence or fruit. On the palate medium body. Not much tannin. Better than the nose. But not much fruit or class.

Château Chasse-Spleen

DRINK UP   12.0

Medium to medium-full colour. Just about mature. Not much nose. A little pinched. Medium body. Rather astringent. Lacks fruit. Poor.

Château La Lagune

NOW–2008   15.5

Medium colour. Just about mature. Mellow, oaky nose. Medium-full body. Balanced and nicely cedary. Quite stylish. Good vigour. Nice fruit. Good plus.

Saint-Julien
Château Beychevelle

DRINK SOON   14.5

Medium-full colour. Just about mature. Some fruit on the nose. Decent balance but lacks a bit of class and depth. Medium body. Quite attractive. No hard edges. Ripe. But not much grip and definition. Quite good plus.

Château Branaire-Ducru

NOW–2010   15.5

Medium-full colour. Still youthful. Rich, ripe, full nose. Abundant. Good tannin. Not quite the grip and class of the best but good fruit. Good plus.

Château Ducru-Beaucaillou

NOW–2009   16.0

Fullish, mature colour. Good class on the nose. Slightly muddy. But not tainted. Fullish. Now just about ready. Reasonable balance and fruit. But not the usual Ducru-Beaucaillou class. Merely very good. (N.B. Bottles of this wine are inconsistent. Some are tainted.)

Château Gloria

DRINK SOON   12.5

Fullish, very purple colour. Slightly green touches, and a little attenuation. A bit weak and short on the palate. Both astringent and attenuated. Poor. Not as dry as some of the Margaux though.

Château Gruaud-Larosé

NOW–2010+   16.0

Full, youthful colour. Big, tannic, rich nose. A bit astringent as well as tannic. But good acidity so this will go. Rich, full and opulent if not much class. Vigorous. Very good.

Château Lagrange

NOW–2010   16.0

Medium-full colour. Just about mature. Good depth and class on the nose. Quite concentrated. Still youthful. Fullish, ripe and abundant. Good grip. Not the greatest class but long and fresh. Very good.

Château Langoa-Barton

NOW–2010   17.0

Fullish, youthful colour. Lovely ripe Cabernet fruit on the nose. Quite accessible. Fullish, harmonious, elegant, ripe and lovely. Now delicious. Will keep well. Very fine finish for once.

Château Léoville-Barton

NOW–2015   18.0

Full, immature colour. Very lovely concentrated Cabernet fruit on the nose. Really profound and classy. Full, rich and profound. Still not quite ready. Splendid dimension. Very Saint-Julien. Fine plus.

Château Léoville-Las-Cases

NOW–2025   19.0

Full, immature colour. Very backward. Very profound. Splendid class on the nose. Full and rich. Immaculately put together. Very classy and very long and complex. This is really very fine.

Château Léoville-Poyferré

DRINK SOON   16.0

Fullish colour. A little development. Ample, rich nose with a touch of spice. A touch of astringency. A little lacking grip. Plump and fruity but a little short. Very good nevertheless.

Château Saint-Pierre

DRINK SOON   14.0

Full, immature colour. Ripe nose. Soft in style, eventually. Slightly astringent on the palate. Not enough grip. Medium to medium-full body. Some fruit but it tails off. Quite good only.

Château Talbot

NOW–2007   15.0

Fullish, mature colour. Bigh, earthy, tannic nose. Medium-full body. Slightly aggressive, somewhat herbaceous tannins. Yet good grip. Ripe underneath and long too. Lacks a bit of style but good.

Pauillac

Château d'Armailhac

NOW–2007   14.0

Fullish, still youthful colour. Slightly lumpy tannins on the nose. But rich underneath. Medium-full body. Rather common. Reduced aspects. A little bitter in the tannic department. Reasonable acidity. It may come round. Quite good.

Château Batailley

DRINK SOON · 13.0

Medium-full colour. A little development. A bit lightweight on the nose. Lacks real concentration and ripeness. Slightly green. Medium body. Pleasant but short and anonymous. Lynch-Moussas is better.

Carruades de Lafite

DRINK SOON · 14.5

Medium-full colour. Some maturity. Ripe but a little thin on the nose. An absence of real concentration and succulence. Medium body. No tannin. Some fruit and good acidity. But lacks real weight. Slight trace of astringency at the end. Yet long and quite classy. Quite good plus.

Château Clerc-Milon

NOW–2010 · 16.5

Full colour. Still immature. Much more sophisticated tannins than d'Armailhac on the nose. This is rich, ripe and profound. Why is this so much better? Fullish body. Still some tannin. Quite concentrated fruit. Good grip. Very Pauillac. Good positive finish. Very good plus.

Château Duhart-Milon

DRINK SOON · 13.5

Medium-full colour. Barely mature. Quite ample on the nose but a little dry. Not much class. On the palate a touch bitter. Medium-full body. Some acidity but lacks generosity and complexity. Not bad plus.

Les Forts de Latour

NOW–2010 · 16.0

Full colour. Still youthful. Lovely nose. Very Cabernet. Ripe and quite rich. Accessible and classy. On the palate the tannins are a bit astringent. But there is good grip and fruit. Finishes positively. Very good.

Château Grand-Puy-Lacoste

NOW–2020 · 18.0

Full colour. Still very young. Very fine classy nose. Lovely concentrated fruit. Very ripe. Very complex. Full, rich, quite tannic and backward. This still needs quite some time. Austere on the attack but rich and potentially opulent at the end. Very long. Real length here. Fine plus.

Château Lafite

NOW–2015 · 18.0

Medium-full, mature colour. Firm, oaky nose. Rich underneath. Quite a big wine. Backward and tannic. The tannins a touch rigid. Good grip. This will still improve. But I don't think it has the richness for greatness.

Château Latour

NOW–2012 · 18.0

Fullish, mature colour. Ripe, opulent, mellow, classy nose. Fullish. Good grip. This is rather more developed and spicy than Latour usually is. Ready. Very fine but not great. Lacks just a little intensity at the end.

Château Lynch-Bages

NOW–2012 · 16.0

Fullish colour. Still young. The nose doesn't have the personality of the Pichon-Longueville nor the class of Grand-Puy-Lacoste. Indeed it seems to lack richness. Fullish. The tannins lack class. Round and ripe but no sophistication. And only adequate grip. Merely very good.

Château Lynch-Moussas

DRINK SOON · 14.0

Medium colour. Barely mature. Soft, ample nose. Some fat. Quite attractive. Medium body. No tannin. Quite fruity if a bit one-dimensional. But reasonable length. Quite good. Better than usual.

Château Mouton-Rothschild

NOW–2015   18.0

Full colour. Only a hint of brown. Rich and
full on the nose but the flavours are a bit
dumb at present. Full, tannic and backward.
It seems to have good grip. Still adolescent.
Certainly fine plus. Could be better.

Château Pichon-Longueville-Baron

NOW–2015   17.5

Full colour. Still very young. Splendidly rich,
ample, opulent nose. Fullish, rich,
chocolatey. Quite tannic. There is however
only an adequate grip, which is a pity. So fine
but not great.

Château Pichon-Longueville, Comtesse de Lalande

NOW–2012   17.5

Medium to medium-full colour. Some
maturity. Ripe and ample on the nose. But
outclassed by Pichon-Longueville. This is a
bit lightweight. Medium-full body. Very
seductive. Fine fruit. Very good acidity. Long
and complex. Most attractive. But not quite
the depth for greatness.

Réserve de La Comtesse

DRINK SOON   14.0

Medium-full colour. Barely mature. Soft,
round, sweet nose. Very attractive if no great
depth or class. On the palate rather dull.
Rather one-dimensional. Decent fruit and
balance but a bit anonymous. Quite good.

Saint-Estèphe

Château Calon-Ségur

DRINK SOON   15.0

Medium to medium-full colour. Just about
mature. Rather tough on the nose. A bit
sturdy and astringent. On the palate medium
to medium-full. Lacks acidity and bite.
Short. Getting astringent. Decent fruit but no
harmony. Yet the finish is not too bad at
present. Good.

Château Cos d'Estournel

NOW–2012   17.5

Full colour. Still immature. Splendidly
seductive, full, rich, abundant nose. Quite
full. Exotic. Good grip. Ample and fruity.
Very enjoyable. But I prefer the classicism of
the Saint-Juliens. Fine though. Very long.

Château Lilian Ladouys

NOW–2010   15.0

Medium-full colour. Still immature. Slightly
robust on the nose, but ripe and fruity and
well-made. Fullish. Quite chocolaty. Lacks a
bit of class but good grip. Very Saint-
Estèphe. Still needs two years to round off.
Good.

Château Meyney

NOW–2012   15.5

Fullish colour. Still immature. Rich, full and
ample on the nose. A good wine. Very rich
fruit and good grip. Less spicy than Lilian
Ladouys. Good substance and depth. Nicely
vigorous. Still needs two years. Good plus.

Château Montrose

DRINK SOON   14.0

Full colour. Mature. Ripe, classy nose. But
not the greatest of depth and concentration.
Medium body. Again it lacks grip. So no
continuation and complexity. Fruity but it
tails off. Indifferent for Montrose.

Château Les Ormes de Pez

DRINK SOON   13.0

Full, backward colour. Slightly dry and
lumpy on the nose. But decent ripe fruit
underneath. Medium body. Lacks a bit of
grip. This detracts from any freshness and
class it has. Bitter finish. Not bad.

1988 VINTAGE

SIZE OF THE CROP:	4,586,788 HECTOLITRES.
VINTAGE RATING:	16.5 (RED WINES).
	16.0 (DRY WHITE WINES).
	17.5 (SWEET WINES).

This was the smallest crop between 1984 and 2001, though by no means short. The average yield was 48.1 hl/ha. The white wine harvest measured 937,117 hl, 20.4 per cent of the total.

Nineteen ninety-eight has always been a sleeper of a vintage. It was a product of a cool summer, one of those which radically divides consumers and critics into those who are prepared to tolerate a certain austerity and admire the elegance and harmony (of which there are plenty in Britain) and those who mark the wines down because there is a lack of richness and substance (of which there are plenty in the USA).

Being a Brit and a classicist I fall, of course, into the former group. I have had many a discussion with others arguing the merit of 1988 over 1989 or the reverse, and many is the time I have compared the same wine in the three vintages of 1990, 1989 and 1988 in front of a group of wine lovers. The 1990 usually wins, but 1988 is as frequently the second preference as 1989, particularly when the wines of the Médoc are compared.

The market, of course, prefers 1989, which leaves the 1988s cheap, to the advantage of those in the classicist camp.

THE WEATHER

It was a very wet winter. Sixty per cent more rain fell from November to April than the average, and it continued raining on and off until the first week of July. 'It could hardly have rained more during the first half of the year', said Gérard Gribelin of Château de Fieuzal in September. Yet, if wet, it was warmer than average. Indeed, there was no real winter at all, and this stored up potential problems in the form of mildew, black rot and insect depredation, making it necessary to spray, spray and spray again to keep the vegetation and embryonic fruit in a healthy condition. After an April and May which were 1.5–2°C warmer than normal (and 40 per cent wetter) there was a very cold and stormy end to May, followed by a sudden warm period at the beginning of June. This was precisely what had happened in 1984, and there were fears that the disastrous Merlot flowering of four years previously would recur. Thankfully this did not take place. The flowering happened very quickly in the second week of June (*demi-floraison* 12th June). There was some *coulure* and *millerandage*, and to the Cabernet Sauvignons as well as the Merlots, but this would only serve to increase the concentration of the remaining fruit by reducing the quantity – *coulure qualitative*, as Alexandre Thienpont of Vieux Château Certan put it. There was also quite a lot of black rot, which further shortened the potential crop, and hail on 29th June which ran through Arsac, Moulis and Listrac and across northern Margaux. Pauillac and the Graves were also affected.

From 5th July onwards the summer was very dry and warm, though seldom hot. July was statistically perfect: almost exactly the equal in temperature and precipitation to the average of the previous 30 years. August was hot and almost totally without rain, 16 mm of rain fell against an average of 64 mm, but no-one can recall exactly when this occurred. At the beginning of September there was a shower or two, but hardly enough to reach the vine roots, and after a heatwave between the 4th and the 15th there began to be fears of drought. A lack of moisture actually has the effect of retarding the progress towards maturity, as any gardener will tell you, and though at the time the fruit turned colour (*mi-véraison* 17th August; similar to 1987 and 1985 but earlier than 1986, 1983 and 1981) a harvest in full swing by Monday 26th September (for the red wines) had been predicted, growers were now speaking of October.

After 15th September the weather cooled, though there was still no rain, and the white wine harvest began around the 19th. It took place in excellent conditions and the fruit was in an exceptionally healthy state.

The curtains then parted for the red wine harvest. When the growers picked, and precisely how ripe the fruit was at the time of harvesting was, as ever, to prove crucial, as was the amount of grapes collected.

It is simplest to summarise the climatic conditions during the month of the harvest as follows:

19th–20th September	Cool nights; sunny days	White wine harvest in progress
22nd–24th September	Cloudy; some light rain	
25th–28th September	Bright and clear; temperatures 20–28°C	Merlot harvest started 26th
29th September	Heavy rain	
30th September –4th October	Sunny and progressively warmer until 4th October	Merlots mainly cropped 2nd–9th both in the Libournais and the Médoc/Graves
5th–6th October	Cloudy; two small showers	
7th–11th October	Warm and fine	
12th October	Heavy rain	
13th–18th October	Warm; dry Sirocco	Cabernet harvest began 13th October
19th–20th October	Rain	
21st–25th October	Hot and clear	Cabernet Sauvignon in optimum condition 21st–23rd October
26th October–3rd November	Cool but fine	

The rain that fell at the end of September seems to have done little harm to the Merlot, certainly in Saint-Émilion and Pomerol, and the grapes, again particularly in the Libournais, were ripe. But the maturity of the Cabernet Sauvignon grapes obstinately refused to progress. The sugar content remained *bloqué* at a potential alcohol level of 10–10.5°C. Some growers panicked after the heavy rain of 12th October and rushed straight out to complete the harvest. Others sat it out. Those who waited at least until the weekend of 15th/16th October before recommencing did better. The fruit picked between the 21st and the 23rd was better still.

Nevertheless it soon became apparent that a significant proportion of the crop *had* been picked, not at the beginning or at the end of the month of harvesting, which would have been ideal, but in the middle. Despite the big gap in optimum maturity between the Merlot and the Cabernet, few properties could afford to leave their pickers standing round idle for a week. The drought particularly affected the Médoc with its well-drained soils. The Cabernet Sauvignon, always the grape that matures the latest, was unwilling to develop to concentration. Moreover, as one grower pointed out, the *véraison*, when the grapes change from green to black in the middle of August, was slow to complete, and so in October the ripeness within single bunches was uneven. As another told me 'I waited and waited. And though my tannins did eventually get riper my Cabernets didn't really increase in sugar or decrease in acidity'. In short the grapes could have been riper. And yet there was one saving grace. There was not a bit of rot.

THE SIZE OF THE CROP

As important as the climatic conditions and the date of the harvest was the amount of wine produced. The simple overall figure hides the real picture. Overall the *appellation contrôlée* red wine *rendement* was 3.64 million hectolitres, the same as 1987 and 25 per cent less than 1986. Yet in Saint-Émilion the harvest was 25 per cent less than 1987! The average yield at *premier grand cru classé* level was 37 hectolitres per hectare. But at Château Latour it was 55 he/ha (though less than 50 in the sections which produce the *grand vin*). Nearby at Château Pichon-Longueville, Comtesse de Lalande, the overall figure was 60. In Saint-Julien 'almost everybody' or 'all except one' of the classed growths, according to my sources, applied for the 20 per cent PLC on top of an already generous *rendement annuel* of 48 hl/ha. And some châteaux still had to send surplus wine away for distillation. Of course every single top proprietor will assure you of the remarkable sacrifices they have gone to in rejecting vats of only marginally inferior wine in the creation of the *grand vin* and some, such as Prieuré-Lichine and Malescot in Margaux, practised a *saignée de cuve*, draining off some excess liquid before proceeding with the fermentation. Nevertheless one can't help wondering if their vines would not have yielded more satisfactory fruit in the first place if they had not been so heavily laden.

THE WINES THEN

This is what I wrote about the 1988s in May 1989:

'Despite the heatwave in September there was a general lack of sufficient warmth during the ripening season. This fact, plus the lack of moisture which retarded the maturing process, has caused an imbalance in the wines. The important thing about tannin is that it should be ripe and backed with sufficient fruit. In 1988 the tannin levels are high; in the main they are not completely ripe; and the concentrated fruit element is low. There is in addition in some cases a lack of acidity. The wines have an outer shell, but inside there is a hollowness, a lack of flesh. Some growers, worried about the high tannin levels, shortened the maceration period, so the wines are not too tannic; but at the same time they are empty. Others, blithe to the consequences, have foisted the wine with the same amount of *vin de presse* as usual and their wines are far too dense. In general the red wines lack charm and generosity. There are certainly very few which show any real breed. It is a vintage where not only is there a wide inconsistency between one property and the next but one where only at the top of the hierarchy is there much to get enthused about. I found few *bourgeois* wines which really excited me.

Nevertheless, in case this should sound unduly damning, the 1988 vintage has its successes. It is at its best in Pomerol. The Saint-Émilions can be recommended, particularly at the top level. There are good Graves, even among the *bourgeois* wines. In Saint-Estèphe, because of a higher proportion of clay in the soil, the effect of the drought was less felt. And as always the superstars – or most of them – of the rest of the Haut-Médoc have done their perfectionistic best.'

THE WINES TODAY

While I fear today that I originally over-estimated the 1988 Saint-Émilions – for I adored Cheval Blanc in cask, and also noted Ausone, Pavie and L'Arrosée, while I under-estimated L'Angélus – I stand by the vast majority of my judgements on the vast majority of the wines. Lafite is the wine of the vintage. At the top of the hierarchy the wines are successful and consistent, proportionately less so as one descends. Wines such as Pichon-Lalande, Léoville-Las-Cases, Léoville-Barton, La Lagune, Malescot, Monbrison, Haut-Bailly, L'Eglise-Clinet and La Fleur de Gay stand out today. But one or two others: Rauzan-Ségla and Cos d'Estournel are the prime examples, seem not so good as they promised at the outset (or did I taste unrepresentative bottles?);

plus of course Ducru-Beaucaillou, potentially a very lovely wine, but sadly – at least in part – tainted during its *élevage*.

The best wines are medium- to full-bodied, ripe if not *that* concentrated, but harmonious and classy and long on the palate. These wines are at least as good – better in the Graves and Médoc and indeed in Pomerol, less so in Saint-Émilion – as the 1989s, for if they lack the weight and richness, they are better balanced and have more finesse. The 1989s are rather more expensive, but the 1988s have a better capacity to continue to age elegantly and successfully. They are now mature. There is much to be enjoyed.

It was also a fine Sauternes vintage. The wines are less lusciously sweet than 1989 and 1990, but concentrated, nobly-rotten and with fine supporting acidity.

PRICES THEN AND NOW

The First Growths, having reduced their prices in the previous vintage, reverted to their 1986 levels of 180 Francs ex-château. Most of the rest of the fashionable wines, especially as the campaign progressed, asked, and got away with it, rather more, but only by a factor of 5 to 10 per cent. This meant, in futures, £265–£300 ($470–$540) per case for the First Growths and £150 ($270) for Ducru-Beaucaillou and Pichon-Longueville, Comtesse de Lalande. Léoville-Poyferré and Grand-Puy-Lacoste sold for £100 ($180), La Lagune for £80 ($140)and Angludet for £58 ($100) per dozen.

Today the First Growths sell for £1200–£1500 ($2160–$2700). Pichon-Longueville, Comtesse de Lalande is £650 ($1170), Gruaud-Larose and Léoville-Barton are £420 ($750), Grand-Puy-Lacoste is £380 ($680)and lesser classed growths can be had for £180 ($320) upwards.

THE TASTING

The following wines were sampled in November 1997.

SAINT-ÉMILION

CHÂTEAU L'ANGÉLUS

NOW–2009	16.0

Good rich full colour. This has concentration and grip. Fullish, positive, ripe nose. Fullish body, still vigorous. Good tannins. Ripe and succulent. Will still develop. This is very good.

CHÂTEAU L'ARROSÉE

DRINK SOON	13.0

Rather a little colour. Mature Merlot, quite fruity but a little feeble on the nose. Similar palate. Not enough richness or grip. Pleasant but blend. The finish is reasonably positive.

CHÂTEAU AUSONE

DRINK SOON	12.5

Medium colour. Quite brown. Rather dank nose. No style. A bit lumpy. Lacks zip again. Some astringency at the back. Medium body. Nothing much here.

CHÂTEAU BEAUSÉJOUR-DUFFAU-LAGARROSSE

DRINK SOON	12.0

Good rich full vigorous colour. Big and barnyardy on the nose. Not much style. Lacks grip on the palate. And not much fruit either. A bit dry at the end. Nothing special.

CHÂTEAU CANON

DRINK SOON	15.0

Medium to medium-full colour. Fully developed. Ripe, vigorous nose. Good fruit here. Nicely nutty. Medium to medium-full body. Some depth and personality here. Lacks a little grip but more richness and succulence. Decent finish though. Good.

CHÂTEAU CANON-LA-GAFFELIÈRE

DRINK SOON	15.5

Medium-full colour. Mature. This has richness and depth on the palate after rather a closed-in nose. Some structure. Better grip than most. This has good depth. Finishes well. Good plus.

Château Cheval Blanc

DRINK SOON   13.0

Medium to medium-full colour. Now mature. Bland nose. Quite fresh yet very little fruit and personality. Dull. Medium body.

Château Figeac

DRINK SOON   15.0

Medium to medium-full colour. Quite brown. Quite pleasant nutty nose. Medium to medium-full. Quite fresh, indeed good acidity, but lacks ripe fruit, let alone concentration. But rather more positive on the finish than most. Good.

Château Larmande

DRINK SOON   (14.0)

Rich, full, vigorous colour. This bottle is corked. But the wine isn't too bad at all underneath. Some body. Good grip. Not the greatest of class but decent fruit and substance and with a positive finish.

Château Magdelaine

NOW–2005   14.0

Good colour. Fully mature. Plump Merlot fruit. Balanced. But not much personality. Medium to medium-full. Good grip. Pleasant enough. Positive at the end. Quite good.

Château Pavie

DRINK SOON   13.0

Medium colour. Fully developed. Pleasant fruit but rather a loose-knit, Merlot-based wine. Medium body. A little astringent. One dimensional. Unexciting but drinkable. Reasonable finish.

Château Le Tertre-Roteboeuf

DRINK SOON   14.5

Fullish, rich, vigorous colour. Pleasant fruity nose. Quite ripe. Some merit here. Medium to medium-full. Some structure. The fruit is a bit one-dimensional but there is more to it than most. Quite good plus.

Château Troplong-Mondot

DRINK SOON   12.5

Medium colour. Fully developed. Fruity nose. Not too aged or bland but a bit neutral. Medium body. Lacks personality. Lurking astringency. Finishes a bit dry.

Pomerol

Château Certan de May

DRINK SOON   15.0

Medium colour. Mature. Slight smell of bonfire on the nose. A bit dry. Quite pleasant – easy to drink. Fruity on the palate. No astringency but no real dimension. Good positive finish though. Good.

Château Clinet

DRINK SOON   15.0

Medium to medium-full colour. Fully mature. Mellow, mature, slightly gamey nose. Good richness and depth. Medium to medium-full body. Lacks grip. Pretty fruit but it doesn't have the structure. Will age fast. Good at best.

Château La Conseillante

DRINK SOON   14.5

Medium to medium-full, mature colour. A little reduced on the nose. Soft, mature, basically Merlot on the palate. Not a lot of style. Slightly burnt, but quite juicy. Quite good plus.

Château La Croix du Casse

DRINK SOON   14.5

Good rich, fullish, vigorous colour. Largely Merlot but of good quality mature fruit. Good depth. Evolved fast in the glass. Medium to medium-full. Very ripe. Not quite the grip. A little over-ripe. Quite good plus.

Château L'Église-Clinet

NOW–2009+   17.5

Very good colour. Still youthful. Ample, profound, very elegant nose. Lots of concentration and quality here. Lots of vigour still. Full. Still some tannin. Rich, concentrated and backward. Very good grip. Splendid voluptuous finish. This is fine.

CHÂTEAU L'ÉVANGILE

DRINK SOON	12.0

Quite an old-looking colour. Lightish nose. Not much substance. Now a touch of volatile acidity. Light, thin, already astringent. Nothing here.

CHÂTEAU LA FLEUR DE GAY

NOW–2009	17.5

Very full colour. Still youthful. Splendidly concentrated nose. Has fine fruit. Very good grip. This is excellent. Still backward. Full body. Backward, oaky, tannic. This is still a bit closed. Lovely fruit. Very fresh. Very long. Fine.

CHÂTEAU LA FLEUR-PÉTRUS

NOW–2007	17.0

Very full colour. Just about mature. Expansive, ripe nose. Very good succulence. Fullish, oaky and cedary flavour. Ripe. Good grip. This is sleek, velvety and elegant. Long finish. Very good indeed.

CHÂTEAU LE GAY

DRINK UP	12.0

Fullish, mature colour. Slightly too much undergrowth on the nose. Dry on the palate. Already astringent. Not nearly enough grip. No.

CHÂTEAU GAZIN

NOW–2007	16.0

Full, opulent, mature colour. Rich, fat, meaty and concentrated on the nose. Fullish, quite tannic and burly. Rich but too muscular at first. Better on the finish. But not really classy. Very good.

CHÂTEAU LAFLEUR

DRINK SOON	16.0

Fullish colour. Now mature. Spicy, ripe Merlot fruit on the nose. Not quite enough grip on the palate. This is a pity. There is good style and concentration here. Very good at best.

CHÂTEAU PÉTRUS

NOW–2010+	18.5

Medium-full, mature colour. Classy fruit here, balanced and succulent. Full, rich, backward. For once real grip and real breed. Very lovely follow-through. Long. Very long. Splendid life ahead of it. Very fine.

LE PIN

DRINK SOON	16.0

Medium-full, mature colour. Nice smoky-nutty nose here. Lead-pencilly. Lots of new oak on the palate. Not quite the grip. But very classy fruit. Easy to drink and enjoy. Very good but not great.

CHÂTEAU TROTANOY

DRINK SOON	14.0

Fullish, vigorous colour. Full, rich and gamey on the nose. Just a little clumsy. Quite sizeable but the fruit is a little dense and bitter. Some astringency. Lacks charm. Will get even more astringent. Quite good.

VIEUX CHATEAU CERTAN

NOW–2007	16.5

Fullish vigorous colour. Slightly animal but ripe and substantial and vigorous. Just a little dense. Quite sizeable. Not a lot of depth though, nor richness. But good grip. Quality here but a little ungainly. Very good plus.

GRAVES

DOMAINE DE CHEVALIER

DRINK SOON	16.5

Medium to medium-full colour. Fully mature. Smoky nose. Ample, stylish, seductive. On the palate this is medium to medium-full-bodied. Open, ripe and succulent. Balanced and long. It doesn't have the greatest of class but is complex and harmonious and attractive. Very good plus.

Château Haut-Bailly

NOW–2010   17.0

Fullish colour. Little maturity. Plump, rich, balanced nose. This has class and depth. Fullish, ripe, still some tannin. Rich and slightly dense at first. But it is still youthful. Very good depth here. Very good grip. Long. Vigorous. Will keep well. Very good indeed.

Château Haut-Brion

NOW–2010+   18.5

Very fine colour indeed. Still youthful. Rich, full and opulent on the nose. Still closed. Fat and luscious nevertheless. Full body. Good grip. Quite intense. Good ripe tannins. Lots of lovely fruit here. But it doesn't add up to any better than very fine. Will still improve.

Château La Louvière

DRINK SOON   14.0

Medium-full mature colour. Fullish, spicy, not much class on the nose. But quite ripe. On the palate medium-full. Rather one-dimensional and a bit lean. Earthy Graves character. Slightly reduced. Reasonably positive at the end. Pleasant. Quite good.

Château La Mission Haut-Brion

DRINK SOON   16.5

Medium-full mature colour. Classy nose. Very youthful still. Slight earthiness. Medium body. A little astringent. The wine is a bit diffuse. Pleasant enough and good grip underneath. Indeed the finish has merit. But there is not quite enough fat. Very good plus.

Château Pape-Clément

NOW–2007   16.5

Medium to medium-full colour. Still quite vigorous. Fullish, ripe but slightly lumpy nose. Medium-full, still a little tannin. Oaky, ripe and better on the finish than the attack. A meaty wine. Still youthful. Very good plus.

Margaux & Southern Médoc

Château d'Angludet

DRINK SOON   13.5

Slightly dense, fully mature colour. A little dense on the nose. Juicy but unstylish. Medium-full. Quite developed and not in a very elegant sense. Slightly dry and tannic on the palate. Lacks succulence and class. Lacks charm. Ungainly. Not bad plus.

Château Cantenac-Brown

DRINK SOON   14.0

Medium to medium-full colour. Fully mature. Quite concentrated on the nose. Balanced and fruity. Almost jammy. Medium body. Lacks a little freshness. Quite ripe but no grip. Will get astringent. But certainly some personality and not too short yet. Quite good.

Château Chasse-Spleen

DRINK SOON   13.5

Good fullish, vigorous colour. Full and rich if slightly chunky nose. But there is some fruit here. Not bad plus.

Château d'Issan

DRINK SOON   14.0

Fully mature colour. A little old. A bit attenuated on the nose. Lightening up on the palate. Had some style once but ageing fast. Medium body. Still a good positive finish but drink quite soon. Quite good.

Château La Lagune

NOW–2010   17.0

Fullish mature colour. Good vigour and class. Very good concentrated fruit. Medium-full. Very elegant. Very harmonious. Gently cedary. This is understated. Very good indeed.

Château Malescot-Saint-Exupéry

NOW–2010+   17.0

Fullish, barely mature colour. Open on the nose. Good fresh fruit. Fullish, rich and concentrated. Very good grip. This is still quite backward but very promising. Lovely ample finish. Intense, even fine.

Château Margaux

NOW–2010+   18.5

Full colour. Just mature. Fine, fragrant, restrained nose. Discreet and lovely. Fully ready. High-toned and spicy. Medium-full. Intense, harmonious and very elegant. This is really lovely and now *à point*. Complex and very distinguished. Very fine.

Château Marquis de Terme

NOW–2008   15.5

Fullish, vigorous colour. Quite ripe and mature on the nose. Medium weight. Succulent. Medium-full body. Good ripe tannins. Fresh. Good grip. This is just about ready. Quite rich. Not the greatest of class. Just a touch dense but good plus.

Château Monbrison

NOW–2010   17.0

Very full colour. Still very youthful. Full, rich, concentrated. Plenty of wine here. This is special. Full body. Still young. Quite a lot of tannin but the tannins very good. Ripe and rich. Lots of finesse. Very fine finish. Very good indeed.

Château Palmer

DRINK SOON   16.5

Fullish mature colour. Ripe. Good Cabernet fruit, mature, balanced and stylish. Fullish, ripe, well-made. Lacks just a little personality. Good fruit though. Finishes well. Very good plus. But will get better. Give it time.

Château Poujeaux

DRINK SOON   14.0

Medium to medium-full colour. Mature. Pleasant fruit on the nose here. Ripe, medium body. No real depth but at least stylish. Fresh and quite good but not a keeper.

Château Rauzan-Ségla

DRINK SOON   12.0

Medium-full mature colour. A little light and blunt on the nose. Undistinguished. Dry on the palate. Unbalanced. No.

Saint-Julien

Château Beychevelle

NOW–2010   16.0

Medium to medium-full colour. Mature. Stylish, vigorous Cabernet on the nose. A full, if not a little solid, Cabernet Sauvignon nose. Good grip. This is firm but fresh. Meaty. Good depth. Good long finish. Very good but not quite the concentration for greatness.

Château Branaire-Ducru

DRINK SOON   15.0

Medium colour. Fully mature. Quite soft and plump but good elegance here. Medium body. Fully ready. Not the greatest of grip or depth but balanced and ripe and long on the palate. *À point*. Good.

Château Ducru-Beaucaillou

\-   -

It may be bad luck – for I am assured that not all the stock was tainted – but I have had many more bad Ducru-Beaucaillou 1988s than 1999 or 2000: six out of eight opportunities since 1994. The good bottles were fine.

Château Gruaud-Larose

NOW–2007   17.0

Full, rich colour. Still youthful looking. A bit dense on the nose. The tannins a little hard. Better on the palate. There is good ripe Cabernet fruit here and plenty of style. Only just ready. Very good indeed.

CHÂTEAU LAGRANGE

NOW–2010	16.0

Full rich colour. Barely mature. Warm and rich on the nose. On the palate the wine is quite chunky. But the tannins are ripe and there is very good grip. Not quite the richness of the best. But still very youthful. Will round up. Will improve. Very good.

CHÂTEAU LANGOA-BARTON

NOW–2008	16.0

Medium-full, mature colour. Not a lot at present on the nose but what there is is elegant and poised. Good oak. Medium full. Very stylish in a feminine sense. Lovely. Real charm here. *À point*. Very good.

CHÂTEAU LÉOVILLE-BARTON

NOW–2007	17.5

Full, vigorous colour. Opulent, ripe concentrated fruit. This is very promising. On the palate a rich wine. Very voluptuous. Fat and ample. Lots of quality and depth. Fine, long, succulent finish. Still a little tannin to resolve. Fine.

CHÂTEAU LÉOVILLE-LAS-CASES

NOW–2010+	18.5

Full, vigorous colour. Opulent, ripe, concentrated fruit. This is very promising. On the palate a rich wine. Very voluptuous. Fat and ample. Lots of quality and depth. Fine, long, succulent finish. Still a little tannin to resolve. Fine.

CHÂTEAU LÉOVILLE-POYFERRÉ

NOW–2008	17.0

Fullish, mature colour. Opulent nose. Rich and flamboyant. Closed and quite tannic. Fat and rich and with very good grip. This is gently oaky and very good indeed.

CHÂTEAU TALBOT

DRINK SOON	14.0

Fullish colour. Fully mature. Rather over-evolved on the nose. Soft and diffuse. Ripe. Indeed over-ripe. Medium to medium-full. Ample, spicy, round. Not enough grip to keep the fruit stylish. *À point*. Only quite good.

PAUILLAC

CARRUADES DE LAFITE

DRINK SOON	16.0

Fullish colour. Well matured. Good ripe fruit on the nose without any real personality. Similar palate. Medium-full. Good Cabernet fruit. Very good but a little dull.

CHÂTEAU GRAND-PUY-LACOSTE

NOW–2008	17.0

Fullish colour. Mature. A little dense-looking. Ripe, soft, voluptuous nose. Both class and fruit here. Luscious. Medium-full, opulent, classy. Spicy. Just about ready. Not quite the grip for great but very good indeed.

CHÂTEAU HAUT-BATAILLEY

NOW–2008	14.5

Good colour. Rather austere, even herbaceous on the nose. Medium to medium-full body. Underneath there is good Cabernet fruit and quite a lot of acidity. It lacks charm.

CHÂTEAU LAFITE

NOW–2020	19.5

Full colour. Just mature. Rich, fat and oaky. Very luscious fruit on the nose. Fullish, quite oaky. Rich and balanced. Concentrated and fine. This has a little more oak than some. Slightly closed still. This will develop. A very lovely wine indeed.

CHÂTEAU LATOUR

NOW–2020	18.5

Very full colour. Still very youthful. Backward nose. Quite tannic. Structured, even a little dense at first. Yet very rich as well. Needs time. Opulent and fat. Rich and ripe. This is very fine.

CHÂTEAU LYNCH-BAGES

NOW–2010+	17.0

Fullish, rich colour. Only barely mature. Firm, rich, vigorous nose. Quite some structure though. A fullish, tannic, meaty wine. Very good depth. Very good grip. Still needs time. Not quite the class for great, but long and complex and very good indeed.

Château Mouton-Rothschild

NOW–2009	16.0

Full colour. Mature. Just a little dull and four-square on the nose. This is the least good of the Médoc/Graves First Growths. Ripe Cabernet fruit, but what it misses is a bit of real concentration. Very good, merely.

Château Pichon-Longueville

NOW–2009	16.0

Medium-full colour. Fully mature. A little slight on the nose. Fresh and fruity but no concentration or dimension. Medium to medium-full. Neat, ripe, stylish. Some depth on the palate, but not a lot; some grip but not a lot. Well made. Very good.

Château Pichon-Longueville, Comtesse de Lalande

NOW–2010+	18.5

Full, mature colour. Fine nose. Very concentrated. Real depth here. Lovely fruit. Rich, fat, concentrated and intense. Brilliant fruit. This is very lovely. Real distinction. Real class. Very fine.

Château Pontet-Canet

NOW–2010	16.5

Medium-full colour. A little old-looking. Ripe, fat nose. Some development here. Fullish, nicely voluptuous. Good grip. This has concentration, balanced and very good length. Nicely cool. Very lovely finish. Good length and distinction. Very good plus.

Saint-Estèphe

Château Calon-Ségur

DRINK UP	(11.0)

Medium-full colour. Fully ready. This seems a bit tired and oxidised on the nose. Loose. Barnyardy. Thin and astringent. No. A bad bottle?

Château Cos d'Estournel

DRINK SOON	15.5

Fullish colour. Still vigorous. Fresh, medium-full nose. A little dumb. Medium body. This is a little loose, even astringent on the palate. There is class here. But not the depth and interest. Good plus.

Château Haut-Marbuzet

DRINK SOON	15.5

Medium to medium-full colour. Well matured. Spicy nose. Slightly diffuse. Slightly rustic. Medium-full. Ripe and nicely spicy but a little common. This is most enjoyable; even seductive. But it lacks class. Good plus.

Château Montrose

DRINK SOON	15.5

Fullish colour. Just about ready. Firm on the nose, if not a little hard. Medium-full. There is a slight absence of charm here. Good style. Good balance but it lacks richness. May get more generous – it isn't hard – as it gets older. Good plus.

Château Sociando-Mallet

DRINK SOON	16.0

Medium-full colour. Fully mature. Rich, youthful and fat and succulent on the nose. Ample on the palate. Still some tannin. Good structure. Fat and rich. Good grip. Very good.

1986 Vintage

SIZE OF THE CROP:	5,615,836 HECTOLITRES.
VINTAGE RATING:	14.0–18.5 (RED WINES – SEE BELOW).
	16.0 (DRY WHITE WINES).
	17.0 (SWEET WINES).

With more than 1 million hectolitres produced than in 1982, 1986 was an immense crop, by a long way a record in modern times, though to be soon overtaken by 1989 and most of the vintages of the following decade. The yield, at 65 hl/ha, is still the highest. The white wine vintage produced 1,101,754 hl (19.6 per cent of the total).

At its best, in Saint-Julien and Pauillac, 1986 ranks with 1982 and 1990 as the best vintage of the decade. Moreover, it is more classic than 1982. The acidity levels are better, even if the wines are not quite as rich. To compare the two Mouton-Rothschilds, as I have done on several occasions, is fascinating. They are both excellent, 20 out of 20 wines even in absolute terms. But they are quite different.

Sadly, outside Saint-Julien and Pauillac, apart for some honourable exceptions, the vintage is quite a lot less good, for reasons which are explained below. In this respect, though not peaking as high, the 1985 vintage is much more reliable.

Having spent an almost over-long period of time in their adolescence, the best 1986s are fully ready. Prices of the top wines are similar to those currently being asked for the 1990s. This means they are around 30 per cent less than the comparable 1982s. The best are certainly not inferior.

THE WEATHER

For three successive seasons – 1987 following 1985 and 1986 – the winter was quite severe in Bordeaux. In 1986 there was no frost damage, as there had been the previous year, but the development of the foliage was retarded, in particular by a very cold April. At the beginning of May the vine was almost a month in arrears. 'If there is one thing that's certain', the locals grumbled to one another, 'it's that we'll be harvesting in October' – a forecast that was to turn out correct only in part.

May, however, brought the hot dry spring everyone had missed, and as this weather continued into June the vegetation rapidly began to catch up. The flowering took place only a few days later than the 20-year average (*mi-floraison* 20th June as against the mean of the 14th) and a large amount of flowers successfully set into embryonic fruit, thus announcing yet again a prolific harvest, particularly in the Merlots.

It continued warm and very dry, producing the driest three months from June to August of the previous 20 years. The *véraison* took place at more or less the usual time (*mi-véraison* 19th August) indicating a harvest which would begin about 1st October. As a result of this lack of rain the Cabernet grapes, though abundant, were smaller than usual, and therefore wider apart.

With the instinctive farmers' nose for the inevitable the Bordelais waited for the rain to come, hoping it would come sooner than later. On 14th or 15th September it rained evenly over the whole *vignoble*; not too excessively and not too late. The effect was beneficial, aiding rather than deterring the process of ripening and concentration. The damage was done nine days later. On 23rd September a violent downpour centred on Bordeaux itself. It was the fact that this time the rain did not fall evenly across the Bordeaux vineyards, coupled with the very high Merlot harvest, which has caused the variation in quality from one commune to another.

The rain fell mainly in Bordeaux itself and to the south and west, that is in the Graves, Entre-Deux-Mers and Libournais. In Bordeaux itself 100 mm was recorded: in Pauillac the precipitation was only 20 mm. Thereafter the fine weather returned. It continued warm and sunny, with increasing periods of morning mist, well into October. The red wine harvest took place without a single interruption for rain.

Most of the top properties found themselves starting the harvest by picking the Merlots, and then stopping for a few days until the Cabernets were absolutely *à point*. At Cos d'Estournel Bruno Prats brought in his Merlot between 29th September and 4th October and his Cabernet between 6th and 15th October. The late Madame Villars at Chasse-Spleen, helped by a mechanical harvester for the Cabernets, began harvesting her Merlot on 6th October and her Cabernet a week later, these dates almost exactly being paralleled by Alexandre Thienpont at Vieux Château Certan, though others in Saint-Émilion and Pomerol picked closer to the rain.

THE WINES THEN

This is what I wrote at the time:

'Broadly, the difference between the quality of the Merlot vats, particularly at those properties which cropped excessively and which vintaged soon after the rain had fallen heavily, and the Cabernet vats, particularly those harvested from old vines in the vineyards which largely escaped the downpour, is enormous. This is a Cabernet year. This is a Médoc vintage.

Overall the wines have a good healthy colour and good fruity aromas. The fruit was in fine sanitary condition when it was brought in and this is reflected in the wine. Acidity levels are not high, if anything in the Graves and the Libournais rather low. Tannin levels *are* high and even in the Saint Émilion and Pomerol areas are 10 per cent more than in 1985. As a result of the excessively low water table caused by the early summer drought, you would expect these tannins not to be soft. This is indeed what you find.

In the Libournais the tannins are rather dry and washed out. I felt with some of the wines that the level of *vin de presse* was noticeable and the effect was one of astringency; as if the wines had been deliberately beefed up by the addition of press wine. In the northern Médoc the tannins are a great deal riper and more succulent.

Where the wines differ, and differ greatly from region to region, is in the density of their composition and in the concentration of their fruit. In the Libournais the wines are overall either somewhat limp and anonymous or a little too dense. They lack richness and grip and therefore definition. There are, of course, exceptions but apart from a few obvious stars (Le Pin, Certan de May, Vieux Château Certan, Pavie and Canon) the level is uninspiring. The 1985 vintage is to be preferred.

I also prefer, by some way, the Graves in this earlier vintage. The 1986 Graves range from the frankly weedy and dilute upwards; but not far upwards. The storm has left its mark.

In Margaux and the southern Médoc the effect of the rain is also apparent. There are some very good wines (Labégorce-Zédé and Angludet among the reasonably priced; Rauzan-Ségla and Palmer among the more expensive, and Château Margaux, of course) but the difference between the top wines of the southern Médoc and the rest is distinct.

Further north in the Médoc the change in style and improvement in quality is marked. Here, from Moulis northwards, and particularly so in Pauillac, Saint-Julien and Saint-Estèphe, the wines have a very full colour, huge amounts of tannin – much more than in 1982 – marvellous Cabernet-based, concentrated fruit and good levels of acidity. Naturally, there are disappointments (though each year one can welcome a few more properties that have turned the corner and are at last making the sort of wine of which they are capable) but overall the quality is very impressive, very impressive indeed.

The quality of these best Médocs is based on this superb, rich, profound Cabernet fruit. In size they resemble the 1982s, and have acidity levels which are similar or better. The Cabernet Sauvignon produces a wine of higher acidity than the Merlot, and in 1986 benefited from a lower yield. Moreover in the Médoc the fruit was picked later, and was able to dry out and reconcentrate after the September rains. Many proprietors, having rejected the least good (Merlot) vats, have made a much more Cabernet wine than usual.

The fruit flavours are less cooked and exotic than in 1982, and the spicy elements – grilled nuts, game, chocolate – less obvious. I find the flavours very classic, and the wines full, harmonious, rich, firm and concentrated. As a result I place the quality of the best Médoc 1986s at a very high level indeed. It is a vintage which will take a very long time to mature, and may well turn out better than in 1982, or where 1983 was better than in 1982, than in 1983. This is high praise.

The Wines Today

Overall, what distinguishes the vintage in the Médoc and at the top levels in the Graves, is a very good ripe acidity. The wines are quite structured, and the best dozen or so are only barely ready for drinking. They also have concentrated fruit. It is this acidity which is keeping everything in equilibrium, and will ensure that the fruit lasts until the tannins finally soften. And of course it gives the wine breed.

Across the board in Saint-Julien and Pauillac, rather less so, sadly, in Saint-Estèphe, but more so than expected in Margaux, there are some very lovely wines. Some (Pape-Clément, Haut-Batailley, Lagrange, Léoville-Poyferré, Grand-Puy-Lacoste, Pontet-Canet, Talbot, Cos d'Estournel and Montrose – none of whom should be more than £480/$860 a case (auction and brokers' prices) – have outperformed their reputation. The remainder, whether Super-Seconds such as Palmer, Rauzan-Ségla, Gruaud-Larose, Léoville-Las-Cases, Pichon-Longueville, Comtesse de Lalande and Lynch-Bages or First Growths, are equally exciting. At the top levels, in these communes, 1986 is a splendid vintage and is living up to its reputation.

The Libournais is another matter. The wines are much more developed, acidity levels are rather lower and there is a lack of class.

In Saint-Émilion, of the wines I have sampled, Cheval Blanc is very good but no better, Canon has fulfilled its early promise as one of the best Right Bank wines, as has Pavie. L'Arrosée and La Dominique are commendable. But this cannot be said for others, such as Ausone and Figeac.

Overall, the Pomerols scored better, though with no greater elegance. Merely better levels of acidity, so they were fresher. I was not struck, even on re-tasting it when I knew what it was, by the Petrus. As usual – and it seems to happen invariably: the wine is obviously to my taste – I gave my highest marks to Vieux Château Certan. I also liked its neighbour, Certan de May. As in the Médoc, there are some Pomerols which will keep well. Choose wisely, and you have a high quality vintage which will age elegantly.

It was a fine Sauternes vintage. The gems are d'Yquem, Climens, Rieussec, Guiraud, Nairac and de Fargues.

Prices Then and Now

The First Growths maintained their prices at 180 Francs per bottle ex-château, but elsewhere prices declined on 1985 levels. Nevertheless, with first growths at £300 ($540) plus, Palmer, Ducru-Beaucaillou and Pichon-Lalande at £175 ($310), Cos d'Estournel at £130 ($230), Lynch-Bages and Gruaud-Larose at £120 ($210), the vintage seemed expensive at the time. Indeed they were cheaper in real terms six years later, in 1993.

Today, of course, it is a different matter. The top 1986s sell for more than the comparable 1985s, much the same as the 1990s. The Premiers Crus range, per dozen, from £2500 ($4500) for Mouton-Rothschild to £1300 ($2340) for Haut-Brion and Cheval Blanc; Léoville-Las-Cases is £1000 ($1800), Pichon-Longueville, Comtesse de Lalande is £800 ($1440), Cos d'Estournel is £700 ($1260), Grand-Puy-Lacoste is £450 ($810) and La Lagune is £300 ($540). Even Château Potensac is £220 ($390).

THE TASTING

The following wines were sampled in May 1998.

SAINT-ÉMILION

CHÂTEAU L'ARROSÉE

NOW–2012	17.0

Medium to medium-full colour. Fully mature. Rich, ample, cedary nose. On the palate this is mellow, oaky and seductive. Good tannins. Good grip. This is an attractive wine with good depth. Not great but very good indeed. Will still improve.

CHÂTEAU AUSONE

DRINK SOON	13.0

Medium colour. Mature. Loose-knit Merlot nose. No great class. Light to medium body. Pleasant but one-dimensional and a bit undistinguished. Will become astringent, I fear.

CHÂTEAU CANON

NOW–2012	16.5

Fullish mature colour. Nice plump nose. Fresh, balanced, stylish. Not too Merlot. Good substance. The tannins properly covered and with unexpected grip for a Libournais this year. Fresh. Good ample fruit. Will still improve. Very good plus.

CHÂTEAU CHEVAL BLANC

DRINK SOON	16.0

Medium-full colour. Mature. Rich, oaky nose. Quite full. Fresh and ripe on the attack. Slightly less to it on the follow-through but certainly very good. Not the greatest of class or intensity. Strangely the Merlot is very apparent. Very good.

CHÂTEAU LA DOMINIQUE

NOW–2008	16.0

Fullish colour. Mature. Rich, full, not too developed nose. Fullish, tannic. Plenty of depth here. A typically opulent wine. Good grip. This is long, lush and positive. Very good.

CHÂTEAU FIGEAC

DRINK SOON	14.0

Good colour. Mature. Rather evolved Merlot nose. Not much depth. Better on the palate. But it lacks class. Ripe, quite fresh. Medium to medium-full. Slightly one-dimensional. Quite good.

CHÂTEAU LARMANDE

DRINK SOON	15.0

Good colour. Still vigorous-looking. Rich, ample Merlot nose. Quite full. Good acidity. Fully ready but fresh and vigorous. No great class but has dimension. Good.

CHÂTEAU PAVIE

DRINK SOON	12.0

Medium colour. Fully mature. Rather dirty on the nose and palate. A little bitter and certainly a bit astringent. Medium body. Lacks class. This is a disappointment. Pavie is usually better than this and has been since the beginning. A badly stored bottle?

CHÂTEAU LE TERTRE-ROTEBOEUF

DRINK SOON	12.5

Medium colour. Fully mature. Rather empty nose. Ripe but lacks grip and substance. On the palate rather dirty. Rather astringent. This is indifferent. Medium body. Unbalanced. Is this a true bottle?

POMEROL

CHÂTEAU CERTAN DE MAY

NOW–2012   16.5

Medium-full mature colour. Rich, full and concentrated on the nose. Lots of depth here. Medium-full. Still tannic, rich, fat and concentrated. Very good grip. Good fruit but not that much volume. Very good plus.

CHÂTEAU CLINET

NOW–2012   15.5

Full mature colour. Opulent, expansive, spicy nose. There is something vegetal about the tannins. On the palate this is fullish, tannic, firm and concentrated. Very good grip. Very youthful. Most impressive at first. Yet over-extracted, I felt on aeration.

CHÂTEAU L'ÉGLISE-CLINET

DRINK SOON   14.0

Good colour. Rather dense on the nose. Medium-full body. Quite ripe underneath. Fresh too. But rather burly and ungenerous. It lacks succulence. Quite good at best.

CHÂTEAU L'ÉVANGILE

NOW–2010   14.5

Medium-full colour. Fully mature. Slightly hard on the nose. But plenty of volume. Ripe, fullish, tannic. A bit four-square and ungainly. Lacks a bit of real class. Quite good plus.

CHÂTEAU LA FLEUR DE GAY

NOW–2008   16.0

Good full colour. No undue maturity. Aromatic, slightly burnt sugar nose. No great weight behind it. But good ripe fruit. Ample and balanced. Medium-full. Still has good grip. Only just ready. Very good.

CHÂTEAU LE GAY

NOW–2010   16.0

Fullish, mature colour. Slightly hard tannins on the nose. A little herbaceous. Fullish. Quite ample but a bit astringent on the palate. It lacks grace as well as class. Rich though. Will it improve? Very good.

CHÂTEAU LAFLEUR

DRINK SOON   14.5

Medium colour. No undue maturity. Rather a simple, insipid nose. A bit more astringent than tannic. Quite ripe. Medium to medium-full body. Decent fruit. Decent follow-through. Quite good plus.

LE PIN

NOW–2012   16.0

Full colour. Some maturity. Open, accessible, cedary nose. Quite stylish, plump fruit. Easy to drink. No hard edges. Voluptuous and seductive. Not great but very good.

CHÂTEAU PÉTRUS

NOW–2008   14.5

Medium-full colour. Mature. Opulent oaky nose. Some Merlot. Pleasant on the plate but rather dense. As much astringent and balanced. A bit one-dimensional but well made. Just about ready.

CHÂTEAU TROTANOY

DRINK SOON   14.5

Medium-full colour. Mature. Slightly over-evolved Merlot on the nose. And on the palate a little weak and one-dimensional. Fruity. Not too astringent but undistinguished. Quite good plus.

VIEUX CHATEAU CERTAN

NOW–2018   18.5

Fullish mature colour. Fresh, concentrated nose. There is good weight and grip here. Lovely fruit. Quite full. Good balance. This is certainly very fine.

GRAVES

CHÂTEAU BAHANS-HAUT-BRION

DRINK SOON   13.5

Medium colour. Mature. Mellow, gently fruity nose. Not *that* clean or classy. Medium body. Some tannin. Rather neutral. Lacks concentration and grip. Will become astringent. Boring.

Château Carbonnieux

DRINK SOON   13.5

Medium colour. Now mature. Pleasant but slightly loose-knit, unclassy nose. Slightly vegetal. On the palate medium body. As much astringent as tannic. Pretty fruit. But one-dimensional and dull. Acceptable.

Domaine de Chevalier

NOW–2008   16.0

Medium colour, fully mature. Mellow, Graves, roast-chestnutty nose. Medium to medium-full. Ripe, uncomplicated. Easy to appreciate. Balanced and charming. Good fruit and style. Good long finish. Very good.

Château Haut-Bailly

DRINK SOON   13.5

Very good colour, just about mature. Reserved, backward, herbaceous nose. Slightly dense and tannic on the palate, and the tannins are not that ripe. Medium-full. Lacks grace. Some fruit here but not enough grip and class. This will never mellow properly. Fair.

Château Haut-Brion

NOW–2010   17.5

Tasted twice: the second bottle slightly less reduced but I gave them identical marks. Medium-full colour. Still youthful. A bit of reduction on the nose. Cleaner, fuller and fresher on the palate. Fullish. Some tannin. Rich, concentrated and profound. Nice ripe fruit underneath. This has class and depth. Fine.

Château La Mission Haut-Brion

NOW–2008   15.5

Medium-full colour. Still youthful. Fullish ample nose. Just slightly sweaty and reduced. There is class here. But it doesn't all add up. The fruit is very ripe and complex. Medium to medium-full. Good grip. Is this sweaty aspect just a phase? Gets cleaner in the glass. Good plus but not great.

Château Pape-Clément

NOW–2018   18.5

Medium-full colour. Still youthful. Full, firm, rich and concentrated on the nose. Ample and impressive. Full, rich, concentrated, lovely cool balanced fruit. This has real grip and depth. Youthful. Harmonious. Very, very long. Very, very classy. Very fine.

Moulis & Haut-Médoc
Château Chasse-Spleen

DRINK SOON   14.0

Full mature colour. Nicely sizeable, quite rich nose. Balance and elegance here. Less elegant, less composed on the palate. Some astringency. Medium-full. A little bitter. This has good size but it lacks charm. Quite good.

Château La Lagune

DRINK SOON   15.0

Full colour, barely mature. Quite rich on the nose. Chunky too, but good ripeness and balance here. Quite tannic. Fullish. Good depth. Nothing too burly on the palate. Good grip. Good richness. Good intensity. Good class. Still youthful. Only just ready. Good.

Château Poujeaux

DRINK SOON   14.0

Medium-full colour. Fully mature. Good rich nose. Plenty of depth. On aeration a lack of real class though. Medium body. Slightly better in its fruit. The tannins a little astringent. Good grip. But the fruit lacks real richness. Quite good.

Château Sociando-Mallet

DRINK SOON   15.0

Purple colour. Full. Refined nose. Good Cabernet. On the palate once again this is as much astringent as tannic, but underneath this rather good fruit. It is a bit too cool and ungenerous for comfort though. Fullish. Good merely.

MARGAUX

CHÂTEAU BRANE-CANTENAC

NOW–2008   16.0

Medium-full colour. Fully mature. High-toned nose. Slightly vegetal. Medium body. As much astringent as tannic, but better fruit and grip on the follow-through. There is fat and generosity here as well as grip. Very good finish. This is very good.

CHÂTEAU D'ISSAN

DRINK SOON   15.0

Medium colour. Some age. Toffee flavours on the nose. Evidence of new oak on the palate. Medium to medium-full. Mellow. Soft. Easy to drink. Aromatic. Quite well balanced. Good but not great.

CHÂTEAU KIRWAN

DRINK SOON   13.0

Medium-full colour. Now mature. Slightly tight and dry on the nose. Ungainly. Over-evolved. Now astringent. Lacks style. Medium-full. Not bad at best.

CHÂTEAU MARQUIS DE TERME

DRINK SOON   12.0

Fullish mature colour. Slightly cooked nose. For once a slight lack of acidity and a hint of attenuation. Evolved palate. Medium body. This has lost some of its fruit. Now rather attenuated. Lacks style. Poor.

CHÂTEAU MARGAUX

NOW–2030   19.0

Very fine colour. Very backward. Very profound nose. Real concentration here. Big; massive, indeed. Very impressive. Enormous depth and power. Yet utterly classy, not a vestige of over maceration or too much tannin. Full, concentrated and tannic. Marvellous fruit. Very, very long and intense. Excellent.

CHÂTEAU MONBRISON

DRINK SOON   15.5

Medium colour, fully mature. Good nose. Slightly lean and reserved but quite classy fresh fruit. An easy to drink wine. Soft, medium body. Ripe. No hard edges. Very pleasant, balanced fruit. But not the depth for serious wine.

CHÂTEAU PALMER

DRINK SOON   17.0

Medium to medium-full colour. Fully mature. Good rich concentrated fruit. There is finesse here. Fully ready. Medium-full body. Balanced. Stylish. Soft. Gentle. This is very good indeed.

PAVILLON ROUGE DU CHÂTEAU MARGAUX (BORDEAUX)

DRINK SOON   15.0

Full colour. Barely mature. Medium weight on the nose. Mellow, ripe and stylish. But not a lot of backbone. Medium body. Acidity shows. The finish is a little better. No undue tannin. But a lack of real backbone, richness and generosity. Good positive finish, though. Not without style. Good.

CHÂTEAU RAUZAN-SÉGLA

NOW–2009   17.5

Very full colour. Little maturity. Very good nose here. Classy fruit. Ripe and balanced. This is really classy and really harmonious. Fullish, mellow. Very good grip and intensity. Consistent from A to Z. Lovely.

SAINT-JULIEN

CHÂTEAU BEYCHEVELLE

NOW–2007   14.0

Full colour. Still youthful. Slightly burly and herbaceous. Fullish. Very tannic. Quite astringent on the palate. A bit lumpy. Plenty of wine here but it lacks grace and charm. A little stewed.

Château Ducru-Beaucaillou

NOW–2020	18.0

I have had one or two samples of Ducru 1986 which have been tainted, but much less frequently than the 1990–1988 trio. At best this is a full-bodied, rich, very classy wine; tannic, profound and backward.

Château Gruaud-Larose

NOW–2020	17.5

Very good colour. Barely mature. Lovely classy Cabernet nose. Lots of depth here. But backward and austere. This is by no means ready. Full, tannic. Rich and profound. Still needs five years. Very good grip. Long. Certainly fine.

Château Lagrange

DRINK SOON	15.0

Medium-full colour. Fully mature. Rich, full nose. On the palate there is very good oaky Cabernet but not quite the grip it should have. This makes the follow-through a bit bland and astringent. Fullish. Good at best.

Château Léoville-Barton

NOW–2009	16.0

Medium colour. Fully mature. Good class on the nose. Slightly less concentrated than some. A more feminine example. Medium to medium-full. Some tannin but some astringency. Essentially soft. Good balance and intensity. Classy fruit. Very good.

Château Léoville-Las-Cases

NOW–2020	18.5

Fullish colour. Still youthful. Very good depth and concentration on the nose here. Fullish. Chocolatey elements. Slightly burly at first. Ripe though. Good clean, long finish because of good acidity. Nice and long. Still very backward – even a bit adolescent – but plenty of concentration. Very fine.

Château Léoville-Poyferré

NOW–2020	18.5

Medium-full colour. Fully mature. Backward but splendidly rich on the nose. Quite a lot of new oak. Full, rich, intense, concentrated and very lovely. Still not ready. This has First Growth depth and class. Very fine.

Clos du Marquis

DRINK SOON	14.5

Medium-full colour. Now mature. Mocha flavoured nose. Aromatic. This is fully ready and it doesn't have the acidity it should have. Quite full, plummy and fruity, but essentially a bit loose-knit. Quite good plus.

Château Talbot

NOW–2009	17.0

Fullish colour. Still youthful. Very good nose. Fullish, Cabernet-based, elegant and balanced wine on the nose and palate. Laid-back. Long. Now ready. This is stylish and well-made. Very good indeed.

Pauillac

Carruades de Lafite

NOW–2008	14.5

Medium to medium-full colour. Just about mature. Good, fullish, ripe concentrated fruit on the nose. Quite a sizeable wine. On the palate it is just a little chunky. It hasn't quite the class and balance. Quite good plus though.

Château Grand-Puy-Lacoste

NOW–2012	17.0

Medium to medium-full colour, now mature. High-toned nose. Good Cabernet fruit. Quite full and tannic. Reasonable grip. Ample. Long finish. Very good indeed.

Château Haut-Bages-Libéral

NOW–2007   12.0

Medium to medium-full colour. Just about mature. Smells just a bit animal (the first sample was corked). On the palate the wine is quite full and quite astringent with the tannin. Not too astringent on the finish but it lacks the richness, grip and intensity of most. Unexciting. Got worse and worse in the glass.

Château Haut-Batailley

NOW–2015   19.0

Medium to medium-full colour. Still youthful. Very, very lovely balanced, classy fruit on the nose. Not a blockbuster but splendid grip and concentration. Excellent fruit. Very long and complex. Very fine indeed.

Château Lafite

NOW–2020   19.5

Medium-full colour, barely mature. The nose is lovely. Gentle (but First Growth 1986 standards) but very ripe and classy. Medium-full body. Some tannin. Very lovely balance. Very lovely fruit. This is long and intense and classy.

Château Latour

NOW–2020   18.0

Full colour, barely mature. Very good blackcurrant nose. Not too much of a blockbuster. Quite oaky. Medium full. A little tannin. Ripe and rich and classy. Very Cabernet. Not quite the depth and intensity of Châteaux Margaux and Mouton-Rothschild. But fine plus.

Château Lynch-Bages

NOW–2010   17.5

Medium-full colour. Still youthful. Good ripe Cabernet on the nose. Quite a gentle wine for a Pauillac. Medium-full. Lush, balanced. Not the greatest of grip and depth but certainly stylish and very good quality. And quite long enough. Long and fine and lovely.

Château Mouton-Rothschild

NOW–2025   20.0

Very full colour. Still purple. Cedary and oaky on the nose. The fruit is very ripe and lush. This is excellent. Splendid grip and intensity. Full, ripe, expansive and beautifully balanced. Very lovely follow-through. Real class. Very special.

Château Pichon-Longueville

NOW–2015   17.5

Full colour. Barely mature. Fat, rich, even opulent nose. Very well covered tannins. This is quite full and has plenty of depth. Good grip. Lush. Mouton-ish. Fine.

Château Pichon-Longueville, Comtesse de Lalande

NOW–2018   18.5

Medium-full colour. Just about mature. Fine, laid-back, concentrated nose. This has plenty of depth and class. Slightly chocolatey. Very good acidity. Lovely, slightly raspberry fruit. This is very fine.

Château Pontet-Canet

NOW–2015   17.0

Full colour, barely mature. A lot of depth on the nose here. Still quite closed. True Pauillac on the palate. A little tough but rich and full and balanced underneath. Good grip. Long finish. Very good indeed.

Réserve de la Comtesse

NOW–2009   16.5

Medium to medium-full colour, just about mature. Rich, fat, lush nose. Medium-full body. Ripe and rich in quite a gentle sort of way. Good oaky depth. Balanced and classy without being a blockbuster. Just about ready. Very good plus.

Saint-Estèphe

Château Calon-Ségur

DRINK SOON   14.0

Medium to medium-full colour. Mature. Slightly burly and dense on the nose. Clumsy. Fresh but lacks richness. Fullish. Slightly astringent. There is decent fruit here but the wine is essentially without grace or balance.

Château Cos d'Estournel

NOW–2020   18.0

Very good, backward colour. Rich, fat and concentrated on the nose. This is very lovely. Fullish bodied, more classic than today. Lots of finesse. Lovely long finish.

Château Haut-Marbuzet

NOW–2009   16.0

Fullish mature colour. Good concentration and class here on the nose. But on evolution got a bit 'tanky' and lost some of its grip and concentration. The tannins a little unsophisticated and there is a lack of dimension. Very good.

Château Lafon-Rochet

DRINK SOON   13.0

Fullish colour. Now just about mature. Not much style on the nose. Not much concentration either. On the palate medium body. Astringent and unstylish. No joy here.

Château Montrose

NOW–2015   17.5

Full colour. Still youthful. Good rich concentrated nose. Fullish, balanced. Very good grip. Lovely ripe fruit. Good grip and intensity. Still youthful. Fine.

1985 VINTAGE

SIZE OF THE CROP:	4,910,890 HECTOLITRES.
VINTAGE RATING:	17.0 (RED WINES).
	17.0 (DRY WHITE WINES).
	14.5 (SWEET WINES).

Though not as large as 1986 was to be, 1985 was a record crop at the time, beating 1982 by over a third of a million hectolitres. The yield was 58 hl/ha, exactly the same. 978,289 hectolitres were declared as AC white wine, 20 per cent of the total.

Nineteen eighty-five is an easy vintage to enjoy. The wines are ripe and healthy, decently-balanced, and have no hard edges. Overall we have much more consistency than 1986 and 1983, but these two vintages can provide, at their best, finer bottles. It was a large crop, and one can see this plethora in some of the wines. Some of the less concentrated wines are now beginning to show some age. The best, though, will still last well.

THE WEATHER

Nineteen eighty-five opened with a spell of really arctic weather throughout France. While the mercury did not completely disappear into the bulb of the thermometer in Bordeaux as it did in Chablis and Champagne, the cold was nevertheless sufficiently severe in pockets to kill off a few young vines, and to restrict severely the potential for the 1985 crop in other locations. Happily most of the fine wine vineyards emerged unscathed (Domaine de Chevalier, sadly, is an exception, but the wine is brilliant) and with the added benefit of a spring and summer free from the usual pests and other depredations the fruit progressed towards maturity without any problem. If it had been only a degree or two colder it would have been a disaster, as in 1956.

March and April were mild but May began cold and wet and ended with hailstorms on the Whitsun weekend, reducing the potential crop in the southern Médoc (particularly, among the top vineyards, at Cantemerle), in the Premières Côtes and in Barsac. June was dry and sunny, if a little cooler than average but the flowering nevertheless took place at the normal time and without mishap.

'Thus' – to quote Peter Sichel in his annual Vintage Report – 'the curtain rose on a summer which was to start well, to improve as it went along, and to finish magnificently.' The 1985 season was characterised by two important and inter-related benefits. It was exceptionally dry, and, from the second half of August onwards, conspicuously and continually warm, without being *too* hot. With the exception of a weekend of rain at the beginning of October there was an almost total drought from 4th July to 21st October. In August and September only 22 mm were recorded, the driest summer since 1929. 1961 was the only other vintage to register a figure of less than 50 mm. In contrast, the figures for 1982 and 1983 were 99.8 and 136.6 mm.

Yet drought did not mean that there was a heatwave. In July the temperatures were about average; August was decidedly cool – only 1979 and 1963 being cooler since 1959, according to the Sichel records, despite an improvement at the end of the month. September, though, was warmer than average. Only in 1961 and 1964 was it hotter, and it was this period of balmy end-of-season weather, continuing, after a brief interruption, well into October, which was the making of the 1985 harvest.

In these dry, warm, climatic conditions the fruit raced towards maturity, both the date of the *véraison*, when the grape begins to change colour, and the date of the harvest being earlier than anticipated, and the picking began on 20th September for the dry white wines and 26th September for the reds, about a week earlier than the date of the flowering would have suggested. The fruit was in magnificent condition. To quote Peter Sichel again: 'It is rare to see Bordeaux vineyards in such exuberant health.'

THE SIZE OF THE HARVEST

If the weather in September 1985 was the making of the harvest, its size was its undoing. If we compare the declarations with 1982 we can see that in Bordeaux Rouge and Bordeaux Supérieur, possibly mainly because of new plantations and the continuing switch from white wine production to red, the rise is over 20 per cent. However, in Pauillac it is a staggering 37 per cent, and in Saint Estèphe it is 23 per cent. In Saint-Émilion and Pomerol the yield was 6 per cent *down*. Overall, the AC red wine crop was 12 per cent more than in 1982. With 3.95 million *hectolitres*, the red wine harvest alone was over half a million hectolitres larger than the total harvest in 1984, white wine and non-AC wine included.

The size of the harvest seems to have caught everyone by surprise. Perhaps because of the January cold, perhaps because the flowering weather was not so obviously magnificent, predictions even immediately prior to the picking were for a crop of 4 million hectolitres overall, hardly significantly higher than in 1984. While the official figure did not appear until March it was already apparent to the producers in October that they had a great deal more wine than they had expected.

As the local paper put it, '*On s'est trompé!*' which I translated when I first reported on the vintage as 'We boobed!'.

THE HARVEST

The harvest began for the Merlot grapes on 26th September. Pétrus, which is to all extents and purposes 100 per cent Merlot, was cleared as usual in three afternoons on 2nd, 3rd and 4th October. The Merlot grapes were in splendid condition, yielding (without the aid of chaptalisation) musts of 12.5° or more of potential alcohol, with a good acidity, round, ripe tannins and plenty of extract. At this stage, however, the Cabernets were not quite ripe and far from concentrated. These grapes were still at the equivalent of 10.50°, and after heavy overnight dew and morning mists at the end of September, this declined to 9.50°. Some proprietors picked part of the vineyard before the rain predicted for the weekend at the beginning of October; others began soon after, when the berries were still to some extent inflated with water, and, equally importantly, when the acidity was temporarily reduced. Thereafter, the fine dry weather returned and those who had courage to wait could harvest a crop with a reasonable potential level of alcohol and at least adequate degrees of acidity and concentration. Paradoxically, the early autumn weather was too good, by which I mean too dry, to enable much botrytis to occur. The Sauternes are full-bodied and sweet, but one-dimensional.

THE WINES THEN

My first impression was of red wines with a good colour and a most appealing, ripe, almost scented fruit. By and large the wines had a sound constitution; they had body, balance, good levels of ripe, round tannin, at least adequate acidity and were positive, accessible and attractive. What the vintage lacked, though of course there were exceptions, were the extra dimension, weight of fruit and concentration that were present in the 1982s.

The wines had a lot of charm – the supreme health of the fruit and the ripeness of the Merlot contributed to this – but all too often this charm appeared to be all on the surface. One was left looking for the almost bitter austerity underneath the varietal fruit, apparent in a young claret of a great vintage. Moreover, few wines were really as full-bodied as they should be, and some distinctly lacked acidity. Equally, though it was more consistent, the vintage lacked the definition and class of the best of the 1983s.

This was, I said in my original report, a variable vintage. The looser wines, once they had lost their puppy fat, their youthful charm, might go the way of the 1976s – develop early, age inelegantly. Others with better acidity might turn out like 1979: pleasant but with the lack of complexity of a prolific vintage.

The best wines, however, were quite different. Where the yield had been kept within reasonable bounds, where the average age of the vines was high, and above all, where a rigorous selection had been made, and all, not just some, of the weaker vats rejected, we had wine which, in Jean-Eugène Borie's opinion, 'starts like 1982 and finishes like 1983' or, as Jacques Hébrard of Château Cheval Blanc put it, a 'a year of finesse, richness and balance'. At this top level the wines were certainly very exciting. Quite a few of these could be found in the Médoc and Graves, more in Saint-Émilion and especially Pomerol where the vintage was clearly better than 1983 (but then the 1983 vintage in the Libournais was not good as it is in the Médoc).

THE WINES NOW

It is generally recognised that this is a very good vintage in the Libournais. The *cuvées* of Merlot were very ripe and round, and this is reflected in the top wines. There is a lot of sweet fruit and a lot of charm. They have more depth and a better grip than the 1983s. The top Pomerols, in particular, are very fine.

Among the lesser Right Bank wines, however, there is a certain imbalance. On the one hand there is a richness and succulence, on the other a lack of concentration and grip: the size of the vintage is apparent. Moreover it is apparent that many wines have been bolstered up by the addition of rather too much *vin de presse*. This leaves a certain unripe astringency, almost a bitter inkiness, lurking in the background and masking the fruit and the attraction of many wines; a characteristic that I fear will not be absorbed with time. There *are* good wines, but in general you will need to go up to *premier cru* level, and its equivalent in Pomerol, to obtain them.

There are one or two odd-balls. Figeac 1985 has never really sung to me. I found an odd flavour in the wine at the beginning, and it has continued to be inconsistent. Ausone is not as good as it appeared at the outset.

The top wines of the Graves and the Médoc are equally as good as the top wines of Pomerol and Saint-Émilion. Latour has always been a disappointment, and Montrose is somewhat insignificant. Giscours is poor and d'Issan has developed a bit too fast, but by and large the vintage has developed well. The top wines have personality, elegance and depth even if at lesser levels the wines have proportionally less interest.

In sum this is a very good vintage. The stellar wines such as La Conseillante and Canon, Domaine de Chevalier, Cos d'Estournel, Léoville-Las-Cases, not to mention Cheval Blanc and Château Margaux, the two best First Growths, are very exciting. At the top levels there are 1985s to match the best of any in the last decade and they can still be kept with confidence.

PRICES THEN AND NOW

With a higher French Franc and a lower £ and $, plus higher prices at source, the 1985s seemed expensive at the time. Prices did not begin to move upwards until 1994 or so. One could have bought the wines then for less money in real terms. The First Growths were £320–£370 ($570–$660), Super-Seconds such as Palmer, Pichon-Longueville, Comtesse de Lalande and Ducru-Beaucaillou £190 ($340), Pape-Clément, Lynch-Bages, Cos d'Estournel and Gruaud-Larose were £120–£130 ($210–$230) but Langoa-Barton, d'Issan and Haut-Bailley no more than £80–£85 ($140–$150) and d'Angludet £55 ($90).

Between 1994 and 1997 many wines tripled in price. They have fluctuated since. The First Growths go for £1300 ($2340) for Latour to £2100 ($3780) for Margaux; Pichon-Longueville, Comtesse de Lalande and Léoville-Las-Cases are £825 ($1480), Palmer is £700 ($1260), Ducru-Beaucaillou is £600 ($1080), Léoville-Poyferré and Rauzan-Ségla are £420 ($750), Haut-Batailley is £300 ($540) and Labégorce-Zédé is £220 ($390).

THE TASTING

The majority of the following wines were sampled in September 1997. I made a further tasting concentrating on those which had not been present in 1997, in December 2002.

SAINT-ÉMILION

CHÂTEAU L'ARROSÉE

NOW–2007	15.5

Good colour. Quite a lot of wood here on the nose. Plump and firm. This is quite marked by the oak. Underneath there is not a lot of intensity. But an attractive bottle. Good plus.

CHÂTEAU BELAIR

DRINK SOON	15.5

Medium colour. This is not a blockbuster but is neat and balanced. Nice fruit. Good style. Balanced. Good plus.

CHÂTEAU CANON

NOW–2015	18.0

Good colour. Lovely ripe, rich, oaky nose. Full-bodied and opulent, almost sweet. But very good grip and very good tannins. Lovely finish. Fine plus.

CHÂTEAU CHEVAL BLANC

NOW–2015	18.5

Good full colour. Less development than most. Lovely nose. Rich, cedary, chocolaty, intense and classy. Fullish. Still not yet ready. Very good grip and vigour. Lovely rich fruit. Ample. Fat. Classy and very fine indeed.

CHÂTEAU FIGEAC

DRINK SOON	14.5

Good colour. Quite toasted oak on the nose. On the palate it lacks a little grip. The fruit is quite classy. The wine medium to medium-full. But it tails off. Will become attenuated. Quite good plus.

CHÂTEAU LA GAFFELIÈRE

DRINK SOON	13.0

Medium colour. Light nose. Lacking concentration and depth. Medium body. No backbone or grip. Merlot-based. Tails off. Essentially weak. Unexciting.

CHÂTEAU PAVIE

NOW–2010	17.5

Good colour. Plump, succulent nose. Good grip and intensity. This is full, ample, cedary and very well balanced. Good follow-through. Long. Classy. Fine. Will last well.

CHÂTEAU TROPLONG-MONDOT

DRINK SOON	14.0

Good colour. Quite closed and chunky on the nose. A little tough on the palate. But good depth here. The tannins are a bit rude but the wine has grip. Quite good.

POMEROL

CHÂTEAU LE BON PASTEUR

DRINK SOON	13.5

Good colour. Quite oaky and not a lot of grip. So now getting a bit astringent. This is not as good as it promised. Fruit but unbalanced. Medium-full. Not bad plus.

CHÂTEAU CERTAN DE MAY

NOW–2009	18.0

Good colour. Fresh, poised, rich and delicious. Better than Vieux-Château-Certan. Still youthful. Full. Very good grip. Rich and intense on the follow-through. Real class too. Fine plus.

CHÂTEAU LA CONSEILLANTE

DRINK SOON   18.0

Good colour. Very lovely fruit all the way
through. 'Old viney' concentration. Laid-
back. Ripe, balanced and elegant. Fullish.
Long. Very fine.

CHÂTEAU CLOS L'ÉGLISE

DRINK SOON   14.0

Good colour. Ample and rich but very
Merlot. Not a lot of class. Medium body.
Reasonable freshness but no great fruit or
dimension. Quite good.

CHÂTEAU L'ENCLOS

DRINK UP   13.0

Good mature colour. Smells of grass. Lacks
grip. Getting attenuated fast. Thin finish.
Not special.

CHÂTEAU L'ÉVANGILE

DRINK SOON   15.5

Good colour. As usual a slight mint-herbal
aspect on the nose. A bit monolithic. Full,
slightly rigid tannins. Good acidity but no
succulence. Four-square. Slight lack of
richness. Lacks charm but good plus.

CHÂTEAU LA FLEUR-PÉTRUS

NOW–2009   17.5

Good colour. Sweet, opulent Merlot nose.
Fullish but mellow. Very rich. Fine
supporting acidity. Ripe and luscious. Lovely
finish. Fine quality.

CHÂTEAU GAZIN

DRINK UP   12.0

A bit thin and cheap on the nose. Astringent
and unexciting on the palate. Mawkish
finish. Mean. No.

CHÂTEAU LAFLEUR

DRINK SOON   16.0

Good colour. As always rather tough on the
nose. Very tannic. Underneath not the grip
or the class of e.g. La Conseillante or others.
I find this a little disappointing. Lumpy
finish.

CHÂTEAU LATOUR-À-POMEROL

NOW–2009   17.0

Good colour. Nicely fresh and round on the
nose, with a touch of mocha. Medium-full
bodied, plump, ripe and rich on the palate.
Long finish. Very good indeed.

CHÂTEAU PÉTRUS

NOW–2012   17.5

Good colour. Quite a dense nose, like the
Lafleur. The Merlot is more evident than real
grip. Fullish, ample, rich and fruity. Good
balance but not the concentration, the
freshness and the grip of Cheval Blanc. Fine.
But a little dense. I prefer Certan de May.

CHÂTEAU TROTANOY

NOW–2009   17.5

Good colour. Full-flavoured. Very ripe
(almost over-ripe) nose but splendid
freshness. Really plummy. Fullish. Balanced.
Ample. Rich. Youthful. Fine.

VIEUX CHÂTEAU CERTAN

DRINK SOON   16.0

Good colour. Rich, full, ample nose. Fat and
succulent and very good grip. Ample on the
palate. Not the greatest of depth and class
but very good.

CHÂTEAU LA VIOLETTE

DRINK SOON   16.0

Good colour. Nice ripe fresh nose. Round
and succulent. Medium to medium-full.
Merlot fruit. Not a lot of class but balanced,
intense and ample. Very good grip. Very
good.

GRAVES

DOMAINE DE CHEVALIER

NOW–2015   18.0

Good full colour. Slightly austere and
herbaceous on the nose at first. Medium-full
body. Ripe, round, generous and classy on
the palate. Smooth but very vigorous. Lovely
long finish. This has been very slow to come
round. Very classy.

Château Haut-Bailly

DRINK SOON	16.0

Good full mature colour. Ripe plummy nose. Good depth. Medium-full body. Ample, succulent. Ripe and almost rich. Nice spice and oak. Good intensity. Very good.

Château Haut-Brion

NOW–2015	18.5

Very good colour. Rich, ample, intensely concentrated nose. This has real depth. Much better than La Mission Haut-Brion. Full, concentrated and with lovely fruit and great class. Very rich. Very opulent. Very fine.

Château La Mission Haut-Brion

NOW–2015	16.5

Good colour. Still quite youthful. Rich, quite full. Still a touch hard. Fullish. Some tannin. Still needs to soften up. Not great but very good plus. Lacks a bit of real richness and concentration.

Château Pape-Clément

NOW–2008	16.0

Medium-full colour. Fragrant, supple, fully mature nose. Medium to medium-full body. Ripe, round, rich and attractive. An easy-to-drink wine with a positive finish. Very good.

Médoc
Château Cantemerle

DRINK UP	12.0

Good, full mature colour. Rather stringy on the nose. Soft on the palate. Medium body. Lacks grip. A little attenuated. This is fading fast.

Château La Lagune

NOW–2009	16.0

Good colour. Rich, oaky, almost exotic nose. Medium-full body. Smooth and velvety on the palate. Balanced. Long. Very good.

Château Potensac

DRINK SOON	13.5

Good full mature colour. Rich but slightly hard tannins on the nose. Still youthful. Fullish. Lacks a little succulence. Just about ready. Not bad plus.

Château Sociando-Mallet

DRINK SOON	14.0

Good fullish mature colour. Ripe and succulent on the nose. Medium-full. Attractive Merlot nose. Not a lot of depth. But pleasant.

Margaux
Château Brane-Cantenac

DRINK SOON	15.0

Good mature colour. Pleasant fruity nose. Some Margaux class here. A bit light and short on the palate. A bit simple. But not bad at all. More fruit and more positive than usual. Good.

Château d'Issan

DRINK SOON	14.5

I loved this wine in cask, and bought some. But it doesn't seem to live up to its early promise. Today it is medium-bodied, fragrant and stylish, but it seems to have lightened up. There is a lack of weight and grip.

Château Malescot-Saint-Exupéry

NOW–2009	15.0

Good colour. Just a little four-square on the nose. Medium-full body. Ripe and rich and reasonably balanced. But not exactly very elegant. But it improved in the glass. Good.

Château Margaux

NOW–2012	17.0

Good colour. Firm, backward nose. This is still closed. Doesn't sing like the Palmer. In fact though it is rich and full and quite tannic and oaky. It seems rather dense. Very good indeed but not fine. I have had much better bottles, and I think this example doesn't do the wine justice: usually 18.5/19.0.

Château Palmer

NOW–2009+	18.5

Good colour. Fullish, rich, fragrant nose. Nicely ample. Full but velvety. Good tannins. Lovely concentrated fruit. Excellent grip for once. This is a splendid example. Real charm. Real depth.

Château Pouget

DRINK SOON   12.0

Good colour. The usual dense, tough unripe tannins on the nose. Pedestrian and tanky.

Château Prieuré-Lichine

DRINK SOON   14.0

Good colour. Ample and fruity if no class or depth. Rather a simple wine. Fully ready. Lacks a bit of grip. Will get attenuated. Quite good.

Château Rauzan-Ségla

NOW–2010   16.5

Good colour. Rich, smooth, silky nose. Fullish bodied, plump and balanced. This has very good depth and class. Long and complex. Very good plus.

Château du Tertre

DRINK SOON   14.5

Good colour. Soft, pleasant nose and palate. Nicely balanced and fruity. But not much class and depth. Quite good plus.

Saint-Julien
Château Ducru-Beaucaillou

NOW–2008   17.0

Good colour. The usual elegant Ducru-Beaucaillou nose. Fresh and positive. medium-full. Nicely cool and austere at first. Not *that* concentrated but classy and long on the palate. Very good indeed.

Château Gruaud-Larose

NOW–2010   15.5

Good colour. Like the Talbot rather smelly and reduced on the nose. Full, slightly dense and tannic. But good succulent if chunky fruit underneath. Still needs time. Slightly ungainly. Lacks a little real concentration but good plus.

Château Langoa-Barton

NOW–2010   16.0

Good colour. Fresh and succulent on the nose. Good substance. On the palate it is a little hollow, but has good freshness and fruit. And good length. Attractive but not great.

Château Léoville-Barton

NOW–2010   18.0

Good colour. Rather better than Langoa. Fuller, richer and better grip. Very lovely concentration. Very ripe Cabernet. This has real depth. Fine plus.

Château Léoville-Las-Cases

NOW–2015   19.0

Youthful colour. Marvellous nose. Rich, concentrated, very classy Cabernet fruit. Full, rich, concentrated and oaky. This has real depth and finesse. Long, composed. Very, very fine. The best wine of the vintage? Will still improve.

Château Léoville-Poyferré

NOW–2010   17.5

Good colour. Rich, opulent nose. Now smooth and silky. Medium-full body. A less classic wine than the other two Léovilles: less austere, more exotic. Harmonious. Long. Fine.

Château Saint-Pierre

NOW–2008   14.0

Good colour. Fresh Cabernet-based nose. Medium-full. A little astringent and a little vegetal on the palate. Fullish but lacks a little grip and succulence. Quite good at best.

Château Talbot

DRINK SOON   12.0

Good colour. Rather reduced on the nose. Rather hard and fruitless on the palate. Astringent. Medium-full. No charm. Ungainly.

Pauillac
Château Duhart-Milon

DRINK SOON   13.0

Good colour. A little dense on the nose. But lacks grip. Will get attenuated. Lacks class. No pleasure here. Medium-full.

Château Grand-Puy-Ducasse

DRINK SOON   12.5

Good colour. A little sweet and attenuated on the nose. Medium body. Rather artificial. Awkward finish.

Château Grand-Puy-Lacoste

NOW–2010+	17.5

Good colour. Fine, stylish, concentrated and youthful. Full, lovely Cabernet fruit. This still has a few years to go. Lots of depth. Classy. Fine.

Château Haut-Bages-Libéral

DRINK SOON	15.0

Good colour. Nice fresh, balanced, stylish nose. On the palate good fruit and charm. Not that much concentrated and flair but good. Just a touch rustic but well made.

Château Haut-Batailley

NOW–2007	15.0

Good colour. Slightly austere on the nose. But good Pauillac fruit on the palate. Good grip. Lacks a little charm but has class, as opposed to the Haut-Bages-Libéral. Good.

Château Lafite-Rothschild

SEE NOTE	16.5/18.5

Fullish colour. Restrained nose. Quite backward and tannic. But on the palate a little thin for a First Growth. There isn't the fat and intensity that it should have. This is a bit ordinary. A second bottle had more to it. More depth (18.5/Now-2009).

Château Lynch-Bages

DRINK SOON	17.0

Good colour. Rich, opulent and spicy on the nose. Concentrated and intense. Fullish, attractive, aromatic. Ripe and fruity. But it lacks a little class. Very good indeed.

Château Mouton-Rothschild

DRINK SOON	18.0

Fullish colour. Lovely fragrant nose. This has good depth if no great weight. Fully ready. Very good ripe fruit, but not the same richness and intensity as Pichon-Longueville, Comtesse de Lalande. Fine plus.

Château Pichon-Longueville

DRINK SOON	13.0

Good colour. Burnt wood on the nose. Earthy *sous-bois* on the palate. Chunky but without succulence and grip. Not special.

Château Pichon-Longueville, Comtesse de Lalande

NOW–2010+	18.5

Good colour. Very lovely succulent classy fruit on the nose. Fullish, ample, splendidly balanced. Really intense. Classy and concentrated. Very fine.

Château Pontet-Canet

DRINK SOON	14.5

Good colour. Fresh, succulent nose. Attractive. Medium body. A little tannin still, which gives a hardness to the centre. But good fruit and acidity. Balanced. Not the class of more recent vintages. Quite good plus.

Saint-Estèphe

Château Calon-Ségur

DRINK SOON	14.5

Medium colour. Slightly dry, *sous-bois* flavours on the nose. Medium-full. Lacks a bit of fat and grip. Finishes reasonably fresh but without class or intensity. Quite good plus.

Château Cos d'Estournel

NOW–2010+	18.5

Fine colour. Splendid concentrated full intense nose. Full, rich, classy and splendidly harmonious. Very good grip. Real depth. Only just ready. This is very fine.

Château Montrose

DRINK SOON	14.0

Good colour. Fresh nose but not the grip or weight of the usual Montrose. Rather stringy on the palate. Lacks class and acidity. Uninteresting.

1983 VINTAGE

SIZE OF THE CROP:	4,114,542 HECTOLITRES.
VINTAGE RATING:	14.0 – 17.0 (RED WINES – SEE BELOW).
	17.5 (DRY WHITE WINES).
	18.5 (SWEET WINES).

Though not as prolific as 1982 or 1979, 1983 was still a very large vintage, only the third in recent times to register over 4 million hectolitres of AC wine. The white wine percentage was 22.3. Overall the yield was 51.5 hl/ha.

Nineteen eighty-three had the misfortune to appear after the great and much-hyped 1982 vintage. It was good, especially in Margaux and the Graves, but not brilliant. Surprisingly, despite higher prices it was well received at the time.

THE WEATHER

The 1983 growing season had periods when all looked as if it was going to be catastrophic. As little as a generation previously it probably would have been. From the end of the 1982 harvest to the beginning of June 1983, the Bordeaux weather was cheerless and exceptionally wet. The spring, particularly, was bleak, damp and cold. Summer then arrived with a bang just when the vines were beginning to flower, and they quickly recovered any delay occasioned by the cool April and May. June was very warm, particularly early on, and, as important, very dry, with only 14 mm of rain (as against an average of over 60 mm). This ensured a successful flowering and guaranteed another large crop, the second in a row.

July was exceptionally hot, with almost half the days registering a maximum temperature of over 30°C. The rainfall was average, but intermittent, the result of storms rather than drizzle. There was some hail, particularly on the 17th, which ravaged part of Fronsac, the Côtes de Bourg and Pomerol, but only had a very small and localised effect in the Médoc.

The weather in August, a month where normally there is little to do in both vineyard and *chai*, and traditionally the weeks of the workers' annual leave, could perhaps in earlier times have wrought irreparable damage to the potential crop. The fact that it did not is a tribute to the advances that have been made in treating the vines against cryptogamic diseases such as mildew, oidium and black rot. Overall it was wet; 100 mm of rain was the average precipitation against a 30-year mean of 61 mm. However, it was also hotter than normal, and the temperature did not cool off markedly during the night. The result was an almost tropical humidity, and the onset of disease was swift and potentially devastating. It was necessary to spray the vineyards ever more repeatedly, particularly as hardly had one finished one treatment when it would rain again and the chemicals would be washed off the vines.

The first two-thirds of September were warm, but reasonably dry, and the vineyards, having survived the August onslaught, were able to progress evenly towards maturity. Nevertheless, though having flowered and reached *véraison* (the date when the grape starts changing colour towards black), at almost exactly the average date for the last 30 years, the ripeness on 20th September was still behind that of 1981, let alone 1982. However, by this time the weather had improved even more. For the rest of the month and well into October – even into November –

there was a long succession of hot, sunny days. For the first time in living memory some proprietors brought in their crop without a single interruption of rain. Though it was hot, it was not as hot as 1982, where the thermometer reached 32°C during the first couple of days of the harvest. In 1983 it was more like 27°C, but continued at this level for longer. Moreover, the previous year's difficulties had encouraged many to install cooling systems. All the major properties were now well equipped to control the temperatures of fermentation. The harvest, which had begun on 16th September for the dry whites, began on the 23rd for Merlot and 1st October for Cabernet. The dry weather had shriveled such grapes as were rotten, and so it was quite easy to eliminate these at the time of cropping, or in the case of whole bunches, to reject them entirely.

THE SIZE OF THE HARVEST

Overall the 1983 red AC crop was 3.20 million hectolitres as opposed to 3.50 in 1982 and 3.32 in 1979. The six vintages between 1985 and 1990 would all be larger – indeed the average over this period was an incredible 4.28 *million* hectolitres. And as all these, bar the 1987s, are at the very least 'good quality', it seems that the Bordelais are capable of producing wines of note on a regular basis even at the very upper end of the yields permitted. This says much for the advances made in the last couple of decades in research into viticulture, vinification and *élevage* techniques.

Three things in particular stand out. Clonal selection has created strains of the local grapes –which can be very productive without a concomitant decrease in concentration and extract. Helped by advice from the University of Bordeaux and the local meteorological office, growers know when and what they have to spray to counteract attacks of mildew and oidium and depredations by insects and other pests. They can, if they can afford it, spray the vines to produce grapes which are more resistant to rot. Finally, the more profitable economic position today enjoyed by growers and owners from *bourgeois* level upwards together with increasing rivalry and competition among these proprietors has led to a position where all – not just the more perfectionistic – are almost duty bound to make a most careful and unselfish selection of only the best vats in the creation of their *grand vin*, and can afford to do so.

Mere statistics of the total harvest, however, tell little about the specific yield among the *crus classés* and their equivalents. The total Bordeaux *rouge* average yield may have quadrupled since the 1950s and doubled since 1970 but it would be ridiculous to assume the same advance among the top growths. Much of the overall increase is due to a change at generic level from making white wine to red. Some is due to a larger area being under vine. Moreover, the famous estates all prune hard and some may even deliberately reduce a large potential harvest by knocking out the odd bunch per vine during August just before the *véraison*. The time to do this, if it is to achieve the desired effect, is crucial.

THE WINES

When I first arrived to taste the 1983s in the spring of 1984, I found wines which surprised me by their fruit, and it is this ripeness which is the key to the vintage. Those who harvested late had made the best wine because the grapes were more mature. Those who benefited most from the glorious autumn made wines which were rich and full, balanced and concentrated, complex and long on the palate. In the case of these wines, 1983 is a classic vintage; better than 1981 and 1979; fuller and richer than 1978 and probably as elegant; less overpowered with tannin and more endowed with fruit than 1975. Nineteen eighty-two is stupendous, but the wines are atypical; yet the best 1983s had great finesse; possibly equally good, if quite different.

What was also apparent was that, geographically as well as hierarchically, 1983 was a variable year. First, as with so many recent vintages, the further up the scale from *petit château* to *cru classé* the better, proportionally, as well as the more consistent, the wines became. Second, while the Médoc was certainly very successful, the wines of Saint-Émilion were less so, in many cases not as interesting as the 1981s. Yet in the Médoc, particularly in the commune of

Margaux, there were wines which were clearly superior to the 1982s, and elsewhere many châteaux had produced a quality which closely approached that of the previous year, though the wines were quite different in style.

A return to Bordeaux in April 1985 confirmed the quality of the 1983s. This was truly, I felt, a classic vintage. There were many excellent wines, and overall, in the Médoc and Graves, I had the impression of more consistency than the 1982 vintage, though as I thought in 1984, the Saint-Émilions and Pomerols were less regular.

The vintage is uninspired (with one exception) in Saint Estèphe, fine in the Graves, very good in Saint-Julien and Pauillac, and at its most inconsistent (as always) in the commune of Margaux. It is *supposed* to be at its best in Margaux. Sadly it isn't: Palmer and Château Margaux itself are very good indeed. Too many of the rest are uninspiring, and have not lived up to their earlier promise. By and large in Saint-Émilion and Pomerol, though there are a few potentially delicious bottles, the wines are ripe, attractive and stylish, but essentially they lack a little weight and depth, sometimes additionally a little length. Overall, despite the inconsistency, it is probably the best of the 1979, 1981, 1983 series. There is still plenty of life in the top Médocs and Graves.

PRICES

Here is a comparison of prices per dozen of the top wines for the 1979, 1981, 1982 and 1983 vintages as of autumn 2003.

FIRST GROWTHS	1982	1979	1981	1983
LAFITE	£3400 ($6120)	£960 ($1720)	£980 ($1760)	£1280 ($2300)
LATOUR	£4000 ($7200)	£1000 ($1800)	£900 ($1620)	£1120 ($2010)
MARGAUX	£3000 ($5400)	£1380 ($2480)	£1200 ($2160)	£2200 ($3960)
MOUTON-ROTHSCHILD	£3400 ($6120)	£900 ($1620)	£850 ($1530)	£1200 ($2160)
HAUT-BRION	£2000 ($3600)	£1000 ($1800)	£820 ($1470)	£960 ($1720)
CHEVAL BLANC	£4500 ($8100)	£900 ($1620)	£1000 ($1800)	£1980 ($3560)
AUSONE	£2400 ($4320)	£800 ($1440)	£700 ($1260)	£980 ($1760)
PÉTRUS	£15,000 ($27,000)	£3000 ($5400)	£3000 ($5400)	£3600 ($6480)
SUPER-SECONDS				
CANON	£920 ($1650)	£320 ($570)	£240 ($430)	£400 ($720)
FIGEAC	£1100 ($1980)	£420 ($750)	£320 ($570)	£620 ($1110)
MAGDELAINE	£700 ($1260)	£265 ($470)	£240 ($430)	£350 ($630)
LAFLEUR	£8750 ($15,750)	£5000 ($9000)	£1000 ($1800)	£3000 ($5400)
VIEUX CHÂTEAU CERTAN	£880 ($1580)	£300 ($540)	£330 ($590)	£480 ($860)
TROTANOY	£2450 ($4410)	£500 ($900)	£440 ($790)	£520 ($930)
DOMAINE DE CHEVALIER	*£320 ($570)	£300 ($540)	£340 ($610)	£480 ($860)
LA MISSION HAUT-BRION	£2750 ($4950)	£780 ($1400)	£600 ($1080)	£720 ($1290)
PALMER	£850 ($1530)	£500 ($900)	£360 ($640)	£1320 ($2370)
DUCRU-BEAUCAILLOU	£1100 ($1980)	£400 ($720)	£420 ($750)	£480 ($860)
GRUAUD-LAROSE	£1080 ($1940)	£350 ($900)	£360 ($640)	£480 ($860)
LEOVILLE-LAS-CASES	£1800 ($3240)	£500 ($630)	£450 ($810)	£540 ($970)
PICHON-LALANDE	£1920 ($3450)	£600 ($1080)	£550 ($990)	£820 ($1470)
LYNCH-BAGES	£1280 ($2300)	£360 ($640)	£390 ($700)	£675 ($1210)
GRAND-PUY-LACOSTE	£800 ($1440)	£290 ($520)	£200 ($360)	£385 ($690)
CALON SÉGUR	£750 ($1350)	£200 ($360)	£240 ($430)	£360 ($640)
COS D'ESTOURNEL	£1270 ($2280)	£460 ($820)	£400 ($720)	£450 ($810)
MONTROSE	£700 ($1260)	£260 ($460)	£250 ($450)	£385 ($690)

* suspect bottles

From this it can be seen that the vintages of 1979, 1981 and 1983 offer some real bargains compared to 1982. Domaine de Chevalier 1983 is an obvious example. So is Château Margaux 1979. Both 1979 and 1981 Haut-Brion and Palmer 1981 and 1979 should be noted and all three vintages of Ducru-Beaucaillou and Grand-Puy-Lacoste snapped up. The message is that you can still thoroughly enjoy fine mature red Bordeaux for under £50 a bottle.

THE TASTING

The following wines were sampled in New Hampshire in October 2001 at a tasting organised by Jack and Thelma Hewitt to compare 1983, 1981 and 1979.

WHITE GRAVES

DOMAINE DE CHEVALIER

NOW–2007	17.5

Fragrant nose. Just a hint of oak. Crisp and peachy/appley. Still very youthful. Now it shows plenty of fruit. Not a bit hard, as it was 10 years ago. Vibrant. Long. Elegant. Lovely.

CHÂTEAU HAUT-BRION

NOW–2007	16.5

Not a lot on the nose, but underneath there is good fruit and concentration. Ripe, stylish and restrained on the palate. Very elegant. Lots of depth. Just a bit richer than Domaine de Chevalier. Still very minerally. I find the Domaine de Chevalier has more interest: more depth as it evolved. But this is very good plus.

CHÂTEAU LAVILLE HAUT-BRION

DRINK SOON	16.0

Rich, fat nose. Buttery, with just a hint of built-in sulphur. Different in character to both Haut-Brion and Domaine de Chevalier. Richer and fatter but less concentration, less depth and grip. Very good but not great.

SAINT-ÉMILION

CHÂTEAU AUSONE

DRINK UP	14.0

Medium-full, mature colour. Soft and aromatic. A touch of age on the nose Pleasant, evolved Merlot flavour but no grip, depth nor great class. One-dimensional.

CHÂTEAU CANON

DRINK SOON	17.0

Medium-full, vigorous colour. Round, fat, rich, spicy-mocha nose. Fullish on the palate. Quite chunky. More Merlot than I would have expected. Good grip. Plenty of life. A little ungainly but sweet at the end. A great success for a Libournais 1983.

CHÂTEAU CHEVAL BLANC

DRINK SOON	16.0

Fullish, mature colour. Fresh, sweet and aromatic on the nose. Much more depth and vigour than the Ausone. Medium to medium-full body. Not a lot of class. Some depth and vigour but now fading. Never that special.

CHÂTEAU FIGEAC

DRINK SOON	14.5

Medium-full, fully mature colour. Fruity nose but a little weak and attenuated. Better on the attack, but the follow-through is a little astringent. Decent fruit underneath. Was 16+/20. Now 14.5.

CHÂTEAU MAGDELAINE

DRINK SOON	14.0

Fullish, mature colour. Surprising fresh nose. Good fruit but a curious character. Medium-full body. Sweet-spicy flavours. Good grip. Plenty of vigour. But not exactly very elegant. Astringent finish. It lacks class.

POMEROL

CHÂTEAU LAFLEUR

DRINK UP	12.5

Medium-full, mature colour. Rather a dried-out, attenuated nose. Not very exciting on the palate either. Sweet but attenuated and astringent. Barely drinkable.

CHÂTEAU PÉTRUS

NOW–2008   17.0

Fine, full, mature colour. Lighter nose than the 1981, but fresh. No great dimension though. Medium to medium-full body. Aromatic, rich and opulent. But it lacks the class of the top Médocs. Better than the 1981 but not as good as the 1979. Very good indeed though.

CHÂTEAU TROTANOY

DRINK SOON   17.0

Full, vigorous, mature colour. Plump, ripe, ample nose. Slightly looser-knit than the 1981, but close. Medium to medium-full body. Soft and attractive. Slightly spicy. No great concentration or complexity but very good indeed.

VIEUX CHÂTEAU CERTAN

NOW–2008   17.5

Full, vigorous, mature colour. Rich, chocolaty elements on the nose. Rather less grip than the 1981 though. Medium-full body. Good freshness on the attack. Good acidity for a Libournais. Classy and full of fruit. Fine.

GRAVES

DOMAINE DE CHEVALIER

NOW–2012+   18.5

Fullish colour. Barely mature. Very fine nose. Lovely complex fruit. Rich depth and class. Still very youthful. Fullish, classy and very composed. Splendidly complex and harmonious. This is very lovely. Great elegance and subtlety, typical of Chevalier. Very fine.

CHÂTEAU HAUT-BRION

NOW–2015   19.0

Fine, full, mature colour. Fine nose but not the depth of Château Margaux. Better than Lafite. Very lovely, balanced fruit. Fullish body. Long and very intense at the end.

CHÂTEAU LA MISSION HAUT-BRION

NOW–2013+   18.5

Very full, barely mature colour. Lovely, profound nose. Still fresh and still vigorous and concentrated. Fullish body. There is a little tannin here. Quite a powerful, masculine example. I find it a touch hot. Much bigger than 1981, but not as graceful. Much bigger than the 1979 too. It needs to mellow at the end. Fine but not great.

MARGAUX

CHÂTEAU MARGAUX

NOW–2020+   20.0

Very fine colour. Still youthful. Amazingly lovely nose. Marvellously concentrated, poised fruit. Fullish body. Still some tannin. Still very young. The fruit is very raspberry-like and still very fresh. Very long. Brilliant!

CHÂTEAU PALMER

NOW–2012   19.5

Very fine colour. Still youthful. Profound and glorious on the nose. Marvellous depth. Fullish body. Everything splendidly in place. This is a great wine. Splendidly concentrated, classy fruit. Excellent grip. Just a little green at the end. A little astringent. Perhaps not the greatest bottle but very, very impressive. Will still improve perhaps. A second bottle was well-nigh perfect.

SAINT-JULIEN

CHÂTEAU DUCRU-BEAUCAILLOU

NOW–2007   18.5

Fine, fresh, full colour. Aromatic nose. More evolved and less classy than Léoville-Las-Cases. Better on the palate. Lots of lovely fruit if without the grip of the 1979. Fat and creamy. Easy to drink. Good length. Very fine.

CHÂTEAU GRUAUD-LAROSE

NOW–2012+   17.5

Very full, immature colour. Some Brettanomyces on the nose but not as much as in the 1981. Full body. Good grip. Good Cabernet fruit. Plenty of substance here and very good vigour. But will it ever get really velvety? Better with food. Fine.

CHÂTEAU LÉOVILLE-LAS-CASES

NOW–2020	19.0

Fine fresh, full colour. Very lovely nose. Ample, balanced, concentrated and full of fruit. Fullish body. Only just ready. Rich and very well balanced. Rather more austere than Ducru-Beaucaillou or the Léoville-Las-Cases 1981 and 1979. A very lovely, classy example. Very fine plus. Will keep for ages.

PAUILLAC

CHÂTEAU GRAND-PUY-LACOSTE

NOW–2013	18.0

Fine colour. Still youthful. Very full. Very lovely nose. Ripe Cabernet fruit. Well balanced. Quite rich. Good structure and very good grip. This will still improve. Profound finish. Lovely. Fine plus. Firmer than Ducru-Beaucaillou but not as fine.

CHÂTEAU LYNCH-BAGES

DRINK SOON	16.0

Full colour. Vigorous looking. Plump nose. A little brettanomyces. This is looser-knit than Grand-Puy-Lacoste and Léoville-Las-Cases and less interesting than the 1979 and 1981. Sweet but not as classy. Decent balance. But no better than very good.

CHÂTEAU LAFITE-ROTHSCHILD

NOW–2015	18.5

Fullish, mature colour. Full, fragrant nose. Lovely raspberry-cassis fruit. Lots of class here. Full, profound, rich and lovely. Quite tannic. Not quite the grip of the 1979 but a splendid wine. Much better than Latour and Mouton-Rothschild. Very fine.

CHÂTEAU LATOUR

NOW–2010	16.0

Fullish, mature colour. This has a good, ripe, accessible nose, but it lacks the grip, vigour and class of Lafite. On the palate fullish body and a little tannin. Quite sweet. Decent length but not the class and complexity of Château Lafite. Very good merely.

CHÂTEAU MOUTON-ROTHSCHILD

NOW–2010	15.5

Full, mature colour. Fullish nose. Good fruit. Quite concentrated. Yet a bit ungainly. Fullish body. No lack of structure but a lack of grip and personality. Decent acidity. Quite long. But curiously anonymous. Pleasant and very drinkable though.

CHÂTEAU PICHON-LONGUEVILLE, COMTESSE DE LALANDE

NOW–2010	18.5

Fine colour. Still youthful. Like many 1983s, though succulent and fresh, the wine on the nose lacks a little zip and there is a suggestion of attenuation. This is not as fresh as the 1979, but it is bigger than the 1981. On the palate ripe, succulent, opulent and very generous. Perfectly enough acidity. Round and complex. Very classy. Lovely. It will still last well.

SAINT-ESTÈPHE

CHÂTEAU CALON-SÉGUR

DRINK SOON	14.5

Medium-full colour. Fully mature. Plump nose. Earthy but good acidity. On the palate a bit chunky. No grace or elegance but good acidity. It will get astringent. Quite good plus.

CHÂTEAU COS D'ESTOURNEL

NOW–2009	17.5

Good fullish, vigorous colour. Ample nose. Rich. Roast chestnutty. Lots of depth and quality here. Quite the best of the 1979, 1981, 1983 Saint-Estèphe flight. Good class. Good concentration. Good depth. Long. Fine. It will last well.

CHÂTEAU MONTROSE

DRINK SOON	14.5

Good medium-full colour. No age. Better than I had expected. Medium weight on the nose. A little one-dimensional but fresh and fruity. Similarly quite pleasant on the palate. It still has a positive finish. Quite good plus.

1982 VINTAGE

SIZE OF THE CROP:	4,550,284 HECTOLITRES.
VINTAGE RATING:	18.5 (RED WINES).
	15.0 (DRY WHITE WINES).
	14.0 (SWEET WINES).

With a total of 1,041,919 hectolitres the white wine harvest formed 22.09 per cent of the total crop. The yield was 58.6 hl/ha, 25 per cent up on the 1970 crop, a record at the time. Much of this increase, however, was at generic level. In Margaux the average yield was only 45.7 hl/ha, and in Pauillac it was 46.3 hl/ha. Moreover, not only were the top châteaux green-harvesting for perhaps the first time, the selection process, dividing the crop into *grand* and *deuxième vin*, was rather more severe than hitherto. At Château Pichon-Longueville, Comtesse de Lalande, less wine was declared as *grand vin* than in 1981.

Much has already been written about the 1982 claret vintage. From the outset its quality was extolled from the rooftops with a consistency of hyperbole which almost suggested hysteria. 'Not the vintage of the century but the vintage of the millennium,' suggested one well-known château proprietor. 'The best wine that this or that estate has ever made ....' It went on and on. Demand, seduced by this relentless enthusiasm, was unprecedented. Greed, fuelled by the demand, was rife. Prices opened high, and as the campaign proceeded they climbed higher still. They have remained on an upswing. Though the 1983s and 1985s were to open higher still, it is the 1982s which fetch much the superior levels whenever they now appear at auction. The 1982s, it seems, were born with a silver *tastevin* in their mouth and whatever might or might not happen to other vintages the 1982s were always likely to be blue chip, a hard currency which would withstand temporary buffets in the marketplace as prices for other years rose and fell.

Tasting a vintage when it is in its infancy is always (if the vintage has any merit) an exhilarating experience. Buzzing around from château to château in late April renewing old acquaintances with owners and *régisseurs*, hearing the gossip and listening to what they have to say about their wines and those of others is one of the delights of a wine buyer's life. Opinions are sought, wines are assessed, judgements are formed, orders are placed. On, perhaps, the basis of a couple of sips in a cold cellar at 9.30 on an April morning, confirmed occasionally by a sample which might be a little tired on a *négociant's* tasting room a day or so later are important decisions made. It is a precarious business. Those with more experience, more flair and an open mind will make a more consistent and successful job of it than others. If we are honest, however, even the best of us must admit that we are considerably aided by the fact that the better properties are themselves remarkably consistent in producing good wine.

Wine is an evolving, daily-changing liquid, particularly in its infancy. It is chemically and bacterially vulnerable. It undergoes a number of treatments and is subject to a series of routines during its *élevage*, the period while it is in cask or vat, and will alter considerably as a result, as well as go through periods when it does not show at its best. Moreover, samples taken from cask have a notoriously short shelf-life. A judgement, and one that is specific enough to attempt to separate the relative qualities of one château from another by a mark which might be as tight as a per centage point must, while the wine is still in cask, be a risky business.

Personally I am convinced that as well as risky, and possibly unfair, it is dangerous to attempt this sort of assessment before the wine has completed its *élevage* and is safely in bottle. The bottling process is fundamentally upsetting to the wine as is the transportation thereafter, so I prefer to postpone making a specific judgement on a particular wine of a claret vintage until three years after the harvest, a year to a year and a half after the bottling.

THE WEATHER

After an unusually mild winter the spring weather prior to the flowering was excellent. April was extremely dry, with less than 6 mm of rain being recorded, and it was mild and sunny. There was no frost, and after the good but by no means prolific harvest of 1981 the vines were healthy and not exhausted, able to throw but an encouragingly, even alarmingly prolific, *sortie* of buds.

The fine weather continued. There was a mini heatwave at the beginning of June which, as Peter Sichel remarked in his annual vintage report the following year, 'provided ideal conditions for a successful flowering as well as setting an early date or the vintage'. Not only did the flowering begin early – about a week earlier than average – but it was uniform and the fruit setting was accomplished very quickly, thus gaining a further week on the norm and ensuring that all the berries would arrive at the fruition at the same time. The large amount of flowers developing into embryonic grape bunches meant that a very large vintage was likely to occur.

July was very hot and for the most part dry. Some much-needed rain began at the end of the month and continued on and off during a rather dull August, thus helping the grapes to ripen further and develop towards maturity at an earlier date than normal. By the 20th of the month, the fruit had finished changing colour from green to black and was already showing a promising amount of sugar if not concentration. The skies cleared at the end of the month and ushered in three weeks of exceptional heat. It was this which made the vintage. Temperatures averaged 29 °C and the thermometer rose even higher – up to 40°C – between 3rd and 5th September and during the 10 days after 8th September. In the great heat the grapes galloped not only towards maturity, but towards concentration. This had four important effects.

1. The exceptionally large harvest could ripen fully. As Peter Sichel later pointed out, without this heat there was no way this amount of grapes would have ripened.

2. There was a danger that the grapes would become too ripe before they could be picked and that the resultant acidity would be too weak. This problem was exacerbated by the enormous size of the harvest. Paradoxically the heat was such that, in fact, the acidity rose during the final few days before the harvest started. The exceptional weather had the effect of concentrating everything – sugar, extract and acidity – as the water evaporated in the berries.

3. During the first week of the harvest the grapes were so warm when they reached the vinification vats that there was a danger of fermentation taking place at too high a temperature. However, many châteaux had made a considerable investment in modern equipment and cooling facilities during the previous decade and were well geared to cope with any excesses.

4. As in 1979, there was a danger that the sheer volume of grapes arriving daily in the *cuverie* would prove an embarrassment: that each batch of new wine would not be able to have enough time to macerate on its skins before the vat was required for a subsequent lot. Again, in retrospect, the lesson had been well learnt. Few wines appear to have this sort of weakness and fragility; though rumours circulated that there had been difficulties at Château Margaux, where some of the crop had to be decanted from the vats to finish its malo-lactic fermentation in cask.

The harvest began on 14th September and was in full swing in both the Médoc and Saint-Émilion two days later – one of the earliest on record and a full fortnight before the norm. The Merlots were picked first, super-concentrated by the great heat, and frequently arriving in the winery with potential alcohol of 13° and above. Château Pétrus was harvested on the afternoons of 17th and 18th September, and the vats produced alcohol levels of 13.2° to 13.6°, unprecedentedly high. For the first time since 1975 it was quite unnecessary to chaptalise.

After 20th September, the heat was less intense, the Merlots were safely in the vats and collection of the Cabernets commenced. At Château Pichon-Longueville, Comtesse de Lalande, and elsewhere the number of pickers was doubled in order to bring in the grapes in optimum condition. At Château Mouton-Rothschild they are said to have completed the picking in seven days, an amazing feat for a 75-hectare vineyard. The Petit Verdot, which ripens last of all, and often not completely, was for once fully ripe. Those properties in the Médoc with a high proportion of these grapes are not often rewarded for their perseverance with this variety! There was a weekend of rain during the weekend 25th/26th September, but this does not appear to have caused any damage.

At the beginning of October, however, there was an abrupt change in the weather. Heavy rain began on the 2nd and hardly ceased throughout the month. Thankfully as a result of the early start to the vintage, the vast majority of the harvest both of red and dry white wine had been collected. Sadly, the Sauternes châteaux, most of whom had only collected about a third of their crop, were left to suffer.

Only a few of the earlier-harvested Sauternes vats showed any botrytis. For the dry wines the early September weather was excessive. The majority lacked freshness and bite.

The Character of the Wine in Cask

The first thing that was remarkable about the 1982s was their colour. Young red wine is always dark and purple, and with modern techniques in the vineyard enabling growers to keep the fruit healthy, we have become used to excellent colour, at least initially, in young Bordeaux, year in, year out. The colour of the 1982s, however, was truly remarkable. Never had I seen wines with such solidity, such density of colour – a deep, almost black purple, right to the rim of the glass.

The next wonder of the 1982s was the amount of ripe, concentrated fruit. The grapes had been picked with the highest level of natural sugar since 1947. The resulting wines had an almost porty richness, which though enveloped by an equal amount of tannin, was immediately evident on nose and palate. The vintage was big, dense and full, backward and high in alcohol, giving the wines a power which had not been seen in Bordeaux since 1959. On top of this, the tannins were round and sweet, not bitter and hard like, for instance, the young 1975s. The effect was a fat, perfumed, creamy character, particularly in the top Pomerols and Saint-Émilions. The best wines of the Haut-Médoc, with a higher proportion of Cabernet, were naturally more austere, yet had an enormous depth and richness of flavour and fruit. At the top levels the wines were balanced and marvellously long on the palate. Though for long keeping, they were, even at the outset, enormously seductive – if in a mind-bludgeoning way!

A fine vintage is always exciting to taste when young. Yet I found the 1982s, because of their sheer size, tannin and concentration, an exhausting experience to evaluate. At the end of each day, having tasted perhaps 50 or more wines, my tongue was black and my taste-buds saturated. Yet, despite the power and body of the wines, I did not consider that this would be a vintage which would need *that* long before it was mature. True, the wines were dense, solid and tannic, but they were neither hard nor harsh. As I wrote at the time, the wines were close-textured, but the strands were soft and ripe, silk rather than steel. As Peter Sichel was to point out a year later, commenting on the 1982s after a year in cask, the normally temperate climate of Bordeaux produces wines with a complexity of flavours (which I add is combined with the predominantly masculine backbone of the claret grapes); after an unusually warm maturation season like 1982 this normal austere complexity was replaced by a greater generosity and fullness of flavour.

THE WINES NOW

I made my first comprehensive survey of the 1982s in bottle in the autumn of 1985. I have since participated in a number of important tastings of the vintage. How do the 1982s show today?

Tasting the top 1982s 20 years on in 2002 confirmed that this is indeed a great vintage. The depth of concentrated fruit, the intensity, the class and the vigour are all exceptional. There are a number of wines: the Médoc First Growths, Léoville-Las-Cases and Pétrus, for instance, which are still not yet at their peak, even 20 years on. Most of the rest, gloriously full of fruit, have many years ahead of them. Wine such as Canon, Magdelaine, Pavie and Figeac, from Saint-Émilion; Vieux Château Certan, Latour-à-Pomerol, Certan de May, La Conseillante and Trotanoy from Pomerol; La Mission Haut-Brion, Palmer, Ducru-Beaucaillou, Gruaud-Larose, Grand-Puy-Lacoste and Cos d'Estournel, not to mention the totally seductive Pichon-Longueville, Comtesse de Lalande, the supremely elegant Haut-Brion, and the voluptuous Cheval Blanc, though *à point* today, will still be alive and vigorous in 2020.

There are other wines which, though in many ways interesting, are better made today than they were in 1982. These include L'Évangile, a little herbaceous in 1982, Lafleur, a little too over-macerated then, and at a lesser level Pape-Clément, Talbot and Montrose. One can include in this category many a Saint-Émilion and Pomerol such as L'Église-Clinet, Clos L'Église, Angélus, Troplong-Mondot and Le Tertre-Roteboeuf.

Where the 1982 vintage did not live up to its early hype is also in this part of the world. Somehow it was assumed that every single Saint-Émilion and Pomerol was splendid. Sadly – and this was evident just 10 years on – many were rich but lacked the correct backbone and grip. They have long dried out. Sadly, too, many of the lesser classed growths of the Médoc and the Graves were never better than a grudging 'quite good' and have never since shown that they were unjustly regarded at the outset. Boring wines: should have done better.

But the best are brilliant. It is a glorious vintage.

PRICES – THEN AND NOW

Opening prices of the properties which were first to announce reflected the interest in the vintage. It would have been short-sighted to expect them to be at 1981 levels, despite the size of the vintage, yet bearing in mind the quality and French inflation, the increases were not unreasonable. Château La Lagune was one of the first big names to come out, and sold on the export market for 39.75 Francs or thereabouts, compared with 35.20 Francs for the 1981. Labégorce-Zédé at 24.55 Francs (22.75 Francs), Angludet at 33.00 Francs (29.00 Francs), Grand-Puy-Lacoste at 48.96 Francs (40.70 Francs) and Léoville-Poyferré 51.30 Francs (37.95 Francs) were equally reasonable. Overall, those who had put their wine on the market by the end of April could be seen to have raised prices by 20–25 per cent over 1981 levels – not the least excessive.

The precedent for more savage rises for the more fashionable wines was set by the First Growths. The 1981 price had been 100–125 Francs (with the exception of Latour); the 1982s came out at 170 Francs. Coupled with higher than normal profit margins imposed by the Bordeaux *négoce* it meant that the cost to the overseas buyer was nearly doubled, at around 225 Francs.

As far as the Super-Seconds were concerned greed over prices was complicated by feelings of jealousy and personal rivalry. Madame de Lencquesaing at Château Pichon-Longueville-Lalande was convinced that her wine was as good as Château Ducru-Beaucaillou and Château Léoville-Las-Cases and was determined that she should sell her wine for as high a price as they. MM. Borie and Delon, meanwhile, were equally determined that she shouldn't. This resulted in an absurd (and to the overseas buyer intensely irritating) game of 'waiting the other out'; neither side wishing to commit themselves before the other. The result as the market demand heated up was very high prices indeed; Pichon coming out at 67 Francs and Ducru and Las-Cases at 70 Francs, and all three finding willing buyers at 100 Francs and above. Again the increase over 1981 was almost twofold.

Today the First Growths sell for between £2350 ($4230) for Haut-Brion and £4500 ($8100) for Latour, Pichon-Longueville, Comtesse de Lalande and Léoville-Las-Cases exceed £2000 ($3600), Cos d'Estournel, Lynch-Bages, Ducru-Beaucaillou and Gruaud-Larose are £1000 ($1800) and more, as are many of their peers in the Libournais. This is 50–100 per cent more than the equivalent 1990s. Only the 1961s are more expensive.

Are They Worth It?

Nineteen eighty-two is not 1961, but then neither is 1986 (in the northern Médoc), 1990, 1998 (in Saint-Émilion and Pomerol), 2000 or any other good year you can care to mention. But it is still a splendid vintage, only dull in Margaux and in the lesser echelons of the Graves *premiers crus*. What it is not is classic, which is why purists (or classicists) such as myself tend to prefer Mouton-Rothschild 1986 if offered a direct comparison, or Haut-Brion in 1989, or Latour in 1990. Yet the 1982 versions of these wines are nevertheless sumptuous. There are even a few which will still get better.

We must also not forget that wine is better made today. I remember asking Christian Moueix, when tasting his 1989 for the first time whether he considered it better than his 1982. His answer was that if he had made 1982 with the increased perfectionism with which he had made the 1989, there would be no question that the 1982 would be superior. This is even truer today. So whether 1982 is 'the best', and worth the premium is a question of taste. You will see my preferences, as far as the top wines are concerned, in the notes below.

The Tasting

I attended two comprehensive 1982 red wine tastings in 2002. At the first, in Chicago in January, hosted by Stephen Kaplan, 40 wines were offered. At the second, organized by Bipin Desai in Los Angeles at the end of April, no fewer than 94 different châteaux were available for tasting. While not all the wines, by any means, were in tip-top condition, it was nevertheless a major event. My heartfelt thanks, gentlemen!

Moreover, at the Bipin Desai event, held over three days, prior to the main tasting, over meals cooked by Josiah Citron of Mélisse and Wolfgang Puck of Spago, we had a separate opportunity to compare, blind, the 1982 with two, sometimes three other vintages of the same property. Sometimes the vintages were older: 1959 or 1961; sometimes they were very much younger: 1996 and 1998. Desai had chosen the competition wisely. It was only rarely that the 1982s were preferred.

The Comparative Blind Tasting

Saint-Émilion & Pomerol

Château Ausone, 1998

2006–2026	18.0

Fullish, immature colour. Rich, ripe and oaky on the nose. Fullish body. Some tannin. A slight lack of real fat and grip and not enough class for great. But there is depth here and a good, positive, long finish. Fine plus. It needs keeping.

Château Ausone, 1990

NOW–2012	17.5

Fullish colour; now mature. Ripe and quite fresh Libournais nose. Decent harmony. Medium structure. Medium-full body. Now ready. Ripe, succulent, balanced and classy. Good long, lingering finish. Delicate but fine.

Château Ausone, 1983

DRINK SOON	16.0

Light to medium colour. Fully mature. Despite the colour, a bit more fruit on the nose than the 1982. But not particularly inspiring. Some ripeness and structure on the palate. Some personality and class. Decent follow-through. But not First Growth concentration. Very good at best.

CHÂTEAU AUSONE, 1982

DRINK UP   13.5

Medium, mature colour. A little dry and pinched on the nose. No great depth. Neither grip nor succulence. Rather fruitless on the palate. Little distinction. Light. Very disappointing for the vintage. I have had better bottles.

CHÂTEAU CHEVAL BLANC, 1998

2010–2035   20.0

Very full, immature colour. Full, rich, concentrated nose. Lots of lovely wine here. But a long way from being ready. As it evolved, marvellous roasted coffee, toast and toffee elements. Rich, ripe, full-bodied and flamboyantly lovely. Very ripe tannins. Very good grip. Long. A really splendid wine, rather better than Ausone. Multi-dimensional. Splendid.

CHÂTEAU CHEVAL BLANC, 1990

DRINK SOON   16.0

Medium full, just about mature colour. Ripe, lush, succulent nose. Quite evolved. There is a strange sweetness in here. Medium-full body. The tannins are fully ripe. A slight suggestion of attenuation. Decent grip. But a lack of real distinction and class. Very good. But I have had better bottles.

CHÂTEAU CHEVAL BLANC, 1985

NOW–2015   18.5

Fullish, mature colour. Aromatic, subtle, high-toned nose. Very seductive. Some evolution now. Medium to medium-full body. Quite loose-knit. Very ripe and lush, but a slight lack of real concentration and zip. Very, very ripe, almost sweet, fruit. Very good acidity. Ripe tannins. Disarmingly gorgeous. Very fine.

CHÂTEAU CHEVAL BLANC, 1982

NOW–2015+   19.0

Medium-full, mature colour. Firm, rich nose. Still youthful. Good depth and vigour here. Medium-full body. The tannins are just about absorbed. Rich and fat. Good acidity. Ripe and vigorous. Plenty of depth. Lush and lovely. Very fine plus.

CHÂTEAU L'ÉVANGILE, 1998

2008–2028   18.5

Full, immature colour. Marvellously rich nose. Balanced, cool, classy and full of succulent fruit. Excellent on the palate. Full body. Excellent tannin. Very fine grip. Marvellously concentrated, quality fruit. Very harmonious. Real depth and dimension here. Fine plus.

CHÂTEAU L'ÉVANGILE, 1985

NOW–2010   17.5

Fullish, mature colour. Rich, full, mature nose. The tannins are just a little hard and evident, a characteristic of L'Évangile. Fullish body. A little muscular. But very good grip and plenty of fruit. Succulent. Very well balanced. Slightly clumsy. Better with food. Fine.

CHÂTEAU L'ÉVANGILE, 1982

NOW–2015   17.5

Full, just about mature colour. High-toned. Individual. Slightly grassy on the nose. It lacks a little charm. Fullish body. Riper on the palate than the nose would suggest. Good grip. Classy. Slightly austere but good distinction. Ripe and long on the finish. Fine.

CHÂTEAU L'ÉVANGILE, 1961

NOW–2020   19.0

Full, mature colour. Rich, mellow, lush and gently oaky. Excellent nose. This is most impressive. Marvellously fresh fruit. Excellent balance. Fullish body. Good tannins. Very good grip. Long and multi-dimensional. Very, very lovely on the finish. Marvellously preserved. A great 1961. Very fine plus.

Château Figeac, 1998

| 2006–2026 | 18.5 |

Fullish colour. A little development but still immature. Fullish on the nose. Some tannin evident. Good classy fruit underneath. A little oak. Potentially very fine. Fullish body. Excellent grip. Aristocratic and harmonious. Profound and lovely. Splendid dimension and intensity here. Very lovely.

Château Figeac, 1990

| NOW–2010+ | (18.0) |

Medium-full, matue colour. A little noticeable volatile acidity here. Cool, composed and classy. A little tainted (TCA) but fullish-bodied, rich and well balanced nevertheless. Good vigour. Good grip. A clean bottle should be rather fine.

Château Figeac, 1982

| NOW–2010 | 17.5 |

Medium-full colour. Now mature. As always with Figeac, just a touch hard and green on the nose as well as, in this case, being quite rich and profound. Good grip. Good vigour. Fullish body. Now just about ready. The tannins are absorbed. This is fine.

Château Figeac, 1970

| NOW–2008 | 18.0 |

Medium colour. Fully mature. Round, rich, ripe and lush. Mature but with plenty of vigour. Lots of depth. Lovely. Medium-full body. Well matured. Good richness and depth. Lush and lovely, but cool and balanced. Very long on the palate. This is fine plus.

Château Lafleur, 1989

| NOW–2019 | 17.5 |

Fullish colour. Only a suggestion of maturity. Slightly adolescent on the nose. A bit tough and tannic. Full-bodied and tannic on the palate. Yet it can be enjoyed. This will always be a wine of structure. But the flavours are rich and it finishes long. Fine.

Château Lafleur, 1982

| NOW–2015 | 17.5 |

Fullish, mature colour. Splendid nose. Lush and succulent. Mature and exotic. Quite structured, even muscular. Full-bodied, very rich and almost over-ripe and pruney. Good grip. Quite tough but fine nevertheless.

Château Lafleur, 1975

| NOW–2009 | 17.5 |

Fullish, mature colour. Cool, balanced and classy on the nose. Distinctive. Fullish body. Quite substantial. Quite tough. On the palate not quite as rich as the 1982, or as big, but balanced and even fresh and elegant at the end. Long finish. Fine.

Château Lafleur, 1961

| NOW–2010+ | 18.0 |

Fullish, mature colour. Rich, full-bodied, ripe and sweet on the palate. Not as exotic as 1982. A full wine. Rich and well-balanced. Cool and more elegant than most Lafleur because there is good acidity. Long. Very lovely. Fine plus.

Château Pétrus, 1989

| NOW–2025 | 19.5 |

Full colour. Not yet fully mature. Very fine fruit on the nose. Full bodied, tannic but not monolithic. Very concentrated and rich. Very fine grip. Full and quite masculine. Still a touch of astringency about it, which would disappear if the wine were decanted. Very fine intensity at the end. Long finish. Very fine indeed.

Château Pétrus, 1982

| NOW–2025 | 18.0 |

Full, well-matured colour. This is now beginning to get accessible. It is ripe and lush and quite concentrated. Yet a little earthy/dead leafy. On the palate full-bodied and full of fruit. A little residual tannin. Good energy underneath. Fat and ripe. Lovely finish. Certainly fine plus. Will still develop.

CHÂTEAU PÉTRUS, 1975

NOW–2025   17.5

Fullish, mature colour. Still quite firm on the nose. Still adolescent. Not the greatest grip and richness underneath. Medium-full body. Ripe and rich on the follow-through. Quite structured still. Still some tannin. Decent grip. But it lacks a little zip. Fine rather than great.

CHÂTEAU PÉTRUS, 1961

NOW–2025   18.5

Fullish colour. Mature – just about. Still quite closed on the nose. Full and rich, of course, but as yet a little monolithic. High quality though. On the palate this is more open: full-bodied, rich and concentrated. Lots of depth. Not too tannic or tough at the end. Good tannins and good grip. Very fine but not great.

CHÂTEAU TROTANOY, 1998

2006–2026   18.5

Fullish, immature colour. Very fine nose. Lots of lovely, lush Merlot fruit. Balanced and concentrated. Fullish body. Very good tannins. Good grip. Distinctive. Potentially very concentrated and very seductive. Excellent fruit. Super.

CHÂTEAU TROTANOY, 1982

NOW–2010   18.0

Fullish, mature colour. This is rich and classy on the nose. Lush, ripe and full of fruit. Fresh. *À point*. Fullish body. Lovely fruit on the palate. Not as rich or as concentrated as 1961 but balanced, profound and rich enough nevertheless. Good energy. Fine plus.

CHÂTEAU TROTANOY, 1961

NOW–2015   19.0

Full, mature colour. Full, rich, opulent nose. Slightly more evolved than the 1982. Fullish body. Aromatic. The tannins are well absorbed. Good grip. So ripe it is almost sweet. Long and velvety. Fully ready. A really marvellous 1961. Holding up well. Very fine plus.

MARGAUX

CHÂTEAU PALMER, 1983

DRINK SOON   15.0

Fullish, mature colour. Quite fresh. But mellow and delicate on the nose. Sturdy for Palmer and slightly astringent on the palate. It lacks class. A bit vegetal. Adolescent. Not a great 1983. But I have had many much better bottles (see page 580).

CHÂTEAU PALMER, 1982

NOW–2010   18.5

Fullish, mature colour. Quite firm on the nose still. Very good depth. Fresh, fullish bodied, soft and plump. Good vigour. Not quite the class of 1961 but very nearly. Very fine.

CHÂTEAU PALMER, 1966

NOW–2006   18.5

Medium-full, mature colour. Soft, mature, mellow nose. Very lovely. Medium-full body. Delicate. Subtle. This is very, very lovely. Long, ethereal and lingering. Very, very classy. Soft and very delicious. Very fine.

CHÂTEAU PALMER, 1961

NOW–2010   19.0

Medium-full colour. Just about ready. Mellow, rich and lovely. A very lovely, classy, round, ripe Palmer. Medium-full body. Fully ready. Very lovely. Very fine indeed.

HAUT-MÉDOC

CHÂTEAU CALON-SÉGUR, 1996

NOW–2015   15.5

Youthful colour. Some tannin but slightly rigid on the nose. Earthy underneath. It lacks a bit of real style. Meaty. Good acidity and decently ripe. But good plus at best.

CHÂTEAU CALON-SÉGUR, 1982

NOW–2010+   16.5

Vigorous but mature colour. Mature on the nose too. Ripe and spicy. Rich and fullish bodied. This hasn't the greatest class but it has good fruit and concentration. Nicely fat too. Good generosity on the finish too. Very good plus.

CHÂTEAU CALON-SÉGUR, 1961

DRINK SOON   16.0

Fully mature if not old colour. Quite aged. A little rustic and dead-leafy. Yet good classy fruit at the same time. Not astringent. Indeed quite fresh. Very good.

CHÂTEAU LA LAGUNE, 1985

NOW–2008   16.5

Fullish colour. Still immature. Medium-full bodied, rich, mature on the palate. Sweet and oaky. Good grip. This is very generous and most attractive. Easy to drink. Plenty of life. Very good plus.

CHÂTEAU LA LAGUNE, 1982

NOW–2010+   15.0

Medium-full colour. Just a little mature. Slightly reduced on the nose. Medium to medium-full body. Ripe but a little astringent. A little dry. It lacks a little zip. Yet the finish is good. Good. But slightly disappointing.

CHÂTEAU LA LAGUNE, 1961

NOW–2008   16.0

Medium, well mature colour. Gently ripe and oaky. Soft and mellow. Medium body. Round, fat and succulent. This is still holding up well. But now needs drinking soon. Ripe, rich and generous. Good vigour. Very good.

SAINT-JULIEN

CHÂTEAU DUCRU-BEAUCAILLOU, 1996

2006–2025   18.0

Fullish, immature colour. Developed, mellow nose. Good vigour and concentration. Lots of fruit. Still quite young on the palate. Fullish body. Just a little tannin. Good energy and dimension. And class too. Long. It could still do with a year or two. Fine plus.

CHÂTEAU DUCRU-BEAUCAILLOU, 1995

2006–2020   16.0

Medium-full, immature colour. A bit closed on the nose but fine and classy. Fullish bodied on the palate. Quite a lot of tannin. This has decent depth and fruit but it doesn't altogether sing. It still needs time. A slight lack of zip and generosity. Slightly dull. Very good at best. I have had better bottles.

CHÂTEAU DUCRU-BEAUCAILLOU, 1982

NOW–2005   15.0

Fullish, just about mature colour. It lacks a little vigour at the end on the nose. Something a bit attenuated lurking. Medium body. Now mellow. A slight lack of freshness and class. And richness. Disappointing for what it is. I have had better bottles.

CHÂTEAU GRUAUD-LAROSE, 1990

2007–2030   17.0

Fullish, just about mature colour. Slightly lumpy as always for Gruaud-Larose at this stage on the nose. Better on the palate. Rich fruit. Some tannin. Slightly earthy. But mellowing into something of class and depth. Very good now. Very good indeed perhaps in 5 years time.

CHÂTEAU GRUAUD-LAROSE, 1982

NOW–2020   17.5

Fullish, mature colour. Good vigorous, substantial wine on the nose. Ripe and rich. Just coming into its own. Full body and plenty of depth. Lovely vigour. Lots of dimension at the end. It will still improve. Fine.

CHÂTEAU GRUAUD-LAROSE, 1961

NOW–2010+   17.5

Medium-full, mature colour. Lovely mature but vigorous nose. A lovely mature wine, but a little astringency left in the middle. Full bodied and rich at the end. Vigorous and long. Lots of vigour. Fine.

CHÂTEAU LÉOVILLE-BARTON, 1996

2015–2045   17.5

Big, backward colour. Big and tannic on the nose. Very backward. Lots of lovely fruit. But a wine in its infancy. Excellent grip. Potentially fine.

CHÂTEAU LÉOVILLE-BARTON, 1985

NOW–2015   16.0

Good fullish, just about mature colour. Slightly rigid. But ripe and just about mature on the palate. This has good vigour and depth. Not the greatest class. But very good. I have had better bottles.

Château Léoville-Barton, 1982

NOW–2015   16.0

Fullish colour. Barely mature. Still a bit adolescent. It is a little awkward. Good fruit and very good grip though. It needs time. Slightly ungainly today but very good. Not fine, though.

Château Léoville-Barton, 1961

DRINK SOON   16.0

Medium to medium-full, well-matured colour. Mellow and classy. But now quite old. It is very good but it lacks the complexity and class it might once have had. Very good.

Château Léoville-Las-Cases, 1996

2010–2035   18.0

Fine, vigorous, immature colour. Youthful, very classy nose. Slightly closed. But very lovely. Full body. The tannins are well absorbed. Rich, concentrated and fragrant. Lovely fruit. Lots of dimension. Excellent grip. This is very fine.

Château Léoville-Las-Cases, 1986

NOW–2030   17.0

Good colour. Still youthful. Soft, rich, fat and meaty. Still a little ungainly. Full body. A little adolescent and a little astringent. But potentially very good indeed.

Château Léoville-Las-Cases, 1982

NOW–2009   17.0

Good colour. Now a hint of maturity. Rich, round and accessible on the nose. Fullish body. Ripe and juicy. Just a little rigid. The wine is better made today but this is still very good indeed.

Pauillac

Château Lynch-Bages, 1990

2007–2027   18.0

Very full, concentrated, youthful colour. Still tight on the nose. Even a little minty. Medium-full body. Some tannin. Not a blockbuster. Classier than 1989. Good grip. Nicely austere. But nicely abundant, complex fruit underneath. Fine plus.

Château Lynch-Bages, 1989

2008–2027   17.0

Full, immature colour. Still a bit tight and tannic on the nose. Full on the palate. Quite ripe and balanced, but not the greatest of complexity or class. Very good indeed at best.

Château Lynch-Bages, 1985

NOW–2020   16.0

Full, vigorous, mature colour. Lovely fruit on the nose. Rich, opulent and succulent. On the palate though a slight lack of grip and depth. Medium to medium-full body. It lacks intensity and real class. Very good at best.

Château Lynch-Bages, 1982

NOW–2020   18.5

Fullish colour. Still quite youthful colour. Ample, rich, ripe nose. This is a big wine but quite accessible. Fullish body. Good structure. Good grip. Long, complex and classy. This is vigorous but now ready. Very fine.

Château Pichon-Longueville, 1990

NOW–2025   17.5

Full colour. Just about mature. Rich, slightly smoky nose. The tannins show a bit but the wine is full-bodied, complex and opulent. This is not a wine of the greatest class though. The tannins are a little unsophisticated if now more or less absorbed. Fullish body. Ripe. Quite powerful. Spicy. Fine but not great. Ready but will still improve.

Château Pichon-Longueville, 1989

2007–2027   17.5

Fullish, immature colour. Quite a solid, chunky, youthful wine on the nose. Good depth. Good freshness. Good fruit. Fullish body. Good tannin. Good grip and well-balanced. Positive. Fine but not great.

Château Pichon-Longueville, 1982

NOW—2012	16.0

Medium-full, well-matured colour. Fully mature, nicely rich, round nose. Ample if not very classy. Medium-full body. Ripe. Lush if with a little astringency. Rich but the tannins are not very elegant. Very good but not great. It should keep well though.

Château Pichon-Longueville, Comtesse de Lalande, 1996

2008—2028	18.5

Fullish colour. No sign of maturity. Lush, succulent, oaky nose. This is very Pichon-Lalande. Still youthful. Fullish body. Very rich. Very lush. Good tannins. Very good grip. Still needs time. But already seductive. Stylish and harmonious. Long. Very fine.

Château Pichon-Longueville, Comtesse de Lalande, 1989

NOW—2015	18.5

Medium-full, mature colour. Fully mature nose. Even just a suggestion of reduction. Fullish body. Well matured. Ripe and concentrated. Lush and succulent. This has excellent grip. Intense and very stylish. Very fine.

Château Pichon-Longueville, Comtesse de Lalande, 1982

NOW—2020	18.5

Fullish, vigorous, mature colour. Cool, slightly austere, slightly herbaceous nose. Nicely ripe, if without *that* much intensity on the palate. Medium-full body. Ready. Quite succulent, fresh and balanced. Good length and class. Very fine in its context.

Saint-Estèphe

Château Cos d'Estournel, 1990

DRINK SOON	14.5

Full colour with a touch of maturity. Quite a firm nose. It has gone into its shell a bit. On the palate a little dry and astringent. Medium-full body. It lacks a bit of zip. Just about ready. Still youthful. But I don't think it will make very good old bones. This is a bit of a disappointment. Quite good plus.

Château Cos d'Estournel, 1989

NOW—2018+	18.0

Full colour. Still youthful. Rich, round, generous nose. Lots of depth. Still young. Full body. Some tannin. A very rich, concentrated, meaty wine. This has lots of rich fruit, plenty of dimension and is long and lovely. Unexpectedly vigorous. A nice surprise. Very fine.

Château Cos d'Estournel, 1988

SEE NOTE	-

Medium-full colour. Still quite youthful. Somewhat corked. Difficult to really taste but it seems to have good class and harmony.

Château Cos d'Estournel, 1982

NOW—2010	17.5

Medium, mature colour. Mellow, rich, fat, voluptuous nose. Fullish body. Good grip. Plenty of depth and concentration. This has depth and good vigour. Nicely spicy. Long. Very typically Cos d'Estournel. Fine. Fully ready but plenty of life still.

Château Montrose, 1990

NOW—2018	15.0

Full, immature colour. Yet rich and aromatic on the nose. Round. Fullish body. A bit of tannin. Very spicy. Not a lot of elegance. But quite substantial. Quite rich. Good.

Château Montrose, 1982

NOW—2010+	17.0

Full, evolved colour. High-toned nose. Classy. Slightly corky. Medium-full body. Very fresh. Slightly corked but there is class here. Full and ample at the end. Very good acidity. Fine.

Château Montrose, 1961

NOW—2010	16.0

Medium-full, mature colour. Decent but a little four-square on the nose. Better on the palate. A little astringent. But ripe and rich. An earthier wine than 1982. Very good.

First Growths (and La Mission)

Château Haut-Brion, 1989
NOW–2025	20.0

Full colour, mature but still vigorous. Fresh, classy, ripe mulberry fruit on the nose. Fullish body. Just a little tannin. This has heaps of class and concentration. Impeccable balance and real dimension. Very, very stylish. Will still improve. Marvellous finish. Splendid.

Château Haut-Brion, 1982
NOW–2010	18.0

Fullish, mature colour. Delicate but very elegant nose. No great power though. Medium-full body. This is fully ready. A fine but not a great wine. Rich and plump. Still plenty of vigour. Long, complex and classy. Fine plus.

Château Haut-Brion, 1961
NOW–2010+	19.0

Full, rich, mature nose. Rich, classy and concentrated nose. Full, open, rich and harmonious. Concentrated, classy and vigorous on the follow-through. Fully *à point*. Very lovely. Very fine.

Château Haut-Brion, 1959
DRINK SOON	18.5

Quite an aged colour. Fullish originally. Well matured on the nose. Stylish though. Good depth. Medium-full body. Quite fresh. Balanced and subtle. Fine. Still intense. But gently fading now. Drink soon.

Château Lafite, 1996
2010–2040	19.0

Full, immature colour. Closed-in, earthy nose. Nutty and profound. But years away from maturity. Fullish body. Quite tannic. Backward. Rich. Vigorous. Potentially very fine but patience is required.

Château Lafite, 1985
NOW–2025	19.0

Medium-full colour. Now mature. Just about mature on the nose. Soft, succulent and fresh. Textbook classy fruit. Very ripe.

Very harmonious. On the palate this is medium-full. There is still a little tannin to be absorbed. Lovely multi-dimensional, harmonious fruit. Long. Very lovely. Still needs a year or two. Very fine.

Château Lafite, 1982
NOW–2020	19.0

Fullish, mature colour. Lovely soft, classy nose. Very elegant. Very pure. Now ready. Excellent fruit. Very complex. Very subtle. Fullish body. Mellow. Very good grip. This is fresh but now mature. It will get even better as it gets more decadent. Very lovely.

Château Lafite, 1959
NOW–2010	19.0

Full and fully mature colour. Rich, full, aromatic, well mature but elegant nose. All the complexity of maturity here. Very classy. Fullish bodied and soft. Very classy. Lovely fruit. An exotic wine now. Still bags of life. Very fine plus.

Château Latour, 1990
NOW–2035	20.0

Full, rich, immature colour. Very lovely, aristocratic nose. Accessible but still very, very vigorous. Just about perfect combination of fruit, depth, grip and structure. Not quite ready yet. Fullish body. Still some tannin. Not a real heavy weight but a wine of real breed and impeccable poise.

Château Latour, 1982
NOW–2020+	20.0

Full, just about mature colour. Rich, ripe and concentrated on the nose. Still very vigorous. But this is complex, profound and very classy. This is really splendid. Full-bodied. Mature. Very good tannins. Very, very profound, concentrated fruit. A powerful wine and a great one. Marvellous potential still.

Château Latour, 1970
NOW–2020	18.0

Full, still quite vigorous colour. Lovely nose. Youthful. Still a little tight perhaps.

Medium-full body. Still some tannin. Good acidity. Classy but it needs time. Still a touch lean. It lacks a little personality. Not the greatest of Latours or indeed vintage but fine plus.

Château Latour, 1961

NOW–2010+   18.0

Fullish, just about mature colour. Good rich nose, but not the greatest of depth or breed. Now fully ready. Better on the palate. Fullish body. Good tannins. Good grip. Ripe, even soft. Good vigour underneath. Plenty of fruit. But not the class of for better than fine plus. I have had better bottles.

Château Margaux, 1996

2010–2030   18.5

Full, immature colour. Ripe and ample but not very positive on the nose. The usual big, tannic, solid, immature Margaux nose we get today. This is going to need time. Meaty, concentrated, but at the moment a bit ungainly. But all the ingredients are here. Very fine.

Château Margaux, 1990

NOW–2020+   18.5

Fullish, just about mature colour. Delicious, fragrant nose with the structure of today's wines. This is mellow, excellently balanced and with real interest. Long and lovely. Very fine.

Château Margaux, 1983

NOW–2025   17.5

Fullish, mature colour. Classy nose. Fragrant. On the palate a little astringent at first. But ripe, rich and attractively fruity on the follow-through. Plenty of life ahead of it. Fine. I have had better bottles.

Château Margaux, 1982

NOW–2023   18.5

Full, just about mature colour. Ripe, rich and fragrant on the nose. Fullish body. Fragrant and lovely on the palate. Lots of depth. This has a great deal of elegance. Very fine. Just about ready.

Château La Mission Haut-Brion, 1989

NOW–2015+   19.0

Fullish, mature, vigorous colour. Ripe, round, rich and opulent on the nose. Very lovely. Just about ready. Full on the palate. Lovely rich, succulent fruit. Very good structure, depth and grip. Still bags of life. This is excellent. Very, very classy. Very fine plus.

Château La Mission Haut-Brion, 1982

NOW–2015+   18.5

Fullish, mature, vigorous colour. Rich, vigorous, virile yet mature nose. Full bodied and rich on the palate. Still some structure here. The tannins now absorbed but the wine is very vigorous. Lots of dimension. This is balanced, complex and classy. Very fine.

Château La Mission Haut-Brion, 1975

NOW–2012   19.0

Fullish, mature, vigorous colour. Aromatic, spicy nose. Just a hint of astringency? Ripe, full-bodied and still vigorous on the palate. The tannins are just a little dry. But the wine is rich and opulent. Best with food. Classy and long. Very fine plus.

Château La Mission Haut-Brion, 1961

NOW–2009   17.5

Fullish, mature, vigorous colour. Rich and full, but sturdy and quite structured. Fullish body. Good tannins. Ripe and vigorous. But essentially quite a masculine wine. Good energy. Not the greatest class of fruit though. Merely fine.

Château Mouton-Rothschild, 1990

NOW–2010+   16.0

Medium-full colour. Just about ready. Not a lot of either volume or depth here on the nose. Strangely unconcentrated and dull for a First Growth. Medium to medium-full body on the palate. Fresh and fruit and balanced but not very rich or concentrated. Puzzling. No better than very good.

Château Mouton-Rothschild, 1986

NOW–2040   20.0

Vigorous colour. Full and rich. Still
immature. Rich, full bodied, youthful and
cedary-oaky on the palate. Very Mouton.
Very lush and succulent and lovely. Just
about ready on the palate. Though still some
tannin to resolve. Fresh fruit. Very good grip.
Very fine class. Long. Excellent. Very
impressive. A wine of real energy. Bags of
life.

Château Mouton-Rothschild, 1982

2008–2040   19.5

Full, rich colour. A touch of brown at the
rim. But still very vigorous. On the nose the
tannins are a little predominant and a bit
hard at that. Better on the palate. Still
immature. Fullish body but very good depth
and class. Very good grip. Good tannins.
This has plenty of vigour underneath and
lovely fruit. This should be very fine indeed.
It needs time.

Château Mouton-Rothschild, 1959

NOW–2020   19.0

A big but old colour. Classy, full, opulent
and very cedar-Mouton on the nose. Fullish
weight. Mature, ripe and seductive. A big,
vigorous wine. Yet with no hard edges.
Velvety. Very good grip. Lovely. Will still
keep well. Not totally brilliant but very fine.

The Main Tasting

Saint-Émilion

Château Angélus

DRINK SOON   13.0

Lightish, evolved colour. Soft, ripe but
slightly weak nose. Light but fruity. Not
astringent. Just a little dilute. Not bad.

Château Ausone

NOW–2007   15.0

Medium colour. Now mature. This is a
better bottle than at the tasting above (see
page 610). Yet nevertheless a little faded on
the nose. Very Merlot. A lack of grip and
depth. On the palate quite sweet and quite
fresh. Good but a little one-dimensional: by
no means great.

Château Beauséjour-Bécot

NOW–2008   15.5

Medium-fullish colour. Fresh, plump, ripe
nose. No enormous structure but rich and
supple. Medium body. Ample. Fresh. Good
fruit. Positive finish. Good plus.

Château Beauséjour-Duffau-Lagarrosse

NOW–2010+   16.0

Fullish colour. Quite firm on the nose. Yet
good fruit underneath. A little residual
tannin. But good depth and class and grip. It
finishes well. This is very good.

Château Belair

DRINK SOON   14.0

Medium-fullish colour. Soft, quite evolved
nose. Seems to be very Merlot. Medium
body. No great grip or depth. A pretty wine
but a bit simple. Quite good.

Château Canon

NOW–2012+   16.5

Fullish, mature colour. Full, rich nose. Some
tannin. As always, you can see the structure.
Full body. Rich and vigorous. Not as
concentrated or as much flair as I have seen
elsewhere. But good fruit and vigour. It
finishes well. This is very good plus. Has
been fine.

Château Canon-La-Gaffelière

NOW–2007   14.5

Medium to medium-full colour. Good fruit.
Slightly muscular. Not the refinement of
today. Medium body. Quite fresh. Decent
fruit. It lacks a little personality but
reasonably fresh and stylish. Quite good plus.

Château Cheval Blanc

NOW–2020   19.5

Medium-full, rich colour. Just about mature. Rich, full, vigorous and concentrated on the nose. This has real depth and is really classy. Full body. Vigorous and very concentrated on the palate. Very lovely fruit. Real depth. Marvellous dimension. Very fine indeed.

Château Figeac

NOW–2015   18.0

Fullish colour. Very classy on the nose. Very Figeac too. Rich, vigorous and concentrated. Ripe and succulent. Fullish body. Good acidity. Great class. Composed, suave and understated. Fine plus.

Château Magdelaine

NOW–2012+   18.0

Fullish colour. Still youthful. Rich, full and succulent on the nose. High class. Good vigour. Fullish body. Lots of depth. Lovely fresh fruit. Balanced and classy. Long and complex. Delicious. Fine plus.

Château Monbousquet

DRINK SOON   14.0

Medium to medium-full colour. Soft, evolved Merlot nose. Ripe but a bit bland. Medium body. Fat and ripe but a little astringency lurks. No great depth but pleasant. Quite good.

Château Pavie

NOW–2012+   17.0

Surprisingly full colour. Rich, full, fat and succulent on the nose. Plenty of vigour and depth. This is fullish-bodied, ample, rich and ripe. Good plump wine. Generous and seductive. Plenty of vigour. Very good indeed.

Château Pavie-Decesse

NOW–2010   16.0

Good fullish colour. A little touch of the rustic but rich and ripe underneath. Medium-full body. Good fruit. Plump and ripe. Not as sophisticated as Pavie. But in the same mould. Very good.

Château Pavie-Macquin

SEE NOTE

Fullish, well-matured colour. Somewhat vegetal on the nose. One bottle was a bit better than the other but neither were specially high quality. Has it gone off?

Château Le Tertre-Roteboeuf

NOW–2009   14.0

Full colour. Still very youthful. Firm, rich, backward but concentrated on the nose. Not the greatest sophistication of tannins. A fullish-bodied, tannic wine. Plump and rich. Youthful on the palate. Slightly tough. But plenty of energy, if no great style. It will always be a bit too muscular. It lacks real class. Quite good.

Château Troplong-Mondot

DRINK SOON   12.5

Full, vigorous nose. Rather tough and unsophisticated. Lumpy. But quite substantial. Fullish body. Good acidity. One can see the terroir but the wine is flawed.

Pomerol

Château Le Bon Pasteur

NOW–2012+   16.5

Fullish, mature colour. Rich, ripe, fresh colour. Lots of depth and vigour. Fullish body. Rich, fat, ripe and luscious. Just a touch of oak. Long and stylish. Plenty of vigour. Very good plus.

Château Certan-Guiraud

NOW–2009   15.5

Medium-full colour. Quite fresh-looking. Decent nose but no real flair. Medium to medium-full body. Nice fresh, plump fruit on the palate. More interesting on the palate than on the nose. Positive finish. Good plus.

Château Certan de May

NOW–2007   15.0

Fullish, mature colour. A little tough on the nose. A bit evolved on the palate. Rich but a touch astringent at the end. Some fruit, but not enough grip. Yet there was still decent fruit as it evolved in the glass. Good.

Château Clinet

NOW–2012+   16.5

Medium-full colour. Well matured. Rich, fat and slighly spicy on the nose. Good rich fruit. Fullish body. Vigorous. Plenty of depth here. This is abundant and complex. Very good plus.

Clos L'Église

DRINK SOON   13.0

Fullish, mature colour. Rich but quite evolved, essentially Merlot, nose. Medium body. A little faded. This is drying up. It lacks grip. Only fair.

Château La Conseillante

NOW–2020+   19.0

Full colour. Marvellous nose. Really perfumed and classy. Aromatic and flowery; violets. Fullish body. Velvety and concentrated. Not a bit tough. Just silky-smooth and very, very concentrated. Really brilliant. Marvellous. Still very, very fresh.

Château L'Église-Clinet

NOW–2010   16.6

Very full colour. Full and rich on the nose but slightly tough. Good depth. Good intensity. Good concentration. Not quite the class of La Conseillante but no lack of profundity or fruit. Very good plus.

Château L'Évangile

NOW–2015   17.5

Full colour. Quite full, even slightly muscular on the nose. Ripe and profound. Fullish body. Rich. Not too ungainly. Substantial, it has to be said. But lovely concentrated fruit. Classy. Very good depth. Vigorous. Long. Fine.

Château La Fleur de Gay

NOW–2009   16.0

Medium-full, mature colour. Soft nose. Ripe and rich if not very complex. A very Merlot wine. Rich and sweet and balanced, if not the greatest of complexity and clas. Very good.

Château Gazin

NOW–2007   15.0

Medium-full colour. Not a lot of class. But quite ripe and vigorous on the nose. Now soft on the palate. A touch one-dimensional. Quite evolved. It lacks a litel concentration and zip. Good finish though. Good.

Château Le Gay

NOW–2008   14.0

Full colour. Tough and chunky on the nose. But, as it is 1982, richer than usual. Quite tannic on the palate. Medium-full body. As usua a bit chunky on the palate too. But there is good concentrated fruit here. Better with food. Quite good.

Château La Grave-Trigant-de-Boisset

DRINK SOON   17.0

Fullish, vigorous colour. Fully mature Merlot nose. It is losing a little of its grip. It is less vigorous than the colour would indicate. Ripe and sweet. Ample and fullish-bodied. Still very enjoyable. No astringency or weakness. Very good indeed.

Château Lafleur

NOW–2015   17.5

Full, concentrated colour. Rich nose. Quite Merlot, surprisingly. It is fat but does it lack a little zip? Fresher on the palate. Rich and concentrated. Still a little tough. But good vigour. A little too muscular. Yet it is fine.

Château Lafleur-Pétrus

NOW–2012+   18.0

Fullish, mature colour. Lovely, rich, concentrated nose. Fine fruit. Elegant and stylish. Fullish-bodied, rich, 'old viney', cedary and very lovely. This has depth, class and vigour. Fine plus.

Château Latour-à-Pomerol

NOW–2012+   17.5

Medium-full, mature colour. Fine nose. Fresh fruit. Good depth and class if not quite the elegance of Lafleur-Pétrus. On the palate it shows medium to medium body and splendid freshness and elegance. A cool wine. Lovely finish. Composed and fine.

CHÂTEAU PETIT-VILLAGE

NOW–2007   15.0

Medium-full, well-matured colour. A little tough on the nose. Not a lot of fruit. Decent on the palate. But fully ready and no great sophistication. Medium-full body. Ripe. Good.

CHÂTEAU PÉTRUS

NOW–2025   18.0

Medium-full, well-matured colour. Still quite tough on the nose. Rich and concentrated. Fat and muscular. Quite dense yet very concentrated fruit. Full-bodied and substantial. Still some tannin. This is still youthful. Rich and concentrated. Very lovely. Perhaps it will be better still after a few years. Fine plus.

CHÂTEAU LE PIN

NOW–2015   18.5

Medium-full, well matured colour. Rich, ripe, plump and exotic. Almost jammy on the nose. Oaky, rich and quite seductive. Surprisingly good acidity. This is disarmingly delicious. Very long. Very lovely. Very fine.

CHÂTEAU TROTANOY

NOW–2015   18.5

Medium-full, well-matured colour. Splendidly sumptuous on the nose. Ample and fruity. Concentrated and lovely. Full bodied, lush, ripe and succulent. Good grip. Plenty of depth. Still very vigorous despite the fact that it developed early. Very lovely. Very fine.

VIEUX CHÂTEAU CERTAN

DRINK SOON   16.0

Medium to medium-full colour. Fully mature. Fat and rich and vigorous despite the colour and the nose. Plump and ripe. Quite evolved on the palate. Good fruit and decent grip on the attack. But a slight lack of concentration on the follow-through. Sweet. No astringency. But only very good. Another bottle had more energy and depth and was very good indeed (17.0/20 and Now–2011).

GRAVES

DOMAINE DE CHEVALIER

DRINK UP   13.0

Medium-full colour. Mature. This is a little thin and pinched on the nose. Similar on the palate. Medium body. Not much structure. Weak and a bit mean. Disappointing.

CHÂTEAU DE FIEUZAL

DRINK SOON   14.0

Fullish, well-matured colour. Medium-full, ample, spicy nose. Not the greatest of class but good ripe fruit. A lack of real breed but ripe and enjoyable. But only quite good.

CHÂTEAU HAUT-BAILLY

NOW–2008   15.5

Medium, fully mature colour. Soft, ripe, voluptuous, almost sweet nose. Very classy and very seductive. Medium-full body. Fully ready. Decent fruit. Some depth. But it lacks a little size and energy. Good plus.

CHÂTEAU HAUT-BRION

NOW–2015+   18.5

Quite an evolved colour. Medium-full, aromatic nose. Lovely fruit. Complex and classy. Mellow and ethereal. Medium-full body. Ripe, plump, stylish fruit. Very well balanced. Very complex. Very fine.

CHÂTEAU MALARTIC-LAGRAVIÈRE

NOW–2010   15.5

Medium-full, well matured colour. Slightly coarse tannins on the nose. Lumpy. But ripe and vigorous. A bit rough and ready but fresher and classier than Châteaux de Fieuzal and Pape-Clément. Not the greatest of class but good plus. A second bottle was fresher in colour and all the way through. It was meaty and succulent and had good class and good depth (16.5/20).

CHÂTEAU LA MISSION HAUT-BRION

NOW–2020   18.0

Full, rich, mature colour. Lovely nose. Plump, classy, vigorous, ripe nose. Medium-full body. Ripe and still with a bit of tannin. Round and complex. Fresh, vigorous and balanced. Plenty of life ahead of it. Fine plus.

Château Pape-Clément

PAST ITS BEST   12.0

Fullish, mature colour. Slightly unclean on the nose. The tannins are a bit coarse. This is pretty poor on the palate. Astringent. Rather fruitless and dried out. Never much good. Now old.

Château Smith-Haut-Lafitte

DRINK SOON   14.0

Medium-full, fully mature colour. Soft and a little sweet on the nose. But a little attenuated. Medium body. Little tannin. Quite sweet and ripe though. Decent freshness. Not much depth or class but pleasant and easy to drink. Quite good.

Château La Tour Haut-Brion

NOW–2015   18.0

Full, rich, very vigorous colour. Somewhat solid on the nose, but rich and full and backward. Plenty of depth. But still it seems it needs time. There is some lovely fruit and plenty of class. Less volume than the Pauillacs (Grand-Puy-Lacoste, Lynch-Bages) but elegant, long and balanced. Fine plus.

Haut-Médoc

Château Cantemerle

DRINK SOON   16.0

Fullish colour. Fully mature. Soft, aromatic, ripe nose. Very attractive but not that much class. Medium body. Mellow, ripe, elegant and even complex. Very good.

Château Cissac

DRINK SOON   14.0

Medium-full, mature colour. Aromatic nose. Medium-full body. Ripe but a little astringent. Decent grip. No great class. But mellow and decent.

Château La Lagune

NOW–2009   16.5

Medium-full colour. Fully evolved. Soft and mellow on the nose. Yet no lack of character. Medium body. Mellow on the palate. Rich, tannic and oaky. This is a lovely example. Very good fruit. Long. Very good plus.

Margaux

Château d'Angludet

NOW–2008   16.0

Fullish colour. A little dull on the nose but a very pleasant and quite classy, mellow Margaux on the palate. Ripe, balanced and long. Fullish-bodied but no hard edges. Quite intense at the end. Very good.

Château Boyd-Cantenac

DRINK SOON   13.5

Good colour. Sweet and ripe but slightly inky on the nose. Ripe but rather dense and tannic on the palate. A bit solid and a bit ungainly on the palate. Vigorous but a bit astringent. Only fair.

Château Brane-Cantenac

DRINK SOON   14.0

Medium-full, now mature, colour. Ripe. Slightly sweaty and *arrières côtes* side to it. It doesn't sing on the palate. Slightly weak. A slight lack of real drive. Drink soon.

Château Giscours

NOW–2008   15.5

Full colour. Ripe, spicy nose. Good depth. Decent structure. Quite rich and fullish and lush. Some tannin behind it. It lacks a little class but decent energy. Good plus.

Château Kirwan

NOW–2008   14.0

Good colour. Slightly lumpy and ungainly on the nose. A little astringent. Ripe, but a little common. Good vigour. Good freshness. Decent fruit. But a lack of elegance. Vigorous though. Quite good.

Château Malescot Saint-Exupéry

NOW–2008   14.0

Fullish colour. Slightly over-ripe and over-evolved on the nose. Full bodied and rich but a bit ungainly on the palate. Slightly solid. But not unduly tannic. Quite good.

Château Margaux

NOW–2019　　　　　　　　　　　19.5

Full colour. Little sign of maturity. Soft, ripe and complex. Fullish-bodied, ripe and multi-dimensional. I find this refined and very lovely. Ripe, rich and round. It finishes long and complex. Very classy. More vigour than Palmer. Very fine indeed.

Château Marquis de Terme

DRINK UP　　　　　　　　　　　12.0

Medium-full colour. Well-matured. A little sold on the nose. Rather tannic on the palate. A bit astringent at the end. Some fruit but rather coarse.

Château Palmer

NOW–2015　　　　　　　　　　　19.0

Medium-full, now mature, colour. Delicious, fragrant nose. This is very lovely. Complex, aromatic, pure and harmonious. Fullish body. Rich, ample and very classy. This is really super. This is better than their 1985.

Château Prieuré-Lichine

NOW–2009　　　　　　　　　　　15.0

Medium-full colour. Round, ripe and mellow if no great finesse on the nose. Medium body. No obvious tannin now. Ripe and balanced. Good grip. A very well-made wine with more class than I thought at first. Plenty of vigour. Good. But not great.

Château Rauzan-Ségla

DRINK SOON　　　　　　　　　　15.5

Medium-full colour. Ripe, mellow, even rich nose. No enormous structure but classy. It got a little attenuated as it evolved in the glass. Medium to medium-full weight. Ripe but it lacks a bit of grip. Slightly chunky at the end. Good plus at best.

Château du Tertre

NOW–2008　　　　　　　　　　　15.5

Medium to medium-full colour. Fully mature. Slightly four-square on the nose. Some tannin which is not quite sophisticated enough, nor yet absorbed. But not astringent. Just a little solid. Good depth and vigour. Good acidity. It lacked generosity at first but got mellower as it developed. Good plus.

Saint-Julien
Château Beychevelle

NOW–2010　　　　　　　　　　　16.0

Good full colour. Ample nose. Fruity but no real Super-Second depth or class. Fullish body. Quite rich, ripe and round. No hard structural elements. Still plenty of vigour. Only very good, as always.

Château Branaire-Ducru

DRINK SOON　　　　　　　　　　13.0

Medium-full, mature colour. Ripe and ample. But not much zip and not much class. Fullish body. Ripe. A little four-square. Some unresolved tannin. A bit astringent at the end. Dull.

Château Ducru-Beaucaillou

DRINK SOON　　　　　　　　　　18.5

Full colour. Little sign of maturity. Classy and fruity. Very good grip. Much better than in the blind tasting. Rich, fat and composed. Very lovely fruit. Long, harmonious and classy. Very fine.

Château Gloria

NOW–2008　　　　　　　　　　　16.5

Medium to medium-full, fully mature colour. Mellow, classy, very Saint-Julien nose. Medium-full body. Ripe and succulent. Stylish and elegant. This is really classy and harmonious. Lovely long finish. Very good plus.

Château Gruaud-Larose

NOW–2010　　　　　　　　　　　17.0

Very full colour. Still youthful. Tough and ready on the nose. Plenty of depth now. Backward, rich, astringent and a bit solid. Some tannin. Yet very good indeed.

CHÂTEAU LAGRANGE

DRINK SOON   12.0

Full, youthful colour. A rather muddy, astringent nose. Medium body. Rather fruitless on the palate. Decent freshness but no grip.

CHÂTEAU LANGOA-BARTON

DRINK SOON   13.5

Medium-full colour. Quite evolved. Elegant but slightly faded, especially after the Léoville-Poyferré. Not entirely clean perhaps. Medium body. Fading a little. Decent fruit but a lack of concentration and grip. Unexciting. A second bottle was fresher, richer and classier, and with much more vigour (16.0/20; Now-2007).

CHÂTEAU LÉOVILLE-BARTON

DRINK SOON   15.0

Medium colour. Now fully mature. On the nose a bit pedestrian compared with some. Medium to medium-full body. Ripe but it lacks concentration. A lack of acidity and a slight suggestion of attenuation. Good at best. A second bottle was much more alive: rich, concentrated and very lovely (17.0/20; Now-2010).

CHÂTEAU LÉOVILLE-LAS-CASES

NOW–2012   18.0

Fullish colour. Little sign of maturity. Rich, ripe, full and very concentrated on the nose. This is still youthful. Lots of depth. Rich, ripe and concentrated. Very good grip. A lovely example.

CHÂTEAU LÉOVILLE-POYFERRÉ

NOW–2009   16.5

Full colour. Full and rich on the nose. Still alive if without a great deal of class. Ample, rich, full-bodied and vigorous on the palate. Ripe, spicy fruit. Plenty of vigour. It lacks a little real refinement but very good plus.

CLOS DU MARQUIS

NOW–2008   16.0

Full colour. Still youthful. Plump Cabernet nose. Still vigorous. Full body. Still some tannin. A little solid. But better with food. Rich underneath. Lots of depth. Very good grip and energy. Long. Very good.

CHÂTEAU SAINT-PIERRE

NOW–2010   15.0

Full, vigorous colour. Aromatic nose. A bit dank and four-square on the palate. Yet plenty of rich fruit underneath. Fullish body. Slightly four-square on the follow-through. Yet rich and succulent. Good.

CHÂTEAU TALBOT

NOW–2009   15.5

Fullish colour. Full, rich and tough on the nose. Quite tannic and quite structured. As so often with Talbot in those days, there is rich fruit but a rather solid, even slightly herbaceous, tannic structure. The fruit is classy. The tannins are coarse. Good plus.

PAUILLAC

CARRUADES DE LAFITE

DRINK SOON   13.5

Good, fullish, vigoorous colour. Slightly tight on the nose. Not the quality of today's Carruades. Medium body. Decent fruit but not much depth or class. Some acidity. But it lacks depth and succulence. A little lean at the end. Only fair.

CHÂTEAU CLERC-MILON

NOW–2010+   16.0

Full, mature colour. Mellow but full, slightly spicy nose. Good depth and class. Fullish body. It has rather more balance and sophistication than Duhart-Milon. Ripe and rich. Good acidity. Still youthful. Very good.

CHÂTEAU DUHART-MILON

DRINK SOON   14.5

Medium-full, mature colour. Rich, full and classy on the nose. No lack of structure. Fullish body. A little solid. Good fruit, but not a lot of succulence or real class. A little astringent at the end. Quite good plus.

Château Les Forts de Latour

NOW–2015+   17.0

Good full, vigorous colour. Lovely full, vigorous, concentrated fruit. Ripe Cabernet. Lots of depth. Fullish body. Still a little tannin. Ripe and classy on the palate. Good depth. Well balanced. Good class and complexity. Plenty of life here. Very good indeed.

Château Grand-Puy-Ducasse

NOW–2010   15.0

Full colour. Ripe but slightly four-square on the nose. A bit dense. Medium-full body. Good fruit. Quite ample on the palate if a little rigid. Yet there is richness underneath. Good acidity too. Good but not great.

Château Grand-Puy-Lacoste

NOW–2015+   18.0

Fullish, vigorous, mature colour. Very lovely nose. Rich, full, mellow and classy. A full bodied, fragrant, harmonious wine. Very ripe. More classy and less exotic than Lynch-Bages. Bags of life ahead of it. Ripe tannins. Very good grip. Splendid fruit. Fine plus at the very least.

Château Haut-Batailley

NOW–2020   17.0

Full, mature colour. Vigorous, classy, fresh Cabernet Sauvignon nose. No lack of depth. Full-bodied, vigorous and classy on the palate. Very good fruit. Slightly austere. But well-made. Lots of energy. Lovely finish. Lots of life yet. This is very good indeed.

Château Lafite

NOW–2020+   19.5

Full, rich, mature colour. Fullish, rich and oaky on the nose. Very classy. Lots of depth. Fullish body. Vigorous. Very good grip. The tannins are fully absorbed. This is very fresh, positive and intense. Elegant fruit. Complex. Marvellously long finish. Lots of life. Very fine.

Château Latour

NOW–2025+   19.5

Very, very full, rich, mature colour. One bottle differed from the other. The cleaner wine was very pure, very rich and very classy. Full-bodied, tannic but not a bit of undue structure. On the palate though this is quite a full, rich, tannic wine still. This is very fine.

Château Lynch-Bages

NOW–2015+   18.0

Fullish, vigorous colour. Youthful, rich, concentrated and very lovely on the nose. Deep, rich Cabernet. More exotic and less classy than Grand-Puy-Lacoste. Fullish body. Ripe, rich and spicy. Very good tannins. Very good grip. This is very lovely. Fine plus.

Château Mouton-Baronne-Philippe

NOW–2009   15.5

Fullish, vigorous colour. Ample and rich on the nose. Softer than Clerc-Milon but good depth. Nicely succulent. Decent attack on the palate. Ripe and quite classy. A little astringent at the end. Medium-full body. Good plus.

Château Mouton-Rothschild

NOW–2025+   19.5

Very full, rich, mature colour. Still a little closed. Full, rich, fresh and profound on the nose. This is very, very lovely. Quite a backward example but one of real power. Fullish body. Still a little residual tannin. Good grip. Marvellously rich fruit. Long, vigorous and classy. Excellent.

Château Pichon-Longueville-Baron

NOW–2020   18.5

Fullish, vigorous colour. This is rich, clean and classy on the nose. This is a rather better bottle than last time out. Still very vigorous. Very clean and pure and concentrated. A true Pauillac. Very classy indeed. Fullish body. Still a little unresolved tannin. Very good grip. This is serious stuff. Unexpectedly long, complex and lovely. Bags of life ahead of it.

Château Pichon-Longueville, Comtesse De Lalande

NOW–2015+   18.5

Full, rich, mature colour. Ripe and rich and aromatic on the nose. One bottle a bit more evolved than the other. The firmer bottle is rich and full-bodied and with plenty of depth and quality. But not the sheer class of the First Growths. Very lovely ripe, rich fruit nevertheless. Long and complex and very fine.

Château Pontet-Canet

NOW–2008   15.5

Fullish, vigorous colour. Quite good nose. Slightly austere. A slight lack of fruit and dimension. But clean and Cabernet Sauvignon in flavour. Full body. Some tannin. A little too much. Some acidity but not quite enough. Not quite enough fruit and succulence. Good plus.

Saint-Estèphe

Château Calon-Ségur

DRINK SOON   16.0

Medium colour. Now fully mature. Ripe, ample nose. Good depth and very good class. Fresh and aromatic. Quite classy on the nose. It got a bit attenuated as it evolved. Ample fruit. No lack of class. Slight tannins stick out here. Very good.

Château Cos d'Estournel

NOW–2009   18.0

Fullish colour. Just a little sign of maturity. Ample and classy on the nose. Rich and succulent. Lots of depth. A great deal of class here. Full-bodied, rich, ripe and concentrated. This is very lovely. Fine plus.

Château Haut-Marbuzet

NOW–2010+   17.5

Medium-full, still youthful, colour. Lush, rich, succulent and sexy on the nose. Round and ripe. Very good tannins. This is full-bodied, rich and concentrated. Lush, succulent and delicious on the follow-through. Smooth and multi-dimensional. Fine.

Château Lafon-Rochet

DRINK SOON   12.5

Good, mellow colour. Quite rich on the nose. But a little rigid. Decent fruit and decent grip on the palate. But slightly one-dimensional. Unexciting.

Château Montrose

NOW–2010+   17.5

Fullish colour. Little sign of maturity. Vigorous, fullish and slightly tough on the nose. But riper and rounder on the palate. Fullish body. Very good grip. Rich, ripe and classy. This is fine.

Château Phélan-Ségur

DRINK SOON   13.5

Fullish colour. Light, quite evolved nose. Slightly attenuated and it lacks vigour. Medium body. A little astringent. Pleasantly fruity but now quite evolved. This is pretty but it needs drinking soon.

1981 VINTAGE

SIZE OF THE CROP:	3,296,476 HECTOLITRES.
VINTAGE RATING:	13.0 – 15.5 (RED WINES – SEE BELOW).
	13.0 (DRY WHITE WINES).
	13.0 (SWEET WINES).

Nineteen eighty-one was considered a small crop at the time. Yet it produced well in excess of 3 million hectolitres of *Appellation Contrôlée* wine. The white wine percentage was 23.3 and the overall yield 42.9 hl/ha.

Nineteen eighty-one was a good but not great vintage: – one for drinkers, especially in restaurants a few years later, for it matured quickly – rather than for collectors or speculators. The Saint-Émilions and Pomerols turned out very well, better than the 1983s. By and large the reverse is true in the Médoc and the Graves.

THE WEATHER

After a cold winter an early start to the vegetative cycle was precipitated by a very warm spell at the end of March. This encouraged the buds to develop about a fortnight earlier than normal, right at the beginning of April. The *sortie* for the Cabernet Sauvignon was particularly good, though for the Merlot and Cabernet Franc not quite as promising, with some potential bunches too far from the main trunk of the vines – it is best if the bunches are close to the sap. Later in April and throughout May the weather was indifferent, wet but not too cold, though there was some frost damage on the night of 27th/28th April.

June brought an improvement. The flowering commenced on the 4th (about average), took place in for the most part excellent conditions – there were two rather cold days which led to a bit of *coulure* – and was almost complete in a fortnight. This meant that the bunches would have an even ripeness, obviously a good thing.

Having given the wines the opportunity to flower satisfactorily, the sun disappeared at the end of the month. The last week of June and the whole of July was miserably cold, wet and sunless. August, though, was completely the reverse. It was extremely hot – not since 1929 had there been so many days with maximum temperatures over 25°C – and very dry, with a precipitation of only 27 mm. The fine weather continued into September, and the growers began to hold their breath: only a few more weeks and 1981 really could be something special.

Sadly, it did not last. Like 1973 and 1976, perhaps the elements felt they had to balance the heat and drought of a baking August and from the middle of September a fair bit of rain fell. Indeed, between 21st September and 15th October, a total of 118 mm was measured at the weather forecasting station in Bordeaux, making 1981 one of the wettest ends to the vintage since the Second World War. Most of this fell in the last 10 days of September.

However, all was not lost. First, unlike in 1976 and 1974, the downpours were not violent. For the most part the rain was gentle and in quantities within the vines' and the soil's capacity to absorb. Second, except for a four-day spell at the end of September, the rain was not continuous. The château proprietors were able to call a halt to the picking and wait until the skies had cleared and the fruit had had a chance to dry out. Third, there was no rot; the August heatwave had thickened the grape skins, and this was aided by the increasingly widespread use of sprays against *pourriture grise*, a technique which had begun to be in common use in the previous vintage. Lastly, by the time the rain commenced, the grapes were more or less ripe. Though rain will inevitably dilute the concentration of the fruit, provided that the fruit is ripe and the rain does not persist, allowing rot to set in, it can do no really serious harm. The rain might have dashed hopes of a great vintage, but it certainly did not spell disaster.

Contrary to the norm, the red wine vintage started first in the Médoc, on 27th September. Though the Pétrus vineyard was cleared in glorious weather in the last two afternoons of September, the Saint-Émilion/Pomerol harvest did not generally get under way until 3rd October. Most of the main properties had finished by 13th October.

Nineteen eighty-one is a vintage where those with sufficient power and resources to remain flexible could amply profit. Château Haut-Brion, handily placed near one of the main campuses of Bordeaux University, was able to double its harvesting team to 180 people and complete the picking in five days. At Latour, they were able to clear the vineyard in a week. Equally, on the smaller estates in Saint-Émilion and Pomerol, not only the Moueix family were able to send in their troops to attack the grapes at the optimum level.

It has been suggested by some that those who started the harvest promptly may have produced the best wine. This, I feel, is a moot point. Lafite did not start until 5th October, by which time Latour had finished, yet Latour currently shows as the best of the Pauillac *premiers crus*. But Léoville-Las-Cases, too, was a late starter, yet its wine is the best of the Saint-Juliens. It is all a question of perfectionism, and of being able to wait until the rain had ceased, for in principle the grapes picked at the end of the harvest were riper than those picked in September, and some grapes were only 9.5° to 10° in potential alcohol at the time picking commenced .

Even bunches picked in the rain can make good wine, if you know how to go about it. I was at Las-Cases when a lorry of grapes arrived. Michel Delon ordered the trailer to be raised, but without releasing the tail-flap. A torrent of water, vaguely tinged with pink, ran out. Not until the very last drop had stopped would he allow the contents of the lorry to be tipped into the reception vat.

THE SIZE OF THE HARVEST

By current standards, the 1981 harvest cannot be considered more than a small average. The total harvest in Bordeaux was four million hectolitres of AC wine, about the same as 1978 and 1975, as against over five million in 1979 – and even more to come in 1982 and 1983 and later on in the 1980s decade. Moreover, since the Second World War the white wine crop had only been smaller in 1977 and had never before represented such a small proportion of the vintage as a whole. However, the quantity of AC red wine produced was 2.5 million hectolitres, substantial by any past standards, for it had only been exceeded previously in the 1979 vintage. Partly this large amount of red wine resulted from an increased area under vine, partly, of course, it demonstrated the progressive switch by growers in the lesser areas of Bordeaux from white grapes to red. While in the 1950s white wine represented two-thirds of the total crop, in the 1980s it was only one-quarter.

While the crop was a quarter as much again as in 1980, the increase was not uniform across the Bordeaux region. The bulk of the rise came from the minor appellations. In the top Médoc properties the harvest was 15–20 per cent more than in 1980, but in equivalent châteaux in the Graves and Saint-Émilion it was 10 per cent less, and in Pomerol more or less the same. At Château Haut-Brion, for instance, while they declared 145 *tonneaux* in 1979 and 120 in 1980, the 1981 crop was less than 100 *tonneaux*.

THE WINES

Unlike 1979 from the quality point of view, 1981 is not an acid vintage. If the less successful of the 1979s can be criticised for having a certain unripe, green background, the mediocre 1981s are merely empty, low in body and substance, and a little short. Most wines, however, are ripe and healthy with a good natural sugar, particularly in the Merlots, but because of the rain, the natural acidity is low, even for those grapes harvested at the beginning, and only the best wines had the substance and real character and length on the palate which made them bottles to keep until this century.

However, at classed growth level, there is plenty of 'best'. Nineteen eighty-one is a vintage like 1978 and 1979 in the sense that there is a wide variation in quality – proportionately wider than prices would indicate – between the hierarchy of classed growths and the *petits châteaux*, but unlike them in that at the top levels the vintage seems more consistent. Among the classed growths of the Haut-Médoc and their equivalents elsewhere in the Bordeaux region there are few disappointing wines. Nearly all are characterised by a good colour, healthy, attractive fruit, and enough length on the palate to finish them off with style and personality. Most still have a life ahead of them, and will keep well for a further six or seven years or so. To sum up what I said at the beginning: this is a consistent, charming, fruity but essentially soft-centred vintage. It will still give a lot of pleasure, and can be bought with confidence.

THE TASTING

The following wines were sampled in New Hampshire, USA in October 2001.

SAINT-ÉMILION

CHÂTEAU AUSONE

DRINK SOON	15.0

Magnum. Full, mature colour. A little chunky on the nose. No lack of fruit, nor acidity but a little over-extracted. Now getting earthy with dead leaves flavours. Some fruit but some astringency. Not as fine as the 1979.

CHÂTEAU CHEVAL BLANC

DRINK SOON	15.5

Medium-full colour. Fully mature. Soft nose. Smooth and ripe and attractive if without great weight or depth. Pleasant medium-bodied wine. No great depth but fresh. Not great, nor even fine but better than Ausone.

CHÂTEAU FIGEAC

DRINK SOON	14.5

Fullish, mature colour. Just a bit more than the 1979. Round and succulent on the nose, but not quite the class of the 1979, nor the zip. Medium body. Soft and pleasant, but it lacks a bit of grip, concentration and personality. Some astringency is lurking.

POMEROL

CHÂTEAU LAFLEUR

DRINK SOON	14.0

Fullish, mature colour. Soft nose. Plumper than the 1979. A bit simple on the palate. No great grip. Slight suggestions of attenuation. Medium body. Pleasant. But a little one-dimensional.

CHÂTEAU PÉTRUS

DRINK SOON	16.0

Fine, full, mature colour. This has now got a bit high-toned and attenuated. Ample nose. But it lacks grip. Medium-full body. Slightly astringent. Ample and fruity but not very well balanced. Nor very elegant. Slightly disappointing.

CHÂTEAU TROTANOY

DRINK SOON	17.5

Magnum. Very full, vigorous colour. Rather plumper and fresher and more stylish on the nose than the 1979. Medium-full body. Fresh, ample and classy on the palate. Now *à point* but still plenty of life. The Vieux Château Certan 1981 has more dimension and better grip but this is fine.

Vieux Château Certan

NOW–2008	18.0

Full, mature colour. Rich and mellow on the nose. Just a bit more vigour than the 1979. Splendid palate. Very fine grip. Full, fat, fresh and concentrated. Plenty of structure for a 1981. Lovely. Fine plus.

Graves
Château Haut-Brion

DRINK SOON	18.5

Full, mature colour. Soft, classy, aromatic nose. This is a lovely example. Medium body. Beautifully balanced. Ripe and succulent fruit. Good grip. Long, intense and very classy on the follow-through. Very fine for the vintage.

Château La Mission Haut-Brion

NOW–2008	18.5

Deep colour. Still barely mature. Lovely nose. Not up to the size and complexity of the 1979 though. Ripe but looser-knit. Medium-full body. Good acidity. Plenty of fruit. This is very stylish. It finishes well and will still last.

Margaux
Château Margaux

NOW–2010+	19.0

Fine, full, mature colour. A very refined nose. Classy and high-toned if without the strength and structure and grip of the 1979. A very lovely 1981. Very lovely, fresh fruit. Good grip. Fullish body. Really long. Splendid.

Château Palmer

NOW–2009	19.0

Medium-full colour. Lovely fresh, fragrant nose. Great class here. Medium-full body. Very ripe. Very fine acidity. Lovely fruit. Ripe and long and very, very classy. As good as the 1979. Marvellously fresh and complex and long at the end. Fine plus.

Saint-Julien
Château Ducru-Beaucaillou

NOW–2007	17.5

Full, vigorous colour. Very good nose. Lovely aromatic fruit if without the depth and grip of the 1979. Medium-full body. Round, ripe and balanced. Cool and classy. Very easy to drink. Good elegant, long finish. Fine.

Château Gruaud-Larose

NOW–2009	15.0

Very full, vigorous colour. Solid nose. Some brettanomyces. Lumpy. A lack of class. But lots of substance. Full, tannic and a little astringent. Barnyardy. Plenty of substance here but no grace. Good merely.

Château Léoville-Las-Cases

NOW–2010	18.5

Full, vigorous colour. Lovely nose. Very pure. Just that little bit more grip and concentration than Ducru-Beaucaillou. Fullish body. Juicy, open and attractive. Very good class and fruit. Harmonious and long. As good in its own way as the 1979. This is very fine for the vintage.

Pauillac
Château Grand-Puy-Lacoste

NOW–2007	17.0

Fullish colour. Ample, succulent nose. Very attractive. Medium-full body. Easier to drink than the 1979. But balanced and classy if not quite the depth of the 1979. Very good indeed.

Château Lafite-Rothschild

DRINK SOON	16.5

Medium-full, mature colour. Fragrant nose. No great weight but plenty of style. Medium to medium-full body. Fresh and stylish if no real grip. This is attractive but it doesn't have much depth. The Latour has much more to it. Very good plus.

Château Latour

NOW–2010   18.0

Medium-full, mature colour. Rich, round, firm but aromatic. Plenty of depth. Fullish body. Some oak. Rather more grip and vigour than Lafite. Lovely fruit. Very good length and class. Long and positive finish. Fine plus.

Château Lynch-Bages

NOW–2007   16.5

Medium-full colour, a little more profound than the 1979. Very aromatic on the nose. Soft and plump. Quite rich. Not the grip of the 1979 but round and succulent and seductive. The Grand-Puy-Lacoste is more classy. Very good plus.

Château Mouton-Rothschild

NOW–2008   15.5

Surprisingly full colour. Ample and fullish. It doesn't seem too stewed. Fullish body. Plump. Good grip. Quite structured. No shortage of vigour and length. But slightly ungainly. Not together.

Château Pichon-Longueville, Comtesse de Lalande

DRINK SOON   18.0

Full colour. Ripe, plump, seductive nose. Good concentration if no great grip. Ample. But now beginning to lose its fruit. Slightly lean at the end. This is soft and charming and fine. But not great. Still stylish and harmonious though. Fine plus.

Saint-Estèphe

Château Calon-Ségur

DRINK SOON   (14.0)

Medium-full, mature colour. Evolved nose. Not entirely clean. Medium body. Now getting a little astringent. Corked. But all the same no better than quite good. Drink soon.

Château Cos d'Estournel

DRINK SOON   15.0

Full, vigorous colour. Curious nose. Not corked but slightly attenuated. Medium body. A lack of punch and zip. It was better five years ago. Some balance and interest but merely good now.

Château Montrose

DRINK SOON   16.0

Very full, vigorous colour. Fullish nose. Quite structured. Good ripeness. This is the best of the three Saint-Estèphes. Medium-full body. Fresh and mellow. Good complexity at the end. Can still be kept.

In addition to the above, the following wines are still vigorous and at least 'very good': Certan de May, La Conseillante, L'Évangile, La Gaffelière, Haut-Batailley, Latour-à-Pomerol, La Tour Haut-Brion, Pavie, Petit-Village, Saint-Pierre and Soutard.

1979 VINTAGE

SIZE OF THE CROP:	4,509,127.
VINTAGE RATING:	15.0 (RED WINES).
	16.0 (DRY WHITE WINES).
	15.0 (SWEET WINES).

Nineteen seventy-nine was a record crop. Never before had even 4 million hectolitres been produced, let alone 4.5. (In addition it has to be said, a further 1.7 million hectolitres of non-*Appellation Contrôlée* wine was made in the Gironde department: most of this was white.) The *Appellation Contrôlée* white proportion was 26.8 per cent. It was also the first time that the average yield exceeded 60 hl/ha. In fact the figure was just under 61.

One of the compelling fascinations about Bordeaux for me is the great variety of different wines, and, moreover, the number of these which attain a very high level of quality. In every Bordeaux vintage there must be at least three hundred different wines, available in commercial quantities without too much difficulty, which at the very least can be termed good: potential bottles for a dinner party or special occasion. A high proportion of these are very great wines – perhaps, (but I'm not going to enter the argument!) more than any other fine wine area in the world.

The taste of a wine, of course, changes. It develops as a wine evolves from infancy through maturity into senility. It varies, perhaps more than we realise, from bottle to bottle, and according to how and where it has been stored. This is another of the fascinations. Every time I return to a wine or a vintage it has changed. Every time I taste a wine I am instinctively measuring it up against my past experience and my current expectation. Frequently I am surprised by the change which has occurred, for better or for worse, since I last encountered a particular bottle. Always, particularly if I have the opportunity to see a wide range of wines from the same property or a single vintage, the experience is interesting, instructive and rewarding.

In September 2002 I was invited by London wine merchants Bibendum (020 7449 4120) to speak to a range of top 1979s. Nineteen seventy-nine was never the greatest vintage; being prolific, the wines never had a great deal of depth and concentration. After well over 20 years, would it be a bit of a disappointment?

THE WEATHER

Like its immediate predecessor, 1978, 1979 was a late vintage. Both vintages were years characterised by poor summers, cool rather than wet, after bad weather in the spring. In both cases the development of the vine started late and never really caught up. However, in each autumn, almost at the last possible minute, the weather brightened up, enabling the fruit finally to attain the correct degree of ripeness.

Following a mild winter, which, as Peter Sichel put it, was wet even by Bordeaux standards, April 1979 was cold. Luckily, the budding was late and the vineyards were spared any damage by frost. It continued wet, the rainfall being almost double the average for each of the months up to May. Peter Sichel again: 'This has little effect on the vine but is not good for the morale'. Thereafter the summer was one of the coldest on record, but also drier than normal. The vines, however, were able to feed on the amount of water in the soil left over from the previous six months of rain, and the water table showed no signs of descending, as it had done in 1964, to levels where the vine could be harmed through lack of moisture.

The vines flowered in mid-June, in perhaps the only period of extended summer weather the Gironde enjoyed this year, and a very large amount of buds set into fruit. July was average in temperature, and dry; August was the coldest for a generation or more, but with only a little rain; and September hardly better, though somewhat less dry.

Overall, some 150 mm of rain were recorded in the four months from June to September; equivalent to 1970, and drier than all the vintages of the previous 20 years except 1961, 1962 and 1967. However, unlike most of these vintages such rain as fell did so in August and September rather than in June and July, and similarly, unlike them, these months were also very cold. While the *véraison* (when the grape begin to turn colour from green to purple) was late, but at about the same date as the previous year, the relatively greater amount of rain during the six or seven weeks prior to the harvest meant that maturity was reached a week earlier than 1978, and the picking generally began in the first few days of October. Though an October *vendange* is commonly thought to be late, the current custom of waiting 110 or 120 days rather than 100 between flowering and harvest normally necessitates waiting until the first week in October. Since this practice of what has been pejoratively called 'waiting for *sur-maturité*' came into being, only in exceptional years such as 1982 and 1989 will we have harvests which largely take place in September. Even in 1981 and 1983, generally regarded as 'normal' harvest dates, most Médoc estates did not commence until 1st October or after.

Towards the end of the growing season the weather brightened up, there were spells of warm, sunny days, and this continued into October. Though the *vendange* was somewhat interrupted by rain, there was not enough humidity to cause any widespread attack of *pourriture grise*. A record crop of healthy, and, for the most part, ripe grapes was gathered in.

THE SIZE OF THE CROP

The essential difference between 1978 and 1979 is the size of the crop. In both years an Indian summer enabled the crop to achieve ripeness after a poor summer. However, in 1978, the weather had been bad during the flowering and the crop was short. In 1979 June had produced the one patch of sun in the whole season. Consequently in 1979 the improvement in the weather had to nourish a much larger amount of grapes.

THE WINES THEN

First reports, dwelling on the size of the crop, indicated at best an average quality vintage, and did not lead one to expect more than soft and pretty wines with a limited amount of richness of fruit for early drinking. My first impression in March 1980 was that the wines were better than that. The colour was good, though at that stage, overall, there did not appear to be a lot of body. In most cases the wines were ripe, fruity and healthy, and had correct levels of acidity. As they had been in 1978, the top wines were proportionately better than the *petits châteaux*. The best of these had finesse and sufficient depth and concentration to make them worth buying, even if one had bought heavily of the 1978s.

THE WINES NOW

Nineteen seventy-nine is a variable vintage. Because of the lateness of the harvest, the size of the crop and the interruptions by rain, the state of ripeness and concentration of the fruit when it arrived in the winery varied considerably. Moreover, for some properties, vat space was at a premium. Some *cuvées*, because of the pressure of the amount of grapes daily arriving at the winery, were not given sufficient time to macerate with the skins, and are, as a result, weak and insubstantial. Léoville-Barton is one of these wines. Elsewhere, where the elimination of the lesser quality vats from the *grand vin* had not been courageous enough, the wines are also loose and indefinite in character. These wines are nearer in character to 1980 than to 1978. There is an inconsistency of quality among the one or two hundred top wines, as there is in 1978. Moreover as a result of the lateness of the harvest, the wines made by the top estates are proportionately better than the *petits châteaux*. The *crus classés* can afford to risk, to delay the picking. In 1979 they were fortunate, for a few extra days gave the fruit a crucial extra degree of ripeness.

The 1979 vintage varies from district to district and commune to commune. At the outset it was thought most successful in Saint-Émilion and Pomerol, even better there in some cases than in 1978. I have never been convinced of this view, and I feel time has borne me out. Not only is the 1979 vintage equally as good in the Médoc and the Graves, in general, but the 1979 Saint-Émilions and Pomerols are inferior to the 1978s, as they may also be to the 1981s. In both these other vintages the harvest was proportionately smaller, and the Merlot grape, predominant in the Libournais, less prolific. The resulting wine, in principle, was hence more concentrated. That said, there are nevertheless many fine bottles among the top estates in these two areas, particularly in Pomerol. There are good wines in Margaux and the Graves. But, as so often, the best wines come from Saint-Julien and Pauillac. The top wines will still give much pleasure.

THE PRICES

Heavy buying of the 1978s was, however, just part of the problem – the growing world recession, high prices, the low level of the rate of exchange between the pound and the franc, and the high cost of money all contributed to the general problem. The 1978 vintage had been very popular and widely bought, certainly at the beginning of the year, but the later half of 1979 and the beginnings of 1980 were sluggish from the export point of view. Nevertheless, having had their best year since the heady days before the crash of 1973–1974, the merchants were short of stock, and ready to buy, provided prices were at reasonable levels.

The merchant and the château proprietor, though, view the word 'reasonable' from opposite points of view. To the former, a large, indeed, record vintage, however good, following a very good one, should be less expensive, particularly in days of high interest rates. Moreover it was considered then that it was always difficult successfully to sell two vintages *en primeur* in a row. The Bordeaux *négociants* could see that their customers would not be rushing to commit themselves, as the latter would feel that they had plenty of time in view of the size of the crop. The merchants expected, or hoped for, a fall in prices from 1978 levels.

The growers, however, had inflation to contend with: higher prices for wages and materials, and particularly for energy. A large crop was a bonus, but Le Bon Dieu, inevitably, would eventually balance this with a meagre harvest, or one which, despite improved methods of vinification and *élevage*, would be considered too poor to merit widespread attention. They hoped they could obtain 1978 prices for their 1979s. The market was slow to open, but, encouraged by the success of *crus* such as La Lagune, which put all its harvest out to the brokers in one *tranche* and had no difficulty in disposing of it in a couple of days, 1978 prices were what the proprietors deemed their wines would fetch.

Thereafter, fashionable châteaux and First Growths sold easily, but lesser wines stuck in Bordeaux. The author, Edmund Penning-Rowsell was told in October 1980, on his annual vintage pilgrimage, that perhaps half of the classed growths still remained unsold in the *négociants'* hands, though prices of the best wines by then were 20–30 per cent up.

Eventually, however, the market for even the lesser 1979s became buoyant. The 1980 vintage was short, and of only fair quality, the 1981s were more expensive, and the 1982 and 1983s were to be more expensive still; considerably so. Meanwhile demand for any and all good Bordeaux continued to surge, and the quality of the 1979s became more widely recognized. Today, good 1979s are much in demand, and prices are getting high, though still some of the best value on the Bordeaux market.

THE TASTING

The following wines were sampled either in London in September 2002 or in New Hampshire, USA in October 2001.

SAINT-ÉMILION

CHÂTEAU AUSONE

DRINK SOON   15.5

Fullish, mature colour. At first good rich, aromatic nose. Fresh. Full of interest. Medium-full body. Soft and well-balanced. Plenty of richness and dimension. Good grip. Long and classy and complex. But later there were forest floor flavours. It faded quickly in the glass. Only good plus.

CHÂTEAU CHEVAL BLANC

DRINK SOON   17.5

Medium-full, quite well-matured colour. The nose is classy, but I think we are getting near the end now. Medium weight. Soft and aromatic. No astringency. No hard edges. Ample and rich. But without the depth of the best Médocs. More generous than La Mission Haut-Brion but less class perhaps. Which you prefer is a question of taste.

CHÂTEAU CANON

DRINK SOON   16.5

Good full, vigorous colour. Nicely rich, 'old-viney' nose. Slight thinning at the end now. Some of the fat has gone. Good full palate. Quite structured for the vintage. Residual tannin and now a little astringent. But good depth and grip. Still vigorous.

CHÂTEAU FIGEAC

DRINK SOON   17.0

Fullish, mature colour. Ripe but at the same time a little lean and vegetal on the nose. Medium-full body. Mellow and classy. Very well balanced. Plenty of dimension and personality. It finishes well. Still sweet at the end. Still much to offer. Very good indeed.

CHÂTEAU MAGDELAINE

DRINK SOON   16.5

Medium to medium-full colour. Possibly lightening up a bit now. Ripe, round nose. Still sweet. Medium to medium-full body. A touch of astringency at the back but good complex, stylish Merlot fruit. Good length. Attractive.

POMEROL

CHÂTEAU LAFLEUR

DRINK SOON   16.0

Fine colour. Rich, fat, concentrated nose. Good acidity but at the end just a little ungenerous. On the palate some tannin. The wine was a bit over-macerated. It dried up in the glass. It was richer and less astringent 5 or 10 years ago.

CHÂTEAU PÉTRUS

NOW–2015   18.0

Full, mature colour. Splendid, rich nose. Opulent and succulent. Very vigorous. Almost sweet. Full, structured, rich and meaty. A fine wine with plenty of life but without the class of the Left Bank First Growths.

CHÂTEAU TROTANOY

DRINK UP   15.0

Fullish, mature colour. Rich, sweet, concentrated, soft Merlot nose. On the palate really quite evolved. Getting thin and attenuated at the end. Sweet but a little simple at first. Then astringent. Good but not great. It was better 5 or 10 years ago.

VIEUX CHÂTEAU CERTAN

DRINK SOON	17.5

Full, mature colour. Splendid rich, classy nose. Very profound. Excellent concentration and grip. Now just about at the end of its optimum drinking. Fullish, fresh, balanced and classy. Lovely pure fruit. But beginning to fray at the edges. Fine.

GRAVES

DOMAINE DE CHEVALIER

NOW–2009	18.0

Fullish, mature colour. Fragrant, composed, mellow, complex, classy nose. Fullish body. Subtle and multi-dimensional. Very stylish and very long on the palate. There is a lot of concentration and great harmony here. Very lovely and still vigorous. Fine plus.

CHÂTEAU HAUT-BRION

NOW–2010	18.5

Fine, full, vigorous colour. Ample, rich, matured nose; mulberry and cedarwood. A lot of class and depth. Plenty of vigour too. Medium-full bodied, warm, generous and succulent on the palate. Mellow and complex and classy. This has a lot of character and quality. Lovely long finish. Very fine.

CHÂTEAU LA MISSION HAUT-BRION

DRINK SOON	17.5

Fullish, vigorous colour. Quite a firm nose. Not as lush as the Haut-Brion. Leaner and less generous. Still a bit of unresolved tannin which will never fully mellow now. The fruit is classy, and there is good acidity. But a slight lack of fruit. A certain astringency now, which would be less apparent with food. But will get drier soon. Good positive finish and high quality though. Fine.

MARGAUX

CHÂTEAU MARGAUX

NOW–2015+	19.0

Very lovely, full, vigorous colour. Quite oaky, certainly concentrated, and almost a little dense on the nose. But very good ripe, rich fruit underneath. Full-bodied, rich, classy, vigorous and opulent. This is certainly a very lovely example. Excellent fruit. Still with bags of life ahead of it. Fine grip. Lovely finish. Complex and classy. Very fine indeed.

CHÂTEAU PALMER

NOW–2010+	19.0

Fine, vigorous colour. Splendidly concentrated nose. Very good grip. Lovely concentrated fruit. Fullish body. Excellent acidity. Mellow tannins. Still very vigorous. Great class. Excellent. Very lovely finish. Will last for ages.

SAINT-JULIEN

CHÂTEAU DUCRU-BEAUCAILLOU

DRINK SOON	18.0

Fullish, fully mature colour. Quite well-matured but classy, Cabernet-based nose. Losing a bit of its fruit now. Medium-full body. Good acidity. This is certainly fine. The follow-through shows plenty of depth and complexity. It is more vigorous than the nose would suggest. Fine plus.

CHÂTEAU GRUAUD-LAROSE

NOW–2009	16.0

Full colour. Still vigorous. Fullish body. Slightly solid. It lacks a bit of charm on the nose. Not too chunky on the palate. Full and fruity but not a lot of nuance. Good grip. But a bit over-extracted. Not astringent though. Very good.

CHÂTEAU LÉOVILLE-LAS-CASES

NOW–2015+	18.5

Full, fully mature colour. Good vigorous, ripe Cabernet nose. Rather more vigour and depth than the Ducru-Beaucaillou. Plenty of succulence and class. A lovely example. Vigorous. Fullish-bodied. Concentrated as well ripe. Excellent fruit. First Growth quality. Aristocratic. Very long. Lots of life ahead of it. Very fine. Not as sweet at the end as Château Margaux. Very fine.

PAUILLAC

CHÂTEAU GRAND-PUY-LACOSTE

NOW–2009   17.5

Fullish, vigorous colour. Fine Pauillac nose. Lots of depth and quality. Ripe and classy. Fullish body. Good grip. Just a touch austere, but not lean. Good tannins. Good long, vigorous finish. Fine.

CHÂTEAU LYNCH-BAGES

NOW–2009   17.0

Medium-full, mature colour. Fullish, plump, oaky nose. Medium-full body. Not as elegant but more seductive than the Grand-Puy-Lacoste. Good length. Very good indeed.

CHÂTEAU LAFITE-ROTHSCHILD

NOW–2015+   19.5

Full, mature colour. Vigorous, concentrated, classy nose. Lovely fruit. Great finesse. Excellent harmony. Fullish body. Mellow but vigorous. Long and complex and very lovely. This has splendid depth and complexity. Intense at the end. Very, very lovely finish. Excellent.

CHÂTEAU LATOUR

NOW–2010   19.0

Very full, vigorous colour. Pure, slightly austere cassis fruit on the nose. Is there a lack of warmth? Another bottle was much better. Classic Latour. Aloof and Cabernet-based. Rich underneath. But not as complete as Château Lafite or Château Margaux. Very fine. (A second bottle was even better than a second bottle of Margaux and Lafite at a meal later – 19.5.).

CHÂTEAU MOUTON-ROTHSCHILD

NOW–2009   16.0

Medium-full, mature colour. A touch astringent on the palate. Medium-full body. I don't think it has the quality of Lafite or even Latour. Decent balance but no real depth, nor much First Growth finesse. Merely very good.

CHÂTEAU PICHON-LONGUEVILLE, COMTESSE DE LALANDE

NOW–2007   18.5

Medium-full, mature colour. Now perhaps beginning to lose its vigour. But lovely nevertheless. It reminds me a little of the Haut-Brion. Mellow, cedary, mulberry and roast chestnuts. But hints that it is thinning out on the nose. Medium-full body. Now mellow. It still has good grip and vigour on the palate. It still has great charm. Excellent harmony and intensity. Lovely.

SAINT-ESTÈPHE

CHÂTEAU CALON-SÉGUR

DRINK SOON   15.0

Fullish, mature colour. Reasonably stylish, ripe nose but not a lot of grip. Medium body. A little one-dimensional, but fresh and fruity on the attack and a positive finish. Good if not great.

CHÂTEAU COS D'ESTOURNEL

NOW–2009   16.5

Full, vigorous colour. Very elegant nsoe. Lots of depth. Plenty of future. Fullish body. Ripe. Good structure. Slightly astringent at the end but good concentration and a stylish, long finish. Very good plus.

CHÂTEAU MONTROSE

NOW–2007   18.0

Full, mature colour. Classy Cabernet nose. No undue astringency. Indeed splendidly ripe, even concentrated. On the palate fullish, a little hard and austere on the attack. Mellow and more succulent on the follow-through. Balanced. Long. Still vigorous. Fine plus.

In addition to the above, the following are still vigorous and at least 'very good': Certan de May, L'Évangile, Haut-Marbuzet, La Lagune, Pavie, Saint-Pierre and La Tour Haut-Brion.

1978 AND 1975 VINTAGES

1978

SIZE OF THE CROP:	3,239,070 HECTOLITRES.
VINTAGE RATING:	16.0 (RED WINES).
	16.0 (DRY WHITE WINES).
	16.0 (SWEET WINES).

Nineteen seventy-eight was a late harvest, but a plentiful one, especially after the short crop of the previous year. The white wine production, at just short of a million hectolitres, was 30.6 per cent of the total, the last time it would represent over 30 per cent. The average yield was 41.3 hl/ha.

1975

SIZE OF THE CROP:	2,757,186 HECTOLITRES.
VINTAGE RATING:	16.0 (RED WINES).
	16.0 (DRY WHITE WINES).
	16.5 (SWEET WINES).

The 1975 crop was of good quantity, but thankfully, in view of the stock position following the 'winegate' scandal and the general economic recession, not too prolific. The average yield was 39.9 hl/ha and just under a million hectolitres (35.8 per cent) was declared as white wine.

I was surprised to find, when I looked at my past reviews of these vintages, that it was as long ago as 1991 that I had last made an important survey of these wines. Both 1975 and 1978 are in some ways flawed, but they remain the most satisfactory red Bordeaux years of that lean period between 1970 and 1982.

Time flies! I had imagined it was a mere five or six years ago. But no! The 1978 vintage was sampled in September 1990, the 1975s by the same team in February 1991.

Following the second tasting in 1991 my professional friends and I were of the view that we had derived more pleasure from the 1975s than the 1978s, though the wines had not been served together. In October 2000 I took part in a parallel tasting, the vintages of each château side by side. Today my preference is for the 1978s over the earlier vintage overall, though naturally there are exceptions. Many of the 1975s exhibit rather dry herbaceous tannins, and do not have enough fruit. Many of the 1978s show a rather lean acidity on the finish: they lack fat. But in both years there are plenty of bottles which had depth, harmony, vigour and elegance. And, by comparison with 1970 and 1982, they are inexpensive.

1978: THE WEATHER

That the 1978 vintage is a good one has been a point of constant surprise and frequent explanation ever since. It was a remarkable vintage. Until mid-August everything went wrong. The ripeness was uneven. Maturity was three weeks behind schedule. Most of the fruit was still green. Growers predicted disaster. One proprietor went on his annual vacation to the West Indies wondering whether to cancel his annual *troupe* of harvesters and leave the grapes to rot on the vines. However, from the third week of August, the weather changed. Thereafter, it could not have been more perfect. From the brink of catastrophe the climate improved and by November some growers were even talking about a *grand millésime*.

The 1978 weather pattern followed that of 1977 and was echoed by both 1979 and 1980 – though not by 1981. The resulting wines are different but one important factor links these four successive harvests. In each the progress of the vine was severely delayed by poor weather in the spring. Where 1978 differs from the other poor years was in the quality of the weather in late summer and early autumn.

The first shoots appeared on the vines towards the end of March, about normal for Bordeaux and, thankfully, not too early as had happened in the previous year. In 1977, the *débourrement* (bud-break) had started on 5th March. Severe frosts and even snow, a rare occurrence in Bordeaux, at the end of the month and 10 days later over the Easter weekend burnt off a lot of the new buds and produced a harvest which was very small indeed.

Thankfully, this did not happen in 1978 but the spring was nevertheless cold and wet and the flowering did not start until 10th June, about 10 days later than average. The cold, cloudy weather continued, the flowering was prolonged and uneven and the cycle became further and further retarded. By the time the grapes began to change colour from green to black, it was mid-August. The vine was three weeks behind schedule; even worse than the 1972 vintage and as much as a month behind 1976.

At the very last minute, though, the sun began to shine and thereafter conditions could hardly have been more perfect. The rest of August and September was hot and dry but not excessively so. A shower or two during the final stage of ripening is important to keep the juices of the plant flowing, to keep the sap lubricated, so to speak.

Nevertheless, it was one of the driest ends to the growing season on record. The rainfall in August and September was measured at 51.5 mm, much the same as 1962 and a figure only bettered in recent years by 1961, 1985 and 2000. Moreover, much of this fell in the first two weeks of August.

The fine weather continued into October during which only 10 mm of rain fell, an unprecedentedly low figure, enabling the vines to complete their maturity without interference and even to catch up on some of the time that had been lost. In the last fortnight, the ripening accelerated, finally removing fears that excessive chaptalisation would be required and the harvest began on 9th October and took place in ideal conditions. Curiously, the vintage began at the same time in both the Médoc and in Saint-Émilion – at Châteaux Palmer and Lafite as well as at Cheval-Blanc – on this or the following day; though at Pétrus and some of the other top Moueix-administered estates in Pomerol they waited a further week.

1975: The Economic Background

Faced with the success of the wines and the economy throughout the 1980s in Bordeaux it seems hard to believe that nearly 30 years ago, Bordeaux, indeed the whole wine trade, was in the throes of a crisis, a crisis that was as much psychological as financial. Nineteen seventy-three and 1974 had seen two largely indifferent but prolific vintages which no-one wanted to buy. There had been a scandal in Bordeaux when one of the oldest and most respected firms had been accused of fraudulent wine labelling. And all this coincided with an artificially induced oil crisis which was forcing up the price of energy, the cost of loans from the bank and the rate and speed of inflation. After two years of madness, when prices quadrupled between the excellent 1970 vintage and the sour, unripe 1972s, the bubble burst. Panic buying changed to panic selling as enormous quantities of very fine wine were unloaded on the market at give-away prices.

In Bordeaux in the spring of 1975 trade was at a standstill and spirits were low. A vintage to restore confidence as well as improve bank balances was badly needed. The cure needed to be as much psychological as economic. Luckily that was precisely what happened.

1975: The Weather

Climatically, 1975 is a curious vintage. On the face of it, it should not be a good vintage at all. The rainfall in August and September measured 216 mm, about twice the average, and this should not have augured well. The previous four vintages with rainfalls of over 200 mm during this period had been 1969, 1968, 1965 and 1960 – not exactly an inspiring run!

The 1975 season began with a winter which was mild and rather wet, and this encouraged the sap to rise and the growing season to begin rather early. As a result, some of the buds had already started to burst open by the end of March, and a sudden cold snap inflicted considerable frost damage, though not as bad as it was to be in 1977. The damage was particularly felt in those part of the vineyards planted in Merlot, for it is this variety which buds earliest.

Spring and early summer were dry and warm, enabling the flowering to take place without mishap, and this was followed by a long dry spell with some extremely hot days at the end of July and the beginning of August. On 31st July the temperature reached 36.6°C.

In the second week of August the weather broke. There were two immense thunderstorms, on the 7th and the 9th, and thereafter for the next six weeks the days were interrupted with more downpours, though the weather in between continued reasonably warm and sunny.

Nevertheless, the fruit was in excellent condition by the end of September. The skins had been thickened by the dry weather in July, there was no rot and the grapes were ripe. Picking began on 25th September and took place under cloudless skies with the exception of a storm on 29th September when some extensive hail damage was caused in Listrac, Moulis and Arcins, vineyards in between the classed growths areas of Margaux and Saint-Julien/Pauillac. The fine weather continued throughout October and for only the second time since 1967 – 1971 was the other vintage – some really good Sauternes were made. The overall crop was small compared with the excesses of 1973 and 1974, but not too tiny: an average of 40 hectolitres per hectare as against 56 in 1973. In all, one and three quarter million hectolitres of *appellation contrôlée* red wine were produced in 1975 in Bordeaux.

The Wines

As with all difficult vintages there is a greater disparity than usual between the best and the rest. This was apparent from the beginning and is even more valid today as many of the lesser wines are now beginning to age.

But at the top levels there is no lack of vigour, nor harmony, nor finesse. Not all 1975s are hard and fruitless; not all 1978s are lean and ungenerous. But you have to stay with the Super-Seconds and the First Growths. Below this there are few pleasant surprises. The majority of the rest now need drinking. The stars will safely keep.

Prices

Supplies of both vintages, naturally, are getting scarce, though Farr Vintners in London still have a fair selection. The First Growths (excluding Château Pétrus) can be obtained for £1000–£1450 ($1800–$2610) the case of 12 bottles for the 1975s, perhaps marginally less for the 1978s. In most of the rest of the wines the 1978s are more expensive. Ducru-Beaucaillou is £540 ($970) for the 1978, £420 ($750) for the 1975; Domaine de Chevalier £380 ($680) for the 1978, £260 ($460) for the 1975. This, as I said earlier, is not expensive. Just choose the wines with care.

THE BEST WINES

These are the wines which I rated 'very good' or better.

1978	1975
AUSONE (BETTER IN 1978); CANON (BETTER IN 1978); CERTAN DE MAY (BETTER IN 1978); CHEVAL BLANC; DOMAINE DE CHEVALIER (BETTER IN 1978); COS D'ESTOURNEL (BETTER IN 1978); DUHART-MILON; L'ÉVANGILE; GRAND-PUY-LACOSTE (BETTER IN 1978); GRUAUD-LAROSE; HAUT-BRION; LAFITE; LAFLEUR (BETTER IN 1978); LATOUR (BETTER IN 1978); LATOUR-À-POMEROL; LÉOVILLE-BARTON (BETTER IN 1978); LÉOVILLE-LAS-CASES (BETTER IN 1978); MARGAUX; LA MISSION HAUT-BRION; MONTROSE (BETTER IN 1978); MOUTON-ROTHSCHILD; PAVIE; PAPE-CLÉMENT; PÉTRUS (BETTER IN 1978); PICHON-LONGUEVILLE, COMTESSE DE LALANDE; TROTANOY (BETTER IN 1978); VIEUX CHÂTEAU CERTAN (BETTER IN 1978).	AUSONE; BEYCEHVELLE; CANON; CERTAN DE MAY; CHEVAL BLANC (BETTER IN 1975); DOMAINE DE CHEVALIER; LA CONSEILLANTE COS D'ESTOURNEL; DUCRU-BEAUCAILLOU (BETTER IN 1975); FIGEAC; GRAND-PUY-LACOSTE; GRUAUD-LAROSE (BETTER IN 1975); HAUT-BRION (BETTER IN 1975); LA LAGUNE; LAFLEUR; LATOUR; LÉOVILLE-BARTON; LÉOVILLE-LAS-CASES; LYNCH-BAGES (BETTER; IN 1975); MARGAUX; LA MISSION HAUT-BRION (BETTER IN 1975); MONTROSE; MOUTON-ROTHSCHILD; PALMER (BETTER IN 1975); PAVIE; PÉTRUS; TALBOT; TROTANOY; VIEUX CHÂTEAU CERTAN

THE GREAT WINES

Both vintages of Petrus are exceptional. Latour 1978, Léoville-Las-Cases 1978 and La Mission-Haut-Brion 1975 are excellent. Cheval-Blanc 1975, Lafleur 1978 and Palmer 1975 are very fine (and Palmer 1978 is not shabby). La Conseillante 1975 is even better. Grand-Puy-Lacoste is splendid in both vintages and must be the best value of the lot.

THE TASTING

The following wines were sampled over three sessions, with food, during a weekend organised by my good friends Jack and Thelma Hewitt in New Hampshire, USA, in October 2000. I offer my grateful thanks to Jack and Thelma and the others who provided the wines.

SAINT-ÉMILION

CHÂTEAU AUSONE, 1978

DRINK SOON	17.0

Fullish colour. Barely mature. Slightly sturdy on the nose. But good depth here. Full body. Good grip. Ripe concentrated fruit. A little solid and a little inflexible. It lacks a bit of charm. Better than the 1975. Longer and fresher at the end.

CHÂTEAU AUSONE, 1975

DRINK SOON	16.5

Full, mature colour. Quite a firm, slightly undergrowthy nose. But rich and classy underneath. Fullish body. Good tannins. The fruit is ripe, the wine wine balanced. But it is not quite integrated, nor really succulent enough. Still vigorous. Very good plus.

CHÂTEAU CANON, 1978

NOW–2008+	18.5

Good fullish, vigorous colour. Still closed on the nose. Plenty of depth and richness underneath. Full body. Very lovely, concentrated, 'old-viney' fruit. Rich and profound. Velvety. Very good grip. Really very youthful. Excellent. A really fine 1978: one of the few.

Château Canon, 1975

DRINK SOON   17.5

Fullish colour. No undue maturity. Ripe, fullish Merlot nose. Not too firm. Fullish, chunky but rich. Very good depth. No undue astringency. Good grip. This has very good fruit. Good style too. Long and mellow on the finish. Fine.

Château Cheval Blanc, 1978

DRINK SOON   18.0

Full, mature colour. This is very classy on the nose. Less opulent than the 1975. Lovely fresh, plump fruit with a touch of cigar boxes. Fullish body. Animal. Not exactly classy but balanced and fresh and highly satisfactory. Not as rich as the 1975. But fine plus.

Château Cheval Blanc, 1975

NOW–2008+   18.5

Full, mature colour. Rich, opulent, well-balanced nose. Exotic but unclassic. Fullish body. Mellow, ripe and very velvety. Very lovely fruit here. This has none of the austerity of the vintage and very good grip. Long. Very vigorous. Opulent. Very lovely.

Château Figeac, 1978

DRINK SOON   15.5

[Sadly we did not taste Château Figeac 1975.] Good fullish, vigorous colour. Plenty of depth on the nose. Ripe, spicy and gently oaky. Medium body. At first fresh and quite classy. Balanced if lacking a bit of weight, fat and concentration. A slight attenuation lurks however. Good plus.

Château La Gaffelière, 1978

DRINK SOON   15.5

Medium-full, mature colour. Pleasant, soft, mellow nose. This is ripe and attractive if without much depth and concentration. Plump. Medium to medium-full body. Balanced. Good plus.

Château La Gaffelière, 1975

DRINK SOON   15.0

Medium-full, mature colour. Good plump, vigorous fruit on the nose. Medium body. Attractive if quite straightforward, mellow wine. Neat, clean and balanced. No undue astringency. Still fresh. It lacks a bit of weight. But good.

Château Pavie, 1978

DRINK SOON   16.0

Good mature colour. Fullish, vigorous-looking. Lovely rich Merlot nose. Fullish body. Rich. Good structure. Plenty of depth. Good acidity. Not as much depth as Canon 1978 but very good and still very vigorous.

Château Pavie, 1975

DRINK SOON   (16.0)

Fullish colour. No sign of age. Badly corked. As far as one can see a good wine with interesting fruit, balanced and stylish.

Pomerol

Château Certan de May, 1978

DRINK SOON   17.0

Medium-full colour. Still fresh. Interesting mocha nose. Medium body. Balanced, good fresh fruit. This is engaging and classy and has a good long, complex finish. Not *that* concentrated though. Very good indeed.

Château Certan de May, 1975

DRINK SOON   16.0

Medium-full colour. Still fresh. Getting a little diffuse on the nose. But good classy fruit nevertheless. Medium to medium-full body. Ripe and balanced. Not a bit astringent. But needing drinking soon: beginning to lose its grip. Very good.

Château La Conseillante, 1978

DRINK SOON   17.5

Full colour. Some maturity now. Lovely nose. Very splendid, complex fruit. Medium-full body. Very fine cool fruit here. Balanced and complex and classy. Long. Better acidity in fact. But not as sweet as the 1975. This is very fine.

CHÂTEAU LA CONSEILLANTE, 1975

DRINK SOON   19.0

Magnum. Very full, rich, vigorous colour. Rich, opulent nose. Lots of very, very ripe fruit. Fullish body. Very lovely fruit. This is rich, fat, sweet and very harmonious. Long and lovely. Lots of vigour. Very fine indeed.

CHÂTEAU L'ÉVANGILE, 1978

DRINK SOON   16.5

Very full colour. Tough. Slightly herbaceous nose. No charm. Medium-full body. A bit dense. Very good fruit and even concentration underneath. One can see the potential. But the exterior is roughly hewn. Merely very good plus.

CHÂTEAU L'ÉVANGILE, 1975

DRINK SOON   15.5

Fullish colour. A bit dense and vegetal. A little sweaty too. Fullish structure but without real charm. Good acidity but it lacks fat and generosity. Merely good plus.

CHÂTEAU LAFLEUR, 1978

NOW–2008   18.5

Full, slightly mature colour. Lovely nose. Plums and mocha. Not a bit too dense. Cool. Opulent. But very good acidity. Slightly porty style. Fullish body. Chocolatey. Not a bit dense. This is rich, exotic and velvety and lovely. No undue tannins. Long. Individual. Fresh and cool. It evolved fast in the glass. Very fine.

CHÂTEAU LAFLEUR, 1975

DRINK SOON   16.0

Full, mature colour. Somewhat dense, tannic, undergrowthy nose. Full-bodied but a lack of charm. This is typical of the old-style Lafleur. Dense and tannic. Over-extracted. Not enough acidity. So astringent and a litte diffuse. Even with food no better than very good. Too dense.

CHÂTEAU LATOUR-À-POMEROL, 1978

DRINK SOON   17.5

Medium-full colour. Fresh nose. Rather more depth and class than the 1975, as well as more vigorous. Medium to medium-full body. Very lovely, fresh, succulent fruit. Not a blockbuster. Neat. Elegant. Quietly successful. Fine.

CHÂTEAU LATOUR-À-POMEROL, 1975

DRINK SOON   15.0

Medium-full colour. Classy nose. Fresh and profound. Quite evolved now though. It aged fast in the glass. Medium to medium-full body. It was ripe, balanced and classy but it is now getting a bit attenuated. Only 'good' today.

CHÂTEAU PÉTRUS, 1978

NOW–2010+   20.0

Magnum. Very fine, very full colour. Slightly less structure on the nose than the 1975, letting the fruit and opulence and richness shine out. This is splendidly impressive. Full body. Not as structured as the 1975. But marvellous fruit and excellent balance. Fat, rich and opulent. This is a very exciting wine. Exhuberant. Very Merlot in character.

CHÂTEAU PÉTRUS, 1975

NOW–2010+   19.5

Very fine, very full colour. Barely mature. Big, rich, very concentrated nose. Very, very fresh and vigorous. Lots and lots of depth here. Full body. Not a bit dense. Quite tannic but splendidly concentrated fruit. Very fine grip. This is a great 1975. Still very youthful. Still improving. Very, very long and complex. Excellent.

CHÂTEAU TROTANOY, 1978

DRINK SOON   18.0

Fullish colour. Very lovely classy nose. Rather more vigour, depth and class than the 1975. Medium-full body. Very lovely fruit. Very classy. A harmonious, complex, lovely, long example. Fine plus.

Château Trotanoy, 1975

DRINK SOON   16.0

Fullish colour. Very seductive, soft, mellow, opulent nose. Round and sexy but a little superficial on the palate. Medium body. Soft as a pillow. It lacks real grip and class. Yet very good.

Vieux Château Certan, 1978

NOW–2008   17.0

Full colour. A little solid on the nose. Very good classy fruit. But a touch solid, if not a bit brutal and austere. As it evolved it got better and better. Still very young. Very concentrated. It doesn't quite have the definition for fine. But certainly very good indeed.

Vieux Château Certan, 1975

DRINK SOON   16.5

Full colour. Fine, full, balanced, classy nose. This seems a serious wine. Fullish body. Balanced. Just a little tough though. Very good grip. Fine with food. Elegant fruit. Will still last well. Very good plus.

Graves

Domaine de Chevalier, 1975

DRINK SOON   17.5

Full, mature but vigorous colour. Lovely ripe, elegant nose. Rich and plump. No undue acidity. Soft but vigorous. Fullish on the palate. Nice and fresh. Complex and harmonious. Good depth. This has class. Long. Lovely. Fine.

Domaine de Chevalier, 1975

DRINK SOON   16.5

Fullish, fully mature colour. On the nose the fruit is good but beginning to get diffuse. No astringency. But an absence of freshness. It got a bit dead-leafy as it evolved. Medium-full body. It is not short. But the succulence and charm are going. Good positive end nevertheless. Very good plus.

Château Haut-Bailly, 1978

DRINK SOON   14.0

Medium colour. A little tired. Soft nose. Not too diffuse. Medium body. But still sweet. Still of interest if a bit on the light side now. Quite positive finish. Good.

Château Haut-Bailly, 1975

DRINK SOON   13.5

Medium-full, mature colour. Mellow nose. Fruity. But beginning to lose its grip. Medium body. A little attenuated on the palate. Fresh still but a touch astringent at the end. It has lost its elegance and interest.

Château Haut-Brion, 1978

DRINK SOON   18.0

Full, mature colour. Soft, aromatic nose. Properly ripe and not a touch of unripe acidity. Slightly drier than the 1975. A little more diffuse. Medium-full body. The nose is showing a bit of age but the wine is vigorous and balanced on the palate. Very good length. The 1975 is more concentrated. This is fine plus though.

Château Haut-Brion, 1975

DRINK SOON   18.5

Full, mature colour. Marvellously aromatic nose. Velvety. Not a bit of 'hard edges'. Medium-full body. Very silky. Harmonious and aristocratic. Long and subtle. Seems lighter than the Cheval Blanc but it is just as intense. But I think it is more evolved. Very lovely. This is both more concentrated and more vigorous than the 1978.

Château La Mission Haut-Brion, 1978

DRINK SOON   17.0

Full, mature colour. Rich, opulent, meaty nose. It smells of vanilla custard. As it evolved it lost vigour and became a little lean. On the palate only medium-bodied. Lacks the richness and concentration of either the 1975 or most of the First Growth 1978s. Very good indeed but not really finely concentrated or very complex.

CHÂTEAU LA MISSION HAUT-BRION, 1975

NOW–2008   19.5

Full, mature colour. This is splendidly profound, and gently oaky. Cedary on the nose. Really exciting. On the palate medium-full-bodied, a touch more astringent than the Haut-Brion. Yet excellent grip, a little more structure, and fresher and with more keeping potential. I find the flavours very, very lovely, and now totally *à point*. No undue structure at all. Very fine indeed.

CHÂTEAU PAPE-CLÉMENT, 1978

DRINK SOON   14.5

Medium-full, mature colour. Good rich, vigorous, slightly spicy nose. Medium to medium-full body. Lighter than the 1975. Less intense. Less vigorous. It has suggestions of attenuation. This is quite good plus.

CHÂTEAU PAPE-CLÉMENT, 1975

NOW–2008   16.5

Fullish colour but a little muddy. Good rich, vigorous nose. Fullish palate. Good grip. This is rich and vigorous. Plump and long on the palate. Plenty of depth. Plenty of life. Very good plus.

MARGAUX AND SOUTHERN MÉDOC

CHÂTEAU CANTENAC-BROWN, 1978

DRINK UP   12.5

Medium, fully mature colour. Rather thin and fruitless on the nose. It lacks style and fat. Thin and astringent on the palate. A little fresher than the 1975 though.

CHÂTEAU CANTENAC-BROWN, 1975

DRINK UP   12.0

Medium, fully mature colour. Rather a fruitless nose. Not much pleasure to be had on the palate. Medium body. Rather astringent. No class.

CHÂTEAU LA LAGUNE, 1978

DRINK SOON   14.0

Medium-full mature colour. Pleasant, cedary nose. Well-made. Still plump and fresh. Medium-full body. This shows a little astringency now but underneath the wine is plump and balanced, though beginning to dry out. It was "good plus", now quite good.

CHÂTEAU LA LAGUNE, 1975

DRINK SOON   15.5

Medium to medium-full, mature colour. Round, ripe, slightly earthy nose. Good vigour on the palate. Medium to medium-full body. Ripe fruit. No astringency. Balanced and attractive. More vigorous than the 1978.

CHÂTEAU LASCOMBES, 1978

DRINK SOON   13.5

Medium to medium-full colour. A little browner but a little richer-looking than the 1975. Medium-full, ripe, spicy nose. Not very classy though. Medium to medium-full body. Some astringency but rounder and more vigorous underneath. Better with food.

CHÂTEAU LASCOMBES, 1975

DRINK SOON   13.5

Medium to medium-full colour. A little undergrowth-y on the nose. Ripe but rather astringent on the attack and slightly corked. Decent balance underneath if no great finesse. Medium-full body. Getting lighter and drier now. It was good once. Now not bad plus.

CHÂTEAU MARGAUX, 1978

DRINK SOON   17.5

Full, immature colour. Rich, oaky, slightly four-square nose. Classy fruit underneath. Compared with the Palmer it is somewhat over-extracted: it doesn't show the Margaux *terroir*. Full body. Very vigorous. Some oak. Rich. Very good grip. It all seems a little too much at first. Will it ever mellow? Long and with plenty of life ahead of it. But it lacks charm and real breed. Got better and better in the glass though.

Château Margaux, 1975

DRINK UP   13.0

Full mature colour. Rather dry and lifeless on the nose. No fruit. Dense. Some unnecessary acidity. Even appley. Poor and stewed. On the palate the wine is not too dry. But there is not much class here. Edgy. Medium-full structure but the acidity is dominating and there is very little elegance.

Château Palmer, 1978

DRINK SOON   18.0

Full, mature colour. Lovely fragrant nose. Rather more flexible than Château Margaux 1978. Classy. Laid-back. Not as rich as the Palmer 1975 though. Medium-full body. Crisp and alive. Good grip. Very stylish, ripe fruit. But it is not as complete as the 1975. But it is long, vigorous and very classy. Fine plus.

Château Palmer, 1975

DRINK SOON   19.0

Full, mature colour. Very lovely nose. A suppleness absent in most 1975s and some very lovely, fragrant fruit. This has a very harmonious structure and lots of class. Medium-full body. Perhaps approaching the end but a most lovely balanced, classy, complex, multi-dimensional wine. Excellent fruit. Very, very long. Very, very lovely. A great 1975.

Château Prieuré-Lichine, 1978

DRINK SOON   14.0

Medium-full colour. Still vigorous looking. A little lean on the nose. It lacks generosity. Quite fresh on the palate. But only medium body. It lacks concentration. Not a great deal of style either. Quite good.

Château Prieuré-Lichine, 1975

DRINK SOON   14.5

Medium-full colour. Still vigorous-looking. Ripe nose. Good substance. Smooth. Medium-full body. Balanced and fruity if no real style. Showing a bit of astringency at the end but quite good plus.

Château Rauzan-Gassies, 1978

DRINK UP   12.0

Medium-full, mature colour. Tired, somewhat astringent nose. Dried-out on the palate. Fresher than the 1975 but pretty disappointing.

Château Rauzan-Gassies, 1975

SEE NOTE

Light to medium, well-matured if not old colour. Thin, tired, sweet-sour nose. Thin. Old. Past whatever 'best' it even had.

Saint-Julien

Château Beychevelle, 1978

DRINK SOON   13.0

Medium to medium-full, mature colour. Older-looking than the 1975. Pleasantly fruity on the nose. But no great depth. Similar on the palate. Now lightening up. Not a patch on the 1975.

Château Beychevelle, 1975

DRINK SOON   16.0

Good vigorous mature colour. Good plump, ripe fruit on the nose. No sign of astringency. There is depth and class here. A fullish, meaty wine. Good character. Vigorous, harmonious, long and even elegant. Very Saint-Julien. Very good.

Château Branaire, 1978

DRINK SOON   14.5

Medium-full colour. Still vigorous. A bit lumpy on the nose. It lacks grace. Some substance. Good fruit. Decent grip. A little astringent but this would be good with food. Slightly ungainly. Quite good plus.

Château Branaire, 1975

DRINK SOON   14.0

Medium-full colour. Still vigorous. Meaty nose. A little firm and astringent underneath. Good fruit on the attack. Medium-full body. A bit lumpy and astringent on the after-taste. It lacks a bit of class. Quite good.

CHÂTEAU DUCRU-BEAUCAILLOU, 1978

DRINK SOON   16.0

Medium-full colour. Strangely blunt on the nose. I have had better examples than this. Better on the palate but not as vigorous as I had expected. Medium-full body. A little astringent at the end. Quite classy fruit in the middle and decent balance. But the wine doesn't sing.

CHÂTEAU DUCRU-BEAUCAILLOU, 1975

DRINK SOON   17.0

Good colour. A little austere on the nose. Medium-full body. This is better than the 1978 but not brilliant. There is a little solidity and astringency, and though the fruit is quite classy, it is not ample enough for fine. Long though. Very good indeed.

CHÂTEAU GRUAUD-LAROSE, 1978

DRINK SOON   15.5

Medium-full colour. Some maturity. Rather herbaceous on the nose. Better on the palate but not a patch on the 1975. Medium-full body. The acidity shows. It lacks a bit of richness and generosity. Good plus.

CHÂTEAU GRUAUD-LAROSE, 1975

NOW–2008+   17.0

Very good colour. Rich, full, fat and ample on the nose. This is very promising. Fullish body. Vigorous. Very good tannins and grip. No astringency. A meaty, quite solid wine. Long, rich and satisfactory. Plenty of life ahead. Very good indeed.

CHÂTEAU LÉOVILLE-BARTON, 1978

DRINK SOON   16.5

Fresh, medium-full colour. Classy nose. More fruit than I expected. Quite round. Medium body. A little dryness at the end. But ripe and pleasant and with the usual Barton elegance. Not great but very good plus. No lack of charm.

CHÂTEAU LÉOVILLE-BARTON, 1975

DRINK SOON   16.0

Good colour. Not a lot of succulence here. Quite evolved. Rather lean. Better on the palate. Medium body. Less body but less austerity than Ducru-Beaucaillou 1975. But less class. Very good nonetheless.

CHÂTEAU LÉOVILLE-LAS-CASES, 1978

NOW–2010+   19.0

Fullish colour. Very classy on the nose. This is very lovely. Pure, rich, concentrated Cabernet fruit. Full, composed and aristocratic. This is still very vigorous. Lots of depth. Very lovely fruit. Very long. Very fine indeed.

CHÂTEAU LÉOVILLE-LAS-CASES, 1975

NOW–2008   17.5

Very good colour. Youthful nose. Quite austere. But quality Cabernet and plenty of depth here. Quite a bit wine. Full and tannic. A touch solid. But rich, ample and classy underneath. This has very good grip, length and vigour still. Fine.

CHÂTEAU LÉOVILLE-POYFERRÉ, 1978

DRINK SOON   15.0

Good vigorous colour. Rather diffuse on the nose though. On the palate medium body. Soft. Some sweetness. A little astringent at the end. Pleasant. Indeed good, because there is class and some length.

CHÂTEAU LÉOVILLE-POYFERRÉ, 1975

DRINK SOON   14.5

Medium-full, mature colour. Some age here. But soft and not too dried out. Only medium body on the palate. It has lightened up and simplified. Pleasant because it is not astringent. But a little simple. Some class though. Not short. Quite good plus.

CHÂTEAU TALBOT, 1978

DRINK SOON   13.3

Medium-full colour. Mature. Decent nose. No great dimension. Not up to the 1975. Medium body. Pleasant fruit. Now lightening up and drying out. It was 14.5, now 13.0.

Château Talbot, 1975

NOW–2008	16.5

Medium-full colour. Still quite youthful. Good full, fruity nose. Not too solid. No astringency. Even rich. Fullish body. Very good grip. Plenty of fruit. Lots of vigour. Good Cabernet flavour. Harmonious and long on the palate. This is very good plus.

Pauillac

Château Duhart-Milon, 1978

NOW–2008	16.5

Medium-full colour. Fully mature. Good fruit on the nose. Good depth too. Very much better than the 1975. Fullish body. Vigorous. Rich, fat and balanced. Slightly earthy but very good follow-through. Fresh. Very Pauillac.

Château Duhart-Milon, 1975

SEE NOTE	

Medium-full colour. Old nose. Dry. A little maderised. Thin on the palate. This is over the hill.

Château Grand-Puy-Lacoste, 1978

NOW–2008	18.5

Full colour. Very youthful. Splendid nose. Excellent fruit. Complex. Very concentrated. Marvellous, 'old viney' fruit and harmony. Fullish body. Very profound. Impeccably put together. Very generous. Very fine.

Château Grand-Puy-Lacoste, 1975

DRINK SOON	17.5

Medium-full colour. Still vigorous. Ripe, succulent, medium-weight nose. This has medium to medium-full body. Very complex, balanced, restrained, old-vine fruit, length and class. A little astringent beginning on the attack, but the finish is fine. Long and subtle at the end. Fine.

Château Lafite, 1978

NOW–2008+	18.0

Magnum. Fine colour. Fresh, fragrant, complex, classy nose. Fullish body, but the structure is very well covered. Ripe even opulent. Very good grip. Very fresh still. This is plump, spicy and multi-dimensional. Lovely finish. It will last for ages. Fine plus.

Château Lafite, 1975

DRINK UP	14.0

Medium-full mature colour. Rather dead on the nose. It lacks vigour and succulence. Medium body. Not too astringent. Just rather neutral, and now a bit over-evolved. Only a vestige of the Lafite breed. Quite good at best.

Château Latour, 1978

NOW–2008	19.5

Full, barely mature colour. Splendidly Latour on the nose. Surprisingly soft on the palate. Fullish, velvety-rich fruit. Very good grip. Above all real breed and complexity. Aristocratic and harmonious. Slightly less voluptuous than the Lafite. The structure is more obvious. But this is classier. Very lovely finish. Excellent.

Château Latour, 1975

DRINK SOON	19.5

Fullish mature colour. Quite a firm nose. But there is depth here. Some of the fruit has dried up a bit. I have had more vigorous bottles. This has some grip and residual ripeness. But it is not exactly rich or profound. Nor is it *that* classy. Very good at best. A bit of a disappointment (18.5 elsewhere).

Château Lynch-Bages, 1978

DRINK SOON	17.0

Fullish colour. Getting a little light and diffuse on the nose. This is very good but it has seen better days. Fresh nevertheless. Medium to medium-full body. Nicely opulent. This is very good indeed.

Château Lynch-Bages, 1975

NOW–2008   17.5

Full, rich, vigorous colour. Good rich, succulent, meaty nose. Fat and generous. Full, opulent, rich and fat on the attack. Not a vestige of astringency or toughness. Quite classy. Long. Very fresh still.

Château Mouton-Rothschild, 1978

DRINK SOON   16.0

Medium-full, mature colour. Not a great deal of depth and personality on the nose. Quite evolved on the palate. Medium-full body. Quite mellow. But it lacks grip and concentration. Pleasant, even some class. But a bit of a disappointment. It now tails off. Perhaps 17.0 once. Now 16.0.

Château Mouton-Rothschild, 1975

DRINK SOON   16.5

Medium-full rather old-looking colour. Soft nose. Quite round and plump. Certainly cedary. Only medium body though. But mellow and attractive, but by no means a great bottle.

Château Pichon-Longueville, 1978

DRINK SOON   15.0

Medium-full colour. Pleasantly fruity on the nose in a slightly lumpy sort of way. Medium to medium-full body. More vigour and more interest than some. Some grip. Decent fruit. No great class or dimension but good.

Château Pichon-Longueville, 1975

DRINK UP   12.0

Medium colour. Fully matured. Medium weight nose. A little one-dimensional. A little dry. Medium body. Rather thin. The astringency dominates. Very nearly past its best.

Château Pichon-Longueville, Comtesse de Lalande, 1978

DRINK SOON   19.0

Fullish, vigorous colour. Very lovely nose. Splendid succulent fruit. Good weight and grip. Still fresh. Fullish body. Very classy fruit. Excellent structure. Good grip. Rich. Very elegant. Very long. Very intense. Very fine.

Château Pichon-Longueville, Comtesse de Lalande, 1975

DRINK SOON   16.5

Full, vigorous colour. A little tough and astringent on the nose, especially after the Lynch-Bages. Good fruit underneath. A little lean now. Medium-full body. Some astringency. Good acidity and fruit but it lacks a little charm. Very good plus.

Château Pontet-Canet, 1978

DRINK UP   13.0

Fullish colour. Only a little maturity. Fruity nose. Mature. It is beginning to lilghten up perhaps. Definitely lightening and drying on the palate. Medium body. Loosing its grip. Not bad at best.

Château Pontet-Canet, 1975

DRINK SOON   14.0

Medium-full colour. Good rich mellow nose. No great depth but balanced and fruity. Medium weight. A bit one dimensional. It is beginning to lighten and dry out. Quite good still. Pleasantly fruity.

Saint-Estèphe

Château Calon-Ségur, 1978

DRINK SOON   14.5

Medium-full, mature colour. A touch farmyardy on the nose. Medium body. Some fruit. A little astringent on the palate. But good acidity. It has lightened up a bit. Yet there is interest here and a good finish. Quite good plus. [We did not sample the 1975 on this occasion.]

Château Cos d'Estournel, 1978

NOW–2008   17.0

Magnum. Very good colour. No undue maturity. The nose is a little dumb but the palate shows real depth and class. Fullish body. No undue astringency. Fine acidity. Really quite rich and expansive. Very good indeed.

CHÂTEAU COS D'ESTOURNEL, 1975

DRINK SOON   16.0

Very good colour. No undue maturity. Quite
rich on the nose. Still vigorous. Fullish body.
Good plump fruit. Slightly astringent now on
the palate. Decent length. But a slight lack of
real definition. A very good wine but not a
fine one.

CHÂTEAU MEYNEY, 1978

DRINK SOON   13.0

Medium-full colour. Rather a muddy nose. A
bit tough and coarse. Not too astringent on
the palate. But I don't like the style. Medium
to medium-full body. No undue age.

CHÂTEAU MEYNEY, 1975

DRINK SOON   14.0

Medium-full colour. No great maturity.
Slightly lumpy and tannic on the nose. Fresh
though. On the palate this is rather
astringent but yet reasonably fresh. Not
coarse. Better with food. There is good
freshness underneath.

CHÂTEAU MONTROSE, 1978

NOW–2008+   17.5

Medium-full mature colour. Quite a tough
nose. Quite rich fruit underneath. Medium-
full colour. Not too tough and tannic on the
palate. Good fruit. Restrained and classy.
Very good grip. Very good length. This is fine.

CHÂTEAU MONTROSE, 1975

NOW–2008+   17.0

Very good colour. Barely mature. Rich and
full but a bit inky on the nose. Better on the
palate. Good grip. Medium-full body. Some
tannin and astringency but not unduly so.
This is better than the Cos d'Estournel for
once. Nice chocolate and caramel aspects.
Long and positive. Very good indeed.

1970 Vintage

SIZE OF THE CROP:	3,375,544 HECTOLITRES.
VINTAGE RATING:	18.0 (RED WINES).
	18.0 (DRY WHITE WINES).
	16.0 (SWEET WINES).

After two poor vintages 1970 was a large and successful crop. It was the first time the 2 million figure for *Appellation Contrôlée* had been exceeded. 1.3 million hectolitres (39 per cent of the crop) was declared as white wine. The overall average yield was 48.5 hl/ha.

I have a very personal interest in the 1970 vintage. It was not only the first vintage I bought as a major professional wine buyer – as buyer-in-chief rather than acolyte – but it was also the subject of the first article I wrote for *Decanter* magazine. It think it appeared in their third issue in the autumn of 1975. Though I had already been to Bordeaux on a number of occasions since doing a *stage* on leaving college in 1964, 1971 was the first year when I made a serious study of a vintage *en primeur*, when it was my decision whether to buy this wine or that, when I committed other people's money and where I was able to follow the development of the wines I had judged at the time to be better or worse than their peers right from six months after the harvest to the present day.

The first comprehensive tasting of the 1970 vintage I made after the wines were in bottle was in early 1975. I have repeated this at roughly three-yearly intervals ever since. Two things have always struck me. First, for the first 15 years of its development the vintage seemed to be more backward as time went on; that is, that one kept putting off further and further into the future the date that the best wines would be at their peak; this is always a sign of a good vintage. Second, that the wines have always had a sunny disposition. The 1970s have never gone through an awkward adolescent phase like the 1966s and other vintages have done and other more recent vintages such as the 1995s and 1996s are doing at the moment; they have always been accessible, generous and welcoming. They also seemed to get better and better, to have more depth, concentration and dimension as time progressed. Unlike vintages such as 1971 and 1976 the 1970s developed better than originally predicted.

THE WEATHER

The key to a vintage, good or bad, is the weather, good or bad. Frosts in the spring; hail, rain, wind or high humidity during the flowering; too little sun to ripen the grapes in the traditional 100 days between flowering and harvest and too much rain in the crucial weeks of September. Each of these can mar a vintage. Their absence in 1970 ensured its success – that there was a warm and sunny June meant that the crop would be large; that there was fine weather in September and October meant that the fruit would be ripe and healthy.

After a late spring, which was probably fortuitous since it lessened the risks of frost, the weather throughout the summer of 1970 and long into the autumn was perfect. From the end of May until the end of July it was warm and sunny. August was indifferent but September was superb with just enough rain in the early part of the month to swell the grapes sufficiently. From then on, throughout the harvest which began late in the month and continued well into October, there was another spell of fine weather. The grapes were gathered in ideal conditions, the berries were large and healthy without a hint of rot anywhere and the crop was large, by far the biggest since the Second World War. The amount of red wine produced was a third as much again as the previous record: 1967.

THE WINES

If the key to the success of vintages in general is the weather, the key to the successful 1970 vintage can be summed up in two words: balance and consistency. The 1970s are beautifully balanced; they have a lot of fruit and they have great style. They are firm – which means that the best will still keep well if properly stored – without being hard. In 1970, the Merlot grape, predominant in Saint-Émilion and Pomerol and equally crucial in the Médoc and Graves, was particularly successful and this has led to a gentle balance of tannin and fruit. In some years when the Merlot fails the resulting wine, with a higher proportion of Cabernet, can have an excess of tannin. These wines can be very hard and austere and will become more and more astringent as they age.

The sheer size of this enormous vintage, coupled with the absence of excessive hardness and tannin, led some to have their doubts about the staying power of the 1970s. Indeed, when they were first sampled in the spring of 1971, they seemed almost too good to be true. They were so agreeable some thought they were too *flatteurs* and would not last. These cynics were quick to point out the size of the harvest (quality being normally inversely proportional to quantity) to substantiate their claim. I have never had such fears. A wine needs not necessarily to have a great deal of tannin and body to keep well; what is required, however, is balance. The 1970s have this is abundance and they have great charm. True, they never had the enormous depth and staying power of the 1961s or 1945s. In character, they most resemble they 1953s – and look how well they turned out!

Another characteristic is their consistency. In this respect they *are* like the 1961s. From the humblest growth in the Côtes de Bourg or the Premières Côtes, to the famous roll-call of classed growths in the Médoc, there are few disappointing wines. Those which, now, do not show as well as their peers, have suffered more probably from bad handling and bottling than through any intrinsic fault in the wines themselves.

When I first sampled the wines, I considered that the lesser classed growths, the good *bourgeois* wines and most Saint-Émilions and Pomerols would be ready towards the end of the 1970s and that the more substantial Médoc *crus classés* would follow in the early 1980s. As I have said, I have revised my view, postponing my 'optimum drinking' time-spans. In 1975, I wrote that all but a few of the really top wines would be ready by 1980, then I found in 1985 that there were *still* a few wines which were not yet ready for drinking and many more which, while they could be drunk and enjoyed, would still improve.

Obviously, a lot depends on how the wines have been stored. A bottle which has been on display in a shop or kept in a cupboard under the stairs will develop much faster than a case in a proper underground cellar or one with temperature/humidity control. There is nothing quite so important as storage. Why pay £500 ($900) a case and then quibble about paying an extra £6–8 ($10–14) per annum in order to have the wine kept in optimum conditions? It is like tilting at windmills.

Now into their fourth decade, the majority of the top 1970s are still fresh and will keep well. Even just below First Growth level: Ducru-Beaucaillou, say, (which I had the other day), or Palmer, the wines are still holding up well.

PRICES – THEN

In view of the much publicised excellence of the vintage, the poor showing of the two previous vintages and the greatly increased interest in wine in America, it is not surprising that the year 1971 opened with an enormous buying boom in Bordeaux. Several American concerns made some very heavy purchases, closely followed by the wine arms of the British brewery groups. Despite the huge crop, demand was unprecedentedly heavy. Prices began to rise and speculators began to arrive, buyers whose intentions was profit, not consumption.

As summer succeeded spring, the hysteria snowballed. While parcels of wine exchanged hands at ever-increasing prices, the châteaux who had announced their second *tranche* prices early watched ruefully as their tardy neighbours got more only a few weeks later and stocks of first *tranche* wine fetched three or four times their original price. It was this that determined them to fix their prices so high for their 1971s and 1972s. Why shouldn't they make some more profit? The price of the wine could obviously stand it.

It was no more comfortable from the buyer's point of view. With prices mounting daily, it was almost impossible to make a cool evaluation of the merits of a number of wines for fear of being gazumped. At the higher levels, the relative qualities of equivalently classed wines were ignored by speculators buying solely on the château name and this led to a further distortion in prices. Those who bought early were fortunate. Those who bought later or who had to return to the market to replace wine already sold were sucked into in this spiral.

On all sides, grower, *négociant* and buyer, greed overcame reason. While the market was rising, any fool could make a lot of money by buying a name today and selling later. Many firms – and there were a lot of new names which suddenly sprang up from nowhere – did make a lot of money whilst the market continued to rise.

The bubble, of course, finally burst and with such savagery that there was hardly a merchant in Britain or France who was not wounded and more than a few who found themselves in acute financial difficulties because they had continued to pay high prices – and, moreover, for the indifferent vintage of 1972 – in anticipation of a further increase in demand which never materialised and were then forced by their accountants and bank managers to de-stock in a great rush.

As a result, there was a time in the mid-1970s when the 1970 and other vintages could be snapped up at little more than their original cost despite the fact that they had several years bottle age, as enormous quantities of classed growths were unloaded onto the market by firms who were forced to release capital or by others frightened that the market would collapse further. This buyer's market lasted until 1977–1978. The 1970s, together with the 1966s, became a good currency to acquire because, of all the wine heaped onto the marketplace, these were the best vintages obtainable at the lowest prices, being available in the largest quantities.

The 1970s are associated with the explosion in wine prices which occurred a few years later but, although this is certainly valid, it was in 1969 that the absurd increases at source really began. Château Mouton-Rothschild, which had offered its 1966 and 1967 at opening prices at 27,000 Francs a *tonneau* (about 27 Francs a bottle and about £21 a case at the then rate of exchange), asked 75,000 Francs for the 1969. Château Lafite was not far behind and where these illustrious names led, the rest soon followed. In 1971, Mouton initially even dropped its 1970 price from the 1969 level in an endeavour to keep prices reasonable but, as its great rival Lafite chose to ignore this initiative, reverted to 1969 prices for its second *tranche*.

In 1972 the 1971 Mouton price leapt to 120,000 Francs, easily five times its 1966 price. Compared with these prices, the opening price of Mouton and Latour 1970, at 36,000 and 40,000 Francs respectively, seem quite cheap. The opening prices of other wines – Château Gloria at 6500 Francs, Château Léoville-Las-Cases at 8700 Francs and Château Palmer at 12,000 Francs – seem even better value.

Prices – Now

Château Latour fetches £3650 ($6570) per dozen, Mouton-Rothschild £1450 ($2610) and Haut-Brion a mere £1000 ($1800); Ducru-Beaucaillou can be acquired for £900 ($1620), Palmer £1400 ($2520) and Trotanoy £2000 ($3600). In comparison with 1961, 1982 and 1990, the 1970s are not expensive.

The Tasting

The following notes are taken from two comparative tastings. The first was hosted by Jack and Thelma Hewitt in New Hampshire, USA, in October 1999. The second, of mainly First Growths, all from the cellar of the late John Tracy, celebrated the 25th anniversary of the South Hampshire (UK) Wine and Food Society in November 2002.

Saint-Émilion

Château Ausone

DRINK SOON	14.0

Fullish colour. Mature but surprisingly fresh. A little bit thin and rustic on the nose. Not too faded though, just not very good in the first place. Medium body. Still sweet but a little astringent on the attack if not on the finish. Quite good.

Château Cheval Blanc

DRINK SOON	15.0

Rich, fullish, fresh colour. Not as sophisticated as all that. But ripe and fruity. On the palate this is rich and sweet and spicy. Fullish body. It lacks real distinction but good. Slightly bitter at the end. It was better a decade ago.

Château Figeac

DRINK SOON	16.0

Medium-full colour. Well-matured. Ripe, almost sweet nose. Suggestions of attenuation behind it. This has good fruit, is medium-bodied – perhaps beginning to lighten up a bit – and a good fresh finish. Interesting flavours: more Merlot than these other wines here but not really a typical Saint-Émilion either. Very good.

Pomerol

Château Lafleur

DRINK SOON	17.5

Very good, full colour. Barely mature. Slightly dense and tannic on the nose. Yet plenty of ripe fruit. Very ripe on the palate. Full, slightly ungainly. Yet really rich and voluptuous. Lacks a little refinement. But the fruit has real vigour and intensity. Very long. Fine. Still plenty of life.

Château Trotanoy

NOW–2009	18.0

Very full colour. Still vigorous. Ample, fresh, full, ripe Merlot nose. Nice and rich. Lots of depth. Fullish body. Classy. No sign of age. Lovely plump fruit. Long complex finish. Fine plus.

Graves

Château Haut-Brion

NOW–2008	18.5

Fullish colour. Good vigour still. Very good Haut-Brion nose. Roast chestnuts and sandalwood and mocha. Just a touch of attenuation now. Fullish body. Rich, opulent and exotic. Long, mellow, complex and classy. Very lovely. Very fine.

Château La Mission Haut-Brion

NOW–2010	17.0

Medium colour. Fully mature. A little bit of volatile acidity here. The nose is a little thin. Better on the palate. Good grip. Not that full bodied. Only medium-full in substance. Good grip. Ripe and fresh. Good follow-through. Not great but very good indeed.

Margaux

Château Margaux

DRINK UP	13.0

Surprisingly youthful, medium-full colour. Slightly dead on the nose but not totally beneath one's dignity. Slightly tired, slightly dry. Yet there is some fruit and distinction on the palate. Medium body. Now a little old. But not too dried-out. A certain charm. But very dull for a First Growth.

CHÂTEAU PALMER

DRINK SOON — 18.5

Fullish, mature colour. Very lovely nose.
Real class. Beautiful fruit. Impeccably
harmonious. Real Palmer silkiness and
fragrance. Fullish and intense. This is really
very lovely. The fruit is very classy. The wine
has real depth and finesse. Indeed it is really
quite full. Excellent, vigorous finish. Very
long. Very fine.

SAINT-JULIEN
CHÂTEAU DUCRU-BEAUCAILLOU

DRINK SOON — 18.0

Good full mature colour. Lovely classy nose.
Medium-full body. Ripe and velvety. This is
laid-back and very intense. Quite developed
now (my own stock is fresher). But still
lovely. Long on the finish. These bottles say
'drink now'. I have seen it more vigorous.
Fine.

CHÂTEAU GRUAUD-LAROSE

DRINK SOON — 17.0

Fullish, mature colour. Somewhat dense and
four-square, yet ripe and rich underneath on
the nose. Less dense, classier as it evolved. In
the end the nose is very good indeed. Lovely,
quite structured Cabernet. Medium-full
body. Nice and ripe. Not as powerful as it
seemed at first. Ample and quite rich.
Suggestions of astringency. This is very good
indeed but needs drinking quite soon.

CHÂTEAU LÉOVILLE-BARTON

DRINK SOON — 16.5

Magnum. Fine colour. Still youthful. Ripe
nose but a little lacking in nuance. Full and
slightly four-square. On the palate a full
wine, leaving a little astringency now. Very
good fruit but somehow a slight lack of
definition and class. No new oak. Possibly
bottled a bit late. Rich finish. Nice and sweet
at the end. Very good plus.

CHÂTEAU LÉOVILLE-LAS-CASES

DRINK SOON — 17.0

Medium-full colour. Mature. Good ripe
nose. Slightly diffuse. On the palate shows
very nice fruit. Nicely smooth. No hard
edges. Classy. Medium-full. Long. Very good
indeed. Will still keep well. After Palmer and
Ducru-Beaucaillou just a little simple,
perhaps.

PAUILLAC
CHÂTEAU GRAND-PUY-LACOSTE

DRINK SOON — 17.5

Full mature colour. Very lovely nose. Old-
vine concentration. Full and rich. Lots of
depth. Chocolate and black-cherry. This is
fine on the palate. Quite structured. The
tannins are still evident at the end. Very
lovely ripe rich fruit. Very good grip. Long
and classy. But quite sizeable. Fine.

CHÂTEAU LAFITE-ROTHSCHILD

DRINK SOON — 15.5

Magnum. Fullish, mature colour. The nose
here lacks class. The wine seems a little dry
and astringent. The fruit isn't too bad but
the net effect is a little coarse. Slightly burly
at the end. No signs of astringency though.
But a little short. Good plus.

CHÂTEAU LATOUR

NOW–2015+ — 20.0

Very full colour. Classic nose. Mature
Cabernet Sauvignon of the highest class.
Rich, mellow, creamy and impeccably
harmonious. Very complex. Full body.
Everything in place. Marvellously rich and
profound. Lots of vigour. Splendid aftertaste.
This is very special. Easily the wine of the
vintage.

CHÂTEAU LYNCH-BAGES

DRINK SOON — 17.0

Full, rich mature colour. A little spicy-burly
on the nose. But full and rich as well.
Medium-full. Slightly astringent again. Ripe
and spicy on the palate. Ample and rich.
Good dimension. Very good balance. Very
good indeed.

Château Mouton-Rothschild

NOW–2010+   18.5

Very full colour. Rich, full and ample on the nose. Not exactly cedarwood though. Slightly burnt and bitter touches. Full-bodied and creamy rich on the palate. A little tough at the same time though. Very good grip. Long and quite powerful. Still very vigorous. Very fine.

Château Pichon-Longueville, Comtesse de Lalande

DRINK SOON   16.0

Fullish, mature colour. Good ripe fruit. But not the depth and class of Pichon today. A little pedestrian, like the Léoville-Las-Cases. Medium-full. Pleasant but a little coarse in this Super-Second company. Decent fruit and acidity. Indeed there is harmony here. But a little astringent and it lacks a little finesse. Very good at best.

Saint-Estèphe

Château Cos d'Estournel

DRINK SOON   16.5

Full colour, barely mature. Ample, ripe, mature nose. Aromatic to the point of a very slight hint of maderisation. Fullish, mellow and balanced. Good depth. Quite classy too. Doesn't quite have the elegance and nuance for fine. But most attractive. No hint of age. Nice and long on the palate.

Château Montrose

DRINK SOON   16.0

Full colour. Barely mature. Slightly burly on the nose. A little dense. Fullish, quite a lot of astringency. The fruit a little cool, but classy nevertheless. Quite a lot of unresolved tannin and the greenness/herbaceaness that goes with it. But very good.

Good Survivors

Looking through my recent notes of 1970s sampled on occasions other than the two sessions above I can recommend the following as being both very good (at least) and still vigorous:

Saint-Émilion	L'Arrosée; Canon; Magdelaine; Pavie
Pomerol	La Conseillante; La Fleur-Pétrus; Le Gay; La Grave (Trigant-de-Boisset); La Pointe; La Tour-à-Pomerol; Vieux Château Certan, and of course Pétrus itself (19.5 on three occasions over the last decade)
Graves	Domaine de Chevalier
Margaux and Southern Médoc	Cantemerle; Giscours; La Lagune; Malescot
Saint-Julien	Beychevelle; Branaire-Ducru; Langoa-Barton; Talbot
Pauillac	Haut-Batailley
Saint-Estèphe and further north	Haut-Marbuzet; Sociando-Mallet

1966 VINTAGE
(AND THE 1967 FIRST GROWTHS)

SIZE OF THE CROP:	3,102,606 HECTOLITRES.
VINTAGE RATING:	17.5 (RED WINES).
	17.0 (DRY WHITE WINES).
	15.0 (SWEET WINES).

Though not as large as 1962 or 1964 (or what 1967 would bring the following year), 1966 was a good-sized crop, with an average yield of over 40 hl/ha. White wines, at over 1.8 million hectolitres, formed nearly 60 per cent of the harvest.

I was worried about the 1966s. Odd results at vertical tastings supplemented by memories of the last time I organised a comprehensive horizontal session made me suspect that many of the wines would be a little past their best, lean rather than succulent, astringent rather than generous, dry on the finish rather than naturally sweet.

I need not have been anxious. On this occasion the wines had come entirely from private cellars, for the most part laid down since original delivery in optimum conditions. Even after 33 years (the tasting was in 1999), the vast majority of the wines were both delicious and still vigorous, proof that a classic vintage – for that is what 1966 is – will keep for far longer than we might imagine if stored properly. It was a splendid tasting, carried out over a couple of days, over three extended excellent meals, in a stately Vermont mansion on top of a hill with 360 degree views.

THE WEATHER

Generally 1966 was a year rather cooler than average, and as far as the summer months were concerned, on the dry side. The *feuillaison*, when the leaves begin to appear on the vines, took place around 15th March, about a week or so earlier than usual, and the flowering began on 25th May, again a little prematurely. So far so good, similar to 1964, but the complete reversal of 1962, when the flowering did not start until 19th June.

The period of the flowering is crucial. Ideally one would like fine, dry weather, so that the setting of the grape can occur quickly, evenly and successfully. Unsettled weather, prolonging this period, and excessive humidity will encourage *coulure*, when the grapes fail to set, and *millerandage*, grape clusters which do not ripen evenly, and which contain some quasi-raisins which remain small, hard and green. Humidity also encourages mildew.

While in 1964 the flowering was over in a fortnight, in 1966 it lasted almost a month, and, though June had been largely fine and warm, July was mixed, sometimes very hot and sometimes rather cool. The ripening of the grapes (*véraison*) began on 25th July, a week or so earlier than average. August was unsatisfactory, cool and cloudy, but it remained largely dry. It was not until September that the weather brightened, with almost uninterrupted fine weather right through to the end of the vintage, which began on 20th September.

The following table may be of interest:

	1961	1962	1964	1966
RAINFALL (MM): AUG/SEPT	36.1	56.1	103.4	75
HARVEST DATE	22 SEPT	9 OCT	24 SEPT	20 SEPT
SIZE OF HARVEST	SMALL	VERY LARGE	LARGE	QUITE LARGE

THE WINES – THEN

Thanks to the fine September, the grapes were in excellent condition when they were picked. A certain amount of *coulure* in June, especially in Pomerol and Saint-Émilion, had reduced the potential size of the harvest, but as often happens, and especially in 1961, this had the effect of enabling the remaining grapes and bunches to ripen more fully. The crop arrived in the press house looking extremely healthy, and the fermentations passed off smoothly and uneventfully.

It was an auspicious start. From the beginning the colour was deep and rich. The wines, though they seemed (rather misleadingly) to be on the light side, had elegance, charm and balance. As The Wine Society reported to its members in the spring of 1967, 'Soft, supple wines of deep colour'. And as Peter Sichel said in his annual vintage report, 'In style they resemble (the 1962s), lighter then 1964 but with sounder balance, more finesse and even more quality'.

THE WINES – NOW

Nineteen sixty-six is at its best in Saint-Julien and Pauillac. Ducru-Beaucaillou is the plum of the first commune, but all the Léovilles, Gruaud-Larose, Branaire-Ducru and Langoa-Barton are all better than very good. Talbot and Saint-Pierre are equally successful.

The wine of the vintage is indubitably Latour, with Mouton-Rothschild a close second (with Palmer). Lafite was in the doldrums at the time and has never been exciting, so Grand-Puy-Lacoste is number three in Pauillac. Grand-Puy-Ducasse, surprisingly (but this is not the first time it has shone) and Lynch-Bages are very good indeed, the Pichons slightly less so. Haut-Batailley is a little ungenerous, but tasted better with food. Les Forts de Latour, the first vintage of this second wine, can also be recommended.

The commune of Margaux, as always, is more variable. Palmer is magnificent, today holding better than the 1961. But there is not much else in the first flight which is truly OK. Like Lafite, Château Margaux was an underachiever at the time. In contrast, all the top Saint-Estèphes can be safely recommended.

Whether you prefer Haut-Brion to La Mission Haut-Brion is a question of taste. We did not taste them side by side. But I see I have given them both 18 out of 20. The former is more succulent, the most seductive; the latter is splendidly balanced and classy. Haut-Bailly, Pape-Clément, and especially Domaine de Chevalier (which we did not have on this occasion) are all very successful.

We sampled a reasonable selection of Pomerols (L'Évangile especially fine; Lafleur, Trotanoy and La Conseillante and to a somewhat lesser extent Vieux Château Certan were also splendid last time out), but few Saint-Émilions. Here the 1966 vintage is at its weakest. Cheval Blanc and Magdelaine showed very well indeed. Otherwise perhaps only Canon is really worth noting. The 1964 vintage is to be preferred.

Which brings me to Pétrus and Yquem. Nineteen sixty-seven is well-known as being a better vintage for Sauternes than its predecessor. What is perhaps less appreciated, though my friend Howard Ripley demonstrated it to me, blind, back in the late 1970s, is that Pétrus is also better in 1967. Indeed, I would put this bottle on a par with all but the top three 1966s.

PRICES – THEN

As the new wines began to settle down after the cold winter, and as the buyers began to arrive in Bordeaux, the market for the 1966 Bordeaux began. One might have assumed with two failures out of the last three vintages that demand would be brisk, but there was still plenty of 1964 around, and the 'campaign' opened with some hesitancy. With the exception of the First Growths, which returned to 1961 levels, prices opened marginally below those of 1964, that is about 50 per cent above the 1962s. Prices at the time were considered a little high, but in retrospect an ex-cellar opening price for Lafite or Mouton at under £2 a bottle – even if one had paid after the sterling devaluation of November 1967 – seems absurdly cheap.

Prices – Today

By comparison with the 1961s, and indeed the 1982s, and in contrast to 1989, 1990, 1995, 1996 and opening prices since, the 1966s are not expensive for what they are, as are the 1970s. Palmer, Latour and Mouton-Rothschild fetch as much as £2850 ($5130) a dozen, and La Mission-Haut-Brion and Cheval-Blanc are not far short of this figure, but Lafite and Margaux are merely £1400 ($2520). Ducru-Beaucaillou fetches £880 ($1580), Pichon-Lalande £750 ($1350), Cos d'Estournel and Montrose either side of £600 ($1080), Léoville-Las-Cases £550 ($990). You could probably pick up the less fashionable Graves (Haut-Bailly, Pape-Clément and Domaine de Chevalier) and the other plums of the Médoc (Grand-Puy-Lacoste, Léoville-Barton, Branaire-Ducru and Calon-Ségur) for less than £400 ($720).

The Tasting

Hosted by Andy and Renée Carter, assisted by Jack and Thelma Hewitt, organised and largely provided by Bob Feinn of Mount Carmel Wines and Spirits, Hamden, Connecticut, the following wines were sampled in Vermont in October 1999. As well as a large range of 1966s, we sampled the First Growths of 1967 as well. My sincere thanks to all (except the gorilla at the Marriot Hotel in Times Square, New York who managed to smash my magnum of La Mission Haut-Brion).

Saint-Émilion

Château L'Arrosée, 1966

DRINK SOON	17.0

Good full, rich, vigorous colour. Concentrated, mellow, ripe, balanced nose, essentially Merlot but good freshness. Medium-full body. Fresh and ripe on the palate. Just a little four-square, but the finish is long and positive. Lovely ripe fruit. Plenty of life ahead of it. Very good indeed.

Château Cheval Blanc, 1967

DRINK SOON	17.5

Fine full colour. Fuller and less brown than the 1966. Ripe and full but just a little dense and over-macerated on the nose. Rich, full and voluptuous on the palate. Still firm. In the background a little too much structure. But balanced and vigorous and long and fine for a 1967.

Château Cheval Blanc, 1966

NOW–2010	18.5

Fullish, mature colour. Not as vigorous as the 1967. Lovely, ripe, rich, intense, fragrant nose. This is luscious and sexy. Fullish body. Very ripe, rich and concentrated. Lovely fruit. Very well-covered tannins. This is very lovely. More ample than Haut-Brion. More alive too. Very long and vigorous.

Château Figeac, 1966

DRINK SOON	16.5

Full colour. Now mature. Very good fresh fruit on the nose here. Classy and oaky. Quite pronounced acidity. Good attack. Ripe, rich and intense. Then it tails off just a little. But the finish is ripe, even sweet, and very long. Very good plus. Still vigorous.

Château Magdelaine, 1966

DRINK SOON	17.5

Medium-full, mature colour. Fully mature on the nose. Very mellow, ripe and soft. Lovely Merlot fruit. Very ripe and very classy. Very well balanced. Medium-full body. Nicely vigorous still. Long, complex and fine.

Pomerol

Château L'Évangile, 1966

DRINK SOON	18.5

Very full mature colour. Full, firm, rich, excellently profound fruit. Full bodied. Some tannin. Very good grip and concentration. Really lovely. Serious stuff here. Bags of life. Really complex and multi-dimensional. Very classy. This is a very fine example.

Château La Fleur-Pétrus, 1966

DRINK SOON	17.5

Full mature colour. Fragrant Merlot nose. Soft and succulent. Medium-full body. Sweet, ripe, mellow and succulent. Lovely fruit. Very harmonious. No hard edges. Long. But not as much grip as Latour-à-Pomerol. Fine.

Château Gazin, 1966

PAST ITS BEST	SEE NOTE

Mid-shoulder fill. Medium-full colour. A little dank on the nose but some fruit here. Decent quality originally if slightly simple. Now rather astringent. Medium to medium-full body. Now a bit old. Was 14.5.

Château Latour-à-Pomerol, 1966

DRINK SOON	18.0

Fullish colour, just about mature. Rich, full, aromatic nose. Hints of caramel and mocha. Full bodied. A meatier wine than La Fleur-Pétrus. More backbone and better acidity. Larger and slightly fresher. Fine plus.

Château Pétrus, 1967

NOW–2007	20.0

Full colour. Fresher than the 1966. Splendid nose. An intensity and luscious succulence unsurpassed by all but the very best 1966s, let alone 1967s. This is most impressive. Oaky-Merlot on the palate. Full but open. Very fat and very, very rich. Splendid balance. Very voluptuous. Very long. Very lovely. The best 1967? Whether you prefer Latour or this is a question of subjectivity. This is 20/20 for 1967.

Château Pétrus, 1966

DRINK SOON	(18.0)

Very full colour. Fuller but not as fresh as the 1967. Big on the nose. Perhaps a little too much structure. Tannic, a little dense. Not nearly as much sex appeal as the 1967. Got rather more corked or musty as it developed. Full and rich, but dense. Not the best of bottles. But if at its best only fine plus (18.0) for 1966 and not as good as the 1967. Plenty of vigour though.

Château La Pointe, 1966

DRINK SOON	15.5

Medium to medium-full colour. Plump, fresh plummy nose. Medium to medium-full body. Fresh and attractive. Not that concentrated or complex but a good wine and a very good example of a middle-ranking Pomerol.

Graves

Château Haut-Brion, 1967

DRINK SOON	17.0

Fullish, mature but vigorous colour. Lovely nose. Elegant, concentrated and still fresh. This shows a little age but is definitely classy. Medium-full body. Good grip. Mellow, complex, balanced and elegant. Long. Very good indeed if not fine for the vintage. Still vigorous.

Château Haut-Brion, 1966

DRINK SOON   18.0

Full colour. Little maturity. Fine nose. Poised, very ripe, plummy and concentrated. Fullish but velvety and round and fat. Not the greatest style perhaps but it has lovely ripe fruit and is long, complex and classy on the finish. Still very vigorous. Fine plus.

Château La Mission Haut-Brion, 1966

DRINK SOON   18.0

Fine colour. Firm, very Cabernet nose. Slightly vegetal yet rich on the nose. Fullish. Some tannin. Aristocratic. Balanced. Very classy fruit. Firm though and slightly austere. Very fine. Bags of life. But Ducru-Beaucaillou and L'Évangile are better.

Château Pape-Clément, 1966

DRINK SOON   16.5

Full colour. Still vigorous. Rich, ample, plump fruit on the nose. Good youthfulness. Medium-full body. Good attack. Lightening up a little on the finish, but still fresh and fruity. Not short. Attractive and stylish. Very good plus.

Margaux

Château Brane-Cantenac, 1966

DRINK SOON   15.5

Medium to medium-full colour. Fully mature. Ample, opulent, elegant, slightly oaky/cedary nose. No undue age. On the palate this is smooth, quite full, just a little lean at the end, but still classy. Good plus.

Château Lascombes, 1966

DRINK SOON   16.5

Full colour. Fully mature. Chunky nose, but rich. Perhaps beginning to lose a little of its fruit. Got fatter and more opulent and classy as it developed. A nice old vine touch here. Full, ripe and still lively. Good positive follow-through. Rich at the end. Still vigorous. Very good plus.

Château Margaux, 1967

DRINK UP   14.0

Medium-full, mature colour. Mellow, soft, slightly coarse nose. Some astringent. On the palate the wine is just about at the end. Medium to medium-full body. Quite fruity, but the finish is a bit dense and awkward. Lacks grace. Not too short though. The class is undeniably there, if overlaid by clumsiness. Still alive.

Château Margaux, 1966

DRINK UP   14.5

Fullish colour. Not very much maturity. Plump, fresh nose. Stylish but it lacks intensity and depth. Still seems fresh. On the palate fullish, fresh and ample. A bit disjointed. Slightly bitter elements. Slightly astringent. Yet by no means disagreeable.

Château Palmer, 1966

DRINK SOON   19.0

Fine colour. Magical fruit here. Very ripe and lush. Soft yet full. Impeccably balanced. Fullish, intense, silky-smooth. Almost sweet. Marvellous concentrated, quality fruit. Totally brilliant.

Château Prieuré-Lichine, 1966

DRINK SOON   15.0

Full colour. Fully mature. Quite full on the nose. Plenty of fruit if not the greatest of class. Slightly stringy. Quite full, but though ripe a little astringent. Slightly clumsy. Positive at the end though. Still holding up. Good.

Château Rauzan-Ségla, 1966

DRINK SOON   15.5

Full colour. Fully mature. Soft, ripe, cedary nose. Good style. Medium to medium-full body. Nicely ripe and full of interest if without enormous grip or concentration. Still fresh. Good finish. Good plus.

Château Rauzan-Gassies, 1966

DRINK UP   12.0

Medium-full colour. Fully mature. Slightly earthy, undergrowthy nose. Lacks a bit of class. Medium to medium-full body. Rather astringent. Never much finesse. Not farmyardy. Just dull.

Saint-Julien

Château Beychevelle, 1966

DRINK SOON   16.0

Magnum. Full colour. Still youthful. Medium-full substance on the nose. Slightly four-square. A lack of flexibility. Medium-full body. Good ripe blackcurrant fruit. Smooth now. Good acidity. Indeed perhaps just a suggestion of leanness at the end. Very good but not great. Still holding up well.

Château Branaire-Ducru, 1966

DRINK SOON   16.5

Medium to medium-full colour. Fully mature. Ample, plump, ripe nose. Good quality. Very good fruit. Fullish on the palate. Slightly chunky but full of old vine fruit. Sweet, ample and long. Lovely finish. Still plenty of life.

Château Ducru-Beaucaillou, 1966

DRINK SOON   18.5

Fullish colour. Very classy nose. Quite lovely fruit. The quintessence of Saint-Julien. Very succulent. Full, very rich and concentrated. This has First Growth quality, class and intensity. Very lovely opulent (yet dignified) fruit. Very long and complex. Head and shoulders above the rest of the Pauillacs (except the First Growths) and Saint-Juliens. Very fine plus.

Château Gruaud-Larose, 1966

DRINK SOON   17.0

Fullish colour. Rich, full, fat, substantial nose. Slightly solid. Slightly tannic. Yet full, sweet and not a bit hard any more. Not perhaps the class of Ducru-Beaucaillou but balanced, long, ample and very good indeed. Long at the end. Very good with food.

Château Langoa-Barton, 1966

DRINK SOON   16.5

Fullish colour. Fragrant, stylish nose. Not a blockbuster. Medium-full body. Quite delicate. Yet very classy. Good fruit. Ripe, mellow and still holding up very well. Great charm here. Very good plus.

Château Léoville-Barton, 1966

DRINK SOON   17.5

Fullish colour. Richer, fuller and fatter than Langoa-Barton on the nose. Plenty of style here. Fullish body. Old vine concentration. More alive and more like the Barton of the pre-1961 period than I expected. Fine Cabernet. Very classy. Very long. Classic.

Château Léoville-Poyferré, 1966

DRINK SOON   17.0

Fullish colour. The nose here is very lovely: ripe, round, subtle and fruity. Very complex. Very lush. Medium-full body, ample and seductive. Old viney. Not quite as attractive and enticing as the nose. Good grip. Lovely finish. Very good indeed.

Château Léoville-Las-Cases, 1966

DRINK SOON   17.0

Full colour. Very classy nose. Not quite as succulent as the Ducru-Beaucaillou. For once neither as good as Léoville-Poyferré or Léoville-Barton. Fullish body. Mellow, quite rich and with very good acidity. Very long. But not quite the interest. Very good indeed.

Pauillac

Château Grand-Puy-Ducasse, 1966

DRINK SOON   17.0

Full colour. Not much sign of maturity. Ripe, mellow Cabernet nose. Fullish, classy, balanced and attractive. Now velvety. Surprisingly fine for the property. Perhaps the one and only really good wine they have ever made recently. Long, nicely Pauillac-y austerity yet still warm and succulent. Still very vigorous. Very good indeed.

Château Grand-Puy-Lacoste, 1966

DRINK SOON   17.5

Fullish colour. Still youthful looking. Rich, classy, mature nose. Lots of depth. Fullish body. Very lovely, ample, old vine fruit. Splendid depth and balance. Very complex. Very classy and classic and indisputably fine. And will still last well.

Château Haut-Batailley, 1966

DRINK SOON   15.5

Medium-full mature colour. Just a little four-square on the nose. But plenty of Cabernet Sauvignon fruit. It has lightened up a little. Quite stylish Cabernet on the palate. Medium to medium-full body. Properly balanced. The fruit is still sweet. But a slight lack of real dimension. Still vigorous. Certainly good plus.

Château Lafite-Rothschild, 1967

DRINK UP   14.0

Light, old colour. Old, attenuated nose. Not much here. Still drinkable but light, fruity and a bit simple. Decent length and cedary-ness. Quite good.

Château Lafite-Rothschild, 1966

DRINK UP   14.0

Medium-old colour. Somewhat coarse, chunky, astringent and reduced on the nose. On the palate medium-full, the sweetness of the fruit has dried up. There is a rather bitter astringency barrier in the middle and the wine is clumsy. Only quite good for a 1966.

Château Latour, 1967

DRINK SOON   20.0

Fullish, mature colour. This is very lovely: mellow, cedary, fresh and classy. A splendid 1967, one of the very best. Velvety, round and fully mature. Very good drive. Lovely fruit. This is open and seductive. Long and inexpectedly classy. Excellent for the vintage. Bags of life. 20/20 for 1967.

Château Latour, 1966

NOW–2010+   20.0

Very full colour. Still youthful. Splendid nose. Very concentrated. Very ripe. Very intense. Very classy. Now mellow, yet pungent and mouth-filling. This is a giant. Marvellous fruit. Very full body. Very rich and concentrated. Tannic but not obtrusively so. Classic Cabernet fruit. Complex and aristocratic. Very, very fresh. Brilliant.

Château Lynch-Bages, 1966

DRINK SOON   17.0

Full, vigorous colour. Ripe, rich, opulent nose. This is really 'poor-man's Mouton' as Lynch-Bages was known in those days. Full, ripe, seductive and sweet. Some tannin. Good acidity. Generous and lovely. Still holding up very well. Very good indeed.

Château Mouton-Rothschild, 1967

DRINK SOON   17.5

Fullish, mature colour. Attractive, opulent, Mouton-style fruit on the nose. Quite full on the palate. Lots of depth and sex appeal. Fuller and chunkier than Latour. Not as smooth and silky. But balanced and ripe and with plenty of depth and class. Very vigorous still. Fine.

Château Mouton-Rothschild, 1966

NOW–2010   19.0

Full, vigorous colour. Splendid nose. Real concentration. Potentially very lush and succulent, yet still seems youthful. Full bodied. Some tannin. Very ripe and concentrated. Nicely austere. Splendidly intense, vigorous follow-through. Lots of wine here and lots of life ahead of it. This is very fine. But Latour is even better.

Château Pichon-Longueville-Baron, 1966

DRINK SOON   15.5

Full, vigorous colour. Just a touch dense on the nose but mellow, rich and 'old viney' underneath. Fullish, just a little over-macerated and old-fashioned. But the fruit is very good and balanced. Lacks just a little class. Slightly astringent at the end.

Château Pichon-Longueville, Comtesse de Lalande, 1966

DRINK SOON   16.5

Fullish, mature colour. Fragrant on the nose. Ripe and stylish. Not the backbone of the Baron. Similarly it is a touch old-fashioned but only medium-full body and sweeter and softer in texture. The fruit is ripe and attractive. Not fine but very good plus. Finishes well.

Saint-Estèphe

Château Calon-Ségur, 1966

DRINK SOON   17.0

Fullish colour. Well-matured. Quite sensual and evolved on the nose but not reduced. Fullish, ripe and mellow. Merlot in evidence. This is rich and opulent. Still vigorous. Long on the palate. Holding up well. Most attractive. Very good indeed.

Château Cos d'Estournel, 1966

DRINK SOON   16.0

Medium-full colour. Fully mature. Fresh, attractive, quite intense nose. Very good ripe fruit. Medium-full body. Just beginning to loosen up, I think. Grab it now as it is fresh, balanced and elegant. Rather less Merlot in flavour than the Calon-Ségur.

Château Montrose, 1966

DRINK SOON   15.0

Full colour. Still vigorous. Rather dense and vegetably tannic on the nose. Typical of Montrose of this period. On the palate medium-full, rich and attractively fruity but overladen by the tannins. Better with food but unbalanced. Too much maceration. Good at best.

Sauternes

Château d'Yquem, 1967

NOW–2010+   19.5

Golden bronze colour. Rich, concentrated, caramelly nose. Lots of depth here. Full and very rich. Plenty of botrytis. Ample, honeyed and splendidly balanced. Very fresh. Very long. Very fine indeed.

Château d'Yquem, 1966

NOW–2006   17.5

Light, golden bronze colour. Fresh, barley-sugar nose. Not a lot of botrytis but some. Medium body. Fresh at first. Heavier and caramelly at the end. Good Yquem intensity. Long and attractive. Fine.

1961 VINTAGE

SIZE OF THE CROP:	1,831,745 HECTOLITRES.
VINTAGE RATING:	20.0 (RED WINES).
	17.0 (DRY WHITE WINES).
	17.0 (SWEET WINES).

Nineteen sixty-one was a pitifully small harvest, especially for red wine. The overall yield was 25.6 hl/ha. Seventy per cent (nearly 1.3 million hectolitres) was white wine.

There is little doubt in my mind that 1961 stands supreme among the vintages of the last couple of generations. For me, it demonstrates in a superlative way all that I look for in a fine wine: ripe fruit, balance, concentration, a 'three-dimensional' quality of flavour and character and, above all, elegance.

All good vintages keep well and the best, on the criteria expressed above, keep the longest. But longevity *per se* is not necessarily a *sine qua non* (to pursue the Latin) of good wine, though frequently they go together. I would rather drink a wine while it retained all its fruit, even if it was still a little raw and even if this broke the 'ten-year rule' for classed growth claret, than experience it dried out some time later. I see little point in deliberately keeping a wine until it becomes a museum piece or, indeed, paying high prices for wines ancient enough to be of dubious sensual pleasure; and I have often wished, when venerable old bottles are kindly put my way, that I had had the opportunity of broaching them earlier in their prime.

Wine from vintages with balanced, ripe fruit and above all a good acidity, do, however, keep remarkably well. The 1953s are a case in point. This was not a structured, tannic, blockbuster vintage, yet it has lasted better than others. Too many wines of the vintages of the late 1940s and 1950s were made too large in size. They had too much body and tannin for their fruit and in the end they became astringent before they had softened up. One could even castigate wines in the celebrated 1945 vintage for this.

Happily the balance of the 1961s is perfect; the wines were not too dense and were able to demonstrate how excellent they were right from the beginning. Unlike other years, they have at no time in my experience been hard to assess or gone through an awkward phase when their quality was difficult to acknowledge. Perhaps this is because though deep in colour, full in body and tannin, they have superbly rich, concentrated fruit.

While always accessible, the 1961s were slow to develop. In 1978 I was invited to a tasting set up by Dr J D Taams, a noted Dutch connoisseur. Dr Taams had assembled a cellar of 1961s and managed to produce, from his own stocks, no fewer than 22 classed growths including all the top wines save Pétrus. The wines were served blind in two flights, with the best of the first group – which turned out to be Ducru-Beaucaillou – going forward to the second group which included all the *premiers crus*. (Ducru eventually came out 3rd equal.)

At this tasting the vintage still showed itself to be in need of many further years of development despite having had 15 years in bottle. Most of the top wines, with the possible exceptions of Palmer and Margaux, were not yet *à point* – though already delicious.

Then in April 1983 I attended an even more comprehensive tasting thanks to the generosity of Keith and Penny Knight of the Houston House Hotel near Edinburgh. Here we tasted 31 top 1961s including Pétrus, the sole Pomerol representative. By this time, one or two of the minor classed growths were getting to the end of their active lives but there were still some bottles – La

Mission, Mouton and Latour – which were not yet ready, over 20 years on. Most of the top wines were *à point*. Few would die before the year 2000.

There have been other occasions: several in the USA, one where we compared 1959s with 1961s; another where we sampled 1961, 1982 and 1990; a tasting in England in 1987 where there were 47 different châteaux represented. On each occasion it was plain to see that 1961 is a great vintage. It is a vintage that stands continually head and shoulders above all the others in vertical tastings. These are wines we should all take the opportunity to linger over, even at today's extortionate prices.

THE WEATHER

The 1961 vine-cycle began early. The spring was mild after one of the wettest winters on record and the vine was already in flower on 20th May, about three weeks earlier than normal. Then disaster struck. On the night of the 30th/31st May, there was a severe frost. Most of the Merlot flowers were 'burnt off', for this variety is always the most precocious. Extensive damage was done to the remainder. Montrose 1961, for example, is, to all intents and purposes, a 100 per cent Cabernet wine. So is Lafite. So is Domaine de Chevalier.

Thereafter, in contrast, the weather could not have been better. July was evenly warm with some rain at the end of the month. August was hot and practically a drought. September was even hotter with over half the days of the month recording a temperature of 30°C. Again, there was less rain than the norm. In all, the rainfall of the crucial last two months, at 30 mm, was the lowest between 1929 and 1985. Only six other years in the last 50-odd – 1955, 1962, 1970, 1977, 1978 and 1985 – show precipitations of less than 80 mm in August and September.

All this drought retarded the harvest which might, by using the normal rule of thumb (100 days after the flowering), have been assumed to begin at the beginning of September if not in August. In fact, it did not begin until 22nd September, paradoxically later not only than 1959 but also, by a week, than 1960, a vintage which had an unexpectedly early start for an indifferent year.

THE SIZE OF THE HARVEST

The harvest took place in fine weather and an exceptionally small crop of exceptionally healthy ripe grapes was gathered. When the statistics had been totted up, it was established that the total A.C. red Bordeaux wine production, at 550,000 hl, was the third smallest since the Second World War. Only 1956, the year of the great February frost, followed by 1957 which suffered equally (for the vine fruits on last year's wood and in 1956 there was so little vegetation that it was inevitable that the successive year would be badly affected) were smaller.

One can further illustrate the short crop of 1961 by comparing this figure with production figures since. In only one other year (1969) in the 1960s decade was the red wine production lower than one million hectolitres. In the decade of the 1970s, the *average* production was two million. In the 1980s the mean was well above *three* million. Today it is six and a half million. The 1984 harvest, at just under two million – four times larger than 1961 – was considered disastrously short.

Right from the start, however, the wine was indisputably of exceptional quality. Not only this but it was also uniformly good throughout the region. 1961 is not one of the years where one can glibly say that Saint-Émilion and Pomerol were better than the Médoc or vice versa; though one can argue that in the Libournais the 1959 and 1964 vintages are as good, if not better in some properties.

How much of this was due to the short crop is a matter for conjecture but there is no doubt that the size of the harvest was an important factor. It seems obvious that a finite amount of nutrient from the soil, ripeness from the sun and so on, if spread over a smaller quantity of grape berries, will produce fruit of a higher quality. The weather, however, particularly in

August and September, has a greater influence, as a comparison of the success of the years of low rainfall cited above, all good to very good with the exception of 1977, which the short years of an equivalent period will show. The small crops, by comparison with their decade's average, are 1952, 1954, 1965, 1969, 1971, 1977, 1984, 1988 and 1991, not necessarily a series of years to conjure with. (I have not included 1956–1959, all short years as a result of the 1956 frost.)

Peter Sichel often made the interesting point in his annual vintage reports that it is the years of drought rather than great heat in August and September which produce the finest, most classic claret – 1982 was a year of high temperatures and the vintage is fine but the flavour is a-typical, 1989 was similar.

THE WINES – THEN

The 1961s were expensive – exceptionally so – but on both quality and quantity counts one can say, in retrospect, justifiably so. The prices of the top growths varied between 15,500 Francs. a *tonneau* (Cheval Blanc) and 27,550 Francs (Lafite).

To put this in perspective and translating earlier years into what were then still very New Francs, one should point out that post-war prices – 1945 to 1954 – were fairly static, with the most expensive wine, usually Lafite, asking about 3,000 (new) Francs. In 1955 this climbed to 5000, in 1957 to 7500 and in 1959 to 11,000, though in this vintage Lafite was a lot more greedy than its rivals. In 1960, despite a larger crop of inferior quality, the Lafite price jumped to 14,000 and Haut-Brion from 7250 to 12,000. Not surprisingly the 1961 prices, in some cases three times that of 1959, caused many buyers to think again despite the already clearly evident quality.

Prospective purchasers, especially in Britain, had a further reason for being hesitant. The wine trade had bought heavily of the 1959 vintage and had not ignored the 1960s despite generally higher prices. This meant that purchases of the top 1961s, as far as Britain was concerned, were in token quantity only.

The wines first appeared on the retail market in 1964 at about £1.00 a bottle for a British-bottled classed growth, up to £1.50 for a château-bottled Second Growth and £3.50 for Lafite and Mouton Rothschild. By 1968, this had climbed to £1.50, £2.30 and £4.50 and by 1972, primed by the auction boom and speculative buying, prices of over £30.00 a bottle were being realised for the top wines.

If £360 ($640) a case seemed expensive in 1972 – and at the bottom of the slump which followed you could pick up 1961 First Growths for as little as £130 ($230)– it was soon to be eclipsed. By 1981, Mouton and Lafite had moved through the £1000 ($1800) barrier – two years later they were making over £2000 ($3600), and they have continued to climb.

THE WINES – NOW

The 1961s are now over 40 years old: well past it, you might have thought. In fact what is remarkable, if the bottles below, all from major private cellars, are any indication, is how much vigour the vintage still possesses. In some cases, a bit of astringency lurks underneath, one or two others are beginning to get a bit attenuated. But in the majority of cases the wines were alive and vigorous, and would continue to be so for many years still. Fiftieth birthday celebrations are already being planned. What this shows is that it is concentration and balance, not bulk, which counts. The continuing great quality of the 1961s demonstrates that the longer one *can* keep a wine, the more complex it gets.

PRICES – NOW

Today, a case of Pétrus 1961 will fetch as much as £30,000/$54,000 – that's over £400 ($720) a glass – and the remaining *premiers crus* anywhere from £3600/$6480 for Ausone to £11,000 /$19,800 for Latour. This is not peanuts. But on the other hand the 1982s are in many cases hardly any cheaper. I know which vintage I would prefer.

THE TASTING

The majority of the following wines were on show at a tasting organised by Jack and Thelma Hewitt in New Hampshire, USA, in October 2003. I have added some notes from the previous occasion on which I saw a wide range of 1961s, at a tasting offered by Dr Peter Baumann and his friends in Linz, Austria, in November 2001. My thanks to all concerned for these invitations and the opportunity to share their precious bottles.

SAINT-ÉMILION

CHÂTEAU L'ARROSÉE

NOW–2010+   16.5

Fullish colour. Rich, concentrated, aromatic, slightly burly nose. Fullish body. Sweet and spicy. Vigorous. Rich. Plenty of fruit and plenty of depth. It lacks a little real class but very good plus. Long and lively at the end.

CHÂTEAU AUSONE

NOW–2010   17.5

Fullish, vigorous colour. Fragrant nose. Plenty of class and interest. No weakness. No sign of undue age. Fullish body. Sweet and aromatic. Very ripe and rich and classy. This is very lovely. No age. Splendidly and unexpectedly fine quality. Yet slightly short compared with the rest of the First Growths.

CHÂTEAU CHEVAL BLANC

NOW–2010   18.0

Very full, vigorous colour. Very fresh, rich, opulent nose. Fat and ripe and very Cheval Blanc. Full body. Rich and slightly spicy. Very exotic. Not as balanced or as classy as the best of the Médoc/Graves. A slight astringency too. But fine plus. But picked a little late. Slightly over-ripe.

CHÂTEAU CANON

NOW–2010+   17.5

Full, vigorous colour. Very rich, very aromatic, almost voluptuous nose. Splendidly concentrated and sweet. Full bodied, rich, concentrated and old viney on the palate. Lovely balance. Lots of depth. A big wine but with lots to it. Fine.

CHÂTEAU FIGEAC

NOW–2010+   18.5

Fullish colour. Very classy on the nose. You can smell the concentrated Cabernet Sauvignon. Lovely. Fullish body. Harmonious, vigorous and profound. Not a hint of age. Very velvety. Very complex. Lots of depth. Very youthful still. Splendid finish. Very fine.

CHÂTEAU FONPLÉGADE

NOW–2008   17.0

Medium-full, mature colour. Quite firm and structured but good ripe, balanced, fresh fruit here on the nose. This is a very attractive wine. Good acidity. Virile ripe fruit. Classy. Fullish body. Ample and fat yet very harmonious and vigorous. Lots of depth. Bags of life. Lovely long, classy finish. Unexpectedly good.

CHÂTEAU LA GAFFELIÈRE

NOW–2010+   18.5

Full colour. Splendidly rich, old-vine concentration on the nose. Full bodied, sweet, concentrated, fresh and harmonious. A voluptuously rich wine. Very lovely fruit. Very, very rich, long finish. Lovely.

CHÂTEAU MAGDELAINE

NOW–2008   16.0

Full, vigorous colour. Good rich nose. But not as exciting as La Gaffelière or Figeac. Medium-full body. A touch of astringency. Ripe but slightly unbalanced. Slightly tight at the end despite the richness. Still very much alive nevertheless. Very good.

CHÂTEAU PAVIE

NOW–2008	15.0

Full, vigorous colour. Ripe and plump but slightly unclean on the nose. Medium to medium-full body. Good fruit. Quite fresh and balanced. But a lack of real complexity, concentration and distinction. Even if clean, no better than good. Yet still fresh.

POMEROL

CHÂTEAU CERTAN DE MAY

DRINK SOON	17.0

Medium-full colour. Still quite vigorous. Soft nose. Not a great deal of grip and vigour, but plump and attractive. A medium-bodied, fresh but quite Merlot-y wine. Ripe, sweet and stylish. Very good balance. Long. Not quite the personality for great. But well-made for a second division Pomerol as it was then. Very good indeed.

CHÂTEAU CERTAN-GUIRAUD

DRINK SOON	16.5

Fullish colour. Good vigour. Fullish but a little inky on the nose at first. Rich, full and ample underneath. Still fresh. Fullish on the palate. A little astringent. But good grip and vigour and style. Finishes long and ample. But a touch lumpy at the very end. Very good plus.

CHÂTEAU GAZIN

DRINK SOON	17.5

Medium-full colour. Still vigorous. Soft but freshly balanced, elegant nose. Medium-full body. Ripe, fat, sweet and succulent. This has good grip and elegance. Long, composed and nicely intense. Lovely finish. Fine.

CHÂTEAU LATOUR-À-POMEROL

NOW–2008	18.5

Medium-full, mature colour. Quite muscular on the nose. Good vigour. Slight austerity and solidity. On the palate this is full, with good ripe tannins. Very good acidity. Lovely full, fresh, balanced, concentrated fruit. Old viney, even sweet. Very Merlot. Vigorous but succulent. Lovely finish. Very fine.

CHÂTEAU NÉNIN

DRINK SOON	17.5

Medium-full, mature colour. Nicely fresh and vigorous on the nose. Classy fruit. Good grip. Very impressive. On the palate this is medium-full, ample, ripe and balanced. There is a touch of astringency at the end but good grip. This astringency would not be noticeable with food. Not the dimension for great. A certain lack of sweetness but fine, if not great.

CHÂTEAU PÉTRUS

NOW–2010	18.5

Practically black, dense colour. The fullest, most dense 42-year-old wine I have ever seen. Very, very rich and meaty and still closed. Almost marmite-ish. After the First Growths of the Médoc/Graves this is caramelly, liquorishy fat and voluptuous. Big. Even muscular. A slight astringency. Ripe and sexy and larger than life. Very fine but overshadowed by the Left Bank.

CHÂTEAU LA POINTE

DRINK SOON	15.5

Fullish, mature colour. Soft and sweet and succulent on the nose. Medium-full weight. Quite Merlot. Just a little bit undergrowthy as it developed. Medium to medium-full body. It has lost a bit of its substance and grip. Balanced though. Still fresh. Good plus. Better five years ago.

CLOS RENÉ

DRINK SOON	16.0

Fullish colour. Good vigour. Essentially Merlot nose. Ample but no great grip. Medium-full body. Plump and fresh. No great tannin and structure but ample, rich fruit. Virile. Good acidity. Finishes stylishly if slightly lumpy at the end. Very good.

Vieux Château Certan

NOW–2010   17.0

Full colour. Rich. Slightly burly. Fat and aromatic if without quite the distinction of the best of the Saint-Émilion flight. Better on the palate. Fullish-bodied, rich and sweet. A trace of astringency but very good follow-through. Ripe and balanced and very good indeed. But not fine.

Graves

Domaine de Chevalier

NOW–2013+   18.5

Splendidly full, vigorous colour. Refined, youthful, intensely flavoured nose. Very lovely fruit. Cool and fragrant. Fullish body. Absolutely no sign of age. It could be a wine of the 1980s. Complex and multi-dimensional. Very long. Very lovely. Amazingly youthful. Very fine.

Château Haut-Brion

NOW–2013+   19.5

Very full, vigorous colour. Intense, round, very classy nose. Multi-dimensional. More aromatic than La Mission. Full body. Marvellous fruit. Very fine balance. Velvety and intense. Magical. Very fine indeed.

Château La Mission Haut-Brion

NOW–2010+   18.5

Very full, vigorous colour. Just a shade fresher than Haut-Brion. Very lovely fruit here. Multi-dimensional again. Not as classy and as complete as Haut-Brion. Fullish body. Very lovely fruit. Almost sweet. Lovely balance. Not quite the complexity and brilliance of Haut-Brion but long and very impressive nonetheless???. Plenty of life.

Château Pape-Clément

NOW–2010   16.5

Fullish colour. Fullish, vigorous, spicy-earthy Graves nose. Good fruit. Not the distinction of La Mission Haut-Brion. Tobacco elements here. Medium-full body. Plenty of spicy fruit. Good grip and concentration. Slightly astringent but no lack of depth. Very good plus.

Château La Tour Haut-Brion

NOW–2010   18.0

Vigorous, fullish colour. Plenty of depth and quality here on the nose. Quite a masculine character: structured and slightly austere. But generous underneath. Still very youthful. Very lovely, very classy fruit. Surprisingly fresh and vigorous. Full body. Very good grip. Very long and very satisfying at the end. This is fine plus.

Margaux and Southern Médoc

Château Brane-Cantenac

DRINK SOON   17.5

Medium, fully mature colour. Soft, ripe, elegant and succulent on the nose. Perhaps just beginning to decline. On the palate only medium body. Balanced and elegant and classy but it was better 5 to 10 years ago. A little astringent at the end. Fine nonetheless.

Château Cantemerle

NOW–2008   17.5

Medium-full colour. Lovely fragrant nose. Now gently fading perhaps. Medium-full body. Balanced. Very classy fruit. More vigour than the nose would suggest. Ripe, complex, intense and classy. Still very long. Fine. Will still keep a few years.

Château Giscours

NOW–2008   15.5

Medium-full colour. Rich, aromatic, quite concentrated nose. Medium-full body. Good freshness if no great complexity or distinction. There is a certain Graves earthiness here. Good follow-through. Balanced. Good plus. Will still hold up.

Château La Lagune

DRINK SOON   17.0

Medium to medium-full, mature colour. Just a touch of volatile acidity on the nose. Ripe. Medium weight. Medium body. This has begun to lighten up but it is still soft, sweet, balanced and juicy. No astringency. Good acidity. Very good indeed.

Château Lascombes

DRINK UP   14.0

Fullish colour. Quite a muscular nose. Not a lot of finesse. Slightly four-square. Fullish body. A little burly. A little astringent now. This is beginning to dry up and to lose its natural sweetness. Only quite good. ·

Château Malescot-Saint-Exupéry

NOW–2008   16.0

Good, full, vigorous colour. Fullish, slightly austere Cabernet nose at first. Good depth. Fullish body. Good tannin. Good acidity and plenty of fruit and depth. Not unduly hard. Indeed ripe and vigorous and very stylish. Very good. I have had better bottles (i.e. 17.5/20).

Château Margaux

NOW–2010   20.0

Full, mature colour. Very, very lovely nose. Ethereal and complex. Very classy and multi-dimensional. Simply lovely. Great finesse. Even better than Lafite. In its own quite delicate way this is well-nigh perfect. The fruit is quite brilliant. Medium to medium-full body. Sweet. Marvellously complex and balanced. Very, very long. Still very, very fresh. Great wine.

Château Palmer

NOW–2010   19.5

Medium-full, mature colour. Very lovely fruit on the nose. Slightly less vigour but perhaps more pure than the Ducru-Beaucaillou. Quite splendid. Medium-full body. Soft, smooth, silky and very ripe. Marvellous balance. Very, very long. Lovely lingering finish. This bottle is still very fresh. Splendid grip. Beautiful fruit. Quite magnificent.

Château Poujeaux

DRINK SOON   17.5

Medium-full, mature colour. Juicy nose. A little reticent at first. Medium-full weight. Stylish. Medium-full body. Balanced. Mellow and most attractive. The follow-through is poised and complex. Very long. Lovely. Fine.

Château Rauzan-Ségla

DRINK UP   15.0

Full colour but really quite developed. The oldest looking of this first flight of Margaux. Some age on the nose too. On the palate medium-full body. A little dry, but there is still class. I find this more enjoyable than the Lascombes. But it is also approaching the end of its life.

Château Rauzan-Gassies

NOW–2008   16.5

Fullish colour. Ripe nose. Good weight and depth. Fresher than Rauzan-Ségla. On the palate altogether more interesting. Medium-full body. Good juicy fruit. Balanced and attractive. Not the greatest class but very good plus. More fat than Giscours. Will still hold up for a bit.

Saint-Julien

Château Beychevelle

NOW–2008   16.5

Medium-full colour. Quite well matured. Very soft and mellow on the nose. No undue astringency. Still elegant and fruity. Medium body. Stylish and balanced if without quite the depth and concentration of the best. Still clean at the end. A little weak though. Very good plus.

Château Branaire-Ducru

NOW–2008   17.0

Medium-full colour. Full, rich, ripe, fresh and classy on the nose. Good vigour here. Attractive fruit too. Unexpectedly good on the palate. Fullish body. Quite burly but ripe, concentrated and the after-taste is clean and civilised. Positive finish. Very good indeed.

Château Ducru-Beaucaillou

NOW–2010   19.5

Medium-full colour. Still quite fresh. Quite delicious, fragrant fruit on the nose. Simply beautiful! Still very vigorous. Ethereal, complex and intense. Medium-full body. Total class and complexity here. By no means a blockbuster but marvellous depth and harmony. Very long. Very fine indeed.

Château Gloria

DRINK SOON   16.5

Full, almost inky colour. Slightly tough nose. A bit astringent. A bit dense. Better on the palate. Rich, 'old-viney' attack. A little dry but fresh and balanced. With the right food, e.g. a rich beef stew, this could be very good indeed.

Château Gruaud-Larose

NOW—2008   17.5

Fullish colour. Good rich, full, meaty, vigorous nose. Fullish body. A slight touch of astringency on the palate. A slight earthy touch too. Yet energetic and fine with food. Just slightly clumsy. Not enough real depth and richness but the finish is long and positive.

Château Langoa-Barton

DRINK UP   14.0

Medium-full, mature colour. Medium weight on the nose. A suggestion of attenuation. A slight lack of grip and vigour. On the palate rather less interest. It has lightened up and dried out. Now empty and astringent. Is this a fair bottle?

Château Léoville-Barton

NOW—2010   18.0

Fullish colour. Classy, mature Cabernet on the nose. Plenty of vigour. Fullish body. Cool and very competent. Lovely balance. Very fresh. The finish is very long and complex. The wine will still last well. This is fine plus.

Château Léoville-Las-Cases

NOW—2010   17.0

Fullish colour. Fresh nose. Clean, pure and classy. But the least depth and concentration of the three Léovilles. Medium-full body. Plump, balanced and fresh. Good class but a slight lack of depth and complexity. It finishes well. Very good indeed.

Château Léoville-Poyferré

NOW—2013+   18.5

Fullish colour. Rich, voluptuous and old viney on the nose. The fattest, richest and most interesting of the Léovilles. Fullish body. Rich, complex and slightly spicy. This is fat, sweet, fresh and positive and very lovely. Very fine finish. Lots of life still left. Very fine.

Château Saint-Pierre

DRINK SOON   15.0

Fullish colour. Rich but a little burly and stewed on the nose. Not too astringent though. A chunky wine. Full-bodied on the palate. Now a little astringent and clumsy. Rather four-square. It lacks a bit of nuance. Good at best.

Château Talbot

DRINK SOON   14.0

Medium-full colour. Well matured. Like the Beychevelle, soft, mellow and fruity without great energy but also without undue astringency. Decent fruit on the palate. Medium body. But a little astringency. Getting a bit light. Losing a bit of its fruit. Was very good, now quite good.

Pauillac

Château Batailley

NOW—2010+   17.5

Full colour. Vigorous. Rich, round, fat, intense and fruity. Like the Beychevelle but with more class and more depth. This is an admirable wine. Fullish-bodied, fresh, harmonious and complex. Medium-full weight. Very good grip. Very fresh. Long. Fine quality. Lots of life.

Château Croizet-Bages

DRINK SOON   15.5

Magnum. Good fullish fresh colour. Soft nose. No hard edges. But no real depth or class either. Ripe and pleasant and still fresh. On the palate this is a lot less rustic than I expected. Medium-full body. Good grip. Good vigour. Quite mellow but positive at the end. A slight lack of fruit as it evolved. Good plus.

CHÂTEAU GRAND-PUY-DUCASSE

NOW–2009   18.5

Fullish colour. Still very vigorous. Just a little dense behind it. Full body. Some tannin. Lots of rich, ripe, concentrated fruit. A shade old-fashioned. Very good grip. A meaty example. But a very fine one. Lovely long finish. Good 'old viney' depth. Very fine. Unexpectedly so. But the 1959 and 1966 are also surprisingly good.

CHÂTEAU GRAND-PUY-LACOSTE

NOW–2013+   18.5

Full, vigorous colour. Lovely nose. Full, rich, concentrated and vigorous. 'Old viney' depth here. Full-bodied, rich, concentrated and vigorous on the palate. Very lovely fruit indeed. Splendid quality. Lots of depth and lots of dimension. Lovely long finish. Very fine. Bags of life ahead of it still.

CHÂTEAU HAUT-BATAILLEY

NOW–2010   17.5

Fullish colour. Ripe, rich and full on the nose. Just a little more austere than Grand-Puy-Lacoste. Medium-full body. Round, ripe, mellow and sweet. Balanced and velvety. Fresh, long and complex. Fine.

CHÂTEAU LAFITE

NOW–2008   19.5

Full, mature colour. Very lovely complex, classy, fragrant nose. There is finesse in spades. Very fresh and harmonious. Let us not forget that this is 100 per cent Cabernet Sauvignon. On the palate this is very fine but it is not as fresh or as intense as the Margaux. Medium to medium-full body. A little more substance but a little more astringency as well. Very fine indeed but not great.

CHÂTEAU LATOUR

NOW–2020   20.0

Absolutely amazing colour. Very, very full. It seems as if it could be a 1956. Amazingly the nose suggests a still unformed wine. One not yet ready. Splendid depth and concentration of fruit. Full body on the palate. A big but velvety wine. Still some tannin but these now mellow and they give size and vigour, dimension and depth. Really aristocratic. Still amazingly youthful. Brilliant. Great.

CHÂTEAU LYNCH-BAGES

NOW–2010   18.0

Full vigorous colour. Very lovely nose. Creamy-rich, ripe and voluptuous. Really concentrated. Splendid depth. Full-bodied, ample, rich and sweet. A little astringent now but still 'old viney' complexity and lots of attraction. Very good grip. Long and lovely. But Grand-Puy-Lacoste is better. Fine plus.

CHÂTEAU MOUTON-ROTHSCHILD

NOW–2010   19.5

Very fine, full, vigorous colour. Almost as youthful as the Latour. Could be a 1990s vintage. Proper Mouton nose. This is the sort of quality Mouton-Rothschild showed more recently in 1982 and 1986. Super rich, fat, ripe and cedary. Quite lovely. Marvellously seductive. Yet very classy too. Fullish-bodied, rich and velvety. Very finely balanced. Really excellent fruit. But not quite up to Latour or Château Margaux. Yet nevertheless very, very lovely indeed.

CHÂTEAU PIBRAN

DRINK SOON   14.0

Double magnum. Fullish colour. Still vigorous. Somewhat dry and inflexible on the nose. A touch of volatile acidity. A little artisanal but good Cabernet Sauvignon fruit. On the palate somewhat chunky, but still fresh. Good grip. Fullish body. Quite vigorous. Some tannin and some astringency. But there is fruit here. Quite good quite rich but a little hard and inflexible. Better with food.

Château Pichon-Longueville-Baron

NOW–2008	17.0

Full, vigorous colour. Good class here. Good vigour too. Fully evolved. Is there now a hint of it loosening up. Older than the Fifth Growths in this flight. Medium-full body. Some astringency. Good finish. Quite classy but very good indeed at best.

Château Pichon-Longueville, Comtesse De Lalande

NOW–2008	18.0

Fullish colour. Gentle, fragrant nose. Quite evolved. Medium to medium-full weight. Subtle and elegant. Medium-full body. Now, like the Pichon-Baron, more evolved than the Grand-Puys and the Lynch-Bages. Elegant fruit. Ripe and lovely. But fine rather than great. Certainly very refined.

Saint-Estèphe

Château Calon-Ségur

NOW–2010	17.0

Fullish colour. Ample, ripe, stylish nose. Good plump, fat fruit. Good style too. Fullish body. Aromatic, sweet and old-viney. Not quite as elegant as the best Saint-Juliens but balanced and warm-hearted. Very good indeed. No hurry to finish up.

Château Cos d'Estournel

DRINK SOON	15.5

Fullish colour. Stylish nose. Not a typical Saint-Estèphe. Nicely fresh. Ripe and attractive. Fullish body. Fresh and decently balanced. But it doesn't have the fat or the concentration of Calon-Ségur. Slightly astringent at the end. Good plus.

Château Montrose

NOW–2008	17.0

Full colour. Slightly firm nose. Quite tannic. And the fruit is drying up. A big wine. Tannic but rich. It was always a little top heavy – a wine for food. But lovely rich fruit. On the follow-through this fruit very nearly matches the tannin. Classy too. Very good indeed.

Château Phélan-Ségur

DRINK SOON	15.0

Medium-full colour. Fully mature. An odd nose. It smells of manure at first. On the palate once again – all the Saint-Estèphes are similar – slight rigidity and astringency. Only a little class. Some length. Decent fresh finish. Finishes better than it starts. Good. I used to have some of this. It was far better in the 1970s and early 1980s.

Sauternes

Château d'Yquem

NOW–2010	-

Slightly pink-edged, medium bronze colour. Sweet but no botrytis on the nose. Simply sweet is all. Not very full or intense either. This is really rather boring. Fresh but simple.

1959 VINTAGE

SIZE OF THE CROP:	1,858,605 HECTOLITRES.
VINTAGE RATING:	19.0 (RED WINES).
	16.0 (DRY WHITE WINES).
	18.5 (SWEET WINES).

As a result of the long-term effects of the 1956 frost, 1959 was a small harvest in Bordeaux, the fourth in a row which failed to exceed 2 million hectolitres overall. The yield was only 27.5 hl/ha. Sixty two per cent of the crop was white wine.

The beginning of the 1960s marked a watershed in Bordeaux's history. If 1959 was the last great year when the wine was made by old-fashioned methods, 1961 saw the start of a change to controlled vinifications, an appreciation of the malolactic fermentation and what it was all about, and the first installation, at Haut-Brion, of stainless-steel vats. These were also the last years when the wine was made entirely with first or second generation, post-phylloxera fruit. From henceforth the replanting of the Bordeaux *vignoble*, made necessary first by the gaps left as a result of economic and war depletion in the 1930s and 1940s and second by the 1956 frost, would increasingly show in the wines. Through the rest of the decade, and well into the 1970s, the Bordeaux *vignoble* declined in average age as yields increased. The quality of the wines suffered. The weather was less kind. Yes, 1966 and 1970 would provide fine wines. But in general the 20 years after 1961 would furnish less great bottles of Bordeaux than the 17 vintages since the end of the Second World War which preceded (and included) it. It would take 20 years and more, until 1982 and after, when a combination of old vines and good vintages would rival what had been produced between 1945 and 1961.

BRITISH (AND OTHER NON-CHÂTEAU) BOTTLINGS

This period also marked the beginning of the end of the quality of British and other non-châteaux bottlings. In the 1940s and 1950s, as hitherto, almost all quality Bordeaux, as well as the lesser wines, was shipped in cask. Top British merchants such as The Army and Navy Stores, Avery's, Berry Bros, Harvey's, Justerini and Brooks and The Wine Society, as well as many other respectable sources which are now defunct, not to forget their counterparts overseas, particularly Vandermeulen in Belgium, would ship their wine in cask – their Léovilles and Pichons and Palmers and Vieux Château Certans, even Cheval Blanc and Margaux, and bottle them themselves. Only a few First Growths insisted on château-bottling their entire production.

While château-bottling, as has been well documented in books on Lafite and Margaux, might have taken place in several stages over a wide spread of months, perhaps when there was little to do in the vineyard, home bottlings were executed by experts, chthonian cellar workers who rarely saw the light of day, who might have known nothing about the whys and wheres and *encépagement* nuances of what they were dealing with, but who had a fundamental craftsman's respect for and understanding of what they were dealing with. These artisans did nothing but bottle wine; sherry and port one week, burgundy the next, a host of *petits châteaux*, and then Ducru-Beaucaillou or Lynch-Bages. A few casks of a wine such as the latter would be siphoned up to a holding tank one day, then bottled by gravity, without filtration, a couple of days later. The speed was archaic, the surroundings probably far from spotless, but the result was fine, often better than that produced by the château. Indeed, if a wine seemed a bit weak, it might be roused up and bottled turbid, so that it could continue to enrich itself on its lees. Even, dare I suggest it, a bottle or two of cognac or vintage port might be added to the blend to enrich it.

A Personal Note

It was about this period that I began to drink fine Bordeaux. They were cheaper in those days: even on a student's grant I could afford a classed-growth claret once a week. In 1964 I spent some months in France and visited Bordeaux as a *stagiaire* for the first time. Some years afterwards I changed jobs, sold a flat in London, bought a house in the country, and with the residual profit on the transaction, 'invested' in wine for the first time. I had a thousand pounds to spend. I wrote round to all the major fine wine retailers and bought a bottle or two, or three, depending on price, of every named Bordeaux I could find. My £1000 bought me one thousand bottles of perhaps 500 different wines of vintages between 1945 and 1959 (the 1961s were not yet on the market). By sampling these wines in a sensible, educative way – three of the same château or three of the same vintage at a time – I taught myself about Bordeaux. I found myself with 40-odd 1959s. I invited some friends to fill in the gaps, and wrote the results up: the first article I ever had published. Thus it all began.

The Weather

By and large 1959 was a fine, hot, dry year. The early spring was particularly fine, with clear skies and high barometer readings, meaning that it was cold at night, crisp in the morning, but, if sheltered from the wind, one could prune in shirt-sleeves in the afternoon. April began well but clouded over after Easter, and there were storms at the end of the month. May began indifferently but improved later, ushering in good weather for the flowering which began at the beginning of June, about a week earlier than normal. July and August are unsettled in Bordeaux, with hail and storms to interrupt the growing cycle of the vine, and with the earlier month frequently colder than June, but in 1959 it was almost entirely warm and sunny, indeed the conditions in July were a real heatwave. September started hot; there was a lot of rain in the week after the 12th but conditions had improved by the time the picking started on the 25th and continued fine and hot throughout the harvest. In all it was a very hot dry year. Though the rainfall statistics for the two crucial pre-vintage months, at 133 mm, bears little resemblance to 1961 and 1985 (both less than 40 mm) and even with 1966 and 1970 (around 75 mm), the rain that fell was almost entirely confined to the week in September mentioned above.

The Wines Now

The majority of the 1959s, even at over 40 years of age, still have much to offer; many are still vigorous.

Beginning with the Libournais, and addressing the wines not tasted below, the Pomerols are one of the high spots of the vintage: a lovely Vieux Château Certan, a fine Trotanoy and an opulent, spicy, larger-than-life Pétrus. I have also enjoyed Latour-à-Pomerol, Lafleur-Pétrus, L'Évangile and La Conseillante. The first-named is the only rival to Pétrus: though Vieux Certan has perhaps the most breed of them all.

Many of the Saint-Émilions are better in 1959 (and perhaps also in 1964) than in 1961. La Gaffelière (then called La Gaffelière-Naudes) was on a roll, after which it dipped, and its 1959 – indeed, nearly all its wines from 1945 onwards – is succulent and 'old-viney'. Pavie is good. Canon better still, if a bit old-fashioned. Magdelaine is rich and refined, as is Belair (though aging now).

The Graves performed particularly well in 1959. Haut-Brion is splendid, La Mission rich and concentrated – see below – but Domaine de Chevalier, at its best, is also a great delight. Up with these I would rate Pape-Clément. And I have fond memories of a profound, 'old-viney' Haut-Bailly.

The commune of Margaux is spotty, as always, but Château Margaux itself is fine and Palmer is superb (see below). Others, such as Lascombes and Malescot-Saint-Exupery, are full, ample and rich, still with plenty of life ahead of them. Most of the rest, though, are perhaps now past their prime.

The best of the 1959s are to be found in Saint-Julien and Pauillac. Beychevelle was very good last time out (though showing age, even in magnum) and Léoville-Poyferré, Langoa-Barton, Saint-Pierre and Branaire are all at least 'good-plus'. The vintage was consistent here.

There are three excellent wines in Pauillac, most of which we tasted below. Most of the rest, except Pichon-Baron, better I think than Pichon-Lalande, will probably be showing age now.

Finally Saint-Estèphe, another successful location for the 1959 vintage. My experience is mainly with the top three in recent years, though I remember Phélan-Ségur from a recent vertical. Calon-Ségur should be good. So is Haut-Marbuzet if you can find it.

Prices Now

The 1959s are now rare, and buying them at auction or on the broker's circuit is unadvisable, unless you can be certain about the provenance. In January 2003 Farr Vintners were quoting Château Margaux (ex-Nicolas) for £6000 ($10,800) per dozen, Pichon-Baron for £1500 ($2700) and Branaire-Ducru for £780 ($1400).

The Tasting

The following wines were tasted in Vermont, check state, courtesy of my friends, Jack and Thema Hewitt in October 1999.

Saint-Émilion

Château Cheval Blanc

DRINK SOON	17.5

Level: mid-shoulder. Aromatic nose. Lush, voluptuous mocha, milk-chocolate touches. Coffee and liquorice. This is full and concentrated, with a touch of spice. Very good grip. Long. Naturally sweet. Very vigorous. Slightly attenuated as it developed. But still fine.

Château Figeac

DRINK SOON	17.5

Level: very high shoulder. Splendidly full, mature colour. Very lovely nose. Sweet, rich, concentrated and ripe. This has real depth. Aromatic and Merlot-y. A true Saint-Émilion, except one with excellent grip and vigour. Medium-full. Very mellow and complex. Spicy-sweet. Fine. Yet didn't hold up *that* well in the glass.

Pomerol

Château Lafleur

DRINK SOON	17.5

Bottled Vandermeulen. Good fill. Full mature colour. Very rich, concentrated nose. Quite dense as usual but the amount of fruit is so voluptuous that it overwhelms the structure. Full and vigorous. Very good grip. Hugely ripe. But basically a very – almost too much – structured wine. The acidity is keeping the wine fresh and vigorous. Fine. But lacks a little nuance.

Graves

Château Haut-Brion

DRINK SOON	17.5

Level: low neck. Quite firm on the nose. Still fresh. Rather aloof, in fact. Slightly rigid on the palate. The finish is fine. Long and fullish. Getting near the end though.

Château La Mission Haut-Brion

DRINK SOON   19.0

Good fill. Very full, mature colour. Splendid nose. Rich, classy, profound. Very lovely fruit. A little tough and herbaceous as it evolved. On the palate rich, very concentrated and very profound. Fullish but no hard edges. Fine grip. This is very lovely indeed. Will still keep really well.

Margaux

Château Margaux

DRINK SOON   17.0

Level: low neck. Splendid aromatic, essentially really very high class on the nose. Very lovely fruit. This had very lovely fruit at first but rapidly began to age in the glass. Slightly rigid. The fruit is long but the wine a bit unbalanced. Didn't hold up in the glass. Slightly earthy at the end.

Château Palmer

DRINK SOON   19.0

Good fill. Full, mature colour. Splendid nose. Velvety smooth, intense and fruity. Gently oaky and very concentrated. Flowery too. Very subtle. This is very Margaux, very Palmer. Medium-full. Smooth and silky. Excellent subtle, balanced fruit. A very, very lovely example. The finish is very complex, and very, very long.

Saint-Julien

Château Ducru-Beaucaillou

DRINK SOON   18.5

Good fill. Fullish, mature colour. Fragrant, classy nose. Lovely but suggestions of astringency. On the palate this is fullish, ample, balanced and shows real finesse. The wine has a lot of dimension, real length on the palate and splendid poise. No sign of age. Yet don't push your luck. It is a lovely example.

Château Gruaud-Larose

DRINK SOON   18.0

Level: very high shoulder. Full, mature colour. Full, rich, concentrated nose. Very lovely Cabernet fruit. Medium-full. Lovely balance and very Saint-Julien. Not a bit burly or dense, like today. Super fruit. Ripe, fragrant, rich and splendidly balanced. Fine plus again.

Château Léoville-Barton

DRINK SOON   18.5

Level: low neck. Full mature colour. Very fine nose. Complex and classy, real depth, splendidly composed. Fullish, more structure evident than the Gruaud-Larose. Very lovely fruit again. Balanced, classy and profound. More of a Pauillac than a Saint-Émilion in its power and richness. Splendid vigour. Will last well. Very, very lovely at the end.

Château Léoville-Las-Cases

DRINK SOON   19.0

Good fill. Fullish, mature colour. Great class and depth here. Fragrant, very lovely nose. Rather smoother and more vigorous than Ducru-Beaucaillou. Very, very lovely, concentrated fruit. Full and ample. No hard edges. Very, very classy. Very, very well balanced. Splendidly long. First class. Will keep very well.

Pauillac

Château Grand-Puy-Lacoste

DRINK SOON   18.0

Level: bottom neck. Full, mature colour. Mellow, fragrant, sweet nose. Splendid depth on the palate, but showing a little astringency now. Underneath very creamy, old wine richness. Excellent grip and great class. Medium-full body. The finish is truly excellent. With food this would be very fine.

Château Lafite-Rothschild

DRINK SOON   19.0

Level: low neck. Splendid nose. This has exceptionally classy fruit. Really lovely depth. Quite fantastic. Rich and voluptuous on the palate. Ripe and inviting on the follow-through. Excellent. As they developed I found the Latour and Mouton-Rothschild marginally better.

Château Latour

NOW–2010   19.5

Level: low neck. Full, very lovely nose. Excellent fruit here. Quite powerful. Higher toned than Lafite. Really classy and elegant. Still very young. Still has some tannin. But marvellous fruit underneath the fat. Long. Very lovely. Quite different to Lafite-Rothschild. Bay leaves. Very fine. Even better than Lafite today.

Château Lynch-Bages

DRINK SOON   17.5

Level: bottom of neck. Very full, mature colour. Really Mouton-y on the nose. Very good oak. Splendid fruit. Still very fresh and vigorous. On the palate this is a full, vigorous, meaty wine. Very fine grip. This is perhaps not quite as classy as the Léoville-Barton, Gruaud-Larose or Grand-Puy-Lacoste but is fat, rich, concentrated and aromatic. Vigorous. Long. Fine.

Château Mouton-Rothschild

DRINK SOON   19.5

Level: mid-shoulder. Very lovely, ripe, classy, velvety, cedary nose. Full, rich, still some tannins. Lots of wine here. Splendidly rich. This is by far the most laid-back of the 1959s. Excellent fruit and grip. Multi-dimensional. Still very youthful.

Château Pichon-Longueville, Comtesse de Lalande

DRINK SOON   17.0

Fill: mid-shoulder. Good full, mature colour. Plump and ripe on the nose. Quite high-toned. Not the greatest of finesse but good volume and vigour. Better on the palate from the point of view of elegance. Medium-full body. Good balance. This is very good indeed. Still fresh. But may begin to crack up soon.

Saint-Estèphe

Château Cos d'Estournel

DRINK SOON   16.5

Level: very high shoulder. Full, mature colour. Fine nose. Full, rich, vigorous and aromatic. Medium-full. Still fresh and complex, though not perhaps for *that* much longer. It is beginning to lose a little of its fat. Good balance and class though. Nicely sweet, with a spicy touch, on the finish. Very good plus.

Château Montrose

DRINK SOON   17.0

Level: high mid-shoulder. Very full mature colour. High-toned nose. This has good fruit and richness. Separately, underneath, a little dense and tannic. An attempt at a blockbuster. Some very lovely fruit here. But all around it the size is apparent. Lots of tannin. Best with food. Very good indeed. How is this going to last? The finish, even without food, is clean, fresh and stylish.

1959 SAUTERNES

The secret to a really great sweet wine vintage is the timing of the arrival of the noble rot. Ideally the onset of the botrytis should start *after* the grape has reached full physiological ripeness. If the fruit is completely ripe and the *pourriture noble* forms on already concentrated berries the resulting flavours will be richer, profounder, more luscious and more complex. The balance will almost certainly be better and the wine more intense and classy.

This was exactly what happened in 1959 and explains why this vintage is more satisfactory than all the others until we get to 1988, 1989 and 1990. It was a long, hot, dry summer, interrupted a week or so before the harvest by some rain. This rain helped create the humid conditions required for the formation of botrytis on fruit which was already fully ripe. The first passages began on 21st September. Every four or five days after that there would be another *tri*, but such was the evenness of the botrytis attack, and the absence of any more bad weather, the Sauternes harvest was complete by the last week of October. There was not a lot of it, but nearly everything was of high quality, worthy of the *grand vin*.

The wines are over 40 years old, but such is the balance and concentration of the vintage few show any age. The best will still last well beyond 2005 – probably beyond 2010. The following wines, though from my own cellar, had been collected over the past five years from a variety of sources. Wines that had not been moved from the outset were in an even fresher condition.

THE TASTING

The following 1959 Sauternes were sampled in London in May 1999.

CHÂTEAU CAILLOU, CRÈME DE TÊTE

DRINK SOON   15.0 (WAS 16.0)

Mid-deep gold colour. Refined nose. Now drying out a little. Soft and gentle on the palate. Peachy in flavour. Balanced. Slightly fading but good class, but got coarser as it developed.

CHÂTEAU CLIMENS

NOW–2009   19.0

Deep colour. Very concentrated. Huge amounts of fruit. Very fine. Full, rich, concentrated. Some oak I am sure. Splendid vigour, class and harmony. Very very lovely, complex, long finish. This is very, very fine.

CHÂTEAU COUTET

DRINK SOON   16.0

Lovely nose. Soft and concentrated and harmonious. This is showing a little age now. It has lost a little fat and a little vigour. Round. Still fresh, still classy. Was 17.5 once.

CHÂTEAU DOISY-DAËNE

DRINK SOON   15.5

Delicate, classy fruit on the nose. Gentle on the palate. Full and with very fine fruit. Quite delicate now. Very good balance. Not a lot of botrytis perhaps. Some alcohol. Good plus.

CHÂTEAU DOISY-VÉDRINES

DRINK SOON   17.5

Very good concentration and balance on the nose. Lovely, subtle, splendidly fresh and complex. Medium-full body. Vigorous, classy and multi-dimensional. Fine.

CHÂTEAU DE FARGUES

NOW–2009   15.0

Deep colour. Concentrated, oaky, barley-sugar nose. Full-bodied, balanced and fresh but somehow a bit one-dimensional. Lacks real concentration and nuance. Plenty of life ahead of it though. Good.

Château Gilette, Crème de Tête

NOW–2005+   17.0

Deep colour. Concentrated, sweet nose, but
little botrytis, if any. Barley-sugar on the
palate. Very sweet. Good acidity. Very
concentrated. Essence of wine. Surprising
refinement and vigour. Very good indeed.

Château Guiraud

DRINK SOON   15.0

Deep colour. Somewhat loose-knit on the
nose. Lacks bite. Soft and sweet. But neither
a lot of class nor a lot of balance. Still fresh
though and not short. Good.

Château Lafaurie-Peyraguey

NOW–2009   18.5

Deep colour. Splendidly fresh, concentrated,
classy, balanced nose. Most lovely on the
palate. Splendid harmony. Full, classy and
complex. Super, yet not that luscious. Very,
very long. Bags of life ahead of it. Very fine.
(Another bottle sampled in Burgundy a few
weeks later was even better.)

Château Rayne-Vigneau

DRINK SOON   16.0

Deep bronzed colour. Just a touch of
oxidation on the nose. Held up well in the
glass though. Caramelly touches. Full, quite
muscular. Good depth and concentration.
Finishes long. Very good.

Château Rieussec

NOW–2009   18.0

Deep colour. Rich, barley-sugar nose. Full,
fat, opulent and concentrated on the palate.
Lovely nobly-rotten character. Vigorous and
balanced. A big wine. Fine plus.

Château Sigalas-Rabaud

DRINK SOON   17.5

Quite a deep colour. Slight touch of resin on
the nose. But not spoiled. Sweet and rich if
not very refined. The sweetness has faded a
little on the palate. Leaving a slightly spicy
bitterness. Fullish. Still most enjoyable. Very,
very concentrated. Youthful. Very good grip.
Fine.

Château Suduiraut

DRINK SOON   19.0

Quite a deep colour. Full, rich, nutty nose.
Touches of caramel. Medium-full body.
Subtle and fine but by no means a
blockbuster. Sweet in a flowery way. Long.
Complex. Very subtle. Lovely finish. Very
persistent. Very fine indeed.

Château La Tour-Blanche

DRINK SOON   15.0

Soft, round, caramelly-sweet nose. Very
velvety. A touch of coconut. A gentle wine
on the palate. Quite sweet. A little one-
dimensional and a little short. Good but not
special.

Château d'Yquem

NOW–2015   19.0

Deep bronzed colour. Splendid nose. Very,
very concentrated rather than greatly nobly
rotten. Very full. Splendid fruit. Still very
fresh. Lovely balance. Very very long and
multi-dimensional. But does it lack a bit of
grip? It is not 'great'. I have had better
bottles. But very fine. Six months later,
alongside – or following – the reds: deep
golden colour. Marvellous nose. This *is* a
great Sauternes. Ample. Barley-sugary,
caramel and honey. Very lush. Very
voluptuous. Beautiful balance. Very
vigorous. Excellent.

1952 VINTAGE

SIZE OF THE CROP:	1,931,457 HECTOLITRES.
VINTAGE RATING:	17.5 (RED WINE).
	16.0 (DRY WHITE WINE).
	17.0 (SWEET WINES).

The 1952 harvest was equivalent in size to 1951, the previous year, but some one-third less than both 1950 and 1953. The average yield was 26.8 hl/ha. The white wine harvest, at 1,077,645 hl, represented 55.8 per cent of the total.

Nineteen fifty-two is a very good vintage. The wines are full and firm, in some cases hard and unyielding. The Médocs and the Graves, where they are not too dry, are classic. They needed time. For once the vintage is better in Saint-Émilion and Pomerol. On the Right Bank the wines are more abundant and generous, less four-square and astringent.

THE WEATHER

Nineteen fifty-two was a hot year which turned cool as the summer progressed. The development of the vegetation was given an early impetus by a warm spring. June was hot, with the flowering taking place under splendidly clear and sunny skies, and July and most of August were also very warm and dry. Then, abruptly, the summer ended. In the next few weeks a lot of rain was to fall, and even when the downpours intermittently ceased the Bordeaux *vignoble* continued to be covered by grey, lowering skies. It was also cold. There is a parallel to be drawn with 1975 here, though in 1975 the precipitation in August and September was even greater (216 mm as against 152). In both vintages the grape skins had been toughened by earlier drought and high temperatures. In both vintages the net result in the Médoc, though to a lesser extent in Saint Émilion and Pomerol, was the creation of wines with somewhat aggressive, unripe tannins which threatened to overwhelm the fruit and which took a long time to mellow.

The vintage began reasonably early, on 19th September. The yield was average, larger than 1949 but smaller than 1948; a long way from the abundance of 1947 and 1950, and, as it would turn out, 1953.

THE WINES – THEN

At the outset the 1952s seemed promising. The colours were good, the wines full-bodied, the fruit attractive, the acidities correct. Fairly soon, though, the tannins began to dominate. They gave rise to the same doubts as with the 1928s, 1934s and 1937s: which would win, the fruit or the tannin? Here we have a pre-echo of the 1975 vintage. Ten or so years later, while the very top wines – Lafite, Margaux, Haut-Brion – were delicious, many of the remaining *crus classés* on this side of the Gironde were eclipsed by the 1953s. The Libournais wines, however, were splendid, continuing the tradition established by the 1945, 1947 and 1949. Not until 1959 and 1964 would we have Saint-Émilions and Pomerols as fine. Twenty-five years on, while the Right Bank wines were still delicious, the sparkle seemed to have left most of the Médocs. They had become dry and dull.

THE WINES NOW

At 50 years old, the 1952s are, naturally, now variable: two bottles from the same case, stored identically, can be quite different. There are still plenty of fine wines, especially in Saint-Émilion, and particularly in Pomerol. But they develop significantly in the glass.

These are wines for food: sturdy, tannic, full-bodied and meaty. In many cases the colours are still very good. But what the wines lack, except the very best, is a sweet succulence on the finish.

The first flight (we started with the Graves and Saint-Estèphes), was a good one. All were still alive, and the Pape-Clément and Cos d'Estournel will still keep. By and large most of the rest of the Médocs were more or less on their last legs. Léoville-Poyferré and Ducru-Beaucaillou were elegant: as Palmer and Pichon-Baron and Cantemerle had once been. The Pontet-Canet was a pleasant surprise.

The next two flights were the Libournais and this is where 1952 was at its best. The Cheval Blanc was a Belgian bottling and did not impress. The Ausone, bottled by the reputable Vandermeulen, was tired but had once been fine. The remainder were most impressive. A simply lovely Vieux Château Certan (which I thought was Pétrus) was my star. The majority of the other tasters preferred Lafleur.

The final flight was the Médoc/Graves First Growths. Latour, despite the recognised success for the wines of the right bank, is for me the wine of the vintage. Apart from the Lafite, all of these five wines showed unmistakable First Growth character.

You will see my notes on the wines above in the following pages. Among the wines that were missing, judging from my notes, I would single out Château La Gaffelière (-Naudes, as it was then called) in Saint-Émilion as a fine success. Châteaux Trotanoy and Latour-à-Pomerol should, if well stored, also give pleasure.

There are fewer wines in the Médoc and the Graves in which I would still have confidence after 50 years: Gruaud-Larose and Talbot, Beychevelle, Léoville-Barton and Langoa-Barton, and (château-bottled) Lynch-Bages.

PRICES

Prices of the First Growths opened at 250,000 Francs per *tonneau* for Cheval Blanc upwards to 350,000 (Lafite) and 375,000 (Mouton-Rothschild and Latour). This was more than the 1949s, a year which had seen an important movement up over 1947 and 1948, but only just. These were old Francs. The retail price in Britain when the wines were released three years later was around 15 shillings (75p per bottle) for the First Growths, 6 to 9 shillings (30–40p) for the important classed growths.

Today the vintage must be 99 per cent drunk up, and is rarely seen on the market. My friends at Farr Vintners estimate £1600–£2500 ($2880–4500) per case for the *premiers crus*, £500–£750 ($900–$1350) for the best known Médoc classed growths and a little more for wines such as Trotanoy and Vieux Château Certan.

THE TASTING

We celebrated the 50th anniversary of the vintage in Linz, Austria in November 2002. My thanks to Dr Peter Baumann and the rest of the 'Linzer Gang'.

SAINT-ÉMILION

CHÂTEAU AUSONE

DRINK SOON — -

Bottled by Vandermeulen. Fullish, quite vigorous colour. Ripe, rich, mocha and chocolate nose. Still very fresh and vigorous. It has lightened a little on the palate. But reasonable fruit and style here once. Was fine.

CHÂTEAU CANON

PAST ITS BEST — -

Medium-full colour. No undue age. Rather a dried-out nose, sadly. A little past its best on the palate. Yet fullish-bodied and with good fruit. The follow-through is the best bit. It was very good plus once (16.5/20).

CHÂTEAU CHEVAL BLANC

DRINK UP — 15.0

Bottled by Pol Mairesse in Belgium. Good fullish colour. Still plenty of vigour. Some Merlot. Mellow and spicy. Not a great deal of class. The fruit is a bit dried-out. Better on the palate. Some astringency but some fruit and sweetness. Not very sophisticated but good. Slight decay at the end. Was splendid in its prime.

CHÂTEAU FIGEAC

DRINK UP — 17.0

Bottled by Sichel. Good fullish colour. No undue age. But slightly astringent on the nose. Better on the palate. Ripe and rich. Good grip. Good Merlot fruit. This is positive at the end. Very good indeed/fine.

CLOS FOURTET

DRINK SOON — 16.0

Medium-full colour. No undue age. Fragrant nose, but a little astringent. Medium-full body. Balanced and classy. Some astringency lurks but the attack is positive, as is the follow-through. Will still keep. Very good.

CHÂTEAU MAGDELAINE

DRINK UP — -

Bottled by Averys. Fullish, quite vigorous colour. Light and fragrant, but not a great deal of depth. Now some astringency. Classy once. Now medium-bodied and drying out. Yet still balanced and sophisticated. It finishes positively. (15.5/20).

POMEROL

CHÂTEAU LA CONSEILLANTE

DRINK SOON — 16.0

Bottled by Eschenhauer. Quite a light colour now. Lead-pencilly. Light and fruitless nose. Light but not too astringent on the palate. Still plenty of fruit. This has balance and character. Not short. Stylish. Unexpectedly good.

CHÂTEAU L'ÉVANGILE

NOW–2007 — 15.5

Full, vigorous colour. A little chunky and maderised on the nose. Some maderisation on the palate. Fullish weight. Some astringency. Underneath decent if slightly austere fruit. As much Cabernet as Merlot. It lacks a bit of charm and sophistication but good plus.

CHÂTEAU LAFLEUR

NOW–2010+ — 18.5

Good vigorous, fullish colour. Ample and generous on the nose. Ripe, rich and fat on the palate. Plenty of life here ahead of it. Full, hefty, tannic, concentrated, rich and muscular. Very good grip. Super but tough.

CHÂTEAU PÉTRUS

DRINK SOON — 17.5

Medium colour. Quite evolved. Flowery and fragrant on the nose. But it has lost a lot of its fruit. Still plenty on the palate though. Medium- to full-bodied, poised and harmonious. Long, classy and positive. This is fine. I thought it was Vieux Château Certan.

Vieux Château Certan

NOW–2010+	19.0

Good fullish, vigorous colour. Rich, ripe, full, sweet and vigorous on the nose. This is very impressive. Full-bodied, rich, concentrated and abundant on the palate. Not as muscular as Château Lafleur. Lots of vigour. Plenty of future and lovely finish. I though it was Pétrus.

Graves
Château Haut-Brion

DRINK UP	17.0

Very full colour. Slightly maderised as well as the usual 1952 chunkiness on the nose. A big, rich, opulent wine on the palate. Slightly over the top. Some astringency. Good grip and positive finish though. It needs food. Not quite classy enough for fine but very good indeed.

Château La Mission Haut-Brion

DRINK SOON	17.0

Fullish, mature colour. Still quite fresh. Firm nose. Just a hint of reduction. Some astringency. Higher-toned than the rest of this Graves/Saint-Estèphe flight. Medium-full weight. Merlot mellowness and spice. Not too dry. This is very good indeed too. But it doesn't have the finish of Pape-Clément or Cos d'Estournel.

Château Pape-Clément

NOW–2007	17.5

Fullish, mature colour. No undue age. Fresh, ripe, classy nose. Good harmony. Lovely on the palate. A big wine, but rich and balanced. Good depth and grip and very good fruit. Alive and vigorous. Long and complex. Fine.

Haut-Médoc
Château Cantemerle

DRINK UP	14.5

Medium to medium-full colour. Well matured. Rather dried out and astringent on the palate. Vestiges of class and interest, especially on the finish. Was fine (17.5), now quite good plus.

Margaux
Château Margaux

DRINK UP	17.0

Medium colour. Well-matured. It has lost some of its fruit on the nose. Soft and fragrant though. Better on the palate. No lack of class. Medium weight but still balanced and with very good fruit and complexity. Better with food. Was fine once. Today very good indeed.

Château Palmer

DRINK UP	14.0

Medium colour. Well matured. A bit of astringency on the nose. The fruit has dried out. Medium weight. Some astringency but reasonable depth and style on the palate. Perhaps still enjoyable with food. Was fine once. Not only quite good.

Château Rauzan-Gassies

DRINK UP	12.0

Medium colour. Well-matured. Dried out, slightly reduced nose. Some sweetness but rapidly overtaken by the acidity. A little over the top. Medium-full.

Saint-Julien
Château Ducru-Beaucaillou

DRINK UP	17.5

Bottled by Deviltz. Medium colour. Well matured. Not dried out but slightly fading on the nose. Medium body. Still sweet in the middle if a little dry at the end. Stylish still. Not short. Fine: just.

Château Lagrange

PAST ITS BEST	-

Medium colour. Well matured. Soft but astringent nose. A little too dry on the palate now. Not undrinkable though. This has merit but it is now beginning to lose its fruit. Was at least 'good', i.e. 15.0.

Château Léoville-Poyferré

DRINK SOON 17.5

Medium colour. Well matured. Good depth
here. Ripe, mocha flavours. Some cedar
wood. Fullish body. Ripe and positive on the
palate. Not too astringent. Good fruit.
Positive finish. Really quite complex. Fine.

Pauillac

Château Lafite

DRINK UP 15.0

Really quite a light colour now. Light and
lead pencilly on the nose. This is light and
pretty on the palate. Not astringent but with
a lack of concentration, dimension and
depth. It doesn't show First Growth
character. Decent balance. Good. I
remember it as being very fine in its prime.

Château Latour

NOW–2010+ 19.5

Good full, vigorous colour. Ripe, rich,
ample, generous nose. No sign of age. Very
classic. Full-bodied. A little tannin still. Not
astringent though. In excellent condition.
Lovely fruit. Very long. Excellent.

Château Lynch-Bages

PAST ITS BEST -

Bottled by Barrière. Full colour. Inky nose.
Somewhat maderised. Very astringent.
Positive on the palate. Yet some residual
sweetness lingers.

Château Mouton-Rothschild

DRINK SOON 18.5

Fullish colour. No undue age. A bit chunky
on the nose. Dense. Some astringency. A bit
four-square. Better on the palate. There is
fruit here and the sophistication of the
château shows through. Better with food.
Fullish weight. Very fine but drink soon.

Château Pichon-Baron

DRINK SOON 16.0

Bottled by Barrière. Fullish colour. No undue
age. Robust, spicy nose. Medium-full body.
Still vigorous. Accessible and fruity. Long at
the end. Very good. Yet it lost it quickly in
the glass. Was fine once.

Château Pontet-Canet

DRINK SOON 17.0

Bottled by Harvey's of Bristol. Medium-full
colour. High-toned nose. Ripe but not too
sophisticated. Better on the palate. This has
more interest than some. Indeed really quite
long and positive at the end. Very good
indeed.

Saint-Estèphe

Château Calon-Ségur

DRINK UP 17.0

Medium-full, well-matured colour. Quite
earthy on the nose. Not too astringent but it
has lost a little of its fruit. Medium-full
weight. A little astringent on the attack but
interesting spices and by no means too dry
on the follow-through. Good depth. Positive
finish if slightly hard at the end. Very good
indeed.

Château Cos d'Estournel

DRINK SOON 17.5

Bottled by Ginestet. Full, mature colour. No
undue age. A little dry and astringent on the
nose. Better as it evolved. Full weight. Good
classy fruit. Plenty of richness and
complexity. Not a bit too astringent on the
palate and not too hard on the finish. Fine.

APPENDICES

Appendix One

Vintage and Price Guide

Please note:
State of maturity:

Bold – not yet ready	e.g. **15.0**
Roman – ready, but will keep	e.g. 15.0
Italic – drink soon	e.g. *15.0*

Ratings (Points):

Wines are rated within the context of the vintage. The vintage is also rated. Some vintages have a split rating, e.g.

1998   15 (Médoc/Graves) – 18.5 (Saint-Émilion/Pomerol)
1996   14 (Saint-Émilion/Pomerol) – 18.5 (Médoc-Graves)
1986   14 (Saint-Émilion/Pomerol) – 18.0 (Pauillac/Saint-Julien)

Ratings are out of 20. In some cases the rating column is blank (–) because I have no recent note on the wine or because the wine had not yet been released.

Prices (Value):

The prices, or value, represent the 'going rate' or an estimated going rate on the wholesale brokers' auction market per dozen bottles, duty paid but excluding delivery and VAT in London in September 2003.

This chart could not have been completed without the generous input on the pricing side of Farr Vintners, Britain's leading wholesalers of fine wine.

	2001		2000		1999		1998		1997	
RATING FOR	15.0		18.5		14.0		15-18.5		13.5	
THE VINTAGE	Value	Points	Value	Points	Value	Points	Value	Points	Value	Points
FIRST GROWTHS										
LAFITE	950	18.5	2850	19.5	850	18.5	1150	19.5	720	19.0
LATOUR	950	18.0	2850	18.5	850	18.0	800	19.0	700	19.5
MARGAUX	950	18.5	2900	19.5	900	17.5	890	19.0	750	17.5
MOUTON	950	18.0	2500	17.0	750	16.0	960	16.5	720	19.0
HAUT-BRION	950	18.5	2500	18.5	750	18.5	1150	19.0	700	18.5
CHEVAL BLANC	1350	17.5	3650	19.5	1080	17.5	2000	20.0	750	18.5
AUSONE	1350	18.0	4200	18.5	1100	16.0	1200	18.5	750	18.5
PÉTRUS	4000	18.5	10,500	18.5	4800	18.5	9000	19.5	3200	18.5
PAUILLAC										
PICHON-LALANDE	350	17.0	880	16.5	250	15.0	250	16.0	250	16.0
PICHON-LONGUEVILLE	275	17.0	550	17.5	230	14.0	210	16.5	220	15.5
DUHART-MILON	195	17.5	210	16.0	130	15.0	145	14.5	125	13.5
BATAILLEY	129	15.5	150	15.5	125	14.0	125	15.5	110	14.0
HAUT-BATAILLEY	130	17.0	180	16.5	125	14.5	125	16.0	100	15.5
GRAND-PUY-LACOSTE	185	17.5	380	18.0	160	15.0	175	17.5	155	16.0
LYNCH-BAGES	240	16.0	620	16.0	265	15.5	250	16.0	240	15.0
PONTET-CANET	185	17.0	330	16.5	150	17.0	150	16.0	150	16.0
D'ARMAILHAC	137	15.0	210	15.5	135	14.5	125	13.5	105	15.0
CLERC-MILON	185	15.5	225	16.0	180	15.0	180	15.0	130	16.0
HAUT-BAGES-LIBÉRAL	115	17.0	175	17.0	120	15.5	120	16.5	100	16.0
SAINT-JULIEN										
LÉOVILLE-LAS-CASES	—	18.0	1300	18.5	420	18.0	440	19.0	360	18.5
LÉOVILLE-POYFERRÉ	195	17.5	465	17.5	180	17.5	180	17.0	170	16.0
LÉOVILLE-BARTON	240	18.0	780	18.5	240	17.5	265	18.0	200	18.0
GRUAUD-LAROSE	215	16.5	520	17.0	210	16.0	220	16.5	185	14.5
DUCRU-BEAUCAILLOU	320	18.0	680	18.5	270	16.5	300	17.5	260	18.5
LAGRANGE	145	15.0	260	15.0	155	14.0	140	15.0	125	16.0
LANGOA-BARTON	180	16.5	240	17.0	160	16.5	160	17.0	130	16.0
SAINT-PIERRE	155	17.5	180	16.5	125	16.0	125	16.0	90	16.0
TALBOT	160	17.5	330	17.0	155	16.0	160	16.5	150	16.0
BEYCHEVELLE	160	16.0	240	16.5	145	15.0	160	16.0	140	13.5
MARGAUX										
RAUZAN-SÉGLA	295	17.0	420	17.5	190	16.0	190	17.0	180	17.0
DURFORT-VIVENS	130	16.5	180	17.0	130	16.5	135	16.0	120	16.0
LASCOMBES	270	15.0	230	17.0	150	15.5	150	13.5	110	14.5
BRANE-CANTENAC	250	16.5	255	16.5	145	16.5	150	16.5	125	16.5
MALESCOT	195	17.5	275	18.0	150	17.0	150	17.0	100	16.5
PALMER	620	17.0	900	18.0	480	17.0	420	18.0	280	17.5
FERRIÈRE	130	17.0	195	17.5	120	17.0	120	17.5	100	17.0
PRIEURÉ-LICHINE	165	14.0	180	15.0	150	15.5	150	13.0	90	14.5

RATING FOR THE VINTAGE	1996 14–18.5 Value	Points	1995 15.5 Value	Points	1994 14.0 Value	Points	1990 18.5 Value	Points	1989 18.0 Value	Points
FIRST GROWTHS										
LAFITE	2000	17.5	1200	18.5	750	17.5	1800	19.5	1580	18.0
LATOUR	1750	18.0	1350	19.5	850	18.5	3300	20.0	1380	18.0
MARGAUX	2000	18.5	1550	19.0	950	18.5	3650	18.5	1750	18.5
MOUTON	1100	18.0	1150	16.0	780	18.0	1280	17.5	1450	18.0
HAUT-BRION	1000	18.5	1100	19.0	700	18.5	1950	19.0	3300	20.0
CHEVAL BLANC	1000	18.5	1100	17.5	720	17.5	4000	18.5	1480	18.5
AUSONE	1100	18.5	1125	18.5	700	16.0	1500	13.0	1050	14.0
PÉTRUS	3200	17.5	5400	18.5	3200	18.5	11,000	19.0	10,000	19.0
PAUILLAC										
PICHON-LALANDE	650	18.0	675	15.0	385	18.0	600	16.5	780	17.5
PICHON-LONGUEVILLE	300	17.0	295	14.0	225	13.5	925	18.0	920	17.5
DUHART-MILON	180	12.5	180	13.0	140	14.5	330	15.5	330	13.5
BATAILLEY	160	–	200	15.5	130	15.0	280	15.5	275	13.0
HAUT-BATAILLEY	200	16.0	200	16.0	155	16.5	360	14.0	300	15.5
GRAND-PUY-LACOSTE	360	18.0	375	18.0	190	16.5	750	17.5	480	18.0
LYNCH-BAGES	440	15.5	420	15.0	300	13.5	950	17.0	1000	16.0
PONTET-CANET	245	17.0	255	16.0	240	16.0	350	14.0	320	14.0
D'ARMAILHAC	165	16.0	185	16.5	150	15.0	360	16.5	350	14.0
CLERC-MILON	225	16.5	270	16.5	160	17.5	380	17.0	380	16.5
HAUT-BAGES-LIBÉRAL	135	15.0	140	15.0	120	16.5	280	16.5	290	13.0
SAINT-JULIEN										
LÉOVILLE-LAS-CASES	1050	19.0	680	19.0	380	18.5	1025	18.5	720	19.0
LÉOVILLE-POYFERRÉ	300	18.0	285	17.5	190	16.0	800	17.5	440	16.0
LÉOVILLE-BARTON	360	18.0	340	18.0	255	17.5	700	18.5	540	18.0
GRUAUD-LAROSE	285	17.0	285	17.0	210	15.0	600	16.5	480	16.0
DUCRU-BEAUCAILLOU	600	18.5	700	19.0	340	18.0	480	17.5	450	16.0
LAGRANGE	230	16.0	240	16.5	150	16.0	540	16.0	420	16.0
LANGOA-BARTON	215	17.0	185	16.5	150	16.5	450	17.0	350	17.0
SAINT-PIERRE	165	14.5	165	11.5	135	15.0	300	16.5	300	14.0
TALBOT	265	17.0	260	16.0	200	15.5	420	15.0	420	15.0
BEYCHEVELLE	200	15.5	225	16.5	185	13.5	470	14.0	480	14.5
MARGAUX										
RAUZAN-SÉGLA	265	16.5	330	17.0	200	17.0	625	16.0	480	13.0
DURFORT-VIVENS	180	15.5	150	14.0	130	13.0	240	14.0	225	13.0
LASCOMBES	160	13.5	160	14.5	150	11.5	320	14.0	335	13.5
BRANE-CANTENAC	200	15.0	210	15.0	150	13.0	380	13.5	350	13.5
MALESCOT	165	16.0	165	15.0	140	16.0	330	16.0	260	16.5
PALMER	450	17.0	480	18.0	320	15.0	760	18.0	975	15.0
FERRIÈRE	175	16.0	135	15.5	135	15.0	240	–	240	–
PRIEURÉ-LICHINE	160	14.0	190	14.5	140	14.5	300	14.5	300	14.0

	1988		1986		1985		1982		1978	
RATING FOR THE VINTAGE	16.5		14.0–18.0		17.0		18.5		16.0	
	Value	Points	Value	Points	Value	Points	Value	Points	Value	Points
FIRST GROWTHS										
LAFITE	1350	18.5	2200	19.5	1500	16.5	3900	19.5	1150	18.0
LATOUR	1225	18.5	1350	18.0	1350	17.0	4000	18.5	1350	19.5
MARGAUX	1500	18.5	2050	19.0	2000	18.5	3500	18.5	1450	17.5
MOUTON	1240	16.0	2500	20.0	1500	17.0	4000	20.0	1000	16.0
HAUT-BRION	1200	18.5	1420	17.5	1450	18.5	2150	19.0	1000	18.0
CHEVAL BLANC	1200	17.5	1380	16.0	2000	18.5	4800	19.0	1050	18.0
AUSONE	900	12.5	850	13.0	850	15.0	2200	16.0	750	17.0
PÉTRUS	4800	18.5	3800	16.5	4800	17.5	17,000	19.0	2700	20.0
PAUILLAC										
PICHON-LALANDE	650	18.5	800	18.5	840	18.0	2200	19.0	750	19.0
PICHON-LONGUEVILLE	480	16.0	480	17.5	440	13.0	840	18.5	260	15.0
DUHART-MILON	300	16.0	320	16.0	360	13.0	540	14.5	225	16.5
BATAILLEY	250	14.0	265	15.5	270	15.0	380	15.5	225	–
HAUT-BATAILLEY	265	13.0	320	17.5	300	15.0	400	17.0	250	14.0
GRAND-PUY-LACOSTE	380	17.0	500	17.0	480	17.5	880	17.5	320	18.5
LYNCH-BAGES	600	17.0	695	17.5	980	17.0	1280	17.0	420	17.0
PONTET-CANET	240	16.5	320	17.0	320	14.5	380	15.5	240	13.0
D'ARMAILHAC	280	14.0	340	16.0	340	16.0	380	15.5	240	16.0
CLERC-MILON	320	17.0	400	17.0	380	17.0	300	16.0	240	14.5
HAUT-BAGES-LIBÉRAL	250	15.0	340	12.0	330	15.0	300	12.5	200	13.0
SAINT-JULIEN										
LÉOVILLE-LAS-CASES	600	18.5	1000	18.5	800	18.5	1950	19.0	600	19.0
LÉOVILLE-POYFERRÉ	320	17.0	440	17.5	420	17.0	780	17.0	280	15.0
LÉOVILLE-BARTON	420	17.5	550	18.5	580	18.0	750	16.0	320	16.5
GRUAUD-LAROSE	420	17.0	640	17.5	540	15.5	1100	17.5	420	15.5
DUCRU-BEAUCAILLOU	420	17.0	670	18.5	600	17.0	1020	18.5	490	18.0
LAGRANGE	350	16.0	420	15.0	380	15.5	400	12.0	250	12.0
LANGOA-BARTON	300	16.0	330	16.0	350	16.0	420	16.0	250	15.0
SAINT-PIERRE	250	15.5	330	14.0	260	14.0	360	16.0	180	16.5
TALBOT	420	14.0	650	17.0	500	16.0	800	16.0	340	13.0
BEYCHEVELLE	420	16.0	500	14.0	500	16.0	650	15.0	330	13.0
MARGAUX										
RAUZAN-SÉGLA	450	12.0	750	17.5	420	17.0	520	15.5	300	14.0
DURFORT-VIVENS	185	11.0	180	14.5	180	14.5	240	15.0	150	14.0
LASCOMBES	285	13.5	300	14.0	350	15.0	425	14.0	220	13.5
BRANE-CANTENAC	260	13.0	360	15.5	400	15.0	380	14.0	220	13.0
MALESCOT	250	17.0	265	15.5	250	15.5	300	14.5	200	13.5
PALMER	580	16.5	660	17.0	660	18.5	850	18.5	640	18.0
FERRIÈRE	200	–	240	13.0	240	–	320	–	180	–
PRIEURÉ-LICHINE	250	14.5	300	14.5	260	14.0	300	15.0	180	14.0

RATING FOR THE VINTAGE	1975 16.0		1970 18.0		1966 17.5		1961 20.0		1959 19.0	
	Value	Points	Value	Points	Value	Points	Value	Points	Value	Points
FIRST GROWTHS										
LAFITE	1300	14.0	1050	15.5	1000	14.0	3600	18.0	7800	19.5
LATOUR	1300	18.0	3650	18.0	2900	20.0	12,000	20.0	7800	19.5
MARGAUX	600	13.0	800	15.5	950	14.5	7000	18.5	4200	17.5
MOUTON	1000	16.5	1450	16.0	1800	19.0	9000	20.0	9500	19.0
HAUT-BRION	1100	18.5	1000	17.5	1450	18.0	7000	18.5	7000	18.5
CHEVAL BLANC	1400	18.5	1250	18.0	1800	18.5	7000	17.5	7200	17.5
AUSONE	500	16.5	720	13.0	900	12.0	3000	17.0	5200	–
PÉTRUS	6800	19.5	7800	19.0	4800	18.0	30,000	19.5	20,000	19.5
PAUILLAC										
PICHON-LALANDE	600	16.5	850	16.0	750	15.5	2500	16.0	2250	17.0
PICHON-LONGUEVILLE	200	12.0	300	13.0	350	16.5	1200	15.5	1500	15.0
DUHART-MILON	200	12.0	200	15.0	240	–	600	12.5	550	–
BATAILLEY	200	15.0	250	15.0	250	–	650	17.5	550	12.5
HAUT-BATAILLEY	210	15.5	300	15.0	320	15.5	750	17.0	720	–
GRAND-PUY-LACOSTE	220	17.5	450	17.5	320	17.5	1000	18.0	900	18.0
LYNCH-BAGES	400	17.5	1050	17.0	750	17.0	2750	17.5	1850	17.5
PONTET-CANET	200	14.0	250	14.0	250	15.0	950	–	780	13.5
D'ARMAILHAC	180	–	250	14.0	300	–	950	16.0	780	–
CLERC-MILON	240	15.0	250	–	320	–	950	–	780	–
HAUT-BAGES-LIBÉRAL	180	13.0	180	–	220	–	600	–	500	–
SAINT-JULIEN										
LÉOVILLE-LAS-CASES	550	17.5	420	17.0	650	17.0	1800	17.5	1800	18.5
LÉOVILLE-POYFERRÉ	250	14.5	280	13.5	280	15.0	1200	15.0	1000	17.5
LÉOVILLE-BARTON	320	16.0	380	16.5	380	17.5	1650	17.5	1250	18.5
GRUAUD-LAROSE	280	17.0	450	17.0	450	17.0	2750	18.5	1500	18.0
DUCRU-BEAUCAILLOU	420	17.0	900	18.5	700	18.5	2750	19.0	1800	18.5
LAGRANGE	220	12.5	180	13.5	220	14.0	600	12.0	600	14.0
LANGOA-BARTON	250	15.0	300	14.0	350	15.5	900	14.0	800	17.0
SAINT-PIERRE	180	15.0	180	16.0	200	15.0	500	16.0	480	16.0
TALBOT	260	14.0	360	14.0	360	16.0	1250	17.0	1000	16.0
BEYCHEVELLE	300	16.0	320	16.0	360	16.0	1500	15.5	1200	16.5
MARGAUX										
RAUZAN-SÉGLA	280	14.0	240	14.5	250	15.5	1200	–	1000	–
DURFORT-VIVENS	160	–	180	–	200	14.0	500	–	480	–
LASCOMBES	220	13.5	250	13.5	280	16.5	750	16.5	700	16.5
BRANE-CANTENAC	230	12.0	200	13.5	180	15.5	1000	17.5	900	16.0
MALESCOT	180	14.0	240	15.0	265	13.5	900	16.0	840	17.0
PALMER	660	19.0	1400	18.5	2500	19.0	9000	19.5	4800	19.0
FERRIÈRE	150	–	180	–	180	–	480	–	420	–
PRIEURÉ-LICHINE	180	14.5	200	14.0	240	15.0	750	15.0	720	

RATING FOR THE VINTAGE	2001 15.0 Value	Points	2000 18.5 Value	Points	1999 14.0 Value	Points	1998 15-18.5 Value	Points	1997 13.5 Value	Points
SAINT-ESTÈPHE										
COS D'ESTOURNEL	350	17.5	560	15.0	240	16.5	250	16.0	250	13.5
MONTROSE	255	18.0	560	17.5	200	16.0	200	17.0	200	16.0
CALON-SÉGUR	180	17.5	500	17.5	150	15.5	170	17.5	150	16.0
HAUT-MARBUZET	165	16.5	225	17.0	150	15.5	150	16.0	120	16.0
HAUT-MÉDOC										
LA LAGUNE	165	14.5	210	16.0	135	13.5	130	14.0	130	14.5
CANTEMERLE	115	16.0	150	14.0	105	14.0	110	15.0	95	13.5
SOCIANDO-MALLET	160	17.0	235	17.0	185	16.0	160	17.0	140	16.0
GRAVES										
HAUT-BAILLY	210	17.5	265	17.5	180	16.5	220	18.0	140	16.5
DOM. DE CHEVALIER	180	18.0	260	18.0	155	16.0	210	17.5	150	17.5
LA MISSION HAUT-BRION	580	18.0	2500	18.0	420	17.5	680	18.0	330	16.5
PAPE-CLÉMENT	350	16.0	380	17.0	240	16.0	350	16.5	190	15.0
LA TOUR HAUT-BRION	235	17.5	310	17.0	150	17.0	240	17.0	160	15.0
SAINT-ÉMILION										
ANGÉLUS	600	17.5	980	18.0	360	16.0	490	17.5	420	17.5
BEAU-SÉJOUR-BÉCOT	250	16.0	380	17.0	180	15.0	275	15.0	170	13.5
BEAUSÉJOUR (D-L)	350	17.0	450	17.5	300	14.0	350	17.5	180	14.0
BELAIR	240	16.0	250	16.5	165	14.0	180	15.5	140	15.5
CANON	360	17.5	360	18.0	200	15.5	240	16.5	140	14.5
CLOS FOURTET	260	16.0	325	15.0	165	14.0	250	17.5	155	14.5
FIGEAC	390	17.5	520	18.0	365	14.0	480	14.0	250	15.0
LA GAFFELIÈRE	260	15.0	280	15.5	165	13.0	200	15.0	125	13.5
MAGDELAINE	375	17.5	350	18.0	175	17.5	340	18.0	150	14.0
PAVIE	950	14.0	1600	14.5	580	12.5	675	15.0	185	12.0
TROTTEVIEILLE	200	14.5	250	15.0	150	12.5	180	14.5	120	12.5
LA MONDOTTE	1250	17.5	2400	18.0	1200	17.0	1750	17.0	1400	17.5
TROPLONG-MONDOT	250	17.5	450	17.5	200	16.5	320	17.0	190	13.5
PAVIE-MACQUIN	300	17.5	520	17.5	330	16.0	495	17.0	220	15.5
TERTRE-ROTEBOEUF	680	17.5	1300	17.5	550	15.0	800	15.0	400	16.0
DE VALANDRAUD	1000	15.5	1620	16.5	1350	14.5	1600	16.0	900	15.5
POMEROL										
TROTANOY	520	18.5	800	18.5	400	18.0	1650	18.5	300	18.0
LA FLEUR-PÉTRUS	440	18.5	500	18.0	320	17.5	620	18.0	280	15.5
LATOUR-À-POMEROL	285	16.5	350	17.5	250	17.0	390	17.5	240	17.0
VIEUX CH. CERTAN	580	17.5	840	18.0	450	17.5	750	19.5	260	17.5
CERTAN DE MAY	440	17.5	550	16.0	300	15.5	495	13.5	200	14.5
LA CONSEILLANTE	490	17.5	1250	17.5	400	17.0	540	12.5	250	14.0
L'ÉVANGILE	880	18.0	1500	18.0	650	17.5	950	19.0	360	18.0
LE PIN	3650	17.5	10,500	17.5	3200	15.5	8500	17.0	2200	16.0
LAFLEUR	900	17.5	5000	18.0	1100	16.5	1450	17.0	650	17.5
GAZIN	320	16.5	300	16.0	200	16.0	385	16.0	180	15.0
CLINET	580	15.5	700	15.5	300	15.5	420	16.5	240	17.5
L'ÉGLISE-CLINET	780	18.0	1400	18.0	750	16.5	1300	18.5	450	17.0
CLOS L'ÉGLISE	735	16.0	1220	17.0	500	15.5	720	16.0	200	16.5

RATING FOR THE VINTAGE	1996 14–18.5		1995 15.5		1994 14.0		1990 18.5		1989 18.0	
	Value	Points	Value	Points	Value	Points	Value	Points	Value	Points
SAINT-ESTÈPHE										
COS D'ESTOURNEL	440	17.0	480	16.5	335	16.0	850	17.5	650	17.5
MONTROSE	375	16.0	360	15.5	285	14.0	1750	17.5	800	14.0
CALON-SÉGUR	265	13.5	360	14.0	190	16.0	520	16.0	425	15.0
HAUT-MARBUZET	190	15.5	235	15.0	165	13.5	420	16.5	280	15.0
HAUT-MÉDOC										
LA LAGUNE	165	15.0	195	14.5	140	15.0	450	15.5	420	16.5
CANTEMERLE	170	13.0	150	12.5	115	12.5	280	14.0	425	12.0
SOCIANDO-MALLET	250	18.0	250	16.5	150	16.0	500	17.0	360	16.0
GRAVES										
HAUT-BAILLY	225	17.0	250	17.0	190	12.5	450	16.0	380	16.0
DOM. DE CHEVALIER	155	17.5	200	15.0	170	14.5	450	17.0	480	17.5
LA MISSION HAUT-BRION	490	17.5	520	18.5	420	17.5	1320	17.0	2500	18.5
PAPE-CLÉMENT	280	17.0	320	17.0	180	13.0	500	16.5	440	16.5
LA TOUR HAUT-BRION	200	16.0	220	—	160	16.5	360	15.5	400	140
SAINT-ÉMILION										
ANGÉLUS	350	17.0	650	16.5	400	17.5	1400	17.0	1200	17.5
BEAU-SÉJOUR-BÉCOT	165	15.0	250	16.0	195	14.5	385	15.5	320	16.0
BEAUSÉJOUR (D-L)	220	14.5	265	14.0	180	13.0	2950	16.0	400	13.0
BELAIR	200	—	200	16.0	140	15.0	320	14.0	325	16.0
CANON	200	12.5	220	13.0	180	16.0	500	17.5	500	17.5
CLOS FOURTET	180	14.0	225	14.0	160	14.5	360	14.5	285	12.0
FIGEAC	280	12.0	420	17.5	240	17.5	850	16.0	550	17.0
LA GAFFELIÈRE	180	16.0	200	15.0	140	15.5	360	15.0	340	11.0
MAGDELAINE	180	13.0	280	15.5	180	12.0	470	16.0	480	16.5
PAVIE	180	16.0	250	12.5	180	15.5	550	17.5	450	15.0
TROTTEVIEILLE	140	—	140	14.0	120	13.5	280	16.0	260	13.0
LA MONDOTTE	1800	17.0	320	—						
TROPLONG-MONDOT	230	17.0	320	16.0	240	16.0	1080	16.5	880	15.5
PAVIE-MACQUIN	220	17.0	200	14.0	190	16.0	420	13.0	360	14.0
TERTRE-ROTEBOEUF	495	15.5	750	15.5	420	15.0	1800	16.5	1350	17.0
DE VALANDRAUD	1500	—	1850	12.0	1700	15.0				
POMEROL										
TROTANOY	360	13.5	620	17.0	360	15.0	1080	18.5	780	18.0
LA FLEUR-PÉTRUS	285	13.0	480	12.5	260	13.0	680	17.5	680	17.0
LATOUR-À-POMEROL	240	12.0	320	14.0	240	17.5	500	17.0	480	17.0
VIEUX CH. CERTAN	390	18.0	420	17.5	280	17.5	680	18.5	520	18.0
CERTAN DE MAY	330	13.5	380	13.0	200	16.5	680	16.0	460	17.5
LA CONSEILLANTE	350	14.0	380	15.0	300	16.0	1550	15.0	1400	13.0
L'ÉVANGILE	395	14.0	620	14.0	400	18.5	1450	17.5	680	13.0
LE PIN	4000	17.0	4700	16.5	3200	17.5	9000	18.5	6000	18.0
LAFLEUR	1000	17.0	1700	16.0	720	14.0	4800	17.0	2850	19.0
GAZIN	240	15.5	320	15.0	180	15.0	500	16.0	400	16.0
CLINET	360	13.5	620	16.5	380	14.0	1200	17.0	2200	17.5
L'ÉGLISE-CLINET	570	16.5	1000	16.0	360	16.5	1150	16.0	950	17.5
CLOS L'ÉGLISE	180	—	200	15.5	150	13.5	250	14.5	250	14.0

RATING FOR THE VINTAGE	1988 16.5 Value	Points	1986 14.0–18.0 Value	Points	1985 17.0 Value	Points	1982 18.5 Value	Points	1978 16.0 Value	Points
SAINT-ESTÈPHE										
COS D'ESTOURNEL	480	15.5	680	17.0	750	18.5	1250	18.5	500	17.0
MONTROSE	420	15.5	550	17.5	450	14.0	750	15.0	350	17.5
CALON-SÉGUR	360	11.0	400	14.0	380	14.5	840	15.0	300	14.5
HAUT-MARBUZET	250	16.0	280	16.0	280	15.5	650	17.5	180	17.0
HAUT-MÉDOC										
LA LAGUNE	360	17.0	360	15.0	380	16.5	650	16.5	275	14.0
CANTEMERLE	240	15.0	265	14.5	300	12.0	300	13.5	200	13.0
SOCIANDO-MALLET	320	16.0	360	15.0	375	14.0	550	16.0	240	
GRAVES										
HAUT-BAILLY	335	17.0	340	13.5	365	16.0	280	15.5	220	14.0
DOM. DE CHEVALIER	390	16.5	400	16.5	480	16.5	320	13.0	380	17.5
LA MISSION HAUT-BRION	720	16.5	780	15.5	820	16.5	2750	18.5	1350	19.0
PAPE-CLÉMENT	400	16.5	485	15.0	420	17.0	280	12.0	280	14.5
LA TOUR HAUT-BRION	300	15.0	300	14.5	320	15.0	1800	17.5	900	16.0
SAINT-EMILION										
ANGÉLUS	680	16.0	420	13.5	420	15.5	300	13.0	200	12.5
BEAU-SÉJOUR-BÉCOT	280	13.0	240	12.0	300	–	260	15.5	150	13.5
BEAUSÉJOUR (D-L)	280	12.0	280	14.0	300	13.5	580	16.0	180	13.0
BELAIR	260	16.0	200	14.5	260	15.5	320	14.0	180	14.0
CANON	360	15.0	460	16.5	525	17.5	920	18.5	360	18.5
CLOS FOURTET	260	15.0	240	14.5	260	13.5	360	14.0	220	–
FIGEAC	450	15.0	600	14.0	600	14.5	1100	18.0	450	15.5
LA GAFFELIÈRE	280	15.0	320	14.0	265	13.0	360	14.0	200	15.5
MAGDELAINE	300	14.0	240	14.5	320	17.5	695	17.5	360	14.0
PAVIE	365	13.0	420	15.0	380	17.0	600	17.0	320	16.0
TROTTEVIEILLE	220	15.0	220	12.0	250	14.0	280	13.0	185	–
LA MONDOTTE										
TROPLONG-MONDOT	450	17.0	300	14.0	340	15.0	250	14.0	200	–
PAVIE-MACQUIN	260	14.5	240	–	280	–	360	12.0	180	–
TERTRE-ROTEBOEUF	820	14.5	720	12.5	920	16.0	780	14.0	400	13.5
DE VALANDRAUD										
POMEROL										
TROTANOY	520	17.0	480	14.5	600	17.5	2400	18.5	400	18.0
LA FLEUR-PÉTRUS	420	17.0	420	14.0	460	15.5	1300	18.0	360	13.5
LATOUR-À-POMEROL	375	16.0	300	14.0	480	15.5	1250	18.0	360	17.5
VIEUX CH. CERTAN	550	16.5	750	18.5	450	16.0	880	17.5	400	17.0
CERTAN DE MAY	660	15.0	540	16.5	720	18.0	2400	18.0	600	17.0
LA CONSEILLANTE	480	14.5	440	15.0	1100	18.0	1320	18.0	420	17.5
L'ÉVANGILE	500	12.0	450	14.5	1100	15.5	2100	18.5	360	16.5
LE PIN	3600	16.0	4800	16.0	6000	17.0	18,000	18.5		
LAFLEUR	1500	16.0	1850	14.5	3000	16.0	9500	18.0	1500	18.5
GAZIN	330	16.0	220	13.5	350	12.0	390	15.0	200	–
CLINET	650	15.0	360	15.5	450	15.5	360	16.5	300	14.0
L'ÉGLISE-CLINET	550	17.5	750	14.5	1320	14.0	680	16.0	500	15.0
CLOS L'ÉGLISE	200	16.0	240	14.0	250	14.0	240	13.0	150	13.0

RATING FOR THE VINTAGE	1975 16.0 Value	Points	1970 18.0 Value	Points	1966 17.5 Value	Points	1961 20.0 Value	Points	1959 19.0 Value	Points
SAINT-ESTÈPHE										
Cos d'Estournel	320	16.0	520	16.5	520	16.0	2100	18.0	1650	16.5
Montrose	265	17.0	820	16.0	540	15.0	1900	15.0	1000	17.0
Calon-Ségur	200	14.5	240	13.5	280	17.0	1000	16.0	850	15.0
Haut-Marbuzet	180	15.5	240	16.0	240	17.0	750	13.0	600	—
HAUT-MÉDOC										
La Lagune	255	15.5	420	16.0	360	16.0	900	17.0	750	—
Cantemerle	165	12.0	180	14.5	240	16.0	720	18.5	600	17.5
Sociando-Mallet	200	.	180	.	180	—	600	17.0	500	—
GRAVES										
Haut-Bailly	240	13.5	360	16.0	360	16.5	950	17.0	900	17.0
Dom. de Chevalier	265	16.5	680	17.5	650	18.0	1800	17.5	1800	19.5
La Mission Haut-Brion	3500	19.5	1050	18.5	900	18.0	6600	18.5	6600	17.5
Pape-Clément	320	16.5	300	14.0	420	15.0	1500	14.0	1500	13.0
La Tour Haut-Brion	900	15.0	500	12.0	780	16.5	1800	18.0	1500	—
SAINT-ÉMILION										
Angélus	200	—	240	14.5	240	15.5	600	15.0	600	13.0
Beau-Séjour-Bécot	180	14.0	180	14.5	200	—	600	12.0	600	—
Beauséjour (D-L)	180	—	180	14.0	200	15.0	600	14.0	600	—
Belair	180	—	180	15.0	200	—	750	—	680	—
Canon	240	17.5	420	16.0	480	16.0	2000	16.0	1800	15.5
Clos Fourtet	240	—	245	14.0	265	14.5	900	12.0	900	—
Figeac	600	15.0	875	16.5	850	16.0	2000	16.5	1800	18.0
La Gaffelière	200	15.0	200	14.5	200	15.0	650	16.0	600	17.0
Magdelaine	385	16.5	400	17.0	400	16.0	1250	16.0	1250	15.0
Pavie	250	16.0	400	16.5	480	14.5	1250	17.5	1200	—
Trottevieille	185	13.0	200	15.0	200	—	650	14.0	600	14.0
La Mondotte										
Troplong-Mondot	240	—	200	14.0	240	—	500	14.0	500	—
Pavie-Macquin	220	—	200	—	240	—	500	—	500	—
Tertre-Roteboeuf										
de Valandraud										
POMEROL										
Trotanoy	1850	16.0	2000	18.0	1000	17.5	6000	18.5	4800	17.0
La Fleur-Pétrus	720	14.0	850	17.5	780	17.0	5000	16.5	4800	16.0
Latour-à-Pomerol	400	15.0	780	18.0	600	16.0	18,000	18.5	6000	18.0
Vieux Ch. Certan	720	16.5	450	17.0	600	16.0	1950	18.0	1800	18.5
Certan de May	680	16.0	450	.	450	15.0	1800	17.0	1800	—
La Conseillante	550	19.0	520	17.0	600	17.5	2800	16.5	2400	15.0
L'Évangile	2000	15.5	750	18.5	600	14.0	3000	14.0	2400	16.0
Le Pin										
Lafleur	6000	16.0	1250	17.5	6000	17.5	9000	19.0	9000	18.5
Gazin	300	—	280	14.5	320	15.0	900	17.5	850	—
Clinet	265	14.5	240	15.5	240	—	480	—	480	—
L'Église-Clinet	1300	15.0	480	—	750	—	1800	16.0	1500	16.0
Clos L'Église	180	12.5	180	—	250	15.5	500	—	500	—

APPENDIX TWO

BORDEAUX'S HARVEST, SURFACE AREA AND AVERAGE YIELD

	RED WINE (Hectolitres)	WHITE WINE (Hectolitres)	TOTAL (Hectolitres)	AC SURFACE AREA (Hectares)	HL/HA YIELD
1961	550,106	1,281,639	1,831,745	71,592	25.6
1962	1,436,038	2,305,412	3,741,450	74,964	49.9
1963	1,236,689	1,737,828	2,974,517	70,750	42.0
1964	1,433,757	1,876,170	3,309,927	74,419	44.8
1965	1,131,641	1,486,028	2,617,669	71,644	36.5
1966	1,282,808	1,819,798	3,102,606	75,676	41.0
1967	1,512,596	1,846,369	3,358,965	76,760	43.8
1968	1,349,901	1,797,887	3,147,788	75,171	41.9
1969	913,662	1,315,684	2,229,346	73,176	30.5
1970	2,061,991	1,313,553	9,375,544	69,628	48.5
1971	1,222,340	912,853	2,135,193	66,104	32.3
1972	1,620,408	1,037,091	2,657,499	69,471	38.3
1973	2,484,723	1,290,373	3,765,096	70,736	53.2
1974	2,237,354	1,136,433	3,373,787	67,364	50.1
1975	1,769,658	987,528	2,757,186	69,028	39.9
1976	2,462,257	1,059,799	3,522,056	70,844	49.7
1977	1,291,700	685,800	1,977,500	76,001	26.0
1978	2,246,382	992,688	3,239,070	78,439	41.3
1979	3,307,839	1,201,288	4,509,127	74,290	60.7
1980	2,047,454	857,773	2,905,227	76,271	38.1
1981	2,528,295	768,181	3,296,476	77,756	42.4
1982	3,508,365	1,041,919	4,550,284	77,687	58.6
1983	3,190,016	917,307	4,114,542	79,941	51.5
1984	1,930,150	907,829	2,838,409	79,682	35.6
1985	3,932,601	978,289	4,910,890	83,779	58.6
1986	4,514,082	1,101,754	5,615,836	86,641	65.0
1987	3,655,535	1,057,099	4,712,634	92,873	50.7
1988	3,649,071	937,117	4,586,788	95,406	48.1
1989	4,869,927	1,034,673	5,904,598	98,205	60.1
1990	4,905,661	1,102,305	6,007,966	101,009	59.5
1991	2,158,913	429,181	2,558,094	106,453	24.3
1992	5,038,311	1,234,138	6,272,449	108,131	58.0
1993	4,840,284	938,804	5,779,088	110,334	51.1
1994	4,830,072	846,787	5,676,859	113,135	50.2
1995	5,494,091	1,044,454	6,538,545	113,230	57.7
1996	5,433,752	979,818	6,413,570	112,217	57.2
1997	5,748,688	933,917	6,682,605	112,877	59.2
1998	5,698,648	884,386	6,583,034	113,384	58.1
1999	5,927,541	879,133	6,806,674	115,109	59.1
2000	5,988,608	815,868	6,804,476	116,902	57.6
2001	5,859,132	701,496	6,560,628	118,424	55.4
2002	4,976,441	636,051	5,612,492	119,817	46.8

Source: CIVB

Appendix Three

Evolution of the Area Under Vine
and the Number of Growers in the Gironde

	Number of Hectares (AC)	Number of Hectares (non-AC)	Total Hectares	Growers Declaring a Vintage
1946	N/A	N/A	136,482	57,907
1951	69,587	62,296	131,883	86,601
1956	67,845	58,359	126,204	46,701
1961	71,592	37,019	108,611	45,685
1966	75,676	34,740	110,416	41,488
1971	66,104	36,251	102,355	33,084
1976	70,844	33,824	104,668	28,630
1981	76,744	19,609	96,353	24,983
1986	87,058	14,714	101,772	20,905
1991	106,453	3444	109,897	15,853
1996	112,218	3020	115,238	12,852
2001	118,424	1245	119,669	11,433

Following the Second World War, the surface area under vine in the Gironde fell until 1984, since when it has risen 25 per cent, as domestic wine consumption has upgraded from non-AC wine to to better, appellation wine. Meanwhile the area and production of non-AC wines, once of great importance, have evaporated to negligible proportions. The number of growers who declare an individual harvest has also fallen substantially, today representing less than one-fifth of those in immediate post-war years. Holdings have been amalgamated and the weekend *vignerons* have decided to sell up.

Source: CIVB

APPENDIX FOUR

EVOLUTION OF RED WINE PRODUCTION
AT THE EXPENSE OF WHITE

	RED WINE (Hectolitres)	WHITE WINE (Hectolitres)	TOTAL (Hectolitres)	WHITE WINE PERCENTAGE
1946	732,971	1,636,157	2,369,128	69.1
1951	732,221	1,204,337	1,936,658	62.2
1956	370,978	847,462	1,218,440	69.6
1961	550,106	1,281,639	1,831,745	70.0
1966	1,282,808	1,819,798	3,102,606	58.7
1971	1,222,340	912,853	2,135,193	42.8
1976	2,462,257	1,059,799	3,522,056	30.1
1981	2,528,295	768,181	3,296,476	23.3
1986	4,514,082	1,101,754	5,615,836	19.6
1991	2,158,913	429,181	2,588,094	16.6
1996	5,433,752	979,818	6,413,570	15.3
2001	5,859,132	701,496	6,560,628	10.7

Just after the Second World War, and continuing well into the 1960s, Bordeaux was chiefly a white wine-producing region. Dramatically since then, the Sémillon and the Sauvignon have been ousted in favour of Merlot and Cabernet Sauvignon. Nineteen sixty-two remains the sole vintage where production of white wine exceeded 2 million hectolitres. The last time the one million figure was exceeded was 1995.

Source: CIVB

APPENDIX FIVE
THE STARRED CHÂTEAUX

THREE STAR

MÉDOC/GRAVES	POMEROL	SAINT-ÉMILION	SAUTERNES
Haut-Brion (Pessac-Léognan)	Pétrus	Cheval Blanc	d'Yquem
Lafite-Rothschild (Pauillac)			
Latour (Pauillac)			
Léoville-Las-Cases (Saint-Julien)			
Margaux (Margaux)			

TWO STAR

MÉDOC/GRAVES	POMEROL	SAINT-ÉMILION	SAUTERNES
Domaine de Chevalier (Pessac-Léognan)	L'Église-Clinet	Ausone	Climens
Cos d'Estournel (Saint-Estèphe)	L'Évangile	Canon	Lafaurie-Peyraguey
Ducru-Beaucaillou (Saint-Julien)	La Fleur-Pétrus	Figeac	Rieussec
Grand-Puy-Lacoste (Pauillac)	Lafleur	Magdelaine	Suduiraut
Laville Haut-Brion (Pessac-Léognan)	Latour-à-Pomerol		
Léoville-Barton (Saint-Julien)	Le Pin		
La Mission Haut-Brion (Pessac-Léognan)	Trotanoy		
Mouton-Rothschild (Pauillac)	Vieux Château Certan		
Palmer (Margaux)			

ONE STAR

MÉDOC/GRAVES	POMEROL	SAINT-ÉMILION	SAUTERNES
Brane-Cantenac (Margaux)	Certan de May	Angélus	Coutet
Calon-Ségur (Saint-Estèphe)	Clinet	L'Arrosée	Doisy-Daëne
Chasse-Spleen (Moulis)	La Conseillante	Beau-Séjour-Bécot	Doisy-Dubroca
Clerc-Milon (Pauillac)	Clos L'Église	Beauséjour-(Duffau-	Doisy-Védrines
Couhins-Lurton	Gazin	Lagarrosse)	de Fargues
(Pessac-Léognan)	La Grave	Belair	de Malle
Durfort-Vivens (Margaux)	Hosanna	Bellevue	Nairac
Ferrière (Margaux)	Nénin	Berliquet	Rabaud-Promis
Haut-Bailly (Pessac-Léognan)		Le Dôme	Rayne-Vigneau
Haut-Batailley (Pauillac)		La Gomerie	Sigalas-Rabaud
Gruaud-Larose (Saint-Julien)		La Mondotte	La Tour Blanche
Haut-Marbuzet (Saint-Estèphe)		Clos de L'Oratoire	
La Lagune (Haut-Médoc)		Pavie-Macquin	
Langoa-Barton (Saint-Julien)		Tertre-Roteboeuf	
Léoville-Poyferré (Saint-Julien)		Troplong-Mondot	
Lynch-Bages (Pauillac)		de Valandraud	
Malescot-Saint-Exupéry			
(Margaux)			
Montrose (Saint-Estèphe)			
Pape-Clément (Pessac-Léognan)			
Pichon-Longueville (Pauillac)			
Pichon-Longueville, Comtesse de			
Lalande (Pauillac)			
Pontet-Canet (Pauillac)			
Poujeaux (Moulis)			
Rauzan-Ségla (Margaux)			
Sociando-Mallet (Haut-Médoc)			
Talbot (Saint-Julien)			
La Tour Haut-Brion			
(Pessac-Léognan)			

APPENDIX SIX

OPENING PRICES

Ex-Château (FF/€)

	CHÂTEAU MARGAUX	CHÂTEAU DUCRU-BEAUCAILLOU	CHÂTEAU GRAND-PUY-LACOSTE	CHÂTEAU SOCIANDO-MALLET	CHÂTEAU CARONNE-STE-GEMME
1981	125	48	37	N/A	14
1982	170	70	42	N/A	16
1983	170	90	48	27	27
1984	170	110	60	33	24
1985	200	110	75	35	25
1986	180	95	65	35	25
1987	130	70	45.20	30	22
1988	180	100	68	35	25
1989	230	125	75	55	28
1990	205	100	63	50	30
1991	160	65	-	45	25
1992	130	58	43	40	25
1993	155	70	53	48	29
1994	180	80	60	56	29
1995	230	115	75	65	32
1996	300	245	120	90	34
1997	500	250	145	115	38
1998	430	210	130	100	38
1999	459.20 (€70)	195	120	100	38
2000	787.10 (€120)	315 (€48)	150 (€23)	108 (€16.50)	40 (€6.10)
2001	557.60 (€85)	203.40 (€31)	118 (€18)	100 (€15.25)	39 (€5.95)
2002	€60	€25	€16	€13.40	€5.95

Source: Balaresque and the properties themselves.

2000/1990	3.84	3.15	2.38	2.16	1.33

Appendix Seven

The Crus Bourgeois Classification of 2003

The most significant change vis à vis earlier classifications of the Crus Bourgeois is that there is no longer any distinction between properties of the Médoc and Haut-Médoc. Hitherto the classifications of Exceptionnels and Supérieurs had been reserved for properties in the Haut-Médoc.

Nine growths have been classed as Exceptionnels, 86 as Supérieurs. Certain properties, notably Châteaux Sociando-Mallet, Gloria, Bel-Air Marquis d'Aligre and Bernadotte, were not put forward for classification.

The new classification applies for the 2003 vintage.

Crus Bourgeois Exceptionnels

Château	Commune	AC
Chasse-Spleen	Moulis-en-Médoc	Moulis-en-Médoc
Haut-Marbuzet	Saint-Estèphe	Saint-Estèphe
Labegorce-Zédé	Soussans	Margaux
Les Ormes de Pez	Saint-Estèphe	Saint-Estèphe
de Pez	Saint-Estèphe	Saint-Estèphe
Phélan-Ségur	Saint-Estèphe	Saint-Estèphe
Potensac	Ordonnac	Médoc
Poujeaux	Moulis-en-Médoc	Moulis-en-Médoc
Siran	Labarde	Margaux

Crus Bourgeois Supérieurs

Château	Commune	AC
d'Agassac	Ludon-Médoc	Haut-Médoc
d'Angludet	Cantenac	Margaux
Anthonic	Moulis-en-Médoc	Moulis-en-Médoc
d'Arche	Ludon-Médoc	Haut-Médoc
Arnauld	Arcins	Haut-Médoc
d'Arsac	Arsac	Margaux
Beaumont	Cussac-Fort-Médoc	Haut-Médoc
Beau-Site	Saint-Estèphe	Saint-Estèphe
Biston-Brillette	Moulis-en-Médoc	Moulis-en-Médoc
Le Boscq	Saint-Estèphe	Saint-Estèphe
Bournac	Civrac	Médoc
Brillette	Moulis-en-Médoc	Moulis-en-Médoc
Cambon La Pelouse	Macau	Haut-Médoc
Cap Léon Véyrin	Listrac-Médoc	Listrac-Médoc
La Cardonne	Blaignan	Médoc
Caronne Sainte-Gemme	Saint-Laurent-Médoc	Haut-Médoc
Castéra	Saint Germain d'Esteuil	Médoc
Chambert-Marbuzet	Saint-Estèphe	Saint-Estèphe
Charmail	Saint-Seurin-de-Cadourne	Haut-Médoc
Cissac	Cissac-Médoc	Haut-Médoc

CHÂTEAU	COMMUNE	AC
Citran	Avensan	Haut-Médoc
Clarke	Listrac-Médoc	Listrac-Médoc
Clauzet	Saint-Estèphe	Saint-Estèphe
Clément-Pichon	Parempuyre	Haut-Médoc
Colombier-Monpelou	Pauillac	Pauillac
Coufran	Saint-Seurin-de-Cadourne	Haut-Médoc
Le Crock	Saint-Estèphe	Saint-Estèphe
Dutruch Grand-Poujeaux	Moulis-en-Médoc	Moulis-en-Médoc
d'Escurac	Civrac	Médoc
Fonbadet	Pauillac	Pauillac
Fonréaud	Listrac-Médoc	Listrac-Médoc
Fourcas-Dupré	Listrac-Médoc	Listrac-Médoc
Fourcas-Hosten	Listrac-Médoc	Listrac-Médoc
Fourcas-Loubaney	Listrac-Médoc	Listrac-Médoc
du Glana	Saint-Julien Beychevelle	Saint-Julien
Les Grands Chênes	Saint-Christoly-de-Médoc	Médoc
Gressier-Grand-Poujeaux	Moulis-en-Médoc	Moulis-en-Médoc
Greysac	Bégadan	Médoc
La Gurgue	Margaux	Margaux
Hanteillan	Cissac-Médoc	Haut-Médoc
Haut-Bages Monpelou	Pauillac	Pauillac
La Haye	Saint-Estèphe	Saint-Estèphe
Labégorce	Margaux	Margaux
Lachesnaye	Cussac Fort Médoc	Haut-Médoc
de Lamarque	Lamarque	Haut-Médoc
Lamothe-Bergeron	Cussac Fort Médoc	Haut-Médoc
Lanessan	Cussac Fort Médoc	Haut-Médoc
Larose-Trintaudon	Saint-Laurent-Médoc	Haut-Médoc
Lestage	Listrac-Médoc	Listrac-Médoc
Lestage-Simon	Saint-Seurin-de-Cadourne	Haut-Médoc
Lilian Ladouys	Saint-Estèphe	Saint-Estèphe
Liversan	Saint-Sauveur	Haut-Médoc
Loudenne	Saint-Yzans-de-Médoc	Médoc
Malescasse	Lamarque	Haut-Médoc
de Malleret	Le Pian-Médoc	Haut-Médoc
Maucaillou	Moulis-en-Médoc	Moulis-en-Médoc
Maucamps	Macau	Haut-Médoc
Mayne-Lalande	Listrac-Médoc	Listrac-Médoc
Meyney	Saint-Estèphe	Saint-Estèphe
Monbrison	Arsac	Margaux
Moulin-à-Vent	Moulis-en-Médoc	Moulis-en-Médoc
Moulin de La Rose	Saint-Julien Beychevelle	Saint-Julien
Les Ormes-Sorbet	Couquèques	Médoc
Paloumey	Ludon-Médoc	Haut-Médoc
Patache d'Aux	Bégadan	Médoc
Paveil-de-Luze	Soussans	Margaux
Petit Boscq	Saint-Estèphe	Saint-Estèphe
Pibran	Pauillac	Pauillac
Ramage La Batisse	Saint-Sauveur	Haut-Médoc

CHÂTEAU	COMMUNE	AC
Reysson	Vertheuil	Haut-Médoc
Rollan de By	Bégadan	Médoc
Saransot-Dupré	Listrac-Médoc	Listrac-Médoc
Ségur	Parempuyre	Haut-Médoc
Sénéjac	Le Pian-Médoc	Haut-Médoc
Soudars	Saint-Seurin-de-Cadourne	Haut-Médoc
du Taillan	Le Taillan-Médoc	Haut-Médoc
Terrey-Gros-Cailloux	Saint-Julien Beychevelle	Saint-Julien
La Tour-de-By	Bégadan	Médoc
Tour de Marbuzet	Saint-Estèphe	Saint-Estèphe
La Tour de Mons	Soussans	Margaux
Tour de Pez	Saint-Estèphe	Saint-Estèphe
Tour du Haut-Moulin	Cussac-Fort-Médoc	Haut-Médoc
Tour-Haut-Caussan	Blaignan	Médoc
Tronquoy-Lalande	Saint-Estèphe	Saint-Estèphe
Verdignan	Saint-Seurin-de-Cadourne	Haut-Médoc
Vieux Robin	Bégadan	Médoc
Villegeorge	Avensan	Haut-Médoc

CRUS BOURGEOIS

CHÂTEAU	COMMUNE	AC
Andron-Blanquet	Saint-Estèphe	Saint-Estèphe
Aney	Cussac Fort Médoc	Haut-Médoc
d'Arcins	Arcins	Haut-Médoc
L'Argenteyre	Bégadan	Médoc
d'Aurilhac	Saint-Seurin-de-Cadourne	Haut-Médoc
Balac	Saint-Laurent-Médoc	Haut-Médoc
Barateau	Saint-Laurent-Médoc	Haut-Médoc
Bardis	Saint-Seurin-de-Cadourne	Haut-Médoc
Barreyres	Arcins	Haut-Médoc
Baudan	Listrac-Médoc	Listrac-Médoc
Beau-Site Haut-Vignoble	Saint-Estèphe	Saint-Estèphe
Bégadanet	Bégadan	Médoc
Bel Air	Saint-Estèphe	Saint-Estèphe
Bel Air	Cussac-Fort-Médoc	Haut-Médoc
Bel Orme, Tronquoy de Lalande	Saint-Seurin-de-Cadourne	Haut-Médoc
Bel-Air Lagrave	Moulis-en-Médoc	Moulis-en-Médoc
des Belles Graves	Ordonnac	Médoc
Bessan Ségur	Civrac	Médoc
Bibian	Listrac-Médoc	Listrac-Médoc
Blaignan	Blaignan	Médoc
Le Boscq	Bégadan	Médoc
Le Bourdieu	Valeyrac	Médoc
Le Bourdieu Vertheuil	Vertheuil	Haut-Médoc
de Braude	Macau	Haut-Médoc
du Breuil	Cissac-Médoc	Haut-Médoc
La Bridane	Saint-Julien Beychevelle	Saint-Julien
des Brousteras	Saint-Yzans-de-Médoc	Médoc

Château	Commune	AC
des Cabans	Bégadan	Médoc
Cap de Haut	Lamarque	Haut-Médoc
Capbern Gasqueton	Saint-Estèphe	Saint-Estèphe
Chantelys	Prignac-en-Médoc	Médoc
La Clare	Bégadan	Médoc
La Commanderie	Saint-Estèphe	Saint-Estèphe
Le Coteau	Arsac	Margaux
Coutelin Merville	Saint-Estèphe	Saint-Estèphe
de la Croix	Ordonnac	Médoc
Dasvin-Bel-Air	Macau	Haut-Médoc
David	Vensac	Médoc
Devise d'Ardilley	Saint-Laurent-Médoc	Haut-Médoc
Deyrem-Valentin	Soussans	Margaux
Dillon	Blanquefort	Haut-Médoc
Domeyne	Saint-Estèphe	Saint-Estèphe
Donissan	Listrac-Médoc	Listrac-Médoc
Ducluzeau	Listrac-Médoc	Listrac-Médoc
Duplessis-(Hauchecorne)	Moulis-en-Médoc	Moulis-en-Médoc
Duplessis-Fabre	Moulis-en-Médoc	Moulis-en-Médoc
Duthil	Le Pian-Médoc	Haut-Médoc
L'Ermitage	Listrac-Médoc	Listrac-Médoc
d'Escot	Lesparre-Médoc	Médoc
La Fleur-Milon	Pauillac	Pauillac
La Fleur-Peyrabon	Saint-Sauveur	Pauillac
La Fon du Berger	Saint-Sauveur	Haut-Médoc
Fontesteau	Saint-Sauveur	Haut-Médoc
Fontis	Ordonnac	Médoc
La Galiane	Soussans	Margaux
de Gironville	Macau	Haut-Médoc
La Gorce	Blaignan	Médoc
La Gorre	Bégadan	Médoc
Grand Clapeau Olivier	Blanquefort	Haut-Médoc
Grandis	Saint-Seurin-de-Cadourne	Haut-Médoc
Granins Grand Poujeaux	Moulis-en-Médoc	Moulis-en-Médoc
Grivière	Blaignan	Médoc
Haut-Beauséjour	Saint-Estèphe	Saint-Estèphe
Haut-Bellevue	Lamarque	Haut-Médoc
Haut-Breton-Larigaudière	Soussans	Margaux
Haut-Canteloup	Saint-Christoly-de-Médoc	Médoc
Haut-Madrac	Saint-Sauveur	Haut-Médoc
Haut-Maurac	Saint-Yzans-de-Médoc	Médoc
Houissant	Saint-Estèphe	Saint-Estèphe
Hourbanon	Prignac-en-Médoc	Médoc
Hourtin-Ducasse	Saint-Sauveur	Haut-Médoc
Inclassable	Prignac-en-Médoc	Médoc
Labadie	Bégadan	Médoc
Ladouys	Saint-Estèphe	Saint-Estèphe
Laffitte-Carcasset	Saint-Estèphe	Listrac-Médoc
Laffitte Laujac	Bégadan	Médoc

CHÂTEAU	COMMUNE	AC
Lalande	Listrac-Médoc	Listrac-Médoc
Lalande	Saint-Julien-Beychevelle	Saint-Julien
Lamothe-Cissac	Cissac-Médoc	Haut-Médoc
Larose Perganson	Saint-Laurent-Médoc	Haut-Médoc
Larrivaux	Cissac-Médoc	Haut-Médoc
Larruau	Margaux	Margaux
Laujac	Bégadan	Médoc
La Lauzette	Listrac-Médoc	Listrac-Médoc
Leyssac	Saint-Estèphe	Saint-Estèphe
Lieujean	Saint-Sauveur	Haut-Médoc
Liouner	Listrac-Médoc	Listrac-Médoc
Lousteauneuf	Valeyrac	Médoc
Magnol	Blanquefort	Haut-Médoc
Marbuzet	Saint-Estèphe	Saint-Estèphe
Marsac-Séguineau	Soussans	Margaux
Martinens	Cantenac	Margaux
Maurac	Saint-Seurin-de-Cadourne	Haut-Médoc
Mazails	Saint-Yzans-de-Médoc	Médoc
Le Meynieu	Vertheuil	Haut-Médoc
Meyre	Avensan	Haut-Médoc
Les Moines	Couquèques	Médoc
Mongravey	Arsac	Margaux
Le Monteil d'Arsac	Arsac	Haut-Médoc
Morin	Saint-Estèphe	Saint-Estèphe
du Moulin Rouge	Cussac-Fort-Médoc	Haut-Médoc
La Mouline	Moulis-en-Médoc	Moulis-en-Médoc
Muret	Saint-Seurin-de-Cadourne	Haut-Médoc
Noaillac	Jau-Dignac-et-Loirac	Médoc
du Perier	Saint-Christoly-de-Médoc	Médoc
Le Pey	Bégadan	Médoc
Peyrabon	Saint-Sauveur	Haut-Médoc
Peyredon-Lagravette	Listrac-Médoc	Listrac-Médoc
Peyre-Lebade	Listrac-Médoc	Haut-Médoc
Picard	Saint-Estèphe	Saint-Estèphe
Plantey	Pauillac	Pauillac
Poitevin	Jau-Dignac-Loirac	Médoc
Pomys	Saint-Estèphe	Saint-Estèphe
Pontac Lynch	Cantenac	Margaux
Pontey	Blaignan	Médoc
Pontoise Cabarrus	Saint-Seurin-de-Cadourne	Haut-Médoc
Puy-Castéra	Cissac-Médoc	Haut-Médoc
Ramafort	Blaignan	Médoc
du Raux	Cussac-Fort-Médoc	Haut-Médoc
La Raze Beauvallet	Civrac	Médoc
du Retout	Cussac-Fort-Médoc	Haut-Médoc
Reverdi	Listrac-Médoc	Listrac-Médoc
Roquegrave	Valeyrac	Médoc
Saint-Ahon	Blanquefort	Haut-Médoc
Saint-Aubin	Jau-Dignac-Loirac	Médoc

CHÂTEAU	COMMUNE	AC
Saint-Christophe	Saint-Christoly-de-Médoc	Médoc
Saint Estèphe	Saint-Estèphe	Saint-Estèphe
Saint-Hilaire	Queyrac	Médoc
Saint-Paul	Saint-Seurin-de-Cadourne	Haut-Médoc
Segue Longue	Jau-Dignac-Loirac	Médoc
Ségur de Cabanac	Saint-Estèphe	Saint-Estèphe
Semeillan Mazeau	Listrac-Médoc	Listrac-Médoc
Senilhac	Saint-Seurin-de-Cadourne	Haut-Médoc
Sipian	Valeyrac	Médoc
Tayac	Soussans	Margaux
Le Temple	Valeyrac	Médoc
Teynac	Saint-Julien Beychevelle	Saint-Julien
La Tonnelle	Cissac-Médoc	Haut-Médoc
Tour Blanche	Saint-Christoly-de-Médoc	Médoc
La Tour de Bessan	Cantenac	Margaux
Tour des Termes	Saint-Estèphe	Saint-Estèphe
Tour-du-Roc	Arcins	Haut-Médoc
Tour Prignac	Prignac-en-Médoc	Médoc
Tour Saint-Bonnet	Saint-Christoly-de-Médoc	Médoc
Tour Saint-Fort	Saint-Estèphe	Saint-Estèphe
Tour Saint-Joseph	Cissac-Médoc	Haut-Médoc
Trois Moulins	Macau	Haut-Médoc
Les Tuileries	Saint-Yzans-de-Médoc	Médoc
Vernous	Lesparre	Médoc
Vieux-Château-Landon	Bégadan	Médoc
de Villambis	Cissac-Médoc	Haut-Médoc

GLOSSARY

ACETIC The sweet/sour smell of vinegar given by a wine which has been affected by vinegar bacteria.

ACID, ACIDITY Essential constituent of a wine (though not in excess!). Gives zip and freshness and contributes to the balance and length on the palate.

AFTER-TASTE The residual taste-impression left in the mouth and memory after the wine has been swallowed or spat out.

ALIOS Hard sandstone rock. A primary subsoil in the Bordeaux area.

AMATEUR French for lover, in the sense of wine-lover.

À POINT Ready for drinking.

APPELLATION CONTRÔLÉE French legislative term referring to the top category of quality wines and the controls surrounding their production.

ARE A unit of measurement. 100 ares = 1 hectare.

ARGILE French for clay.

AROMA The smell or 'nose' of a wine.

AROMATIC Flavours/constituents of smell: more than just the grape variety.

ASSEMBLAGE The blending together of the constituent parts of a wine.

ASTRINGENT Dry taste and finish of a wine which has lost some of its fruit or is too tannic.

AUSTERE Restrained, 'shy' taste – of a Médoc as opposed to the more open, accessible taste of a Saint-Émilion.

BACKBONE Structure of a wine, implying body and grip.

BAKED Slightly burnt flavour resulting from a very hot dry vintage.

BALANCE The harmony of a wine; its balance between body, fruit, alcohol and acidity.

BARRIQUE Wooden barrel size (usually 225 litres) frequently associated with Bordeaux.

BÂTONNAGE Stirring up of the lees of a very young wine in a cask. Applies to white wine more than red.

BEAD The 'tears' formed by a ripe, full wine on the side of the glass.

BIEN NATIONAL Term given to estates sequestered and then sold by the state at the time of the French Revolution.

BIODYNAMISM A philosophical approach to viticulture, derived from the theories of Rudolf Steiner, involving homeopathy and the movement of the planets.

BITTER Self-explanatory, but if not in excess, not necessarily a bad thing in an immature claret.

BLACKCURRANTS Said to be the characteristic fruit taste of Cabernet Sauvignon.

BLOWSY Fat but without enough zip, or acidity.

BODY The 'stuffing' or weight of a wine.

BOISÉ Excess of a woody taste, resulting from a prolonged use of new oak.

BOTRYTIS CINEREA A fungus which attacks grapes and which can cause 'noble rot' in certain climatic conditions. Noble rot is responsible for the luscious sweet white wines of Sauternes and elsewhere.

BOUQUET The smell or 'nose' of a wine. A term used for mature rather than immature wine.

BOURGEOIS Denoting a wine of lower than 'classed growth' status. Applies particularly to properties in the Médoc and Haut-Médoc.

BOURGEOIS SUPÉRIEUR The best of the above.

BREED Finesse, distinction. Cabernet Sauvignon One of the classic – if not the classic – grapes of Bordeaux.

CAILLOU French for pebble.

CALCAIRE French for limestone.

CANTON A French administrative district within a department.

CAVE French for cellar, whether below or above ground.

CÉPAGE French for vine variety.

CÉPAGE AMÉLIORATEUR A quality or 'noble' grape variety.

CHAI Outbuildings, cellars, where wine is made and matured.

CHAPEAU The 'cap' of grape skins etc., which tends to rise to the top of the must during fermentation.

CHAPTALISATION Addition of sugar to the must with a view to increasing the eventual alcoholic content of the wine.

CHARACTER The depth or complexity of a wine.

CHÂTEAU French for 'castle', but also means a country house or villa; and also a wine estate including its outbuildings and vineyards, no matter how big or small.

CLOS French for 'enclosed'; in wine denotes a vineyard enclosed within a wall.

COARSE Lacking finesse and possibly not very well made.

COCKS AND FÉRET Authors of the 'Bible' of Bordeaux. *Bordeaux et Ses Vins* lists all the main properties and other information. Has been republished in a number of editions since its first publication in 1850.

CODE NAPOLÉON The French law of succession abolishing primogeniture.

COLLAGE Fining.

COMMUNE French for parish.

CORKED, CORKY An off, oxidised and dirty smell owing to a defective or diseased cork.

CÔTE French for slope or plateau.

COULURE Failure of a vine's flowers to set into grapes. Results from poor, humid weather during the flowering.

COURTIER French for wine broker – the 'middle-man' between the grower and the *négociant.*

CREAMY A richness and concentration in a wine's character and flavour as a result of old vines.

CROUPE French term for a gravel ridge or mound. Highly suitable soil for vines, particularly in the Médoc.

CRU French term for 'growth', or vineyard and the vines thereof.

CRU CLASSÉ Officially classed growth: see introductory chapters. Often further qualified, as in *premier* and *deuxième* and so on.

CUVAISON The (length of) time a red wine must macerate with the skins.

CUVE French term for 'wine vat'.

CUVÉE The contents of a wine vat: used to denote a blend or particular parcel of wine.

CUVIER, CUVERIE French for the vat house or part of the cellar where the vinification takes place.

DÉBOURBAGE French term for the process of allowing must to settle and deposit soil particles and other sediment before fermentation is allowed to commence.

DÉBOURREMENT French term for 'bud-break'.

DELICATE Charm and balance in a wine of light style.

DÉPARTEMENT French administrative area, equivalent to a county.

DEPTH Subtlety, 'dimensions' of flavour.

DEUXIÈME CRU Second 'growth' in a classification.

DEUXIÈME MARQUE/VIN Second wine: hence the produce of the less good vats or less mature wines.

DRY Opposite of sweet. Sometimes, when used of a wine, indicates a lack of ripe fruit.

DULL Boring, uninteresting, absence of character and complexity.

DUMB Used for an immature wine which has character but is still undeveloped.

EARTHY Character deriving from the nature of the soil. Not necessarily a pejorative expression.

ÉCLAIRCISSAGE Crop-thinning by removal of buds or embryonic grape bunches.

ÉCOULAGE French term for the process of draining wine of the residual skins, pips etc. after *cuvaison* is completed.

ÉGRAPPAGE À LA MAIN Hand destalking.

ÉGRAPPOIR Machine which de-stalks.

ELEGANT Style, finesse.

ÉLEVAGE Literally the 'rearing'. In wine used to denote the length of time and processes undergone between vinification and bottling.

EN FERMAGE Tenant farming.

EN FRICHE Land lying fallow.

EN PRIMEUR Sale of the young wine within the first few months of the harvest.

ENCÉPAGEMENT Proportion of grape varieties.

FAT Full in the sense of high in glycerine, ripeness and extract.

FEUILLAISON Coming into leaf.

FINESSE Style, breed, distinction.

FINING A process, like filtration, to remove impurities from a wine. At the top properties white of egg is used. This helps precipitate matter which would otherwise not settle out of its own accord.

FINISH The 'conclusion' of the taste of a wine on the palate.

FIRST GROWTH In Bordeaux the top wines in a classification. Traditionally used for the four wines: Lafite, Latour, Margaux and Haut-Brion, so classed in 1855.

FLAT Dull, lacking in zip of acidity.

FLORAISON Flowering of the vine. Usually takes place in June.

FOUDRE Large oak vat.

FOULOIR-ÉGRAPPOIR Crushing and de-stalking machine.

FRANCK, W M Author of *Traité sur les Vins du Médoc*. First published in 1824, and revised several times during the next generation, this was one of the first comprehensive works on the wines of the Bordeaux area.

FULL (-BODIED) Ample body. High in extract and (probably) alcohol and tannin.

GELÉE French for frost.

GENEROSITY Used of wines to describe something which is ripe, round and attractive.

GOÛT DE TERROIR Earthy, though not necessarily in a pejorative sense. Denoting literally a 'taste of soil'.

GRAND CRU 'Great Growth': without the qualification of 'Classé' need not necessarily mean anything.

GRAND CRU CLASSÉ 'Classed great growth', a term used in the official classifications of the Graves and Saint-Émilion.

GRAND VIN The first wine, i.e. product or blend which will eventually be bottled under the château name. Can also be used, of course, simply in its literal, complimentary sense.

GRAVES French for 'gravel'.

GREEN Used to describe an unripe flavour, possibly also denotes the produce of immature vines.

GREEN HARVEST Removal of excess bunches of grapes before *véraison*.

GRÊLE French for hail.

GRIP Opposite to flat or flabby. Satisfactory acidity level which 'finishes' the taste-impression off well. Applies particularly to wines with a level of youth in them.

GUYOT Eponymous system of long-cane pruning.

HARD Firmness of an immature wine normally denoting plenty of body, tannin and acidity as yet un-mellowed.

HARSH As above, but in a fiery way, i.e. perhaps to excess.

HEAVY Denoting a full, alcoholic wine; could be used where it is rather too full-bodied, perhaps out of balance and 'stewed'.

HECTARE International measure of area; equivalent to 2.471 acres.

HECTOLITRE International measure of capacity; 100 litres equivalent to 11 cases of wine or 22 Imperial gallons.

HOGSHEAD English name for the traditional Bordeaux barrel, holding 49.5 Imperial gallons or 225 litres.

HORIZONTAL TASTING Tasting of a group of wines of the same vintage.

INAO Institut National des Appellations d'Origine. French government body which legislates vine-growing and winemaking controls.

INDIVISION Joint possession (of a property) between a large number of heirs.

INKY A rather stewed, metallic taste.

LEAN The opposite of generous; an absence of roundness and ripeness, warmth and attraction. Usually indicates quite high acidity.

LEES Sediment or deposit of dead yeast cells, tartrate crystals etc. which settles out of a wine.

LIEU-DIT Place-name.

LONG (on the palate) Finish continues for some time and has complexity and interest.

MADERISED Combination of oxidised and volatile acidity flavour in a wine which has been badly stored or is over the hill.

MAÎTRE DE CHAI Cellar master or manager.

MALBEC One of the main grapes of the Bordeaux area – see introductory section.

MARNE Marl, a clay-limestone soil.

MEATY Full, rich, fat wine, normally used of a wine still young, with a tannic grip - almost a chewable quality.

MELLOW Round, soft, mature – no longer hard, firm or harsh.

MERLOT One of the most important grapes of the Bordeaux area, particularly in Saint-Émilion and Pomerol.

MESOCLIMATE The climate of a specific geographical area.

MICRO-OXYGENATION/ MICROBULLAGE A device which releases small quantities of oxygen into the wine in the vat.

MILDEW A cryptogamic or fungus disease of the vine. Counteracted by the application of copper-sulphate solution. Also known as 'downy' mildew.

MILLERANDAGE Shot berries. As a result of poor flowering some of the berries fail to develop.

MILLÉSIME Vintage year.

MUST Grape juice which has not yet fully fermented out and become wine.

NÉGOCE Collective term for

the wine trade or merchants in Bordeaux or elsewhere.

NÉGOCIANT A wine merchant.

NEUTRAL Self-explanatory: absence of character but without any positive defect save that.

NOBLE Top quality, breed, distinction.

NOBLE ROT The beneficial fungus needed to make luscious sweet wine. Also called *Botrytis cinerea*.

OENOLOGY Science of wine and winemaking.

OFF-TASTE An alien smell or flavour.

OÏDIUM Or 'powdery' mildew. A cryptogamic or fungus disease of the vine. Counteracted by the application of sulphur.

OUILLAGE Literally ullage: applied to the *élevage* of wine it means the regular topping up of the barrels to replace wine lost through evaporation.

OXIDISED Flat, tired taint in a wine which has at some time had excessive exposure to air.

PALUS Alluvial land closest to the Gironde estuary. Not suitable for the production of fine wine.

PASSAGE A visit to a row of vines to pick those clusters at their optimum ripeness. Several *passages* will indicate that the vineyard has been picked over several times.

PHYLLOXERA A parasitic disease of the vine caused by a member of the aphid family. The problem is held at bay by grafting European vines onto phylloxera-resistant American rootstock.

PIGEAGE The treading down

and the breaking up of the cap or *chapeau* of grape skins.

PIJASSOU Professor René Pijassou of Bordeaux University has done an immense amount of pioneering research into the history of wine and the major estates in Bordeaux.

PLAFOND LIMITE DE CLASSEMENT (PLC) The ceiling yield for any appellation, normally a maximum 20 per cent above the permitted base yield.

PORTE-GREFFE Rootstock.

POURRITURE GRISE 'Grey rot' caused by the same fungus that is responsible for 'noble' rot in Sauternes and elsewhere, but occurring in wet, humid weather. The grape skins can now be to some extent rendered resistant to rot by sprays.

POURRITURE NOBLE French for noble rot or *Botrytis cinerea*.

PREMIER CRU (CLASSÉ) First (classed) growth.

PROFOUND A wine having depth.

PUISSANCE Literally power, but when used of wine it means more than that, more the kinetic energy of a youngish wine.

RACK (ING) To pump out or empty off and separate the clear wine in a cask from its lees.

RÉCOLTE Harvest.

RÉGISSEUR Bailiff, estate manager.

RENDEMENT Quantitative harvest, the yield.

RÉSERVE DU CHÂTEAU Specially selected superior *cuvée* created by some

Bordeaux properties.

RESINOUS Not, in the case of Bordeaux, used literally! Indicates a suggestion of resin.

RICH For red wines, doesn't indicate sweetness, more a combination of fullness of body, abundance of ripe fruit, extract and probably alcohol.

RIPE The result and a confirmation of healthy fruit picked in a ripe condition, giving richness and fullness of flavour to a wine.

ROBUST Full not round, slightly tough, hard and perhaps earthy; possibly also a bit coarse.

ROCADE A French word for a by-pass.

ROOTSTOCK The American base onto which European vines have been grafted since the phylloxera epidemic.

ROUND Soft and mellow, a characteristic of a mature wine.

SAUVAGE French for 'savage'; also a somewhat raw, youthful wine, with as yet unrefined character.

SEVERE Hard, austere, unforthcoming. A characteristic of an immature wine.

SHARP An excessive, normally youthful, acidity, possibly sour.

SILKY Soft yet rich-textured, implying ripeness and fullness.

SMOKY A self-explanatory description of particular aromas.

SMOOTH Round, no hard edges, even silky.

SOFT Looser-textured than the above, round, mellow, normally mature.

SOUS-BOIS French for 'undergrowth'; a tasting term

implying a damp, vegetative smell.

SOUS-SOL French for subsoil.

SOUTIRAGE French for racking.

SPICY Richly aromatic, strong-flavoured.

STAGE Colloquial French word for a period of time worked as a student with a French *négociant* or grower.

STALKY A 'green' rather raw, possibly stewed flavour particularly noticeable in young wine. Can derive from overlong maceration with the stalks.

STYLE/STYLISH Breed, finesse, character.

SUCCULENCE Rich, very ripe and juicy. A wine with an abundance of fruit.

SUPERFICIAL Lacking depth and complexity.

SUPPLE Absence of hard edges, round, yet not without vigour and grip.

SUR SOUCHE Purchase (and sale) of wine in advance of the harvests.

SUR-MATURITÉ An optimum ripeness, which may be associated with a marginal deficiency of acidity.

SYRAH Classic grape variety of the northern Rhône, planted in the Gironde up to the first half of the nineteenth century, but no longer authorised.

TABLE DE TRI Conveyor belt on which the grapes are laid out so that *triage* can take place.

TANNIN An essential constituent of young red wine. An acid deriving from the skins of the grape which leaves an astringent, chewy taste in the mouth. Adds to the weight of the wine. Broken down and mellowed by ageing.

TARTARIC ACID Natural acid in grapes, and the base by which the acidity is measured.

TEN-YEAR RULE Drink good classed growth red Bordeaux when the wine is 10 years old and not before.

TERROIR A French term used to denote the general physical environment of a vineyard: climate, soil, altitude, exposure and so on.

TÊTE DE CUVÉE Literally, French for the juice of the first pressing, and therefore the best. Indicates the grower's best wine.

THIN Deficient in body and substance, watery.

TONNEAU Measure of the production of a Bordeaux estate; equivalent to four hogsheads or 1000 dozen bottles.

TONNELLERIE Part of the *chai* where hogsheads are made and mended.

TOUGH Full-bodied, hard, tannic, perhaps robust; if young, may soften when mature: also used of overbalanced older wines.

TRANCHE Literally 'slice'; a portion of the yield.

TRIAGE The process of eliminating the bruised, unripe and rotten from healthy fruit.

ULLAGE The gap of air between the cork and the wine in a bottle.

VELVETY Silky, opulent, rich, smooth.

VENDANGE Harvest.

VENDANGE VERTE Removal of excess bunches of grapes before *véraison*.

VÉRAISON The point at which the ripening grapes begin to turn into their mature colour, i.e. from green to black in the case of a red wine estate, usually in August.

VERDOT (PETIT) Important but subsidiary red Bordeaux grape.

VERTICAL TASTING Tasting of a number of vintages of the same property.

VIGNOBLE Vineyard area.

VIGOROUS Lively, balanced flavour with grip and some element of youth.

VIN DE GOUTTE The free run juice racked off after maceration.

VIN DE PRESSE Wine produced from pressing the skins, pips etc., after the free-run juice has been tapped off. Usually high in tannin and acidity, the incorporation of a judicious amount of *vin de presse* can add backbone to the blend.

VINICULTURE Everything to do with the production of wine.

VINIFICATION The process of winemaking.

VINOTHÈQUE Library or collection of wine bottles.

VINTAGE The year of the harvest.

VITICULTURE Everything to do with the growing of vines and the production of its fruit.

VOLATILITÉ (ACIDITY) Present in all wine; yet when used refers to an excess, a whiff of sweet-sour vinegar.

WELL BALANCED Harmonious, the constituents of the wine.

WOODY Normally used in a pejorative sense not so much referring to an excess of oak-ageing (new or old) as to an off-taste due to a faulty stave.

BIBLIOGRAPHY

ALLEN, H. WARNER *The Wines of France*, 1924 (London); *The Romance of Wine*, 1931 (London); *Natural Red Wines*, 1951 (London); *Through the Wine Glass*, 1954 (London); *A History of Wine*, 1961 (London).

AUSSEL *La Gironde à Vol d'Oiseau*, 1865.

BARTON, ANTHONY and PETIT-CASTELLI, CLAUDE *La Saga des Bartons*, 1991 (Paris).

BAUREIN, ABBÉ J. *Variétés Bordelaises* (originally published in 6 volumes) 1784-86; 2nd edition G. Meron, 1876 (4 volumes).

BENSON, JEFFREY *Sauternes*, 1979 (London); and MACKENZIE, ALASTAIR *The Wines of Saint-Émilion and Pomerol*, 1983 (London).

BERRY, CHARLES WALTER *Viniana*, 1929 (London); *A Miscellany of Wine*, 1932 (London); *In Search of Wine*, 1935 (London).

BERT, PIERRE *In Vino Veritas: L'Affaire des Vins de Bordeaux*, 1975 (Paris).

BERTALL (real name ARNOUX) *La Vigne: Voyage Autour des Vins de France*, 1878 (Paris).

BOLTER, WILLIAM *The Red Wines of Bordeaux*, 1988 (London); *The White Wines of Bordeaux*, 1988 (London).

BROADBENT, J. MICHAEL *The Great Vintage Wine Book*, 1980 (London); *The Great Vintage Wine Book II*, 1992 (London); *Vintage Wine*, 2002 (London).

BROOK, STEPHEN *Liquid Gold*, 1987 (London).

BUTEL, P. 'Grand Propriétaires et Production des Vins du Médoc au XVIIIème Siècle, article in *Le Médoc*, 1964.

CAMPBELL, IAN M. *Wayward Tendrils of the Vine*, 1947 (London); *Reminiscences of a Vintner*, 1951 (London).

CASSAGNAC, PAUL DE *French Wines*, translated by Guy Knowles, 1930 (London).

COATES, CLIVE *Claret*, 1982 (London); *Grands Vins, The Finest Châteaux of Bordeaux and their Wines*, 1995 (London); *An Encyclopaedia of the Wines and Domaines of France*, 2000 (London).

COCKS, CHARLES *Bordeaux, Its Wines and the Claret Country*, 1846; and FÉRET, ÉDOUARD, *Bordeaux et Ses Vins*, various editions in English and French, 1850-2001 (Bordeaux).

CRESTIN-BILLET, FRÉDÉRIQUE *Les Châteaux du Médoc*, 1988 (France); *Les Châteaux de Saint-Émilion*, 1989 (France); *Les Châteaux de Sauternes et Graves*, 1990 (France).

D'ARMAILHACQ, A. *De la Culture des Vignes dans le Médoc*, various editions, 1855-1867 (Bordeaux).

DANFLOU, ALFRED *Les Grands Crus Bordelais*, 1867 (Bordeaux).

DION, ROGER *Histoire de la Vigne et du Vin en France des Origines au XIXème Siècle*, 1959 (Paris).

DOUTRELANT, PIERRE-MARIE *Les Bons Vins et les Autres*, 1976 (Paris).

DOVAZ, MICHEL *Encyclopédie des Crus Classés du Bordelais*, 1981 (France); *Encyclopédie des Crus Bourgeois du Bordelais*, 1988 (Paris).

DUIJKER, HUBRECHT *The Great Wine Châteaux of Bordeaux*, 1975 (London); *The Bordeaux Atlas and Encyclopaedia of Châteaux*, 1997 (London).

ENJALBERT HENRI *Comment Naissent les Grands Crus*, Annales ESC 1953 (ed); *Great Bordeaux Wines, Saint-Émilion, Pomerol, Fronsac*, 1985 (Paris).

EYRES, HARRY *Wine Dynasties of Europe*, 1990 (London).

FAITH, NICHOLAS *The Winemakers*, 1978 (London); *Château Margaux*, 1980 (London); *Victorian Vineyard*, 1983 (London); *Château Latour*, 1992 (London); *Château Beychevelle*, 1991 (France).

FÉRET, ÉDOUARD *Saint-Émilion et ses Vins*, 1893 (Bordeaux).

FORSTER, ROBERT 'The Noble Wine Producers of the Bordelais in the Eighteenth Century', article in the *Economic History Review*, 1961.

FRANCIS, A.D. *The Wine Trade*, 1972 (London).

FRANCK, WILHELM *Traité sur les Vins du Médoc et les Autres Rouges du Département de la Gironde*, various editions, 1824-1871 (Bordeaux).

GALET, P. *Cépages et Vignobles de France*, 1958 (Montpellier).

GINESTET, BERNARD *La Bouille Bordelaise*, 1975 (Paris); *Margaux*, 1984 (Paris); *Saint-Julien*, 1984 (Paris); *Pauillac*, 1985 (Paris); *Saint-Estèphe*, 1985 (Paris); *Saint-Émilion*, 1986 (Paris); *Pomerol*, 1984 (Paris); *Barsac, Sauternes*, 1987 (Paris).

GUILLON, ÉDOUARD *Les Châteaux Historiques et Vignobles de la Gironde*, 4 volumes, 1867-1870.

HEALY, MAURICE *Claret and the White Wines of Bordeaux*, 1934 (London); *Stay with Me Flagons*, 1940 (London).

HENDERSON, ALBERT *The History of Ancient and*

Modern Wines, 1824 (London).

HIGOUNET, CHARLES (editor) *Histoire de Bordeaux*, 6 volumes, 1962-1969 (Bordeaux).

HYAMS, EDWARD *Dionysus: A Social History of the Vine*, 1965 (London).

JAMES, MARJORY *Studies in the Medieval Wine Trade*, 1971 (Oxford).

JOHNSON, HUGH *The Story of Wine*, 1989 (London); and ROBINSON, JANCIS *The World Atlas of Wine*, 5th edition, 2002 (London).

JULIEN, A. *Topographie de Tous les Vignobles Connus*, 1832 (Paris).

JULLIAN, CAMILLE *Histoire de Bordeaux*, (2 vols), 1985 (Paris).

KAY, BILLY and MACLEAN, CAILEAN *Knee Deep in Claret*, 1983 (Edinburgh).

KRESSMANN, EDOUARD *Le Guide des Vins et des Vignobles de France*, 1975 (Paris-Bruxelles).

'G.A.K' *Clarets and Sauternes*, 1920 (London).

LACHIVER, MARCEL *Vins, Vignes et Vignerons, Histoire du Vignoble Français*, 1988 (Paris).

LAFFORGUE, GERMAIN *Le Vignoble Girondin*, 1947 (Paris).

LAWRENCE, R. DE TREVILLE, SR (editor) *Jefferson and Wine*, 1973 (Virginia, USA).

LICHINE, ALEXIS *Guide to the Wines and Vineyards of France*, revised edition 1987 (London); *Encyclopedia of Wines and Spirits*, revised edition 1985 (London).

LITTLEWOOD, JOAN *Mouton-Baronne-Philippe*, 1982 (London); *Milady Vine*, 1984 (London).

LORBAC, CHARLES (real name ABROL) *Les Richesses Gastronomiques de la France: Les Vins de Bordeaux*, 1867

(Strasbourg).

MALVESIN, FRANZ *Histoire de la Vigne et du Vin en Aquitaine*, 1919.

MALVESIN, T. and FÉRET, E. *Le Médoc et Ses Vins*, 1876 (Bordeaux).

MALVESIN, THÉODORE *Histoire du Commerce de Bordeaux*, 1892.

MARCHIOU, GASTON *Bordeaux sous le Règne de la Vigne*, 1947 (Bordeaux).

MARKHAM, ROGER *The 1855 Classification*, 2000 (New York).

MONSEIGNEUR LE VIN (GEORGES MONTORGUEIL), *Le Vin de Bordeaux*, volume 2, 1925 (Paris).

MOTHE, FLORENCE *Graves de Bordeaux*, 1965 (Paris).

OLNEY, RICHARD *Yquem*, 1985 (Paris).

ORDISH, GEORGE *The Great Wine Blight*, 1972 (London).

PAGUIERE, M. *Classification et Description des Vins de Bordeaux et des Cépages Particuliers au Département de la Gironde: Mode de Culture*, 1828, facsimile edition, 1977 (Bordeaux).

PARKER, ROBERT *Bordeaux*, 1986 (London) 2nd edition, 1992 and various editions since.

PENNING-ROWSELL, EDMUND *The Wines of Bordeaux*, 6th edition, 1989 (London).

PEPPERCORN, DAVID *The Mitchell Beazley Guide to the Wines of Bordeaux*, 2003 (London); *Bordeaux*, 3rd edition, 2002 (London).

PEYNAUD, PROF. ÉMILE *Le Goût du Vin*, 1980 (Paris); *Connaissance et Travail du Vin*, 1981 (Paris). The photograph on the cover is of Léon Thienpont in his *chais* at Vieux Château Certan.

PIJASSOU, RENÉ 'Un Château du Médoc: Palmer', published in the journal *Le Médoc*, 1964 (Bordeaux); *Le Médoc*,

2 volumes, 1980 (Paris).

PLUMB, PROF. J.H. *Men and Places*, Chapter 12: 'Mr. Walpole's Wine', 1966 (London).

RAY, CYRIL *Mouton Rothschild*, 1974 (London).

REDDING, CYRUS *A History and Description of Modern Wines*, 1833 (London).

RHODES, ANTHONY *Princes of the Grape*, 1975 (London).

RIBADIEU, HENRI *L'Histoire des Châteaux de la Gironde*, 1856; *Histoire de Bordeaux pendant le Règne de Louis XVI*, 1853 (Bordeaux).

ROGER, PROF. I.R. *The Wines of Bordeaux*, English edition, 1960 (London).

ROTHSCHILD, BARON PHILIPPE DE *Vivre la Vigne*, 1981 (Paris).

SAINTSBURY, PROF. GEORGE *Notes in a Cellar Book*, 1920 (London).

SEELY, JAMES *Great Bordeaux Wines*, 1986 (London).

SHAND, P. MORTON *A Book of French Wines*, 1928 (London); revised edition by Cyril Ray, 1964 (London).

SHAW, THOMAS GEORGE *Wine, The Vine and the Cellar*, 1863 (London).

SICHEL, ALLAN and PETER *Yearly Vintage Reports* (1961-1993).

SIMON, ANDRÉ L. *History of the Wine Trade in England*, facsimile edition, 1964 (London); *Bottlescrew Days*, 1926 (London); *Vintagewise*, 1945 (London).

TERS, DIDIER *Haut-Médoc*, 1985 (Paris); *Moulis and Listrac*, 1990 (Paris).

VANDYKE PRICE, PAMELA *Guide to the Wines of Bordeaux*, 1977 (London); *French Vintage*, 1986 (London); *Wines of the Graves*, 1988 (London).

YOUNGER, WILLIAM *Gods, Men and Wine*, 1966 (London).

INDEX